MW00379519

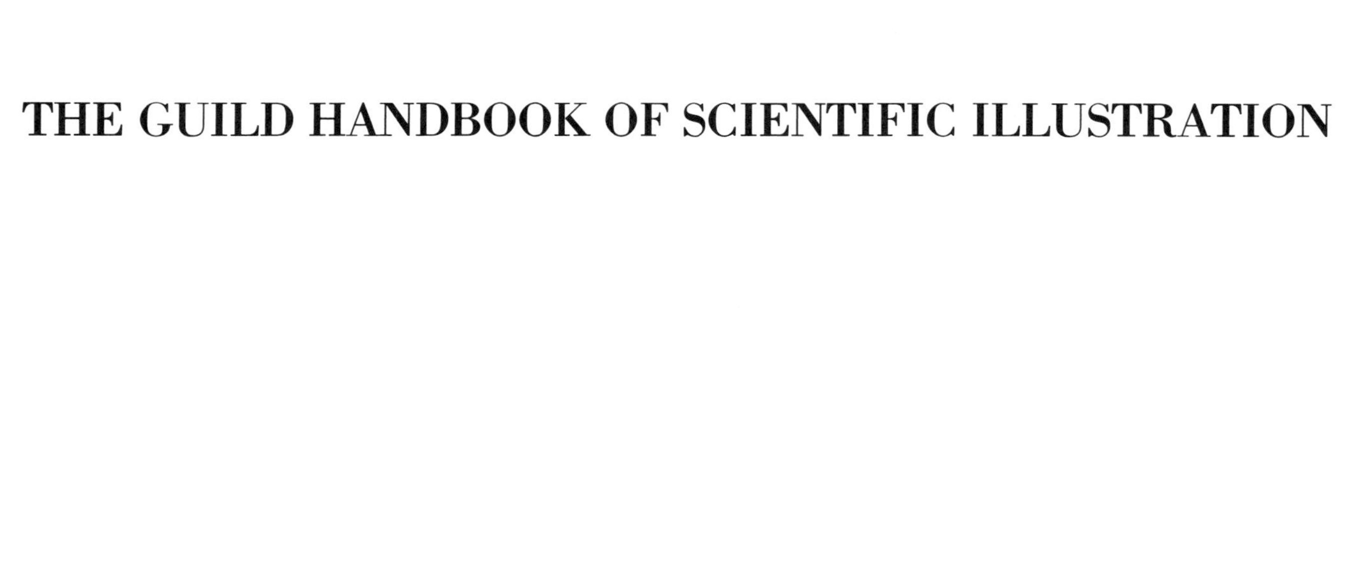

THE GUILD HANDBOOK OF SCIENTIFIC ILLUSTRATION

NAP

The Guild Handbook of SCIENTIFIC ILLUSTRATION

Edited by

Elaine R. S. Hodges

with
Lawrence B. Isham
Marsha E. Jessup
G. Robert Lewis

JOHN WILEY & SONS, INC.

New York Chichester Weinheim Brisbane Singapore Toronto

Designed by East End Graphic Arts

This book is printed on acid-free paper. ♾

Published by John Wiley & Sons, Inc.

Published simultaneously in Canada.

Library of Congress Cataloging-in-Publication Data:

The Guild handbook of scientific illustration.
Bibliography: p.
Includes indexes.
1. Scientific illustration—Handbooks, manuals, etc.
I. Hodges, Elaine R. S., 1937- II. Guild of Natural Science Illustrators (U.S.)
Q122.G85 1988 502.2 88-10599
ISBN 0-471-28896-9

Printed in the United States of America

10 9 8

Contents

Authors

Kraig Adler, Professor of Biology, Cornell University, Ithaca, NY
Karen L. Allaben-Confer, Bird Artist, Northwoods Art, Brooktondale, NY
Arly Allen, Vice President and General Manager, Allen Press, Inc., Lawrence, KS
Terry L. Chase, Scientific Illustrator and Model Maker, Chase Studio, Cedar Creek, MO
Chip Clark, Photographer, Smithsonian Institution, Washington, DC
Daniel G. Cole, Cartographer, Smithsonian Institution, Washington, DC
Jennifer Loynd Cowherd, Scientific Illustrator, Alexandria, VA
Marion J. Dalen, Scientific Illustrator, Port Orford, OR
David M. Dennis, Biological Illustrator and Photographer, College of Biological Sciences, Ohio State University, Columbus, OH
L. Michael Druckenbrod, formerly Scientific Illustrator, Department of Entomology, Smithsonian Institution, Washington, DC
Candy Feller, Scientific Illustrator, Washington, DC
Elsie Herbold Froeschner, Scientific Illustrator, retired from Department of Entomology, Smithsonian Institution, Washington, DC
Carolyn Bartlett Gast, Scientific Illustrator, retired from Department of Invertebrate Zoology, Smithsonian Institution, Washington, DC
T. Britt Griswold, Scientific Illustrator, Fairfax, VA
Nancy R. Halliday, Scientific Illustrator, Wilmette, IL
William Hamilton IV, Medical Illustrator, Ferrisburg, VT
Charles O. Handley, Jr., Curator, Department of Vertebrate Zoology, Smithsonian Institution, Washington, DC
Gerald P. Hodge, retired Professor and Director, Medical and Biological Illustration, University of Michigan, Ann Arbor, MI
Elaine R. S. Hodges, Scientific Illustrator, Department of Entomology, Smithsonian Institution, Washington, DC
Francis M. Hueber, Curator, Department of Paleobiology, Smithsonian Institution, Washington, DC
Jane Hurd, Medical Illustrator, Bethesda, MD
Lawrence B. Isham, Scientific Illustrator, retired from Department of Paleobiology, Smithsonian Institution, Washington, DC
Joel Ito, Medical Illustrator, Oregon Regional Primate Research Center, Beaverton, OR
Marsha E. Jessup, Director, Media Resources, University of Medicine and Dentistry of NJ—Robert Wood Johnson Medical School, Piscataway, NJ
John W. Karapelou, Chief Medical Illustrator, College of Physicians and Surgeons, Columbia University, New York, NY
Karen Klitz, Scientific Illustrator, Museum of Vertebrate Zoology, University of California, Berkeley, CA

Lloyd E. Logan, Scientific Illustrator, University of Georgia, Athens, GA

Patrick J. Lynch, Associate Director, Department of Biomedical Communications, Yale University School of Medicine, New Haven, CT

Vichai Malikul, Scientific Illustrator, Department of Entomology, Smithsonian Institution, Washington, DC

David Mascaro, Associate Professor, Medical Illustration Graduate Program, Medical College of Georgia, Augusta, GA

Elizabeth Morales-Denney, Scientific Illustrator, Inverness, CA

Trudy Nicholson, Scientific Illustrator; Medical Illustrator, National Institutes of Health, Bethesda, MD

Rosemary Nothwanger, Scientific Illustrator, Bethesda, MD

Gregory S. Paul, Scientific Illustrator, Baltimore, MD

Kenelm W. Philip, Research Associate, University of Alaska, Fairbanks, AK

Arwin V. Provonsha, Curator and Scientific Illustrator, Purdue University, West Lafayette, IN

John B. Randall, Senior Scientist, Entomology Research Department, S. C. Johnson & Son Inc., Racine, WI; Scientific Illustrator

Barbara N. Rankin, Medical Illustrator, Cleveland, OH (deceased)

Lewis Sadler, Associate Professor; Acting Director, Department of Biocommunication Arts; Director, National Research Center for the Identification of Missing Children, University of Illinois, Chicago, IL

Jack R. Schroeder, Scientific Illustrator, Crisfield, MD

Marion Ruff Sheehan, Scientific Illustrator; Assistant Professor, University of Florida, Gainesville, FL

Christine A. Smith, President and Director, Conservation of Art on Paper, Alexandria, VA

Wayne Trimm, Art Director, *The Conservationist Magazine,* Albany, NY

Stanley H. Weitzman, Curator, Department of Vertebrate Zoology, Smithsonian Institution, Washington, DC

Richard E. White, Research Scientist, Systematic Entomology Laboratory, U.S. Department of Agriculture, Washington, DC

Acknowledgments

A collection of information as diverse and encyclopedic as that in this handbook requires help from many people in addition to the authors and illustrators. Sincere gratitude is owed to all of them. L. Michael Druckenbrod and Keiko Hiratsuka Moore were early members of the editorial board, and their excellent efforts over several years are much appreciated. James F. Mello, David Challinor, S. Dillon Ripley, Wayne N. Mathis, Ronald J. McGinley, Donald R. Davis, Stanwyn G. Shetler, Porter M. Kier, Richard S. Fiske, James C. Tyler, and Robert S. Hoffmann, all of the Smithsonian Institution, made this book possible with their invaluable support and encouragement, administrative as well as personal.

Many generously contributed ideas to various chapters: Karen Ackoff (chapter 2); Arly Allen (chapter 1); Marcia D. Bakry (chapter 2); Frederick M. Bayer (chapter 15); Sally J. Bensusen (chapters 29 and 30); William L. Brudon (chapters 4 and 7); Terry L. Chase (chapter 2); Daniel G. Cole (chapter 2); John O. Corliss (chapter 15); L. Michael Druckenbrod (chapters 2 and 5); Candy Feller (chapter 12); Elsie Herbold Froeschner (chapter 2); Margaret Fulford (chapter 12); Carolyn Bartlett Gast (chapters 1 and 2); T. Britt Griswold (chapter 2); John Gurche (chapter 14); William Hamilton IV (chapter 30); Gerald P. Hodge (chapters 2 and 6); Steven E. Hodges (chapters 2 and 4); Regina O. Hughes (chapter 12); Ralph Idema (chapter 15); Pat Kenny (Introduction to part 2); George Robert Lewis (chapters 2 and 21); Patrick J. Lynch (chapter 2); Mary S. Monsma (chapter 12); Ellen Paige (chapter 2); David L. Pawson (chapter 15); Whitney Powell-Cummer (chapter 21); Arwin V. Provonsha (chapters 2, 6, and 27); John B. Randall (chapter 2); Barbara N. Rankin (chapter 1); Jane Redmann (chapter 6); Anne E. Richardson (chapters 1 and 15); Klaus Ruetzler (chapter 15); Molly Kelly Ryan (chapter 1); Sue Seif (chapter 1); Marion Ruff Sheehan (chapter 1); Stanley Snyder (chapter 30); Young T. Sohn (chapter 2); Ann Szymckowicz (chapter 29); Alice R. Tangerini (chapters 6 and 12); George L. Venable (chapters 1, 2, and 6); Stanley H. Weitzman (chapter 2); Wendy B. Zomlefer (chapter 12). Richard E. White added many valuable concepts to the section on insect illustration in chapter 15. Elaine R. S. Hodges was responsible for the part introductions.

Each chapter was reviewed by specialists in the subject: Edmond S. Alexander, Karen L. Allaben-Confer, Scott T. Barrows, Bret Beall, Sally J. Bensusen, Patricia Bonamo, Dieter Brill, William L. Brudon, Martin A. Buzas, Fenner A. Chace, Jr., Mary E. Challinor, May S. Cheney, Jonathan Coddington, Joel Cohn, Bruce B. Collette, John O. Corliss, R. Henry Cowherd, Ronald I. Crombie, Ranice W. Crósby, John Crowell, Arthur Cushman, Bijan Dehgan, R. C. Douglass, William J. Dress, Don Richard Eckelberry, Clifford Evans, Ellen R. Farr, Priscilla Fawcett, Sara Fink, Dick Fisher, Henry Frieswyck, Elsie Herbold Froeschner, Kristian Fauchald, Alfred L. Gardner, Weston D. Gardner, Carolyn Bartlett Gast, Gary Gill, Philip Gingerich, Linda Golder, Robert Golder, M. P. Goodkin, Inc., J. Douglas Grierson, Walter Gumpertz, John Gurche, Nancy R. Halliday, William Hamilton IV, Biruta Akerbergs Hansen, Aline Hansens, J. William Hardy, Robert Higgins, Horton H. Hobbs, Gerald P. Hodge, Steven E. Hodges, Jeanne Holgate, Cliff Hopson, Nikki Horton, Nicholas Hotton III, Regina O. Hughes, Jane Hurd, Jasper N. Joiner, Christina L. Jordan, Walter S. Judd, J. W. Kimbrough, Louise Kurtz, Anne E. Lacy, Denis Lee, Gary P. Lees, Clare Walker Leslie, Lloyd E. Logan, Lowe, Bressler and Kaufman, Charles McCutchen, David Mascaro, Jay Matternes, Betty J. Meggers, Mary S. Monsma, Ronald Moretti, Mitsu Nakayama, Trudy Nicholson, Rosemary Nothwanger, Donald J. Ortner, Laurence A. Pace, David L. Pawson, Anthony M. Pazos, Whitney Powell-Cummer, John B. Randall, Clayton E. Ray, Klaus Ruetzler, Lewis Sadler, Alan Savitsky, Donald B. Sayner, Laurel V. Schaubert, Susan Seif, Marion Ruff Sheehan, Kathy Shuster, Virginia M. Simon, Tom Sims, Lois Sloan, Stanley Snyder, Victor G. Springer, Art Sylvester, George

Talbot, Lucy C. Taylor, Hans Thewissen, F. Christian Thompson, Richard W. Thorington, Wayne Trimm, Richard P. Vari, George L. Venable, James H. Wallace, Jr., William Westwood, Richard E. White, Donald R. Whitehead, Joseph W. Wiedel, Roger B. Williams, George R. Zug, Richard L. Zusi, and Frances W. Zweifel.

Special thanks go to T. Britt Griswold for his creative, well-designed and well-executed drawings and graphics that are throughout the book. In addition to drawings done by some authors for their own chapters, other illustrators prepared illustrations especially for this book and are credited by their work: Thomas M. Evans, Sara Fink, Caroline Herbert, Lawrence B. Isham, Irene Jewett, Ken Lee, Charissa Baker Lounibos, Sally Parker, Nancy A. Payzant, Stasia Penkoff, Barbara N. Rankin, Deborah Leather Roney, Karen Schmitt, Marilyn Schotte, Alice R. Tangerini, Jo-Ellen Trecartin, George L. Venable, and Wendy B. Zomlefer. Others spent time locating and/or checking artwork: Donald Baird, Martin A. Buzas, Stephen D. Cairns, Fenner A. Chace, Jr., A. H. Cheetham, Ranice W. Crosby, William A. Deiss, Richard E. Grant, Roman Kenk, Gary P. Lees, David L. Pawson, Harold A. Rehder, Susan Lynn Richardson, Clyde F. E. Roper, Jerry Russell, Ray T. Rye, Donald B. Sayner, Kathleen P. Smith, and George E. Watson.

Valuable expertise, information, and other services were offered by Robert E. Dierker, Noreen M. Dinndorf, Frank A. Florentine, Weston D. Gardner, Art Graham of Grumbacher, Carolyn S. Hahn, Mort Hallwig, Susan Sare Hodges, John M. Kingsolver, Eve Kloepper of Animals, Animals/Earth Sciences, James G. Mead, Beth M. Norden, Laurence A. Pace, Gary Raham, Ruth F. Schallert, Joel J. Snyder, Paul J. Spangler, Phyllis M. Spangler, Mary R. Tanner, William M. Winn, and Harvey Zuckman. The Smithsonian Office of Printing and Photographic Services handled much of the photography through the considerable talents of Chip Clark, Joe A. Goulait, Victor E. Krantz, Mary Ellen McCaffrey, Llewellyn Thomas, and James H. Wallace, Jr. Alice R. Tangerini prepared most photostats, and she, Mary S. Monsma, and Jo-Ellen Trecartin helped with illustration copy preparation. For the second and third printings, Dick Rauh corrected the entire Appendix, which was researched for the first edition in part by Roni Freeman and Audrey Grissom.

The excellent and intelligent typing of Jan S. Ballard, Sally Gagné, Micky Goldstein, Stuart Halliday, Mavis Klueter, Charissa Baker Lounibos, Carol Randall, Phyllis M. Spangler, Lisa Klueter Sulick, and Marilyn Weitzman made sense out of challenging, rough copy. On occasion Ms. Klueter spent all night and early mornings typing material into a word processor to meet deadlines.

Some who were especially generous with their encouragement, enthusiasm, and interest in this project over the years, particularly at critical low points, are J. F. G. Clarke, Candy Feller, Richard H. Foote, Sally Gagné, Weston D. Gardner, Gerald P. Hodge, Larry B. Hodges, Lester and Elma Hodges, Trudy Nicholson, Marilyn Schotte, Samuel and Pat Snyder, M. Alma Solis, and Frederick M. Stehr. They helped keep me going.

The Guild of Natural Science Illustrators financed the handbook, a considerable expenditure for a nonprofit group with low dues. I hope the royalties will recoup their costs. Members of the GNSI have been incredibly patient, tolerating delays with understanding and sympathy. Members of the editorial board—Larry Isham, Marsha Jessup, and Bob Lewis—devoted years to reading and evaluating chapters through many revisions. Their patience has been sorely tested.

Everyone at Van Nostrand Reinhold Company has been most pleasant and helpful. Nancy N. Green, who signed me with VNR, and Lilly Kaufman, Sponsoring Editor, have insisted on quality above all else, a contagious attitude. Copy editor Kathleen Brandes masterfully imposed consistency on this long and complicated manuscript, despite its many cross-references. She found errors overlooked by many readers, for which I am immensely grateful. Linda Venator oversaw the book through the editorial, design, and production process and has been a patient and enthusiastic supporter. Although I initially protested some changes she requested, they all turned out to be beneficial. Her stewardship and encouragement maintained progress at a steady pace.

I owe many thanks to editor Barbara Ravage who, through her example, taught me a great deal about good editing. She made me more conscious of how small changes in language increase or decrease confusion. For about three years she put up with my complaints about her requirement for consistency. Her insight has made this a better book.

I am especially indebted to my husband, Ronald W. Hodges, for his encouragement and support. He took over most household chores and prepared sumptuous meals for thirteen years, sacrificing his own entomological research time, so that I could devote nights and weekends to this book. In addition, he answered many scientific and editorial questions and provided valuable leads to information and specialists.

Elaine Rita Snyder Hodges

Introduction

"Guild" in this handbook's title refers to the Guild of Natural Science Illustrators (GNSI), a nonprofit organization of scientific illustrators and others devoted to improving the quality of scientific illustration through shared ideas. Starting with luncheon meetings at the Smithsonian Institution in 1966, the guild was formalized by a constitution in 1968 with twenty-one charter members, mostly scientific illustrators from the Smithsonian's National Museum of Natural History but also including some medical illustrators from nearby medical schools. By word of mouth and a newsletter, GNSI has grown into an international association of over 1,000 members providing written and workshop training.

Scientific illustration is the production of drawings of measured accuracy and other graphic images that help the scientist-author to communicate. These illustrations should convey to the reader the same concepts that are in the mind of the author. Because they communicate subtleties and eliminate the ambiguities of language, scientific illustrations are an important, often necessary, element in precise communication.

In this communication process the illustrator should produce accurate work that is also pleasing to the eye in terms of balance and artistic handling of the subject. This obligation is well expressed by two quotes:

> If the technical illustrator will just keep in mind that the product and its components have already been designed and his main job is to present it accurately and with emphasis as required he will have easy sailing.—Anthony D. Pyeatt *(Technical Illustration*, 1960, Higgins Ink Co.)

> . . . aesthetic qualities will give to the illustration life and a measure of charm. These will help to put over the facts and to fix them more firmly in the readers' memories.—Geoffrey Lapage ("Making Science Readable," *Medical and Biological Illustration*, 1962, 12(2):114–20.)

The scientific illustrator, whose training, ability, and interests extend into both art and science, applies discipline to creativity so that the images produced do not merely decorate, but serve science.

The natural sciences use scientific illustration in most publications. Drawings are essential to depict diagnostic characters that differentiate one taxonomic group from another. The skilled scientific illustrator can clarify infinite focal depth and overlapping layers, emphasize important details, and reconstruct broken specimens on paper—results unattainable through photography (figs. I-1, I-2; see also figs. 13-16, 13-17). The techniques of art, when refined to meet the needs of science, can be used to show structure and detail through cutaway drawings, transparencies, and exploded diagrams. Many steps may be required to achieve accuracy (fig. I-3). In the quest for nature's details, the illustrator, using microscopes and other instruments, enters a world that few people know or appreciate and describes it to others through drawn images.

Future developments in electron microscopy and computer graphics may well bring changes to the illustration of natural-science subjects. Although electron micrographs supplement scientific drawings, they have the same limitations as photography. Computer graphics techniques may become useful as their costs decrease but still will require interpretation to clarify structures. Because of space limitations, these two topics are not covered extensively in this book, but there are many references that the reader can consult.

Medical illustration differs from other types of scientific (biological) illustration in that it does not always require measurement and exact depiction; it allows more latitude for artistic license. But both biological and medical illustrators use similar drawing techniques. Several schools offer degrees in medical illustration.

Wildlife illustration, another branch of scientific illustration, also requires a thorough knowledge of natural-science subjects; however, it is not bound by the requirement of exact presentation. Wildlife illustrators have more of the freedom of the fine artist and are able to work in color, whereas other scientific illustrators use color less often because of cost restrictions.

The successful scientific illustrator must have a penchant for precision, great tolerance for and appreciation of detailed work, and the patience to stare into a microscope for hours hunting for a minuscule hair. Although some may complain about the tedium—and such work is often monotonous—all may take pride in the finished work: a beautifully rendered drawing or painting that is as true as possible to its subject and that, upon publication, will supplement a body of scientific information.

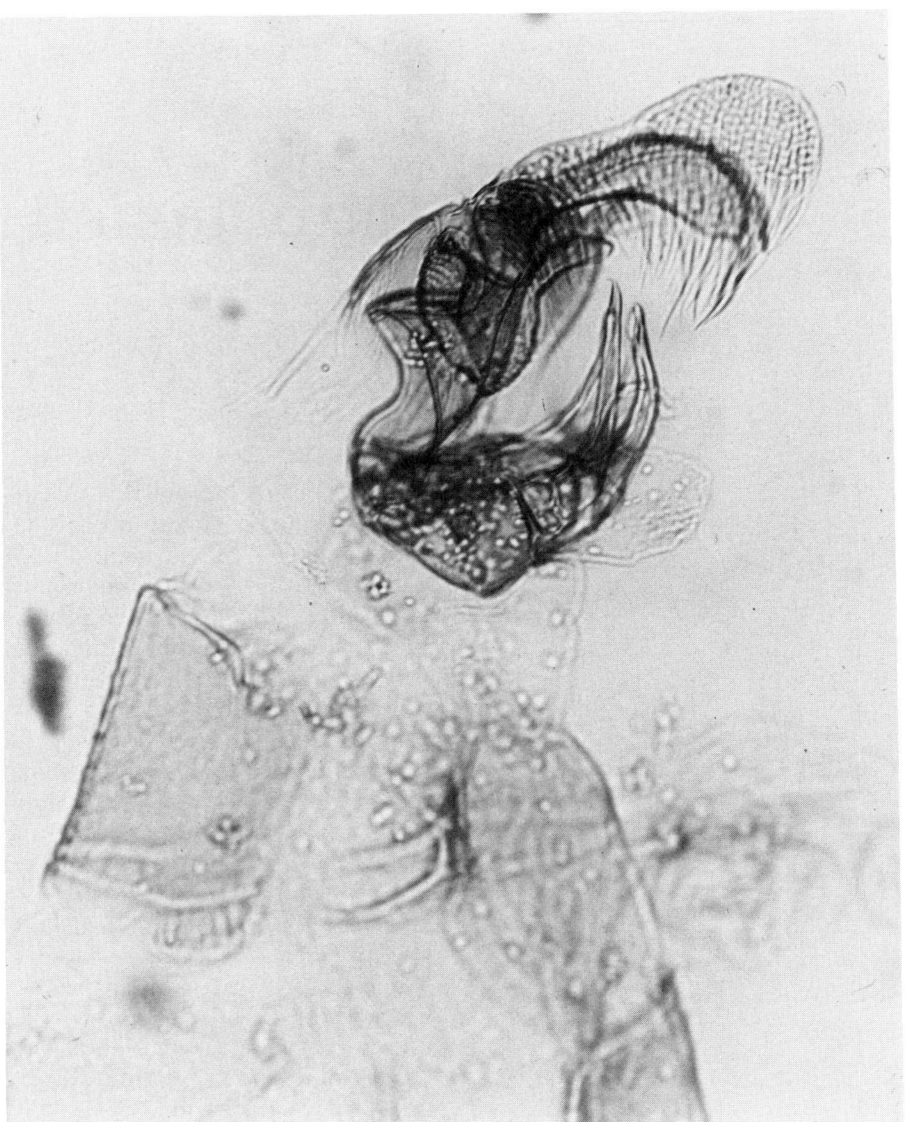

I-1. A photograph frequently cannot show clearly and unambiguously structures that attach to one another and overlap. In this photograph the large abdominal plates, flattened laterally, are unclear and must be represented in dorsal view to show their shapes. The aedeagus is fused to the rest of the genitalia so that it cannot be dissected. It shows faintly in the center of the dark structure, between two projections (brachia). The eighth sternum is folded around the genitalia; its structure and the center connecting piece (shown in fig. I-2 (c) as dashed) are obscured. *Asymphorodes ergodes* (Lepidoptera: Cosmopterigidae), holotype, male moth genitalia, lateral view, partially attached to abdomen. Photo by Vic Krantz.

This book is designed to be a reference for the scientific illustrator, other artists, and scientists who do their own drawings or hire illustrators.

Part 1 includes the basics that cover what every scientific illustrator should know, regardless of technique or subject. The steps, materials, and tools required to produce almost any illustration are discussed. Emphasis is placed on the preservation of drawings, especially through the choice of materials, so that works of art will not deteriorate before they can be

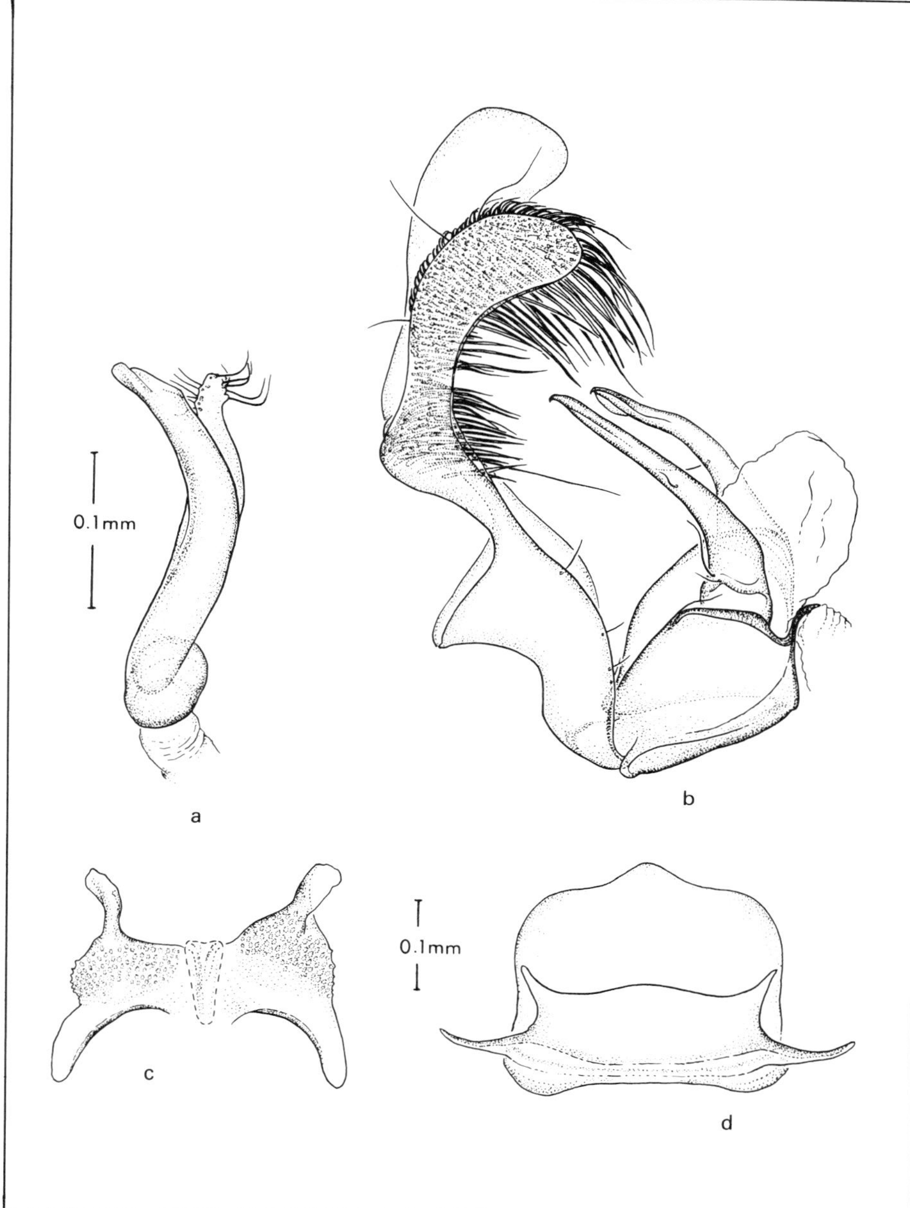

I-2. Drawing of the same specimen as in fig. I-1. The aedeagus *(a)* has been drawn separately from the structure *(b)*. The eighth sternum *(c)* and seventh tergum and sternum *(d)* have been visually unfolded and drawn from a dorsal view. Articulations have been clarified. Gillott 659 pen nib and ink on hot-press Bristol board, by Elaine R. S. Hodges. Courtesy of J. F. G. Clarke.

reused or reach an archive. How light affects forms and is in turn affected by them is elucidated; this interaction is a quagmire for most people, who find it very difficult to render what they see.

Part 2 covers the rendering techniques most likely to be used in scientific illustration. In addition to traditional materials and methods, these techniques use modern materials, including plastics, airbrush, and other media and surfaces not available to illustrators earlier in the twentieth century.

Chapters in part 3 discuss the subjects of scientific illustration: plants, animals, and people and their artifacts. Each author explains the pertinent field, basic anatomy and terminology, how to achieve accuracy with each group, and how to handle each type of specimen. The subject-matter chapters are organized in an evolutionary hierarchy. Here, those areas of biology that use scientific illustration extensively are treated in commensurate detail.

The illustrator of animals in their habitat applies procedures explained in other chapters to develop basic, accurate preliminary drawings. How to take these drawings and make them into successful wildlife art is covered in chapter 20.

Subjects of medical illustration are not mounted, handled, and measured as are other types of specimens because medical illustration often is more a conceptual than a literal depiction of the subject. The medical illustrator must be trained in the anatomy of humans and domesticated animals, subjects too extensive to be discussed in this book. There are many references on these subjects, some of which are listed in the Bibliography.

Part 4 begins with a chapter on optics to explain the basic tool of most scientific illustrators, the microscope. Other chapters deal with graphic considerations; graphs, charts, and maps invariably are needed to communicate scientific concepts. Illustrators need to photograph their work for portfolios, so techniques are presented for doing this properly. Reproduction in print is the eventual fate of most scientific illustrations; the critical aspects that both the illustrator and scientist should understand are discussed in the chapter on the printing process.

The last section, part 5, is devoted to business concerns, addressing primarily the needs of the freelance illustrator—a large group because most scientific illustrators are self-employed. The scientist-author-employer-client also would

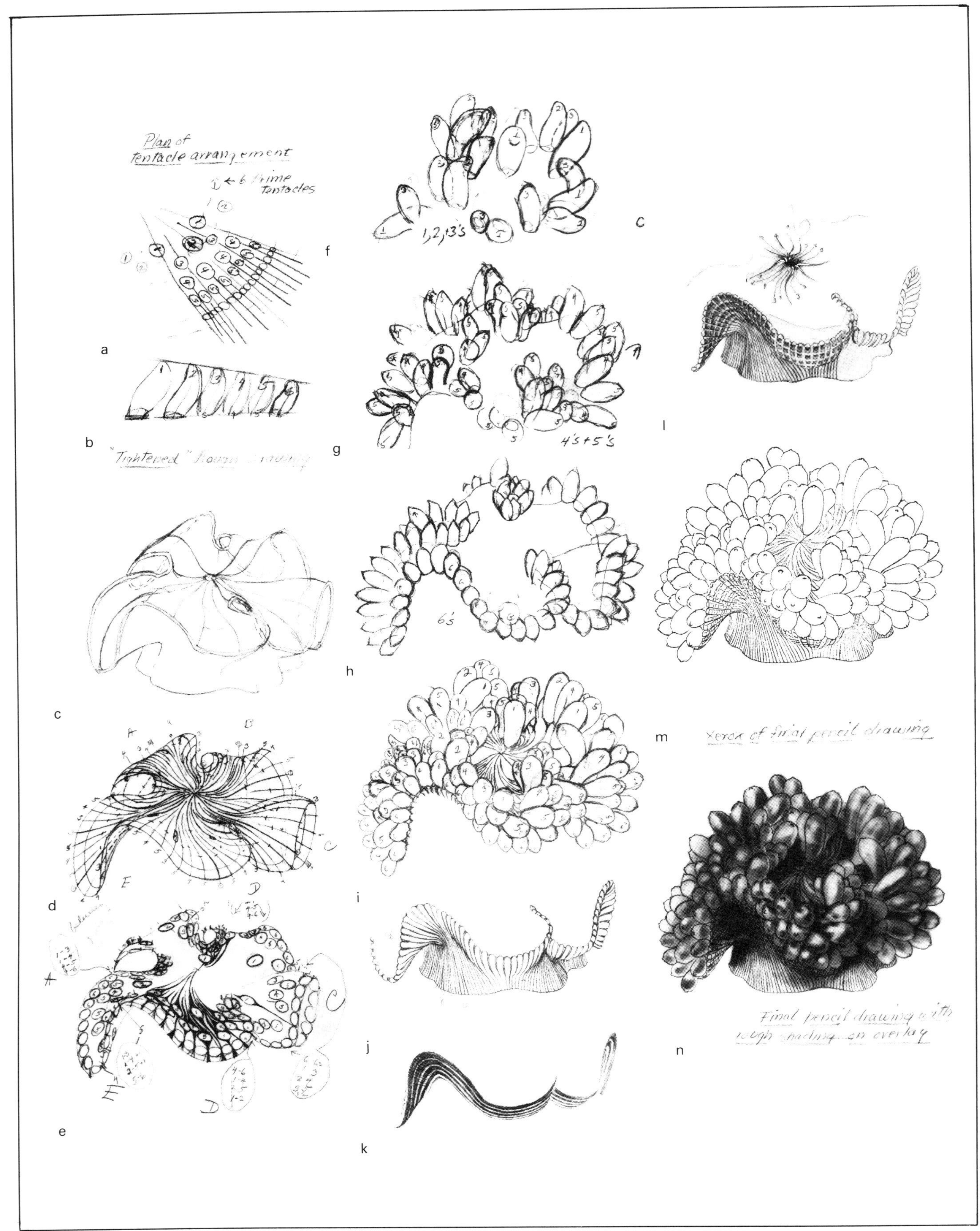
Plan of tentacle arrangement
← 6 Prime tentacles
a
b
"Tightened" rough drawing
c
d
e
f
1,2,+3's
C
g
4's+5's
h
6's
i
j
k
l
m
Xerox of final pencil drawing
n
Final pencil drawing with rough shading on overlay

benefit from the chapters on contracts and copyright.

At the end of this book is the Appendix, including a list of suppliers who can provide materials and instruments mentioned in the chapters. The Bibliography, organized by chapter title, provides further reading for those who want to pursue a topic in more detail.

Scientific illustration, a respected and demanding profession since the first scientific books were published, has suffered from a lack of suitable training programs and adequate texts and reference works. It is the intention of the editors and authors that this volume help fill this void.

Lawrence B. Isham
Elaine R. S. Hodges

I-3. The process of accurately drawing a complicated specimen in mixed media. This sea anemone, *Entacmaea quadricolor*, was drawn by Carolyn Bartlett Gast from a living specimen. After a rough preliminary sketch, *(a)* a plan of the tentacle arrangement was devised, *(b)* the tentacles were numbered 1 through 6 according to size; *(c)* a tightened rough drawing established a composition based on one pose of the living, moving anemone; *(d)* rays of tentacles were numbered; *(e)* bases of each tentacle were drawn; *(f)* a drawing of the 1, 2, 3 sizes placed their location, then *(g)* the 4s and 5s and *(h)* the 6s; *(i)* an amalgamation of the sizes arranged the tentacles; *(j)* the base of the anemone with its vertical pattern was drawn, and then *(k)* its horizontal pattern; *(l)* the base and radiating central core were combined; *(m)* final pencil drawing ready to be transferred; *(n)* rough shading on an overlay covering the outline drawing. The finished painting is figure C-1.

Part I Basics

What are the essential elements in the production of a scientific illustration? Knowledge of the anatomy of the subject and the techniques for rendering the final drawing are among them, but no less important are the process, tools, and background information that enable the illustrator to produce a detailed drawing on which the rendering is based. It is these aspects that are covered in this first section.

The steps to be followed in producing any scientific illustration are described in chapter 1. The scientist gives the illustrator a specimen and instructions, and they discuss the basic details of the project. The illustrator, armed with knowledge about the subject offered in part 3, first studies the specimen and then produces a proportionally accurate but rough drawing, using the tools and methods introduced in chapter 2. From this, the illustrator produces a detailed drawing for checking, and after that begins rendering, using one or more of the techniques described in part 2.

Some debate exists over the terminology used to describe the drawings that precede the rendering, drawings that may represent various levels of detail and completeness. The last one that forms the basis for the rendering may be a completely finished publishable drawing. However, it usually is in graphite pencil and most likely on tracing paper. Pencil is an excellent rendering technique, but it may not be desirable for all publications or all subjects. This last detailed drawing usually is to be finally rendered in ink, paint, or some other medium.

Because these early drawings are preliminary to the rendering—even to a final pencil rendering—they are termed *preliminary* and divided into two types: rough and detailed. Further description of these stages appears in chapter 1.

Choices of surfaces and media for the rendering should be influenced by archival considerations, especially if the drawing or painting is to endure. Chapter 3 describes the factors to be considered when making these choices. Sometimes the drawings required are simple "quickies"—not meant to last beyond the trip to the printer—but when much effort, time, and talent go into an illustration, its components should reflect that quality and be able to survive for reuse and display.

A basic understanding of how light affects form is another of the essential elements in the production of a scientific illustration. A drawing, no matter how beautifully rendered, will not look convincing if the highlights and shadows are placed unnaturally. Chapter 4 demonstrates through diagrammatic, photographed, and illustrated examples the many different types of light and shadow and how they are most effectively reproduced in two dimensions.

With understanding of these basic concepts, the illustrator has a foundation from which to build a solid and successful drawing.

1/Generalized Steps in Scientific Illustration

Elaine R. S. Hodges and John B. Randall

The scientific illustration is a joint effort by the scientist and illustrator to communicate scientific concepts to a specific, usually professional, audience. Drawing a specimen is the best way for either scientist or artist to understand its structure and to see its details. Because the illustrator may spend more time intently gazing at the specimen than the scientist does, the illustrator might discover new aspects of the specimen overlooked by the scientist. In the best of circumstances the scientist and illustrator share the discovery of some aspect of the subject matter and the documentation of this discovery in an artistic rendering. Or, as Lawrence Isham described the collaborative process:

> The actual mechanics of the process include a sketchy preliminary drawing, subsequently covered by a series of tracing-paper overlays (each overlay representing some kind of skirmish between author and illustrator) on which changes and additions accumulate until the preliminary drawing is no longer visible. At this point it is discovered that the preliminary bears no resemblance to the top overlay. Finally the author and illustrator agree that the process has been carried far enough (a decision usually triggered by a publication deadline) and a final drawing is rendered. At this point the author arrives, from ambush, with some changes he has been considering, and a bit out of breath. A discussion is held which includes strong language, threats of bodily harm, and the word "deadline" is heard mentioned in tones of operatic hysteria. When the dust settles, everyone congratulates everyone else, and some time later the illustration appears on the printed page—inadvertently reduced to column width! (GNSI *Newsletter*, March 1976)

THE INITIAL MEETING: GETTING THE ASSIGNMENT

If errors are to be prevented, both scientist and illustrator must ask the right questions and provide adequate information for each other. The illustrator should approach each new interview with pencil and paper, ready to take detailed notes rather than relying on memory; instructions are usually complex, and the possibility of later confusion is great if care is not taken in the initial meeting. The illustrator must be willing to swallow any embarrassment or pride and ask for definitions of unfamiliar terms. During the discussion, textbooks with diagrams are useful as references for anatomy and terminology.

An illustrator working for several clients or on a long-term assignment should find out how much time each scientist needs to prepare specimens for illustration. Dissections may be required, specimens may have to go through a series of chemical baths, slides may need to dry, material may have to be borrowed. Some scientists want two to three weeks' notice before the illustrator starts work or switches specimens; others are happy with one day's warning. From the point of view of the illustrator, enough specimens and instructions should be ready in advance to keep him or her occupied. Time is money to any worker or employer, but especially to a contract artist.

The illustration should be checked by the scientist at least twice during the drawing process: after the detailed preliminary drawing is completed and after rendering is done. It is helpful if the artist and scientist can work near one another to permit more frequent checking and interplay of ideas during the drawing process. When this is not possible, initial arrangements may be made by phone, mail, or in person. See suggestions for this situation under Checking the Drawing.

The following factors of concern to both illustrator and scientist should be covered in the first meeting to avoid any future misunderstanding of the assignment.

The Specimen

Identification: Obtain the specimen's scientific name or number or both. The scientist should note whether the specimen is a *type*, especially a *holotype* (the single specimen that is the standard for a species). Where there is a choice, specimens with as little damage as possible should be used for illustration, so that reconstruction and interpretation time are minimized. The scientist should also provide a list of specimens to be drawn, if there are more than one, with instructions on what to include in each drawing. Alternatively, the illustrator should organize the job in consultation with the scientist.

Care of the specimen: The illustrator should ask if the specimen requires any special care. Specific information on handling various types of specimens can be found in the individual chapters of part 3. In general, specimens fall into three categories, microscope slide mounts, unmounted, and live, and each requires special considerations. If the microscope mount is a freshly made or wet one, it should be kept level and protected from dust at all times. Unmounted specimens may have to be adjusted for better orientation, and responsibility for that task should be arranged before the illustrator accepts the specimen. It is wise to ask the scientist to handle and position delicate or rare specimens; if the illustrator is to do so, the scientist should provide precise instructions. Handling live specimens and holotypes is of utmost concern to the beginning illustrator, and it is essential that the scientist fully inform him or her of all details. All specimens (not only types) are valuable; they must be protected and handled with great care.

If the specimen is accidentally broken during the drawing process, carefully collect all pieces and show them to the scientist. Remember that accidents happen to everyone, including the scientist.

Taxonomic characters: The illustrator must know what to look for, what is important and unimportant. The scientist should explain in detail what is to be delineated and perhaps provide the taxonomic description of the species, if it exists, so that the illustrator can see what characters are important. If any parts of the drawing should be emphasized, it is the scientist's responsibility to say so.

Specimen series: Like people, individuals within any species may vary. Providing several examples of a species makes it possible for the illustrator to see what variations occur and better judge the normal condition.

Existing distortion: Any distortion in the specimen that needs correction in the illustration should be pointed out by the scientist and a drawn example of a restoration provided.

The Drawing

A rough sketch provided by the scientist of what needs illustration can prevent much misinterpretation of verbal instructions.

Representation: The scientist must decide, in consultation with the artist, how several questions are to be answered: Is the whole animal, plant, or object to be drawn (habitus view) or just a detail of it? Should the drawing be an exact portrait of the individual specimen or should it be generally representative of the species, idealized or diagrammatic? Is the specimen to be shown as symmetrical? A simple outline drawing may communicate information most clearly, but in some cases a more detailed rendering may be desirable. The artist should keep in mind that when scientists say a simple outline drawing would be sufficient, they might in fact appreciate more detail. With every technique, judicious use of line, tone, and texture can suggest form and inspire aesthetic satisfaction without too much extra investment of time. (See figs. 5-7, 5-8, 5-24, 5-25.)

Conventions: Each specialty has its traditional ways of representing the specimen. The illustrator should ask the scientist what they are. Among the questions to be asked are: What views are needed (lateral, dorsal, ventral, three-quarter, sagittal, cross section, exploded)? In what positions should the specimen be drawn? For taxonomic illustrations, for example, animals are often drawn facing left. Should dotted lines be used to indicate internal structures? A sample drawing for that discipline should be obtained. Maintaining consistent conventions permits the work of several illustrators to be easily compared and ensures that an illustration will be "read" accurately.

Technique: The method of reproduction, paper quality, and publication guidelines may determine the rendering technique. Does the intended publication require line art or halftones? What is the printing quality of linework and halftones? On what kind of paper does the publication print its artwork?

Convention or the subject itself may determine the medium. Hard-surfaced subjects may be well represented with lines, soft-surfaced subjects with gray tones. Most subjects, however, can be depicted with any technique.

Reconstruction: If there are broken, missing, or distorted parts, the artist must know if they should be drawn in their imperfect state or reconstructed. It should be agreed which of various conventional ways to represent reconstructions—such as with dots, dashes, a blank space—is to be used, or whether the specimen is to be drawn as though it were perfect (fig. 1-1; see also fig. 13-16). Should the subject be made to look alive, as is commonly done with pressed plants?

The Publication

The style of publication for which the artwork is intended can influence early planning or later stages of the drawing or both. The illustrator should try to obtain a copy before starting the project; often the inside of the back cover carries guidelines for authors and illustrators. It is useful to file copies of author's guidelines from various journals for future reference. A copy of the publication itself and the guidelines can answer many important questions for the illustrator. Others will have to be answered by the scientist, who may in turn have to check with the editor of the publication.

Plate proportions and reduction: What is the page size? Does the journal or publisher recom-

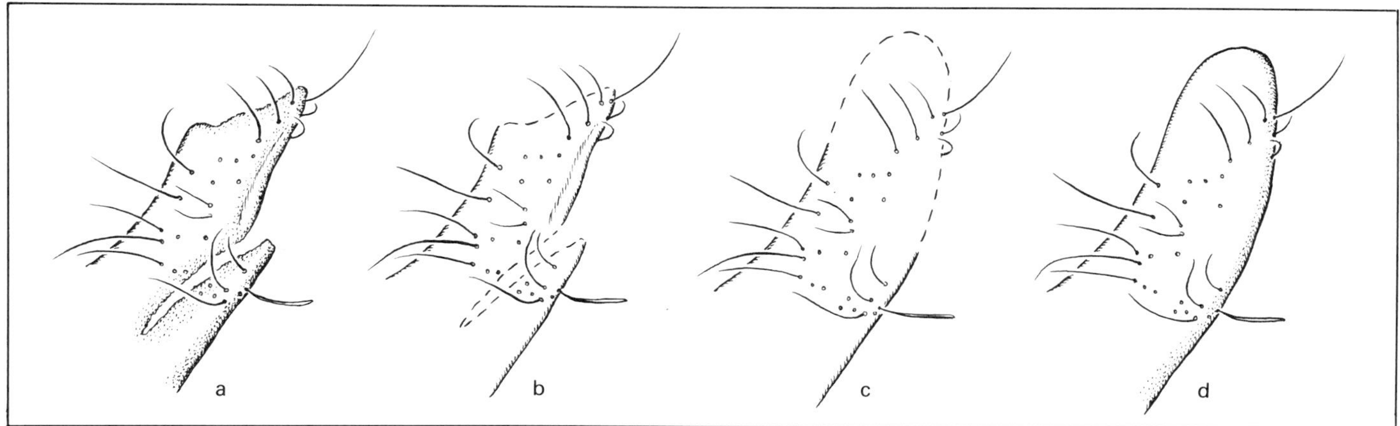

1-1. Studies of reconstruction: *(a)* "portrait" of a broken specimen; *(b)* dashes used to indicate broken areas; *(c)* reconstruction with dashes; *(d)* reconstruction as though unbroken. Valve of male moth genitalia. Pen-and-ink on Bristol board, by Elaine R. S. Hodges.

mend a particular reduction? Is the drawing to be reproduced as a full bleed (without margins) or is it to fill the same area as text? Could the illustration occupy the width of one column on a page with a two-column format? Answers to these questions may determine the size of the drawing.

Number of drawings per plate: How many drawings are to be placed on a page? Are these drawings to be designed and drawn as a single plate from the start (often done in botany) or mounted later? Some scientists have a system of drawing sizes that they feel produce the best reduction for the published format.

Labeling: Is labeling—words, figure numbers, leaders (arrows), scales—to be applied by the illustrator or by the publisher? If by the illustrator, is there a preference by the author or journal for a type size or style? Although the author provides the text and sometimes a rough indication of placement, the illustrator decides the final position of labels after drawings are completed and mounted. If labeling is critical to the illustration and its layout, it might be planned before illustration begins and even applied to the final rendering surface or overlay so the illustration can be designed around it. But this is uncommon.

Mounting: Does the publisher or printer have special requirements for the way artwork is mounted? For example, if laser or other color separation methods are used, the artwork is bent around a revolving drum, which requires a flexible surface. The artist who sends artwork on inflexible board to such a printer risks having the upper layer stripped from the board to yield a flexible surface. Knowledge of this in advance means the illustrator can choose a flexible material and send it on a temporary mount or do the stripping with utmost care before sending it to the publisher.

PREPARATION FOR THE WORK

After consulting with the scientist, settling points in question, and obtaining specimens, the illustrator is ready to begin the drawing process (fig. 1-2). This process may involve drawing the specimen four or more times.

After studying the specimen, the illustrator does a preliminary drawing. Usually this involves two steps: a rough drawing and scale obtained with one of the measurement devices discussed in chapter 2; and a detailed but still preliminary drawing for the scientist to check. How an accurate rough drawing is produced is determined by the nature of subject; each of the subject matter chapters recommends the best projection or measuring devices to use for its particular specimens. If the specimen is bilaterally symmetrical, a second rough drawing may be necessary to make both sides identical. The preliminary drawing usually is transferred to a surface before rendering, becoming the third (or fourth) drawing, and at last the rendering is produced, the fourth (or fifth) drawing of the specimen.

Depending on the experience and the skill of the illustrator, the rendering method, and the drawing surface, one or more of these steps can be skipped. For example, if film is used for the final rendering, the drawing can be traced as it is rendered, skipping the transfer step. A very complicated specimen, on the other hand, may require many more preliminary study drawings (see fig. I-3).

Studying the Specimen

Before applying pencil to paper, the artist *must* study the subject in detail. This point cannot be emphasized enough: *know your subject*! Take as much time as needed to study the subject thoroughly before starting to draw. Study the underlying geometric forms that give

SCIENTIST	ILLUSTRATOR
Provides material description specimen	Requests information Records information Studies specimen Makes rough drawing Makes detailed preliminary drawing
Checks detailed preliminary drawing	Corrects preliminary drawing
Checks corrections	Produces rendering
Checks rendering	Labels drawing
Checks labeling	Returns specimen
Makes copies before shipping original	
Stores copies	
Sends original to editor or publisher with instructions to return it to scientist	
Gives reprint and possibly original to illustrator	
Stores original	

1-2. The responsibilities of the scientist and the illustrator. Chart devised by Alice R. Tangerini and Elaine R. S. Hodges.

the subject its characteristic shape. A reducing lens or a lower microscope magnification will help by reducing the image of the subject, thus compacting the geometric shapes and making them more visible. The highlights (those spots that appear to be the brightest) can be studied by squinting at the subject to visually eliminate extraneous details and reduce the subject to simple lights and darks. Texture, the angles where different forms join, perspective, and foreshortening all must be carefully studied and understood. (See chapter 4.)

Many cases require thorough knowledge of the living subject if natural postures and surroundings are to be rendered accurately. Sometimes the subject can be brought into the studio and observed in an artificially arranged environment. To achieve the best results, an illustrator may need to spend hours studying the subject of an illustration, consulting literature, other drawings, and photographs, and making observations of the subject in its natural habitat. Sometimes complicated anatomy can be clarified with a sketch using different colors to represent layers or direction of rows, such as the rows of anemone tentacles shown in figure I-3. Strips of paper or fabric can be twisted to form a three-dimensional model of a complex structure, the strips following the directions and layers of intertwined anatomic parts.

Cleanliness

Cleanliness is vital for both the work area and the illustrator. Work areas must be free of dust, liquids, and anything that has the potential to spill on or smudge the illustrations.

Skin oils can be absorbed by paper, altering its surface quality. Hands should be thoroughly clean and dry. During the course of drawing, wash your hands often. To protect the drawing surface, try keeping a piece of paper under the heel of your drawing hand as you work. Or wear white cotton gloves (available from photography suppliers) and cut off the ends of the thumb and first one to three fingers for better control, leaving the little finger intact, since it has most contact with the drawing surface (see gloved hand in fig. 22-10). Or cut a paper cover sheet or mask to cover all but the drawing (fig. 1-3). Do not use a plastic or acetate mask; static electricity will cause dirt and eraser crumbs to adhere to the cover. Or use a wooden or plastic bridge as a hand rest (fig. 1-4). Clear plastic bridges have the advantage of being transparent; any bridge can double as a ruling guide.

Pencil dust frequently accumulates on drawings. Instead of blowing it off and possibly spraying drops of saliva onto a delicate rendering, use one of the dust removers described in chapter 2 to provide clean jets of air.

Physical Considerations

After years of leaning over drawings at a desk or drafting table and peering into a microscope, the illustrator is likely to develop eyestrain and neck and upper back problems. In addition to using an adjustable chair and good lighting, described in chapter 2, some simple measures and exercises may minimize or prevent problems.

While working, focus periodically on an object in the distance to relieve the strain of focusing close up on drawings. Have regular eye examinations. Farsighted people will need reading (magnifying) eyeglasses. Tinted glasses may reduce fatigue caused by the contrast in black-and-white inking, and magnifiers such as clip-on magnifying eyeglasses or headbands with mag-

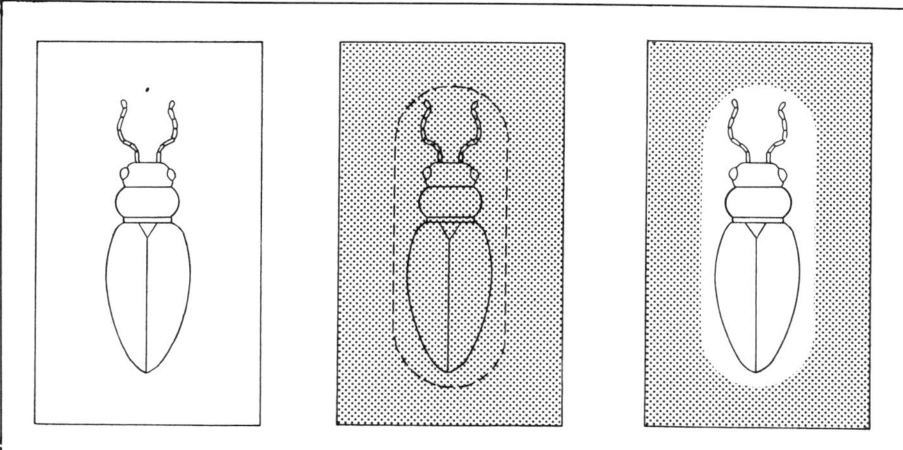

1-3. Steps in making a cover sheet. Draw a rough outline of the drawing on the cover sheet. Cut out this outline and tape the cover sheet to the drawing surface. Pen-and-ink and shading film on Bristol board, by Caroline Herbert.

1-4. Clear plastic bridge over drawing with cover sheet. Bee. Carbon dust on no. 00 Ross board, by Elaine R. S. Hodges. Photo by Vic Krantz.

nifiers may help with very detailed close-up work (see Magnifiers in chapter 2).

For the neck and upper back, exercises will help strengthen and relax tense muscles. Symptoms of neck strain or neck arthritis may be headaches or earaches, not just "pain in the neck." A doctor and a physical therapist should be consulted for proper diagnosis and exercises.

To reduce neck and back strain aggravated by bending over drawings, work at a slanted surface as much as possible. Although camera lucida drawings will have to be done on a flat surface if the microscope is sitting on a flat surface, an inclined surface such as a desk easel or small portable drawing board can and should be used in most other circumstances.

Long periods of sitting present other problems of poor circulation and reduced flexibility with the passage of time—even at a relatively young age. Frequent breaks for stretching and walking are important, as is regular exercise suited to your age and physical condition.

Sizes of Drawings

Once the subject is chosen, the size of the drawing must be decided upon. Will it fill a one- or two-column format?

In considering the size of the drawing, the artist should know the exact size of the illustration area (minus the caption) in the proposed publication. This will give the proportions and suggest the amount of reduction to plan. Estimating the space for a caption is usually guesswork. In general, the more drawings on a plate, the larger the caption. If the caption can go on a page facing the illustration, the entire area of print can be allotted for the illustration.

Depending on drawing technique and specimen, the general rule is that drawings should be slightly larger than the proposed reproduction; they may be up to three times larger, but usually no more than two times larger is desirable. There is a point of diminishing return. A drawing many times larger than the proposed size of reproduction will require a great deal more time to complete. Moreover, much of the detail may disappear when reduction is greater than 50 percent. Another consideration is that some journals require illustrations to be 8½ by 11 inches, the same size as the text page, to facilitate storage and shipping. If the illustration cannot be rendered that small, a reduced reproduction should be sent to the journal.

To determine how large to make the drawing, use a proportional scale to calculate reduction percentages (see fig. 2-6). Another method is demonstrated in figure 1-5. Making the drawing larger than

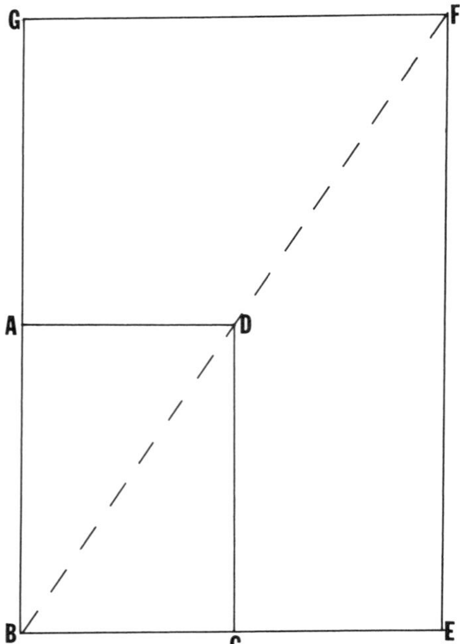

1-5. Technique for calculating drawing size. Suppose rectangle ABCD is the size of the proposed reproduction and a 50 percent reduction is intended. The reproduction will be one-half its original size; that is, the drawing must be twice as big as the printed version. Extend line AB its same length to point G and extend line BC its same length to point E. Then extend diagonal BD out to point F. Complete the larger rectangle by connecting points EF and FG. The rectangle thus created by points BEFG with the diagonal BF is exactly twice the size of and proportional to the proposed reproduction. The same procedure can be used to calculate any proportional reductions or expansions of drawing size by dropping perpendiculars from the diagonal BDF. Pen-and-ink on Bristol board, by John B. Randall.

the final printed size enables the illustrator to include greater detail, working at a more comfortable size. When the illustration is reduced for printing, coarseness disappears and a finely detailed illustration results—assuming the printer does a good job. No amount of reduction, however, will improve a poorly done illustration.

Layout

Placement of drawings must be considered when more than one drawing is to appear on the same page. There are no hard-and-fast rules for layout; each plate will have its unique problems. Although aesthetics are a major concern, other considerations affect the layout and may take precedence over aesthetics. Sometimes the drawing elements should be arranged to match their sequence in the author's manuscript. For instance, if drawings of parts of both sexes are to be mounted together and females are discussed first in the text, their drawings ideally should be in the upper left so that the arrangement reads from left to right. Some disciplines have conventions of how certain parts are arranged, and the artist should be informed of any conventions that might pertain. Important elements should not be covered up when parts must overlap. These considerations should be discussed with the author. After they have been taken into account, if necessary, aesthetic principles can be applied. Some of these are suggested below.

If the finished drawing is to be done over the preliminary drawing (by tracing, or if the preliminary drawing has been done directly on the final rendering paper), placement of the drawing is important from the start. Plan ahead. Draw all the objects in the final arrangement on rough drawing paper or draw each object on a separate piece of paper, arranging them when the drawings are transferred or traced. Inked drawings or drawings on a black background can be cut out and mounted after rendering (see fig. 6-2). The printer can eliminate cut edges when reproducing the drawing. Be sure to plan placement of labels at this time too, if any are planned.

Strive to fill all available space without overcrowding. The goal is to achieve a clear, balanced, uncluttered arrangement. If the relative sizes of the objects vary, arrange them on the page with the larger, heavier object(s) in the center or in bottom corners of the page, filling the remainder of the space with smaller objects.

Assess the balance of composition by turning the plate upside down or holding it up to a mirror. It should look balanced upside down and in reverse as well as in its correct state. Inconsistencies between the sides of a subject, especially if it is meant to be symmetrical, will be evident from these checks. Squinting at a drawing also helps to check the composition by highlighting basic shapes.

Some specimens have long projections such as antennae, legs, stems, or leaves that must be arranged in the most economical and graceful manner on a plate. One way to plan such an arrangement is to photostat, photocopy, or trace the preliminary drawing; cut apart segments of the copy; and arrange these paper parts until the solution is suitable. Tape the paper pieces in place and trace the arrangement. Note, however, that photocopy methods often reduce or enlarge slightly, even when set for 100 percent, and could, therefore, lead to inaccuracies in size. Another method is to cut narrow charting tape to the length of the projecting part, arrange the tape as desired, and use it as a guide for arrangement of the final drawing.

THE PRELIMINARY DRAWING

From the preliminary drawing, the final work evolves. In many situations, the preliminary is as detailed as the finished work. In some cases, the specimen shown in the preliminary drawing may be lost or broken before the final drawing is complete; in the case of living plants, the specimen may change in a matter of hours or even minutes because of growth or the opening of a bloom. The preliminary drawing and any notes the illustrator or scientist may have made thus serve as the only references for the finished product. That is why it is very important to make the preliminary drawing as complete as possible. There are exceptions, of course, such as when all that is required is a representation of the basic forms and proportions, with details to be added during the final rendering.

Before starting the rough drawing, select the position in which the subject is to be drawn. This depends on the view to be illustrated, subject matter conventions, and preferences of the illustrator, the scientist, or both. Also before starting, situate the subject in a manner that minimizes glancing from the subject to the paper. This simplifies returning to the original viewing position. Accuracy is increased if the artist's line of sight to the specimen remains the same with or without a microscope. The relationship of lines and shapes to one another changes with even a slight shift in the angle of view.

Basically, work from the general to the specific, making overall shapes accurate and then inserting details.

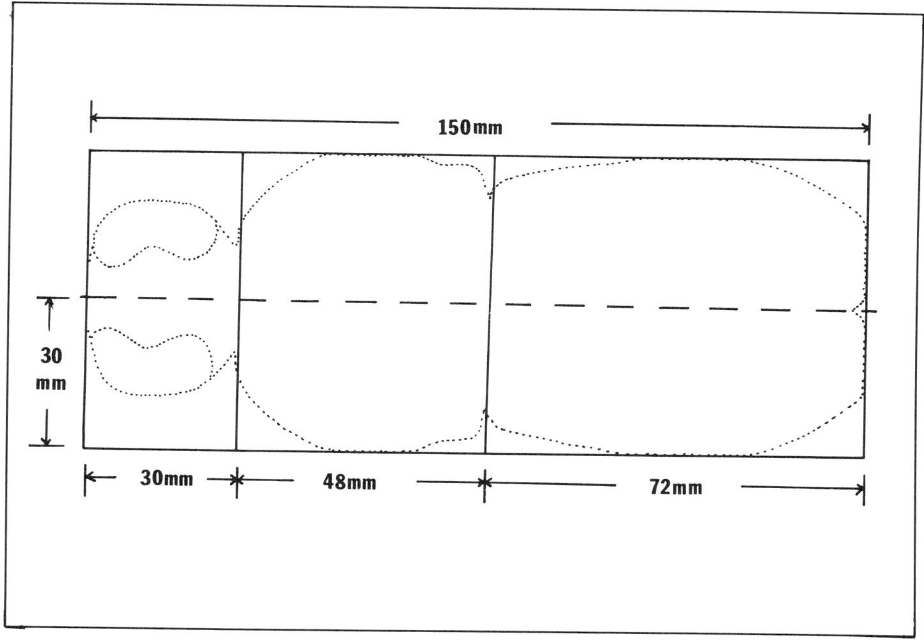

1-6. Method of calculating drawing size in relation to specimen size. Pen-and-ink on Bristol board, by John B. Randall.

Rough Drawing

The first step is to draw an accurate outline of the specimen's main structures on plain bond or tracing paper. Depending on the size and type of specimen, the outline can be produced with grids, dividers, camera lucida, microprojector, 35mm slides, telescope, ruler, or another device. Put the specimen's name or number and a labeled scale on the drawing after drawing the outline (see figs. 2-28, 2-29). Obtain the scale with a ruler or stage micrometer, depending on the size of the specimen (see Measuring Devices in chapter 2). The scale is useful even if it is not to appear on the final drawing because it makes it possible to return quickly to the same projected or magnified size if additions or corrections must be made (see figs. 1-4, 1-7).

If the subject can be measured with a ruler or dividers, use its measurements to calculate the size of the drawing. If the drawing is of a beetle that is 50mm in length, for example, and it is to be drawn three times actual size, or 150mm, mark off a space 150mm long on the drawing paper. If the beetle is 20mm wide, mark off a width of 60mm on the drawing paper. If it is 10mm from the anterior tip of the head to the posterior part of the head, mark off 30mm for the head, and so on. If the animal is bilaterally symmetrical, add a line to bisect the length of the rectangle just formed (fig. 1-6).

Concentrating on one body segment at a time, visually block in the major geometric forms and begin the drawing by outlining those forms within the constraints of the rectangles already drawn. Note how various shapes and lines relate to one another, their relative sizes and lengths, distances between and from their constraining rectangles. When these forms and their proportions are correct, you can add detail, working from large to small. Always use a ruler or some other instrument like proportional dividers to check measurements; if something does not look right, measure again and recheck calculations.

If the rough drawing is not the right size for the eventual publication, as can happen with camera lucida drawings, enlarge or reduce it with a grid, dividers, or opaque projector (see chapter 2).

Bilaterally Symmetrical Subjects

There are shortcuts for doing preliminary drawings of subjects that have bilateral symmetry. Draw one half, flip it over, and transfer it to the other side. Or draw a straight line on tracing paper to bisect the subject, then draw half of the subject on one side of the line. When the first half of the drawing is complete, fold the paper along the line and trace the second half of the subject, using the first half as a template. Take care that the fold of the paper, by its thickness, does not add extra width to the subject. This technique can be modified, especially for distorted specimens, as in figures 1-7 through 1-10. Be very cautious when making drawings symmetrical since not all subjects or their parts are completely bilaterally symmetrical.

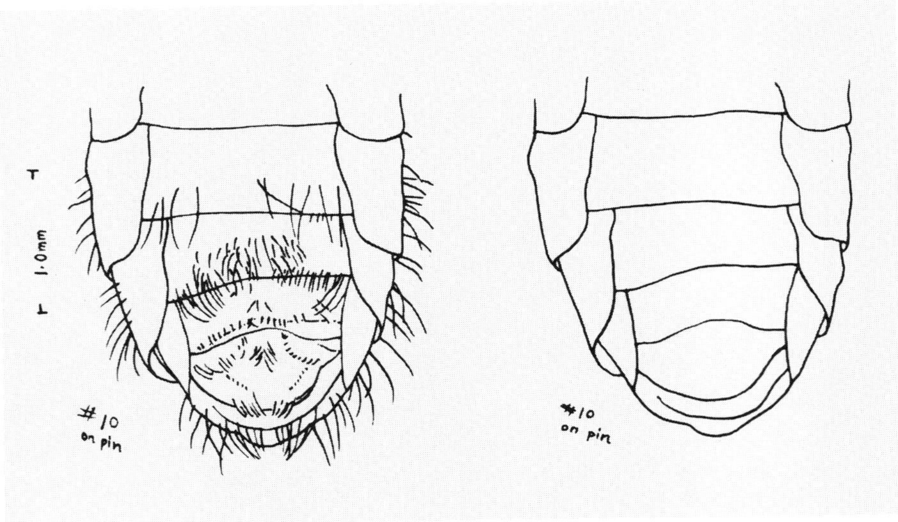

1-7. Making a drawing bilaterally symmetrical. The outline of the rough drawing is traced and the tracing paper folded down a median line with the drawing inside. The two halves will not match. The original camera lucida drawing is on the left and its tracing on the right.

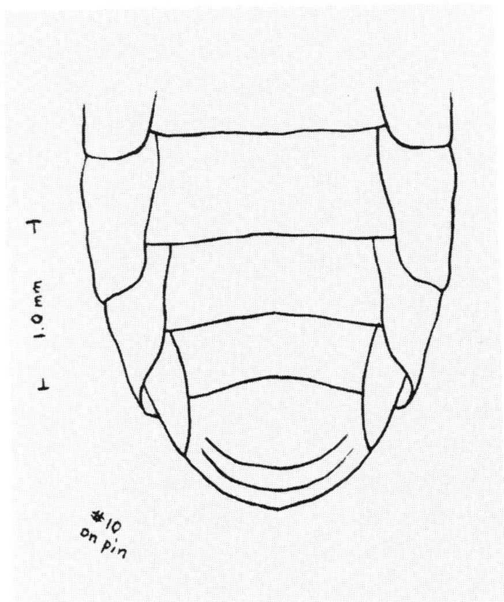

1-10. The paper is refolded and the compromise drawing traced onto the blank half, producing a symmetrical drawing when the paper is unfolded. The width of this symmetrical reconstruction should be compared with the width of the original drawing from the specimen. Widths at several points should match. Penciled diagram of bee abdomen, by Elaine R. S. Hodges. Photos by Vic Krantz.

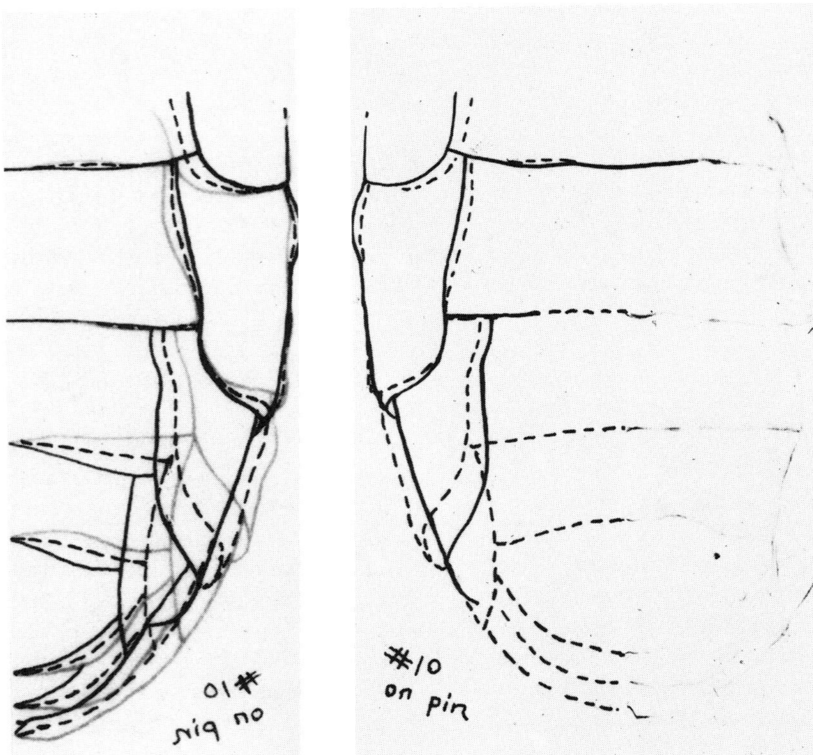

1-8. On the *back* of one half, compromise lines are drawn (here dashed for clarity), evenly spaced between the two original lines.

1-9. The drawing on the inside is erased, leaving only the compromise drawing. (Drawing shown is incompletely erased.)

Detailed Preliminary

Once you have prepared the correctly sized and proportioned rough preliminary, add details on tracing paper placed over the rough drawing. Complete the drawing with constant reference to the specimen. Using layers of tracing paper, trace on each overlay what is correct from the drawing beneath, adding improvements to each new sketch. This way, nothing is lost, as it would be if lines were erased. If you are using a surface such as good Bristol board that can take a lot of erasure, do the rough drawing in final size directly on it. Then do the detailing, erasing, and refining over the rough preliminary. Eventually the rendering covers the detailed preliminary.

The finished detailed preliminary drawing should show a smoothed outline and all important details and should include the scale and the specimen name or number. It should be clear and unambiguous, so that the scientist is able to determine how structures have been interpreted, thus reducing the possibility of error or need for major changes after the drawing is rendered.

Checking the Preliminary Drawing

Although the scientist and the illustrator share responsibility for the accuracy of the drawing, the accuracy of all published material is ultimately the scientist-author's responsibility. Therefore, it is most important that the scientist thoroughly check drawings against specimens, particularly during stages preliminary to final rendering, even if the illustrator is experienced and knowledgeable.

To prepare the preliminary for checking, cover it with tracing paper. Match register marks on the drawing and the overlay and explain to the scientist the use of the register marks (see Lettering and Other Graphics in chapter 2). If the drawing is on the final surface, inform the scientist that corrections and comments should be made lightly (with a no. 2 or softer pencil) on the cover-overlay to prevent surface indentations, ink, spills, and fingerprints, which may be difficult to remove. Questions and answers can be written lightly on this cover and retained as a reference after the drawing is completed (fig. 1-11). Figure 1-12 shows the completed rendering.

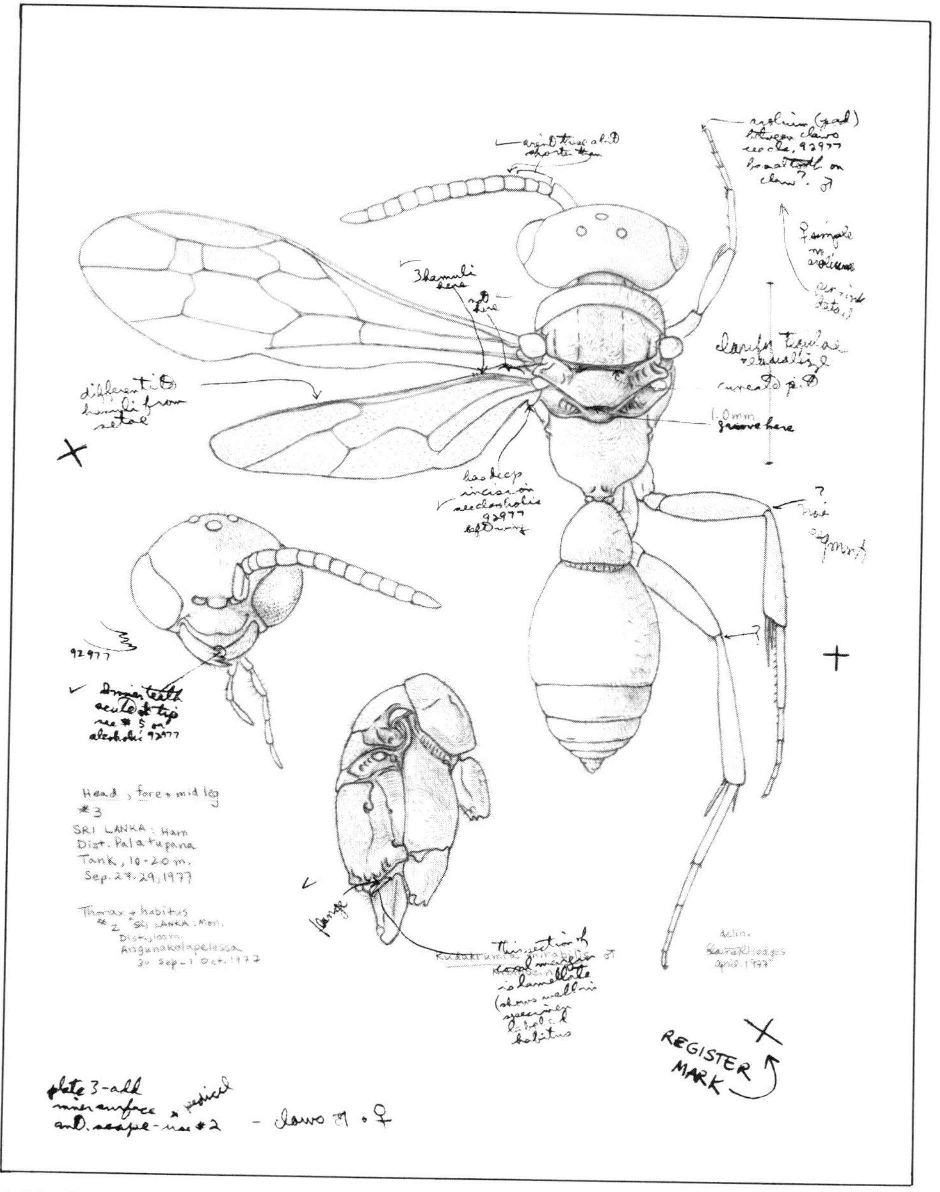

1-11. Correction of the detailed preliminary drawing. With the aid of a stereo microscope, the artist added details to the tracing of the rough preliminary shown in figure 2-29. The tracing paper overlay bears questions from illustrator and corrections by scientist. Pencil on tracing paper, by Elaine R. S. Hodges.

A very common problem occurs when the scientist looks at the detailed pencil sketch in a perfunctory manner, approves it for completion, and then, after it is rendered, discovers errors or decides to change a few "little" things. It is very difficult, time consuming, and expensive for the artist to correct a drawing after it has been completely rendered. With some techniques, corrections are impossible and the drawing must be redone if an error is found or a change requested after completion.

When checking the preliminary, the scientist should note whether important characteristics are sufficiently emphasized. Will these and other details survive reduction? Is it clear how the final rendering will develop and differ from the preliminary drawing? When all corrections are made, the scientist should initial the overlay so there is no question that the drawing was checked. If disagreements arise over interpretation of a microscopic specimen, the illustrator should view the specimen through the scientist's microscope (and the scientist through the illustrator's, if possible) to see if the image differs. Varied lighting and optical qualities affect what is visible.

Allow sufficient time for the scientist to examine the drawing. If you obtain enough specimens and instructions at the beginning of the project, you can plan your work schedule so that while some drawings are being checked, there are

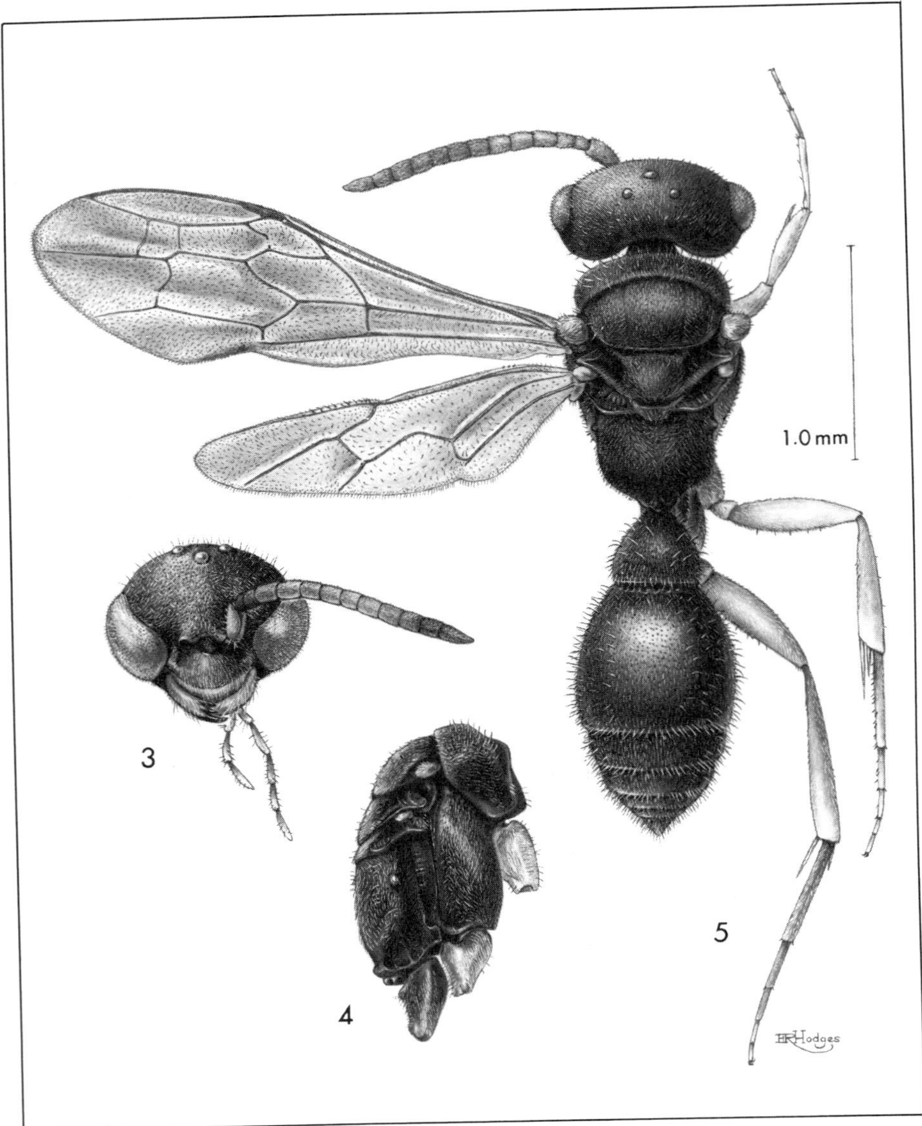

1-12. Completed, shaded rendering of drawing in figures 1-11, 2-28, and 2-29. Carbon dust on no. 00 Ross board. Details drawn with sharpened soft graphite pencils and no. 16 X-Acto blade. *Kudakrumia mirabilis*, male wasp, by Elaine R. S. Hodges. Courtesy of K. V. Krombein.

others on which work can be done.

If contact must be by mail, avoid frequent shipping of original artwork by sending the scientist two sets of good-quality photocopies of the drawings. The scientist can make corrections and comments on one set of photocopies and return it to you, retaining the other set. Ideally—one might say necessarily—the drawings should be checked against the specimen, although it is risky to ship specimens back and forth. If the scientist does not have representatives of the species that is being drawn, an alternative is to have a knowledgeable colleague in the illustrator's locality check the drawing. Photocopies still should go to the client, however, to ensure that the drawing interpretation is correct.

Be sure the scientist gets a final look at the corrected preliminary drawing just before rendering begins, to minimize (or eliminate) the number of changes requested after rendering is completed.

The scientific illustrator and the scientist should be perfectionists in their aim for accuracy, but some scientists are more demanding than others. Do not let an artistic ego block acceptance of corrections; an inaccurate drawing reflects on the illustrator as well as on the scientist.

TRANSFER METHODS

After the preliminary drawing is completed and checked, the next step is to render the drawing for the final illustration. The surface used will depend on the rendering technique. If the preliminary drawing has been done on the final surface—for example, Bristol board—the drawing can be inked directly over the preliminary, with no need for transfer. If, however, the drawing is to be rendered on a different surface, one of several transfer methods can be used.

With all transfer methods, use a sharp pencil to achieve a thin line. Thick lines may resist some media, such as watercolor. If there is a center line for a symmetrical subject or a scale, align this parallel to the sides or perpendicular to the top or bottom of the paper to which the transfer is being made before beginning the transfer process. Otherwise, the drawing or scale will be crooked.

Direct Trace Technique

The direct trace method is the simplest transfer technique: a transparent paper is placed over the preliminary drawing and the drawing is traced (fig. 1-13a). Several drawings can be arranged and traced onto a plate. Tracing boxes or light boxes facilitate tracing onto more opaque papers (see Drafting Aids in chapter 2). Tape the preliminary drawing on the light box, then the drawing paper over it; or tape the two papers together so they can be moved around conveniently while tracing. To avoid picking up graphite on the back of the rendering surface, cover the preliminary drawing with transpar-

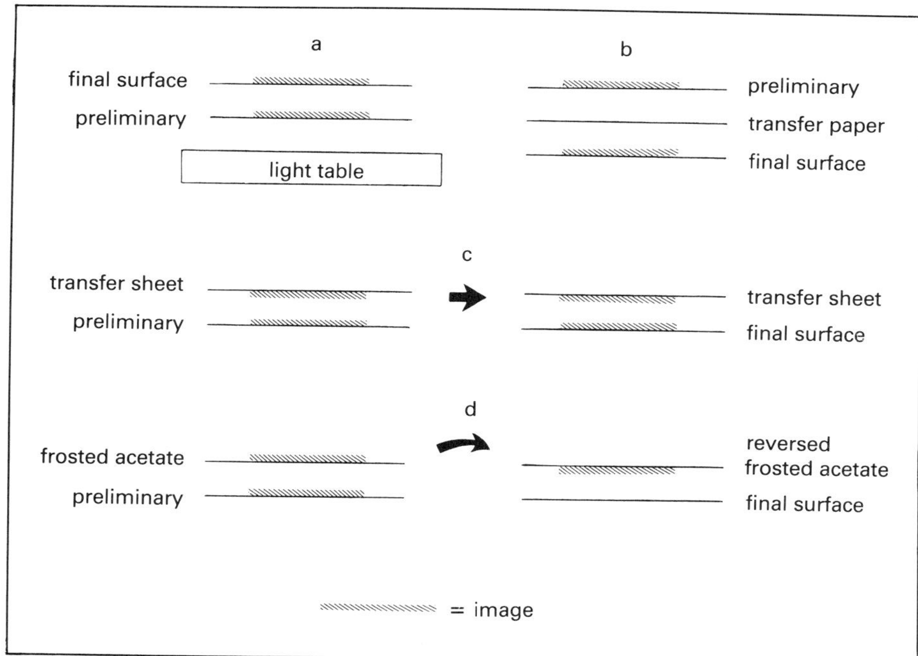

1-13. Tracing and transfer methods: *(a)* direct tracing; *(b)* use of transfer paper; *(c)* double transfer; *(d)* double transfer with frosted acetate. Pen-and-ink and shading film on Bristol board, by Sally Parker.

ent film, then lay down the rendering surface. Slip opaque white paper between the preliminary and the tracing periodically to check progress.

Graphite or Carbon Techniques

For surfaces too opaque to make use of the light box (such as scratchboard or clay-coated papers), one of the graphite or carbon transfer techniques may be used.

A simple one is to rub a soft graphite pencil or stick over the back of the preliminary drawing (either over the entire surface or only on the outline), then place this over the final surface and follow the lines of the drawing, with a pencil or embossing tool, applying even pressure. The graphite on the underside will adhere to the final surface, thus transferring the drawing.

Carbon pencil or pastel chalks may be used in lieu of graphite and may be preferred for certain techniques and colors and because they are less greasy than graphite. Excess carbon or chalk can be removed by rubbing with tissue, cotton balls, or a kneaded eraser.

Studio-made transfer papers avoid the need to blacken the back of the preliminary drawing. Rub a soft graphite pencil (or carbon pencil or chalk) all over the back of a sheet of paper. Position the preliminary drawing over the final surface and tape along one edge. (3M's Scotch no. 811 [Magic Plus transparent] tape will not damage most surfaces.) Slip the transfer paper, graphite side down, between the two surfaces and scribe the lines on the preliminary drawing (fig. 1-13b).

A method of making reusable transfer paper was described by Gail W. Guth in the summer 1977 GNSI *Newsletter*. Form a masking-tape border around a piece of tracing paper to keep the paper from tearing. Rub a graphite stick all over one side of the paper, applying the graphite as smoothly and solidly as possible. Moisten a piece of tissue or cotton with rubber-cement thinner or turpentine and very lightly blot and rub the surface of the paper. Use the solvent sparingly; too much will remove the graphite from the paper. Remember that rubber-cement thinner is extremely flammable; keep the can covered (see chapter 2). Dry the paper thoroughly. Repeat to fill any thin areas. This transfer paper can be used repeatedly until the graphite wears off.

Commercially prepared transfer papers, some of which come in a variety of colors, tend to leave a greasy line that is difficult to erase and may cause an uneven flow of the chosen medium over the transferred line. Graphite also is greasy, tends to smudge, and may alter the surface quality of some papers. It is wise, therefore, to keep the transferred image pale enough to follow in rendering but with a minimum of graphite. Although less greasy, carbon and chalk are too powdery to make reusable transfer paper.

Never use carbon paper intended for typewriter use. It will interfere with the rendering media and is difficult to erase.

Double-Transfer Techniques

As the name implies, this technique involves twice transferring the preliminary drawing, first to an intermediate paper (transfer sheet), then to the final surface. Lay a transfer sheet (tracing paper or frosted acetate with frosted side down) over the preliminary drawing. With a burnishing instrument (the most readily available and possibly most efficient is the thumbnail), rub (burnish) the transfer sheet, going over each line of the preliminary carefully to transfer the drawing to the underside of the transfer sheet (fig. 1-13c, left). Place the transfer sheet over the final surface and again burnish over the lines, transferring the drawing to the final rendering surface (fig. 1-13c, right; see fig. 8-6). It should be noted that each time the drawing is transferred, the image will be lighter, because some graphite or carbon is lost at each stage of the procedure. This can be remedied by redrawing the lines on the transfer sheet with a relatively soft pencil between transfers. Using a soft pencil for the preliminary drawing permits a darker transfer.

If tracing paper is used as a transfer sheet and it begins to tear, place a piece of clear acetate over it before burnishing. Acetate can withstand a great deal more abuse than tracing paper. Harder burnishing may be necessary, however, through the added layer of acetate.

If the image does not transfer well to a transfer sheet, a reverse double transfer can be made. Directly trace the drawing with soft pencil onto the frosted side of acetate. For burnishing, turn the acetate frosted side down over the final surface (fig. 1-13d). The resulting image, of course, will be reversed. This can be avoided if the preliminary drawing is on a translucent paper and can therefore be reversed before being traced. The reverse transfer will result in a correctly oriented drawing.

Once a drawing is transferred, refine the lines lightly with a pencil to make sure all important details are present, checking against the specimen and the preliminary drawing. Do not apply too much pressure; indentations in the paper may be difficult, if not impossible, to remove. And, like any other abnormality on the paper surface, they will interfere with the rendering technique.

RENDERING

Directions for specific rendering techniques appear in the relevant chapters in part 2. Here we offer general suggestions.

Practice

Before applying any rendering technique, practice on a separate sheet of the proposed rendering surface. Practicing takes a little extra time but is time well spent. By doing this, you may discover that the technique originally chosen is not satisfactory. It may, in some cases, be difficult to decide exactly which technique or combination of techniques will work best for a particular subject. With experience, you will know exactly what rendering technique to use before even starting the preliminary drawing.

To save money, a thinner, cheaper material with the same surface quality can be used—such as one-ply Bristol for practice instead of the three-ply used for the rendering. Old drawings, drawings with mistakes, or scraps of rendering papers or films make fine practice surfaces.

Shading and Details

Like the preliminary drawing, the detailed drawing should be worked from large to small, from general to specific. It is vital to capture the underlying form of the subject before adding details. To avoid any perceptual illusions or distortions when comparing the drawing with the specimen, orient the drawing in the same direction as the specimen.

Shading can progress from light to dark, or vice versa. It is wise to leave the lightest areas white or blank until the end of the rendering. This adds a sparkle to the drawing and avoids the grayness sometimes produced by erasure. Any detail needed in the lightest areas can be added last.

The time to add the finest details is when the illustration nears completion. To include fine detail, study the specimen millimeter by millimeter. Check the drawing with a reducing lens to estimate what will be visible after reduction in the published form. This is a very important stage in the evolution of an illustration. It is easy to become impatient when so close to completion, but such attention to detail can make a drawing especially accurate and attractive (see fig. 1-12).

As a last step, go over the entire background with a kneaded eraser to remove any unsightly marks.

FINAL CHECKS, CORRECTIONS, AND LAST STEPS

After the rendering is completed, have the scientist give it another check before any labeling is applied. The completed, rendered drawing usually looks different (if only as a darker version) from its precursor, and the scientist may see things not noticed during earlier checking. The final drawing frequently does differ to some extent from the preliminary since the illustrator tends to make adjustments and corrections during rendering. Providing a photocopy reduced to reproduction size, especially of a line drawing, helps the scientist visualize the printed result and the illustrator ensure that lines do not disappear or reduce to a black mass.

To enable the distant scientist-client to check the rendering, a good photocopy or photostat of line work can be mailed. A finely screened photostat of a tone drawing may be an adequate substitute for the original drawing, at less cost in time and money than a photograph. If necessary, the original drawing can be sent by registered mail, private express delivery firm, or some other safe method. The scientist can return the original the same way if changes are requested.

The rendering technique and drawing surface determine how corrections are made. The technique chapters in part 2 offer specific advice on making corrections.

Fixatives and Cover Sheets

With friable media such as pencil, charcoal, and carbon dust, and with any technique where smudging is a possibility, fixation of the final drawing usually is necessary. Fixatives are designed to more or less fix the medium to the paper and provide a barrier film that somewhat protects the illustration from smudging, fingerprints, and moisture. Workable fixative usually is used. Always test the fixative over the medium on a scrap of the drawing surface. Different brands of fixatives react differently with different surfaces and media, sometimes creating special effects, which may be desirable or disastrous.

Regardless of whether fixative is used, *all* finished drawings and even photographs should be protected by a cover sheet. Use tracing paper or cockle-finish bond paper to cover the entire illustration. The cockle finish provides some cushioning when illustrations are stacked. Do not use materials that produce static electricity, such as acetate, since they may pick up transfer lettering from the illustration, lift off part of a drawing in friable media, and attract dirt. Conservation supply sources sell acid-free papers and envelopes that can be used for covering illustrations (see Appendix).

Mounting

Mounting artwork on board helps to eliminate warping of the rendering surface and adds rigidity and strength that may be an advantage if the drawing will be mailed. In some techniques, such as those using clay-coated papers, the drawing surface is mounted securely before the preliminary drawing is transferred to it (see chapter 3, Adhesives). It is a good idea to mount all small drawings on a piece of board the size of the envelope or box in which they will be mailed. When mounting drawings, line up any scales or center lines of symmetrical subjects parallel to the side of the board or perpendicular to the top or bottom. Leave a margin of at least 1 inch (2.5cm) around the image.

As mentioned earlier, because many printers require artwork to be flexible for mounting on a revolving drum, it is a good idea to mount artwork so that the mount is easily removable without damage to the rendered surface. The publisher or printer's requirements should be ascertained at the initial meeting with the scientist.

Labels

Ideally, the illustrator will know from the initial meeting with the scientist if the job includes labeling the drawing, and if so, the size and style required by the publication. Consecutive labeling—such as a, b, c—should follow the author's manuscript and be placed in a logical, readable, and legible manner, consistent with other drawing series in the manuscript.

Also, because a common mistake made by printers is to confuse two different plates that have a similar size and similar numbering, the illustrator should not repeat numbers or letters in a sequence of plates or figures. Instead of numbering figures 1 a,b; 2 a,b; 3 a,b,c; number them 1,2; 3,4; 5,6,7. The printer is less likely to confuse two plates labeled 3,4 and 5,6 than two that are labeled a,b and a,b. Thus, advance planning by the illustrator and author may prevent errors.

Labels can be placed on the original artwork, particularly on line work. The most common method, however, especially for tone or colored drawings or those that might be exhibited, is to place labels on transparent registered overlays (see figs. 2-42, 2-43). These then can be photographed apart from the drawing, using line film to produce the sharpest image. Over friable media, insert a sheet of paper between the drawing and the transparent overlay to protect against static electricity.

The letter style should be simple and should, as far as possible, be compatible with type on other drawings in the publication. The most common type styles are Helvetica Regular or Helvetica Medium, with a reduced size no smaller than 8 point. Publishers who prefer to typeset their own labels want the artist to indicate placement of labels, or "call-outs," on a tracing paper overlay.

There are many methods available for lettering: hand lettering, lettering using templates, Leroy-type lettering sets, cutout and dry-transfer lettering, Kroy, Merlin, and phototypesetting (see Lettering and Other Graphics in chapter 2). If drawings for the same manuscript require different reductions and the labels are supplied by the artist, the point sizes of type should vary so that the reproduced labels end up all the same size in print; i.e., large drawings receive large letters, small ones, small letters (see chapter 27).

All labeling, leaders, and scales should be checked by the scientist.

Leaders

Leaders are lines or arrows with or without arrowheads or bullets (bullet- or ball-shaped heads at the ends of the leader) used to point at —or lead to—labeled or important parts of an illustration (see figs. 15-4, 15-14b and c, 15-36). They usually are solid lines but sometimes are dashed (see figs. 15-33, 15-34). Dashed lines should be used cautiously, because they can make an illustration look too busy. Some illustrators maintain that leaders with heads shaped like arrows should be used only to indicate direction (see fig. 1-16) and that leaders used for labels should have either no head or only a bullet- or ball-shaped head.

Leaders can be inked, cut from charting tape, or applied with cutout or dry transfer lines or arrows. The tape, cut-out, or transfer versions are available with white edging on one or both sides of the line, which automatically separates the leader from the drawing it covers, avoiding confusion between the leader line and a drawing line. When the white is only on one side of the line, that side can be placed toward the upper left of the drawing whenever possible to simulate light from the upper left (see fig. 15-9). Inked leaders can be separated from their underlying drawing with white paint carefully painted along the edge of the leader or by scraping away a bit of the drawing line that is being covered by the leader. Scraping works best on coated boards and films; paint is recommended for paper.

Magnification Scales

Magnification scales, if used, should always be included as part of the drawing or photograph, not relegated to the caption. For printing production as well as for editorial reasons, it is often necessary to alter the reproduction size of illustrations. If the magnification scale is in the figure legend only, a change in the illustration size creates an error. If the scale is in the illustration itself, a change in size will not affect the data (see figures throughout this book).

Artist's Signature

After placing labels, determine where your signature would best add balance to the drawing or plate. Sign the drawing unobtrusively. A signature should not be too large and should take into consideration what the published size will be. In federal government publications, the Government Printing Office removes signatures that look too large for the size of the drawing. If you intend to register the artwork with the copyright office or if the publication will do it for you, write the copyright symbol, ©, and the year after the signature (see chapter 28).

Masking the Image

To keep a white background in the printed reproduction of a tone drawing so that it will look as much like the original as possible, a drop-out or highlight halftone can be requested from the printer. When the printer photographically "drops out" or "knocks out" the gray from the background, however, light grays in the drawing also disappear, changing the effect created by the illustrator and possibly losing important information (see fig. 27-7). This can be avoided by cutting a mask for the drawing from translucent orange or red masking film. Ulano Amberlith and Rubylith are common brands (see figs. C-2, 27-8). Be sure the film base is polyester and therefore dimensionally stable (will not react to changes in temperature and humidity). Masking the image permits the photographer to prepare two negatives for the printer: one of the drawing with a screen that breaks the grays into corresponding densities of black dots and one of the mask that creates a window for the gray area and black for the areas that are to be white. What the masking film covers becomes a clear window on the negative. Anything left uncovered, or any holes in the colored film, will reproduce as white. When the two negatives are sandwiched and printed, the result is a gray (or tonal) drawing on a white ground (see figs. 2-45, 2-46). The printer can do the masking, but if the illustrator cuts the mask, printing costs are reduced and the illustrator can control the quality of the mask (see Masking Materials, in chapter 2, for instructions on cutting a mask).

The Mechanical

At this point, the illustration or plate with several illustrations (possibly photographs) can be considered a *mechanical*, the term used by printers for camera-ready artwork. Any needed overlays with labeling and masking film are in place. The overlays bear register marks precisely aligned with identical marks on the artwork. If any cropping is to be done—that is, if not all of the illustration is to appear in the reproduction—crop marks have been drawn on the mounting board or on the overlay. The use of register and crop marks is explained in more detail in chapter 2, under Lettering and Other Graphics, and in figures 2-42 and 2-43. Instructions to the printer are clearly provided on an overlay or in the margin, outside the area to be reproduced.

Identification of the Illustration

Once a drawing leaves the illustrator and the scientist, anything can happen to it. To avoid some of the more predictable pitfalls, on the back of the mounting board, provide the title of manuscript, name of the person for whom the drawing was done, name and address of the illustrator, date, rendering technique, name of the subject, and the scale of the drawing if relevant. Indicate on the back of the illustration or photograph, as well as by a cover letter, that illustrations are to be returned to the author or illustrator. Illustrations are likely to be destroyed after one year unless the publisher receives this request. This provision is written into most publishing contracts. Some illustrators order a rubber stamp that states the information or provides space for it, as shown here:

Title of manuscript:
Illustration of:
Drawn for:
Address:
Drawn by:
Address:
Date:
Technique:
Scale:
Return to:

The percent of reduction expected in the final printing sometimes is written on the cover sheet. If the drawing is one of a sequence of figures to be mounted on one board, pencil on the back of each drawing the figure number, author, and the publication. Thus, if the drawing becomes separated from its board at the printer's shop, it can be associated with the correct project.

Copies of Illustrations

There are a number of reasons why it is useful and valuable to make copies of the finished work, for the artist, the scientist, and the publisher.

Whether through accidental destruction, loss, or contractual agreements, the illustrator may never see the work again after it has been delivered. It is highly recommended, therefore, to make photographs, photostats, or 35mm slides of *each* completed major work. Make two or three copies of each illustration, at least one copy for personal records and additional copies to be used in portfolios for securing future illustration assignments. Photocopies are less expensive than photographs and are quite adequate for most line drawings. In case of loss, the photocopy can be used for redrawing, replacing several of the preliminary steps. A rough sketch of the final plate layout with figure numbers is helpful if a photocopy or photograph of the entire plate is not kept. This will simplify mounting the plate if the original is lost.

The scientist, too, should retain photocopies, photographs, and/or slides in case the original is lost. Photocopies also are valuable to send to reviewers of the manuscript.

Some publishers or editors actually prefer copies over originals for reproduction. Photographs or photostats may give good results with line work; slides or transparencies are often preferred for color reproduction, especially if the original is on a rigid support.

In most situations, the client will be glad to supply the illustrator with one or more copies of the printed illustration when it appears in publication. If such an offer is not forthcoming, request a copy and specify this provision in future contracts, whether verbal or written.

Record Keeping

Careful records of all assignments are invaluable as reminders of how and when a project was done and also for tax purposes for the illustrator. Whether the records are in the form of a logbook, card file, or some other system, the goal is to retain essential information. Figure 1-14 illustrates some categories from a logbook: name of client, species name, specimen numbers, type of drawing, magnification, medium, return of specimen, record of photocopy or photograph made of drawing, and dates for each step of the drawing process. A brief section (contents) at the beginning of a logbook might synopsize each job on one line with name of client, date of job, brief description, and page number indicating where detailed data begins. (A form for a card-file system appears in figure 1-15.)

Keep all preliminary drawings and illustrations from each assignment. These are useful as guides for future jobs, especially if notes on magnification and media used and photocopies of the finished drawings are retained. The preliminary drawings act as additional insurance against loss of the final rendering.

The scientist should keep copies of lists of specimens given to the illustrator, drawings requested, and instructions. This facilitates communication with the illustrator and prevents repetition of drawings. When many new species are being illustrated, it is easy to forget what was drawn and to find that the same species was inadvertently illustrated more than once.

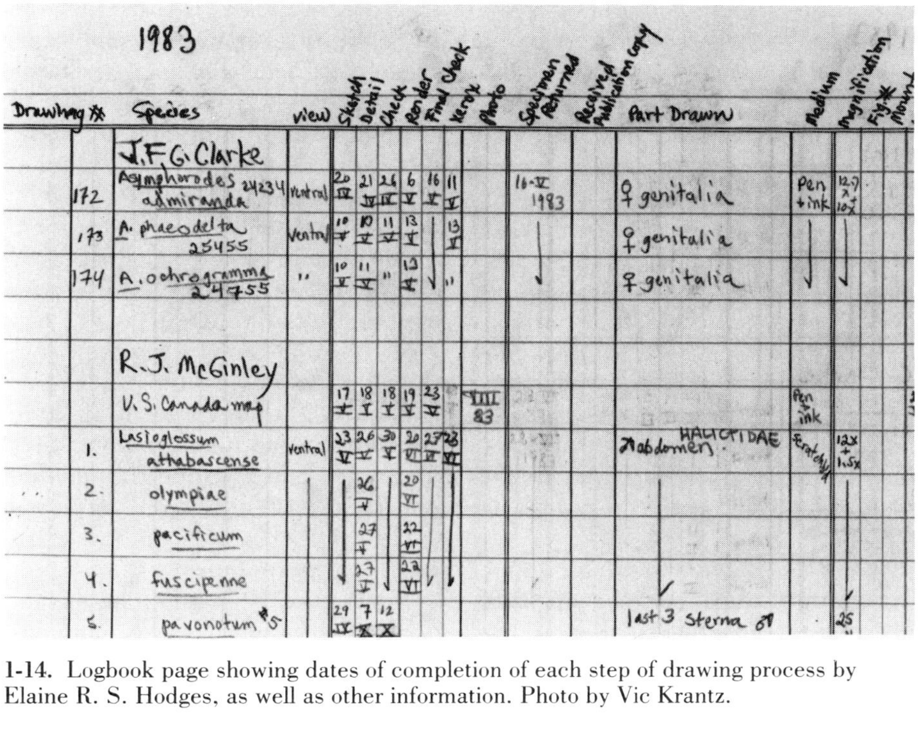

1-14. Logbook page showing dates of completion of each step of drawing process by Elaine R. S. Hodges, as well as other information. Photo by Vic Krantz.

Job no.: ______ Subject: ______________ Div.: ______ Scientist: ____________
Request received, date: __________ Requested completion date: __________
Copy or specimens received, date: __________ Work begun, date: __________
Completion date: __________
WORK PHOTOS ordered, date: __________ Quantity: ______
Proofs received, date: __________ Final work photo received, date: __________
JOB DESCRIPTION, quantity: ______ Figures on each of ______________ plates
Medium: ______________
To illustrate:

To be published in: __________________ Page size: ________ H ________ W
Record photo ordered, date: __________ Received, date: ______________
Chairman's approval: ______________________________
Specimen returned, date: ______________

1-15. Record keeping: example of a card file system. Modified from file card by Carolyn Bartlett Gast.

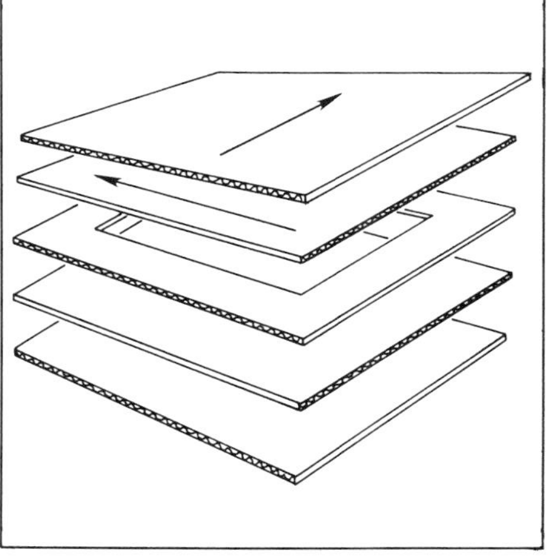

1-16. Packing unframed artwork for shipping. Cut five to seven pieces of corrugated cardboard several inches larger than the matted work. Discarded boxes can be used. In one, cut a window the same size as the artwork. Place the window piece in the center of the stack with the artwork in the window so that the other boards form a sandwich around the art. This will prevent the art from shifting, protect its corners, and provide rigidity. Alternating the direction of the corrugations adds strength. For thick artwork, additional window layers may be cut. Pen-and-ink on film, by Karen Schmitt. Based on suggestion by George L. Venable.

Handling and Shipping Illustrations

Usually the scientist packs and ships illustrations to the publisher or editor, but sometimes the illustrator has this responsibility or must ship illustrations to a distant client or to an exhibit. Portfolios of slides or drawings sometimes must be shipped. (See chapter 30 for more information about portfolios and the shipping of slides.)

All illustrations, including photographs, should be packed carefully for shipping with no sharp materials like paper clips or staples anywhere near them. Indentations, scrapes, creases, tears, bent corners, and smudges will show up in the reproduction of tone copy and may distort line copy. Such sloppiness also looks unprofessional. If you must attach something to the illustration, do so with removable tape applied to the overlay or to the margin of the mounting board. Do not place photographs or drawings face to face; any abrasive or moisture caught between the two will ruin both.

Multiple plates should be about the same size; a mixture of sizes may result in the smallest ones slipping out and being misplaced. If the illustrations are not the same size, mount them all on the same size mounting board.

Pack the illustrations securely. This cannot be overemphasized. Sandwich the illustrations between heavy cardboard layers with their corrugations alternating at right angles to one another. Acid-free cardboard and wrapping paper are available for special illustrations. For extra protection, cut a hole the size of the artwork in a central cardboard layer (fig. 1-16). Cover with a waterproof material such as a plastic freezer bag or small garbage bag. Place this package into a suitable flat, sturdy box, such as an X-ray or other film box or a flat metal container used for shipping motion pictures, or in one specially constructed to fit the illustrations. Some conservation and art-supply companies sell reusable boxes designed for shipping artwork. Enclose a second mailing label within the package in case the outer label is ruined. Do not forget to include your return address on the inner and outer labels. Tape the outside box closed with a strong material such as self-adhesive polyester tape, strapping tape, or duct tape.

If a framed or matted illustration is being shipped, perhaps to an exhibit, be sure to pad the corners of the frame or mat. Avoid shipping glass-covered art, but if it is necessary, cover the glass with strips of masking tape so that, if the glass breaks, the tape will hold the pieces in place and keep them from marring the drawing. Layers of bubble plastic are good insulation for glazing of either glass or acrylic. Large, framed illustrations should be shipped in a wooden crate.

Insure the illustrations to the maximum allowed by the carrier, whether U.S. mail or a private firm. Request a signed return receipt, if available. Remember that the U.S. Postal Service will not accept private carrier packages addressed to a U.S. post office box. However, private carriers may send a postcard to the post office box notifying the recipient that a package is being held for delivery.

Private delivery firms and Express Mail can be used for fast transport. Save time by obtaining a supply of forms and envelopes from the U.S. Postal Service and several private express delivery services, so that you can prepare necessary paperwork before going to the post office or before a scheduled pickup. Some private carriers will set up an account for customers, simplifying pickup and billing. Check current mailing regulations for U.S. mail and private firms before a critical need arises.

Concluding the Job

Expression of appreciation for work well done always improves human relationships. This is as true between scientist and illustrator as in any other case. Praise from the scientist for an exceptionally good drawing or extra research and overtime by the illustrator is always welcome. Thanks from the illustrator for the scientist's loan of equipment or thoughtful critique of work in progress is similarly appropriate.

The scientist—or other client—and the illustrator depend on one another to achieve a successful collaboration. The scientist counts on the skill of the artist to convey the concept or appearance of the subject. The artist relies on the scientist for the subject matter and information about what must be represented. Together they help build the structure of scientific knowledge.

2/Studio Basics

Elaine R. S. Hodges

Producing a scientific illustration requires some of the art supplies any illustrator needs, but more specialized tools are required for certain activities, particularly those involved with achieving accurate depictions of animals or plants. Specialized tools used for specific areas of subject matter are described in the chapters where they are most relevant. This chapter presents general information about surfaces, media, tools, and miscellaneous items that might be used in the process of illustrating several areas of subject matter. Not all items are essential; choice depends on the requirements of the technique used and the preference of the illustrator. Surfaces and media are discussed in more detail and from the standpoint of conservation in chapter 3.

In general, buy the best-quality materials you can afford. Good brushes, pens, pencils, and paper prevent the aggravation of frayed hairs, splayed tips, broken points, and uncorrectable surfaces that impede the production of a good drawing. Price is not always the determinant of good quality, but it may be a clue. Experience will best determine what works.

For the most part, tools are described here in their usual capacities, but keep in mind that the usefulness of a tool is limited only by the ingenuity of its user. Follow the manufacturer's recommendations for the care of any equipment. Especially important are maintenance procedures such as regular lubrication and cleaning where applicable. Never force an implement to work. If resistance begins to develop in a knob or crank that used to move freely, stop using it and have the tool checked by a reputable technician or the manufacturer. Continued pressure on a part that needs lubrication or cleaning might result in costly damage, perhaps requiring replacement instead of a little machine oil. Use tools with respect, and keep them clean.

Many illustrators invent their own tools and techniques. In creating new tools, or new uses for old ones, use principles of physics and measurement that will result in proportional, accurate depiction with no distortion. Also remember that scientific illustrations are intended for reproduction; any graphic application must not interfere with a clean, clear image in print or on film.

SURFACES

Individual chapters will specify the kinds of surfaces best suited to a given medium or technique. In the world of art, drawing surfaces may be called by different names —ground, primary support, or substrate—but they all refer to the surface on which a drawing or painting is produced. Sometimes *support* may refer to a board or canvas on which a drawing surface —a *ground* such as gesso—is prepared before the application of media. (See chapter 3 for a fuller discussion of archival considerations and the nature and uses of various surfaces.)

There are many kinds of drawing papers, and the choice an artist makes among them is determined by the medium and effect desired. They basically are smooth (hot press) or rough (cold press), but many variations exist within each type. Acid-free papers are always the best choice for longevity. Smoother papers permit more tightly rendered drawings because there is little or no texture to impede the depiction of detail. In some cases, a particular texture may convey the effect of the specimen. For instance, when a pebbly texture is rubbed with colored pencil, it resembles the texture of angel-wing begonia leaves. Colored papers provide instant colored backgrounds and create wonderful effects, especially with light-colored media. Oriental textured papers normally are not used in scientific illustration but might be considered for special situations.

Tracing paper is used in layers for correcting and refining a drawing from the rough through the detailed preliminary. It also can be used to make precise transfers and to cover and protect drawings. For these purposes, inexpensive thin tracing paper, sometimes called parchment, is preferable to heavier translucent vellums. The heavier, all-rag tracing papers can be used for ink or pencil renderings.

Smooth white paper is useful for rough drawings and for slipping between layers of translucent papers and films to provide a white background. White bond paper also makes a good cover sheet.

Bristol board is widely used for scientific illustration—smooth high- or plate-finish for ink and pencil and rougher medium- or kid-finish for pencil and wash. Named after the town of Bristol, England, it is constructed in laminated layers (plies) ranging in thickness from one-ply to five-ply. Two-ply is translucent enough for tracing a sketch taped beneath it on a light box or table. Two-ply is adequate for drier methods and ink line, but three-ply or heavier weight Bristol should be used for wash. All-rag Bristol, such as that made by Strathmore in its 500 series, is essential for best results, especially with pen-and-ink (see chapter 5). It withstands erasure and heavy burnishing.

Coquille board is a soft paper with a coarse or fine embedded texture. Rubbing a pencil across the surface deposits tone on the peaks of the raised texture, leaving the crevices white. It creates an instant stippled effect (see chapter 7).

Grafix (Duo-shade and Unishade) are chemically treated papers for shading; they must be painted with a liquid developer to bring out the tones. The papers come in a variety of textures, such as stippling or parallel lines; the developer instantly produces the effect of texture. The tones are very fugitive, however, so such papers should be used only for projects scheduled for prompt publication and should be stored covered in a dark place (see chapter 5).

Illustration board is suitable for all media, depending on the surface of the board; it is fabricated by laminating drawing papers to one or both sides of a board that may or may not be acid-free. The better boards are made with high-quality acid-free papers and an acid-free core. The surface may be smooth or rough. The advantage of illustration board is that it will not buckle when exposed to wet media and, thus, for watercolor does not need to be stretched. Its lack of flexibility poses a problem, however, for color reproduction using curved laser drums (see chapter 27).

Museum and mat board are substitutes for cold-press illustration board. Museum board is acid-free and comes in a limited array of colors. Mat board may be acid-free and is available in many colors and textures. Both generally come in three weights—single, double, and triple thickness—depending on the color. Not specifically intended for drawing, the surfaces of these boards may be less resistant to erasure and may be more absorbent than the surface on illustration board. Their main advantage for illustration is the array of color and texture available.

Coated boards and papers permit scratching of sharp white details and corrections on either a very smooth or a textured surface. Varieties of clay, silk-screened paint, or chemicals create the coatings, the thickness of which differs among brands. A thicker coating permits more scratching and reworking. Coatings created with chemicals (Crescent Line Kote) and silk-screened paint (Chroma-Rama, Color-Aid, ColorMatch) tend to be thin. The silk-screened papers come in white, black, and various grays as well as other colors and also are available with adhesive backings, useful for attaching to a board or for collage effects. Their paper support, however, is acidic.

Standard scratchboard (called scraper board in England) has a very smooth surface and is used primarily for ink drawing, but a wash technique on scratchboard is described in chapter 9. Scratchboard comes in white or black (see chapter 5). It is too smooth for pencil dust to adhere to, so it is unsuitable for carbon and other dust techniques.

Slightly textured coated boards, such as those listed in chapter 8, will hold dust and can be used with black and colored pencils, carbon and graphite dust, pastels, and mixed media. Line Kote works well with pastel dust.

Scratchboards made by British Process Boards (Ess Dee brand) in England have graphic textures such as crosshatching, parallel lines, and coarse stipples. These textures emerge when black ink is washed across the white board or a knife scrapes across the black version. United Process Boards is the American distributor. (See Appendix.)

Drafting film is translucent; made from polyester or cellulose acetate, it is used for ink line and pencil but not usually for wet media. It is described as frosted or matte to differentiate it from clear, transparent films that will not accept pencil or most inks. Some clear acetate films, called wet-media acetate, are treated to accept ink and paint.

Many films are available as matte (coated) on both sides or matte on one side and glossy (uncoated) on the other, each type having advantages for certain techniques described in this book. As explained in chapter 3, polyester films are dimensionally stable (will not shrink or stretch), whereas acetate films are not and therefore may buckle and not lie flat, especially in large sizes. Most matte films are coated with acrylic and silica, but DuPont's Cronaflex, designed for photographic use but used in many techniques, is polyester coated with a gelatin and silica emulsion. Before 1980, rice starch was used instead of silica, giving it a yellowish color. Its surface will come off if it is soaked. Paint applied lightly with an airbrush or dry brush, however, can be used on Cronaflex. There are several kinds of Cronaflex, most of which are used in photography. The one designated in this book is labeled U-C Tracing Film, with thickness indicated as UC-4 (4 mil) or UC-7 (7 mil).

Unlike paper, most films have a nonabsorbent surface; the pen glides more smoothly over them. Nonetheless, because of the silica, pen points wear out faster on film than on paper, so technical pens for use on film should have jewel or tungsten carbide points rather than stainless steel ones. It is possible to scratch the film surface with a very sharp blade to create details or make corrections, but the scratched line is finer and weaker than on scratchboard. Some films permit scratching and then inking over the scratched surface better than others. Denril (Borden and Riley) is particularly good in this respect.

The coating on film creates a tooth that holds pencil line and dust very well. But films vary in how black a line can be made with graphite, carbon, or plastic pencils, or in whether colored pencils are accepted. For instance, General's charcoal white pencil appears very white on Cronaflex but hardly shows at all on Denril, whereas Prismacolor white works well on both of these brands.

Film that is matte on both sides permits tentative drawings to be outlined on the back so that they can be erased or washed off without affecting the rendering on the front surface. Lines that are to be retained can be traced on the front to make them as dark as the rest of the drawing. But drawing or painting on the back of film can also be planned as an integral part of the halftone or color rendering, utilizing the dulling effect of the film's thickness (see figs. C-4, C-29, C-30, and chapter 10). Shadows are effectively placed on the back of film (see fig. C-18).

Because line reproduction requires as black a tone as possible, all ink work should be on the front of the film. Most films are slightly gray or yellowish and will photograph as gray; backpainting the entire back of a halftone drawing with white acrylic or latex paint results in more contrast between the image and its background, and it eliminates any shadow created by the image when the film is placed on a background. Of course, backpainting also makes it impossible to change colored backgrounds by using backgrounds of colored paper.

All films build up static electricity. This may help in holding friable media to the surface, but it also will hold stray particles and dirt, so backgrounds must be checked carefully for unintended marks. Some polyesters have chemicals added to the resin to reduce static electricity buildup; they are labeled as "anti-stat."

When using films, it is important to protect the surface from skin oil. Wearing cotton gloves while working is a good way to protect the surface, as are the other strategies described in chapter 1 under the heading Cleanliness. Some artists find it helpful to wash the film surface gently with a drafting powder such as Pounce, household detergent, or soap and water, using a soft cloth or cotton, to remove any oils before inking. However, even this very slight abrasion can damage the surface so that it will not accept ink. Test such a cleaning method on a scrap of the intended surface. (Flammable liquids such as rubber-cement thinner are not recommended. The friction of rubbing can ignite the vapors.)

Films can be used for tracing, but they are more expensive than tracing paper, especially polyester, and their static electricity attracts and holds erasure crumbs. More durable than tracing paper, frosted acetate is recommended for some transfer techniques (see Transfer Methods in chapter 1).

Canvas is used for oil and acrylic paints; it comes sized with a white coating or as raw canvas that must be sized with a glue mixture or acrylic gesso before use to prevent the acid in oil paints from soaking into the canvas and hastening its deterioration. Sizing seals the surface of canvas; a material such as gesso can serve double duty as both sizing and ground. (A helpful reference here is *The Artist's Handbook of Materials and Techniques,* by Ralph Mayer—see Bibliography.)

In scientific illustration, canvas is used mainly for wildlife paintings, sometimes for museum dioramas. It must be stretched and tacked to a frame that is properly reinforced for its size. Mounted canvas and canvas boards are available, but canvas boards are not recommended for work that is to last, since the quality of the materials is likely to be inferior to stretched canvas.

Hardboard (Masonite) is a board made of wood fibers pressed together. Hardboard sometimes is used for large acrylic or oil paintings because it is strong and thick and will not readily warp. Ordinary wood does not share these characteristics and should not be used for paintings. Hardboard is available tempered or untempered. Usually the untempered hardboard is recommended for paintings because additives used in tempering might seep through to the surface of the painting. Some people claim, however, that the high heat used in the tempering process probably inactivates the additives. The disadvantage of untempered hardboard is that it is less sturdy; the edges can crumble on impact. When untempered board is framed, therefore, its edges and corners should be cushioned with felt inside the frame.

Whether tempered or untempered, hardboard should be coated on *both* sides and on the edges with a ground such as gesso to prevent moisture from seeping into the wood and to provide a smooth, nonreactive rendering surface. Coating both sides prevents warping, which might occur if one side is treated differently from the other. To apply the ground properly, first brush the panel with acetone and wipe it off to remove grease. Sand the surface to roughen it. Then apply the ground, which also may require sanding to provide a toothed surface for retention of the paint.

Gesso is a coating painted onto canvas, hardboard, and other surfaces to provide a ground for paint. Traditional gesso is made from glue plus a whitener such as chalk (calcium carbonate or whiting) or gypsum (calcium sulfate). Acrylic gesso contains, as its name suggests, acrylic, a form of plastic. Either type can be tinted with some of the paint to be used. Traditional gesso is best under oil paint and is preferred for use on hardboard panels. Acrylic gesso can be used under oil or acrylic paints but is the best choice with acrylics, permitting similar materials to adhere to one another.

After gesso is applied and thoroughly dry, it should be roughened to provide a tooth for the paint to adhere to, especially oil paint. (Further suggestions for applying gesso are offered in chapter 10.)

White mounting board serves as a backing for many illustrations, either temporarily for layers of tracing paper or as a permanent mount. Black board might be used for drawings with black backgrounds. Mounting board also is used as a secondary support, backing another board to provide additional protection. The quality of the board should be considered in relation to its use (see chapter 3).

MEDIA

Although all the media used by artists, particularly commercial artists, can be used in scientific illustration, those that create highly detailed, smooth effects that reproduce well are used most often. To this end, adaptations of some traditional drawing media have been developed in some techniques. For instance, using a dry brush to apply dust made from charcoal pencils produces the tonal realism of a photograph, unlike the coarsely textured strokes made with the pencils themselves. Colored pencils can create smooth effects when each layer is burnished with a white pencil, which also changes the colors and makes them more brilliant.

Pencils

Pencils fall into three general categories distinguished by the way they feel when used as well as by their constituents—waxy clay type, charcoal, and grease. Pencils from each group can be intermixed only with care and in the sequence of fat over lean, meaning that the greasy pencils should be used only on top. Clay-based and charcoal pencils will not cover grease-based pencil marks. Charcoal will not easily cover clay-based or plastic pencil marks (see chapters 6, 7, and 8). Black charcoal and clay-based pencils usually are graded in degrees of hardness from B to H (soft to hard). They all may have some graphite (a form of carbon) and wax as constituents. There is a white "charcoal" pencil (made by General) that is soft and powdery but is not graded (see White Pencils, below).

Clay-based pencils and leads are made with graphite, clay, or plastic, among other things, sometimes including wax. These pencils leave a slightly shiny mark and burnish to a sheen; they can be sanded to make dust for use with a brush.

Graphite Pencils and Leads

Graphite pencils and leads in grades B to 4H are used for preliminary as well as final drawings; additional grades are available for rendering. The leads 2H to 4H are most commonly used for preliminary drawings; they are soft enough to provide a dark line yet need sharpening less often than softer leads (see chapter 6). The same grades of lead are available in pencils or for use in mechanical lead holders. The hardness of the lead is designated at one end of the lead or pencil (fig. 2-1); do not, therefore, sharpen that end. Some lead holders have a slot at the end that can be turned to expose a number and letter, indicating what lead is being used.

Maintain a very fine sharp point on leads by sharpening them on fine sandpaper or with one of the commercially available lead pointers or pencil sharpeners. To produce a fine point on a wooden pencil lead, use a knife to shave away the wood to expose ¾ to 1 inch of the lead. (see fig. 2-1), which will then fit a lead pointer.

Graphite Sticks

Graphite sticks are available in 2B, 4B, and 6B grades. They are used for making transfer paper (see Transfer Methods in chapter 1).

Mechanical Pencils

Mechanical pencils are available with lead diameters as fine as 0.3 mm and in varying hardnesses, like graphite (see fig. 2-1). These pencils offer a consistent point, thus eliminating the constant repointing required with lead holders and wooden pencils.

Colored Pencils

Colored pencils are useful for differentiating structures when interpreting complicated anatomy. They also are effective as rendering media. (See chapter 6 for a full discussion.)

White Pencils

White pencils may be clay-based (waxy) or charcoal. They are used instead of or with paint and scratching for highlights or white hairs when a soft effect is desired, and also for drawing on dark backgrounds. Waxy white pencils layered with colored pencils produce more brilliant colors. Different brands produce unpredictably different results on various surfaces, so experimentation is advised. For instance, on Denril polyester, Prismacolor white is much whiter than Mongol white, although both have waxy textures, and Koh-I-Soft RP 4700 appears whiter than General's equally powdery charcoal white. Conté white is very faint on Denril. On frosted acetate, Koh-I-Soft and General's charcoal white are whitest, Prismacolor and Conté next, and Mongol faintest. Fixatives make some white pencil marks translucent (see chapters 1, 6, and 8).

Film Pencils

Film pencils are made of plastic (polymer) and are designed for use on film. These look and handle like graphite and can be used like

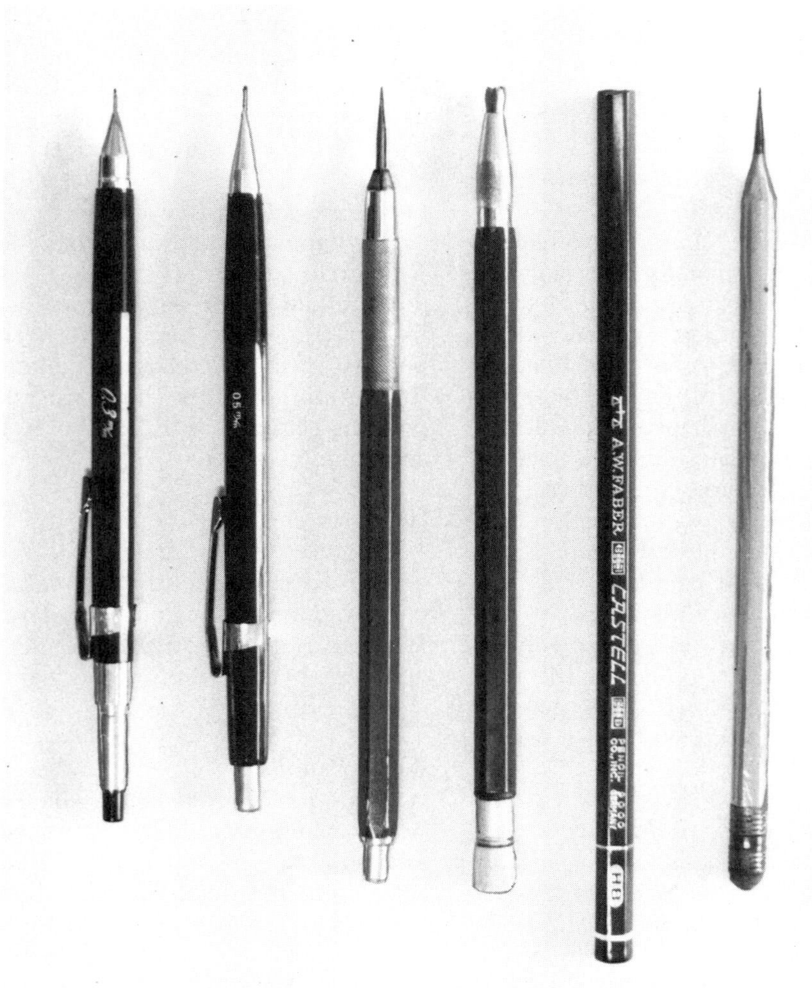

2-1. Types of pencils and lead holders. From left to right: two mechanical pencils with very thin leads, 0.3 and 0.5mm; two lead holders; an unsharpened pencil bearing its lead designation at one end; a wood-encased pencil in which the lead has been exposed by shaving with a sharp knife. Photo courtesy of John B. Randall.

graphite on film or paper. Film pencils are available in fewer hardness grades than graphite pencils are, and the hardness of lead is designated by different letters (such as E, N, H, or K) according to the manufacturers.

Charcoal-based pencils are for rendering in carbon dust, on coquille board, and for creating dark transfers. Some brands are Wolff's carbon, Conté à Paris Charcoal no. 728, Conté Pierre Noire no. 1710, General's Charcoal no. 557, Eberhard Faber Koal Blak no. 230, Ritmo Charcoal, and similar pencils made by Grumbacher, Lyra (Alvin Co.), and Weber. How black a mark they make depends on the drawing surface and the grade of pencil, with the softest grades being blackest and most powdery (see chapters 7 and 8). Experimentation is recommended. The British Wolff's carbon pencil has been a standby of the scientific illustrator since the early 1900s and is recommended in several chapters. Unfortunately, it was discontinued in the mid-1980s. The Conté Pierre Noire, Conté à Paris, and the new Italian-made Ritmo pencil—especially the 3B for making dust—seem to be fairly good substitutes. Conté pencils are generally available in art-supply stores; Ritmo is sold by Jerry's Artarama (see the Appendix).

Grease-based pencils are used for coquille-board drawings. These include lithographic crayons, Staedtler-Mars Omnichrom, and similar pencils that will mark on glass. They create an intense black but are not easily erased.

Pastels

Pastels are used for pastel dust and for detail in mixed media. Soft, powdery pastels are used to make dust. The wood-encased, pencil-shaped pastels such as Carb-Othello permit the rendering of details. The chunky shapes of hard and oil pastels might be useful for large, loose drawings, but they cannot render details (see chapters 7 and 9 and fig. C-5).

Inks and Paints

India ink is the ink most often used in scientific illustration. It contains lampblack or other blacks, glue or shellac, and other additives. Paints are pigmented mixtures usually used for full-color paintings. Techniques for their use are covered in chapters 9, 10, and 11. Methods of application range from a wash for broad areas to tiny strokes with a dry brush for detail.

Ink is used for rendering with pen and brush on smooth paper, film, or scratchboard. India ink is intensely black and waterproof, but brands and types vary in blackness and in whether they are designed for paper or film. Both technical pens and conventional dip pens such as crowquill should be available to the illustrator because they create different effects (see chapter 5 and figs. 5-1, 5-3). Ink used as a wash is discussed in chapter 9. Colored inks seldom are used in scientific illustration because their colors traditionally have not been intense or permanent. Because they are liquids, inks are convenient for airbrush use; however, the shellac in india ink can clog an airbrush if it is not cleaned thoroughly (see chapter 11).

Watercolor is referred to as transparent; it is the most commonly used paint in scientific illustration. It is particularly effective when used in translucent, thin washes but is often applied more thickly with a dry brush (see chapter 9).

Dyes are used like watercolor. The two advantages of dyes are their intense color and their liquid formulation, which makes them easy to use in an airbrush. They are, however, very fugitive. Paintings done with dyes must be protected from light to preserve them until reproduction; they cannot be expected to retain their color intensity once exposed to light.

Gouache is watercolor that has been made opaque with the addition of whiteners, gum arabic, dextrin, or other additives. Designer colors, sold in tubes and pans, are gouache, as are Grumbacher Gamma retouch gray paints in tubes used for retouching photographs. The opaqueness of gouache gives it certain advantages over transparent watercolor (see chapter 10).

Casein paint is made from skimmilk curd combined with preservatives and other additives; it is available in tubes. Water-soluble when wet, casein becomes insoluble when it dries. It does not shift color after drying, and the colors are lightfast. It is very brittle when dry and therefore should be used only on a firm support such as a hardboard panel or illustration board. This becomes a concern if a flexible surface is required by the printer; but a color transparency can be submitted in place of the original. If applied very thinly, casein can be used on heavy paper. Thinned paint will have reduced brilliance, however. Casein may be used like gouache (see chapter 10) and in an airbrush (see chapter 11). Shiva is a major manufacturer of casein.

Acrylic paint is a very fast-drying plastic paint. Although water-soluble when wet, acrylics become hard and insoluble after drying. They can be handled like watercolors or oils (see chapter 10).

Oil and alkyd paints are slow drying and soluble in oil or turpentine. The slow drying time permits changes to be made easily. Oils are used primarily for wildlife paintings, with which deadlines are less often an issue. Because of their limited use in scientific illustration, the technique of oil painting is not described in this book. Nonetheless, a way to combine them with acrylics is explained in chapter 10, and they are suggested in chapter 20 as a medium for underwater sketching. Alkyd paint dries much faster than oil but slower than water-based paint. In addition to turpentine, alkyds are thinned with alkyd resin media. As a relatively new medium, alkyds have not been used much in scientific illustration but deserve more attention (see Gerald P. Hodge's article "Alkyd Paint for Scientific and Medical Illustration" in the *Journal of Biocommunication*, listed in the Bibliography).

White ink and paint are used to cover errors and to create highlights. Do not use typewriter correction white (such as Liquid Paper or Wite-Out), because it dries too fast and may flake off. For pens, use liquids such as Pen-Opake and FW non-clogging waterproof ink (both Steig); for brushes, use a thicker-consistency paint such as Gamma all-purpose white (Grumbacher), Pro White (Steig), Bleed Proof White (Dr. Ph. Martin's), and Steig Graphic White.

DRAWING TOOLS

Pens

Both conventional (dip-type, such as crowquill) and technical (such as Rapidograph) pens belong in the studio and their techniques in the repertoire of the scientific illustrator. In chapter 5, pens for drawing and their use are covered in detail. Two other types are discussed here.

Lettering pens are used for lettering or for drawing broad strokes. Both of these uses are rare in scientific illustration. The lettering pen may consist of a holder plus a nib (point) with a reservoir that can be filled with ink or paint from a dropper (an eyedropper or one that sometimes is built into an ink bottle cover), or they may be fountain pens. The nib has a slightly slanted, sharp, flat tip rather than a point. This tip can make sharply edged thick lines when the flat edge is placed squarely on the paper and pulled toward the artist, or it can make thin lines when the pen is turned so that the tip is sideways. The ability to convert quickly from thick to thin lines makes these pens ideal for calligraphy. About six nib widths and a left-handed version with the slant reversed from the right-handed style are usually available.

Ruling pens are designed to draw lines. They are metal units consisting of a handle with two long prongs (the nibs)—one straight and one slightly curved—connected by a threaded bolt with a wheel on one side; when turned, the wheel screws onto the bolt, pulling one of the nibs closer to the other, thus creating a smaller space between the two, or unscrews, creating a larger space. The space between the nibs determines the width of the drawn line. Ink or paint is dripped with an eyedropper into the space, which constitutes a reservoir. The pen is placed so that both nibs are on the paper with one nib against a straightedge or curve, and the pen is pulled toward the illustrator. A variation of the ruling pen is the *railroad pen*, which essentially is a double ruling pen with three nibs. It draws precisely parallel lines, for instance, for roads or railroads on maps.

Because line widths cannot be

repeated predictably and the pens must be refilled frequently if broad lines are being drawn, ruling pens have been replaced by technical pens for drawing lines with ink. Few people use ruling pens today. If lines must be drawn with paint, however, a ruling pen is useful because it cannot clog like a technical pen.

Sharpeners

Honing or sharpening surfaces include Arkansas oilstone, emery cloth, or fine sandpaper, all of which are used to sharpen knives and conventional pen nibs (see fig. 5-1d).

Sandpaper is used for pointing pencils and conventional pen nibs, sharpening knives, or creating dust for certain techniques such as carbon dust. For creating the dust, the finest grit is best; rough sandpaper has large particles that can come off and contaminate the dust, eventually scratching the drawing surface. Emery cloth, crocus cloth, or no. 400 or finer sandpaper have very fine grit.

Pencil sharpeners are used for sharpening conventional pencils. Electric sharpeners save time if a rendering is being done with wood-encased pencils, especially colored ones.

Lead pointers are used for sharpening pencil leads or conventional pencils with the lead exposed after whittling back the wood. Some adjust for variable-point tapers (fig. 2-2). Keep a piece of foam or carpet nearby for wiping off excess pencil dust.

Cutting Tools

Knives and blades are used for corrections or creating sharp lines on film or coated boards; cutting drafting and other tapes; cutting masking, shading, and other films; lettering; and performing assorted studio activities. The X-Acto knife, with its many shapes of blades, is versatile, with nos. 16, 10, and 11

2-2. Lead pointer. Photo courtesy of John B. Randall.

blades most recommended (Fig. 5-1j). The stainless steel no. 21 blade, shaped like no. 11, may hold an edge longer than the other blades. The pointed shapes of the no. 11 and no. 21 blades are very useful for lifting edges of tape and film. Surgical knives and blades accomplish the same goals (fig. 5-1k). Disposable frisket knives hold an edge quite well. Always use a sharp blade. For safety, discard dull blades in a box or jar.

Scratch knives, also called scrapers, are pointed to make lines and curved to scrape broad areas (see fig. 5-1i). They are designed for use on scratchboard. A no. 16 X-Acto knife works well as a scratch knife for lines and dots, as does an engraving tool (fig. 5-1l).

A mat knife is valuable for cutting mats and boards and for trimming photographs.

Single-edged razor blades sometimes are used for small cutting jobs, including plant dissection and scratchboard drawing.

Many types of knives are available; some make double cuts with twin blades, others swivel to cut around curves and are used to cut masking film.

Scissors, both long and short bladed, are useful for various cutting and trimming chores.

Paper cutters are used for reducing large papers and boards to manageable size and for trimming paper edges to right angles. Most paper cutters are expensive, and a mat knife used with a metal straightedge can accomplish the same end, but a paper cutter is a great time saver. Some have safety features to prevent accidents.

Erasers

A wide variety of erasers is available, and some are better suited to specific media and surfaces than others. The most useful for all purposes are the kneaded rubber eraser and pencil-shaped soft erasers of the sort designed for use on offset master or multilith plates. Both can be used for drawing as well as erasing. In some techniques presented in part 2, the eraser does as much drawing as a pencil or pen. Regardless of the type of eraser used, if the medium smears while being erased, rub the eraser on scrap paper to clean it before continuing to erase.

Pencil-shaped soft erasers are relatively soft and wood-encased. They can be sharpened in a pencil sharpener to produce a sharp point for drawing or for erasing tiny areas. The opposite end can be cut into a chisel shape to draw sharp lines or to erase close to an edge. The best kinds are labeled for use on offset master or multilith plates, such as the Eberhard Faber Kleen-Off no. 41 and the AM Multigraphics Division no. 40-2547.

Kneaded rubber erasers leave almost no crumbs, and their soiled surfaces can be kneaded and embedded, exposing a clean eraser surface. Softer kneaded rubber types (such as a blue version) can be kneaded together with the harder gray type to create a more workable hybrid, a method developed by illustrator T. Britt Griswold. The kneaded rubber eraser also is useful for propping specimens, both dry and in alcohol.

Artgum erasers are rectangular golden blocks that crumble easily. They are used for general cleanup around drawings. The crumbs, however, are a nuisance and, as they roll around, may erase spots in drawings made from friable media such as carbon dust. This property may be used deliberately to create texture. Kneaded rubber is a better choice for cleaning purposes.

Pink Pearl and Ruby erasers are oblong blocks for general pencil erasure. The Pink Pearl is softer and more pliable than the Ruby eraser.

Fiberglass erasers are brush-type erasers consisting of glass-fiber bristles in a plastic holder (spelled "Fyberglass" by one manufacturer). The screw-out handle allows for extension of bristles when the brush wears down. It is designed to remove ink or paint from matte-surfaced paper and illustration board without destroying the surface texture. Some burnishing may be required to restore a uniform surface (see chapter 10).

Specialized erasers include the liquid-imbibed type for erasing ink from film, plastic (vinyl) erasers for film, and erasing liquids.

Electric erasers are used primarily for removal of ink or paint. Invaluable for making corrections, the electric eraser erases smoothly, sometimes leaving the condition of the drawing surface better than it was originally. Its motor rapidly revolves an eraser plug, available in different grades for different surfaces. The electric eraser should be moved back and forth, not held in one spot so that a hole is worn through the surface. The white or pink eraser strips or plugs are least likely to leave marks on paper and will erase ink just as well as the harsher "ink" eraser does. Some models can be operated by a switch, others by a mercury battery that starts the motor when the eraser is turned over; still others are cordless (fig. 2-3).

Cleaning pads and drafting powders are used to remove oils from films and papers. The cleaning pads are filled with an absorbent powder like those sold in loose

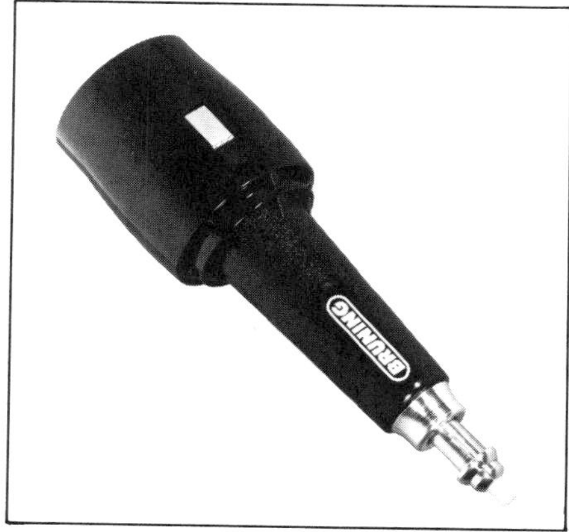

a

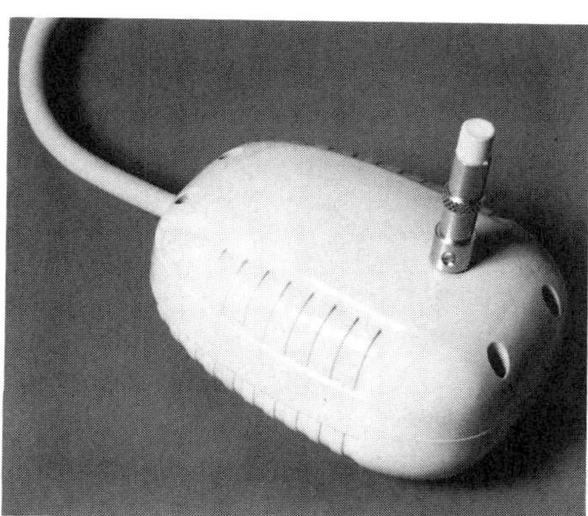

b

c

2-3. Electric erasers: *(a)* Bruning model operated by switch (courtesy of Bruning); *(b)* type with mercury switch, by Apollo or Teledyne Post, which operates when it is turned over (courtesy of Teledyne Post); *(c)* cordless electric eraser by Peerless (courtesy of Pierce Business Products).

form. The powders should be thoroughly brushed off so no residue interferes with rendering media.

Erasing shields are templates with holes, used to restrict erasures to areas being erased, protecting the rest of the drawing. Commercial shields are made of metal. A piece of heavy paper also can be used as an erasing shield.

Blenders

Stumps (stomps) and tortillions (tortillons) are used for smudging and blending pencil tones. They are cylinders of blotting paper rolled in various thicknesses with a point at one or both ends, depending on how they are rolled. Tortillions tend to be rolled diagonally; stumps are rolled straight. They come in assorted lengths and thicknesses, numbered according to size, with the smallest being tortillions, usually no. 1. The numbers are not consistent among manufacturers, however, and some no. 1 models have larger points than others. Stumps and tortillions can be sharpened and cleaned by rubbing them on sandpaper or by trimming them with a sharp knife.

Cork can be cut into small pieces and inserted in a lead, pastel, or charcoal holder. Soft cork (such as Champagne corks) can smooth pencil tones or, cut to a sharp edge, can be used to draw with pencil dust.

Chamois is soft suede leather for erasing or applying pencil dust, leaving soft edges. Chamois works best on film. Dampened chamois also cleans pen nibs without leaving lint behind.

Brushes such as those with soft sable bristles, especially flat (bright) brushes, blend pencil very well on paper, coated boards, or film. Various kinds of brushes are needed for media described in part 2.

Drafting Aids

Straightedges are used as guides for cutting with a blade. A very heavy metal straightedge, at least 30 inches (76cm) long, is most useful for cutting mats and boards. A shorter metal straightedge serves for smaller projects. There should be no measuring marks, as on a ruler, since their rough edges may

---

Patrick J. Lynch contributed to the text on drafting aids.

interfere with the blade's smooth progress.

T squares and drafting machines are useful for aligning lines of type and edges of photographs and for drawing right angles. The T square should be used with a metal edge on a drafting board to ensure even contact of the T with the board. Metal edges can be bought separately, but some boards come with them. Boards can also be bought with an attached parallel rule that moves along the board with cables and takes the place of a T square. A more expensive alternative is a drafting machine, which can be attached to a drafting table. It permits precise alignment of materials and can function as a triangle, T square, scale, and protractor.

Triangles are used with a T square or parallel rule for drawing elements (such as center lines of a specimen or millimeter scales, and in producing charts) and for mounting materials at right angles to an edge. They are also useful for measuring large specimens along a perpendicular, a technique particularly useful for anthropological artifacts (see chapter 21). A selection of clear and colored plastic triangles of different angles—as large as 18 inches (45cm) and as small as can be found—is useful. An adjustable triangle adds versatility, going from 45 to 90 degrees and any angle in between. Triangles intended for inking should have beveled or raised edges to keep ink from "crawling" under the edges during linework (see French curves, below). Those intended as a guide for cutting should have metal edges or be made entirely of metal, since one slip of a blade with a plastic triangle renders the edge useless. Examine all triangles (as well as French curves and templates) when buying (and frequently in the studio) for rough, nicked, or damaged edges, which will produce imperfect lines.

French curves are helpful in inking smoothly curved lines; they are available in a variety of shapes. Also available are adjustable curves, snakelike plastic devices that can be bent into large-diameter curves (but not tight bends). Look for curves with beveled edges that prevent ink from seeping under them. If they are not beveled, lift the edges by gluing on slices of eraser plugs or applying layers of transparent tape (trim the tape parallel to and 2 to 3 millimeters in from the edge). For duplicating organic shapes, illustrator Carolyn Bartlett Gast recommends Airmate no. 6, Dietzgen 2152-10, and Lutz no. 8.

Templates are patterns with circles, ellipses, squares, and other shapes used to draw parts of specimens and to outline enlargements of details. Beware of poorly cut or poorly marked templates; many have rough or ragged edges, centering marks out of register, and neither bevels nor raised edges for ink work. Some templates can be saved by careful sanding of rough edges with extra-fine sandpaper or an emery board. Ink seepage can be prevented with an ink riser to lift edges off the drawing surface; this plastic rectangle slips under the template and has holes that fit under template holes, permitting the pen to reach the paper.

Drafting compasses are used for a variety of circular tasks. Be sure to select a good-quality one with a secure locking mechanism that holds the selected radius without slipping. At least one arm of the compass should "break" or "bow" for large-diameter work. Other handy features are the ability to hold a technical pen in place of the drawing lead (for map- and chart-making) and to hold small blades for cutting circles in film or paper.

Burnishers are used for rubbing down films or transfer and other lettering. A plastic or wooden burnisher—or your thumb—is less likely to leave marks than a metal burnisher when used directly on the artwork. To improve adhesion, burnishing should be done a second time over a cover sheet, ideally the slick backing that comes with most lettering sheets.

2-4. Tracing box. Acculight, courtesy of Knox Manufacturing Company.

Dust removers are used to wipe eraser crumbs from drawings. A draftsman's dusting brush is most basic, but a soft complexion brush works for very small areas of drawings. To blow off pencil dust cleanly, use a baby's bulb ear syringe (from a pharmacy), atomizer, or commercial cans of gas (such as Dust-off from photo and art stores). There is even a tiny, battery-operated vacuum cleaner designed for this purpose (sold by Daniel Smith Inc.). Avoid blowing on artwork; saliva spots are likely to result.

Light boxes (tracing boxes or tables) are for tracing, using lights projected upward through glass. The material to be traced is taped to the glass and tracing paper taped over all (fig. 2-4). Wood or metal boxes or tables containing fluorescent bulbs under a glass-paneled top can be purchased or made. Check to see that the light source provides an even glow over the entire surface, not strips of light and dark. Even lighting is likely to be provided by more than two bulbs and a thick frosted glass. Fluorescent bulbs stay cool and use less energy and are therefore preferable to incandescent bulbs. Other tracing-table variations include a glass insert in a desk or table or in a desk drawer or a plastic or glass sheet on a table easel, under each of which a lamp provides light (fig. 2-5).

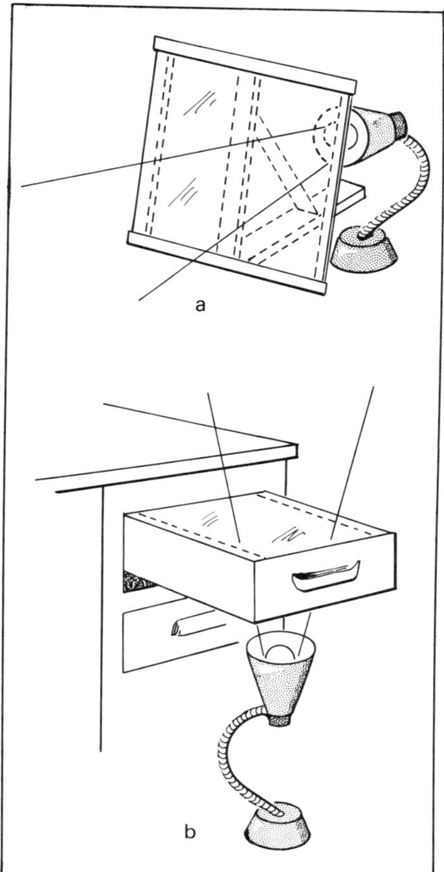

2-5. Tracing surfaces: *(a)* a table easel with acrylic support for drawing, behind which a light shines to permit tracing; *(b)* a desk drawer converted to a light table. The bottom of the drawer has been replaced with translucent Plexiglas and the drawer returned to its compartment upside down. Pen-and-ink on paper, by Barbara N. Rankin.

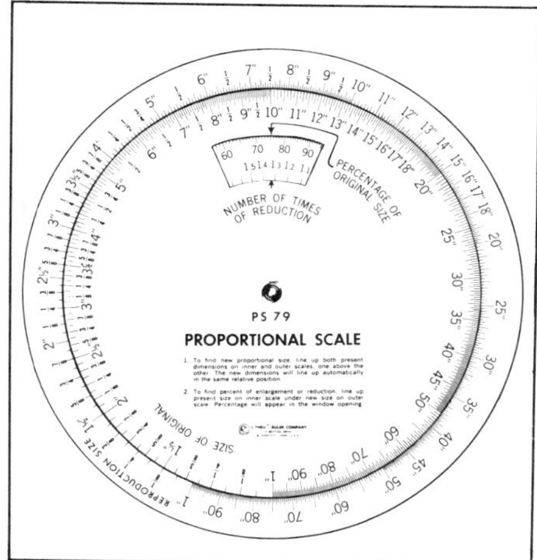

2-6. The proportional scale is used to compute enlargements or reductions. Photo by Judith Guenther; scale, courtesy of C-Thru Ruler Company.

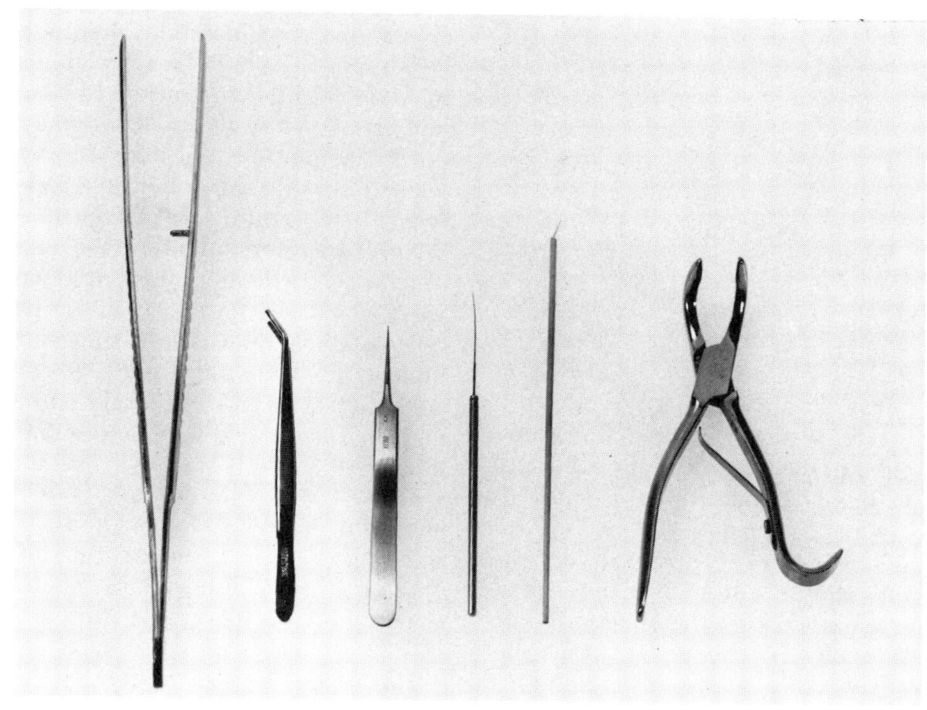

2-7. Instruments for handling specimens. From left to right: bottle forceps; bent-nosed forceps; no. 5 jeweler's forceps; metal probe or dissecting needle; minuten probe; pinning forceps. Photo by Vic Krantz.

Circular proportional scales are used to determine enlarged or reduced sizes (fig. 2-6). Two wheels with measurements on their perimeters are attached so that they revolve independently. One wheel indicates the size of the original, the other indicates the size of the proposed reproduction. A cut-out window toward the center provides the percentage of reduction or enlargement for any setting. To determine the percentage the original will be reduced (or enlarged), move one wheel to match a measurement of the original drawing (for example, its width) with the width of the printed page on the other wheel. If there is a choice of sizes, a larger proportional scale might permit more precise computations than a smaller scale.

SPECIMEN-HANDLING TOOLS

Tools are necessary for manipulating specimens, especially those too small or too delicate to handle with fingers. Specimens must be moved into position, mounted, or turned so that all sides can be studied. Sometimes this is done under the microscope, or the specimen may be in fluid. Each instance and each type of specimen require different methods of handling; these requirements should be explained to the illustrator by the scientist. Some tools that are useful, especially for work with invertebrate specimens, are shown in figure 2-7. Their applications are described in the individual subject-matter chapters in part 3. The minuten probe (fig. 2-8) can be made by soaking a 3/32-inch (3mm) balsawood dowel or matchstick in water until it softens and then inserting in one end the coarser tip of a fine minuten pin or needle. When the wood dries, it will hold the minuten securely.

Small, soft sable brushes (nos. 5×0 to 3) and eyedroppers are useful for transferring tiny specimens in liquid from one container to another. Practice in creating the cor-

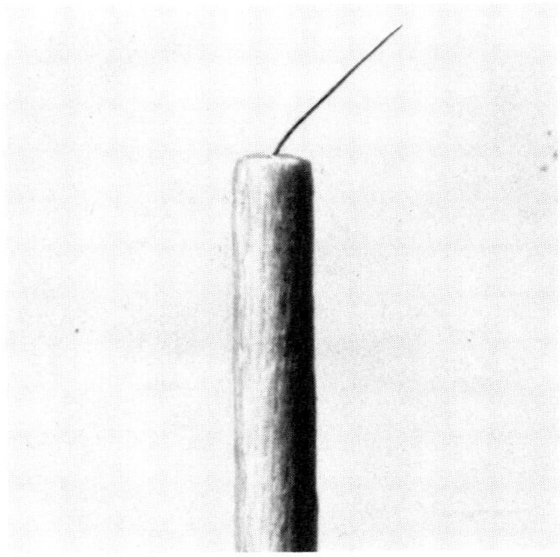

2-8. Enlargement of the tip of a minuten probe. Photo by Vic Krantz.

rect amount of pressure on the bulb of an eyedropper is important, to avoid sucking the specimen into the bulb.

Not quite a specimen-handling tool, but very useful with alcohol-immersed specimens, is the polyethylene "wash" bottle designed for holding alcohol. It has a screw top for filling and a tubular nozzle through which alcohol is dispensed drop by drop or in a stream. This design minimizes or even prevents evaporation and reduces the risk of ignition. It allows small quantities of alcohol to be dispensed with a certain amount of precision into small dishes, a frequent requirement under the microscope. Wash bottles, available from biological supply houses (see Appendix), are very inexpensive.

PROPPING MATERIALS

The method used for holding the specimen in place is determined by its nature (animal, vegetable, or mineral), size, shape, fragility, and susceptibility to staining, as well as by whether it is in fluid (and what kind of fluid) or under a microscope (and whether the microscope is stereoscopic or compound). Often the support material used is an innovation of the scientist or illustrator, with consideration first for the safety of the specimen.

Each chapter in part 3 contains recommendations on propping specimens. For instance, methods for supporting plants are explained in chapter 12, Illustrating Plants, and those for very small animals, particularly under the microscope, are extensively described in chapter 15, Illustrating Invertebrates. Several chapters mention the use of clay (specifically plasticine) or wax. Because there are different types of clay and wax, and they can be used for many different types of specimens, some general comments about these substances follow.

Clay, the nonhardening modeling type, is used for supporting specimens such as bones and for making three-dimensional reconstructions (see figs. 14-19 through 14-22).

Plasticine is most widely available (in toy and variety stores) and is fine for holding insect pins, but it contains oils that may stain or leave a residue on specimens. Most plasticine clays are a mixture of clay and powdered sulfur with a vehicle of various oily substances. The sulfur inhibits the curing of silicone rubber used for making molds of reconstructions and thus is not a good choice in that case (see chapter 14, Modelmaking). Newer composition clays have no sulfur and are ideally suited when rubber molds are used. They use microcrystalline wax as a base along with a vehicle. Some microcrystalline-based modeling clays are Klean Klay, Permoplast modeling clay, Leisure Craft clay, and Jolly King Plasteline (see Appendix). Klean Klay is soluble in ethyl alcohol; the others listed are not. Leisure Craft clay is best for old bones but will leave a slight oil residue (but less than Klean Klay does) on the specimen if left in contact for several days. All four clays are available in a white or off-white color that will not stain surfaces over a short period, although all will leave oil marks on porous surfaces. They are nontoxic, very malleable, and more sanitary than traditional plasticines.

Wax—paraffin, beeswax, and dental wax—are all harder and more brittle than nonhardening clays. Paraffin is melted onto the bottoms of pans for large specimens or small petri dishes for microscopic specimens, and pins are inserted in the wax to keep the specimen in place. Paraffin is flammable, so high heat never should be used to melt it. It is available in supermarkets and wherever home canning supplies are sold. Beeswax can be warmed and softened in the hand and shaped into a support to fit the specimen, but nonhardening clays are easier to shape. Dental wax, made from paraffin, microcrystalline wax, beeswax, and additives, retains its malleability almost indefinitely. It varies in hardness, with those containing more microcrystalline wax tending to be softer. Dental wax is used by mammalogists to support teeth but could be employed for other specimens. Microcrystalline wax contains oil, which might stain specimens, as might some colored dental waxes, although this has not been a problem in mounting teeth. One type, called Spru, is relatively soft and likely to be uncolored. Dental wax is available from dental supply sources.

Terry L. Chase contributed to the text on clays.

MEASURING DEVICES

Rulers are used to measure specimens, drawings, and drawing surfaces, among other things. Both metric (subdivided into centimeters and millimeters) and English (subdivided into inches and sixteenths) rulers are necessary, from 6-inch (15cm) to 18-inch (46cm) lengths. A yardstick is useful for measuring large sheets of paper. Clear plastic rulers with beveled edges permit viewing what is being measured and facilitate inking. Rulers with the zero mark set in from the edge, not flush with it, are more likely to yield an accurate measurement.

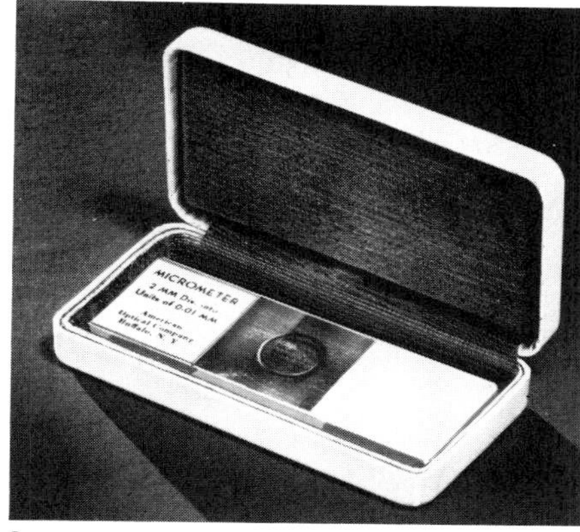

a

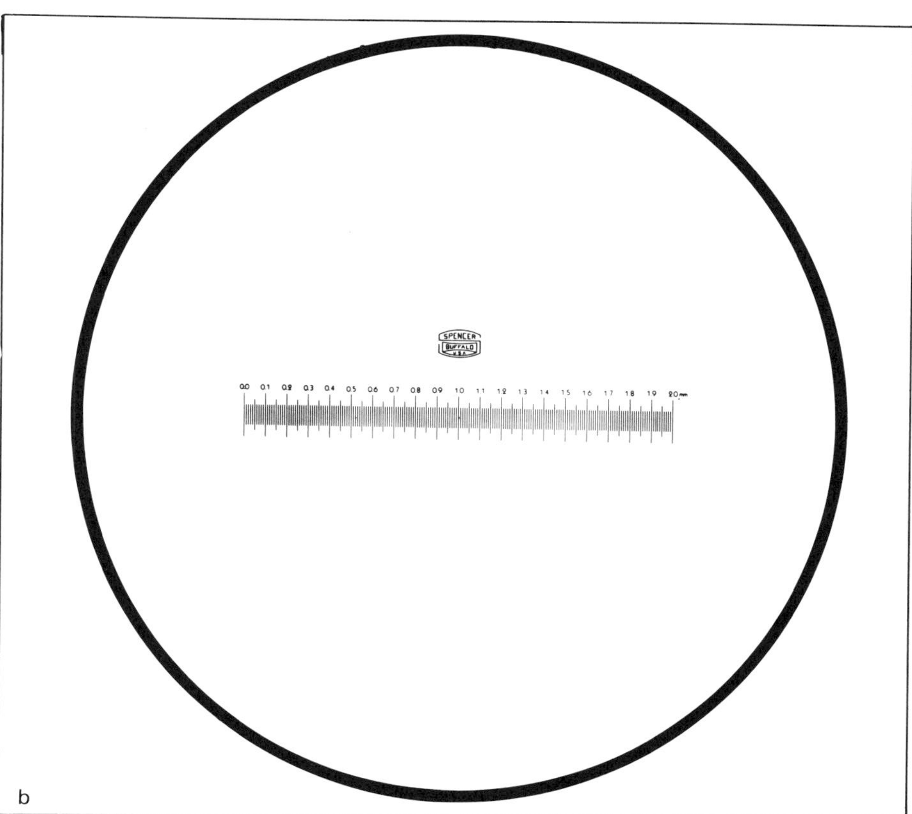

b

2-9. Stage micrometer: *(a)* the slide in its case; *(b)* the scale with labeled divisions, as it appears through the microscope. Courtesy of American Optical Scientific Instruments, Warner-Lambert Technologies, Inc.

Micrometers are very small measuring scales, usually divided into tenths of millimeters and used for specimens that must be measured with optical enlargement. Measurements are always made at the same magnification as the specimen was drawn.

The ocular micrometer is a millimeter scale engraved on a small, round piece of glass (reticle) that fits in the microscope ocular, or eyepiece (see Reticle, below).

The stage micrometer is a glass microscope slide with a mounted scale, usually 2 millimeters long (fig. 2-9). It can be used with a microprojector or compound or stereoscopic microscope. After a drawing is traced from a microprojector image, the stage micrometer replaces the specimen, is projected from the stage of the microprojector, and is traced onto the drawing. Under the microscope, the stage micrometer can be traced with the camera lucida or drawn using the ocular grid (see below). The stage micrometer should be at the same level as the specimen under the microscope. Focusing the image (changing focal depth) slightly does not change magnification as long as the image is made sharp. An image that is out of focus, however, is at a slightly different magnification than when focused.

A stage micrometer with labeled divisions, visible upon magnification, is most useful. Those that are identified only on the slide label, with no indication on the line itself, can lead to incorrect labeling on the drawing.

It is sometimes necessary to calibrate the stage micrometer with an ocular micrometer (reticle) to measure a specimen under the microscope. There are two methods of doing this.

Eyepiece Scale Value Method

This method should be used if the value of the eyepiece micrometer scale is not known. Looking through the microscope, determine the number of divisions in the ocular micrometer that match a given value on the stage micrometer. To determine the value of one eyepiece scale interval, divide the value of the stage micrometer interval by the number of eyepiece scale intervals contained in the image. For instance, if 0.1mm of the stage micrometer covers five divisions of the ocular micrometer, then one division of the ocular micrometer equals 0.1mm/5 = .02, which becomes the value of each division of the ocular scale. To determine the length of a specimen, multiply the number of divisions of the ocular micrometer that the specimen covers by 0.02mm. Thus, an object that covers 2.5 divisions would be 0.05mm long.

Magnification Factor Method

When both stage micrometer and ocular micrometer are graduated in the same units, the number of times a specimen is magnified can be determined by the objective. The size of the specimen, as shown on the ocular micrometer, will be that dimension divided by the magnification factor. To determine the exact magnification factor, divide the dimension in the ocular micrometer by the actual dimension on the stage micrometer it

---

The text on calibrating micrometers is by Bausch & Lomb, modified, with permission; with contributions by Elsie Herbold Froeschner.

covers. For example, if 0.1mm on the stage covers 1.5mm on the ocular micrometer, the magnification factor is 15.0 (1.5/0.1 = 15.0). If an object is measured as 0.25mm in the ocular, its actual size is 0.25mm/15.0 = 0.0166mm.

Grids are surfaces evenly divided into squares. The grid might be considered the mainstay of the scientific illustrator. Before camera lucidas and microprojectors, it provided a way to derive an accurate depiction of a specimen; it still serves that purpose for little cost. The grid is placed over the specimen, and what appears in each square is copied freehand into corresponding squares ruled on paper. The size of the drawn squares determines the size of the drawing. An ocular grid is on a glass disc called a crosshatch lens, or reticle, that fits in a microscope ocular (fig. 2-10, and see Reticle, below). A grid can be used for reconstruction of a specimen using parts from various specimens to make a single drawing. See instructions under camera lucida, below.

A large grid is needed for drawing macroscopic specimens. The line of sight must always be perpendicular through each square to the specimen. This is more easily accomplished with a double grid, one directly above the other. The part of the specimen being drawn should be viewed through two precisely aligned, superimposed squares, which will compensate for the viewer's parallax view. When two squares are aligned, all the others will be out of alignment. After drawing what shows in one set of squares, move ahead to line up the next set, and so on. (Instructions follow for making a double grid.) Squares can be numbered on one edge and lettered on another edge, marked on both the drawn grid and on whatever type of grid is placed over the specimen. This helps the artist to coordinate and identify individual squares, and thus keep track of what is being drawn.

Another grid construction uses

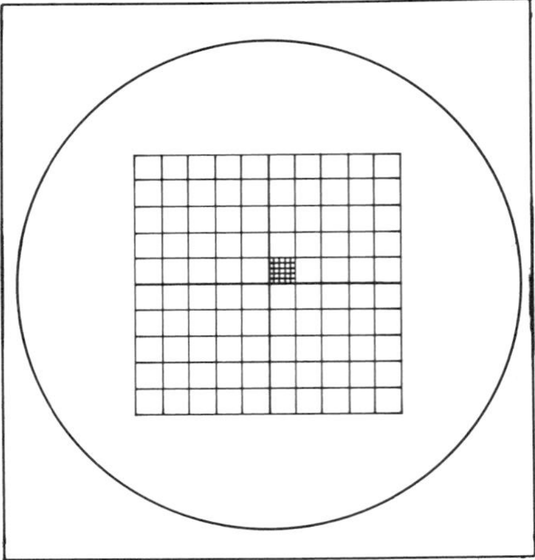

2-10. A grid in a reticle that fits in a microscope ocular lens. This Whipple grid has a smaller grid within the large one, which permits drawing or measuring more detailed areas of a specimen moved into the field of view under the smaller grid. Pen-and-ink on Bristol board, by T. Britt Griswold.

intersecting threads (one or two layers) on a box in which the specimen sits. Evenly spaced slots or holes in the box's edges hold the threads. A door in the side of such a box permits adjustment of the specimen. Variations on grid constructions are limited only by the imagination.

How to Construct a Double Grid

Constructing a double grid on Plexiglas is an elegant solution that minimizes perspective distortion and ensures a certain degree of accuracy in drawings of macro specimens. The more detail required, the smaller the grid divisions should be. Generally, divisions of ¼ inch (0.5cm) are adequate.

Matching grid patterns are engraved with a knife on both sides of a Plexiglas panel ¼ inch thick and of sufficient length and width to cover typical specimens. An 8- by 10-inch or 11- by 14-inch (20 by 25cm or 28 by 35cm) area generally is large enough. The ¼-inch thickness separating the grids will be enough to allow the artist to judge when upper and lower squares are aligned and the eye is directly in front of a particular part of the specimen.

Before removing its protective paper covering, cut the Plexiglas to the desired size; make sure you cut as perfect a rectangle as possible or the squares engraved will not be square. On a heavy piece of card stock or illustration board, slightly larger than the Plexiglas, draw an accurate grid. Use drafting equipment (a parallel straightedge and triangle, or a drafting machine). Remove the protective papers from the Plexiglas and place it on top of the drawn grid. Put one corner of the Plexiglas on a corner of the grid, align the two, and tape them together securely.

To engrave lines that are positioned exactly like the drawn grid, square the paper and Plexiglas to the parallel straightedge. Secure the paper and Plexiglas so they will not move. Use a triangle placed upright along the vertical edge of the Plexiglas; line up the 90-degree base angle with the first grid line on the pattern. By sliding the parallel straightedge up to meet this, you can score right above the paper grid line (fig. 2-11). Use a knife; an X-Acto with a no. 16 blade is suitable. Do not bear down hard, as Plexiglas scratches easily and a deep line is not necessary. After completing one set of parallel marks, rotate the Plexiglas and paper pattern 90 degrees, again squaring them to the parallel straightedge, and complete the grid. Then flip the Plexiglas and register the scored grid with the drawn grid; resecure the two and repeat the scoring process on the reverse side.

Once the grid is duplicated on both sides of the Plexiglas, rub ink into the lines to make them more visible. To protect the Plexiglas, make a slipcase of cloth or cardboard taped, sewn, or glued together.

In some instances, a stand to hold the grid may be helpful. Cut

---

T. Britt Griswold wrote the text on constructing double grids, with contributions from L. Michael Druckenbrod and George L. Venable.

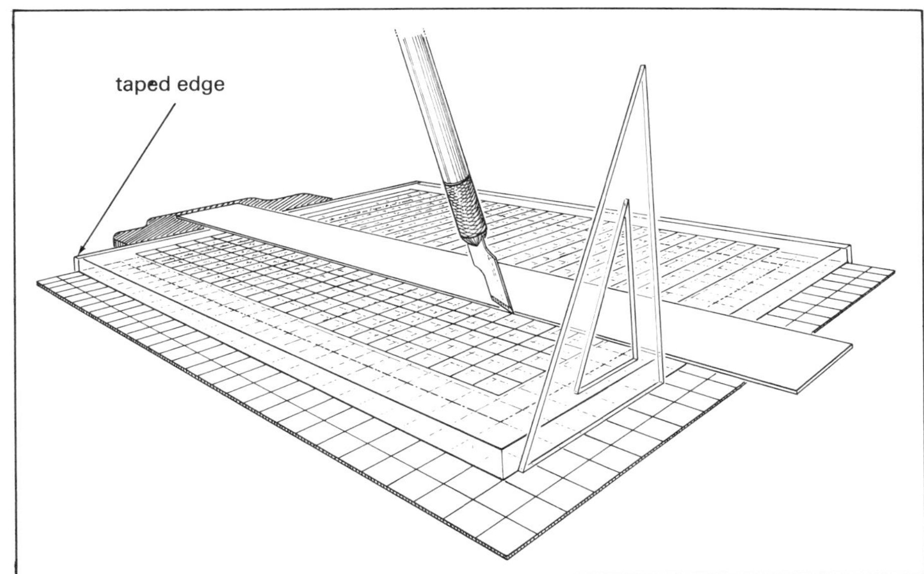

2-11. Making a double grid. Scribe grid lines directly above the grid lines on the opposite side of the Plexiglas, using a straightedge and triangle. Pen-and-ink on vellum, by T. Britt Griswold.

slots at several different angles into two pieces of wood or Plexiglas. To make it even more flexible, hinge the grid to a frame, like a door turned up on its side. It can then be adjusted with a support to any suitable angle.

Grid under the Drawing

Placing a grid under a translucent drawing surface is a substitute for using graph paper or drawing grid lines on the sketch. Inked grids in different sizes produce drawings of various sizes. Graph paper may be used, but several homemade grids may be designed to produce a more useful range. Experimentation and experience will determine the best sizes to use.

Ink the grid precisely on smooth white board, such as Bristol board, and back it with heavy mounting board if necessary. Heavy clear plastic taped over the surface will protect the grid and permit drawing paper to be taped onto it.

Proportional dividers are used to take measurements and transfer dimensions. Navigational dividers are hinged at one end and open to form a V so that measurements taken between the points may be transferred to a map or drawing. Proportional dividers pivot in the middle and open to form an X with points at both ends. Both ends are used to take measurements and transfer dimensions from specimen to drawing. The advantage of proportional dividers is that they may be set to enlarge or reduce the dimensions measured, the points used at one end to measure a specimen and the other end to install or check the dimensions of a drawing. When the knurled knob (a) in figure 2-12 is loosened, the index bar (b) slides within the slot, and the index mark may be lined up with the calibrations scribed on the divider leg (c). The dividers should

2-12. Navigational and proportional dividers. Navigational dividers *(top four)* transfer points directly; proportional dividers *(bottom two)* can be set to enlarge or reduce dimensions. A knurled knob *(a)* loosens to permit an index bar *(b)* to line up a mark with the calibrations *(c)* scribed on the divider leg. Pen-and-ink on Bristol board, by Lawrence B. Isham.

Lawrence B. Isham wrote the text on proportional dividers.

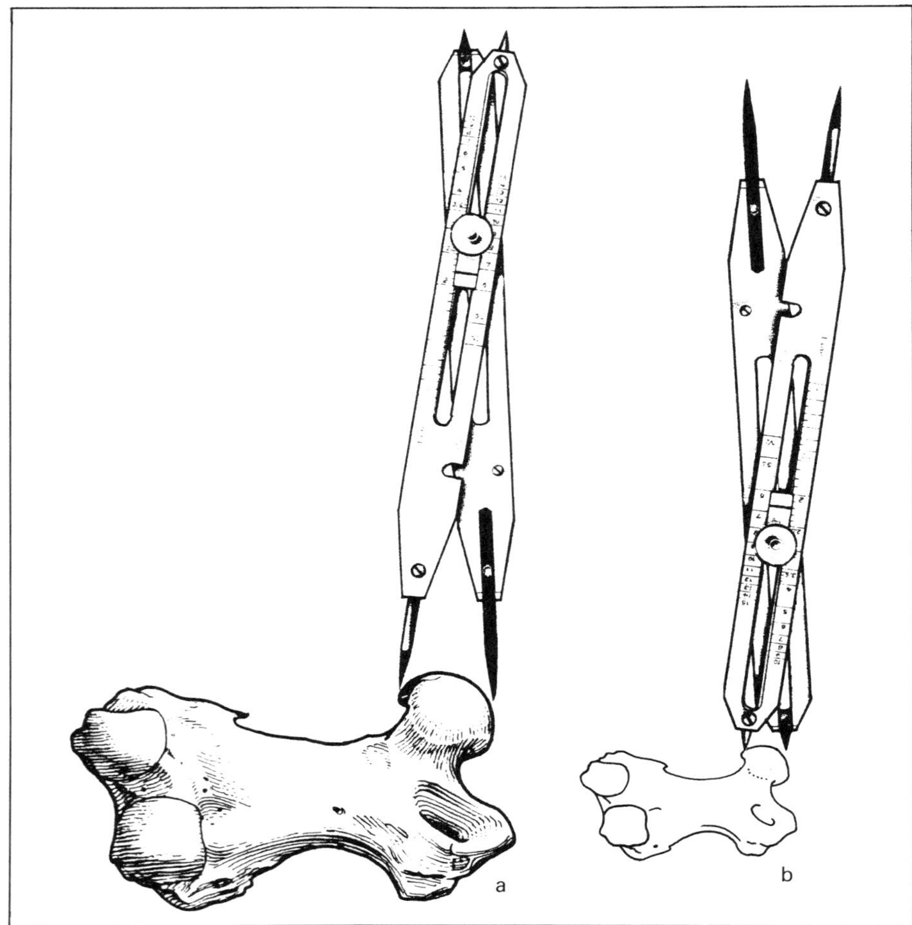

2-13. The dividers are set at a ratio of 1:2. *(a)* The large end of the dividers measures the diameter of a process on a bone. *(b)* The small end transfers the halved measurement to the drawing. Pen-and-ink on Bristol board, by Lawrence B. Isham.

be fully closed when the index bar is moved.

Most proportional dividers have two calibrated scales, one labeled *lines* and the other labeled *circles.* Since we are dealing only with linear measurements, we will consider here only the scale marked *lines.*

Some proportional dividers have a second knob that, when turned, moves a gear along a rack in the slot. This facilitates accurate settings and is preferable to the sliding-bar method.

Procedure

Moving the index bar in the slot allows a wide range of measuring ratios. In figure 2-13, for example, the dividers are set at a ratio of 1:2; the specimen is measured with the large end of the dividers, and the measurement is transferred to the drawing (at half natural size) using the small end of the dividers. Note that it is necessary to take measurements with one end of the dividers and transfer those dimensions to the drawing with the opposite end. To eliminate possible errors, use a finely divided ruler (millimeter scale) to check the actual measurement ratio when setting it.

Regard the specimen as two-dimensional and measure as though it were a photograph: hold the dividers so that a line between divider points is perpendicular to your line of sight. When the two end points of the measurement being taken lie in the same plane as the drawing, no error will be introduced; if a dimension is measured over the curve of the specimen so that the end points of the measurement do not lie in the same plane as the drawing, error results. An accurate drawing, therefore, is an orthographic projection. Figure 2-14a shows a dorsal drawing of a skull, with the desired measurement indicated in brackets. The side view (fig. 2-14b) shows the dimension being taken incorrectly; an error of about 17 percent will be introduced because the dividers are measuring down over the curve of the skull instead of measuring horizontally. The correct measuring method is shown in figure 2-14c (see also fig. 16-10).

Divider Scales

Proportional dividers with the gear-and-rack setting method may have a Vernier scale scribed on the index bar, instead of merely a line, to set against the regular calibrations on the divider leg. The Vernier scale (after Pierre Vernier, seventeenth-century French mathematician) greatly increases the accuracy obtained in fractional or decimal settings between whole numbers. Bowen and Tacro are firms that make dividers with a Vernier scale.

The Vernier scale is scribed on a separate bar of metal that slides along the unit scale on the divider leg as the divider fulcrum is moved to change settings. In figure 2-15 four different settings are shown, and in each the Vernier scale is the upper set of calibration marks. The ten divisions of the Vernier scale are equal in total length to nine divisions on the unit scale (the lower set of calibration marks), so that as the Vernier scale is moved, only one of its calibration lines can be exactly aligned with a similar line on the unit scale. (The unit scale is much longer than the Vernier scale; in figure 2-15, only part of it is shown.)

The zero mark on the Vernier scale is read to obtain the setting. Reading top to bottom in figure 2-15, the upper setting is 20: the zero calibration is aligned with the 20 on

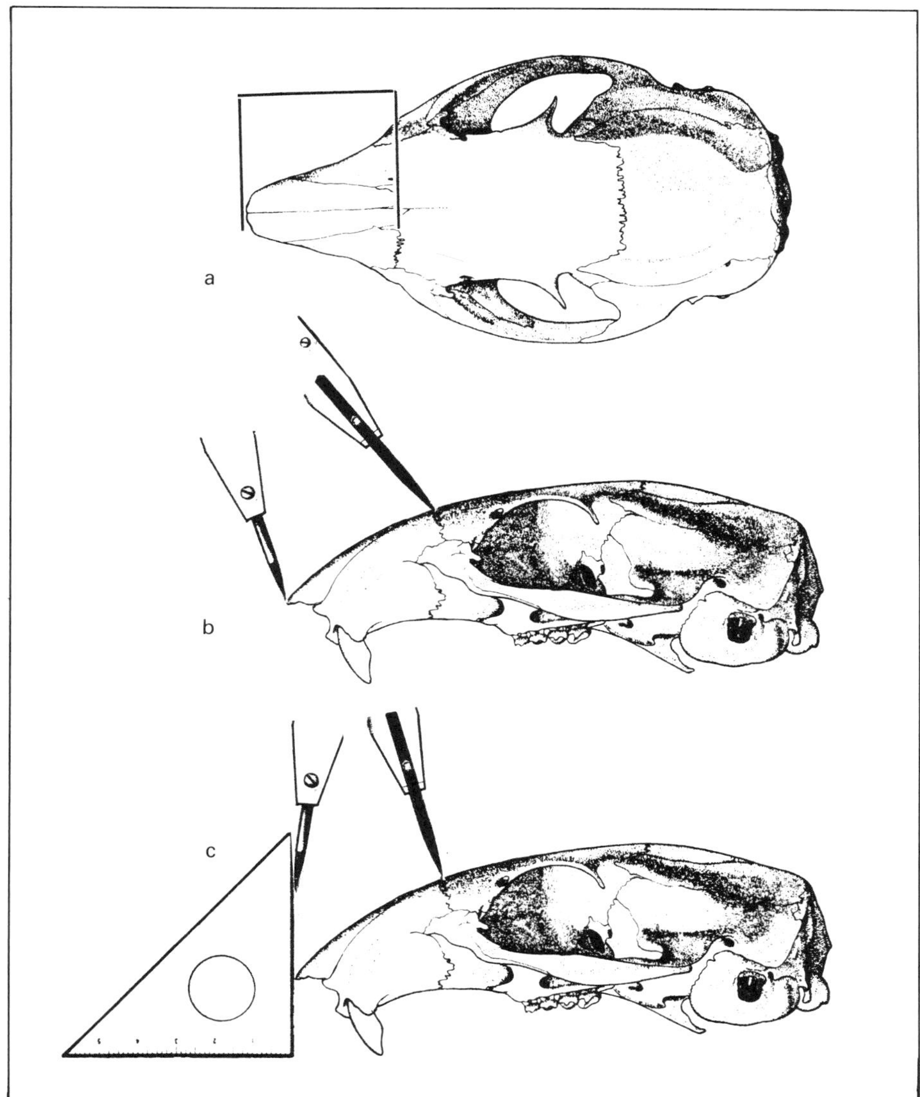

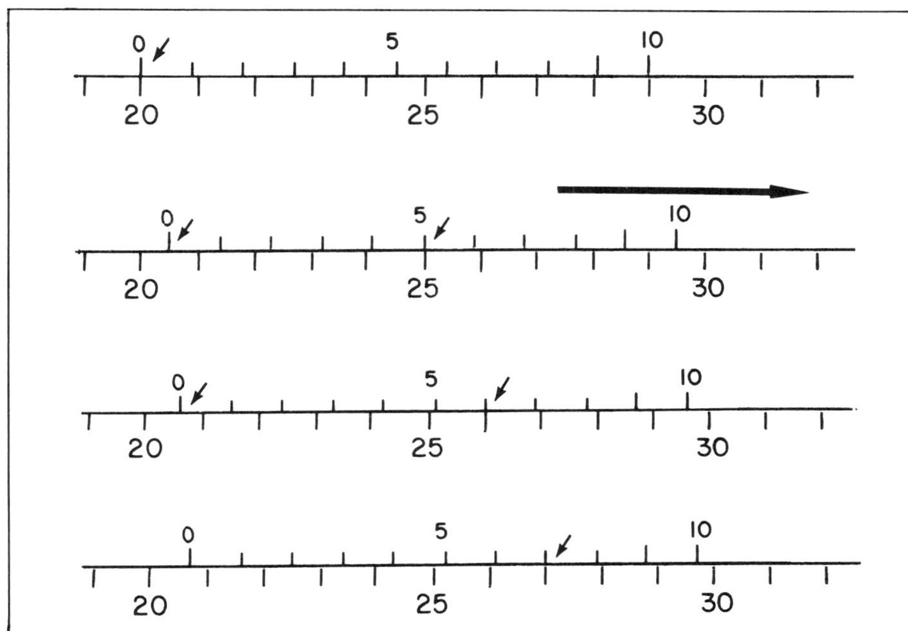

the unit scale. Accurate whole-number settings such as this are easily obtained, but as the Vernier scale is moved to the right to obtain fractional settings above 20, it will be noted that since there are no fractional calibrations on the unit scale against which to align the Vernier zero line, such readings are approximations. If the Vernier scale is moved carefully to the right until its zero calibration is halfway between 20 and 21 on the unit scale, the 5 calibration on the Vernier scale will be the one most closely aligned with any line on the unit scale. If these are exactly lined up, an accurate fractional setting of 20.5 is obtained. Continuing down figure 2-15, where the Vernier 6 is lined up with a mark on the unit scale, the setting is 20.6; and where the Vernier 7 is lined up with a unit scale calibration line, the setting is 20.7. In each case an approximate fractional setting is made using the zero line on the Vernier scale; this setting is refined by carefully adjusting the Vernier scale so that the appropriate calibration line falls exactly opposite a line on the unit scale.

In proportional dividers with Vernier scales, the calibrations on the unit scale do not represent par-

Top:
2-14. Method of measuring a curved surface: *(a)* dorsal view of skull with desired measurement shown in brackets; *(b)* incorrect way to measure this distance; *(c)* correct method of measurement. Dividers are held with points parallel to surface on which specimen sits, or perpendicular to viewer's line of sight to the dorsal view. Pen-and-ink on Bristol board, by Lawrence B. Isham.

Bottom:
2-15. Calibrated scales. Four Vernier scale settings are shown. Reading top to bottom, a setting of 20 is obtained where the zero calibration on the Vernier scale is aligned with the 20 calibration line on the unit scale below it. Successive settings shown are 20.5, 20.6 and 20.7, indicated by that particular calibration on the Vernier scale that exactly lines up with a mark on the unit scale below it. Pen-and-ink on Bristol board, by Lawrence B. Isham.

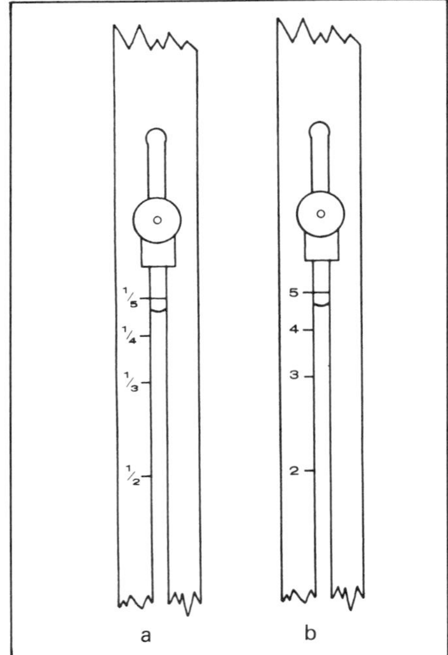

2-16. Types of markings on proportional dividers: *(a)* 1:2, for example, is represented by the fraction ½; *(b)* 1:2 is represented by the whole number 2. Pen-and-ink on Bristol board, by Lawrence B. Isham.

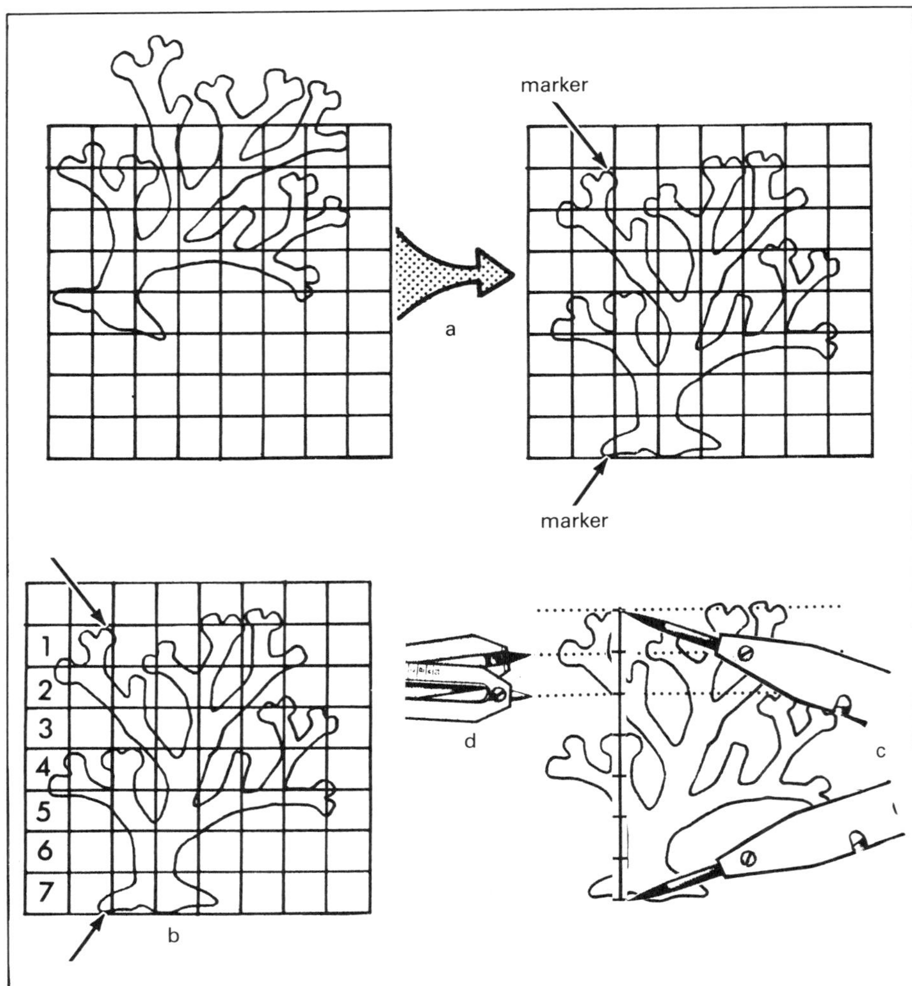

2-17. Use of proportional dividers with an ocular grid to construct a matching grid on paper: *(a)* move the specimen or grid until two distinctive markers intersect horizontal grid lines and lie along a vertical grid line; *(b)* count the squares between markers and set dividers for, in this case, 7:1; *(c)* place the divider points with the large opening on the drawing between the two markers, and mark these points with a pencil; *(d)* with the small opening of the dividers, mark off the squares between markers and construct any further grid squares as needed. Pen-and-ink on Bristol board, by Lawrence B. Isham.

ticular ratios but refer to a table of settings provided by the manufacturer. The table has a wide range of settings to arrive at any desired ratio for reduction or enlargement. It also has settings for conversions such as centimeters to inches, feet to meters, yards to meters, and miles to kilometers.

Proportional dividers with a single line scribed on the index bar and no Vernier scale may be set directly for the desired proportions scribed on the unit scale. Figure 2-16a shows an example of this type of scale (manufactured by Kern and Co.), set for a proportion of 1:5 (indicated as 1/5). Settings for proportions that lie between these numbers may be arrived at by careful adjustment and checking against a millimeter rule.

Although the markings on the Kern dividers appear as fractions (fig. 2-16a), other brands of dividers are marked with whole numbers (fig. 2-16b)—Keuffel and Esser, Hago, Dietzgen, Charvoz, Tacro. The fractions that appear on Tacro and Charvoz dividers all lie between the settings 1:1 and 1:2 and are marked to facilitate settings between 3:5 and 11:12 (appearing as 3/5 and 11/12, respectively).

Use of Proportional Dividers with Microscope

A rough drawing obtained by microprojector or camera lucida is usually refined by using a microscope to view the specimen. If the microscope has an ocular grid, proportional dividers may be used to construct a matching grid on the drawing. By this means, features on the specimen that do not appear on the camera lucida or microprojector drawing may be added accurately to the drawing (fig. 2-17).

Move the grid or specimen until two distinctive points, or markers, near opposite ends of the specimen intersect horizontal grid lines and lie along a vertical grid line. Count the squares between markers. With x number of squares, set the dividers for x:1 (7:1 if there are 7 squares, and so on). Place the divider points with the large opening extending between the markers on

Young T. Sohn contributed to the text on using dividers with a microscope.

the drawing. Use the small opening of the dividers to step off the squares between markers, and use this fixed measurement to construct further grid squares beyond the markers on the drawing. Use a triangle to draw horizontal grid lines perpendicular to the vertical line between the two markers. Construct intersecting vertical lines to complete the grid.

If the microscope magnification is changed, a new grid must be made.

Proportional dividers, in combination with an ocular micrometer or grid, also may be used to check measurements on a drawing. When a part of a specimen, such as an insect leg section, is measured with the grid or micrometer scale, the yield is a number that has no direct measurement value but is part of a proportion or ratio. If, for example, a hair on the insect is then measured with the ocular device and it measures one-half the length of the leg section, the proportional dividers, when set for 1:2, may be used to determine the correct length of the hair on the drawing. If the large opening on the dividers is set to the length of the drawn leg section, the small opening is the correct length of the hair.

Care of Dividers

Dividers should be kept in their case when not in use and should not be subjected to rough treatment, which may result in loss of accuracy. If the points become bent or broken, replacement points may be purchased. Carefully check the accuracy of the dividers after points are replaced. If cleaning is ever necessary, gently rub the dividers, especially the toothed rack, with a clean, dry toothbrush.

If, for some reason, you disassemble the dividers, take care not to reinstall the index bar in a reversed position; all resulting settings will be incorrect. Should this occur, remove the knurled knob and the bushing beneath it, remove the index bar (actually two thin facing bars), and rotate the entire assembly so the index line is toward the other end of the dividers.

Spacing dividers are available in two sizes (fig. 2-18). Used for marking off equidistant points, they can space latitude and longitude lines, typography and grids, or the proportional points in scales.

Calipers are commonly used for making measurements in biology. There are several kinds of calipers based on the principle of a pair of arms or jaws, one fixed and the other movable, with which to measure the distance between two points. (Instruments with two movable arms, known to biologists as dividers, are by dictionary definition also calipers.) At the present, dial calipers (fig. 2-19) are the most widely used. They are easy to handle and simple to read. Caution: the indicator needle of some dial calipers makes a complete revolution in 5mm, others in 10mm. The latter is less likely to cause recording errors. Obsolete and less accurate, but still found in some labs, Vernier calipers require that measurements be calculated from sliding scales. At the other extreme is a new breed, electronic digital calipers. This instrument is more accurate than its predecessors, has a memory, and can be plugged into a computer so that measurements can be fed directly into a database. Giant calipers, known as an anthropometer, are used for measuring whale skulls and other large objects.

Most calipers come with blunt jaws, which are good for measuring nuts and bolts and mechanical parts but are unsuited for fragile objects such as tiny skulls and bones. Thus, before calipers are used for the first time, the jaws must be ground down to fine tips.

Whenever a part of an object is measured, two points must be touched by the tips of the jaws of the calipers. These two points define a measurement. The reference point is the point of the pair that can be most accurately and securely touched by the tip of the fixed jaw of the calipers. With the fixed tip on the reference point, the movable tip is closed down carefully until it touches the other point. Each measurement is repeated until there is a consistent result.

Charles O. Handley, Jr., wrote the text on calipers.

Reverse (spring) calipers are used to measure interior width and thickness of walls of pottery vessels.

Procedure

1. Rule a piece of paper to the same measurements as on a ruler that will fit inside the vessel.
2. Screw the calipers closed to insert into the vessel.
3. Set the ruler vertically within the vessel.
4. Screw the calipers open inside the vessel until the tips of the caliper arms just touch the sides of the vessel (fig. 2-20). The nut that is screwed holds the arms open to a fixed point.
5. Note where the top of the calipers measures on the ruler. Pinch the calipers closed to remove them from vessel. When the calipers are released, the tips spring back to the preset point.
6. Measure between these tips and record at the point on the paper where this measurement was taken.

Repeat the process at another level in the vessel, and so on. Measuring at regular intervals gives an interior profile of the vessel, plotted by a series of points. The comparison of interior measurements with exterior measurements taken at corresponding points shows the thickness of the vessel walls. Allow for the thickness of the vessel base while taking exterior point mea-

Marcia D. Bakry and George Robert Lewis contributed to the text on reverse calipers.

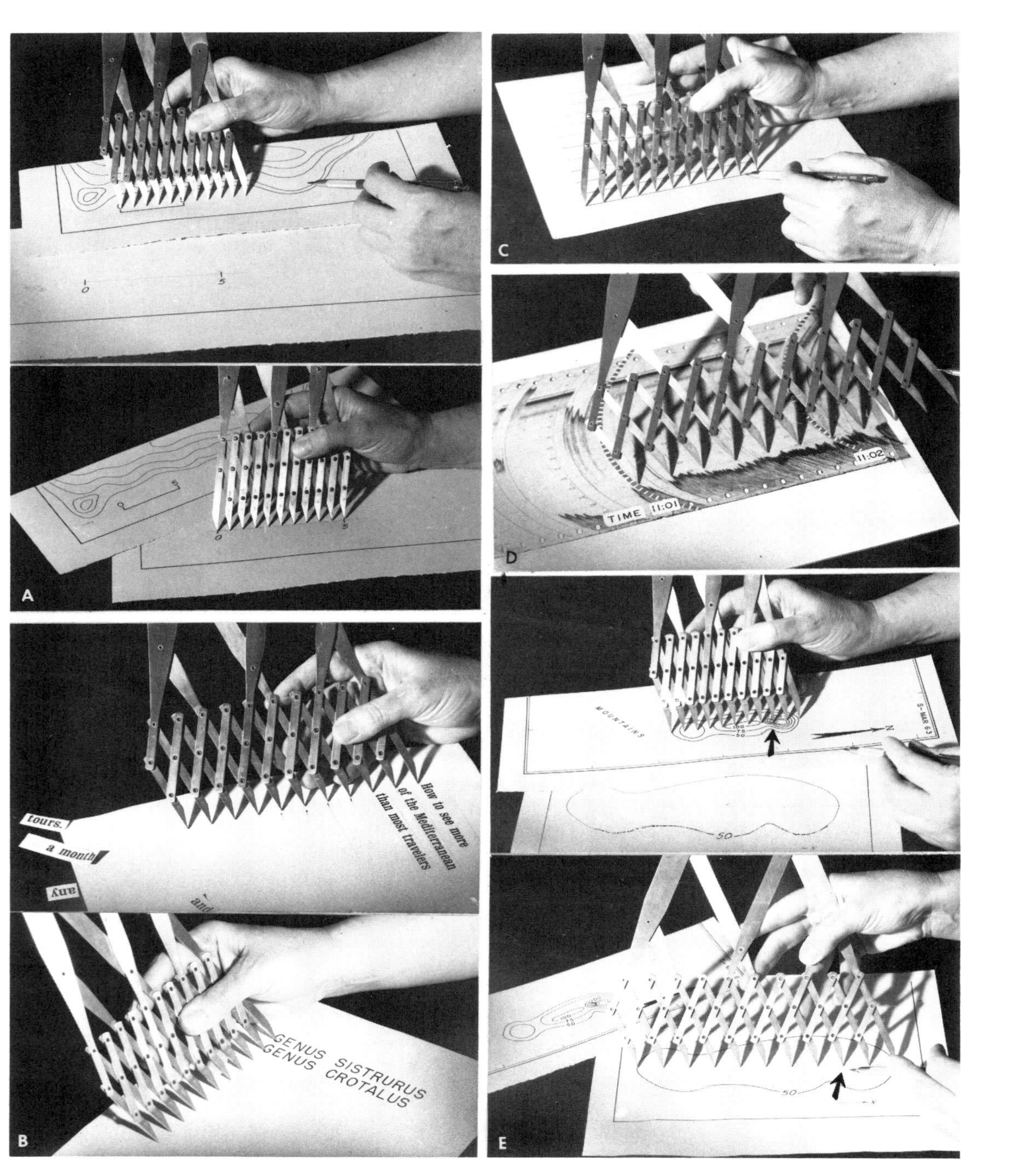

2-18. Several ways to use spacing dividers. *(A)* Graphic scales can be redrawn proportionally. In this example, the scale in the upper photograph is being doubled in the lower photograph. *(B)* The spacing of phototypography or other lettering can be laid out accurately. *(C)* Grids of arbitrary size, such as unplotted townships on a map, can be marked off. *(D)* Fathograms and other electronic charts can be interpreted in terms of either amount or time. The photograph shows the setting that provides a depth reading for every ten seconds, the points being extended from zero to six on the time scale of sixty seconds. *(E)* The relocations of plots from a map of one scale to another of a different scale can be established by the adjustable points. This process is useful for proofreading the work of cartographers or illustrators. Photos and caption by Donald B. Sayner, from his booklet, written with Gladys Bennett Menhennet, *Drawing for Scientific Illustration*, "Professional Aids and Devices," © Donald B. Sayner, 1969 (University of Arizona, 1969).

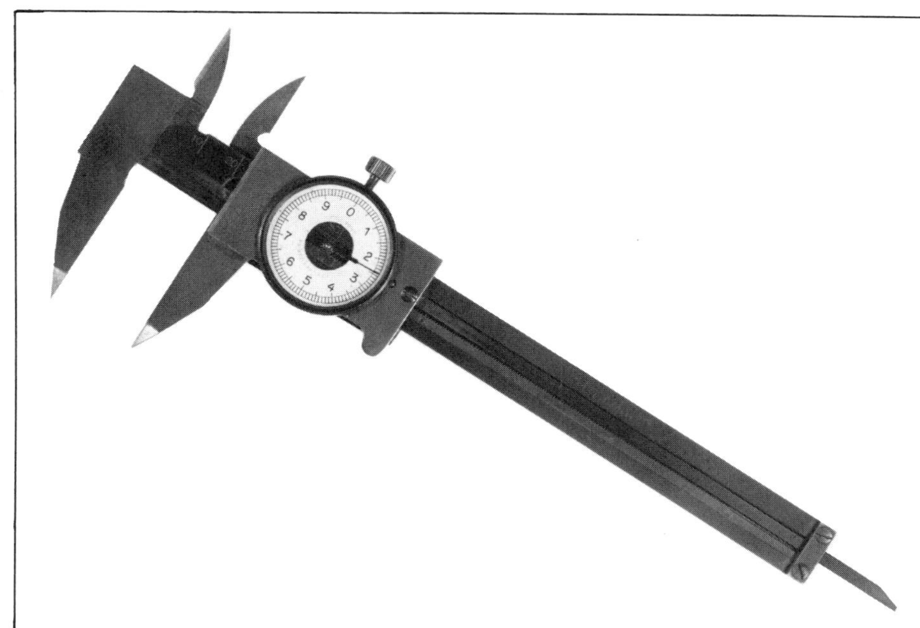

2-19. Dial calipers with sharp-pointed jaws, measuring to tenths of millimeters—the standard tool for measurement of mammal skulls and bones. Photo by Vic Krantz.

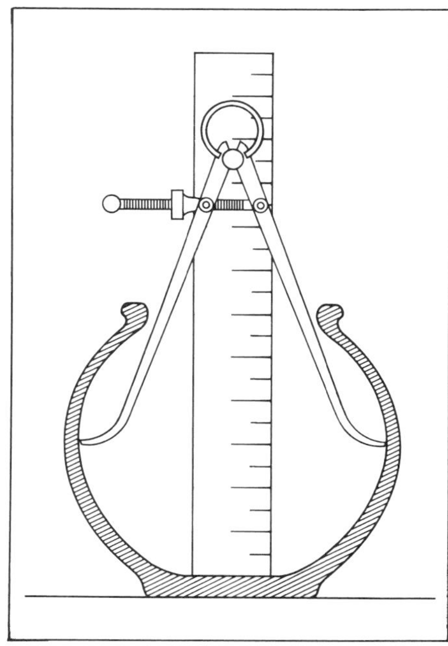

2-20. The use of reverse calipers and a ruler to measure the interior of a pot, shown in shaded cross section. Pen-and-ink on Bristol board, by George Robert Lewis.

surements by noting on the inserted ruler the difference between interior and exterior height of the vessel base rim.

Carpenter's molding gauges, contour gauges (Form-a-Gauge) consist of numerous parallel metal wires that slide freely between two slats, taking on the outline of whatever they are pressed against (fig. 2-21). Originally intended for use by carpenters to reproduce ceiling and other trim moldings, they aid anthropological illustrators in obtaining the outline of pots. After the wires duplicate the shape of the object to be drawn, they are placed flat on paper and the outline is traced. Very large gauges can be handmade to duplicate the shape of large pots.

Perspective machines (Perspektomat) are used for geographic and geologic illustrations. The Perspektomat P-40, model D, is used to convert topographic and bathymetric maps into parallel, perspective views as well as geologic block diagrams. With the help of a simple, supplementary attachment, the artist can make these block diagrams into stereographic pairs. Block diagrams designed for stereo viewing also can be used in chemistry and crystallography. A series of profiles of the terrain can be drawn very quickly by using a blocking device that stops the machine at the correct angle.

The Perspektomat apparatus is a steel precision instrument (fig. 2-22). It combines the systems of a pantograph and a parallelogram, with the arms guided along a fixed horizontal rail. A portion of the map is secured with magnets to a metal plate, and the drawing paper is attached to a board covered with a revolving rubber band. This board has a knurl attachment that can be graduated for each contour tracing to provide the vertical elevation.

Landscape panoramas prepared with a Perspektomat are drawn in parallel perspective. That is, all the straight lines parallel to the main rail transfer to the drawing in their actual length, but those perpendicular to it are foreshortened. The ratio of foreshortening depends on the sine of the angle of projection. A panorama illustrated with the use of the Perspektomat is therefore different from an illustration done from an aerial photograph, because it has a mathematically accurate perspective. Changing the angle of view—or the sine of the angle of projection—can produce a diagram very similar to an aerial photo. This can be done by dividing the map into zones so that the viewer has a steep view of the foreground, but the middle distances and background appear progressively more horizontal. The parallel perspective still will be accurate.

Although this apparatus is fairly easy to use, it can be very tiring, tedious, and time consuming. It also requires considerable cartographic skills, some knowledge of calculus, and artistic acumen to be able to render relief forms of the landscape from contours. Many hours of careful drawing are

---

Ellen Paige contributed to the text on gauges.

Rosemary Nothwanger wrote the text on perspective machines.

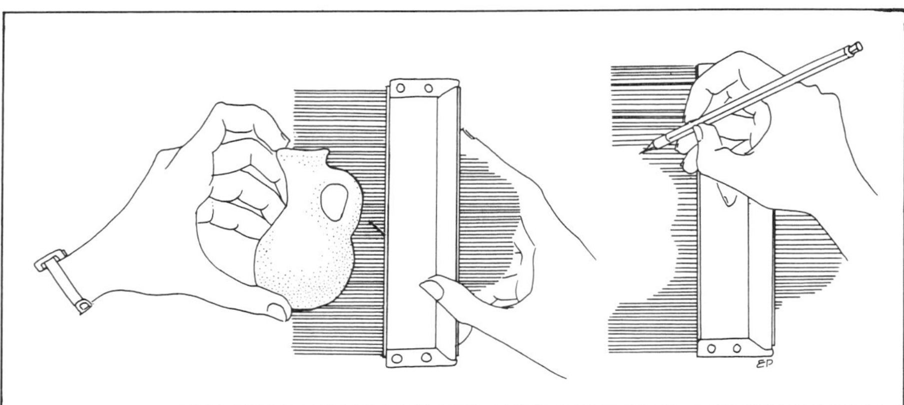

2-21. Form-a-Gauge, used for copying the shape of an object. The metal wires take on the outline of any shape against which they are pressed. The shape created by the wires is traced; if the pot is symmetrical the reverse can be drawn by flipping over the gauge. Pen-and-ink on Bristol board, by Ellen Paige.

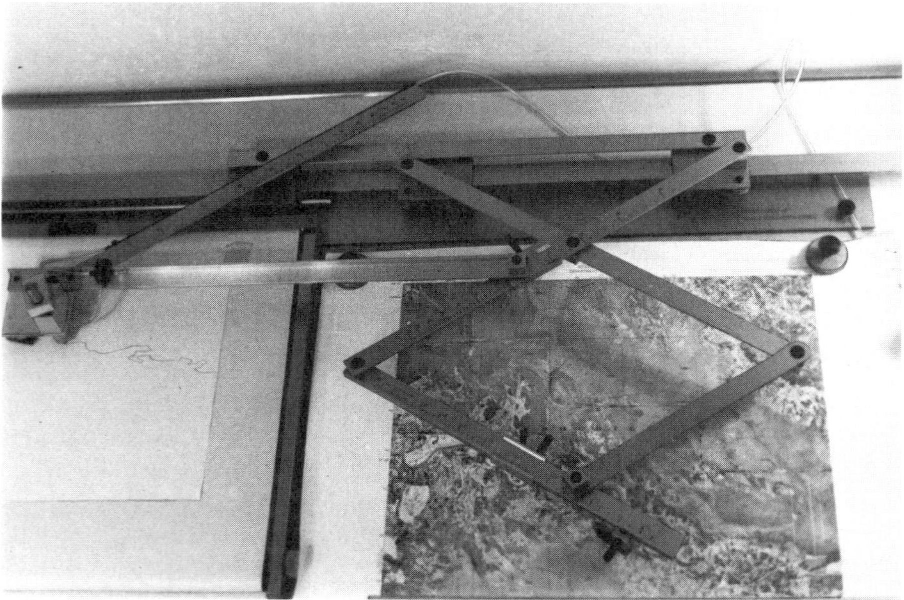

2-22. The Perspektomat P-40, a device for converting topographic maps into parallel perspective views. Photo by Rosemary Nothwanger.

needed to produce a panorama such as shown in figure 2-23.

The Perspektomat P-40, along with other types of perspective machines, is produced and sold by F. Forster Apparatebau (Mathematical Instruments). (See Map Sources, Symbols, and Scales in the Appendix.)

Optical Devices

The ultimate and most important optical device for the scientific illustrator of small subjects is the microscope. (Its use and principles of operation are explained in chapter 23.) Simpler optical devices are also used in many circumstances. Two of them, the camera lucida and the reticle, attach to a microscope. In using any optical device, draw what appears in the center two-thirds of the field of view only; the outer third is the most distorted by lens curvature.

Compound and stereoscopic microscopes: Although it provides a much lower magnification than the compound microscope, the most commonly used microscope in scientific illustration is the stereoscopic (also called dissecting) microscope. It is designed so that the two oculars view the specimen from different angles through separate objectives or a series of lenses, creating parallax and resulting in a stereoscopic view of the specimen, just like viewing it with two eyes directly (see fig. 23-13). The stereoscopic microscope also affords considerable space beneath the objectives so that whole specimens in dishes or on pins can be manipulated. In contrast, oculars of the compound microscope view the specimen in a single straight line through one objective (see fig. 23-12); a single image is seen by both eyes. Only specimens on microscope slides will fit under the compound microscope's higher magnification objectives. Shallow dishes will fit under objectives with magnification up through 10×.

Under the stereoscopic microscope the specimen looks three-dimensional and is seen in the same orientation as it is without magnification. With the compound microscope, the specimen looks flat and is reversed, top to bottom and left to right. A needle being inserted under a compound objective to move the specimen from the left will be seen coming from the right, so it is necessary to work backward when manipulating a specimen under the compound scope.

Early compound microscopes were monocular, having only one eyepiece, but today both stereoscopic and compound microscopes are binocular.

Most microscopes sit on a base in front of the user, with the specimen placed on the microscope stage. To permit viewing of details on specimens too large to fit on the stage, stereo microscope bodies can be attached to an arm that either clamps onto a table or is attached to a stable base (fig. 2-24). The microscope then can be swung over the table to focus on any portion of the specimen.

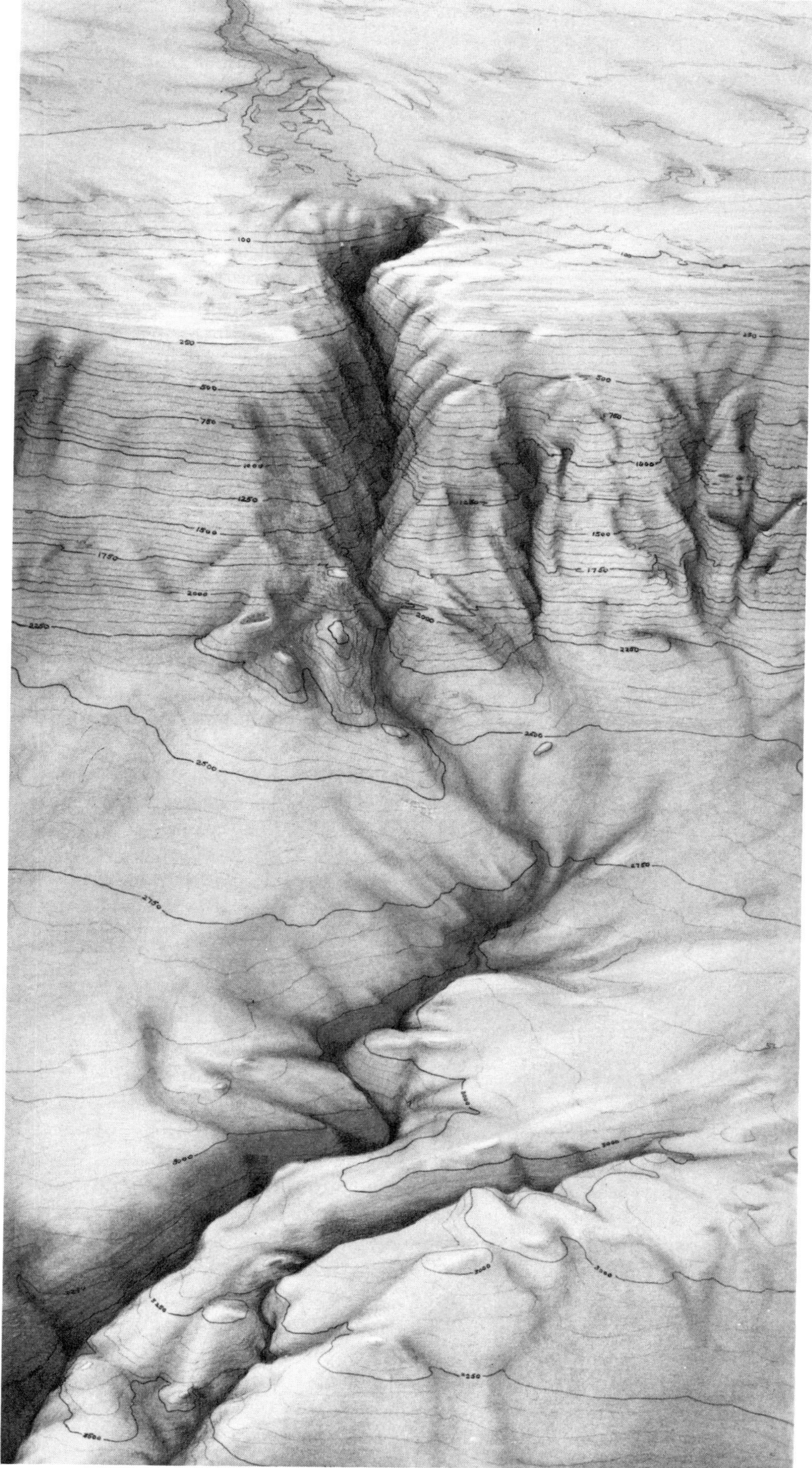

2-23. Hudson Canyon and the Heezen Plateau with the Hudson and Carsten valleys, a sea-floor panorama with accurate perspective created using the Perspektomat. Blue Col-erase and Prismacolor pencils on blue mat board, by Rosemary Nothwanger.

Microscope lighting is either transilluminated (coming from below and through the specimen) or reflected (shining toward the specimen from above or the side). Transillumination usually is created by a light bulb that fits into the base of the compound or stereoscopic microscope, but reflected lighting can be directed onto a mirror in the base to send light up through the specimen, creating transillumination. With the stereoscopic microscope, reflected lighting is used most commonly. The lamp housing may be a freestanding unit or may attach to the microscope body in a fixed position or on movable arms (see figs. 2-24, 23-12).

Microscope bulbs (also called lamps) often are powered by a small transformer with a rheostat or multiposition switch, which reduces the intensity of the light by reducing the power available to the bulb, or with a diaphragm, which reduces the intensity simply by covering up part of the bulb. With a diaphragm the bulb brightness and color are constant regardless of how low the light intensity. Because microscope bulbs are expensive, a true rheostat or switch is preferable to a diaphragm for drawing purposes, since it extends the life of the bulb. If, however, photographs are to be taken through the microscope, the diaphragm system is desirable because the constant color of the light produces consistent photographic results.

Most often transilluminated light is incandescent, whereas reflected lighting may be incandescent or fluorescent. The incandescent source may be a bulb that shines directly on the specimen or a fiber-optic system in which the light is transmitted through a bundle of glass fibers. Quartz halogen incandescent bulbs are increasingly used. The bulb envelope is made

---

Steven E. Hodges contributed to the text on microscope lighting.

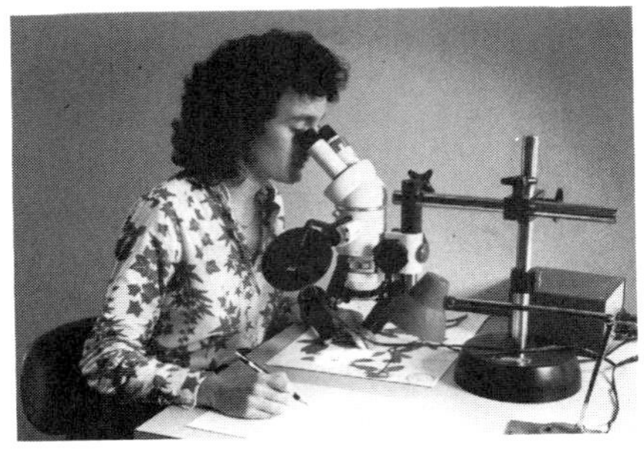

2-24. Mounting a microscope body on a movable arm permits viewing of specimens too large to fit a standard microscope stage. This photograph of botanical illustrator Wendy B. Zomlefer shows an ideal setup for viewing a herbarium sheet (or any other large subject), since the microscope can be moved above the specimen with ease. Photo by Paloma Ibarra.

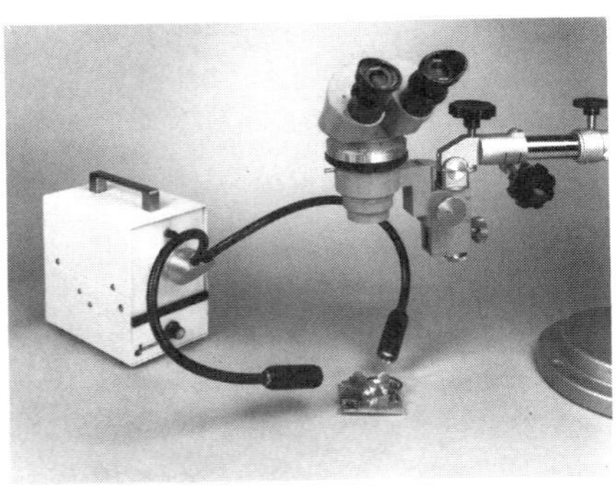

2-25. Fiber-optic transformer with two light guides. This model has a true rheostat to adjust light intensity. The stereoscopic microscope shown is mounted on an arm. Courtesy of Dyonics, Inc.

of quartz, a crystalline form of silica (fused silica), which transmits light better than common glass (amorphous silica), and the bulb is filled with a halogen gas (versus a vacuum in conventional bulbs), which produces brighter light. Unfortunately, they also produce a lot of heat.

The best stereoscopic microscope lighting for most scientific illustration is a fiber-optic system, because much of the heat of the source is absorbed by the glass fibers (fig. 2-25). The resulting cool, intense light will not heat up the specimen or vaporize preserving fluids, as direct incandescent illumination will do. A disadvantage of fiber optics is that the glass also absorbs a significant amount of light, so some of the lamp light does not reach the specimen.

The glass fibers are spirally wrapped in metal so that they are flexible enough to bend into the best position for viewing a specimen; these so-called light guides have focusing lenses at the ends to concentrate the light. Usually two light guides (bifurcate) are used, but a unit with three light guides (trifurcate), available from some manufacturers, will provide light from three directions or for two microscopes when it is necessary to work with more than one microscope at a time. This latter situation usually occurs only when reflected light is being used for both stereoscopic and compound microscopes, an uncommon event. When the light is split between microscopes, less light is available for each subject.

Although fluorescent lights also are cool, they are not as intense as other light sources. Furthermore, the mercury vapor gas they contain is flammable, making them undesirable for use with specimens in alcohol in the event of breakage. Nonetheless, a small, freestanding fluorescent lamp (with two tiny bulbs) is useful. Directed at a specimen from the side (raking light), it shows punctures very effectively.

Another type of microscope lighting is the ring light; it attaches to the objective of a stereoscopic microscope. Ring lights may be solid rings of light (made from fluorescent bulbs or fiber optics) or may project as four pinpoints of light. They provide an even, diffuse light that is good when viewing dark, shiny objects such as beetles or wasps.

When specimens are to be depicted in color, the color of the microscope lighting may be of concern. Most incandescent light is yellowish to reddish, but quartz halogen light is quite white. Fluorescent light is bluish or greenish.

Microscope and other catalogs provide information about various light sources (see Appendix).

Magnifiers are used to check detail in drawings or make corrections, particularly to ink drawings, and to study specimens that are not so small as to require microscopy. A hand magnifying lens is useful, but most helpful is a lighted magnifier that clamps to a desk. The latter frees both hands, especially if it will stay in place by itself when moved into position. Magnifying lenses that clip on to eyeglasses or are attached to a headband are also valuable (see Appendix).

Reducing lenses are used for checking how a drawing will look when reduced. Although it looks like a hand magnifier, this lens makes images look smaller.

Reticles (reticules, graticules) are round glass discs on which are engraved scales or patterns for measuring purposes. The pattern might be a plain or numbered grid, cross-hair design, or a design for specific types of measuring. The reticle fits on a ledge of sorts inside the microscope ocular. Oculars designed to hold reticles are focusable and usually unscrew to permit the reticle to be dropped in. Do not leave an ocular unscrewed and open very long; dust will migrate inside. And always handle a reticle by its edges to keep off fingerprints.

Put the reticle into the ocular corresponding to your stronger eye; this will make it more likely that the grid will remain clearly in view, superimposing the specimen. Reticles are made in different diameters to fit oculars of different sizes, and adapter rings are available to fit a smaller reticle into a larger ocular.

Microscope camera adapters are devices that connect microscopes to cameras to permit photography through microscopes. The microscope must have a vertical, extra ocular opening to which the adapter connects. Microscope photography is often done by biological photographers (see chapter 19). The Biological Photographic Association is a source for information on techniques and publications (see Appendix).

Camera lucidas (tracing devices, drawing tubes) are devices that attach to binocular microscopes (stereoscopic or compound) and, through the use of prisms or mirrors, allow visualization of the specimen and the drawing paper simultaneously (fig. 2-26). In the past, this principle was employed with a suspended prism and mirror that simply reflected the image of a distant object onto a drawing surface. Today, Wild, Leitz, Nikon, Olympus, and Zeiss are among the manufacturers that provide removable camera lucidas for their microscopes (fig. 2-27).

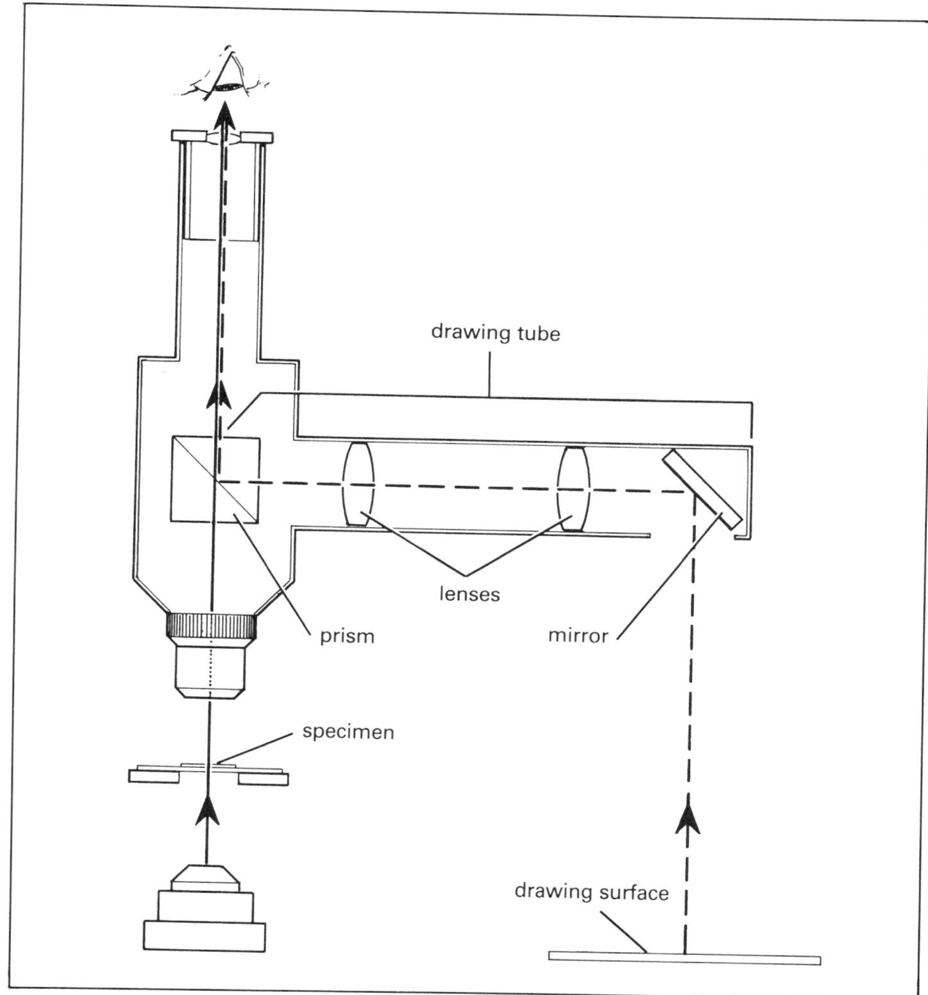

2-26. Diagram of the camera lucida, or drawing tube, with microscope. The mirror reflects the drawing paper and pencil via a prism into one ocular while the specimen is viewed. In the resulting image, the specimen appears to be on the paper and can be traced. Diagram concept courtesy of E. Leitz, Inc. Redrawn with pen-and-ink on Bristol board, by T. Britt Griswold.

When using the camera lucida, the viewer's two eyes see three images. Both eyes see the specimen on the microscope stage, but the eye closest to the camera lucida's prism or mirror also sees the lighted drawing surface and pencil. The specimen appears to be on the drawing surface, permitting its image to be traced with the pencil.

Theoretically, anything that fits under a compound or stereoscopic microscope can be drawn with a camera lucida. There are exceptions, however, such as specimens too small to be enlarged sufficiently with the stereoscopic microscope camera lucida but too opaque to permit interior details to be seen with transmitted light on the compound microscope. Yet, such a specimen may require higher magnification than can be used with reflected light on the compound scope, because the objectives with higher magnification are so close to the specimen that there is not enough space for reflected light to reach the specimen. The specimen also may be too opaque to be drawn from a microprojector. With such specimens, a finely lined ocular grid might work better than a camera lucida.

Specimens that extend beyond the field of view in the microscope at its lowest power must be drawn in sections, with adjoining sections matched precisely as the specimen is shifted. If this becomes so clumsy that it lessens accuracy, proportional dividers or a grid (depending on the specimen's size) might be preferable. Another option for the stereoscopic microscope is a reducing objective (0.3×, 0.5×); this can bring a specimen down to a comfortable size in some cases. Of course, a camera lucida drawing that comes out too small or too large can be enlarged or reduced with an opaque projector, photostat machine, photocopier, or grid.

Whether a specimen is too small or too large to be drawn with the camera lucida and particular microscope depends on the specimen, what must be drawn, and whether a method is available to make size corrections. If only an outline drawing is needed of an opaque specimen measuring one-tenth of a millimeter, and equipment is available to enlarge the drawing, it can be drawn with the stereoscopic microscope. That same specimen may be too small to be drawn with that microscope if a large, detailed drawing is needed and enlarging the camera lucida drawing is impractical.

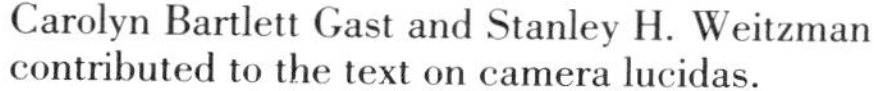

Carolyn Bartlett Gast and Stanley H. Weitzman contributed to the text on camera lucidas.

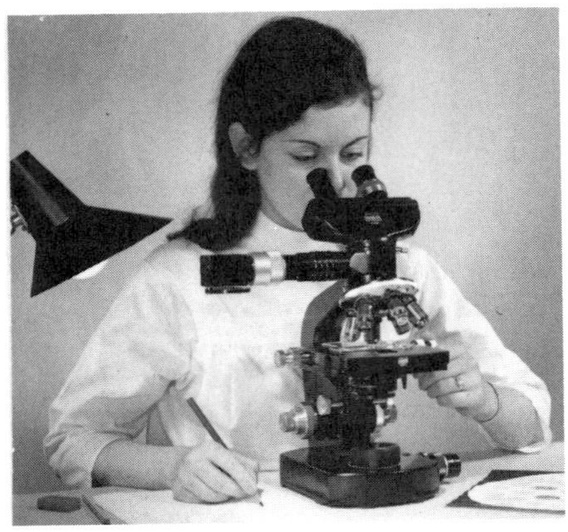
a

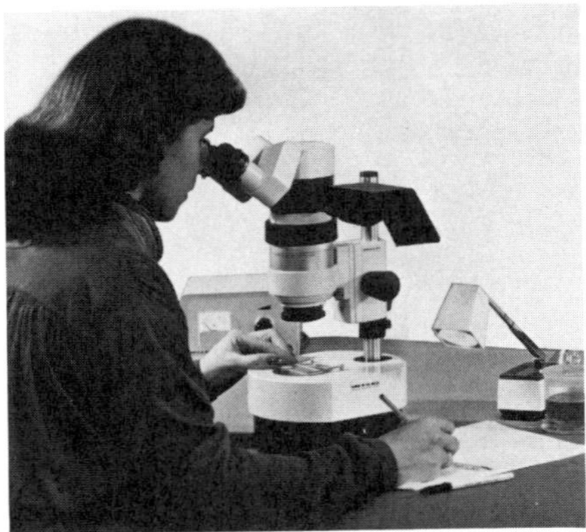
b

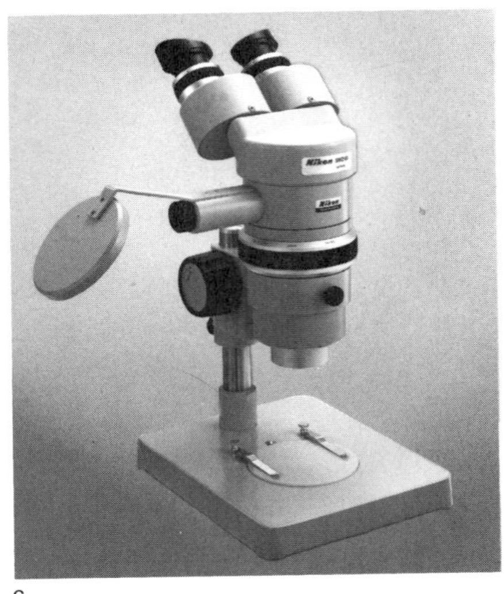
c

2-27. Various styles of camera lucidas. *(a)* A Leitz (Wild) compound microscope with camera lucida that has an eyepiece. Different magnifications of the eyepiece and extension of its tube determine the size of the drawing area. *(b)* Wild zoom stereomicroscope with low-slung binocular body. *(c)* Nikon stereoscope with drawing tube. *(a)* and *(b)* courtesy of E. Leitz, Inc; *(c)* courtesy of Nikon, Inc., Instrument Division. Photo retouching by George L. Venable.

Size of Drawing

Because the camera lucida is mounted below the eyepieces, the size of the image is determined by the objectives, the level of the drawing surface, and the camera lucida itself, not the ocular(s). Therefore, changing ocular magnification will make the specimen look larger or smaller, but the size of the drawing will not be affected. Camera lucidas designed like those manufactured by Leitz (see fig. 2-27a) have removable eyepieces, which fit into the tracing device. Their different magnifications, plus the extension of this eyepiece tube, establish the size of the drawing area.

To further adjust the size of the drawing may require raising or lowering the microscope or drawing surface, as with a microprojector. Raising the drawing surface (with books or boxes) will reduce the size of the drawing. To enlarge the image area beyond magnification provided by stronger objectives, raise the microscope or lower the drawing surface by moving the microscope to the edge of the drawing table and extending the camera lucida mirror or drawing tube over the edge and over a lower surface that still can be reached for drawing. Boxes and books can be combined to achieve a correct drawing size. A record on the drawing of which boxes or books were used will help if a return to that size is necessary.

Recording Magnification

In calculating the total magnification of the microscope, it must be considered that some camera lucidas inserted between the eyepieces and objectives may increase the total magnification of the microscope (eyepiece times objective magnification times camera lucida magnification). For future reference, always record the magnifications used on every preliminary drawing, including any accessory objectives—for example, "10× (ocular) by 12× (objective) by 1.5× (accessory objective)," or "180×." Total magnification would include the camera lucida, perhaps 1.25×, making this total magnification equal 225×. The most useful information is the magnification of the objectives, since they are a variable in determining the drawing's size. Some stereo microscopes provide the total ocular/objective magnification on the magnification increment settings by assuming 10× oculars.

Derive a scale for the drawing by placing a stage micrometer or ruler under the microscope at the same magnification as the specimen and tracing it (see Stage Micrometer, discussed earlier).

Checking Distortion

When purchasing a microscope–camera lucida system, compare the models available and choose the system with the least amount of distortion. Such distortion can be detected by use of a microscope reticle with a grid pattern of equal squares since the squares in these reticles are nearly perfect and the lines are parallel and straight. Place the reticle under the objective of the microscope and adjust the magnification so that ten to fifteen series of squares are lined up across the entire diameter in all directions of the optical field. The square projected in the middle of the field will be somewhat distorted —more so in poorer optical systems, less so in better systems. Using the camera lucida and a fine pen, trace onto a piece of tracing paper the image of the square in the middle of the field, being careful to make the tracing as exact as possible. Do the same for a square at the periphery of the field. Mark on the paper which corner of the peripheral square is nearest the border of the optical field. Then place one square over the other, attempting to make the squares congruent. The image at the periphery of the field will have somewhat curved sides compared to the central square; the corner of the peripheral square closest to the border of the field will be larger than the corner of the central square. Again, there will be less distortion in better optical systems.

Procedure

When using the camera lucida, set an adjustable light source for the microscope, preferably with a rheostat on a transformer, so that it clearly defines the outlines of the specimen. Position a second, bright light, such as a high-intensity lamp, to cover the entire drawing area. Balancing of the lights is important for obtaining a clear image of the specimen. Generally the microscope light must be turned down. Sometimes adjustment of the device that turns on the camera lucida—that is, exposes the mirror to the prism—will help balance the lighting between specimen and drawing. This device may be a knob or a sleeve, depending on the make of the camera lucida. A less-than-full opening may improve the image.

1. The drawing surface and microscope base should be in the same plane: if the microscope sits flat on the drawing table, the drawing surface must be flat; if one is inclined, the other must be at the same angle. Otherwise the drawing will be distorted.
2. Position the specimen under the microscope. Focus on the part to be drawn, usually the margin of that part.
3. Adjust lighting on the drawing area.
4. While looking through the microscope with the camera lucida turned on, find where the drawing paper should be best situated to encompass the entire image. Tape the drawing paper in place under the mirror.
5. Focus the camera lucida (following manufacturer's instructions) on a pencil point held on the paper or on a pencil mark.
6. Balance the lighting between specimen and paper so that both pencil line and image are clearly visible.
7. Start by drawing the outline. Draw everything that is in one plane before focusing to a new level. This ensures that everything on each plane is accurately in proportion. Use a sharp pencil. If your eyes have to adjust every time you look in the microscope, if the image looks double, or if the image and pencil line do not match after being drawn, check whether the camera lucida is properly aligned with the microscope.
8. Keep the image centered in the ocular and draw only what is in the center two-thirds of the image area. Periodically check that the specimen and the paper have not moved.
9. To keep the image and pencil line visually aligned, hold your head very still while drawing. Do not hold the microscope's focusing knob while drawing; pressure on that knob tends to shift the microscope enough to change the drawing image.
10. Focusing may make the specimen appear to shift in position. The drawing can be moved to align it with the specimen. Before moving the paper, however, refocus on parts that were already drawn. If they still match the drawing, the paper probably should not be moved. If they do not match, adjust the drawing until it aligns with the specimen.
11. A camera lucida drawing that does not appear to be accurate can be checked by redrawing the specimen with a grid and comparing the two drawings.
12. Never touch the camera lucida mirror. If there are fingerprints on it and it needs cleaning, use a soft cloth (not paper or lens tissue) with alcohol and rub *very* gently.

Reconstruction of a specimen can be done with the camera lucida and tracing paper. Draw a number of views or parts from several specimens of the same size using the same magnification. Then combine selected views or parts to form an ideal drawing (figs. 2-28, 2-29). Mark reference points on one view to guide the attachment of parts drawn from other specimens or parts that are in different positions on the same specimen.

To determine where an appendage connects ventrally to a specimen such as an arthropod, draw the dorsal view with the camera lucida, then invert the specimen so that appendage attachments are visible. Match the dorsal outline drawing to the ventral body outline and mark where the appendages connect. Separate drawings of the appendages (at the same magnification) can be connected, using layers of tracing paper (fig. 2-30). Use this same procedure for reconstruction with a grid.

If parts from specimens of different sizes must be combined, the opaque projector helps (see that section and fig. 2-34).

Microprojectors are essentially upside-down compound microscopes. Light comes from above or laterally, depending on the design, and passes through the specimen on a stage, then through an objective and perhaps an ocular to the drawing table or wall, where the image is traced. More magnification is possible with a microprojector than with other methods for achieving a proportionally accurate rough drawing because of this capacity for projection; the farther the projected image, the larger the magnification. Until 1983, Bausch & Lomb produced a relatively simple, efficient, and inexpensive microprojector, the Tri-Simplex, which works vertically or horizontally. Used ones may still be available. A similar microprojector is the Ken-A-Vision (fig. 2-31). Another manufacturer is Aus Jena.

As with any compound micro-

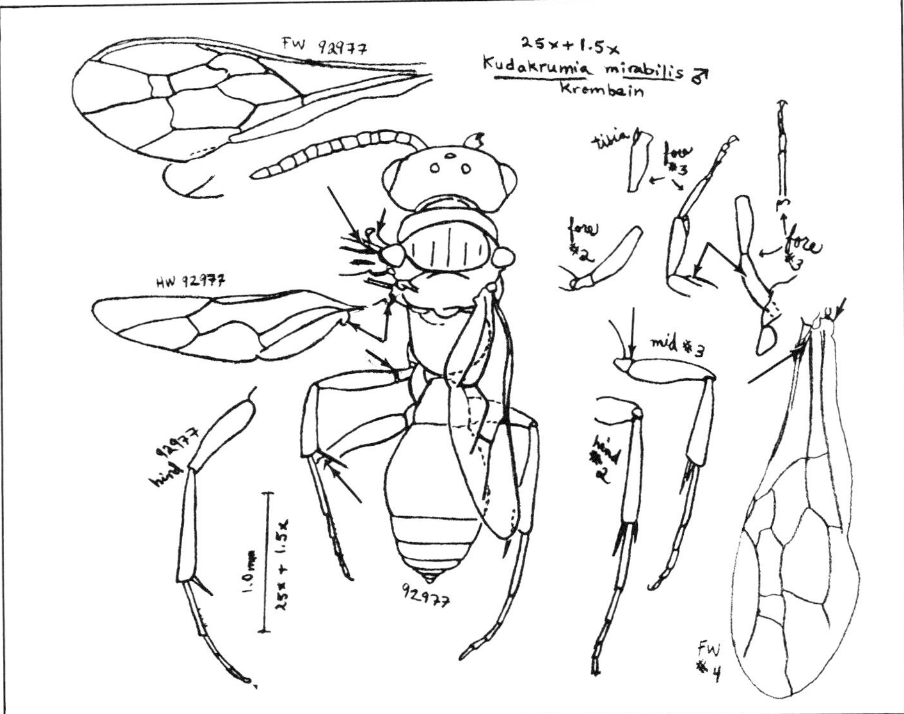

2-28. Reconstruction with the camera lucida. Parts are drawn from different specimens of a wasp and in various positions but include reference (common) points for attachment (marked by arrows). Pencil on tracing paper, by Elaine R. S. Hodges.

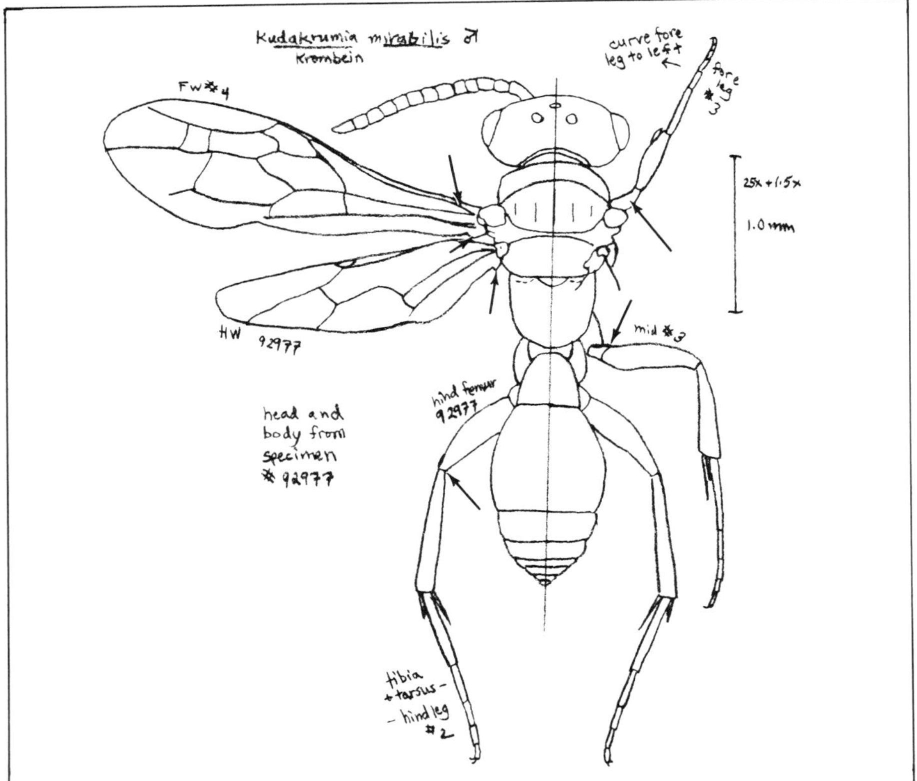

2-29. Complete (but still preliminary) drawing of wasp with appendages attached. If specimens are different sizes, parts must be enlarged or reduced to match the reference points, marked by arrows (see fig. 2-35; see also figs. 1-11, 1-12). Pencil on tracing paper, by Elaine R. S. Hodges.

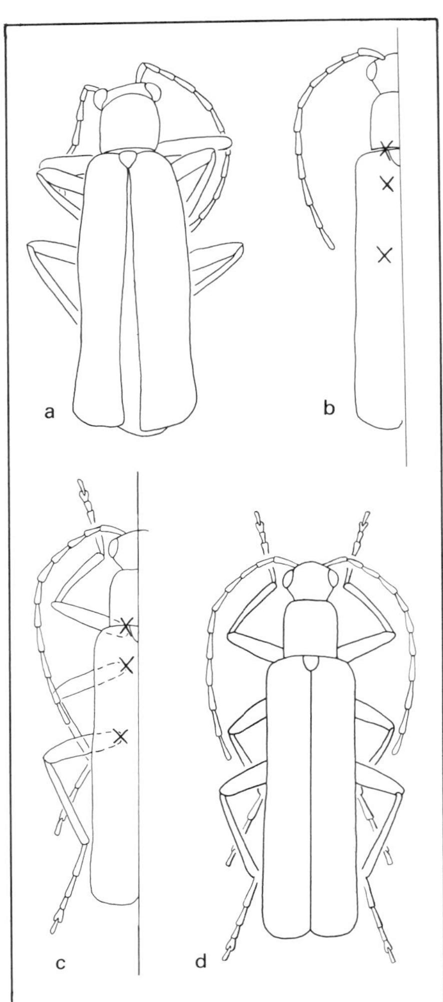

2-30. Use of the ventral view to find the correct attachment points for appendages to be shown in a dorsal view. *(a)* Dorsal view of beetle as it really appears. *(b)* Crosses on back of beetle mark where leg bases attach on ventral side. Beetle has been straightened and made symmetrical. *(c)* Legs drawn into position with bases attached at crosses. *(d)* Finished drawing. Pen-and-ink sequence by Richard E. White.

scope, the specimen must be translucent, and it should be mounted on a microscope slide. Dry (permanent) slides can be turned over so that the objective focuses only through the cover slip, most important when using a high-power objective such as 43×, but care must be taken not to damage the cover slip. Be aware that reversing the slide also reverses the drawing. If the drawing is on tracing paper, turning it over will correct the reversal.

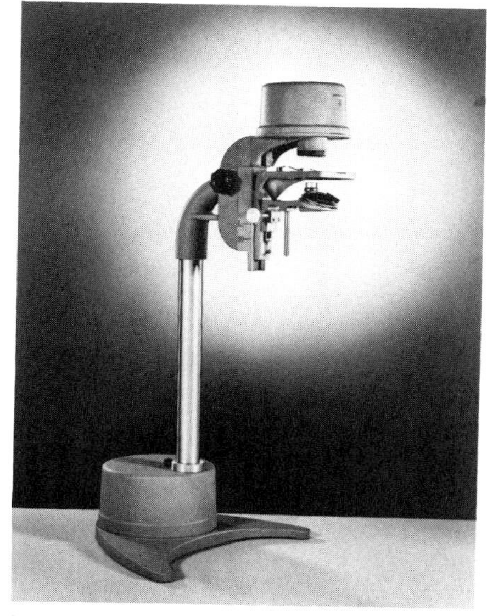
a

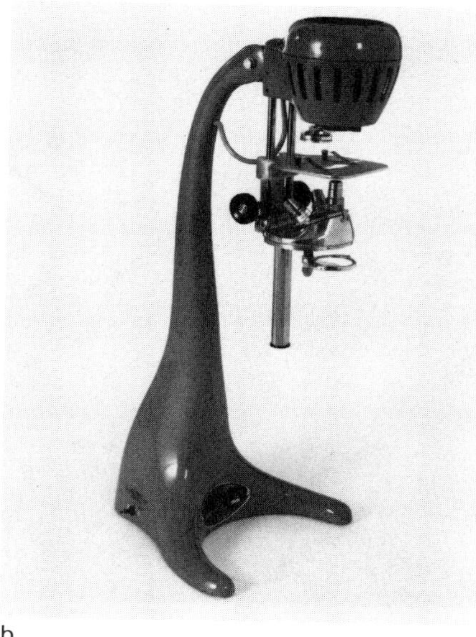
b

2-31. Microprojectors. *(a)* Bausch & Lomb Tri-Simplex. One objective is shown below the microscope stage. An eyepiece tube, which holds oculars of varying magnification, can screw into a hole below the objectives, further increasing magnification. *(b)* Ken-A-Vision microprojector. Courtesy of Ken-A-Vision.

Wet (temporary) mounts must be set on the stage right side up. Because even supposedly dry slides may not be completely dry—balsam mounting medium takes months or years to dry thoroughly—it is safest to use a microprojector that can hold the specimen horizontally, projecting its image vertically or down to the drawing surface. Brands differ in how they hold the specimen.

Procedure

The microprojector should be used in a dark room. A condenser lens increases light intensity and is an option with some models.

Magnification can be varied in several ways, depending on the style of projector. Objectives and oculars can be changed, the projector or the drawing surface, or both, can be shifted, perhaps raised or lowered with books or boxes. A shelf for the projector or the drawing surface can be made movable with pulleys or other means if the projector projects downward. The Tri-Simplex and Ken-A-Vision can project below their bases to a low table or the floor to increase magnification. Projection to a wall extends magnification even more. A microprojector drawing can be enlarged further by a grid or an opaque projector. If the specimen will not fit into the field of view, it can be drawn in sections. A scale is obtained by projecting a stage micrometer at the same magnification as the specimen.

To prolong the life of the bulb, plan a session of continuous work so that the bulb need not be repeatedly turned on and off. To change the bulb, unplug the projector and allow the bulb to cool first. Shield eyes in case the bulb breaks. Clean and dry the new bulb before inserting it.

Opaque projectors or viewers ("lazy lucis") are for enlarging or reducing images that are projected from the original object to a drawing or viewing surface by a mirror or lens and then traced. Some of these instruments accept only flat material; others also hold books or specimens. With some designs it is possible to pin a specimen onto the surface where paper is usually placed and to project its image for tracing. Be certain, however, that the specimen can take the intense heat from the projector's bulbs.

There are many types of opaque projectors with differing capabilities and prices. In general, they are either direct or indirect. A direct projector projects the artwork to a work surface, permitting opaque papers to be used; it must be used in a darkened room. An indirect projector—the "luci"—projects an image from below a sheet of glass, on which a translucent paper is used to trace the image. Indirect projectors usually are floor models with a cloth drape to create a dark space around the illustrator (fig. 2-32). A horizontal or tilting shelf holds two- or three-dimensional objects. For the latter, light should be directed at an acute angle toward the specimen.

The Postoscope is an inexpensive direct projector; however, it will only enlarge. Of other types that both reduce and enlarge, some are wall-mounted and some freestanding; others clamp to a drawing table (fig. 2-33). A wall-mounted version should be installed so that its projected field of view is not too far from the front of the table to be used. Otherwise, you will have to bend far over the table to draw. To prevent distortion of the projected image, carefully follow the manufacturer's installation directions in aligning the projector. The crank of wall-mounted styles should be greased periodically.

Some direct projectors can be used in reverse to accommodate a large three-dimensional specimen. Tape a piece of glass to the part of the projector where the original material ordinarily goes. Set the specimen on the table where tracing would otherwise occur. In a darkened room, direct an intense, perhaps raking, light on the specimen, but *do not* turn on the projector light. The image of the specimen will appear on the glass and can be traced onto tracing paper placed over this glass (fig. 2-34). The usual precautions must be observed for mounting a specimen

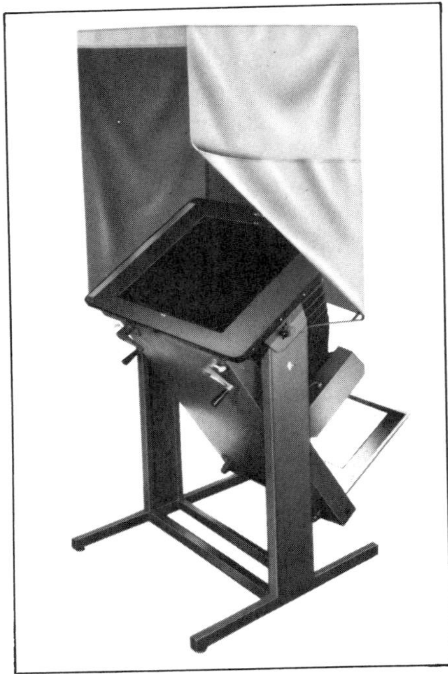

2-32. "Lazy luci" indirect opaque projector. On this Goodkin swivel-top projector, the drawing to be enlarged or reduced is below the bellows and is projected up to the glass drawing surface. Courtesy of M. P. Goodkin Company.

2-34. Use of a wall-mounted direct opaque projector in reverse. Light on the specimen (a lobster claw) is reflected as image onto glass or clear acrylic taped over the area where a drawing normally would be placed for projection. The image is being traced by Marilyn Schotte. Photo by Vic Krantz.

2-33. A direct opaque projector clamped to drawing board. Courtesy of Artograph.

so that an undistorted image is traced. Pertinent chapters contain advice on mounting each subject.

Another use of the opaque projector is for reconstruction, combining parts of different-sized specimens of the same species into one drawing. This may be necessary when parts from one specimen are deformed or missing. In addition to the parts needed from each specimen, draw common parts so they can be matched. For instance, if a wing of an insect is needed from a supplementary specimen that is smaller than the basic specimen, draw the thorax as well as the wing of the supplementary specimen. Place the basic drawing on the drawing surface of the opaque projector. Enlarge the supplementary drawing until its thorax matches the basic specimen's thorax. Then trace the wing in its proper place. The result should have an accurate proportional relationship (fig. 2-35).

Cameras, 35mm, record specimens in slide or print form to provide supplementary (or the only) information about color, natural position, environment, and other details. Sometimes a photograph taken with a telephoto lens provides the best undistorted view of a very large specimen, such as large dinosaur bones. Prints can be enlarged on the opaque projector for tracing.

Slide projectors are used for projecting images to study or trace. Although standard 35mm projectors can project the image to a wall for tracing, it is easier to work on a horizontal surface. Figure 2-36 shows a simply made device for tracing drawings from 35mm slides. The mirror should be set at a 45-degree angle.

If the slides are to be used for reference only, and a vertical nearby image is preferred, the projector can be set in a box with one translucent side onto which the image projects via a mirror. The viewer sees the image from outside the box on that translucent panel—in effect, behind the screen (fig. 2-37). This can be installed near a work area. Such rear-projecting devices are available commercially.

A microfiche can also be used to enlarge 35mm slides for viewing.

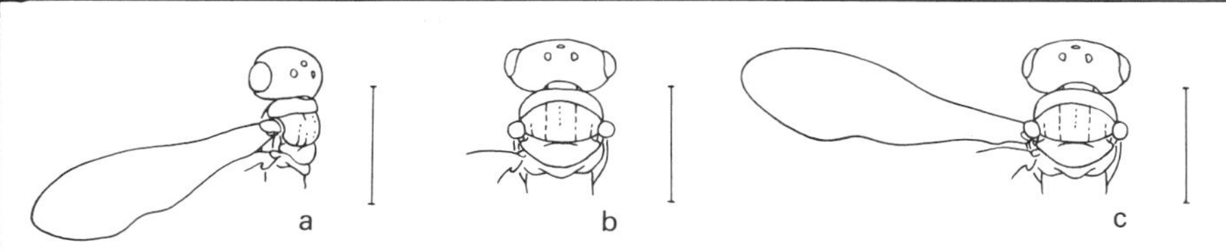

2-35. Combining parts from specimens of different sizes: *(a)* supplementary specimen drawn at same scale as basic specimen; *(b)* basic specimen; *(c)* wing of supplementary specimen enlarged and attached to drawing of basic specimen. Usually only the scale of the basic specimen would be shown in the final drawing. Wasp. Pen-and-ink on Bristol board, by Elaine R. S. Hodges.

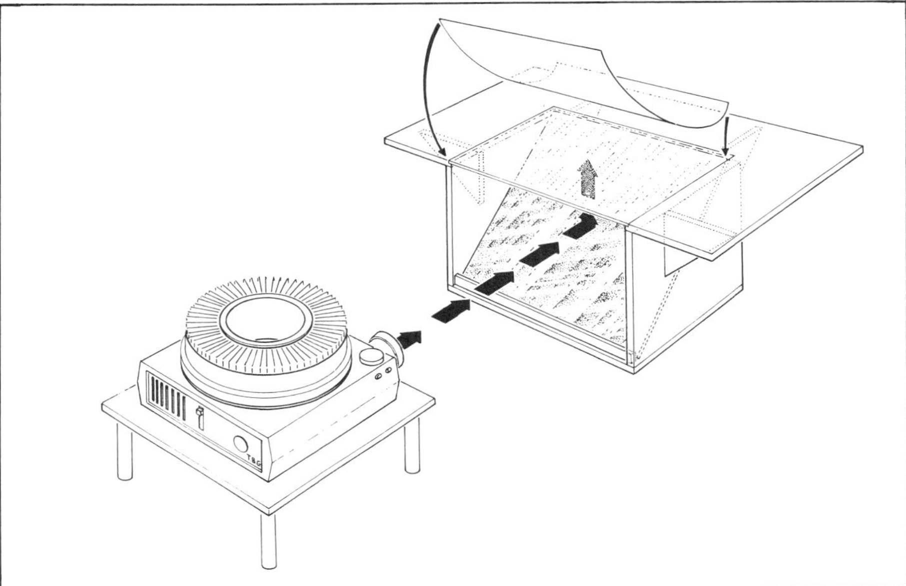

2-36. Device for drawing from 35mm slides. Pen-and-ink on Bristol board, by T. Britt Griswold, from a design by Donald B. Sayner.

2-37. Device for viewing 35mm slides for reference. The open lid shows the 35mm projector and mirror. A translucent panel forms the screen. Designed by Warren A. Cutler, Jr. Photo by Office of Graphics and Exhibits, U.S. National Zoological Park, Smithsonian Institution.

MISCELLANEOUS

Adhesives

Adhesives are needed to mount drawings temporarily during the drawing process and more or less permanently for reproduction or viewing. They present serious and difficult problems for the illustrator interested in having a drawing last for years, until it is either printed or placed in archival storage. Often the manuscript for which drawings are done is not published for anywhere from two to twenty or more years. Many adhesives such as rubber cement or masking tape lose their adhesive properties and leach acids through the drawing surface, leaving yellow stains that can destroy the image. Unfortunately, the worst offenders are the easiest ones to obtain. For an illustration that is also a work of art, use only adhesives that will not damage the image or its support and that can be safely removed from the artwork.

To mount a good drawing that was done on paper, hinging with archival-quality tape or paper hinges and starch paste is safest. This is fine for exhibition but often is not practical for sending a drawing to the printer unless the drawing is on one board rather than on bits of paper requiring mounting onto a plate.

When an illustration is purely utilitarian, archival considerations may not be involved. The following discussion will cover adhesives suitable for both archival and utilitarian uses.

Pastes, from vegetable sources, are generally weaker than glues, which derive from animal or synthetic sources. A good paste, however, is very strong. For use with all but the heaviest papers, starch paste is the preferred adhesive. Starches are carbohydrates occurring in plants as tiny white gran-

---

Christine A. Smith and Elaine R. S. Hodges wrote the text on adhesives.

ules. Flours are mixtures of starch and gluten, a material that is useless in forming adhesive bonds. Since flour pastes become insoluble with age, whereas starch pastes remain indefinitely soluble, strong, and harmless to both paper and design, conservation pastes are made with starch, not flour. Commercially available library paste consists of dextrin (a simple, converted form of starch) plus a preservative, plasticizer, fluidizer, and fragrance. Because these additives might cause undesirable chemical reactions, pure starch pastes should be used on objects of value.

Starch pastes are cooked mixtures of either wheat or rice starch and water, with the possible addition of a fungicide to retard mold growth. When cooked, the starch granules absorb water and swell. Eventually, the absorbed water bursts open the granules, creating a continuous, creamy medium: paste.

Rice starch granules are smaller than wheat starch granules, so rice paste tends to be creamier. A wheat paste that is noticeably granular is undercooked. Wheat starch is somewhat stronger than rice starch. Only experience can teach when a stronger or more delicate paste is necessary. On very thin or translucent papers, wheat starch paste sometimes leaves a faint gray shadow, so rice paste often is preferable for such papers.

Because pastes are hygroscopic (moisture absorbing), they expand and contract to a limited extent when dried, unlike tapes and some glues. This movement permits the natural expansion and contraction of paper. An adhesive that restricts paper from moving causes cockles or tears in the restrained areas.

The disadvantages of pastes are their vulnerability to deterioration by molds (they should not be used for longer than one week after being cooked) and the need to work with them a while before gaining confidence and understanding their subtleties. Nonetheless, artists who regularly need high-quality paper adhesives will be amply repaid for the time spent learning to make and use starch paste. Ingredients may be obtained from conservation supply houses (see Appendix).

Recipe for Starch Paste

- 10 grams wheat starch (4 teaspoons)
- 120 ml distilled water (4½ fluid ounces)
- 8 grams thymol (fungicide crystals, may be available from a pharmacist) (2½ teaspoons)
- 10 ml grain alcohol (ethanol) (2 teaspoons)

Put the starch in the top of a small double boiler and add enough distilled water to mix the powder to a yogurtlike consistency. Heat tap water in the bottom of the double boiler. Bring the remaining distilled water to a boil in a separate vessel and add it to the starch mixture, stirring rapidly to prevent lumping. Cook the mixture, stirring constantly, for about thirty minutes (maintain heat of water in double boiler with medium-high heat) until it is thick and glassy, not thin and chalky. Do not cook beyond this point; overcooking weakens paste. Allow to cool, stirring occasionally to prevent formation of a skin. Break up lumps by beating or straining through a nonmetal strainer.

To keep the paste beyond one day, dissolve the thymol crystals in the alcohol and stir a few drops of this solution into the paste. Store the excess alcohol/thymol mixture in a narrow-necked, stoppered glass bottle to reduce evaporation. It can be saved and used for the next batch of paste. Store the paste in a glass container with a nonmetallic lid, both of which have been rinsed inside with thymol solution. Do not refrigerate. Discard the paste if it separates into liquid and solid, discolors, or smells sour, putrid, or yeasty.

To use the paste, remove some from the jar and either force it through the strainer again or knead it with a stiff-bristled brush. Then slowly work in distilled water (tap water contains metals and other materials that catalyze paper deterioration) until the paste is completely homogeneous in texture and as thin as cream. Thick layers are likely to crack when humidity drops, whereas thin layers can be brushed into the interstices of the papers, forming a very close, strong bond.

Glues are neither necessary nor desirable for most paper objects. Many glues become completely insoluble with age or require very strong solvents to be released, and they can discolor objects either by staining them directly or by darkening and becoming visible through thin papers. Glues may be acidic and are also likely to restrain the hygroscopic movement of paper, causing the sheets to draw or wrinkle. In some situations, however, glues are preferred, such as when joining sheets of two-ply Bristol weight or heavier supports. Conservation supply houses stock glues that will not stain or chemically damage paper objects, but the illustrator needs to develop a sense for the strength of different adhesives appropriate for different jobs.

Although only glues that meet archival standards should be applied to valued objects, illustrators may be interested to know the components and characteristics of other common glues.

White glue (for example, Elmer's) is an emulsion of polyvinyl acetate (PVA) and water that becomes virtually insoluble after some aging. Various formulations are more or less acceptable for archival applications, so an illustrator who intends to use a PVA glue should choose one designed for

---

Marjorie Cohn at the Center for Conservation and Technical Studies, Fogg Art Museum, Harvard University, formulated this recipe for starch paste.

these purposes. They should not be used on thin papers such as one-ply Bristol because wrinkling may occur when the paper dries. The virtues of good PVA glues are long-term strength and flexibility with almost no discoloration.

Rubber cement is liquefied rubber in volatile organic solvents, used for quick-and-dirty methods. It darkens, stains, generates sulfuric acid, becomes brittle, and loses its bonding ability. It is inappropriate for all but throwaway projects. With that in mind, the artist can use it for photographs (of which there are duplicates or negatives) and simple utilitarian drawings that will not be reused or retained. Putting the cement on both mounting surface and the back of the illustration, letting them dry to tackiness, and then mounting the illustration results in the strongest bond and does not permit easy shifting of position. If cement is brushed on just one surface and mounting is done immediately while wet, the illustration can be peeled off relatively easily, which may be desirable in case a rearrangement is needed.

Although widely available, plastic jars for rubber cement are not recommended, as they are porous and permit the cement to dry out quickly. Glass jars should be used.

Rubber-cement thinner (Bestine is a common brand) is used to thin rubber cement to a proper consistency, that of slightly thickened gelatin that still will run off a brush. Squirted under an illustration glued down with rubber cement, it will help dissolve the adhesive. Thinner also is useful for cleaning off various adhesive residues. Be aware that the liquid and its vapors are highly flammable and can spontaneously ignite merely from the friction of vigorous rubbing or from an electrical spark. It also is considered carcinogenic. For the sake of studio safety, have only a small quantity around and keep it in a tightly closed can. To prevent the buildup of volatile vapors and to reduce your exposure, never leave the can open for more than a minute. Cans with nozzles, sold in art stores for dispensing thinner, reduce the amount of vapors emitted.

A square of hardened rubber—called a rubber cement pickup—can be purchased or made from rolled-together balls of dried rubber cement. It is invaluable for cleaning up excess cement that invariably oozes out from edges of illustrations.

Wax adhesives range from pure wax to combinations of wax, plasticizer, and adhesive; they are used for relatively temporary mounts. Pure wax is a chemically inert adhesive, but it provides a brittle bond and can make paper more translucent. Waxes that are altered with plasticizers and adhesives form more secure bonds but are not of archival quality.

The wax coater spreads a thin film of melted wax on drawings or photographs to act as an adhesive for mounting. A heating element melts the wax in the coating machine. Tabletop models have rollers into which the paper is fed (fig. 2-38). Hand-operated waxers are held like a pistol to roll the wax onto the surface (fig. 2-39). Waxed items are just slightly tacky and can be repositioned. After burnishing, lightweight papers stay in place rather well. Although waxing is preferable to rubber cement for the durability of the artwork, some waxes may seep into and stain the surface of certain drawings after a period of time, depending on the drawing surface used and the conditions of storage or exhibition. Wax should not be used on very thin papers because it will soak through. Use a waxer that applies a solid coating of wax, not the kind that applies wax in stripes, since the stripes of wax tend to be messier and sometimes bleed through to the surface of photographs or thin papers, where they will appear, stripelike, in reproduction. Brushing wax on will produce a thick coat that may make paper translucent and may soak through the illustration. A waxed illustration should be burnished down with paper protecting the surface from the burnishing tool. Even after burnishing, however, a waxed illustration, especially if it is small or on relatively heavy paper, may shift or come off if it is handled too much.

2-38. Tabletop waxer has rollers into which paper to be waxed is fed. Courtesy of M. P. Goodkin Company.

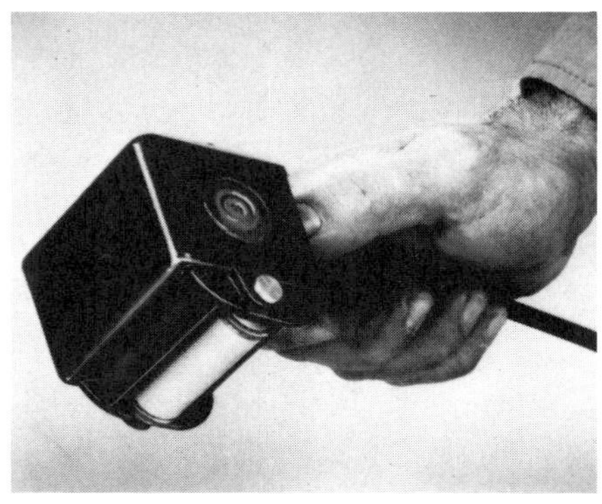

2-39. Hand-held waxer can spread or tack wax in small areas. Courtesy of Lectro-Stik Corporation.

Spray adhesives are made from a variety of glues. Their advantages or disadvantages can be determined only on a case-by-case basis. All spray adhesives, however, are propelled as minute, solid particles, so light they remain airborne. Both the propellants and the materials propelled may be toxic to the artist—in fact, deadly—because their fine mists can travel quite far (including deep into the lungs). If they must be used, good ventilation is mandatory—ideally, under an exhaust hood—and a respirator (designed to filter the specific material being sprayed) is strongly advised. The safest procedure is to avoid using spray adhesives.

Tapes are used for fastening *edges* of drawings; they are generally unacceptable for direct contact with objects intended to last. Tapes are likely to create stains, become insoluble, induce acid damage, and prevent paper from moving with humidity changes. Included in the group of unacceptable tapes are stamp-hinge glassine tapes, which respond dramatically to water and are too weak to be reliable; gummed brown-paper tapes, which are acidic and lose their bonding ability; pressure-sensitive tapes, which stain; and any other tapes not known specifically to meet archival standards. Conservation supply houses do sell some tapes, but because they are intended for differing uses, it would be wise to consult a conservator before using a tape in the construction of scientific illustrations.

On the other hand, it does seem safe to use 3M's Scotch double-sided adhesive tape (no. 415) to join mounting boards or to use outside the image area. On boards 11 by 14 inches (28 by 35cm) or smaller, apply strips of the double-sided tape along two opposite edges of the back of the board so that it can be set in place parallel to the edges of the mounting board. Using few strips and only two edges permits some reactions to atmospheric effects on the boards. Remove protective strips from tape, exposing the sticky surface, and carefully tilt and press the drawing board into place. No shifting is possible. Do not use double-sided tape for thin papers or for larger boards, which will warp.

White artist's tape, such as 3M's Scotch no. 285, or transparent tape, such as Scotch no. 811 (Magic Plus), which have a "low tack" (lift off readily), are extremely useful in temporarily holding down overlays during the drawing process. They leave little or no immediately visible residue and rarely tear the drawing or drawing board surface; however, no. 285 has been known to damage drafting table covers, and both tapes will leave a residue on photographs

Both coated boards and thin materials, including drafting films, can simply be taped on the edges to mounting board with a tape such as Scotch no. 810 (Magic transparent).

Mount films with the convex surface down to reduce shadows of the drawing on the mounting board. Line drawings can be arranged on a plate with tiny strips of tape; if the tape edges show in the eventual photographic negative, they can be painted (opaqued) out on the negative by the printer. (A special dark red paint, called opaquing fluid, is used for this purpose.) Tape should not be placed too close to inked lines, or the photo retoucher will not have enough space to paint out any tape that shows. No. 811 tape permits repositioning but also might come off during handling by the printer. More permanent tapes, such as Scotch no. 810, might be safer.

Tape should not be used near a tone drawing image or on photographs because it will show in reproduction and cannot be opaqued out of the negative. If there is plenty of room around the central image, tape may be used to attach edges of a tone illustration to a mounting board. If necessary, slit the tape to remove the drawing. Do not tape solidly around the edges, however, since room for expansion and contraction of drawing surface and mounting board is necessary to prevent warping. Tape on two edges or four corners usually is sufficient.

Drymounting is a process using adhesive-impregnated tissue between the back of the object to be mounted and the front of the mounting board. Once the sandwich has been assembled, heat or pressure or both activate the adhesive, resulting in overall attachment of the mounted drawing. This is an unacceptable method for mounting illustrations drawn on hygroscopic supports because the mount impedes contraction and expansion, adhesive staining is possible, and damaging chemical reactions may occur. Conservation-quality secondary supports, however, can be adhered to each other by drymounting, either to build thickness or for aesthetic reasons. The illustration then would be hinged to this mount. In the event of problems caused by the drymounting, the drawing can be cut away at its hinges. No currently available commercial drymounting tissues can be considered archival.

One of the more recent drymount innovations is 3M's Scotch C-35 PMA system, which does not require heat. The illustration is burnished by hand or run through a special press to activate an adhesive sheet, Positionable Mounting Adhesive no. 568, that glues the illustration to a mounting board. One advantage of this system is that it requires two burnishings for permanent mounting: the first run through the rollers applies a tacky adhesive somewhat like wax, which makes the illustration repositionable until the second burnishing. But both this system and drymounting with heat fasten materials permanently, so they cannot be considered archival because the mounting cannot be reversed (see Appendix).

Fixatives are liquids sprayed onto a drawing or lettering to "fix," or seal and protect, the surface. A fixative is an adhesive in the sense that it helps media adhere to the drawing support. It can stain. Spray cans of fixative ("fixatif") come in a wide variety of commercial preparations, the most widely used being a workable fixative. As the name implies, the workable fixative allows for continued erasure and drawing if need be. Other types do not afford such flexibility and only provide protection.

Some permanent fixatives contain hazardous substances such as toluene; read the labels. An effective, inexpensive fixative for clay-coated papers is 80 percent ethanol (ethyl alcohol). The alcohol sets the dust of graphite or carbon into the paper surface but does not harm the paper, since the alcohol evaporates quickly. A small atomizer may be used to apply the alcohol. An airbrush is ideal for application, as the density of the mist can be controlled. Again: be aware that all fixatives are flammable. Use them with good ventilation, ideally under an exhaust hood.

Lettering and Other Graphics

Lettering techniques using ink freehand or with lettering guides, such as a Leroy set, are most permanent; these, however, require skill to use. Freehand lettering is not acceptable to most journals or publishers, although excellent calligraphy might be suitable in some cases. Other graphics include symbols, shading screens, and charting tape.

Dry transfer, cutout lettering, lettering on tape (Kroy, Merlin), shading screens, and charting tapes are backed by adhesives. Because these products are relatively new, long-term effects of their adhesives on drawing surfaces are not known. Thus far, dry transfer does not seem to stain surfaces, but in the past, cutout type has left yellow stains when removed. It is safest not to place any adhesive-backed materials directly on valuable or original drawings, those considered works of art. Apply the graphics to an overlay.

Leroy is a brand of lettering set that has ruler-shaped templates with incised alphabets of different sizes into which the point at one end of a scriber fits while its other end holds a pen. When the scriber's point is moved along the shape of the letter, the pen draws the letter. There is only one choice of lettering designs, and, by modern standards, the look of Leroy lettering is not considered attractive.

Dry-transfer or cutout type consists of alphabets, numbers, arrows, and symbols on plastic sheets; these are available in a wide variety of typefaces and sizes. Dry-transfer type is attached to the back of a plastic carrier sheet and is rubbed into position. The figures on cutout type are also on the back of plastic, but the plastic is transferred with the type and protects it. Cutout type must be cut and lifted from its carrier sheet and placed in position. Both should be burnished with a paper between the type and the burnisher. To prevent cracking of the type, a larger burnisher should be used with larger type.

Dry-transfer type (also called transfer or instant type) is widely used because of its availability, variety, and ease of application. It is not without problems, however. Type may chip or come off the sheets as subsequent figures are applied to a drawing; type may transfer to the cover sheets; and some dry-transfer type may shrink after application. The older the sheet, the more likely the figures are to chip. Some brands may become dry after one or two months' storage, depending on the local climate. Newer brands of dry-transfer type are improved. Some brands found to work well are Prestype,Geotype, Zip-A-Tone and Chartpak (see Appendix). Use care when spraying fixatives on dry-transfer type. Some fixatives tend to dissolve the material of which it is made, and the characters "bleed" on the paper.

Cutout type, such as Formatt brand, is much more durable. There is, however, a backing similar to transparent tape around each letter, which may show in halftone reproduction, especially on black areas.

Lettering machines may be mechanical, electronic, computerized, or photographic. These save time by producing entire words or sentences, which can be cut out and applied as a unit. Small machines, such as the Kroy and Merlin brands, type out carbon figures on an adhesive-backed tape from which a backing tape is peeled (fig. 2-40). Because the type is on top of a plastic carrier tape and can be scratched or smeared, the tape should be sprayed lightly with workable fixative before use. After the type is placed in position, burnish it as you would transfer type.

Many type styles and sizes are available on the machine's interchangeable discs or templates, and various sorts of tape can be chosen, such as black and white on a translucent background, shiny or matte, or black or colors on white. Diazo tape may adhere better to film than Photo-Quality tape, but adheres poorly to treated papers such as Clearprint tracing paper. Beware of cheaper off-brands of tape sold for use in lettering machines. Contrary to claims, they may not work in the machine, or they may produce inferior type.

A trimmer is available from the machine's manufacturer to trim the width of tape with 18-point or smaller type neatly. Test a strip of tape with the type size you plan to use to make sure that the type edges are not cut off.

The electronic and computerized machines are much faster and more convenient to use but also are much more expensive than the manual versions. Although lettering machines are invaluable for producing words, transfer or cutout type may be faster for individual letters and numbers that so often are needed for labeling plates.

Phototypesetting machines produce type on a tape by a photographic process, all of which is done inside the machine (fig. 2-41). The tape must be waxed, trimmed, and pressed into place. Such machines, including the headliner

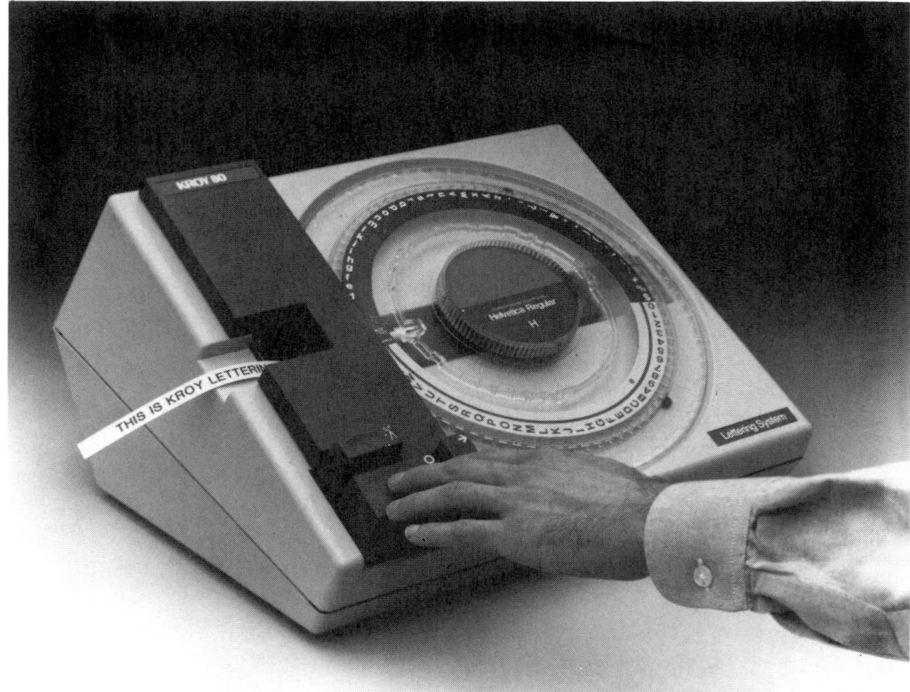

2-40. Kroy lettering machine. Shown is the relatively inexpensive manual version. One model with a computerized keyboard (made by Kroy or VPS Lettering Company) speeds production considerably. Courtesy of Kroy, Inc.

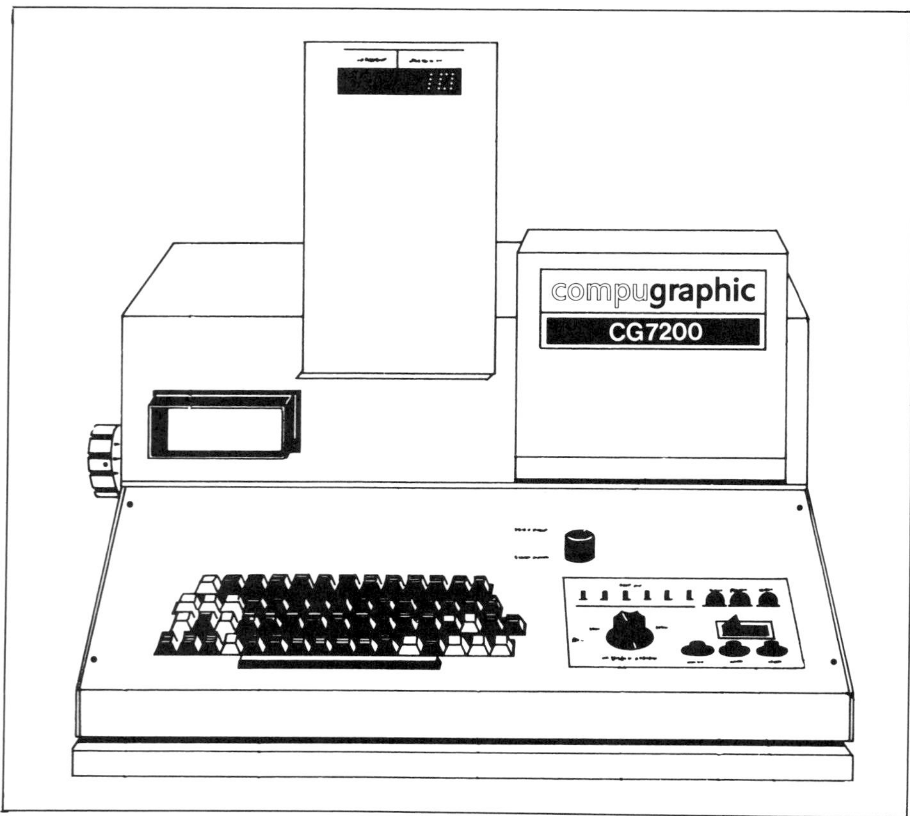

2-41. Phototypesetting machine from Compugraphic Corporation. Diagram courtesy of Compugraphic Corporation.

types, Varityper, and Compugraphic, are quite expensive. Increasingly, they are computerized. For large projects and large budgets, type can be set on a compositor, a machine likely to be found in printing and typography shops or perhaps in large institutions. Almost any style or size of type can be ordered. The strip or block of type then has to be attached to an illustration or overlay with wax or some other adhesive.

Computers can produce type on adhesive-backed paper or plain paper or film, to be attached to an illustration or overlay. When an illustration is created on a computer, typography is created as an integral part of it (see chapter 24). The variety and quality of type depend primarily on the software (computer programs) and the printer.

Shading films (shading screens) are adhesive-backed and provide patterns, colors, and tones for drawings and maps. The black-and-white versions reproduce as line. They take the place of drawing by hand when areas must be covered with precisely drafted, repetitive designs, but even random stipple patterns are available (see Patterned Surfaces in chapter 5).

Charting tapes are thin, preprinted, adhesive-backed tapes on rolls that come in various widths, colors, solids, and patterns. Glossy or matte versions can be chosen to match the rest of the artwork; glossy may be preferable for printed reproduction, matte for slides. The tape is used to form lines and bars on graphs, outlines for maps and charts, and for many other applications depending on need and creativity. Some tape is even flexible, designed to create curved lines.

Although tape can replace inking, it is less permanent than ink; it may shift, peel, and shrink. Therefore, it should be used for jobs that will be photographed or printed promptly. In fact, for black-and-white work it is a good idea to photograph or photostat the finished artwork immediately and send the reproduction to the printer in case problems develop with the original. The main advantage of charting tape is its clean-cut, mechanical look: edges are sharp, patterns precise. For patterned or colored bars, it is faster to use tape than ink or paint. For lines, it may take longer to cut and miter corners of tape than to rule them, but the effect with tape is likely to look more professional. (See chapters 5 and 24 and the Bibliography for additional information on how to use tapes.)

Printer's Guides

Register marks are crosses or crosses in a circle, either hand drawn or commercially printed. They permit the printer to align overlays precisely with the drawings. At least three register marks each should be put on the art and the overlay. The marks should be at different angles, perhaps two at 90 degrees and one at 45 degrees to the vertical and horizontal, or placed asymmetrically to prevent accidental flopping of the negative (figs. 2-42, 2-43; see fig. C-2). Place the register marks on the illustration first; then securely tape an overlay—usually clear acetate or polyester—to the top (or left side) of the support for the illustration. Make sure it lies flat; then hold its free edge down with a small piece of removable tape (artist's, masking, or Scotch no. 811) at the bottom (or right side) of the support to prevent shifting. Using an X-Acto blade, forceps, or other tool (or pen for drawn register marks), place register marks on the overlay precisely over the marks on the illustration. Some brands precisely align registration marks to both illustration and overlay simultaneously, using a dry-transfer system. If you use commercial register marks on film (cutout, dry transfer, or on tape), they may creep over a period of time. Placing Scotch no. 810 Magic transparent tape over them increases the adhesive area, thus reducing the possibility of change. Register marks should be placed outside the area of the drawing to be reproduced but close enough so that they will show in the photographic negative, within an inch of the illustration area to be reproduced (see Labeling on Overlay in chapter 27).

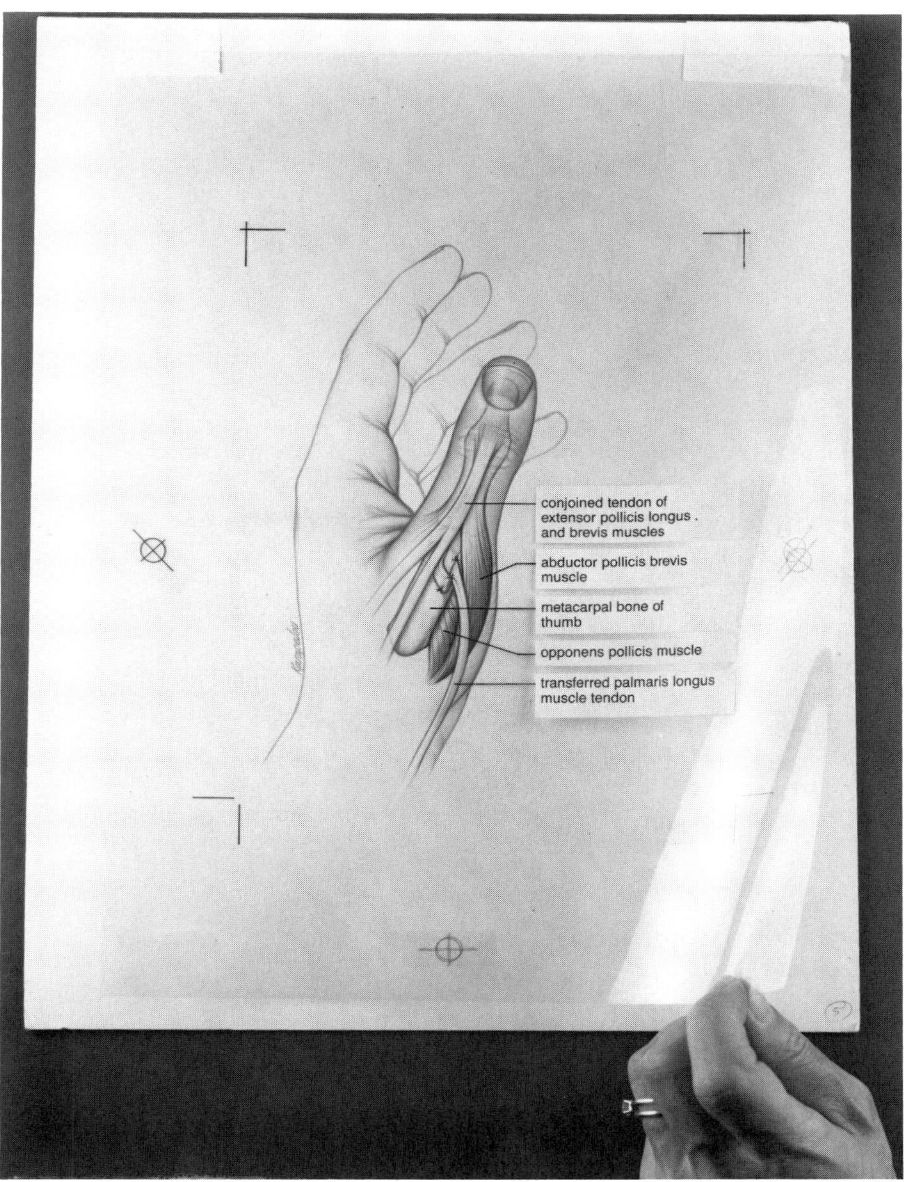

2-42. Placement of register and crop marks and labels on an overlay. Two different ways to draw crop marks are shown at the top and bottom of the overlay. Figure 2-43 shows the reproduction of figure 2-42.

Crop marks are hand-drawn short lines at right angles to each other that tell the printer how much of the illustration is to be reproduced. They are placed outside the area to be reproduced, in the margins of a photo or drawing. The printer then uses a triangle or T square to determine where the right angles would intersect if they actually were drawn across the illustration, and thus knows how much to cut off the negative. Nothing is drawn directly on the illustration itself. Crop marks can be drawn on an overlay, as in figure 2-42, but care must be taken not to create an indentation on the illus-

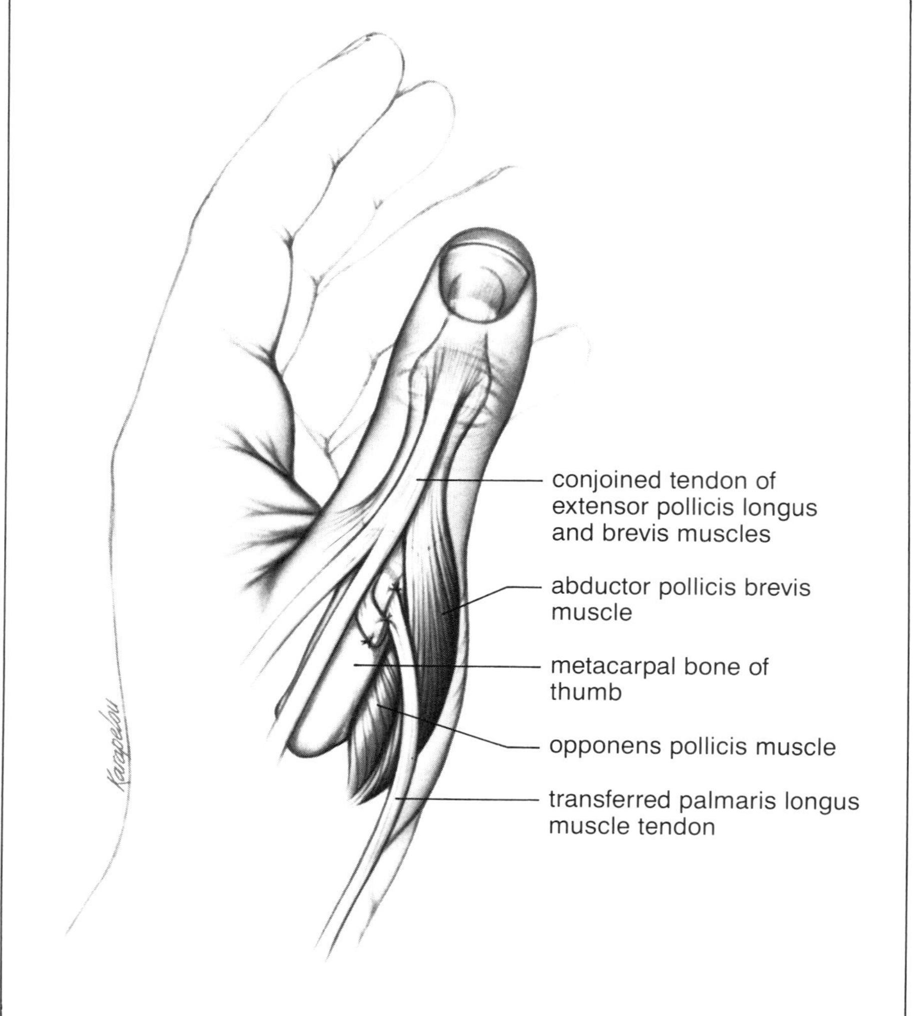

2-43. Printed version of figure 2-42. The labels were printed from a line negative and the art was printed from a halftone screened negative. Note that the crop and register marks do not appear in the reproduction. The overlay is acetate, .005 inch thick; crop marks and leader lines were inked with technical pens. Labels were phototypeset using the Compugraphic MCS system with an 8200 optical strobe printer, and were attached to the acetate with adhesive wax coated on the back of the typesetting paper. Register marks are precut and on a dispenser tape, made by X-marx Process Company. An orthopedic surgical procedure rendered in transparent ivory black watercolor with brush and airbrush and opaque watercolor applied with brush on Crescent no. 215 hot-press illustration board, by John W. Karapelou.

tration (see Cropping in chapter 27).

Pin (or punch) register systems involve the use of a system of pins (also called pegs), usually metal, to align a base drawing precisely to overlay materials so that when the overlays are placed on the same pins as the illustration, all parts will be in register. A registration punch works like a loose-leaf paper punch to make the holes for registering the artwork and overlays. Strips (header strips) or tabs with prepunched holes can be attached to the materials to accomplish the same end. The Acme registration system shown in figure 2-44 is designed for use with animation cels—the individual films with drawings for each step of an animation sequence. It or a similar system can be used in the darkroom to guarantee alignment of all photographic overlays; it also is used in cartography. All overlay materials are punched, or prepunched header strips or tabs are attached to the overlays, before they are used.

Labels are used to identify overlays on drawings and photographs for the printer, slides for portfolios, and specimens for photography. They should provide a good writing surface. Adhesive-backed labels, available in stationery stores, and strips of white artist's tape are handy for identifying overlays, photographs, and slides. Adhesive-backed matte, transparent tape such as Scotch no. 810 also may be used to label photographs. On the back of a photograph, a label should be placed away from the image area to ensure it does not show through or its edges do not create an imprint on the image. Write on the label before it is affixed to the photograph; if anything must be added afterward, minimal pressure should be used to avoid making an impression on the surface. On the front of the photograph, the label can be cut to fit in the white border. (When ordering photoprints, specify a border wide enough to provide room for labels.) If the printer is to see instructions or identifications on the line negative, labels on the illustration should be handwritten in black ink or typed.

Labels for 35mm slides can be typed in a very small font, printed very small by some computer printers, fed through a reducing photocopy machine, or hand-printed with ballpoint pen or pencil, depending on the slide mount.

Some opaque labels on slides do pose one problem: curled edges and added thickness can snag in a projector. This is less likely, however, in slide trays designed for fewer slides—for instance, carousels that hold 80 slides instead of 140.

Daniel G. Cole and Karen Ackoff contributed to the text on pin registration systems.

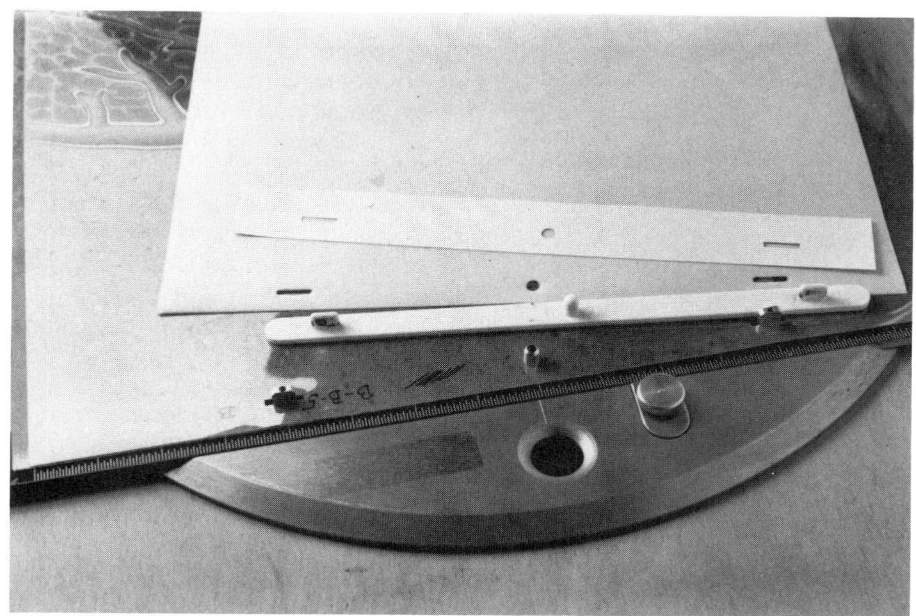

2-44. Pin registration allows precise alignment of overlay materials that have been punched for that particular registration system. Shown here are punched header strip, tracing paper, and cels, along with plastic and metal registration pins. The metal pins are affixed to an animation drawing disc. These examples are of the Acme registration system. Courtesy of Steven J. Harrison.

Not a printer's guide, but an aid to the illustrator, are labels on index or other white cards, used when large specimens are photographed to serve as the reference for a preliminary drawing (see chapter 14). White cards with black printing placed next to the specimen will clearly identify the species in the photograph.

Masking Materials

To protect surfaces temporarily from media or to cover areas to achieve certain printing results, a mask of some sort often is needed.

Friskets—acetate film, liquid, or adhesive-backed film—are used for temporary coverage. Frisket usually refers to materials used to protect part of a drawing from airbrush spray. Friskets also are used in watercolor wash painting to keep an area white when paint is brushed broadly over a surface. Because liquid friskets dry clear and invisible, some have color added to make them visible. Colored liquid friskets should be tested before use on a surface because the color may stain. Film frisket has an adhesive backing. It should not be left on a drawing overnight because it may become too firmly attached to remove. When acetate or some other temporary loose material is used as a mask, it should be weighted down. Rubber cement may be applied to the mask and allowed to dry before use, forming a low-tack surface that will come off easily. If the drawing is on a thin material and can be placed on a metal board, magnets will hold down the mask. The specific applications of friskets are discussed in chapters 9 and 11.

Masks for printing are usually overlays of commercial films. Masks permit the printer to create a white background or to isolate parts of a drawing that are to be printed with different colors, tones, or patterns. A mask should be a thin orange or red film on a polyester base for dimensional stability—meaning there will be no shrinking or stretching of the overlay before the illustration is printed. The orange is easier to see through than the red film, but red more completely blocks the drawing from the camera. Amberlith and Rubylith (made by Ulano) are common brands with a polyester backing. If the illustration is not on a dimensionally stable material, it may change size and eventually not match the overlay, so it is always best, though not always feasible, to prepare overlays just before the illustration goes to press. To reduce its exposure to varying humidity and temperatures, store the art in one room until it goes to the printer.

To prepare the mask, tape the masking film flat onto the upper edge of the mounting board. With a sharp blade or swivel knife held perpendicular to the film, cut carefully around the drawing image so that the knife does not slice through the clear polyester into the drawing. To protect the drawing, place a sheet of clear acetate between the drawing and the masking film. Use light pressure. Peel the colored film from the background; red or orange should completely cover anything to remain gray or black (figs. 2-45, 2-46; see fig. C-2). Bright white highlights can be created with shapes deliberately cut in the film. These should be done judiciously, possibly in areas where they would be surrounded by some light gray and therefore not appear too harsh. Crisp edges can be softened by stippling into the clear area with opaquing fluid or india ink and a brush or pen, or with a felt-tipped opaquing pen designed for this purpose.

If the subject has projecting hairs or other fine detail that is difficult to cut around, paint or draw them on the film with black india ink or opaquing fluid. If these liquids crawl, place a piece of Scotch Magic transparent tape (which has a polyester base) over the area, extending from the masking film, and paint details on the tape. Ink designed for use on plastic film should adhere well.

As with overlays, put at least

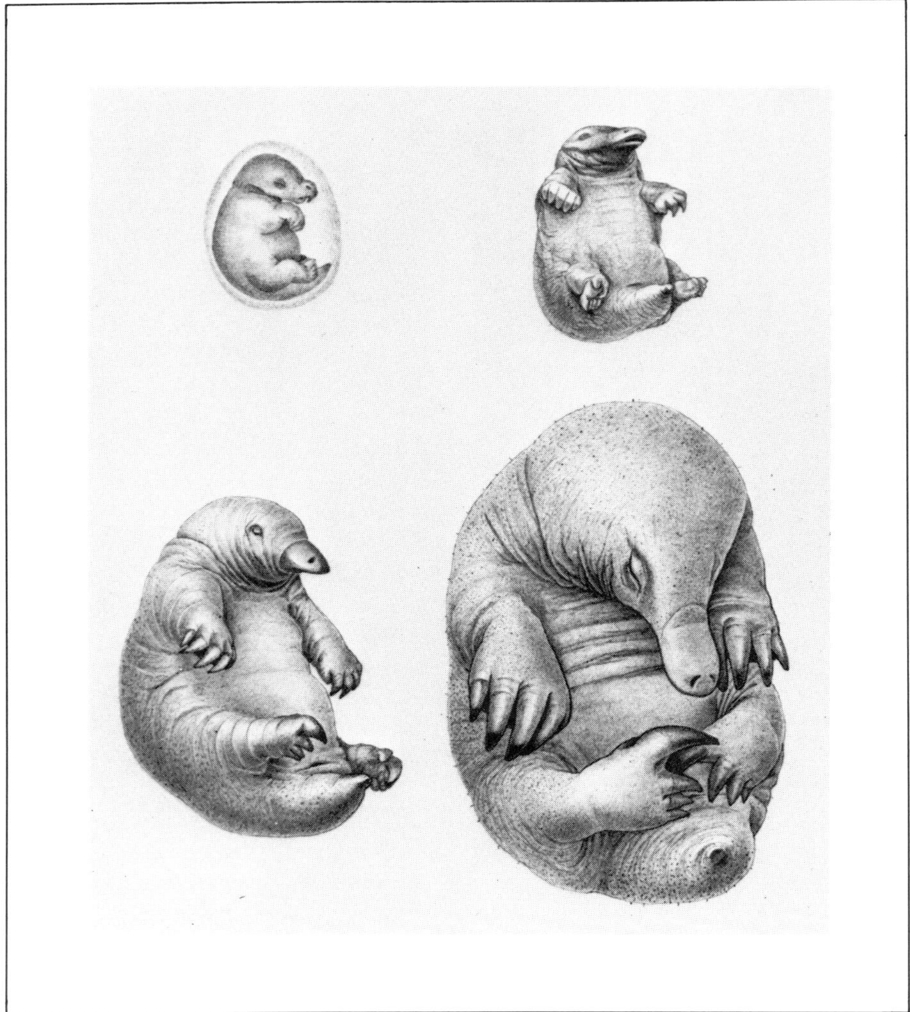

2-45. Drawing reproduced without being masked. Note gray tone in background. (See figs. 2-46 and C-2.)

three register marks each on the art and the masking film so that the two elements can be aligned precisely (see Register Marks, above, for hints on how to position them correctly).

Light-sensitive masking film is used in drafting maps. Two brands are Peel Coat and Peelrite; "peel coat" tends to be used generically. The red polyester film resembles Rubylith, but areas to be removed are etched by the action of intense light rather than being cut. The film is placed under a sheet of scribe coat—a specially formulated colored, coated polyester film—that has been etched with a scriber (see chapter 25, under the headings Instruments and Materials, and Technique). Light goes through the etched line and exposes the masking film, etching it in turn. The etched areas, which are likely to be lines representing boundaries, roads, and rivers, are finally peeled off.

Daniel G. Cole contributed to the text on light-sensitive masking film.

Furniture and Lighting

Drawing tables support drawing or painting. Both flat and slanted surfaces are necessary. A flat surface should be available for microscope and specimens and for drawing from the camera lucida (if the microscope is on a flat surface; see camera lucida procedure). For detailing and rendering drawings, a slanted surface is important to relieve neck strain. Techniques such as wash utilize a slanted surface to achieve certain effects. An adjustable table easel can be set up next to specimen and microscope, providing a comfortable working angle that can be removed when a flat surface is needed. Some drafting tables with adjustable tops have adjacent flat areas on left or right sides.

For drafting charts, diagrams, and maps, a sturdy drafting table at least 31 by 42 inches and fully adjustable for height and board angle is desirable. Cover it with a self-mending vinyl surface made especially for drafting boards.

Adjustable chairs permit backrest and seat height to be changed to suit the individual and the particular job. Ideally, the chair should quickly and simply adjust to different heights with a hand lever, pneumatically, so that it can be raised or lowered to keep your back straight when working at a microscope. The height of the microscope changes when attachments such as a camera lucida or accessory objects are added.

Lamps are used to illuminate a drawing area. Lamps combining fluorescent and incandescent bulbs or special fluorescent bulbs simulate daylight and are essential for work in color. A lamp clamped to the side of the desk or table leaves the drawing area clear. For camera lucida work, a second small lamp, such as a high-intensity lamp, is needed to shine on the drawing surface. To avoid working in the shadow of your hand, position a second lamp opposite your drawing hand.

Large-specimen lighting is used to examine colors of specimens such as mammals and birds. For drawings or paintings in color, the specimen must be viewed in light

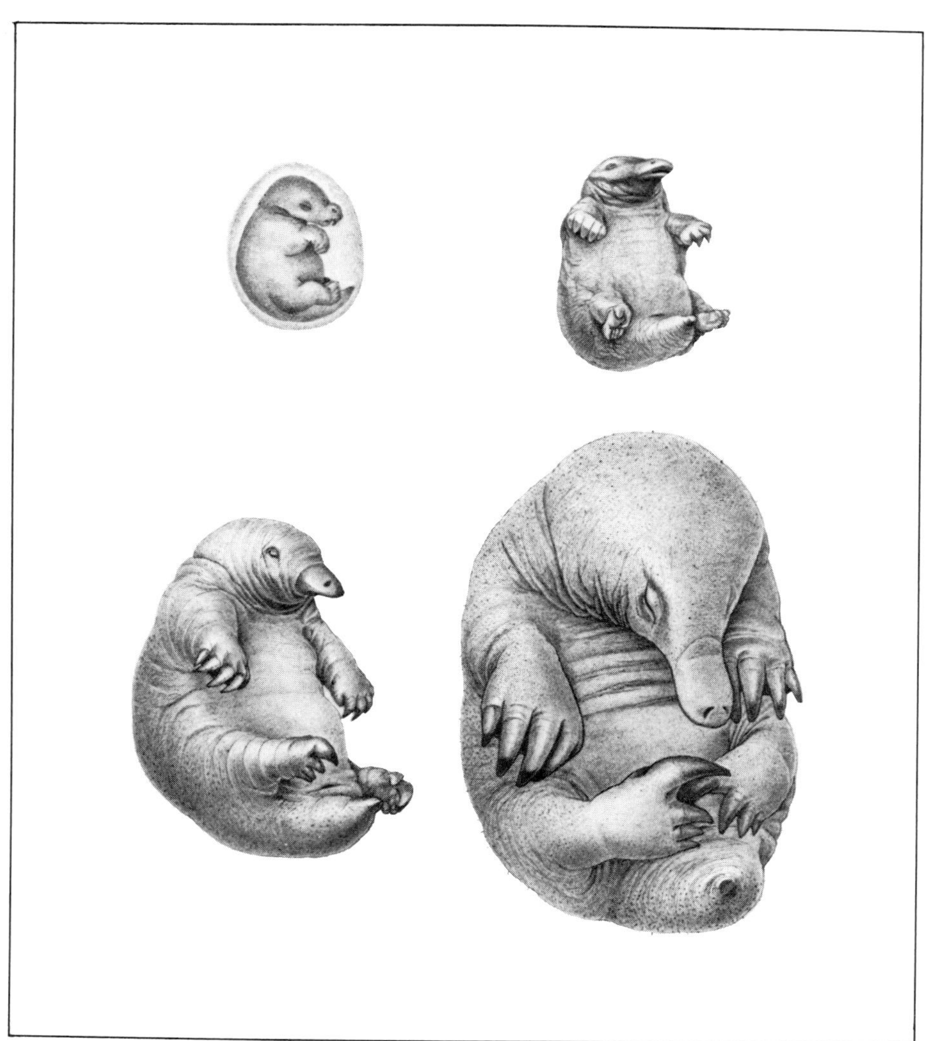

2-46. Reproduction from drawing with Amberlith mask, resulting in a white background (see figs. 2-45 and C-2). Stages of development in spiny anteater. Wolff's carbon pencil on Strathmore five-ply Bristol board, hot-press, by Margaret L. Estey. © Time-Life Books, L.N.L. (Life Nature Library).

as close to natural daylight as possible. Examolite fixtures, or another combination of fluorescent and incandescent bulbs, can duplicate daylight. Be aware, though, that specimens are prone to fading in artificial or natural light. It is important to block as much ultraviolet light as possible, since this is the most damaging component of light. One method is to cover fluorescent bulbs with plastic sleeves designed to block ultraviolet rays. The same principles apply to protection of artwork, described in chapter 3. (See Appendix for sources of light-filtering devices as well as Examolite.)

This chapter has described tools and materials mentioned throughout the rest of this book. Not all are required or appropriate for every job; some are specialized for certain subject matter or particular techniques. You may never need some of these items, whereas you might use others every day. Regardless of how often you use these tools and materials, knowledge about them is worth having, both to have a greater understanding of scientific illustration as a discipline and to gain ideas that might be creatively applied to your own work.

3/Materials, Construction, and Care of Scientific Illustrations

Christine A. Smith

Preservation of scientific illustrations concerns most artists who devote their efforts and time to creating simultaneously informative and beautiful drawings. Several years may pass before a drawing is actually reproduced, it may be needed a second time long after its completion, it may be requested for exhibition, it may become part of an archive or other collection.

The well-being of artwork must begin long before it is finished, for no work is any stronger than the materials of which it is composed. The illustrator must select individual materials for maximum stability and must understand how combining them affects the work's longevity. After a drawing is completed, how it is stored and exhibited affect its preservation. This chapter provides a very brief survey of the problems involved in making and preserving scientific illustrations. The reader is urged to consult the Bibliography for sources of additional information.

An archival-quality material is defined as one that: (a) causes neither physical nor chemical damage to an object either when the material is applied or in the indefinite future; (b) retains its desired characteristics for the indefinite future; and (c) remains removable or reversible for an indefinitely long time, should some future circumstance require the object's disassembly.

Not all art materials meet all these criteria, however. For instance, carbon inks sink into soft paper fibers and sometimes cannot be removed completely without damaging the surface. On the other hand, since they are fundamental parts of an illustration, there is little expectation that their reversibility would be desired. In contrast, many colored inks are very fugitive, and their inability to retain their desired characteristic (color) is a major deficiency. Consequently, they cannot be considered for archival use. The definition cannot, therefore, be applied absolutely, but it provides a perspective of safety, endurance, and reversibility against which every material should be judged.

When buying materials, it is essential to be as informed as possible about criteria for quality and to ask pertinent questions. Art-store personnel and catalogs do not usually have complete or correct technical information. Both paper conservators and manufacturers' representatives, however, may be able to provide tips about handling products or recommend alternative materials, but they will be more inclined to consider a problem if questions are specific and indicate a basic understanding of the materials involved. It is a good idea to rank the requirements for a material or project; since no product or process is perfect, deciding which characteristics are most important aids in making an informed choice.

Test or otherwise investigate all materials before buying in quantity. Manufacturing formulas are changed periodically, and a product may be either improved or adulterated. Some companies manufacture products in both student and artist grades, so relying solely on a company's name is risky. And the cliché about getting what you pay for is valid for artists' materials: there is generally a reason why bargains are cheap. Any object is only as strong as its weakest material, so it does not make sense to put fugitive ink on excellent paper or to apply a staining adhesive behind a completed project.

THE NATURE OF PAPER

Scientific illustrators need to understand the general nature of paper, basic paper categories, and some of the criteria for selecting archival papers.

A sheet of paper is made by agitating a slurry of approximately 97 percent water and 3 percent fibers on a screen through which the water will drain, leaving behind the fibers. This randomly matted structure, which resembles felt cloth, is turned onto an absorbent surface for drying and pressing. In addition to fibers and water, pulp may contain any number of additives: sizing (a very thin adhesive, which controls ink absorption), dye, fungicide, filler (clay added to increase opacity or extend a given quantity of fiber), and more.

The basic sheet can be varied by exaggerating or eliminating texture, by laminating into board, by adjusting the surface's response to water, by adding a surface coating, or by any number of other functional or aesthetic modifications (fig. 3-1). The surface character is influenced by how it is pressed. Cold-press (rough) paper may be pressed only with felt material, the texture of which is imprinted into the paper. For example, very rough watercolor paper owes its texture to rough-textured felt. Hot-press (smooth) paper is pressed between

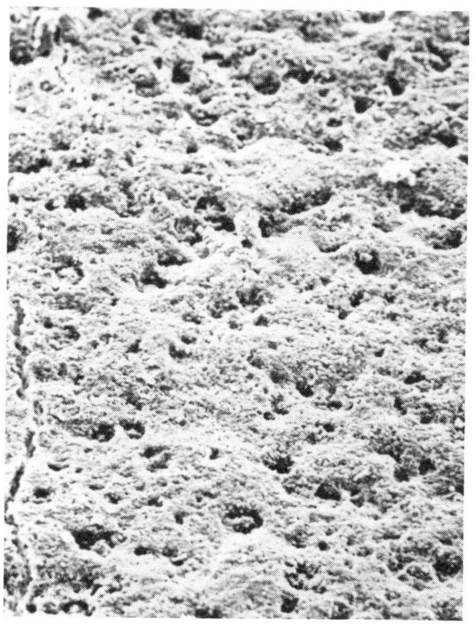
a

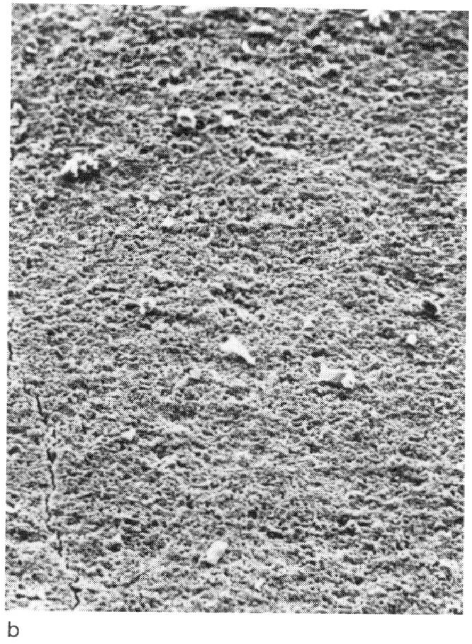
b

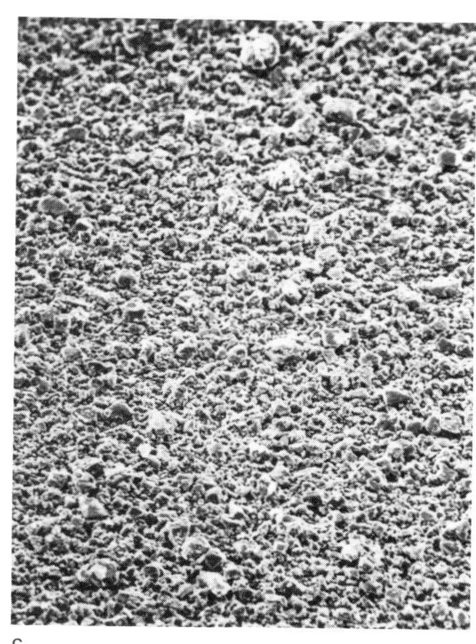
c

3-1. Clay-coated boards and paper magnified 150 times with the scanning electron microscope: *(a)* Ross 00 board, no longer made; *(b)* dull-finish stipple board, Medical Models Laboratory; *(c)* Video Media paper. SEM photos by Mary-Jacque Mann, designed by George L. Venable and Carolyn Bartlett Gast

metal rollers, several times for very smooth surfaces such as high-finish Bristol board. The repeated passes through the rollers generate heat—hence hot press (fig. 3-2).

The sheet is held together mostly by physical entanglement of the fibers, somewhat by chemical bonds between the fibers, and usually with the assistance of sizing. The longer the fibers, the greater the distances they span and the more they interlock with other fibers; long fibers help make strong paper able to flex without breaking.

Whether a surface is stipple board, Bristol board, or mat board, it is likely to be made from one of four types of paper: groundwood, chemically pulped wood, chemi-groundwood, or rag. For archival purposes, the important differences among papers are not so

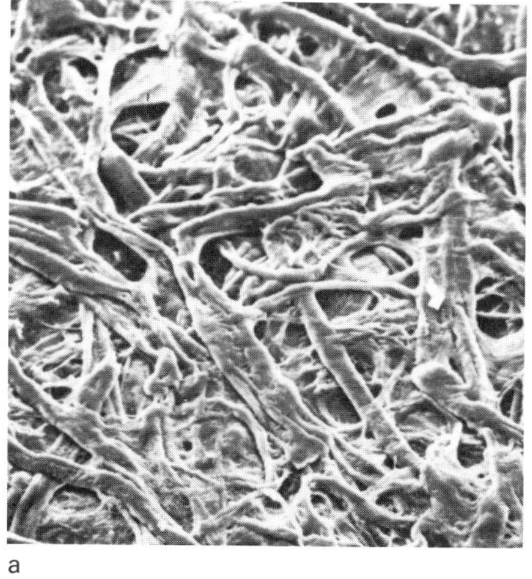
a

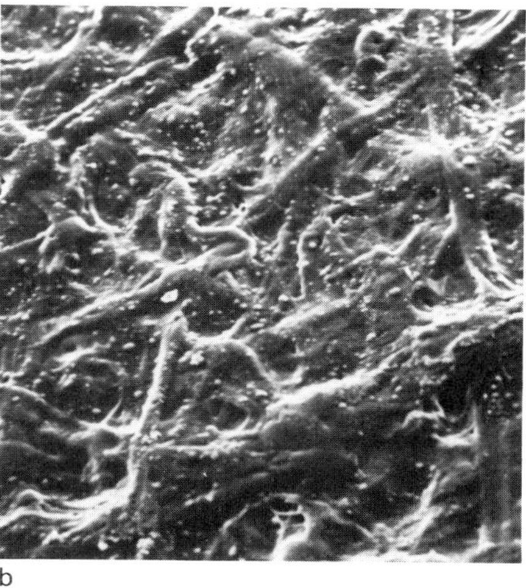
b

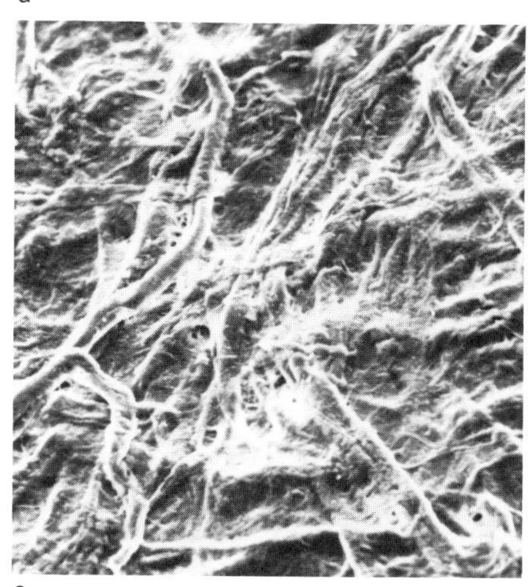
c

d

3-2. Papers magnified 150 times with the scanning electron microscope: *(a)* Strathmore hot-press (plate finish) Bristol board; *(b)* Keuffel and Esser Albanene tracing paper; *(c)* Clearprint tracing paper; *(d)* Bienfang Satin Design "vellum." SEM photos by Mary-Jacque Mann, designed by George L. Venable and Carolyn Bartlett Gast.

much the surface finishes as the sources of the fibers and the methods of manufacture.

Groundwood Paper

The pulp for groundwood paper, also known as mechanically pulped wood paper, is made by grinding debarked logs against a stone with water. Because water is the only processing substance used and the raw material is merely ground up, the product is very inexpensive. Since materials extraneous to paper formation are not removed, the sheet is bulky and opaque. Among the materials not removed is lignin, the matrix in which the cellulose fibers are embedded in their natural state. Lignin causes several reactions in the presence of light or moisture, or both, which rapidly break cellulose fibers into increasingly shorter lengths, making them progressively weaker and less flexible. The sheet becomes brittle and darkens markedly. This change is familiar to us in newspapers left in a sunny spot for a few days. Groundwood papers may or may not be bleached. They are fine for throwaway projects but absolutely unacceptable for objects meant to last more than a few weeks.

Chemical Wood Paper

Chemically pulped wood paper is made by several processes, some of which meet archival standards. In all of them, chips are reduced to pulp using chemical solutions, high temperatures, and pressure. The strong chemicals and long cooking remove lignin and wood resins.

Chemically processed wood fibers have the potential to make excellent papers since the fibers are not cut up during pulping but merely freed from the lignin matrix by the cooking liquor, leaving them at their full lengths. Although not as long as rag fibers, they are much longer than groundwood fibers. Their length, the delignification process, and the lower cost of wood as compared to cotton place chemical wood papers between groundwood and rag papers in both price and quality. If the papers are processed carefully, they can rival rag papers.

Chemigroundwood Paper

As its name implies, this is a combination of the two previously described processes. Whole logs are treated chemically at high temperature and pressure and then reduced to fibers by grinding. Because grinding shortens the fibers, chemigroundwood paper is too weak for archival purposes.

Rag Paper

Rag fibers come not from a wood source but from cotton or linen. Although rags were originally used to make this pulp, today most rag paper is made with fibers from the cotton plant or from cuttings off new textiles. Because raw cotton and linen fibers are nearly pure cellulose and therefore require relatively little treatment, and because they are much longer than wood fibers, rag paper has the potential to be superior to all other Western papers if it is processed skillfully. Contrary to popular opinion, however, "rag paper" per se does not denote high quality; poorly processed rag paper will deteriorate almost as quickly as ordinary chemical wood paper.

Many papers contain mixtures of several fibers, which may have been pulped by several methods. The possible combinations are vast, making it impossible to evaluate specific papers without subjecting them to scientific analysis. Other sources of paper fibers (straw, bark, nylon) are not discussed here since they are unlikely to appear in papers used for scientific illustrations.

CRITERIA FOR EVALUATING PAPER

For scientific illustrators, the most important criteria for evaluating paper quality are its pH; the presence of sizing, residual bleach, and fiber-source impurities; and the nature of secondary materials (dyes, laminating adhesives, surface coatings) used in the manufacture of the paper. These criteria contribute to a paper's suitability for archival use, its permanence—not to be confused with its durability, which is a different matter altogether. According to *The Dictionary of Paper*, by the American Pulp and Paper Association (see Bibliography), *durability* refers to a paper's physical nature, its ability to retain "its original qualities under continual use." The paper from which a grocery bag is made is an example of a durable paper. *Permanence* refers to a paper's chemical nature, its ability to retain "significant use properties, particularly folding endurance and color, over prolonged periods." Good Japanese tissue is an example of a permanent paper. A paper can be durable without being permanent, permanent without being durable, neither permanent nor durable, or both permanent and durable.

In general, one can find reliable information about a paper's qualities from the packaging itself, technical literature supplied by the manufacturer, or a technical sales representative employed by the manufacturer. The artist can perform some simple tests on papers under consideration for use, either with kits or with readily available substances under studio conditions.

pH

A pH value is a numerical indication of the concentration of free or potentially reactive ions in an aqueous solution. It is as a measure of the freedom to react with other materials that pH is such an important indicator of a paper's stability.

The pH scale extends from 0.0 to 14.0 (fig. 3-3). Solutions that register at the midpoint of 7.0 are neutral, neither acidic nor alkaline. The closer a solution gets to 0.0, the more acidic it is; the closer to 14.0, the more alkaline it is. Those two points are the theoretical extremes of acidity and alkalinity, although in reality they are never quite reached. The mathematical basis for this scale makes a change of one pH unit (for example, from 6.0 to 7.0) a *tenfold* change in the concentration of acidity or alkalinity.

Papers are manufactured in a wide range of pHs, from approximately 3.5 to approximately 8.5. A paper intended to last indefinitely should have a pH in the range of 7.0 to 8.5. Such papers are somewhat difficult to find and are expensive because of more careful and extensive processing, but they are essential if finished artwork is expected to retain original color, character, and strength. (See Appendix for a list of some suppliers of conservation-quality papers.)

Why is acidity damaging to paper, and why is some alkalinity beneficial? Acids attack the bonds of cellulose molecules, breaking the fibers into shorter lengths. This damage is permanent and irreversible. The paper becomes progressively less flexible and more brittle. As a by-product of this scission, degradation products form and darken the paper. Acid can migrate from one spot on a sheet to other areas and from one sheet to adjacent sheets.

To counteract acidic degradation, an alkaline (base) buffer (usually calcium carbonate) is added to pulps designed for archival papers. It neutralizes acids that threaten the paper's stability, whether they come from internal or external sources. A given concentration of base can neutralize an equal concentration of acid, but the effective life of the same buffer varies in different sheets depending on the pH of the pulp; how much buffer was added; the pH of mounting, matting, and framing materials; the intensity of acidic air pollutants; and the amounts of moisture, heat, and light to which each paper is exposed. Since high alkalinity can damage paper as much as high acidity, buffers are usually limited to pH 8.5. (High alkalinity swells the more reactive portions of cellulose molecules, exposing them more to chemical attack. In addition, any lignin within a paper will react with alkali at room temperature, resulting in weakened, yellow paper.) Manufacturers' technical sales literature should specify both pH and alkaline reserve, which is the amount of buffer a sheet contains expressed as a percentage of the sheet's weight.

Because paper cannot escape contact with acids (see Other Environmental Considerations, at the end of this chapter), it is advisable to purchase alkaline, instead of neutral, papers. Note, however, that pH 8.5 is not safe for all paper-based objects. Current research on the conservation of photographs suggests they require a neutral pH. A few pigments may be affected by alkalinity—for example, Prussian blue and Hooker's green.

Sizing

A very dilute adhesive that controls the amount of ink paper absorbs, sizing also helps to bind the fibers and prevent dust from becoming embedded in the paper surface. Sizing can be made from a variety of materials, including gelatin, starch paste, a combination of alum and rosin, wax, or a wide range of synthetic materials. It can be added to pulp, the formed sheet, or both; but today it is most often mixed into the pulp. Its functions and its presence throughout the sheet distinguish it from coatings, which are applied only to the surface of a sheet and serve to create or eliminate texture or provide opaque, uniform color.

Many modern papers contain alum-rosin sizing, which leaves a residue of sulfuric acid on the fibers. Sulfuric acid is a very strong, nonvolatile acid that lowers the pulp pH to about 4.5. As a result, this sizing is one of the major sources of acid deterioration in paper. Moreover, it is incompatible with calcium carbonate buffer. The presence of alum-rosin sizing makes a paper absolutely unacceptable for archival use.

Bleach

Most paper pulps are bleached, usually with chlorine derivatives. By a variety of continuing, irreversible oxidation reactions, these bleaches eventually destroy the very paper they helped create. However, bleaches can be used successfully if they are chosen wisely, used gently, and *removed completely* once bleaching is completed. Perhaps the easiest way to judge the care with which a paper was bleached is by association: if the end-product is free of acid and alum-rosin sizing and buffered to

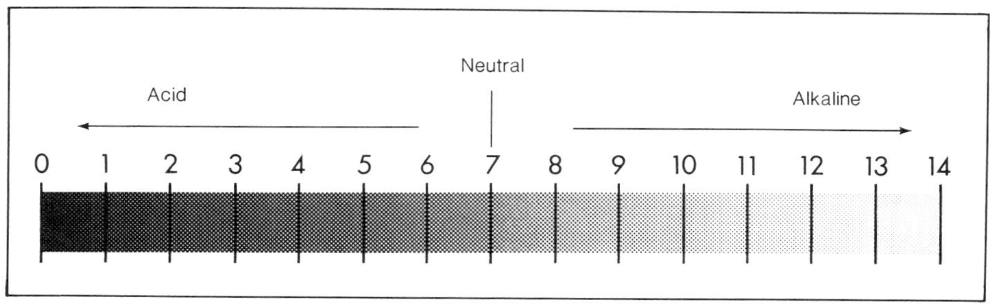

3-3. A pH scale showing the acidity range from acid at 0 to alkaline at 14. Neutral is 7.0. Diagram by T. Britt Griswold, using gradated shading film.

be permanent, it is probably safe to assume that the bleaching was also done carefully.

Fiber-Source Impurities

By far the most hazardous impurity that paper may retain from its fiber source is lignin, which is present in all wood fiber sources (trees) but absent from cotton and linen. Other possible fiber-source impurities are specks of bark, seeds, fiber knots, and mineral or metal traces.

Metallic traces are most likely to originate with the papermaking machinery, and some of them can cause serious damage to paper. Iron, copper, cobalt, and manganese catalyze cellulose oxidation in both pulps and finished sheets unless they are deactivated by magnesium or calcium compounds, which may be added to the pulp or even to a finished drawing (in the latter case, by a conservator). A technical sales representative can provide information about deactivation.

Secondary Materials

Secondary materials used in manufacturing, such as laminating adhesives, dyes, backings, or coatings, also affect the longevity of paper. Secondary materials may expose the paper to acids and may themselves contain reactive metals, be fugitive in light or be degraded by it, or be water-soluble. If they absorb water, these materials can be tested with pH strips (see below). Consult the manufacturer's representative regarding light stability, or expose a sample in a southern window, saving another sample for later comparison and noting the date of first exposure. To test for water solubility, thoroughly wet the sample in question, press it briefly between white blotting papers, and then check for migration of color or change in surface character. If a material is soluble, it may be advisable to choose another paper, since water damage may occur after a drawing has been completed even if none of the media is water-based.

Testing

All materials under consideration for use in illustrations intended to last should be tested for both working characteristics and longevity before being purchased in bulk or actually used. An invaluable and inexpensive three-bottle Tri-Test kit permits easy testing for three major weaknesses in papers: acidity, lignin, and alum-rosin sizing. These criteria are so important that a paper failing any one test must be considered unacceptable for archival use.

More refined acid-base measurements than the Tri-Test kit can be obtained from pH indicator strips. These paper strips change colors at various pHs and are available in a range of sensitivities. Some indicate the entire pH scale in whole units (such as pH 3 or pH 9); others indicate more limited ranges (such as pH 3.0 to 6.0) in increments of 0.5 pH units. The 0-to-14 scale should be used first to locate the approximate pH and then the appropriate finer scale used for a more precise reading. Strips with nonstaining dyes permit monitoring of finished illustrations. Strips with three or four indicator colors are much easier to read than those with only one color chip. The strips are affected by atmospheric pollutants and have a finite life span, so they should be stored in airtight containers—preferably glass or aluminum—and replaced every two years.

To test the pH of a paper sample, lay the sample on clean, dry glass (to prevent the strip from responding to materials under the paper) and wet the sample with deionized or distilled water. To be measured, the free hydrogen ions, or acid, must go into water solution. For that reason, wet the sample thoroughly but avoid excess water, which will dissipate the ions. Press the test strip against the wet area as long as possible, short of the water's drying, then compare to the color scale in the kit. This measurement will be remarkably close to what would be obtained by more elaborate methods: the margin of error is approximately ±0.3 pH units. If the sample is coated or highly calendered (pressed smooth with metal rollers), tear it to expose the interior, and test both the interior and the exterior surfaces. Likewise, test board composed of different core and surface materials at both locations to get an indication of cumulative acidity. Then measure the pH of the water itself and calibrate the reading taken from the paper sample.

OTHER SURFACES

Vellum

True vellum is treated animal skin, a proteinaceous material with a long and well-documented history as the finest form of parchment. It is rarely used today and is not what is meant when the word is used to refer to a commercially available drawing surface. What is now called vellum is made by impregnating cellulose fibers with synthetic resin to achieve a translucent sheet and embedding in the surface finely ground silica particles, which provide a slight tooth to help hold drawing media. This material appears to be very promising as an archival drawing support; companies manufacture it using cotton fibers and very stable resins. Be aware, though, that one manufacturer claims the resin will not not yellow, whereas another says it will yellow "very slightly" over a long period of time. Whether the differing claims are due to use of different resins or different definitions of yellowing is unclear (see fig. 3-2).

Still another material marketed as vellum is paper made translu-

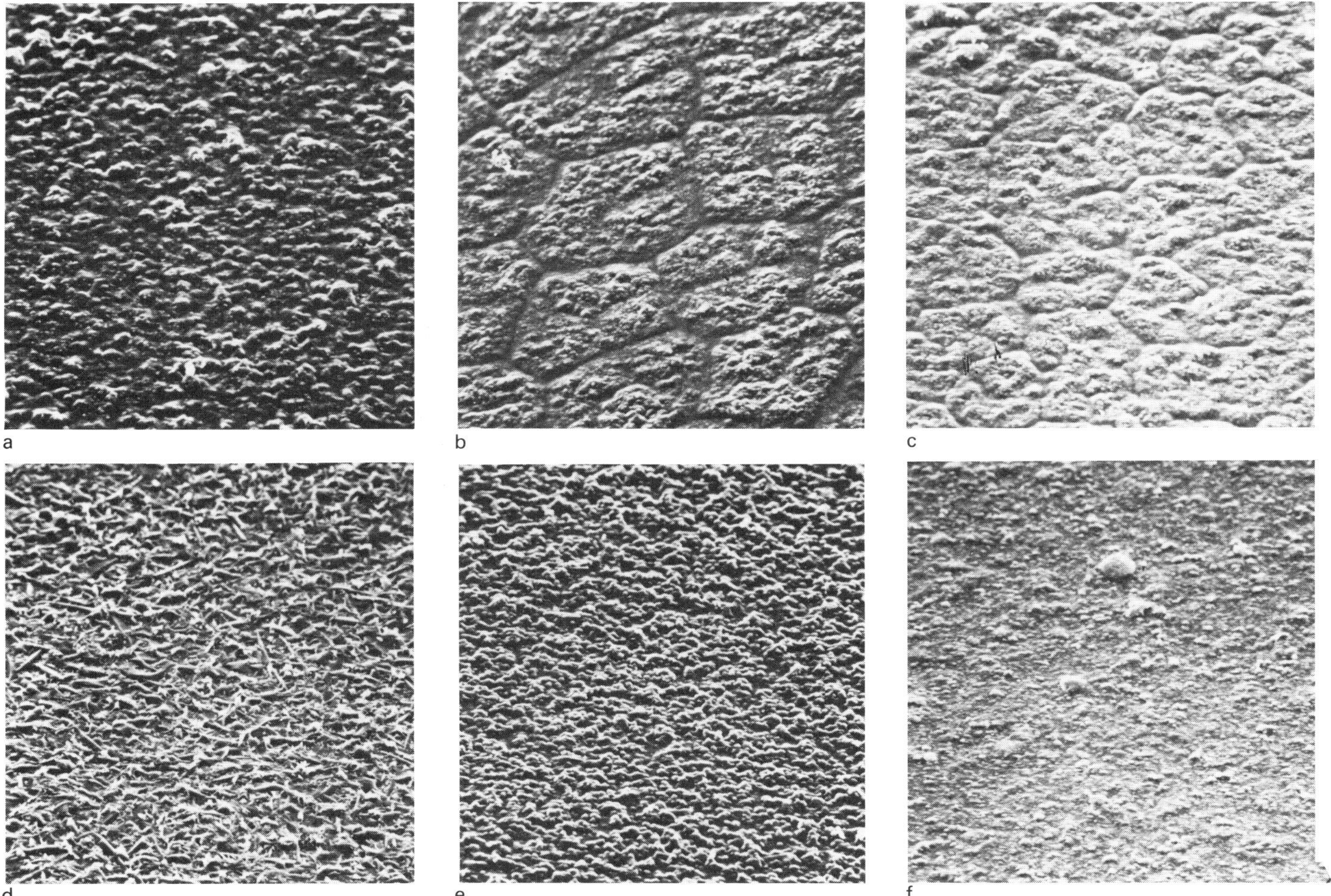

3-4. Films magnified 150 times with the scanning electron microscope. All but *(d)* are polyester. *(a)* Dietzgen Ageproof; *(b)* Koh-I-Noor Rapidraw; *(c)* Bruning Sure-Scale; *(d)* Bienfang Protectoid frosted acetate; *(e)* DuPont Cronaflex UC-4; *(f)* Denril. SEM photos by Mary-Jacque Mann, designed by George L. Venable and Carolyn Bartlett Gast.

cent by beating pulp longer than usual, in the presence of sulfuric acid. The extensive beating and the acid, which shorten and weaken the fibers, make this third vellum too unstable for archival use.

Drafting Film

There are wide variations among drafting films (see chart 8-2). In general, the core of these films is cellulose or polyester. In each type, the malleable material is extruded through rollers into a smooth sheet, which hardens as it cools. Cellulose acetate films require plasticizers to make them flexible; polyester films do not. To enable media to adhere to their otherwise slick surfaces, drafting films are coated in various ways. Some surfaces are more granular than others, so there are distinct differences in their reactions to media (fig. 3-4).

Cellulose acetate is an altered form of cellulose, with acetic and sulfuric acids used in the manufacturing process. The acetate's long-term stability is affected greatly by the degree to which these acids are removed after processing. In addition, all cellulose acetate film becomes very brittle with time, as the added plasticizer either oozes from the film (possibly staining adjacent materials) or crosslinks with itself, forming larger, stiffer molecules. Some plasticizers are additionally vulnerable to attack by fungi or insects. All cellulose acetate films have fairly low resistance to abrasion, are permeable to water vapor, and tear easily. Like paper, they are more vulnerable to chemical and photochemical degradation in the presence of water, whether liquid or vapor. The greatest amount of deterioration to these films is usually caused by ultraviolet light, whether from daylight or fluorescent tubes. Some films are described by their manufacturers as withstanding light well, but this is meaningless without reference to the type of light, its intensity, and the duration of the test exposure.

Polyester looks very much like cellulose acetate but is far superior for use in the construction and storage of scientific illustrations.

There are many brands of polyester, including Mylar, which is simply DuPont's brand name. Because polyester does not need a plasticizer for flexibility, the problems of acidic degradation, embrittlement, and staining are avoided. As long as it hasn't been treated with special coatings, impregnants, or dyes, the material is chemically inert and very stable over a long period of time. Its tensile properties are essentially equal in both directions, so it maintains a flat, unstretched surface. It is extremely difficult to tear. The surface is susceptible to abrasion. It has a high charge of electric static, which may be an advantage or a disadvantage. The charge in combination with the film's ability to absorb impact can hold in place and physically protect the most brittle papers when polyester is used as a cover sheet. However, the charge can pull away from a drawing any media such as graphite, charcoal, or chalks that are not held to their support by a binder.

DRAWING MEDIA

Since some pigments are lightfast and others are fugitive, and since some artists' materials are made less expensive by the incorporation of fillers or extenders, the quality of a certain product line should be investigated thoroughly before purchase or use. Ascertain that the color comes from the named pigments only and not partially from extender pigments of lesser quality. Learn what materials are used as fillers and extenders. Books listed in the Bibliography will aid in this, and most manufacturers will answer questions about their products. Labeling is becoming increasingly informative.

Broad Media

The broad drawing media are useful and beautiful for their abilities to render tones and textures. They demand careful handling, however, because they are held to their supports only by being caught mechanically in surface irregularities instead of being attached securely by binding agents (oil- or wax-bound crayons are exceptions). Therefore, the choice of substrate is critical to the survival of these drawings: if the surface is not sufficiently roughened, the media can be disturbed extraordinarily easily. Even on substrates designed specifically for their use, works done in broad media must be handled and stored with extreme care. If they are jarred, rubbed, or pressed, the media are easily disturbed or lifted (fig. 3-5).

3-5. Graphite mark on Japanese tissue paper, magnified 50 times. Note how the graphite sits on top of the long paper fibers. Photo by Martha E. Goodway.

Because they are so fragile, drawings using the broad media require deep window mats or spacers to protect their surfaces from contact with other surfaces. In addition, picture-frame glazings must be glass, never acrylic sheet, which has an electrostatic charge strong enough to pull unbound particles off the drawing surface and onto the glazing.

Charcoal is an impure form of carbon made by simply heating twigs or vines in a sealed atmosphere so they char instead of burn. Natural charcoal is by far the most fragile of the broad media, since its marks are merely particles of charred wood splintered away from the stick by pressure. Although the other broad media are not bound to their supports, they are somewhat less easily disturbed than charcoal due to a minimal amount of binder in them that holds powdery pigments together in a drawing stick.

Compressed charcoal avoids the uneven marks characteristic of natural charcoal, which result from variations in the source wood. It is made by grinding charcoal finely, adding a binding agent (traditionally glue), compressing the mixture into a stick, and baking the stick slightly to improve its working strength. Various hardnesses are created by adjusting the amounts of binder and baking. Charcoal pencils are compressed charcoal in wood casings.

Graphite is a form of pure carbon in which the crystals slide over each other and separate readily, making it an excellent marking material. Originally obtained from mines, it is now produced synthetically and combined with fine clays and a slight bit of wax. Clay modifies the marker's hardness—the more clay, the harder and less lustrous the mark—and wax increases the permanence and smoothness of the mark. What we call lead pencils are, in fact, graphite. Referring to graphite marks as lead seems to date from the late sixteenth or early seventeenth century, when both natural graphite and lead were used for drafting and one word was used to describe either medium. (Lead, of course, is a very soft and malleable metal.) Since graphite can mark more finely than lead, lead seems to have passed from use as the manufacture of graphite pencils evolved during the eighteenth century.

In all the preceding media, the pigmenting agent is carbon, an extremely stable material that can withstand exposure to visible and ultraviolet light, moisture, acids, alkalis, and air. It can be destroyed only by burning at high temperatures and is therefore excellent for use on drawings that must last.

Pastel sticks and **Conté crayons** are made from one or more dry pigment powders, gum or glue binder, and white clay for tints. Again, hardness of the sticks is controlled by the proportion of ingredients and the extent of firing. In addition to the vulnerabilities of the broad media already described, pastels are especially prone to mold growth because of the large amount of gum or glue they contain. They must be stored in an environment with controlled humidity.

Pastel pencils are wood-encased pastels with extra binder, which enables them to withstand the added pressure of being used as pencils.

Colored pencils are wood-encased mixtures of pigments, binder, and a slight amount of wax used to increase the smoothness of their marks. The quality of the pigments used varies greatly, and the illustrator must compare individual products, not just manufacturers. The pencils also exhibit various responses to water: some bleed or set when moistened, effects that may or may not be desirable.

Inks, Watercolors, and Dyes

Inks, watercolors, and dyes are similar (at times identical) media. An ink is a liquid used for drawing, writing, or printing. It may be colored by a pigment or a dye, which may be suspended in water or oil; a binding agent of glue, gum, or synthetic resin is usually added. Pigment consists of finely divided, discrete coloring particles suspended in a vehicle for application. In contrast, the coloring material in a dye is soluble in its vehicle, so a dye solution acts simultaneously as coloring and binding agent, staining into a support instead of sitting on top of it and being held by a binder. A watercolor is pigment suspended in water with a gum or other binding agent. When white pigment is added to make the watercolor opaque, it is called gouache. A lake is a pigment made by precipitating an organic dye onto an insoluble, finely divided, inorganic, inert substrate such as alumina hydrate or clay. (Refer to *Painting Materials: A Short Encyclopedia*, by R. J. Gettens and G. L. Stout—see Bibliography.)

Drawing inks are usually suspended in water and colored by a combination of pigment and dye, although some are made using either pigment or dye. A good drawing ink will flow out and color evenly and with uniform texture, whether taken directly from the bottle or diluted to a wash; and therein lies one of the criteria for choosing black ink.

Carbon particles are so small that the grinding process is intended not to pulverize them but to disperse them in binder. Further, with proper formulation the particles will remain suspended. Some black drawing inks are made with carbon pigment only, many are pigment and dye combinations, and some are dye only.

All ink dyes, including black, are decomposed by ultraviolet light. Colored drawing inks are usually made with dyes, but ink technology is moving toward a norm of colored inks made with pigments, since they can provide lightfastness. It is important to understand, however, that even with pigments of the highest quality, the degree of lightfastness varies from pigment to pigment; for example, cobalt blue is characteristically more lightfast than indigo. In terms of working qualities, a good colored ink must have a combination of chromatic and value strength, so it can give either a strong, intense color or a wash.

Modern india ink, also known as Chinese ink, consists of lampblack pigment suspended in water and bound with resin (although the traditional binder was gum or glue). Lampblack is impure carbon that is somewhat oily or resinous and bluish in tone. To increase gloss, the concentration of binder is increased; to make the ink waterproof, a solution of shellac and borax is added to the water.

Good watercolor paints allow the artist to achieve effects of color and texture not possible with inferior materials, while simultaneously increasing the likelihood of a design surviving as conceived. Too much or too little pigment grinding causes separation of the solution or pigment agglomeration (mineral pigments cannot be made to stay in solution). Too little binder causes a dry, particulate appearance and results in lost pigment; too much binder can lead to cracking. Binder and pigment must be thoroughly mixed to obtain easy wetting. To achieve a wash of uniform color and texture, this dispersion must be maintained from the time that paint is diluted until it has dried. Once the water has evaporated, a good binder holds pigment securely to the support.

Ink or watercolor drawings are mechanically stronger than drawings in the broad media since binders attach inks and watercolors to their supports; but the binders may be subject to insect or mold attack. Many pigments are quickly and irretrievably faded by exposure to visible or ultraviolet light or are affected by exposure to air pollutants or changes in pH. Despite the binder, watercolor surfaces are fragile enough to warrant protection by deep window mats.

Acrylic Paints

Acrylic paints consist of pigments ground and dispersed in an emulsion of water and an acrylic resin. It is possible to thin the emulsion with water while working, but once the water evaporates, the pigment is bound within a continuous acrylic film that is insoluble in water. Available only since the 1930s, these paints are too new to have been evaluated after natural aging, but they are assumed to be very stable since the manufacturing process stabilizes those parts of the original molecules that are reactive. Acrylic paints adhere well to most surfaces, remain flexible, resist deterioration by visible and ultraviolet light, and do not yellow or darken. Besides drying much more quickly than oil paints, acrylics have the virtue of not needing a ground to separate them from the support material.

GENERAL STORAGE CONDITIONS

Storage for materials and finished artwork should be designed carefully and then monitored regularly to provide objects with the greatest possible protection. New wood shelving should be sealed with three coats of polyurethane, since fresh woods contain volatile acids. Metal storage shelves should be lined with blotting paper to absorb shock or any condensation that might occur on the metal. The storage area should have a temperature range of 65° to 72°F, ±5 degrees, and a relative humidity range of 45 to 55 percent, ±5 percent. From season to season, a gradual change of ±10 percent is acceptable. These conditions must be maintained at night and on weekends as well as during the workdays. In a museum, filtered air protects objects from acidic air pollutants. Darkness retards light damage, but since many microorganisms, insects, and rodents like darkness, the area must be kept well ventilated, clean, and absolutely free of food crumbs. Although a storage area should be out of the line of daily traffic, which disrupts the constancy of environmental conditions and brings light and dirt into the area, it should not be so isolated that insects and rodents are attracted and the air becomes still and damp. Containers of objects or framed pictures should never be stored directly on the floor, which is cooler and damper than the rest of the room and thus subjects the artwork to the dangers of mold growth, "foxing" (brown spots), and flood. A planned storage arrangement makes it easier to locate objects, and labeled boxes save time and frustration and minimize handling of the objects.

Attention, scientists: do not wrap drawings in any kind of nonarchival paper envelopes for storage. These will leach acid into the drawing. Archival-quality wrapping papers and corrugated boards are available from companies listed in the Appendix.

Light

Light is a form of electromagnetic energy categorized by the length of its repeating waves. Three types of light affect illustrations: visible light (the spectrum to which our eyes respond), ultraviolet light (UV), and infrared light (IR) (fig. 3-6). Shorter wavelengths have more energy than longer ones and therefore generate more reactions in materials they strike. UV light provides the energy for many reactions that are highly destructive to illustrations, both media and supports. Visible light near the UV area of the spectrum is destructive in the same way. Damage caused by these reactions is irreversible, so control is of the utmost importance. Infrared light is not energetic enough to cause damaging photochemical reactions, but it generates heat, another form of energy. Heat increases the rate of chemical reactions already begun and causes physical damage to objects.

No light level is low enough to prevent damage to illustrations. With less light, the damage will only occur more slowly. Theoretically, serious damage to paper occurs after 50 to 100 hours of full sun, which emits radiation in all three spectra of concern; but temperature and humidity are very important to the actual rate of degradation. The level of visible light recommended for display of paper objects is five footcandles, and display areas should be monitored periodically with an incident light meter (a photographer's meter that measures only reflected light is unsuitable). Illustrations should never be displayed across from windows or otherwise in the path of strong light, and drapes or blinds should be closed whenever an exhibition room is not being used.

Exposure to light can bleach paper or yellow it, depending on whether light or heat predominates as the paper is exposed. If heat predominates, the paper will yellow; if light predominates, it will bleach.

Artificial light in museums and homes is usually provided by incandescent and fluorescent fixtures. Fluorescent lamps consume very little power, are available in a range of colors, and emit very little heat. They do emit considerable UV light, however, and must be fitted with filtering sleeves when used near valuable objects. Incandescent lamps do not emit UV light, but they do generate large amounts of heat. They must either be placed far enough from objects so the heat dissipates before reaching them or be fitted with infrared light filters. Preventing UV and IR light from reaching objects does not make viewing those objects any more difficult, since the human eye cannot see in the UV and IR bands.

Effects of UV light can be reduced by framing objects with specially formulated acrylic or glass (such as Denglass) that blocks most of these rays, the amount depending on the type and brand of acrylic or special glass. Unfortunately, both of these alternatives are very expensive.

To minimize damage to both design media and supports, objects should not be exhibited for more than three or four months at a time. It is a discouraging and still unexplained phenomenon that after exposure to light, paper experiences continued deterioration when returned to dark storage.

Heat and Humidity

Although heat and humidity damage objects individually, their effects are closely interconnected. Air that is warm can hold a fairly large amount of moisture; when the temperature drops, the air is unable to hold the same amount of moisture and releases some, causing the relative humidity (RH) to rise.

Although controlling both temperature and relative humidity is important, uncontrolled humidity causes more damage than uncontrolled temperature. High humidity promotes mold growth and some chemical reactions and sets the stage for others that could not occur in a drier environment. On the other hand, excessively low humidity (below 30 percent RH) seriously embrittles paper, making it much more vulnerable to physical damage.

Heat affects paper physically when it withdraws moisture. As the paper contracts, it can draw into ripples or tear in areas that are restrained or weak. The low end of a temperature range is determined by human comfort since no temperature is too low for the well-being of scientific illustrations.

Because paper constantly seeks equilibrium with its surroundings, the environment must be controlled and monitored constantly: turning off air-conditioning equipment at night and during holidays negates its usefulness. In fact, it is better to maintain paper in a constant imperfect environment than in an environment that fluctuates between perfect and imperfect, keeping the object in a continuous state of movement. If these movements are radical enough or occur for long enough, the paper will weaken sufficiently to tear. Furthermore, the stresses of humidity changes seem actually to weaken the cellulose bonds. Artwork that is to be moved from one environment to another should be conditioned gradually over a period of four to seven days, not taken directly from one environment to another.

Artwork should not be hung over registers, radiators, fireplaces, or air ducts where it will be blasted with hot air, cooled air, dry air, and soot. Nor should it be hung on exterior walls, which become damp and cold during winter months. Mold, "foxing," and moisture condensation are likely to occur under such conditions.

Other Environmental Considerations

As mentioned above, molds, insects, rodents, and air pollution can affect illustrations. Molds that

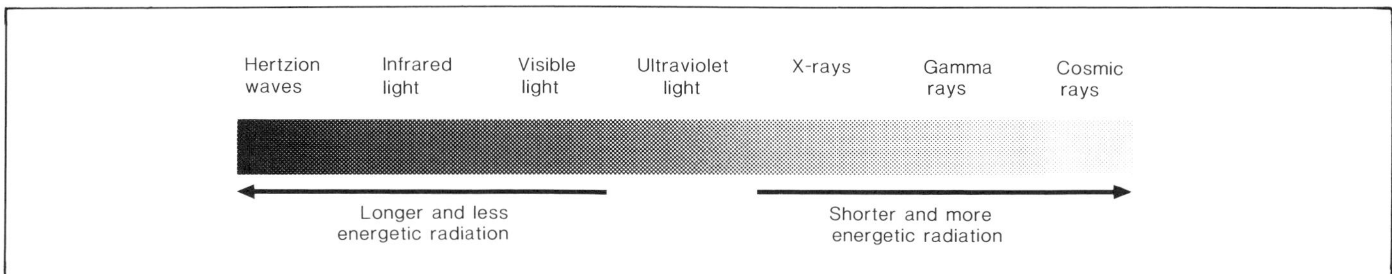

3-6. Range of light waves. Shorter wavelengths are more destructive to materials than long ones. Diagram by T. Britt Griswold, using gradated shading film.

affect paper become active when the RH exceeds 68 percent at room temperature. Paper attacked by mold is physically weakened and defaced in ways that often require radical restoration. Reducing humidity, maintaining good air circulation, and regular cleaning (dust contains mold spores) will deter mold growth. Some insects and rodents are attracted to paper and its adhesives. Good housekeeping helps prevent infestations. For serious problems or more information, contact the National Pest Control Association, 8100 Oak Street, Dunn Loring, Virginia 22027. Do not permit any poisons to be placed on stored objects; stains or chemical reactions may occur.

Sulfur dioxide, nitrogen oxide, ozone, and aerosols all degrade art objects, but there is little the individual can do about air pollutants. The best protection is to be sure doors and windows fit tightly, keep them closed, store objects in closed containers, and replace air filters as needed.

This chapter has been merely the briefest introduction to the materials and care required for scientific illustrations that are intended to endure. It is hoped that the reader has become intrigued by the complexities of the materials and processes involved. Although choosing materials and caring for completed objects requires continuing self-education, perseverance, and energy, the reward of a stable collection will make the effort worthwhile.

4/Light on Form

Marsha E. Jessup and David Mascaro

In learning how to shade a specimen, it is helpful to understand different types of lighting and their general effects. Most important, however, is the objective study of how each lighting situation affects each specimen. Suggestions offered here are meant to be guidelines, not rules. Observe carefully how different kinds of light and shadow occur on various materials and textures

GENERAL THEORY

A source of light, either perceived in the artist's mind or actually observed, must be present to reveal the optimum form of objects to be drawn or painted. Light flowing across a form creates different values (areas of lightness or darkness) on that form. If these values on the object are judged incorrectly, the object(s) to be drawn may look flat rather than three-dimensional. The values on an object, including shadows, are influenced mainly by the strength of the light source and the texture of the object, its local color, and its planes.

The word *plane* refers to the flattened area(s) of a form or to the areas of value on a curved form that the illustrator abstracts into planes or facets. This abstraction is done in order to place areas of various values to show best the shape of the whole form.

When the illustrator does not have a specimen from which to work, the rendering becomes conceptual and is, at least in part, created from the illustrator's imagination. Thus, the illustrator must be well trained in the accurate depiction of form. It is particularly helpful if the illustrator can imagine the basic planes of each object to be drawn.

In scientific illustration it is customary to locate the primary source of light at the upper left front at about 45 degrees to the object. To help give an object three-dimensionality, or form, locate or assume the location of a secondary light source or reflected light at the lower right. Figure 4-1 shows a ball lighted in this fashion and identifies the values that occur on the shape. This provides a good ratio of light (three-fourths light, one-fourth shadow) on the object. This direction and its consistency from drawing to drawing will help the viewer "read" the form correctly.

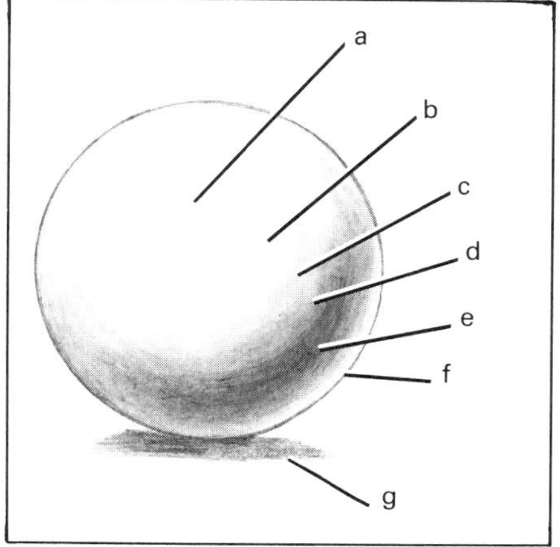

4-1. Lit from the upper left front position, this ball demonstrates the following idealized phenomena of light and shadow: *(a)* the highlight or crest light; *(b)* the range of the light or light-struck area; *(c)* the range of the halftone or half-light area; *(d)* the object shadow; *(e)* the core of the object shadow; *(f)* the reflected light or bounce light; *(g)* the cast shadow (umbra and penumbra—see fig. 4-8). Graphite pencil on cold-press board, redrawn by Marilyn Schotte from a sketch by David Mascaro.

The Highlight or Crest Light

The highlight, or crest light, is the lightest area or edge observable on any object. Although highlights are bright, they are not always equally light, nor are they always the same color as the object upon which they occur. The brightness of a highlight is affected by the object's overall value and by its texture. A piece of glass and a piece of wood may both be influenced by the same light source; the glass, however, will exhibit much brighter highlights because of the reflective quality of its surface. On a colored object, the color of a highlight may differ from the object's surface color if that object is glazed, polished, or wet. Such shiny highlights are called specular, and they may be as bright as their light source. An example is a black glazed vase sitting in the sunshine. The vase will have highlights, but the highlights may be the blue-white of the sky being reflected by the glazed surface of the vase, which acts as a mirror. A touch of specular highlight conveys high sheen and at times even wetness, adding sparkle to a drawing. Specular highlights should be used judiciously because too many bright spots make a drawing look choppy, visually overactive. All other highlights (those on duller and dry surfaces) are chromatic; they become lighter in value and color as the planes of the object face more directly toward the light source.

William L. Brudon made invaluable contributions to this chapter.

The discussion on general theory is adapted from "On the Use of Color in Medical Illustrations," by David Mascaro, in *The Journal of Biocommunication* vol. 9, no. 1, ©1982. Reprinted with permission of *The Journal of Biocommunication*.

The Light-struck Area

The light-struck area is that area of an object whose planes face the light at *nearly* right angles, and, therefore, is not as bright as the highlight itself. The light area surrounds the highlight, generally shows the least amount of texture, and, on rounded objects, blends imperceptibly into the halftones.

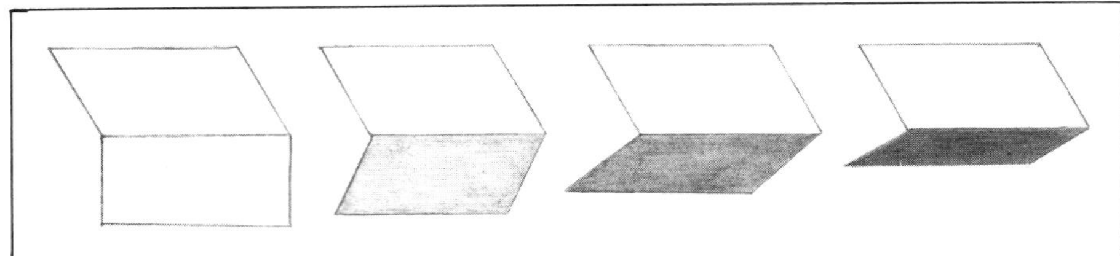

4-2. A top light is assumed to be illuminating a piece of paper folded at different angles. In each case, the top portion is fully lit; the bottom, folded portion ranges, left to right, from light halftone through middle halftone and dark halftone to shadow. By moving the lower plane of a similarly folded and lighted paper while looking into a mirror in a semidarkened room, one can see a visual "click," the halftone area developing and getting darker, as the fold goes into shadow. Aim for this same visual "click" in illustrations of all objects except those that are nearly flat. Graphite pencil on cold-press board, redrawn by Marilyn Schotte from a sketch by David Mascaro.

The Halftone or Half-light Area

Halftones are middle values located halfway between the light and object shadow (fig. 4-2). Viewed with the eyes squinted, halftones are eliminated and an object is reduced to light and shadow. Halftone areas are unnecessary for object recognition but indispensable when a three-dimensional effect is desired.

Texture in the Halftone

Texture is usually most evident in the halftone area and most remarkable at the halftone edge just before it goes into shadow (fig. 4-3). Texture in the light-struck area that is perpendicular to a light source is flattened visually because shadows, which normally help to reveal texture, are nearly eliminated. Even if darks do occur in the light-struck area, their presence should be minimized in order to maintain the integrity of the highlight and light-struck areas.

As the planes of a form turn from the light source, and as the angle of illumination becomes more oblique, lengthening of each texture's cast shadow will occur until at the halftone (where the angle of illumination is at its most oblique) the cast shadows are at their longest. At this point, the textural projections themselves are still receiving direct light, but the surface upon which they rest is now a middle or dark halftone. This contrast between the lighted textural projections and the darker ground upon which they lie makes the halftone area appear more active visually. Without question, the halftones are by far the most varied tonal areas in a rendering. Halftones are the connecting values that bring unity to any form, and, as such, are usually the most difficult areas to paint or render correctly.

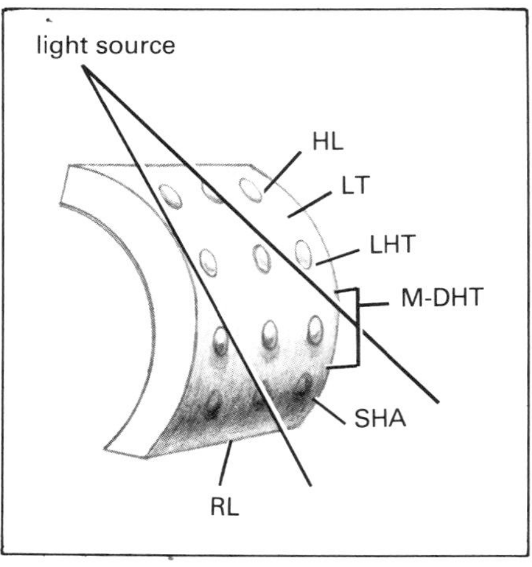

4-3. Texture on a curved surface. HL = highlight; LT = light; LHT = light halftone; M-DHT = medium to dark halftone; SHA = shadow; RL = reflected light. Graphite pencil on cold-press board, redrawn by Marilyn Schotte from a sketch by David Mascaro.

The Object Shadow

The planes of an object that are turned away from the light source and consequently receive no direct light become the object shadows. The darkest portion is the core (see fig. 4-1). In addition to factors mentioned earlier that affect values and shadows, any background and the reflective quality of that background or the environment surrounding the object or both will affect the darkness of shadows. The brighter the light, the darker the shadows will appear. In any rendering, all elements should be lighted consistently, unless the intention is to spotlight a selected area. The closer an object shadow is to the viewer, the darker it should appear. Conversely, in deep space that is dark, the object shadows tend to blend with their backgrounds and become less distinct or lost completely.

Backgrounds offer yet another critical consideration. One needs only to look at the value and texture of surrounding structures to get an idea of how much light will reflect back into a given object shadow. If, for example, two tissue areas are next to each other, one being very dark (such as a spleen) and the other light (such as the peritoneum), it is quite possible that the shadow side of the spleen could be well illuminated if the light source were reflected back into it by the juxtaposition of the peritoneum. An artist with choices to make may choose not to complicate an area by eliminating this reality or may choose not to be exact because the point is better made without this distinction. The artist must be aware of these possibilities and add or delete with expert judgment.

The Reflected Light or Bounce Light

The reflected light bounces back or is reflected back into the object shadow from a secondary light source or from an object's surroundings. It is most easily observed at the edge of a form just before that form meets its cast shadow. Although a reflected light is absolutely necessary in most instances to enhance the dimensional quality of a form, it is one of the most misused phenomena in the tonal scale.

With a dark edge and without a reflected light (fig. 4-4, left), the shadow side of an object could look as though it were cut out, like a black-paper silhouette. Not only does this look harsh, but it can make the object's shadow side appear to come forward.

Nonetheless, great restraint must be exercised in rendering reflected lights if the integrity and solidity of the subject is to be maintained. If reflected light is rendered as slightly lighter than the shadow but darker than the halftone, the correct tone has probably been achieved. A safe method of judging reflected light is by squinting, almost shutting the eyes. If the reflected light nearly disappears, it is probably just right for the situation.

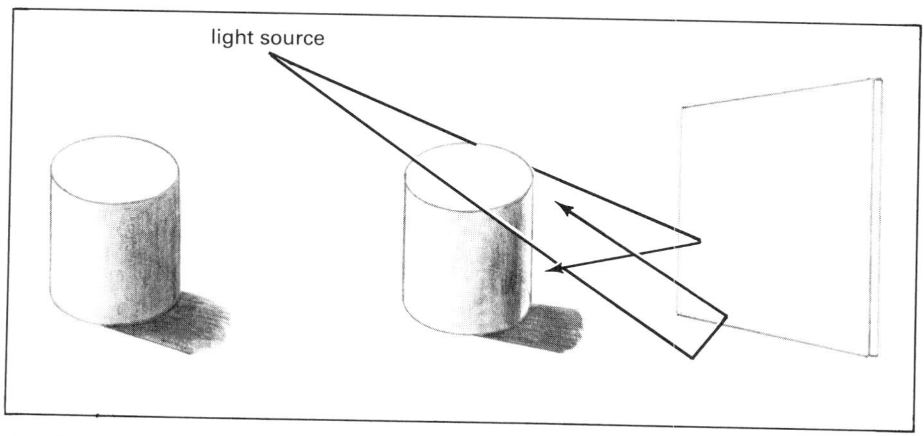

4-4. Light hitting an object *(left)* without reflected light and *(right)* with reflected light. Graphite pencil on cold-press board, redrawn by Marilyn Schotte from a sketch by David Mascaro.

The Cast Shadow

The cast shadow is an effect created by the interruption of light rays by an object cast onto another plane. Shadows may vary in their degree of darkness depending upon the strength of the light source and the value of the area upon which they are cast. Cast shadows will change value and color slightly as they cross areas of different value and color (fig. 4-5); all cast shadows must conform to the shape of the surfaces upon which they are cast (fig. 4-6). In illustrating cast shadows from imagination, be careful not to make them look too much like the object that is casting them. In reality, cast shadows rarely mimic the exact shapes of the casting objects (fig. 4-7). Rather, the shadows will undulate with the surface upon which they are cast and appear thinner or broader depending upon the angle at which they are viewed.

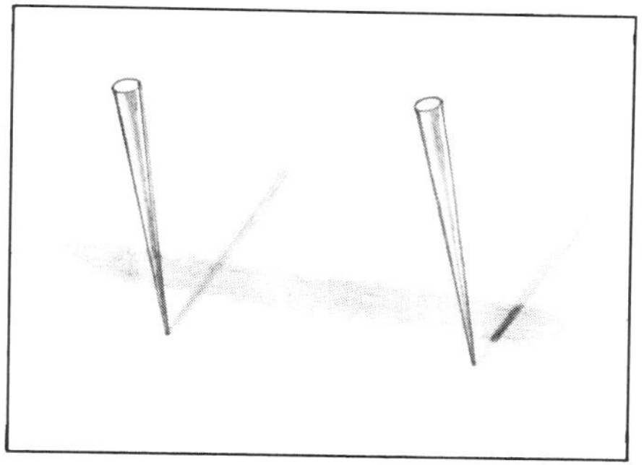

4-5. Cast shadows should change value, become lighter or darker, as they cross areas of different values. The shadow on the left is drawn incorrectly; the one on the right, correctly. Graphite pencil on cold-press board, redrawn by Marilyn Schotte from a sketch by David Mascaro.

The cast shadow consists of two areas: the umbra, its darkest part, and the penumbra, its softer and lighter outer area (fig. 4-8). In most cases, the distinction between these two areas is a theoretical one. What should be remembered is that the cast shadow generally contains the darkest values in a rendering and that the darkest value within this dark area occurs where the shadow meets the object that is casting it, the point of deepest accent.

As a cast shadow moves away from its object, the edges are crisp, and as light begins to infiltrate it, the edges become softer and lighter until the limit of the shadow is reached. Depending upon the angle of illumination, cast shadows can be shorter or longer than the object that is casting them. Generally, the more perpendicular the illumination is to the lighted object, the more restricted the cast shadow (fig. 4-9).

Do not render shadows so opaquely or darkly that they appear or even hint at being solid. The deepest, darkest cavity should still suggest that air exists within it; let the shadows breathe.

No lights within the shadow, except a possible wet light, should compete in lightness with any areas within the light. Regardless of what he or she sees, the artist must control this situation. One of the laws of simultaneous contrast states that a light within a dark area takes on an extra brilliance because of the sharp contrast of values that exists. When improperly rendered, this contrast of values can create a visual hole in the drawing.

At times, actual holes in an otherwise dark area or structure (the sacral foramen on a sacrum in light and shadow, for example) or holes

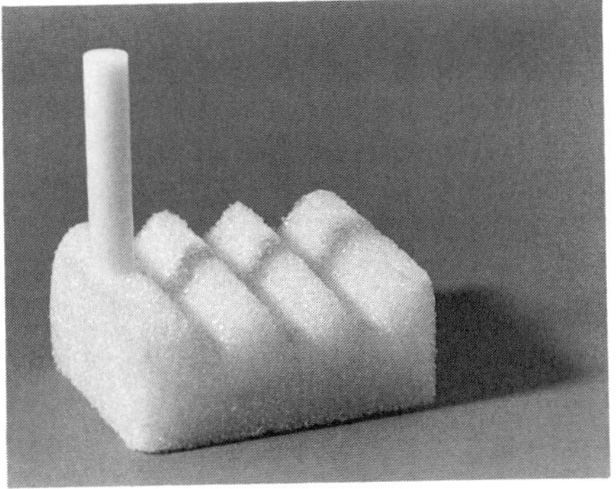

4-6. Cast shadows must conform to the shape of the surfaces upon which they are cast. Photo by Michael Kantor.

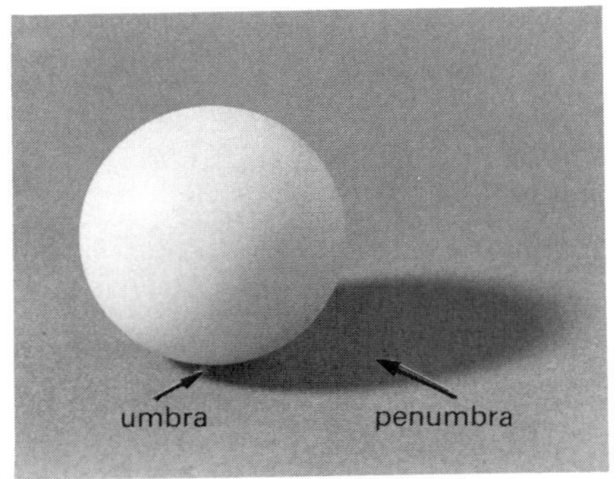

4-8. Cast shadow of a sphere. Photo by Michael Kantor.

4-7. A study in shapes of cast shadows with some reflected light. Photo by Michael Kantor.

4-9. Length of cast shadows: *(a)* short shadow—light source close to perpendicular; *(b)* long shadow—light source more angled. Photo by Michael Kantor.

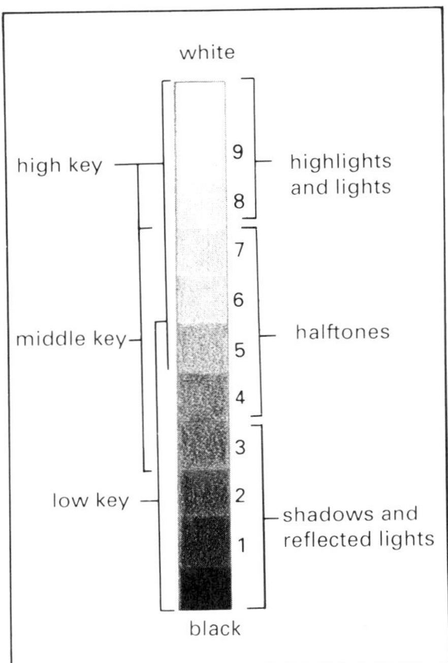

4-10. Standard nine-value gray scale. Graphite pencil on cold-press board, by David Mascaro.

created by adjoining structures (bones of the shoulder joint) might need to be arbitrarily toned down from white (if the surrounding area is white) so that they do not assume an unreasonable visual importance in the overall value scheme.

Finally, shadows are the quiet areas in any realistic composition and should remain so. The values within a general shadowed area tend to merge toward a limited scale of low values. This merging is very evident if a nine-value scale is placed in a well-lighted room and the illumination slowly lowered (fig. 4-10). The darker values from 5 down to black begin to merge or become less distinct as the illumination decreases. Conversely, the light values from value 5 up to white maintain their individuality to a much greater degree under the same lighting differences. This value-merging phenomenon causes any shadow area to be much less active visually than the neighboring halftone and light areas.

SPECIFIC LIGHTING CONDITIONS

Shadows in Concave Areas

Concave structures are curved or rounded inward and appear as indentations or depressions on a surface. Any depression or indentation identifies itself with shadow as much as a convex or outwardly curved structure does. In rendering a concave surface, note that the edge above and surrounding the shadowed depression area is lighter in value; the shadow core occurs just below the edge; and the object shadow, halftone, and light areas of the concave surface appear in that order as they move away from the direction of the light source (figs. 4-11, 4-12, and 4-13). An intense or close light source will often create a highlight on the rim opposite the light source. Shiny, highly reflective, and wet surfaces will show more contrast between the highlight and surrounding surface areas. In conventional lighting situations, the order of light and shadow on a concave surface may be said to mirror the effect of light and shadow on an opaque sphere. The arrangement of light and shadow would be different if the light source emanated from within the concavity or was directed into it as a narrow beam of light.

When a pitted surface occurs on a rounded form, the concave structures or pits conform to the same rules as demonstrated earlier with the convex or raised surface (see fig. 4-2), especially with textures in halftones and the object shadow (figs. 4-14, 4-15). Figure 4-16 illustrates concavities on a flat plane.

The perceived angle of light can affect the viewer's interpretation of concave structures on a flat plane. When lighted with a conventional upper-left-quadrant light source, the cups in figure 4-17, left, appear as cups. Generally, if the light source appears to come from below the horizon, the cups appear as spheres. This is because we are accustomed to viewing illustrations that depict conventional lighting conditions with a light source from above. Placing an object upon the surface of the paint palette, however, dispels the optical illusion (fig. 4-18).

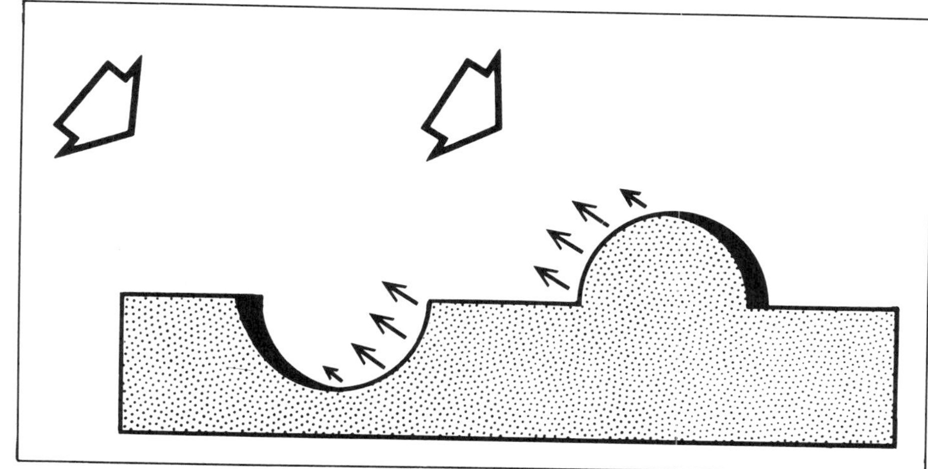

4-11. Comparison of light and shadow on concave and convex forms. The large arrows represent the light source; small arrows indicate reflected light. Pen-and-ink with shading film on hot-press illustration board, by William L. Brudon.

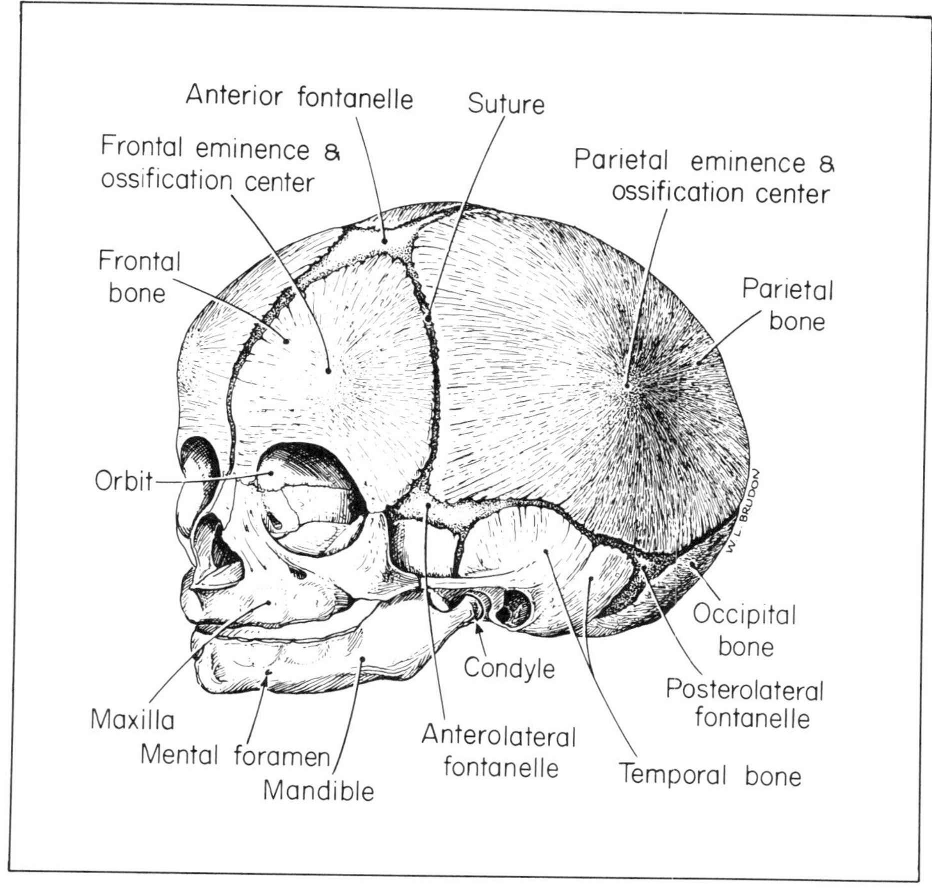

4-12. Line drawing study of concave and convex surfaces. Newborn human skull. Pen-and-ink on hot-press Bristol board, by William L. Brudon. From *Essentials of Human Anatomy*, 8th ed., by R. T. Woodburne (© 1988, Oxford University Press). Reprinted by permission.

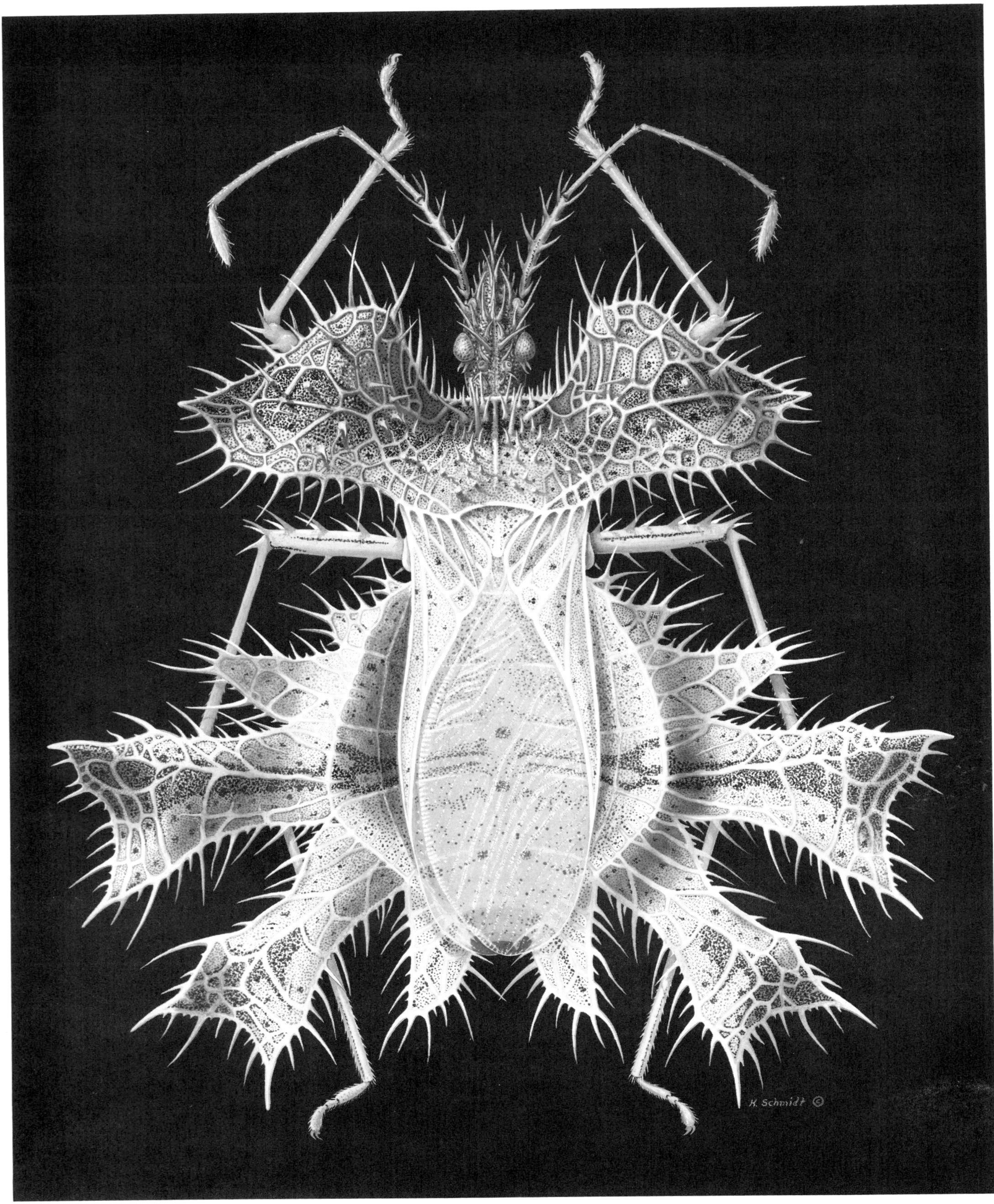

4-13. Broad convex and concave surfaces. *Pephricus paradoxus* (Hemiptera: Coreidae). White tempera, dilute ink, and smudged Conté no. 3 pencil on black paper, by Kathleen A. Schmidt.

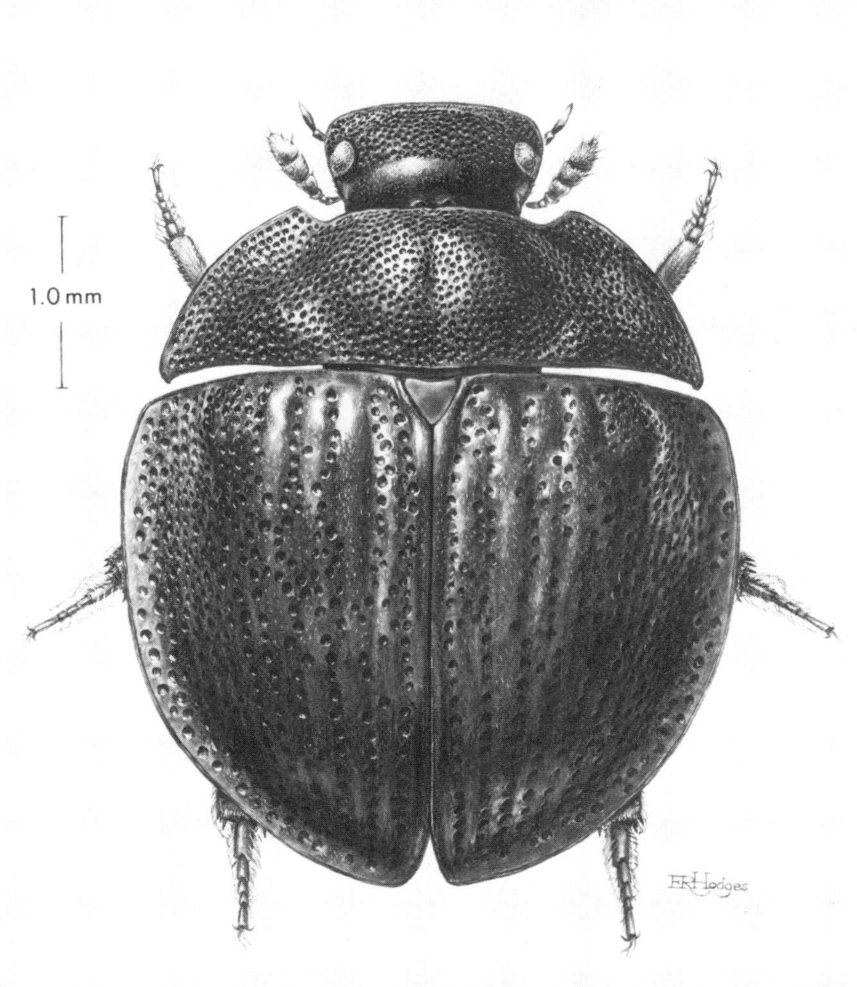

4-14. Small concavities. *Kruia chrysopelma* (Coleoptera: Hydrophilidae). Carbon dust and retouch gray paint on no. 00 Ross board by Elaine R. S. Hodges. Courtesy of Paul J. Spangler.

4-15. Pits on a rounded surface. Photo by Michael Kantor.

4-16. Pits on a flat plane. Photo by Michael Kantor.

4-17. Cups in *(a)* have light coming from the upper left. The same picture turned upside down *(b)* appears to show convex instead of concave shapes. From *Scientific Illustration*, by Phyllis Wood (© 1979, Van Nostrand Reinhold). Reprinted by permission.

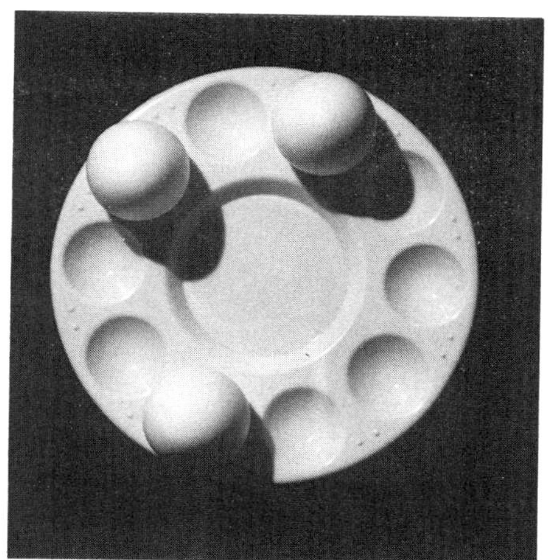

4-18. Objects placed in the palette cups dispel the optical illusion regardless of how the photograph is turned. From *Scientific Illustration*, by Phyllis Wood (© 1979, Van Nostrand Reinhold). Reprinted by permission.

Light and Shadow on Cubes, Cylinders, and Cones

A cube is a series of flat planes. If these are evenly lighted and are the same color, any variation of tone on the planes is caused by cast shadows or reflected light from adjacent surfaces. Reflected light produces a very subtle lightening of tone on the affected area, and shadows darken it. The most brightly lighted surface (lightest tonal value) of the cube will be the flat plane perpendicular to the light source. The plane farthest from the light will be the darkest and the remaining plane will be an intermediate tone between the other two (fig. 4-19). Structures on the three visible surfaces of a cube will be more closely related tonally to the plane that they rest on than to structural components on either of the other planes (fig. 4-20).

Cylinders and cones are similar in shape; indeed, a cone may be thought of as a cylinder that tapers at one end. Unlike the parallel shading configuration on a cylinder, the shading on a cone tapers proportionately to its shape as it converges toward the tip. Foreshortened cylinders resemble cones and, as with spheres, the arrangement of tonal values on cones or cylinders with highly reflective surfaces differs markedly from their counterparts with dull, matte surfaces (fig. 4-21).

A number of organisms and structures in nature resemble cylinders and cones. They appear flat-

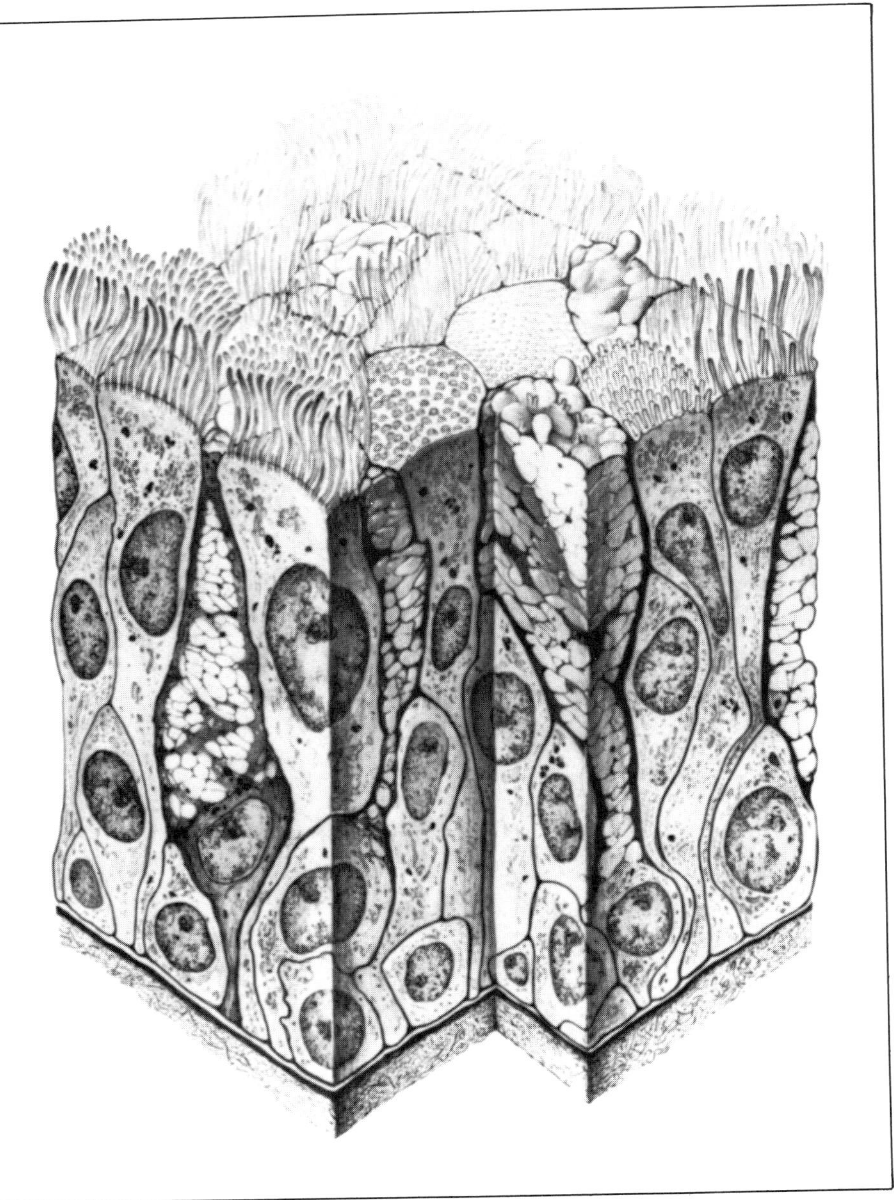

4-20. Cuboidal section of a human epithelial cell. Although the right-hand planes are in shadow, the shading is just suggested so that details are not obscured. Graphite pencil on Video Media paper, by William L. Brudon. From unpublished work by Johannes A. G. Rhodin.

4-19. Tonal relationships of planes of a cube to each other and to the surface below. Photo by Michael Kantor.

a

b

4-21. Comparison of *(a)* dull and *(b)* highly reflective surfaces. Photo by Michael Kantor.

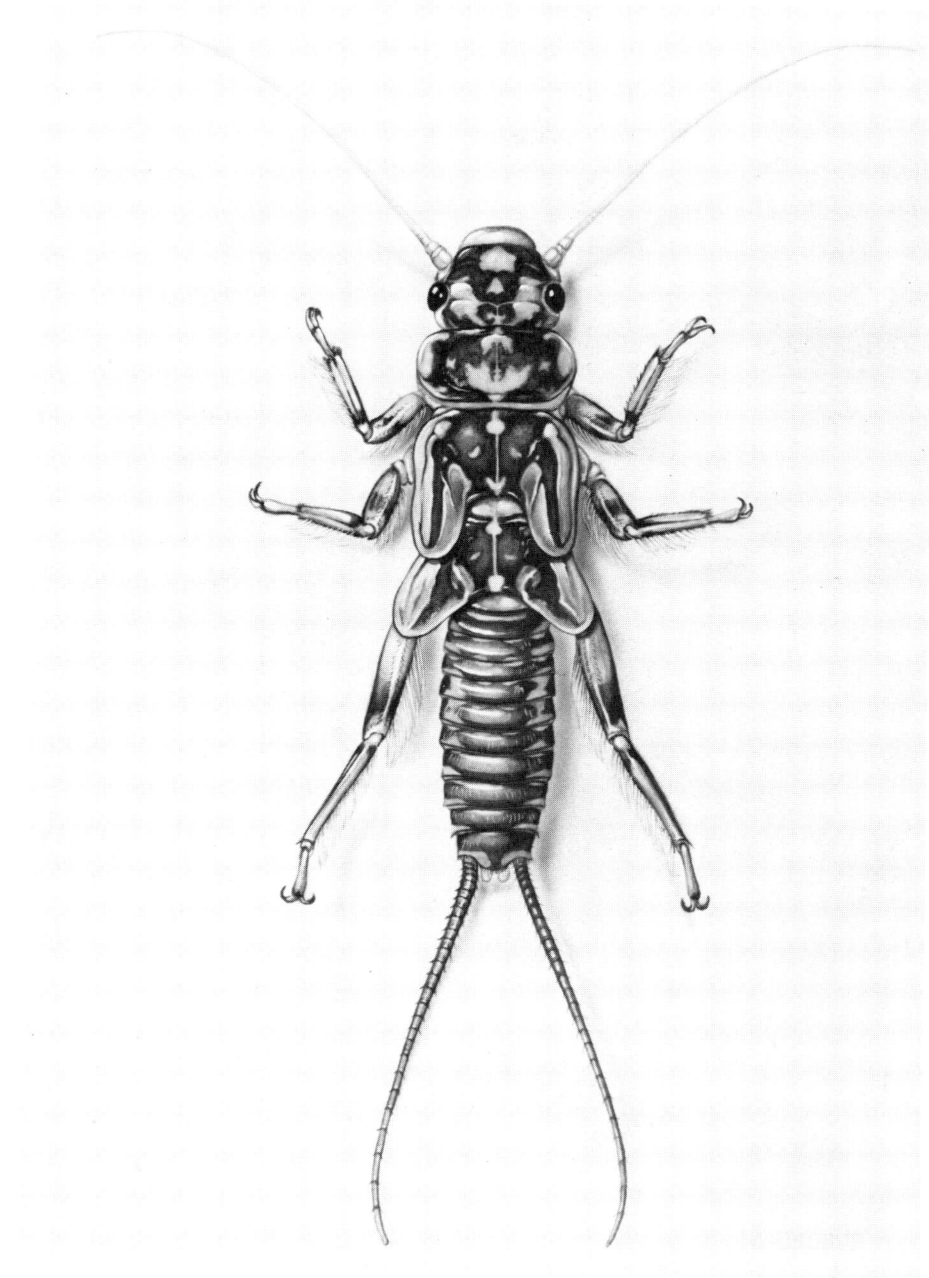

4-22. Segmented, semicylindrical form. Stonefly nymph, *Plecoptera*. Airbrush and watercolor on Strathmore watercolor board, by Marsha E. Jessup.

tened to varying degrees, as in the case of some fish or insect bodies and crustacean appendages (fig. 4-22; see figs. 15-43, 15-44). If the cylinder or cone is segmented, each segment must be rendered secondarily to the overall form. Consequently, the light and shadow areas on the entire cylinder or cone are rendered before the top and bottom edges of each individual segment are clearly delineated. The resulting effect is that the overall form is dominant over any individual segment.

Light and Shadow in Biological and Medical Illustration

Since biological illustrations most often depict isolated specimens or structures, it is important that conventional lighting be used —unless, of course, the structure of the specimen is difficult to see under such lighting. In that case, alternate light sources can be used, provided they do not confuse the viewer's perception of the depicted form. (Alternate light sources are discussed later in this chapter.)

The use of conventional light sources in biological illustrations is even more critical because cast shadows are rarely used by biological illustrators in journal publications (where most of their work appears) because cast shadows might obscure taxonomic characters. Medical illustrators make greater use of subtle cast shadows in their work; they are more likely to be illustrating concepts than details of specimens. In both fields, however, it is important to develop an understanding of cast shadows, since they can often define structure and depth in a way not possible by any other means.

In medical and biological illustration it seems best to use artistic license to curtail the use of cast shadow and to soften or lose those shadows that do exist; the artistically untrained eye may misinterpret a cast shadow (particularly one that is overstated) as another form or structure rather than a simple interruption of light. When information and technique conflict, technique must always be given secondary importance.

Transparency

If a transparent specimen or structure is to be illustrated without something that can be seen through it, specific artistic liberties must be taken to ensure that the viewer perceives the degree of transparency desired. Although there is no formula for approaching this, certain effects are known to work. For example, the highlight on a transparent sphere is rendered with the shadow core (darkest shadow) surrounding and immediately adjacent to it. The remainder of the sphere fades to a

4-23. Transparent lucite sphere. Photo by Michael Kantor.

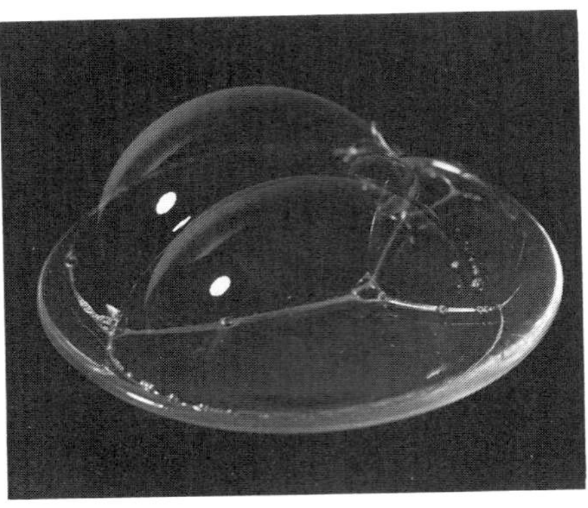

a

b

4-24. Transparent forms on *(a)* dark and *(b)* light backgrounds. Photo by Michael Kantor.

4-25. Examples of tonal ranges in translucent forms. Photo by Michael Kantor.

much lighter value until it reaches a brighter reflected light area equal in intensity to the highlight and hugging the lower edge of the sphere (fig. 4-23). The reflected light area is usually crescent-shaped and is diametrically opposite the highlight. On light or white backgrounds, there is usually a darkening on the edge of the sphere, and it becomes a little heavier on the edge farthest from the light source.

If a cast shadow can be used, a light area of the same intensity as the highlight and approximately that size would appear within the cast shadow and opposite the highlight. The light area in the cast shadow, if bright enough, would also be reflected back to some degree onto the lower edge of the sphere. In color illustrations, it is a little easier to create transparency, since the background color shows through the object. Figure 4-24 shows a transparent form on dark and light backgrounds.

Subtleties of transparency, such as detail in reflections, can be shown more easily with continuous tone than with line. Line renderings can only suggest the range of tones possible in continuous tone. The inversion of objects seen through a transparent sphere, or the reversal of images seen through a transparent cylinder, would be difficult to capture in line. Figure 4-25 shows the range of tone evident in transparent and translucent forms photographed under conventional lighting conditions.

If structures can be seen under or behind a transparent object, the illustrator's task becomes much simpler. The object beyond is rendered first in full detail and then disappears as it approaches the external edge of the transparent form (figs. 4-26, 4-27).

IRIDESCENCE

Trudy Nicholson and T. Britt Griswold

Iridescence is the changing colors of an object's surface observed when the angle of view changes. Iridescent colors look different from the other colors seen in nature. Indeed, they are different in that iridescence is color due to macroscopic structure (the shapes of objects), whereas other colors are pigmentary or due to their molecular structure. Pigments absorb

---

Steven E. Hodges contributed to the text on iridescence.

light. All wavelengths of light (color) are absorbed to some degree. What is seen is the color that is absorbed the least.

Iridescent colors are produced by a phenomenon known as interference, the interaction of light waves, which may be constructive (when light waves coincide and produce a brighter color) or destructive (when light waves cancel each other and produce no light). Constructive and destructive effects are seen, for example, when light is reflected off the inner and outer surfaces of a very thin transparent layer (fig. 4-28). The layer's density and thickness (approximately one wavelength thick) are the factors that affect light. Light of the proper wavelengths reflects from one surface and either constructively or destructively interferes with light reflected from the other surface(s). Wavelengths that interfere constructively seem to be enhanced, whereas those that interfere destructively appear to vanish. Examples of this phenomenon are the iridescent reflections of soap bubbles and oil slicks. Both constructive and destructive interference can occur simultaneously at a single position for different colors and simultaneously for the same color at different points. This is why the relationship of iridescent colors does not change as a specimen is turned, even though the colors of a part of the specimen appear to do so. For instance, a pink will stay next to a green in more or less the same place even though the pink may change to tan and the green may become blue as the specimen is turned.

Multiple transparent layers will reflect more light than a single layer, with each layer reflecting a percentage of the light not reflected by the layer above it. With enough layers, a metallic appearance will result (fig. 4-29). This effect is seen, for example, on some insect exoskeletons and fish scales. If the layers are of uniform thickness, only one bright color will be re-

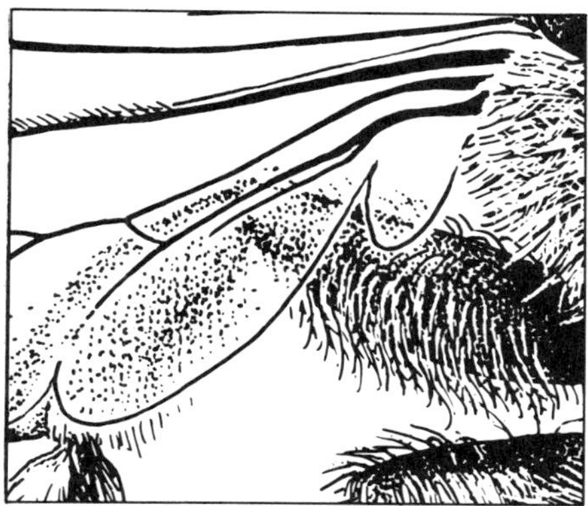

4-26. Linear rendering of transparent structure. Detail of bee wing over leg. Ink on scratchboard, by Elaine R. S. Hodges.

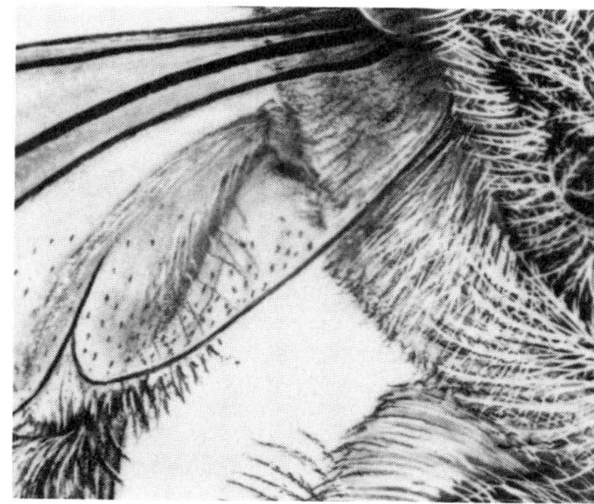

4-27. Continuous-tone rendering of transparent structure. Detail of bee wing over leg. Carbon dust on no. 00 Ross board, by Elaine R. S. Hodges.

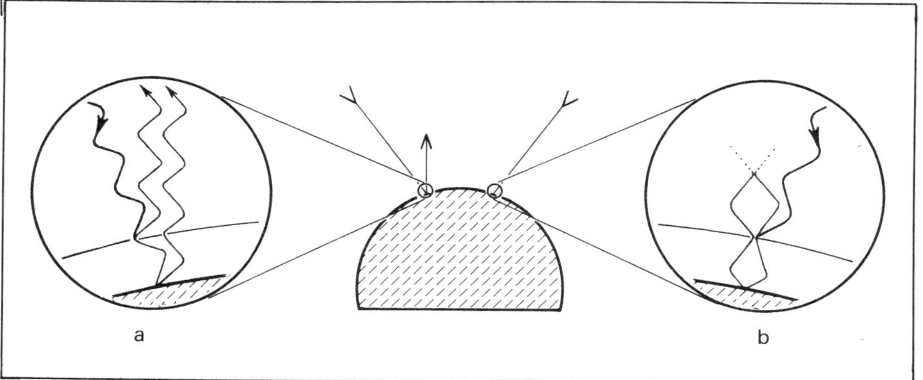

4-28. Interference: *(a)* constructive and *(b)* destructive. Light waves are reflected off the inner and outer surfaces of a transparent layer that coats an object. Pen-and-ink with shading film on hot-press Bristol board, by T. Britt Griswold.

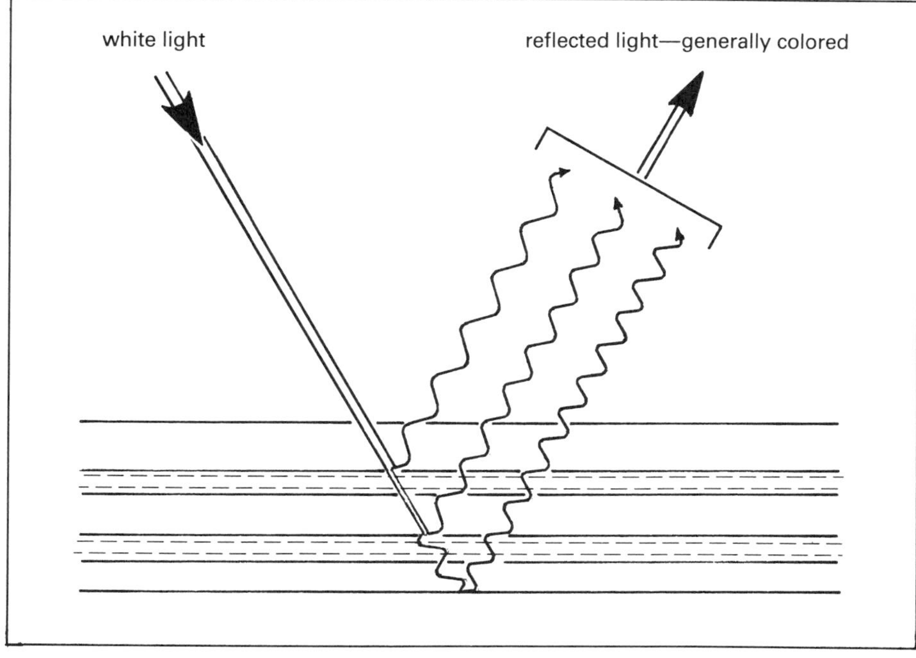

4-29. Bright, metallic appearance produced by light reflected by multiple transparent layers. Pen-and-ink on hot-press Bristol board, by T. Britt Griswold.

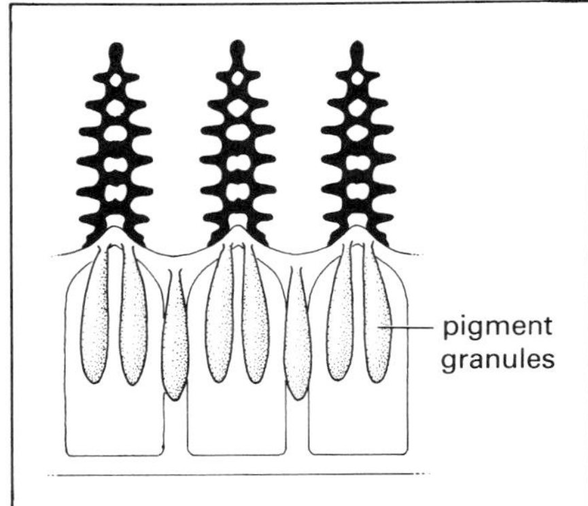

4-30. Reflection gratings. A cross section of a small portion of a Pierid butterfly wing scale of the male *Eurema lisa*. Each vertical ridge has several horizontal ridges to form an even finer reflection grating than normal, reflecting iridescent effects in the ultraviolet range—undoubtedly for other insects to see. Sacs of yellow or white pigment lie within the scales. Pen-and-ink on hot-press Bristol board, by T. Britt Griswold.

flected. If the layers are of varying thicknesses, many colors are reflected and white silvery reflections result.

Iridescence produced in a second way is found on some butterflies, beetles, birds, and reptiles. Thousands of tiny, closely spaced parallel ridges make up a reflection grating that behaves in a fashion similar to transparent layers. That is, each ridge reflects light waves that interfere with the light waves reflected from adjacent ridges (fig. 4-30).

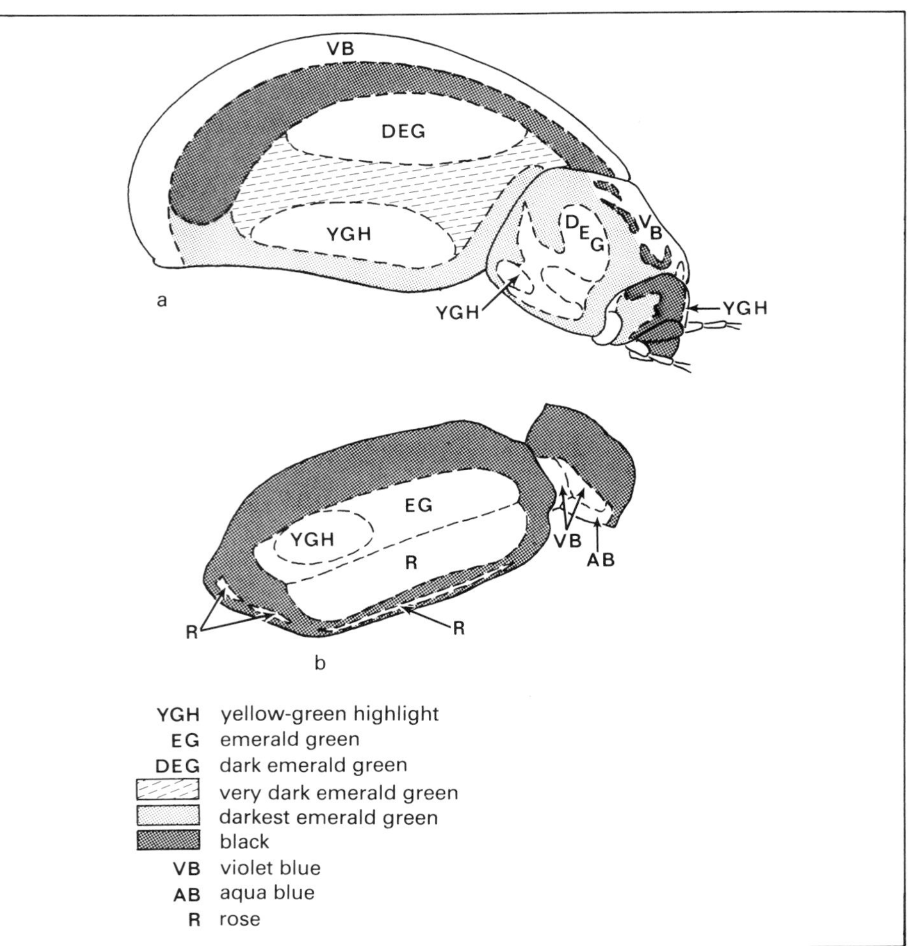

4-31. Examples of iridescent color placement: *(a)* the tergal plate, wing case, and head of a leaf beetle showing areas of color with a light source assumed at upper left (compare with fig. C-4); *(b)* the tergal plate and wing case of *Carabus sycophanta*, a carabid beetle. These creatures were hunted almost to extinction for their beautiful, iridescent colors. Pen-and-ink with shading film on Denril, by Trudy Nicholson © 1975.

Illustrating Iridescence

The artist is limited in illustrating iridescence, since no drawing using pigments, even iridescent ones, can convey all the flashing changes of iridescent hues when reproduced. Metallic and fluorescent media will not reproduce in print without greatly adding to the cost, and they do not, in any case, duplicate iridescence: fluorescent paint gives off a light that does not resemble iridescent colors, and metallic paint alone on a flat surface does not produce the shiny, bright metallic reflections of a three-dimensional object. There are, however, several ways to suggest iridescence, with its unusual color relationships and striking reflective powers (see fig. C-3). First, brilliant colors placed adjacent to each other, by their position on the structure and their softened edges, imply iridescence without being confused with color patterns seen on pigmented specimens.

In addition, iridescence is characterized by intense colored highlights and deep blacks next to suddenly emerging brilliant color. This differs markedly from pigmentary color, which gradually darkens to the core of the shaded area, where the color still may be seen but is faded and darkened. Even continuous-tone rendering, without color, can convey some characteristics of iridescent color, including metallic sheen and high reflectivity, by juxtaposing lights and darks somewhat sharply rather than with gradual shading. Because iridescent colors are more intense than pigmentary colors, and their darks and sometimes color are related to viewing angle rather than a gradual decrease in light, contrast is increased. Iridescent dark areas, which are intensely dark, are placed somewhat differently in relation to the structure of the specimen than are shaded areas in pigmentary color.

The diagrammatic analysis of the coloring of two iridescent beetles exemplifies some of the characteristics discussed above (fig. 4-31). When painted, these beetles can be made to look distinctly iridescent (see fig. C-4). In the leaf beetle (fig. 4-31a), yellow-green is the brightest color of the portion of the animal viewed perpendicularly. This changes to dark emerald-green as shapes curve away from the observer's eyes, blending into a narrow band of black where all reflecting colors have canceled each other. As the shape curves farther down and away from the observer, a band of violet-blue borders the farthest edge of the wing case and tergal plate. Yellow is canceled at the most oblique angles of view where the colors violet and blue are enhanced. The carabid beetle (fig. 4-31b) also has a yellow-green highlight on emerald-green, but the green changes to a rose color.

To create the illusion of iridescence, carefully study the specimen to duplicate precise colors and tones as they occur in relation to each other. In figure C-4, notice that there are no white highlights. Highlights are a more intense green, a bit more yellow. The brilliant green moves immediately into an intense shading so dark that no color is evident at all. These colors and shadows were copied as accurately as possible, using acrylic emerald-green, adding a little yellow for highlights, and blue lightened with white for the light area at the farthest edge.

ALTERNATIVE LIGHTING CONDITIONS

In some situations, conventional lighting conditions make it difficult to see certain structural aspects of a specimen or conceptualization, and alternative lighting may provide a better view. For instance, raking (acute-angle) light emphasizes texture that might be obscured by conventional lighting (see figs. 4-41 and 4-44b). Most uses of alternative lighting, however, are reserved for creating unusual or dramatic spatial concepts and attracting attention. Illustrations of this nature are common in medical advertisements directed to medical professionals.

Several lighting concepts are illustrated in figures 4-32 through 4-57. In the diagrams, the large arrow represents the direction of light from the light source; the small arrows indicate by their size the amount of light reflected back from the object.

4-32. Diagram of 45-degree conventional (upper left) lighting on a convex surface. Pen-and-ink with shading film on hot-press illustration board, by William L. Brudon.

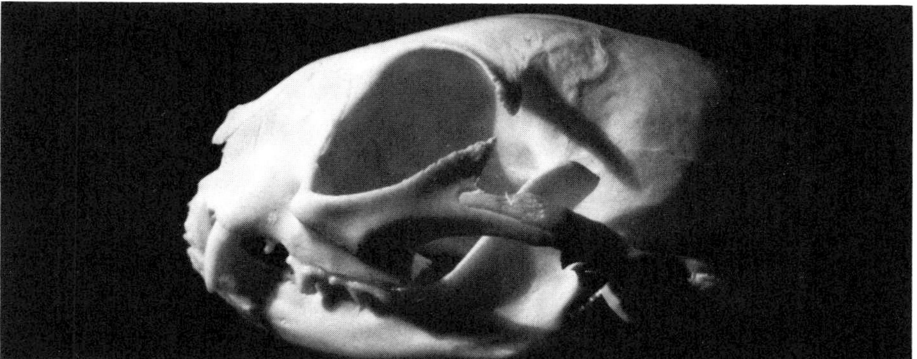

4-33. Cat skull with 45-degree conventional lighting. Textures, overlapping structures, and unusual biological architecture can be interpreted in an otherwise confusing field of view when highlights and shadows are where they are expected to be. Photo by William L. Brudon.

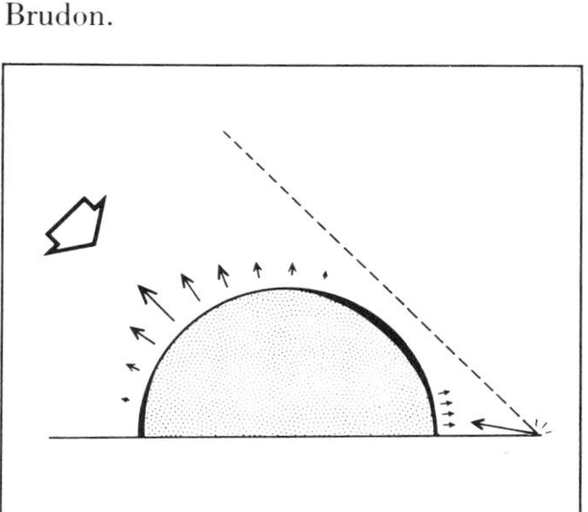

4-34. Diagram of 45-degree conventional lighting on a convex surface with light reflected into the shadow area. Pen-and-ink with shading film on hot-press illustration board, by William L. Brudon.

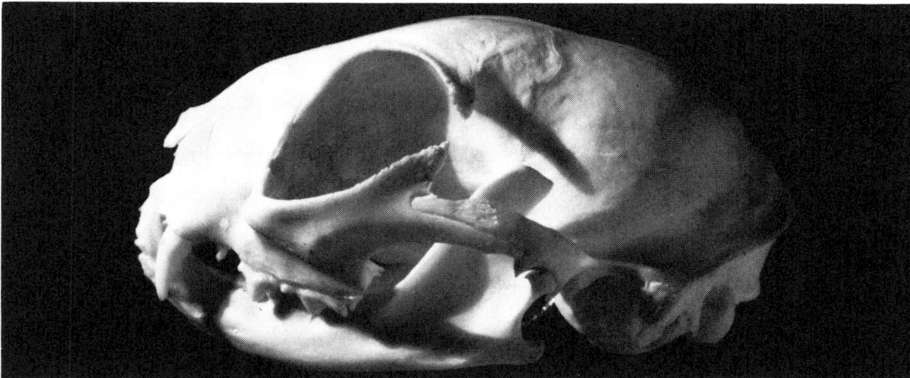

4-35. Cat skull with reflected light. Additional reality is achieved when light is assumed to reflect from the surface upon which the subject rests (without showing the reflecting surface). The degree of reflectance is in proportion to the intensity of the original (main) light source, and considerable loss of that original intensity takes place in the reflection. Photo by William L. Brudon.

a

b

4-36. Reflected light. Comparison of *(a)* textured with *(b)* smooth, highly reflective surface. The metal ball exhibits specular highlights. Photo by Michael Kantor.

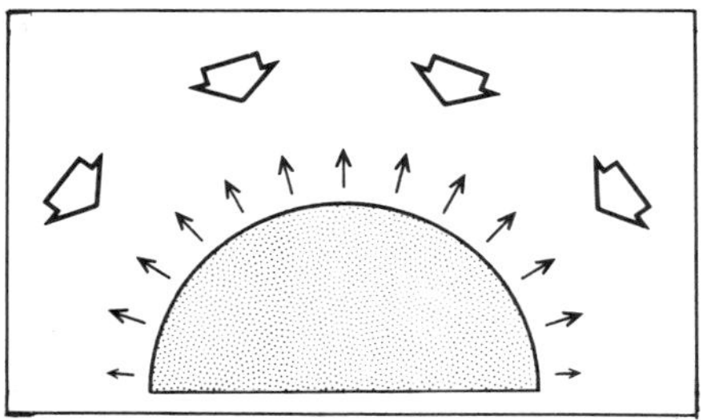

4-37. Diagram of diffused lighting. Pen-and-ink with shading film on hot-press illustration board, by William L. Brudon.

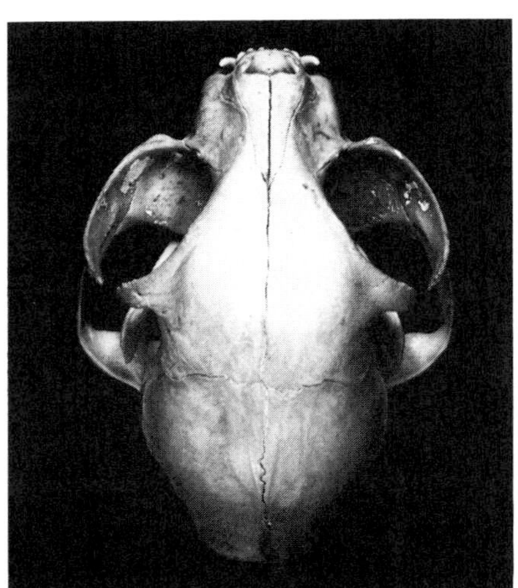

4-38. Cat skull in diffused light. Light aimed at the subject from several angles or sources simultaneously diminishes modeling and definition of contours. Color, general shape, and comparison with other objects in the picture plane may have to convey the subject-form message. When such component messages are important in the visual story, diffused lighting is ideal. Photo by William L. Brudon.

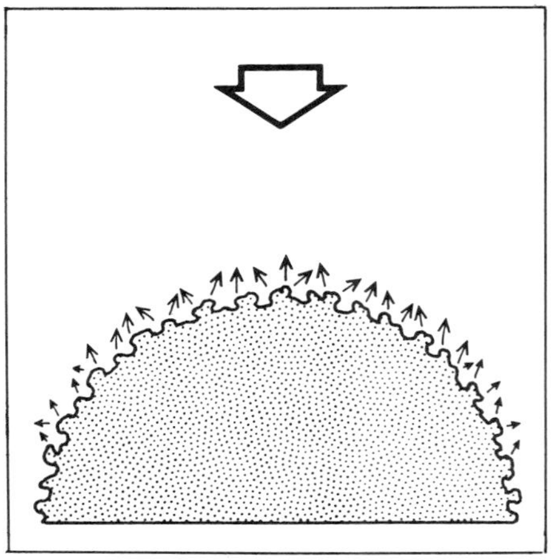

4-40. Diagram of diffused lighting on a textured surface. When a rough-textured surface is illuminated with a diffused light source, reflection from individual components of the texture further diffuses the light (see figs. 4-36 and 4-43). Here light comes from the zenith; however, light from any angle will produce the same effect on such a textured object. Pen-and-ink with shading film on hot-press illustration board, by William L. Brudon.

Left:
4-39. Diffused light rendering. Note how the light is almost totally absorbed and very little modeling is apparent so that the form is almost silhouetted. The cast shadow helps suggest form. Salamander. Airbrush and transparent watercolor on no. 00 Ross board, by William L. Brudon.

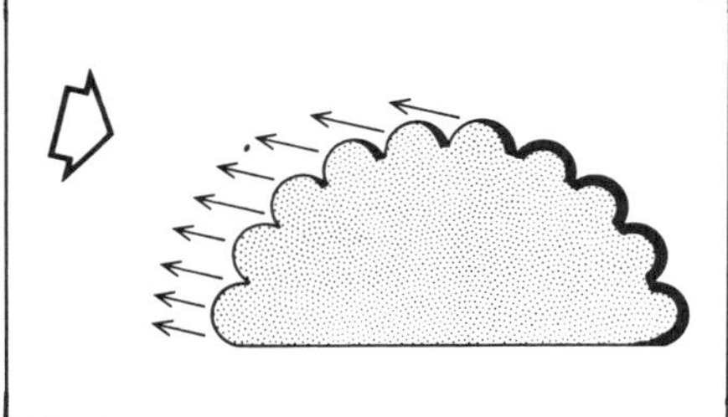

4-41. Diagram of raking light. Pen-and-ink with shading film on hot-press illustration board, by William L. Brudon.

4-43. Although texture may invite the illustrator to portray detail slavishly, total objective form must not be sacrificed. Overall highlights and shadows often are most important. Note that raking light on a broadly curved surface leaves a small halftone area between highlight and shadow areas. Photo by Michael Kantor.

4-42. Cat skull in raking light. When a light source is aimed at an object acutely, textured details are better defined since individual components reflect individual highlights and cast their individual shadows. Note the broad, flat highlight on the left and equally flat shadow on the right. Photo by William L. Brudon.

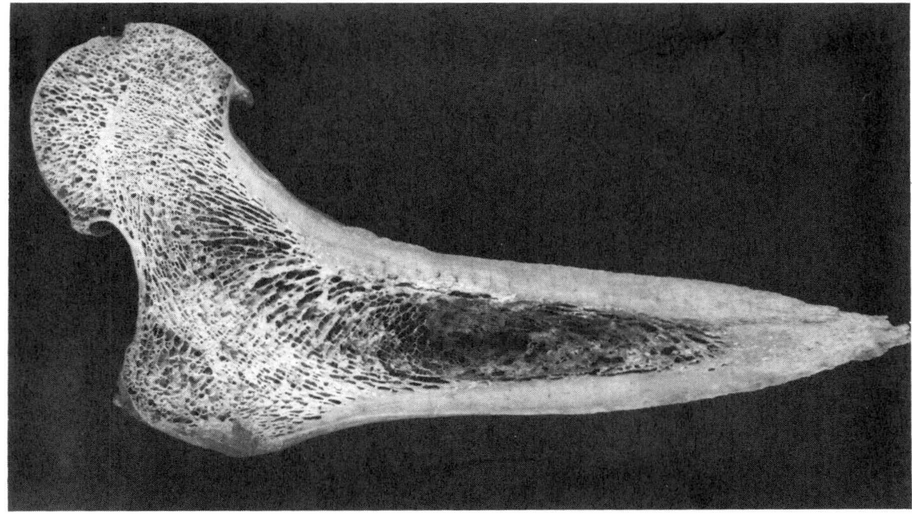

a

b

Right:
4-44. These photographs of sagittal cross sections through the human femur dramatically demonstrate the effects of acute-angle illumination (raking light) on a flat, textured surface: *(a)* direct illumination of the surface results in an almost single-toned pattern; *(b)* raking light produces a more distinct two-toned effect. Photo by William L. Brudon.

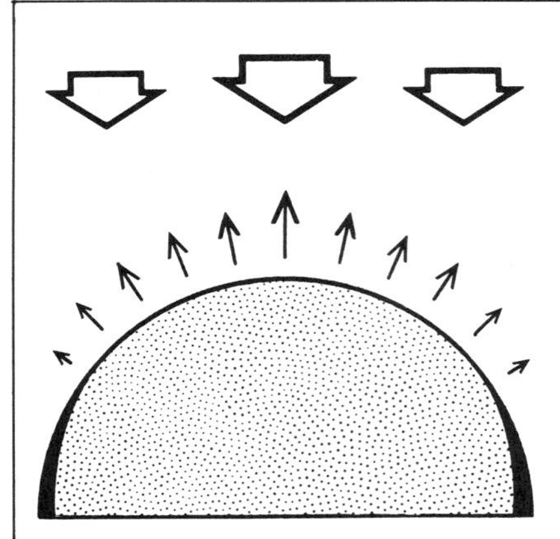

4-45. Diagram of rim shadow lighting. Pen-and-ink with shading film on hot-press illustration board, by William L. Brudon.

4-47. Diagram of plateau lighting, a variation of rim shadow lighting. Pen-and-ink with shading film on hot-press illustration board, by William L. Brudon.

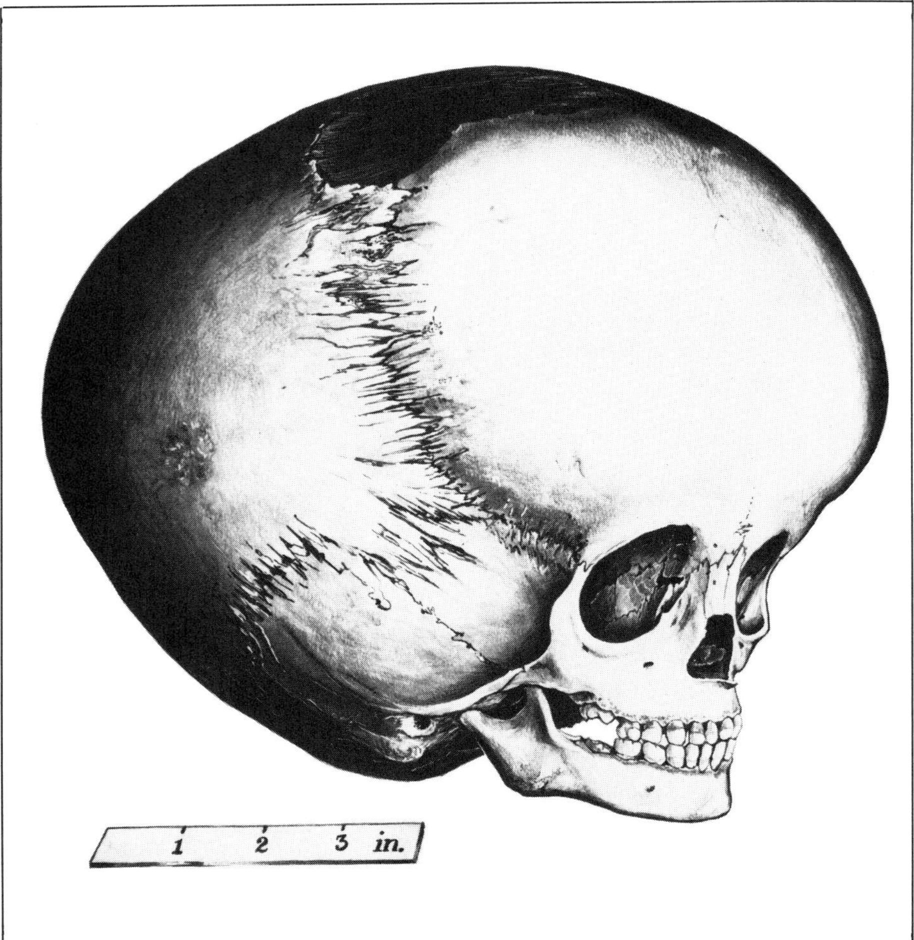

4-46. If a narrow, intense beam of light strikes an object, an effect called "rim shadow" may result. The periphery, receiving no direct light rays, will be in shadow. The method used to depict this effect is to render nearer areas of the subject lighter and more distant parts darker. This technique has special value when minimal shading or color patterns are important. Hydrocephalic skull. Wash on illustration board, by William L. Brudon. From *Elementary Human Anatomy*, by A. Berger (John Wiley and Sons, 1964). Reprinted by permission.

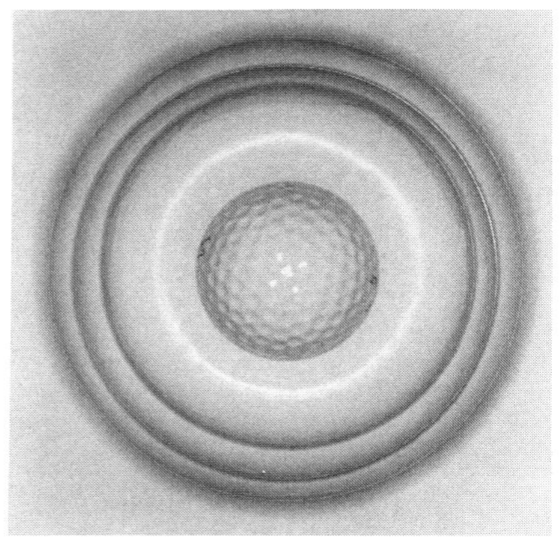

4-48. In plateau lighting, the layers (or echelons) of individual form are individually rim shadow–illuminated. Photo by Michael Kantor.

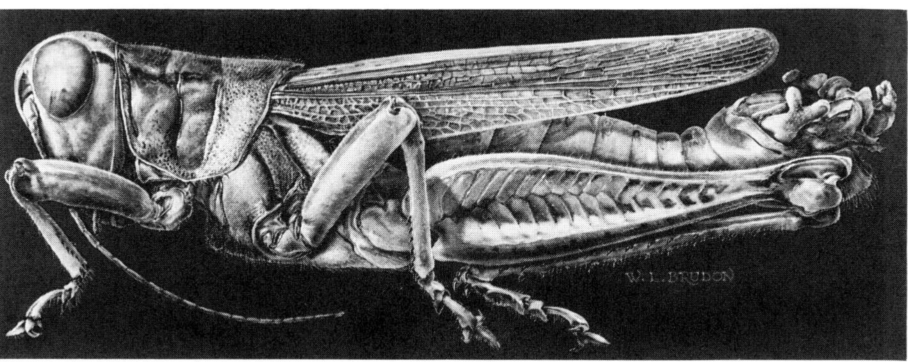

4-49. Use of plateau lighting, especially notable on the grasshopper's eye, in modeling of the head and legs, and on the wing venation. *Melanaplus differentialis*, family Acrididae. Rendered with airbrush and wash on scratchboard, by William L. Brudon. Courtesy of T. H. Hubbell.

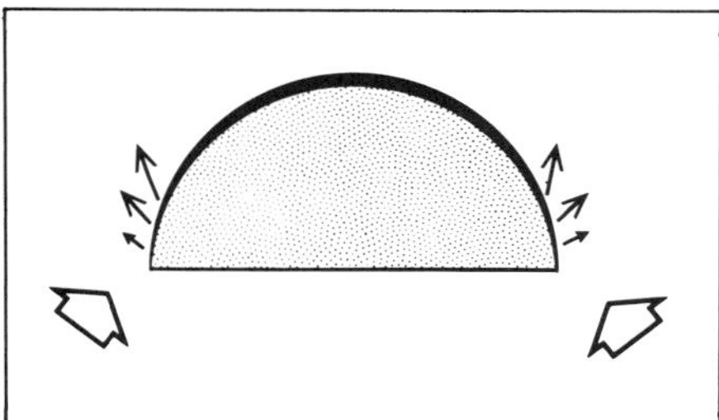

4-50. Diagram of backlighting of an opaque object. Pen-and-ink with shading film on hot-press illustration board, by William L. Brudon.

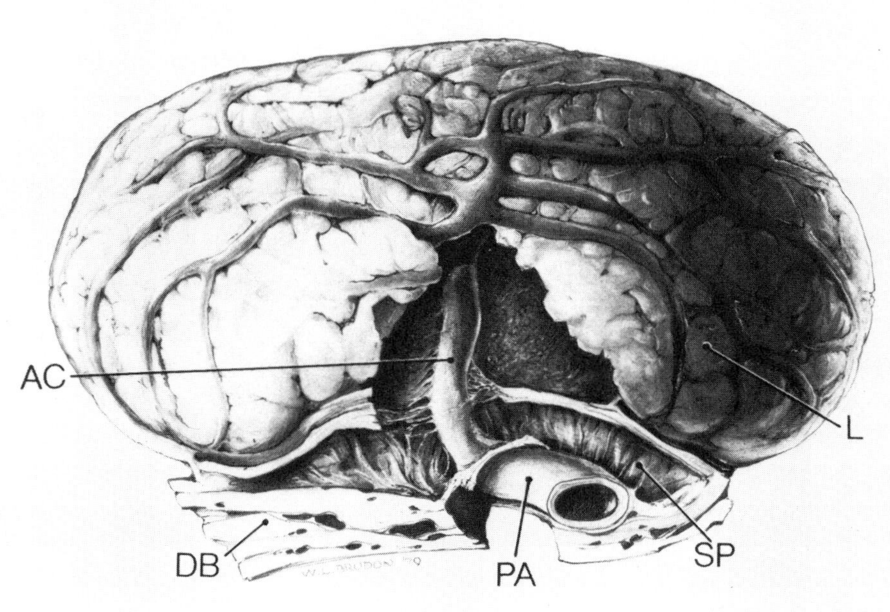

4-52. The apparent distance or depth created by suggesting a light source that originates far behind the picture plane provides an atmosphere obtained in no other lighting situation. Note that the forward areas of the subject are naturally in shadow. Beaver placenta. Graphite on Video Media board, by William L. Brudon. From "Placentation in the American Beaver *(Castor canadensis)*," by T. V. Fischer (*American Journal of Anatomy*, vol. 131, no. 2, 1971). Reprinted by permission.

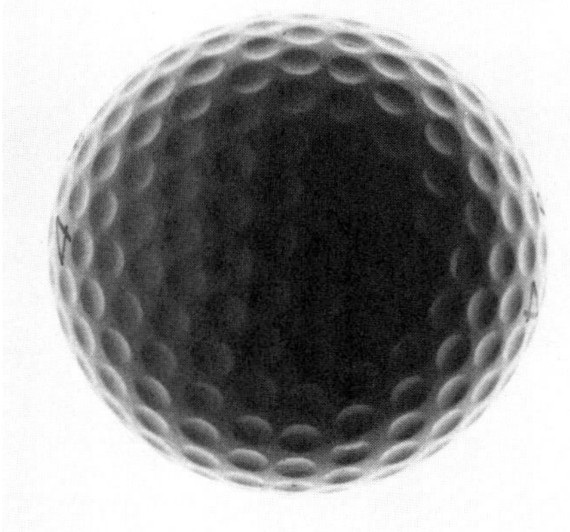

4-51. Backlighting, illuminating the subject from behind, creates a dramatic appearance. A raking effect usually results, especially in highlight areas. Photo by Michael Kantor.

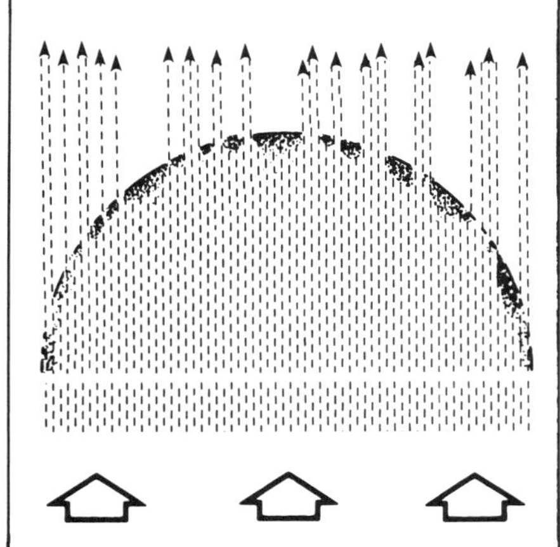

4-53. Diagram of transillumination, the backlighting of transparent and translucent objects. Pen-and-ink with shading film and dry-transfer arrowheads on hot-press illustration board, by William L. Brudon.

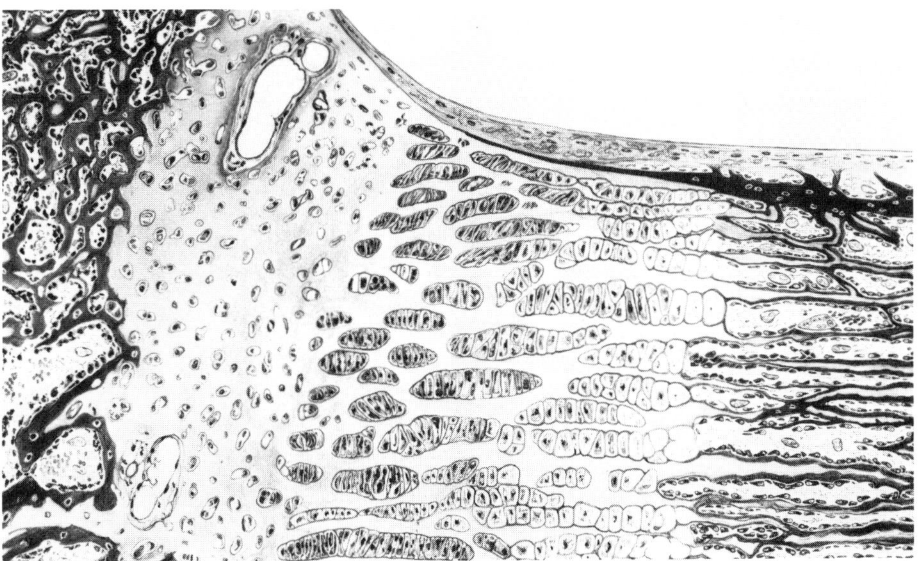

4-54. Light passes through portions of a transilluminated object. Microscopic transillumination, or substage lighting, is the classic application of this principle (see figs. I-1, 15-42). Densities, shadow or phantom effects, and enriched colors are characteristic of this lighting method. Microscopic slide section of human bone. Graphite and wash on Video Media board, by William L. Brudon.

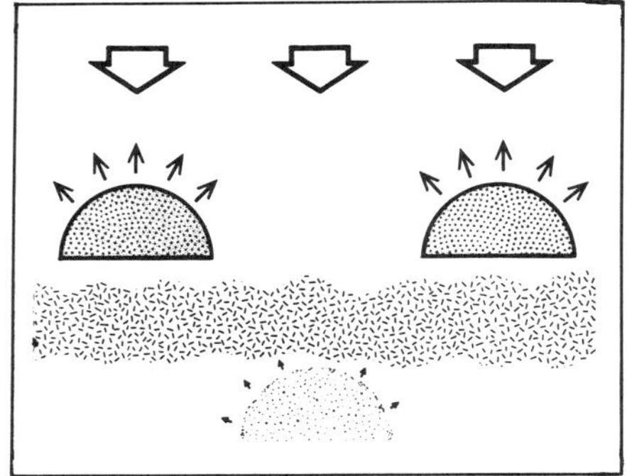

4-55. Diagram of atmospheric lighting. Pen-and-ink with shading film on hot-press illustration board, by William L. Brudon.

4-56. In aerial perspective, objects in the foreground are sharply defined and those farther away are less distinct, with hazy edges. Scattered elements of a pictorial entity may be shown separated by air or space. Atmospheric interruption (such as fog or smoke) of forward-to-distant elements can enhance this effect to whatever degree is desired. Great blue herons, *Ardea herodias*, flying over water. Transparent watercolor on Arches smooth paper, by Barry Flahey © 1983.

Below:
4-57. In limited space, the forward elements may be rendered with extremes of contrast while more distant objects are rendered in a limited range of tones. Space separating forward and rear objects enhances the perception of perspective. The aging mandible. Pen-and-ink line on hot-press Bristol board, by William L. Brudon. From *Elementary Human Anatomy*, by A. Berger (John Wiley and Sons, 1964). Reprinted by permission.

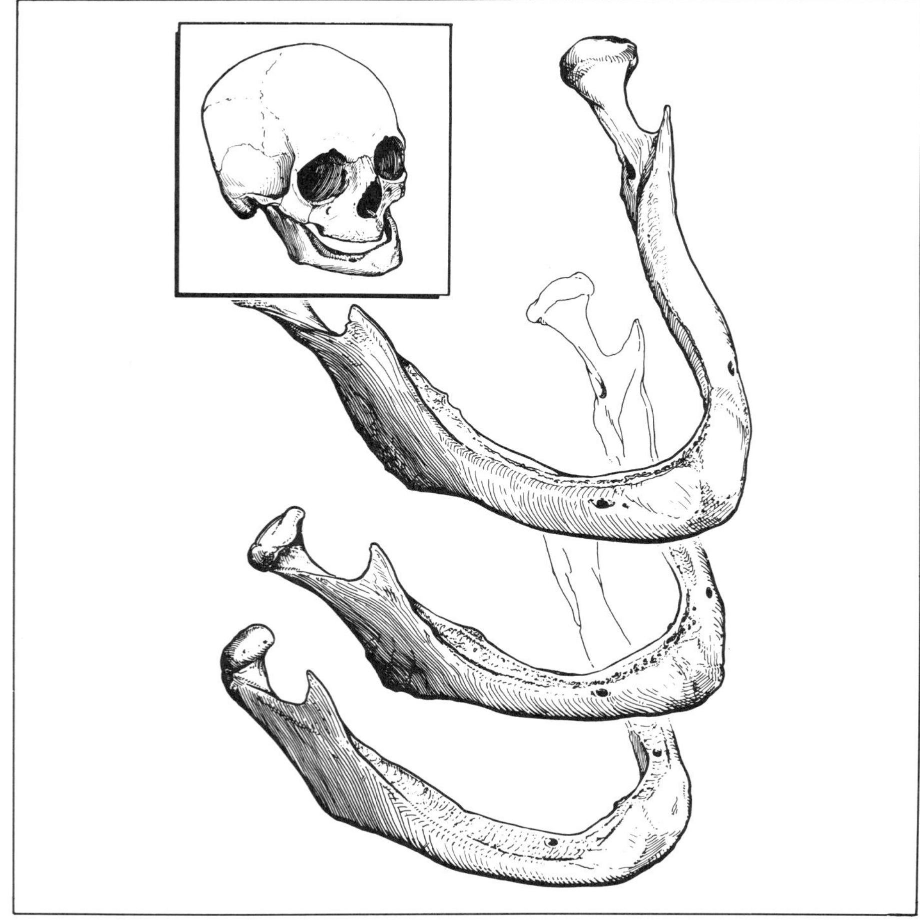

SELECTIVE EMPHASIS IN ILLUSTRATIONS

One aspect of manipulating pictorial elements is compensating for the limitations of lighting situations. Illustrators who have occasion to use raking light, for example, must compensate in their drawings for the lack of contour definition that occurs on the shadowed side of the specimen. Lights and darks may also have to be adjusted to some extent. In diffuse light, surface texture may be more obvious, but contours may be undefined. A light background may allow a shaded edge to show and a dark background will define a light edge, but on a white background, light contours must be reinforced with tone or line.

A comparison of the photograph of the skull in figure 4-58 with the illustration in figure 4-59 shows the artistic license taken to ensure that the viewer perceives all of the pertinent information required about contour, mass, and texture. What should be apparent from looking at

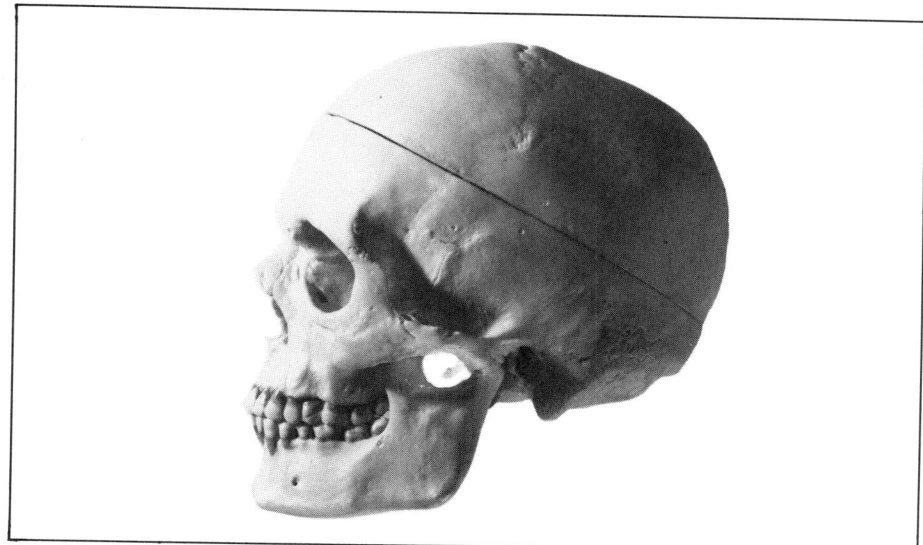

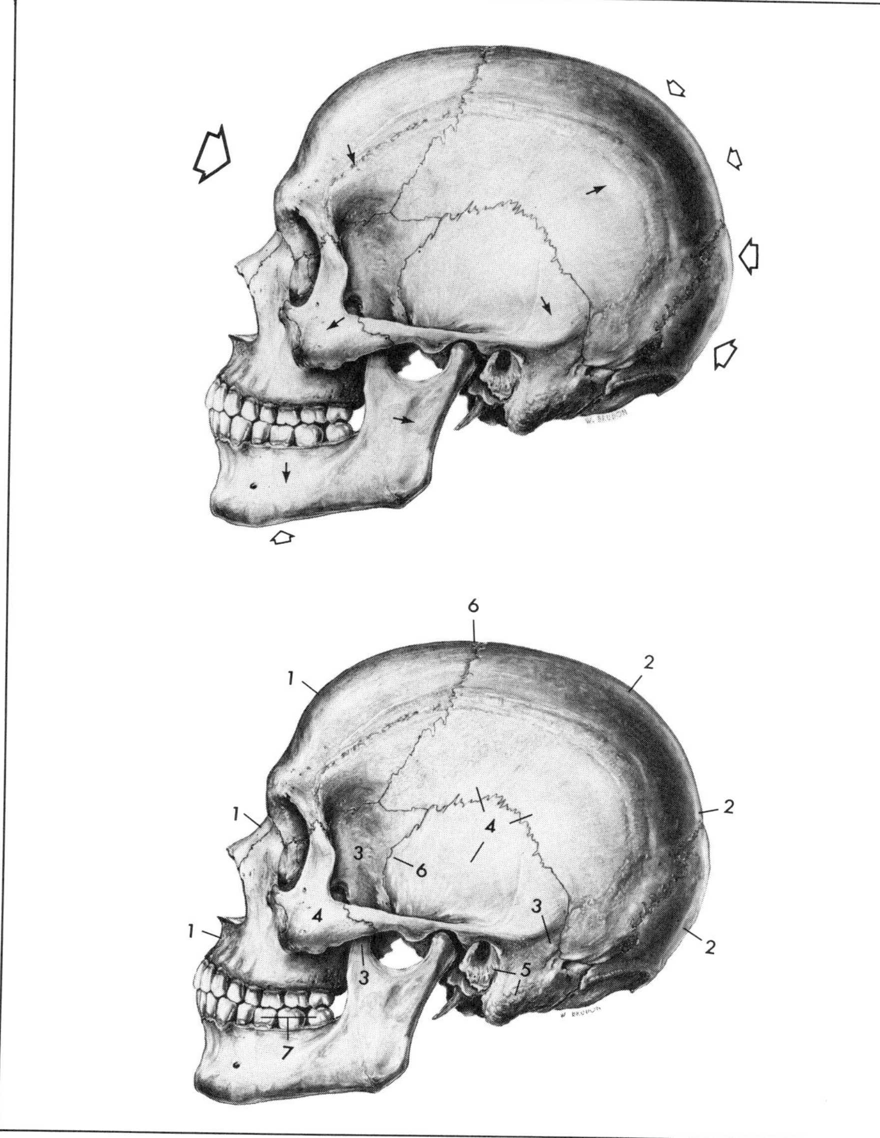

the various photographs of actual specimens in this chapter is that photographs taken under different lighting conditions selectively emphasize different qualities of a specimen. An illustrator thus can be guided in choosing lighting that would best show structural details that are difficult to depict using conventional lighting. Photographs also can help establish the value of lights and darks to be used in an illustration. One illustration can combine the attributes of several photographs, an advantage that makes illustration invaluable.

Aside from the manipulation of the effects of light, several techniques are used by illustrators to achieve a specific pictorial objective. They include isolation of the subject and selective emphasis of detail. Subjects in a field of other objects can be isolated or made more dominant by rendering them larger, with more detail or contrast,

Top left:
4-58. Human skull. Photo by William L. Brudon.

Bottom left:
4-59. Application of light-on-form principles. *(a)* Arbitrary illumination. The illustrator may control lighting in the illustration to clarify detail, regardless of how the specimen is illuminated. The size of the arrow indicates the volume of light striking this skull as *visualized* by the artist/viewer—for instance, strong upper-left lighting with lesser reflected light shown on the back of the sphere. Intricate interior lighting is indicated by small black arrows. Light rakes local areas to produce a juxtaposition of lights and darks, which heighten texture and form. *(b)* 1 = highlight edges developed with rim shadows; 2 = shadowed areas as in 45-degree reflected light to indicate texture; 3 = structural shadows eliminated except to suggest overlapping structures; 4 = highlight areas retained in low tones or plateau lighting; 5 = textural details heightened with pseudo-raking light; 6 = sutures emphasized by raking light in figure 4-58 are minimized; 7 = small structural details are developed individually. Airbrush with watercolor and wash on no. 00 Ross board, by William L. Brudon. From *Essentials of Human Anatomy*, 8th ed., by R. T. Woodburne (© 1988, Oxford University Press). Reprinted by permission.

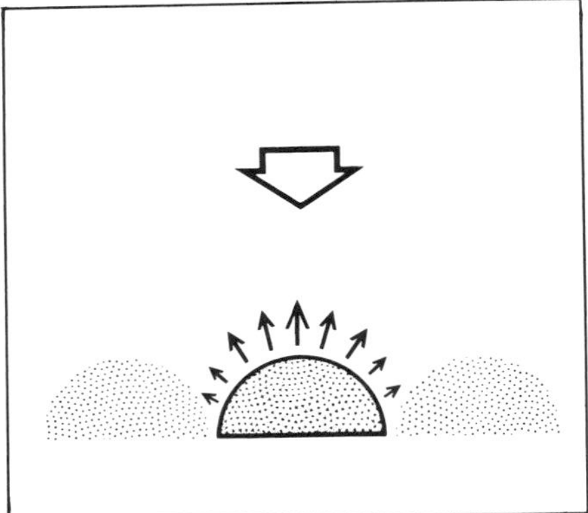

4-60. Isolation of subject. Pen-and-ink with shading film on hot-press illustration board, by William L. Brudon.

4-61. Isolation of subject. With elements in foreground and background out of focus, the central theme is unchallenged. Fringed gentian. Photo by Elaine R. S. Hodges.

or both, than the objects surrounding them (figs. 4-60, 4-61). In color, brighter and more saturated colors stand out next to paler or more subdued colored objects or backgrounds. The eye can be drawn to an area of greater detail by vignetting—allowing the edges of a structure or subject that is attached to an unimportant structure to fade away to nothing (fig. 4-62; see figs. 8-5, 8-19, 20-14).

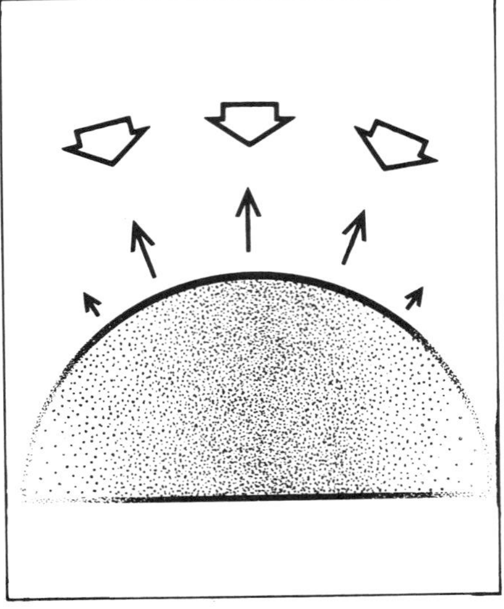

4-62. Diagram of vignetting. (See fig. 20-14.) Pen-and-ink on hot-press illustration board, by William L. Brudon.

Line Interpretations of Light on Form

Although techniques for rendering line art with pen-and-ink are detailed in chapter 5, a word should be said here about the limitations and strengths of interpreting form through line. The scope of possibilities is narrower than that of continuous tone, but line artwork often saves on rendering time and cost of reproduction. It can be an appropriate and effective means for communicating certain types of information in certain circumstances.

Lacking the range of tonal variations to imply patterns of color, such as that available with continuous-tone drawings, line illustra-

4-63. Depiction of color pattern while still showing lights and shadows with pen-and-ink rendering. *Hydaticus subfasciatus* (Coleoptera: Dytiscidae). 4×0 technical pen and Gillott 659 nib on plate-finish Bristol board, by Elsie Herbold Froeschner. Courtesy of Paul J. Spangler.

tions can simulate pattern and differentiate it from shading through alteration of the distance between dots (stipples) and lines as well as variation in the direction of the lines. This can be tricky for the artist to accomplish, since both the way the light hits the object and the pattern of color on the object must be suggested without conflicting visually with each other. Figure 4-63 shows a successful example of this.

The most elementary means of interpreting form is the simple outline, of which there are several kinds. An outline with lines of consistent weight shows no particular emphasis. It is more effective in comparing variations in contours among objects than full rendering. Accented outlines (figs. 4-64, 4-65) suggest various light conditions. Lines are made heavier in shadow areas, lighter in light-struck areas, and broken in areas of strong highlights, giving a lost-edge appearance. Lines in shadow areas can be made heavier by being thickened, feathered, or serrated. Primary-secondary line techniques involve the use of a bold, consistent weight of line for external contours and lighter consistent-weight lines for a secondary structure within the form (or contour) (see fig. 5-38). Any combination of these techniques can be used to interpret light on form in a linear fashion.

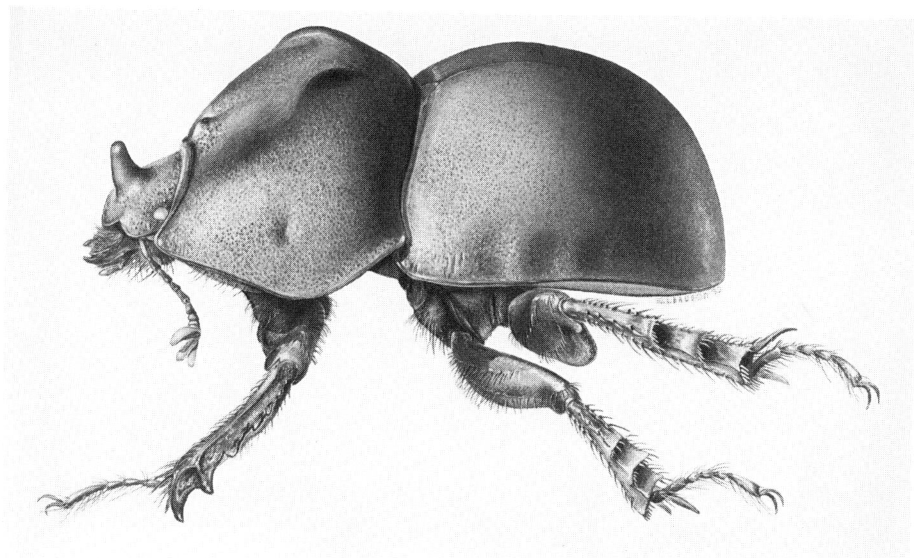

4-64. Tone version of dung beetle in figure 4-65. *Mycotrupes lethroides* (Scarabeaeidae). Airbrush, wash, carbon dust on no. 1 Ross board, by William L. Brudon. From University of Michigan Museum of Zoology, Misc. Publications, no. 84 (1954). Courtesy of T. H. Hubbell.

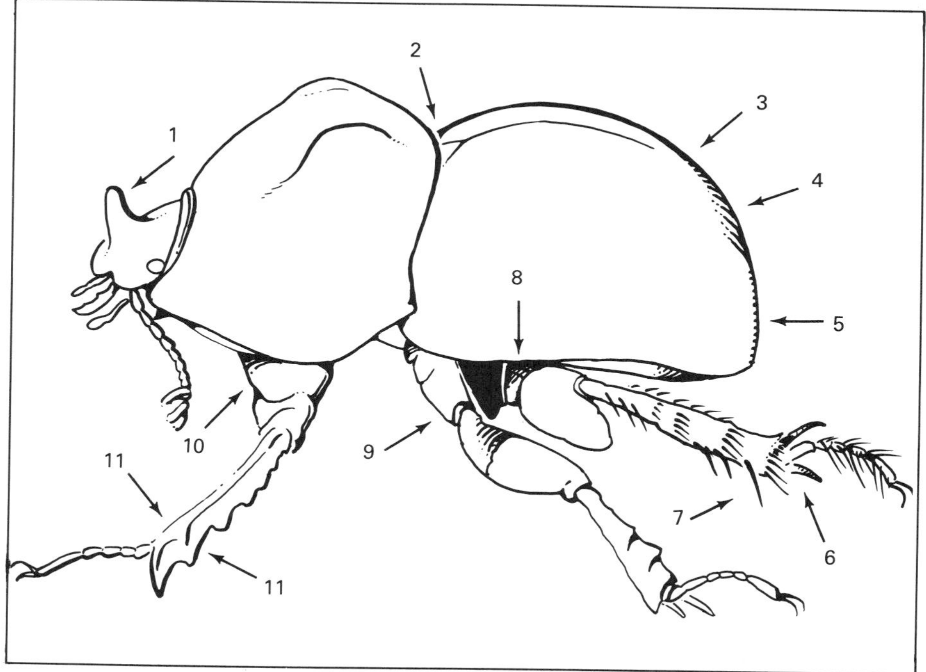

4-65. Analysis of line drawing. 1 = strong shadow emphasis; 2 = broken junction of lines (aerial perspective); 3 = shift in shading method; 4 = woodcut shadow; 5 = serrated shadow; 6 = lost edges, lines, and structures; 7 = broken edges (highlights) on both sides of small, superficial structure; 8 = deep shadow shading; 9 = shadow edges outlined with heavier line; 10 = "Snodgrass" effect (triangle of black to indicate shaded juncture); 11 = lost edges, strong shadow emphasis. Pen-and-ink on hot-press Bristol board, by William L. Brudon © 1970.

The study of how light molds form is a challenging one. Great effort is required to develop sensitivity to nuances of lights and darks, to where and why they appear. But this sensitivity is essential, for it is the realistic depiction of highlights and shadows that makes a drawing meaningful aesthetically and scientifically. The understanding of light on form becomes invaluable when the illustrator must create realistic shading where—because of artificial lighting, for instance, under the compound microscope—none exists. Constant practice in carefully looking at objects, studying their lights, darks, and grays, and drawing them is the best way to develop an understanding of light as a basic perceptual clue to the shapes of forms and their relationships to each other.

Part II
Rendering Techniques

The chapters in this part deal with individual media and surfaces and the basic rendering techniques for each. Included in the discussions are variations and modifications derived from experiences of the authors in applying the technique to scientific illustration; many of the techniques are original with the authors. A tight, realistic rendering is customarily required in scientific illustration, and these techniques have been developed to achieve this. But each reader can introduce further modifications to produce different, perhaps looser effects, as needed.

Many of the media and illustration techniques that have been covered in individual chapters can be combined. Such mixed-media techniques may involve wet-with-wet, dry-with-dry, or wet-with-dry media on a variety of surfaces. Aside from imagination, the only limiting factors are which media combine readily, effectively, and safely, and which will be lasting—either until reproduction or for centuries, depending on the goals of the artist and the client.

Sometimes unorthodox combinations save time or produce a texture or effect suited to a particular job. But be forewarned: mixing media does not always save time, and unexpected disasters may occur when unfamiliar materials are combined. Try out ideas on a scrap of the intended drawing or painting surface to see what will work. Sometimes the basic technique is faster, and perhaps safer for the longevity of the drawing. However, if time is not a concern, experimentation may yield an invaluable learning experience that will add to an artist's repertoire.

Experimentation is all the more important because new materials are constantly coming onto the market. Some of these, such as polyester films, have distinct advantages and inspire new techniques such as those discussed in the following chapters. To keep up with these changes, try out these new materials, and keep in touch with other artists and publications for artists.

One problem artists face is that manufacturers of art supplies are frequently bought and sold, with the result that the quality, names, and availability of their materials change constantly. To complicate matters, manufacturers and store catalogs are inconsistent among themselves in grade and size designations and spellings of art supplies. For example, the same size of small, pointed, diagonally rolled paper stump is variously called a tortillon and a tortillion, and its size designated as 1 or small. In the same paragraph of an art store's catalog, the same drafting film is referred to as both polyester and acetate. The best defense for the illustrator is to learn the characteristics of materials by reading and experimenting. Letters to manufacturers and dealers pointing out inconsistencies will alert them that knowledgeable artists expect accuracy and consistency.

Some art materials, including many that have been in use for hundreds of years, contain hazardous substances. Increasing numbers of manufacturers are avoiding these substances, however, and the Art and Craft Materials Institute, Inc., has set up safety guidelines to which many manufacturers subscribe. Materials conforming to these guidelines are so marked on their labels. *The Art Hazards Information Newsletter* (see Appendix under Safety) and *Artist Beware*, by Michael McCann (see Bibliography) are good references on this topic. Flammability is another concern, and it is addressed in chapter 11.

Some materials do not mix well or at all or should be used only in certain sequences. For example, slow-drying media such as oil paint should not be used under or mixed with fast-drying media such as acrylic or watercolor because the topmost medium will crack and shrink as the underlying layer dries. Slow-drying media can be applied on *top* of fast-drying media *after* the latter have dried. On frosted acetate, watercolor tends to puddle unless dry-brushed. It is difficult to correct colored pencil on frosted acetate and polyester. See chapter 3 and chapters on specific media, and read the labels and product inserts for more information on the properties of materials.

There is no single correct way to draw or paint. Techniques develop according to each artist's ability and needs. Learning these techniques with their creative modifications establishes a foundation of knowledge that can be expanded continually by artists who take what they learn from others, modify, add to it, and apply their experience with new materials. As a result, scientific illustrators in particular, but also artists in general, benefit.

5/Line and Ink

Gerald P. Hodge and Elaine R. S. Hodges

Line illustration refers to drawings that can be reproduced without a halftone screen, as is required for continuous-tone drawings done with pencil or wash, for example. The most common type of line illustration is done with pen-and-ink, the use of which is the most important technique for the scientific illustrator to master.

It is a challenge to translate the tonal gradations and color of an object into black-and-white lines and dots (see figs. 4-63, 21-14). Sometimes a line drawing can be created faster than a comparable tone drawing, especially if it is a simple outline or if areas intended to represent tone are shaded with line instead of dots, or with preprinted shading films. But a complicated ink rendering can take as long as a tone rendering. Reproduction of line, however, is likely to be better and cheaper than reproduction of tone drawings.

It is easier to control the quality of line if drawings are smaller than 11 by 14 inches (28 by 35.5cm). But an ink drawing should never be so small as to require an enlargement, because whenever a drawing is printed, the ink tends to spread on the paper, thus making the most regular lines appear heavy and irregular in an enlargement. The size of pen nib used, and consequently the width of the line, should be determined by the amount of reduction planned. It is best to work for no more than 10 to 50 percent reduction, meaning the reproduction would be 90 to 50 percent of the size of the original.

This chapter explains various ways to produce line drawings: standard pen-and-ink technique on paper, film, and scratchboard, and Grafix surfaces. Specific rendering techniques, including stipple, eyelash, and crosshatch, also are described.

MATERIALS

Surfaces

See charts 8-1 and 8-2 for useful information about various opaque and translucent surfaces.

Bristol and illustration board: hot-press, high surface or plate finish, 100 percent rag (such as the Strathmore 500 series), and neutral pH. Two-ply is an adequate thickness and less expensive than thicker plies.

Coated board (scratchboard): clay-coated, such as the British Ess Dee brand scraper board (distributed in the United States by United Process Boards); chemically coated, such as Line Kote (Crescent). Thicker coatings facilitate corrections. All coated boards are subject to cracking. Some of the backing boards are so thin they require mounting on heavier board; other coated boards are quite heavy.

Tracing paper: medium or heavy weights that lie flat, 100 percent rag; should be archival quality and suited for inking, such as Micro 75 or 105 (Charvoz-Carsen), Canson Vidalon (Morilla), Albanene (Keuffel and Esser).

Drafting film: frosted acetate or polyester, such as Denril (Borden and Riley), Cronaflex and Crovex (DuPont), Rapidraw (Koh-I-Noor), Ageproof (Dietzgen), Sure-Scale (Bruning).

Grafix (Duo-shade or Uni-shade): chemically treated film, paper, or board requiring liquid developers to produce a pattern.

Mounting board.

Media

India ink: designed for conventional (dip) or technical pens or both, and various types formulated for paper or film. For instance, Pelikan ink with the yellow label is excellent on paper but is not black enough on some films, for which Pelikan blue- or green-labeled ink is designed. The Pelikan inks work well in most technical pens. Rapidraw 3084 is very opaque and excellent on film but does not adhere well to paper. Higgins Black Magic is fine for both paper and film, but it may be too thick for some technical pens. Manufacturers of technical pens often supply their own brand of india ink, usually in non-refillable cartridges.

India ink is used for scientific illustration because it is waterproof and the blackest of inks and thus best for reproduction. Old ink may lose its opacity because the carbon has settled, so shaking the closed bottle periodically and before each use helps keep the ink well mixed. An open bottle in frequent use permits evaporation, resulting in ink too thick to flow easily. Dilute such ink with a bit of water, or add a drop or two of ammonia or liquid dishwashing detergent to the bottle to make the ink flow more easily and reduce crusting of dried ink on the pen point. Periodically clean the inside of the neck of the ink bottle with a scalpel and a tissue or damp cloth to keep pieces of dried ink from falling into the bottle.

White ink and paint: for drawing and corrections (see chapter 2).

Grafix liquid developers: for use with Grafix papers.

Shading film: for creating instant line textures.

Tools

Conventional pen nibs and holders: a conventional pen nib is the point that slips into a dip pen holder and is dipped into ink, or a drop of ink is placed on the curved back of the nib with an ink dropper (in some ink bottle covers) (fig. 5-1). A split leading from a hole down to a sharp point carries ink to the drawing surface. With pressure, the split point spreads apart, making lines of varying widths depending on the size of the nib and how far apart the two halves of the nib will spread. More flexible nibs can make a greater range of line widths, but they are more difficult to control than firmer nibs (fig. 5-2). Firm nibs make uniform dots.

Usually nibs are purchased separately from holders. Not all holders will fit all nibs, so be sure to check this before purchase. Look carefully at pen nibs to see that the two halves of the point meet perfectly and that they are not twisted or spread apart.

The nibs listed below make fine lines and thus are particularly useful for scientific illustration.

- Gillott 290 and 291: very fine and very flexible
- Hunt 100: very fine and very flexible
- Gillott 1950: fine and moderately flexible
- Esterbrook 354 and 355: fine and moderately flexible
- Gillott 659: super-fine and moderately flexible; firm enough for stippling
- Hunt 104: very fine and stiff; good for stippling at 20 percent reduction (meaning 80 percent of original size) when new, greater reduction when worn
- Hunt 102: moderately fine and stiff; for stippling at up to 50 percent reduction

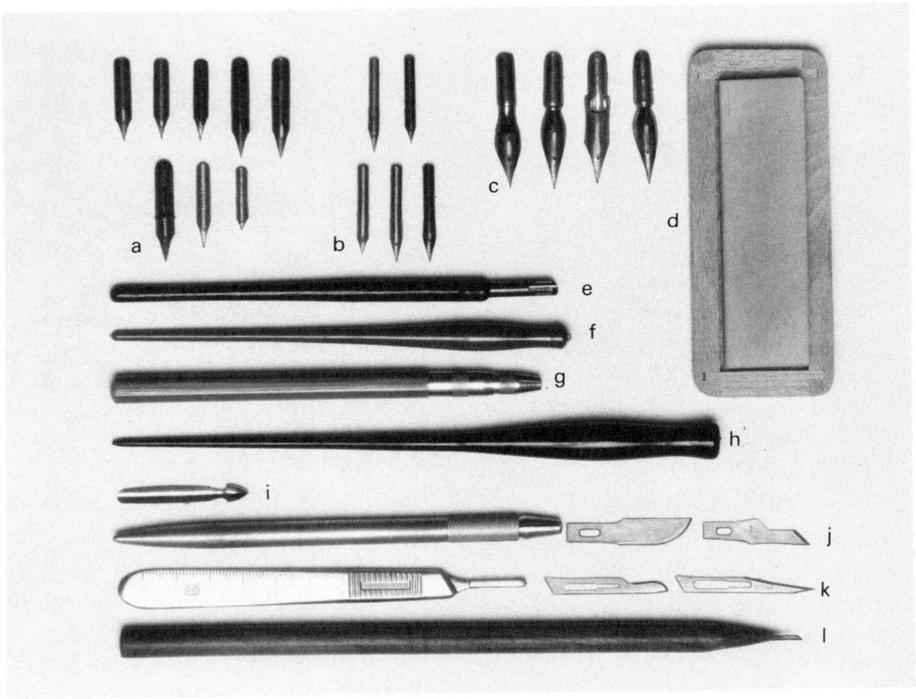

Technical or mechanical pens: plastic holders with pen-point assemblies threaded in at one end. The point or nib terminates in a hollow tube containing a steel wire plunger (wire plus cylindrical weight), which, under the pressure of drawing and by capillary action, allows ink to flow down the wire and onto the drawing surface. The smaller the diameter of the tube and wire, the finer the inked line (fig. 5-3). Widths of points vary from 6×0 or 0.11mm (the finest), to 7, or 2.0mm (the largest). The most commonly used for small scientific drawings are 4×0, or 0.18mm: 3×0, or 0.25mm: and 2×0, or 0.30mm. They may be purchased in sets of three to eight pen sizes for maximum economy. Because the points or nibs of technical pens are not flexible, they make lines and dots of uniform widths. When changes in drawings are made, using the same size point ensures a line of precisely the same width as those already drawn. However, technical pen points wear down when used on frosted film and eventually will produce a broader line than when new. More expensive, but generally more durable, are jewel or tungsten technical points; for those who often work on drafting film, the additional expense may be worth it. Lines and dots look crisper and more mechanical than lines made with conventional nibs (fig. 5-4). There are many brands of technical pens, and more appear each year. Some have refillable ink cartridges; others use disposable

5-1. Basic tools for pen-and-ink illustrations. *(a)* Standard small pen nibs. Top row: Gillott 170, 290, 291, 303, 1068; second row: Hunt 56, 103, 104. *(b)* Crowquill nibs. Top row: Gillott 659, 850; second row: Hunt 102, 107, 108. *(c)* Nibs for broad ink lines. Esterbrook Flyer 531, Hunt Globe 513, Gillott Hollow Points 13 EF, 14 EF. *(d)* Arkansas oilstone for sharpening nibs and knives. Nib holders: *(e)* for the smaller of the standard nibs; *(f)* for crowquill nibs; *(g)* adjustable for crowquill nibs and nibs such as Hunt 104; *(h)* for larger nibs. Scratchers and etching tools: *(i)* Hunt 113 scratchboard knife; *(j)* X-Acto handle and blades no. 10, no. 16 *(k)* Bard-Parker surgical knife handle with Bard-Parker blades no. 15, no. 11; *(l)* engraving tool.

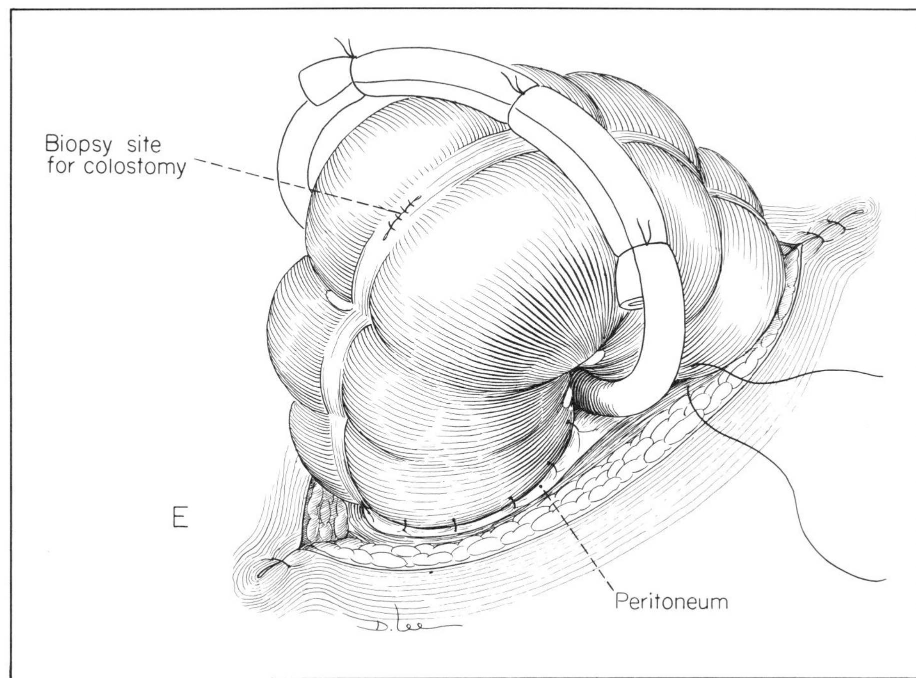

5-2. Drawing with conventional pen point, Gillott 290 nib, on scratchboard. The eyelash technique (thick/thin lines) effectively shows form with lines that create both shading and reflected light. Surgical procedure for a colostomy in regard to Hirschsprung's disease, by Denis C. Lee. Courtesy of A. G. Coran, D. M. Behrendt, W. H. Weintraub, and D. C. Lee, *Surgery of the Neonate* (Little, Brown and Company, 1978).

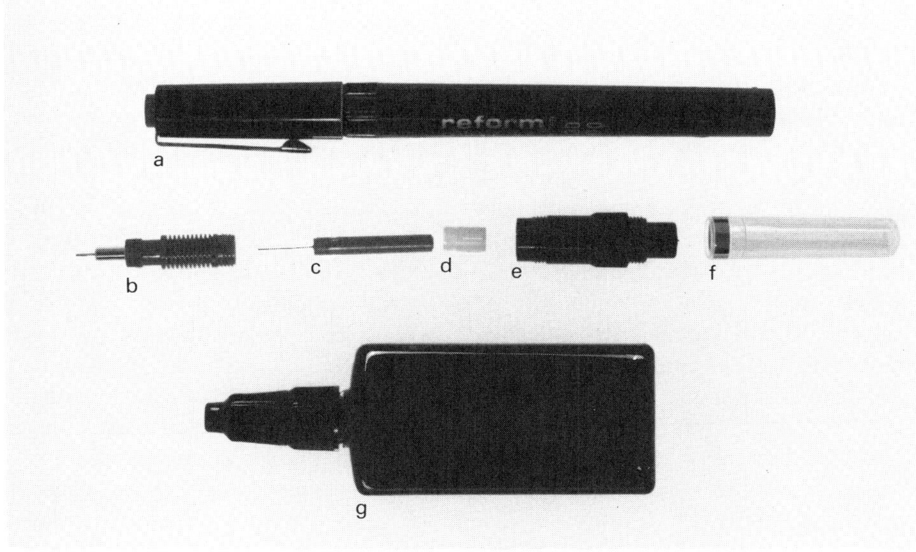

5-3. Construction of a technical pen: *(a)* complete, closed pen; *(b)* point (point tube or nib) into which *(c)* wire plunger (needle plunger, wire weight) slips; *(d)* safety cap, which keeps wire plunger in the point; *(e)* body, which connects the point to *(f)* cartridge for holding ink; *(g)* squeeze bottle of ink designed with small nozzle to fill ink cartridge. Pen shown is a Reform Refograph (Alvin Co.).

cartridges of ink, which prick open when they are connected to the pen. This sort of connection is airtight and may reduce clogging of the point by dried ink. Some pen brands can use either type of cartridge. Two brands that do not clog easily are Rotring (Koh-I-Noor) and Reform Refograph (Alvin Co.). Rotring is designed differently from other technical pens and works exceptionally well.

Brushes: for drawing and for painting black areas, Winsor & Newton Series 7 red sable watercolor, 3×0 to 5; Grumbacher Spotrite 5×0; or other brands of similar quality. (See chapter 9 for guidelines on selecting brushes.)

Erasers: for removing penciled guidelines and ink; must be suited for each purpose and for the drawing surface. Kneaded rubber, plastic, and pencil-shaped erasers remove pencil from any surface. Plastic fluid-imbibed erasers are excellent for removing ink from drafting films. Various liquids are available for this purpose, but water also will remove fresh ink from some films. Removal of ink with liquid can be messy and cause smears. A Pink Pearl eraser is used to polish and harden scratchboard.

Electric erasers: essential for erasing ink from paper. Eraser inserts or plugs for these machines are made of various materials, in various textures. To leave a smooth, unstained surface, use the pink or white eraser inserts (see chapter 2).

Chamois, sponge, or other lint-free material: used wet or dry, for cleaning nibs; dry chamois or soft cloth for cleaning coated boards.

Engraving tools: for correcting inked lines on drafting film or scratchboard and etching-drawing on scratchboard (see fig. 5-1). X-Acto handle with no. 10 or no. 16 blades. Surgical knives: Bard-Parker handle with no. 11 or no. 15 blades; Feather handle with no. 22 blades. Scratchboard or etching knives.

Honing or sharpening surfaces.

Miscellaneous

Tap water: for washing brushes, thinning paint and ink.

Liquid dishwashing detergent or ammonia: for thinning ink.

Red Conté crayon: for transferring to black scratchboard.

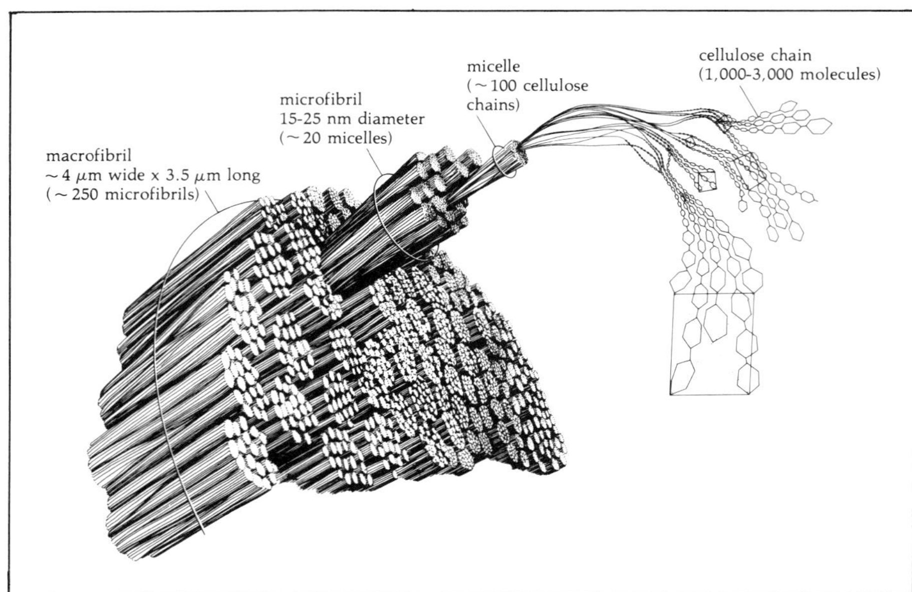

5-4. Drawing produced with technical pen points 2×0, 3×0, and 4×0 on hot-press plate-finish Bristol board. Structure of cellulose by Chris Mari van Dyke. From *Plant Physiology*, 4th ed. (© 1983, PWS Publishers). Reprinted by permission of Willard Grant Press.

Drafting powder: Pounce or Pelikan Inking Powder for cleaning oils from tracing film and scratchboard; to polish erased paper and new scratchboard.

Ultrasonic cleaner: loosens ink in clogged technical pens by vibrating liquid.

Household cleaners: Formula 409 or Fantastik, for cleaning pen points.

Magnifying glass: to check blackness of ink and clarity of lines. A magnifier surrounded by a fluorescent light that clips onto a work area permits delicate corrections and additions to be made most accurately.

Reducing lens: to show how work looks when reduced, particularly whether small details still will be visible.

CARE OF PENS

Keep two or three containers of tap water near the work area: one for rinsing off black ink, one for rinsing off white paint, and one with clean water for thinning paint and ink. Japanese waterwells with three compartments are ideal (available from Daniel Smith, Inc.; see Appendix).

New conventional pen nibs have a thin coating of oil to prevent rusting; this must be removed to allow the ink to flow easily. Dip the nib in boiling water, or in ammonia or household cleaner, for a few seconds, then wipe dry. Or briefly hold a lighted match to the dry point. In use, the nibs should be rinsed, then wiped with lint-free material before each dip into ink.

If ink will not run from a full nib, the problem may be dried ink blocking the tiny hole in the center of the nib. Scrape off accumulated crusts of ink with a knife or dissolve them by soaking the nib in a household cleaner. If that does not improve the flow, the ink may have thickened in the bottle. Thin it with a drop or two of ammonia or tap water, stirred in well. If the ink level is very low, start with a new bottle, because too much liquid in relation to sediment will have to be added.

Conventional pen nibs vary in their ability to maintain a sharp point. Replace or sharpen the point as soon as it dulls and the lines begin to thicken. Conventional points can be sharpened on emery cloth, super-fine sandpaper, or a fine sharpening stone.

Rinse and wipe technical pen nibs before setting them aside temporarily or capping. To help prevent clogging, keep the point loosely capped every time you lay down the pen. When storing a filled pen for a week or more, put a drop of water in the cap before screwing it on the pen and store the pen, point up, in a jar with a damp sponge on the bottom. The high humidity helps prevent ink from drying in the point. Do not let any metal parts such as pocket clips sit in water; they might rust. Keeping the ink cartridge over half full will also increase humidity.

Clean pens thoroughly every one or two weeks, or whenever they are to be unused for more than a week. (This is unnecessary for Rotring brand pens.) Unscrew the point and clean the threads with a toothbrush and soapy water. Rinse the point well and blow excess water from both ends of the point's tube. Empty and rinse the ink-holding cartridge.

When a pen becomes seriously clogged, disassemble the nib, if possible. If the wire plunger is bent, straighten it by drawing it carefully between thumb and index fingernails. Soak all parts in a household cleaning solution or hot water, or use an ultrasonic cleaner with water, an ammonia-detergent mixture, or other cleaning solution. In an ultrasonic cleaner, the nib can be left assembled but the pen parts should remain in the fluid no more than ten minutes at a time: in some ultrasonic cleaners heat builds in the vibrating liquid and can soften and destroy some plastics. As little as one minute may be enough to loosen and dissolve clogged ink. After soaking, remove the parts, rinse in clear tap water, and wipe dry. If the point is still clogged, hold the wire firmly near

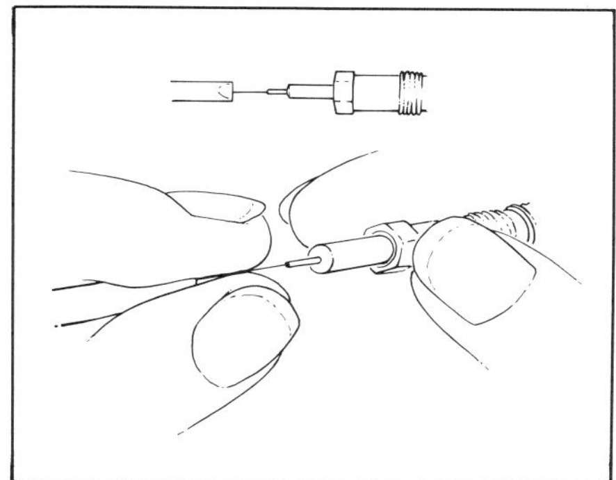

5-5. Unclogging a technical pen point by inserting wire plunger in reverse direction. Gillott 659 and Hunt 104 nibs on Bristol board, by Elaine R. S. Hodges.

the tip so that it will not bend and carefully push it into the point's tube from the reverse direction until it slides through without obstruction from dried ink (fig. 5-5). Repeat the soaking and blowing through the tube. Let all the parts dry thoroughly before reassembling and adding fresh ink; otherwise, the ink will be thinned and gray. To reinsert the wire, hold the point vertically and gently drop the wire into the point. Do not push, but lightly tap the point until the wire slides into the central opening of the tube. Some nibs cannot be disassembled; soaking and blowing dry the intact point is the only recourse. If all else fails, replace the point.

Care of brushes is discussed in chapter 9.

BASIC TECHNIQUES

To obtain maximum control with pens or brushes, work on a surface that is at a comfortable height and either flat or slightly tilted. You should be able to swing your drawing arm smoothly and evenly from elbow or wrist without tremor or a need to exert irregular pressure. Sit with both feet on the floor, not with legs crossed. These habits are especially important when using flexible nibs and brushes.

As with other rendering techniques, the preliminary penciled drawing should be transferred to the final opaque drawing surface or traced onto translucent materials (see chapter 1). This keeps the final surface free of corrections and erasures and preserves the preliminary drawing for reference. If a preliminary drawing on good-quality plate Bristol board is fairly clean, however, inking can be done directly over it to save the time of transferring. Before touching the drawing, make practice strokes on a scrap of the same drawing surface to ensure that the ink flows freely and no fibers or dirt are adhering to the point.

Several considerations apply to any line drawing. Avoid the tendency to fill in everything, which results in too much overall gray; leave some white areas for visual interest and contrast.

Taking advantage of what the human brain is used to seeing in nature, the artist can create perceptual illusions with line replacing continuous tone (fig. 5-6). The quality of the line, used as outline or for modeling (shading), conveys information to the viewer about light, shade, and structure.

For good design and balance, the lines of a drawing have to be weighted properly. For example, if the subject matter is illuminated from the upper left, the portions of the subject receiving light (top left of each structure) should have thinner lines than those on the shadow side (fig. 5-7). Small, thin-walled structures require lighter lines than larger, dense objects. For example, a delicate insect wing should have thinner lines than the insect body. Placing a little extra ink at the junction of lines that form an angle adds substantial form to the drawing as well as a few "punctuation marks" for variety (fig. 5-8). The style is sometimes called "Snodgrassing," named for Robert E. Snodgrass, an excellent insect morphologist and artist who used it in his illustrations of insect anatomy (see fig. 4-65). The weight of the modeling lines as well as of the outline are important in depicting near or distant objects. In general, outlines and modeling lines that are heavy and far apart make the object appear close to the observer; thin outlines and fine, closely placed modeling lines extend the apparent distance from the observer, as demonstrated by the flexible tubes in figure 5-6.

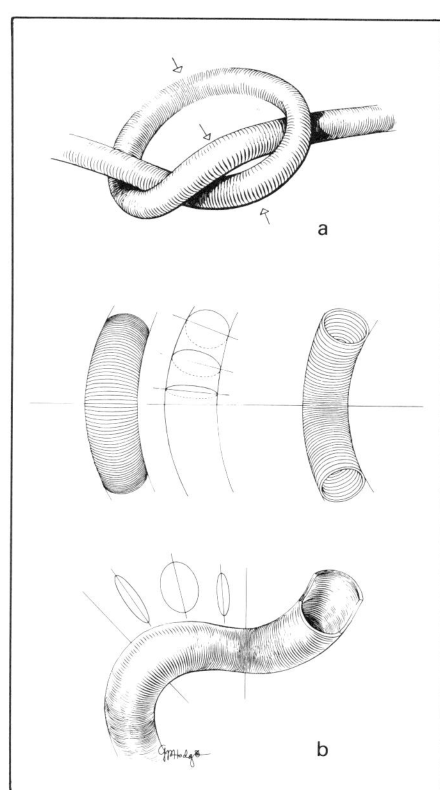

5-6. Line direction. *(a)* Arrows point to where the object is farthest from and closest to the observer. Where the object is farthest, the exact center receives a nearly straight line, the modeling (shading) lines are thin and close together, and the outlines are either very thin or nonexistent. Where the object is closest, the exact center also receives a nearly straight line, but the modeling lines are thicker and farther apart, outlines are thicker, and highlights are larger. *(b)* The shapes of the ellipse lines vary according to the curve of the structure. Gillott 290 nib on hot-press illustration board, by Gerald P. Hodge © 1979.

Overlapping structures can be represented to suggest atmospheric perspective and lighting. When fine details such as hairs (called pubescence) overlap an outline, ink these first and then break the outline on one or both sides where it passes under the hair. Another solution is to ink everything

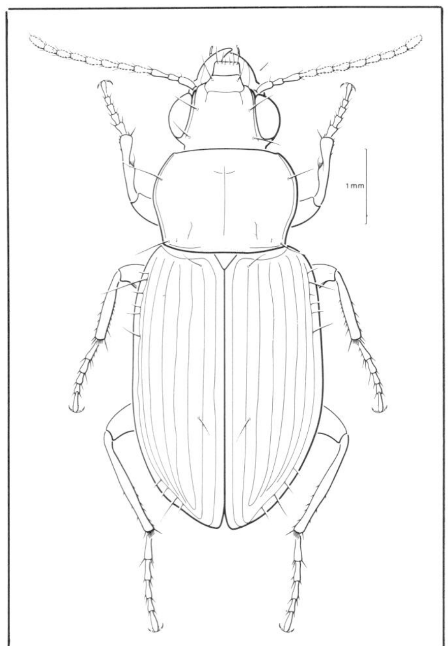

5-7. If the subject is a simple one, an outline with no shading is clear and effective. The variation in line width adds interest and suggests light from the upper left and shadow on the right side. On Cronaflex polyester film, a Hunt 100 nib was used for hairs on legs; technical pens (nos. 4×0 to 3) produced lines and longer hairs. Carabid beetle, *Abaris splendidula*, by Go Sato. Courtesy of Yves Bousquet, Agriculture Canada.

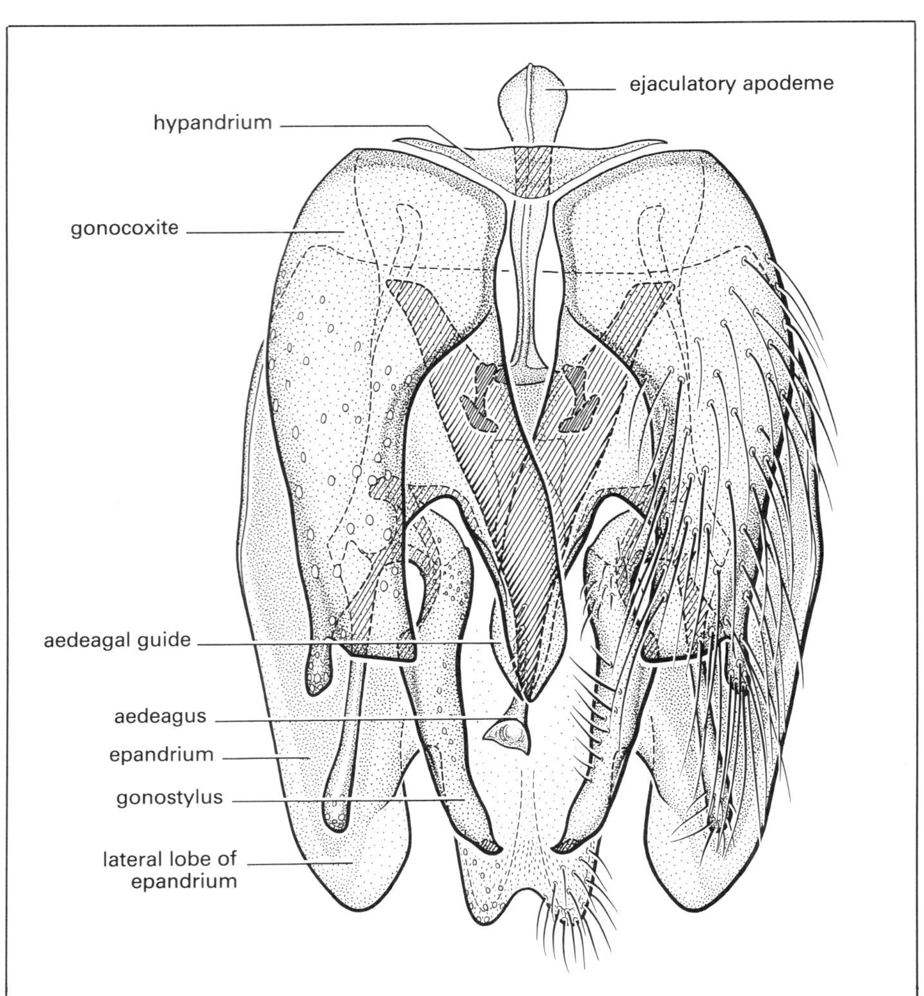

5-9. Breaks in outline. A knife etched white lines to highlight the hairs and outlines. The leaders have a white edge that also breaks the outline. The use of a drawn line pattern is an effective way to show diagrammatically an inner structure. Note that these lines taper from thick to thin. Crowquill pen on DuPont UC-7 film. *Spiriverpa* (fly) male genitalia, by Ralph Idema. From *Manual of Nearctic Diptera*, vol. 1, by J. F. McAlpine et al., Research Branch Agriculture Canada Monograph no. 27, 1981. Reproduced by permission of the Minister of Supply and Services, Canada.

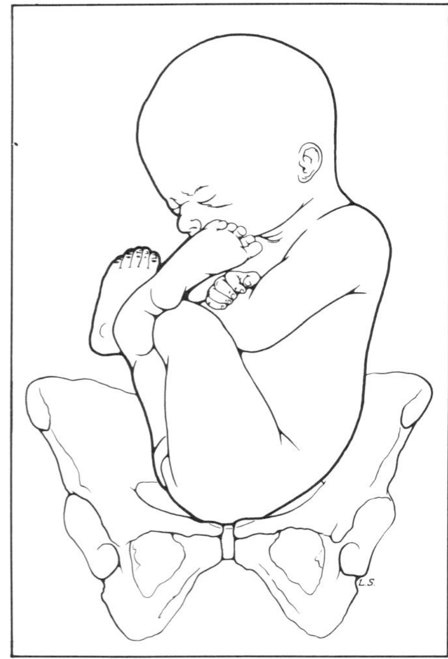

5-8. Note the extra ink in the angle at the junction of any two or more lines. This lends the drawing more contrast and form. Breech birth, by Lewis L. Sadler © 1979.

solidly and then paint the breaks in outline with white paint or to scratch them out. The breaks in outline suggest distance between the overlapping structure and the outline; the larger the space, the greater the distance. Breaks on the lighted side also can represent highlights (fig. 5-9). Dense pubescence normally will obscure the lateral margin of the body; make the line of the body margin incomplete (fig. 5-10).

To depict transparency, slightly strengthen an object with heavier lines or shading before it enters another form; then eliminate all evidence of the first object for a short distance. Gradually have the internal structure come into sufficient intensity to show any texture or details (fig. 5-11).

Penciled lines from the preliminary or transferred drawing may show on a completed rendering. After the ink is completely dry, gently erase this pencil and any smudges with a kneaded or soft plastic eraser. If this erasure removes so much ink as to leave gray instead of black lines, some lines may break up or even disappear when the drawing is reproduced. Check the blackness of the ink with a magnifying glass; drafting films can be held up to a light to check opacity of the ink. Re-ink any lines that are not totally black or opaque.

A reducing lens helps in judging whether lines and dots look gray or will be too close together or too far apart after reduction. If they are too close together for eventual reproduction, they might reproduce as black blobs. See the discussion of stippling (later in this chapter) for suggestions on how to avoid this.

When any ink line has been scratched out or erased (except with an electric eraser), the drawing surface is disrupted and it is difficult to redraw smooth lines that do not bleed. On paper (but not film) this can be remedied somewhat by burnishing the affected area, applying drafting powder, and then spraying with a workable fixative through a paper cutout.

Conventional Pens

Hold a conventional pen loosely between thumb and index finger; point the nib either away from or toward the body (fig. 5-12).

To draw along the edge of a ruler or French curve with a dip pen, slant the tip away from the edge. Take care not to overload the pen; wipe excess ink from the side that will touch the ruler or curve. To draw a continuous line in sections, lightly touch the pen or brush to the end of each completed section (preferably while the line is still wet) and continue the line with the same pressure used for the preceding section.

Too much work in a wet (ink) area will soften paper fibers, which will be picked up by a pen. If the paper feels soft under the point, let that area dry thoroughly before reworking. When repairing a break or nick in a line, do so if possible while the original ink is still wet and use a finer nib or point than was first used. Lightly touch the break with the pen or brush tip so that capillary action draws the new

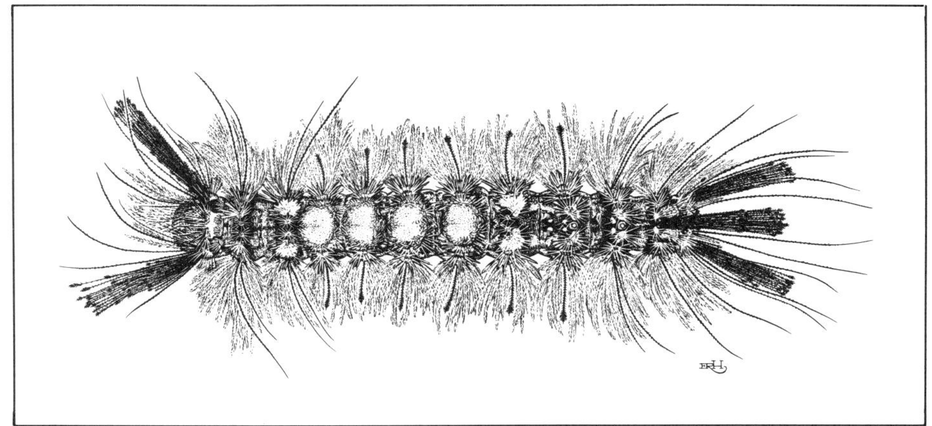

5-10. Thick pubescence obscures the body's outline. To isolate and elevate certain hairs above the others, white outlines were left around them. Hunt 104 nib and X-Acto no. 16 blade on scratchboard. Moth caterpillar, *Dasychira dorsipennata*, by Elaine R. S. Hodges. From *Moths of America North of Mexico*, Fascicle 22.2, by D. C. Ferguson (E. W. Classey Ltd and the Wedge Entomological Research Foundation, 1978).

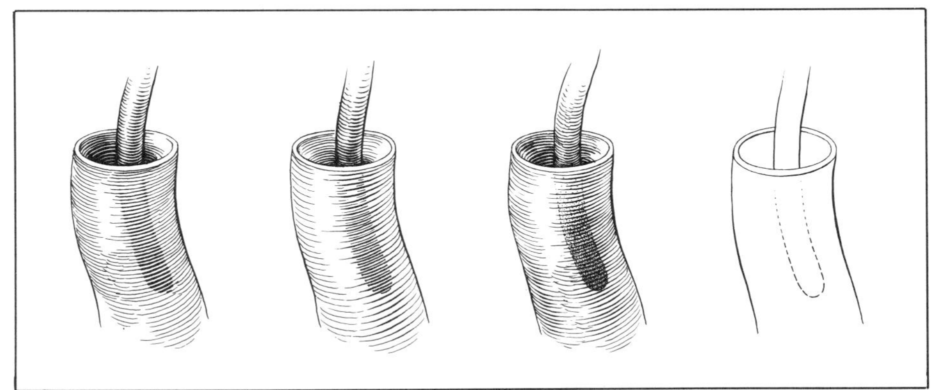

5-11. Depicting transparency. Note the different shading with lines alone in the two left-hand drawings. In the third, stippling combines with line to show the internal object, and in the fourth drawing, outline alone suffices. Gillott 290 nib on scratchboard, by Gerald P. Hodge.

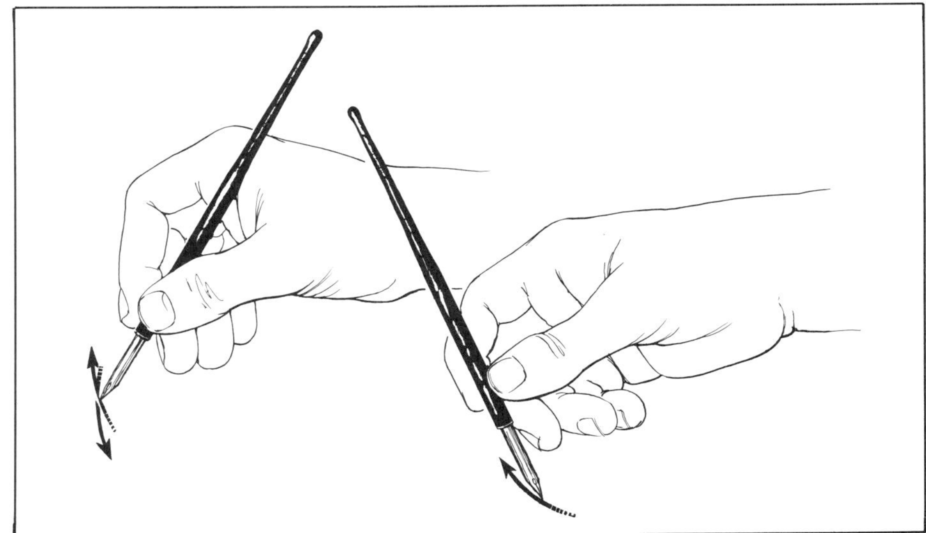

5-12. Two ways to hold a pen. Left: pen nib pointed away from body; right: pen nib pointed toward body. No. 1 red sable brush on hot-press illustration board, by Gerald P. Hodge © 1982.

ink into the damp ink on the paper. If the ink is dry, touch the broken area with the pen or brush point, allowing ink to flow into the space.

Technical Pens

To help in choosing the proper line width for each drawing, make yourself a chart of lines from each pen nib size. This will act as a reference for visualizing what sizes will go together to create specific effects or to meet reduction requirements.

A technical pen should be held almost vertically so that the rim of the point tube does not scrape over the drawing surface. Hold the pen lightly, yet with control. Pressing down hard impedes the ink flow. To start the flow of ink, gently shake the pen for a few seconds. (Violent shaking could bend the wire plunger.)

Although a conventional nib or brush is best for drawing tapered continuous lines, it is possible to produce slightly tapered lines with a technical pen by changing the angle of the pen, drawing speed, or point sizes, or a combination of the three. Slanting the pen at a more acute angle or slowing hand movement as the line is drawn thickens it. (Both increase the ink flow.) Changing to the next larger point will further widen the line. To taper a line to a relatively fine point, start slowly at the thicker end and increase drawing speed rapidly, terminating the line with a flick of the pen off the drawing surface at the thinner end.

The long, straight, tubular nib of a technical pen is ideal for use with rulers and French curves and is less likely to leak ink under the drawing edge than is a conventional pen nib.

Brushes

Brush-drawn lines can be identical to or considerably different in style from pen-drawn lines (figs. 5-13, 5-14). A brush will achieve a clean line on a rough, soft, or delicate surface, such as coquille board, on which a pen would scratch or leave an irregular line.

The size of the brush used is determined by the width of the required line. Using too fine a brush to make a broad line will require painting parallel edges and filling in the center. Furthermore, the smaller the brush, the less ink it will hold and the more frequently it will have to be dipped into ink. All the same, a range of line widths can be drawn with a 0 brush by applying more or less pressure to increase or decrease line width. For drawings under 10 inches square (25.5cm), nothing larger than a 0 brush is generally used.

Because it is difficult to dip any brush into a small-mouthed ink bottle without getting ink on the ferrule (the metal cylinder that clamps the hairs together), it is better to work from drops of ink in the depression of a watercolor tray. The ink evaporates quickly, so dilute it with tap water (one drop of water to eight drops of ink), occasionally adding another drop of water as evaporation takes place. Do not overdilute; it is essential that the ink lines on the drawing be jet black. Repoint the brush after each dip into ink by twirling it lightly on scrap paper.

Although some artists draw away from the body with the brush, most find it more natural to brush toward the body. The brush should be grasped more firmly than a pen. And only the wrist should move, with the heel of the hand acting as a pivot.

Drawing with a brush requires practice. To gain control, practice parallel lines. Rather than attempting right away to draw long lines in one stroke, make several series of short straight and curved lines, then connect them into a single line (fig. 5-15a). Taper lines by pressing

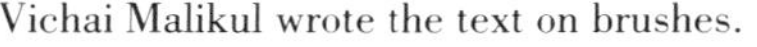

Vichai Malikul wrote the text on brushes.

5-13. Brush lines can appear almost identical to the finest of pen lines. Brush and ink on smooth illustration paper, Pine cones, *Pinus monticola*, by Frederick A. Walpole. Courtesy of Hunt Institute for Botanical Documentation, Carnegie-Mellon University, Pittsburgh; indefinite loan from the Smithsonian Institution.

the tip of the brush at the broader base of the line and then gradually lifting it higher near the end of the line (fig. 5-15b).

When the hairs of a brush flare out, the brush can be trimmed with a knife into a full cone shape, which will hold more ink than an overtrimmed brush, yet have a very fine point. Do so by dipping the brush in ink a few times to note the location of any disarranged hairs. Flatten the brush on a piece of cardboard and carefully trim the shortest those hairs that are nearest to the ferrule (fig. 5-16). While rotating the brush, trim the hairs equally all around to create a cone shape. Again, dip into ink to see that the hairs are forming a point. Every hair originally set into the ferrule will be needed at whatever the trimmed length to support the body of the pointed tip. Practice trimming on an inexpensive brush.

Ink is harder on brushes than paint is. A brush that feels inflexible and on which the fine point no longer can be maintained has too much ink built up in its base and needs to be washed (see Care of Brushes in chapter 9). Do not use soap; the bristles will become too dry.

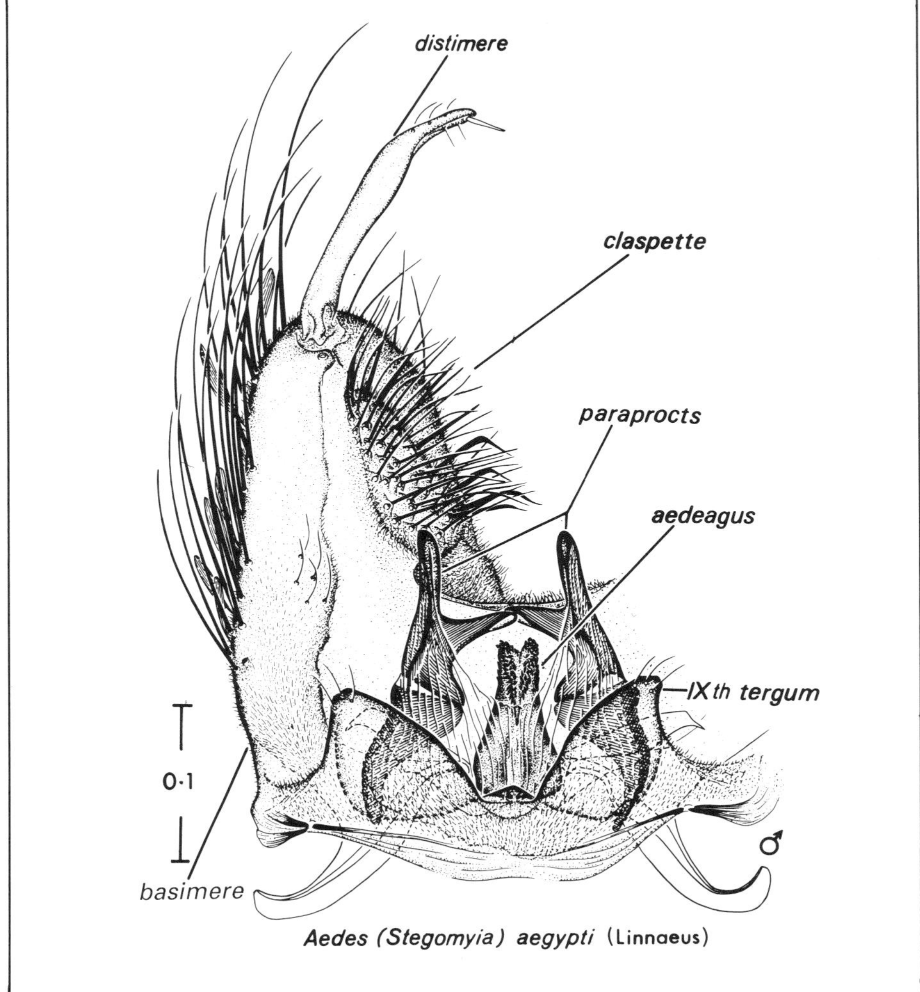

5-14. Brush rendering. Everything but the long lateral hairs (setae) was drawn with a brush, including the stippling. Note how transparent membrane was rendered. Ink on hot-press, plate-finish Bristol board. Mosquito male genitalia, *Aedes (Stegomyia) aegypti*, by Vichai Malikul. Courtesy of Bruce Harrison and Walter Reed Biosystematics Unit.

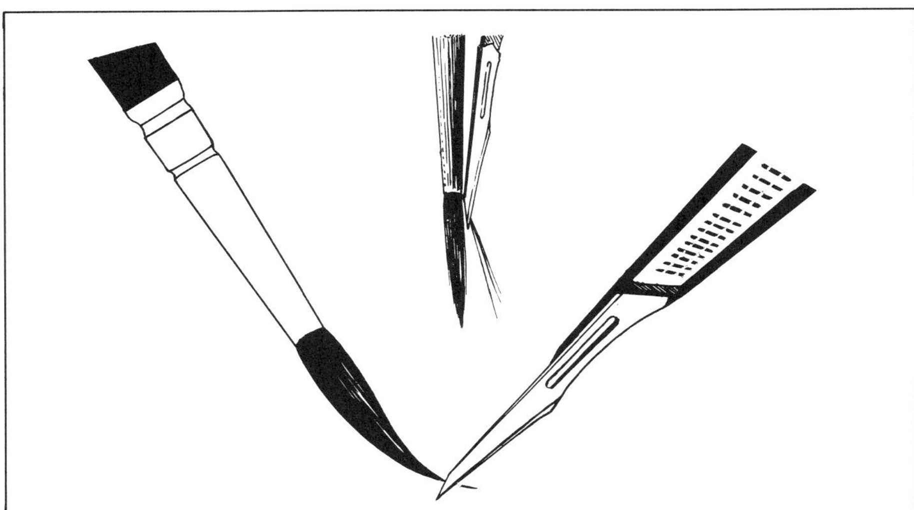

5-16. How to trim a brush to a cone shape, tapered to a perfect point. The full base holds a large quantity of ink to carry to the fine point. Ink, brush, and technical pen on Bristol board, by Vichai Malikul © 1980.

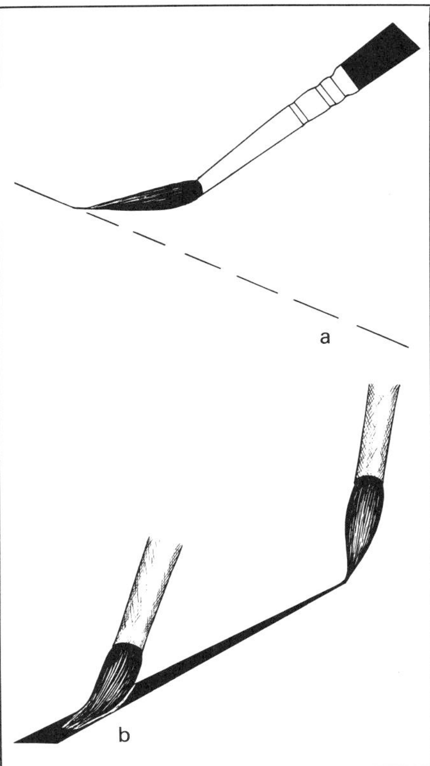

5-15. Connecting and tapering lines. *(a)* Sometimes it is preferable to connect a series of short lines rather than attempt to draw a long, precise line in one stroke. *(b)* To taper a line, press the tip of the brush down at the broader base of a line, then gradually lift the brush as the end of the line is approached. Ink, brush, and technical pen on Bristol board, by Vichai Malikul © 1983.

Scratchboard

5-17. Scratchboard—white on black. Many thousands of strokes were etched into the surface of black scratchboard with a hand-sharpened engraving tool. Middle dorsopelvic feather tract of white turkey (Beltsville), by Raynard LeNeil.

Scratchboard is a black or white coated board that lends itself to drawings requiring dramatic contrasts, an engraved or woodcut effect, or white lines on a black background (figs. 5-17, 5-18, 5-19; see figs. 12-37, 20-1, 20-3, 20-5).

Scratchboard technique generally involves drawing with a sharp-bladed engraving tool, usually in conjunction with a pen or brush or both, on a black-painted clay- or otherwise coated surface. It also can be used for conventional pen-and-ink or brush-and-ink drawings; its coated surface permits the pen or brush to glide smoothly and errors to be scratched out. Although both white and prepainted black scratchboards are available, scientific illustrators most commonly use the white board and paint black only those areas they choose.

First mount the scratchboard, if necessary, to protect it from cracking (see chapter 2 for mounting methods). Polish and harden the surface by rubbing briskly and firmly in several directions with a Pink Pearl eraser. This reduces the likelihood of pen nibs gouging the surface or picking up and clogging on particles from the coating. Brush away all eraser residue and wipe with a clean chamois or soft cloth. To polish the surface further, rub on drafting powder and wipe off the excess. Transfer the preliminary drawing (see chapter 1). If transferring to black scratchboard, coat the back of the drawing with red Conté crayon and burnish the outlines onto the board. Or use graphite transfer paper or direct drawing with an HB graphite pencil; the graphite lines will be visible since they reflect light off the black.

On white scratchboard, roughly establish the cast shadows, dark structures, or areas to be rendered white on black. Paint these with thin coats of india ink diluted so that it takes about three applications to make a solid black: the less concentrated the pigment, the smoother the etched lines. Maintain an irregular outline to make blending of inked and scratched lines unobtrusive, since straight edges of solid black areas tend to remain artificial looking even when stippling is applied to the edge (fig. 5-20). While the ink dries, outline and render the rest of the drawing with pen or brush or both.

After the areas painted with ink are completely dry, begin drawing with an engraving tool (fig. 5-21). To recover guidelines on these

5-18. A linear, woodcutlike style was used on scratchboard with crowquill pen and a knife. Five-lined skink, *Eumeces fasciatus*, by Don Luce.

inked areas, transfer again from the preliminary as suggested above for black scratchboard.

With the preliminary drawing nearby for reference, etch into the black areas, matching the weight, style, and direction of the original lines. White lines and dots should break up the black to give the impression of gray tone. Re-ink black lines that are inadvertently broken, and correct overlapping or ragged inked lines with the etching tool. Ink-drawn, black-on-white parts of the rendering should blend with the blade-drawn, white-on-black portions so that it is difficult to differentiate between them. On

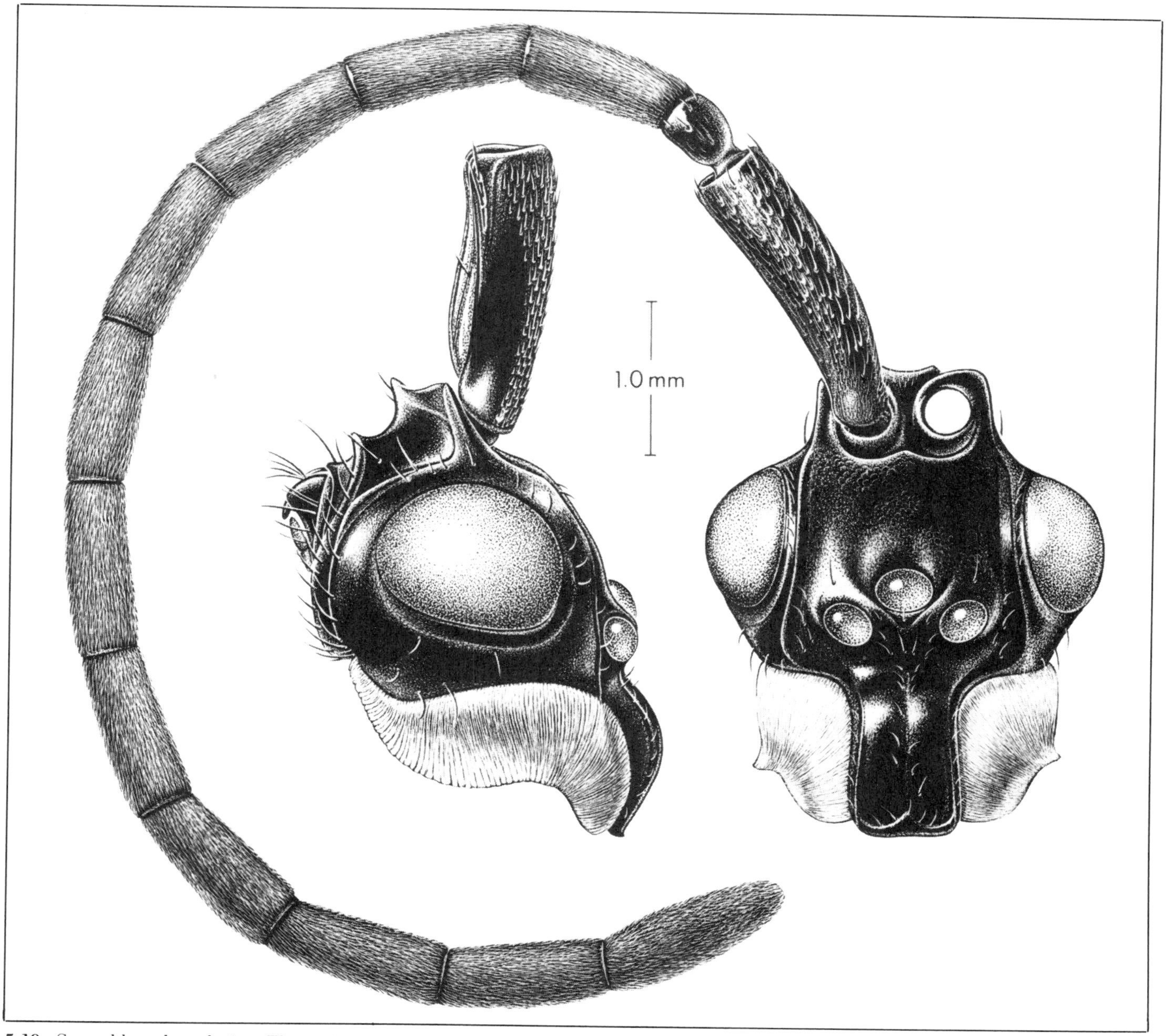

5-19. Scratchboard rendering. The entire structures were painted black on white scratchboard; the white details, including stippling, were added with a no. 16 X-Acto blade. Wasp heads, *Loboscelidia atra*, by George L. Venable. Courtesy of K. V. Krombein.

5-20. Irregularly shaped black areas permit inconspicuous blending of ink-drawn and knife-drawn parts. Examine the leaf under the bird. Bard-Parker no. 15 blade and Gillott 659 nib on scratchboard. Baby bird on rhododendron leaves, by Trudy Nicholson © 1979.

scratchboard, sizable areas of drawing can be removed by scraping carefully with a razor blade. To reharden the surface, erase with a Pink Pearl eraser or polish with drafting powder, or both.

Patterned Surfaces

In addition to inked black lines on white paper (or the reverse), preprinted, patterned surfaces such as Grafix papers and shading films can be used for line reproduction.

Grafix

These chemically treated papers are especially suitable for quick diagrams or other simple drawings that do not require subtle shading. With the application of Grafix developing liquids, patterns emerge, much like in children's coloring books in which colors "magically" appear after being painted with water. Grafix paper may be purchased in either transparent (like vellum) or opaque (like Bristol board) sheets, both of which are well suited for india ink. They come in a variety of line or stipple patterns, which reproduce as line in 1:1 or various reductions. The Uni-shade type develops only one tone; Duo-shade uses two devel-

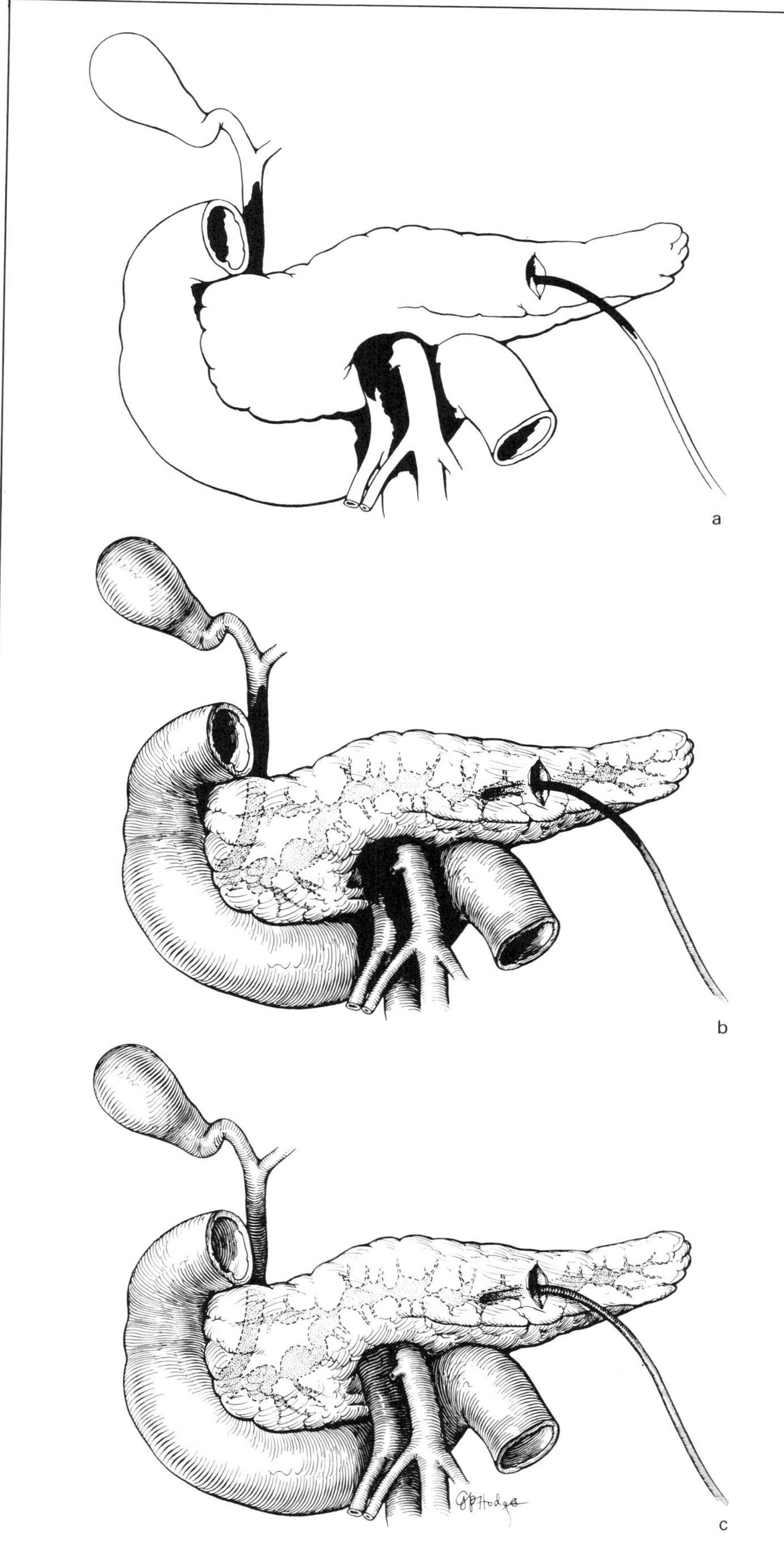

opers to give two tones of the same pattern.

After transferring the detailed preliminary to the Grafix surface if necessary, use either a dip or technical pen to draw the outline with india ink. Then, with a clean brush (the size depending on the area to be shaded), shade with the light-tone developer. With Duo-shade, it is customary but not essential to follow with the dark developer (fig. 5-22). Either dark or light developer can be used alone. Because perspiration can develop unwanted areas, keep some paper under the drawing hand. Use a different clean brush for each developer and apply it liberally. Blot excess developer with any absorbent material as the drawing progresses. The developing fluid dries very quickly, but be sure the paper is completely dry before applying the second developer. Although a brush is easiest to use, dip or technical pens are useful for achieving controlled thin lines in tone. If a technical pen is used, the reservoir can be filled with the developer. Clean the pen by flushing it with water.

Drawings on Grafix papers should be stored in a dark place. Even so, they may not last more than a few months since the tones fade quickly when exposed to light. The drawings will last considerably longer if covered with black paper or dark red masking film. Reapplication of the developers will temporarily reactivate the chemically printed patterns and is a good step to take just prior to sending illustrations to the publisher.

5-21. Steps in scratchboard drawing. *(a)* Outline the transferred drawing with ink. Then establish dark areas (often shadows) and paint in the blacks with brush and diluted ink. *(b)* Complete the modeling lines with pen or brush. *(c)* Etch with a knife into the dry black areas, blending the white etched lines with the black lines. Gillott 290 nib and Bard-Parker no. 15 blade. Fogarty irrigating catheter inserted into a dilated and constricted pancreatic duct, by Gerald P. Hodge © 1980.

Shading Film (Shading Screen)

Shading films, commercially available as Zip-A-Tone and Par-A-Tone, among other brands, are adhesive-backed transparent plastic sheets printed in a large assortment of screens and patterns for application to papers or drafting films. Some transfer by burnishing; others must be cut out and stuck on (fig. 5-23).

Prepare an inked drawing and outline the area to be shaded. Place the sheet of shading film over the outlined area. Drawing lines covered by the film still will show and reproduce clearly. With the cutout type of film, use an X-Acto or swivel knife to cut around the edge of the area, just a bit larger than the outline; take care not to cut through the backing film into the drawing. Remove the sheet and, with sharp forceps or tweezers, lift the cutout shape from its backing and position it over its area. Smooth the film into place, rubbing out any air bubbles, and burnish with a broad burnisher or a fingernail. Stubborn bubbles can be pricked to release air and then pressed flat. The film must have no bumps or ridges, for these will show up in reproduction. Use the knife to trim carefully any film extending beyond the outline. Although it is possible to render with ink on the film surface, it is not advisable to ink along its edge, since ink will seep under it.

With transfer-type films, use a plastic, metal, or wooden tool to

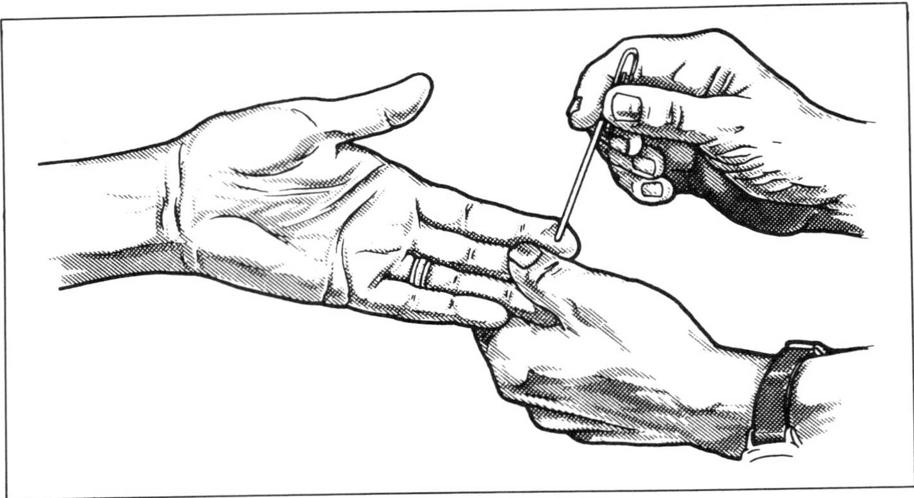

5-22. Use of Grafix prepatterned Duo-shade paper. Note darker tones, such as on watchband and in shadow areas, and lighter ones; each was painted with a different developer. The drawing is outlined in ink on the chemically treated surface, then the light and dark tone developers are applied with a brush or pen. Blood sampling using capillary tube, by Lewis L. Sadler © 1981.

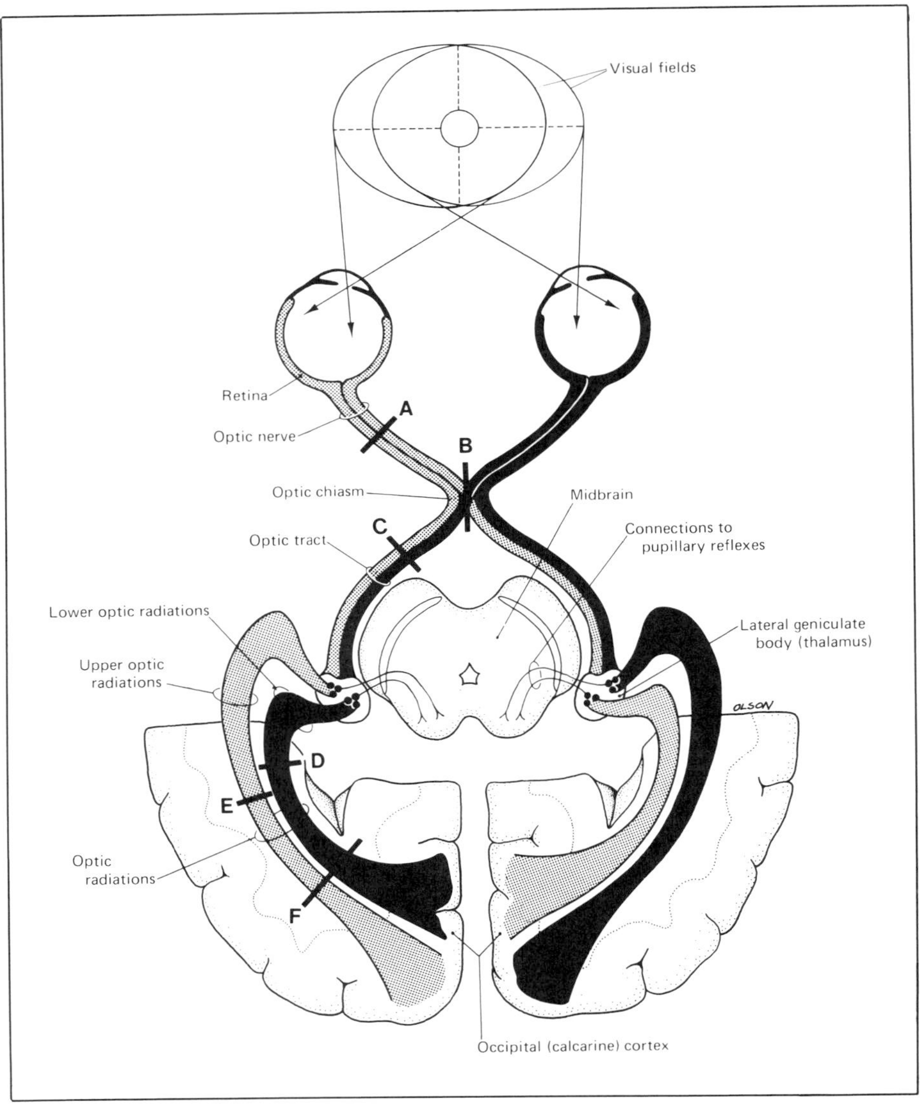

5-23. Use of shading film. The cutout type of shading screen in a dot pattern used for the gray areas enhances the visual effect of the diagram and also isolates areas for clarity. The drawing was outlined and stippled with a technical pen on hot-press, plate-finish illustration board. Visual pathways in the brain, by Mary Ann Olson. Courtesy of K. R. Magee and J. R. Saper, *Clinical and Basic Neurology for Health Professionals* (© 1981, Year Book Medical Publishers).

burnish the pattern onto the area to be shaded. To improve adhesion, burnish again over a clean, plain sheet on top of the drawing (preferably the backing sheet that accompanies the transfer film) after the transfer sheet is removed. To protect the pattern from chipping, spray the finished art with workable fixative and protect it with a paper cover sheet rather than plastic or acetate, which might lift off part of the pattern with static electricity.

Creative effects can be achieved with the different patterns or combinations of them (fig. 5-24). Superimposed dot screens can be rotated to create a moiré pattern for a diagrammatic highlight (see fig. 15-52).

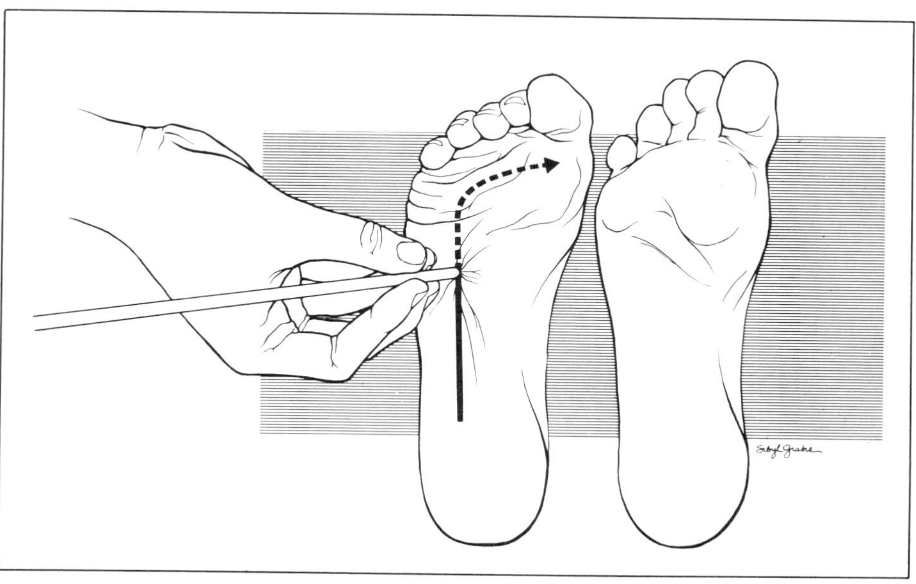

5-24. Shading film in a line pattern was used to tie the three elements of the drawing into one unit. The drawing was outlined with a Gillott 290 nib on heavy tracing paper, then shading film was applied. Plantar reflex, by Sibyl Graber © 1982.

INK RENDERING STYLES

An outline only, with no shading, may suffice to finish a simple drawing (see figs. 5-7, 5-8). If, however, it is necessary to show additional information—such as texture, volume, or transparency—or if a more realistic drawing is wanted, greater detail may be provided with stippling, eyelashing, and crosshatching. A timesaving compromise that is often acceptable is to detail only the most important part (fig. 5-25). Shading with lines—for example, crosshatching or eyelashing—is faster than stippling. This technique is, however, more difficult to control, and subtle form is not easy to depict with linear methods. Care should be taken with any rendering style to avoid suggesting nonexistent textures on the specimen; lines in particular tend to suggest ribbing or segmentation if not handled sensitively. Lines imply harder textures, and directional lines effectively suggest form (see figs. 5-13, 5-30). Small stipples can connote softness, while larger ones spaced far apart can suggest hardness (figs. 5-26, 5-27). Sometimes it is effective to combine two or more styles of rendering with ink line (see figs. 5-9, 5-32, 5-36).

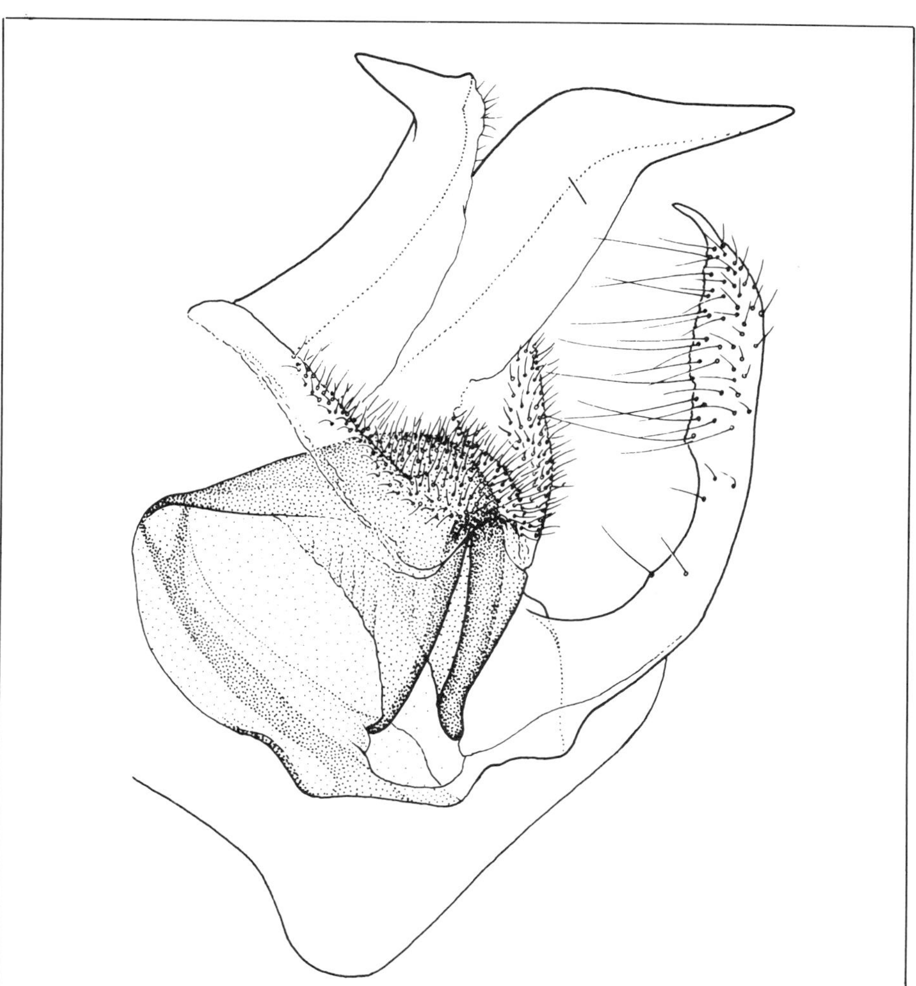

5-25. To draw attention to a portion of the drawing and to save time, the artist stippled only the most critical area, using a technical pen on Bristol board. Moth genitalia, male, ventro-lateral ¾ view, by Biruta Akerbergs Hansen. Courtesy of D. R. Davis.

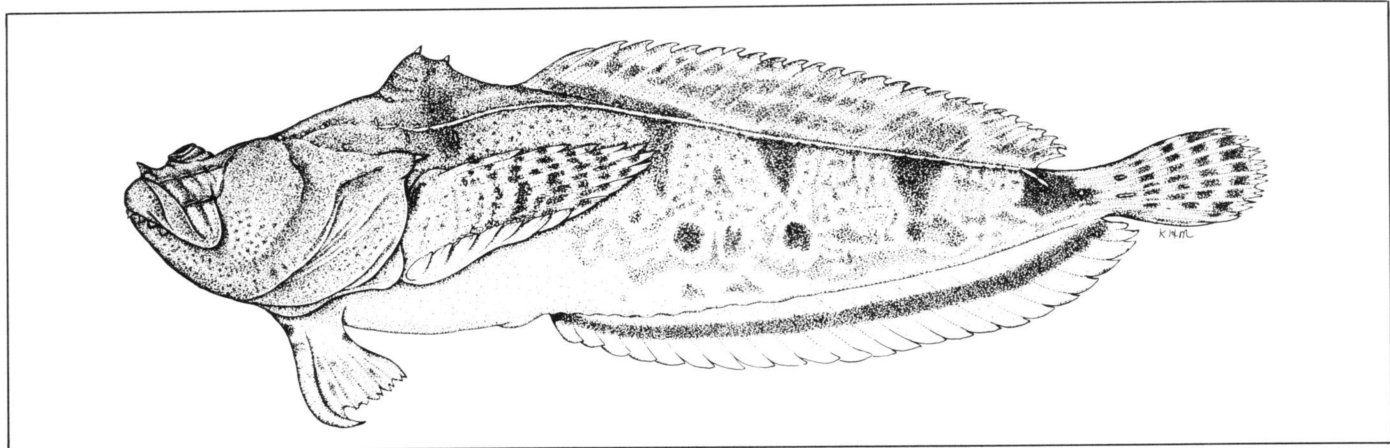

5-26. Stippling. Relatively small, closely spaced stipples represent the soft, unscaled flesh. Technical pen on hot-press, plate-finish Strathmore Bristol board. Colombian venomous toadfish, *Daector quadrizonatus*, by Keiko Hiratsuka Moore.

5-27. Stippling. Relatively large, evenly spaced stipples convey the feeling of hardness. A strong outline around this drawing also strengthens the image. Technical pen on Cronaflex film. Stone figure from San Agustin, Colombia, by George Robert Lewis.

Stippling

Stipples are dots. Almost all subjects for scientific illustration can be rendered with stipples, which suggest form in naturalistic gradations of tone. Done properly, stippling is very time consuming.

For drawings that will be reduced no more than 25 percent, the technical pen with a 2×0 or 3×0 point is very good for stippling; dots on scratchboard, however, usually thicken slightly as they soak into the coating, so a 3×0 or 4×0 point is preferable for that. The Gillott 659 and Hunt 104 are also fine for stipple drawings (especially of fine detail) that will be reduced no more than 25 percent (fig. 5-28). For up to 50 percent reduction, use 0 or 2×0 technical pens or a Hunt 102.

It is difficult for the inexperienced person to judge the proper scale and spacing of individual stipple dots; seeing the work reproduced and reduced provides the ultimate lesson. The beginner will find it hard to keep stippling consistent; first attempts at this technique usually result in stipples that are unevenly formed and spaced and either too fine or too coarse. When drawn too small, the dots will become very pale or will drop out entirely in reproduction; if drawn too close together, they will merge into areas of solid black.

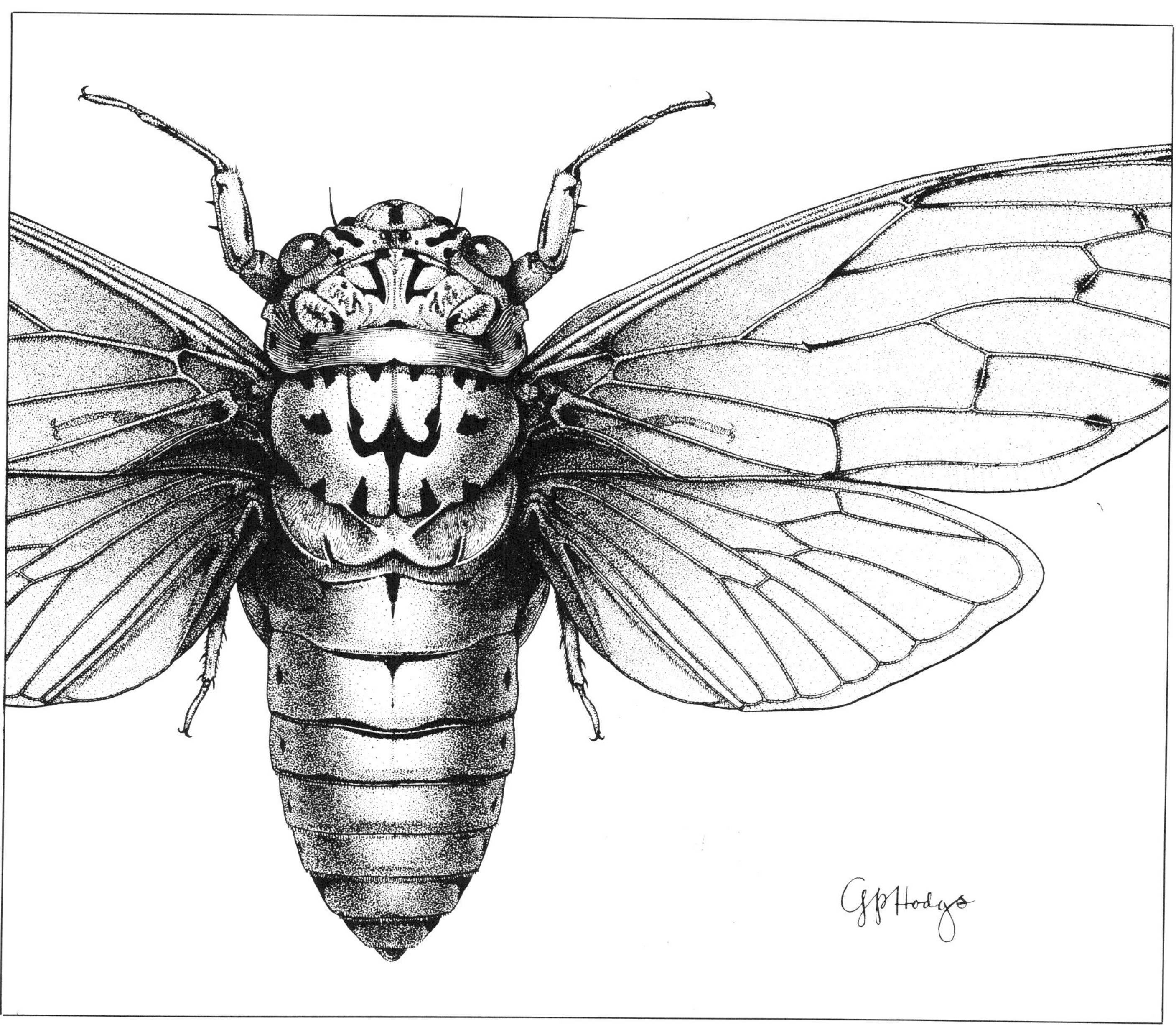

5-28. Small, even stipples with a conventional pen nib. The effect is visual vibration. Some areas are stippled almost to black. Gillott 659 nib on hot-press, plate-finish Strathmore paper. Cicadidae: *Pomponia imperatoria*, male, from Malaysia, detail, by Gerald P. Hodge © 1979.

Very smooth paper is essential for even stippling: the smoother the paper, the more consistent the stipple. Begin by placing some dots randomly, then gradually fill in. Be sure the dots are dots, not dashes. Avoid arranging the dots in obvious irregular or circular chains. Start stippling by placing the dots in groups of three or five and work out from there. Aim for an even gradation of tone. Like a pointillist painting, the drawing will appear to vibrate slightly (see figs. 5-27, 5-28). Stipple only as necessary to depict the tonal values of the subject. Every dot should have a purpose, and there should be neither too many nor too few. With experience, a certainty will develop as to when and where to add them.

To retain the identity of closely placed dots after reduction of 50 percent or more, leave space between adjacent dots or lines at least equal to the diameter of the dot or width of the line. When dots become overcrowded or if a few are too large, scrape them off, trim them with an etching tool, or touch up with opaque white ink and a fine-pointed brush.

In areas of shadow, stipples may be overlapped to almost 100 percent black, approximating the darkest tones; but the totally black areas should be kept to a minimum to avoid a muddy reproduction. White ink or paint may be stippled

over black-painted areas of paper or white dots etched onto black areas of scratchboard (fig. 5-29).

Eyelashing

An eyelashed line—thick in the middle and thin at each end—is used frequently in medical illustration (see fig. 5-2). Firm nibs and technical pens are unsuitable for eyelashing. Flexible pen nibs or pointed brushes are recommended, and the most sensitive and precise lines are drawn with fine, very flexible nibs such as Hunt 100 and Gillott 290 and 291. The stiffer Gillott 659 is easier to control, but because of its stiffness, the line produced will not be as wide as those from the more flexible pens (fig. 5-30). Size of brush depends on how thick the lines are to be, but a 3×0 or smaller should suffice.

Start the line with light pressure, then gradually press the pen or brush harder to widen the line; release this pressure to taper the line back to fineness (fig. 5-31; see fig. 5-15b).

Crosshatching

Crosshatched lines cross each other to form a pattern called hatching. A much more common rendering technique in the nineteenth and early twentieth centuries than it is today, crosshatching is a generally loose style because the shading is built up at random according to the size of the drawing and the artist's skill (fig. 5-32). It can be a quick and effective rendering technique for drawings intended to be so reduced that the crosshatching suggests modeling of

Facing page:
5-29. Stippling with white. A black background was prepared by airbrushing full-strength india ink onto museum board. Then white stipples were applied with Hunt 99 and 104 pens and black stipples were added to modify the white stipples. Bottlenose dolphin, *Tursiops truncatus*, by Pieter A. Folkens © 1979.

5-30. Eyelashing. A sketch was prepared using the exact number of lines shown, and this was double-transferred onto scratchboard. The lines with the broad centers were made with a Gillott 290 nib; those that are consistently fine were made with a Gillott 659 nib. Note addition of stipples. Amaryllis, *Hippeastrum vittatum*, by Gerald P. Hodge © 1979.

5-31. Eyelashing to delineate opaque and transparent spheres. Note the different placement of the thick and thin parts of the lines in relation to the highlights. The thin/thick line is made in one stroke with a flexible fine nib such as the Gillott 290. Ink on Cronaflex film, by Gerald P. Hodge © 1980.

form and not the specimen's actual texture.

To avoid a monotonous gray effect, plan in the preliminary drawing to leave some sizable white areas for contrast. By itself, with no border, crosshatching gives the effect of fuzzy edges, so an outline is important to hold everything within bounds. After completing the outline, place the heaviest modeling lines first. Apply the next series of crosshatched lines at oblique angles, with each tiny space between lines forming an elongated diamond shape (fig. 5-33). This will produce more subdued shading than the distracting checkerboard or screen-wire effect of right-angle crosshatching (fig. 5-34). Sketch the third and fourth series of lines at random, in groups of three to eight lines, wherever more modeling is needed. Finally, wherever white space seems too large, fill in with dots or short lines (fig. 5-35). If the convergence of many lines has created a noticeably dense spot, etch through or correct with white paint.

5-32. Crosshatching with short lines has been built up in a way to blend the owl into the background. Seychelles Island owl, *Otus insularis*, by D. M. Reid-Henry. From *Extinct and Vanishing Birds of the World*, by James C. Greenway, Jr. (Dover Publications, 1967. Originally Special Publication no. 13 by the American Committee for International Wildlife Protection, 1958).

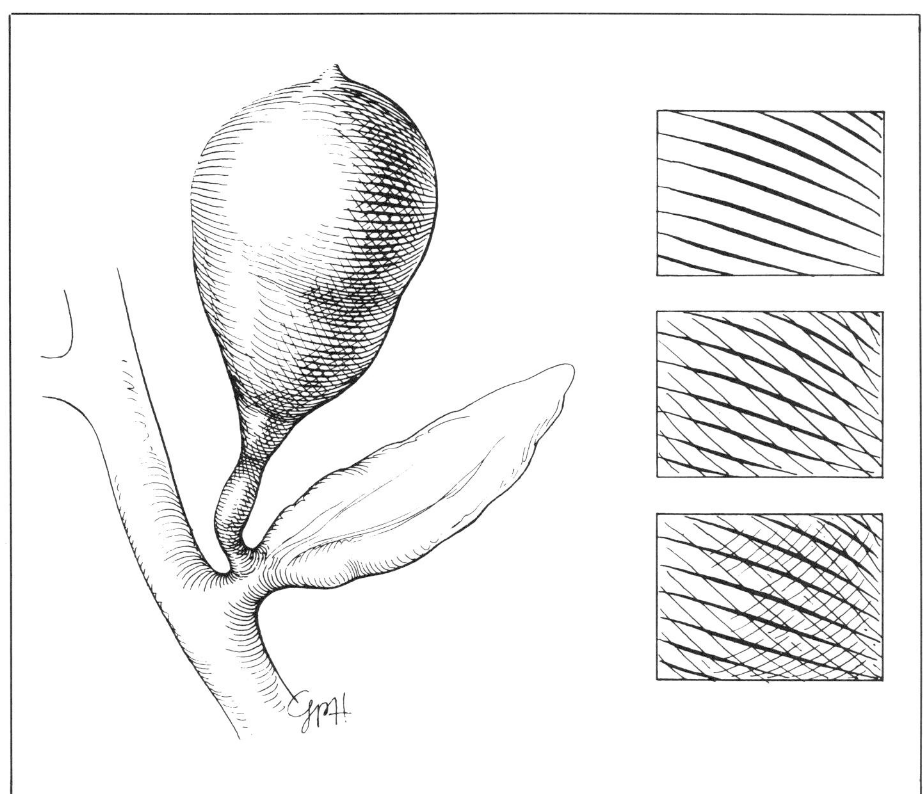

5-33. Principles of crosshatching. The first set of lines should be the main modeling lines and may be eyelashed, as in this instance. The second group of lines should be placed obliquely rather than at right angles and can be thinner than the first set. The third group of lines may be shorter than the others and placed randomly to emphasize form. A fourth set of lines, necessary for dark areas, is usually made up of groups of very short lines. Finally, any disconcerting white spaces are filled in with dots or short dashes. Gillott 290 nib on tracing paper, by Gerald P. Hodge © 1981.

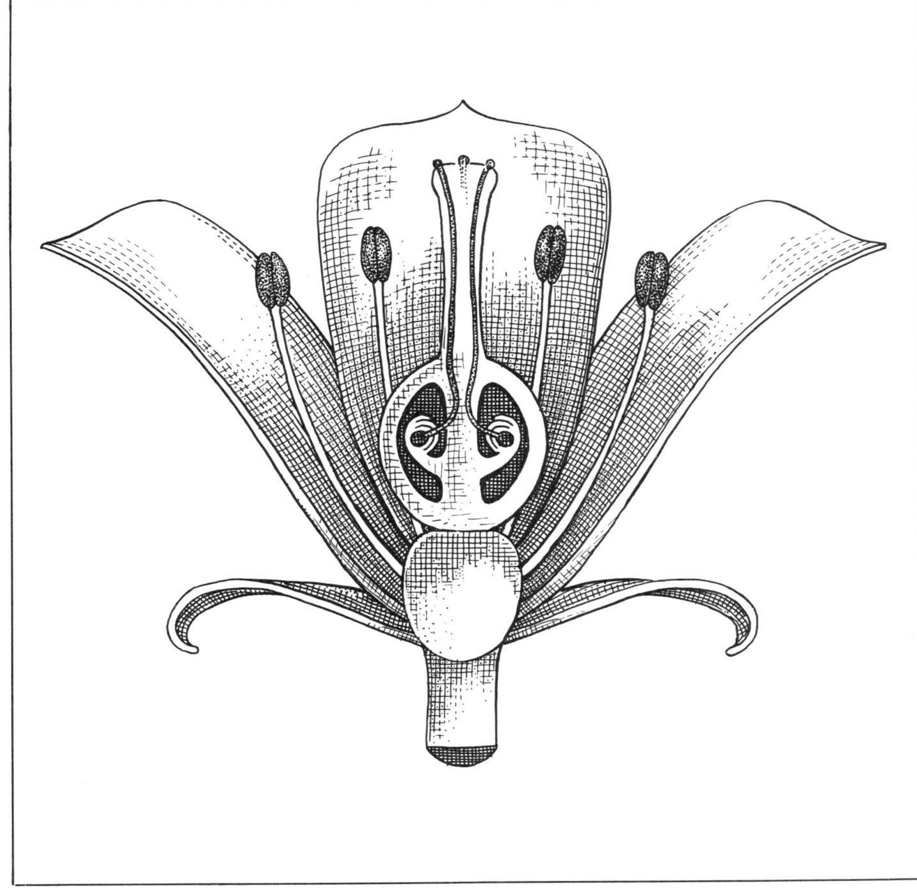

5-34. Crosshatching at right angles forms a distractingly regular pattern that does not look natural for shading. Addition of stippling softens the overall effect. Gillott 659 nib on Denril film. Position of parts in hypogynous flower type, by Gerald P. Hodge © 1985.

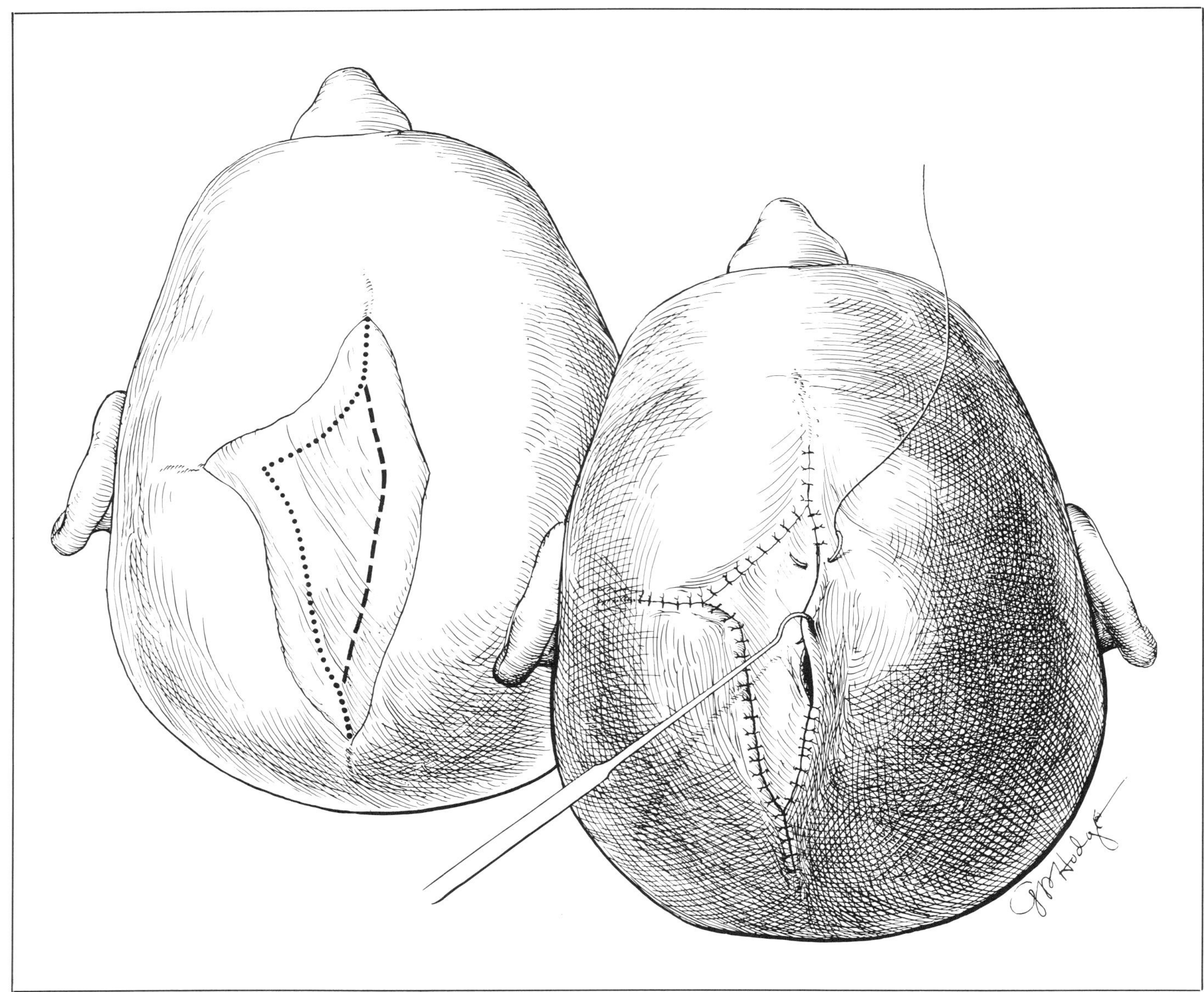

5-35. The first layer of crosshatching was eyelashed and the next several layers were applied at oblique angles, with care taken not to block up any areas. Note that the lines are long compared to those in figure 5-32. Gillott 659 nib on scratchboard. Surgical repair of the scalp, by Gerald P. Hodge. Courtesy of W. C. Grabb, J. W. Smith, *Plastic Surgery* (Little, Brown and Company, 1979).

Miscellaneous Ink Styles

Short-line Drawing
This style involves shading with short, straight lines about ⅜ inch (1cm) in length. The short lines allow for some crosshatching and can simulate a great variety of textures (fig. 5-36; see figs. 5-20, 5-32).

Serrated-edge Line Drawing
This calls attention to special areas and can emphasize heavy outlines in shadow (fig. 5-37a).

Double-line Drawing
This softens or blurs outlining with a thin line inside and adjacent to the heavier outline (figs. 5-37b, 5-38).

A wide variety of ink techniques may render almost any subject matter as long as the technique does not overpower or obstruct the scientific value of the drawing (fig. 5-39).

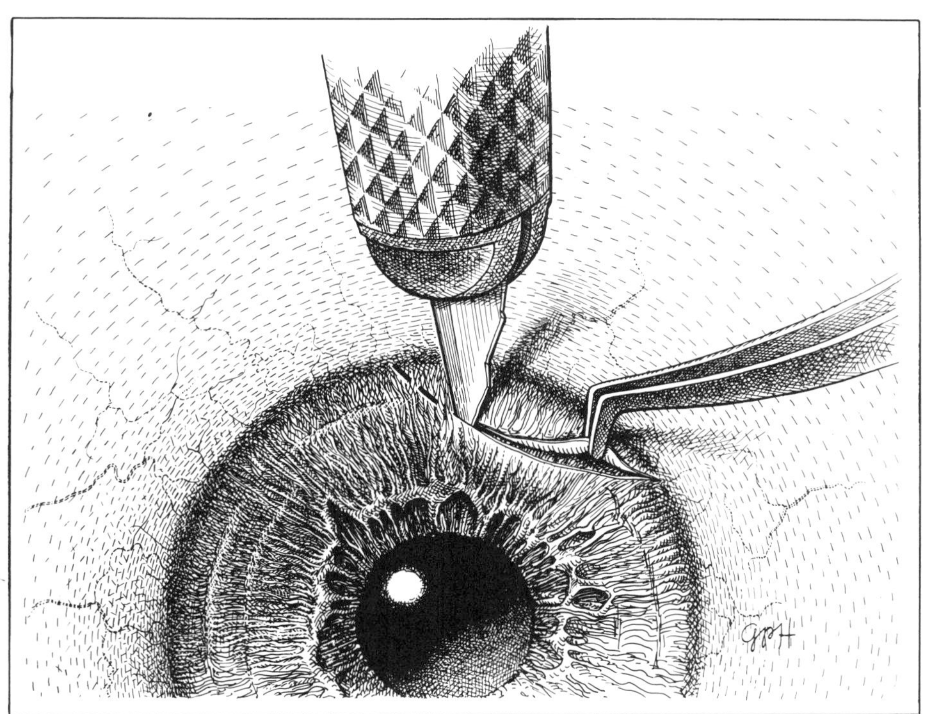

5-36. Short-line technique with some of the lines crosshatched on knife and in pupil. Hunt 104 nib on scratchboard. Incision in cornea: filtering trephine operation for glaucoma, by Gerald P. Hodge © 1978.

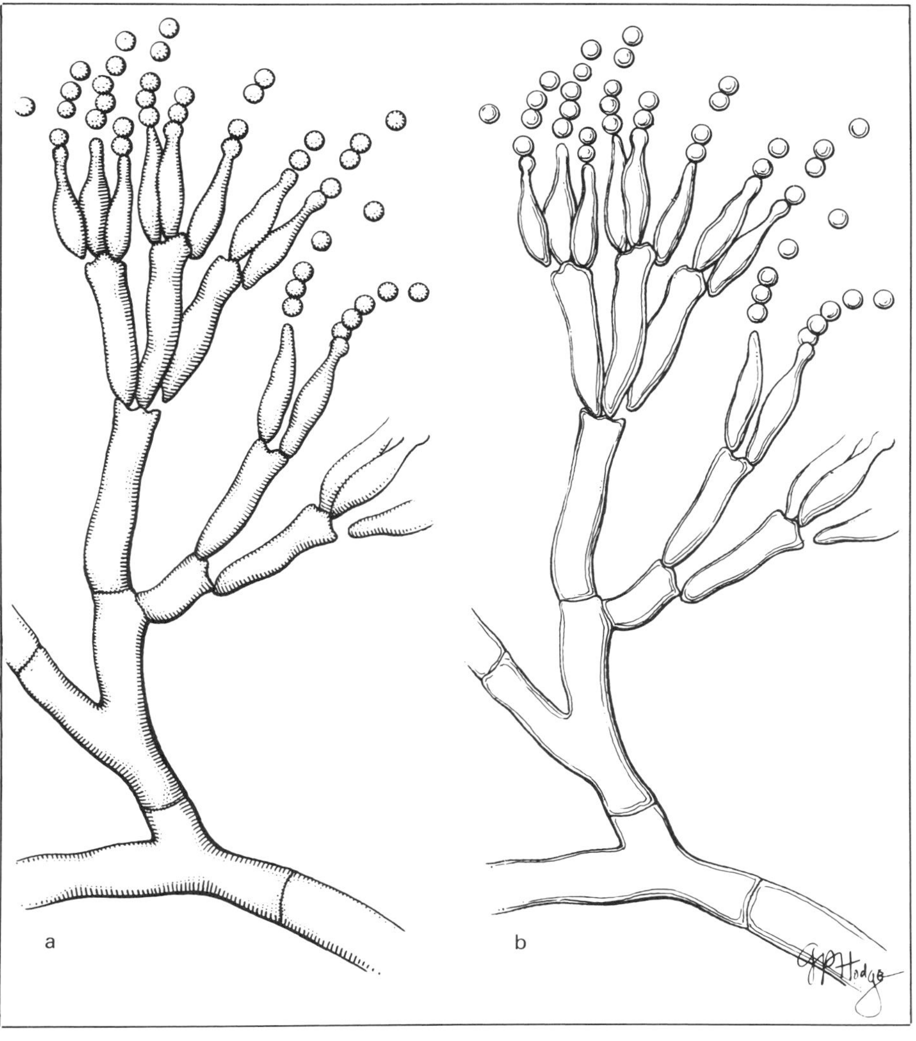

5-37. Comparison of two linear styles on the same subject: *(a)* serrated edge; *(b)* double line. Both styles enhance outline and impart form. Gillott 659 nib on Vidalon tracing paper. A form of *Penicillium*, by Gerald P. Hodge © 1980.

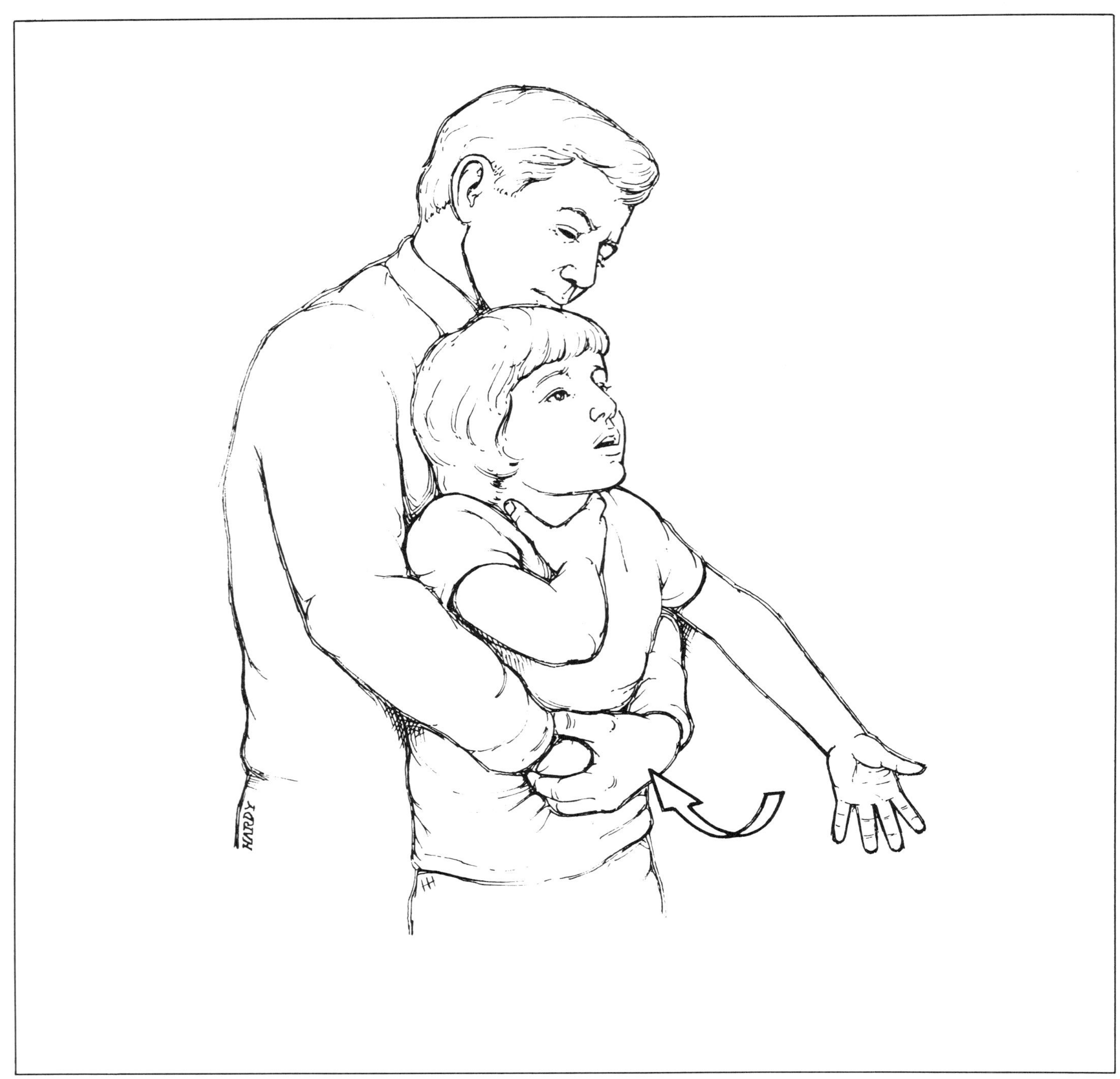

5-38. Double-line drawing style. The double line creates a soft (out-of-focus) effect and also helps give form. 3×0 technical pen on hot-press illustration board. Heimlich maneuver, by Neil Hardy © 1977. Courtesty of J. Shiller, *Childhood Injury* (Stein and Day, 1977).

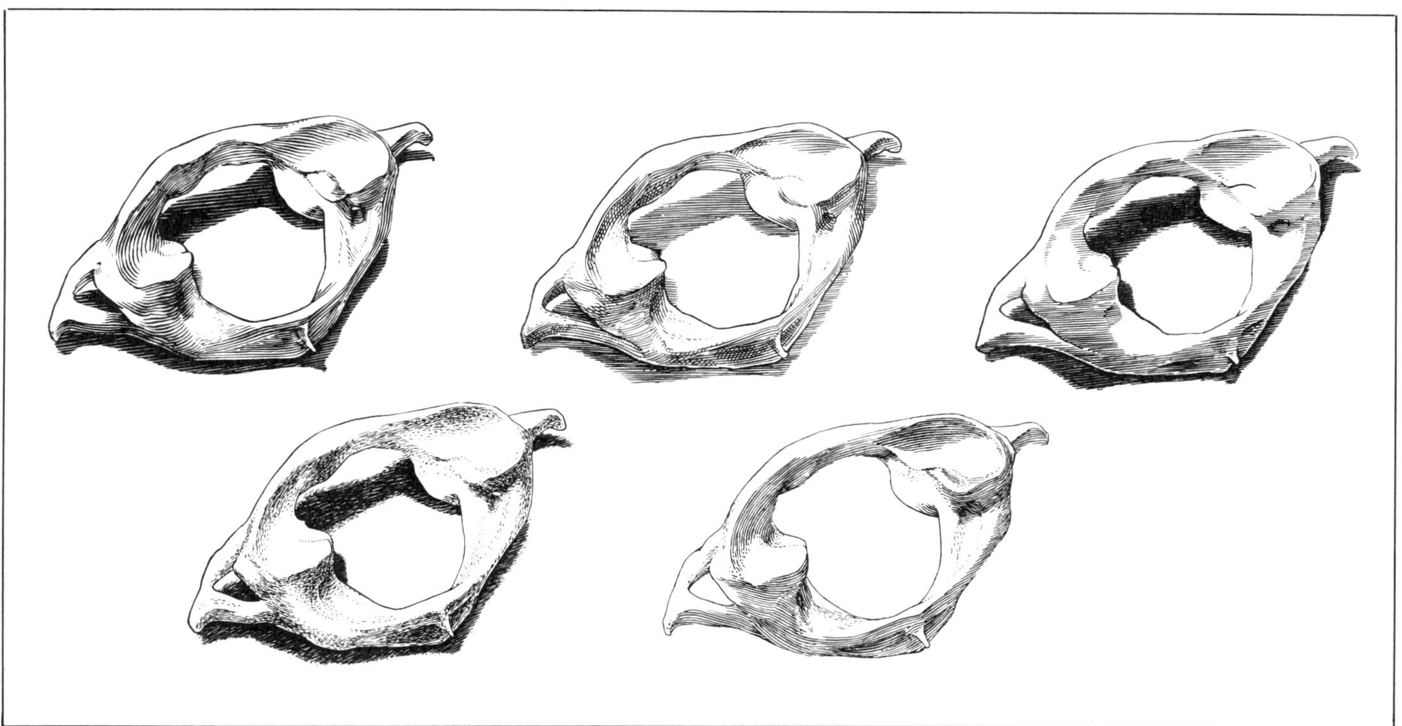

5-39. The same structure successfully rendered in various ink line styles. Identify these styles and note that all the renderings follow (model) the form of the object except the one at upper right. Compare the effects with and without a cast shadow, omitted from drawing at lower right. Gillott 290 nib on scratchboard. Cervical vertebrae, by Trudy Nicholson © 1974.

6/Pencil

Lawrence B. Isham

Elsewhere in this book, pencil has been taken for granted as a medium for drawing specimens. It is almost always used for preliminary sketches, for outline and blocking in, in preparation for other media. The pencil on its own, however, can be used effectively to produce fully rendered, finished illustrations.

Many pencil types are available —among them graphite, plastic, colored, white—with which different effects can be produced on various surfaces. Three pencil techniques are discussed here in detail: graphite pencil on paper, plastic pencil on drafting film, and colored pencils on various surfaces.

Graphite Pencil

The intent of the artist in using this method with graphite drawing pencils is to produce an illustration in which the "evidence of the medium" is suppressed. The directional quality of pencil shading is obscured by smudging so that pencil strokes may not be interpreted as grooves or other surface texture. In order to achieve this, the artist performs a sequence of operations to preserve the surface quality of the paper. If it is blemished or disturbed in the early stages by rough treatment, the surface will not lend itself to a smoothly rendered drawing. For that reason, all internal and middle-tone shading is applied with graphite-loaded paper stumps, and all erasures are carefully done with a clean kneaded eraser. The highlight areas are seldom erased; rather, they are left free of graphite from the beginning.

MATERIALS

Surfaces

See charts 8-1 and 8-2 for useful information about various opaque and translucent surfaces.

Bristol board: medium (cold-press) finish; two- or three-ply is ideal. If a drawing paper shows much reflected glare in the light, it is hot press and too smooth for this purpose, although rubbing it in several directions with a clean kneaded rubber eraser will make it acceptable. A slightly rougher paper can be used with carbon pencils.

Drafting film: can be used but its texture is abraded by heavy use of stumps, so flat sable brushes are recommended instead.

Media

Pencils: graphite, grades 2H, B, 2B, 4B; carbon (Wolff's or similar type; see Charcoal Pencils in chapter 2). A minimum of four grades of pencil is usually necessary in this technique. Grades 2H and B may be used as leads in mechanical holders, but since 2B and 4B leads are quite fragile, wood-encased pencils are used instead. It is sometimes desirable to use harder graphite, such as 4H or 7H, for delicate shading in small areas, but a carefully handled 2H will do. Any graphite softer than 4B has a tendency to spread into areas where it is not wanted. The 4B is little used.

Carbon pencils may be used with this technique provided the drawing paper has enough tooth or texture. This is appropriate for larger drawings, but the paper texture might prove distracting in small drawings.

White ink and paint: for corrections and highlighting. Higgins white waterproof ink and titanium white acrylic or white gouache such as Dr. Ph. Martin's Bleed Proof White or Steig Pro White may be used.

Tools

Lead holders: if leads are used instead of pencils.

Tortillions and stumps (stomps): rolled paper used to apply and to smudge graphite. Size numbers 1, 2, and 3 are most useful. Several stumps of each size are needed. If the ridges of the rolled paper show on the tapered end, carefully shave them with a sharp razor blade to provide a softer, fibrous surface, eliminate the ridges, and clean the working surface of the stump. Stumps are not advised for use on polyester film, although figure 6-4 shows a successful result of stumps used with care.

Cork: to blend and smooth tones.

Brushes: flat sable brushes of various sizes. Used to apply graphite if plastic film is used instead of paper. A small brush is needed for applying white ink for highlights.

Crowquill pen: for highlights.

Chamois, cotton, facial tissue: nonabrasive materials used to remove excess graphite.

Erasers: kneaded rubber eraser as primary erasing tool. Also convenient to pick out small light areas is a pencil-shaped eraser. Do not use an abrasive typing eraser, but the softer kind intended for offset master plates. Sharpen one end to a point, the other to a chisel edge.

Miscellaneous

Razor blade.

Workable fixative: Krylon works well for this technique.

Paper: for preliminary drawings and protective masks during rendering; as an abrasive surface for sharpening pencils and collecting pencil dust.

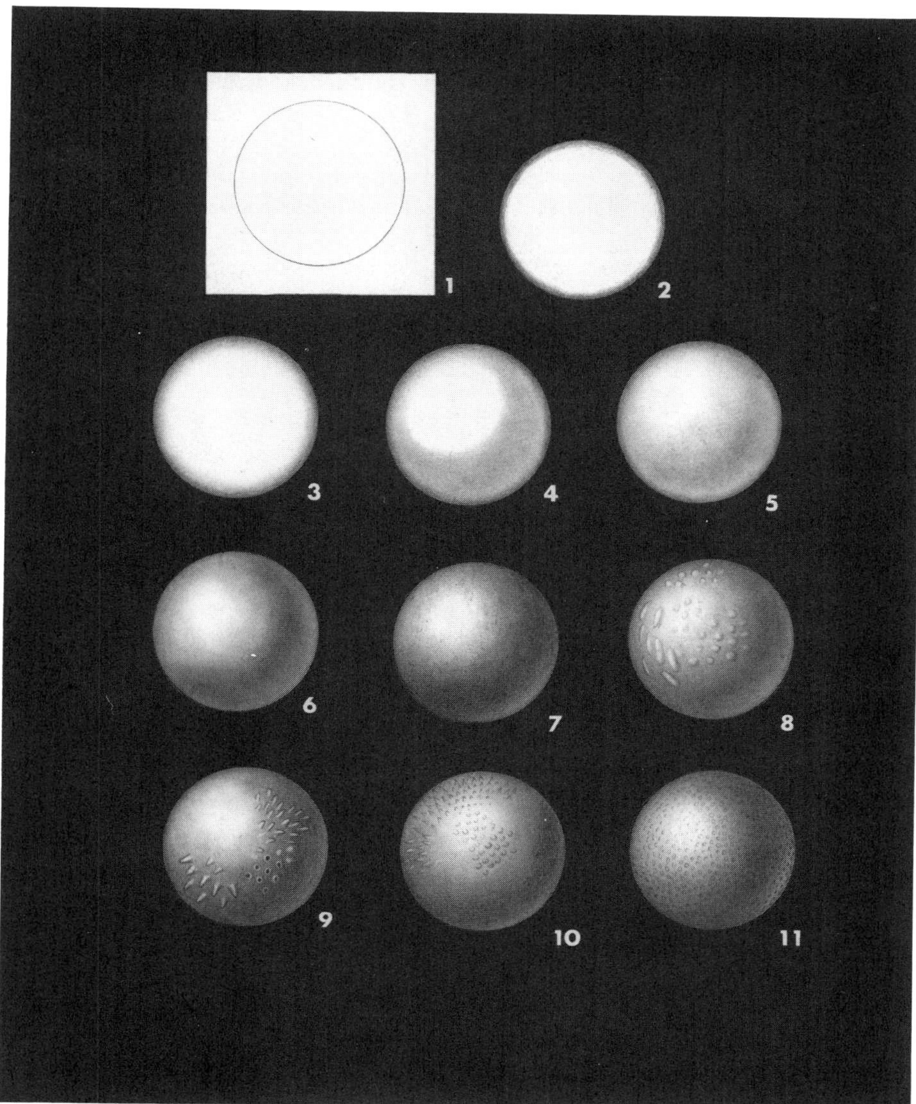

6-1. Steps 1 to 11: successive stages in the progress of a pencil drawing. Lawrence B. Isham.

TECHNIQUE

Make a preliminary line drawing carefully on any inexpensive white paper, using a very sharp B or HB pencil to show accurately only the outline of the specimen and some of its main features. Do this tightly with a thin line, free of lost edges or other ambiguities of outline.

Transfer the preliminary to Bristol board (see chapter 1 for transfer techniques). Remove any smudges on the transferred drawing by dabbing with a kneaded eraser, and refine the quality of the line with a very sharp B pencil (fig. 6-1, step 1). The preparation of a separate preliminary drawing and transfer keeps the final drawing surface free of heavy erasures, divider scratches, and other damage that could seriously affect later stump shading. Protect the transferred drawing by covering it with a paper mask with a window cut out over the work area (see fig. 1-3).

Use a well-sharpened 2B pencil, held at a very low angle to utilize the side of the graphite rather than the point, to establish a uniform band of dark tone, 1/16 inch (2mm) wide, just inside the outline. Use a sharp B pencil in the same manner to place a narrow band of tone just inside and overlapping the first one. Repeat the process with a 2H pencil, so that the outline is accented with three overlapping narrow values, decreasing inward, having a total width of 3/16 inch (3 to 4mm) (step 2). If the specimen is flattened or has a sharp periphery, this shading should be confined to a narrow area, but if the subject is spherical or rounded, enlarge the band of tone at the edge. Do not permit bands of tone to become too wide or overpowering. Avoid rubbing so hard with the pencil that the paper is indented or ingrained with too much graphite to permit corrections.

With a clean soft stump, smudge and blend the bands of dark tone, using strokes parallel to the outline as far as the profile of the specimen allows. Avoid circular movements and short, choppy strokes. If some graphite moves outside the outline, remove it with the kneaded eraser. Blur the local variations in value and directional texture left by the pencil with a no. 2 or 3 stump, leaving a band of graded tone about 1/4 inch (5mm) wide around the edge of the drawing, the margin of the light inner tone being very indistinct (step 3).

Before proceeding, decide where the major highlights are to appear and avoid shading those areas. This does not apply to the representation of small surface details, which should be ignored until the general shape of the specimen in the drawing has been established.

For drawing small details or fine lines, sharpen the pencil to a needle point by rubbing it on a piece of scrap paper. The residue on the scrap paper will provide the graphite to be picked up eventually on the stumps. Pencils may be sharpened on a sandpaper pad, but care must be taken not to let stumps come in contact with the pad or they might pick up loose sand from it. A stump contaminated with an abrasive will produce a network of directional scratches that will darken with graphite and ruin the drawing.

To create the middle tones of the interior of the drawing, load a soft stump with graphite by rubbing it on the paper on which graphite dust has collected; remove the excess graphite by stroking the stump on a clean piece of paper. Use this moderately darkened stump to apply the middle tones gently, working inward from the outline. Leave the areas to be highlighted slightly larger than they are to appear in the final form, allowing some space for transition from middle tone to highlight (step 4). The highlights will be more definite and their edges softer if they are left clear in this fashion rather than being erased later.

Adjust the transition from middle value to highlight area by blending with a *clean* stump. If the subject has a dull finish, the highlight must have soft edges, with a gradual transition into the middle tones (step 5). Do not move graphite too far into the highlight.

Use a clean stump also to remove some graphite if the previously installed middle tones seem too dark. At this point, the drawing is fairly weak with a heavy outline, showing only profile, middle tones, and highlight.

Now load a stump heavily with graphite, testing it for darkness on scrap paper, and apply the darker areas on the drawing. Use long, gentle strokes, and keep these darker areas smaller than is the final intent. Where appropriate, use a separate stump cautiously to blend these dark values into the middle tones. Do not use a clean one for this purpose, as it will remove too much graphite. At this stage, the drawing is outlined, smoothly shaded, in three basic values, but rather weak for publication (step 6).

This method of graphite rendering may need to be altered if the area to be shaded is either very large or extremely small. If an extensive area is to be shaded, the stumps may not be large enough to apply tone smoothly. Instead, small pieces of chamois may be folded over a finger and used as a swab to apply and spread the graphite. Clean chamois will remove excess graphite and lighten an area. Other soft, nonabrasive materials, such as cotton or facial tissues, are also suitable.

When the area to be shaded is very small and the shading must be subtle, it is useful to use hard pencil (grades 4H to 7H) for light tones instead of stump-applied graphite. For blending and smoothing tones in small areas, use a piece of cork shaped and sharpened to a small point or edge instead of a stump. Cork holds a sharp edge or point better than a stump. Tape it to a handle or stick it on the end of a dissecting needle or shape it to fit a mechanical holder. Keep the piece of cork sharp. This sort of shading is difficult to erase, but delicate highlights may be added with a pen and white ink.

Most shading done thus far lends itself to changes or removal with the kneaded eraser. The only real commitment is the outline and its shading. The next step is to add the darkest tones, starting with the main shadows, making long strokes with the side of a 2B pencil. Place the darks as smoothly as possible, and accent them with the 4B pencil where necessary. Again, keep shadows slightly smaller than would seem adequate; subsequent use of the stump to smooth the darks will expand them slightly.

Keep one or two large stumps very heavily loaded with graphite from a 4B pencil (rub pencil on paper and pick up the graphite with the stump). Use it to apply graphite in more liberal amounts. For this purpose it is preferable to choose old stumps with softer working ends and less densely packed fibers. Smooth the pencil-shaded areas with the very dark stump, blending them into natural gradations of tone. Work with pencil and stump to bring all the main shadows to their final form (step 7). Avoid the highlight areas and clean up outside the margin of the drawing with the kneaded eraser. Now indicate some of the larger surface detail by dabbing out small lights with the kneaded eraser and shading small darks with the pencil or a loaded no. 1 stump (step 8). There should be sufficient contrast to render shapes convincingly.

Handle the surface texture last to avoid interfering with broader shading intended to show the general shape of the specimen. Where it is necessary to depict detail on those areas already darkened, use the sharpened offset eraser to lighten small areas, touching up with pencil or ink to produce the effect of spines, pores, or other texture (step 9). If erasing is not practical, use white ink or paint, diluted with water to avoid too much contrast in the shadows, which would create a harsh appearance. If de-

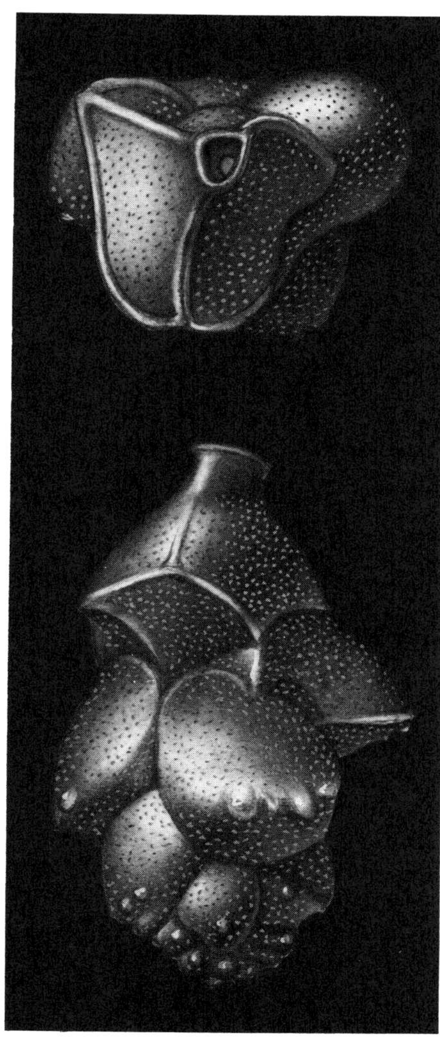

6-2. Graphite pencil drawings on Bristol board, painted black around the image. White ink defines sharp highlights and details on the right, shaded sides of the subjects. The cutout drawings were glued on black poster board, the white edges of the board painted black. Foraminifera, by Lawrence B. Isham. Courtesy of Martin A. Buzas.

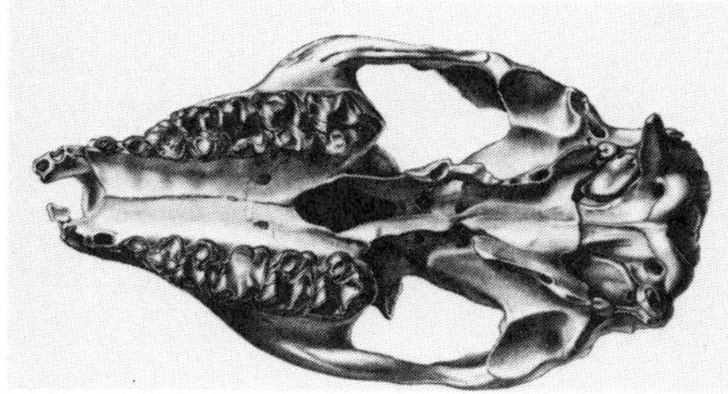

6-3. Graphite pencil on cold-press Bristol board. Ventral view of the skull of *Meniscotherium chamense*, by Lawrence B. Isham. From C. L. Gazin, *Smithsonian Miscellaneous Collections*, vol. 149, no. 2, 1965.

tails so drawn seem too white after drying, darken them with a stump or pencil.

Surface texture usually should be merely suggested rather than drawn in detail. Use dots, circles, or crescents to suggest pores. Small crescent-shaped shadows represent bumps, and angular shadows and lines give the impression of a spiny surface (step 10). Use the harder pencils in the lighter areas of the drawing, and avoid allowing the surface texture to interfere with the shadows and highlights, which define the shape of the specimen (step 11).

Among a range of materials to use to apply white for highlights on a shaded drawing of this kind, first choice would be white acrylic or gouache diluted with water for pen or brush; second would be white drawing ink. The better grades of Chinese white watercolor are suitable, but they may become powdery if applied too heavily. Dry methods such as chalk, pastel, Nupastel, and white pencil are not recommended because they do not adhere to a paper surface polished by the application of graphite.

When the drawing is finished, remove the paper mask, clean the area around the drawing with a kneaded eraser, and give the drawing a protective coat of workable fixative.

Figures 6-2, 6-3, 6-4, and 13-24 illustrate the graphite technique. Figures 6-4 and 13-24 were done with graphite pencils on polyester film; figure 6-5 was done with carbon pencils on Bristol board.

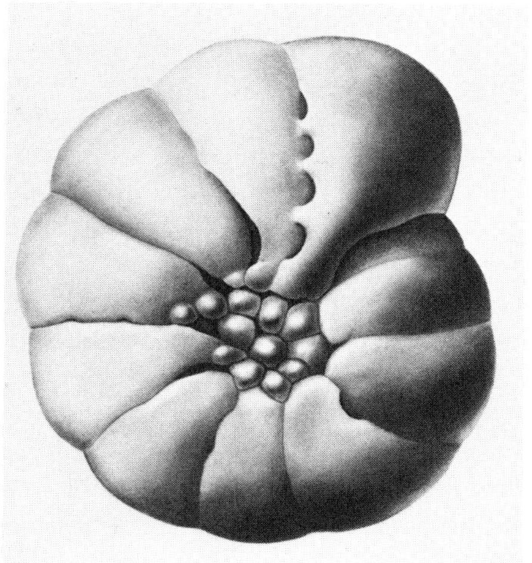

6-5. Wolff's carbon pencil on Bristol board. Foraminiferan, by Lawrence B. Isham. Courtesy of *Nature* magazine.

6-4. Graphite pencil on polyester film. A stump was used lightly to blend the pencil. Drawing based on 35mm slides and preserved legs. Striped-back wren, Venezuela, by Kathy Shuster.

Plastic Pencil on Drafting Film

Jack R. Schroeder

The use of film as a drawing surface is discussed in chapter 8, where it is used with a dusting technique in which a brush picks up and paints with ground, dry carbon, or graphite. Here the pencil point builds tones on a translucent surface. The surface, polyester film, is washable, will not tear, and its microscopically granular coating (see fig. 3-4) accepts pencil very well. The medium, plastic drawing "leads," has been developed to complement polyester (plastic) films. The leads are graded like graphite from soft to hard, although the hardness designations vary with the manufacturer.

Plastic leads or pencils leave a blacker line on frosted plastic films than do graphite pencils but otherwise look and handle just like graphite. They can be smudged with a brush (or very carefully with a stump) using the technique described earlier. The main technique described here, however, does not involve blending; smooth effects result from closely spaced pencil lines. A second technique uses stumps sparingly.

MATERIALS

Surfaces

Polyester drafting film: coated (frosted) film such as Bruning Sure-Scale (no. 44-122, 2 mil thick), coated on both sides to prevent curling. Other polyester films may be used. The thinner films are more translucent and thus make tracing easier. Because pencils produce a blacker line on some brands than on others, experimentation is advised. (See chart 8-2 for useful information about some of these surfaces.)

Mounting board.

Media

Plastic pencils or leads: sometimes listed in art-supply catalogs as "film" pencils. Different manufacturers use different designations for degree of hardness; for instance, Staedtler-Mars Duralar pencils and leads range from K1 through K5; others use the letters B, H, F, P, N, or E plus numbers. When a system other than B and H is used, the lowest number, often 0, is softest, and there usually are no more than six gradations, to 5, the hardest. When B and H indicate the grades, B levels are the softest, H levels the hardest, with F indicating middle hardness.

India ink, lampblack watercolor: for detailing.

Opaque white paint: for highlighting; gouache or acrylic, as listed under Graphite Pencil, earlier.

Tools

Lead holders: if leads are used instead of pencils.

Aluminum roofing nail: 2 to 3 inches (5 to 8cm), with point filed flat; for detailing.

Erasers: kneaded rubber, plastic, and pencil-shaped soft erasers.

X-Acto or other sharp blade in handle: for scratching details.

Brushes: 5×0 or larger for applying highlights, details, and outlines.

Tortillions and stumps (stomps): use (rarely) for final blending of pencil lines.

Miscellaneous

Paper: for protective mask during rendering; smooth surface for the preliminary drawing and as a slip sheet between the preliminary and the film.

Clear acetate sheet: to cover preliminary drawing.

Facial tissue: use dampened to remove mistakes.

Workable fixative.

White acrylic paint: in a spray can, for backpainting finished work.

TECHNIQUE

After preparing a preliminary drawing, spray it with fixative or cover it with clear acetate to keep it from rubbing off onto the back of the film. (Static electricity will attract the pencil granules to the polyester.) Tape the preliminary drawing to a white board and cover it with the film. No transfer is necessary since the preliminary can be seen through the film, but eventually the preliminary will be removed and placed nearby for reference. Cut a paper mask to cover the film (as described in chapter 1) or use a scrap piece of film in the same way. To aid evaluation of the tones, have smooth white paper ready to slip between the film and the preliminary as rendering progresses.

It is important to use smooth paper for both the preliminary drawing and slip sheet because any texture on the underlying material will show on the film, particularly a very thin one. The result is an embossed "rubbing" created by the pencil. Paper texture may be used to advantage if it matches that of the specimen, but in general the texture should be drawn with the pencil.

Outline the subject and its internal details, if outlines are desired, with a medium-hard pencil. To

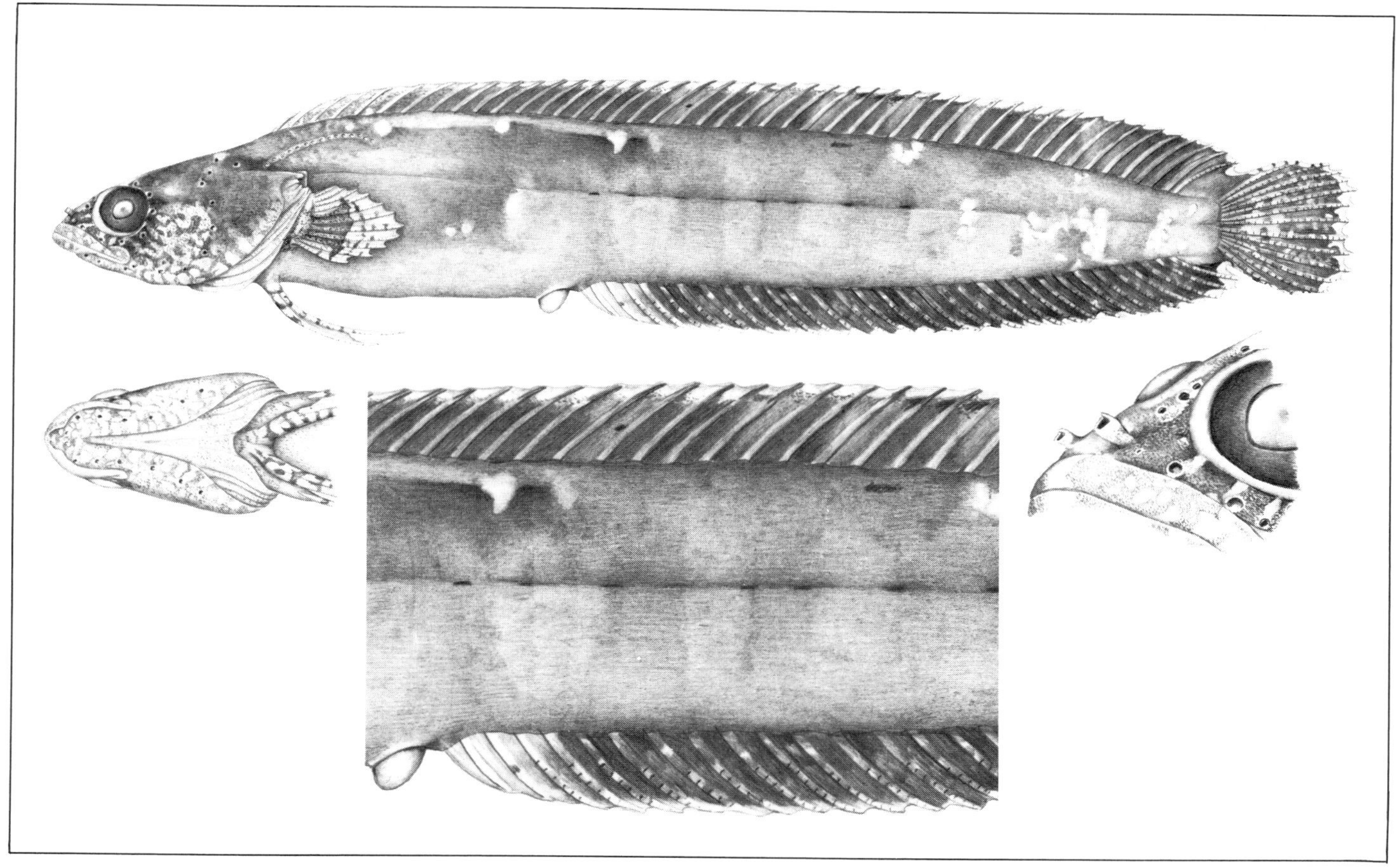

6-6. Closely spaced lines drawn with plastic pencil on polyester film. The enlargement shows the lines. *Ophiclinus ningulus*, by Jack R. Schroeder. From the files of the Division of Fishes, Department of Vertebrate Zoology, National Museum of Natural History. Courtesy of Victor G. Springer.

mold shapes or indicate pattern, use the sharpened point of the pencil to shade with closely spaced lines of even weight. Choose the hardness of pencil to match the needed tone: in the hard range for light, soft for dark. Keep even pressure on the pencils to achieve a smooth tone. Then use a very sharp pencil to fill in between the first lines. Any light areas in need of touch-up will be visible through squinted eyes. A very light tone requires only a few passes; several layers of pencil will create a darker tone (fig. 6-6). A roofing nail, held in a lead holder, can create light lines in a dark area or pale preliminary lines.

Brush on opaque white paint for sharp, bright highlights and use the erasers for both soft highlights and corrections. Scratch delicate, sharp white highlights and details with a sharp blade. For slightly less sharp-edged effects, cut one pencil-shaped eraser to a chisel point. A second, blunt-ended eraser rubbed lightly over an area lightens the tone. To erase an area completely, use erasers or a dampened tissue.

Contrasts in the drawing will be heightened if the film is sprayed on the back with white acrylic; this prevents a cast shadow on the mounting surface. Make sure the film is clean before spraying it. Remove any lint, smudges, or eraser crumbs with a kneaded eraser or damp tissue. Allow backpaint to dry completely (if used), then mount the finished drawing on white mounting board.

Use of Stumps

A variation of plastic pencil technique is shown in figure 6-7. As in the graphite technique, stumps are used to blend together pencil lines, but very sparingly and only as a final step. No further pencil work can be done on top of the stumped areas because the surface has been smoothed too much to accept more pencil. After the blending step, lampblack watercolor is applied with a brush to reinforce outlines and dark areas and to add linear details. Opaque white paint is used to create the sharp highlights. The liquid adheres better to a layer of pencil than to bare or lightly penciled plastic. Soft highlights are rubbed out with a plastic eraser.

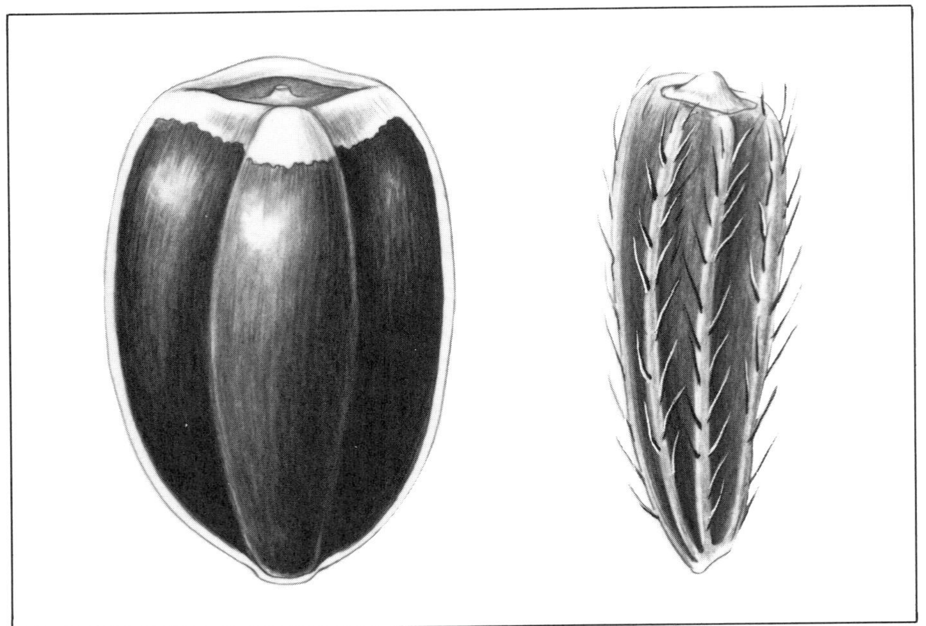

6-7. Plastic pencil blended with stumps and intensified with lampblack watercolor on polyester film. Achenes of some Heliantheae, by Alice R. Tangerini.

Colored Pencil

Arwin V. Provonsha

Although colored pencils are familiar to most of us from our youth, many illustrators do not take full advantage of them as a professional illustrating tool. If handled properly, they can give textural and color effects very difficult to achieve with any of the conventional wet color media. The equipment needed is minimal, and in many instances, a colored pencil rendering can be completed in much less time than would be required for other color media (see figs. C-18, C-19). Pencils also can be utilized effectively in conjunction with other color media such as acrylics, gouache, pastels, or transparent watercolor (see figs. C-1, C-5, C-6, C-28, C-29, C-30, C-31).

Gerald P. Hodge, Jane Redmann, and George L. Venable contributed to the text on colored pencil.

MATERIALS

Surfaces

Paper, board, film: any surface with a good tooth and random texture such as 100 percent rag mat board, kid-finish (cold-press) illustration board (100 percent rag), Video Media paper, kid-finish (cold-press) Bristol board, Line Kote board, or coated (frosted) drafting film may be used. See charts 8-1 and 8-2 for useful information on various opaque and translucent surfaces. Black or very dark surfaces can be effective backgrounds.

Media

A set of at least twelve pencils is recommended. Brands vary in their characteristics.

Berol Prismacolor, FaberCastell Venus Spectracolor: soft leads that produce brilliant colors but do not hold a point well; water resistant.

Berol Verithin: relatively hard leads that do not produce colors as brilliant as Prismacolor and Spectracolor, but they hold a sharp point well and also are water resistant. The sharp point is useful for inserting small details.

Mongol: about the same brilliance and hardness as Verithin and thus hold a point well. They are water soluble, permitting blending with water.

Other brands, such as Conté, Derwent, and Castell, are also good.

White gouache or acrylic paint: for highlights and bright white details (see chapter 2).

Tools

Brushes: small sable watercolor for dry-brushing highlights.

Erasers: Pink Pearl, Red Ruby, plastic erasers, among others.

X-Acto blade and holder, scratch knife: for working on scratchable surfaces such as Video Media board or frosted film.

Miscellaneous

Workable fixative.

White acrylic paint: in a spray can, for backpainting finished work on frosted film.

Matte acrylic media: see chapter 10.

TECHNIQUE

Transfer the detailed preliminary to the desired drawing support, using a light-hued colored pencil to coat the back of the tracing paper (see chapter 1). Graphite is not recommended for this, as colored pencils may not take well over it.

For most areas, particularly those that need to be brilliant or light in color, and especially if the background is dark, it is necessary first to cover the background evenly with white pencil, then overlay with colors. If film is used, backpainting it with white acrylic after rendering is completed also intensifies color.

Although the side of the pencil may be used for some effects, color should be applied in most cases with the point of the pencil. Use tiny, closely spaced strokes. These may be applied as crosshatching, side by side, at random, or in any combination. Do not smudge or blend the strokes with a stump because this will produce a shiny surface that will no longer accept pencil.

Begin with middle tones, working toward the darker and lighter values. Use combinations of colors to build up brilliant effects, such as yellows, yellow-greens, and blues to make a bright green. Lighten when necessary with white pencil on top of the other colors. In general, apply lighter colors over darker ones.

Avoid overworking. If the support becomes very shiny, that means it is saturated with pencil and no more color, especially lighter values, can be added, even after a workable fixative is applied. Careful erasing will dull the shiny pencil surface and remove enough dark tones to allow the area to be lightened. Coating with a thin glaze of matte acrylic medium also will provide a new working surface to which more pencil can be applied.

It may be difficult to render primary or wet highlights with pencil alone where pure, intense white is required, especially when they lie on a darker surface. Build up the highlights as well as possible with white pencil; avoid overworking them, which may result in muddy color. Then very delicately drybrush with white paint to increase the highlights to pure white. This will add greatly to the brilliance of the drawing. Unless this is done, the technique loses much of its effectiveness.

Many colors, especially in certain brands of pencils, will develop a dull, waxy film ("bloom") shortly after completion. This bloom is similar to the whitish coating on grapes or plums. Brilliance can be restored to the drawing after it is completed by spraying it with workable fixative. Test the fixative on a sample before spraying an illustration, since some fixatives will dissolve the colored pencil, make colors bleed, or change the entire effect.

There are, of course, many other techniques besides the three outlined that use pencils of various types for rendering, either alone or in combination. See chapter 7 for a technique that employs pencil on a specially textured surface called coquille board.

7/Coquille Board

Candy Feller and Elaine R. S. Hodges

Coquille board is a textured, uncoated drawing paper about the weight of three-ply Bristol board. The texture or grain is impressed into the paper during manufacture. It is commonly used for quick sketches, often for artwork in newspaper ads. With a little more attention, however, it can be used for scientific illustrations, producing aesthetically pleasing as well as functional results (fig. 7-1). It depicts color patterns very successfully (fig. 7-2; see also fig. 19-19).

Coquille board drawings are usually rendered in black and white, but the surface is also suitable for pastels and colored pencils. A technique using color is described toward the end of this chapter.

Two factors favor using this technique: time and money. Compared with other methods of showing form, color pattern, and habitus, rendering on coquille board takes very little time to learn or practice. It costs little to produce coquille board drawings, not only because it takes less time than such techniques as pen-and-ink and carbon dust to cover an area with shading, but also because the materials are relatively inexpensive. Such characteristics make it particularly useful to freelance illustrators as well as to scientists who do their own drawings. These drawings can be made to simulate the characteristics of other techniques (pen-and-ink stippling, halftone, lithography). If the artist emphasizes blacks and whites and minimizes grays, coquille board drawings can be photographed for printing as line art; hence, the printer avoids the additional expense of preparing halftone copy (fig. 7-3).

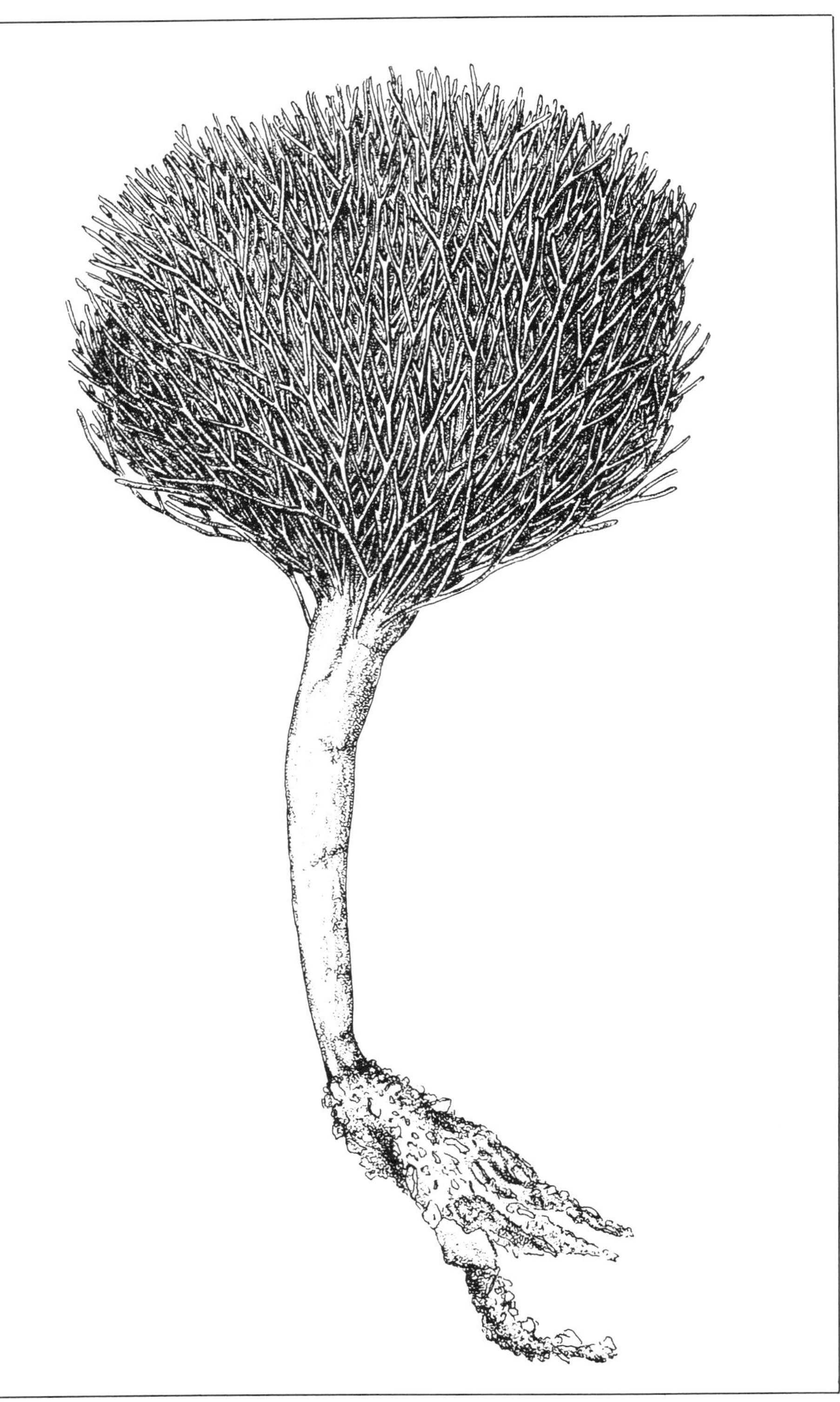

7-1. Conté pencils on fine coquille board. Alga, *Penicillus lamourouxii*, by Candy Feller. Courtesy of James Norris, Smithsonian Institution.

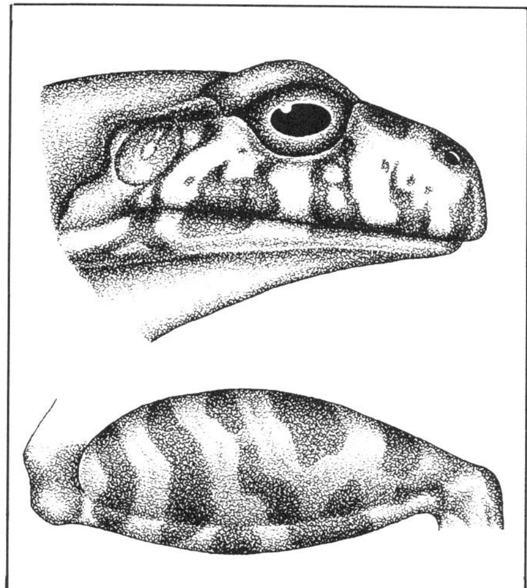

7-2. Conté pencils on fine coquille board used to render patterns. Ink was used for eye, nostril, and outline. Frog parts: head of *Leptodactylus labyrinthicus*, tibia of *L. flavopictus*, by Fran Irish. Courtesy of W. Ronald Heyer, Smithsonian Institution.

a

7-3. Venus Spectracolor no. 1406 pencil on coarse coquille board. Original is 13 inches (33cm) square. *(a)* Halftone reproduction. *(b)* Line reproduction. *(c)* Much-reduced line reproduction. Lichens, *Pilophorus robustus*, by Lucy C. Taylor © 1978. Courtesy of Department of Botany, University of Wisconsin, Madison.

b

c

Coquille board is not appropriate for all scientific illustrations, however. If very fine detail or a very smooth surface must be depicted, other techniques should be chosen. All the same, small details can be shown even on coarse-grained board if the work is done on a large scale. If shading is in the middle to dark values, there is little loss of detail despite great reduction (see fig. 7-3c). Normally, reduction should be no less than 50 percent of the original, but this depends on the drawing's detail. With specimens that have very delicate details—insects, for example—little or no reduction usually should be made. As when other techniques are photographed for printing, the lights tend to become lighter and the darks darker; therefore, it may be desirable to keep marks in a middle range of gray and to incorporate the white of the paper to show details, rather than shading very lightly. A gray value of less than 30 percent black tends to disappear in reproduction. Labeling should be done on an overlay (see Labels in chapter 1) because coquille board is so soft that any attempt to change a label will destroy the surface.

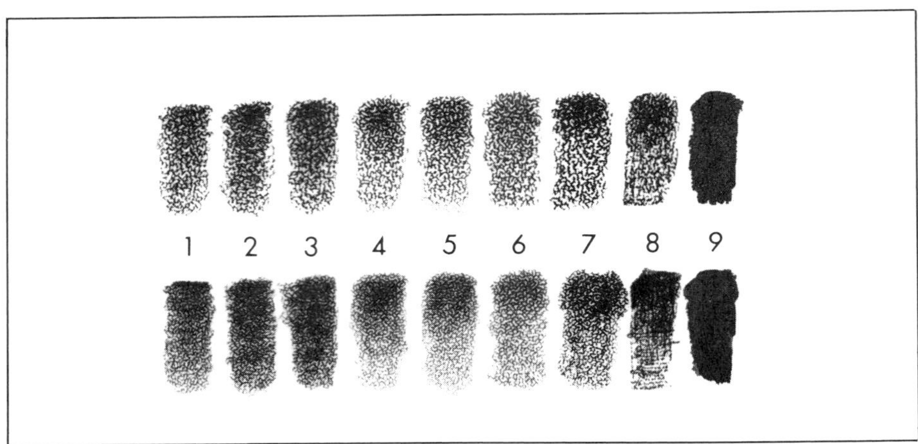

7-4. Samples of various media on coquille board. Top: coarse; bottom: fine. (1) Wolff's carbon B; (2) Wolff's carbon BBB; (3) Conté 3B; (4) Prismacolor 935; (5) Spectracolor 1406; (6) graphite 4B; (7) "China-Riter" grease pencil; (8) BIC felt-tipped marker, fine point; (9) india ink with brush.

MATERIALS

Surfaces

Coquille board: two grain sizes are available, fine and coarse (fig. 7-4). The size of the drawing and the degree of reduction, as well as the specimen, will determine which grain to use, but in general fine-grained coquille board is the choice for scientific illustrations. Coquille board has a right side and a wrong side; the drawing surface has more evenly distributed, deeper impressions with higher ridges than the back side. Occasionally a sheet of coquille board has imperfections such as bald spots, which interfere with the uniformity of the texture, and some will not take ink without bleeding. Since such flaws will interrupt the stipple effect of the rendered drawing, examine the drawing surface of each sheet before buying, if possible, or before drawing on it. Ask to test a sample in the store.

Because coquille board is not presized, it should be sprayed with several coats of workable fixative before pen-and-ink work begins. Otherwise, the soft, spongy surface might not accept ink well. Some sheets are worse than others, and occasionally only a portion of a sheet will be too soft. If such an area is found after a drawing is underway, turn the board over, tape down the edges, spray enough to soak the back with fixative, and allow to dry for at least thirty minutes. The fixative penetrates and strengthens the paper, making it more workable.

Media

India ink.

Pencils: four basic types of black pencils generally are used with coquille board: carbon (Wolff's HB and B, Conté Pierre Noire no. 1710 HB through 3B, Ritmo Charcoal 3B, or other soft chalky pencils; see Charcoal Pencils in chapter 2), graphite, carbon/wax (Venus Spectracolor 1406, Berol Prismacolor 935, and other black colored pencils), and grease, marking, or lithographic pencils (Staedtler-Mars Omnichrom 108–9). As described in chapter 2, the principle of fat over lean should be followed for large areas: more greasy or waxy pencils should be used only on top of drier pencil marks. Therefore, if the different types of pencils are combined in one drawing, the carbon type should be used first, then the graphite (except for outlines), then the carbon/wax, with the greasy types used last. Graphite usually is used first for transferred outlines, but it does not interfere in this case with overlying drier media such as carbon pencils because the area covered by an outline is very small.

Carbon pencils should be corrected with a kneaded rubber eraser. For black colored pencils, use a pencil-shaped eraser; the kneaded rubber is too soft. The grease-based pencils, such as lithographic or marking pencils, are very difficult to correct except with opaque white paint.

Conté and Ritmo pencils produce richer tones, and the texture of the lead goes into coquille board better than that from Wolff's carbon pencils does, but Conté and Ritmo pencils produce more dust than Wolff's carbon pencils do and are therefore messier. The dust, however, is easily removed with a kneaded eraser. Graphite pencils should be used only in the 3H to 7B range, since harder leads will abrade the surface. Because of their light tones, graphite renderings require halftone reproduction. Grease-based pencils achieve rich tones, but after several years they are likely to develop a waxy, gray, or whitish film on their surface. Spraying with workable fixative may prevent this problem.

Pencils used for details must be sharpened frequently. To sharpen by hand, use an X-Acto blade to whittle the wood about ½ inch (12mm) back off the lead. Direct the blade away from you and toward the tip of the pencil. Keep at least two pencils sharpened: one with a finely pointed tip and one with an acutely beveled tip. Use a sandpaper pad or other sharpener frequently to keep the tips shaped and sharpened.

Felt-tipped markers: as black as possible; can be used by themselves or with the pencils listed above. Must be corrected with opaque white paint; cannot be erased.

White paint: gouache or acrylic for highlights and corrections (see chapter 2).

Tools

Pens: technical (3×0, 4×0); fine-pointed conventional pens.

Brushes: 0 to 5×0.

Erasers: kneaded rubber; soft pencil-shaped eraser such as Magic Rub or Kleen-Off.

Embossing tool: should have a small, smooth point, such as an old dental probe or old, dry ballpoint pen.

X-Acto blade in handle.

Sandpaper pad or other pencil sharpener.

Miscellaneous

Workable fixative.

TECHNIQUE

Prepare a detailed sketch of the specimen on tracing paper. Work out all tonal problems on the sketch, keeping in mind the percentage of black each area represents. Make certain the original drawing is accurate before transferring to avoid the need for correcting on the coquille board. Transfer the outlines and details of the sketch with graphite paper (see chapter 1). The hard rubbing required for double-transfer methods impresses the coquille board and should not be used, but other single-transfer methods may be used. When taping the tracing-paper sketch and graphite paper to the coquille board, be careful that the tape touches only the edges. Most tapes will pull the surface off the paper. Remove the sketch and graphite paper. Go over the drawing with a relatively soft graphite pencil (3H or softer) to strengthen the lines. Do not use much pressure or the surface will dent or abrade.

Throughout the work, handle the drawing surface as little as possible and with clean hands. Keep paper under your drawing hand. These precautions are necessary because skin oil makes smooth, even shading impossible.

Ink all hard lines, including setae or hairs, on drawings of hard-edged specimens such as insects (fig. 7-5a). Touch the surface with the pen very lightly to avoid nicking it, since this will cause the ink to bleed into the surface. Using a brush instead of a pen eliminates this problem. For some drawings it may be advisable to add noncontinuous ink lines after pencil shading. The softer effect of a penciled line may add to the sense of depth (atmospheric perspective), whereas a hard line could flatten the form.

Use the pencils to shade in details, leaving white or highlighted areas blank. Sharp highlights may be produced by using an embossing tool at this point to push down

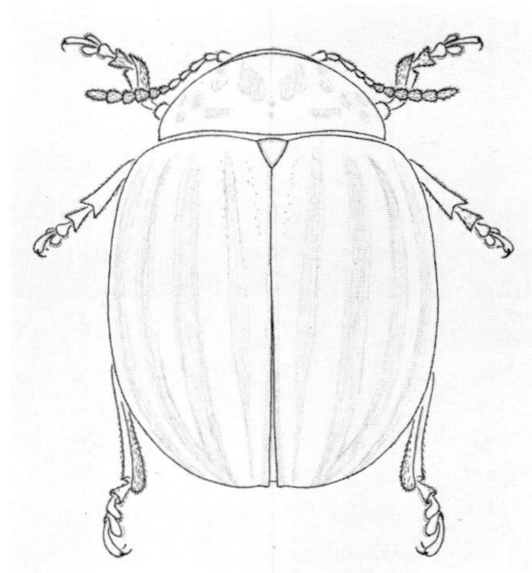
a

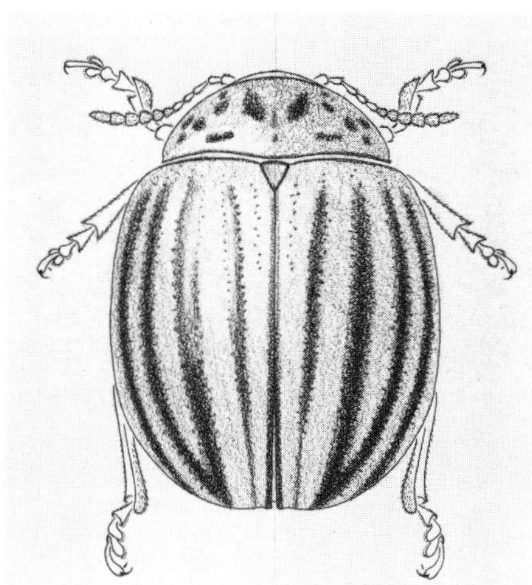
b

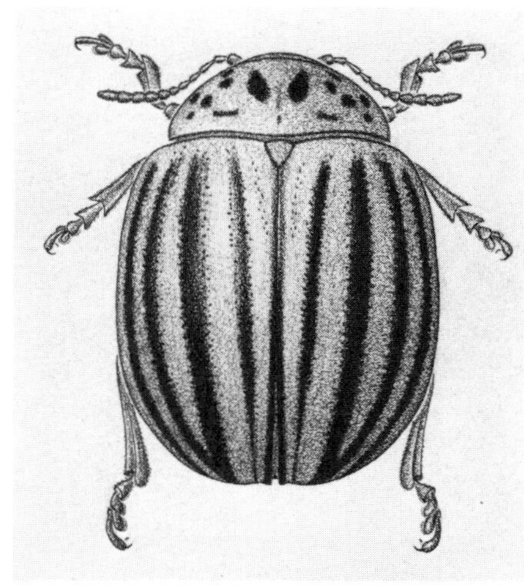
c

7-5. Conté pencils and ink on fine coquille board. *(a)* Ink outline and hairs on transferred and reinforced drawing; *(b)* color pattern established with highlight area left light or white; *(c)* shading added to complete drawing. Chrysomelid beetle, *Leptinotarsa* species, by Candy Feller © 1982.

the surface so that pencils skip the indented areas, leaving them white (fig. 7-6).

Establish the color pattern, if there is one, as though the specimen were flat, ignoring form for the moment (fig. 7-5b). To prevent carbon from spreading outside the shaded outline, do not blend carbon or carbon/wax pencils all the way into the outline; stop just before the edge. Then delicately stipple with ink, matching the coquille pattern, from the pencil shading to the inked outline (fig. 7-7). Apply shading, simulating the texture of the specimen. Work carefully near the highlighted or white areas to keep them clean.

After the color pattern is established, continue working with the pencil, now adding contrast to give form to the illustration. Work carefully to avoid damaging the surface. If very dark or black areas are needed, carefully build up these tones with the pencils. Darker shades can be attained by stippling or painting ink in the dark areas, applying a fine felt-tipped marker or grease pencil, or brushing on black watercolor with very little water (fig. 7-5c). If grease pencil is used, it should be applied last.

Additional highlights can be added with white paint and a fine brush on top of the pencil. Correct or lighten with erasers. Cut pencil-shaped erasers to a sharp wedge to make crisp edges or details on carbon/wax penciling. To correct shading with carbon pencils, a gentle "pickup" motion with a kneaded eraser will remove tone or excess carbon without damaging the paper surface or smudging the carbon.

Corrections can be made with white paint. However, try not to shade over painted areas because the paint fills in the grooves of the board, producing a different effect when pencil is applied over it. An electric eraser can be used very carefully for inked lines, but it will remove the textured surface. If that happens, it is possible to simulate the texture with careful pencil or ink stippling or both.

When the shading is completed and all smudges have been removed with a clean eraser, spray the drawing with two or three coats of workable fixative. Cover it with paper for added protection.

7-6. Embossing tool used to create white areas to be skipped over by the pencil. Photo by Vic Krantz, Smithsonian Office of Printing and Photographic Services.

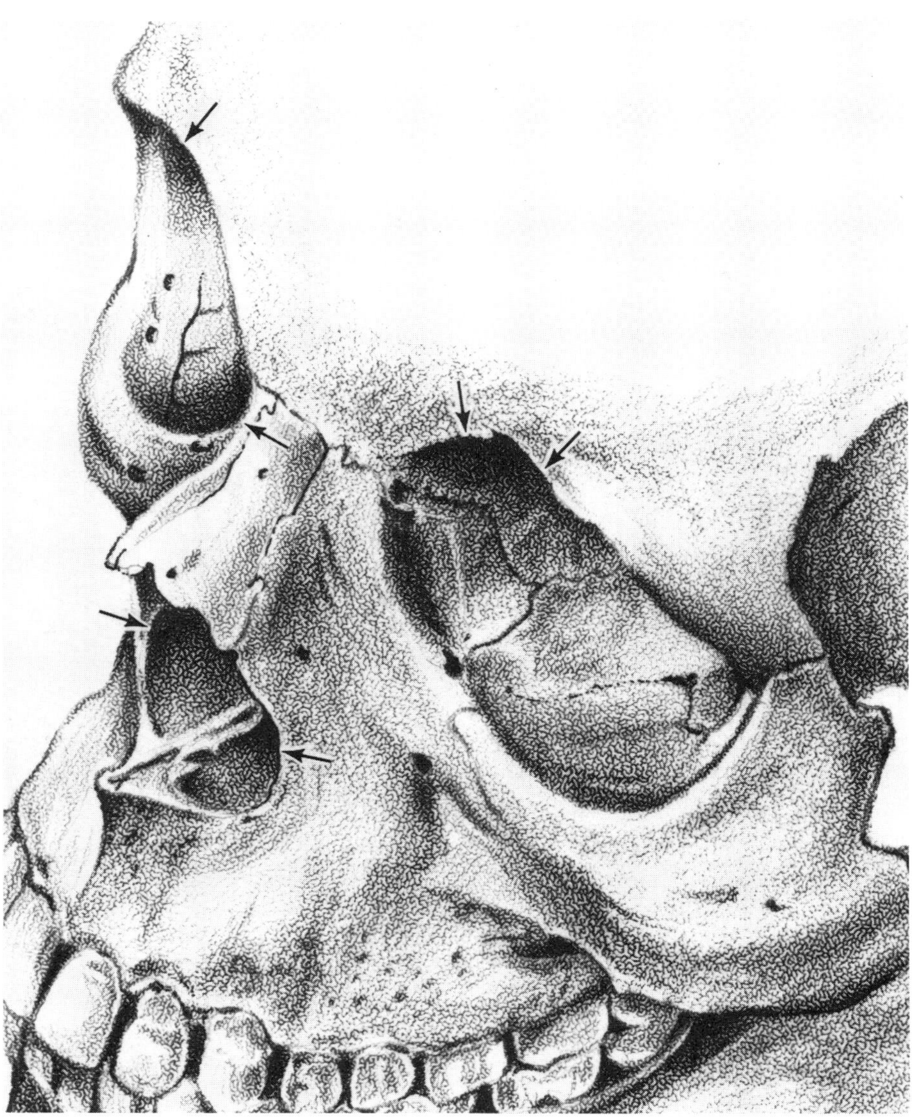

7-7. Hardmuth Negro no. 3 pencil on fine coquille board. Ink was stippled to edges of dark areas (note arrows). Detail of skull, by William L. Brudon. From *Essentials of Human Anatomy*, 8th ed., by R. T. Woodburne (Oxford University Press, 1988). Reprinted by permission.

Pastels, Pencil, and Paint on Coquille Board

Karen L. Allaben-Confer

Pastels can be applied to coquille board in several ways. They adhere well to its textured surface, while producing extremely soft tones. In contrast, paint convincingly renders hard objects such as a bird's beak. Paint fills in the texture of coquille board, creating a smooth surface on which fine detail can be drawn with any pencil, and pastel dust is accepted uniformly (fig 7-8; see fig. C-6).

MATERIALS

Surfaces

Coquille board: fine or coarse texture.

Media

Pastels: Carb-Othello pencil pastels, which are relatively hard and therefore retain a point, permitting greater control over rendering of fine details; softer stick pastels.

Paint: watercolor or acrylic.

Ink: india and colors.

Pencils: graphite, H to 6B.

Tools

Tortillions and stumps (stomps).

Brushes: small, flat, sable, like those used for carbon dust.

Eraser: kneaded rubber.

Abrasive surface: fine sandpaper, such as 400-grit or crocus cloth.

Miscellaneous

Workable fixative.

TECHNIQUE

Transfer the preliminary drawing as described for the first technique in this chapter. Do not spray the board with fixative, however, before beginning to draw. Draw directly onto the coquille board with pencil pastels carefully sanded to a fine point or beveled for broader lines. The texture of the paper softens the colors at first, but as the pastels are built up, richer tones will result. To produce opaque colors with very rich hues, lightly spray each layer with workable fixative. The fixative tends to strengthen the surface of the coquille board while raising its tooth, and ensures that when the next layer of color is laid down, the first layer will not be removed or softened more by the overworking. The light spray of fixative also allows some blending of colors where desirable.

Apply additional layers of pastel in a manner similar to that used with carbon dust. Use the softer pastel sticks and sand them carefully on sandpaper to produce colored dust. Apply with small brushes, using a different one for each color to prevent unwanted mixing. As in the carbon dust technique, tones are built by layers.

Alternatively, use tortillions to apply dust to the paper. Achieve detail by drawing fine lines with the sharp point of the tortillion.

All three means of applying the medium produce very soft tones and allow subtle blending of colors and gradual shading; careful manipulation of the stump can produce sharp, hard tones as well. Leaving the paper white at the high points of curved surfaces makes

7-8. Pastel and graphite pencils on coquille board, with pastels used like carbon dust. The eyes were painted with black ink. "Scarlett's Hungry Eyasses" (peregrine falcons), by Karen L. Allaben-Confer © 1980.

clear and crisp highlights and reflections. Watercolor or ink can be applied judiciously to areas of darkest shadow or intense detail.

A fourth approach is useful when dark, rich tones are needed. For instance, to achieve a velvety black, put down a fairly dark but very thin layer of watercolor over the areas requiring the rich black. Do not get the surface too wet because the coquille board might begin to disintegrate. The coquille board may buckle slightly when wet but will return to its former shape when it dries. Let the watercolor dry completely (blowing with a hair dryer may help) to a flat, one-dimensional hue. Fill in the dried, dark regions with black pastel. As it covers the watercolor, the pastel creates a velvety texture. To insert a slight sheen or highlight, spray the black pastel with a good dose of fixative, let it dry, then carefully blend a bluish-gray or other light pastel over the highlighted areas.

Graphite pencils create soft detail. As with pastels, soften the penciled areas with the tortillion or stump and blend watercolor or ink into the darkest tones. You can achieve a more realistic result by leaving edges soft. Be sure, however, to clean the background close to the outline of the drawing with a kneaded rubber eraser so that the subject is cleanly presented and does not appear out of focus.

Although coquille board is not suited to all styles, subjects, and media, it is clearly worth exploring. The speed and economy gained by using it, as well as the range of effects made possible by the textured surface, make it a useful and versatile material for the scientific illustrator.

8/Carbon Dust

Elsie Herbold Froeschner and
L. Michael Druckenbrod

Rarely can we trace the development of a particular drawing method over a long period of time, but the carbon dust technique is an exception. It gained prominence in America through the drawings and teachings of Max Brödel, the first director of the Department of Art as Applied to Medicine at the Johns Hopkins University (fig. 8-1). Since 1911, when Brödel began teaching, the carbon dust technique has become widely used in medical as well as general scientific illustration. Essentially, the technique involves drawing images with carbon pencils and working up three-dimensional form by application of carbon dust with dry brush. Direct drawing is done by carbon pencils. Highlights are either scratched out or painted on, depending on the surface used. It is a flexible technique that allows for great tonal development well suited to the various interpretations required by many scientific disciplines. By employing graded tones—from palest gray to rich, intense black—on a stipple-surfaced coated paper or other surfaces, toothed or plain, it is possible to express three-dimensional form and surface texture and also to translate the tonal values of color patterns. The same technique can be used with graphite dust, but the end product displays a more limited range of grays and no rich blacks unless a darker medium such as diluted ink is added (see fig. 8-18).

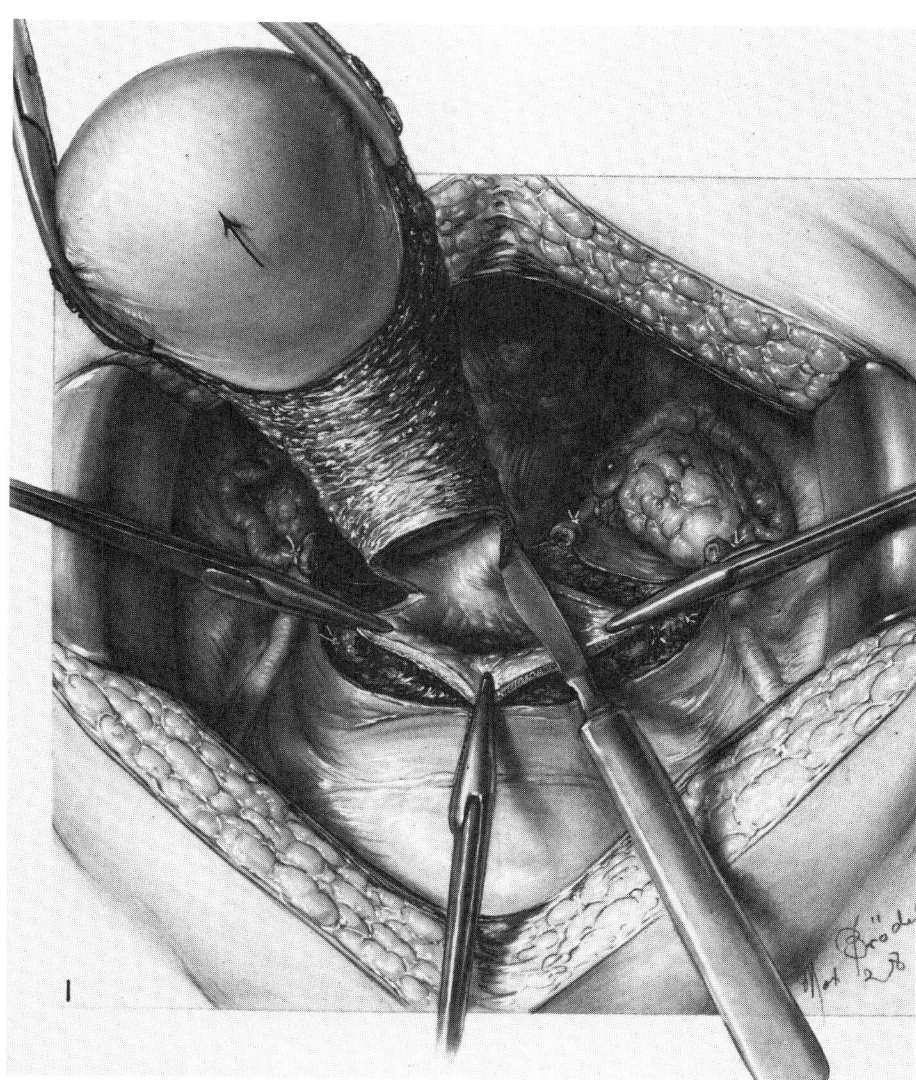

8-1. The carbon dust technique as developed by Max Brödel. Carbon dust, pencil, and india ink on Ross stipple board no. 8, scratched highlights. Conservative total hysterectomy: amputation of uterus and cervix across the vaginal vault. Courtesy of Art as Applied to Medicine, The Johns Hopkins Medical School, Permanent Collections (no. 823 Brödel Collection).

For well over fifty years, the carbon dust technique was used on Ross stipple boards, ranging from no. 00 to no. 27. The most popular one was the no. 00 illustration board (fig. 8-2; see fig. 1-12), a white calcium-coated board with a finely stippled surface. After Ross board ceased to be manufactured in 1971, the technique continued to be used on a variety of paper and boards such as Media, Video, and Anjac, all of which appeared and disappeared in a relatively short time span (figs. 8-3, 8-4, 8-5) to be replaced by others. Today it is applied to a variety of surfaces, such as board, paper, and drafting film. Thus the technique lives on with modifications dictated by the surfaces available.

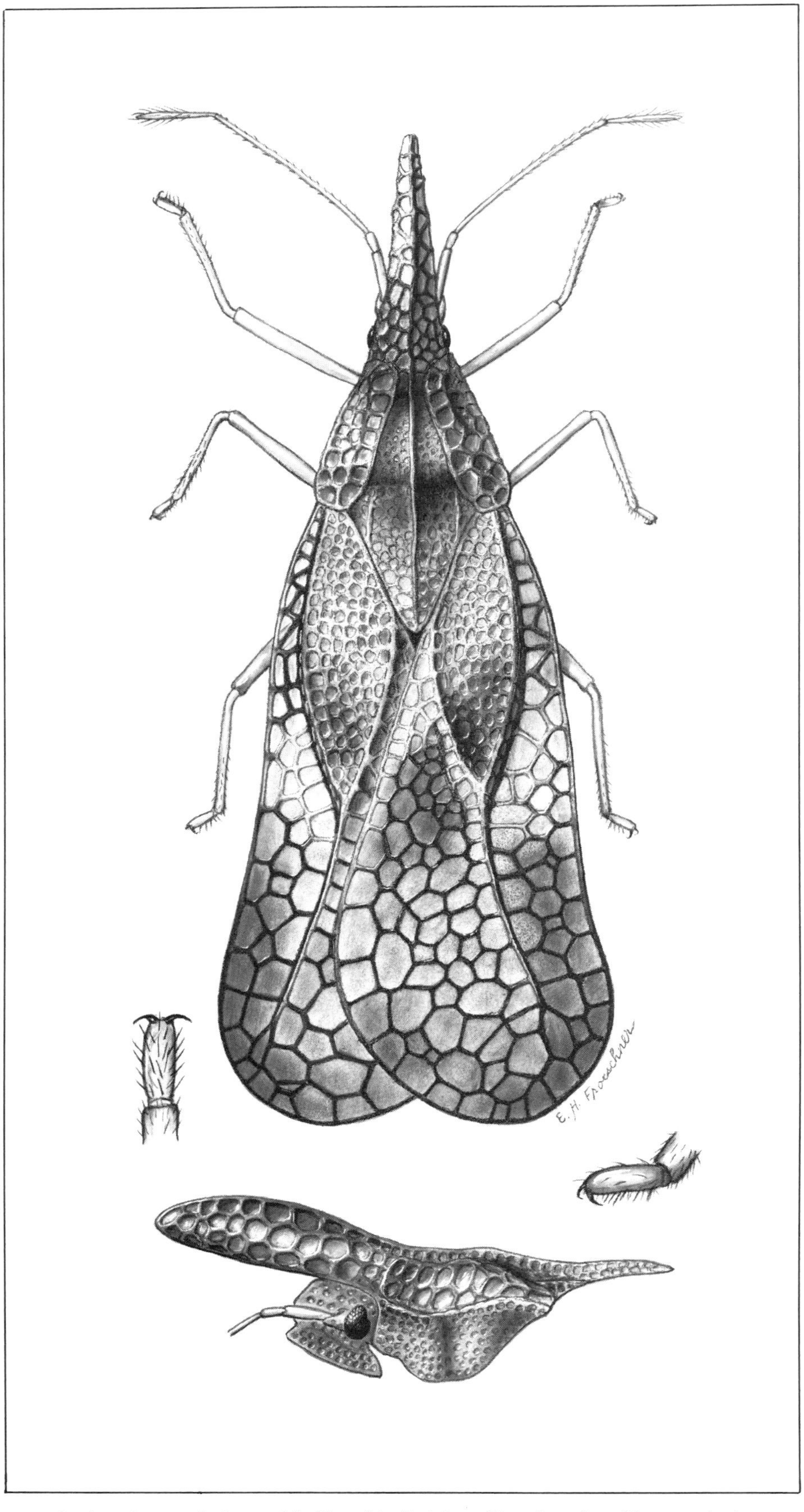

8-2. Carbon dust technique with diluted india ink on Ross board no.00, scratched highlights. Lacebug, tingid, *Aepykorys proekes*, by Elsie Herbold Froeschner.

This chapter will describe the classic black-on-white carbon dust technique on both opaque and translucent surfaces as well as an innovative application of the technique using white on black.

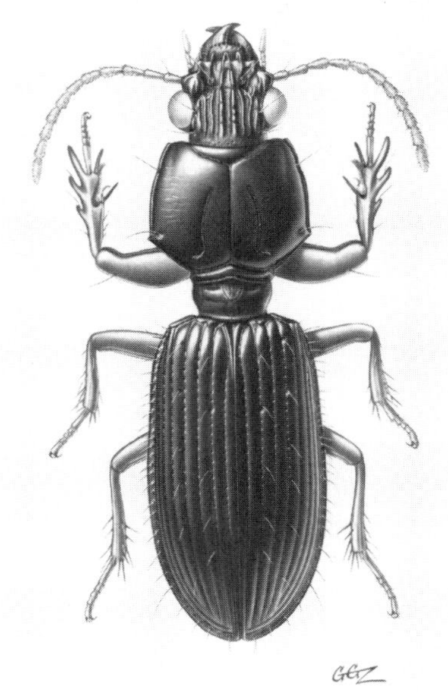

8-3. Carbon dust technique on Video board. Pencil used directly on surface, then smudged with a stump, produced the deep blacks. Beetle, a species of *Schizogenius*, by Gloria Gordon Zimmer. Courtesy of Terry Erwin.

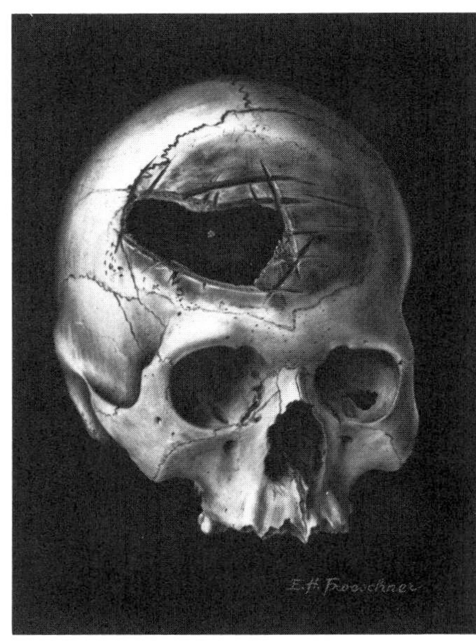

8-4. Carbon dust technique with lampblack watercolor on Anjac board, scratched highlights. Trephination in ancient Peruvian skull, by Elsie Herbold Froeschner.

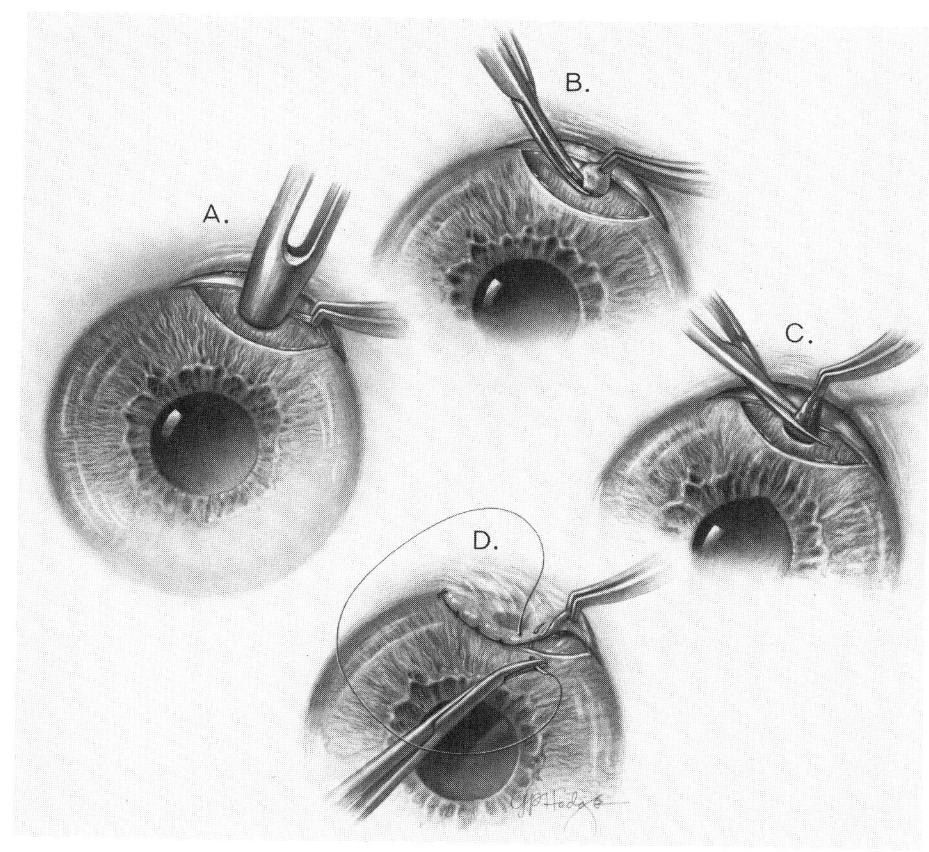

8-5. *(A)* Silver point, lampblack watercolor, graphite pencils, and carbon dust on Media paper. *(B)* Carbon dust was applied first to establish the dark areas; then graphite was used to finish most of the drawing. *(C)* Silver point created some of the delicate strands of the iris; lampblack watercolor was added for contrast and to define details. *(D)* The faded edges of the eyes exemplify vignetting. Filtering corneal trephine operation for glaucoma, by Gerald P. Hodge. Courtesy of the University of Michigan.

Carbon Dust on Opaque Surfaces

MATERIALS

Surfaces

Calcium-, acrylic-, or clay-coated board or paper: see chart 8-1. Closely examine the surface of the board or paper chosen for the final rendering. Coated boards must be free of cracks, fingerprints, or surface irregularities, and must be mounted on a fairly heavy board to maintain rigidity.

Mounting board.

Media

Pencils: several types needed:

- Carbon drawing pencils—see Charcoal Pencils in chapter 2: Wolff's HH through BBB, Conté Pierre Noire no. 1710 H through 3B; Ritmo charcoal HB, B, 3B. The Conté pencils tend to produce a richer black than do the Wolff's pencils, especially the Conté 3B, which is the softest and grinds to a very fine, soft dust, finer particles than those from Wolff's pencils.
- Graphite pencils: 2B, HB, 3H, 8H, 10H.
- White pencil: for highlights, such as those listed in chapter 2.

White paint: for highlights (see chapter 2).

Lampblack watercolor and diluted india ink.

Silver wire: for delicate details.

Tools

Abrasive surface: for creating dust, such as emery cloth, metal file, or silicon carbide paper, 3M no. 400. Do not use coarse sandpaper because grit will come off and scratch the drawing (Figures 8-7 and 8-9 show a sandpaper pad being used; this is not recommended.)

Brushes: large squirrel or camel round brush (for large areas); flat short-haired sable nos. 2, 3, 4, 6 (nos. 12 and 20 if needed for large work). Carbon dusting is a dry-brush technique, and some illustrators use only brushes that have never been moistened before, believing that moisture destroys the bounce necessary for smooth tones. Others believe good results can be achieved with brushes washed with care and allowed to dry thoroughly.

Chart 8-1. Comparison of Opaque Surfaces

Name	Surface Type	% Black with Carbon Pencil[1]	% Black Carbon Dust with Brush[1]	Shading with Brush	Lightening with Chamois	Lightening with Eraser	Scratched Highlights
Dull-finish stipple board (Medical Models)	thick clay coating	dark, about 95%; stumps fairly smoothly	75%	smooth; some texture	effective	effective	sharp
ChromaRama (Prestype) (white and colors)	acrylic smooth surface	dark, about 95%; stumps well	75%	smooth; dark tones	fair	effective	sharp and crisp; do not dig deeply
Color-Aid (Color-Aid Corp.) (white and colors)	very light coating (fine tooth)	dark, about 85%; does not stump very well	70%	smooth	not as effective	effective	sharp
ColorMatch (Ohio Graphic Arts) (white and colors)	light clay coating (fine tooth)	dark, about 95%; does not stump very well	70%	smooth	not as effective	effective (Pink Pearl)	sharp
15B medical board (Ess Dee)	clay coated	dark, about 80%; stumps fairly well	75%	smooth; shows stipple	effective	effective	sharp
14B suede board (Ess Dee)	thin clay coating	dark, about 85%; stumps fairly well	75%	fairly smooth; some grain	fairly effective; possible sheen	effective	sharp and crisp
Brite-white #205 and #215 (Crescent)	hot-press illustration board	dark, 85%; stumps fairly well	70–75%	fairly smooth	effective	effective	will not scratch cleanly
Line Kote #210 and #220 (Crescent)	thinly coated illustration board	dark, 90%; stumps well	70–75%	fairly smooth	fair	effective	can scratch sharply but may gouge
Coated cover dull 100 lb. (Wedgwood)	cover stock; fine tooth; light coating	not very dark; stumps fairly well	60%	difficult to get smooth	not very effective	fairly effective	sharp
Smooth ledger paper	smooth surface	dark, 90%; stumps well	70–75%	can get smooth	effective	effective	will not scratch sharply
Video Media (Crestwood Paper Co., Arthur Brown Co.)	smooth surface	dark, 95%; stumps well	75%	uneven; difficult	effective	effective	not sharp and crisp

1. This represents the percentage of black obtainable without fixing the surface. Spraying once or twice with alcohol or workable fixative and then dusting over will increase the richness and darkness.

Erasers: Pink Pearl, plastic (vinyl), kneaded rubber, Kleen-Off eraser (Eberhard Faber no. 41).

Tortillions and stumps (stomps): various sizes.

Cork: soft fine grain; in pastel or charcoal holder.

Chamois: small round piece gathered in tip of pastel, lead, or charcoal holder. Narrow strips or ear-shaped pieces in drinking straws or other holders.

Cotton swabs.

Scraper: any type of sharp-edged scratcher or scriber, such as Hunt curved-edge scratch knife; no. 15 Bard-Parker surgical blade and holder; etching tool, sharpened at an oblique angle; or no. 16 X-Acto blade in handle.

Miscellaneous

Fixative: workable fixative or ethyl alcohol in atomizer.

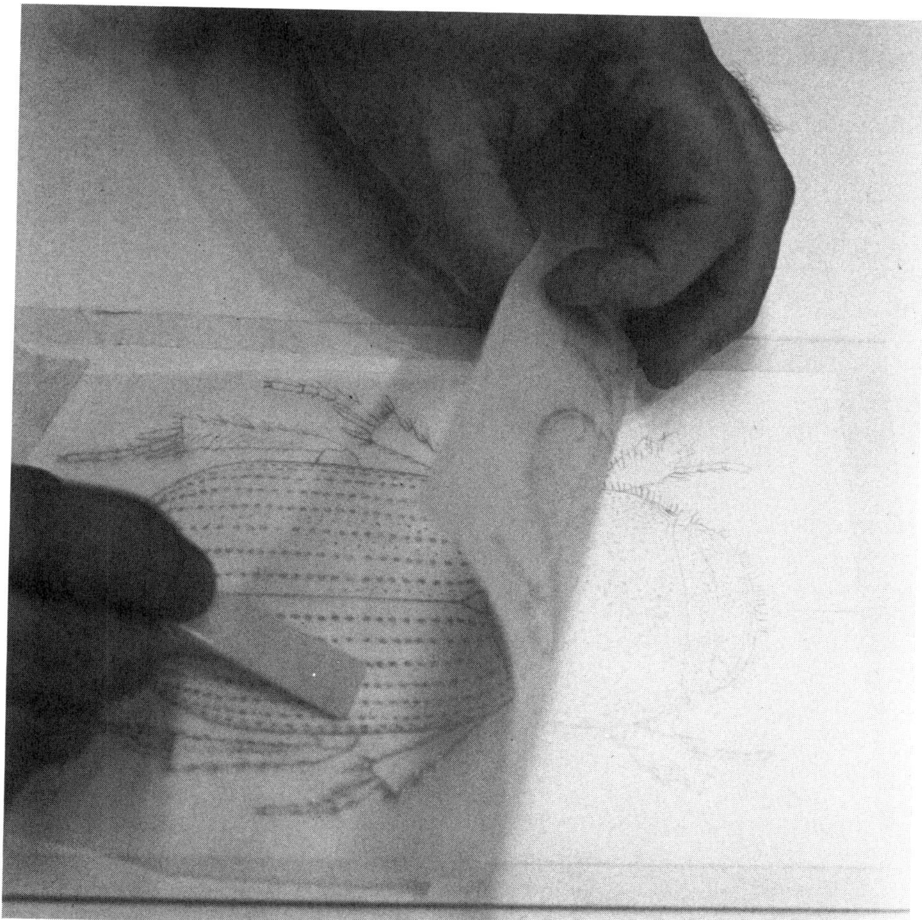

8-6. Transferring the preliminary drawing with a burnisher. Note pale lines of final image. Photo by T. J. Spilman.

TECHNIQUE

Skin oils in fingerprints attract carbon dust, and fingerprints can show in the printed image. It is important, therefore, to protect the drawing surface throughout the work. Handle it as little as possible, touching the edges only. Take the precautions described in chapter 1: mask the surface and use a slip of paper under your drawing hand or wear cotton gloves with the fingers cut off.

In this technique, the coated surface is mounted *before* the work begins. Choose a mounting board of the appropriate weight and use double-adhesive tape or fine-grade white paste on the edges (see chapter 2). In high-humidity environments, it may be necessary to dry the coated surface before mounting it so that tones will brush on most evenly. Do this by placing the board or paper briefly in a drymount press set at medium heat or under a warm light, or put it in an oven (150° to 200°F) for a few minutes. If possible, work in an air-conditioned room or near a dehumidifier.

Transfer the preliminary drawing by the double-transfer method or use graphite paper (fig. 8-6, and see chapter 1).

Strengthen weakly registered image lines using H or HB carbon pencils applied evenly but not heavily. Reinforce all details that should not be lost under the carbon dust, especially structural details specific to the subject. These can be veins, nerves, hairs, scales, or a variety of pits and protuberances. Do not sharply darken any lines that should not appear as a hard line in the final rendering.

If some of these lines later become obliterated by the dusting, place the original sketch over the drawing surface with a clean sheet of nonoily tracing paper or thin drafting film, matte side down, between the two. Make sure everything is lined up accurately. With a sharp pencil, go over all details, pressing firmly but not too hard. The lines again will become apparent on the drawing surface, but this time as light negative lines where the dust was lifted onto the paper or film sandwiched between.

Applying Dust

Make a supply of carbon dust by rubbing the softest grades of carbon pencils on an abrasive surface and collecting the resulting dust in a small box. Or pick up the dust directly and lightly from the abrasive with a brush as you "paint." Take care that no carbon flakes or other particles are in the dust.

For large areas, dip a large camel or squirrel round brush into the dust, then tap out the excess on chamois thumbtacked to a work surface or on scrap paper. This knocks off particles that might streak. Apply the dust in a very light, thin, and even layer (fig. 8-7). Build the layers of dust gradually to achieve the desired darkness. Putting on too much dust too fast may result in a streaky and blotchy tone. Never scrub hard; this may damage the surface and make later application of the dust difficult.

If the surface will not accept more dust but a darker tone is required, create a new base by spraying with ethyl alcohol in an atomizer or with a workable fixative. Be sure first to mask the parts that are not to be sprayed, then spray the dark areas. Repeat to achieve a deep, velvety black with additional applications of dust.

Use sable flat brushes of various sizes to work carbon dust up to the outlines with a side-to-side motion (fig. 8-8), then continue to give form by softly brushing, blending thin layers of dust into dark or light areas. Leave the general highlight area unshaded or lightly shaded. Sharp, crisp highlights can be scraped out or painted on later.

Keeping the overall specimen in mind, build up all areas of the drawing to maintain a tonal balance. Smooth blending between light and dark areas enhances the drawing. If an area becomes too dark, lighten it carefully with a piece of clean chamois in a holder or a cotton swab. If too much dust has accumulated, stand the drawing on one edge and tap lightly or gently blow off dust.

It is possible to build small areas of tone quickly by directly shading with very soft carbon pencils, smudged smooth with brushes and stumps (see fig. 8-3). However, it is usually difficult to achieve the smoothest texture and remove streaks on large areas unless a very light pencil touch is maintained. The safest way to produce very smooth tones is with a slow buildup of brushed dust.

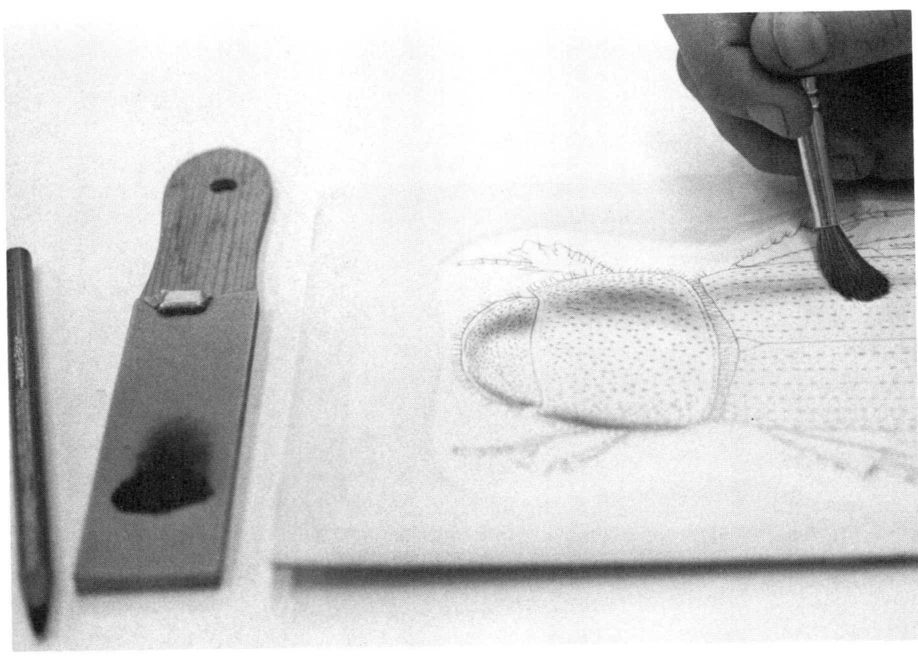

8-7. Applying carbon dust to large areas of deeper tone with a large round brush. Note paper mask. Photo by T. J. Spilman.

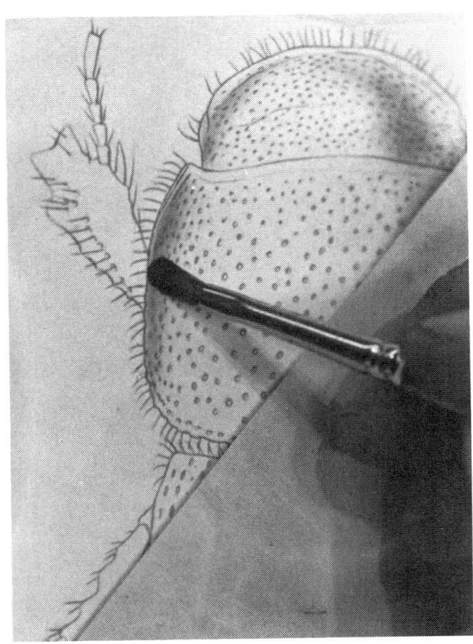

8-8. Modeling form by using a small flat brush in a side-to-side motion to apply carbon dust close to the outline. Photo by T. J. Spilman.

With the three-dimensional form established, it is time to work on surface texture and tonal values of color patterns. The techniques employed become a matter of preference for the individual artist. Among the options are brushes, pencils, chamois, or eraser edges cut to a chisel shape. Sometimes using a chisel-shaped eraser (in effect, drawing in reverse) works nicely to create white or light lines and areas. But never erase a large area with plans to reapply dust if a smooth effect is desired, especially on clay-coated papers. If the area is still too dark or does not erase smoothly, use charcoal white pencil, white pastel, or a white Conté stick. Add areas of dark by dipping a pointed cork in dust and applying as lines or spots. Use stumps or well-worn brushes to apply small areas of dark or to smooth tonal areas or lines (fig. 8-9). If a suitable worn brush is unavailable, use a blade to trim the hairs on a new brush to a shorter length or singe the hairs by holding the brush horizontally and quickly rotating it past a match held under the hair edges.

Use a carbon pencil (HB, B, or BB) directly for emphasis or to delineate such details as pits, protuberances, grooves, or an abrupt line where value changes (fig. 8-10). Use the cork, brush, or stump

8-9. Depicting grooves by using a small worn brush to widen the carbon pencil lines. Photo by T. J. Spilman.

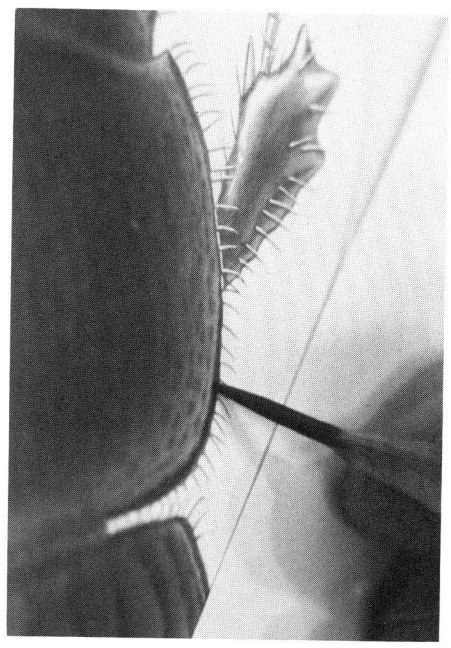

8-10. Using a sharp pencil to delineate details such as narrow edges, pits, dark hairs, and lines of demarcation. Photo by T. J. Spilman.

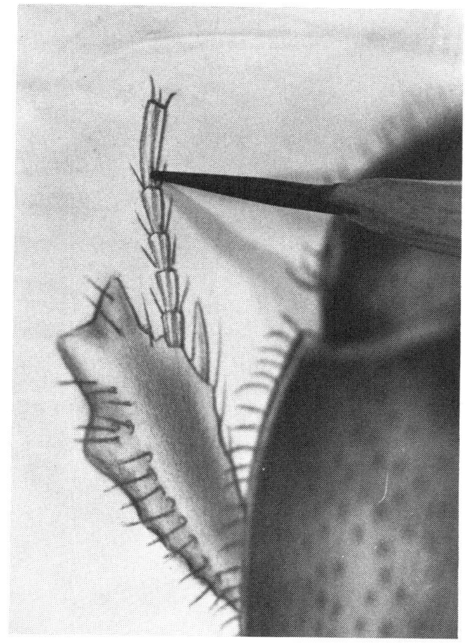

8-11. Direct use of carbon pencil to indicate shadowed area in a small structure. Photo by T. J. Spilman.

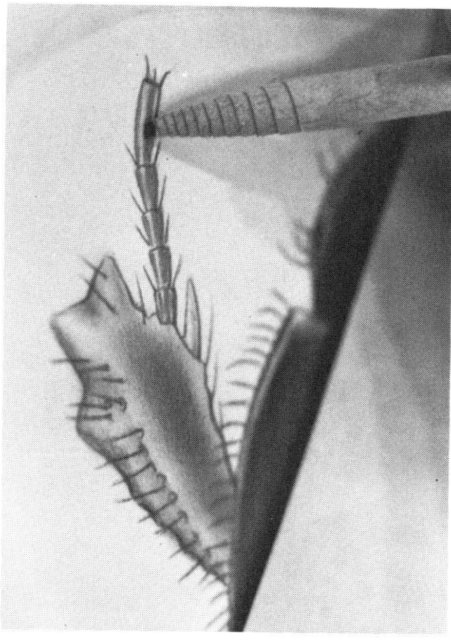

8-12. Using a tortillion to widen the shaded area in a small structure. Photo by T. J. Spilman.

to smooth lines, but do so judiciously to avoid creating a streaky texture.

In small areas such as insect legs, plant stems, or small blood vessels, shade with a carbon B or BB pencil (fig. 8-11), then blend with a pointed cork, small flat brush, or stump (fig. 8-12). Hard graphite pencils, 8H to 10H, register quite darkly on some clay-coated papers and can be used for emphasis. Use softer grades of graphite pencils on other papers or boards.

Some artists add silver point for very fine, pale, sensitive detailing (see fig. 8-5), using heavy-gauge silver wire (about 1⁄16 inch or 1.5mm thick) in a mechanical lead holder. Because they are so delicate, such lines may be lost in reproduction unless handled by a very good printer. Eventually the lines on the original drawings may darken as the silver oxidizes.

Highlights and Accents

Create highlights by removing the dust from an area with chamois or by light, careful erasing. Make sharp, bright highlights with a sharply cut, chisel-shaped plastic (vinyl) eraser or the Kleen-Off pencil eraser. The very sharpest highlights on coated boards are those scraped off from a darker background (fig. 8-13). Scraping with a sharp tool is particularly well suited for depiction of hairs, spines, and protruding surface structures (fig. 8-14). Scrape carefully and do it last: an error can be difficult to repair! Use a sharpening stone to keep a sharp edge on blades and points, ensuring crisp lines.

If sharp highlights cannot be scratched, paint them on with one of the opaque white paints. For highlights that are sharp but should not appear bright white, scratch or paint them and then lightly brush with carbon dust.

Add emphasis, if needed, with lampblack watercolor or diluted india ink applied carefully with a brush. Sometimes fine pen-and-ink work is appropriate. Experiment with these modes of emphasis before applying to a final drawing.

For light-colored specimens such as bones, fossils, and pale plants, a dark background may be desirable. First cover the drawing of the specimen with a mask of tracing paper that has been cut to match the outline of the drawing. Using square brushes (brights), dust in the background, carefully working around the masked drawing. Use smaller square brushes when working close to the edge of the drawing. To obtain rich, velvety tones, spray workable fixative lightly between layers of dust. Such colored coated papers as Color-Aid, ChromaRama, and ColorMatch also can be used to provide a contrasting background.

Corrections, Repairs and Completion

An unwanted scratch or gouge can be darkened with an extremely sharp soft carbon pencil. If the scratch is large, wait until the drawing is completed and touch up with diluted lampblack watercolor, being sure to match up tonal values.

If a fingerprint shows up in the shading, carefully dab it with a soft clean cloth moistened with rubber-cement thinner. (Remember how flammable this thinner is, and cover the can tightly after pouring out the needed amount.)

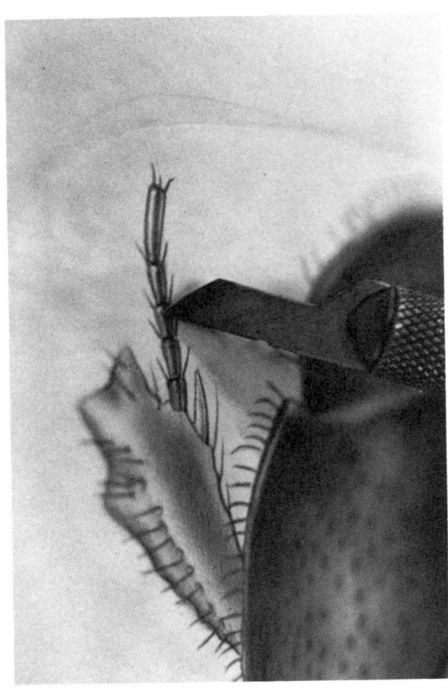

8-13. Scraping with a sharp blade to create highlights on coated paper. Photo by T. J. Spilman.

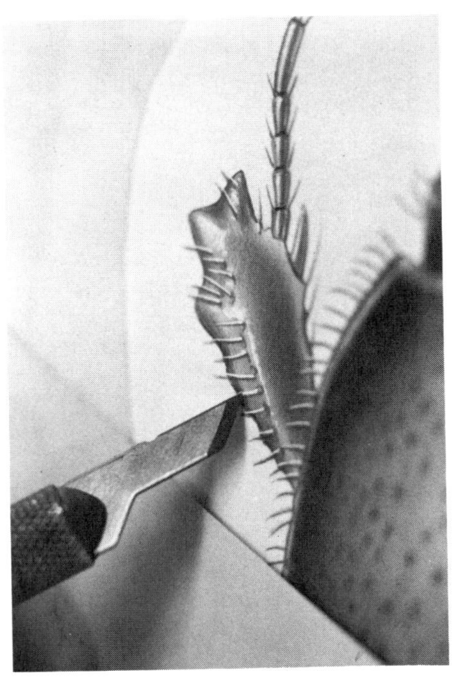

8-14. Sharp-pointed blade shown scraping spines. Note that tips of spines are scraped across the outline of the structure to make them stand out. A narrow pencil stroke under each scraped line beyond the margin completes the spine. Photo by T. J. Spilman.

8-15. Using an eraser to clean up the background. A pencil-type eraser cut to a chisel shape can be used for small areas that need cleaning. Photo by T. J. Spilman.

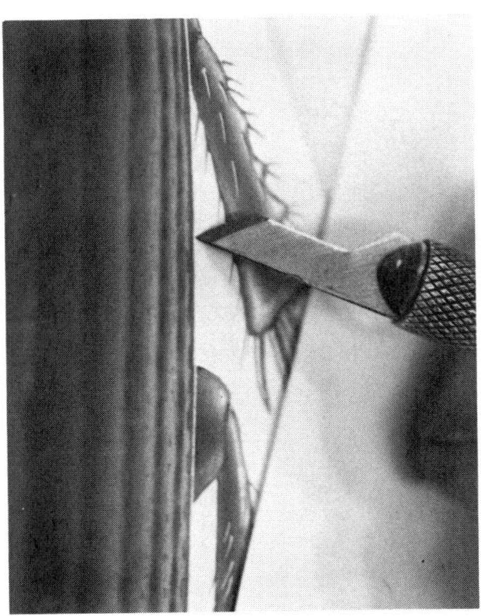

8-16. Using a sharp blade to cut a clean edge on a coated board. Photo by T. J. Spilman.

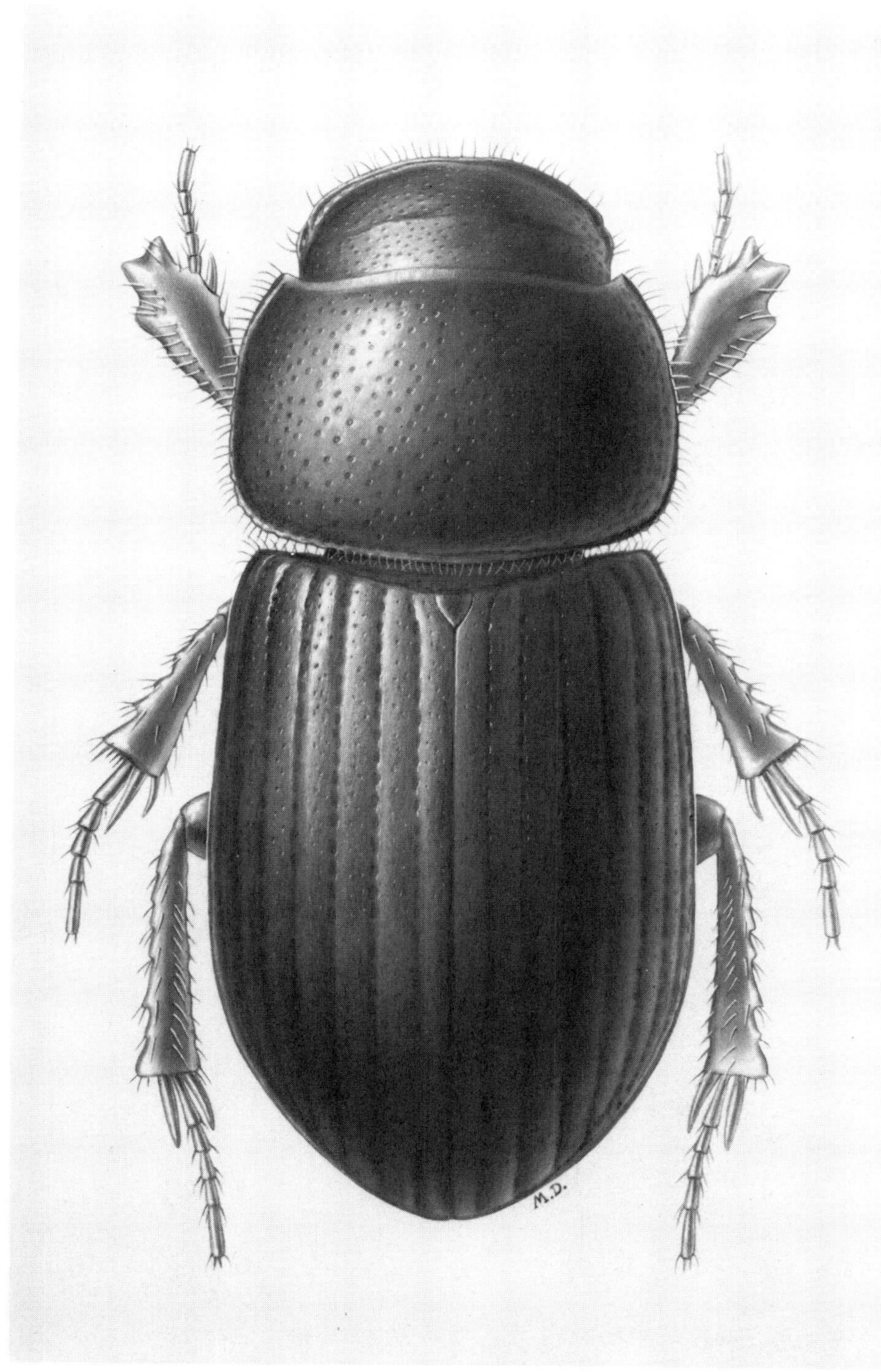

8-17. Finished carbon dust drawing with scratched highlights on Video board. Beetle, *Aegialia terminalis*, by L. Michael Druckenbrod. Courtesy of Robert Gordon.

Dried moisture droplets (from blowing dust off the drawing) tend to collect dust and become darker than surrounding areas. These can be eliminated by dampening a soft cloth or cotton swab with water and dabbing lightly; do not get the surface too wet. Allow it to dry thoroughly before carefully reapplying dust. If droplets are small, wait until the drawing is completed and then very lightly scratch with a fine-pointed blade in a crosshatch pattern. Do not scrape deeply.

When the drawing is completed, clean up the background and around the edges of the image with an eraser (fig. 8-15), a scraper (fig. 8-16), or both.

After signing the drawing, spray it at some distance with workable fixative so that further work can be done if necessary. The matte finish of the workable fixative maintains the beautiful gradation in the shading; a glossy fixative could diminish some subtle tonal gradation. On the cover sheet instruct the photographer or printer not to touch the drawing surface.

Carbon Dust on Translucent Surfaces

The use of drafting film has broadened the scope of what can be achieved with the carbon (or graphite) dust technique (figs. 8-18, 8-19; see fig. 27-3). Unlike other surfaces, such as clay-coated board, on which a 10H pencil appears almost as dark as an HB, differences in hardness show up on acetate or polyester film as differences in value—from 10H graphite (approximately 50 percent black) to HB graphite (approximately 80 percent black) to BB carbon (approximately 95 percent black). This is a great asset in the subtle shading of fine details.

MATERIALS

Surfaces

Drafting film: see chart 8-2 and chapter 3 for details and a full discussion of generic differences among films.

Mounting board.

Media

Pencils:
- Plastic pencils or leads: Staedtler-Mars Duralar, grades K1 to K5; Koh-I-Lar 3B to 4H; Eagle Turquoise Filmograph E0, E1 to E5.
- Graphite pencils: various grades 10H through 2B.
- Carbon pencils: all grades as listed under opaque surfaces.

Liquid watercolor: black or gray transparent, such as Dr. Ph. Martin's dyes.

Retouch gray paint: for black specimens only.

Tools

(For details, see list for opaque surfaces.)

Abrasive surface.

Brushes.

Erasers.

Cork.

Chamois

Cotton balls and swabs.

Scraper.

8-18. Graphite dust with diluted india ink on Cronaflex polyester film, backpainted white to eliminate shadows. Fly puparium, *Dagus dominicanus*, lateral view, by Elaine R. S. Hodges. Courtesy of W. N. Mathis.

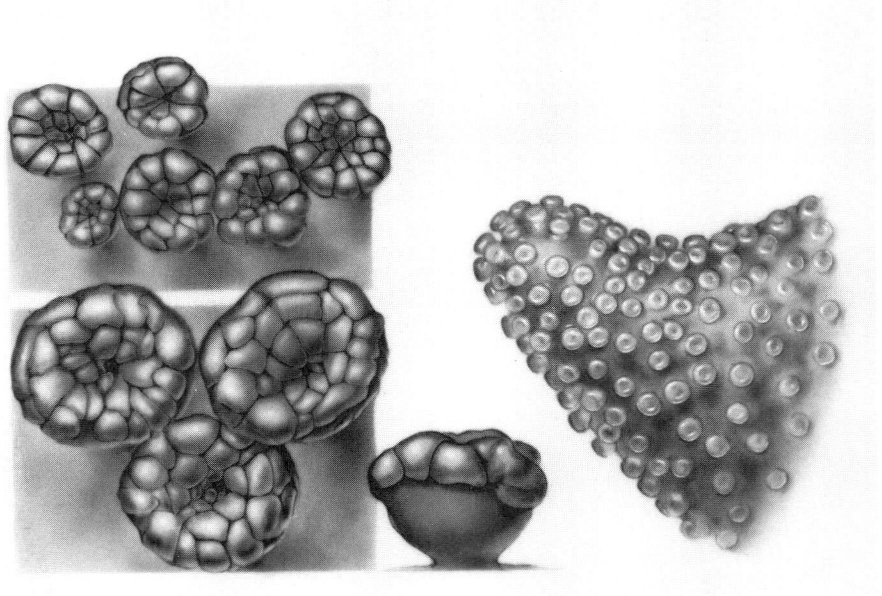

8-19. Carbon dust on Cronaflex UC-4. After the outline was established with black dye, carbon dust and graphite were used to render the drawing. Note vignetting of lateral view on right. Sipunculid papillae, by Carolyn Bartlett Gast. Courtesy of Mary Rice.

C-1. The steps followed in producing this drawing from a living animal are shown in figure I-3. The drawing was double-transferred using colored pencils and frosted acetate. Black (mixed with a little white) polymer paint was painted around the image area. Diluted Higgins colored inks were applied in a damp wash technique, then colored pencils and pastels used to reinforce tones and details. Whites were scratched out, some scratches colored intense pink. Brushstrokes that showed in the black background were sanded off with no. 400 sandpaper. Sea anemone, *Entacmaea quadricolor*, in mixed media on white scratchboard, by Carolyn Bartlett Gast. Courtesy of C. Cutress.

C-2. An Amberlith mask cut out over a tone drawing to be used for a line negative. Pen and india ink were used to cover the small projecting hairs. Register marks align the overlay mask with identical marks on the drawing. This negative combined with a halftone negative of the drawing image will result in a white background in reproduction. (See figures 2-45 and 2-46 and chapter 2.) Stages of development in spiny anteater. Wolff's carbon pencil on Strathmore five-ply (hot-press) Bristol board, by Margaret L. Estey. © Time-Life Books, L.N.L. (Life Nature Library).

C-3. Yucatan jay, showing iridescence. Watercolor, by Nancy R. Halliday. From the *Wilson Bulletin*, "Behavioral Ecology of the Yucatan Jay," by R. Raitt and J. W. Hardy, 1976.

C-4. An example of iridescent color. An analysis of the colors is in figure 4-31. After the drawing was rendered in carbon dust on the frosted side of acetate film, acrylics were painted on the shiny side of the film in reverse order: top colors or highlights first, background last. The cast shadow was airbrushed with black watercolor onto a backing of Color-Aid paper and touched up with carbon dust. (This backpainting technique is described in chapter 10; also see figures C-29, C-30.) Leaf beetle (Coleoptera: Chrysomelidae), by Trudy Nicholson © 1975.

C-5. Mixed media, including soft pastels used like carbon dust, colored pencils, and acrylic wash. The light and dark colors were planned in a rough drawing. Petals were numbered in sequence. An outline of the rough drawing was placed under Cronaflex UC-4 film. Over this went acetate, curled side down, to be cut into templates for each petal. White board under the film layers provided a white background. Under the board was a galvanized metal sheet, which permitted the layers to be held down with magnets. Following completion of the shaded rough drawing, each template was lifted individually for work on that area, then replaced. Pastel dust was applied first with flat and pointed natural-fiber brushes. It collected at edges, intensifying the colored outline. Colorbrite or Col-erase pencils permit smudging and were used for veins and final shading. When the drawing was nearly done, highlights were scratched and final details added. Small areas were dry-brushed in acrylic wash without medium to permit corrections. With the back of the flower painted white, background colors or details could be added on the front or back of the film. Poppy, by Lois Sloan © 1983.

C-6. Coquille board used for mixed-media rendering: pencil, pastels, and watercolor on coquille board. "Wanderings of a Gallinule," detail, by Karen Lynn Allaben-Confer © 1983.

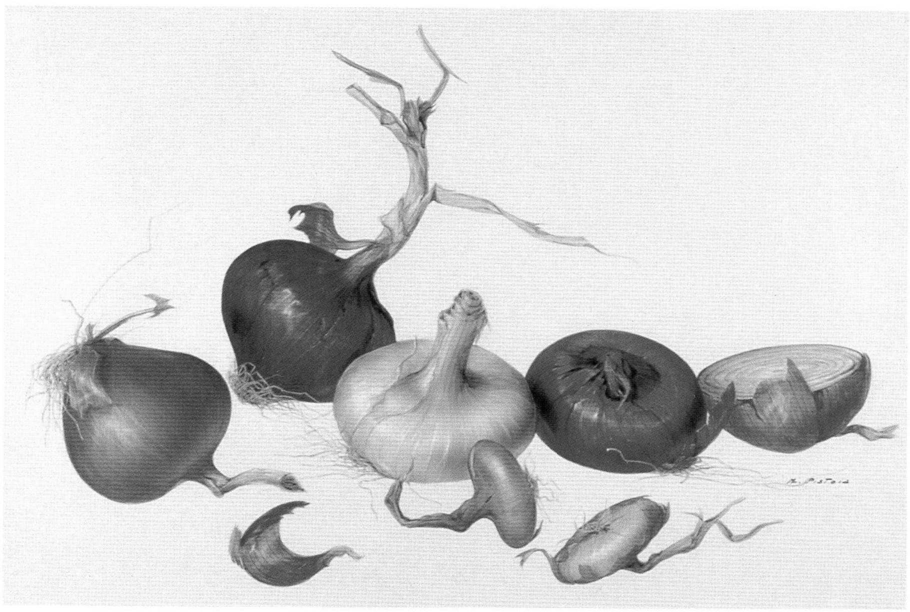

C-7. Watercolor in a dry-brush style. Onions, *Allium cepa*, by Marilena Pistoia. Courtesy of the artist and Hunt Institute for Botanical Documentation.

C-8. Dry-brushed Winsor & Newton transparent watercolors on Strathmore cold-press paper, 140-pound weight. No white was used. Blue parrot tulips, drawn from life by Jeanne Holgate.

C-9. A fully rendered background. Drawn from live birds with photographs as reference for details, the quail were painted first and the background was added around them, with the result that the birds seem to be relatively inconspicuous amid the orchids, grasses, palms, and pines in the habitat. Bobwhite quail, *Colinus virginianus*, and various native orchids including *Calopogon*, *Cleistes*, and *Pogonia* species in a typical habitat for these birds in the southeastern United States. One purpose for this illustration was to encourage conservation of wild species. Winsor & Newton watercolors and Series 7 brushes on four-ply Strathmore drawing board, medium surface, by Marion Ruff Sheehan © 1983.

C-10. An example of a watercolor painting handled in a very tight and meticulous style with the use of very little water. Scorpion, by Bernard Durin. From *Insects, Etc.: An Anthology of Arthropods Featuring a Bounty of Beetles*, Hudson Hills Press (© 1980 by Schirmer/Mosel Verlag Gmbh and Bernard Durin; © 1981 by Hudson Hills Press).

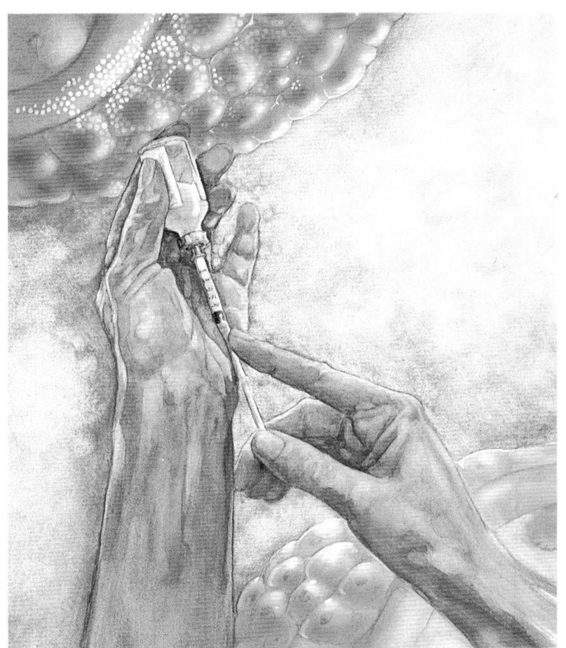

C-11. A conceptual medical watercolor painting. To create the translucency, Winsor & Newton gouache was airbrushed on top of the dry watercolor. Then areas of the dried gouache were rubbed off with a damp ⅛-inch Winsor & Newton Series 680 flat nylon brush. "Diabetes," by Carol Donner. Courtesy of *Today's Pharmacist*. Art Director: Robert Herald.

C-12. Procedure for applying watercolor (from top left to lower right). Washes of the lightest values are applied over the entire area. Form is developed using stronger color (more pigment) in slightly drier washes. Full form and depth have then been attained and some details have been added. Final details, surface patterns, and highlights complete the painting. *Rhododendron simsii* hybrid (azalea). Winsor & Newton and Schmincke watercolors on Strathmore drawing board, medium surface, four-ply, by Marion Ruff Sheehan © 1983. Photo by Joe A. Goulait.

C-13. To depict a shining highlight in a watercolor painting, the paper has been left white in a crisp shape. Tomato, by Marion Ruff Sheehan © 1983. Photo by Joe A. Goulait.

C-14. Highlight and texture have been created with Chinese white watercolor on top of transparent watercolor. Lemon, by Marion Ruff Sheehan © 1983. Photo by Joe A. Goulait.

C-15. A soft, dull surface is depicted by using color over the entire surface, keeping it lighter in the highlight area but not white or bright. Winsor & Newton and Schmincke watercolors on Whatman cold-press watercolor paper. Peach, by Marion Ruff Sheehan © 1983. Photo by Joe A. Goulait.

C-16. Soft highlights on the cicada's wings were produced by erasing the well-dried watercolor with a Klenzo ink eraser. The gray background was airbrushed with the subject area masked with frisket. Pelikan transparent watercolors and Winsor & Newton brushes on Arches smooth paper, in both wet and dry-brush techniques. *Tibicen linnae*, by Barry Flahey © 1978.

C-17. Texture, painted with Permanent Pigment watercolor on Crescent no. 300 cold-press illustration board using Gyros red sable brushes. *Hyla trux*, by David M. Dennis. From "New Tree Frogs of the Genus *Hyla* from the Cloud Forests of Western Guerrero, Mexico," by Kraig Adler and David M. Dennis (Occasional Papers of the Museum of Natural History, University of Kansas, no. 7, March 1972).

C-18. Prismacolor pencils on Cronaflex film. Image was backpainted white, then shadows added with carbon dust on the back of the film. Details were enhanced with knife and graphite pencil. Lady beetle, *Adalia bipunctata*, by George L. Venable.

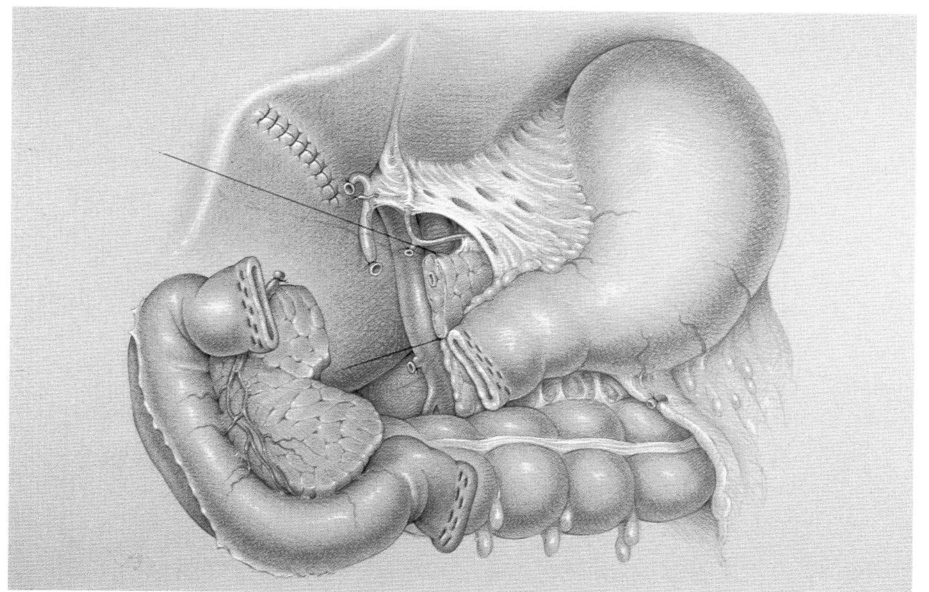

C-19. Berol Verithin colored pencils on Crescent coral charcoal paper with white gouache added for highlights. Pancreatoduodenectomy for cancer of the pancreas, by William B. Westwood. © 1982, 1983 by Learning Technology, Inc. Reprinted by permission of Smith Kline and French Laboratories and Learning Technology, Inc.

C-20. Permanent white added to the colors creates a milky effect. Gouache on light gray ColorMatch paper. Leopard gall on oak leaf, by Gerald P. Hodge © 1984.

C-21. Winsor & Newton Designers Gouache with brush and airbrush on Bainbridge no. 80 cold-press board. Mount St. Helens cross section, by Jaime Quintero © 1980. From *Science 80*, vol. 1, no. 6. Courtesy of Rodney Williams and Jaime Quintero.

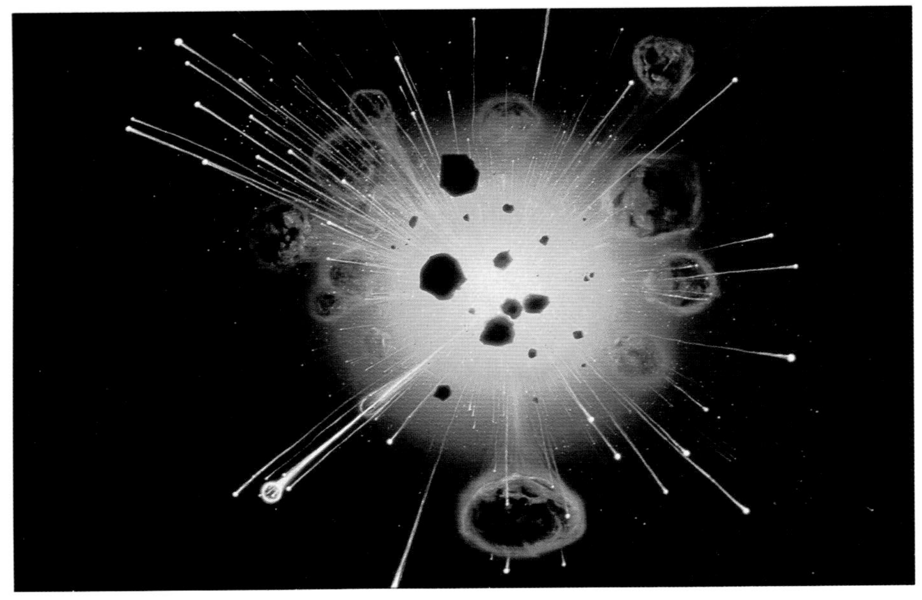

Above, left:
C-22. Acrylic applied with brush and airbrush on black Crescent poster board coated with washes of ivory black acrylic. The bright central blast was airbrushed first as red, orange, yellow, and, finally, white. Rocks were hand-painted afterward. A toothbrush was used to apply smallest stones and dust particles. Finally, gases and dust particles surrounding some of the largest chunks of rock (comets-to-be) were airbrushed. "The Origin of Comets," by Sally J. Bensusen © 1982 (published in *Mercury* magazine).

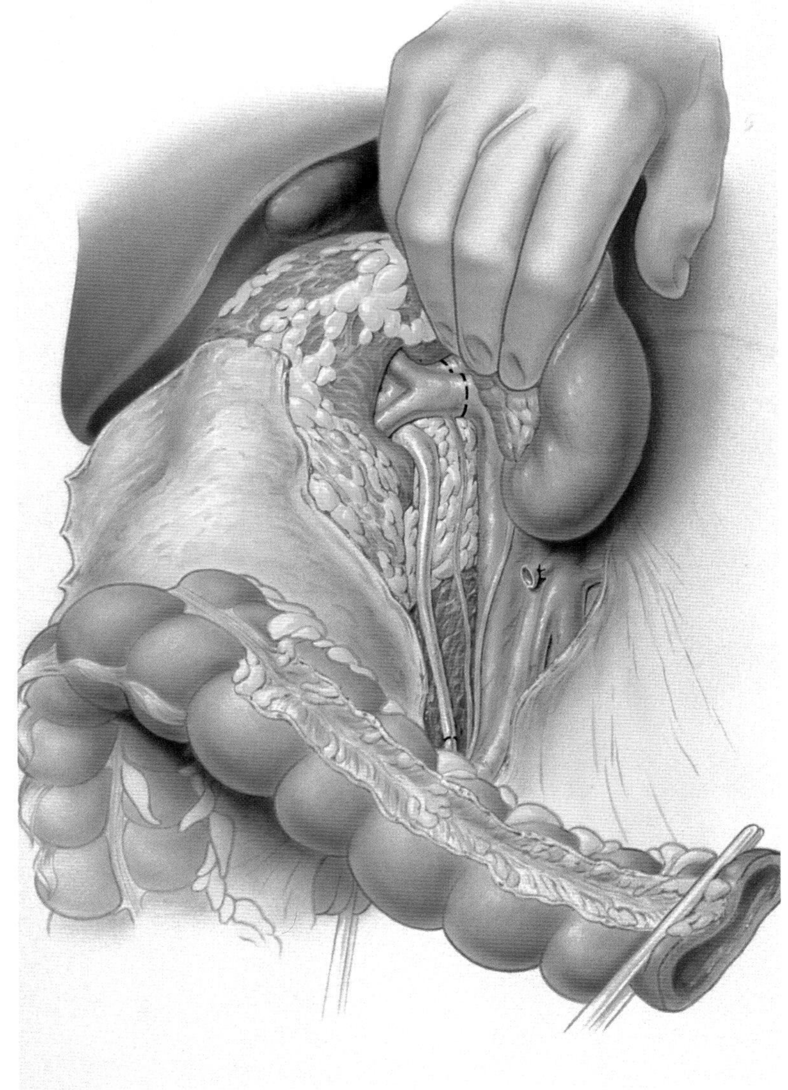

Facing page, right:
C-23. Airbrush with diluted jar acrylic was used to create background water. The drawing was based on many photographs taken by the artist, the composition arranged from enlarged and reduced photocopies of the photographs to capture their tonal quality during planning. Stuffed or frozen birds provided detail and proper color. The ducks were painted on Strathmore cold-press illustration board with transparent, tube watercolors diluted with a mixture of half acrylic medium and half water. Acrylic medium kept the watercolor pigment from washing out under final glazes. Light areas and highlights were painted with acrylic paint; shadows and form were created with glazes of watercolor and acrylic medium. Ring-necked ducks, *Aythya collaris*, by Hoyt Smith. Winner of the 1984 Oklahoma Duck Stamp competition. © Oklahoma Department of Wildlife Conservation.

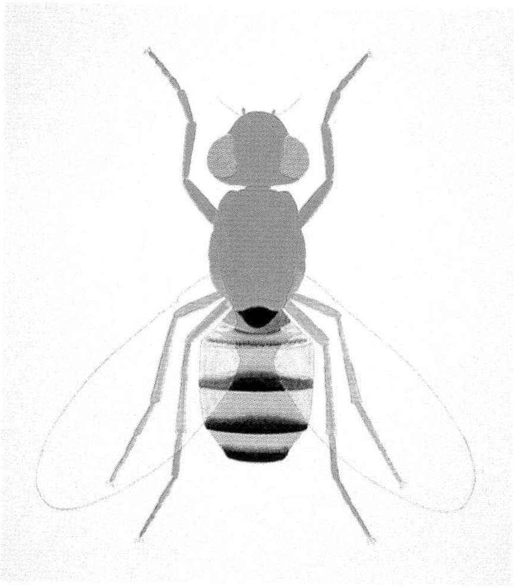

C-25. A first step in an acrylic painting: The base color is applied in flat tones.

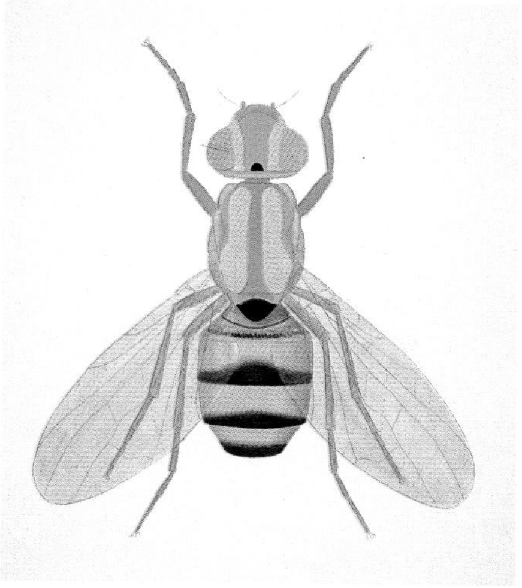

C-26. The refinement of color pattern and shadows is begun; the wing membrane is glazed.

Facing page, bottom:
C-24. Acrylic with brush and airbrush on Crescent no. 110 illustration board. One of a series of medical paintings produced by two illustrators. Trudy Nicholson worked with the doctors and prepared the composition and pencil drawing; Jane Hurd rendered the color painting. Resection of tumor in right retroperitoneal space, from *Manual of Soft Tissue Tumor Surgery*, by W. Lawrence, Jr., J. P. Neifeld, and J. J. Terz (© 1983, Springer-Verlag, Inc.).

C-27. Color pattern and shadows are further defined.

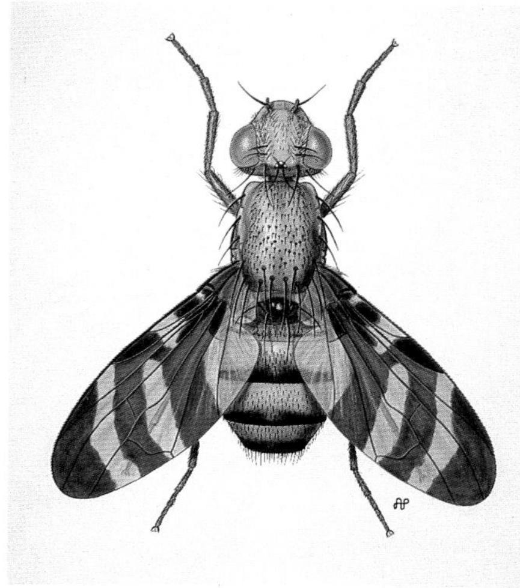

C-28. Shadows and highlights are finished. Setae and general outlining were added with pen-and-ink. In the shadows, colored and graphite pencils were applied over the dried acrylic. *Tritoxa pollinosa* (Diptera: Otitidae). Acrylic, Prismacolor pencil, pen-and-ink on gesso-coated illustration board, by Arwin V. Provonsha.

C-29. Backpainting on film: the back surface of an illustration on Cronaflex frosted on both sides, left incomplete for demonstration purposes. The paint and colored pencil applied to the back show through the Cronaflex, adding color to the front surface. The leaves on the left of this view have been opaquely painted in several layers with Liquitex artists' acrylic paint, Value 5 green. This flat color takes on the effect of blended hues when seen through the carbon dust rendering on the front (see fig. C-30). (More details about specific media are described in fig. 10-5.) Rhododendron leaves and blossoms, by Trudy Nicholson © 1987.

C-30. Backpainting on film: the front surface of the demonstration illustration shown in figure C-29. All gray and black shading is rendered with carbon dust technique on this front surface. The color is applied primarily on the back surface, leaving the carbon dust rendering undisturbed. Note the effects of different-colored papers placed behind the Cronaflex and the carbon dust rendering, giving the effect of full color to the entire illustration. A few small details are colored on the front with colored pencil and acrylic. (A full description of the media used to create different color effects is provided in fig. 10-5.) Rhododendron leaves and blossoms, by Trudy Nicholson © 1987.

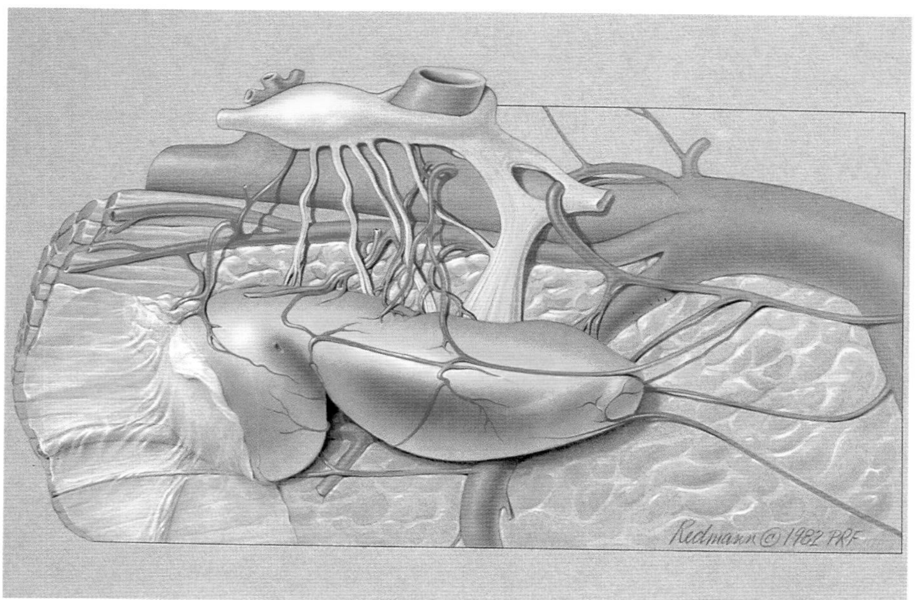

C-31. Prismacolor pencil and acrylic on mat board. Dog adrenal with blood supply, by Jane S. Redmann. © Purdue Research Foundation.

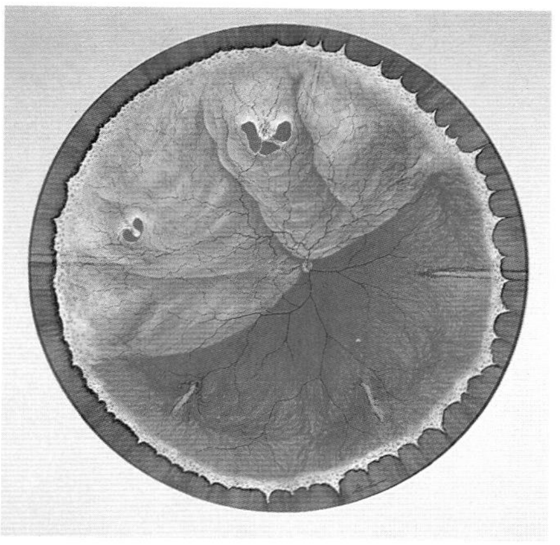

C-33. An illustration produced after examination of the patient by the artist using a binocular indirect ophthalmoscope and scleral indentation. Retinal detachment with two retinal tears. Winsor & Newton watercolors on no. 500 Strathmore illustration board, medium surface, using Strathmore brushes and airbrush, by William J. Stenstrom © 1983.

C-32. Oil and acrylic paint. Highlights were applied with oil paint over dried acrylics on polystyrene board. *Thrincopyge alacris* (Buprestidae), by Richard E. White. From *A Field Guide to the Beetles of North America*, © 1983 by Richard E. White (published by Houghton Mifflin Co.).

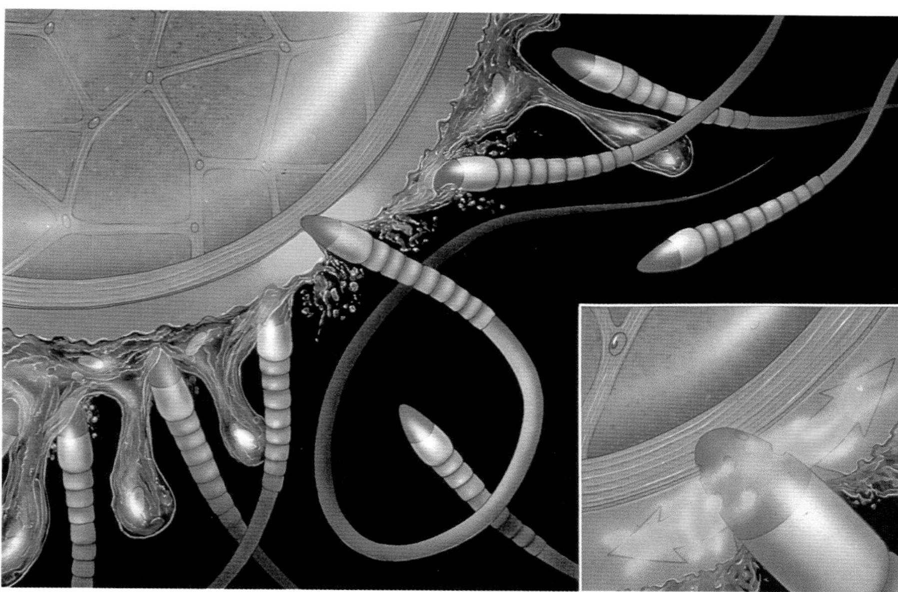

C-34. Cel vinyl paint on acetate. After black outlined the subject on the front of the cel, cel vinyl was used as a wash on the zona radiata (bluish projections around the ovum). The gray sperm and the yellow and purple colors were airbrushed, and toothbrush spattering added texture to the center of the purple ovum. Wash and airbrush were applied to both back and front of the cel. Finally, the black was brush-painted on the back. "Sperm Entering the Zona Pellucida," by Edmond S. Alexander © 1981. This illustration won the Ralph Sweet Award, Association of Medical Illustrators, 1981.

a

b

C-35. Mechanical color separation for spot color printing. Black line cut *(a)* with one additional color screened to produce 20 percent, for the background *(b)*, and 60 percent, for the bee *(c)*, of Pantone 021 orange. In *(d)* screened colors and the drawing are combined. No colors are actually on the original art (see fig. C-36). Bee, pen-and-ink, by Arwin V. Provonsha © 1983.

c

d

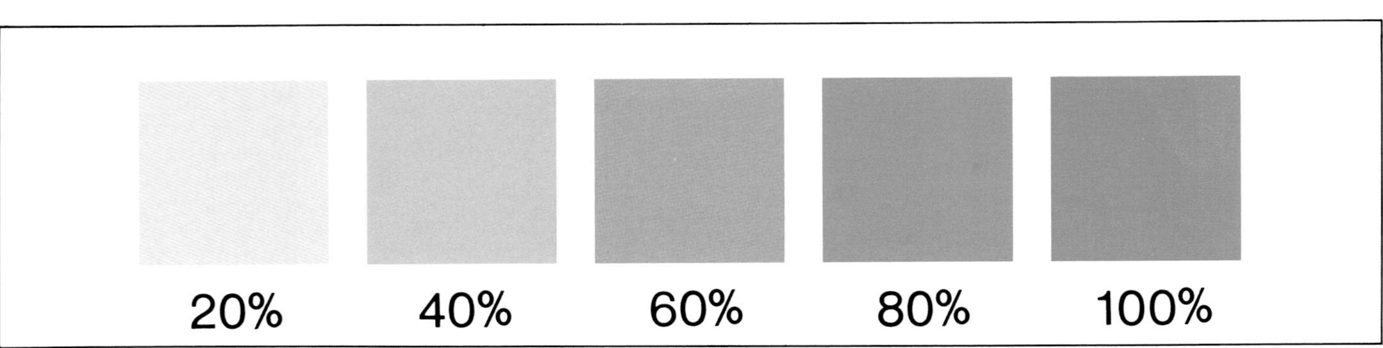

C-36. Examples of screening percentages. The illustrator selects and marks percentages of color on overlays to tell the printer which intensity of color to print in each area of an illustration. Courtesy of Arwin V. Provonsha.

Miscellaneous

Workable fixative.

Cotton gloves.

TECHNIQUE

The use of drafting film entails some modification of the technique used on opaque surfaces.

Start with clean film without fingerprints or other blemishes. Handle it carefully between two sheets of paper and with cotton gloves to keep skin oil off the surface. If necessary, the film can be cleaned by wiping gently with soft cloth or cotton moistened with rubber-cement thinner.

After the preliminary drawing is ready, spray it with workable fixative or put a sheet of clear acetate over the drawing to prevent it from rubbing off onto the back of the drafting film for the final rendering. Line up the preliminary drawing and tape it on one side to a smooth board. Place the rendering film over all and tape it, curved side down to minimize shadows, on the same side. Finally, tape a protective mask with a window exposing the drawing area over the final rendering film. The reason for taping on one side only is to allow a white opaque paper to be slipped between the preliminary drawing and the rendering to check progress of tonal buildup. Tones of the rendering cannot be judged accurately over the preliminary drawing. Also, the preliminary drawing must be removed when it no longer can be seen clearly. Keep it nearby for ready reference.

Outline with a well-sharpened graphite pencil, plastic pencil, diluted india ink, diluted transparent black or gray watercolor, or retouch gray. A wet medium gives a clear outline and does not smear. Most plastic pencils also do not smear, and graphite smears less than carbon. Carbon dust gathers on retouch gray to make it intensely black, which may be too dark for most drawings but is excellent for rendering a black drawing (see fig. 4-14). Lines may be trimmed carefully with a sharp knife blade. Test the outlining media on a scrap of the film, try scraping the line, and apply carbon dust to see how it adheres to the outline.

The same procedures for applying dust to opaque surfaces are applicable for film. Apply dust sparingly and lightly, a thin layer at a time. Add the details of interior structures with very sharp pencils of hard plastic or graphite. Create highlights with a plastic (vinyl) eraser cut to a chisel point, by scraping carefully with a sharp knife blade, or by applying opaque white with brush or pen.

Corrections and Repairs

Lighten tones that are too dark by gently wiping with clean chamois. A continuous tone can be reestablished over an area lightened with chamois.

In erasing or scraping on plastic film, use a light touch to avoid removing tooth or texture, because the shiny plastic underneath is not receptive to further work. Stumps

Chart 8-2. Comparison of Translucent Surfaces (Drafting Films)

Name	Surface Type	% Black with Carbon Pencil[1]	% Black Carbon Dust with Brush[1]	Shading with Brush	Lightening with Chamois	Lightening with Eraser	Scratched Highlights
Cronaflex UC-4 (DuPont)	good rough tooth	about 95%	65–70%	very smooth	effective	effective but can wear tooth	crisp and sharp
Frosted acetate	rough tooth	about 95%	65–70%	smooth	effective	effective but can wear tooth	crisp and sharp
Ageproof #138-4 (Dietzgen)	rough tooth	about 90%	65%	smooth	effective	effective but can wear tooth	hard to get sharp
Sure-Scale #44-122 (Bruning)	medium to fine tooth	about 85%	50%	very smooth	effective	effective but can wear tooth	hard to get sharp
Rapidraw (Koh-I-Noor)	fine tooth	about 95%	50%	smooth	effective	effective but can wear tooth	very hard to get sharp
James River Drafting Film JR300 and JR330	fine tooth	about 95%	65–70%	smooth	effective	effective	crisp and sharp

1. This represents the percentage of black obtainable without fixing the surface. Spraying once or twice with workable fixative and then dusting over will increase the richness and darkness.

are not recommended with film because they abrade the tooth and thus prevent the surface from accepting dust. Do not use a pencil-shaped eraser, which will cause streaks. Instead, use a kneaded eraser with a light touch. Dust must be reapplied over an erased area lightly and carefully so a darker spot does not emerge. If the area is still too dark, white pencil, white pastel, or white Conté stick can be used. Charcoal white on film may disappear when sprayed with fixative. Test on a scrap.

Most drafting films are washable. Should a mistake be made in the pen-and-ink work, remove ink lines with a water-dampened piece of cloth or tissue over the tip of the finger. Re-ink when the area is dry. Rubber-cement thinner may be used to remove pencil shading and smudges, but care should be taken not to remove part of the drawing.

After the drawing is done, tape it to the mounting board. Backpainting of the figure with several coats of white acrylic helps eliminate shadows when film is mounted.

White and Gray Carbon Dust on a Black Ground

Carolyn Bartlett Gast

A drawing rendered in shades of white, gray, and color on the frosted side of an acetate film backpainted black captures the transparent quality of some creatures, especially certain invertebrates (fig. 8-20). Keep in mind, however, that some printers find it difficult to print solid black backgrounds.

MATERIALS

Surfaces

Drafting film: polyester for detailed preliminary drawing; frosted acetate, frosted on one side, 0.005 inch thick (see chart 8-2). Tape edges to prevent tearing.

Black paper or red masking film: as large as acetate drawing surface.

Clear acetate: temporary barrier to keep working drawings from rubbing onto overlay.

MEDIA

Pencils:

- Charcoal white.
- Carbon or charcoal, HB, B through BBB.
- Prismacolor, white and grays, colors.

White paint: water-soluble opaque. Steig GraphicWhite, Johnston's Snow White Ink.

Black paint: acrylic or lacquer in spray can or airbrush.

Tools

Brushes: 3×0 brush or smaller for white paint; assorted brushes for black dust; additional brushes for white dust.

Eraser: kneaded rubber.

Miscellaneous

Fixatives: Krylon Workable, Krylon Crystal Clear, Grumbacher Tuffilm.

Abrasive surface: silicon carbide 400 (black so white dust is easily visible).

TECHNIQUE

Prepare the detailed preliminary drawing in pencil on translucent stock (polyester film or frosted acetate) so that when it is under the drawing in progress, a black sheet or red masking film can be slipped beneath both layers to check the white rendering. Tape frosted acetate, frosted side up, on top of the preliminary. Draw white lines at least 1½ inches (4 cm) from the work area to mark the margins.

Trace the drawing with charcoal white pencil, which erases and also fades somewhat when sprayed with fixative, thereby permitting changes and a blending into the eventual rendering. Trace more permanent outlines and details with white ink or paint or white Prismacolor pencils, all of which are hard to remove. (They can be scraped off, but this may damage the acetate's frosted surface.) Slip black paper under the film to check the drawing periodically and when the tracing is completed.

Turn the final rendering surface face down on a light box and spray black paint on the glossy back until it extends beyond the white margins of the drawing. Let dry thoroughly.

With the detailed preliminary and specimen nearby for reference, render with brushes in standard carbon dust technique using charcoal white pencil dust created by rubbing on very fine black sandpaper. Apply the white dust quite generously, even if it seems too white, because it will tone down when sprayed with fixative and also can be darkened with carbon dust and gray pencils.

To build intense but soft whites, fix the first layer with workable fixative. When dry, brush on more white dust. Work either from dark to light or light to dark in duplicating the tones of the specimen. Tighten details with carbon and gray Prismacolor pencils and white paint or ink. Clean the background with the kneaded eraser.

Fix the completed drawing with Tuffilm for a waxy surface or Krylon Crystal Clear for a shiny effect. Both make the acetate become more transparent where there is no drawing. The background then looks more intensely black.

Adding Color

A colored overlay for the drawing can be made on another sheet of frosted film, to be used for slides and other color use, while retaining the black-and-white drawing for separate reproduction. Place the film, frosted side up, over the rendering, with a clear piece of acetate between the two to prevent dust from the original rendering from rubbing off onto the overlay during the coloring process.

Render in color with Prismacolor pencils. The lines and details of the original rendering should be clearly apparent through the glow of color to provide the detailed characters of the specimen. The clear darker colors become transparent when sprayed with fixative, so that the drawing shows through, but the lighter opaque colors may have to be scraped away to reveal lines in the base drawing.

Spray the finished colored rendering with Krylon Crystal Clear, making the background of the overlay transparent and the black underpainting of the original rendering more intense again.

Photograph the combined films and then separate them.

Carbon dust technique can be mixed with other media such as ink, watercolor, pastels, colored pencils, casein, airbrush, damp wash, and black or colored backpainting (see fig. C-4). Colored illustrations can be produced by substituting dust ground from colored pencils or pastels (see chapter 7 and figs. C-5, C-6, 7-8). With its many variations, the carbon dust technique produces beautifully graded tone drawings, enabling an artist to interpret the myriad nuances of light and shade.

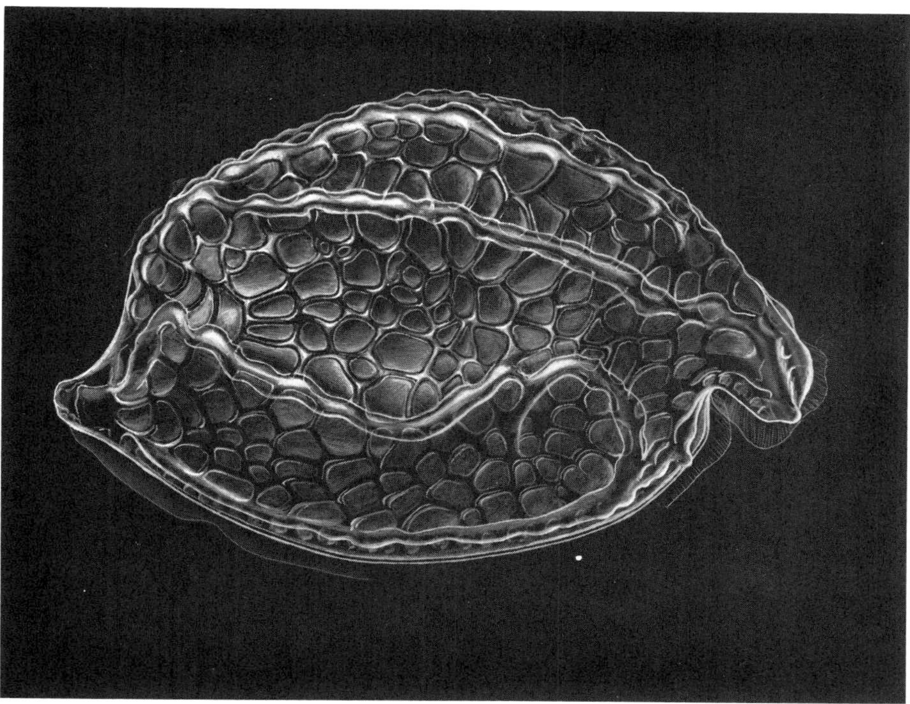

8-20. Charcoal white pencil dust, carbon and Prismacolor pencils, and white paint on frosted acetate. Black paint was sprayed on the back of the acetate. Ostracod, *Anarthron evexum* Kornicker, by Carolyn Bartlett Gast. Courtesy of Louis Kornicker.

9/Watercolor and Wash

Marion Ruff Sheehan and Jane Hurd

A watercolor or a wash is essentially fluid containing pigment that is pushed, pulled, or made to flow in a controlled, organized, and predictable manner to achieve a continuous range of tones, creating the illusion of three-dimensional form. The term *watercolor* implies full color, the term *wash* implies black and white (as well as a way to apply paint), but the media for both are applied similarly.

The wet quality of the medium is particularly suitable for rendering biologic subjects, which often are wet, shiny, translucent, or transparent (fig. 9-1). Surface pattern, texture, and sculpturing are readily depicted as well. The clear, bright and often vibrant colors obtainable with watercolor are well suited to copying nature, making this a very desirable technique to master for full-color drawings (figs. C-7, C-8, C-9). The technique permits versatility, ranging from extreme control of gradations for highly detailed, meticulous illustrations (fig. C-10) to very loosely drawn forms with drips, bleeds, and free strokes with hard edges, as with traditional watercolor (figs. C-9, 9-2, 9-3). The wash technique has long been used in scientific and medical illustration. Tom Jones, one of the great early medical illustrators in the United States and

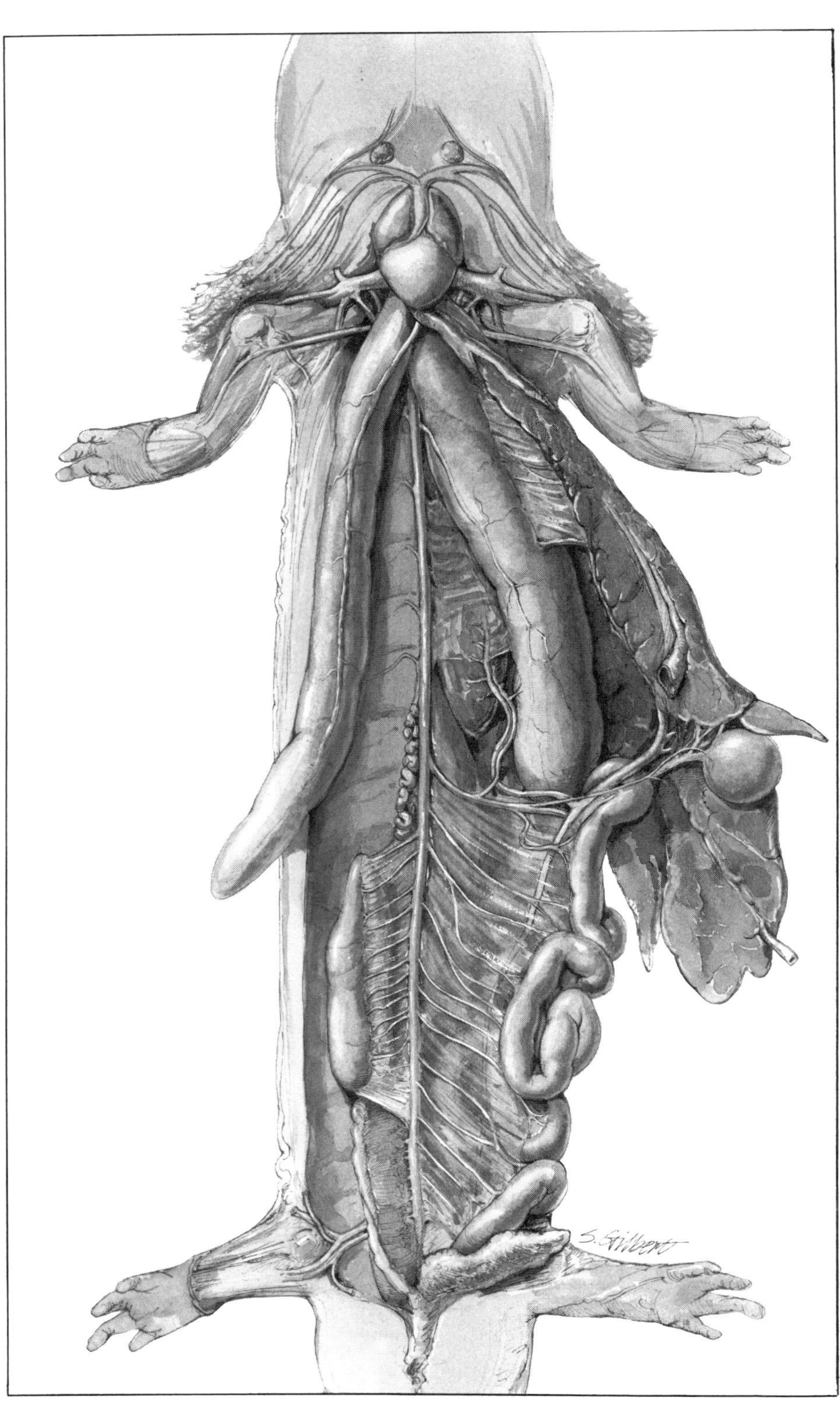

9-1. Smooth tones contrast with intricate detail. Delicate lines are drawn on the limbs with a brush. Note the roughly textured opaque white painted on membrane to give it a translucent and wet quality. Winsor & Newton lampblack watercolor on J. Whatman drawing board no. 1 (medium tooth). Ventral view of the dorsal aorta in a male Necturus, by Stephen G. Gilbert. From *The Pictorial Anatomy of the Necturus*, by Stephen G. Gilbert (University of Washington Press, 1973).

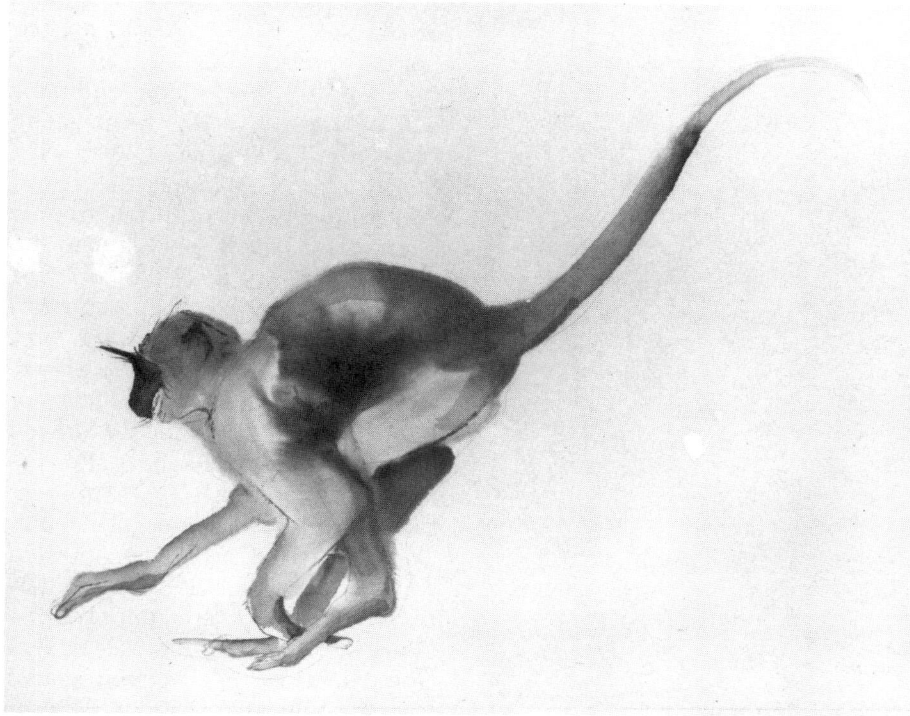

9-2. Loose application of wash with wet-on-wet technique. Lampblack watercolor on rice paper. Gray langur *(Presbytis entellis)*, by Joel Ito © 1980.

founder of the School of Medicine Illustration at the University of Illinois, was a master of wash (fig. 9-4). As a result of his teaching, this technique was firmly established in this field.

There are two basic ways of applying wash (regardless of color) to a surface: wet-on-wet and wet-on-dry. The wet-on-wet technique ensures good control, even tones, smooth gradation, and a softer overall drawing; wet-on-dry offers a high degree of control and the ability to render fine detail and pattern meticulously.

Most watercolors are transparent when spread on paper, but when the base contains additives such as white fillers, as does gouache, the color becomes opaque, producing an entirely different effect (see chapter 10). Either transparent watercolor washes alone or combined with opaque paints may be necessary to achieve a desired effect. The latter combination allows the greatest versatility in copying natural subjects.

Conventional wash techniques are the subject of this chapter, with an addendum explaining the use of wash on scratchboard as a specialized technique.

MATERIALS

Surfaces

Surfaces in general should have the following qualities:

1. Smoothness but with some tooth (cold-press) or extreme smoothness with no tooth (plate finish, hot-press), according to preference. The choice is determined by the amount of detail necessary in the drawing. Generally, the more detail needed, the smoother should be the surface selected for a drawing.
2. Substantial thickness to withstand multiple washes (sometimes several layers of paint are applied over one area), erasures, and general working over. A very soft or thin paper may disintegrate under hard use.
3. Durability to withstand long-term exposure to light, moisture, dust, and temperature variations, conditions often prevalent during storage of illustrations. A surface that is 100 percent rag or part rag matte-finish and acid-free is recommended.

Paper and illustration board: paper may be bought unmounted or mounted. Unmounted papers may be single sheets or laminated (two or more sheets glued together, like plywood). Two-ply is acceptable; three- to five-ply is better, but more costly. Laminated papers take considerable erasure and correcting without damage to the surface. Nonlaminated papers are categorized by weight: 140-pound is good; 300-pound is excellent but expensive. Heavy papers usually do not buckle when wet.

If it is necessary to work on thin paper that will buckle when wet, such as two-ply or papers less than 140-pound, thoroughly soak the paper with water, then tape along all four edges to an unwarpable board. When completely dry, the paper will be evenly shrunk, providing a drum-tight, nonbuckling surface.

Some thin papers need mounting on heavy card or illustration board. Use a liquid adhesive of archival quality, as sold by conservation supply houses. (See chapters 2 and 3 for advice on glues, mounting boards, and papers.)

Illustration board is a paper glued to a card backing. All face papers are thin, but backing comes in medium or heavy weight. Only a limited amount of correcting and very little erasing are possible because of the thinness of the paper layer, but these boards are satisfactory and create no buckling problem.

Recommended are Strathmore drawing board, three-, four-, or five-ply, or illustration board;

9-3. Graded wash loosely applied with wet-on-wet technique. Lampblack watercolor on Crescent watercolor board. Human fetus, by Anthony Pazos © 1976.

Arches cold- or hot-press watercolor paper; Fabriano/Crescent papers, 100 percent rag watercolor or illustration board; Whatman cold- or hot-press 140-pound or 300-pound paper or board.

Handle paper by the edges only. Store it flat, wrapped in an acid-free material for long-term storage.

Mounting board.

Media

Transparent black pigment, india ink: for black wash drawings. Winsor & Newton ivory black and lampblack spread evenly and are fairly permanent. India inks spread well and are permanent. Different brands of ink have different characteristics, however; look for inks that have the same desirable characteristics as those listed for watercolor paint, below.

Watercolor paint: may be purchased as either moist pigments in tubes or as dry colors in metal pans or cups (cake colors). Tube paints have the advantages of staying clean and pure and providing a readily mixed strong concentration of pigment. With cake or pan colors, the entire palette is in view, there is little or no waste, and pans can be replaced. On the negative side, color mixing is slower, as it takes time to moisten the paint, and some artists have trouble keeping the cakes clean, as they do not take time to wash brushes properly between color pickups.

When choosing any watercolor, buy the best brand you can afford. Recommended brand names for tube colors are Winsor & Newton (excellent), Grumbacher, Permanent Pigments, Aquarell, Schmincke Horadam, Dr. Ph. Martin's Radiant concentrated watercolor (which is often impermanent and may fade quickly), and Winsor & Newton Designers Gouache (opaque). Recommended cake brands are: Pelikan, Winsor & Newton, Prang, and Grumbacher Symphonic.

Color choices for full-color watercolor renditions depend on the needs and preferences of the illustrator. Subject matter may dictate the choices. Nonfading permanence should play an important role in selection. Since watercolors differ in transparency, this might be a consideration. How readily a color reliquefies and picks up when painted over may be very important since most artists work over previously applied paint several times in the process of preparing an illustration. Another very important consideration is how well paints mix with each other to produce the desired color effect. One final consideration is the preference for having a few basic colors that mix well and mixing most of the colors desired versus the choice of having a great many colors ready to squeeze out of tubes or pick up from pans ready to apply. Each company offering watercolors has between 50 and 100 (or more) choices.

All paints should possess the following qualities for all types of wash and color work:

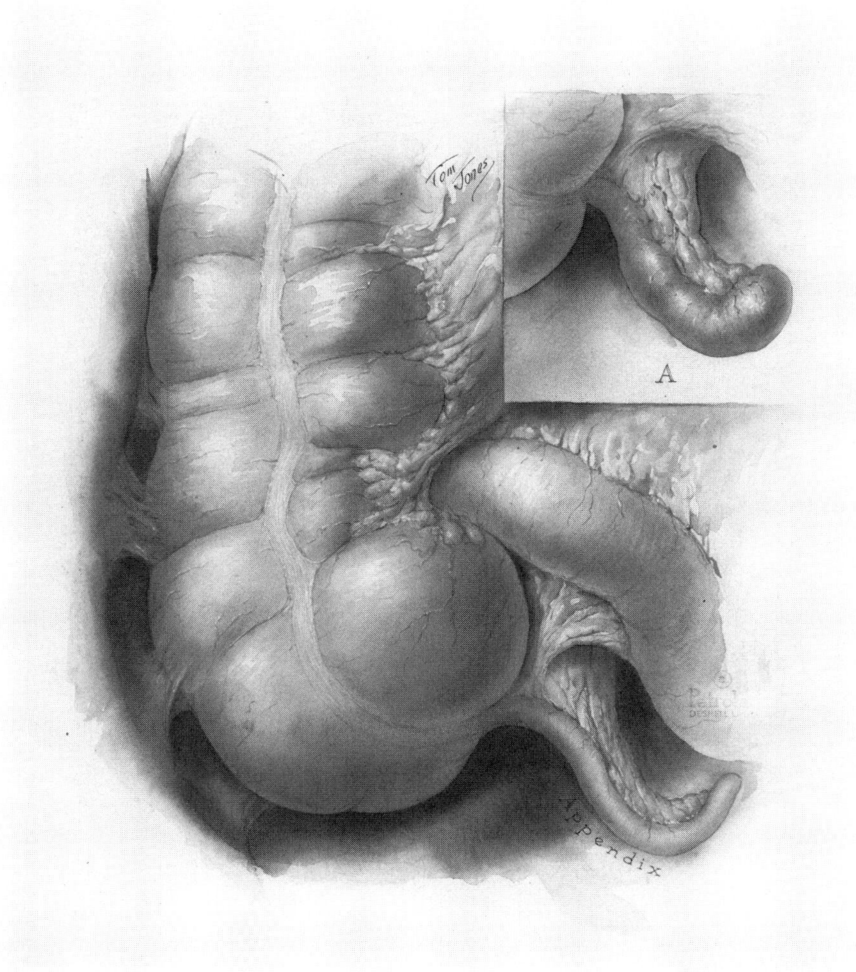

9-4. Note the smoothness and spontaneity of wash. A knife was used to scratch out a few small highlights. Talens photo retouch colors on cold-press illustration board. Anatomy of the caecum and appendix; inset showing enlarged appendix, by Tom Jones for Petrolager, Deshell Laboratory, Inc. © Petrolager, Deshell Laboratory, Inc.

1. Even texture and color, no undissolved pigment.
2. Consistency, neither hardened nor separated into liquid and pigment in the tube.
3. Trueness to color; good name brands will be the same from tube to tube.
4. Permanence (nonfading, especially important for full color work); most manufacturers provide a key indicating whether the paint is permanent or semipermanent, or whether it will fade in time. Permanent colors should be used, because scientific illustrations may sit for years before being published. If the work is exposed to light, nonpermanent colors, such as dyes, will fade.
5. Ability to spread smoothly or evenly.
6. Adherence: how tightly it binds to the painting surface, whether repeated layers of wash pick up or loosen the previously dried pigment. *Note:* Lack of strong adherence can also be a desired quality, however; a pigment that can be lifted after drying allows corrections or removal of pigment to suggest texture.
7. Granularity: the size of the pigment particles and whether they clump or build up at the edges.

Soft pastels: for creating some background effects.

Oxgall: to help paint go over oily spots; available as a solution or powder in some art stores. It may be added to colors in minute quantities to eliminate surface tension, allowing the color to cling to the surface and spread without bubbling or running.

Tools

Brushes: finest-quality round red sable (or Kolinsky) brushes are essential for maximum control and ease of handling of watercolor wash. Brushes should have the following qualities:

1. Ability to hold a fine point when wet, which allows for sharp detail and outline.
2. Good water-holding capacity, which allows the artist to cover larger areas with a single stroke. Avoid using brushes that do not pick up and hold much paint.
3. Enough resilience to hold a symmetrical, pointed shape when wet. The brush that has so little body it assumes a "new-moon" curve and holds it when wet is virtually useless, as it cannot be controlled (fig. 9-5).
4. Good closure of the metal ferrule around the hairs.
5. Hairs of the brush securely fastened so that none come loose. Brushes should be tested individually before purchase.

The choice of sizes to buy depends on the preference of the artist and the type of illustration being done. Sometimes the size of brush used depends on the size of the area to be covered in a single wash. In general, use numbers 5 and 6 for large areas, 1 to 4 for medium areas, and 5×0 to 0 for fine detail. Number 3 or 4 can be used to render an entire drawing; buying one of the best-quality brushes available is wiser than buying a variety of sizes of poor-quality brushes.

A large camel-hair brush is useful for painting backgrounds or laying a large area of wash. Another excellent brush for watercolor and wash rendering is the flat type in sable or oxhair. This brush allows the illustrator to lay a broad flat wash or to achieve a fine line by turning it on edge, perhaps in the same stroke. It is especially useful for curved areas. Recommended sizes are ¼ inch, ⅝ inch, and 1 inch (6, 15, and 25mm).

Many feel that Winsor & Newton Series 7 is the best brand of brush available, but other companies make a similar top-quality red sable brush, and personal preference enters into the choice of which brand to use. There are some excellent artificial sable brushes offered, and again, the choice is highly personal. Brushes differ primarily in controllability and pigment-holding ability. A good-quality brush may be a big investment, but it should last a long time with proper care.

Palette: among the many types of palettes commercially available, the well-and-slant type, ceramic or plastic, is most suitable for wash. The advantage of the slant over a flat compartment is that the washes do not spread out and therefore do not dry out as fast. Ceramic does not stain, but plastic is lighter in weight. A large white ceramic plate or platter makes a good palette; it cleans up well and offers plenty of space for color mixing.

Erasers: Artgum or kneaded eraser for general erasing; ink eraser and plastic (vinyl) eraser to correct mistakes; electric eraser and Pelikan plastic imbibed eraser no. PT20 for cleaning up paint droplets or paint outside the drawing lines, or for removing color to lighten an area; fine-grained, soft eraser plugs for electric eraser.

X-Acto blade in handle: no. 11 blade; or similar knife for some corrections and for scratching fine lines.

Miscellaneous

Water container: a low jar, bowl, or glass. (A wide top opening is preferable.) If working with white paint for details, have a second container for use with it exclusively, as it "muddies" the water, making it unusable for transparent colors.

Paper towels, napkins, facial tissues, absorbent gauze, cotton: for removing excess water from the brush; creating special effects in wet paint; or cleanup.

Frisket: either paper or liquid; to mask highlights, keeping them white.

Eyedropper: for transferring water to the palette.

Workable fixative: if pastels are used in conjunction with watercolor.

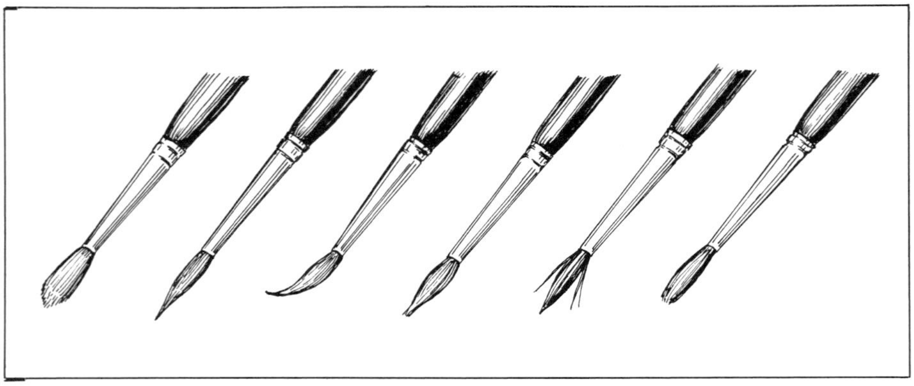

9-5. Good and bad watercolor brushes. From left to right: good dry—dull, tapered; good wet—pointed; poor—no resilience; poor—no sharp point when wet; poor—straying hairs; poor—no point. Pen-and-ink on Bristol board, by Marion Ruff Sheehan.

CARE OF MATERIALS

Brushes

Clean brushes by washing in cool or cold water with mild soap or detergent. Never use hot water, as it can melt the glue holding the hairs in place. Gently rub bristles on the palm of the hand to loosen deep-set paint. To clean inner hairs, part them with the fingernails, keeping the hairs extended in one direction. When the hairs are clean, point the bristles by sharply shaking the brush and/or shaping the point with your fingers. As an alternative, after cleaning, coat the brush with soap and bring it to a point. When dry, the soap will hold and maintain the point. Avoid bending the hairs while they are fixed in soap, and gently rinse out the soap before the next use.

Always store brushes upright or flat, with bristles protected. Never leave a brush standing on its bristles in or out of water for even a few seconds. More than one brush may be transported by securing them together with bristle ends alternating against the handles. The handles thus will protect the bristles.

Paints and Palette

All tubes and other types of paint containers should be stored closed tightly. If a cap refuses to come loose, flame it briefly unless it is plastic—in which case, try hot tap water. Dried paint in tubes or jars need not be discarded. Tear open the tube and use the paint as in cake form. Most dried paint can be reliquefied for immediate use by putting a chunk of it into a small amount of water and heating before using. Keep cake paints clean by covering them when not in use and by washing each brush well between changes of color.

It is not necessary to clean the palette after each use, especially if usable quantities of paint remain at the end of the work period. The next time, simply wet dried blobs of dissoluble paint on the palette. If the paints flake or if dust has accumulated between uses, however, it is necessary to clean the palette before reuse. Dry particles of paint can cause serious problems if they are picked up by the brush along with moist pigment. They often soak up moisture when placed on the wet drawing and cause dark or undesirable dots of color that are hard to remove.

TECHNIQUE

In general, work proceeds from upper left to lower right (left-handed people working from upper right to lower left). This allows the artist to go on to the next section with no fear of damaging a still-wet area. Work on a slanted surface to enhance the flow of a wash if a flow is desired; the excess moisture from each stroke will settle at the bottom of the stroke, making it easier to pick up a wet edge in subsequent strokes. Work on a flat surface if the paint should not flow. Do not tape the drawing to the work table or board as it is better to be able to turn it in any direction while the painting progresses, allowing the hand to move in a relaxed, natural way.

Make a preliminary drawing on thin white tracing or drafting paper. It must be completely detailed, showing outline of form, planes, and all features. Work out lighting and shading and consequent tonal relationships so that, at the wash stage, all attention can be devoted to this dynamic technique.

Corrections are very difficult with the wash technique so it is important to have an accurate preliminary sketch and to apply washes carefully from the beginning. Because the white of the surface is the source of lightness in the tones, it is almost impossible to retrieve it if covered.

Transfer the sketch to the final surface (see chapter 1). A soft lead (2H to HB) is least likely to leave indentation. Prepared carbon or graphite transfer papers generally are not suitable for watercolor work, as the grease in them leaves a paint-resistant film on the paper. Saral brand graphite paper works for wash drawings. Keep the sketch close at hand for constant reference when doing the final rendering. Clean up smudges and incorrect or extra lines and lighten dark or broad lines gently with a kneaded eraser before beginning the wash rendition.

Prepare for the rendering process by setting up supplies and tools. Have ready before starting a water container, tissue or toweling, and paper to mask the entire drawing (or to place under the drawing hand), or cotton gloves, if preferred. If using tube paints, squeeze out small (¼-inch or 6mm) dabs of paint on the palette. (It may be desirable to put out two or more dabs of each color for mixing ease.) For black-and-white renderings, mix several solutions of pigment and water of varying intensities in the slant sections of a well-and-slant palette. These may need redissolving during the course of the painting. Wash, especially ink, taken from partially dried areas may contain dried clumps of pigment, which will result in specks in the painting. Prevent ink from evaporating completely.

Before beginning, consider the kind of background and the stage at which it should be added. If a flat background color is desirable, it may be applied either before or after the subject is painted. A landscape (habitat) background may be worked simultaneously with the featured subject, such as a bird or animal in its natural environment (fig. C-9). (See Backgrounds, below.)

As with any other technique, the most important consideration is to work on the illustration as a whole. It is the relationship among various areas of tone, texture, and detail that creates the illusion of three dimensions (fig. 9-6; see fig. 9-1). To keep the proper relationships, all areas should be built up gradually and alternately using several layers of wash. If one area alone is concentrated on while others are neglected, it may become apparent that the first area does not fit in properly, requiring that the others be adjusted in an undesirable manner to work with the first. Before beginning, any white or highlight areas should be defined and an effort made to avoid putting pigment over them, as a white surface provides the very best white highlight there is.

The first washes generally are done on wet paper with usually the lightest value of the subject being placed first. As each successive wash is laid down, use less fluid to avoid picking up the previous washes. Remove excess liquid by scraping the brush on the edge of the water container or paint well. When even less water is desired, scrape the brush first, then touch the brush to paper toweling or cloth to remove even more water before returning to the drawing.

A form can be almost completed quickly by applying the strokes of color in the direction in which the subject matter is shaped. For example, apply color for a petal or leaf in the same direction as the growth pattern, or around the curve of a rounded subject (figs. C-7, C-8). Even though much of the color becomes suffused, this method of application still renders a convincing shape or texture.

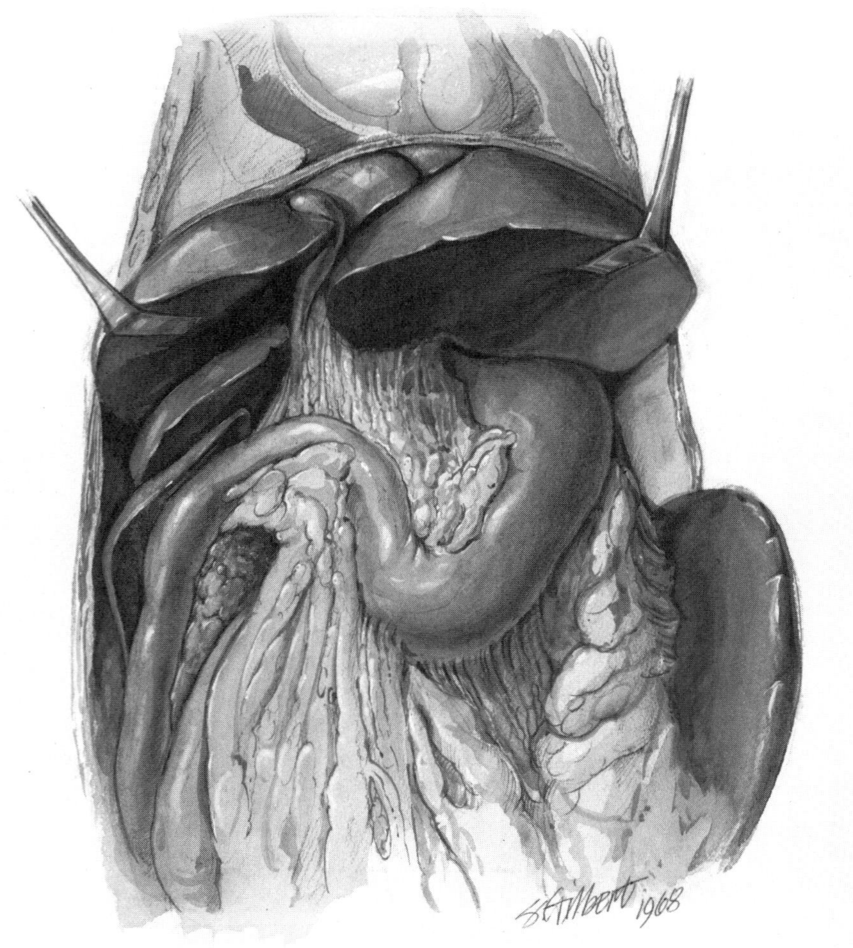

9-6. Note rendering of individual forms in relation to the entire dissection field. The pencil sketching was purposely left to add texture, and a few highlights of white gouache were applied. Winsor & Newton lampblack watercolor on HiArt illustration board, no. 79 (heavyweight). The stomach, liver, and spleen of the cat, ventral view, by Stephen G. Gilbert. From *The Pictorial Anatomy of the Cat*, by Stephen G. Gilbert (University of Washington Press, 1968).

Because wash is developed from light to dark and is difficult to reverse, it is important not to get too dark. Darkness is relative, however. Laid down on a brilliant white surface, any tone, when first applied, appears dark.

While one area is drying, start on another, nonadjacent area; adjacent areas must be allowed to dry to prevent bleeding. Proceed with flat or graded washes on dark and light middle-tone areas, developing core shadows, reflected light, shade areas, and texture while leaving highlights. When all areas except highlights are covered with tone, continue with repeated washes, further developing form. Continue repeated washes until proper tonal relationships, form, and details develop.

Small details—such as blood vessels, nerves, pigmentation patterns, texture lines, small shadows, cut edges, and hairs—may be added with a small brush by a wet-on-dry technique.

For final touches, opaque white may be used for details or for small, sparkly highlights, or for highlights that have been lost. Most types of opaque white will dissolve again if gone over with water. Because of this, subsequent tonal washes may cause the white to lift and produce a muddy effect when mixed with the black or colored pigment. White should therefore be added as a final step. Some whites, such as acrylic or cel-vinyl, will dry permanently and will not bleed with repeated washes. Acrylic, however, will blend with the watercolor pigment and become muddy if it is applied too wet or with too much brush action. Any white should be applied gently to avoid lifting or mixing with the underlying wash. Figure 9-7 shows an effect using opaque white that would be difficult to achieve in a pure wash. Whites also can be achieved by scratching off the tone with any sharp instrument to reveal the underlying white surface (fig. 9-8; see fig. 9-4). Experiment with different types and applications of white to suit particular needs.

Graphite, carbon, or other pencils also may be used in combination with watercolor and wash (see figs. 9-6, C-6). Pencil lines and shading can be used at any stage to build up tones or accentuate detail. However, on illustration board, pencil will not give as sharp a line as wet-on-dry wash with a fine brush (see fig. 9-1). If wash is to be applied over the pencil, make a test first to be sure that the particular pencil will not bleed or smear with the wash technique being used.

Wet-on-Wet (Wet Surface)

In this technique, clear water is applied to a dry area before pigment is applied. Three factors control the movement of pigment: the layer of water, the brush, and gravity. The wet area is a plane of water through which applied pigment travels by capillary action, spreading out naturally and evenly with gravity giving a predictable direction to the spread (see figs. 9-2, C-12, C-13). The direction and speed of the brushstrokes, as well as the manner in which the brush con-

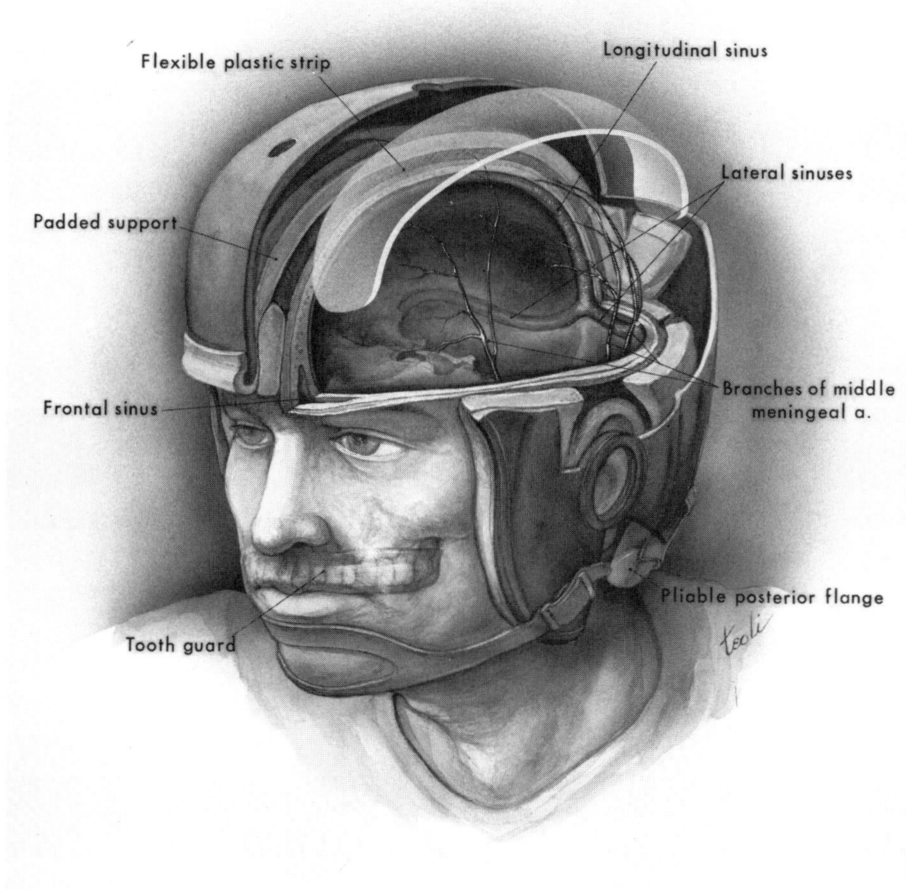

9-7. The flexible plastic strip was airbrushed with white gouache. The rest of the painting was done with Winsor & Newton lampblack watercolor on cold-press double-weight illustration board. White tempera created small highlights. This illustration successfully accomplishes the illusion of three dimensions while dealing with many structures cut at different angles to demonstrate the significant anatomy. Modification of football helmet to prevent injury to the middle meningeal arteries, by Alfred P. Teoli. Courtesy of Richard C. Schneider, *Head and Neck Injuries in Football* (Williams and Wilkins, 1973).

tacts the surface, will control the deposition of pigment. The degree of tilt and the degree of wetness will further affect the flow of the wash on the surface and the resulting appearance of the wash. As the water soaks into the surface, the pigment becomes embedded in it. When the water evaporates, the pigment remains.

A variety of effects can be achieved with wet-on-wet technique, depending somewhat on the wetness of surface at the time pigment is applied. Usually the water is allowed to permeate the surface so that the sheen has disappeared and no freestanding water remains before pigment is brushed on. Otherwise, a spiderweb appearance results and movement of pigment cannot be controlled. Achievable effects include smooth, flat, consistent tones; smooth tones grading from dark to light; soft edges; hard edges; and textures.

To prepare a surface for this type of rendition, use a clean brush and apply an even coat of clear water to the area to be rendered. To achieve a sharp, neat result at the edges, carefully and precisely bring the water all the way to, but not beyond, the transferred outline. The water will be contained by the graphite line. It is important to produce an even layer of water. Picking up and tilting the surface in various directions will help spread the water evenly. Check under a light to be sure there are no dry spots. The degree of wetness desired depends mostly on the size of the area to be covered. However, the surface should never be so wet that the water runs or drips. For areas under one square inch (2.5cm square), the surface must be only slightly damp. If a large area is to be covered, it should be wet enough so that it does not dry before the wash is applied. If any area begins to dry too soon, it may be remoistened at this stage, but not after the wash is begun. The whole area must be kept wet throughout the application of the wash.

Pigment applied as a wash is composed of water and paint or ink. A flat wash is a uniform application of a premixed pigment over a given area with no fluctuation of tonal value (fig. 9-9; see fig. 9-8). A graded wash is one in which there is a smooth transition between varying tonal values, the simplest of which is an even transition from light to dark.

Flat Wash

To apply a uniform flat tone, mix sufficient pigment and water to cover the area generously. Wet the area to be rendered with clear water, as described above. Before beginning the wash, make sure there are no drops of clear water on the brush handle or ferrule that will run down into the wash and create a lighter blotch. Dip the brush in the desired premixed wash solution. Starting in the upper left corner (upper right for left-handers), put the brush to the surface so that it bends slightly, with about two-thirds of the brush surface in con-

9-8. The background, basically a flat wash with minor tonal variations, was rendered while liquid frisket covered the light areas. Pigment was allowed to build up and outline the swan's body. Note the subtle suggestion of texture in the chick feathers. Scratching was used where the feet and grass enter water. Permoblack on Crescent no. 110 board. Trumpeter swan, by Biruta Akerbergs Hansen © 1981.

9-9. Note smooth gradation of wash incorporating texture into the overall form in this very controlled wash. Opaque white was used for bright highlights. Winsor & Newton lampblack on Arches 140-pound watercolor paper. Haitian land snail, *Lucidella manni* Clench, by Nancy R. Halliday. Courtesy of F. G. Thompson, Florida State Museum.

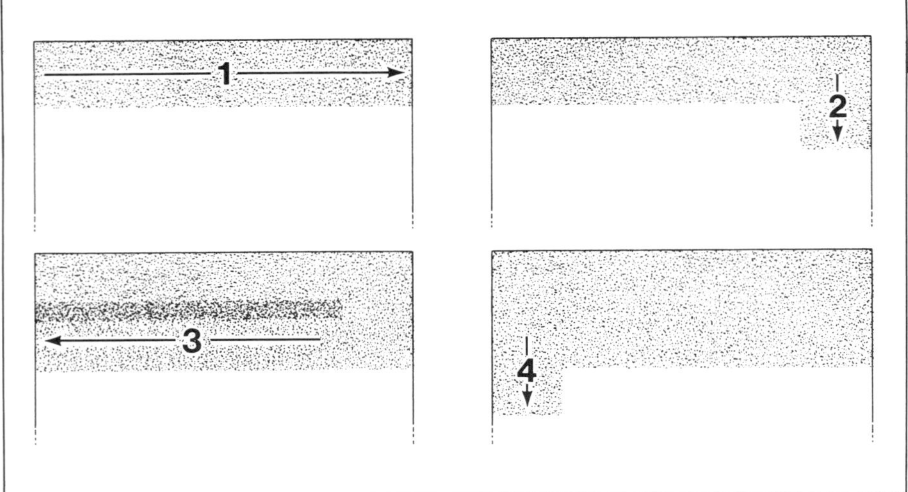

9-10. Progression of strokes in the basic wash application. Diagram by T. Britt Griswold, using hand stippling on top of randomly stippled shading film.

tact with the rendering surface. Sweep the brush horizontally to the right edge. Without lifting the brush, bring it down vertically about two-thirds the width of the first band, and then bring the brush back across from right to left, overlapping the lower border of the first stroke by about one-third. When the left edge is reached, move the brush down vertically and continue back to the right, overlapping the previous stroke in the same manner (fig. 9-10). Continue this procedure, without lifting the brush, until the area is covered. Do not move the surface while the wash is still wet, or a backwash may develop. If the correct size of brush for the area is used, it should not be depleted of wash before the area is covered. If the brush does run out of wash, pick it up at the end of a horizontal stroke, dip it in solution again, and replace it in the same spot to continue. This must be done quickly, with care taken not to get too much solution in the brush, which would create a darker stroke. Even with care, there is frequently a puddle at the end of the last stroke. Correct this by quickly blotting the brush with gauze or a paper towel, then gently touching the puddle edge to absorb the excess.

Streaks, blotches, or other imperfections may interrupt a flat wash. Horizontal streaks may be caused by too much water, using only the tip of the brush, or insufficient overlap of previous strokes. Make sure that enough of the brush is touching the surface and that the overlap of the previous stroke is sufficient.

Vertical streaks can be avoided by reducing the table tilt and/or the amount of liquid in the water layer or wash.

Radiating streaks are caused by a change in the tilt or position of the surface during the procedure or before the wash has dried; too much or uneven water; or water or wash droplets falling into wet tone.

Blotches result from an uneven layer of water; stopping, slowing down, or picking up the brush during a stroke; a water or wash droplet falling into the tone; or a damaged or soiled surface.

Ragged edges result from imprecise application of water or wash at edges.

If hard lines appear within the area of tone, a portion of the water layer has dried before the wash was finished or a wash stroke has dried before being overlapped by the following stroke.

If pigment builds up around edges, the pigment was applied too close to the graphite outline. Allow the layer of water to spread the pigment evenly to the edge; do not bring the brush that close. Sometimes, however, this dark edge can be a deliberate effect (see fig. 9-8).

When dry, the tone will appear lighter. If a darker tone is desired, repeat the procedure. Wait until the first wash is thoroughly dry (two to six minutes, depending on original wetness), apply a layer of clear water (taking care to stay within the edges), then apply a wash solution as before. Repeated washes should be as dark as or darker than the previous one. For very dark tones, a smoother, less grainy wash is achieved by building it in several (three to five) progressively darker washes, rather than doing a very dark wash in a single application. A grainy tone may be the result of too much water or the type of pigment used.

Graded Wash

Graded wash is done in the same way as flat wash, except that the intensity of the wash solution is changed during its application or the first stroke of pigment applied is drawn out to a lighter value through use of clear water (fig. 9-11).

9-11. Note the graded wash on the back of the frog, starting dark at the posterior and grading lighter toward the anterior. The texture and pigmentation spots are convincingly incorporated into the overall form. Some fine dry-brushed strokes were used for final detail. The medium probably is Talens photo retouch black, the surface a cold-press board. *Eleutherodactylus insignitus* Ruthveni, by E. N. Fischer, 1917. Courtesy of the University of Michigan.

One method for a black-and-white drawing using graded washes begins with mixing three or four wash solutions in the palette. The first should be very dark, with each successive solution a bit lighter. Wet the area to be rendered with clear water. Turn the rendering surface so that the darkest part will be at the top. Dip the brush in the darkest solution and proceed as with flat wash. At the end of the second or third horizontal stroke, pick up the brush, blot it quickly, then dip it in the next-lighter solution. Quickly replace the brush in the position from which it was lifted, catching the puddle from the previous stroke, and continue the procedure, being sure to overlap about one-third of the above stroke. After a few more strokes, again pick up the brush at the end of a stroke, blot it, and dip it in the next-lighter solution. Replace the brush, catching the puddle, and continue, following this procedure until the tone reaches the lightest value desired. If it is to be graded to white, the last few strokes should be done with clear water. The number of strokes made with each tone depends on how fast the gradation proceeds from dark to light and the size of the area. A small area may require fewer premixed intermediate tones, and perhaps a small brush. If there is a large area that requires a very gradual gradation, more horizontal strokes with each solution or a larger brush may be needed. Also, more premixed tones with subtler changes may facilitate a smoother, slower gradation, avoiding or correcting an effect of tonal stripes.

After the wash has dried, the procedure may be repeated, if necessary, to make it darker or smoother. Wet the entire area with clear water again and repeat. Any uneven areas may be treated selectively. For instance, if there is a light streak, simply add the required amount of tone to that area only. If there is a dark streak, add more tone above, blending down to (but not onto) the dark streak, as well as underneath the streak if necessary to produce an even gradation from dark to light.

An alternative method may be used for either full color or black-and-white. To achieve a graded color by this method, the first brushful of pigment should be fairly strong in color or value. After making the first stroke on the darkest side of the subject in the drawing, immediately dip the brush in clear water. Do not agitate it; some pigment should remain. Scrape the brush on the water vessel edge and quickly catch the wet edge of the previous stroke. The pigment should spread from the first stroke into the second, creating a dark-to-light effect. If additional strokes are needed to cover the desired area, dip the brush in clear water before each one. Do not touch the work until the first application is dry. The process may be repeated if necessary, but ideally, the color should be mixed and enough pigment picked up to achieve the desired result with a single application.

Another way to achieve graded wash uses the length of the brush only. Dip the brush in water and scrape it on the container edge to remove the excess. Then dip the tip in the premixed pigment. The pigment will travel through the moist bristles, creating a gradation of value within the brush. Place the tip against the dark side of the subject and hold the brush as flat as possible against the painting surface during application. The result is a narrow graded wash. This is very useful for small or narrow areas. (See Damp Wash on Scratchboard, below.)

Wet-on-Dry (Dry-surface Painting)

In the wet-on-dry surface technique, the pigment solution is applied directly to the dry surface. This approach is often used for small areas, but entire paintings can be done this way. It can be used to create a smooth tone, but because there is no water to facilitate movement of the pigment over the surface, each stroke must follow the previous one very quickly to ensure that the edge does not dry between strokes. It takes a sure and swift hand to cover a large area successfully with a smooth application of tone, either flat or graded. For this reason, it is advisable to reserve this technique for areas less than about 4 inches (10cm) in each direction. On the plus side, working on a dry surface is a little faster, since it eliminates the premoistening step.

Dry-surface (also called drybrush) painting can be, and often is, combined with wet-on-wet work after the first one or two wet applications have been made and are completely dry. All additional color is applied in layers using short brushstrokes to grade colors from the lightest to the darkest until the final variations in tone have been achieved (fig. 9-12; see fig. C-8). Very little water is used. Some artists employ this technique from the beginning and do not even apply basic washes, but rather work entirely with strokes (figs. C-7, C-10).

9-12. Dry-brush technique (wet-on-dry) using watercolor with Chinese white on Arches paper. *Magnolia tripetala* fruiting branch, drawn from life, by Esther Heins ©.

Special Effects

Highlights

Highlights may be achieved by:

1. Leaving white surface (do not wet highlight areas if using wet-on-wet technique). This approach is good for depicting shiny or glossy surfaces (see fig. C-13).
2. Covering highlight with frisket or thinned rubber cement. After applying pigment, remove covering material to reveal white surface (see Damp Wash on Scratchboard, below, and fig. 9-8).
3. Adding a spot of pure white or tinted opaque paint over color (see fig. C-14).
4. Lightening the overall color or using very pale solution in the highlight area to create a dull highlight (see fig. C-15).
5. Removing paint by moistening and blotting away or erasing a spot. To avoid damage to the surface, make certain it is completely dry before attempting to erase paint. This approach is good for dull effects (see fig. C-16).

Textures and Patterns

Textures and patterns occur in all of nature. Texture may be thought of as small forms on a larger form. A few examples are warts on a toad, hairy vestiture on leaves, the bumps on a scorpion's claws (see figs. C-10, C-17). Patterns are areas of a different color or a lighter or darker value of pigment superimposed over the basic color of the subject. A few examples are the markings on shells, stripes or dots on animals, the variegated colors of flowers (see fig. C-9). The techniques for rendering textures and patterns are generally the same, but the appearance of texture is usually structural or sculpted, whereas pattern tends to be part of the uppermost layer of the surface (see figs. 9-8, 9-11).

When rendering texture, the

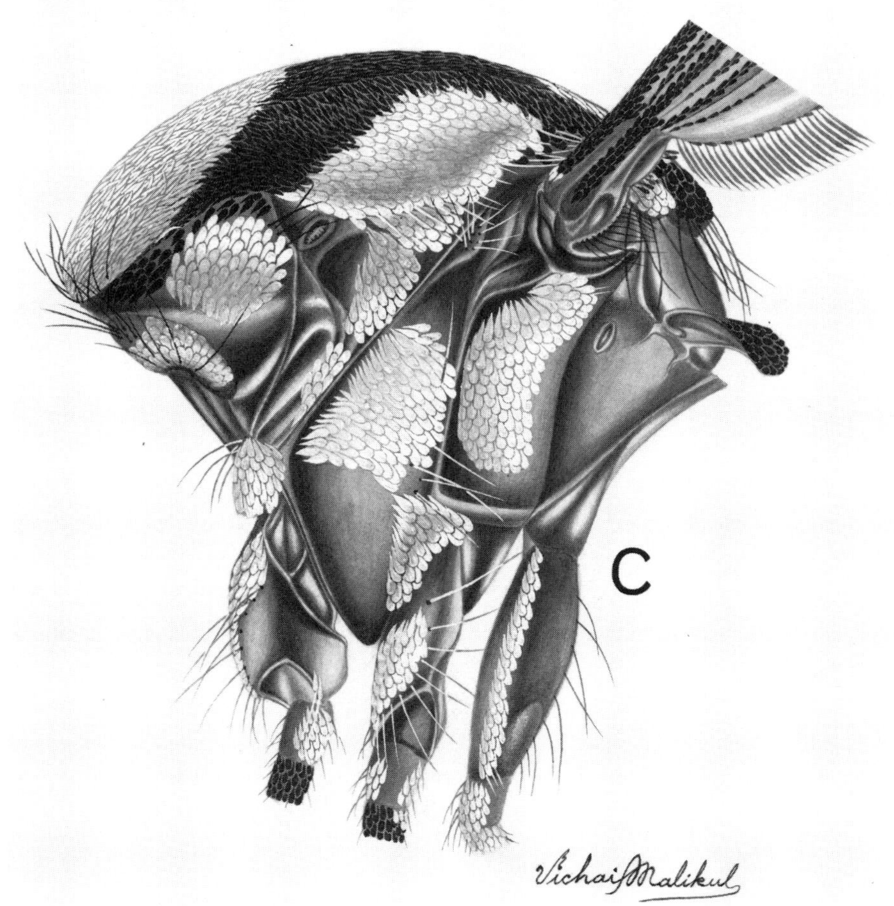

9-13. Extremely controlled wash technique using india ink on Bristol board. Many fine wet-on-dry brushstrokes were made with opaque white for white scales. Mosquito thorax, lateral view, by Vichai Malikul. Courtesy of Bruce Harrison, Walter Reed Biosystematics Unit.

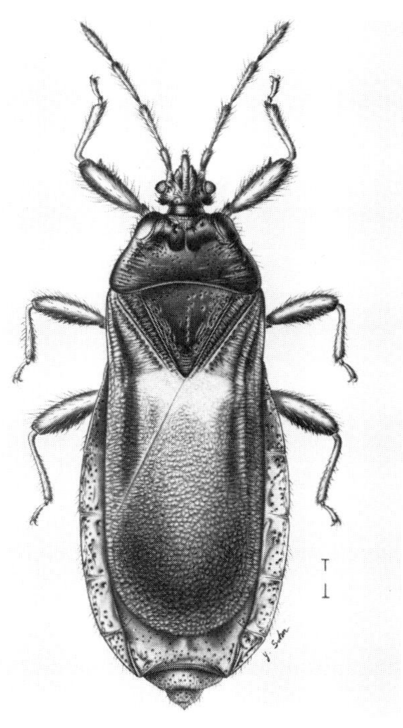

9-14. Tight wash with india ink on Bristol board. Opaque white was used for some fine white hairs and in the highlight. Note how texture is incorporated into the overall form, the small textural highlights and shadows remaining secondary to the form as a whole. Hemiptera, *Isodermus gayi*, by Young T. Sohn. Courtesy of R. C. Froeschner.

idea is to suggest it, not to paint every bump or hair. Observe carefully the shapes created when light hits the texture. Some shapes will be negative spaces, shadows between closely placed hairs (fig. 9-13), and some shapes will be small highlights and shadows of the small textural forms (fig. 9-14). Keep the lights and darks of the texture in proper relation to the lights and darks of the larger form (fig. 9-15). In the wash rendering, texture should be developed concurrently with the overall form.

To start, it may be necessary to reinforce the transferred lines slightly with delicate wet-on-dry wash application so that they will not be lost with the overall wash form. Alternate between painting texture and laying wash over whole objects to develop form. This will create a unified appearance rather than having the texture seem to just sit on top of the object. For areas where the texture is to be sharp, use the wet-on-dry application (see figs. 9-9 and 9-13). Where texture is to be subtle and softer (highlight, shaded or distant areas), use the wet-on-wet approach (see figs. 9-8 and 9-11). Since most texture will be accomplished with small, delicate lines, let the water layer become only slightly damp so that the pigment does not spread too much. This may be done as part of the overall wash. As the tonal wash becomes almost dry, add the texture strokes.

For lighter texture lines, use a clean, blotted brush to pick up tone from the tonal wash while it is still slightly damp. With less permanent pigments, use a clean, wet brush to remove small areas of tone from a previously dried wash. For sharp, delicate, bright whites, opaque white may be needed.

Fur and hair details may be added one hair at a time with a fine-tipped brush, or they may be applied with the following dry-brush method. Pick up pigment with a damp brush and squeeze the base of the brush to fan the bristles, or scrub the brush on paper to form a fan of bristles. Bristles spread apart in this way will paint several hairs at a stroke. Refill the brush with paint and fan again as needed. Vary the placement of strokes so that this pattern looks natural and not too repetitive.

Sometimes texture may be created effectively with cotton, a sponge, stiff-bristled brushes, sand or salt sprinkled on the surface, and so on.

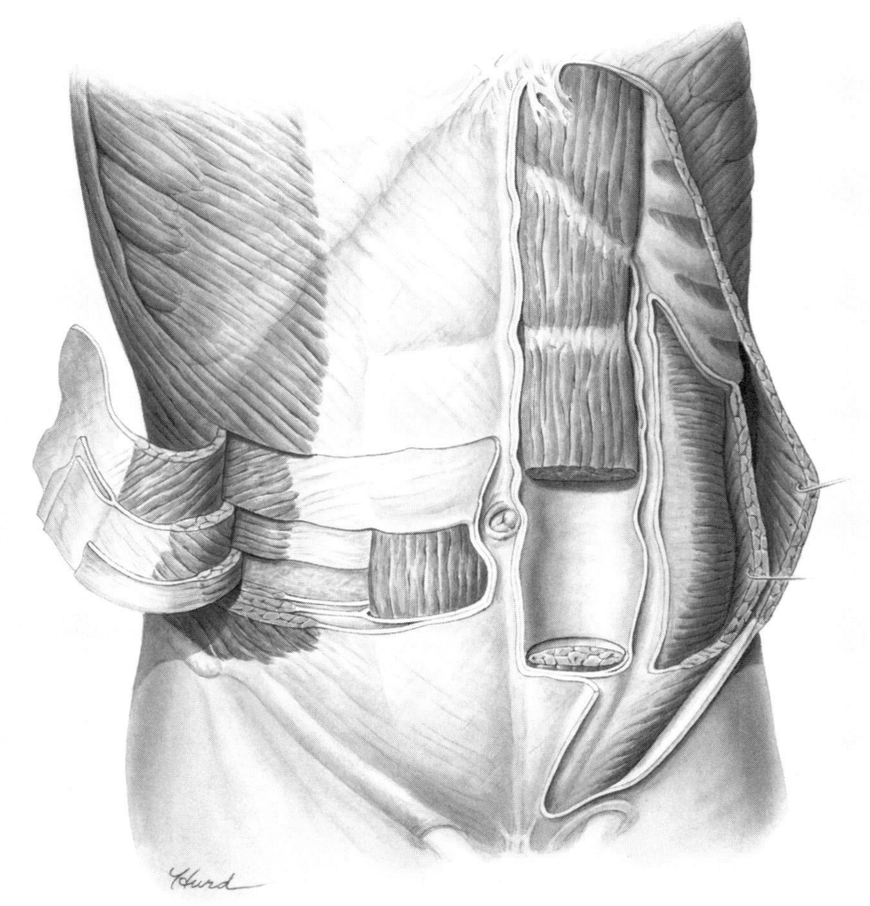

9-15. Texture, tonal differences of tissue, and a variety of cut edges are incorporated into the overall form. Permoblack on Crescent no. 110 illustration board. Muscles of the abdominal wall, by Jane Hurd. Courtesy of *American Family Physician*, March 1976 ("The Unrecognized Spigelian Hernia," Timmes, Rocko, Harper, and Zolli).

Surface patterns should be indicated in the initial sketch, leaving only the mixing of paint to match the markings. Apply the lightest base color first, then the color pattern on top, as it is easier to work up from light colors, even if dark colors predominate. For example, in a variegated leaf with light veins and a dark major pattern, cover the drawing with the subordinate light green first, then apply the darker dominant patterns, leaving the vein areas light. This ensures that the light part of the pattern is clear and true to color. Patterns may be handled and applied in much the same way as texture, although because pattern usually is flat on the surface, applying it may be the last step in a painting.

A full-color painting may need to simulate the iridescence found in many subjects in nature (see fig. C-3). Iridescence takes special planning and an understanding of the principles involved (see chapter 4).

Outlining

If outlining is desired, it always should be the final step in the painting process. Use a slightly darker value of the subject color for the outline; do not use black, no matter whether the background is white, precolored, or painted in after the subject is completed.

A subtle outline defines light areas, as shown in figures 9-14, 9-16, and 9-17. Shading that gradates to the outline makes it less obvious (see fig. 9-11). The outline can also be created by shading around rather than inside the subject. In figure 9-8, pigment in the background was built up around the frisketed subject, creating a dark outline outside the edges of the swan, so that its feathers remained stark white.

Backgrounds

Painted backgrounds may be necessary to set off the subject. Background color (flat color) is especially useful to accentuate a pale or white subject, particularly when there is an objection to outlining. Pale or white flowers, for example, are difficult to handle in full color without the use of a background or shadows. The use of colored paper as a painting surface generally is ruled out, as transparent colors cannot be used on colored paper unless the paint colors are darker than the paper. Opaque watercolors may be used successfully on colored papers; however, the pigments either must be darker than the paper or mixed with light colors or white so that they show up well against the background.

If the background is to be painted first, cover the subject area with paper or liquid frisket to prevent pigment from coming into contact with it. Then paint the background with an airbrush or large brush, trying to produce as smooth a tone as possible. Do not premoisten the background or the frisket may buckle, causing pigment leaks onto the subject.

As an alternative, use soft pastels for the background. Again, protect the subject area with frisket. Either make a powder of the pastel and apply with a cotton ball for a smooth look, or apply pastels directly and blend after application. Spray with fixative before removing the frisket.

Before painting the subject, protect the background by covering it with tracing paper and cutting an opening to expose the subject. It is virtually impossible to remove any paint spatters or other marks from a painted, airbrushed, or pastel-covered background. (A paper mask is also useful to protect an unpainted background.)

If the background is to be painted *after* the subject is completed, again the subject must be protected from spatters. Use a paper frisket, since liquid frisket might damage the paint. When the background has been added last, tonal qualities of the subject's edges adjacent to the background may have to be adjusted (see figs. C-9, C-16).

Shadows

Cast shadows add an illusion of three-dimensionality to a drawing, accentuating form and depth of the subject. Shadows may be of an allover, even tone with sharply defined edges, thus rendered easily with a flat wash. More often, however, they are smooth gradations of tones as angles of light rays and surfaces create shadows that gradually become lighter and more fuzzy-edged as they move away from their source (see figs. 4-8, 4-9). This latter type of shadow is produced with the standard graded wash, the only difference being that the edges of the shadow must gradually become less sharp as the tone becomes lighter. To achieve this, turn the surface so that the darkest part of the shadow is at the top. Starting at the edge of the object, gradually extend the water beyond the intended edge of the shadow as it moves away from the object casting it. Begin the graded wash at the darkest part of the shadow, then brush each successive stroke farther into the water layer to spread the soft shadow. The pigment should bleed out into the water layer to the intended edge of the shadow, but not to the edge of the water. If it should spread too far, quickly blot the brush and pick up the excess seepage. The result should be a very soft edge on the periphery of the shadow. The wetness of the water layer will determine the extent of the pigment spread and the fuzziness at the edge. More wetness produces more softness. Best results require several repetitions of this process. Each time, the water may be spread less or more to create the desired effects. Grayed colors such as gray-blue, gray-green, and gray-purple should be used for adding cast shadows with full-color drawings.

FULL-COLOR RENDITION

Using full color to render an illustration requires different pigment choices, an understanding of color mixing, and perhaps the addition of a full background to the drawing. For desirable qualities of paints, see the discussion of paints under Materials, at the beginning of this chapter.

Because tube colors and cake or pan colors differ on paper, the artist should make color swatches and keep them for ready reference. Use a strip of the paper usually used for color illustrations since various papers soak up color differently, and paper color and fiber content affect colors applied. Another helpful reference shows the effects of colors when applied on top of each other: paint a ½- to 1-inch-wide (1.3 to 2.5cm) stripe of each color in one direction on a square of paper large enough to accommodate all the desired colors. Then paint equally wide stripes of each color perpendicularly across all the first. A second chart reversing the order of the stripes will show the different way the colors appear, depending on which pigment is on top. The two charts also pinpoint those paints that pick up readily when a second paint is applied on top and those with good adhesive qualities.

Choice of a Palette

The range of colors available is enormous, and an illustrator's choice is a matter of personal preference. Even so, most illustrators consider several colors essential to the basic palette: those that usually intermix well and are useful for most scientific illustrations. The first five in chart 9-1 can be intermixed to produce a wide range of colors. However, if a red-purple is needed—perhaps for orchids—magenta red should be added to the palette, for it is difficult to mix.

Color Mixing

Color selection will be modified as an artist gains experience at color mixing or works with diverse subject matter. Learning to mix colors takes practice. A few basic rules follow.

Start by placing a small amount of water in a clean area of the palette. Wet the brush thoroughly by immersing it in the water jar, then tipping it against the edge to remove excess water before it is touched to the pigment. Pick up the pigment and transfer it to the pool of mixing water on the palette. After cleaning the brush in the water jar, pick up a second pigment, add it, and so on. Add pigment until the desired hue, value, and intensity are obtained. Test on a scrap of the same surface to be used for the drawing. Before proceeding, let the test surface dry to reveal intensity and truest color. It is important to mix enough paint to cover a given area without running out, as it is difficult to remix a color exactly.

Some standard rules for mixing basic colors:

- Browns: mix red and yellow with black, blue, or green.
- Purples: mix reds and blues.
- Oranges: mix reds and yellows.
- Greens: mix thalo-green or blue with cadmium yellow; add touches of red or black (judiciously) to copy the exact color.
- For lighter values: thin paint with more water.
- For darker values and shadows: use complementary colors, not black, which will tend to make a light color look dirty. Browns, purples, blues, and Payne's gray

are safer additives for the beginner.

- For bright color: add more pigment to the water. The more pigment in the mix, the more brilliant the color produced.

CORRECTIONS AND CLEANUP ON PAPER AND ILLUSTRATION BOARD

If you notice oil spots on the rendering surface while you are painting, work a paint- or water-filled brush over the spot persistently until paint or water soaks into the surface; or stop work, allow the surface to dry, and clean spots using an eraser or cleaning pad. An alternative to erasure is the addition of oxgall to the paint, which helps cover oily spots.

To remove pigment, try lifting it with water. This is easiest with less-adhesive pigments. Wet the entire area with water and, moving from top to bottom and side to side in the same manner used for applying a wash, go over it with a clean blotted brush, soft paper toweling, or facial tissue to absorb the water and any pigment that has been loosened. Repeatedly rinse and blot as pigment is lifted. The process may be repeated several times, but be gentle and avoid scrubbing, which may damage the surface. If there is no surface damage, the area may be reworked successfully with wash. Areas where the surface is damaged will absorb more pigment and subsequent washes will appear grainy.

If water does not work, try using a soft eraser or an electric eraser with a fine-grained, soft eraser plug, with a gentle, even motion. Be sure the surface is completely dry, never damp. Try not to damage the surface if it is to be reworked. A plastic imbibed eraser is sometimes effective in removing the tone without damaging the surface. For small areas, a knife or a very sharp instrument may be used to scratch off the pigment. The scratched area will not be suitable for subsequent smooth washes.

If there are dark blotches in an area of tone, try lightening them with a soft eraser. An easier method is to darken the area around the blotches to match them. Wet the entire area and apply tone selectively to areas around the blotches. Make sure that the proper amount of wetness is used so that additional pigment does not spread into the already dark blotch.

Opaque white may be used to cover undesired areas of tone. It may be applied straight and thick for bright whites, or as a tinted wash to merely lighten a tone. Painting over errors, if done carefully, will not show in reproduction.

When the painting is finished, allow it to dry thoroughly, then erase any remaining pencil lines through an erasing shield to protect colored edges, and erase or touch up spatters. If the background is spattered, moisten and blot, or gently use an ink or electric eraser (use the finer-grained eraser plugs), or carefully scrape off with a very sharp knife.

If watercolor paper has buckled, very carefully moisten the background around the drawing, then moisten the back of the drawing. Place it between blotters under a board or other flat object. Weight the board and allow to dry.

Mount the drawing on heavy board (if not already done) and cover with acetate or tracing paper to protect the now-completed drawing.

If any labels are to be used on a watercolor/wash drawing for publication, best results (crisp, black type) are achieved if the type is on a separate, registered overlay (see figs. 2-42, 2-43).

Chart 9-1. Watercolor Paint Qualities

Color	Opacity or Transparency	Colorfastness
Thalo-green or Winsor green	transparent but intense	stable
Thalo-blue or Winsor blue	transparent but intense	stable
Winsor red or Grumbacher red	slightly opaque	stable
Ivory black (a warm black)	transparent	very stable
Cadmium yellow medium or light	slightly opaque	very stable
Chinese white	tends to be opaque	very stable
Vermilion	slightly opaque	stable
Cadmium orange	transparent	stable
Cerulean blue	slightly opaque	very stable
Ultramarine blue	transparent	stable
Raw sienna	slightly opaque	stable
Burnt umber	transparent	stable
Cobalt blue	transparent	very stable
Alizarin crimson	transparent	stable
Cadmium red, pale and deep	slightly opaque	stable
Magenta red	slightly opaque	fair
Raw umber	slightly opaque	very stable
Viridian	transparent	very stable
Payne's gray	slightly opaque	stable
Violet	slightly opaque	stable
Lampblack (a cool black)	transparent	very stable
Terre verte (soft greenish brown)	transparent	very stable

Damp Wash on Scratchboard

Carolyn Bartlett Gast

Damp wash on scratchboard is a multimedia technique that uses basic wash methods with modifications. It combines diluted india ink applied with a blotted damp brush, pencil lines, and knife-scratched details on a high-quality clay-coated scratchboard surface. Sometimes a final toning with carbon dust is added just before details are scratched out. It is a technique well suited to preparation of illustrations requiring smoothly graded tones in very small areas that include tight rendering and sharp white detail. The result is an almost photographic drawing (figs. 9-16, 9-17).

MATERIALS

Surfaces

Scratchboard: Ess Dee suede board, Ess Dee regular scratchboard for ink. (See chart 8-1 for useful information on these surfaces.)

Acetate: frosted on both sides; for preliminary drawing.

Mounting board: heavyweight.

Media

India ink: Pelikan yellow label; prepare three dilutions in clean ink bottles or others of similar size:

1. A few drops of ink in a bottleful of water (pale gray).
2. One part ink to ten parts water (medium gray).
3. One part ink to three parts water (dark gray).

Pencils: graphite, 2H to HB.

Carbon dust materials: see chapter 8.

Tools

Brushes: Winsor & Newton Series 7 watercolor brushes or equivalent quality of another brand.

Scratch knife: with holder.

Eraser: Eberhard Faber Kleen-Off no. 41.

Abrasive surface: to create dust; emery cloth, metal file, or silicon carbide paper (3M no. 400).

Miscellaneous

Facial tissue.

Liquid frisket: optional.

Frosted mending tape: such as Scotch Magic (no. 810).

TECHNIQUE

Mount scratchboard on a slightly larger heavyweight board, using the frosted mending tape over all four edges for rigidity. Tape may be readily slit if it becomes necessary to remove the scratchboard from the backing. On frosted acetate, prepare a highly detailed preliminary drawing that includes everything that will appear in the final rendering.

Transfer the preliminary drawing to the scratchboard. External and internal details may be drawn on separate acetate sheets and each set transferred separately as the rendering progresses. Reinforce details and dark lines with an HB graphite pencil.

Apply the damp wash by dipping a clean brush into water, blotting the tip only, then dipping the brush into an ink dilution and blotting the entire length of the brush until it is only damp. The pigment is mostly in the brush tip while the base of the brush, where the pigment is more diluted, leaves softer tones. Swish the brush over the scratchboard so that the tip covers the darker areas of the subject. The result is a minute graded tone, brush tip to brush base in width. If the brush is handled correctly, there should be a dark bead along the edge that fades to white. Use this procedure to grade tones away from the graphite-pencil lines.

Build darker tones through several applications of pigment, using the appropriate dilution for each one. If the surface turns yellow, it means the clay has become saturated with water. Wait a few minutes until it dries and turns white again, then continue building up tones.

If the tones are too dark, lighten the area but still retain the relative values by erasing gently on the dry drawing. A moistened Kleen-Off eraser will completely and safely remove the drawing.

To keep details such as tubercles or bumps lighter than the background, paint them with liquid frisket before doing washes so that the background can be washed

9-16. Damp wash technique using diluted india ink with HB graphite pencil on scratchboard. Reconstruction of fossilized, fragmented coral that was partially embedded in rock, using photos and diagrams, by Carolyn Bartlett Gast.

over them to two-thirds of the eventual background darkness. After the wash is dry, rub off the frisket with clean fingers. The masked details will be very white; mute the white with additional overall washes to bring background to its full tone. Scratch sharp highlights and details through the dried wash.

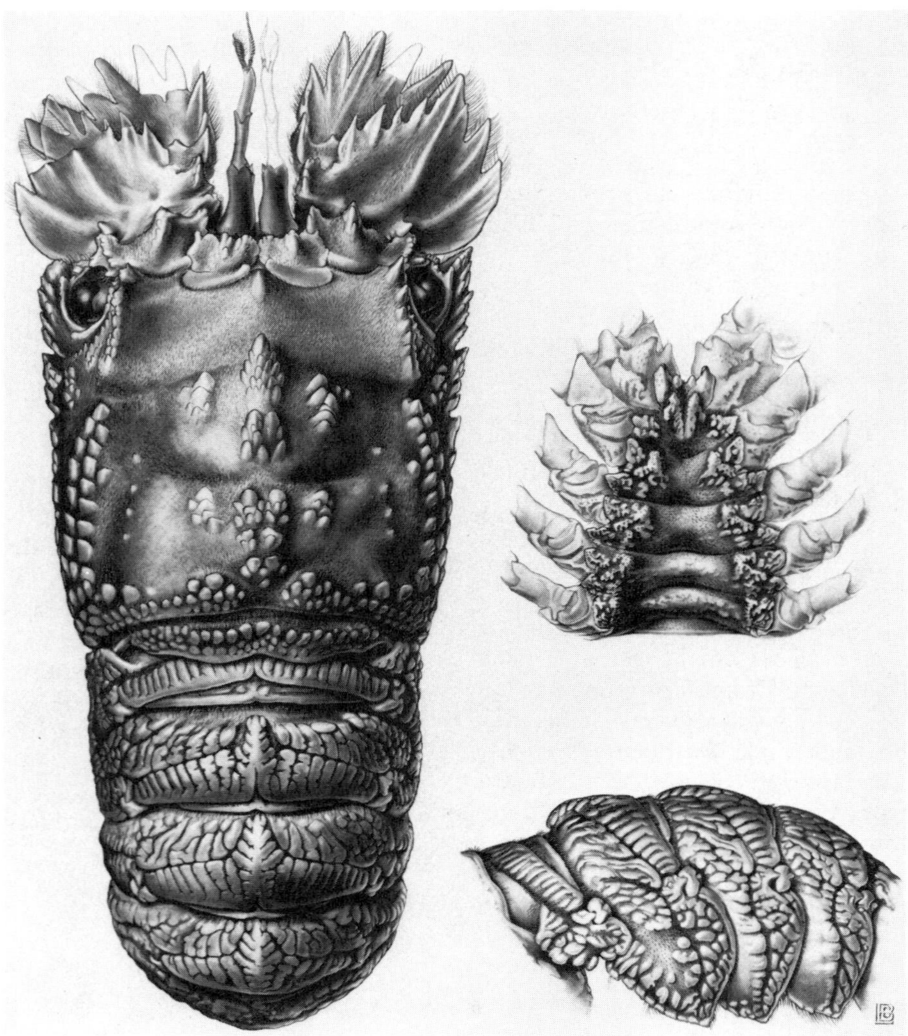

9-17. Damp wash technique using diluted india ink and HB graphite pencil on scratchboard. The bumps were masked with liquid frisket to keep them white under the first wash application, then colored with later washes. Scyllarid lobster, by Carolyn Bartlett Gast. Courtesy of R. Manning.

A modest application of carbon dust just before the last step of scratching will soften or pull together the drawing.

A modification of this technique is to use colored inks for the washes, then colored pencils and pastels for reinforcement (see fig. C-1).

CORRECTIONS FOR DAMP WASH ON SCRATCHBOARD

To make changes or to remove or lighten a toned area, wet the area thoroughly (it will turn a pale yellow) and gently agitate the surface with the smoothest, softest eraser available. The dark tone will rise to the surface of the puddle, where it can be blotted off. Wet again and repeat the process. When the board turns a very bright yellow, blot and wait an hour, or until the area is once again clear white. Then repeat the wetting and blotting. If carefully done, the area will not be damaged and may be rendered as though it were new.

Watercolor and wash techniques range from black-and-white to full color, can be used for very loose, impressionistic wash styles as well as tighter, nearly photographic renderings (as in the scratchboard technique), and ideally depict transparency and translucence. Colors range from pale to brilliant, and both watercolor and black wash combine well with other media, including pencil and dusts.

10/Gouache and Acrylics

Arwin V. Provonsha

This chapter deals with the wet media of gouache and acrylics. The main value and application of these two media is in the rendering of subjects in color, whether it be natural or only schematic. These two media have in common many functional applications, as well as many technical approaches. And many of these also closely parallel those used for traditional transparent watercolor, so chapter 9 should be consulted for additional information. These three media may, and freqently are, used in combination with each other, as well as with various other media. This "mixed media" approach is touched on in this chapter because it has become an integral part of color illustrating. In addition to the many attributes shared by gouache and acrylic paint, each also possesses its own unique qualities, uses, and approaches in application, which are covered in detail.

It is important to be aware that there is seldom one single way to use these media. The techniques described in this chapter are generally the preferred approaches of the contributing authors. What works for us may not work as well for others, and we encourage experimentation with different approaches.

For the illustrator who has traditionally worked in black-and-white, color presents an entirely new set of challenges and satisfactions. In addition to the mastery of the techniques used in rendering gouache and acrylics, a basic knowledge of color theory is also essential. It is not within the scope of this book, however, to cover this lengthy but very important topic. Many articles and books have been written on the subject, and a number of these are listed in the Bibliography.

One problem faced by all artists working in color is the light source. Anyone who has looked at paint chips in a paint store is aware of the different ways that incandescent and fluorescent lighting affect color. The problem becomes most acute for the illustrator who is painting under fluorescent room lighting but viewing the subject under an intense incandescent microscope light. In this case, incandescent light should be added over the drawing. Where possible, the subject and painting should be viewed under the same type of lighting. A combination of incandescent and fluorescent lighting best duplicates daylight.

The high cost of printing in full color has traditionally limited the amount of color artwork appearing in scientific publications. With new advances in printing technology, however, the differences in cost between color printing and black-and-white reproduction have decreased, and it is possible that, in the future, the use of color in scientific journals will become economically feasible. The commercial sector has long recognized the value of color in selling its product. Trade magazines and textbook publishers—as well as companies that supply biological materials or related instruments, equipment, or services—also represent major potential clients for the scientific illustrator who can produce full-color artwork.

Gouache (Opaque Watercolor)

Gerald P. Hodge

Gouache is composed of opaque pigments that have been ground in water and thickened with a gum substance. The chief advantage of gouache over other media is that its opaqueness will allow a light color to cover a dark color completely in one stroke. Because of its covering power, gouache often is used advantageously as an underpainting for semitransparent media such as acrylic. Some artists are pleased with the milky effects that occur when permanent white is added to colors (see fig. C-20). Others prefer to keep the clarity of pure colors or the clear tints of color lightened by zinc white (fig. 10-1). Gouache, with its fine texture, opacity, and smooth-flowing capability, is ideal for use in airbrushes and in ruling and lettering pens (see fig. C-21). Its opaqueness and brilliance particularly suit it for use on colored or gray papers.

MATERIALS

Surfaces

Illustration board, paper: medium-smooth illustration board is recommended for most work, but certain subjects might be rendered better on a rough or a high-finished (smooth) surface. If the board is thinner than single weight (about 1/16 inch or 1.5 mm), it will curl, so it should be mounted on a thicker

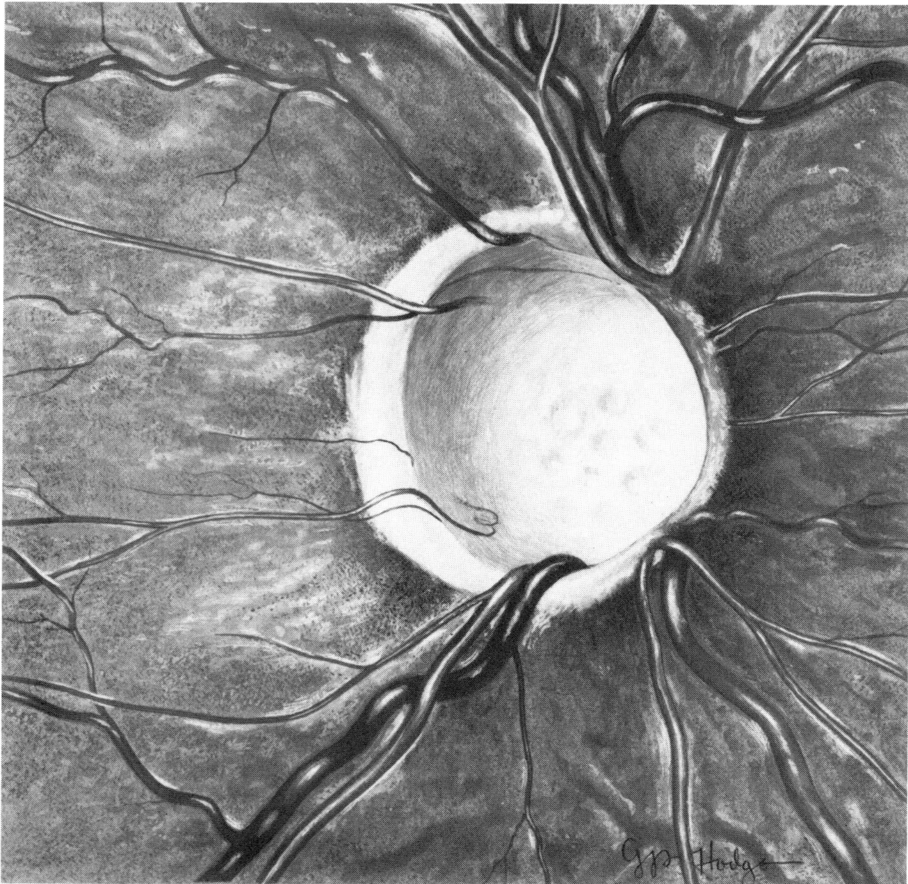

10-1. Gouache. Bright orange Mi-Teintes paper was used as the base color for the retina. The vessels, optic nerve, and surrounding details were dry-brushed with gouache, and zinc white was used to lighten colors. Depression of the optic disk due to glaucoma, by Gerald P. Hodge © 1984.

board. Gessoed panels and some heavy papers and boards such as Video Media and Line Kote are also satisfactory. Good choices for colored papers or boards include Mi-Teintes (see fig. 10-1), Color-Match (see figs. 10-4, C-20), Color-Aid, and tinted Crescent or Strathmore papers or boards. Avoid papers that are quite thin. They will become permanently rippled from the wet gouache. Drafting film also is unsatisfactory, because the dried gouache will crack and flake off if the film is lifted and curled.

Mounting board: use where needed.

Media

Paints: recommended brands in tubes are Winsor & Newton Designers Gouache watercolors and grays; in pan sets are Marabu and Pelikan opaque watercolors and Grumbacher retouch grays. Various other brands also are acceptable.

Because fairly large amounts of paint are needed for backgrounds or large objects, tube colors are preferable for such subjects; however, the sets of pan colors are useful for modeling and detailing. Occasionally, the clear binder fluid separates from the pigment in the tube. Too much of this fluid, when mixed with a relatively small amount of pigment, will cause the paint to dry too slowly, even to the point of remaining tacky. Should any of the fluid run out of the tube, replace the cap quickly and squeeze the tube back and forth until the pigment and binder are thoroughly mixed.

Although the colors required to complete a rendering may vary somewhat depending on the subject matter, the recommended list for transparent watercolors (see chart 9-1) serves well for selecting the basic palette of paints. Add to that the following: jet black, for the most intense black; ivory black, for warm grays when mixed with white; zinc white, for lightfast tints; permanent white, for greatest opacity. Keep in mind that gouache colors look different when wet than when dry. This is true also of the grays used for photo retouching—the lighter grays seem to dry darker and the darker grays may dry lighter.

The degree of permanence (nonfugitive—see chapter 3), opacity, and staining tendency varies significantly from color to color. Some colors are very opaque, while others are quite transparent. Most colors are nonstaining, but a few are highly staining; if used as a base coat, they will stain the surface and errors cannot be washed out with water. Staining colors may also bleed through superimposed colors and therefore should be used only as the final layer. Winsor & Newton has produced a chart that rates all of its Designers Gouache colors with respect to these three important but highly variable characteristics. Individual ratings also appear on the individual tubes.

Tools

Brushes: use only the finest red sable watercolor brushes, such as Winsor & Newton Series 7 or the best quality from Grumbacher or Raphael. For a detailed painting up to about 11 by 14 inches (28 by 35cm), a ¾- to 1-inch (2 to 2.5cm) bright (flat) is recommended for large areas; no. 3 round for medium-sized dry-brushed areas; no. 1 round (or smaller) for small dry-brushed areas and modeling of details.

Miscellaneous

Containers: for storing mixtures of paint. Small (one- to two-ounce) wide-mouthed bottles with screw-on lids (which can be purchased at pharmacies), plastic 35mm film containers, or coin bottles in quarter and half-dollar sizes (available in coin stores) are convenient sizes.

Plastic wrap: placed under the lid of a container of mixed paint to retard evaporation of water.

Consult the acrylic section and chapter 9 for additional materials useful in rendering with paint.

TECHNIQUE

As with any new technique, it is advisable to do some practice exercises before embarking on an important drawing. The beginner should practice putting in a background to develop a feel for how thick the paint must be and how fast to work. A few preliminary exercises in dry-brushing are recommended for learning how to build up pigment for bleeding and modeling (fig. 10-2).

Usually the background should be painted first, as it would take too long to fill in carefully around an already finished illustration and still achieve an essential smoothness of tone (fig. 10-3). To be smooth, the background must be painted rapidly. If the painted background is blemished for any reason, try going over it again with a watered-down application of the same paint mixture.

For large, flat, even areas (including backgrounds), dilute tube paint with water to the consistency of light cream. It should be just thick enough to cover completely. Paint that is too thick will lump and may crack and flake off. It will also leave brush marks. If the paint is too thin, the effect will be uneven. For dry-brushing, the paint must be thinned to a watery consistency.

10-3. Placing the image over the background. A gray-green background in gouache was applied to Crescent cold-press no. 100 illustration board. Then the feather was dry-brushed and stippled with gouache. First flight feather of great horned owl, detail, by Gerald P. Hodge © 1984.

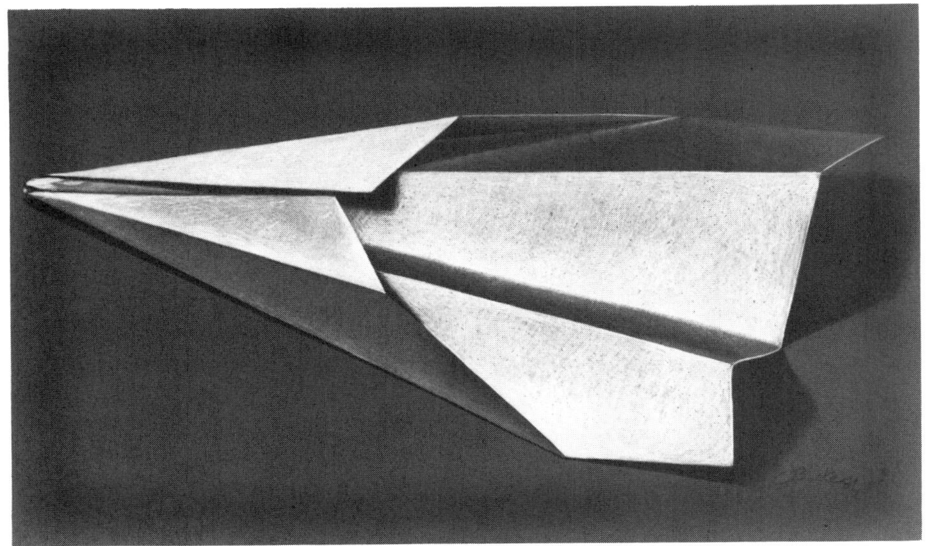

10-2. Practice exercise of paper airplane in gouache on Crescent cold-press illustration board, medium surface. After the approximate flat values in grays were painted, a dry-brush technique of crosshatching was used to blend the values. The gouache for the background should be the consistency of light cream, and the paint for dry-brushing should be thinned with water. Christopher J. Burke © 1981.

Since the paint dries fast, it is necessary to work rapidly in several directions, crisscrossing back and forth, in order to eliminate all brushstrokes. To achieve a smooth tone, paint a thin first coat, allow it to dry thoroughly, and then quickly paint a second thin coat over the first one.

Avoid painting over damp spots. Underlying paint may lift off when an additional coat is applied if the underlying coat is still damp. Be patient and allow the undercoat to dry thoroughly before proceeding. If lifting does occur, stop immediately, let the paint dry thoroughly, then blend the undercoat by dry-brushing clear water over the area. If lifting is severe, adding a watered-down coat of the base color may be necessary. Save some of the original paint mixture for this purpose as well as for repairs to the background (which often are necessary after all rendering is finished).

After the background is thoroughly dry, use one of the transfer techniques described in chapter 1 to transfer the preliminary drawing to the painting support. Protect the background by taping over the painting a cover sheet through which an opening slightly larger than the outline of the sketch has been cut (see fig. 1-3).

Use the dry-brush technique to blend colors and build the form of the subject on the background. Dip the brush in paint that has a watery consistency, then remove most of the paint by pressing and stroking the brush a few times on a piece of practice paper. This also will fan out the brush. For extremely subtle dry-brushing, follow the same procedure, then squeeze out even more of the paint between thumb and index finger, being careful to keep the brush fanned out.

Some artists dry-brush consistently in the same direction—diagonally up from left to right or diagonally down from right to left. Others prefer dry-brushing in several directions, crosshatching their strokes and constantly changing the position of the paper until the effect is uniform. If dry-brushing appears too textured, the effect can be softened or completely eliminated by finishing with clear water dry-brushed over the area. The brush must not be too wet—just damp or fairly dry, depending on the desired result. This procedure will blend the adjacent and underlying paint together (fig. 10-4).

Paint the subject in several values with the intent to blend them together later. Determine the middle value to be painted by imagining the actual three-dimensional modeling of lights and shadows as variously toned flat patterns. Mix colors to approximate these tones, outline the areas to be painted, then quickly fill in with the same mixture.

For the light area of the subject, mix white with the middle color for a tint about 15 percent lighter. Dry-brush this mixture on the area to be lightened. Add more white and dry-brush again (if necessary) to lighten further. For the shadow side of the subject, mix a small portion of black (used judiciously and in minute amounts) or a darker value of the same hue or a complementary color to the original mixture, and dry-brush it on. Add more of the darker pigment and dry-brush again if necessary to darken further.

To increase the color range of the painting, dry-brush some pale tints of warm colors such as yellow, orange, or pink on the light side of the painting, and cooler shades such as blue, green, or purple over the shadow side. These tints and shades should be made very thin with water before applying. This method of increasing the color range may not apply to all subject matter.

The appearance of a shiny or wet surface is created by a hard highlight. Apply a brilliant opaque white as a final touch; the paint must be just thick enough to flow from the brush easily. If it is applied too thinly, the highlight will not be pure white when the paint is dry because some of the underlying color will show through. To soften the edges of a highlight, dry-brush some thinned white around the hard highlight. Subtle, soft highlights may be added with colored pencil, as described under the section on acrylics (see fig. C-28).

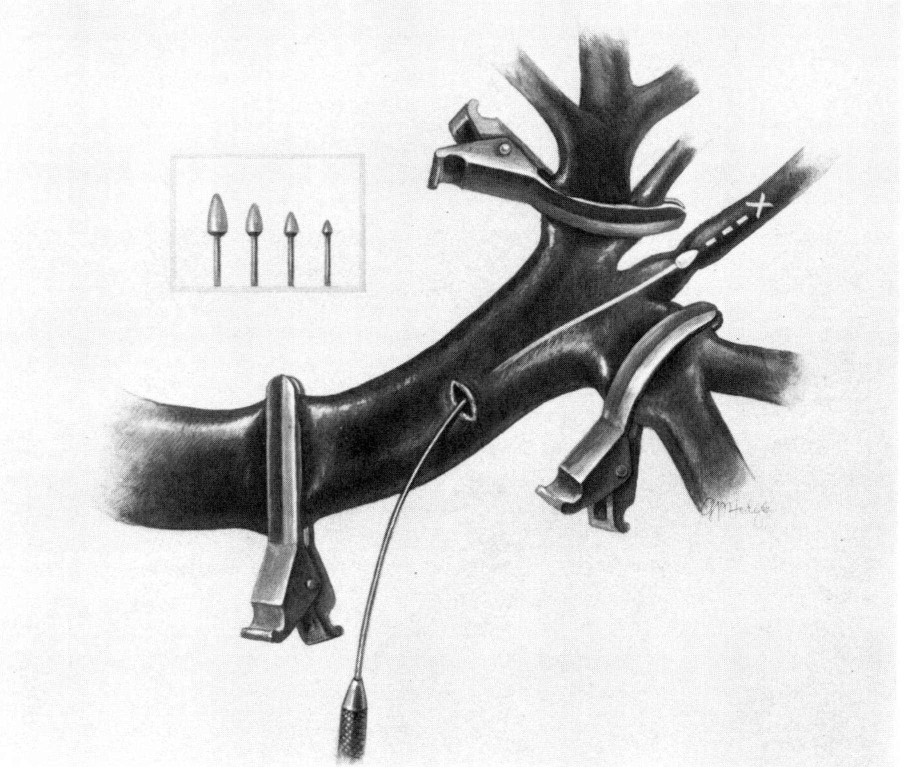

10-4. Smooth effect with gouache. Texture is sometimes unwanted for small drawings. After the preliminary dry-brushing has been finished, dry-brush again with water only. This will soften or eliminate any existing brushstrokes. Gouache on light gray ColorMatch paper. Renal vessel, by Gerald P. Hodge © 1984.

Protection and Repair

Because gouache paintings are so easily damaged, it is wise to protect all finished work with some type of covering. (See chapter 1 for recommended procedures.) Do not use varnish, lacquer, or fixatives of any type without experimenting first, as they may make the painting semitransparent and blotchy.

When dry, gouache is very rigid and brittle. If applied to a thin surface that has not been properly mounted on a sturdier board, rolling, bending, or rough handling will cause the paint to crack or flake off. Cracking may also occur if the paint is too thick when it is applied and/or if it is force-dried by exposing it to excessive heat. In any of these situations, prevention is the best cure. If cracking does occur, it may be repaired by lightly and very carefully dry-brushing over the cracks with clear water to reblend the paint.

Acrylics

Arwin V. Provonsha

Acrylic paints consist of fine particles of water-insoluble acrylic plastic suspended in water, forming an emulsion. The addition of a catalyst causes the particles to polymerize into a resin as the water vehicle evaporates, forming a tough film (thus the term *acrylic polymer emulsion*). The film contains microscopic pores, making it water permeable but not water soluble.

Acrylic paints provide an extremely versatile medium with many noteworthy qualities. Their strong adhesiveness and flexibility make them suitable for working on a broad range of surfaces, from paper to drafting film. Acrylics can produce a very smooth or textured surface with either a matte or a glossy finish. The hues are exceptionally brilliant and will not yellow or fade with time (see fig. C-22). They dry rapidly and, when dry, are water insoluble, allowing the application of additional coats without affecting the underlying layers. They can be applied in a wide variety of techniques, including transparent washes (as in watercolors) or opaque overlays (as in gouache or oil paints), with airbrush, or in a variety of other ways that cannot be duplicated with any other medium (see figs. C-23, C-24). To achieve special effects, they may be mixed or used in conjunction with many other materials such as pastels, watercolor, pencil dust, and sand.

The acrylic painting method described here combines techniques used for transparent watercolor and gouache. Chapter 9 should be consulted for additional information that can be applied to painting with acrylics.

MATERIALS

Surfaces

Illustration board: three- or four-ply, matte finish (cold-press) board. A slight matte finish allows for better and more uniform adhesion of the paint, and erasures and other cleanup procedures are less noticeable on this type of board than on a smooth-surfaced (hot-press) one. Acid-free 100 percent rag paper resists yellowing; standard student illustration board is less expensive but yellows with age and exposure to light. However, if the board is to be treated with gesso, it is not necessary to use the more expensive rag board.

Untempered hardboard: ⅛- or 3/16-inch (3 or 4.7mm) thick; Masonite and other brands. If the rendition is to be especially large (more than 12 by 16 inches/30 by 40cm) and a gesso surface is desired, untempered hardboard is recommended over illustration board.

Drafting film: polyester or acetate, frosted on one or both sides.

Gesso: provides a smooth, uniform surface that is especially receptive to acrylic paint. It also provides a very white background, and errors can be corrected easily by covering the area with more gesso.

Media

Paint: acrylic paints are available in tubes or jars. Of the two, the more widely used and readily available is tube paint, which has the consistency of toothpaste and needs to be thinned with either water or acrylic medium for most techniques. Its opacity varies greatly from color to color. Jar paints are most convenient when large quantities are needed. They lie flatter and have greater covering capacity than tube paints; however, there are fewer colors available. Only jar paints are advised for use with an airbrush. Jar and tube paints may be mixed.

Most of the better brands of acrylic polymer paints perform equally well. Some brands, such as Liquitex, come in "modular colors," providing a broad range of premixed values that greatly reduces the amount of mixing time required. Within the standard and modular systems, there are more than seventy-five tube colors from which to choose. Although the basic palette will vary somewhat depending on the subject matter, a suggested general list of colors appears in chart 9-1.

Soak the top of hard-to-open containers in very warm water for ten or fifteen minutes, then twist the cap with a firm, even, and prolonged pressure. The problem can be minimized by getting in the habit of using a damp paper towel to wipe away traces of paint or medium from the lid and neck of the container before replacing the lid.

Mediums: although acrylic paint may be thinned with water, most manufacturers produce liquid painting mediums for this purpose. These acrylic polymer latex emulsions are mixed with acrylic colors to increase their transparent qualities and produce a uniform surface.

Three formulations are useful in painting scientific illustrations:

1. Matte medium: when mixed with paint, will produce a satin finish. It may also be applied as a final varnish whenever a matte finish is desired, but it tends to dull the colors slightly in the process.
2. Gloss medium: has similar properties to matte medium but produces glossy characteristics. When used as a final varnish, it tends to deepen and brighten the colors slightly.

   Gloss and matte mediums may be mixed in various proportions to produce the desired finish. Most brands of medium come in jars; however, Vanguard (Hunt) matte and gloss mediums come in squeeze bottles, making measuring very easy.
3. Gel medium: versatile medium that comes in tube form and has the same consistency as the tube colors. Like the other mediums, it is milky white but dries to a clear, transparent film. Although it may be used as a final varnish, it is generally mixed with tube colors to increase their transparency while maintaining the pasty consistency of the paint.

Retarder: in most instances, the quick-drying characteristic of acrylic paint is advantageous; if it dries too fast for handling proper blending of colors, however, a retarder may be added to extend the drying time and prolong the workability of the paint.

Pencils: graphite.

Pastels: soft, chalky type, not oil pastels.

Tools

Brushes: use good-quality red sable brushes in size nos. 6 and 8 for laying in general color; nos. 3 and 2 round for details; no. 10 bright (flat) for wetting and filling in large areas of color. Other useful brushes are nos. 0, 00, or 000 spotting brush for very fine details; one- or two-inch (2.5 or 5cm) bristle or camel-hair brush for applying gesso; no. 6 or 10 lettering brush for long, crisp edges. (See chapter 9 for discussion of brush quality.)

Erasers: Artgum or kneaded rubber for general erasing. A fiberglass eraser works well for removing drops of paint from the background on illustration board not treated with gesso. An electric eraser is also effective for this purpose.

Miscellaneous

Palette: a well-and-slant palette with at least ten sections. Because of the adhesive quality of acrylics, the palette used must be made of a material to which the paint will not permanently adhere. Nylon and polycarbonate plastic are best; glass, Formica, and white enamel are suitable but harder to clean if paint has dried.

Containers: small bottles for storing mixed paint. (See Gouache, Miscellaneous, for details.) Plastic ice cube trays or chambered plastic boxes similar to those used by fishermen for storing lures also may be used for mixing and storing. Since these boxes are usually made from acrylic plastic, they should be sprayed with silicone before using to prevent chemical bonding of the paint. Two small jars for water are also needed, one for cleaning brushes, the other for adding clean water to the paint.

Paper towels, facial tissues: for cleaning and blotting brushes.

Sandpaper: extra-fine, for sanding gesso coating.

Register marks: for aligning the tracing for repeated transfers of drawing.

Liquid frisket: painted on with a brush to protect a part of the work or to maintain a blank area while additional color is added; peeled or rubbed off after the paint has dried. Use commercial friskets, such as Miskit by Grumbacher; thinned rubber cement may yellow a paper surface by introducing acid.

Workable fixative.

Spray bottle: filled with plain water to dampen paint on palette.

TECHNIQUE

Preparation

Illustration Board

If the subject is to be rendered with general watercolor techniques, uncoated illustration board provides an excellent surface. When the painting is to be done directly on 100 percent rag board, no preliminary preparation of the surface is necessary. However, after the outline drawing has been transferred to the board, the area within the confines of the drawing should be wetted with clear water to prepare the board to receive the paint.

Illustration Board Coated with Gesso

Apply one to three coats in a mixture of approximately one part water, one part matte medium, and three parts gesso. The addition of medium to the mixture will help seal the board and prevent any eventual yellowing from bleeding through to the surface of the painting. The gesso should be about the consistency of cream. If brushstrokes are noticeable, it is too thick; add more water. If two or more coats are used, apply them in alternate directions. Each coat should be allowed to dry thoroughly, then lightly sanded with extra-fine sandpaper to produce a smooth and uniform surface. It is usually necessary to apply an equal number of coats of gesso to the back of the board to prevent warping. Gesso may also be applied with an airbrush with excellent results.

Hardboard Coated with Gesso

The surface should be sanded and cleaned of dust before gesso is applied, as above, to both sides of the board. Three or more coats are usually necessary to cover the brown hardboard completely.

Transfer

Transfer the preliminary drawing to the support using one of the techniques described in chapter 1. During the initial transfer, it is not necessary to include small details that will be obscured when paint is added. After the basic colors have been applied, the tracing paper with preliminary drawing may be replaced over the painting and these details transferred at that time. Register marks placed outside the area of the drawing will help in realigning the tracing for this procedure.

Backgrounds

Many technical illustrations require a white background, but, where feasible, background color can add interest to an illustration and enliven the main subject. This is true whether the background color is solid and uniform, uneven, only a splash, or a fully detailed natural setting.

A uniform background color can be achieved by mixing acrylic pigment with gesso. Be sure to reserve some of this background color for touching up any errors later on. To produce an uneven effect, simply brush acrylic pigment into the gesso while it is still wet. Splashes of color are most effectively applied with an airbrush and acrylic jar paint. A similar effect can be achieved with pastels. If pastels are used, spray with workable fixative or thinned acrylic medium (with water, approximately one to one) in an airbrush before painting the main subject.

In most cases, it is easier to paint the background before beginning work on the main subject. If the background color is fairly uniform, it is not likely to show through the final painting. If, however, a detailed or uneven background containing various light and dark areas is used, there may be some interference, especially if the main subject is fairly light in color. This problem can be solved by drawing the outline of the main subject before painting the background and applying a liquid frisket or frisket film to this area. Or it can be done by drawing the outline of the main subject after the background is painted and filling it with an opaque coat of medium-gray acrylic paint to obscure all background color.

Paint Preparation

This is one of the most critical aspects of full-color scientific illustration. If the colors are not at least reasonably close to those of the subject, the main purpose of the illustration may never be realized.

As a first step, mix the basic ground color (local color) of the subject, looking for a point of reference where the values are least altered by highlights or shadows. For this basic undercoat, thin the paint with plain water or water and a small amount of matte medium until it is about the consistency of poster paint. Even though acrylics have an exceptional ability to even out when they are dry, it is better to apply the paint thinly in two coats than in a single thick coat, which may leave permanent brushstrokes. Any texture on the surface may distort colors applied later.

Although a little paint goes a long way, make certain to prepare enough to finish the job. It can be extremely frustrating to try to match a color exactly when you are halfway through a painting.

While working, it may be occasionally necessary to spray a fine mist of water over thick paint on the palette or to add a few drops of water to thinned paint to keep it from drying out. Small amounts of acrylic tube paints squeezed onto a damp paper towel will remain moist for hours. If the painting must be set aside for a period of time, cover the palette with plastic wrap. First ring the lip of the palette wells with paint to ensure airtight adhesion of the plastic wrap.

One of the few disadvantages of acrylics is that they change color slightly (usually darkening) as they dry, so it is important to test colors on a scrap of the same support material being used, letting them dry thoroughly.

When mixing colors on the palette, use a clean area each time to avoid picking up particles of dried acrylic paint.

Applying Color

Do not fasten down the painting. As work progresses, turn it to whatever position is necessary to allow comfortable and controlled strokes.

Block in the basic areas of color

with flat, opaque tones (see fig. C-25). Use as large a brush as is practical for the central areas, switching to a smaller brush only as needed. Do not worry about highlights or shadows at this point.

As with watercolors, the opacity of acrylics varies from color to color. It may take several coats to obtain the desired uniform coverage. It is best to start with the lightest colors and work to the darkest. Although acrylic paint has good covering qualities, it is often difficult to mask a darker area completely with a lighter color.

In areas where the edges of color patterns are graded rather than sharply defined, extend the lighter color to the point where it is completely dissipated. As you add darker color, blend the edges using the basic wet-on-wet watercolor technique: wet the area with clear water (not excessively wet, just damp), then apply the paint along the dark edge and let it bleed into the lighter area. Smooth any uneven spots gently with a light touch of a damp brush. If a good base coat has been laid down, the paint will not soak into the surface too rapidly and can be moved about quite freely until it begins to dry. The addition of a little matte medium will help retard the drying time slightly; however, fast work is necessary. Once the paint starts to set, stop! Any alterations attempted at this point will lift out small remaining puddles of wet paint, creating a blotchy effect.

By looking at the drawing surface at an angle, you can usually see the shine reflected by any remaining moisture. If a puddle of paint does lift from the surface, it is often difficult to repair, since, unlike watercolors or gouache, acrylics cannot be moved around with a damp brush once they are dry. The only solution may be to repaint the damaged area completely.

Refining the Colors

The next step is to develop small color differences, value shifts, and shadows (see figs. C-26, C-27). After the base colors have dried thoroughly, replace the tracing over the painting, making certain that it is perfectly aligned. Retrace all details that have become obscured by the base coat.

Once again, the paints should be rather thin and built up with several semitransparent coats, a process called *glazing*. By definition, a transparent glaze, whatever its color, should rest on a surface that is lighter colored than the glaze.

To prepare a glaze, mix equal parts of medium and water with a small amount of pigment. First, dampen the area to be glazed with clear water to ensure an even application of glaze, then add the glaze with even, smooth, and rapid strokes. Blend the edges with a clean, damp brush. Now you have only a few seconds to decide whether you like what you have done. If necessary, the entire glaze may be lifted quickly from the painting with a slightly damp brush, or washed out with a wet one. However, once the color has dried, such corrections are not likely to be successful. Any small imperfections may be corrected by dry-brushing pigment over the problem area with a fine spotting brush.

Glazing is also an excellent way to depict translucent structures such as insect wings (see fig. C-26) or other thin membranes. A slightly glossy medium (mixed matte and gloss) is a more effective vehicle for this type of glaze than is a matte medium. First paint any underlying structures, rendering them in a somewhat translucent fashion, not in totally opaque tones. This is easily achieved by working wet-on-wet. Allowing the edges to remain a little ill-defined will help add to the translucent effect when the overlying membrane is glazed in.

Highlights

After adding all structural color and shadows (see fig. C-27), start working on the highlights (see fig. C-28). Achieving effective highlights can be difficult, especially for the beginner. Do not be timid about indicating them, however. They are often essential in conveying the proper texture and form of the subject.

Highlights will vary from a slightly lighter value of the local color to pure white, depending on the texture of the subject and the angle of light on the surface area where the highlight appears (see fig. C-23). In the case of certain iridescent organisms, highlights might have to be indicated in an entirely different hue (see chapter 4).

The process of adding a lighter opaque color on top of a darker one is referred to as *scumbling*. Prepare the paint for scumbling in highlights in the same way as that used in glazing—approximately one part water to one part matte medium; however, a little more pigment is usually required for proper coverage. Here, too, a little paint goes a long way. After dampening the area to be highlighted, pick up only a small quantity of paint on the brush. It may be necessary to remove most of this paint on the scrap of support material to produce a fairly dry brush. Try to apply the paint in a single stroke. The edges may be gently blended, but avoid overworking the area as this will result in an uneven blotching, which is more noticeable in scumbling than in glazing. If the surface is dampened properly, the highlights will flow on smoothly and will bleed out just enough to minimize the amount of blending necessary. If the surface is too wet, however, the pigment will puddle around the outside of the highlight—a situation difficult to correct or conceal once the paint has dried. If the surface is too wet, it is best to lift the entire highlight from the painting and start over. As with shadows, small imperfections in highlights may be touched up with very thin paint applied with an almost dry spotting brush. It is best to build up the scumbled highlights gradually, using several coats to achieve the brighter primary highlights.

The use of other media, such as oils, pastels, and colored pencils, can be of great help in rendering realistic shadows, highlights, and many slight color shifts.

Small Details and Outlining

Most small details, such as setae (hairs) and punctations (small pits) can be added with a no. 1, 0, or 00 brush. When drawing fine lines, make certain that the paint is not too thick and that there is not too much paint in the brush, either of which will result in uneven, overly heavy, or broken lines.

Adding some outline can make the work crisper and provide sharper definition and technical clarity. Outlines generally should be done with a slightly darker value of the base color they border.

Corrections and Cleanup

If the subject has been rendered on white, uncoated illustration board, mistakes may be covered with value 9 neutral gray paint, which matches the color of the board more closely than does a pure white paint. Small unwanted splatters of paint outside the subject area also may be removed with an electric eraser or a brush-type fiberglass eraser. Never try to scrape away unwanted lines or marks with a razor blade or knife, as this will destroy the texture of the board and may create a flaw more obvious than the original mistake.

If a uniform white or tinted gesso background has been used, lightly sand any spatters of paint, then cover the area with additional gesso. After it has dried, sand again to match the texture of the original background. With a colored background, use the reserved tinted gesso for touch-up.

Although it is advisable to clean the palette immediately after use, dried paint usually will peel off with little difficulty if a suitable palette is used. A brief soaking in warm water will loosen any stubborn spots.

Clean brushes immediately with soap and warm water. Be sure to remove all paint from the base of the inner bristles. Dried paint is difficult to remove from a brush; soaking it in ethyl or isopropyl alcohol may help.

Acrylic paint may be used in conjunction with many other media. A few of the more commonly used "mixed media" approaches are discussed below. Materials and techniques, however, are limited only by the imagination of the user. Some experimentation may be required to find the most suitable combination for the individual artist and the subject matter being rendered.

Backpainting on Film

Trudy Nicholson

Color can be added to a continuous-tone drawing rendered in carbon dust on frosted polyester or acetate film by applying acrylic paint and colored pencil to the back surface of the film, and by placing a background of colored paper or board behind the film. Before color is added, however, the carbon dust illustration should be photographed against a white background as a continuous-tone print for publication. Once color is added, the drawing becomes a highly rendered, full-color illustration for colored slides, display, or prints (see figs. C-4, C-29, C-30).

MATERIALS

In addition to the basic carbon dust materials described in chapter 8, the following will be needed:

Surfaces

Drafting film: polyester or acetate, frosted on one or both sides (see chapter 8 and chart 8-2).

Mounting board: white.

Colored board or paper: to create background colors.

Media

Colored pencils: Prismacolor or other soft brands; adheres only to frosted surface.

Acrylic paint: adheres to frosted or unfrosted surfaces.

Tools

Brushes: for painting back of film with acrylic.

Airbrush: optional, for background or rendering effects.

Toothbrush or other stiff brush: optional, to create spatter effect.

Scraper: no. 16 X-Acto blade and holder or other blade, for removing acrylic paint.

Miscellaneous

Soft facial tissue or cotton wads: to clean film

Alcohol, soap and water, or household detergent: to clean film if necessary (see chapter 2, under Drafting Films).

Tape: artist's or translucent, to tape edges of acetate.

Transparent acetate: to sandwich between preliminary sketch and rendering film.

TECHNIQUE

Examine the film angled to the light, holding it carefully by the edges, to be sure there are no discolorations or scratches deep enough to affect the rendering. Remove any dirt or fingerprints by the method recommended in chapter 2, under Drafting Film. Once carbon dust has been applied, the film cannot be cleaned without smearing rendered areas. Tape the edges of the acetate to prevent its tearing (unnecessary with polyester film). To protect the surface from skin oils or other dirt, cover the film with a sheet of tracing paper cut out only where rendering is to be done, and always keep a tissue under your hand or wear gloves.

Tape the film, frosted side up, over the pencil sketch. Transparent acetate inserted between the sketch and the film will keep pencil from the sketch from adhering to

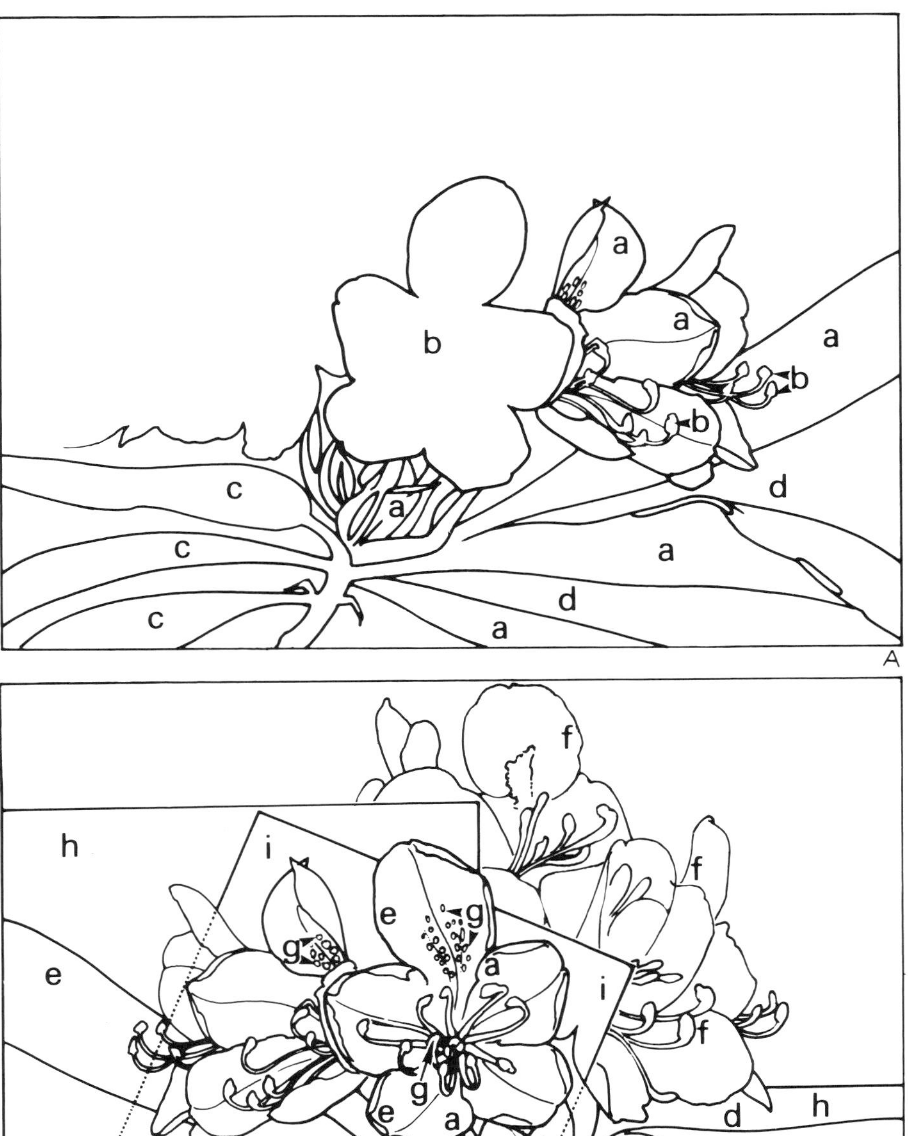

10-5. Backpainting on film. *(A)* Diagram of the back surface of the demonstration illustration shown in figure C-29. *(B)* Diagram of the front surface in figure C-30. Media used for shading and for color are designated by letters described in the following key:
(a) Prismacolor pencil applied to the back surface. *(b)* Winsor & Newton artist's acrylic paint, titanium white, applied opaquely in several layers to the back surface over Prismacolor pencil. *(c)* Liquitex artist's acrylic paint, value 5 green, applied opaquely in several layers to the back surface. *(d)* Black areas created by applying Wolff's carbon pencil BB directly on the front, then smoothed with paper stumps. *(e)* Gray shading created by a light application of Wolff's carbon dust BB and HB with paper stumps and tortillions of different sizes. *(f)* Pencil sketch placed under the Cronaflex. *(g)* Prismacolor pencil applied to a small area on the front surface. *(h)* Blue Color-Aid paper (no. B T3) placed under the finished portion of the illustration. The completed illustration will have one sheet of Color-Aid for the entire background. *(i)* Orange Color-Aid paper (no. OYO HUE) used in this demonstration to show the effect a bright color has on subjects that have not been opaquely colored. It has altered the color of the leaves on the left, the calyx, and the blossom petals on the left. The colors of the central blossom, the stamens, and the pistil, which have been opaquely painted on the back, are not changed by the introduction of color placed behind them. Pen-and-ink on Denril film, by Trudy Nicholson © 1987.

the back of the film. Render in carbon dust technique (see chapter 8).

After rendering, reverse the drafting film so the unrendered side is up. Clean the reverse side gently with a tissue to be sure that any dirt or pencil residue from the sketch is removed, as static electricity makes particles adhere to film. Place the film, rendered side up, on a white board for photographing. If the illustration is handled carefully, it is unnecessary to apply fixative. After any necessary black-and-white photographs of the carbon dust rendering have been taken, coloring may begin.

Position the film with the unrendered side up and the rendered side down on a clean, flat surface. If you are using colored pencils, the film must be frosted on both sides since the pencil will not adhere to an unfrosted surface. Acrylic paint, on the other hand, will adhere to either frosted or unfrosted film. It can be painted over colored pencil or directly on the unrendered surface in flat colors within the edges of the subject (fig. 10-5A; see fig. C-29). It is difficult to blend these colors effectively with a brush, but the carbon dust rendering will add a remarkable effect of shading to the flat acrylic colors when viewed from the rendered side. Several layers of acrylic are necessary to achieve an opaque color so the color of the backing board will not show through the acrylic, affecting its color (fig. 10-5B; see fig. C-30). Acrylic paint can be spattered or airbrushed onto this unrendered side to blend colors or to achieve certain texture effects. Other textures, as well as small color areas, can be created with colored pencil before the acrylic is laid down. When working on the reverse (unrendered) side, color areas in reverse order, placing small details of color, such as highlights, first, and then painting general color areas over these. It helps to plan the sequence before applying paint.

Be sure to consider the effect that colors will have on the carbon dust rendering through which they will be seen. As a test, apply a small patch of paint to the unrendered side; let it dry, then reverse the film to determine the color's effect. If it overpowers the carbon dust rendering, remove the acrylic by dampening it and then very gently scraping it off without scratching the film. It will peel off as a thin skin. Try a lighter color.

When the coloring on the reverse side is complete and dry, return the film to its original position, with the carbon dust rendering up. Apply finishing touches such as fine highlights, light hairs, or veins on the carbon dust side. Acrylics or watercolor (painted or airbrushed) or colored pencil add subtle color changes when applied on top of the carbon dust, but care must be taken to avoid disturbing the carbon dust rendering.

To provide a colored background for the rendered subject, place colored board or paper under the completed illustration (see fig. C-30). Cast shadows or other background effects may be rendered on this backing surface using airbrush, carbon dust, or other technique (see fig. C-4). The assembly of the backpainted film over the background colors completes the final color illustration.

Colors applied to the reverse, unrendered side can be easily removed. Colored pencil can be gently scratched off without totally removing the tooth of the frosted surface, permitting reapplication of colored pencil. Acrylic can be peeled off as previously described.

This technique provides opportunities for color changes and experimentation. Colored pencil, used on the reverse frosted side to color large areas, creates a different color effect from that produced by acrylic paint. Colored paper, cut to the shape of the subject, gives an overall color and produces yet another effect (see fig. 10-5B). All of these media can be combined in various ways.

Acrylic Paint with Pencils, Pastels, and Ink

Arwin V. Provonsha

In addition to the backpainting approach described above, acrylic paint may be used in combination with carbon and graphite pencils, as well as colored pencils and pastels, in a more direct approach. These other media can be used to advantage in rendering highlights, shadows, and small details, as well as in laying down major areas of color. This approach can save the artist a tremendous amount of time over rendering the same subject matter completely with acrylics in a more traditional approach.

MATERIALS

In addition to the basic materials listed at the beginning of this chapter, the artist should have the following:

Prismacolor pencils.

Conté pastel pencils.

Graphite pencils: 2H through B.

Carbon or charcoal pencils: HB, B.

India ink.

Technical and/or conventional pens.

Tortillions and stumps (stomps).

Workable fixative.

TECHNIQUE

Acrylic paint may be used to provide a rather minimal colored underpainting, with pencil being used to complete all color shifts and details (see fig. C-31). This approach is here referred to as a "partial" rendering. At the other extreme, acrylic paint may be used to produce all major color patterns and the majority of details, with pencil used only to enhance the acrylic rendering (see fig. C-28). This approach is referred to as a "complete" rendering. The artist may find that the best results lie somewhere between these two extremes.

Partial Rendering

The painting support can be any coarse, nonglossy board in whatever color will best enhance the illustration, and of a quality that will last for the needs of the project. Mat board (100 percent rag) provides an ideal surface for this type of rendering.

Apply the basic colors of the subject in uniform, flat, transparent acrylic washes (see chapter 9 for technique details). Refine all color variations, shadows, highlights, and most details with colored pencils (see chapter 6 for techniques). Areas of color that are blotchy or cloudy can be rendered effectively with pastel dust applied with a stump. A heavy undercoating of colored pencil may prevent proper adhesion of pastels; a coat of clear acrylic matte medium will help solve this problem. Touch up primary highlights and small sharply defined details with acrylic paint.

Complete Rendering

Use any painting support suitable for acrylics. If a gesso-coated board is used, make certain that it is smooth and free of brushstrokes or other flaws, as they will have an adverse effect on the application of pencil.

Prepare a fully developed acrylic painting, complete with basic shadows. To blend and improve shadow areas, use Prismacolor pencils in the same hue as the underlying colors. These areas may be blended slightly with a clean stump, but the waxy nature of the pencil prevents its being moved around very much. Slight variations in color or a coarsely textured quality can be obtained by gently rubbing the flat side of the pencil point over the appropriate areas of the painting.

Realistic highlights can be achieved by laying down white Prismacolor pencil, blending it with a stump, adding more pencil to the primary highlight areas, and then blending in titanium white acrylic paint. Use a dry-brush technique with a no. 00 to no. 1 brush. Work from the center of the highlight outward in a stippling fashion until you cannot tell where the paint stops and the pencil remains.

On very dark subjects, the effect of reflected light may be added by applying white or light-colored Prismacolor or pastel pencil dust with a clean stump. (Sand a pencil point to collect dust.)

A very thick underpainting of acrylics may result in a surface too slick for the pencil to adhere to. A coat of clear matte medium will provide a better working surface.

Graphite or carbon pencils may also be used effectively in rendering shadows. In most cases, graphite is best suited for this purpose as shadows often contain some gray-blue colors, which are closely approximated by graphite. Apply the graphite pencil directly and then blend with a stump, or apply it as graphite dust gathered on a stump (see fig. C-28).

After pencil has been added, spray with workable fixative or coat with clear acrylic medium to prevent smudging. Once the pencil has been sealed, additional acrylic glazes may be added if necessary.

The addition of some pen-and-ink outlining to an illustration adds crispness, definition, and clarity to the subject. Technical pens, flexible pen nibs, or fine brushes can be used.

If the painting is to be coated with a final varnish after ink has been added, be certain that the ink is thoroughly dry first. Load the brush with varnish and let it flow over the surface with light, uniform strokes. Avoid going back over an area once the varnish is laid down, as this may occasionally cause the ink to run.

Acrylic Paint with Oil Paints

Richard E. White

Oils may be used to modify acrylic colors, add subtle tones, and create highlights. Smooth, uniform, evenly graded shadows can be obtained much more easily with oils than with acrylics alone because of their longer drying time and superior blending capacity. Oils effectively depict translucence or iridescence. They must be applied only *on top of dried* acrylic paint (see fig. C-32).

MATERIALS

In addition to the basic materials listed at the beginning of this chapter, the artist should have the following:

Opaque white plastic (polystyrene) sheet: .02 inch (approximately 0.5 mm).

Oil paints: fast-drying Winsor & Newton transparent oils.

Japan drier: for speeding drying.

Thinner: Linseed oil or faster drying mediums, such as turpentine.

Turpentine: or equivalent for cleaning brushes and thinning oils.

Brushes: two sets, one for acrylics, one for oils.

TECHNIQUE

Do not use illustration board or other paper products as a painting support since oils will "bleed" into the board, leaving a yellow ring around the illustration. Although the recommended white plastic support needs no preparation, most types have a slight blue or yellow cast and may require a coat of gesso if a pure white background is desired.

Add water and retarding medium to the acrylic that will form the base color. This base layer must be thick enough so the painting support will not show through, but it must not show brushstrokes after it has dried. When applied properly, it will take some hours to dry thoroughly. The acrylic will be semirunny, so lay it flat for drying.

To shade with oils, use the complementary color of the underlying surface, or very little black. Apply sparingly; a little goes a long way. Thin the paint with linseed oil to provide a glaze over the acrylics. Start with the darkest shadows and work away from them. Blend and thin the oils into the nonshaded areas of the subject.

For highlights, use white oil paint for shiny areas, other colors for secondary highlights on nonshiny surfaces and iridescent areas. Proceed in the same way as for shading. Use thicker white oils for sharp highlights. Pubescence and other fine details may be applied with a fine brush.

Glazing is especially effective for rendering transparent or semitransparent membranes (such as insect wings). Over the dry acrylic paint, brush very thin translucent, zinc white oil paint. Very thin black oil color will indicate vague wing shadows. In order to produce an iridescent effect, paint a white oil background and let it dry. Then add a very thin layer of transparent Winsor & Newton oil color over the white. The white background with the thin transparent oil over it creates intense color.

Oil can take days or longer to dry. Drying time seems to vary with brand and color. Manufacturers can provide a list of colors with their drying times.

In addition to their excellent qualities in brush-worked color renderings and when mixed with other media, gouache and acrylics are well suited to airbrush application. Chapter 11 explores various airbrush techniques as they relate to scientific illustration.

11/Airbrush

Joel Ito and Lewis Sadler

An airbrush is a sophisticated spray gun designed to apply paint to a surface by means of air pressure. The spray can be controlled to produce the fine lines, soft tonal gradations, translucency, tints, and stippling required in scientific illustration (see figs. 9-7, C-11, and C-21 through C-24). In scientific illustration, airbrushes are used primarily for rendering and retouching. Rendering is usually done with a variety of paints on drawing paper; retouching involves use of retouch grays or colors to alter photographs (fig. 11-1).

Museums such as the American Museum of Natural History in New York City use the airbrush in exhibits for such diverse assignments as coloring in large areas on flat and relief maps and adding shades of green to plaster of paris leaves on trees and shrubs for permanent displays. Completed resin or fiberglass casts of many animals, especially reptiles and fish, are airbrushed with lacquers or acrylics. Then conventional brushwork adds such details as sharp lines, small spots, and scales. The airbrush also is used to restore colors to mounted specimens that have faded over time, and in some cases the airbrush creates subtle shadows on specimens in display cases.

The main attraction of airbrush rendering is that the finished product reproduces so well. Its ability to duplicate reality—with its smooth look and clean, sharp edges—makes it perfect for many assignments, and the application of color or shading is quick. A disadvantage is the time-consuming process of cutting masks and waiting for the paint to dry between sprays of color. The smooth, mechanical appearance of some airbrush renderings, moreover, can be atypical of most living creatures. Therefore, airbrush techniques are more useful for simple diagrams or when combined with other media. Texture and volume may be rendered with traditional techniques using pencils, pens, and brushes, with airbrush used to add quickly the effects it creates best (figs. 11-2, 11-3).

This chapter attempts only to introduce the airbrush as it applies to scientific illustration. Much more has been written about airbrush use and applications. (See Bibliography for books that treat the subject more thoroughly.)

MATERIALS

Surfaces

Paper, illustration board, drafting film: the spray of airbrushes adheres to any number of different papers and film, including vinyl or acetate cels used to produce overhead or other projection media. Therefore, the choice generally depends on additional media used and effect desired. Any good grade of paper or illustration board suffices, but paper that is too thin buckles and its surface becomes marred when paints and friskets are applied. Three-ply Bristol and

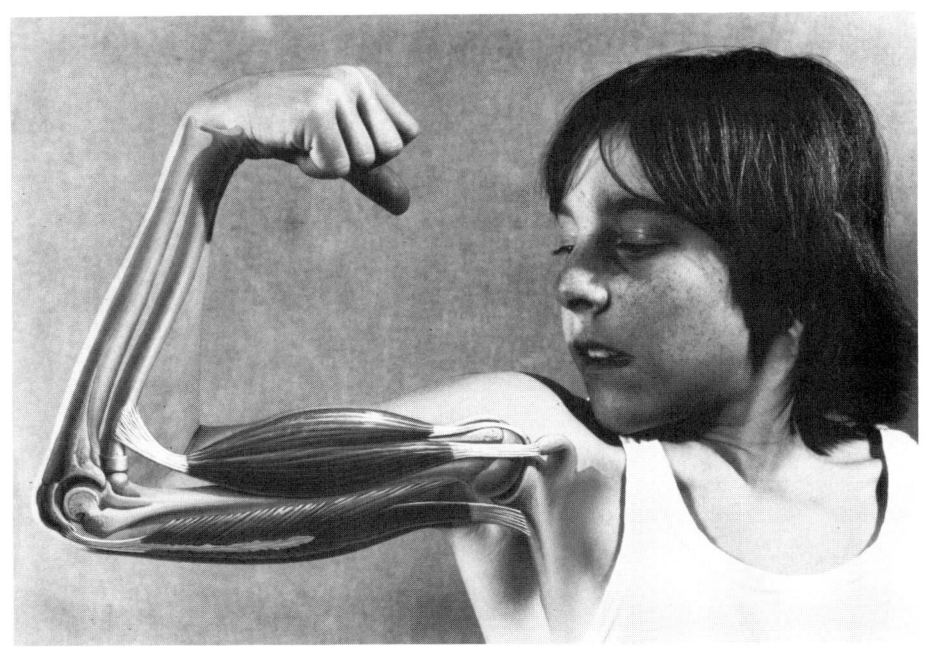

11-1. Retouching ("drawing") on a photograph. Acrylic paint was first airbrushed onto a matte, colored print; then details were added with a sable brush. Frisket covered areas not to be airbrushed. Opposing muscles in the upper arm, painted by Jane Hurd on a photograph by Wendy Cortesi © NGS (National Geographic Society).

11-2. The sketch was drawn with a sepia pencil on frosted drafting film. After light values were airbrushed, watercolor linework was added with a no. 0 watercolor brush. Then the middle and dark values were airbrushed and the figure was completed with charcoal pencil, colored pencils, and permanent white gouache. Chimpanzee, by Joel Ito © 1984.

illustration board are commonly used. Frosted drafting film is a durable material that can be placed over the preliminary sketch to eliminate the need for transferring. Clay-coated boards are useful because highlights can be scratched out, but care must be taken to avoid spraying too much paint, which tends to run on smooth surfaces.

Media

Almost any liquid can be sprayed through an airbrush. The most common media for scientific illustration are listed below; lacquers, which are toxic and can easily clog an airbrush, are not recommended.

Colored inks and dyes: brilliant and undoubtedly the easiest and most convenient of all the media to use. Their effect is transient, however, as they fade within hours or days when exposed to light. For this reason, they are not recommended for scientific illustration. India ink is permanent and therefore acceptable.

Transparent watercolor: most often chosen by scientific illustrators; easy to use; has the advantage of easy cleaning from the airbrush, even after drying. Pans and tubes work equally well, and watercolor can be applied over or under other media. The disadvantages are extreme transparency (requiring multiple applications to achieve saturation) and the tendency of some colors to fade when exposed to light.

Opaque watercolor (gouache): can be used in its usual form or diluted to a transparent wash. Like transparent watercolor, gouache cleans easily from the airbrush. To avoid a "chalky" look, use zinc white instead of permanent white when mixing tints of colors. Use a very dilute mixture and spray fairly close to the surface to avoid formation of "dry beads" of pigment, which are difficult to paint over, are easily abraded, and are picked up by frisket paper.

The major disadvantage of opaque watercolor lies in the characteristic color shift between wet and dry paint. This difference is especially disconcerting when white is sprayed over a highlight area. What appears perfect when the gouache is wet often disappears during drying, and several additional applications are necessary. Another disadvantage is that the surface of the finished painting is very delicate and can be marred or scratched easily.

Casein: when thinned, more transparent than gouache; when used opaquely, more dense. Casein colors are more saturated than gouache colors, and the pigments do not undergo a color shift as they dry. When freshly applied, the paints are soluble in water, but when dry, they are insoluble and permanent.

Acrylics: excellent for use in airbrushes. They mix well with other water-based media, are relatively permanent, and are not easily

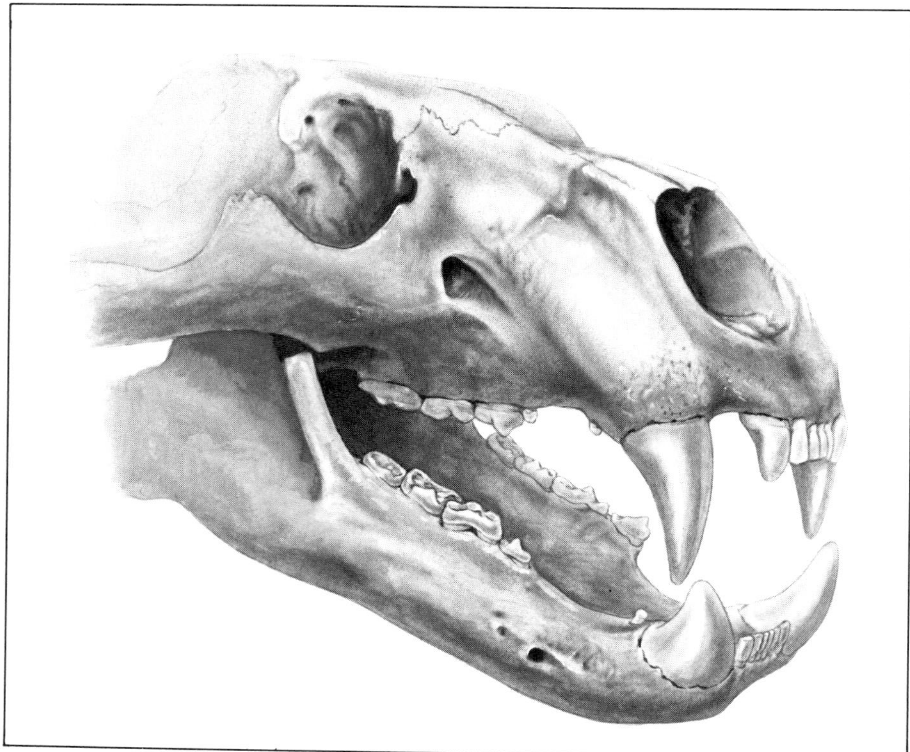

11-3. To preserve the white background, a frisket cut from 5-mil unprepared acetate was held in place over the drawing by magnets. (A sheet of galvanized metal was placed beneath the drawing.) Neutral-tint watercolor was painted with a sable brush on Crescent no. 100 illustration board. This developed the full tonal rendering. Colored gouache was then applied freehand over the tonal underpainting with a Paasche AB airbrush. The preliminary hand painting broke up the slickness of the airbrush rendering. Highlights were added by hand with pure white gouache. *Thalarctos maritimus*, by Lewis L. Sadler © 1985.

soiled or pulled up by friskets. Use acrylic jar colors, which are formulated to flow easily at an even consistency. Many artists use acrylics in dilute form, with a mixture of half water and half gloss (or matte) medium, which helps prevent breakdown of the emulsion binder when overthinning.

Several companies make acrylic colors especially for airbrush work. These extremely finely ground, lead-free pigments are water soluble when wet, waterproof when dry, nontoxic, and dry quickly on the work surface. However, they are designed to be used thinly; if applied thickly with a conventional brush, they may remain tacky. They can be used directly from the container without thinning and work well on illustration board, paper, canvas, acetate, and plastic. They are available in one-ounce bottles in transparent and opaque forms.

Acrylics tend to clog some instruments; they are less likely to clog external-mix airbrushes. Immediate, thorough cleaning after each use helps prevent clogging.

Tools

Airbrushes: several brands of airbrushes are suitable for use by artists. All models are similar in size and method of operation. They differ in the way paint flow is controlled (that is, by single-action or double-action) and in whether the paint and air are mixed internally or externally.

With a single-action airbrush (such as Paasche models H and F), the artist initiates the paint flow by pressing down on the finger lever. The spray width cannot be altered except by altering the distance between the instrument and the paper. This simplified mechanism is not designed to produce varied, gradated tones. Single-action brushes cover large areas quickly but are suitable only for producing flat backgrounds, elementary airbrush art, and flat backpainting on translucent materials.

The artist controls the spray pattern from a double-action airbrush by pressing down and pulling back the finger lever. The farther back the lever is pulled, the greater the amount of paint in the spray. Because its infinite combinations of air and paint allow anything from thin lines to broad washes, the double-action brush is a valuable tool for illustration (figs. 11-4, 11-5).

Internal-mix models use either gravity or suction to combine the paint and air inside the brush heads. External-mix models combine the air and paint in side- or top-mounted cups outside the brush heads; they operate on a suction-fed system and generally are not so sensitive as gravity-fed models, but they offer the advantage of holding larger quantities of paint and allowing quick changes of color and easy cleaning. Examples of double-action brushes are Thayer and Chandler model A, Paasche models VL and VJR, Wold models A2 and V2, Iwata models HPH, HP-B, HP-C, and HP-SB. More models arrive on the market every year.

Special mention should be made of the Paasche model AB airbrush. Although it has a double-action finger lever like those already mentioned, it is quite different from other brushes. It operates on an air-powered turbine with an offset nozzle. Depressing the lever controls the amount of air flowing into the instrument. Part of the air runs the turbine (up to 20,000 RPM), which causes the needle to oscillate. The rest is diverted to the air

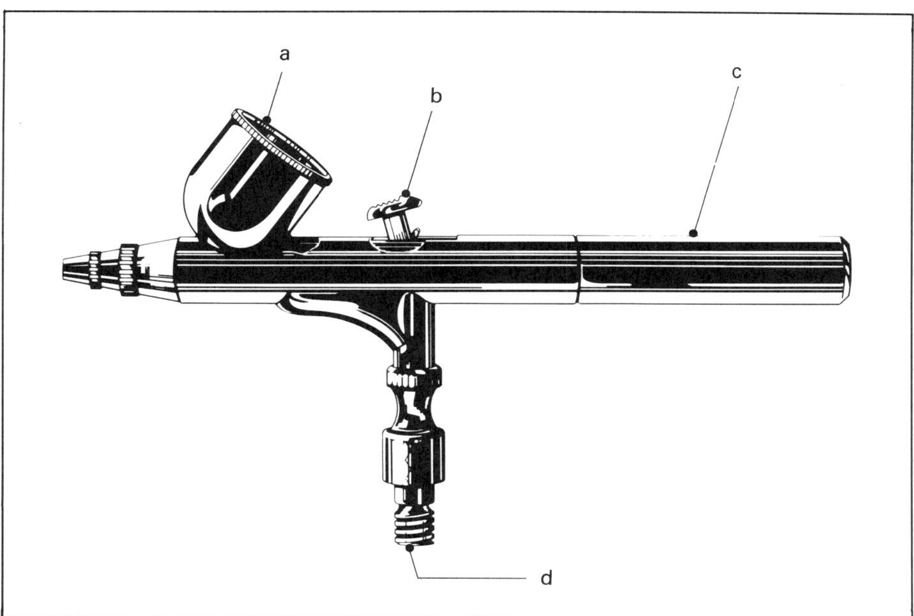

11-4. Double-action, internal-mix airbrush: *(a)* color cup; *(b)* finger lever; *(c)* handle; *(d)* air hose connector. Ink on frosted drafting film, by Katie Simon.

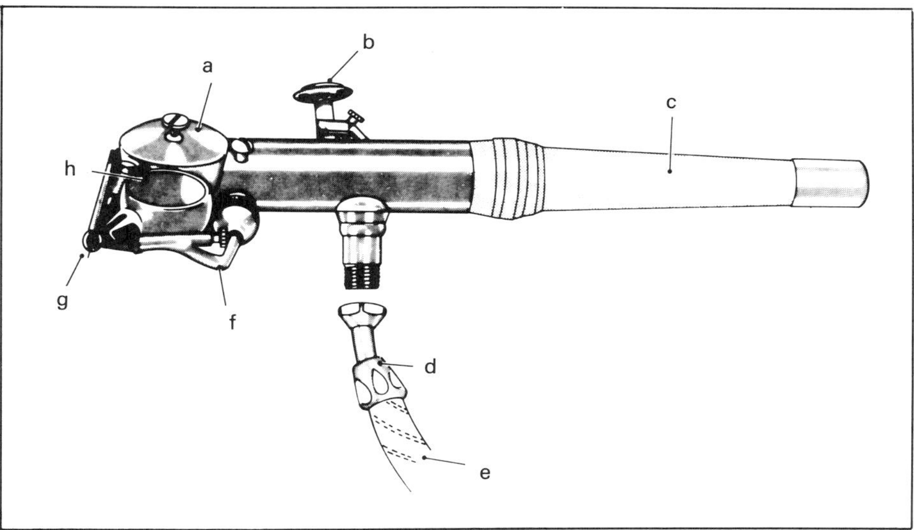

11-5. Generalized diagram of a double-action, external-mix airbrush: *(a)* power wheel and shaft assembly; *(b)* finger lever; *(c)* handle; *(d)* hose coupling assembly; *(e)* connected to air source; *(f)* air blast tube; *(g)* needle; *(h)* color cup. Ink on frosted drafting film, by Kathy Kerr.

nozzle, to blow the paint off the needle and onto the painting. The second action of the lever (backward and forward motion) controls the travel of the needle and allows more or less of it to be exposed to the air jet, so that more or less paint can be blown onto the drawing. In action, the paint flows by gravity, from the color cup into the needle guide, where a thin film of paint is picked up by the needle and moved out into the air blast emitted from the air nozzle. The needle then returns to repeat the process over and over again very quickly. The operator can control this speed, as well as the amount of needle surface being exposed with each pass. This feature allows the ultimate control needed to produce the shades, lines, tints, and stippling demanded in scientific illustration. Because it is a precision instrument, the Paasche model AB is expensive and delicate; it requires some maintenance and tuning as well as operating skill. Nevertheless, it has no equal for sensitive rendering.

Propellant system: the source of air or gas required to operate the airbrush. A regulator allows the artist to adjust the pressure delivered to the brush without regard for the actual pressure developed in the propellant system. The regulator can be regarded as an additional variable in adjustment of the system. At high pressures (40 psi, pounds per square inch), a few millimeters of lever action span 0 to 40 psi, whereas at lower pressures (20 psi), the same few millimeters of lever action span 0 to 20 psi. Therefore this "coarse adjustment" of pressure results in a much more sensitive, controllable instrument, permitting finely detailed work.

Pressure for the airbrush can be supplied by carbon dioxide or oxygen, obtainable from metal cylinders or from an air compressor. Tank sizes range from ten to fifty pounds (weight of gas, not the tank). Tanks of gas, available and refillable from soda-fountain supply companies and carbonic gas companies, provide about thirty hours of continuous operation for each ten pounds of gas in the tank. Because most work does not consist of continuously holding down the finger lever, a ten-pound tank can last a long time. The major disadvantage in using compressed gas is the delay that occurs when a tank suddenly is empty. An extra tank is a wise investment to prevent missed deadlines.

An alternative to carbon dioxide or oxygen cylinders is the air compressor. The continuously operating models are turned on by means of electric switches. An air valve and regulator are necessary for steady air pressure. Simple compressors lacking reservoirs and regulators cannot be used for fine, detailed work. The lack of a reservoir allows pump pulsations to be transferred to the brush and thus to cause a series of dots instead of fine lines. Unlike carbon dioxide cylinders, which are noiseless in operation, most compressors do make some noise. There are "silent" compressors on the market with oil (for lubrication) reciprocating piston motors, reservoirs, and adjustable air-pressure regulators that operate without pulsation, but they are expensive.

Hoses and couplings: to deliver propellant to airbrush; hoses can be transparent, colored, braided, or coiled. Clear hoses offer the advantage of allowing easy inspection of the line for oil, moisture, and other foreign debris. Braided hoses are sturdy and will give the longest service without replacement. Regardless of the type selected, it should be no shorter than eight feet and no longer than ten feet from regulator to airbrush. This seems a minor point, but the regulator pressure reading will mean little or nothing if the hose varies much from these standard lengths. Couplings must fit the particular airbrush on one end and have a standard design to fit the air compressor or tank on the other. Adaptors are available to standardize fittings if several brands of airbrush are to be used on a single hose. There should be no air leaks.

Traps or filters: in air hose to prevent oil and moisture originating in a compressor from reaching the airbrush and drawing.

Miscellaneous

Friskets: anything that blocks the spray of paint from areas that are not to be airbrushed immediately. They usually are thin masks placed on or glued to a drawing. Protective masks often are needed to shield areas around the drawing from overspray. For straight edges or simple curved shapes, rulers, pieces of paper, French curves, or drafting tape can be employed. For more complicated masks, commercial frisket film or acetate sheets can be cut to suit the subject or liquid frisket applied.

Commercial frisket usually is adhesive backed and comes in high- or low-tack (degree of stickiness). Low-tack frisket is used for delicate surfaces to prevent pulling up the paper and previously painted areas. High-tack frisket can be applied when this would not be a problem and when extra sticking is required, such as when rough or irregular surfaces are being painted. Commercial friskets are not recommended for use on photographs or slick surfaces because the carrier sheets (used to keep the adhesive from drying out) are coated with silicone, which leaves a thin film on the adhesive, which in turn is transferred to the surface, rendering it waterproof. Such transfer can be a problem when water-soluble paint is being used.

Unprepared frisket looks like tracing paper but is specially formulated to resist curling when rubber cement is applied. Two thinned coats of rubber cement should be applied to the paper, the second coat at 90 degrees to the first. Then the glue should be allowed to dry. This type of frisket is always fresh and has a low tack. A rubber cement pickup should be used with a dabbing, not a rubbing or stroking, motion to remove adhesive remaining on the drawing after the frisket is cut.

Liquid frisket often is chosen for small or intricate shapes that would be difficult to cut if other frisket materials were used. Made of liquid latex, it is applied with a brush that has been well lathered with soap. It can be rubbed off with the fingers or a rubber cement pickup. Some liquid friskets have added color, which may stain the paper.

Dry friskets or masks are usually made of 5- or 7-mil acetate sheets, either clear or frosted. They usually are held down by hand or with weights; if the rendering surface is placed on a metal sheet, magnets can be used.

For uncomplicated shapes, masks can be prepared from drawing, blotting, or tracing paper. Paper masks can be used only once for a specific area because they curl when wet. The paint should be directed over the edge, not into it.

Weights for friskets: erasers, watercolor tubes, coins, long lead strips (fishing sinkers). Magnets and a galvanized metal sheet placed under the drawing are excellent for hard-edge effects.

Knives: to cut frisket. Any very sharp blade can be used, such as a scalpel or X-Acto blade or the Ulano swivel knife.

Brush: for liquid frisket. Any inexpensive natural-hair or synthetic-fiber brush may be used as long as it holds a point. Liquid frisket can ruin the brush, so special care should be taken to clean it thoroughly.

Airbrush holder: to keep airbrush securely on the table. Some clamp onto the drafting table or desk. A useful type is the drop-lock holder made by ArtCadi (see Appendix).

Facial mask: An inexpensive particle mask will prevent inhalation of airborne paint but will not protect against solvents other than water.

AIRBRUSH CLEANING

Total cleanliness is essential when using any airbrush because pigment such as waterproof ink and acrylics can harden in the tiny inside channels and clog the mechanism. For most water-soluble paints, including acrylics, rinse the parts with water and then a solution of water and ammonia, or a glass or window cleaner. When using acrylics, any sign of clogging or blockage should be followed by a flush with denatured alcohol. Stronger solvents such as acetone have been recommended. However, when atomized, these solvents can turn the studio atmosphere into a potential bomb; any electrical spark or open flame can ignite them. Acetone and strong solvents should *never* be atomized. If they must be used, the brush should be disassembled and the parts soaked outdoors. Several ammonia-based commercial airbrush cleaners on the market for acrylics also may be used for other water-based paints. Do not use toluene, rubber-cement thinner, xylene, or benzene because they are health hazards as well as very flammable. After thoroughly cleaning the airbrush at the end of the day, leave it disassembled to dry overnight.

TECHNIQUE

Clear off all nearby surfaces before beginning a work session, especially when larger washes will be done. Atomized paint particles travel for a surprising distance in the studio, covering everything within range with a fine film of paint. These atomized pigment particles also pose a health hazard as they are inspired and ingested. Many pigments, especially those derived from metal compounds, pose a hazard to the artist, so painting should be done only in a well-ventilated space, and a mask should be worn.

Work on a slanted surface (about 30 degrees). Unless the area to be painted is broad, the color cup should contain only a small amount of paint. In the time it takes to refill the cup, the artist can reexamine the work and decide how much additional paint is needed. Airbrush effects are rarely achieved in one quick stroke; the proper tone usually is built up gradually.

Learning to mix paint properly is important to avoid working with paint that is too dilute. The resulting spray requires many passes to lay down much pigment, soaking the paper and causing it to warp or buckle. In the case of water-soluble paints, the spray may wash away previously painted areas.

With the Paasche model AB system, running a filled no. 1 or no. 2 brush over the needle gives enough paint for several quick passes. Always test the spray on a scrap of paper to ensure that the color is correct and the brush is functioning properly.

Operate the airbrush in the following manner:

1. Set the hand in motion.
2. Press the finger lever down to release air but not paint.
3. Gently pull back the finger lever to release paint.

Keep the hand in motion during spraying. If steps 2 and 3 are run together, a blob of paint forms at the beginning of each stroke. If a smooth, even passage is required, it is important not to turn the wrist, dip the hand, or change the brush angle. Start and stop the paint spray on the frisketed area or a scrap of drawing surface instead of the drawing surface itself.

A number of problems may arise during testing of the airbrush at the beginning of a session. If a grainy spray or spitting develops, check the air pressure to make sure it is sufficiently high for the viscosity of the paint being sprayed (usually 20 to 30 psi). Check the paint mixture to make certain it is not too thick. Inspect the cone and needle for dried paint, excessive wear, or damage. Clean or replace these parts as necessary. In the case of the Paasche model AB, make sure that the needle is centered in the air jet and that the stipple-adjusting screw is loosened (turn counterclockwise).

A splatter at the beginning of a stroke can be caused by the finger lever not returning to its resting position before starting a new stroke. With the Paasche model AB, it can be caused by a color cup positioned at too great an angle or by paint that is too thin being allowed to flow too quickly into the path of the air jet. Another problem caused by too much paint is a centipedelike effect that occurs when a line or dot is sprayed. In this case, paint is being delivered properly, but at too great a pressure for the distance to the surface. Either reduce the air pressure or move your hand farther from the surface being painted.

Any part of the drawing or the background that is not to be sprayed immediately should be masked with frisket (see chapter 2, under Masking Materials). Personal preference determines whether an artist uses a frisket that adheres to the drawing surface or a mask that must be held down by hand, tape, or other means. Let freshly painted areas dry before applying any frisket. Commercial frisket film or frisket prepared with rubber cement never should be left on a drawing overnight. After about twenty-four hours, the laminate is permanent and cannot be removed without damage to the drawing surface.

When an acetate mask is to be made, use only unprepared acetate (not "wet media"). Score the acetate along the outline of the drawing underneath with a sharp straight or swivel knife. It is not necessary to cut through the acetate, but it is important to place the blade in the same cut at the end of each knife stroke so that the cut will be continuous. Remove the acetate from the drawing surface and bend it along the scored area so that it cracks along the cut. Pull up a short length of the cut at one time, and be careful going around sharp corners and curves. Occasionally sandpaper is needed to smooth edges of the mask. Acetate can be cut to various shapes and used for stock masks, singly or in combination to fit particular areas. Acetate masks can be lifted up to

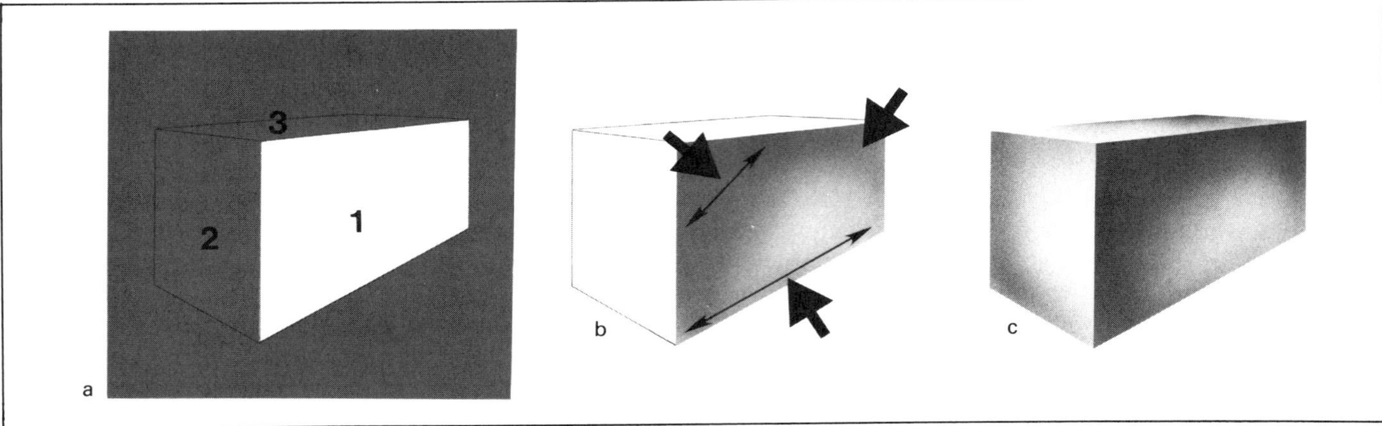

11-6. Rendering a hard edge. *(a)* The entire figure is covered with frisket paper and then the first area to be sprayed is cut out. The numbers indicate the painting sequence. *(b)* After the first area has been painted, it is re-covered. Then the frisket is removed from the second area, and it is painted. Heavy arrows indicate the direction in which the airbrush was pointed; light arrows trace the stroke pattern. *(c)* The finished cube. Lampblack watercolor with airbrush on illustration board, by Joel Ito.

check the areas being worked on against previously painted areas.

There are many refinements in airbrush techniques. Experience and practice are essential to satisfactory results.

Rendering a Hard Edge (Cube)

See figure 11-6. Apply frisket to the entire subject and over the background. Cut out frisket covering each plane to be painted in sequence and replace it before spraying the next plane (unless the first plane is to be darkened or colored with the paint applied to subsequent planes).

Start with the darkest plane in order to provide a comparative value for other planes. All planes should be smoothly graded in value from the darkest area to the opposite corner. Continually turning the surface makes it easy to spray the darkest corner nearest the artist and to fade out to the corner diagonally opposite. Start each pass at the darkest corner, gradually building the tone until the desired result has been achieved. As each plane is completed, allow paint to dry thoroughly, then reattach the cut frisket or cover the area with a new frisket. Take care to compare frequently the sprayed area with its neighboring planes so that the drawing maintains an overall balance. Friskets distort the values, making the plane appear lighter than it really is.

Rendering a Sphere

See figure 11-7. Draw a circle and apply frisket over the entire illustration area. Cut and remove the frisket from the sphere, and airbrush a very faint tone all around the edge of the sphere. Airbrush a shadow along the right side, keeping the highlight on the upper left of the sphere as white as possible.

Gradually build tones within the frisket opening in a freehand manner. Short strokes, applied in all directions, are easier to control than long ones. Keep the tone as even as possible, fading it out gradually with each stroke.

Rendering a Soft Edge

See figure 11-8. A soft or fuzzy edge is produced with a torn paper or an acetate or paper shield held a

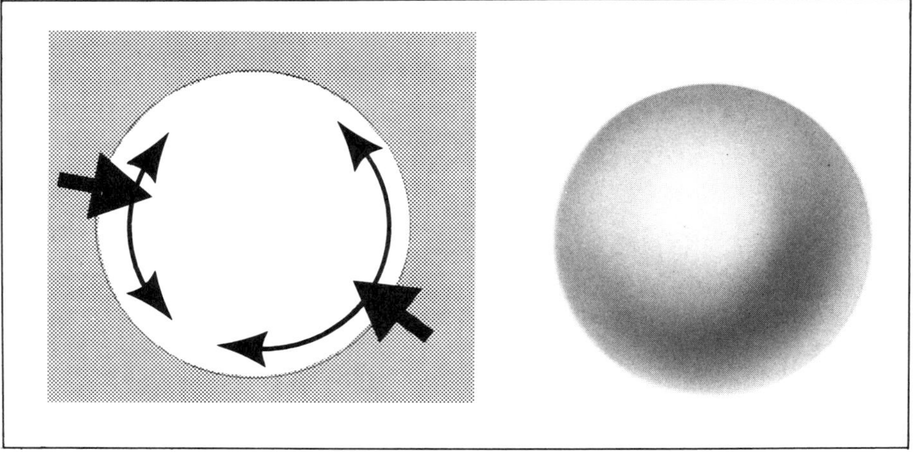

11-7. Rendering a sphere. Heavy arrows indicate the direction in which the airbrush was pointed during spraying; light arrows trace the stroke pattern. Lampblack watercolor with airbrush on illustration board, by Joel Ito.

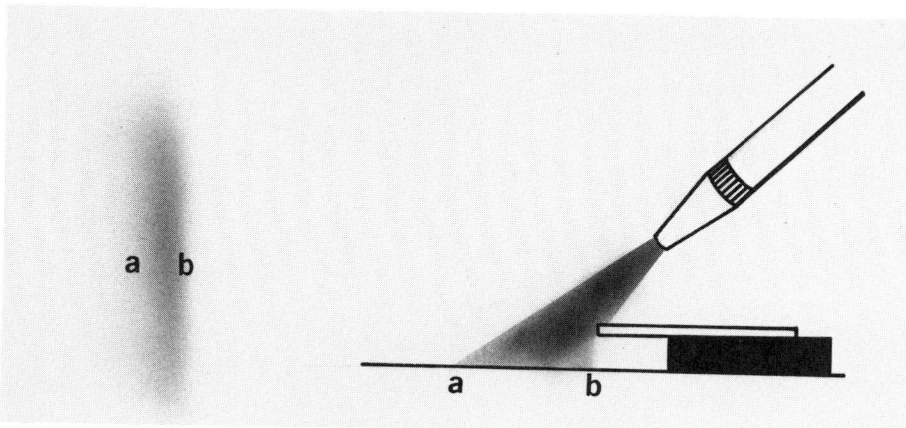

11-8. Soft edge achieved by spraying over a raised mask. Depending on the distance and angle of the airbrush to the masks, varying degrees of softness will result on the free surface *(a)* and around the masked area *(b)*. Lampblack watercolor with airbrush on illustration board, by Joel Ito.

11-9. Lampblack watercolor airbrushed over a graphite pencil line sketch done on Crescent Line Kote board. Cut acetate shields were held while watercolor was sprayed around the knee and on the face. Lampblack then was applied with a brush to the tail and face for emphasis, and highlights were scratched out with a knife. *Lemur catta*, by Joel Ito © 1982.

short distance away from the drawing surface. Various degrees of softness can be attained by changing the distance of the brush to the raised mask and the angle at which the spray is directed. The soft effect results from some of the pigment passing under the mask (b). Airbrush a few strokes by first working almost vertically with the brush and then turning it slightly upward, aiming at the edge of the mask. The soft-edge look of figure 11-9 was achieved in this way.

Airbrush with Other Media and Techniques

The airbrush can be used in the initial stages of a carbon dust, graphite, or other tone drawing to determine the basic form of the structure. Large areas can be covered quickly and easily. Refinements and detailed structures then can be added by conventional pencil or paint techniques (see fig. 11-2).

The airbrush also is an excellent accompaniment to watercolor, pencil, pastel, and charcoal linework. Airbrushing done over line drawing helps tie general areas together; the line beneath provides texture and gives the impression of great solidity. Linework can be added on top of the airbrush painting to finish the rendering (fig. 11-9; see fig. 11-3).

The airbrush can be successfully incorporated as part of a multimedia approach to scientific illustration; airbrush application of paint or ink is compatible with several other media (see chapters 8, 9, 10). The versatile airbrush can be utilized for underpainting, backgrounds, shadows, backpainting translucent surfaces, as a finishing touch over line work, and to blend and smooth traditionally hand-painted areas.

Part III
Subject Matter

How to handle specimens and draw subjects of natural history accurately are explained in the following chapters. Each discipline has distinctive problems and procedures requiring different approaches. However, some basic points can be made about all subjects, and a few that the illustrator and scientist should know will be covered here.

The first and most important is that all specimens should be treated with care as directed in their respective chapters. They should be kept covered when not in use and should be protected as much as possible from accidental damage. Furthermore, small wet specimens of all sorts should be kept submerged while being drawn to protect them from drying out and also to prevent distracting reflections from parts that break through the fluid surface, including pins holding the specimen in place.

Scales do not always appear on the drawings because they are not always necessary. Even in drawings done for research papers, a scale may not be pertinent because of wide size variations among the specimens and because the measurements are discussed in the text.

Drawing animals and plants accurately is like making a portrait of a person. In people the relationship of a nostril edge to the pupil of the eye to the mouth corner defines each individual's identity, creates the likeness. When objects of research are the subject, the same loving attention must be given to subtle curves of line and spatial relationships between points. The scientific illustrator creates portraits of animals (including humans) and plants, or parts thereof.

Almost any media and technique can be used to render the subjects of these chapters. Pen-and-ink is most often used because it is cheapest and easiest to reproduce well. In some fields there are traditions of emphasizing certain techniques, and there are even conventions encouraging a certain appearance for a drawing (see chapter 15), but both illustrator and scientist should keep an open mind about the way a subject might be best depicted, depending on the reproduction factors discussed in chapter 1 and other chapters in this book, as well as the nature of the "critter," as many organisms are fondly called by their researchers.

The science defining relationships among organisms, the study of biological diversity, which includes describing and naming organisms, is called *systematics*, or *taxonomy*. When describing a new species, the systematist assigns it a two-part name, one for the genus and one for the species. This is the binomial system devised by Carolus Linnaeus in 1753 for plants and in 1758 for animals. For example, the name applied to humans is *Homo* (genus) *sapiens* (species). Genera fit into families that in turn fit into higher categories such as superfamilies, orders, classes, phyla, and kingdoms. Generic and specific names are always underlined or italicized. Specific names are not capitalized, whereas names of genera always are. Family names for animals end with "-idae," such as Hominidae for the human family. Plant family names usually end in "-aceae," such as Rosaceae, which includes roses, but there are such exceptions as Compositae, which includes daisies and sunflowers, among others. Family names are not italicized or underscored but are always capitalized.

The systematist selects one specimen, the holotype, to be the sole voucher, a reference for the new species, with which other specimens are compared. The holotype is unique. Sometimes it is the only known specimen of its kind. When the holotype is selected, if more than one specimen of the new species exists, one or more paratypes may be designated. In most disciplines and museums, the holotype receives a red label, or, in the case of plants, is stored in a red-marked folder; an older specimen may have only the word *holotype* on its label. Different disciplines and museums treat paratypes differently: some label them in blue, others in yellow or even red. Other types are designated for special situations. When the holotype is lost, for example, a neotype is designated. A red or blue label on a specimen commonly indicates it has special scientific importance, and extreme care must be observed when handling it.

Systematics, as every field, has its own jargon. The word *character* refers to a qualitative or quantitative aspect of a species. To say that a character shows *species specificity* means that the characteristic differentiates one species from another—perhaps an anatomic part that is rounded in one species but pointed in a closely related species. In some species males and females look alike, but in others they have one or more different characters; for example, the tail fan of the male peacock distinguishes it from the female. This circumstance is called *sexual dimorphism*. Many other terms could be discussed; some are explained in the following chapters, and others can be learned from science courses or books.

Every systematist also must be a *morphologist*, a student of form, sensitive to nuances of shape, structure, color, and pattern *(maculation)*. The scientific illustrator should have the same sensitivity. Morphology, literally the study of form, involves the study of anatomy. The word *morphology* is used in systematics commonly but incorrectly when reference is made to an animal's "morphology" instead of its anatomy. Whatever the word, both illustrator and scientist must be accurate observers. Knowledge of the subject's anatomy is important whether the drawing is for a taxonomic research paper or for a wildlife painting.

Although the scientist should indicate those features of a specimen that are to be particularly noted and illustrated, there still remains latitude for the illustrator to determine what is extraneous (perhaps an artifact such as dirt) and what is an inherent part of the specimen or species. For instance, where a membrane is wrinkled, how much wrinkling should be shown? Such a question can be answered by the illustrator with experience or training or both. Beyond the anatomic questions come artistic ones. If the amount of wrinkling is not critical to describing the species, then the illustrator must choose what lines to include that will suggest wrinkling yet not distract from more important information or obscure other features. Often, too many lines are included. Of benefit to the scientific illustrator are courses in comparative anatomy, animal or plant morphology, and graphic design—the choice depending on the illustrator's specialization.

Another decision for the illustrator involves choosing how to show highlights and shadows on the subject. It is mentioned frequently that scientific illustration has a convention of showing light coming from the upper left. This is generally true except for wildlife art, a branch of scientific illustration described in chapter 20, where a more flexible, fine-arts approach may be taken than in other types of scientific illustration (see figs. C-9, C-23, 4-56, 20-1, 20-5, 20-11).

One specialization not treated separately in the following chapters is geological illustration. The primary types of drawings needed in geology are explained in chapters 2 (perspective machine); 21 (archaeological soil sections or profiles); and 25 (maps and block diagrams).

Each subject-matter chapter includes a list of materials and instruments useful for working in that particular discipline. These are for handling specimens, achieving accuracy, and producing a preliminary drawing. Materials needed to create the final rendering are listed in the chapters on techniques in part 2 of this book.

In the process of handling specimens, the illustrator will be around flammable materials such as alcohol and perhaps toxic substances such as arsenic-treated animal skins, Formalin, or xylene. Be sure that ventilation is adequate in such situations. Protective measures are recommended in pertinent chapters.

12/Illustrating Plants

Marion Ruff Sheehan

For centuries scientists have studied plants. Botanists examine plant classification, structure, and function; horticulturalists add studies of plant cultivation and utilization. Botanical illustration serves these sciences and their contributions toward understanding the plant kingdom.

Plants, especially their flowers, have been favored artistic subjects throughout history. In fact, the first known impressions of plants were made during the Paleolithic period. *Codex Vindobonensis*, by Dioscorides, the earliest-known existing illustrated botanical book, appeared in A.D. 512. (There are references to earlier works, but none has survived.) Since then, illustrations have enhanced the value of scientific books about plants. Moreover, botanical illustrations have been incorporated into illustrations of other subjects, such as when animals are depicted in their natural habitat.

Botanical drawings most often illustrate writings on plant taxonomy and identification. They also are utilized in other botanical and horticultural studies such as anatomy, cytology, ecology, and morphology. Botanical illustrations are often found in such nontechnical works as wildlife journals, popular books and magazines, and advertisements. Regardless of the purpose for which the drawing is intended, technical accuracy is essential. Generally, the genus or species must be identifiable from a botanical illustration.

Botanical illustrations usually include representations of habit (whole or partial plants showing form and growth type) and reproductive structures. Drawings may be prepared from specimens that are living, freshly cut, pressed and dried, or preserved in liquid. Microscopic structures are generally illustrated from prepared slides or microphotographs, and more rarely from scanning electron microscope photographs (made from specially prepared material, usually greatly enlarged).

Most botanical illustrations are done in black-and-white, with pen-and-ink most often used for line drawings. Pencil and wash are commonly used for continuous-tone drawings. Full-color drawings are usually rendered in watercolor, gouache, or acrylic, although some artists prefer colored pencils, pastels, or, more rarely, oil paints (see color plates).

The vast array of organisms in the plant kingdom may overwhelm the beginning botanical illustrator. Preparation for becoming an illustrator should include some course work, beginning with general botany. Courses in morphology and anatomy will provide an understanding of plant structure in more detail. Taxonomy provides an understanding of relationships between and among plant groups and teaches the student how to read plant descriptions. Reading a description and understanding it or trying to visualize the whole or partial plant from words can be difficult for the experienced botanist and may completely befuddle the novice illustrator.

Because of the large scope of the plant kingdom, most illustrators specialize in one division of plants, and, within that, they may limit themselves to one section, a few genera, or even a single genus. Courses in specific botanical subjects are helpful for specialization. There are courses limited to algae (algology), fungi (mycology), lichens, liverworts, ferns, and so on.

In addition to course work, access to and understanding of botanical literature is essential. The artist must know how to locate accurate illustrations as well as information about the subject at hand. The artist must know how to use a herbarium and how to handle pressed specimens, as most botanical drawings are made from such material.

In preparation for having botanical illustrations made, the botanist, horticulturist, or other client generally outlines the needs as a guide for the artist. A list or even crude sketches may be presented to the artist along with suggested views, scales of enlargement or reduction, and sources for or actual specimens to be used. Dissections may be prepared by the client or, depending on the skill of the artist, may be left for the illustrator to prepare. Only a very experienced artist is expected to choose what to illustrate, views, and scale with little or no input from the client. For all drawings, the client is expected to check sketches for content and accuracy before the final rendering is completed.

It is often helpful for the illustrator to keep backup material handy on the drawing table—a reference book, the manuscript with the description, an illustration, or a handwritten list of characteristics. Before beginning an illustration, the artist should note all characteristics mentioned in the literature and in descriptions, or shown in illustrations, since many abnormalities occur in the plant kingdom, and subjects showing deviation from the norm should not be used. Common aberrations include missing or extra parts, fusion, abnormal forms, and abnormal sizes. Fungi may have grown on the specimen and could look like hairs.

INSTRUMENTS AND MATERIALS

In addition to the art materials used for the chosen media and techniques, a botanical illustrator will most likely use some of the tools and supplies listed below.

Optical Devices

Stereoscopic microscope: for preparing botanical drawings of small subjects and for making dissections. Sufficient working space under the objectives is especially important when the artist must examine plants mounted on herbarium sheets. (A good setup is shown in figure 2-24.) Ideally, the microscope body should be mounted on an arm clamped to a table instead of the usual stand, so that the body can swing out over a large specimen.

Reducing objective: to permit more of a plant to be seen under the stereoscopic microscope.

Compound microscope: may be needed for drawing cell structure and microscopic specimens such as pollen and spores.

Camera lucida: for preparing rough basic sketches of small specimens and slide-mounted material.

Reticles: with grid, micrometer, as needed. The grid can be used instead of a camera lucida. The micrometer is used for measuring through the microscope (see Optical Devices in chapter 2).

Microprojector: useful for drawing slide-mounted specimens.

Opaque projector: for enlarging and reducing drawings and herbarium specimens.

Stage micrometer: for obtaining a scale.

Magnifiers: hand-held, and one with a light that clamps to drawing board (see Optical Devices in chapter 2).

Reducing lens: to visualize reductions of specimens or drawings.

Camera: 35mm single-lens reflex, to photograph live plants at desired stage for illustration. Slide or print film can be used, depending on the system available for viewing the results.

Macro lens: for camera, to permit close-up photographs.

Photocopy machine: to provide quick images of pressed plants that can be used as the rough sketch, an invaluable timesaver. Reduction and enlargement capabilities of a machine permit the drawing size to be adjusted.

Measuring Devices

Metric rulers: metal or opaque plastic, 15cm (6 inch) and 30cm (12 inch).

Proportional dividers: 8 inch (20cm).

Grid: drawn on acetate, for producing enlarged, reduced, or one-to-one drawings.

Drafting Aids

Light table: for tracing herbarium specimens or transferring preliminary drawings.

French curves.

Specimen-handling Tools

Forceps.

Dissecting needles: sewing needle mounted in a handle or metal probe.

Dissecting knives: scalpel, razor blade.

Eyedropper and wash bottle: for adding moisture to dissected or dried material.

Specimen Props

Florist's foam: such as Oasis, Filfast; brick-shaped foam blocks with high water-holding capacity, used to hold stems in position; available from florists or craft stores.

Florist's clay: sticks to surfaces under water; used to hold flower holders ("frogs") securely or for direct support of stems or other specimens that must be kept in water; available from florists or craft stores.

Plasticine, kneaded eraser, beeswax.

Flower holders: can be purchased from florists, gift shops, or variety stores.

Minuten pins.

Tapes: transparent, masking, or double-sided, for holding small, sturdy specimens such as seeds.

Paper towels, facial tissues: dampened or submerged in fluid to support delicate plant tissue.

Containers

Petri dishes and larger dishes: for floating specimens.

Crucibles: for boiling dried specimen parts.

Containers for fresh flowers: vases, jars, tubes with rubber ends to hold single stems (available from florists, orchid suppliers).

Microscope slides: for holding small dissections.

Wetting Agents and Preservatives

Alcohol: 95 percent ethyl.

Glycerin: for mixing with water (one drop to one teaspoon) to prevent specimens from drying out.

Pohl's solution or Pohlstuff: for reconstituting portions of herbarium specimens (see below).

Cut-flower preservatives: products such as Floralife, Bloomlife; citrus soft drinks containing sugar diluted one part soft drink to two parts water; lemon and sugar, used at the rate of one teaspoon each to one cup water. Use of floral preservatives prolongs the lives of cut flowers.

Miscellaneous

Plastic bags: for reviving wilted live plants or for storage of live plants in the refrigerator.

MAJOR DIVISIONS OF THE PLANT KINGDOM

The plant kingdom is divided into several sections, each with distinct characteristics. The classification of plants is interpreted differently by botanists around the world. A uniform and definitive organization of the world's flora has yet to be completed, but the sections can be differentiated on the basis of morphologic and anatomic differences. A major division can be based on reproductive mechanisms: plants that reproduce by fission or spores and plants that reproduce by seeds. Each division can be further divided based on such characteristics as presence or absence of vasculature. The botanical artist should understand basic vegetative and reproductive structures. Illustrations and brief explanations of each division will provide characteristics of plants in each taxon, but further study will be necessary before the illustrator can prepare drawings of a particular subject.

Algae

The algae are aquatic, chlorophyllous plants with a thallus (undifferentiated body) composed of cells with little specialization. Some of the larger seaweeds are differentiated into a holdfast (anchoring basal portion), stipe (stalk), and blade (fig. 12-1b). Reproduction is sexual or asexual. The various algal groups, which exhibit every type of life history, are probably more diverse than any other major division of the plant kingdom. The habits range from minute unicellular forms to large seaweeds more than several meters long. Since generalizations about algal morphology are difficult to formulate, an illustrator must research each particular group.

Usually a habit illustration is required with details of various reproductive structures. Many algae must be drawn from material on microscope slides. The substance of macroscopic plants can range from membranous or gelatinous to very rigid and firm. The texture can be slimy, stringy, spongy, lumpy, spiny, and sometimes smooth. Each of these characteristic textures and habits must be captured in the illustration.

Other diagnostic details usually are at the cellular level and require specimens mounted on slides. A cross section of the stipe or axis or a close-up of the cells of the plant

a

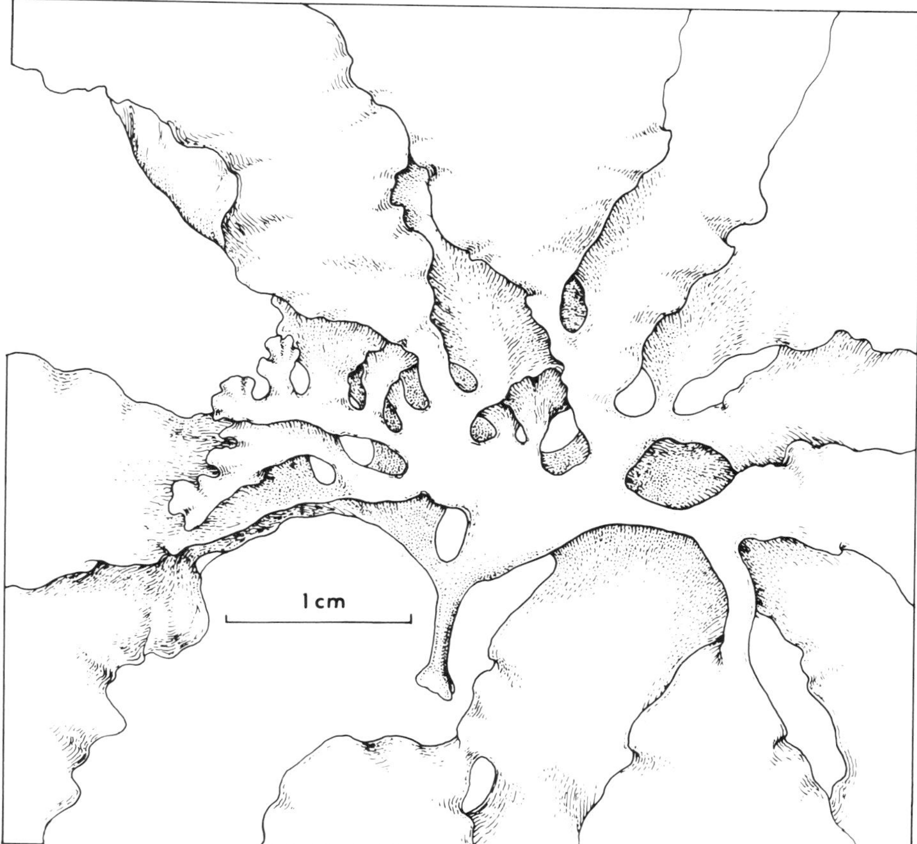

b

12-1. Algae. *Platoma abbottiana: (a)* photograph of a dried specimen from which illustration was made; *(b)* detail of branching pattern showing holdfast, stipe, and base of blade. Gillott 659 pen and ink on Cronaflex film, by Alice R. Tangerini. Courtesy of J. N. Norris.

Candy Feller contributed to the text on algae.

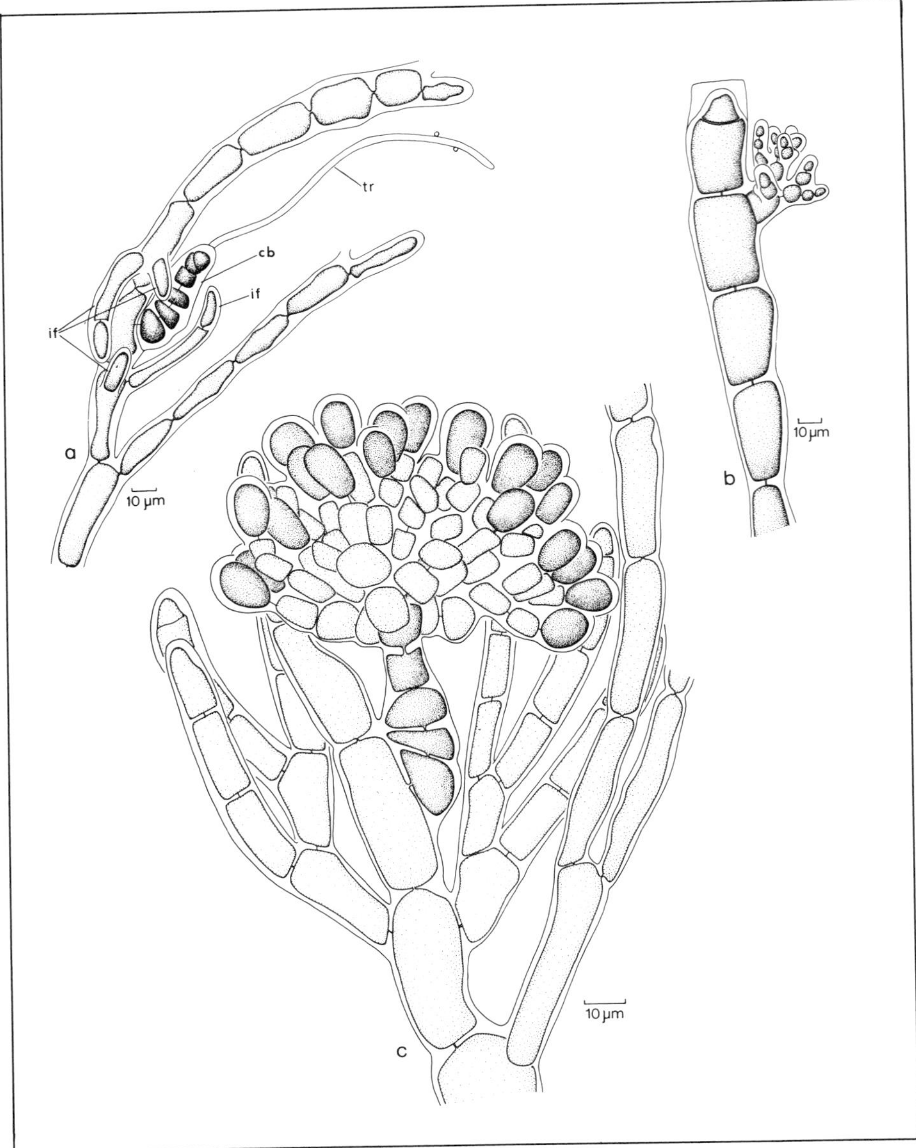

12-2. Algae. *Liagora pinnata*, details of reproduction: *(a)* carpogonial branch (cb) with trichogyne (tr) showing developing involucral filaments (if); *(b)* assimilatory filament bearing lateral spermatangia; *(c)* mature cystocarp. Technical pen and ink on Bristol board, by Candy Feller. Courtesy of J. N. Norris.

might be included. Usually characters of the gametangia, gametes, zygote, and zoospores are illustrated. These reproductive structures should be shown in relation to the vegetative portions of the plant (fig. 12-2). Some reproductive structures such as the conceptacles (the flask-shaped structures containing gametangia) of the *Phaeophyta* (brown algae) or carpogonia (the female sex organs) of the *Rhodophyta* (red algae) can be complex.

Fresh algae should be suspended in water to remain in good condition. Dried algae may be moistened and removed from a herbarium sheet and then floated in water while being drawn. A helpful trick is to place a piece of glass across the top of the container and use a technical pen to trace the form on the glass. Some large mounted dried specimens (fig. 12-1a) may be placed directly on an overhead projector for drawing or reducing or both.

Fungi

Fungi are spore-bearing, achlorophyllous plants generally with a thallus composed of branched filaments (hyphae). The cell walls contain chitin or cellulose or both. Reproduction is sexual or asexual. This very diverse group includes molds and mildews, slime molds, yeasts and cup-fungi, rusts and smuts, mushrooms and puffballs. Like algae, the various fungal groups defy gross generalizations, so an illustrator must become familiar with the diagnostic features of each group. Many of the more minute examples can be drawn only from microscope slides.

A number of classes of fungi have microscopic thalli, and illustrations commonly include features of the sporangia, zoospores, and resistant (resting) spores (fig. 12-3). The sporangium can vary in shape (globose to cylindrical), surface texture (smooth to ribbed), and mode of dehiscence (mode of opening, by pore or lid); the resistant spores have a characteristic ornamentation, pigmentation, and wall thickness. The habits of other fungal groups may be drawn with a dissecting microscope, although some features require still higher magnifications.

The thalli of the more complex Ascomycetes (yeast and cup-fungi) and Basidiomycetes (rusts, smuts, and mushrooms) vary from microscopic to large and conspicuous. Illustrations of the Ascomycetes usually include features of the spores, asci (saclike structures within which spores are formed), and the ascocarp (fruiting body) (fig. 12-4). Often a longitudinal section of the ascocarp is illustrated to show the microscopic nature of the hyphae (fungal threads) making up the stroma (tissue) (fig. 12-5, top).

The Basidiomycetes contain the majority of conspicuous fleshy fungi commonly known as mush-

Wendy B. Zomlefer contributed to the text on fungi.

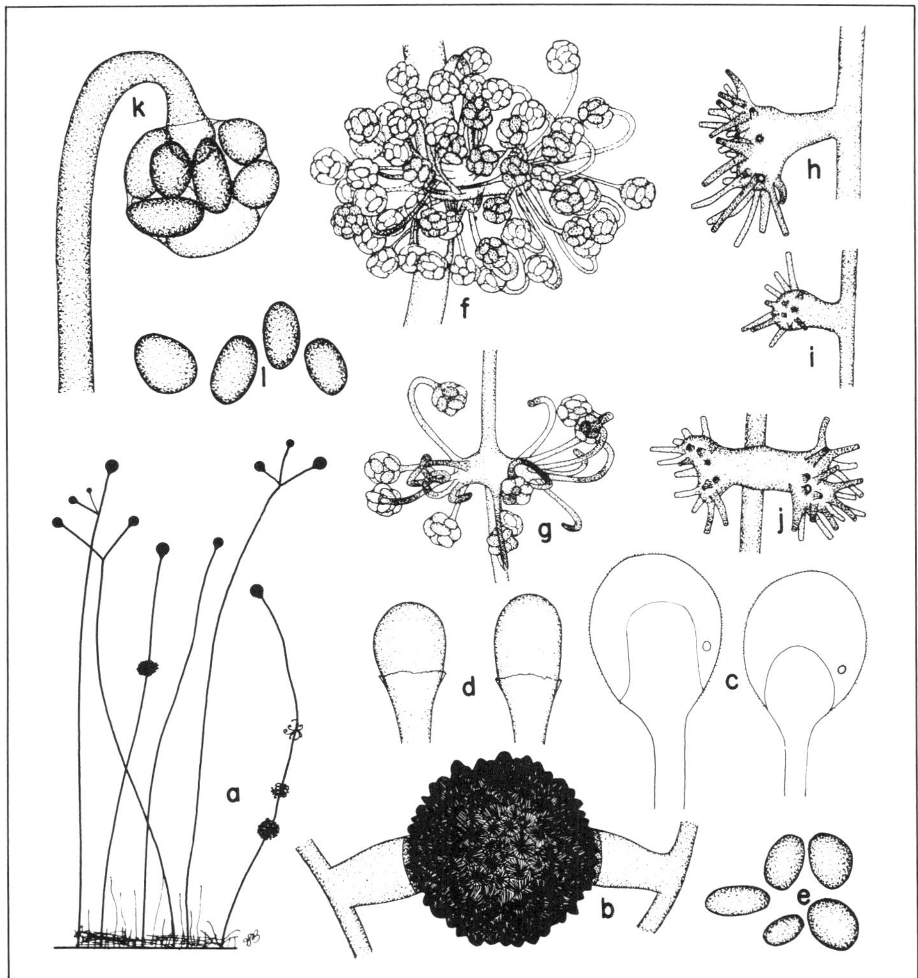

12-3. Fungi. *Thamnostylum nigricans: (a)* habit of sporophores; *(b)* typical zygospore and its suspensors; *(c)* sections of two primary sporangia showing variation in shape of columellae and relative size of sporangiospores; *(d)* columellae of two primary sporangia showing basal collars and apophyses; *(e)* sporangiospores from a primary sporangium; *(f), (g)* portions of two sporophores showing variation in number of sporangiola in heads; *(h), (i), (j)* portions of three sporophores; *(k)* a sporangiole and the distal portion of its reflexed pedicel; *(l)* sporangiospores from a sporangiole. Pen-and-ink on Bristol board, by Gerald L. Benny. From *Observations on Thamnidioaceae* (Aliso, vol. 8, no. 3, 1975).

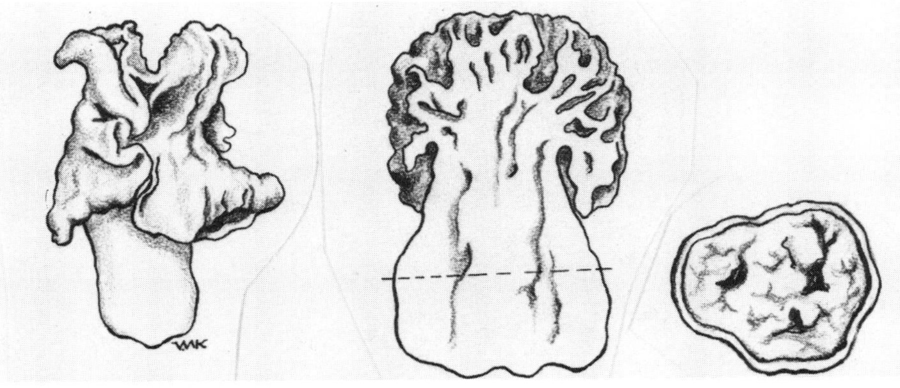

b

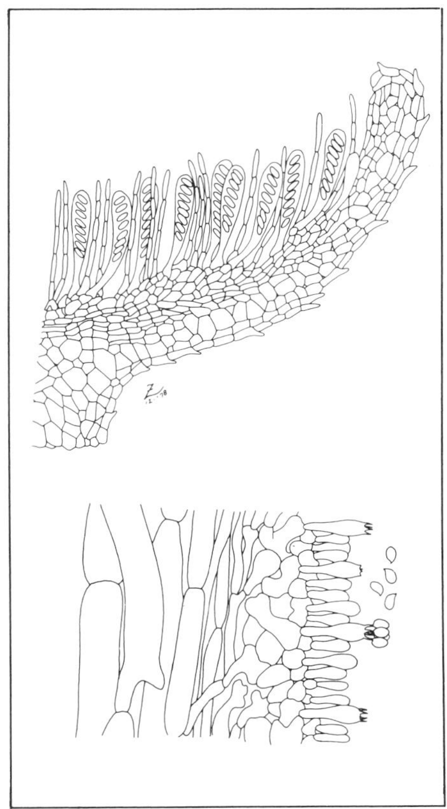

12-5. Fungi. Top: longitudinal section through a cupulate apothecium of an Ascomycete; bottom: longitudinal section through the hymenial layer of a gilled Basidiomycete. Technical pen and ink on Satin Design paper, by Wendy B. Zomlefer.

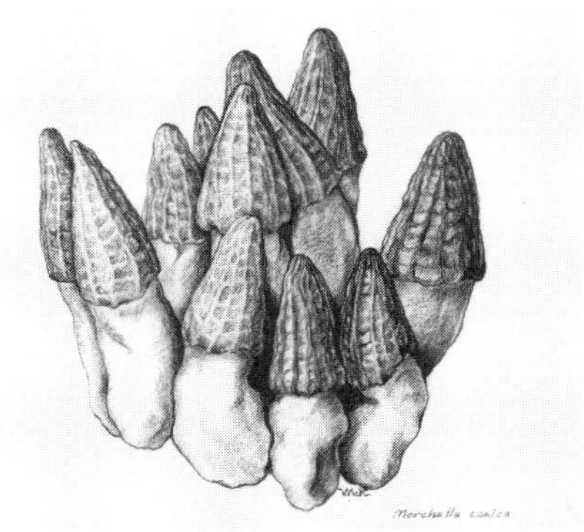

a

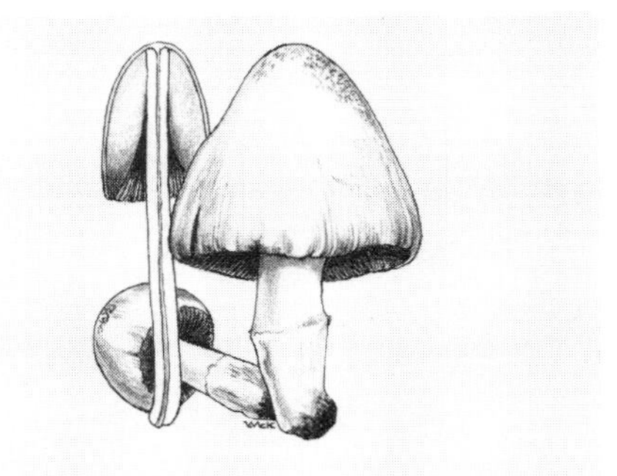

c

12-4. Fungi: *(a)* Ascomycete, *Morchella conica;* Wolff's BB pencil on medium-surface Strathmore Bristol board; *(b)* Ascomycetes, *Gyromitra* species; Stabilo pencil and pen-and-ink on medium-surface Bristol board; *(c)* Basidiomycete, *Coprinus atramentarius.* Stabilo pencil and pen-and-ink on coquille board. All by Vera B. McKnight.

rooms or toadstools. Illustrations stress features of the habit, basidia (club-shaped structures that bear exposed spores), and spores. The vegetative form varies from amorphous blobs (jelly fungi) to platelike shelf fungi or mushrooms with a distinct stipe and cap. The hymenium (fertile layer) can occur in pores, gills, folds, or teeth formed on these different fruiting bodies. For example, with the gilled fungi, an illustration of a longitudinal section of the basidiocarp is often included to show the attachment of the gills to the stalk (fig. 12-5). Other examples of diagnostic vegetative characters are the volva (cup) and annulus (ring) of the gilled mushrooms, which represent the remnants of protective membranes. Also important are color and surface features of the cap and stipe, such as scales, pubescence, reticulations, and zonate patterns. Besides the basidia and spores, other microscopic details commonly illustrated include the cellular nature of the cuticle and gills.

A lichen consists of two plants, an alga and a fungus, living in close association. The thallus may resemble leaves or mosses, or appear to be a gray or green covering on a tree trunk or rock. Illustrations may be of the thallus and reproductive structures (see fig. 7-3).

Liverworts and Mosses

Stemlike and leaflike structures without vascular tissue and a lack of true roots characterize these plants. Reproduction is by spores produced on the conspicuous sporophyte plant (fig. 12-6).

Habit drawings generally are

Margaret Fulford contributed to the text on liverworts.

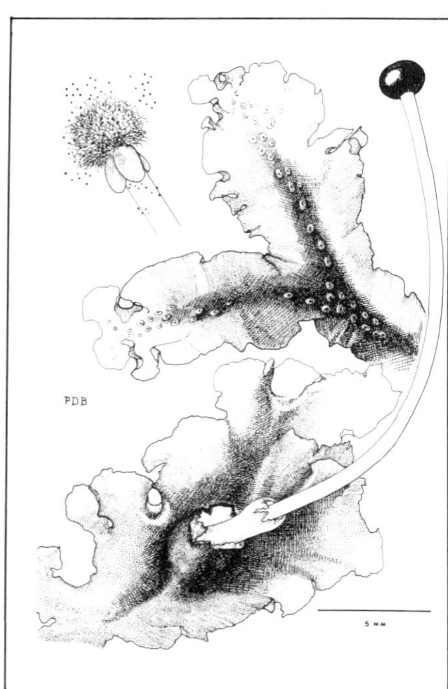

12-6. Liverworts. *Pellia neesiana:* (top) upper surface of thallus showing antheridial chambers; (bottom) thallus with sporophyll. Upper left, dehiscing capsule showing valves, elaters, and spores. Technical and crowquill pens and ink on Strathmore drawing board, drawn from fresh material, by Patricia Drukker Brammall. Courtesy of W. D. Schofield, University of British Columbia.

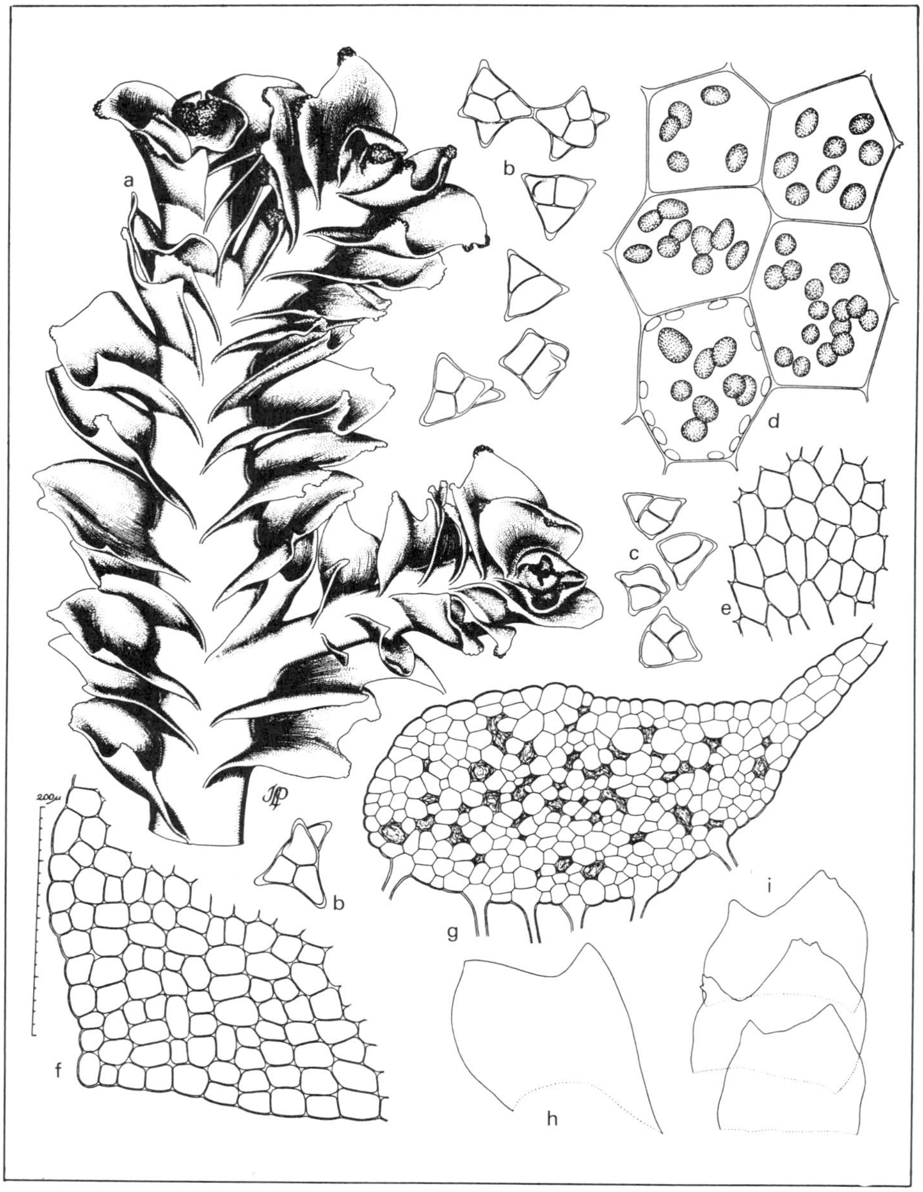

12-7. Liverworts. *Lophozia excisa* var. *elegans: (a)* gemmiparous shoot with two *Radula*-type branches; *(b), (c)* gemmae; *(d)* median cells; *(e)* median cells, much enlarged; *(f)* cells of lobe apex; *(g)* stem cross section; *(h), (i)* leaves. Pen-and-ink, by Joseph Palazolla. From *The Hepaticae and Antherocerotae of North America*, by R. M. Schuster, 1969. Courtesy of Columbia University Press.

made from herbarium specimens that readily revive in water. The small size of these plants requires that they be examined under a microscope. Details are taken from slide mounts usually prepared by the botanist. Many botanists prepare their own drawings because of the degree of precision required in the illustration and the fact that knowledge of morphology and anatomy of these plants is essential (fig. 12-7).

Leafy liverworts are illustrated to show habit, leaf arrangement and shape, and leaf cells. Reproductive parts usually illustrated include:

1. For perianth, number of angles, form of mouth, male and female bract and bracteoles, and stalk of the antheridium.
2. For sporophyte, shape of foot, cross section of stalk; structure of capsule valves; inside and surface views; cross section of the valve (from slides).
3. Spore-coat markings (from slides or scanning electron microscope photographs.)

Drawings of mosses show stems, attachment, arrangement and shape of leaves (fig. 12-8; fig. 12-9E, F, G), and stem cross sections. The reproductive structure is a capsule (fig. 12-8, upper right; fig. 12-9B). Enlarged details are generally of attachment, shape, the operculum, and peristome (including correct number of teeth).

Horsetails, Club Mosses, Selaginella, Quillworts, Isoetes, and Ferns

These plants have a vascular system, roots, stems, and leaves but lack flowers, fruits, and seeds. Spores are produced in small cases called sporangia.

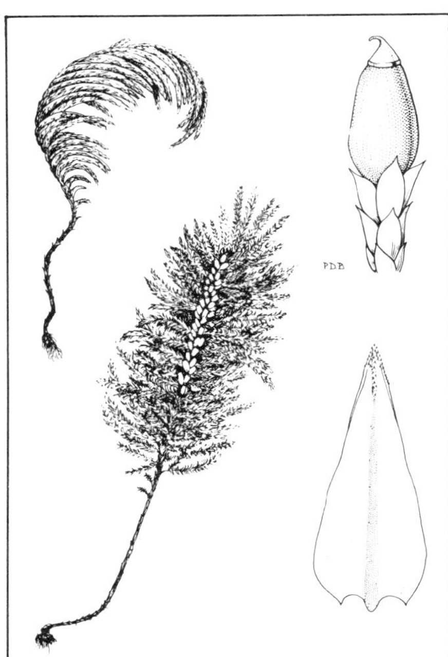

12-8. Mosses. *Dendroalsia abietina:* (top and bottom left) habit drawings; (upper right) capsule; (lower right) single leaf. Technical and crowquill pens and ink on Strathmore drawing board, prepared from live material, by Patricia Drukker Brammall. Courtesy of W. D. Schofield, University of British Columbia.

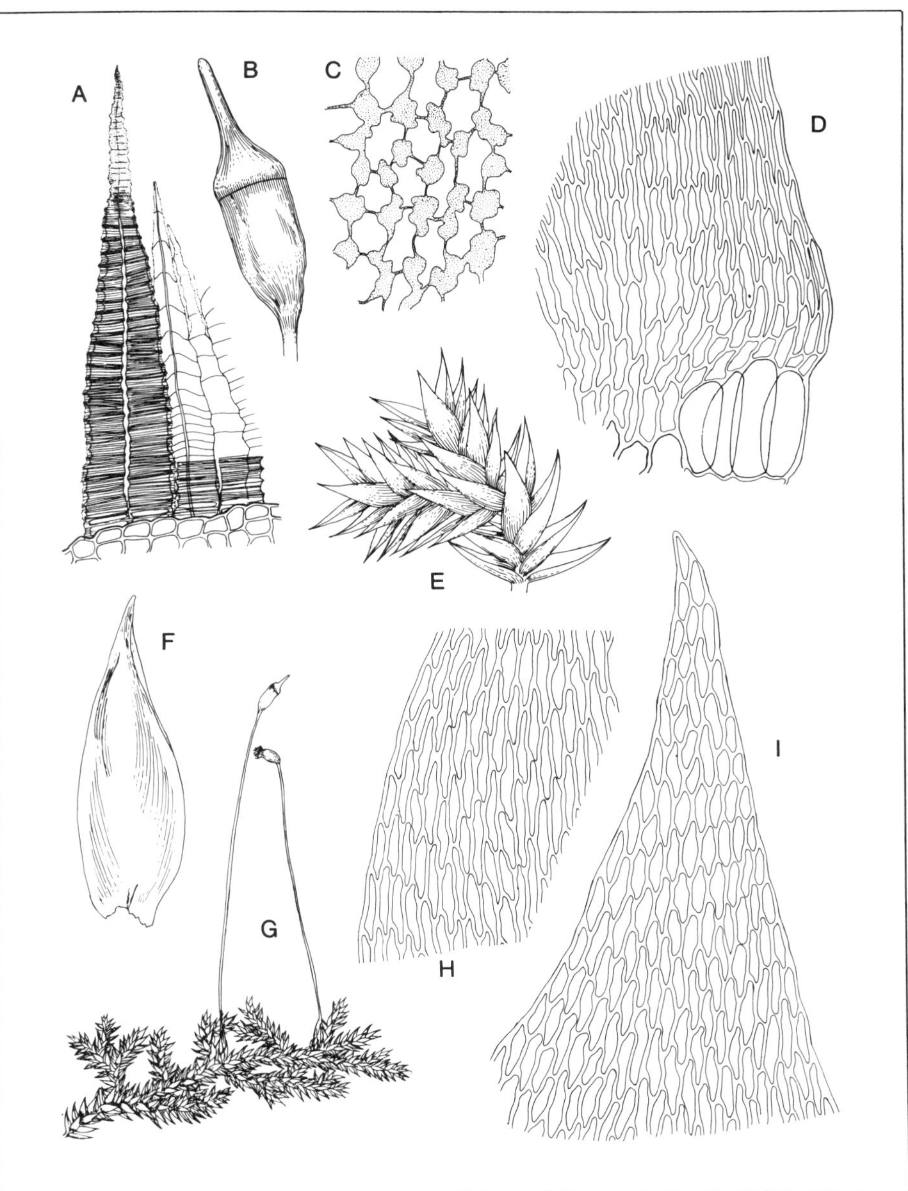

12-9. Mosses. *Acroporium smallii: (A)* portion of peristome; *(B)* capsule; *(C)* exothecial cells; *(D)* cells at leaf base: *(E)* portion of stem and branch; *(F)* leaf outline; *(G)* habit; *(H)* cells above leaf middle; *(I)* cells at leaf tip. Pen-and-ink. Artist unknown. From *Mosses of Eastern North America*, by H. A. Crum and L. E. Anderson (Columbia University Press, 1981).

In addition to habit (fig. 12-10–12-14), reproductive structures are important in this group. *Psilotum* sporangia may be shown open. The strobili of *Lycopodium*, *Selaginella*, and *Equisetum* generally are cut in half longitudinally to show arrangement of the sporangia (figs. 12-11d, 12-12f). Individual mega- and microsporangia may be shown (fig. 12-13d,e; see fig. 12-12d,e). The sporangiophore, spores, and stem of *Equisetum* are distinctive and often are shown in detail (fig. 12-13).

Ferns comprise a large and diverse group divided into several families, and plants range in size from minute to large and treelike. Vegetative parts are always illustrated to show size and division of the fronds (leaves) and the method of attachment to the rhizome (stem) (fig. 12-14). Rhizomes are important diagnostic features because of the presence or absence of vestiture such as hairs or scales and therefore usually are illustrated. The reproductive structures, thinly stalked sporangia, are borne on the backs of the fronds, where they are usually collected together in lines or clusters called sori. They may be under a rolled leaf edge, under an umbrella-like cover (indusium), or unprotected. Sori may be shown as individuals from a top view or cut vertically to show details such as the position of the indusium and number of sporangia present. The individual sporangium is drawn in detail to show the annulus (a zipperlike mechanism of dehiscence), stalk, and size. Spore detail may be illustrated from scanning electron microscope (SEM) photographs.

Most ferns are illustrated from herbarium specimens, but sometimes fresh plants are available. Many ferns immediately curl up when cut, making them useless for illustration. A potted plant, perhaps dug from the wild, provides the best subject. When illustrating sporangia and sori from fresh plants, select fronds with sori that

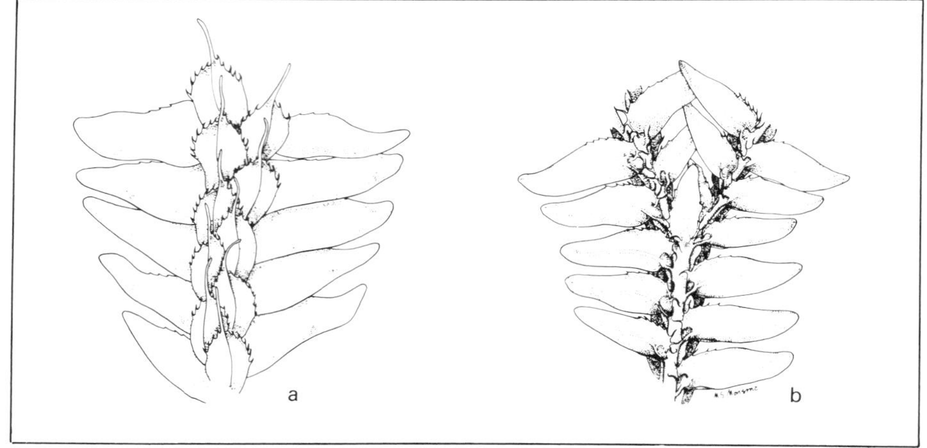

12-10. Spike mosses. *Selaginella martensii:* upper *(a)* and lower *(b)* surfaces of portions of branches and leaves. Crowquill pen and ink on Cronaflex film, by Mary Monsma. Courtesy of D. B. Lellinger.

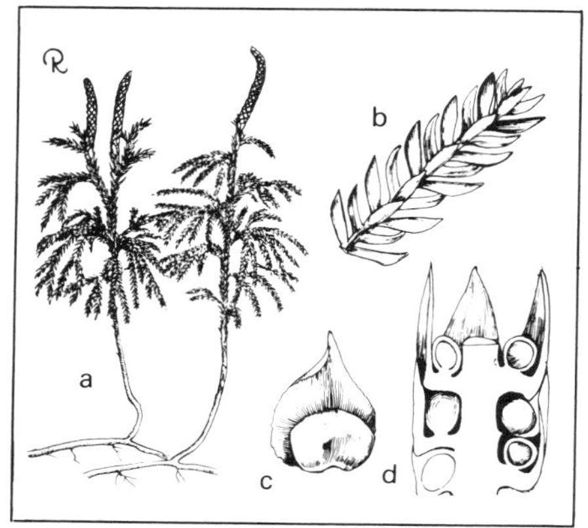

12-11. Club mosses. *Lycopodium obscurum: (a)* habit; *(b)* sterile branch showing leaves; *(c)* sporophyll; *(d)* longitudinal section of fertile branch showing sporangia (strobilus). Crowquill pen and ink on Bristol board, by Marion Ruff Sheehan. Reproduced with permission of the publisher, from *Taxonomy of Vascular Plants*, by G. H. M. Lawrence (© 1951 by Macmillan Publishing Company, renewed 1979 by M. B. Lawrence).

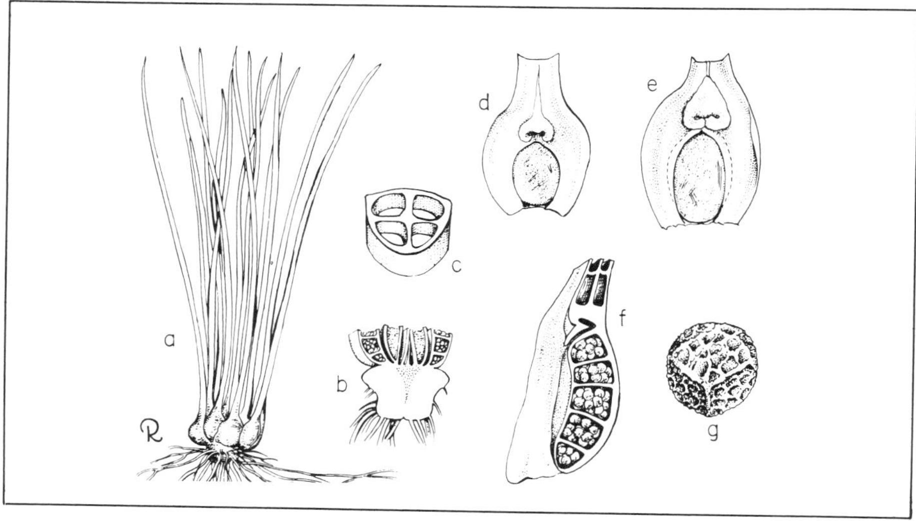

12-12. Quillworts. *Isoetes Engelmannii: (a)* habit; *(b)* vertical section through rhizome and leaf bases; *(c)* cross section of leaf; *(d)* leaf base showing microsporangium; *(e)* leaf base showing megasporangium; *(f)* leaf base in longitudinal section; *(g)* megaspore. Crowquill pen and ink on Bristol board, by Marion Ruff Sheehan. Courtesy of the L. H. Bailey Hortorium, Cornell University.

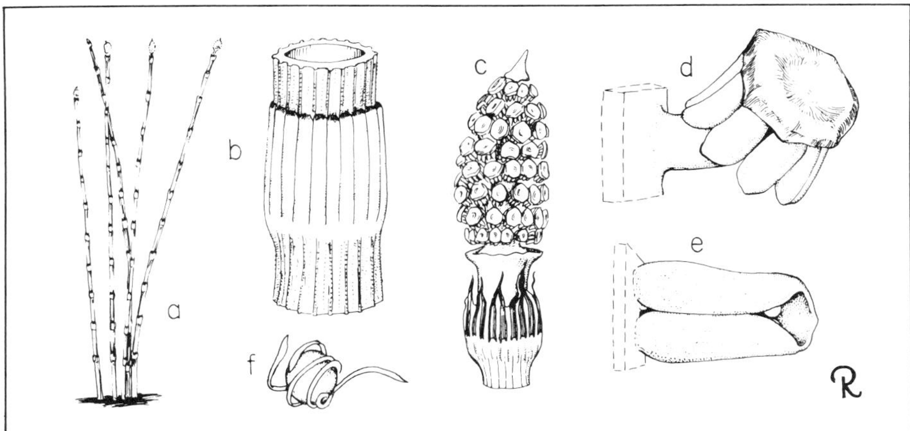

12-13. Horsetails. *Equisetum hyemale: (a)* habit; *(b)* stem section at node showing leaves; *(c)* strobilus; *(d)* sporophyll; *(e)* single sporangium; *(f)* mature spore with elaters. Crowquill pen and ink on Bristol board, by Marion Ruff Sheehan. Reproduced with permission of the publisher, from *Taxonomy of Vascular Plants*, by G. H. M. Lawrence (© 1951 by Macmillan Publishing Company, renewed 1979 by M. B. Lawrence).

are mature in size but not quite ripe enough to split open normally. Those ready to shed spores will do so at the slightest touch or with minor amounts of heat from microscope lamps, leaving no unopened sporangia to illustrate.

Gymnosperms

Plants having roots, stems, leaves, a vascular system, and exposed or naked seeds (not in an ovary) are called gymnosperms. They include trees, shrubs, and herbs. Male and female reproductive organs are always contained in two separate structures, monoecious (on one plant) or dioecious (on two plants) (fig. 12-15).

Drawings of vegetative structures always show leaf arrangement and structure. Leaves may be scalelike (see fig. 12-40), or needlelike (fig. 12-16), or resemble those in angiosperms (flowering plants). The reproductive structures are usually arranged in cones (strobili). The strobilus may be sectioned longitudinally to show the arrangement of male (microsporophylls) and female (megasporophylls or ovuliferous scales) sporophylls. Individual sporophylls are usually illustrated. The seeds generally are grouped in cones, which are usually shown as mature and opened to disseminate seeds (see fig. 12-15). Immature cones do not always show all the desired characteristics.

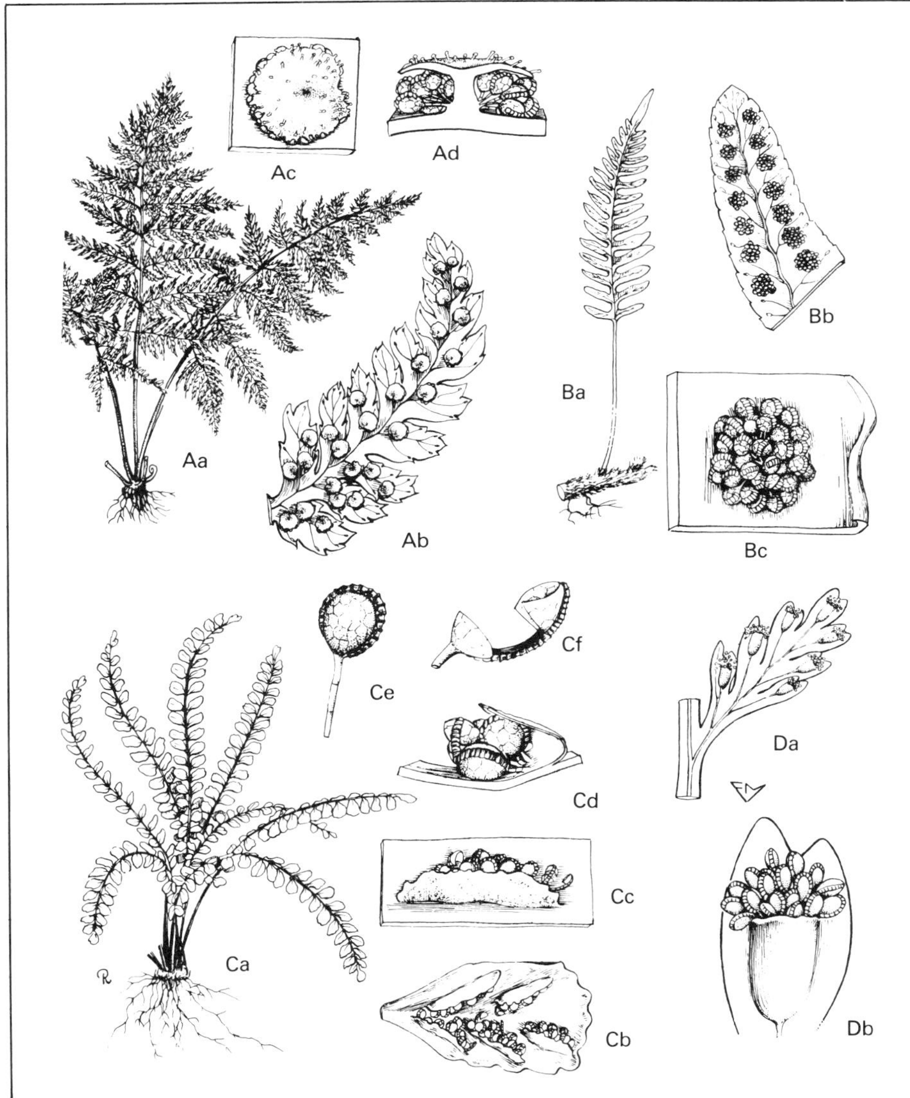

12-14. Ferns. Polypodiaceae, some leaf and sorus types. *(A) Dryopterus austriaca* var. *spinulosa: (Aa)* habit; *(Ab)* pinnule; *(Ac)* sorus: *(Ad)* sorus, vertical section. *(B) Polypodium virginianum: (Ba)* habit; *(Bb)* pinna; *(Bc)* sorus. *(C) Asplenium trichomanes: (Ca)* habit; *(Cb)* pinna; *(Cc)* sorus; *(Cd)* vertical section through sorus; *(Ce)* sporangium; *(Cf)* sporangium dehisced. *(D) Davallia trichomanoides: (Da)* pinnule; *(Db)* sorus. All pen-and-ink on Bristol board. *(A), (B), (C):* Marion Ruff Sheehan, *(D):* Florence McKeel Lambeth. Courtesy of the L. H. Bailey Hortorium, Cornell University. From *Manual of Cultivated Plants*, by L. H. Bailey (Macmillan Publishing Company, 1949).

Pinus elliottii

a

b

c

d

e

h

g

f

i

j

PF

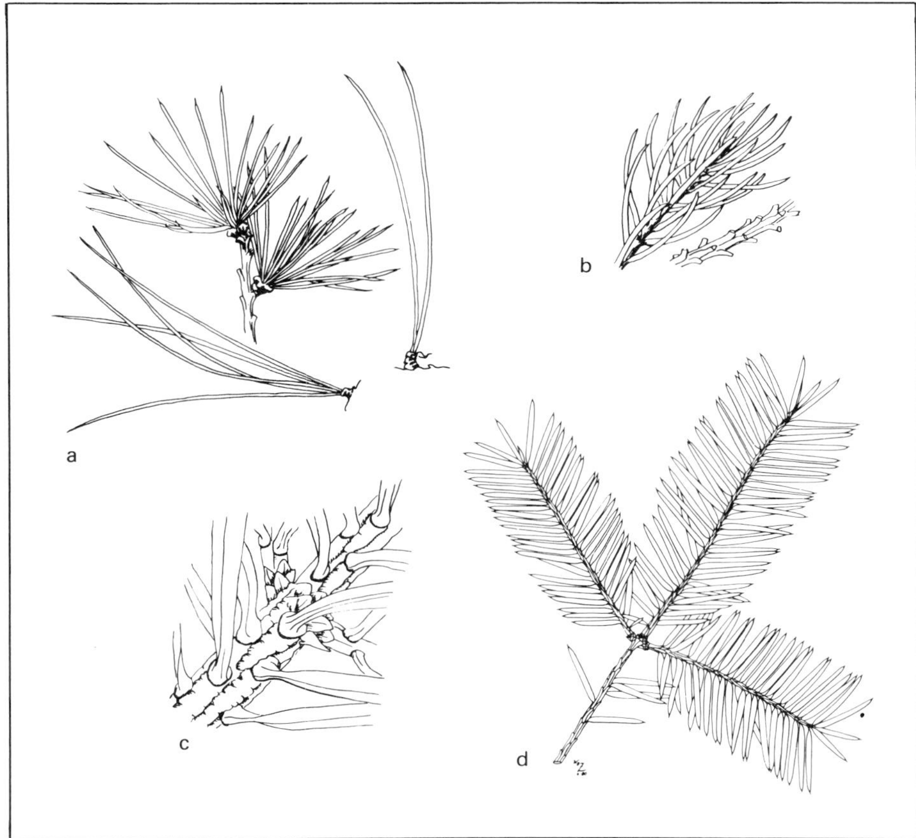

12-16. Gymnosperms, some foliage types. *(a)* Top left: tamarack, *Larix;* right: pine, *Pinus;* bottom: *Pinus strobus. (b)* Spruce, *Picea. (c)* Fir, *Abies homolepis*, leaf base detail. *(d) Torreya taxifolia. (a), (b), (c)*: Gillott pen and ink on Albanene paper, by Bente Starcke King, courtesy of the L. H. Bailey Hortorium, Cornell University; *(d)*: crowquill pen and ink on Bristol board, by Wendy B. Zomlefer.

Facing page:
12-15. Gymnosperms. *Pinus elliottii* var. *densa: (a)* female conelets: *(b)* cluster of pollen cones; *(c)* single pollen cone; *(d)* pollen-bearing scale, with pollen sac, from above and below and in longitudinal and transverse section; *(e)* pollen; *(f)* ovule-bearing cone at time of pollination: *(g)* detail of young cone; *(h)* detailed single-scale complex, from above, to show bract scale supporting the ovuliferous scale with its two ovules; *(i)* developing cone; *(j)* old cone with winged seed. Gillott 1950 pen nib and ink on Strathmore drawing board, high surface, by Priscilla Fawcett. From *The Biology of Trees Native to Tropical Florida*, by Dr. P. B. Tomlinson, 1980. Courtesy of the author.

Angiosperms

Plants having roots, stems, leaves, a vascular system, and seeds enclosed in an ovary are called angiosperms. Male and female reproductive organs may be separate or combined. (See figs. 12-22, 12-34, 12-35.)

The habit (whole plant or representative segment) may be drawn life-size, enlarged, or reduced, depending on specimen size. When only a portion of the plant must serve, it should be of sufficient size to portray necessary characteristics of the plant (see figs. 12-32, 12-34a). To draw the habit, measure height and width and block these off on sketch paper at the desired scale. Determine the direction of the main axis and draw a line to represent it, remembering that plant stems are usually curved, if only slightly. Make secondary measurements of the major parts, branches, inflorescence, and so on, and mark them on the main axis line. Draw the axis of each part first, then the plant tissue around each line.

If the whole plant is very large or complex, it may be simplified in the illustration. Represent only major branches, sufficient leaves, or other vegetative parts to show characteristics (see fig. 12-35A). View a large subject through a reducing lens to estimate the effect of reduction.

Leaves and Other Vegetative Structures

Critical factors when drawing leaves and similar structures include disposition on the stem and angle of divergence, as leaves may be held erect, at right angles, downward, or anywhere in between (fig. 12-17). Leaf curvature is an important characteristic and varies from almost straight to strongly recurved. Because of their disposition on the stem, most leaves are seen in perspective and must be illustrated foreshortened (see figs. C-30, 9-12, 12-33, 12-34).

Most leaves are composed of petiole and blade, although many other forms exist in nature. To draw a leaf correctly, first draw the entire petiole and central vein (midrib or midvein), noting changes as the midvein emerges and angles or curves away from the stem. It should be possible to follow the midrib to its end in an unbroken

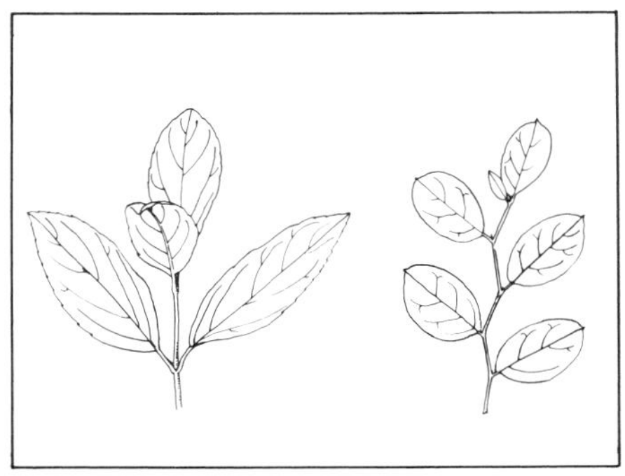

12-17. Disposition of leaves on stem. Left: opposite; right: alternate. Crowquill pen and ink on Bristol board, by Marion Ruff Sheehan.

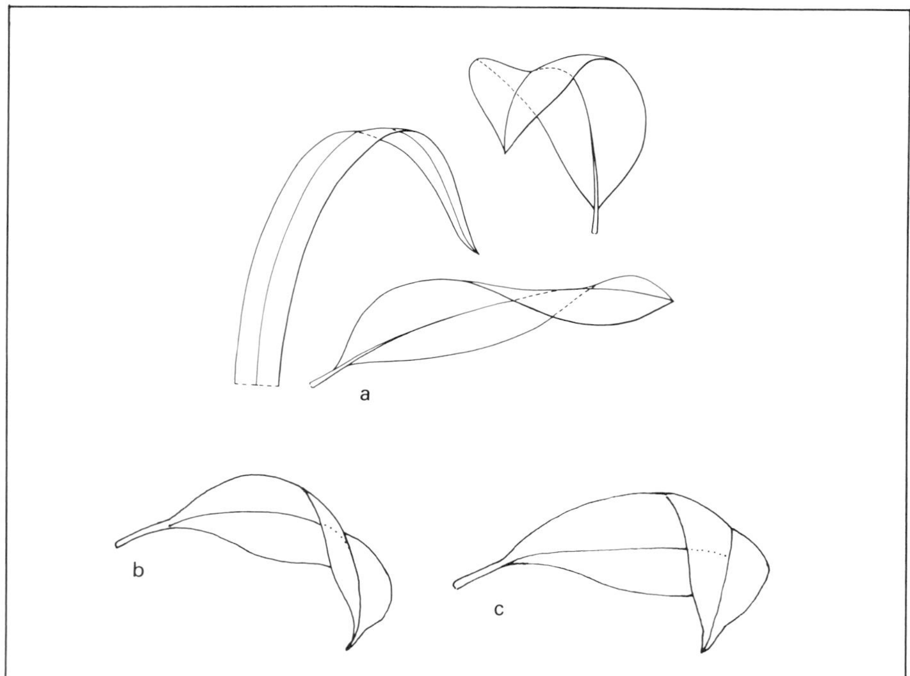

12-18. Curvature in leaves: *(a)* leaves in different positions to show proper curvature; *(b)* leaf correctly drawn to show curvature, the midvein being a continuous line; *(c)* leaf incorrectly drawn; midvein is discontinuous and cannot be followed as a line from one end of the leaf to the other. Crowquill pen and ink on Satin Design paper, by Wendy B. Zomlefer *(a)*; on Bristol board, by Marion Ruff Sheehan *(b,c)*.

and smooth line if the drawing has been prepared correctly. Add the leaf blade as a continuous line around the midvein (figs. 12-18, 12-19, 12-20). Count and add major secondary veins next, noting positions and divergence. Where possible, match veins with major lobes or serrations on the leaf margin (fig. 12-20, bottom). Inattention to this aspect ruins many otherwise well-done botanical drawings. For compound leaves, draw the midvein of each leaflet and then outline the blade as for single leaves. Proper foreshortening follows naturally when this procedure is followed, as focusing on the position of the midvein automatically positions the leaf properly.

Flowers

An inflorescence must be placed squarely on the stem, its point of emergence and type accurately delineated. Flowers must be drawn correctly positioned on the peduncle (figs. 12-21, 12-22-1a). The flared portion of the corolla (limb) must be correctly positioned on the lower portion (tube) (fig. 12-23-2a).

12-19. Leaves. Drawing the leaf midvein first ensures proper position and direction. Blades are added around the midvein. Top: linear leaves; bottom: a rosette of leaves properly positioned. Crowquill pen and ink on Bristol board by Marion Ruff Sheehan.

12-20. Leaves. Top: compound leaf—sketch at left, completed drawing at right; bottom: two types of leaf venation and margin showing vein curvature and relationship to teeth on margins of leaf. Crowquill pen and ink on Bristol board, by Marion Ruff Sheehan.

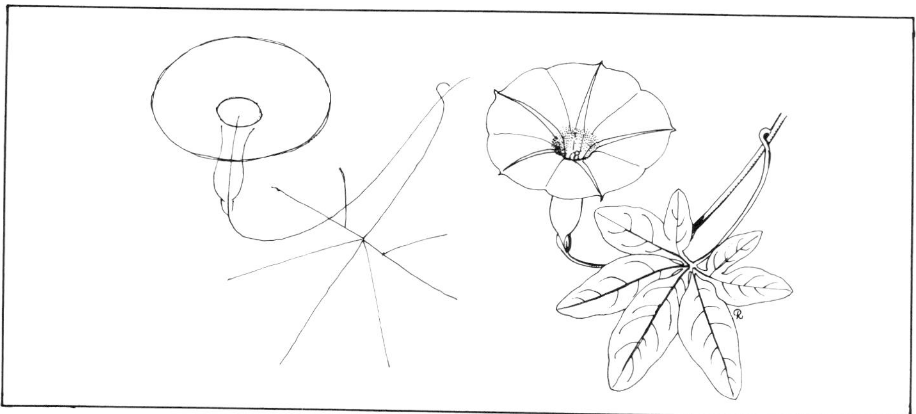

12-21. Drawing flowers. Left: line sketch properly positions flower on stem and leaflets on leaf; right: corolla is completed and leaf blade added. Crowquill pen and ink on Bristol board, by Marion Ruff Sheehan.

The opening in the limb must match the diameter of the lower portion of the flower, whatever its shape (figs. 12-23, 12-24).

When drawing the calyx (outermost flower whorl, the sepals), note the position and number of lobes (figs. 12-22, 12-23, 12-25). Frequently, the calyx lobes number the same as the petals and are alternate to them, but many other arrangements are found.

Examples of flowers incorrectly drawn are legion. Careful observation leads to accurate illustration.

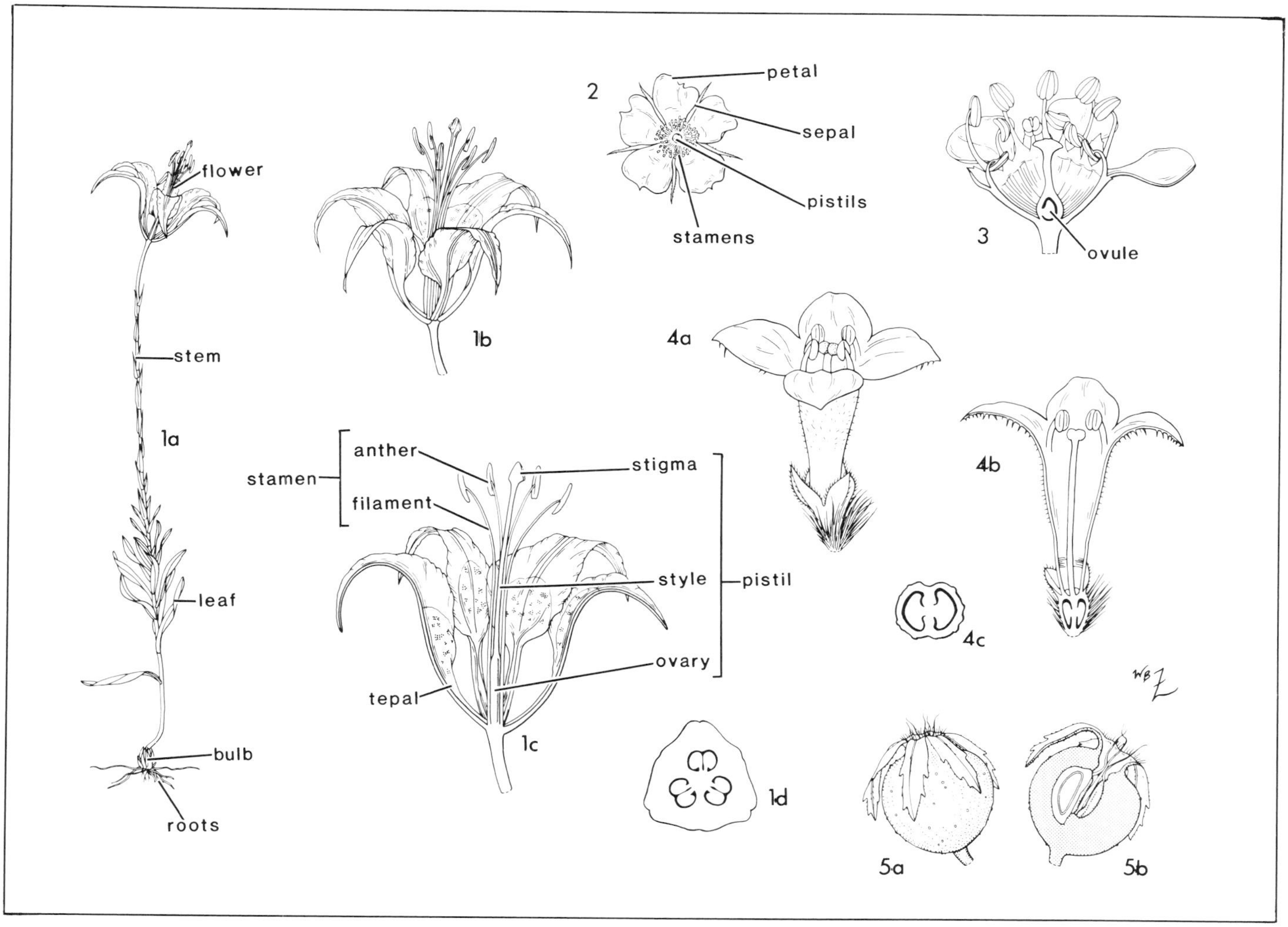

12-22. Angiosperms. Vegetative and reproductive structures. *(1) Lilium catesbaei: (1a)* habit; *(1b)* flower; *(1c)* longitudinal section of flower; *(1d)* cross section of ovary. *(2) Rosa palustris:* flower. *(3) Prunus serotina:* longitudinal section of flower. *(4) Diodia teres: (4a)* flower; *(4b)* longitudinal section of flower; *(4c)* cross section of ovary. *(5) Crataegus uniflora: (5a)* fruit (pome); *(5b)* longitudinal section of pome. Crowquill pen and ink on Satin Design paper, by Wendy B. Zomlefer.

1a
1b
1c
1d
2a
2b
2c
3
4a
4b

12-24. Drawing flowers. Top: sketches of a composite (Asteraceae) head to show basic circle and ellipses used to define the shapes before completing the drawings. Center: three steps in drawing a tubular-shaped flower *(Alstroemeria):* basic shape is an ellipse and a cone; second step indicates position and direction of petals; final step adds petal shape. Bottom: a drawing of *Impatiens* is begun with the outline, which is then divided into the number of petals and their correct width; next, petals are outlined; to the right is a side view of the same flowers showing the extreme foreshortening of the face. Pen-and-ink on Strathmore drawing board, high surface, by Marion Ruff Sheehan.

Facing page:
12-23. Drawing flowers. Perspective in flowers. *(1)* Flower shape: *(1a)* ellipses; *(1b)* circle; *(1c)* cylinder; *(1d)* cone. *(2)* Drawing tubular flowers: *(2a)* flower with tube and limb (flared portion of the corolla) correctly drawn; *(2b)* tube and limb incorrectly aligned; *(2c)* opening in limb too small in relation to tube diameter. *(3)* Face and side views of the same flower showing differences depending on position. *(4)* Bilaterally symmetrical flowers: *(4a)* pansy; *(4b)* orchid, with a dashed line showing the correct cut to use for bisection. Crowquill pen and ink on Satin Design paper and Bristol board. *(1a–d), (4b):* Wendy B. Zomlefer; *(2a–c), (3), (4a):* Marion Ruff Sheehan.

To draw a flower, begin by sketching the geometric shape, usually a circle (ellipse in perspective) and a cone, tube, or variant of either (see figs. 12-23, 12-24). For example, an Easter lily in three-quarter view is basically an ellipse and a cone. Find and add the central axis line and then the central axis for each petal or sepal. This divides the flower into the correct number of segments. Add petals around these lines just as the leaf blades were added to the leaf midvein. The tube of a tubular flower may be drawn as a separate unit to the point where the corolla flares. Drawing flowers as if they were transparent ensures perfect alignment of parts. Flowers that are bilaterally symmetrical, such as orchids, should be drawn with the two sides equally proportioned, images of each other (see figs. 12-23, 12-24).

Details and Dissection of Flowers

To dissect a flower completely, first remove the calyx, then the corolla (fig. 12-25). Either may be composed of separate or fused segments. Remove single sepals and petals one at a time, severing thick ones at the base with a cutting tool. Remove fused sepals and petals as a unit, cutting around their base to free them; some corollas break free readily without cutting. Free single sepals and petals may be illustrated in any of several ways: singly (see fig. 12-25); as a series artificially arranged; or as a complete series arranged as they appear on the flowers (fig. 12-26). Fused sepals and petals may be shown in top, side, three-quarter, or back view, depending on diagnostic characters, such as the degree of fusion or shape. Tubular corollas may be split, either between lobes or by bisecting a lobe, spread open, and illustrated to show inner aspects such as glands, staminodes, stamens, and vestiture (fig. 12-27d). A tubular flower with an irregular shape must be cut so that the inner features are equally distributed on both sides when the corolla is opened. The corolla should be spread as flat as possible, anchored on a bit of clay or by a small nail laid across it to hold it open. Any crinkling due to spreading of the petals can be smoothed out in the drawing, retaining true measurements and shapes. Free petals at the top may appear as overlapped in the drawing. This method is also useful for opening other tubal structures such as staminal tubes of composites.

Stamens and Pistil

Stamens are illustrated in side (lateral), face (ventral), or back (dorsal) view (see fig. 12-27e). For ease of handling, place individual specimens on slides, supported by clay in position for drawing. Anthers are ideally illustrated just before anthesis (open to shed pollen), when the form and shape are still evident, but some situations require that they be at anthesis to show the manner of opening (see fig. 12-34j). After floral envelopes (sepals and petals) and stamens have been removed, the pistil is readily visible and may be drawn in situ or removed (see figs. 12-34f, 12-38q).

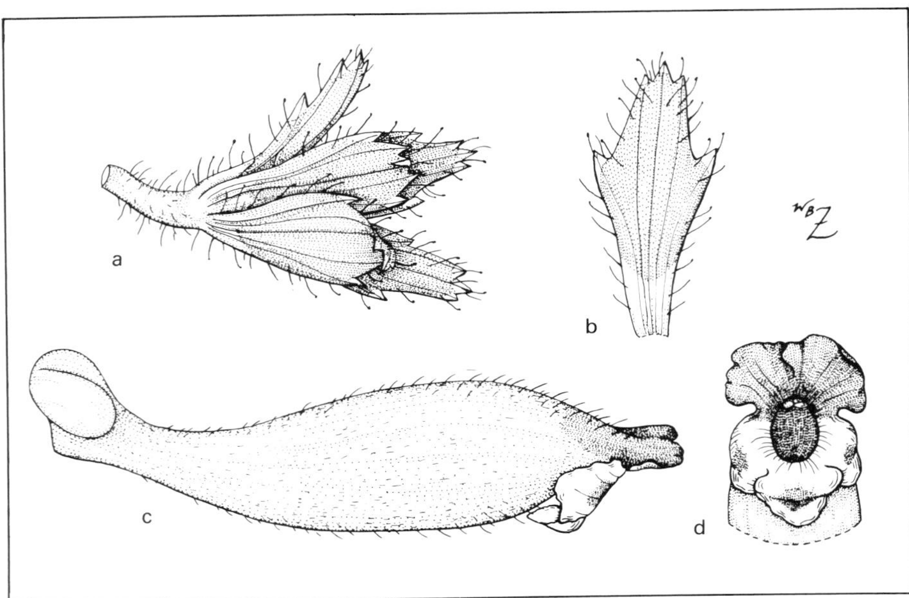

12-25. Floral dissections. *Bucinella nariniana: (a)* complete calyx removed; *(b)* single calyx lobe, face view; *(c)* entire tubular corolla removed, side view; *(d)* face view of upper portion. Crowquill pen and ink on Strathmore drawing board, by Wendy B. Zomlefer.

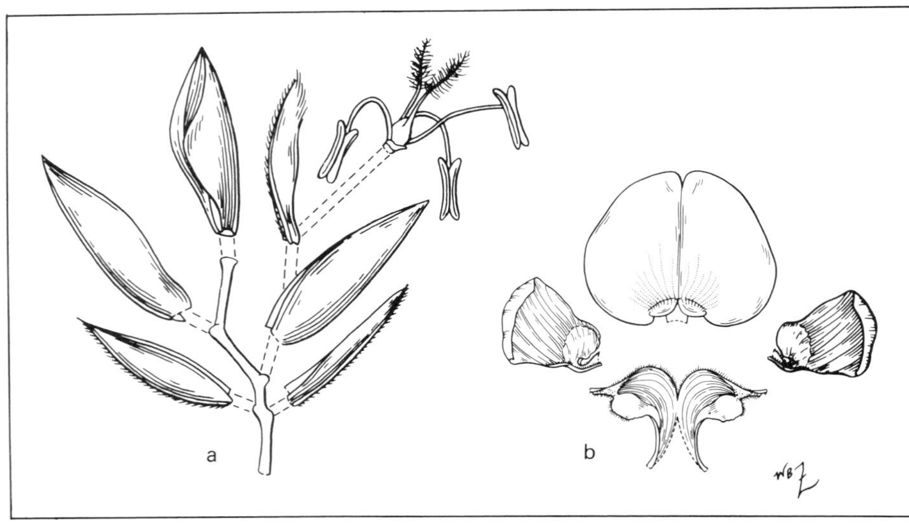

12-26. Dissections. *(a) Eragrostis spectabilis:* expanded grass spikelet with one expanded floret. *(b) Crotalaria spectabilis:* exploded legume flower showing relative size and shape of petals. Pen-and-ink on Satin Design paper, by Wendy B. Zomlefer.

To prepare a vertical section, use a clean sharp tool, as any small bit of debris on the blade edge may tear tissue. To make a perfect cut, study the ovary, observe any lobes, and find the widest area for the dissection since the number of locules and position of ovules usually can be best determined from these external features (see fig. 12-27h,i). Ovules are usually attached at the widest point of the ovary. A perfect cut of an ovary with one locule or an odd number of locules will reveal one open cell (see fig. 12-22-1c, -3; and figs. 12-27g, 12-34h). A perfect cut of an ovary with an even number of locules will show two open cells, one on either side (see figs. 12-22-4b, -4c). The ovules and their means and place of attachment should clearly show in all vertical sections. A cross section is made at right angles to the vertical axis, usually at the widest point (fig. 12-27h). Exceptions to this include where a uniform thickness allows for a cut anywhere along the axis (orchids) or where the ovule is basally attached but the ovary swells higher up (palms). These exceptions illustrate the need for study and understanding of the specimen before dissecting. A thin slice of the pistil may be removed and placed on a slide with droplets of plain water or water with a small amount of Pohl's solution (see formula under Dried Specimens) or glycerin added to prevent drying (see fig. 12-27i). The space around the ovules, the open locule, may be drawn as solid black (see figs. 12-27g, 12-34g,h) or darkened with shading to show the ovules clearly. The stigma is often shown in enlarged detail, but dissection is usually unnecessary.

Vertical Sections

A vertical cut through the whole flower is generally the most difficult type of dissection. A true vertical section perfectly bisects the flower; but this is no easy task to perform, especially when the flower is delicate or small. Flowers with an odd number of parts should show one bisected petal and one bisected sepal, on opposite sides. Flowers with an even number of parts are usually cut to bisect two petals, but may be bisected between petals (see fig. 12-22-2; and fig. 12-27a,b,c). The pistil must be perfectly cut and the stamens must be equally divided by the cut, perhaps one being cut in half (see fig. 12-27f,g,h,i). Bilaterally symmetrical flowers must be cut exactly in half (see fig. 12-23-4b).

Sometimes sections are made of imbedded structures such as inflorescences in pits (see fig. 12-38a) or deeply imbedded flowers. The cut to show this should bisect the imbedded structure to show attachment and arrangement of parts.

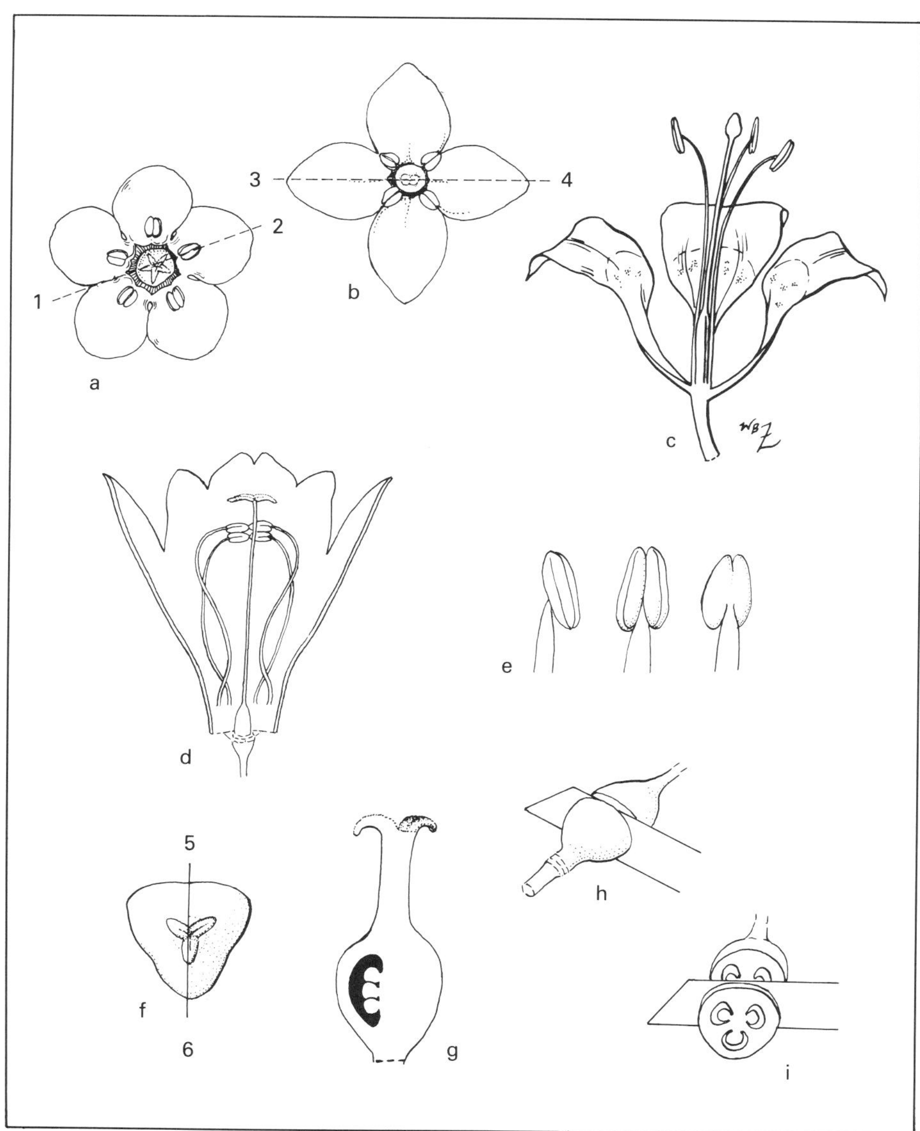

12-27. Floral dissections: *(a)* line 1-2, correct cut to prepare a vertical (longitudinal) section of a flower with odd number of parts; *(b)* line 3-4, the correct cut to section a flower with an even number of parts; *(c)* a flower with even numbers of parts divided between corolla parts, a cut sometimes used but less desirable; *(d)* tubular flower cut through a lobe and expanded to show inner features evenly distributed on both sides, ovary in place; *(e)* stamens: side, face, and back views; *(f)* line 5-6 shows the cut that perfectly bisects a gynoecium; *(g)* perfectly cut gynoecium with an odd number of cells in the ovary, only one open cell showing; *(h)* cut made at the widest part to prepare a cross section; *(i)* for clarity, a thin slice is removed for illustration. Crowquill pen and ink on Strathmore drawing board, high surface. *(a)*, *(b)*, *(d)* through *(i)*: Marion Ruff Sheehan; *(c)* Wendy B. Zomlefer.

Fruits and Seeds

Fruits are the reproductive bodies of seed plants. They consist of one or more seeds encased in protective structures. Fruits should be illustrated when they are fully developed and the seeds mature. Fleshy fruits must be illustrated when fully ripe or almost so (see fig. 12-22-5a, -5b). Dry fruits may be drawn as dehisced (see figs. 12-15j, 12-34k) or indehisced (see figs. 12-29, 12-32), depending on the requirements of the illustration. It is sometimes necessary to illustrate a vertical or cross section of a fruit. It must be perfectly cut through the center (see fig. 12-38u,z). Some very hard fruits, such as those of palms, must be cut with a hacksaw or a pair of heavy shears or wire cutters.

Vestiture and Texture

It is often necessary to show an enlarged detail of the surface or vestiture of a specimen (see fig. 12-37). A segment may be drawn as if excised from the specimen or an enlargement may be shown with no apparent boundaries. Vestiture can be portrayed in top, side, or three-quarter view, carefully observing and drawing angles of divergence, curvature, spacing, width, segmentation, and presence or absence of glandular tips (fig. 12-

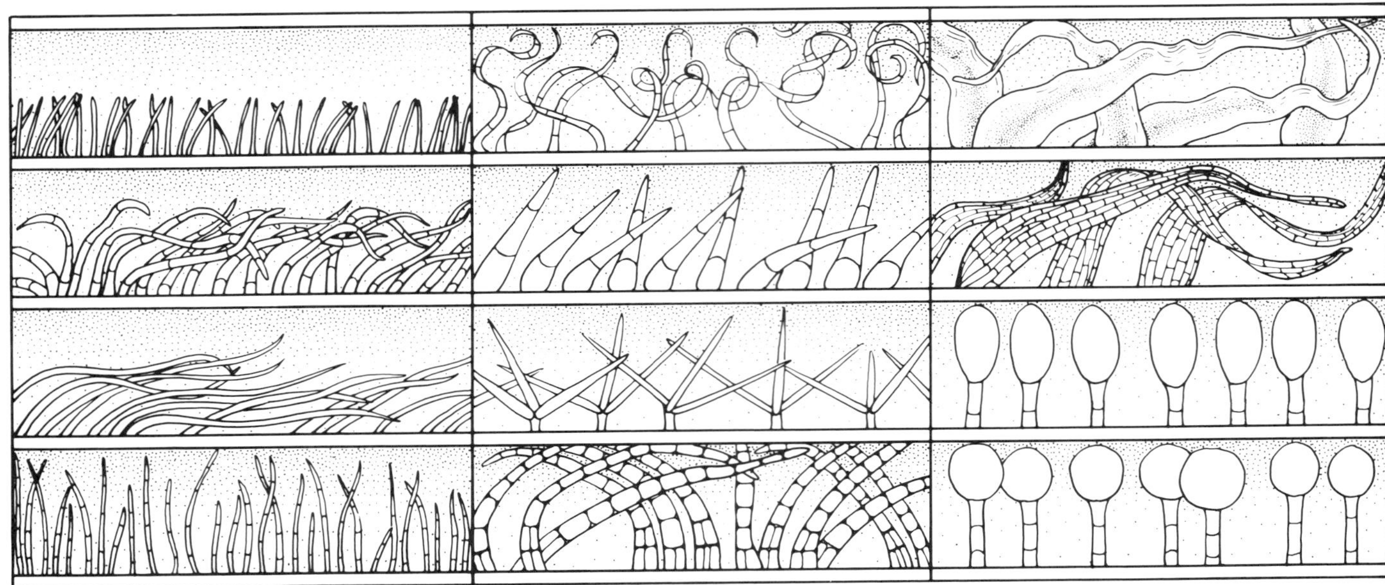

12-28. Vestiture, side views. Hair, scale, and gland types on ferns. Technical pen and ink on Cronaflex film, by Mary Monsma. Courtesy of D. B. Lellinger.

28). Stellate hairs are drawn in top view with the proper number of radiating points shown.

Expanding Structures

Complex structures (such as grass flowers) may need to be dissected and the parts spread apart for illustrating. This technique also is used to illustrate complex floral envelopes, stamens in series, whole flowers, inflorescences, strobili, or any other parts compressed in a tight arrangement (see fig. 12-26b).

CARE AND HANDLING OF SPECIMENS

Each type of specimen, whether fresh or preserved, requires special handling, and the botanical artist is responsible for its care while a specimen is in use or in the studio.

Live Specimens

Drawing live specimens has advantages and disadvantages. Nothing is as satisfactory as live material for ease of illustration and for imparting realism and three-dimensionality (fig. 12-29; see figs. C-5, C-8). On the other hand, live material, whether growing or cut, is constantly changing: buds may pop open; flowers turn, open more fully, fade, or close. The bloom may open for only a few hours or for a single day. Nothing is more disheartening than to start work on a flower and find that it has closed forever or fallen apart. Leaves turn toward the light, unfurl, grow, and reposition themselves in many ways. The illustrator must very quickly capture the specimen at its

12-29. Drawing from live specimens. *Acer saccharum:* a fruiting branch rendered in a combination of line (fruits) and stippling. Various pen nibs (Hunt 104; Gillott 850, 290; Esterbrook 357) and ink on Strathmore drawing board, by Nancy Hart. From *The Morton Arboretum Quarterly*, 1977.

peak of perfection, sketching and noting features for future reference.

It is helpful to take a series of photographs of habit, flowers, fruit, leaves, stems, and other features for future use, especially if the final rendition of the drawing must be done after the plant is no longer available or when the flowers are dead. Notes on textures, patterns, and other details, plus some pencil shading, also help. If a color drawing is being prepared, color slides are imperative. Quick color studies or patches of color on the sketch will provide good references for future rendering if it is impossible to complete a drawing with the specimen in hand. When working on a flowering plant, sketch the whole plant and then concentrate on the flowers, especially if they are short-lived. The leaves usually will last longer and can be detailed later.

Potted Plants

A living potted plant must be given proper care to ensure its continued growth or blooming condition or both. A plant in the studio might suffer from low light and low humidity. Ideally, the plant should be returned to its former environment or to a greenhouse each night. If it must be kept in the studio two or more days, check the soil for moisture. If it is dry to the touch, add water until it runs out the bottom of the pot, allow the pot to drain, and place it on a saucer to catch excess moisture. If the plant wilts when brought indoors, add water, cover with a plastic bag, and place in a cool spot until the plant revives. If a plant is to remain indoors for several days, it may need supplemental light from a bright window. It should be kept out of direct sunlight, which may burn it. Additional light can be supplied from lamps, which can be left on all night. Never place the plant closer than 15 inches (40cm) from the light bulb to prevent burning and drying of the leaves and flowers.

Set live specimens growing in containers upright or spread plants on a stable support to establish the view desired. If a stem needs to be elevated for illustration, prop with a forked stick or a table fork (tines up), the handle inserted in the soil. Vines or other pendant plants should always be supported or hung so that the stems fall naturally. For the artist dealing frequently with live plants, a standing coatrack or permanently mounted ceiling hook is a good device for suspending specimens. Fit the pot with a sling or pothook, available from a garden supply center. Any such support, however, should not obstruct the natural position of the stems.

Cut Flowers and Stems

Freshly cut specimens usually are brought to the artist in a plastic bag or vasculum (collecting container used by botanists). While they may keep for a short time in this way, it is better to place them in a container of water immediately or to refrigerate the specimens in a plastic bag to prolong their freshness. If the specimens arrive badly wilted, recut the stems, place them in deep warm water, 100° to 110°F (39° to 42°C), and cover the specimens with a plastic bag. Warm water is taken up more quickly than cold. Refrigerate immediately in the bag, if possible, as the cool, moist atmosphere in a refrigerator aids recovery by slowing respiration. Recut the stems daily to remove any decaying matter and to open clogged water-carrying tubes. For longer preservation, add florist's preservative (Floralife, Bloomlife) to the water or use a solution of one teaspoon sugar and one teaspoon lemon juice to one cup of water. Citrus soft drinks containing sugar also will serve as preservatives when diluted with water to one-third strength. Refrigerate cut specimens when not in use, or place them in their container in a cool place, avoiding areas near air-conditioners or heat vents, which will dry out the plant tissue.

Stand slender to medium upright material in a narrow-necked flask. Larger and heavier material may be placed in a wide-necked jar, supported by any of the devices used in flower arranging. Florist's foam (Oasis, Filfast), available from any florist shop, holds its own water supply and needs only to be placed on foil or a plate after being saturated with water. It will support inserted plant specimens securely in the exact position desired and may be dried between uses or stored wet in a refrigerator. Such foams eventually crumble with use and must be replaced.

Keep individual flowers, leaves, and small stems in a small bowl or crucible in shallow water or in plastic tubes with rubber-capped ends, available from a florist. Fill the tube with water, place the cap over the open end, and insert the specimen. Anchor the tube in clay or foam. Support individual leaves and flowers on clay or paper toweling. Place fragile specimens, such as the petals or other parts of flowers, on soft tissue, either arranged or allowed to assume their natural positions.

Preserved Specimens

Plants are easily preserved in liquid, but the containers usually take up more space than most herbaria can spare. However, very fleshy or large specimens (cacti and certain fruits) may require it. A botanist may preserve some field collections in liquid, especially if it is anticipated that illustrations will be needed. The combination of preserved and pressed specimens is invaluable to the artist.

Preserved specimens for illustration should be kept moist and returned to the storage container as soon as possible. If several specimens must be removed for the selection of one for illustration, return the others before beginning the drawing. Keep the selected specimen in a crucible, petri dish, or other suitable container. Add some water or some of the liquid in which the specimen was preserved to prevent it from drying out completely. The addition of a small amount of glycerin to the liquid used will prevent drying, but it will also make the specimen sticky and shiny. It may be necessary to allow partial drying to reveal features, but complete drying can ruin a subject. Dissections dry very quickly under microscope lights, less so under fiber-optic lights. Strong light may fade specimens taken out of liquid, so avoid long exposure. Cover specimens when not in use.

All pieces of dissections should be returned to the storage jar. Separating them into a small vial inside the large jar will keep them readily identifiable and available for future use. It will also prevent cluttering of the preservative and remaining specimens with bits of debris.

Specimens in collection jars become distorted, folded, or collapsed, but it is often possible to rearrange distorted structures in a natural position on moist tissue. Bits of clay or kneaded eraser also will support small specimens in the proper position for illustrating. Support larger specimens on crumpled paper toweling made wet with water or preservative and molded into shape. Float very soft specimens in liquid. Small specimens may have to be secured to prevent movement and can be pinned with minutens into white beeswax that has been melted into the bottom of a petri dish. The beeswax is translucent enough to allow some light to pass through and the minutens are small enough not to obstruct the view. Cover with water to prevent glare.

Subjects such as large flowers might have to be drawn while still in the jar, since they may collapse if removed. If the specimen must be removed, float it in sufficient liquid from the jar to retain its shape.

Preserved specimens lose all color, and some become almost transparent, especially those with thin tissues. It is difficult to see structures in translucent material. Also, vestitures and surface textures may not be visible on wet preserved specimens. Partially drying the specimen will reveal some features such as prominent venation and suture lines. Usually hairs will spring back to a more natural state on partially dried specimens.

Microscope lighting may have to be modified for preserved materials. Directing light from the side (raking light) often reveals details. A dark substage or black paper under a translucent or very pale subject clarifies details and structure.

Dried Specimens

Pressed and dried plants (herbarium specimens) have lost all three-dimensional qualities and most of their substance. In approaching the drawing of an herbarium specimen, it is important to have a clear understanding of the botanist's illustration requirements as well as whether the assignment involves producing a strict depiction of the specimen as it appears pressed flat or a reconstituted rendition of the plant as it appeared living.

Herbarium sheets are prepared by arranging plant specimens on paper to fit within an area of about 11 by 16 inches (28 by 40.5cm), covered with more paper, interleaved with blotting paper, pressed and dried, and then mounted by means of special adhesives and tapes on heavy 100 percent rag paper (fig. 12-30; see fig. 12-1). Loose parts are enclosed in packets attached to the sheet. After labeling, the sheets are systematically filed within rag folders and stored in dust-, insect-, and light-proof herbarium cases.

Alice R. Tangerini and Mary S. Monsma contributed to the text on dried specimens.

Dried specimens are brittle and easily damaged. When removing specimens from the storage case, remove the entire folder first, then the desired sheet and specimen. Never pull a single sheet from a closed folder, as damage is very likely to occur, perhaps to several specimens. Herbarium sheets should be supported from beneath to prevent twisting and bending of the specimen. Specimens should not be turned upside down except when being photocopied. Place unused specimens in herbarium folders to keep them clean and to prevent damage. If it is necessary to remove parts for dissection, do so only with the consent of the botanist. If permission is granted for removal of material, note on the sheet (on a label, if available) what is removed, the remover's name, and the date. Indicate where the drawing is to be published, if known. It may be necessary to replace removed parts, which may be redried, remounted, or folded in a packet and the packet fastened to the herbarium sheet to retain the complete specimen for future reference.

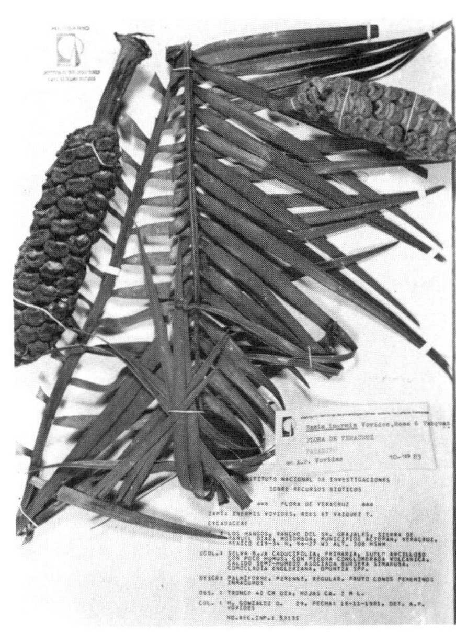

12-30. Typical herbarium sheet from which an artist might work. Leaflets of this cycad have been folded and partially trimmed away so that the specimen fits the sheet.

Dried specimens mounted on herbarium paper need no special support for illustration as the whole sheet is placed under the objectives of the microscope for study and illustration. Parts that are removed for illustration or dissection are supported in the same ways as fresh and preserved material (on clay or tissue or with the other methods detailed earlier). A strip of cellophane, masking, or double-sided tape anchored at both ends will hold small seeds and other minute material immobile and in the desired position for illustrating. This system is not recommended if the material is fragile and must be returned to the herbarium sheet, as it may not be possible to remove the specimen safely and completely from the tape.

Herbarium specimens are flattened, sometimes wrinkled, often folded, and perhaps even rearranged in an atypical way to fit the paper. The artist cannot tell by looking at the specimen whether it was thick or thin when alive. Careful study of the literature before beginning a drawing of a dried specimen is therefore essential.

Drawings depicting the dried specimen are usually not meant to resemble the living plant. The botanist and artist must decide if parts should be drawn as folded on the sheet or unfolded. Depth is imparted by shading to avoid too flat a look (fig. 12-31). Specimens to be rendered at natural size can be pencil-traced on vellum or frosted acetate with the aid of a light table. Specimens too brittle to be traced directly without breaking under the pressure of the hand may be photocopied and the resulting copy traced easily. If reduction is required, the desired scale can often be achieved by a reducing photocopier, opaque projector, or grid. The opaque projector, enlarging photocopier, camera lucida, or a grid will enlarge the drawing. Direct tracing or photocopying the specimen must be approved by the botanist, as some specimens are too fragile to be photocopied or traced safely. In this case, the illustrator must use measurements or a grid to prepare the drawing.

Direct measurements of the entire width and height are made first, then of the main axis of the subject; these are marked on the drawing paper at the proper scale. Additional measurements are made of the secondary axis, major parts of the plant, and finally, smaller parts. To draw a folded stem or leaf as unfolded, measure each fold and add the measurements together. The measuring device should never be inserted under leaves or stems, especially of fragile specimens. A proportional divider works well when drawing from herbarium specimens.

An easy way to draw an herbar-

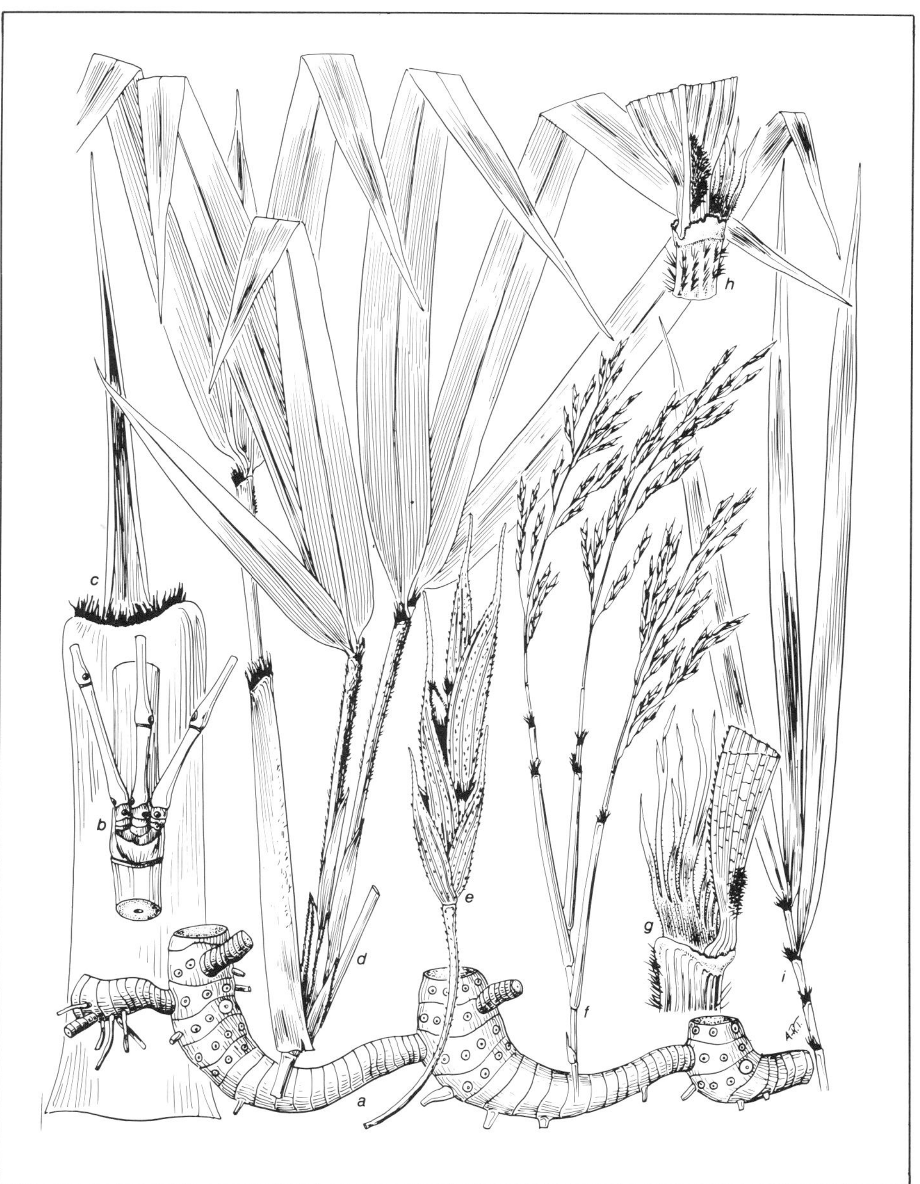

12-31. Drawing prepared from an herbarium specimen without lifelike repositioning of parts. *Otatea fimbriata:* habit and details. Parts have been drawn folded and overlapped to show as much as possible in a limited space. No important parts have been obscured by doing so. Ink lines on leaves go from base almost to tip to accentuate and depict parallel venation found in monocots. Gillott 659 pen and ink on Cronaflex film, by Alice R. Tangerini.

ium specimen is by using grids. Prepare two acetate sheets (.003 or .005 weight) 11 by 16 inches (28 by 40.5cm) in size. Using either ½-inch or 1cm spacing, ink lines in both directions. (Try tracing the grid of printed graph paper to simplify this operation.)

Place one acetate over the specimen and one under thin tracing or sketch paper (the see-through kind). To draw natural size, copy the specimen square by square onto sketch paper. To reduce by one-half, copy what appears in four squares on the specimen into one square on sketch paper. Do the opposite to enlarge by 2.

Whatever the method of preparing the sketch, it is necessary to refer constantly to the specimen when finishing structure and details by viewing with the binocular microscope or hand lens. On dried specimens, such details as texture and venation may be more visible when wet, but a specimen should be studied dry, when other surface details are more visible, before it is moistened. Alcohol is a safe wetting agent: it dries without residue, thus protecting the specimen; it does not reconstitute or soften tissue in any way but does highlight structural details. To soften and reconstitute a portion of a specimen, either mounted or removed from the herbarium sheet, Pohl's solution (developed by Richard Pohl of Iowa State University and available from Fisher Scientific—see Appendix) may be used.

Pohl's Solution (Pohlstuff):
Dioctyl sodium sulfosuccinate (Aerosol OT) 1 percent
Distilled water 74 percent
Methyl alcohol 25 percent

This clear solution does not stain herbarium paper, so it may be applied directly to the mounted specimen with a dropper to soften plant parts that may not be removed. Blot the excess liquid with tissue.

Remove parts with a blade and forceps. To soften and reconstitute, place in a petri dish or crucible with water and a drop of glycerin and boil gently for a few minutes. If Pohl's solution is available, add a few drops to cover the specimen before adding water and boiling. A cover will minimize evaporation. The softened material can be removed to a slide for examination and dissection with razor blades or microscalpels. If needed, use supports as discussed earlier. The dissected parts should be returned to their herbarium packet or a new packet should be made for them.

If lifelike interpretation of an herbarium specimen is requested, it must retain the characteristics of the specimen, be accurate in measurement, yet reveal the subtle forms and three-dimensional arrangement of the living plant (fig. 12-32). This is a difficult task requiring study of other illustrations, photographs, sketches, field notes when available, and any other information that would provide a clear concept of the plant as it appeared in its living state. Studies of numerous specimens will often provide vital information about angles of emergence of branches, leaves, and inflorescences. The botanist can help by making suggestions for improving the drawing as it progresses. The most difficult aspect of preparing a drawing from a flattened specimen is disposing the parts in space as they appeared in life.

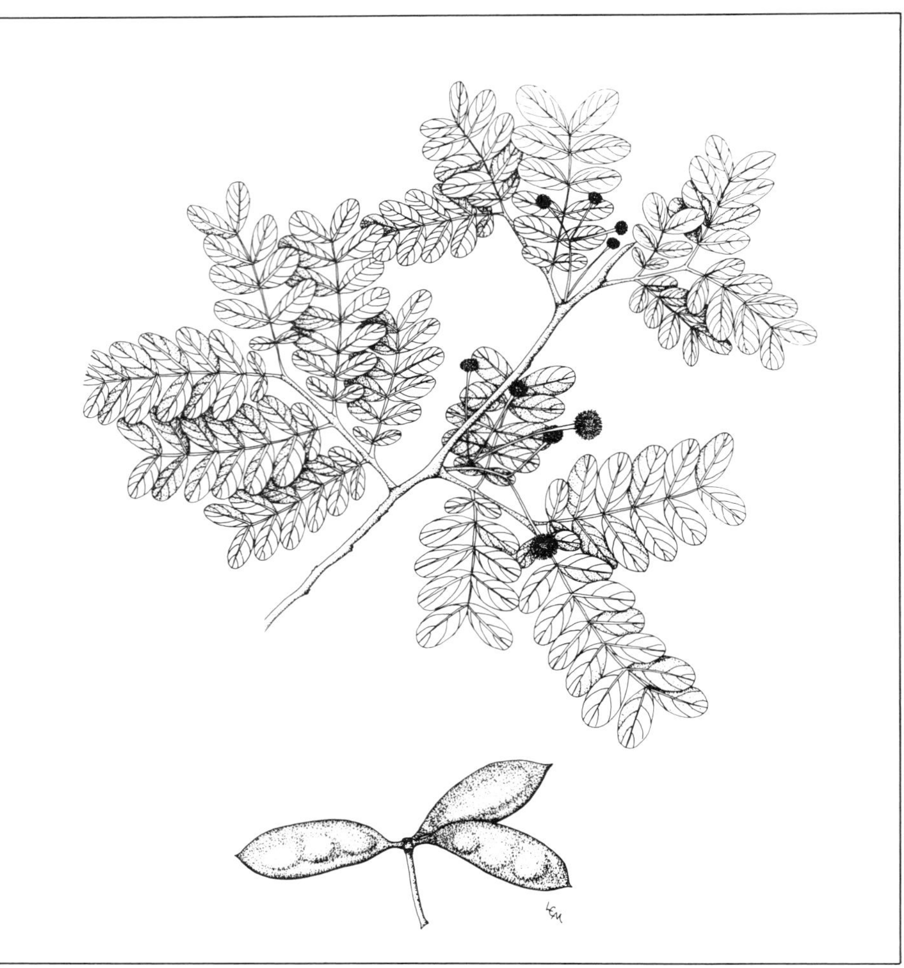

12-32. Drawing prepared from an herbarium specimen with parts repositioned in a natural posture. *Acacia choriophylla:* habit and fruit. Technical pen and ink on Strathmore drawing board, by Lisa Megahee. Courtesy of D. B. Ward.

Preparing a drawing of this type

begins as usual with tracing, photocopying, or measuring the specimen to establish size and position of its parts. Next, leaves, stems, flowers, and other structures are repositioned in a more natural way, some aiming toward the viewer and some away from the viewer. The artist must understand the principles of foreshortening to prepare such a drawing successfuly. Attempting to impart a three-dimensional look by aiming a single part toward the viewer, leaving the rest drawn flat, results in a poor drawing at best. It would be better to draw the entire plant as a flat specimen.

MEASUREMENTS

All measurements are metric and are usually made with a metric ruler. A proportional divider is also useful. Be sure to note the scale used for each drawing as it is prepared. Measurements may be made directly, yielding a true flat measurement, or they may be foreshortened to produce a three-dimensional representation of the specimen.

True Measurements

Small, essentially flat or shallow objects, such as grasses, leaves, flat algae, and dissections, can be measured directly with a ruler. The specimens may be live, freshly cut, or preserved in fluid. Dried herbarium specimens may also be measured directly since all perspective is eliminated by virtue of the drying and pressing the specimen has undergone. In all of these cases, no consideration is given to foreshortening or perspective, and the resulting flat, single-plane drawing is an accurate representation of the specimen.

Foreshortened Measurements

When a three-dimensional representation is desired, however, foreshortened measurements must be made with a ruler or with a proportional divider, because true measurements would result in a flat-looking drawing. Plant parts should be oriented in space in a characteristic arrangement. A leaf viewed from its top side will show its full width and length, but turning it to a lateral view shows only true length, the width being foreshortened (fig. 12-33). As the leaf is turned toward or away from the viewer on its central axis, it becomes increasingly foreshortened lengthwise, finally showing width only, the length being obscured. Any depth showing in an end view of the leaf will be due to curvature. This principle applies to any three-dimensional subject or portion of the subject. A circular flower becomes an ellipse of diminishing width as it is turned away from or toward the eye, so the true side

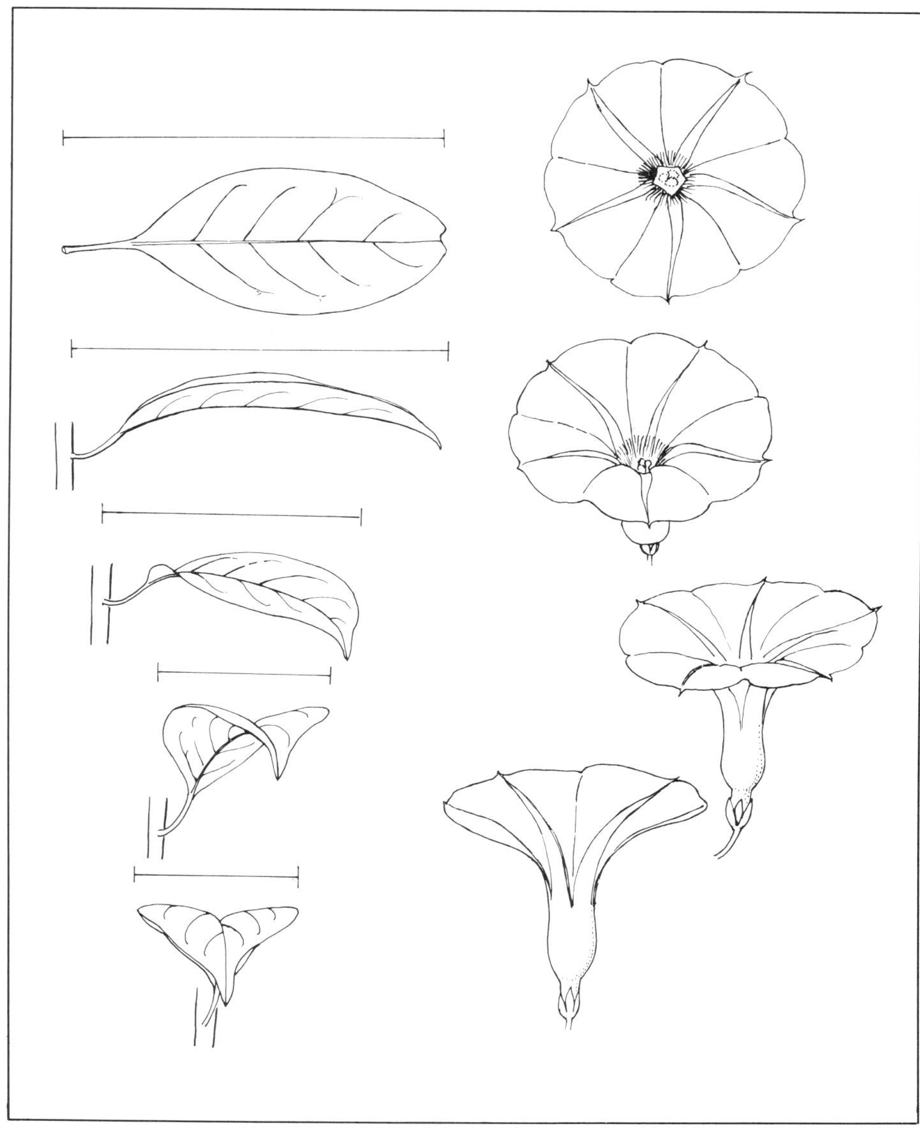

12-33. Foreshortening and measuring. Left: foreshortening as it affects leaf measurement. Full width and length show in face view at top, but only true length is evident in the side view immediately below it; remaining views from middle to bottom show how the length diminishes as the leaf is turned away from view, finally showing only the width. Right: foreshortening as it affects flowers. Full face view at top reveals a circle; as the flower face is turned away from view, it becomes an ellipse of diminishing width. Crowquill pen and ink on Satin Design paper, by Marion Ruff Sheehan.

view of a circular flower shows a relatively straight line instead of a circle.

Many botanical subjects are composed of conical or cylindrical forms, all of which must be drawn with series of ellipses of diminishing or increasing width, the most distant one being the widest. If all ellipses are drawn the same width, distortion results, a very common problem in botanical drawings.

To be accurate, all measurements must be made in the same plane, parallel to the eyes of the artist, and at a uniform distance from the subject. An easy way to arrive at this is to imagine a piece of glass between yourself and the subject. Take all measurements holding the ruler against this imaginary pane of glass, the picture plane. For very small subjects, make measurements close to the plant's axis. For larger plants, measure parts that are in the foreground. Measurements taken at different distances from the axis of the subject (that is, at varying depths) will result in distortion. The parts at the back or front of the plant will appear too large in comparision with the center. Differences should be minimal and only as needed for good perspective.

CONVENTIONS

The means of depicting a plant subject vary depending on the division of the plant kingdom under study and the purpose of the illustration. Some general conventions apply to all plant illustration, with specific ones applying to each division. The many common conventions observed for illustrating the spermatophytes (seed plants) are given strong emphasis here, as this division represents roughly 250,000 of the approximately 390,000 species of plants of the world, with about 200,000 being angiosperms (flowering plants).

Plate Organization (Composition)

Botanical illustrations are frequently preplanned in their entirety. This is desirable because of complex composition and the varied sizes of the components on the plate (see figs. 12-35, 12-36, 12-38, among others in this chapter). It is important for the artist to know the anticipated reproduction size so that the drawing can be prepared in the proper proportion. Drawings are most frequently ×2 (twice printed size), ×1½ or ×3, but rarely ×1 (printed size). A drawing larger than ×2 is not generally recommended because of the greater amount of time required to cover the greater area and the fact that any black-and-white technique must be rendered coarsely at that scale if it is to be reduced successfuly by two-thirds. Nonetheless, the ×3 drawing is occasionally useful for large or coarse subjects such as palm leaves and fruits.

Scale of Components

The drawings should be large enough to show all diagnostic characteristics clearly, but not so large as to be out of proportion to others on the same plate (see fig. 12-38). Very small subjects are the most difficult to handle, not only because of manipulation problems but also because a minor error in measuring can result in a distorted drawing at a large scale. Often the enlargements of plant parts are determined by the size necessary to show distinctive characters. Very small details such as hairs or glands may have to be greatly enlarged. On the other hand, bringing very large subjects down to plate size can often result in erroneous proportions. The most common error from reduction results in oversized leaves, flowers, or other reproductive parts in proportion to the whole plant, a common feature of the exaggerated drawings often produced for advertising seeds and plants. Careful measurements will avoid this.

A well-planned plate should use the entire space to good advantage, with its components drawn as large as space will allow within reason. As a general rule, ¼ inch (5 to 6mm) between parts on the printed plate prevents a cluttered look. If the individual parts seem oversized, the entire plate should be made smaller and the components drawn at a smaller scale to be reduced less in print. Small drawings floating in too much space and drawings that are overcrowded are both undesirable, but overlapping may be necessary with complex plates or when drawing very large plants or those with greatly elongated parts (see fig. 12-31). When this is done, the parts covered by the overlap must be clearly represented elsewhere.

Planning the Arrangement

In planning the arrangement of the plate, always consider the largest drawing first, usually the habit (see fig. 12-6, 12-11, 12-12, 12-32, 12-34, 12-35, 12-36). Aesthetically, it should be placed low or centered to avoid a top-heavy appearance. However, a vining or drooping plant is placed at the top left of the plate, to allow for natural positioning of the cascading stems or flowers. Group additional details around the habit in a logical sequence. In order to plan the final arrangement and scales of components, make some preliminary measurements and draw rough shapes on tracing paper to represent each part. Move these shapes about within the plate size. It will be obvious at once if the scale chosen is wrong, and adjustments can be made before the final drawings are begun. For ease of comparison, all views of a part, such as vertical section and cross section of an ovary, should be drawn at the same scale. Details of any part should be placed in proximity to the source (for example, flower views near inflorescence). Progressive details or dissections of a single part should be placed left-to-right in logical sequence (see figs. 12-34, 12-38). Dioecious plants require special composition if the staminate and pistillate plants differ in habit as well as in sexual characteristics. In these illustrations, the male and female components should be placed to form integrated groups (fig. 12-35; see fig. 12-38).

Scales of enlargement or reduction must be noted either on the drawing in the form of a scale or numbering, or in the legend (the most commonly used method), so it behooves the artist to keep careful record of this information, usually as a notation in the margin alongside each component of the plate. Scales (see figs. 12-1, 12-2, 12-6, 12-7, 12-8, 12-35) or numbers may be placed on the completed plate directly or, preferably, on an overlay. Bar scales are impractical on a complex plate as so many might have to be used as to be confusing.

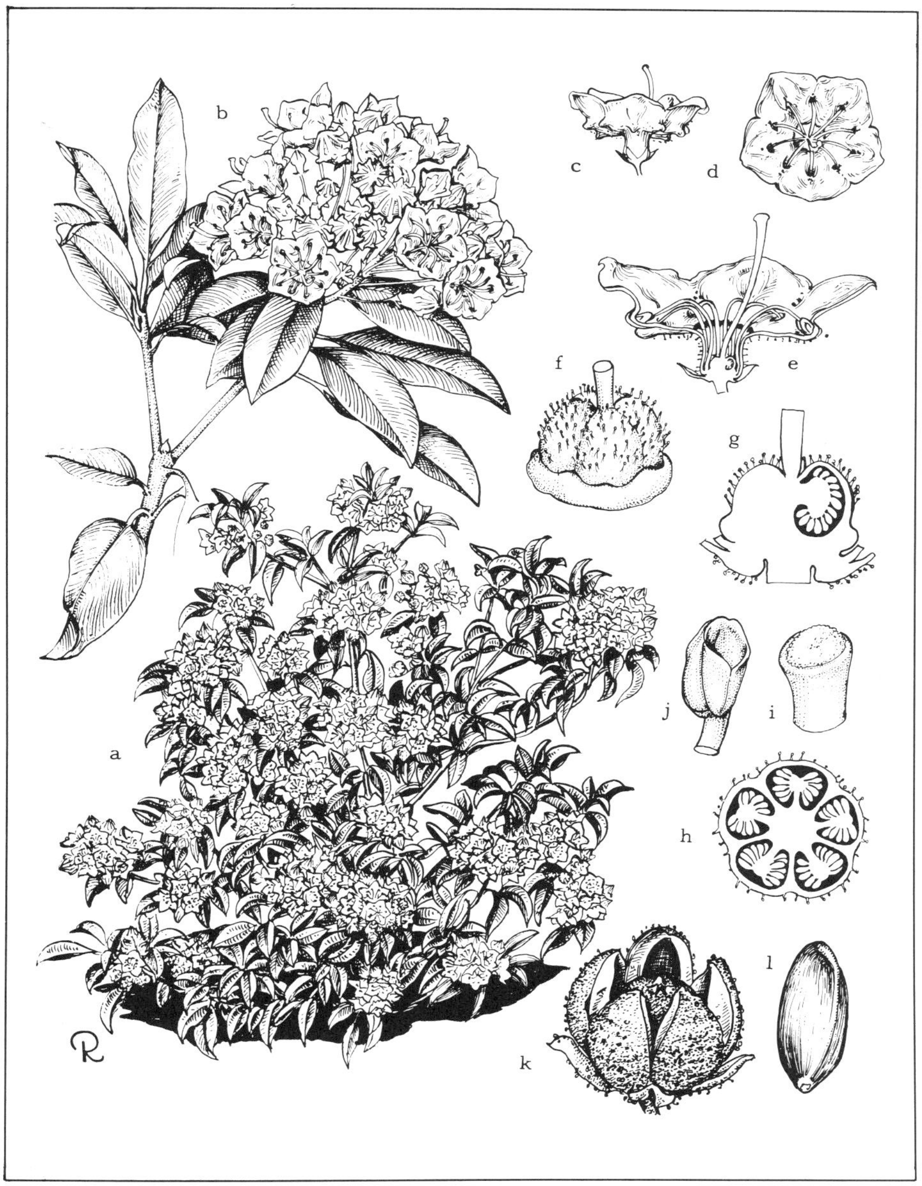

It is a matter of personal preference whether sketches and final drawings are done within the plate size outlined on sketch paper or on individual pieces of paper to be organized into a plate when they are ready for transfer. If a pen-and-ink or other rendering is to be done on translucent drafting paper or film, the corrected sketches may be traced with ink or inked directly on the sketch and the individually inked pieces mounted with tape and then labeled. Or the sketches may be organized and mounted into a plate, a large piece of drafting paper, or film placed over the arrangement, and the drawings then rendered as an entire plate without further mounting. If a drawing is to be rendered on opaque paper, the sketches may be arranged and taped to tracing paper marked with the plate size and then traced to the rendering surface using a light table, or transferred using graphite paper. Whatever the system, organization and preplanning for enlargements or reduction are essential. Check the plate for good balance, as recommended in chapter 1.

12-34. Plate organization and usual parts drawn—angiosperms. *Kalmia latifolia:* *(a)* whole plant in flower; *(b)* portion of a stem and inflorescence; *(c)* flower, side view; *(d)* flower, face view; *(e)* flower, vertical section; *(f)* ovary; *(g)* ovary, vertical section; *(h)* ovary, transverse section; *(i)* stigma; *(j)* anther; *(k)* fruit; *(l)* seed. Crowquill pen and ink on Strathmore drawing board, high surface, by Marion Ruff Sheehan. Courtesy of the L. H. Bailey Hortorium, Cornell University.

Consistency

Many botanical drawings are prepared in series form, each plate having the same components. When this is necessary, establish a format and follow it consistently, using the same approach to organization and to handling of the chosen technique. Scales of enlargement or reduction must also be considered in a series, as it is sometimes necessary to use a consistent scale throughout.

Dissection Drawing Conventions

Cut edges are shown as double lines indicating the thickness of the tissue (see figs. 12-11, 12-12, 12-22, 12-27, 12-34, 12-38). Dashed lines are used to show where a part has been removed (see fig. 12-38). Stippling may be used to indicate tissue differentiation where there is no obvious suture line (see fig. 12-38).

RENDERING TECHNIQUES

Shading clarifies shapes and textures but should not be overdone. It should not suggest texture or pattern that is not present. See the relevant chapters for each technique.

Line

Pen-and-ink effectively portrays any botanical subject matter with both intermittent and continuous line and stipple shading. Flexible pens provide subtle variations in line width and a lively, natural appearance. Use contour lines following the curvatures of the specimen (see figs. 12-14, 12-22, 12-26, 12-37). Space lines closely for dark areas and farther apart for light areas. Thick/thin or tapered lines and crosshatching are sometimes used (see figs. 12-6, 12-35, 5-30). For most monocot leaves, make lines in the direction of the main veins, usually from leaf base to tip (see fig. 12-31). Shading dicot leaves with lines running at right angles to the midrib or main secondary veins or both will avoid confusing shading lines with veins (see figs. 12-34, 12-37). Shade flowers by placing lines along the length of the petal rather than crosswise. Generally, stippling gives a soft effect to flowers (fig. 12-36). When drawing algae, stipple reproductive parts more heavily than vegetative parts to differentiate the two.

Scratchboard is a highly effective material for illustrating hairy or spiny subjects or those with much surface texture or pattern, or complex structures such as cactus aereoles (fig. 12-37; see chapter 5).

Coquille board is less commonly used than it deserves to be for doing fast, effective botanical illustration of large or coarse subjects where a stippled effect is desirable. It is especially effective for simulating the enormous variety of textures found in algae and lichens (see figs. 7-1, 7-3).

12-35. Plate organization with dioecious plants. Sexes are grouped. *Lychnis alba:* *(A)* habit, branchlet of staminate (male) plant; *(a)* staminate (male) flower; *(B)* habit, branchlet of pistillate (female) plant; *(a)* pistillate (female) flower; *(b)* capsule; *(c)* seeds. Pen-and-ink on Strathmore drawing board, high surface, by Regina O. Hughes.

Continuous Tone

Pencil is the choice of many botanical artists. Very complex plates

12-36. Stipple technique. *Diastema* sp.: habit drawing and details stippled to impart a soft and dull surface effect to the subject. Stippling with technical pen and lines drawn with Gillott 659 pen nib and ink on Cronaflex film, by Alice R. Tangerini. Courtesy of L. Skog.

may be more easily and quickly rendered with this highly controllable and correctable technique. Plastic pencil on film is especially good for producing dark line and tone (see fig. 6-7).

Both watercolor and ink wash are used for their superior rendition of form and surface features such as sculpturing. These can be quick methods of rendering but are not easy to master (fig. 12-38; see chapter 9).

Full Color

Watercolor is the finest medium for capturing the color intensity,

transluce
found in
particula
C-8, C-1
its super
(see cha
the adv
ease of
color. C
by some
color and
to achiev
6, 10). G
produce
flower ill
used (see

RECON

Recon
piecing t
tial plan
rials. It n
any divis
larly wh
are the s
specimen
some sor
mounting
a particu

12-37. Scratchboard. Upper left: *Passiflora edulis*, habit; lower right: *Nautilocalyx bullatus*, habit; lower left: face and side views of flower. Ess Dee scratchboard and india ink, rendered with a flat scratch knife, pen-and-ink details on flowers at lower left, by Marion Ruff Sheehan. Bottom: from *African Violets, Gloxinias and Their Relatives*, by Harold E. Moore, Jr. (Macmillan Publishing Company, 1957). *Passiflora* courtesy of the artist © Marion Ruff Sheehan.

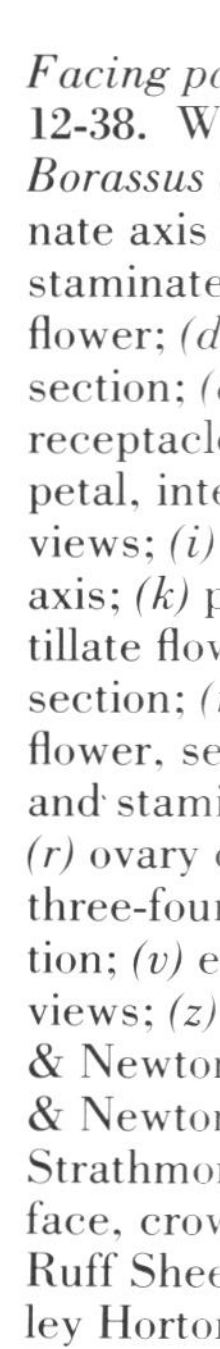

Facing pa
12-38. W
Borassus
nate axis i
staminate
flower; *(d)*
section; *(e*
receptacle
petal, inte
views; *(i)*
axis; *(k)* p
tillate flow
section; *(n*
flower, se
and stami
(r) ovary
three-four
tion; *(v)* e
views; *(z)*
& Newton
& Newton
Strathmor
face, crow
Ruff Shee
ley Horto

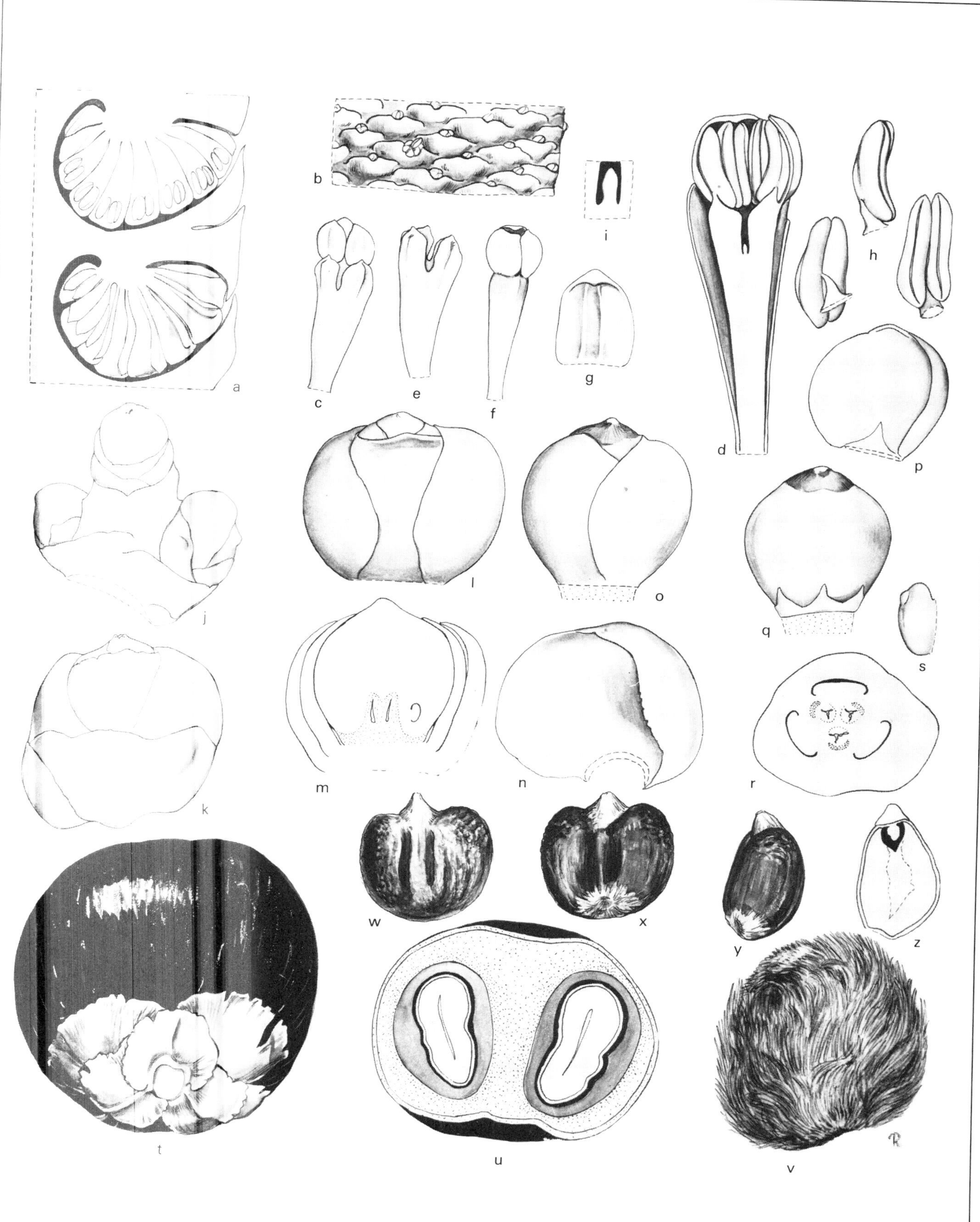
a
b
c
d
e
f
g
h
i
j
k
l
m
n
o
p
q
r
s
t
u
v
w
x
y
z

or missing parts so that the artist may have to replace or visually correct those parts, basing reconstruction on what remains plus research and advice from the botanist. Preserved materials often break or collapse.

Live plants may need reconstruction as well. Damaged leaves and flowers are common but usually must be drawn as perfect. Sparse flowering or foliage may need supplementing to depict the ideal plant. A common way to achieve this effect is to use the existing parts as subjects more than once, drawing them in different positions to complete an inflorescence or fill out foliage.

How much reconstruction is possible depends on the availability of other specimens for study, drawings, and photographs of the plant. Other specimens or illustrations used to develop a drawing must be authenticated and authorized by the botanist before use. Citations of substitute specimens should accompany the drawing.

SPECIAL PROBLEMS IN BOTANICAL ILLUSTRATION

Spirals

Many botanical structures have a spiral arrangement, the spirals being discernible in two directions. A pine cone is a good example of this (see fig. 5-13). To draw a subject of this nature, count the rows of spirals in one direction, noting their direction, and draw lines to represent each row (fig. 12-39). Study the subject to determine placement and direction of the rows in the opposite direction and draw lines for each row. At the intersection of each set of lines, draw the part found there on the specimen (the bract tip in the case of the pine cone). Sometimes it is desirable to draw lines to separate sections rather than locate centers; then the desired structure is drawn between the spiraled lines (for example, flowers of an aeroid inflorescence). Many inflorescences are spiral in arrangement, the spirals radiating from the edge to the center. This same method of drawing applies, using two sets of spirals in opposite directions, which may result in very small intersections at the center of complex inflorescences such as those of the Asteraceae (Compositae or daisy family). Since the flowers open from the

12-39. Spirals. *(a) Camellia japonica:* spiraled petal ar
Ruff Sheehan. *(b) Sequoiadendron giganteum;* gymnosp
arrangment. Pen-and-ink on Albanene paper, by Bente
arrangement of composite flowers. Buds and flowers tenc
enlarging toward the margin. Pen-and-ink, by Marion R

outer
most
velop
small

Tree
Subj

Th
be ap
typic

of specimens should be studied and sketched or photographed. The best and easiest way to draw a tree is to use a composite of several sketches of features from photographs, which may need to be combined to produce the ideal tree. Important characteristics are the position, angle, and number of branches; the size of leafy crown in relation to total height and width; the size and direction of the trunk; its texture; and leaf density, distribution, and texture. Tools are available for measuring the height of trees, amount of clear trunk, and size of crown. The most commonly used ones are the Abney level and Merritt hypsometer. Other devices include surveying equipment, the Relaskop, or a simple stick about four feet or one to two meters long. Instructions on using these devices are available from anyone concerned with forestry.

The drawing may be a simple black silhouette indicating outline and texture (fig. 12-40). For a shaded drawing, prepare a sketch based on preliminary studies and measurements. First, shade the entire tree, making the right side darkest, so that the tree's basic shape is established before detail is added. Draw leaf masses indicating texture: fine (small leaves), coarse (large leaves), or other. Add flowers or inflorescences where necessary. Pines and other conifers need special treatment to indicate needles. Develop more detail on the leaf masses closest to the viewer. The remainder of the leaf masses should contain only a suggestion of texture with light and shade. Each leaf mass (usually the end of a branch) should be treated as a unit and shaded from dark to light. More shadow will appear in the masses on the dark side of the tree (fig. 12-41).

When necessary, add individual leaf detail last in the foreground. It is not always possible to do detailed leaf drawings on an entire tree, so suggestion of texture and size may suffice. Keep in mind what detail is

12-40. Tree illustration. *Juniperus chinensis* var. *columnaris:* tree is shown as a silhouette with a detail of a branch. Pen-and-ink on Strathmore drawing board, by Marion Ruff Sheehan.

12-41. Tree illustration. *Cinnamomum zeylanicum:* sketch shows overall shape, clear trunk, and foliage masses on a small, dense tree. Pencil on Denril film, by Marion Ruff Sheehan.

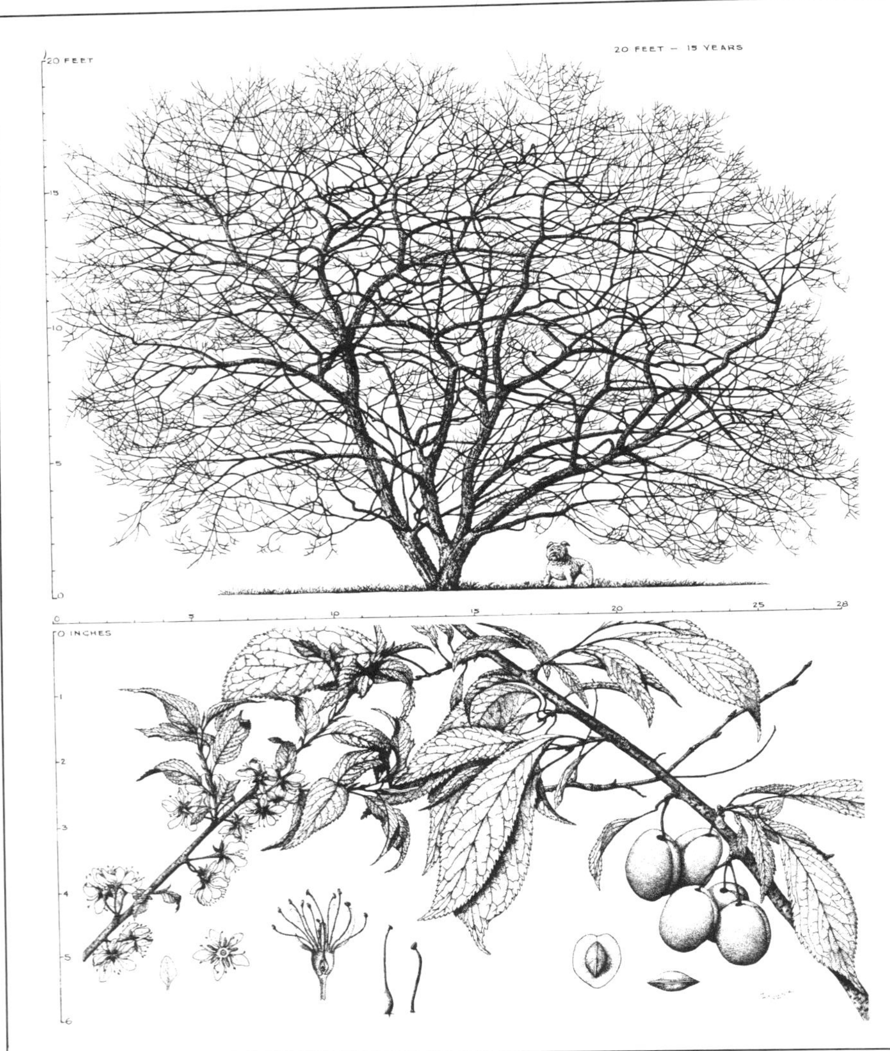

12-42. Tree illustration shaded by stippling and light strokes. *Prunus americana:* drawing done from a tree specimen during a full year, showing flowering and fruiting details and the dormant tree. Gillott titquill pen nib and ink on Strathmore drawing board, medium surface, by Anthony Tyznik. From *The Morton Arboretum Quarterly*, 1975.

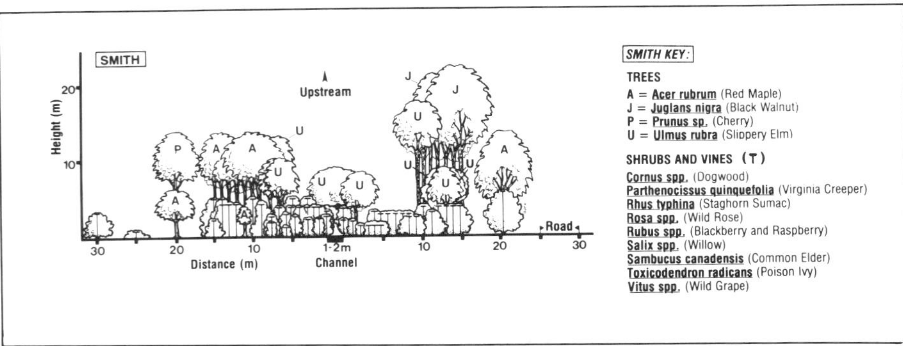

12-43. Plant profile. Community metabolism and autotrophic-heterotrophic relationships of woodland stream riffle sections. Technical pen and ink on Strathmore high-surface drawing board, by Gail W. Guth. Courtesy of Donna King.

likely to
and repr
largemen
sometim
drawing

Plant P

A pla
of repre
munity
habitat
43).

All th
the sam
specim
tablish
either i
rangem
include
The me
scribed
sureme
to be i
trees a

The
its hig
sents
portio
It is t
matte
tors t
perha
plants
ploye
ical d
to ma
artist
techn
forta
Withi
matt
lustr
caree
find

13/Illustrating Fossils

Lawrence B. Isham, Karen Klitz, and Francis M. Hueber

Fossils are the subject matter of paleontological illustrations; they may be botanical, invertebrate, or vertebrate. The drawings may be used for scientific papers, popular publications, museum dioramas, or murals. They may range from simple line clarifications of photographs through complicated line or tone reconstructions to full-color restorations of an entire ancient habitat (fig. 13-1). Three-dimensional reconstructions of extinct life forms, usually for museums, are another type of paleontological illustration. Paleontological specimens are in many cases unique, incomplete, and fragile—all of which present special problems in illustration.

The sections of this chapter complement one another. Some ideas in each apply to the others; therefore the beginner in this subject should read all the sections, even if only one type of palentological illustration is to be pursued. Reconstruction of extinct animals into lifelike poses is treated in chapter 14.

For some groups, taxonomic characters of fossils and methods of mounting and measuring them are likely to be similar to those of extant relatives discussed in other chapters. Fossils, however, are hard, generally have no soft parts or internal organs preserved, and may remain partially obscured by matrix, preventing all but one view; the characters that can be studied and drawn may therefore be limited. Nevertheless, it is helpful for the paleontological illustrator to study living relatives of the fossil animal or plant and to read relevant chapters on their illustration.

The illustrator of fossils should take courses in paleontology, geology, zoology, and perhaps in specialized areas such as botany or invertebrate zoology if certain types of specimens are likely to form the bulk of work.

In Lawrence B. Isham's words:

> The illustrator of fossil specimens should provide the author with a drawing of measured accuracy in which the basic shape and necessary taxonomic details are visible. The distortions, scars, and blemishes imposed on the specimen by the weight of geologic time should be minimized where they obscure features critical to the text. While drawing only "what is there," the illustrator can, without distorting facts, emphasize features whose visibility has been weakened by bad fossil preservation. The illustrator owes the author this service, and it is this skill in alliance with that of the author that makes valuable contributions to the scientific literature.

INSTRUMENTS AND MATERIALS

What is used to handle fossils depends on the size and condition of the specimen. The only surface and medium specific to fossil illustration are black poster board and black poster tempera paint used in invertebrate paleontology to create a black background against which certain microfossil drawings, especially of foraminifera, are mounted.

Optical Devices

Stereoscopic microscope: most often used.

Reducing objective: to permit more of a specimen to be seen under the stereoscopic microscope.

Compound microscope: seldom needed.

Camera lucida: for stereoscopic microscope, and compound microscope if used.

Reticle: with micrometer for measuring specimens.

Microprojector: for microscope slides.

Opaque projector: indirect type that permits large specimens to sit on a shelf for tracing (see chapter 2).

Stage micrometer.

Camera: 35mm single-lens reflex, with fine-grained (low ASA rating) film.

Camera lenses: telephotos of different lengths plus one 52 to 55mm lens.

Measuring Devices

Metric rulers: metal or plastic, 15 cm (6-inch) and 30cm (12-inch), perhaps longer ones for very large specimens.

Dividers: proportional dividers, 8-inch (20cm) and 10-inch (25cm); calipers with a Vernier scale (see Proportional Dividers, Calipers in chapter 2).

Grid: drawn on plastic, acetate, or graph paper to use with a grid drawn on transparent plastic or acetate held over any specimen that is too large to fit under the microscope; box with a grid made

from inte
opening (
chapter 2

Metric
beled in
men that

Specim

Forceps
steel, fo
stiff pap
eyelash
gles tap
for man

Picking
ries 197
nipulati

Specin

Knead
wax or
square
of bir
specim

Soft c
specim
case t

Cushi
cloth,
wood
pegs,
larger

Cont

Card
verte

Boxe
sizes
foam
men
ile,
spec

13-1.
John
Smith
Maso
tat of
by Cl
Instit

Wetting Agents and Preservatives

To wet specimens and make them translucent or to increase contrast.

Alcohol: 70 to 90 percent as needed

Glycerin.

Anise oil.

Clove oil.

Mineral oil.

Xylene: considered carcinogenic and is flammable; use only with good ventilation, ideally with an exhaust hood.

Miscellaneous

Ammonium or magnesium oxide powder: for coating specimens to clarify features. (For more information, consult "Whitening Fossils," by P. M. Kier, R. E. Grant, and E. L. Yochelson in *Handbook of Paleontological Techniques*, edited by Bernhard Kummel and David Raup, and "Illustration of Fossil Vertebrates," by E. H. Colbert and C. Tarka—see Bibliography.)

Copy stand: for photographing smaller vertebrates.

Ladder: to which a camera can be clamped for photographing larger vertebrates.

Fossil Plants

Francis M. Hueber

Paleobotany is the science of description and interpretation of the evolution of the plant kingdom through geologic time based on fossil evidence. Prerequisites for paleobotanical research are a background in plant morphology, anatomy, and taxonomy, as well as training in stratigraphy, sedimentology, and to some extent mineralogy. Ideally, the paleobotanical illustrator should have some undergraduate training in plant morphology and anatomy. In lieu of specialized training, the illustrator should have a basic understanding of or feeling for plant form and structures and be able to recognize and depict significant and at times subtle detail.

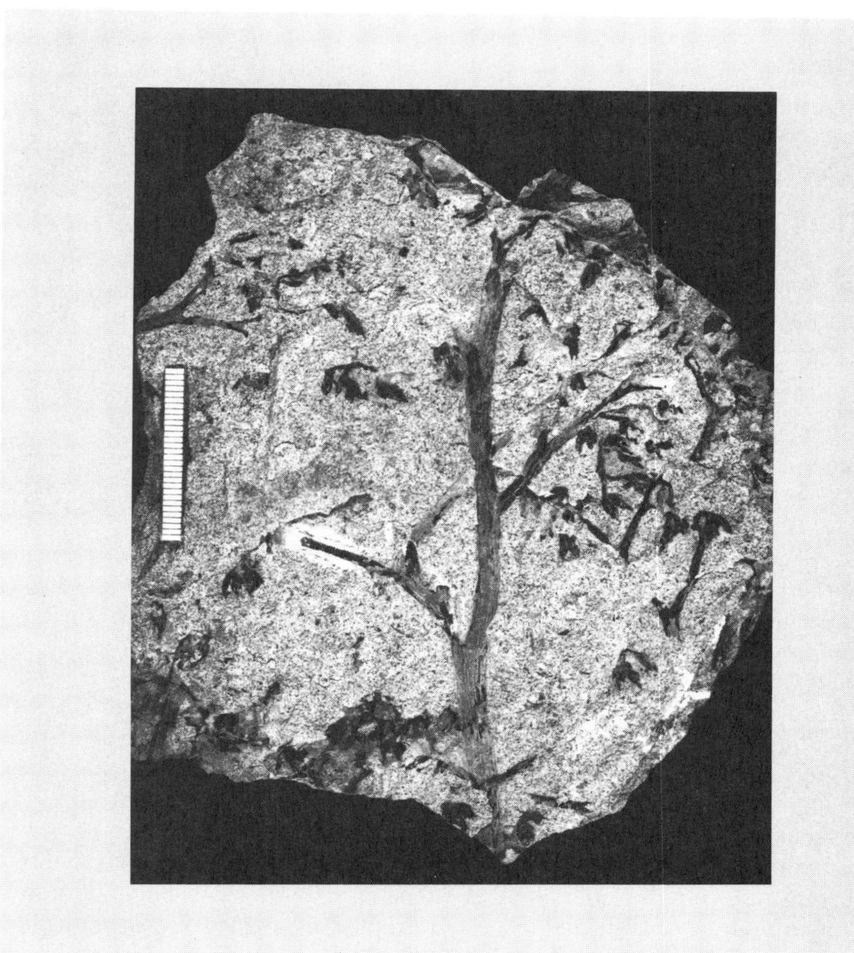

13-2. Compression of *Psilophyton* Dawson from the Devonian of Gaspé, Quebec, Canada, showing carbonized remains of a 375-million-year-old plant. × 1. Photo by J. P. Ferrigno.

NATURE AND CONDITION OF SPECIMENS

The subject matter for illustration will be fossils, nearly always fragments of larger entities. Very rarely is a whole plant found preserved.

Fossil plants are preserved in a variety of forms but basically are of three types. Most common is a compression in which carbonized organic residues of the original

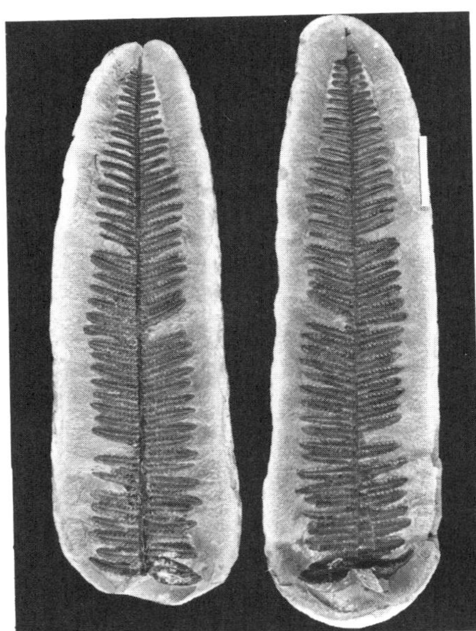

13-3. Compression-impression of the fern genus *Pecopteris* in which none of the original plant material remains. From Pennsylvanian strata in Illinois; about 250 million years old. Scale equals 3cm. Photo by J. P. Ferrigno.

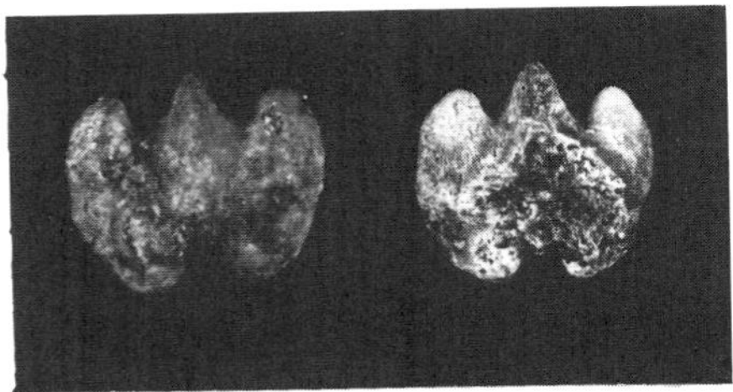

13-4. Chalcedony casts of walnut kernels about 25 million years old, from Sioux County, Nebraska. × 1. Photo by J. P. Ferrigno.

13-5. *(a)* Natural sandstone mold of the surface of *Sigill* Pennsylvanian strata in Pennsylvania. *(b)* Silicone-rubbe × ½. Photo by J. P. Ferrigno.

13-6. Polished surface of the cross section of an oak l log, from Eocene strata in Oregon, is about 45 million Ferrigno.

plant tissues or organs or both are preserved (fig. 13-2) or a mere compression-impression without organic residues (fig. 13-3). Both are fragile, the former more than the latter, so the surfaces should not be touched or rubbed. The second type of preservation is a cast or mold. Here the original plant fragments rot away, leaving a void in the surrounding mud or sand. The void may be filled subsequently with sediment of a different grain size or a mineral precipitate, creating a cast (fig. 13-4), or it may remain empty after the surrounding sediments have turned to stone (lithified), creating a mold (fig. 13-5). The fragility of this type of specimen depends on the hardness and texture of the rock matrix itself. The third and most rare type of preservation is permineralization (petrification), in which minerals precipitate within the buried plant tissues and preserve minute anatomical as well as morphological details (fig. 13-6). Such specimens seldom are fragile, but because

they
ones.
store
paste
They
trate

Spo

Ar
leob
of sp

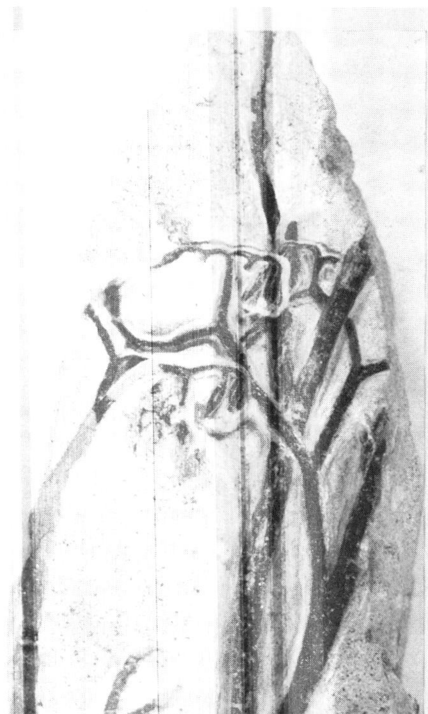

13-7. Stem bearing a fertile lateral branch that was uncovered with steel needles to reveal the three-dimensional aspect of the plant. × 1. Photo by Francis M. Hueber.

13-8. Stems of the Devonian plant *Sawdonia ornata* (Dawson) that Francis M. Hueber removed from the sandstone matrix with acid and then embedded in plastic for protection and observation. This type of preservation clarifies the specimen for the illustrator. × 1. Photo by Francis M. Hueber.

development of this particular field of research, as with any other descriptive endeavor, details of the structure of spores and pollen were illustrated with pen-and-ink drawings, washes, or renderings in charcoal. With the advent of improved photomicrographic equipment, drawings were supplanted by photographs, and today the scanning electron microscope has revolutionized the illustration of the structural details found and used in the descriptive studies of spores and pollen. The illustrator more often will be called upon for help with graphics (phylogenetic charts, distribution maps) than for illustrating descriptive taxonomic studies.

CARE AND HANDLING OF SPECIMENS

The methods of preparation and study of fossil plants by the scientist or technician vary with the type of preservation, quality, and quantity of the specimens at hand; preparations are not the responsibility of the illustrator. In the case of carbonized compressions, measurements and morphological detail can be obtained directly from the specimen as collected, with no preparation (see fig. 13-3). If parts of the fossil are covered with matrix, sharpened steel needles are used under a dissecting microscope to pick away the enclosing sediment. Care must be taken to ensure that the removal of matrix is controlled and the potential of damaging the specimen reduced (fig. 13-7). When a large number of well-preserved specimens is available, the fossil plant material may be freed from the matrix with appropriate acids such as hydrofluoric for siliceous matrix and hydrochloric for carbonate-rich matrices. The fragments obtained by this means are washed, dehydrated, and mounted on microscope slides or embedded in plastic for observation and description (fig. 13-8). Some three-dimensional details are clearer in this type of preparation and are a great aid to the illustrator in the rendering of drawings or reconstructions. In the case of compression-impression types of fossils, the illustrator is obliged to work directly from the specimen.

When possible, and depending entirely on the quality of preservation of detail, cellulose acetate film pulls or latex or silicone casts can be made from the fossil surfaces when study of minute detail is required. Fortunately, natural casts and latex replicas from natural molds offer little problem to the illustrator as they are direct replicas of plant organs, may be handled for purposes of measurement and observation, and give clear three-dimensional feeling for the plant or plant part in question.

Although permineralized fragments of plants require the most time and tedious work to prepare, they yield the best detail for study and illustration. Two techniques of preparation are used—the ground thin-section and the cellulose acetate peel. Although it is of value for the illustrator to understand how specimen fragments are prepared, it is always the client's responsibility to prepare or have prepared the specimens before giving them to the illustrator.

Ground Thin-Section

First a diamond saw is used to slice the fossil specimen very thinly in specific planes of orientation. The individual slices are permanently mounted on microscope slides and then ground to microscopic thinness using varying grades of abrasive powders. The time required to complete a thin-section may vary from an hour to days, depending on the size of the section and the toughness of the mineral that impregnated the plant tissues during the process of fossilization.

Cellulose Acetate Peel

The specimen is sliced thickly with a diamond saw, and the sawed surfaces are smoothed and flattened by grinding with fine abrasive powder (fig. 13-9a). Then the surfaces are washed clean and a dilute acid solution is applied to remove a very small amount of mineral matter. That leaves the cellular tissues of the fossil plant projecting slightly above the surface (fig. 13-9b). The etched surface is very gently washed with water and allowed to air-dry. At this point, touching the surface will crush the delicate structures. The surface is then flooded with acetone and, while still flooded, covered with a sheet of cellulose acetate, .003 inch thick (fig. 13-9c). The acetate dissolves in the acetone, filling and embedding the cell structures exposed as a result of the etching process. When dry, the cellulose acetate sheet is carefully peeled from the surface; it will be seen to contain all of the fossil tissues (fig. 13-9d). The process is repeated, and each peel is numbered serially. As many as a thousand peels per inch can be obtained, and

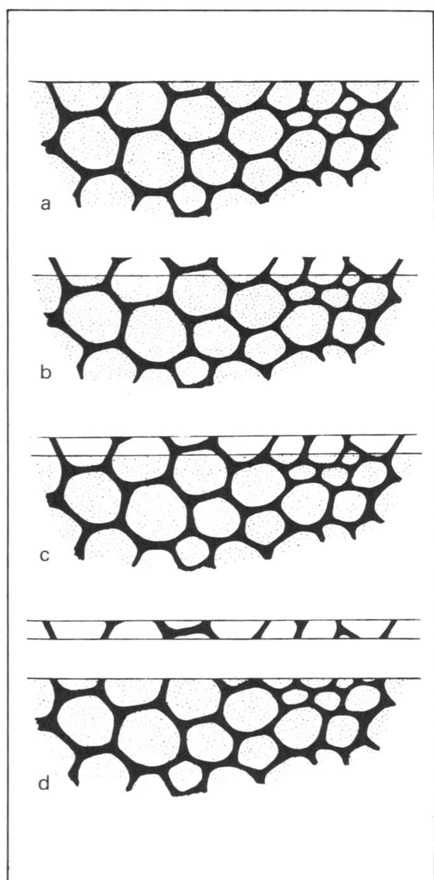

13-9. Diagrammatic representation of steps in the peel technique for preparation of permineralized plant remains; stippled areas represent mineral that has penetrated and filled the lumens of the cells; cell walls are represented in black. From A. Wesley, A Short Synopsis of Some Microscopical Methods in Palaeobotany (Leeds Philosophical and Literary Society [Scientific Section], vol. 6, 1974).

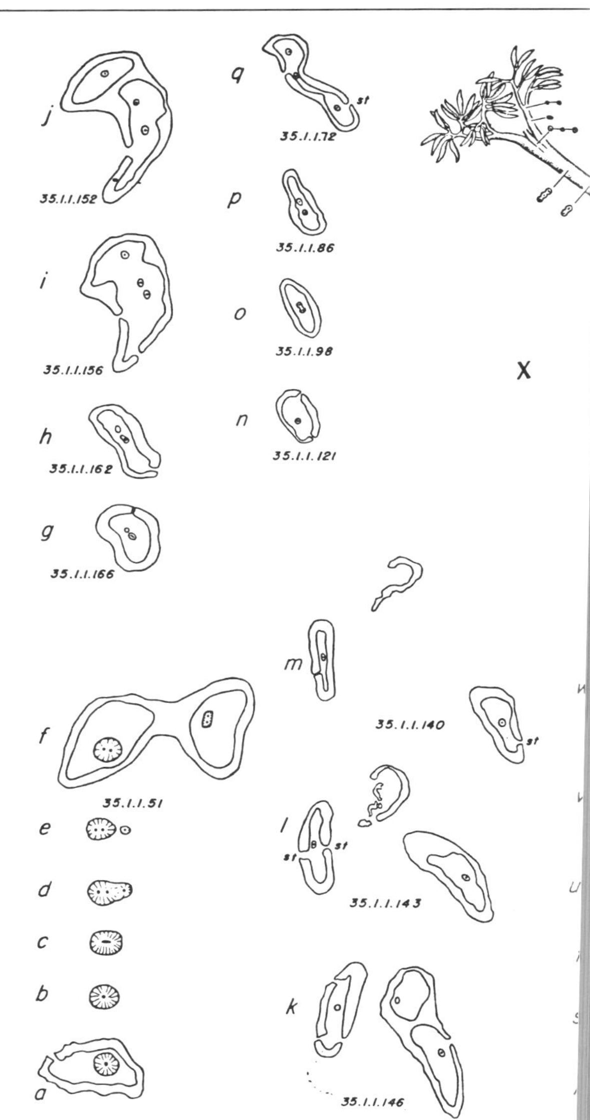

13-10. Camera lucida drawings derived from a series of p… permineralized stem of *Psilophyton dawsonii* Banks, et a… recorded during the preparation of the peel series permit… of the plant as shown in *(x)*. The form of the xylem stran… drawings along the margins of the reconstruction. Court…

by mai…
ments o…
peeling…
constru…
possible…

Measu…

Meas…
the res…
or scie…
Accura…
during…
stages…

13-11. Composite reconstruction derived from several series of peels, degagements (material revealed through removal of matrix), and microscopic observation of compressed, carbonized stems. This pen-and-ink line drawing on Bristol board by Elfriede Abbe is based in part on figures 13-7 and 13-10.

thin sections of the fossils or in the preparation of serial peel sections. This is done to establish linear spacing of the finished sections. In the rare event that the illustrator is asked to make measurements of specimens for the purpose of reconstruction, such measurements should be made with calipers fitted with a Vernier scale or by means of an ocular micrometer, the choice dictated by type, size, and condition of the subject. In general, for compressions, use the calipers; for thin-sections, use the ocular micrometer (see chapter 2).

RECONSTRUCTION

The illustrator's primary task in paleobotany is interpretive reconstruction based on prepared and unprepared specimens. This may entail working from compressions alone or from a combination of specimens and preparations. The object of the whole process is to render a reconstruction with a lifelike appearance and one that is fully believable on the basis of the material at hand. It is the responsibility of the researcher to supply the illustrator with correctly annotated and prepared materials and to be available to interpret weaker lines of evidence in the reconstruction. Secondary to the reconstruction process, the illustrator will probably be asked for help in inking projected images, such as camera lucida drawings and photographic negatives.

Orientation

In all illustrations, the orientation of the drawing is along the vertical axis of the plant, whether it be tissue (wood) or organs (branches, flowers, leaves). In some instances it is difficult to determine which end is up. Details such as this should be determined by the researcher and submitted to the illustrator in annotated form.

MEDIA AND TECHNIQUES

Reconstructions in paleobotanical literature are predominantly drawn with traditional line and stipple techniques. Carbon dust rarely is used except in illustrating some palynological studies. Recently, watercolor and oil have been used to very attractive advantage in the reconstructions of early flowering plants. The colors of the flowers are arbitrarily agreed on by the researcher and the illustrator.

Fossil Invertebrates

Lawrence B. Isham

NATURE AND CONDITION OF SPECIMENS

The very small—often microscopic—size of invertebrate fossils presents problems different from those encountered with plant and vertebrate fossils. The foraminifera represent a good example of invertebrate microfossils, and suggestions for handling them apply generally to others. Foraminifera are protozoans, almost entirely marine, and they build tests (shell-like structures) of varied sizes and complexity. These tests may be fossil or Recent, and may be chitinous, calcareous, or composed of agglutinated materials such as sand grains or spicules. Most of the living species are smaller than a millimeter in size, although there are exceptions, and some fossil forms measure several inches in diameter. These latter types and other invertebrate fossils such as bryozoa and corals are usually illustrated by photographs of thin-sections, except for diagrams of structures (fig. 13-12). Details such as apertures, supplementary apertures, keels, tooth plates, and sutures vary greatly among species; and illustrators should become familiar with these through study of a book such as *Foraminifera*, by Joseph A. Cushman (see Bibliography).

The smaller foraminifera usually are kept in cardboard well-slides, as are ostracods, and are glued down with a water-soluble gum (tragacanth, arabic), since their size and weight are such that a light air movement could cause them to be lost if the cover slide

13-12. Left: photographs of thin-sections of foraminifera; right: diagrams of structure of foraminifera. Pen-and-ink on Albanene paper, by Lawrence B. Isham.

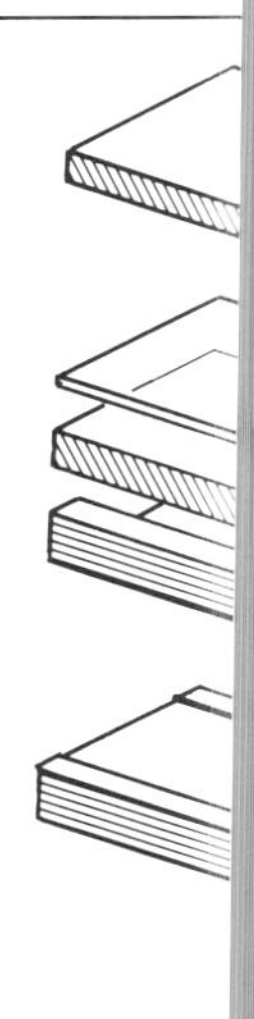

were removed (fig. 13-13). The well of the cardboard specimen slide has black paper at the bottom to facilitate locating the specimen under the microscope. The specimen slide is stored between a glass cover slide and a tightly fitted aluminum holder to prevent loss of a specimen and to keep out dust. These are usually removed for viewing the specimen.

The invertebrate phyla that occur as fossils often require sectioning or other processing for study. These sections are mounted on glass slides for interpretation and drawing. The illustrator may be furnished, for example, with a sequence of thin-sections of a bryozoan from which the animal's "shell" or skeleton must be reconstructed, or a series of acetate peels of a coral for reconstruction. In figure 13-14 (left) are photographs of bryozoan thin-sections. A transverse section is shown at top and a longitudinal section at bottom. The diagram at right is obtained by referring to transverse sections *(a)*, longitudinal sections *(b)*, and tangential sections *(c)*, and interpreting them to arrive at the mode of growth of this cylindrical bryozoan.

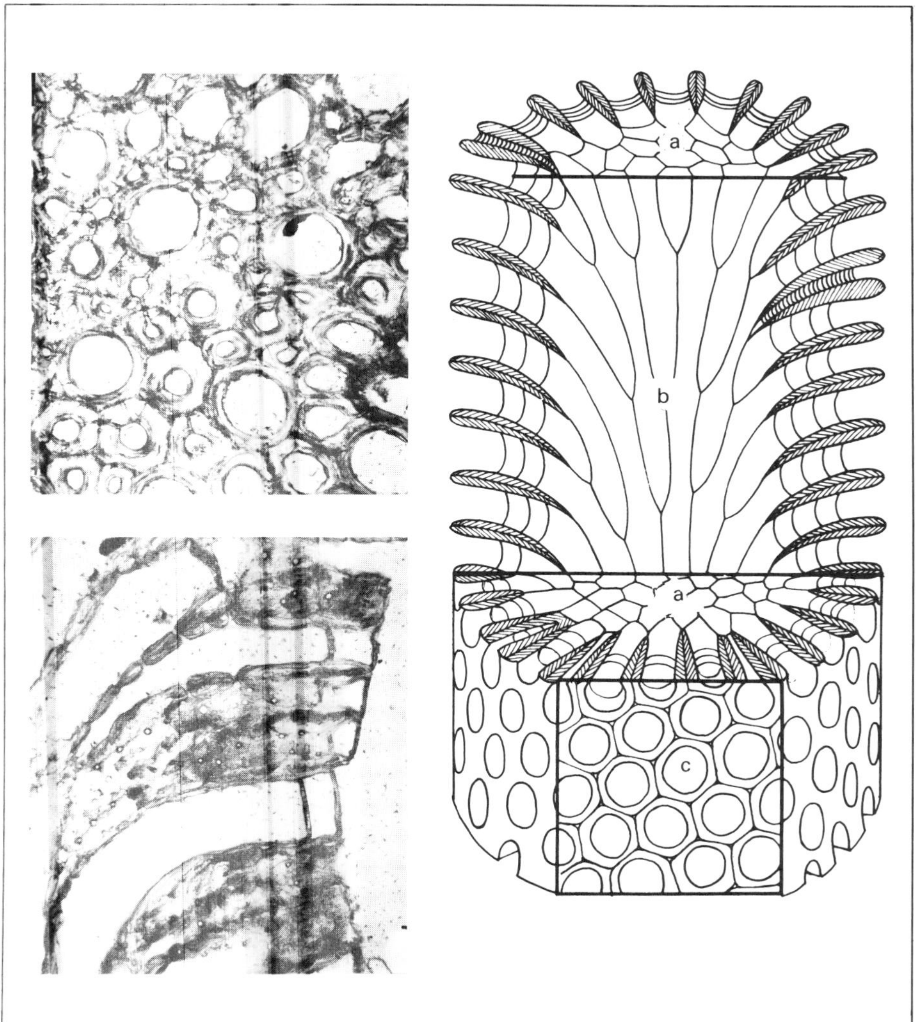

13-14. Left: thin-sections of a bryozoan; right: sections diagrammed in pen-and-ink on Albanene paper, by Lawrence B. Isham, to show structure of bryozoan. *(a)* Transverse sections; *(b)* longitudinal section; *(c)* tangential section.

It is unwise to use fingers to pick up or move fragile specimens. Thin forceps of spring steel are ideal, but it is often necessary to improvise tools to deal with delicate specimens: forceps cut from stiff paper (three-ply drawing paper, manila folders), a scoop made from paper to slide under the specimen to move it, or a single eyelash attached to a toothpick. Manipulate or move microfossils under the microscope with a small picking brush dampened with water. Use the brush carefully to soften the gum with which the specimen is mounted; then roll or stand the fragile specimen on end to obtain the required view and hold it in position with the damp brush as the gum dries. This technique requires practice. Specimen loss or damage during this process is usually due to a dry brush.

Even with some larger invertebrate fossils (such as pelecypods or lophophore supports of brachiopods), the illustrator's concern is the safety of the specimen while it is being oriented to obtain the proper view. A large invertebrate fossil may be placed in a box of birdshot to hold it in position and to provide a heavy base resistant to accidental movement. Modeling clay may be used as a prop, but it tends to leave an oily residue that can stain the specimen. A better choice is kneaded eraser, pieces of which may be pinched into wedges or molded into a cradle to hold the specimen. If this is done on a cardboard base, the specimen may be moved and rotated, base and all, under the microscope or without it. A simple ring or doughnut of the material will suffice to support small mollusks and brachiopods. The very slight adhesive quality of the latex eraser helps to hold the specimen in the desired position.

It is sometimes necessary for the illustrator to extract more information than is readily visible on the dry specimen. It may be rendered more translucent by applying an oil, with the permission of the scientist. Clove oil and anise oil, both relatively volatile, evaporate in the heat of the microscope lamp but help to locate sutures and other details, especially the tiny early chambers of coiled foraminifera. Where it is desirable to keep the specimen damp for a longer period, glycerin or water may be used, although either might soften glue or gum and allow the specimen to move.

Measurement

The best method of measurement always provides the most accurate preliminary drawing in the least time. For microscopic fossils, the initial drawing is done with a camera lucida, which usually requires adjusting light sources and moving the microscope lamp to see detail. The camera lucida setup can be checked for distortion with a stage micrometer or a grid. Specimens may be measured with an ocular micrometer, which must be calibrated with a stage micrometer. Comparisons of measurements of the specimen with measurements of the finished drawing allow a confident statement about magnification.

For larger specimens, dividers and proportional dividers provide

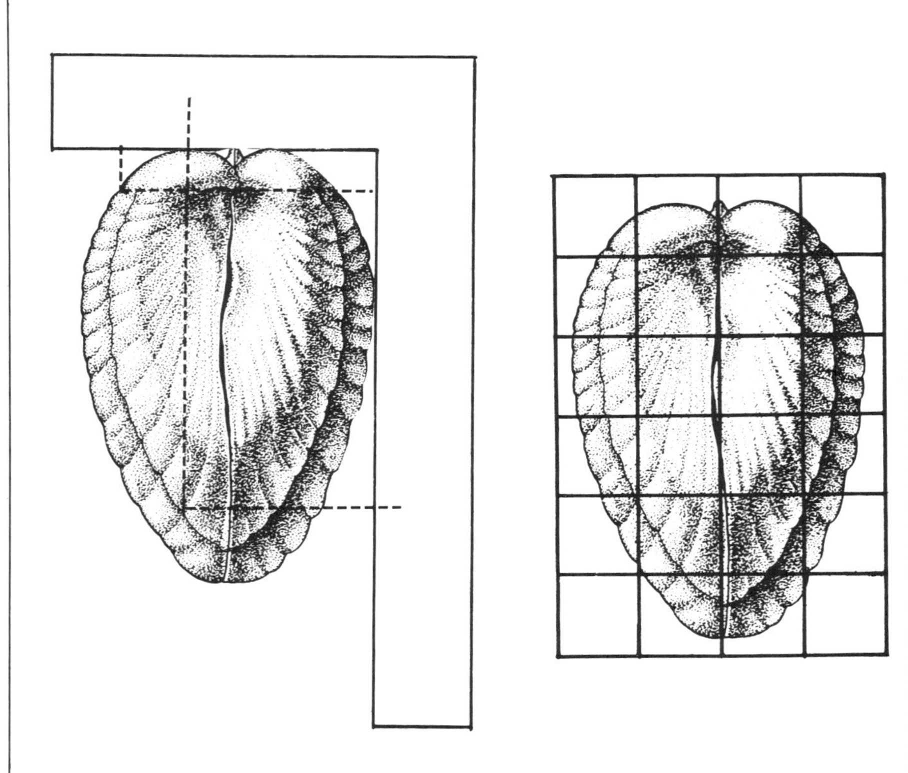

13-15. Left: coordinate measurements of a pelecypod specimen; right: grid superimposed on specimen for measurement. Pen-and-ink on Albanene paper, by Lawrence B. Isham.

measurements (see Measuring Devices in chapter 2). A coordinate method may be used by framing the specimen with a cardboard square tangent to its outline and taking measurements from this reference to points on the specimen. In figure 13-15, measurements taken at right angles to the cardboard square give coordinates for visible points on the specimen. The specimen shown is a bivalve, anterior view. Viewing the specimen through a grid drawn on plastic or glass may aid in obtaining the preliminary drawing, as will setting the specimen on grid paper or in a box with threads stretched over the top to form a grid. Using two grids, one above the other, gives even more accurate results (see Measuring Devices in chapter 2).

A camera lucida separate from the microscope may be used, but there is a high risk of peripheral distortion. A photograph of the specimen may be traced to provide a preliminary drawing, which then may be corrected by measurements. A projector or microprojector may be used to obtain a preliminary sketch of a thin-section mounted on glass (but be aware that plastic peels may soften near a projector bulb). Or, if the specimen is flat enough, the fossil itself may be placed in an indirect opaque projector to save time in drawing the outline.

RECONSTRUCTION

Illustrators working with fossils for the first time tend to exaggerate extraneous and distracting details such as cracks, adhering matrix, tool marks, and plaster patches. These features, whether natural or artifactual, may obscure the more important details of the specimen. It is best to minimize the visual impact of those details known to be

unimport
emphasiz
cant. If
symmetri
torted by
is no ser
size that

In figu
cates a
men, whi
of fairly
notices a
tion of th
the tend
this may
13-16b).

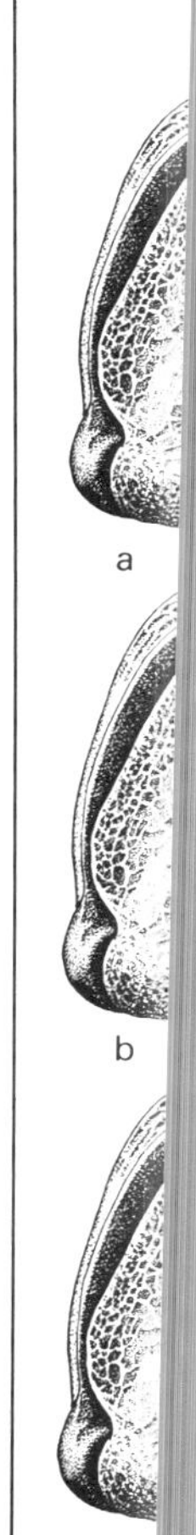

13-16. (
(echinod
with da
with bro
on Strat
(hot-pre

ment, it would be preferable, using the information available from the unbroken side of the specimen, to draw it as complete (fig. 13-16c).

At times it is necessary to reconstruct a specimen on paper. An echinoderm, for example, may become flattened, its plates and spines scattered in the matrix. The various units may be drawn on separate pieces of tracing paper and a series of pasteup overlays made to put together this jigsaw puzzle. When the best fit is obtained for the plates or groups of plates, a final tracing is transferred to drawing paper (fig. 13-17).

Orientation

The orientation of drawings of invertebrate fossils follows life habit, so that echinoderms would be drawn with the oral surface down, and branching bryozoa with the attachment down. Most foraminifera are drawn with the aperture toward the top, although the spiral forms are usually shown with the last, largest chambers upward, which may mean that the aperture faces to one side. It is important that opposing views of the same specimen be oriented consistently. Generally, the orientation of the drawing is best determined by consultation with the scientist.

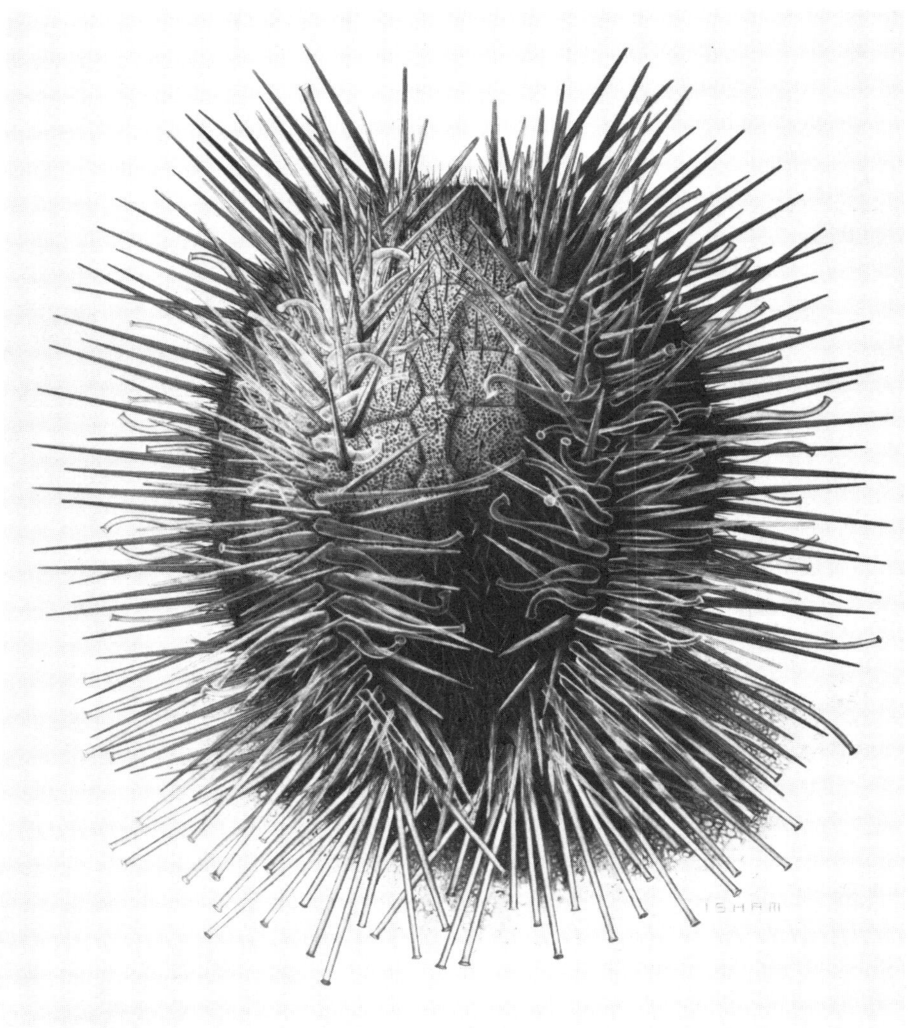

13-17. Fossil echinoderm restoration from fragments. Mixed media: airbrush, ink, acrylic, carbon pencil on Strathmore three-ply Bristol board (hot-press), by Lawrence B. Isham.

MEDIA AND TECHNIQUES

In general, the illustrator working with fossil invertebrates will be expected to produce an accurate image that looks better than the specimen. The choice of a medium to accomplish this will be influenced by the condition of the specimen, the page size and print quality of the publication in which it will appear, and the illustrator's relative skill in the various techniques. Also, the choice must be consistent with the wishes of the scientist. Expense also may dictate the choice of technique where, for example, sufficient funds are available for a simple line diagram but not for a more time-consuming detailed stipple drawing.

Tone drawings of microfossils usually have been done in graphite because it can be easily controlled, corrected, and changed. In the case of foraminifera, the margins of the small drawings are usually painted with black poster tempera, to be mounted in groups on black poster board (see figs. 6-1, 6-2). This has been traditional because the specimens are always viewed on a black background in their cardboard well-slides and also because the black background conceals the shadows of the pasteup job when the plate is photographed for publication. For larger tone drawings, carbon dust, wash, and airbrush also are used (see fig. 6-5).

Line illustrations of microfossils usually have been stipple drawings but also have included line-shading, coquille board, and scratchboard. In the past, engraving and lithography have also been used to produce these illustrations. Although these techniques are no longer in use, good examples of them will provide the perceptive illustrator with sharp lessons concerning light on form and the use of page space.

Fossil Vertebrates

Karen Klitz

NATURE AND CONDITION OF SPECIMENS

Fossils of vertebrate animals are scarce compared to those of invertebrates, although they may be locally abundant. They include a size range from dinosaurs and mastodons to insectivores and lizards. Generally only the hardest parts of their bodies have survived thousands or millions of years. Bones and teeth of fishes, amphibians, reptiles, dinosaurs, and mammals are the typical subject matter provided to the illustrator. Very rarely found are impressions or remnants of soft parts such as skin, fur, or feathers. The illustrator needs a background that includes vertebrate morphology or osteology and experience with the condition of fossils.

Fish fossils of sufficient diagnostic interest to be illustrated are isolated bones, spines, braincases, scales, complete skeletons, and molds of skeletons. Fish skeletons have usually been compressed and often fractured or even pulverized in place. Those specimens may show the overall size and shape of the taxon better than the morphology of individual bones, which may be hard to distinguish (fig. 13-18).

Amphibian, reptilian, and dinosaur fossils are most commonly isolated bones, although the many spectacular finds of articulated dinosaurs have contributed to their accurate restoration (see chapter 14). Skulls and jaws are most useful for identification (they are said to be "diagnostic"), followed by limb and foot bones and pelvic and shoulder girdles. Dinosaur elements are abundantly drawn because of the public interest in them.

Although recent work has greatly increased the collections of

13-18. Photograph of whole fish skeleton, *Priscacara*, fr[…] Although body form and size are clearly shown, a detaile[…] individual bones is quite difficult. Photo by George Junne[…]

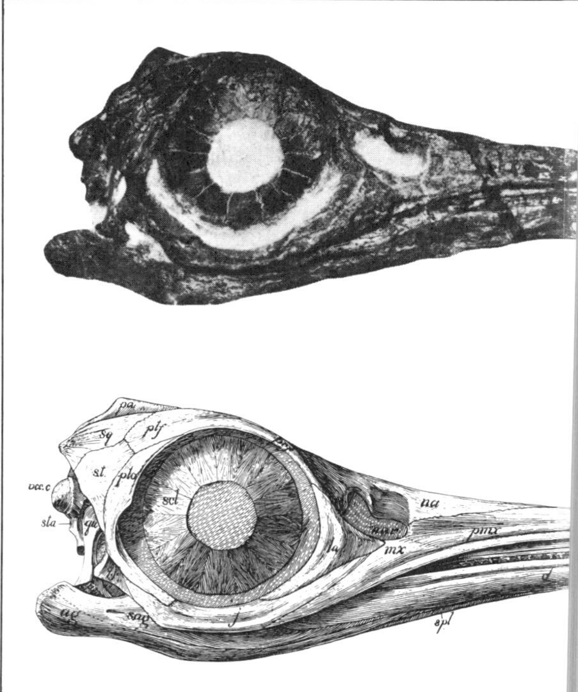

13-19. Top: Even well-preserved, relatively undistorted[…] photographs. Bottom: In the pen-and-ink line drawing […] *Osteology of Baptanodon*, by C. W. Gilmore, 1905), no[…] the individual skull bones and the treatment of the mis[…] *Ophthalmosaurus (Baptanodon) discus*, a Jurassic ichth[…]

fossil bird material, fossil birds are rare compared to other vertebrates because of the fragile nature of their skeletons. The most commonly illustrated fossils are limb bones and pelves.

Mammal fossils are represented most often by isolated teeth and jaw fragments, which is fortunate, since teeth are the single most diagnostic element. Limb and foot bones may be abundant but have variable diagnostic value. Skulls are rare and, when found, are often crushed.

Illustrations are superior to photographs in that they can deemphasize the irrelevant distractions of the preservation process and can be made from specimens that are difficult to illuminate properly for a photograph. When photographs are used, they often require explanatory illustrations (figs. 13-19, 13-20). An accurate and selective drawing, on the other hand, can stress the largest number of relevant details.

CARE AND HANDLING OF SPECIMENS

Before examining a fossil to be drawn, the illustrator should be aware of its preparation and condition. Besides being fragmentary and often crushed, the specimens may be discolored, partially embedded in matrix, translucent, twisted, or otherwise distorted. In spite of many hours of cleaning and preparation, most fossils remain fragile. Many of them have been cracked, and apparently whole bones and skulls may actually be small fragments held together by internal or surrounding matrix. For this reason, a preparator paints or soaks fragile specimens with an adhesive or hardener to minimize breakage and separation of the fractures.

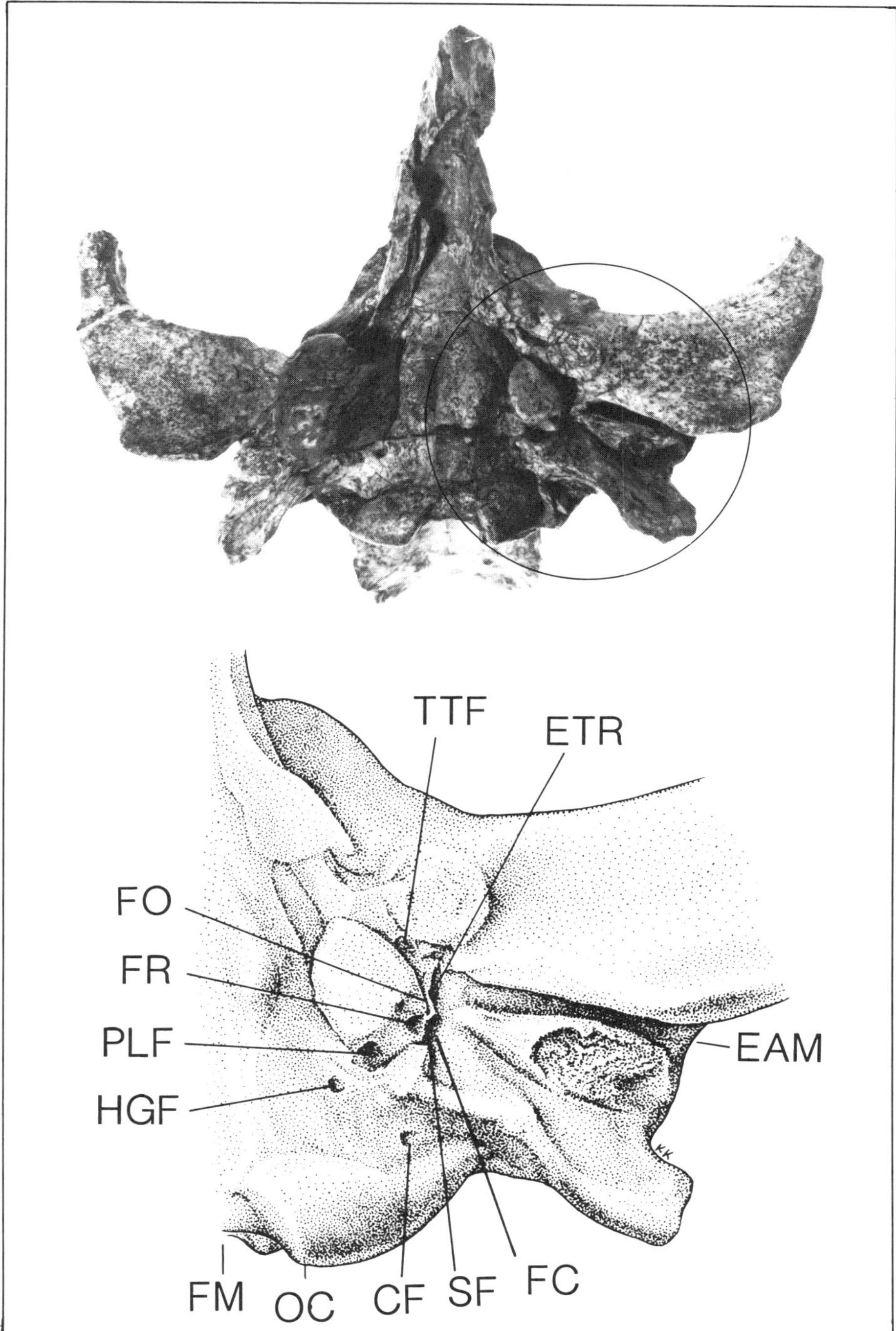

13-20. Top: Photograph. Bottom: Pen-and-ink stipple drawing of enlarged area of interest with only slight restoration, clearly showing morphological details without the discoloration and crack and chip distractions of the original specimen. Ear region of basicranium of *Pakicetus inachus*, an Eocene whale from Pakistan. Photo by George Junne. Drawing on Strathmore Bristol board, by Karen Klitz. Courtesy of P. D. Gingerich.

The preparator may embed in plastic resin some fossils that are soft or are to be sectioned. Large specimens and articulated skeletons may be embedded in plaster or left in the block of matrix, with only one side accessible, to avoid further damage. If a fossil is difficult to discern in the matrix, the illustrator may, with the scientist's permission, immerse it in water, alcohol, glycerin, anise oil, mineral oil, or xylene to increase the contrast. The fluid used depends on the chemical content of the fossil and matrix. Care must be taken that the particular immersion fluid does not dissolve the adhesives or hardeners present. Note that xylene is considered a carcinogen and must be used, if at all, under a vent. It will dissolve many substances.

Fossil bone may be fluorescent, permitting it to be photographed under ultraviolet light to show detail. Infrared radiation and X rays have been used to reveal important structures that are obscured by matrix. (The section on Radiation and Related Techniques in the *Handbook of Paleontological Techniques*, edited by Bernhard Kummel and David Raup—see Bibliography—is helpful.) The success of radiographic techniques depends on the relative densities of the fossil and matrix.

Sometimes valuable material in other institutions or countries is available for study or illustration only as casts. The use of casts in place of the original specimen eliminates the problems of variable coloration and translucence and reduces handling of the original. Disadvantages of using casts are shape change and possible loss of small details of structure. In some cases the original variation in color or surface finish provides additional clues; for example, it indicates the enamel-dentine boundary on teeth.

Fossils that are dark, badly discolored, or translucent may, with the scientist's permission, be coated by the illustrator with a very light layer of white powder, such as ammonium or magnesium oxide. Surface detail is thereby accentuated and shadows become clearer. (See *Handbook of Paleontological Techniques*, mentioned above.) This procedure does not damage the fossil; the powder washes off with water or can be blown or brushed off. Nonetheless, the oxide should not be left on for weeks because it may interact with the surface of the fossil.

Vertebrate fossils present problems in handling because of their fragility and extremes of size. Fossils too small or delicate to be handled easily and safely can be glued on a pin by the preparator, or more temporarily pressed on a cylinder of wax. Paper triangles taped on the ends of tweezers or a small wetted brush may be used to manipulate small and delicate specimens under the microscope. The specimen number should be written on the mounting cardboard when the fossil is positioned there. Once small fossils are mounted, they should be kept in a lidded box or drawer when not in use. Large fossils and delicate small ones should be kept on foam padding, sponges, cotton, or similar material to protect the weight-bearing areas. A small fossil can be pressed gently onto a piece of kneaded eraser on a small square of cardboard. The eraser should first be indented to the shape needed to hold the specimen. Wax also will hold fossils firmly enough in any orientation but may leave stains if in contact for more than a few weeks. Plasticine shapes more easily, but this becomes a disadvantage under hot lights: dark fossils absorb much heat and have been seen sinking into the substrate! Furthermore, the oil from plasticine will stain light-colored fossils. It can be removed with acetone or carbon tetrachloride, but these chemicals may also dissolve the glue that holds the specimen together. Isopropyl alcohol will dissolve shellac, which may have been used on old specimens. Staining may not be a concern on dark or large fossils, where it will not be noticeable.

Measurement

Accurate preliminary drawings of small specimens are most easily based on a camera lucida drawing. Depending on the amount of relief, the size of the fossil, and the detail required, photography, indirect projectors, and other methods also may be used (see Optical Devices in chapter 2). To prevent distortion of specimens with very high relief, it may be necessary to photograph

tation. Stability is the foremost concern. Use blocks, wedges, wooden pegs, and shot-filled bags as support when the specimen is correctly positioned. The supports may be visible but must not obscure the edges of the fossil.

Determine the position of the camera by the size, type, shape, and fragility of the specimen. If the fossil is not too big, a regular copy stand works well. Take dorsal views of large fossils from a vertical position a few feet above them. Good results have been obtained by clamping the camera onto a ladder. A centered camera position is adequate for all except the very wide specimen, in which case it may be desirable to take two parallel shots from a closer distance, rather than the one required to fit the specimen in a single shot without distortion. Placement of the scale depends on the visible depth of the fossil from the camera position. If it is six inches (15cm) or more deep, place the scale in a plane halfway back from the nearest surface to the edge. Shallower specimens will not change significantly in magnification from front to back, depending on the distance and focal length used.

Distance between subject and film is perhaps the single most important factor in recording an accurate and overall sharp image. Distortions of perspective inherent in normal viewing distances can be minimized by recording the subject from a greater distance. When the subject is too close, the nearer parts are magnified more than the distant parts. Large fossils should be photographed from at least ten times their depth. The image can be reenlarged to optimum drawing size on the print.

At any single distance, lens focal length determines the size of the image on the negative and, along with aperture, the depth of field. Large fossils of shallow depth can be photographed with small telephoto lenses. For example, a 150mm lens can be used to record specimens 1.5 inches (3cm) deep or less. Deep specimens such as large skulls can be taken with normal lenses of 50 to 55mm. The inverse relationship between lens size and specimen depth has to be balanced with overall specimen size. Depth of field is maximized by using small apertures of f/10 or greater. Where to focus a plane within this field is determined by the areas of critical detail. The depth of field extends a greater distance behind the plane of focus than in front. The proper lens, aperture, and distance to the subject should maximize the depth of field sufficiently to get sharpness of detail throughout.

The above requirements of distance and small aperture mean that obtaining enough light becomes a concern. Light should be almost uniform but slightly directional to enhance relief. There should be sufficient contrast between the edges of the specimen and the background, both of which may be in shadow. Large specimens that can be moved safely are often best photographed outdoors on overcast days. The small apertures and available light will determine the necessary accommodations in shutter speed and film speed. Fine-grained film retains sharp images that can be enlarged to drawing size without loss of detail definition. Since fine grain requires a slower film speed, increased light on the specimen is required, but the result will reward the effort.

RECONSTRUCTION

The accurate placement, shape, and size of all the characters of the specimen are the foundation of the drawing to be developed at this stage. The amount of detail and the degree of restoration to be portrayed are decisions that usually are made by the paleontologist. The uniqueness of the specimen and the condition it is in will suggest what degree of restoration is appropriate. The paleontologist and the illustrator may together decide the best technique and size for the drawing (fig. 13-21). If several specimens are to be compared to scale on the same plate, the largest and smallest ones should be drawn at a trial magnification to find the best compromise between fit and detail.

The illustrator in paleontology is always working with probabilities of the original appearance and must know how to deal with breakage, distortion, and matrix interference. These are minimized in a drawing that conveys all the relevant scientific information, even when breakage is shown (fig. 13-22). A drawing always shows some degree of restoration compared to the fossil's appearance in a photograph. It is the job of the illustrator at this stage to separate the visual information into what must be retained and what can be minimized or discarded.

The amount of visual restoration depends on the purpose of the drawing. Most paleontological illustrations show a particular specimen because it makes a significant contribution to what is known. All morphological details, as well as breakage, are shown. Sometimes evidence of significant fractures is important to indicate possible distortion. Comparison with other material may help the illustrator find or see features in a poorly preserved specimen. Animals thought to be closely related may provide the basis for including a dashed outline of missing parts. This type of illustration is restored to the extent that discoloration, small breaks, and translucent characteristics are omitted (fig 13-23).

If a new specimen adds to previously known morphology, then a composite drawing may be developed to show the complete bone or dentition. Because of bilateral symmetry in vertebrates, material from the same species may be reversed from the other side to supply missing pieces in a composite drawing. Sometimes a size difference requires adjustment. The paleontol-

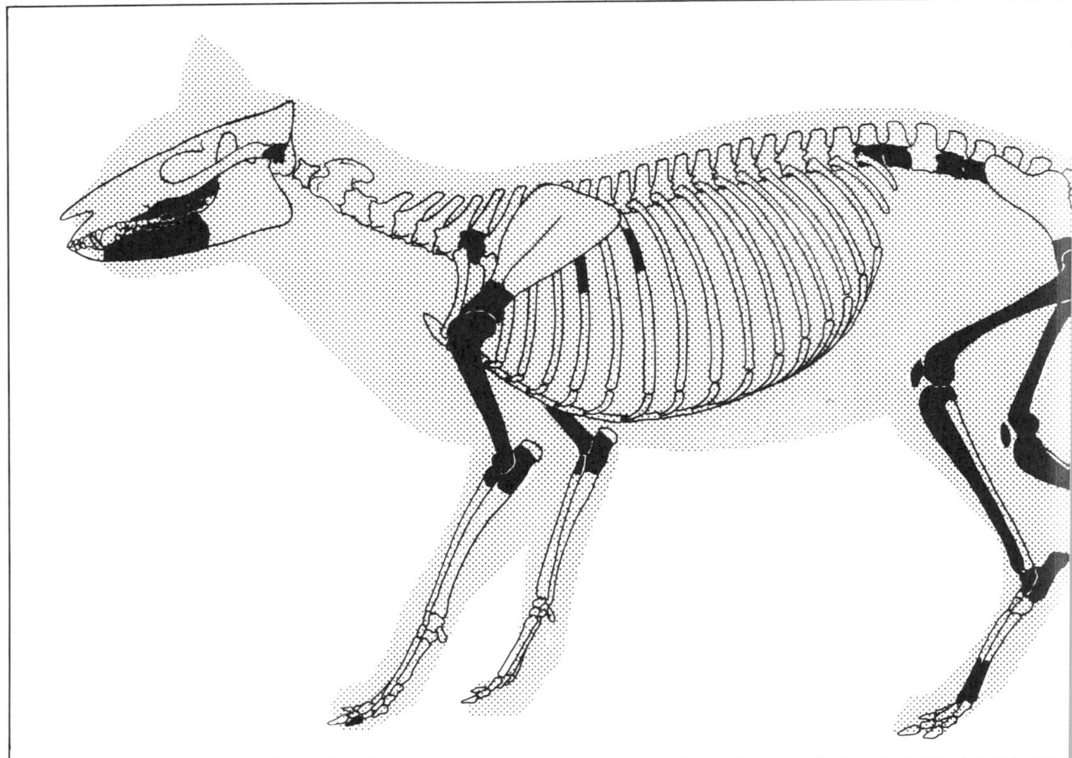

13-21. Partial skeleton (black bones) of *Hyracotherium grangeri*, an Early Eocene horse from Wyoming. The new specimen is restored to its natural position and given scale by superimposition on a cat silhouette. The small size of the new material, compared to other *H. grangeri*, is the most important feature to illustrate. The amount of skeletal material found is also useful to support scientific conclusions. Since the anatomy of individual bones does not differ from previously known larger specimens, simple outlines are sufficient. Pen-and-ink on Cronaflex film (with shading-film silhouette on the back), by Karen Klitz, courtesy of P. D. Gingerich. Skeleton was based on a drawing published in *Hitherto Unpublished Plates of Tertiary Mammalia and Permian Vertebrata*, vol. 3, by E. D. Cope (American Museum of Natural History, New York, 1885).

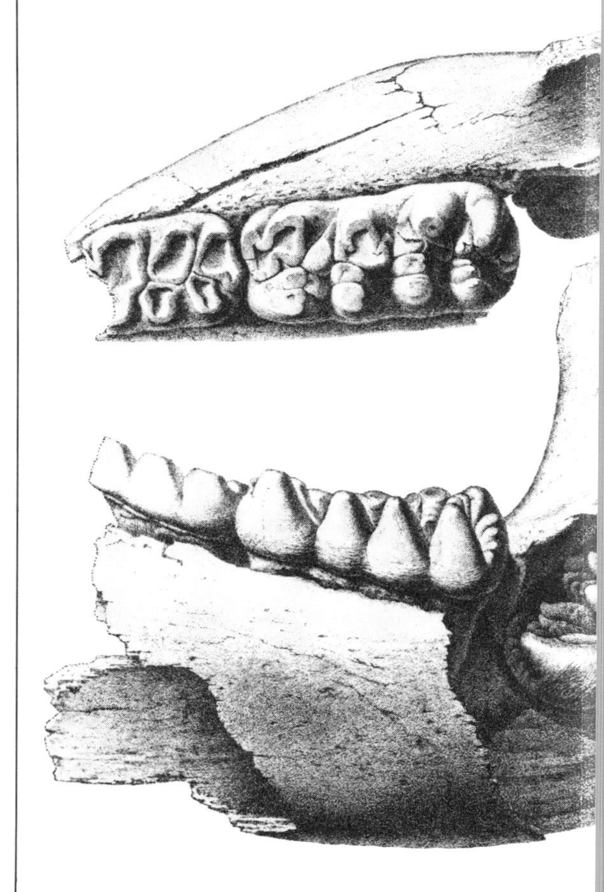

13-22. The molars command attention, but all areas, including breakage, have been rendered. The side of the jaw was cut away to show the third molar in the crypt, a pocket that would have been difficult to illuminate for a photograph. Jaw fragment of "*Mastodon*" *dissimilis*, from the Pleistocene of France. Drawing (medium unknown) and lithograph by L. Gauthier from *Recherches sur les Mastodontes*, by L. Lortet and E. Chantre, 1879.

ogist has the responsibility of providing the appropriate specimens for substitution. One risk of composite drawings is the possibility of masking real differences between specimens. Careful records must be kept to indicate each specimen's contribution. Occasionally drawings are needed that give lifelike form to fossil material where much of the skeleton is missing. The fossil may be so twisted or crushed that reconstructing the original form must be based on a series of assumptions and comparisons that involve risk. The text and/or illustration clarify where the morphological evidence is poor or lacking (see chapter 14).

13-23. Reconstructions of leg movement can be based on these detailed surfaces and natural relative positions. Rugosities are emphasized so that muscle attachments can be studied; cracks are minimized. Left tibia, fibula, and astragalus in anterior and medial views of *Brontosaurus (Apatosaurus) excelsus*. Drawing (medium unknown) by Frederick Berger and lithography by E. Crisand under Marsh. From *Marsh's Dinosaurs*, by J. H. Ostrom and J. S. McIntosh. 1966. Courtesy of Yale University Press.

Orientation

Orientation of the fossil depends on its type more than its size. Some views may be restricted by matrix and the fragility of the fossil in it. Teeth, either separate or in mandibles and maxilla, are most often drawn in occlusal view (looking down on the chewing surface). Other views are buccal (outside surface of the teeth) and lingual (from the tongue side). A dentition should be set up so that the teeth, and not the bottom of the jaw, are level (fig. 13-24).

Limb bones typically are figured in lateral and medial views. Skulls often are drawn in lateral, dorsal, and ventral views, occasionally in anterior and posterior views. Other angles of orientation sometimes are required to show particular features.

MEDIA AND TECHNIQUES

A wide variety of line and tone media have been used to illustrate vertebrate fossils. In addition to the usual considerations of purpose and available time are the condition of the specimen, techniques traditionally used, and the ease with which changes can be incorporated. As the research continues and as new fossils are found or borrowed, the illustrator may have to make additions or changes of detail or emphasis. Bones and teeth are traditionally rendered in line or stipple technique. Carbon dust, graphite, and more rarely, scratchboard and wash illustrations also are used.

With any fossil illustration, we can imagine a progression of illustrations based on a significant fossil find. First a faithful rendering of several views of the specimen is published, showing fractures and missing areas. Some years later, after some of the missing pieces are supplied, a composite drawing appears showing little or no breakage. When another researcher uses it for comparison, the composite may be redrawn, often in a simplified style, as part of a skull or complete vertebrate skeleton. Finally, the animal may be drawn in a lifelike pose, with scales, feathers, or fur, in a reconstructed environment from an ancient time. An exciting aspect of illustrating fossils is the possibility of new discoveries proving correct—or incorrect—our visual and taxonomic assumptions.

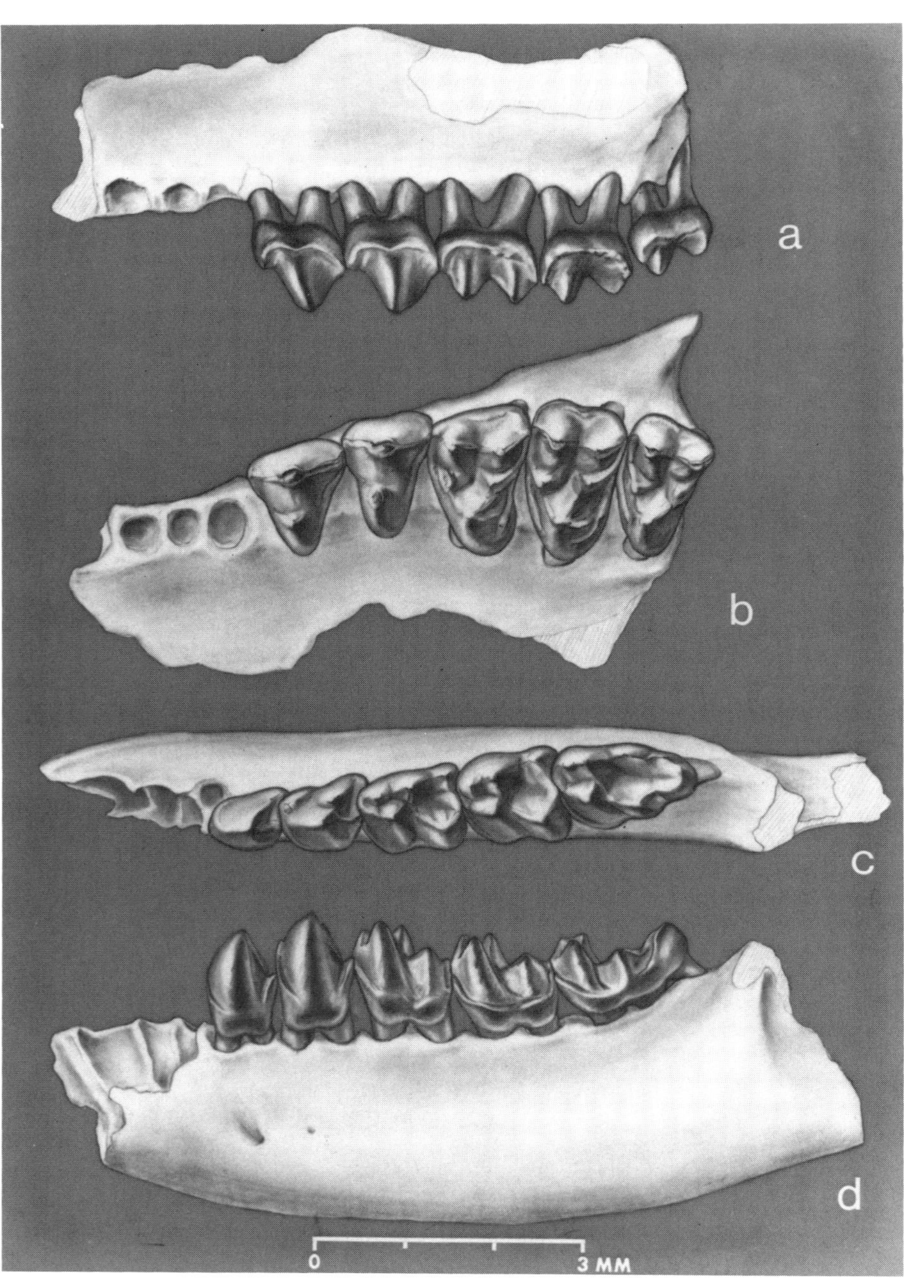

13-24. Jaw fragment of *Altanius orlovi*, an Eocene primate from Mongolia. Maxilla in buccal *(a)* and occlusal *(b)* views. Mandible in occlusal *(c)* and buccal *(d)* views. Note that the buccal views are in life position and the occlusal views are aligned with and close to the teeth in buccal view. Graphite on Cronaflex film, by Karen Klitz, courtesy of P. D. Gingerich.

14/Reconstructing Extinct Vertebrates

Gregory S. Paul and Terry L. Chase

The development of paleoecology, the study of relationships among ancient animals and plants, has intensified the demand for paleontological reconstructions in the form of dynamic illustrations, sculpture, and films that re-create the appearance, habits, and often the habitats of prehistoric animals and plants. To the illustrator of prehistoric subjects, reconstructions are illustrations, models, and sculptures that reproduce the appearance of an extinct animal's bones, skeleton, habitus, and often the habitat in which it lived. For more than a century, reconstructions have been used for murals and models in museum galleries as well as for illustrations in popular books on paleontology. Only recently, however, has there been substantial demand in the scientific literature for paleontological reconstruction, usually in the form of block diagrams showing fossil communities or as illustrations of individual organisms that show the function of skeletal anatomy, soft anatomy, life habits, and growth forms. This chapter will discuss the various kinds of useful information available from the fossil record and some procedures for gathering and translating these data directly into a vertebrate paleoreconstruction.

To prepare a paleoreconstruction, the artist must be able to synthesize basic scientific data. A thorough knowledge of the form and function of the paleontological subject, as well as familiarity with the anatomy and ecology of its living relatives, is usually essential. It is also important to understand the progression of geologic time. The artist who is not a paleontologist or biologist ought to be able to communicate and work closely with those scientists who can supply the basic information needed to reconstruct a fossil organism accurately. The ability to gather much of this information independently could be a significant advantage to any artist. Courses in comparative anatomy, vertebrate and invertebrate zoology, paleontology, and botany are helpful, as are apprenticeships. Independent study is important.

Dissection and study of various modern animals will help the artist to build an understanding and appreciation of body structure. Familiarity with relationships among organs, skeletal structure, muscles, fat deposits, and skin can be applied judiciously to reconstruction of extinct forms. It is further important to know where muscles are attached, how they change shape when body parts move, and how thick they are (when probed with a needle). Specimens for dissection can be obtained from biological supply houses, zoos, and animal laboratories. For reference, observations should be recorded with drawings and photographs during several steps of dissection—for instance, when the skin is pulled back, when muscles are cleaned of fat, as certain muscles are removed, and when bones and organs are exposed. If reconstruction will involve plants, modern and fossil plant structure should be studied. The accuracy of observations and reconstructions based on dissections or other information should be checked with a paleontologist, anatomist, or other specialist in the pertinent field. Especially important to restoring extinct vertebrates is the use of modern analogues, living animals that are most like the extinct subject. These can be relatively close relatives—such as modern horses when restoring fossil horses—or they can be animals of similar form—such as elephants when working on a giant brontosaur.

Although the illustrator is seldom responsible for preparation of the skeletal reconstruction from which the rendering is to be made, it is important to understand how errors can arise. Errors in a finished reconstruction resulting from inaccuracies in the prepared skeleton or a misinterpretation of the skeleton occur for at least three basic reasons:

1. The reconstruction was based on an incomplete or deformed skeleton.
2. The original interpretations of the skeletal reconstruction were in error but became so ingrained in scientific thought that they were perpetuated long after new evidence indicated that they were wrong.
3. The fossils were assembled erroneously.

There are many cases in which errors in assembling vertebrate skeletons have led to persistently inaccurate reconstructions.

The artist not only must be able to interpret paleontological and biological evidence, but also must possess the imagination to visualize the fossil as a living organism and the technical and artistic skills to translate this mental image into graphic form accurately and convincingly. Whereas the rendering techniques used to prepare paleoreconstructions are the same as those used to produce other forms of scientific illustrations, the procedures used to produce the preliminary drawing are quite different. Frequently a sculptured three-dimensional model is created as a guide for the two-dimensional rendering (see figs. 14-19 through 14-22). Creating a reconstruction is, in some ways, similar to preparing a scientific research paper (which it may accompany), except that the results are expressed in pictorial rather than written form.

Renderings can be done in any medium and on any surface, although pen-and-ink is used most commonly. Because reconstructions sometimes are done in mural form, they present the opportunity to work in media such as oils or acrylics on a larger scale than is customary in other fields.

INSTRUMENTS AND MATERIALS

In addition to the art materials used for the chosen media and technique, the reconstruction of extinct vertebrates will require the use of some of the following items. (There is some overlap with the list of Instruments and Materials in chapter 13, and reference should be made to that chapter.)

Surfaces

Tracing paper, drafting film: inexpensive for early rough drawings and better quality for later stages.

Graph paper: various scales such as 8/inch, 10/inch, to compute enlargements and reductions.

Optical Devices

Stereoscopic microscope: for very small fossils.

Reducing objective.

Camera lucida.

Reticle with grid: used when camera lucida is not available.

Opaque projector: indirect for enlargement and reduction of drawings or of the actual fossil; direct for projection of drawings, but can be used backward to draw some fossils (see fig. 2-34).

Camera: 35mm single-lens reflex, with slide and print film.

Lenses: telephoto and macro, for camera.

Slide projector: to enlarge slides of specimens for tracing and study.

Measuring Devices

Proportional dividers: large and small sizes, depending on the sizes of the fossils likely to be drawn—8-inch (20cm) will accommodate most small fossils.

Metric measurers: for measuring specimens and drawings—tape measures for curved surfaces, rulers from 15cm (6 inches) to a yardstick or one-meter stick. Rulers should be both clear plastic for use in drawing and white opaque plastic with black markings to be placed next to specimens for photography.

Protractor.

90-degree triangle.

Specimen-handling Tools

For very small specimens that require microscopy, the same instruments listed in chapter 13 are needed.

Specimen Props

Sandbox: in which to articulate bones.

Microcrystalline (dental wax) (petroleum based and somewhat sticky): for holding bones together or to support them in position; available from dental suppliers. Plasticine also may be used (see Clay, Wax in chapter 2, and Appendix).

Soft cloth fabric: to place under specimens for protection.

Cushions
cloth, Sty
wooden b
pegs, shot-

Containe

Boxes: ca
smaller sp
padded w
sponge fo
Very large
wooden cr
ally handl
cians.

Miscellan

Scissors: l
pieces as
A paper cu

Calculato
ships amo

Plasticine
modeling
structions
layers as g
tion. Klea
plasticine
(see Appe
Klay).

Index car
larger; to
labels plac
photograp

Felt-tippe
ing cards.

Transpar
ish that ac
810, for e
ing paper

PROCEI
RECONS
SKELET

After a
carefully
treated w
prevent d
cedures a
tent pre
combined
preparato

necessary for full reconstruction of the animal from the skeleton embedded at the discovery site to an illustration or model of the animal's appearance in life.

Even though the illustration techniques apply to all land vertebrates, including early hominids, the large predatory tyrannosaur dinosaurs of the group Theropoda will be used here as the primary example in an outline of basic procedures for preparing a paleoreconstruction. Such features as the relationship of bones to each other, evidence of muscle attachments, and fossil footprints are all clues to an animal's anatomy, life-style, and habitat. This kind of information should be sought whenever an animal is to be reconstructed. The same principles of interpretation apply to invertebrate animals and plants.

Fieldwork

When a large skeleton or bone bed is uncovered in the field, a quarry map or chart of the remains is often prepared, documenting the position of the bones as found (in situ) (figs. 14-1, 14-2). Such drawings and supporting photographs help in reassembling the skeleton in the laboratory and are critically important for understanding how and why the specimens came to be preserved. Photographs should be made of the exposed fossil using the archaeological-type grid system with a camera suspended over the quarry. The grid allows for correction of parallax in the subsequent drawing. (See chapter 21 for a description of quarry mapping.)

Illustrating Related Bones

After fossils have been excavated and then cleaned in the lab, they may be illustrated as either isolated bones or an articulated skeleton left half-buried in the matrix (death pose) (see fig. 14-2). Because these bones or skeletons may be massive or may be stored in some remote location, camera lucida and other reproduction tools may not be practical or available. Slides (35mm) of the specimen in several standard views (lateral, dorsal, ventral)—shot with a telephoto lens to reduce parallax and with a metric scale next to the specimen—can be projected and the specimen's outline and gross characters traced. The subject may photograph more clearly if it is evenly white. To that end and with the permission of the scientist, some specimens can be coated with chemical powders (see chapter 13). Sometimes, to minimize handling of a fragile specimen, a cast is made for illustration or photography. Additional details are drawn from the specimen or, if the specimen is not available, from photographs. Standard views facilitate comparative study. Additional views may be necessary for some purposes. The scientist may also require more complex drawings showing such features as the functioning of various joints and cross sections through elements.

Skeletal Restoration

A full skeletal restoration is the next step in the reconstruction of an animal. If a good freestanding skeletal mount of the animal is not already available, this stage can be accomplished by a series of studies. It now becomes essential to understand the anatomy of the animal being drawn. The most reliable way for the artist to develop a reconstruction is to build up on paper from bones or photographs a pencil reconstruction, preferably in multiple (lateral, top, front) views. Reconstructing an animal from several angles forces the illustrator to examine how various elements relate to one another in three dimensions and may reveal errors that are not apparent in reconstructing the skeleton in lateral view alone. Each of these views shows the full extent of certain bones, depending on the angle, and they may be combined to make a full and accurate analysis of the animal. Restorations that depict a living animal in its habitat may require more complicated poses with foreshortening. Here artistic experience and knowledge help the illustrator estimate what each part of the organism should look like and what its size should be when seen from various angles. When the skeletal reconstruction is complete, a separate drawing is made of muscle and fat layers attached properly to this skeleton. In a third drawing, skin is added and, finally, any cuticular details such as hair and texture.

Sometimes changes are required after the final rendering is done. If the final drawing is to be inked, it should be on good tracing paper or thin film so that it can be changed if necessary by cutting and repiecing. A line reproduction will not show the cut edges.

A Bone Library

Reconstruction begins with a series of tracings that constitute a "library" of skeletal parts, a disarticulated paper skeleton that will be used to reconstruct the whole skeleton. First determine the scale to be used. For example, if the length of the original bone was 1300mm and it is drawn at 130mm, the scale is 1/10. Next calculate the length of the other skeletal elements at that same scale. On a sheet of tracing paper, mark the dimension for any given element and use an opaque projector, grids, or proportional dividers to achieve the desired size of that element for tracing (see chapter 2).

If the skeleton is to be restored in multiple views, select and draw the elements in those views that will be reconstructed. Only the overall outline of each bone and a few major topographical contours should be drawn. Details clutter and confuse the already complex skeletal reconstruction.

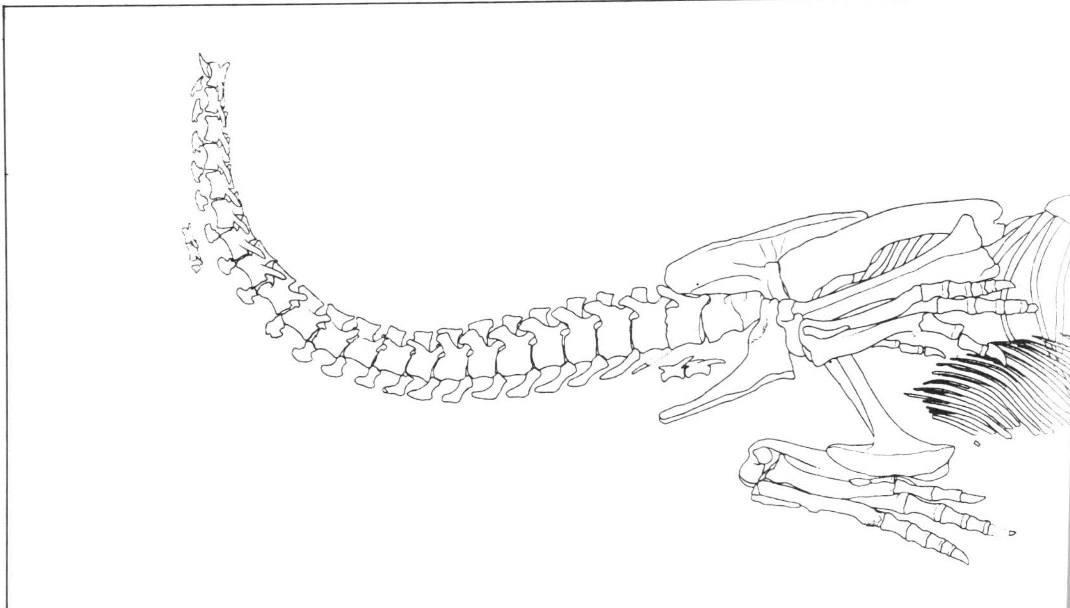

14-1. Quarry of a well-preserved tyrannosaurid skeleton *(Albertosaurus libratus)*, showing the placement of the bones as originally found. Pen-and-ink. Artist uncertain. From Geological Survey of Canada, Memoir 100, 1917. Courtesy of National Museum of Natural Sciences, National Museums of Canada.

14-2. Shaded study of the opposite side of the same skeleton shown in figure 14-1 still in the matrix. Pen-and-ink, by Arthur Miks. From Geological Survey of Canada, Memoir 100, 1917. Courtesy of National Museum of Natural Sciences, National Museums of Canada.

Combining Unequal Skeletons

A problem that frequently arises is that no single complete skeleton exists for reference and assorted partial skeletons of the same or similar species differ in size. Sometimes what is missing on one side of a specimen can be found on its other side. Elements from various individuals must be scaled to a common size by comparing the dimensions of those bones that are found in more than one skeleton and scaling up or down the associated remains. Caution is necessary here: the proportions of the reconstruction will be accurate only if the size differences of various individual elements are not too great, because body proportions may change radically as size changes during growth. On the other hand, a skeletal reconstruction that shows the overall design of a fossil with only approximate proportions may be useful.

Reconstructing the proportions of a species from multiple fragmentary specimens requires a calculator and a list of measurements of the specimens' bones. First, choose the most complete adult specimen available to form the core or primary specimen for the restoration. Then select sections or parts from the other specimens, and rescale and compile them to make a complete individual. Some elements often are shared between the primary and secondary specimens, facilitating this kind of assembly.

To start the reconstruction, take measurements of long limb bones if possible; if not, girdle bones and sections of the vertebral column will suffice. Calculate the ratio between lengths of an element shared between the primary and secondary specimens. If the primary specimen has a femur 1300mm long and the length of the femur of a secondary specimen is 1000mm, the ratio is 1.3:1. Do the same for some other elements shared between the two skeletons and, with the scientist's guidance, decide which ratio is best or whether an average of the various ratios is more suitable. If the ratio is as above (1.3:1), all parts from the secondary specimen should be scaled up, that is, multiplied by 1.3, to fit into the primary specimen. If the elements are absent from both the primary and the secondary specimens, find a third specimen and repeat the process.

The task becomes more difficult when, for example, elements are missing from the primary specimen and are present in a secondary specimen, but the two specimens lack shared elements, and a third specimen shares some elements with each, but not the ones the primary specimen is missing. Such complicated situations are common. In this case the size ratio between the second and third specimens must be calculated. Then the elements of the secondary specimen that are absent in the primary one must be scaled to the size of the tertiary specimen. The size ratio between the tertiary and primary specimens is calculated, and the elements scaled into the tertiary specimen from the secondary specimen are again rescaled, this time from the tertiary to the primary specimen. This procedure may have to be repeated with other specimens to complete the primary specimen's proportions. If changes in bone size are great, some adjustments to the proportions of the bones themselves may be necessary. For instance, bones from larger individuals tend to be, but are not always, more stoutly constructed than those of smaller juvenile specimens of the same taxon.

If more than one specimen is needed to restore a single individual, but no parts are shared among the specimens, careful guesstimates must be made of the animal's proportions. These should be checked by the scientist.

ARTICULATING AND RESTORING THE SKELETON

Although other species are shown here to illustrate certain principles, *Tyrannosaurus rex* is used to illustrate the basic reconstruction process. *Tyrannosaurus rex* presents relatively few problems. An almost complete specimen with skull is known. Only part of the tail, some ribs, shoulder girdle, forelimb, and hindlimb are missing. Fortunately, another specimen identical in size is known from a nearby location; this specimen provides the shoulder girdle, humerus, and hindlimb. The missing tail, lower forelimb, and toe bones are reconstructed and scaled in from other tyrannosaurs. Modern analogues provide clues to probable structure. In the case of tyrannosaurs, the best modern analogues are birds, both because of their similar form and because birds are direct descendants of small theropods related to tyrannosaurs.

Lateral View

Vertebral Column

Because the vertebral column is the axial element on which the other bones are attached, it is a logical point to begin the reconstruction. To illustrate a vertebral column, one of two basic approaches can be used: each vertebra can be drawn separately to scale and articulated on paper; or the vertebrae themselves can be articulated in a sandbox or on the framework of a mount as it is being constructed, then photographed or sketched in sections (fig. 14-3a). When some vertebrae are missing, as is commonly the case, the original number must be estimated. The appearance and size of the missing vertebrae can be extrapolated from the vertebrae that are present directly behind or in front of them (fig. 14-4). When the end of the tail is missing, as in the *Tyr-*

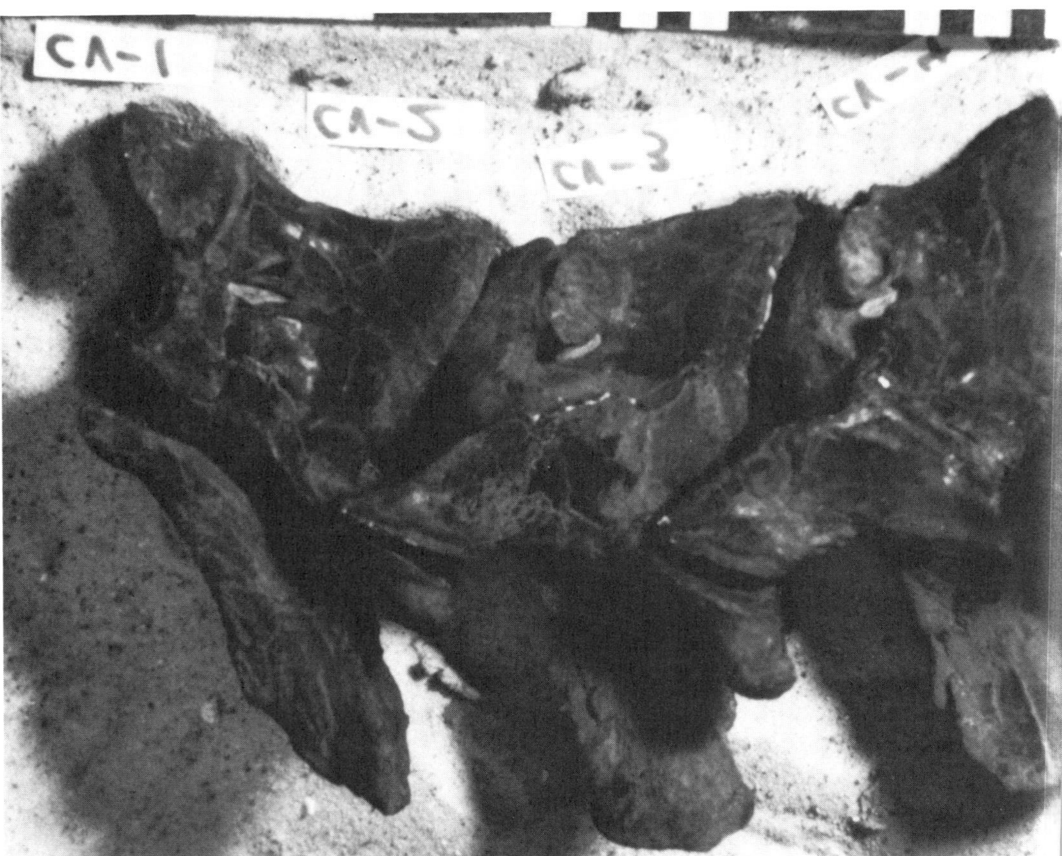

a

transverse process
diapophysis
parapophysis
prezygapophysis
parapophysis
postzygapophysis

b

14-3. *(a)* To determine the posture of the vertebral column of the dinosaur *Allosaurus*, the vertebral centra have been aligned face to face, separated slightly to allow room for the cartilaginous intervertebral discs (not preserved) and the zygapophyses.
(b) Schematic drawings of *Camptosaurus* vertebrae to show the positions of the zygapophyses. Left: anterior view; center: side view; right: posterior view. Pen-and-ink on Cronaflex film, by Karen Klitz.

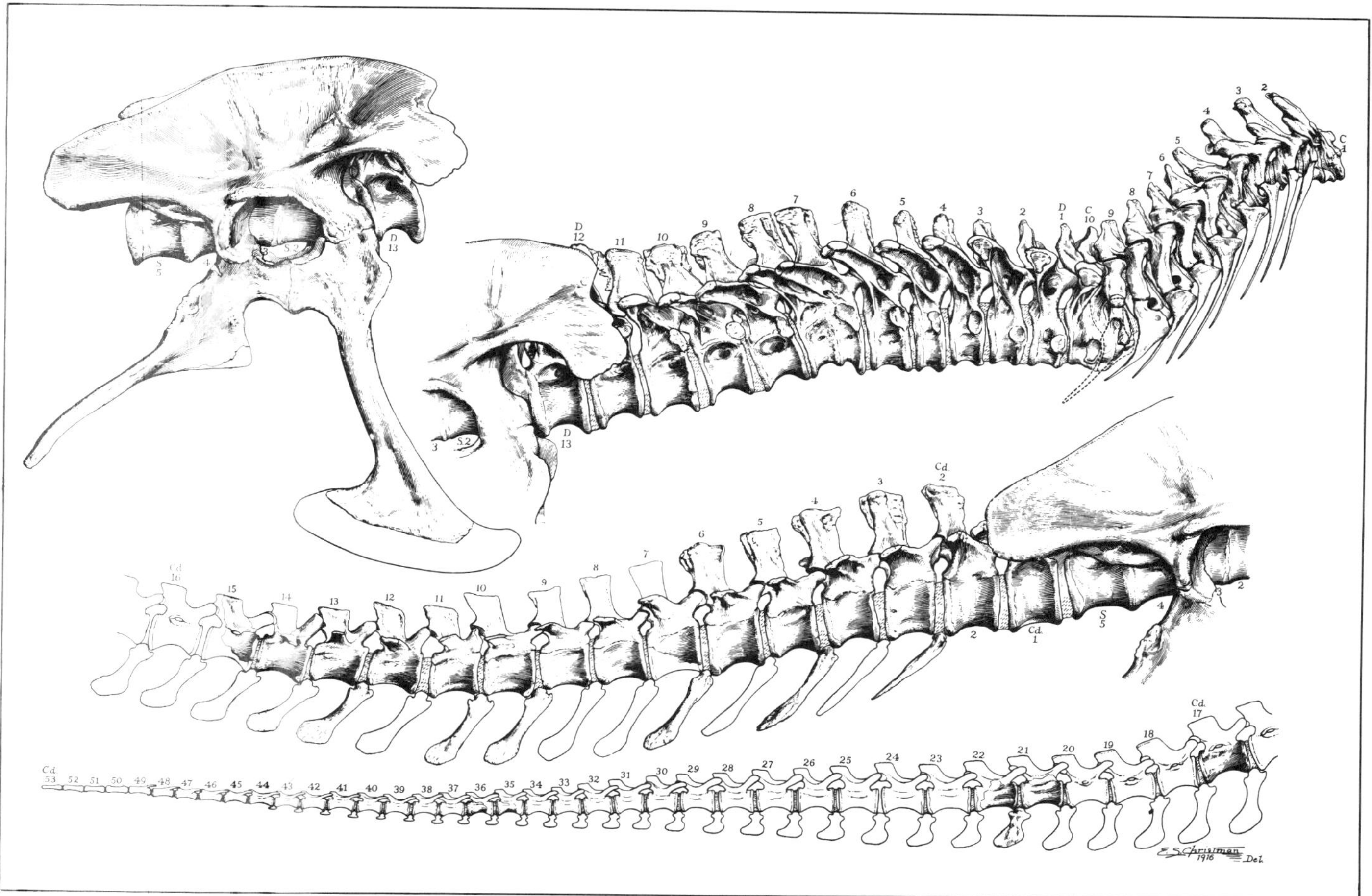

14-4. A study of the articulated vertebral column of a *Tyrannosaurus rex* specimen upon which the final reconstruction is based. Note the curvature of the neck and back. Two vertebrae *(D 7* and *D 8)* in the back have fused together, a pathological condition. One error has been made: the tail, incomplete, has too many vertebrae added to it. More complete tails show a total count of fewer than forty. The neural spines on the back show remnants of ossified interspinal ligaments, evidence of a rigidly braced trunk. Pen-and-ink on Bristol board, by E. S. Christman (*Bulletin* of the American Museum of Natural History, 1916).

annosaurus specimen, estimating the original length can be a problem.

To connect the vertebrae, articulate the zygapophyses (the small interlocking articular surfaces on each vertebra, shown in fig. 14-3b) and align the face of each centrum parallel to the next. Keep the centra separated from one another by about 10 percent of the average length of either adjacent centrum. In life, this space was filled by a flexible intervertebral cartilaginous disc. Broad zygapophyses and the curvature suggest that the neck was very flexible. Small zygapophyses and ossified interspinal ligaments indicate a very rigid trunk column, as in birds. The vertebrae in the pelvic region are rigidly fused to one another. The tail emerges either straight from the pelvic region or, more commonly in tyrannosaurs, with a slight upward bend given by the upturned faces of the last few pelvic centra. If drawings of a portion of the vertebral column seem unsatisfactory, they can be cut apart and rearticulated. This is true for any stage of the penciled reconstruction. The final pencil reconstruction may consist of many pieces of paper fastened together with transparent tape.

Rib Cage

The rib cage is important to restoring the shape of the subject, but a crushed specimen rib cage, which is quite common, makes the work difficult. In the tyrannosaurid dinosaurs, the ribs sweep down and backward from the vertebrae as they do in other dinosaurs, birds, and crocodiles. The varying shape and direction of each rib are to be noted. The rib-to-sternal connections and some of the sternals, which were cartilaginous and usually not preserved, can be reconstructed by analogy with living vertebrates, in this case birds.

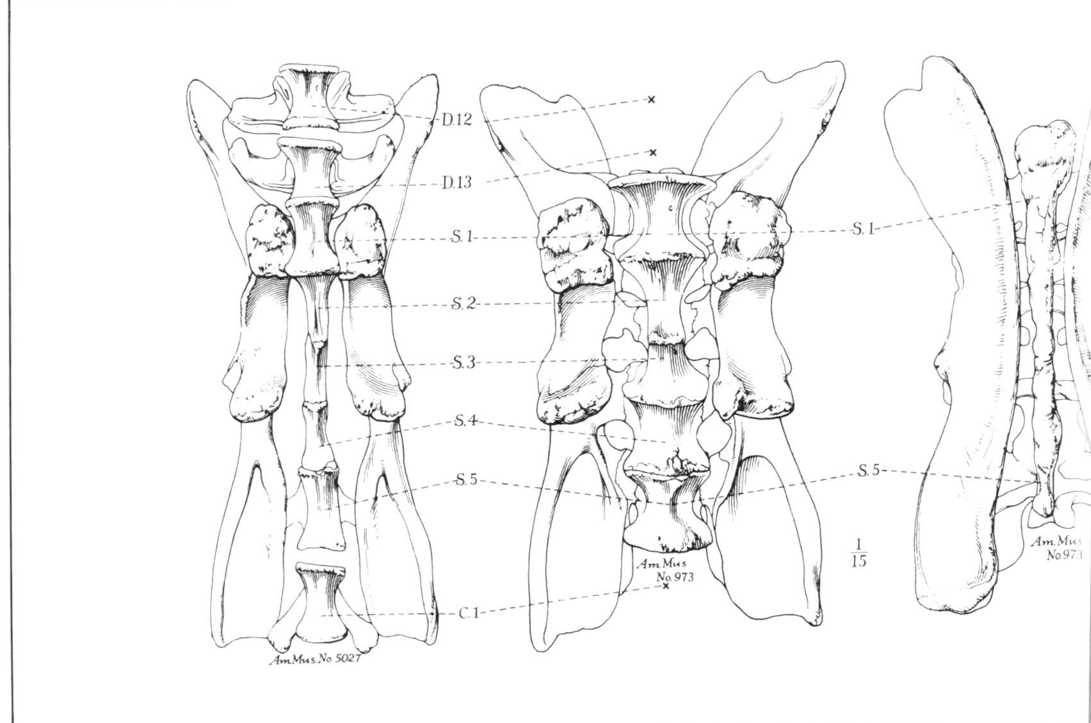

a

b

14-5. Pelvis *(a)* and hip vertebrae *(b)* of the two *Tyrannosaurus rex* specimens used in the final reconstruction. These drawings illustrate a problem of paleobiology: the pelvis was unnaturally crushed and narrowed by the weight of thousands of feet of overlaying sediments. Pen-and-ink on Bristol board, by E. S. Christman (*Bulletin* of the American Museum of Natural History, 1916).

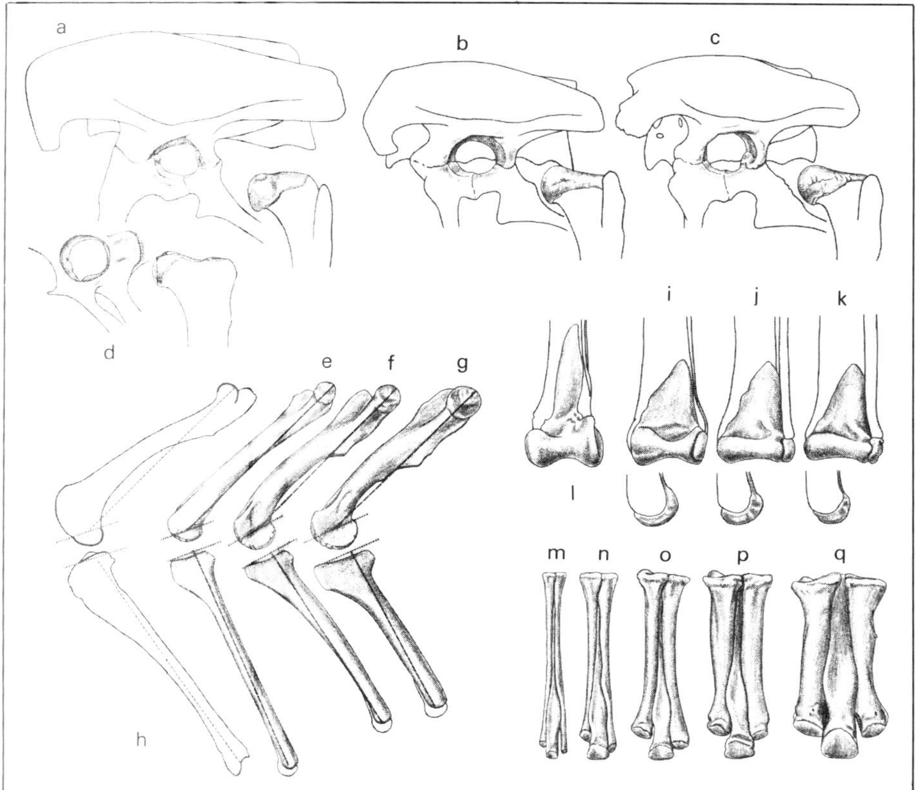

14-6. Chart comparing the structure of the hindlimbs of tyrannosaur species of varying sizes to that of the very similar, small, struthiomimid theropod dinosaurs. The shapes remain little changed. To show proportional changes, the elements have been drawn to standard dimensions. China marker, Stabilo pencil, and ink on coquille board, by Gregory S. Paul. *(a), (e), (i), (m), (n)*: struthiomimids; *(b), (c), (f), (g), (j), (k), (o), (p),* and *(q)*: tyrannosaurids; *(d)* and *(l)*: ostrich; *(h)*: gazelle.

Limbs

The placement of the shoulder girdle upon the rib cage is a most difficult point in reconstructing fossil skeletons because the girdle is a free-floating system attached to the ribs only by muscles and cartilaginous sternal elements, neither of which are preserved. The position of the shoulder girdle is best estimated by noting its placement in well-articulated specimens, by estimating the most plausible position of the girdle and the sternal elements relative to the first dorsal ribs, and by comparison with the similar shoulder girdles of related taxa. In quadrupeds, shoulder girdle position is a major determinant of overall body posture, an important point for the illustrator to remember. Much extra work can be avoided by accurately locating the shoulder girdle in the lateral reconstruction so that subsequently prepared views, based on the lateral, will not require repositioning. It may be worthwhile to do a preliminary reconstruction of the anterior rib cage and the shoulder girdle, following the directions for reconstructing the front view outlined below.

It is easy to locate the placement of the pelvic girdle and hindlimbs on the skeleton. The pelvis attaches directly to the sacral vertebrae through massive buttressing ribs (fig. 14-5).

Function and movement, as well as construction, of the fore- and hindlimbs must be understood to restore an animal as a moving dynamic being. Careful study of the limb joints provides information for accurate reconstruction. Comparative studies (fig. 14-6) show little change in body and limb design from half a ton to ten tons; only the proportions changed. Tyrannosaurs have limbs very like those of birds, and as in birds, the restricted action of cylindrical hindlimb joints limited tyrannosaurs to a fully erect gait in which the limbs were always held directly under the body. This is confirmed by the narrow, slightly sinuous fossil trackways made by predatory dinosaurs.

Measurements of the articular surfaces of the knee suggest that *Tyrannosaurus* had highly flexed knees like those of horses and ostriches rather than the straight knees of elephants (figs. 14-6, 14-7, 14-8). The extensive hip-joint articular surfaces suggest that the femur swung from about 30 degrees below horizontal to just past vertical during fast locomotion (less at slower speeds) and that the ankle was fairly straight, as it is in big ground birds. All of this data can be used to reconstruct the limb action in a motion series study (fig. 14-9).

To finish the penciled skeletal reconstruction in side view, select a reconstructed limb posture that allows both limbs and the pelvis to be seen. Drawing the limbs on separate pieces of tracing paper and taping them to the skeleton drawing makes it possible to try various poses without having to erase and redraw the limbs repeatedly.

Animals with limbs held directly beneath their bodies are relatively easy to draw in lateral view. Drawing the limbs of sprawling gait animals, such as lizards and salamanders, in which the limbs splay out from the body, may be more difficult. This requires a good eye for freehand sketching of oblique (foreshortened) views of limb bones, guided by some pertinent measurements in the proper positions. For some examples of and solutions to the problem, read the chapters on reptilian fossils in *Vertebrate Paleontology* by A. S. Romer (see Bibliography).

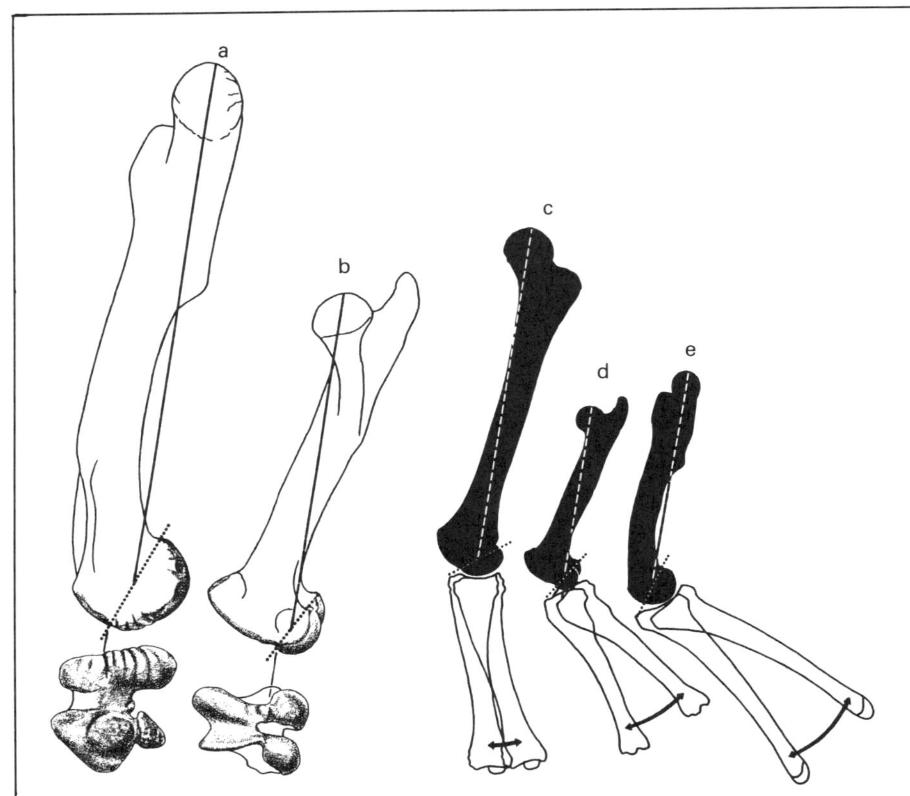

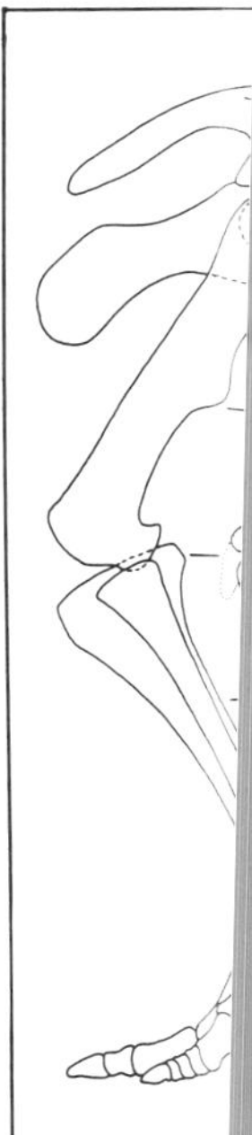

14-8. A stu[...] hindlimb of [...] ink on traci[...]

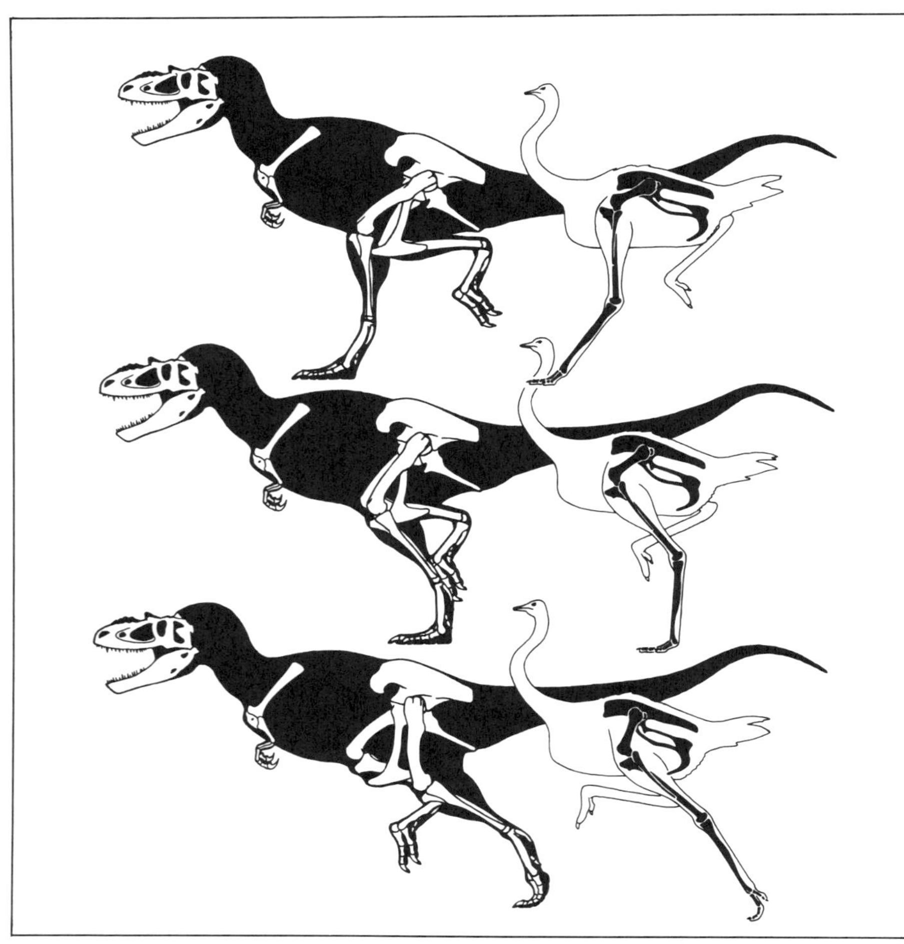

Top left:
14-7. Diag[...] flexion is e[...] and *(b)* ho[...] the articul[...] shaft of th[...] compares [...] locomotin[...] The same [...] tyrannosa[...] pencil, an[...] Gregory S[...]

Bottom le[...]
14-9. Fro[...] limbs, me[...] flexion, a[...] vertebrat[...] conceptio[...] worked c[...] illustrate[...] of a runni[...] Pen-and-[...] S. Paul.

Top and Front Views

Having completed the penciled sketch of the side view, the artist must next restore the skeleton in top and front views. A back view is also useful, but since this is done with the same techniques as the front view, it will not be discussed in depth here.

Figures 14-11, 14-12, and 14-13 show a blueprintlike plan of the skeleton in three nonperspective views—from directly above (perpendicular to the ground), from directly forward of the skeleton (line-of-sight parallel to the ground), and in the direct side view (lateral)—already reconstructed. In effect, each part of the skeleton is triangulated and plotted on the top and front views. It is not a perfect blueprint: some leeway will be allowed in posing the different views (The process of triangulation is explained in chapter 16 and in figs. 16-9 and 21-23.)

To start, cut out two sheets of tracing paper large enough to hold the skeleton drawing in top and front views. Draw in the baselines shown in figure 14-10. These are the ground lines in front and side view, lines describing a transverse plane cutting through the base of the tail (posterior face of the last sacral centrum) in side and top views, and lines representing the vertical body midplane that splits the animal into left and right halves (sagittal section) from front and top views. These baselines describe the three basic planes—ground, body sagittal (midplane), and a transverse plane—needed to triangulate the skeletal elements. Note that the line marking the body midline in top view may be either perfectly straight or slightly curved to re-create the flexion of a vertebral column in a moving animal. The former is a little easier to do and slightly more accurate in measurements; the latter is more realistic. Do not attempt to show curvature of the vertebral column in front and back views; it is difficult and unnecessary.

Complete the reconstruction of the trunk in the multiple views before restoring the skull, neck, and tail in those views. Restore the vertebral column in front view first. Do this by placing the tracing paper with the front view over the lateral view reconstruction. Referring to figures 14-10 and 14-11b, align the ground lines with one another. Then slide the front-view sheet until the body midline runs across the top of the first dorsal's neural spine. Mark off the very top of the neural spine on the body midline. Using this reference point, take the front-view sketch of the first dorsal vertebra from the "bone library" and draw it in place, taking care to adjust for any tilt of the vertebra. Do the same for each succeeding dorsal vertebra that can be seen in front view, drawing in only those parts not obscured by the vertebra before. After this, restore the dorsal column in top view (fig. 14-11c). Follow the same method used for the front view. Overlay the top-view sheet on the side-view reconstruction, aligning the transverse plane lines with one another. Mark out the positions of tips of the neural spines and transverse processes relative to the body midline. Then use the front view of the vertebral column to mark out where the tips of the transverse processes are astride the body mid-

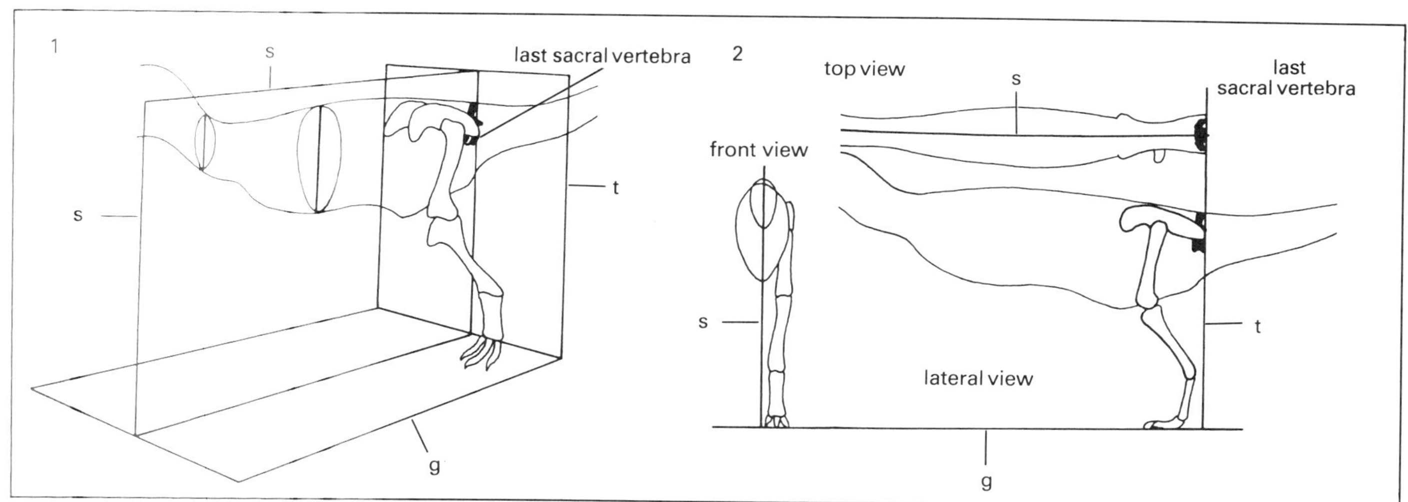

14-10. A schematic representation of the three planes needed to triangulate a skeleton in three or more views. *(1)* Three-quarter view showing all three planes in relation to the skeleton: a ground plane *(g)*, a body sagittal plane *(s)*, and a transverse plane at the base of the tail *(t)*. *(2)* These planes as represented by lines in the lateral view (only the ground line and transverse line are seen here), sagittal line in front view, and the sagittal line and transverse line in top view. These lines and planes form the base for the multiview reconstruction shown in the rest of the figure. Pen-and-ink on tracing paper, by Gregory S. Paul.

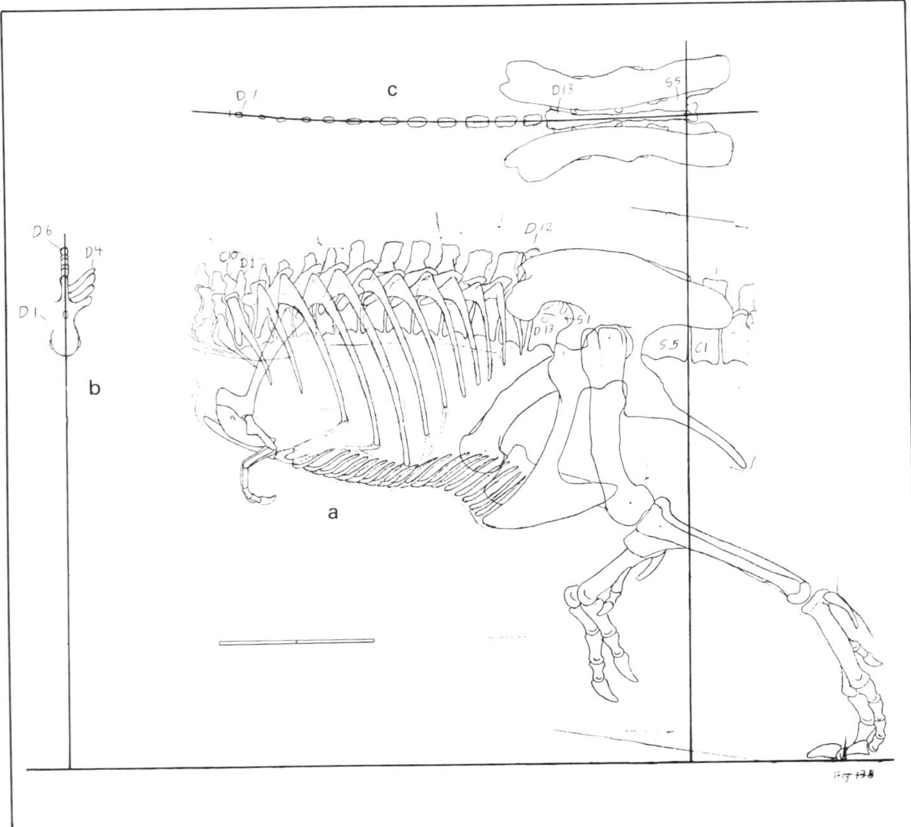

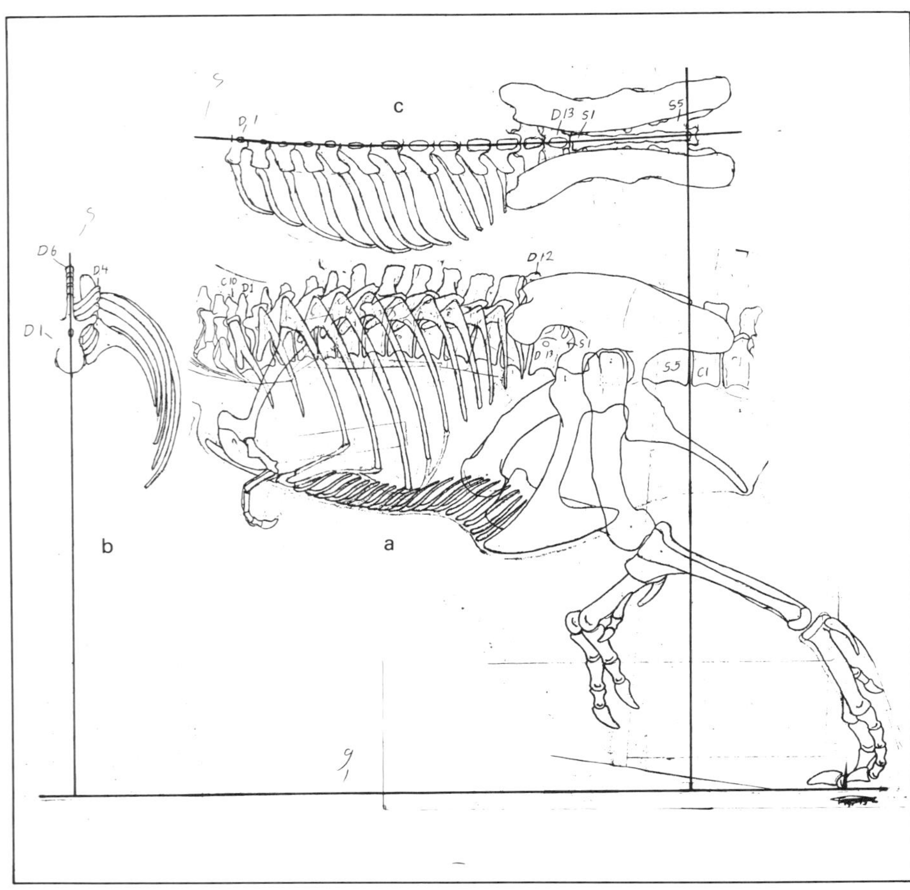

line. Plot
zygapophy
draw in ea
Use these
to plot out
centra, th
and limb e
views (figs
one side
the latera
animals
symmetric
be flipped

The rib
present t
cause the
ticulation
difficult t
that requ
expert.
construct
Articulat
the verte
lated sp
cages aid
It is best
front vie
lateral

Top left:
14-11. Th
top and fr
penciled
ground li
plane cut
have bee
ground li
the body
drawn in
as outlin
cil in the
flexed li
and a tra
cutting t
been dra
artist ha
baseline
verse pr
and pelv
Pencil
Paul.

Bottom
14-12.
view *(b*
front ar
has bee
view *(c*
Gregor

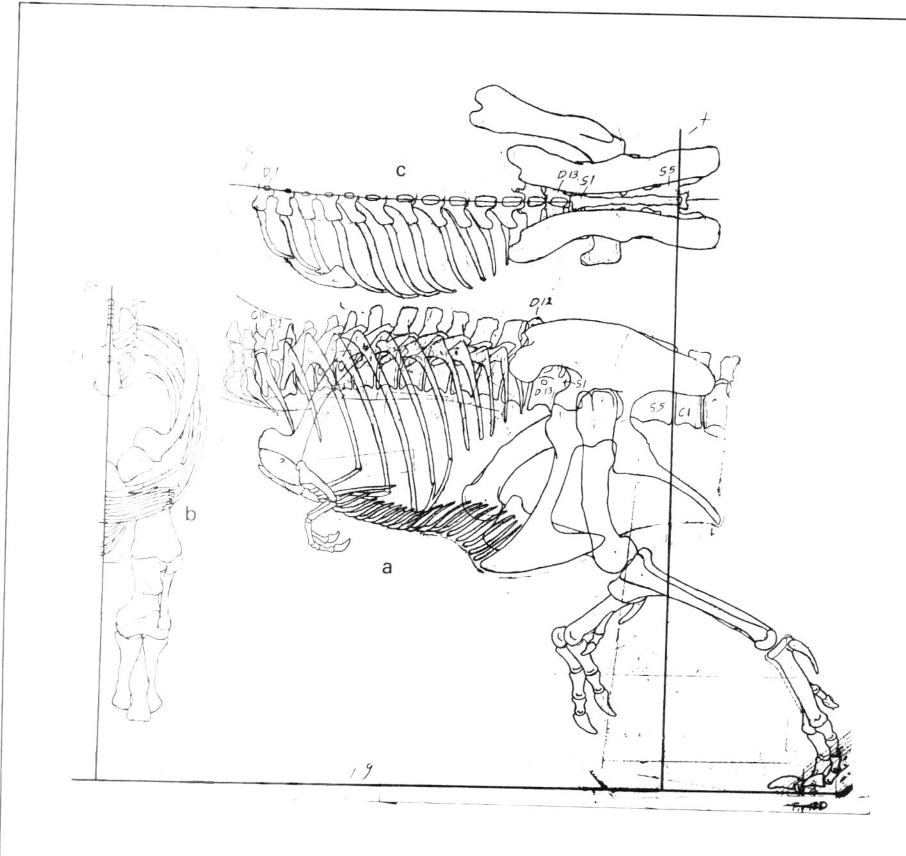

14-13. The shoulder girdle restored, first in front view *(b)* and then checked in top view *(c)*. The forelimbs and the hindlimbs have been added in both views. Pencil on tracing paper, by Gregory S. Paul.

check its appearance in top view (see fig. 14-12). Sometimes the top view will show that the front and lateral views are restored incorrectly. For clarity, draw in only those parts of the ribs not obscured by other ribs. Next restore the shoulder girdle front and top views (see fig. 14-13). Further alterations to the rib cage may be required. This is a potential point of crisis in reconstructing a quadrupedal animal since the front and top views of the shoulder girdle may reveal that the lateral reconstruction of the girdle is in error. If so, the shoulder girdle may have to be shifted upon the rib cage, changing the whole posture of the animal relative to the ground. In turn, the top and front views may have to be redone completely. But such errors will occur. Note that the shoulder girdle was shifted posteriorly in the restoration in figures 14-11 and 14-12 from figure 14-13; however, since the tyrannosaur is a biped, the posture of the body and hindlimbs was unaffected.

Once the dorsal-sacral column, rib cage, shoulder girdle, and pelvis are properly restored in top view, the limb elements can be triangulated into the front and top views (see fig. 14-13). Use the elements from the "bone library" as guides to trace or sketch in the limbs, showing only the parts that would be visible from whichever view is being drawn.

Having finished the trunk and limbs, restore the neck and tail in top view with the same basic methods used for the dorsal column. It is best not to restore the neck in the front view or the tail in a back view, however, since doing so is inordinately difficult and will obscure the trunk and limbs. Although a back-view restoration of the skeleton follows the same methodology as the front view, it is easier because the pelvis is usually a solidly built structure that is fairly simple to reconstruct.

The Skull

The last part of the skeleton to be considered is the skull. In a sense the skull is a separate entity from the rest of the skeleton. Skulls are very complex structures; the relationship of the mouth roof elements to one another, in particular, may not be as obvious as, for example, the relationship of each vertebra to another, so the skull may require as much effort to reconstruct as the entire rest of the skeleton.

If the skull being restored is partial and disarticulated but the missing parts are duplicated from other individuals or closely related species, use the techniques outlined above for the rest of the skeleton. The individual bones of the skull may be illustrated separately. It is useful to do skull reconstructions simultaneously in multiple views, side and top at least, in order to avoid serious errors that may occur if the skull is reconstructed in one view only. In addition to the standard lateral, posterior, and dorsal views of a completed skull, a three-quarter view is invaluable for explaining the complex structure of a skull to the reader (fig. 14-14).

To add the skull to the skeletal reconstruction, prepare a simplified pencil sketch of the outer skull and jaws showing the suture lines in lateral and top views at the proper scale. In tyrannosaurs, a spherical "condyle" of the skull's braincase articulates with a cup that is formed by the first, or atlas, vertebra. This is a simple ball-and-socket joint and permits the head to revolve. Pick a suitable pose for the skull and jaws and add them to the top and lateral skeletal reconstructions.

OTHER ELEMENTS IN RECONSTRUCTION

Musculature

Once the reconstruction of the skeleton is complete, the contours of the head and body may be reconstructed with the addition of appropriate soft parts, primarily the muscles. There are two basic types of muscle restorations. One consists of detailed, muscle-by-muscle restoration for specific scientific purposes. Only a few specific muscles may be restored, or the animal's whole musculature may be built up in detail by the illustrator. To do so requires examination of the bones for muscle scars that mark points of insertion, for important processes that anchor or guide certain muscles, and extrapolation from the musculature of analogous living vertebrates. Estimating the bulk of specific muscles depends on the size of insertions and the probable power requirements. The process of interpreting clues from bones for reconstruction of soft parts should not be represented as a hard science. Sometimes definite statements can be made; in other instances, only guesses are possible.

The other type of muscle restoration is for artistic purposes. Here the principles are the same as those just outlined, but the artist is concerned only with the contour muscles, which determine the external shape of the live animal. These restorations can be quite informal but can and must be functional and reflect the animal's shape in a realistic manner (fig. 14-15).

Body Covering

The scientist decides how the skin pattern, texture, and color will be depicted, based on whatever

evidence e
trators m
input or
skin patte
many foss
sions hav
for all of t
groups, i
Some ski
saic patt
scales an
iously siz
tubercles
small the
pear to re
dotherms
rhinos, a
saurs, ar
moregula
Tyrannos
as an adu
hatchling
substanc
rough ar
over the
skull (se
the foot

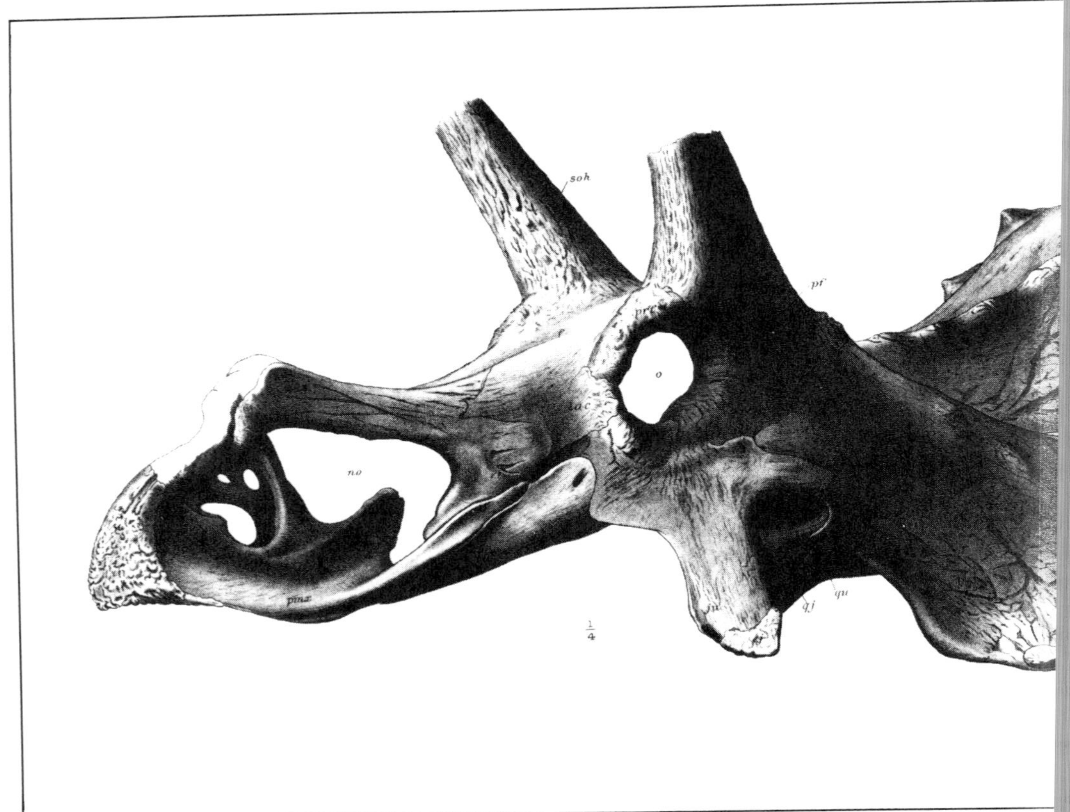

14-14. Three-quarter view of the skull of the horned dinosaur *Triceratops horridus*. Pencil, by Frederick Berger (U.S. Geological Survey Monographs, 1907).

14-15. Muscle restoration of the tyrannosaur *Albertosaurus libratus*, with superficial and major contour muscles shown. (Scale bar equals 1 meter.) China marker and Stabilo pencil on coquille board, by Gregory S. Paul.

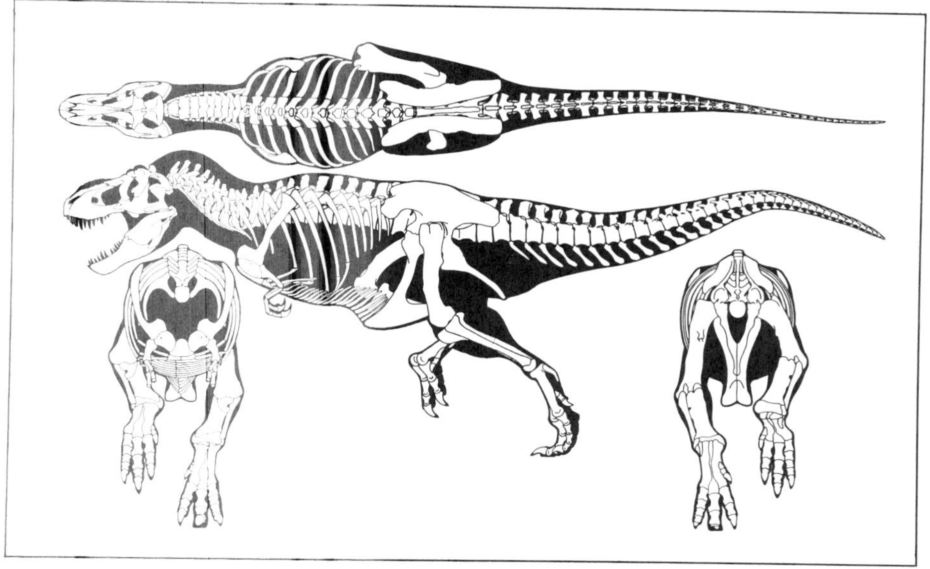

14-16. Completely restored skeleton of *Tyrannosaurus rex* in multiple views. Pen-and-ink on tracing paper, by Gregory S. Paul.

structed with confidence from fossil trackways.

Color is the least knowable and also the least important aspect of dinosaur reconstruction. Nonetheless, the question most frequently asked an illustrator is how he or she knew the animal's color. Large dinosaurs, like most large modern-day animals, may have been dun, earth, or green colored; small dinosaurs, like modern-day small mammals, reptiles, and birds, may have been brightly colored. It is probable that camouflage patterns, sometimes bold, were often present. Like their reptile ancestors and probable bird descendants, dinosaurs likely had color vision. Special color patterns concentrated around the head and neck may have been important as display devices. The designs and variations in color may have been arranged symmetrically with relation to the whole body, analogous to most animals of today.

Representation

The final reconstructions may be depicted as drawings, paintings, or diagrams. The form of representation is determined by what most clearly communicates the concept being illustrated, and this is best decided by the scientist and illustrator together. In order to show the relationship between the skeleton and the reconstructed flesh, a drawing of the skeleton surrounded by an outline of the body may be prepared. One way to clarify and dramatize such illustrations is to draw white bones against a solid black background of flesh (fig. 14-16). When this is done, it is best to keep detail on individual bones to a minimum. The skeletons can be drawn to a standard size (the length of the femur is a good constant), and all animals of similar form can be posed in the same manner. If carefully done, such skeletal restorations are valuable comparative tools for examining differences and similarities. A scale bar may or may not be included. Occasionally the artist has the opportunity to prepare a painting or drawing of the subject against a reconstructed landscape (fig. 14-17).

Any rendering technique that suits the purpose of the drawing can be used. Reconstructions for scientific journals are usually prepared in one of the various black-and-white drawing media to illustrate a particular technical feature. The form of representation may determine the technique chosen—for instance, pen-and-ink to represent white bones on a black background. Pencil on coquille board was chosen for several of the illustrations in this chapter largely because it is a fast way to shade and it effectively conveys the feeling of bone texture.

Behavio

In ord
realism.
somethin
havior an
lationshi
surround
render fa
of the an
sential; t
lifelike p
tured. U
nical inf
common
attempt
the subj
the limb
cast of t
alism, t
much a
mal's e
food an
tors or
animals
its dem
mation
suggest
fossil re

The
wealth
in reco
and fe
mamm
and gri
teeth c
adapte
incisor
the ca
(Chapt
tail.)

FINA

In c
and b
ical a

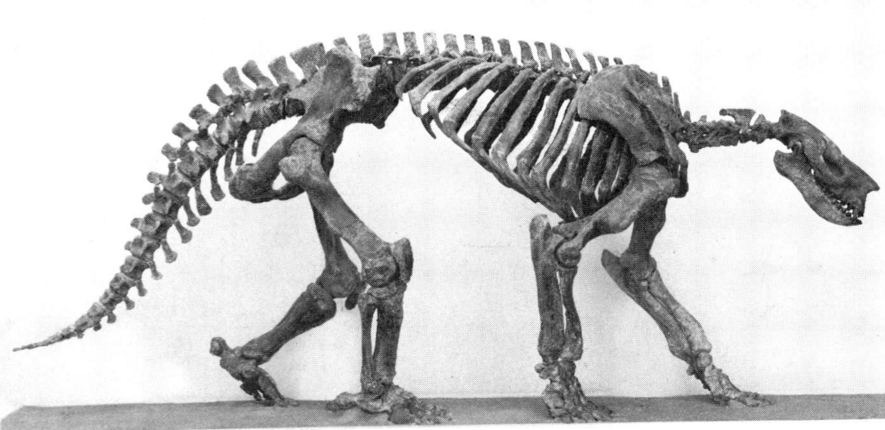

a

b

14-17.
habitat
Paleoc
illustra
Court
tory a
sity. F
the U
Philos

can be gathered, a plausible conception of the appearance and behavior of the extinct animal can be imagined by the illustrator and the final steps in the preparation of a reconstruction may be attempted (fig. 14-18).

First, it is good practice to sketch the animal in a variety of positions and activities before deciding on the final pose. While drafting these initial sketches, the artist should be mindful of the presumed or probable habits and temperament of the animal. The reconstruction may be blocked out by preparing a drawing of the skeleton in the desired position, then making a series of tracing-paper overlays of the muscle structure and skin.

Modelmaking

It is often helpful to construct a plasticine or Klean Klay model as an aid to visualizing the relative breadth or foreshortening of the animal's head and trunk in various oblique views. For greater accuracy, such a model can be built up over a scaled-down, sculpted facsimile of the skeleton, or templates can be used as guides to the dimensions of the trunk and other parts. A skeletal framework or templates can be made from such materials as balsa wood, wire, and Styrofoam. Charles Knight, who painted numerous large murals of prehistoric life for the Field Museum in Chicago and the American Museum of Natural History in New York in the 1930s and 1940s, constructed such models as an aid to proper distribution of light and shadow in his paintings.

The process of building a three-dimensional reconstruction from skull through musculature, cartilage, fat, glands, and skin is illustrated in figures 14-19 through 14-22. This reconstruction by John Gurche was based on knowledge he gained through dissections of modern human and ape cadavers; the same research process is used to reconstruct other animals. Marks on the fossil bones indicating origins and insertions of muscles provided clues as to the locations and sizes of muscles. Klean Klay was used because it permits the use of silicone as a molding material.

Whatever techniques are employed, the successful completion of any paleoreconstruction utilizes the skill and knowledge of both the artist and the scientist, a mutual effort that can result in paleobiological reconstructions that are both technically as accurate as the state of the science allows and artistically pleasing to the eye.

14-18. Reconstruction of the 2.5-ton duckbill dinosaur *Hypacrosaurus casuarius*. This reconstruction is uniquely accurate because it is based upon a virtually complete skeleton found in a very lifelike pose similar to that shown here; much of the skin and body profile, the frill along the back, the long vertical shoulder skin folds, the ossicles beneath the hips, and the skin texture were preserved as impressions. China marker and Stabilo pencil on coquille board, by Gregory S. Paul.

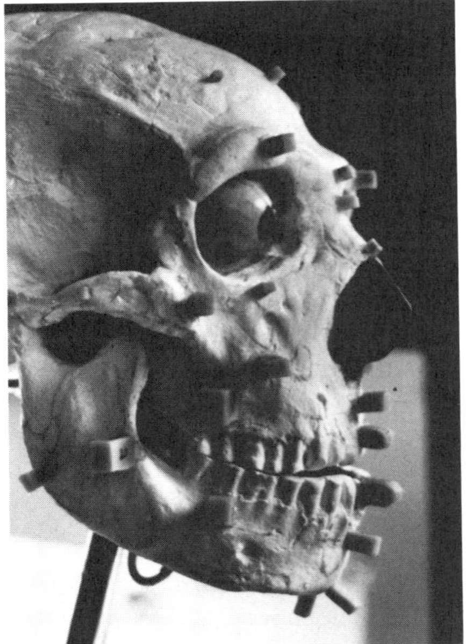

14-19. Three-dimensional reconstruction of the face of Shanidar I, a Neanderthal man from Iraq. A cast of the original fossil was reconstructed with plaster and epoxy putty to restore missing or damaged portions. Acrylic eyeballs were placed in the orbits, their size based on relative size in modern humans, their position based on dissections of human and ape faces.

Blocks of Artgum eraser representing tissue thickness data taken from modern cadavers were glued to the plaster skull as a general guideline, to be overridden when muscle markings on the bone indicated stronger or weaker muscles. To add a cartilaginous nasal septum, a line is projected from the distal third of the nasal bones, following their direction. The point of attachment of the base of the nasal septum (the nasal spine in later hominids) is located, and a line drawn from this to form an angle close to 90 degrees to the first line. The intersection of these lines approximates the point at which the nasal septum dives deeply into the nose toward its point of basal attachment. This does not represent the tip of the nose. Klean Klay reconstruction by John Gurche. Photo by Chip Clark. Courtesy of the Smithsonian Institution.

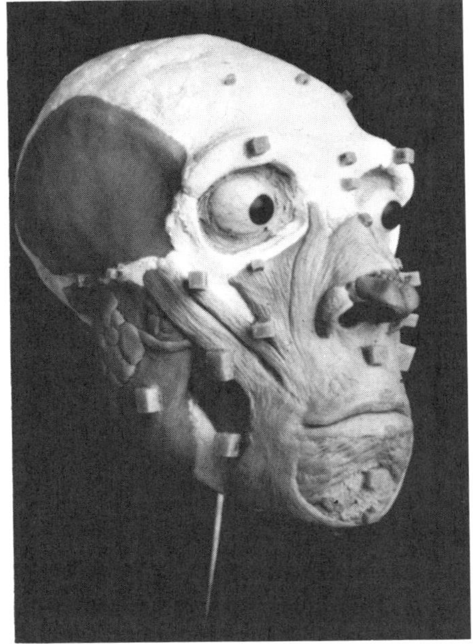

14-20. The masticatory muscles, overlying fascia, and parotid gland have been added, as well as many of the facial muscles. The lower lateral cartilages of the nose have been added, extending beyond the nasal septum, as in modern humans and apes. The fibrofatty tissue and muscle fibers making up the lateral wings of the nose can be placed with some reliability, as these muscle fibers always originate just medial to the origin of *levator anguli oris*, a muscle that lifts the corner of the mouth. Other clues to the nose's form are the projection of the nasal bones, the sloping of the borders of the piriform (nasal) aperture, and the position of the nasal spine. Klean Klay reconstruction by John Gurche. Photo by Chip Clark. Courtesy of the Smithsonian Institution.

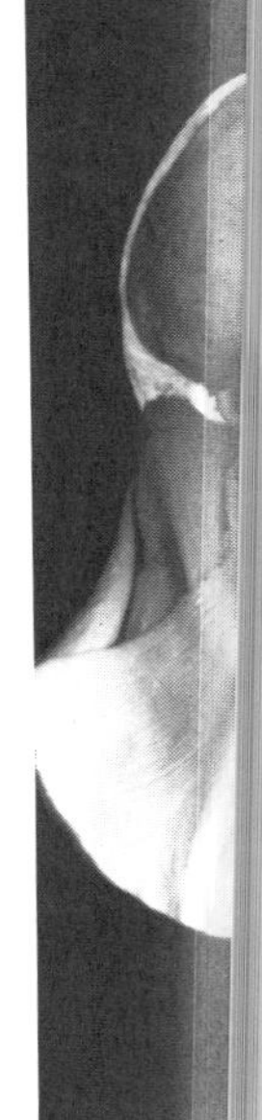

14-21. Th
been add
bit more
mans, ba
on the sk
has been
the neck.
tebrae cl
muscles,
culature,
modern h
tion by J
Clark. C
tution.

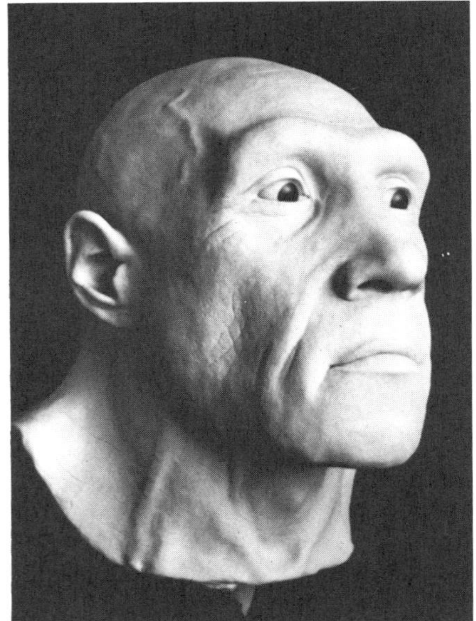

Left:
14-22. S
lowing t
mans. T
and alm
modern
the bro
cal data
them a
area de
edge-to
most m
oped ch
are no
of the
Klean K
Gurche
of the S

15/Illustrating Invertebrates

Elaine R. S. Hodges

Invertebrates have no true internal skeleton: as their name suggests, they have no spinal cord or vertebrae. They include animals as diverse as butterflies, clams, sea anemones, lobsters, microscopic mites, and fifty-foot giant squid. The groupings and discussions of animals in this chapter reflect the complexity of methods for handling them rather than their biological classification. Hence the phylum Arthropoda, especially class Insecta, is treated separately and extensively because there is such variation among the animals' sizes and methods of preservation.

The illustrator of invertebrates should read texts about invertebrates in general to get a "feel" for the entire group and more specialized material about each type of animal to be illustrated. The six volumes of *The Invertebrates*, by Libbie Hyman, and *Animals Without Backbones*, by Ralph Buchsbaum (see Bibliography), provide good general coverage. Some more specialized reading material for the nonscientist is available on certain groups such as insects, spiders, and mollusks that are collected by the lay public. The scientist client may be able to provide further pertinent reference material.

A way to appreciate invertebrate behavior and body movement is to observe live animals in insect or invertebrate zoos, found in some museums and traditional vertebrate zoos, or to collect and keep live animals for study. Books on insect flight will be helpful for accurately depicting this behavior. Courses in invertebrate zoology, entomology, and insect morphology are invaluable, providing an organized and firm foundation for understanding invertebrates. If associated plants or habitats are to be drawn, study of the structure of these organisms and environments is advisable.

A wide range of media can be used to illustrate invertebrates, although for research publications pen-and-ink is most commonly used. Some media are better suited than others for producing specific effects; for example, carbon dust, wash, and graphite lend themselves to the realistic depiction in black-and-white of the textures and translucency of many invertebrates such as the bells of jellyfish, the carapaces of ostracods, and the wings of insects. In some specialties conventions exist that encourage specific media and styles. For instance, many spider specialists not only want coquille board drawings but they expect such drawings to achieve heightened contrast with white edging separating structures (fig. 15-1). The scientist should inform the illustrator about any conventions to be followed.

Although the character of the animal and complexity of detail that must be shown, as well as conventions of a given specialty, may influence the choice of media, perhaps more important factors, as with all scientific illustration, are time available and the expected reproduction quality. For instance, although carbon dust technique might best duplicate the smooth texture and transparent anatomic layers to be shown in a worm, if the drawing is to be printed on uncoated stock in a journal with poor reproduction, pen-and-ink would be a safer choice. If time is a critical factor, stump-smudged pencil or coquille board techniques could be used. Examples of all black-and-white media renderings of invertebrates are found in this chapter and throughout the book.

Many invertebrates catch the popular interest or have economic importance and thus are illustrated in books for the layman, providing

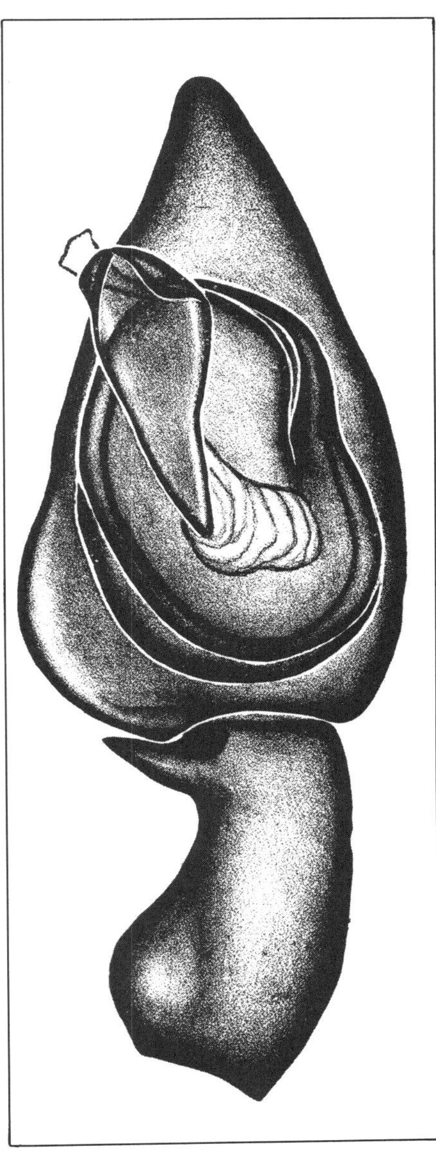

15-1. Ventral view of male spider palp showing convention of white outlining to define structure. *Acanthoctenus spinigerus*. Pencil on coquille board, by R. R. Forster. From "The Spiders of New Zealand," Part 4, *Otago Museum Bulletin*, 1973, by R. R. Forster and C. L. Wilton.

opportunities for color work. Watercolor has been most often used in these instances, but acrylics, oils, colored pencil, and mixed media also successfully depict invertebrates (see figs. C-1, C-4, C-10, C-16, C-18, C-28, C-32).

INSTRUMENTS AND MATERIALS

Because of the great range in size among invertebrates, the instruments and mounting materials used will depend on the group to be illustrated.

Optical Devices

Stereoscopic microscope: the most useful tool for the illustrator of invertebrates. There should be good working distance under the objectives, and the optics should be of good quality.

Reducing objective: to permit more of a specimen to be visible under the microscope.

Compound microscope: for use with minuscule invertebrates that must be mounted on microscope slides and require high magnification. Good-quality optics are important (see chapter 23). Special options such as phase contrast or dark-field illumination and polarizing attachments may be helpful or even necessary to see some features of very tiny animals.

Camera lucida: for both stereoscopic and compound microscopes.

Reticles: with grid, micrometer, as needed. The grid can be used instead of the camera lucida to create the rough drawing.

Microprojector: can be used instead of a camera lucida to create the rough drawing of slide-mounted specimens.

Opaque projector: either direct or indirect for enlarging or reducing drawings. The direct opaque projector can be used backward for drawing larger animals (see fig. 2-34). The indirect projector has a shelf that can hold a large specimen for tracing.

Stage micrometer: for obtaining a scale line on the drawing. Substitutes are a small piece of millimeter ruler on the microscope stage or in the specimen dish for camera lucida tracing, or a measuring reticle in the ocular. The stage micrometer can be projected from a microprojector or used with transmitted or reflected light with the compound or stereoscopic microscope (see fig. 2-9).

Measuring Devices

Rulers: clear plastic, 6 inch (15cm) and 12 inch (30cm), with millimeters and inches indicated, for measuring specimens and drawings.

Proportional dividers: at least 8 inch (20cm) or larger, for obtaining accurate proportions of invertebrates too large to outline under the microscope (see chapter 2).

Grid: an alternative for obtaining an accurate rough drawing of larger animals when an opaque projector and proportional dividers are unavailable (see chapter 2).

Specimen-handling Tools

Forceps: straight, finely pointed jeweler's; bent-nosed with serrated tips; long bottle type; pinning (see fig. 2-7).

Dissecting needle probe: size depending on specimen. A delicate probe can be made from a dowel and shortened, stiff hair from a camel- or sable-hair brush (no. 0). Commercially available probes with stiff metal needles are useful for large, hard-bodied invertebrates. Chapter 2 explains how to make a probe by mounting a minuten pin or needle in a dowel (see fig. 2-8).

Eyedropper (medicine dropper, pipette): one used for glycerin

only, othe
Long pipe
23cm) are
very small
tainers be
hood that
sucked in
available
sources; th
arately.

Specimen

Insect pin
less steel
used in flu
of all sizes

Sand, glas
slides, kn
bits, cover
mens.

Birdshot,
and nuts,
ceans in fl
large crust

Cardboard
cine: for d

Specimen
specimens
the micros

Container

Dishes: tra
and with
mens in flu

Aquarium
dishes: for

Covered b

Microscop
dinary flat
depressions
hold fluid.

Slide trays
porting mic

Clean glas
for live mat

Wetting A Preservati

Alcohol: 7(

Liquid glycerin.

Liquid household cleaner: such as Formula 409, Fantastik; for precipitating small crustaceans and for softening insect joints.

Mounting Materials

Glycerin jelly: texture like hard gelatin, must be heated to soften; for temporary slide mounts. Available from biological supply sources (see Appendix).

Paraffin wax: melted on the bottom of glass or metal containers to permit the positioning of specimens with pins inserted in the wax. Usually such specimens are in fluid.

Clear fingernail polish, white glue: to mount broken parts from dried insects.

Beeswax, kneaded rubber eraser: molded into shapes to support specimens.

Miscellaneous

Matches, laboratory hot plate: for softening glycerin jelly.

Paper scraps: black and white, to place under specimens, especially under the microscope.

Lens tissue: to clean microscope slides.

Mothballs: for storage of dry insects.

CARE AND HANDLING OF SPECIMENS

All invertebrate specimens are subjected to some kind of fixing or preservative process to keep them from deteriorating. Many also require special preparation of one kind or another to reveal the taxonomically important characters that the illustrator will be required to depict. Methods for handling dry specimens in each invertebrate group tend to be specialized and are discussed with each group.

Liquid Storage

Many invertebrates are too large to be mounted on a slide and are usually stored and studied in alcohol or other fluids. Invertebrates in wet media can be viewed from many directions, and structure can be more easily interpreted than if the specimen were fixed on a slide. Never allow wet specimens to dry out; keep them covered with liquid.

The illustrator should learn to recognize the characteristic odors of liquid preservatives and should keep additional quantities on hand. Labels accompanying specimens may or may not indicate which one is in use, and it is essential to replenish the specimen's fluid with the same fluid. The most widely used liquid preservative is ethyl alcohol (ethanol). Liquid glycerin also is used for some specimens such as beetle genitalia. A dilute aqueous solution of formaldehyde, called Formalin (formol) is the principal liquid preservative for certain groups of animals such as some crustacea, medusae (jellyfishes), and for mixed plankton. Because Formalin has a weak acid reaction, it must be buffered by the scientist to prevent damage to specimens with calcareous parts. Formalin can "freeze" some animals into awkward positions and make them very brittle and fragile.

Formalin gives off fumes that are hazardous to breathe. It is usually permissible to transfer specimens kept in Formalin to a tray of water during illustration. If the scientist feels the specimen must be kept in a tray of Formalin, maintain adequate ventilation at all times. This is especially important when drawing specimens with the camera lucida attachment on a microscope, because formaldehyde fumes will tend to rise directly into the observer's nose and eyes. A plastic bag placed over the microscope and specimen—with holes cut for the oculars and focusing knob—will contain most fumes.

Alcohol and water evaporate quickly under hot microscope lights, so check the liquid level frequently and make it a habit to cover the specimen container securely whenever you leave the drawing board.

Glycerin does not evaporate readily. On the contrary, it tends to absorb moisture from the air, becoming more fluid and increasing in volume. If the fluid level rises too high, there is a danger that the specimen will float out. Specimens remain still better in fresh glycerin because it is at its most viscous when fresh. Adding a small amount of glycerin to alcohol will help keep the specimen soft. (Obtain the scientist's approval before adding it, or anything else, to preserving fluid.)

At the end of each day, it is best to return the specimen to its storage container. If you do not want to move the specimen out of position, it is permissible to leave it in the observation container if the following precautions are taken: add as much liquid as the container will safely hold and cover it. Taping the cover to the container further reduces evaporation for a day or more, but the taping process may disturb the specimen. Experience will determine how fast evaporation from each size of container and specimen occurs.

Wet specimens can be manipulated for study with forceps, dissecting needles or probes, minutens (see fig. 2-8), and brushes. An eyedropper or pipette, fine sable-hair brush dipped in the preservative, or fine forceps will shift tiny specimens to and from storage bottles. Always check under magnification to see that no part of a tiny specimen has been left on the tool. Ask the scientist which implement is preferred for each specimen.

Always *lift* the specimen into and out of containers. Avoid pulling it over the edge of a container, especially a dish with a ground-glass edge. A rough edge could damage the specimen.

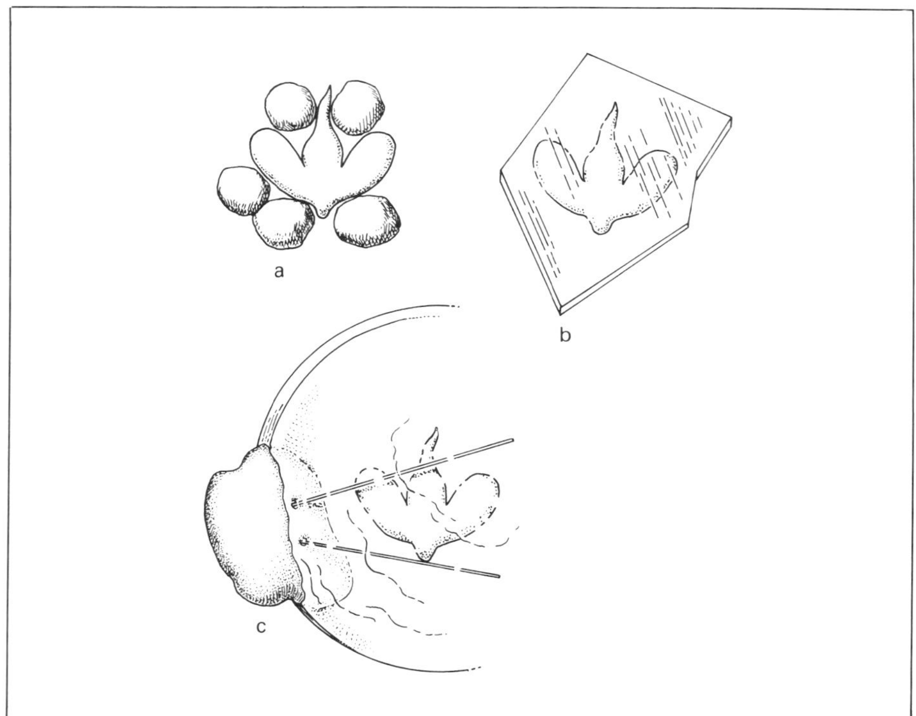

15-2. Methods of securing microscopic specimens in liquid: *(a)* glass beads or sand grains; *(b)* piece of cover slip atop specimen; *(c)* a "fence" created with hairs extending from plasticine pressed into the side of a well-slide. Gillott 659 pen and ink on Bristol board, by Elaine R. S. Hodges.

Whether a transparent or opaque, light or dark container is used depends on the character of the specimen and what you want to see. A white container will reflect light and increase its intensity around the specimen, which is especially helpful for dark specimens. The outline of a very light specimen is sometimes easier to see against a dark background. If the specimen is translucent and internal structures are important, a transparent container will permit visualization with substage lighting (transillumination).

Mounting the Specimen

To hold a small specimen in place in liquid, one or more of the following can be used, depending on the specimen, the liquid medium, the need for transparency, and the scientist's preference: light or dark sand grains, tiny glass beads, broken pieces of microscope slides or cover slips, bits of kneaded rubber eraser, or minuten pins in paraffin wax (see Slide Mounts, below). Ask the scientist before using any material that might leave residue on the specimen. Sometimes one part of a dissected specimen can be balanced on another separated part. Pieces of slides or cover slips dropped on top of microscopic specimens will secure them. Plasticine pressed onto the edge of a well-slide can support one or more hairs from a brush or two eyelashes, which then act as a "fence" supporting the specimen (fig. 15-2).

For larger, opaque specimens, use paraffin melted on the bottom of a metal or heatproof container. Position the specimen with pins. Do not stick pins through the specimen without the permission of the scientist.

Regardless of the propping method used, all specimens should be cleaned when the drawing is finished by teasing off any debris that may have drifted into the liquid. Use minutens or forceps very gently. Do not try to remove debris that was on the specimen origi-

pared with balsam or other mounting media. Temporary slides might be made with glycerin, lactic acid, water, or no fluid. A medium between permanent and temporary is glycerin jelly; it holds specimens in place very well and does not heat up quickly under microprojector lights as liquid glycerin does. The specimen should be cleared (internal organs dissolved chemically) by the scientist before it is put into glycerin jelly so structure will not be obscured by muscles and other soft anatomy. Glycerin jelly requires very low, carefully controlled heat on a laboratory hot plate or from a lighted match under the slide to soften it enough to insert, move, or remove the specimen. Experiment to determine the optimum heat: the ideal consistency is like soft molasses. If the jelly becomes too hot, it will form air bubbles, which enter and obscure the specimen. Bubbles can be gently removed with a needle after the jelly is cooled and then reheated slightly. A cover slip is not necessary over the jelly, and the slides can be stored vertically if room temperature is not too warm.

Handling Slides

Keep fingers off the slide's cover slip or where the specimen lies. If the slide is less than one year old (note date on label or ask the scientist), the specimen still can shift, so be especially careful to keep the slide flat and do not stack it. Even permanent mounts may take a year or more to dry completely; thicker slides take even longer. Temporary slide mounts are wet (usually with glycerin) and especially prone to picking up dust on the sticky edges of their cover slips (which cannot be cleaned without moving the specimen). All slides not in use should be kept in a covered box to prevent dust accumulation.

Permanent, dried slides are relatively sturdy and can be cleaned before each drawing session with lens tissue. While holding the slide with the specimen uppermost, gently polish the cover slip and the bottom of the slide under the specimen. Permanent slides still should be protected; they are glass, thin, and easily broken if dropped or dropped upon.

Studying the Specimen on a Slide

It is sometimes possible to overcome the rigidity of the single view presented by a permanent slide by tilting it as the focus on the microscope is adjusted. The slide can be kept in this position for drawing by balancing it on supports such as pennies or erasers while it is on the microprojector or under the microscope. Check with the scientist to be sure that this is not a distorted view.

For a rear view, turn the slide over, balancing its label spaces on two pennies to keep the cover slip from contacting the microscope stage. Be sure to remove it very carefully so that the cover slip does not hit the stage. Do not tilt or reverse a freshly mounted or temporary slide.

So much of a slide-mounted specimen is visible internally and externally under the microscope that it confuses the beginner. Repeatedly focus up and down to distinguish what is above from what is below, and their interrelationship. Change from substage lighting to reflected light with white, black, or ground-glass stage plates. Try to obtain additional unmounted specimens of the same species for manipulation. Make sure that the specimen is mounted right side up for drawing; if it is not, reverse the slide or the drawing.

It is important to learn to distinguish the important from the unimportant. The illustrator need not draw everything in view. Sometimes only the surface structures are drawn, and sometimes everything is shown, but with varying lines and textures. For instance, learn to differentiate folds from sutures, the internal edge of a telescoping abdomen from external color pattern, distortions and broken parts from correct anatomy. Rarely are parts in perfect position for illustration, hence the animal often must be repositioned for each feature to be drawn. Each view can be drawn on a separate piece or part of drafting film or tracing paper, the pieces to be compiled later (see chapter 1).

In general, invertebrate parts, sutures, edges, and setae are more or less symmetrical, so a clue to the authenticity of a structure's appearance is provided by the presence or absence of a comparable structure on the other side of the specimen. If a similarly shaped or placed structure is on both sides of the animal, it is less likely to be an artifact, such as dirt or a deformity. If the structures are symmetrical, they usually should be drawn identically on both sides of the animal. It is important to remember, however, that asymmetry may exist and sometimes is important.

When a drawing of a very detailed surface is required, it may save time to have an ordinary or electron microscope photograph of the specimen as a reference. Punctures and other details can be counted or even traced from the photo.

Major invertebrate groups and appropriate techniques for handling them are described below. A complete discussion of invertebrates for illustration might include two groups now considered to be separate from the kingdom Animalia: Prokaryota and Protista.

PROKARYOTA

Organisms that have no discrete nuclei in their cells—bacteria—compose what some scientists today call the superkingdom Prokaryota. Within the cell, there are no membrane-bounded structures or organelles such as mitochondria

---

John O. Corliss contributed to the text on Prokaryota and Protista.

or chloroplasts. Despite their lack of a "true" nucleus, they often have a single strand of DNA and small ribosomes are found in the cytoplasm. Usually a rigid wall surrounds the single cell, and any flagella that are present differ radically from the flagella of eukaryotes (organisms with membrane-bounded nuclei and other organelles).

Because of their very small size, bacteria must be observed under the higher powers of a compound microscope (often using phase contrast and dark-field optics) or preferably with electron microscopy. (Refer to "Electron Microscopy as a Tool for Scientific Illustrators," by Mary-Jacque Mann and Elaine R. S. Hodges—see Bibliography.)

Since the specimen is likely to be on a microscope slide, apply the rules for handling slide mounts. If the specimen is photographed or viewed through an electron microscope, the scientist or a technician is likely to handle and position it. If only electron micrographs are available for reference, drawings can be made from these (see fig. 15-4).

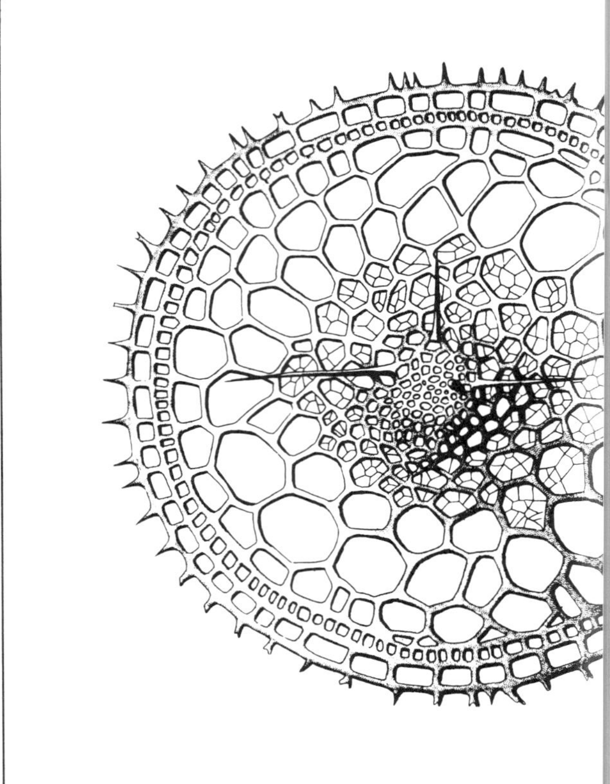

15-3. A radiolarian, *Eucecryphalus gegenbauri*. From *Die* … Haeckel. Drawing by Ernst Haeckel. Medium unknown.

PROTISTA

Organisms that constitute the kingdom Protista are (lower) eukaryotes, have only one tissue type, and usually are unicellular and microscopic. Even the larger multicellular protists do not have differentiated tissue types. There are more species of protists—some 120,000 have been described—than any other animal or plant group except insects. Some are parasitic, causing diseases in animals and plants. Many protists are found in water and were first discovered by early microscopists curious about the invisible forms of life about them. Drawings from the eighteenth and nineteenth centuries are still among the most beautiful to be found (fig. 15-3).

The Protista generally are thought to include such common forms as the amoebae, various simple algae, euglenoids, flagellates, radiolarians, diatoms, ciliates, foraminiferans, certain spore-forming parasites (sporozoans), slime nets, slime molds, and other funguslike eukaryotic microorganisms. Many of these organisms are often considered to be protozoa. Foraminifera are discussed in chapter 13 because they usually are drawn as fossils. Algae, although considered members of the Protista by many biologists today, usually are studied by botanists and drawn by botanical illustrators; thus they are covered in chapter 12.

The groups of protists are differentiated by kinds, shapes, and numbers of various cytoplasmic organelles or inclusions, cilia or pseudopodia, method of obtaining nutrition, presence or absence of cell walls or skeletal systems, method of reproduction, and other anatomic or life-cycle characteristics. Either the exterior (the test) or

the interr
ton) of so
material t
and comp
of the cel
of locom
plasmic
to illustra
sion (TE
electron
invaluabl
structures
light mic
graphs of
for drawi

Small
often are
scope slid
times on
best silho
pecially if
tions (op
These car
a stereo
camera l
suppleme
power of

if the preparation is not too thick. If the specimen is two or more millimeters in any dimension, the scientist might place it in alcohol or glycerin like any small part of an invertebrate. The scientist or illustrator can position it on sand grains or glass beads. The smallest protists might be provided on a slide, fixed (prepared chemically), and stained, or living in a drop of water under a cover slip. If the total preparation is thin enough, an oil immersion objective (with oil) will provide the highest compound microscope magnification (see chapter 23). Several hundred specimens might be on a single slide. Often a composite drawing is produced, using the best views of several specimens.

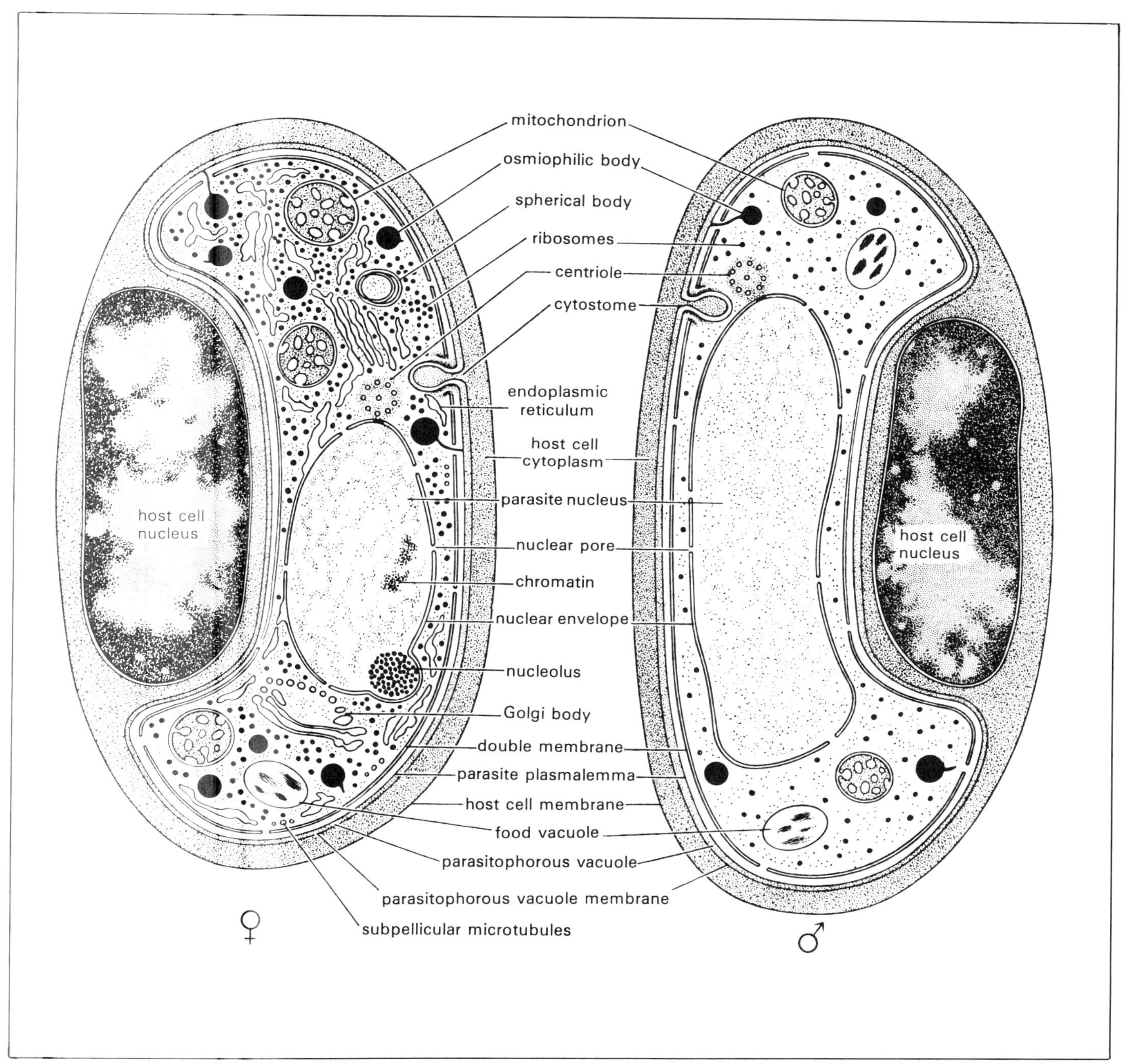

15-4. Sexual stage of avian malaria parasite in host red blood cell. This stage transmits the parasite from avian host to mosquito vector. The drawing is based on several electron micrographs of cells and is a composite, rather than a drawing of one cell. Pen-and-ink on Denril film, by Trudy Nicholson. From *Textbook on Malaria*, in press (Churchill Livingston, Edinburgh). Courtesy of Richard Carter, National Institutes of Health.

Nonarthropod Invertebrates

Invertebrates that are not arthropods do not have jointed legs. Otherwise they encompass a wide variety of animals of different shapes, textures, sizes, and lifestyles. Included in this group are sponges, gorgonians, stony corals, bryozoans, brachiopods, shelled mollusks, starfishes, brittle stars, anemones, sea cucumbers, and sea urchins, among others. Drying may obscure or obliterate important characters in some of these groups, so some of the specimens may be preserved in a liquid in order to retain features lost in drying.

SPONGES

Sponges form the phylum Porifera, "pore bearers," named for the microscopic pores through which food is carried by water currents created by the pumping action of collared cells (choanocyte chambers). One way to differentiate the various classes of sponges is by different skeletal framework materials. The calcareous sponges contain calcium-carbonate spicules; the glass sponges are characterized by six-rayed silica spicules. A third class, the demosponges, include horny sponges that have no spicules but have spongin fibers instead (the commercial sponges used for cleaning), or spongin fibers reinforced by sediment grains (fig. 15-5), and sponges containing some spongin as well as siliceous spicules that are not six-rayed.

Care and Handling

Large sponges often are preserved dry and are quite rugged, posing no special problems in handling. Fluid-preserved sponges are best kept immersed since their porous structure allows fluids to drain from them quickly. An all-glass aquarium of appropriate size serves well to permit undistorted observation from the side while keeping the specimen immersed.

Should drawings of spicules or stained sections (to show skeleton structure) be required, suitable slide preparations ordinarily will be provided by the scientist. Preparation of spicule mounts is a specialized procedure best accomplished by the scientist or trained technician. A compound microscope with both dark-field illumination and an oil-immersion objective may be needed for drawing siliceous spic-

ules wit
larizing
attachm
serving
spicules
The
minute
spicules
etrate th
so it is p
handling
must be
to delica

COEL

The r
terates
(hence
a mout

15-5. Sponge: *(a)* entire animal; *(b)* cross section showing reinforcing fibers and cortex tissue. *Psammocinia* species micronormo. 13 technical pen and ink on Mellotex book p *Marine Sponges—Forty-six Sponges of Northern New Zea* Battershill, P. R. Bergquist, and V. Ward (Leigh Laborat

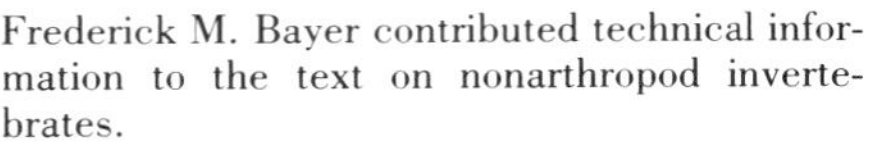

Frederick M. Bayer contributed technical information to the text on nonarthropod invertebrates.

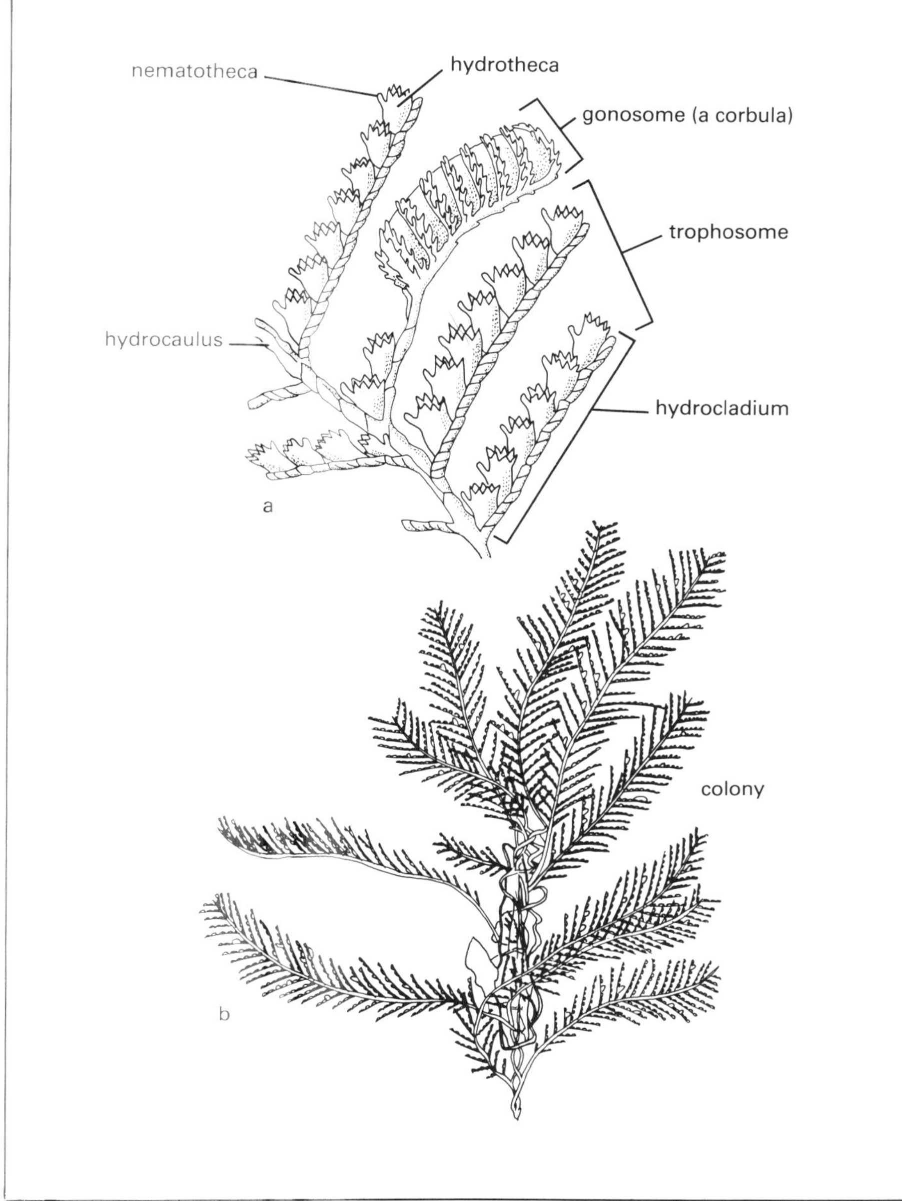

15-6. Coelenterata: plumularian hydroid. *(a)* Detail; *(b)* colony. Redrawn with technical pen and ink on Ageproof film with modifications, by Irene Jewett, from *British Zoophytes*, by G. Johnston (John Van Voorst, London, 1847).

This phylum (Coelenterata or Cnidaria) contains diverse animals such as hydroids, anemones (see fig. C-1), corals, and sea fans. Sometimes there is confusion between the names *hydroid* and *hydra*. Hydroids are branching colonial coelenterates (fig. 15-6), whereas the hydra is a small freshwater polyp, one stage of development in some coelenterates. A sessile form, the polyp is often an elongate cylinder fastened at the aboral end (the end opposite the mouth), with the mouth and tentacles at the free end. At another stage of development in some coelenterates, a free-swimming medusa forms, expanding radially into a bell, bowl, or saucer shape with tentacles around the margin. Jellyfish are medusae (fig. 15-7). Hydroids have both polyp and medusa stages.

In coelenterates, the whole animal, the skeleton, or parts may be illustrated (fig. 15-8). Optical magnification may or may not be required, depending upon the size and structure to be illustrated. Coelenterates are preserved in a variety of ways.

Care and Handling

Hydroids

Hydroids are preserved wet more commonly than dry, as only in this way are the polyps kept in good condition. Great care must be used in handling specimens, as the polyps can be damaged easily, and the reproductive structures often are so scarce that loss or damage through carelessness cannot be tolerated. Handling and positioning of specimens should be done with fine jeweler's forceps under constant observation with the dissecting microscope. Caution must be used in replacing the specimens in vials or bottles, to prevent damage by the sharp edges of labels in the containers.

Not infrequently, parts of hydroid colonies are prepared as stained whole mounts on glass slides, and these rather than the whole wet specimens are used for the preparation of drawings.

The terminology of the major hydroid structure that the illustrator may be expected to know is shown in figures 15-6 through 15-9.

Medusae

Medusae (jellyfish), the free-swimming stage of many hydroids and scyphozoan polyps, are usually preserved in Formalin and should be observed only in Formalin or water. Transferring to alcohol will damage tissue. Because of their delicate structure, jellyfishes should not be picked up (the sharp points of forceps will irreparably damage them); if possible, they should be poured carefully into the observation dish or tray, into which some fluid already has been poured. If necessary, small specimens can be picked up with a spoon and sufficiently small ones can be picked up

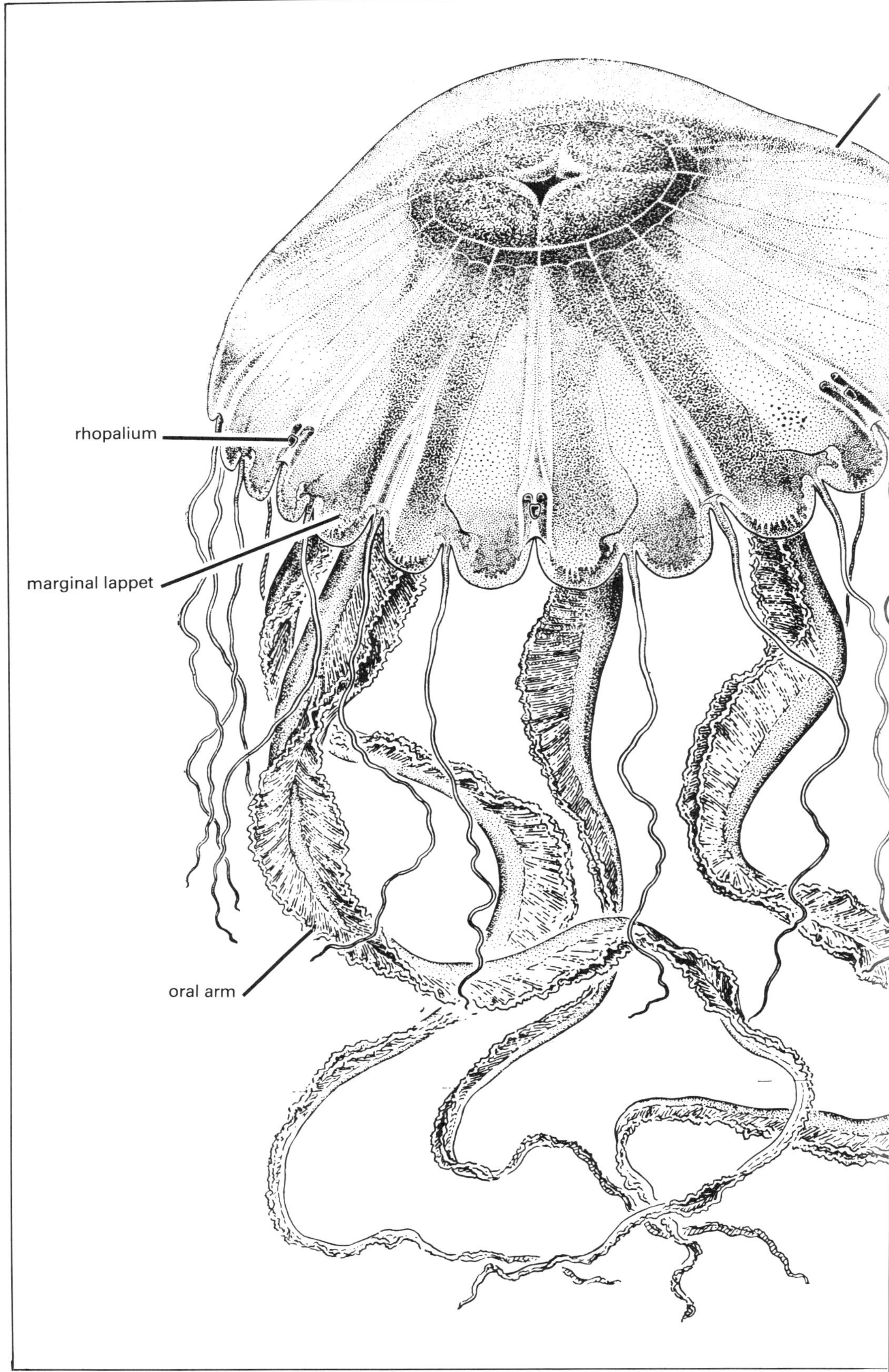

15-7. Coelenterata: Scyphomedusa. Artist and medium unknown. From *Scyphoid Medusae of the Seas of the USSR*, by D. V. Naumov (Isdatelstvo Akademii Nauk SSSR, 1961).

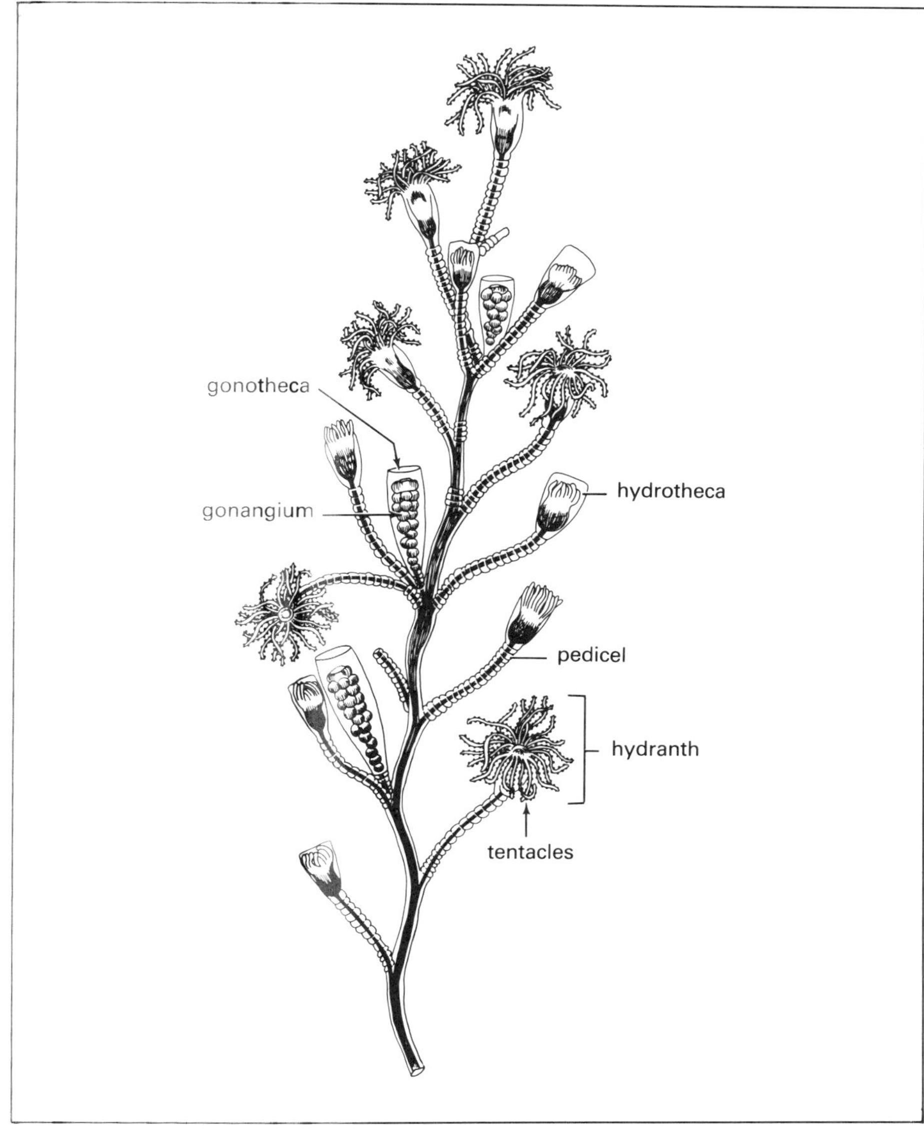

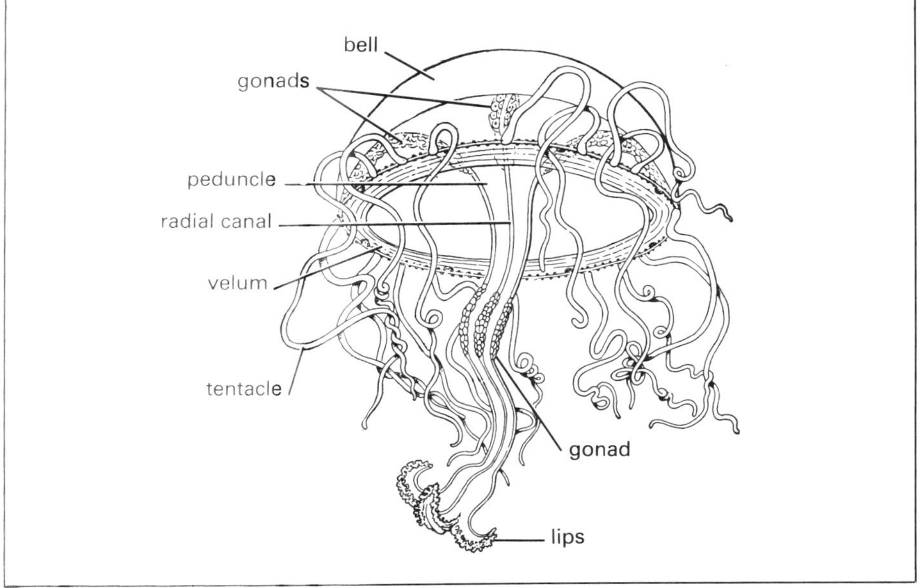

with a pipette. Needless to say, specimens should be replaced in their storage containers with equal care.

Stony Corals

Stony corals (Madreporaria or Scleractinia), if small, may be extremely delicate and should be handled with great care under the dissecting microscope (figs. 15-10, 15-11). Do not use modeling clay to hold the specimen in position because remnants of the clay may lodge in interstices of the coral skeleton and be difficult if not impossible to remove. Props and wedges of cardboard, wood, or glass are suitable supports. The same precaution pertains also to the stylasterine corals, which taxonomically belong to the Hydrozoa and are more closely related to the hydroids than to the stony corals.

Photography has for the most part supplanted drawing for the illustration of most kinds of corals, although certain structural details may lend themselves better to drawings.

Gorgonian Corals

Gorgonian corals (Octocorallia) —the sea fans, sea plumes, precious corals, and their relatives— are sometimes preserved in alcohol, sometimes dry, depending usually upon size. When dried, all of them are brittle and must be handled with care. The whole colonies ordinarily are illustrated by photography, but the distribution and form of polyps and the natural relationships of various kinds of

Top:
15-8. Campanulate hydroid colony. Redrawn with technical pen and ink on Ageproof film, by Irene Jewett, from *British Zoophytes*, by G. Johnston (John Van Voorst, London, 1847).

Bottom:
15-9. Coelenterata: Hydromedusa, *Eutima campanulata*. Pen-and-ink. Artist unknown. From *Medusae of the World*, by A. G. Mayer (Carnegie Institution of Washington, 1910).

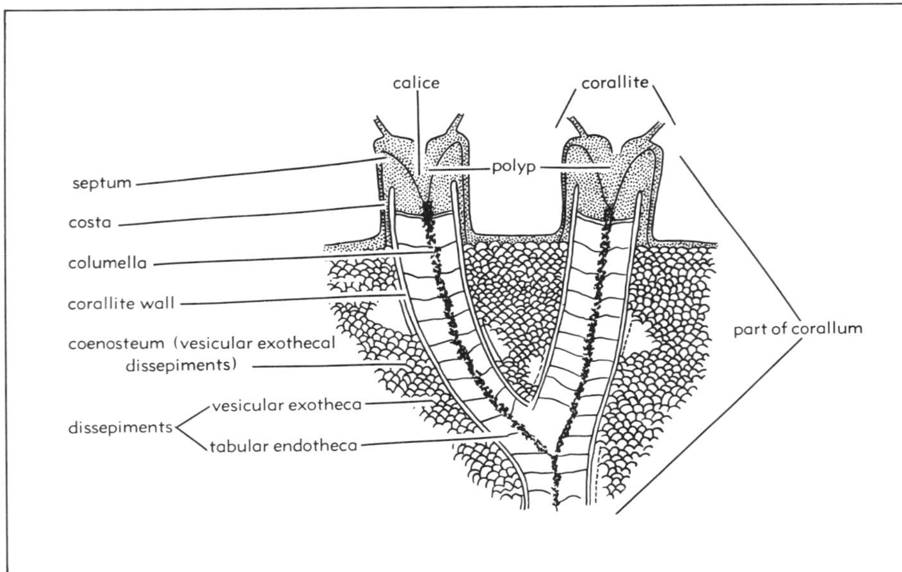

15-10. Coelenterata: coral. Scleractinia skeletal structure. Pen-and-ink. From *Treatise on Invertebrate Paleontology*, Part F. Courtesy of the Geological Society of America and the University of Kansas.

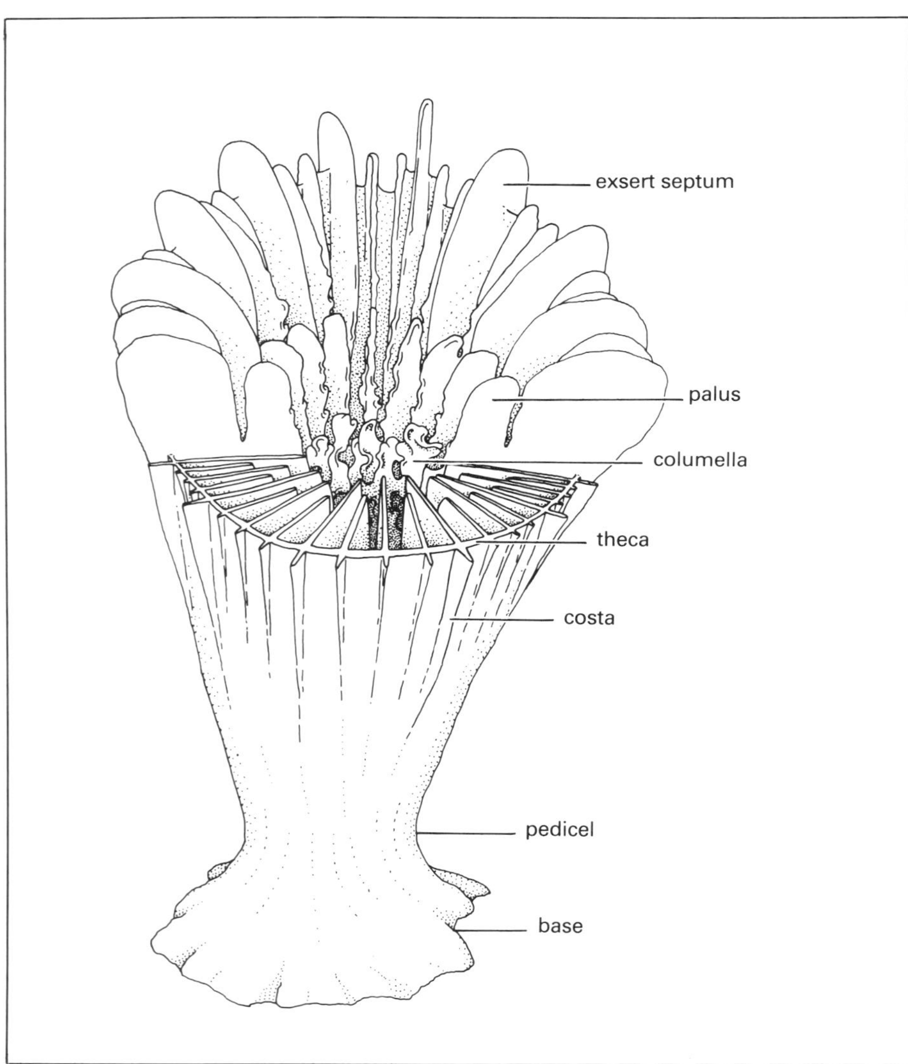

calcareous
visible at
men are b
ing (fig.
illustrator
lected sa
men, with
a small p
sary to w
great care
sitioning
under the
signment
scope m
stand is
2-24).

Wet w
kinds of
ble and
tray with
very brit
judicious
bers of t
fig. 15-1
with larg
cately a
as a brit
skeleton
delicate.
specime
of detac
minimiz
required
in the j
Scannin
(SEM) i
lustratin
at mode
75×).

Isolat
prepare
slides fo
ple tec
these, t
lustrate
tative s
15-13.

15-11. S
Technic
Charles
Stephen
Fauna o
(NOAA.

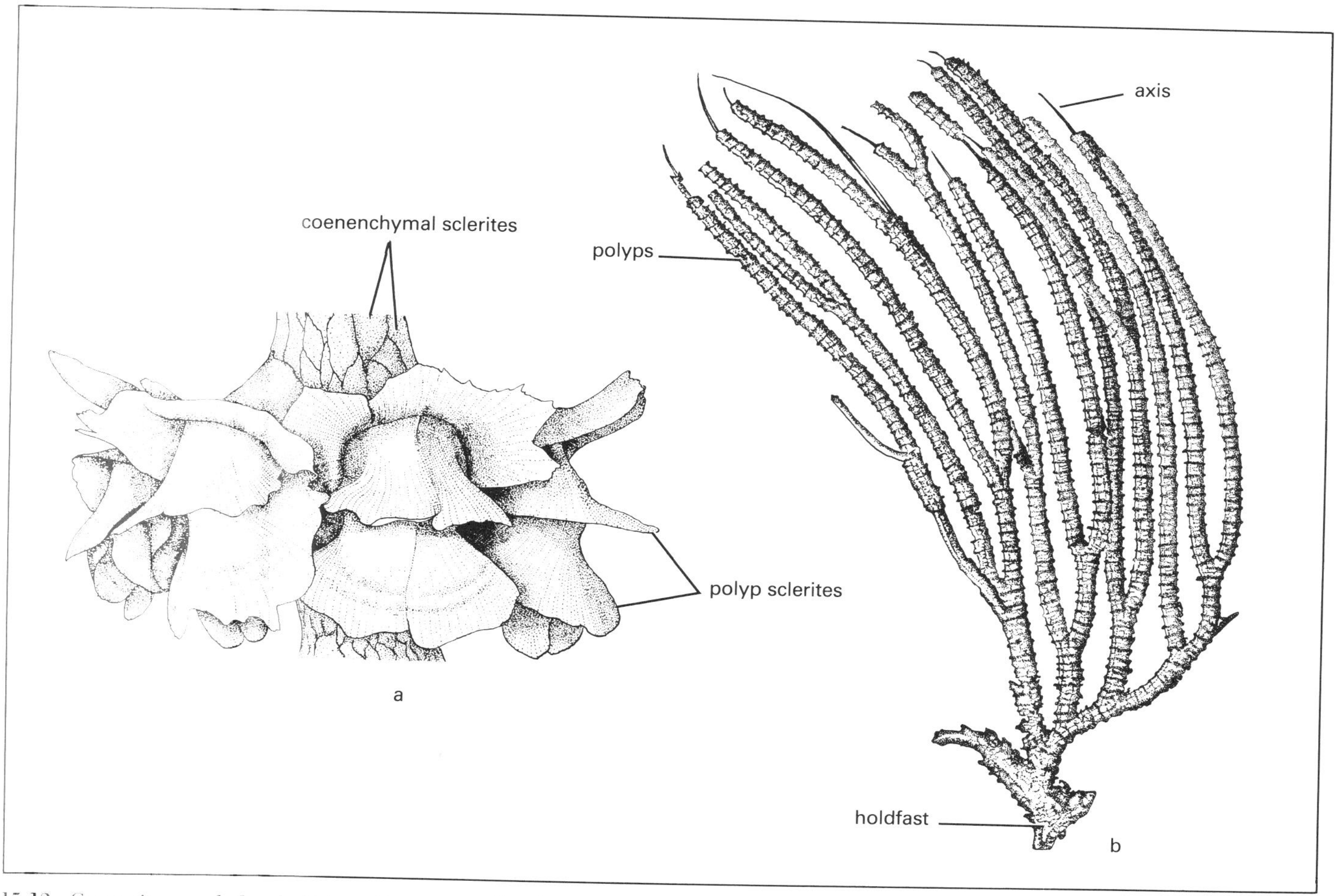

15-12. Gorgonian coral, family Primnoidae, genus *Narella*. *(a)* Whorl of polyps. Crowquill pen and ink on Bristol board, by Frederick M. Bayer. *(b)* Colony. Redrawn with Hunt 102 pen and ink on Bristol board, by Sally Parker from *Three Cruises of the Steamer Blake*, by A. Agassiz (*Bulletin* of the Museum of Comparative Zoology, Harvard University, 1888).

15-13. Octocoral sclerites: various species and magnifications photographed with the scanning electron microscope (SEM).

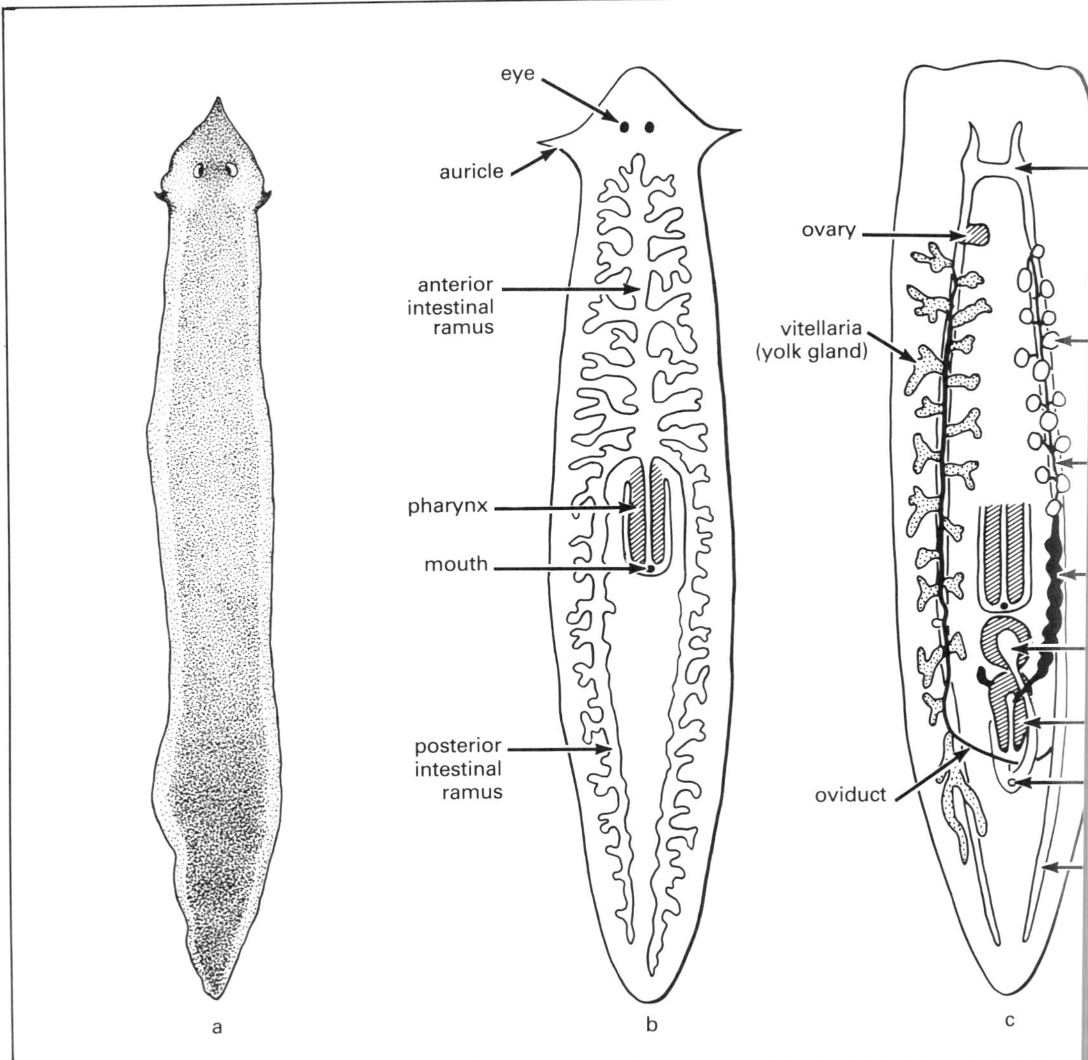

15-14. Platyhelminthes: planarian or flatworm. *(a)* Habitus view, from photo. Gillott 659 pen and ink on Bristol board. *(b)* and *(c)* Anatomy—outlines show two different types of flatworms, redrawn from diagram. Hunt 104 and Gillott 659 pens and ink on Denril film, by Elaine R. S. Hodges. Courtesy of Roman Kenk.

FLATWORMS

This phylum (Platyhelminthes) includes the flatworm *Planaria*, as well as a host of other terrestrial, aquatic, and parasitic flatworms. The important taxonomic characters of many flatworms are anatomical and must be illustrated from histological sections, usually serial, on microscope slides prepared by the scientist (fig. 15-14). Such preparations are treated with the same care and precautions as standard microslides. Large specimens may be loose in a liquid preservative (most likely alcohol) and smaller ones may be permanently whole-mounted on glass slides. Wet specimens may be as delicate as jellyfishes and must be handled accordingly.

Care and Handling

Since a principal character of many marine polyclad flatworms is the color in life, the artist may be called upon to illustrate the natural color pattern from living material. The animal probably will be delivered to the artist in a container of water su
rectly or
croscope
clean gla
hold it,
imprope
injurious
A suppl
used wi
Formalin
able if
handled
erwise, t
living sp
tainer to
is compl

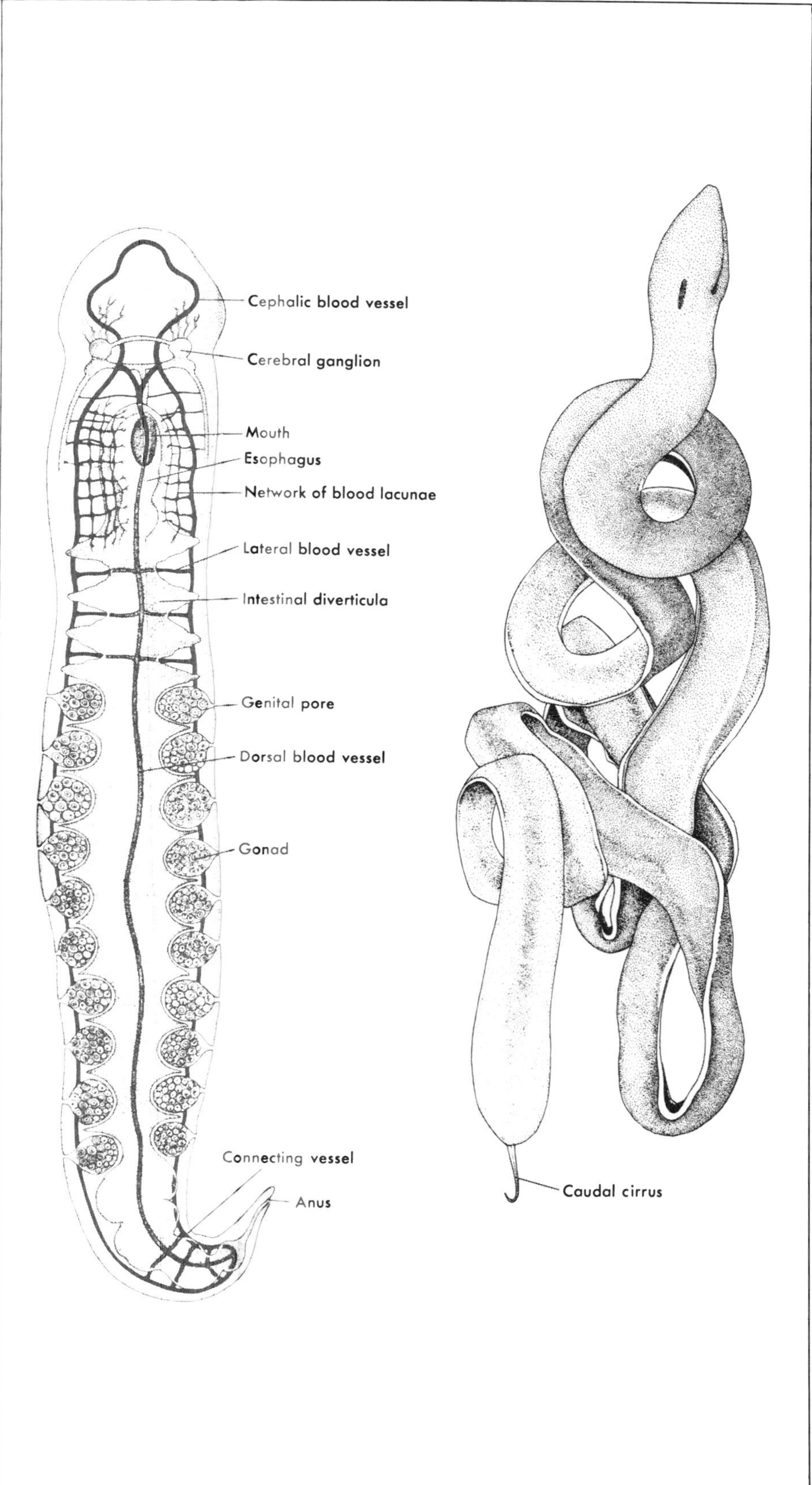

15-15. Nemertean. The whole animal is shown on the right, its internal anatomy on the left. Pen-and-ink, by Peter Loewer. From *The Free-Living Lower Invertebrates*, by Frederick M. Bayer and H. B. Owre (Macmillan, 1968). Courtesy of the authors.

NEMERTEANS

Nemerteans (phylum Nemertea or Rhynchocoela) are unsegmented worms commonly known as ribbon-worms or bootlace worms because of their extremely elongated form (fig. 15-15). As in the case of flatworms, the artist may be expected to produce color drawings of living animals as well as anatomical drawings of sections mounted on glass slides.

Care and Handling

The same precautions should be taken with nemerteans as with flatworms, but it should be remembered that many nemerteans are even more unmanageable in life than are flatworms, and they often tend to autotomize (break up in small pieces) if handled too roughly.

BRYOZOANS

The so-called moss animals, bryozoans (phylum Bryozoa) form delicate branching or encrusting colonies on dock pilings, boat bottoms, and other submerged objects in salt water (fig. 15-16). Scientific illustrations of bryozoans are likely to include both colonial forms and details of individual zoecia, the chitinous or calcareous tube in which the animal lives.

Care and Handling

Entire colonies are usually preserved in alcohol, occasionally dry; parts of colonies to show zoecial characters, such as sculpturing or the form of the colony, are sometimes whole-mounted on slides. Handle arborescent specimens in the same way as hydroid colonies, taking care to avoid damage. Slide mounts ordinarily will be accompanied by special precautions as well as details required in the artwork.

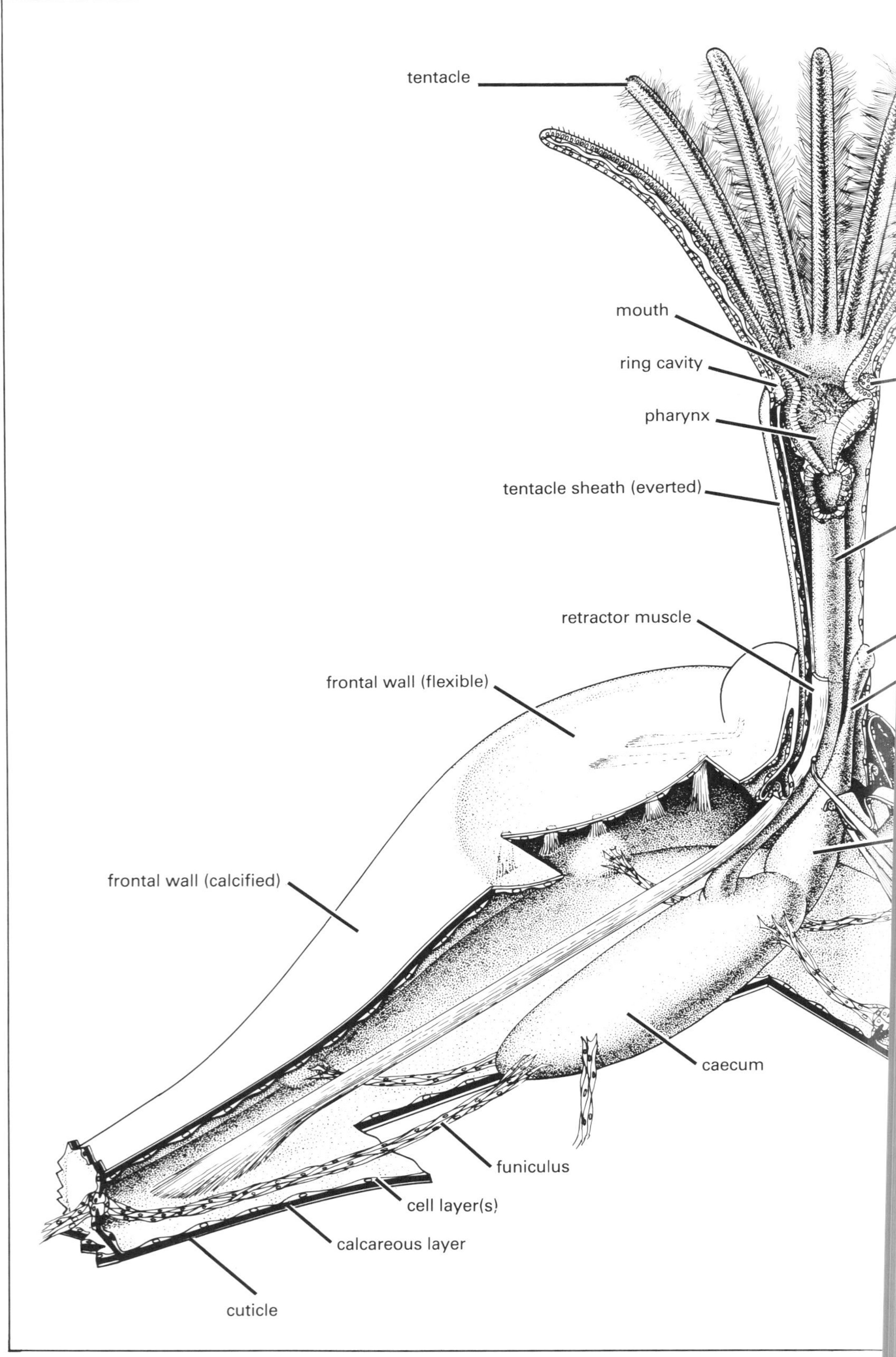

15-16. Bryozoan with lophophore extended. The lophophore consists of the tentacles and tentacle sheath. Pen-and-ink on film, by Lawrence B. Isham. From *Treatise on Invertebrate Paleontology*, Part G, *Bryozoa Revised*, vol. 1, 1983. Courtesy of A. H. Cheetham.

BRACHIOPODS

Brachiopods (phylum Brachiopoda) are the so-called lamp shells that have a bivalved shell superficially resembling a clam but fixed in place by a fleshy stalk that passes through an aperture in the ventral valve.

Care and Handling

Dry shells of brachiopods can be mounted just as mollusk shells for illustrative purposes (fig. 15-17). Most are around 50mm in size and can therefore be studied with the lower powers of a stereomicroscope. Immature brachiopods are under 1mm, whereas fossils can be as large as 20cm. Characters of interest may be internal or external. Specimens kept in alcohol to preserve the lophophore apparatus (the "loop") should be opened and positioned by the scientist (fig. 15-18).

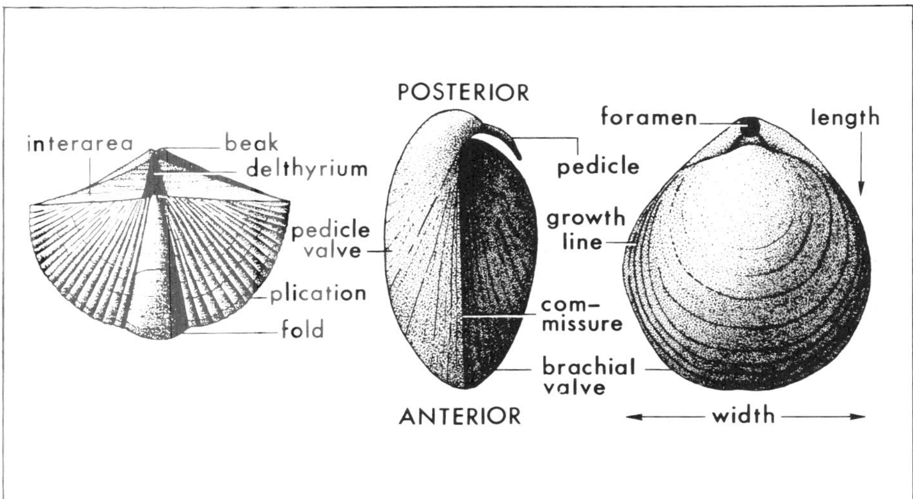

15-17. Brachiopod: external anatomy. Pen-and-ink on K & E Crystalene tracing paper, by Terry L. Chase. From *Environments Through Time: A Laboratory Manual in Historical Geology*, 2d ed., by R. L. Anstey and Terry L. Chase (Burgess Publishing, 1979).

ANNELIDS

This phylum (Annelida) contains worms with bodies divided into segments that have more or less conspicuous chitinous setae. They include the common earthworm and marine worms such as the common clam-worm and lugworm. The features of polychaete annelids most commonly illustrated are the parapodia and associated setae, details of the setae, head and appendages, jaws, and posterior extremity. Most of these require dissection and mounting by the specialist, so the illustrator may deal mainly with prepared microscope slides. Occasionally, drawings of the entire worm may be required (fig. 15-19).

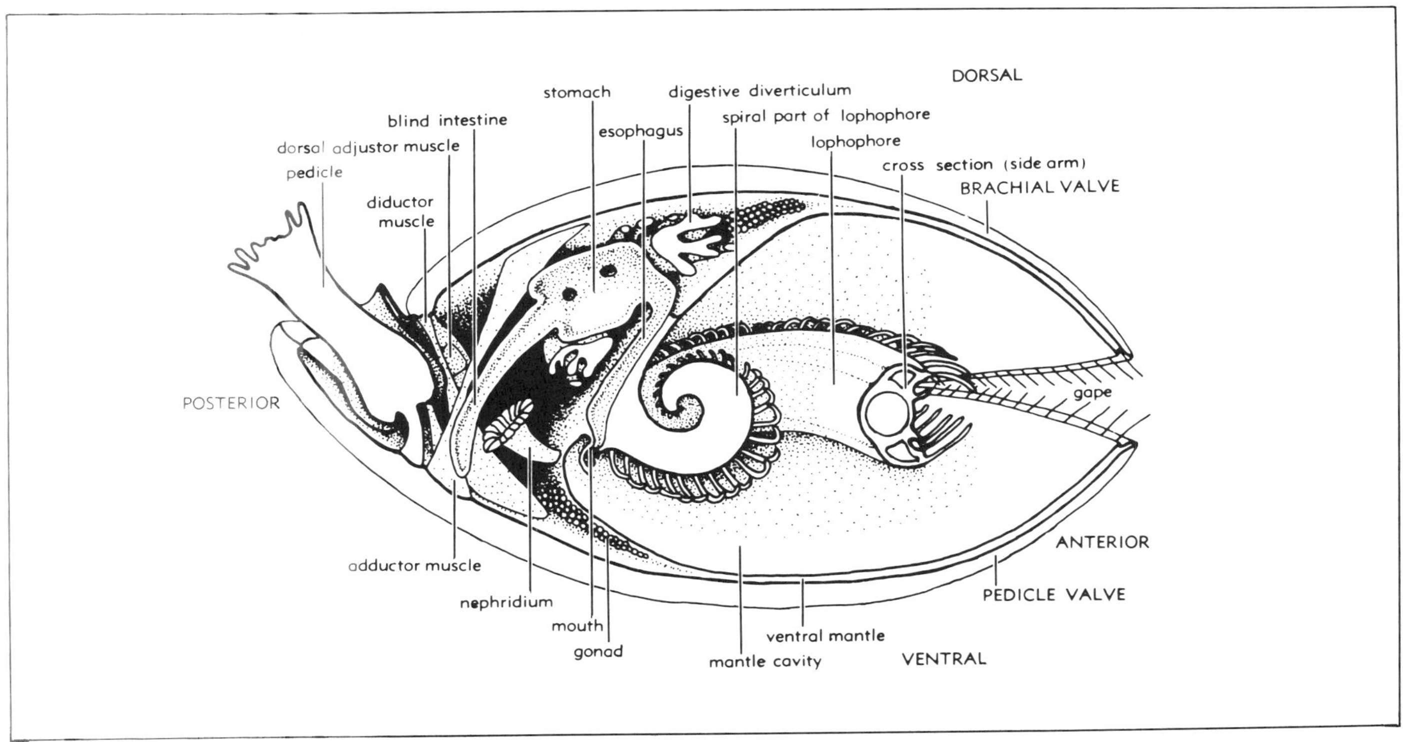

15-18. Brachiopod: internal anatomy. From *Treatise on Invertebrate Paleontology*, Part H. *Brachiopoda*, vol. 1, 1965. Pen-and-ink. Artist unknown.

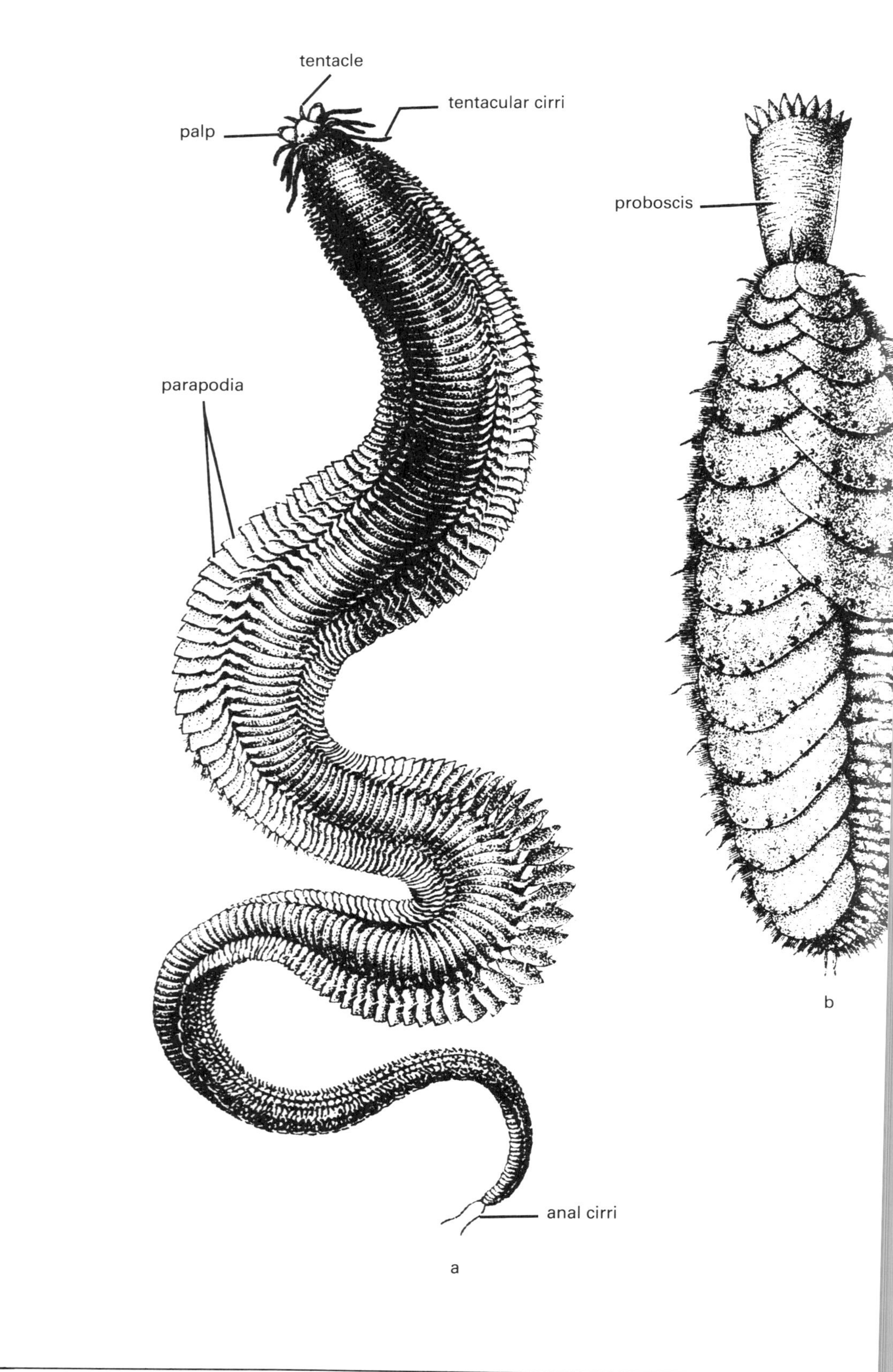

15-19. Annelid worms: *(a)* polychaete—note parapodia that aid worm's movement; *(b)* polynoid polychaete, or "scale worm." Artist and medium unknown. From ***Atlas of the Invertebrates of the Seas of the Far East of the USSR***, 1955.

Care and Handling

Whole specimens are preserved in alcohol and most are of sufficient size to permit handling with fine forceps. Small strips of glass cut from a microscope slide are useful for holding specimens in place if they tend to drift about in the viewing dish. Polynoid polychaetes (scale worms) have delicate scales, or elytra, that may detach readily if handled carelessly.

MOLLUSKS

Included in the phylum Mollusca are the familiar clams and snails, as well as slugs, the octopus, squid, and pearly and paper nautilus. Colorful, soft-bodied forms such as opisthobranchs may be drawn in color from living specimens, although color photography is now more commonly used for this purpose.

Care and Handling

As a rule, shelled forms pose no special problem for the illustrator (figs. 15-20, 15-21). Elaborately sculptured shells should not be positioned with plasticine if this is likely to stick in the sculptural detail. Specimens with frilly, hairy or feltlike periostracum (the outer skinlike coating of many kinds of shells) must be handled with care and also should not be positioned with plasticine. Molded beeswax or a kneaded rubber eraser can be used. Many snail shells have an accessory piece, the operculum, either shelly or horny, which closes the aperture more or less completely. This may require illustration in addition to the shell proper. In the dead animal, the operculum is likely to be loose, so care should be taken to keep the correct operculum with its shell if numerous specimens are being handled at the same time.

Cephalopod specimens (squid and octopus) are usually preserved in alcohol and may be rather large, so they can be handled and drawn in much the same way as fishes (see chapter 16). The aim of the overall drawing is to present the form of the animal in reasonably natural attitude, with the arms (and tentacles if present) positioned to show form, proportion, and relative lengths (figs. 15-22, 15-23, 15-24). Specimens frequently are distorted in preservation, so positioning and holding the various parts of the specimen in place may test the artist's ingenuity. A wax-bottomed dissecting pan often is a useful

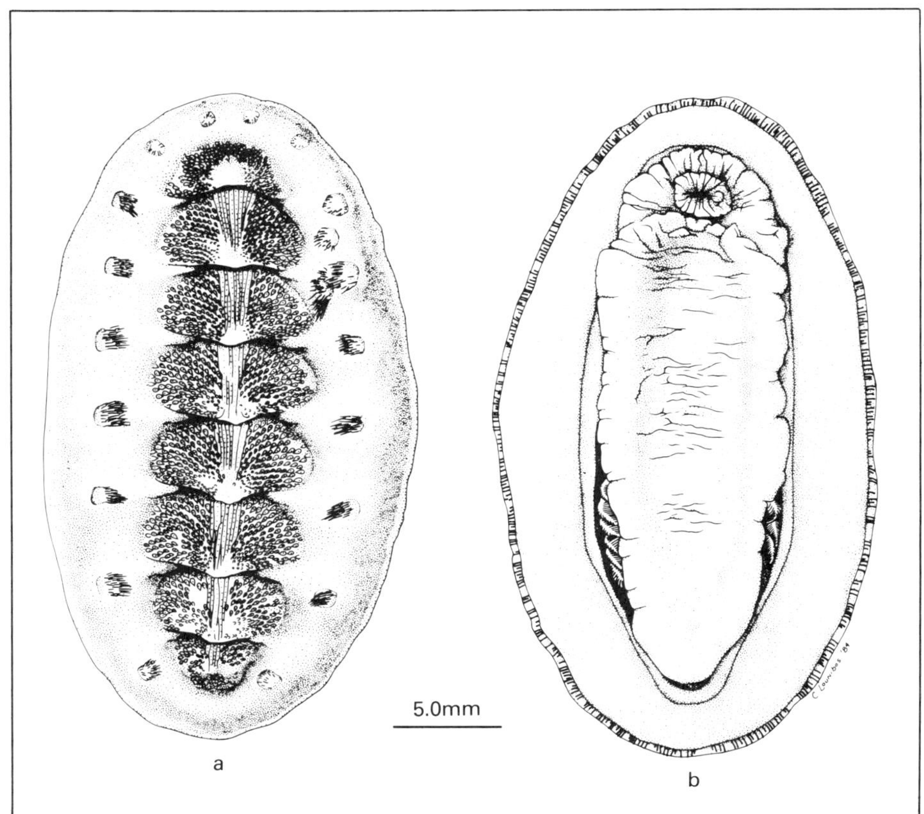

15-20. Mollusk, Polyplacophora: chiton, *Acanthochitona spiculosa*. *(a)* Dorsal morphology. *(b)* Ventral view. Technical pen and ink on Cronaflex, by Charissa Baker Lounibos.

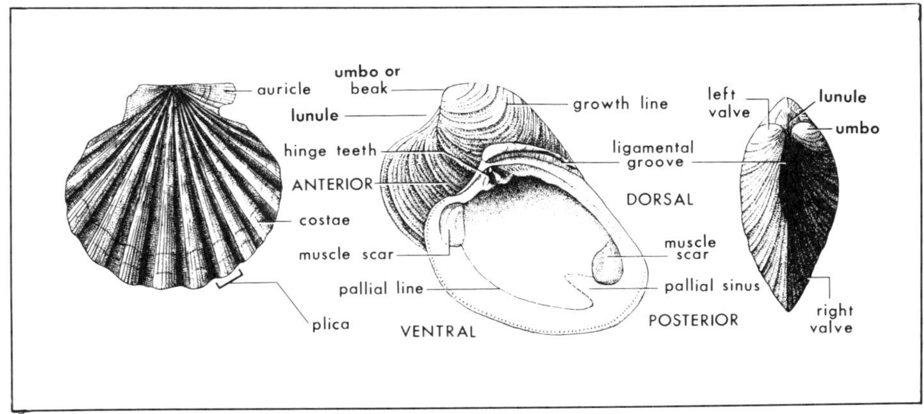

15-21. Shells of bivalve mollusks. Pen-and-ink on Crystalene tracing paper, by Terry L. Chase. From *Environments Through Time: A Laboratory Manual in Historical Geology*, 2d ed., by R. L. Anstey and Terry L. Chase (Burgess Publishing, 1979).

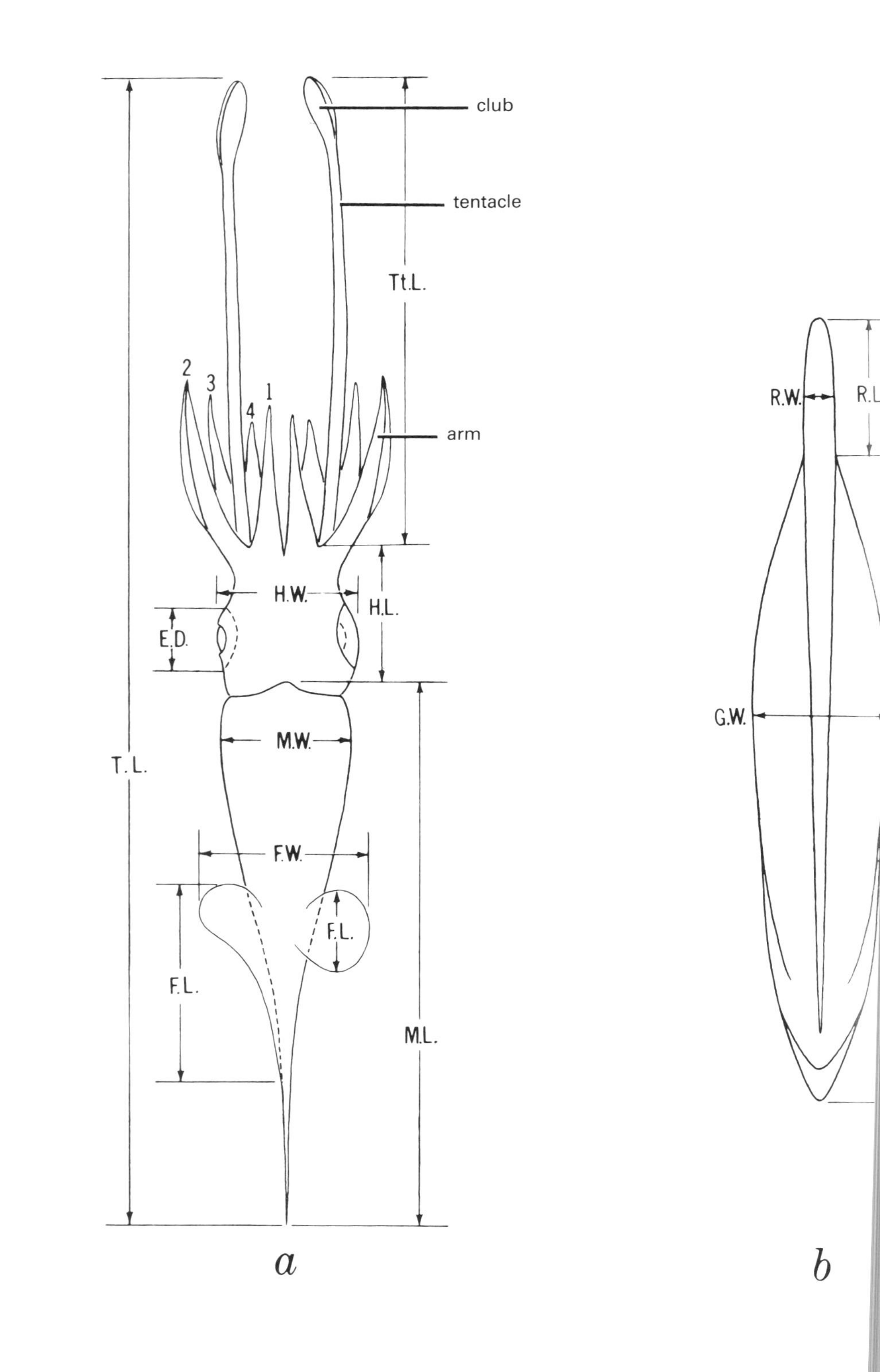

15-22. Cephalopod mollusk (Octopoda). Teuthoidea, measurements. *(a)* Dorsal view: ED = eye diameter, FL = fin length; FW = fin width, HL = head length, TtL = tentacle length; left eye = oegopsid eye, right eye = myopsid eye. *(b)* Gladius, ventral view: GL = gladius length, GW = gladius width, RL = rachis length, RW = rachis width. Hunt 104 pens and ink on Albanene tracing paper, by Carolyn Bartlett Gast. From *Memoirs* of the National Museum of Victoria, vol. 44, 30 June 1983. Courtesy of Clyde F. E. Roper and Gilbert L. Voss.

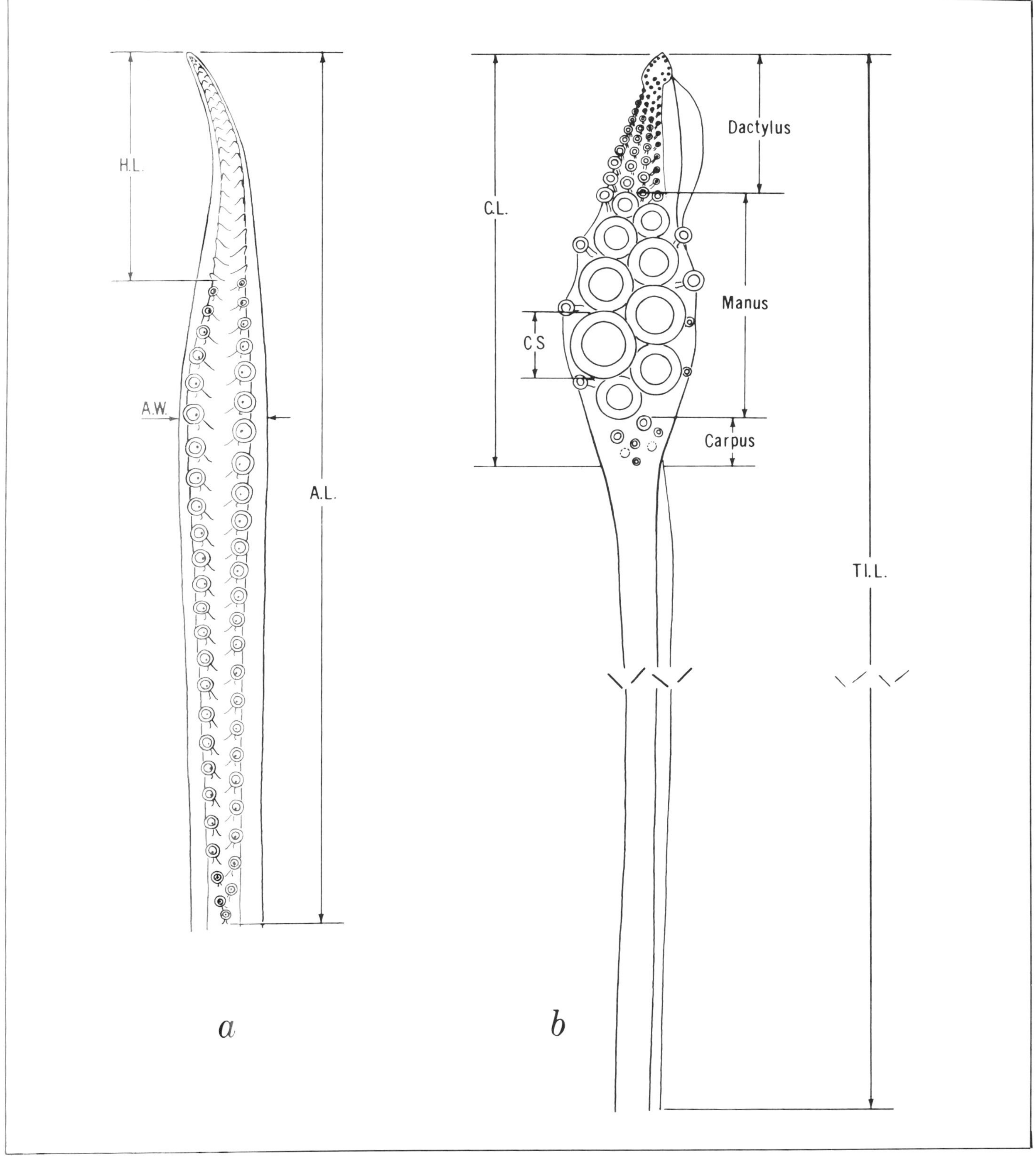

15-23. Cephalopod mollusk (Octopoda). Teuthoidea, measurements. *(a)* Hectocotylized arm: AL = arm length, AW = arm width, HL = hectocotylus length. *(b)* Tentacle and club: CL = club length, CS = club sucker (largest), TtL = tentacle length. Hunt 104 pens and ink on Albanene tracing paper, by Carolyn Bartlett Gast. From *Memoirs* of the National Museum of Victoria, vol. 44, 30 June 1983. Courtesy of Clyde F. E. Roper and Gilbert L. Voss.

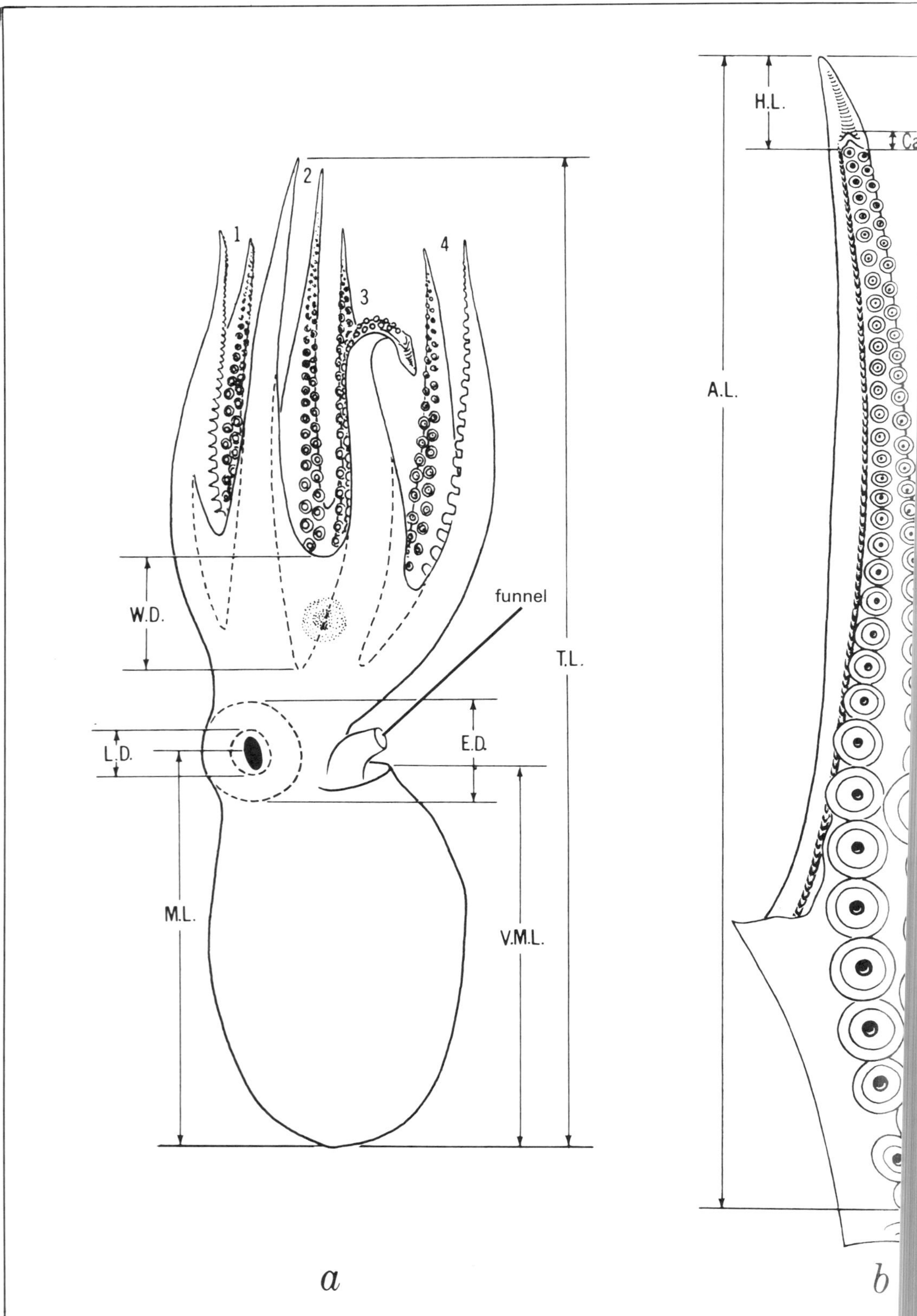

15-24. Cephalopod mollusk (Octopoda). Incirrata, measurements. *(a)* Lateral view: ED = eye diameter, LD = lens diameter, ML = mantle length, TL = total length, VML = ventral mantle length, WD = web depth. *(b)* Hectocotylized arm: AL = arm length, CaL-calamus length, ES = enlarged sucker, HL = hectocotylus length, LL = ligula length. Hunt 104 pens and ink on Albanene tracing paper, by Carolyn Bartlett Gast. From *Memoirs* of the National Museum of Victoria, vol. 44, 30 June 1983. Courtesy of Clyde F. E. Roper and Gilbert L. Voss.

container: the body and arms of the specimen can be held in place with crossed pins or dissecting needles. One pinning and straightening method is to insert a stainless steel insect pin through the tip and into the cavity of an arm, parallel to its length, then brace other pins against this pin, not against tissue, as they are pushed into the wax. Check with the scientist before inserting any pins into a specimen. The tray may be too shallow to permit covering the specimen with liquid, so it may be necessary to use a cloth dampened with preservative to cover the specimen at all times when measurements or observations are not being made. A deeper dissecting tray can be improvised by adding a paraffin layer to an appropriate tray or dish. The greater volume of fluid may hamper measuring with dividers, but the specimen certainly will be kept in better condition.

ECHINODERMS

The currently living members of this phylum (Echinodermata) are distributed among six classes: the sea stars (Asteroidea) (fig. 15-25), brittle stars or serpent stars and basket stars (Ophiuroidea) (fig. 15-26), feather stars and sea lilies (Crinoidea) (fig. 15-27), sea urchins (Echinoidea) (fig. 15-28), sea cucumbers (Holothuroidea) (fig. 15-29), and the very rare sea daisies

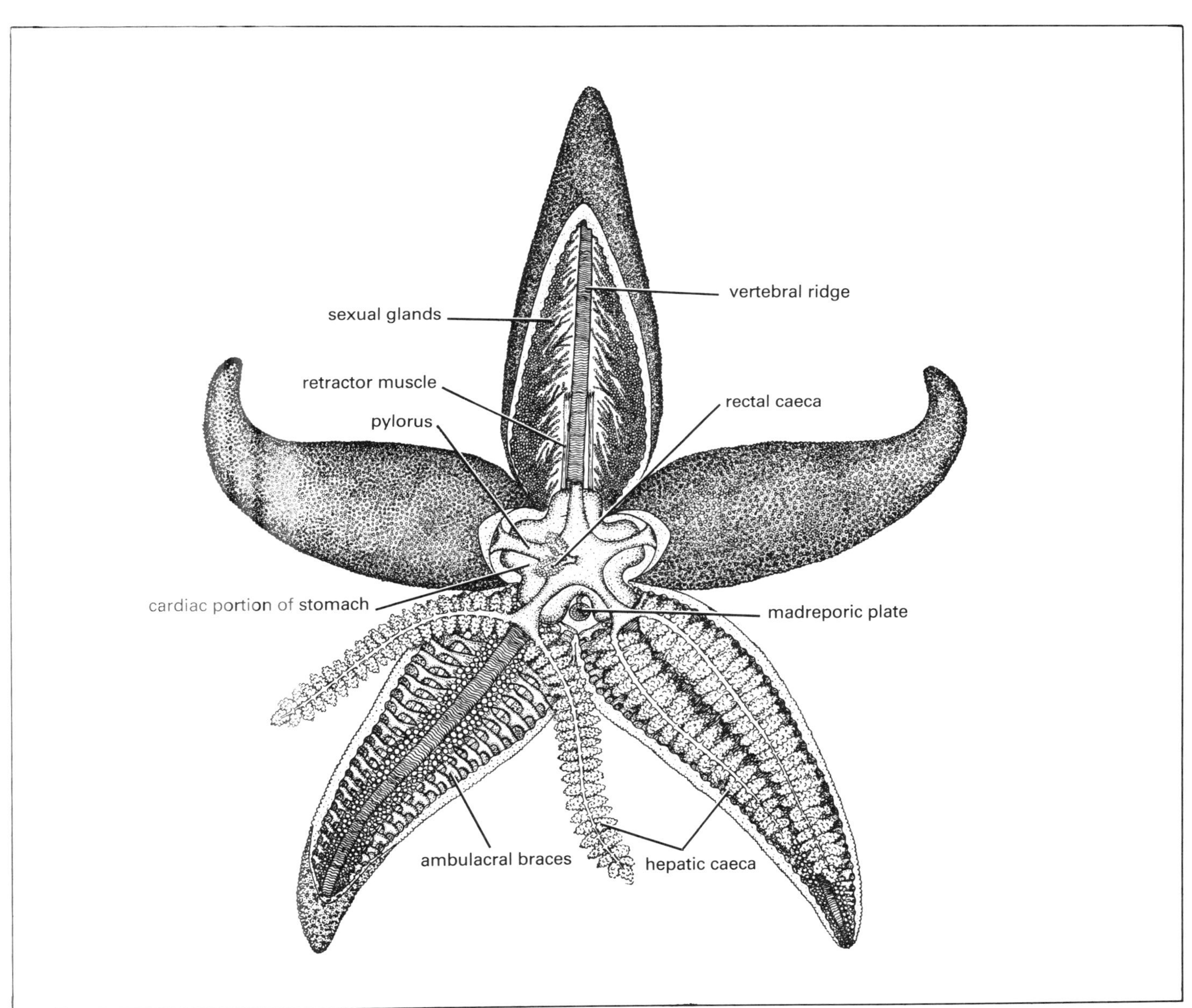

15-25. Echinoderms: Asteroidea. Anatomy of sea star. The lower right ray shows the viscera in their natural position. In the lower left ray, the sexual glands and retractor muscles have been removed. Hepatic caeca have been removed from the upper ray. Pen-and-ink. Artist unknown. From *Echinoderms of Connecticut*, by W. R. Coe (State Geological and Natural History Survey, Hartford, 1912).

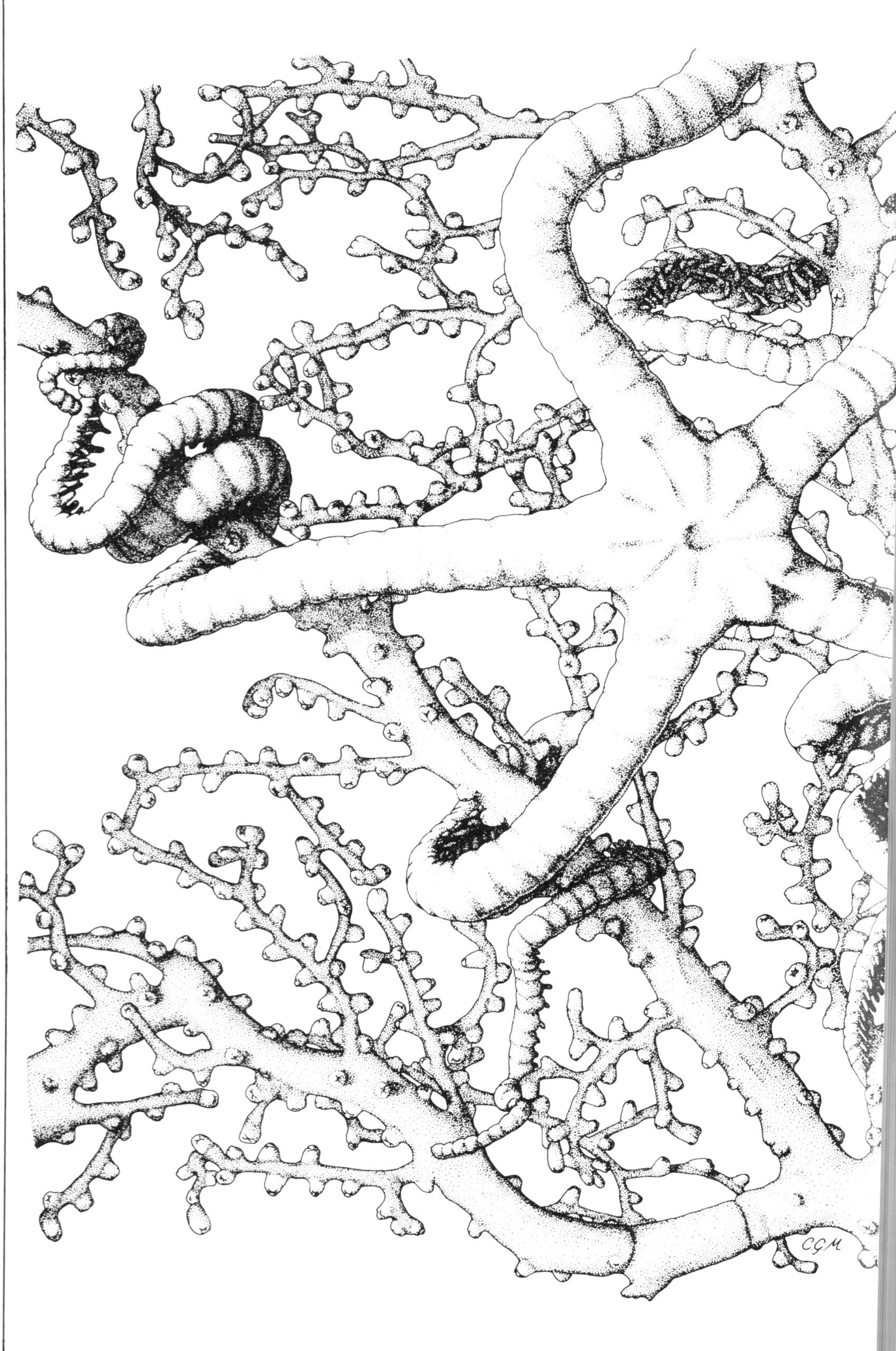

15-26. Echinoderms: Ophiuroidea. Living *Asteroschema* species, basket-star, on a gorgonacean. Technical 4×0 pen and ink on Strathmore plate-finish Bristol board, by Charles Messing © 1975.

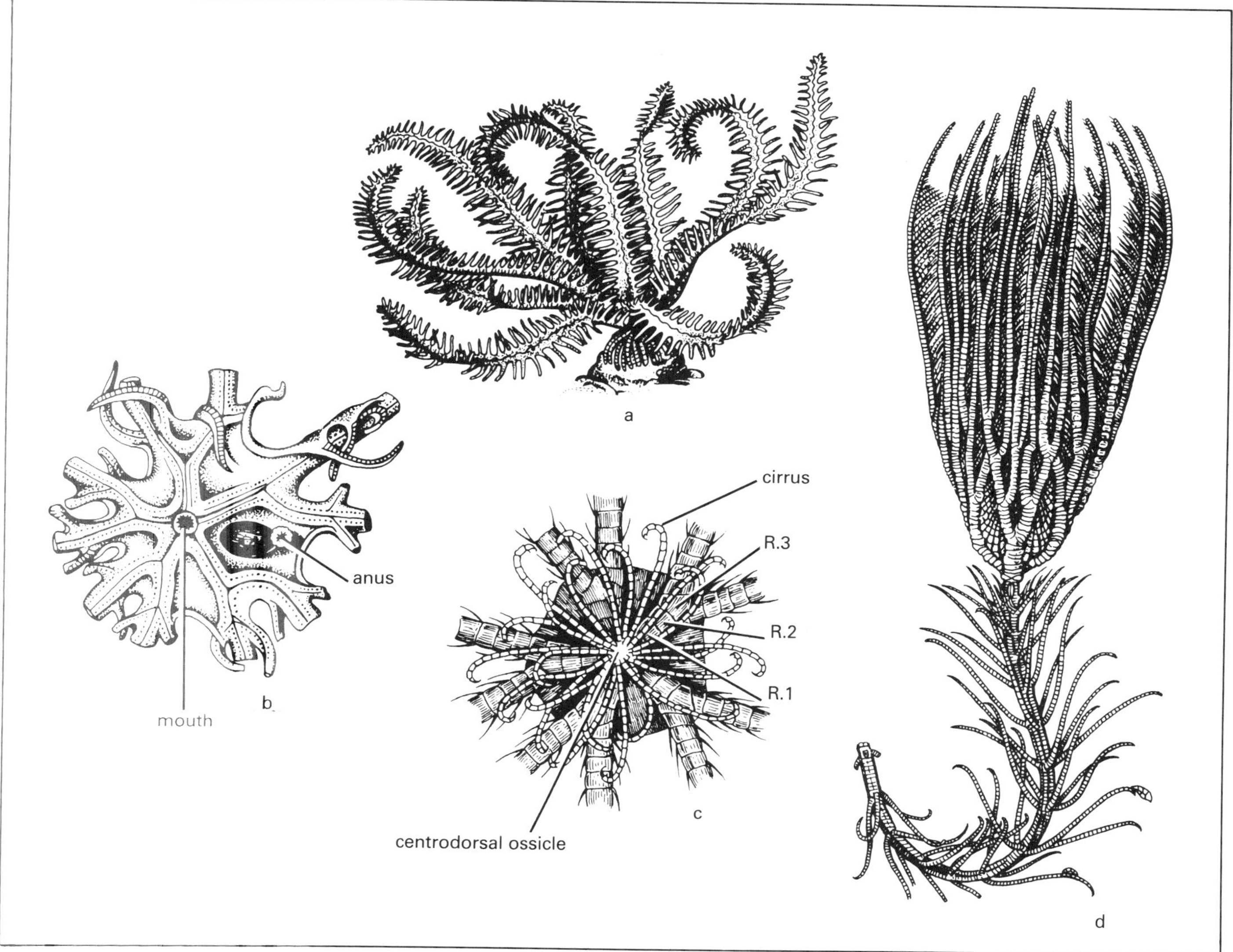

15-27. Echinoderms: Crinoidea. *(a)* Feather star, or comatulid crinoid: lateral view of whole animal (from Leuckart and Nitsche). *(b) Antedon*: oral view—upper surface of the central disc (from Vogt and Jung). *(c) Antedon*: aboral view. R.1, R.2, and R.3 are the three radial plates of one column (from Macbride). *(d)* Sea lily or stalked crinoid, *Metacrinus interruptus* (from P. H. Carpenter). All in pen-and-ink; courtesy of W. D. Williams and Elsevier Science Publishing Company, *Textbook of Zoology, Invertebrates*, 1972.

(Concentricycloida). Of these six groups, specimens of the last two are almost without exception preserved in alcohol, whereas the others may either be kept in alcohol or dried.

The terminology of the generally radial basic features of the various echinoderm classes is essentially the same, but the details peculiar to each differ to some extent. Major characters are shown in the accompanying figures.

The sea cucumbers, usually soft-bodied, sluglike creatures of 1.2 to 1.5 inches (3 to 4 cm) to more than 3.3 feet (1m), are classified by the shape of small, calcareous ossicles in the body walls and by anatomical details and structure of the tentacles and tube feet, if present. Although drawings of these anatomical and structural details may be required, they often can be revealed only by dissection, which must be done by the scientist, so specimens for drawing usually will come to the illustrator already prepared, either as wet preparations that must be kept immersed or, in the case of calcareous ossicles, mounted on glass slides. The latter should be treated like similar preparations of sponge spicules and gorgonian sclerites.

Care and Handling

Echinoderms generally are large and therefore relatively easy to align for examination and drawing. They can be treated like mollusks

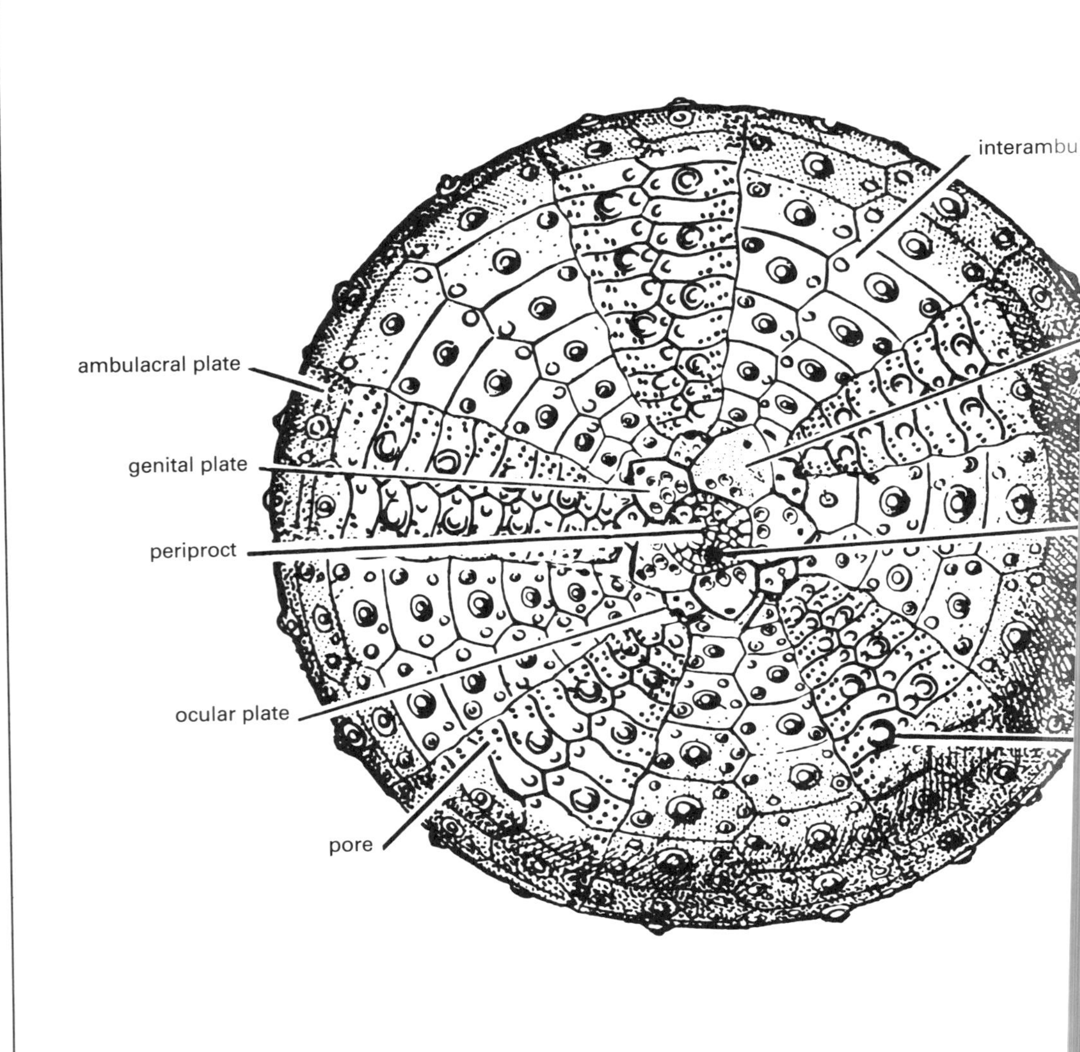

15-28. Echinoidea, sea urchin *Echinus*. Upper or aboral view showing arrangement of fused, calcareous plates on the test or skeleton. Spines have been removed. Pen-and-ink. Artist unknown. From *A Textbook of Zoology*, edited by A. J. Marshall and W. D. Williams (MacMillan Press, London, 1972).

or corals. Pieces of glass slides or cover slips can support smaller animals in alcohol; shaped kneaded rubber erasers, glass, wood, or cardboard can be used to prop dried echinoderms.

Certain characters of some echinoderms are visible only on dried specimens. Therefore, those that are stored in alcohol must be dried briefly (with the permission of the scientist), contrary to advice given about most wet specimens. Do not let the specimen dry so long that its soft parts become brittle. Depending on the size of the specimen, this can occur in fifteen minutes or in hours. Periodically feel the soft parts with a needle to see that they remain flexible. If the specimen dries too much, it may be necessary to keep it as a dried specimen rather than returning it to alcohol. It is possible, however, to reconstitute the specimen by softening it in liquid dishwashing detergent/water solution (proportions about 1:10) for up to thirty minutes. Check the condition of the soft parts by looking at them and by poking gently with a needle to see if they are flexible again. After reconstitution,

they ca
cent alc
Sea
special
bounda
see (se
clarifie
red ink
per or
manen
obtaine
attemp
there a
can be

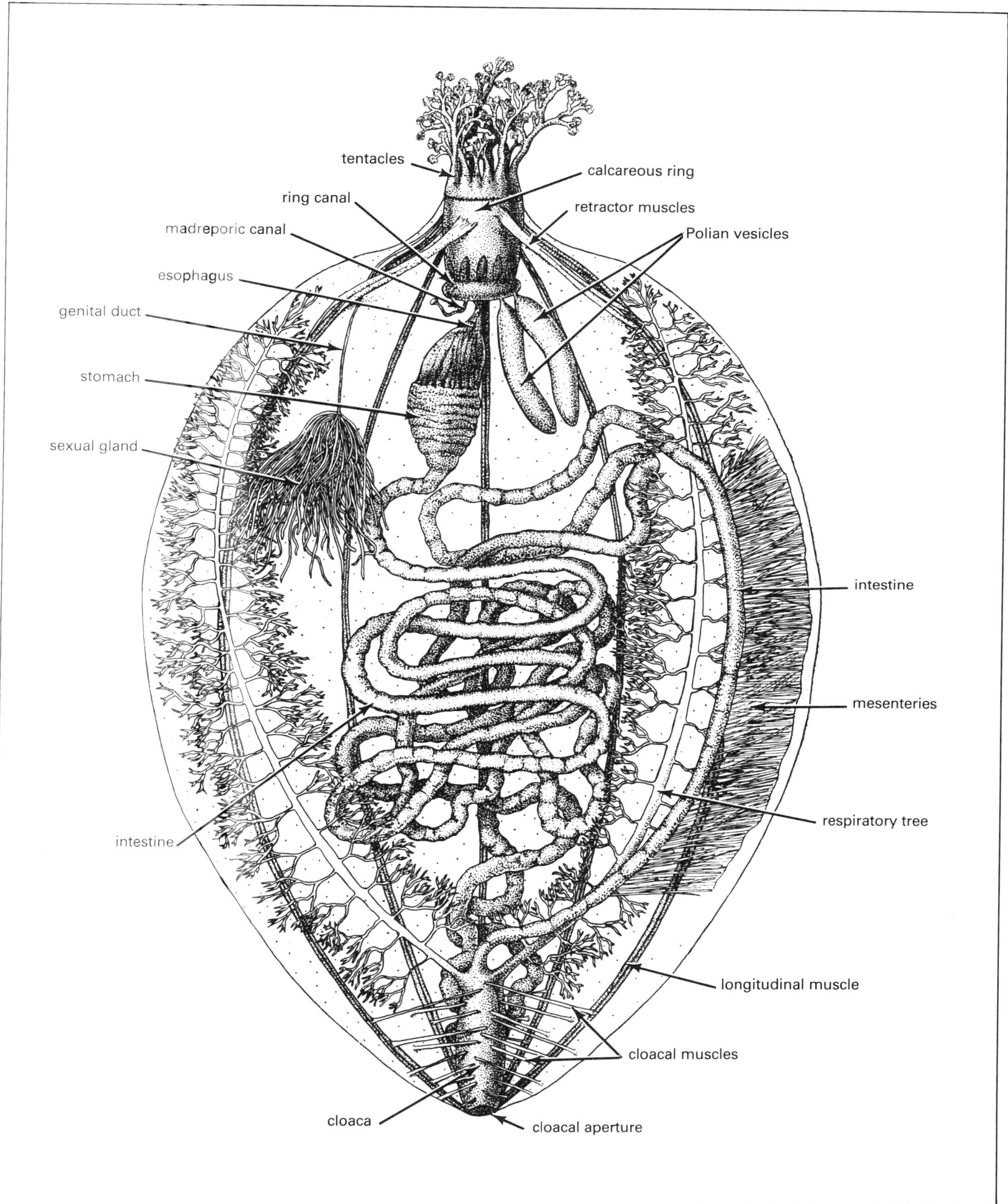

15-29. Echinoderms: Holothuroidea, sea cucumber. Internal anatomy of *Thyone briareus*. Pen-and-ink. Artist unknown. From *Echinoderms of Connecticut*, by W. R. Coe (State Geological and Natural History Survey, Hartford, 1912).

Arthropods

Arthropods include crustaceans, arachnids (see fig. C-10), millipedes, centipedes, and insects, as well as smaller, lesser known or illustrated groups. Only the major groups will be discussed in detail here. The principles of handling apply to all arthropods that match in size, fragility, and storage method the group that is specifically covered.

To reflect methods of handling them, crustaceans are discussed separately from the other arthropods. Crustaceans include the largest arthropods, such as lobsters, which can weigh more than twenty pounds, and spider crabs, with a possible 5-foot (1.5m) spread across legs, but also include animals as small as or smaller than most insects. Whereas crustaceans are almost always stored in liquid, insects are stored dry, in liquid, or on microscope slides. Millipedes, centipedes, and some arachnids such as spiders are stored in alcohol, but very small arachnids such as ticks and mites often are mounted on slides. The size and fragility of the specimens, as well as their storage methods, determine how they are mounted and handled for illustration.

Members of the phylum Arthropoda have jointed legs as well as other body segments. The exoskeleton is chitin, an almost indestructible substance that is both strong and elastic. "Chitinized" and "sclerotized" refer to the tissues of arthropods that are hardest and often darkest. Their muscles connect to the body wall instead of to a true internal skeleton, as is the case with vertebrates.

There is an "internal" skeleton of sorts that really consists of invaginations of the exoskeleton. These invaginations may form ridges or rods to which muscles attach or that act as struts for support (see fig. 15-43b, apophysis

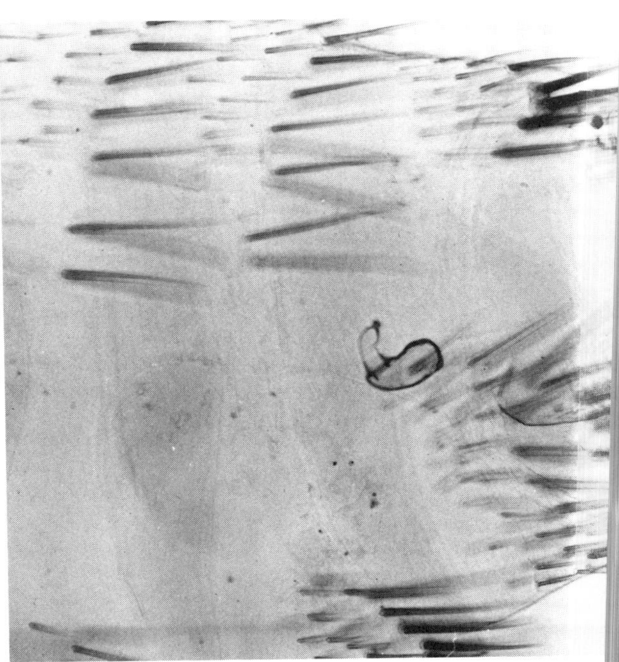

15-30. Determining which segment edge is on top is somet
flea abdominal section, by Deborah Leather Roney. Court

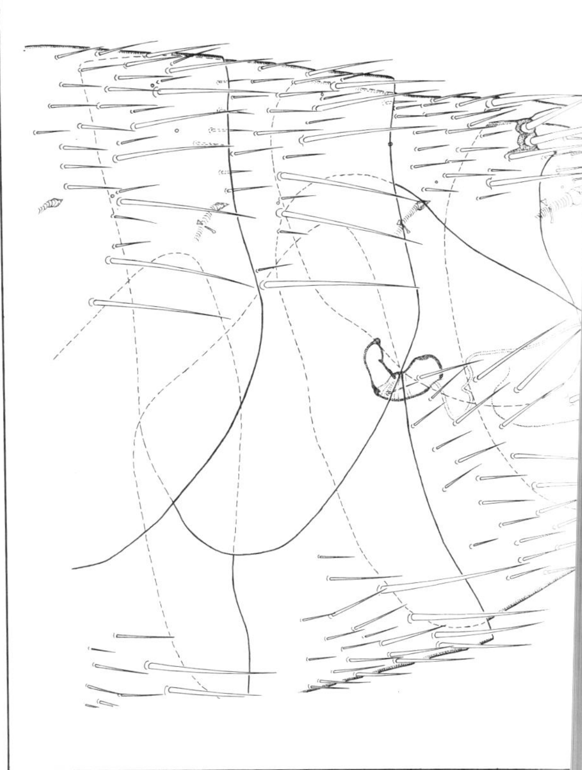

15-31. Drawing of specimen in figure 15-30 clarifies rela
on Bristol board, by Deborah Leather Roney. Courtesy

posterioris and apophysis anterioris). The invagination sometimes is visible externally as a pit, seen in figure 15-52 on the front of the moth head between the antennae and the mouth appendages.

To visualize the arthropod's body, think of it as a series of cylinders. Flexibility results from membranous connections between these segments, especially in the abdomen, where muscles telescope the segments into one another (see fig. 15-37). Sometimes this telescoping is visible and may be confusing to the illustrator when the top (anterior) edge of a segment shows through the transparent preceding segment (figs. 15-30, 15-31). Turning the specimen on its side to silhouette the segment's profile while manipulating the lighting will make it easier to differentiate the segments.

Other types of body divisions are defined by sutures, lines that may or may not delimit a true segment or plate edge. It is usually important to draw these sutures (fig. 15-32).

The immature arthropod may bear no resemblance to its adult. Among both adults and young, there are great variations in sizes and characteristics.

CRUSTACEANS

Carolyn Bartlett Gast

Members of the class Crustacea have two pairs of antennae and breathe with gills. Figures 15-33 and 15-34 show typical crustaceans in conventional positions, with anatomic parts and structures important for illustration labeled. (A detailed external drawing is shown in fig. 8-20.) Genitalia drawings are needed for some groups (fig. 15-35).

Care and Handling

Because the appendages are extremely brittle and can break off easily, heavily calcified specimens (such as crayfish and lobsters) are ideally positioned head down in jars of alcohol. The legs naturally tend to point toward the head, making it safe to remove the specimen without breaking the legs. Formalin is used occasionally and makes the connection tissue at the joints rigid, rendering the specimen even more fragile. To remove the animal, grasp it with forceps by its middle—without disturbing appendages, if possible—and gently pull it from the jar. The specimen should be replaced head down, feet first, in the container for future easy removal. Crustaceans with more delicate exoskeletons (most shrimps) are usually maintained head up to avoid injury to the rostrum, the beaklike protuberance between and in front of the eyes. When the animal is head up, the appendages should be teased into position toward the mouth of the jar before an attempt is made to remove the specimen by grasping the body. Never handle or haul the animal around by its appendages. For study, promptly submerge the animal in an observation dish full of the same liquid that was in its storage jar. All crustaceans except those previously dried or mounted on slides are drawn while completely submerged in liquid to prevent the animal from drying out and to avoid distorting refractions and reflections. Very small crustaceans may be mounted on microscope slides permanently or in glycerin or lactic acid temporarily, usually by the scientist.

Positioning

One of the major problems encountered when drawing unmounted crustacea is positioning the animals for proper views and keeping them in position long enough to complete the drawing. The easiest way to hold specimens in place is to pin them to a wax-bottomed container (melt paraffin and pour into dish) with stainless steel insect pins cut in half. Other metals will rust and discolor and, in some cases, damage the animal. The smaller the pins, the less damage will be done and the less chance there will be that the upper ends will break the surface of the liquid.

Two pairs of forceps are needed: a bent-nosed pair with serrated tips, held with the tips horizontal to grasp firmly, insert, and remove the pins; and a jeweler's pair to position the specimen while the pins are being inserted. Pinning forceps or curved-nosed pliers are essential for pinning heavily calcified animals (see fig. 2-7). The straight forceps also are used to straddle the puncture and press down lightly while the pins are being removed to prevent any tissue from sticking to the pin and tearing. Sometimes twisting a pin before removing it will loosen the tissue without tearing it. Pins should be inserted so that they do not interfere with visibility of the specimen.

15-32: Sutures: *(a)* hypothetical suture lines viewed from above; *(b)* cross sections of sutures, each constructed differently. Hunt 104 pen and ink on Bristol board, by Elaine R. S. Hodges.

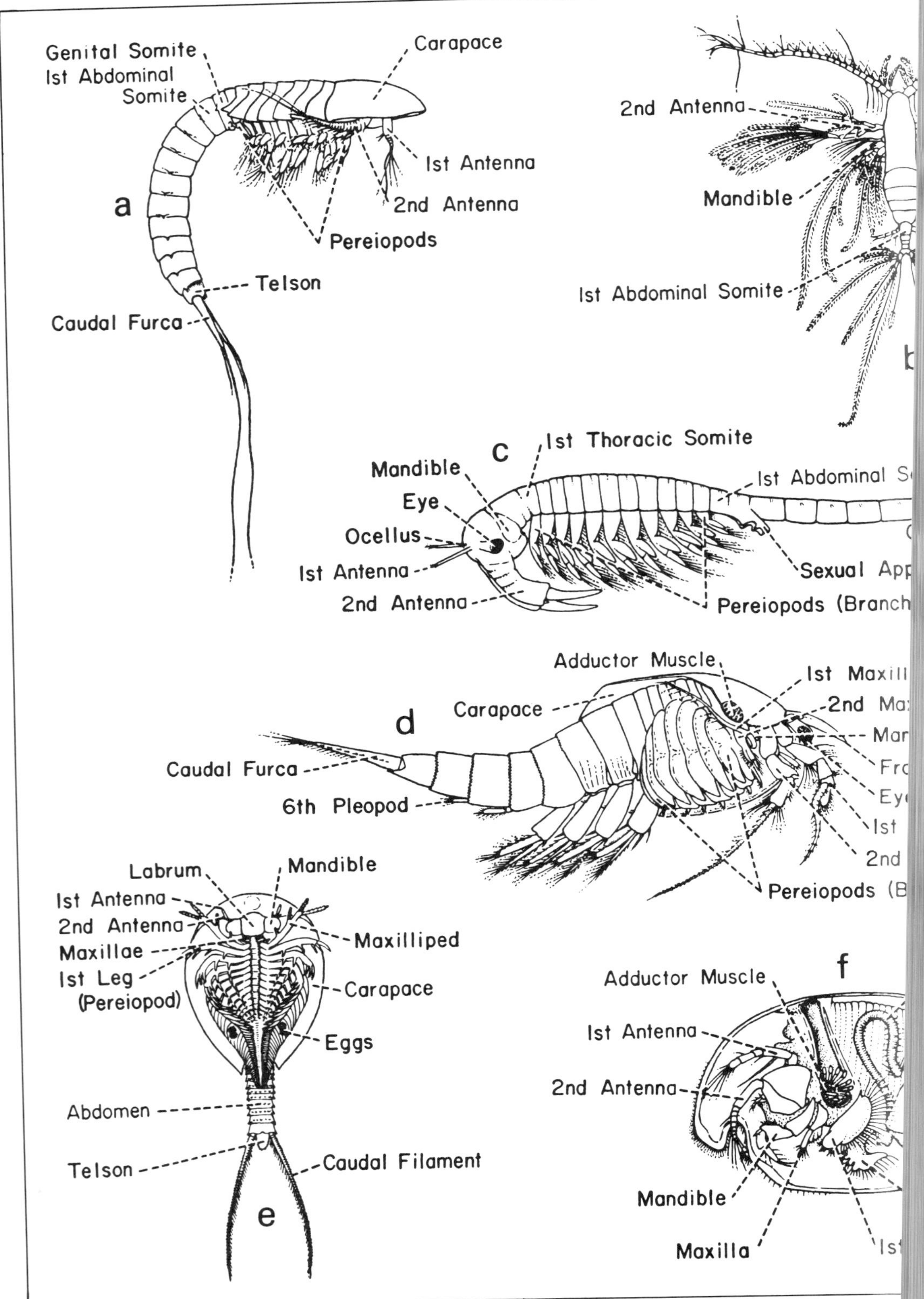

15-33. Crustaceans. *(a)* Cephalocaridan, *Hutchinsoniella macracantha*. *(b)* Calanoid copepod, *Euaugaptilus filigerus* (redrawn from Giesbrecht). *(c)* Anostracan branchiopod, *Branchinecta paludosa* (redrawn from Sars). *(d)* Nebaliacean, *Nebalia bipes*, with right half of carapace partly removed (modified from Sars). *(e)* Notostracan branchiopod, *Lepidurus arcticus* (redrawn from Sars). *(f)* Myodocopan ostracod, *Philomedes globosus*, with left shell removed (redrawn from Snodgrass). Crowquill pen and ink on Bristol board, by Fenner A. Chace. From *The Physiology of Crustacea* (© 1960 Academic Press).

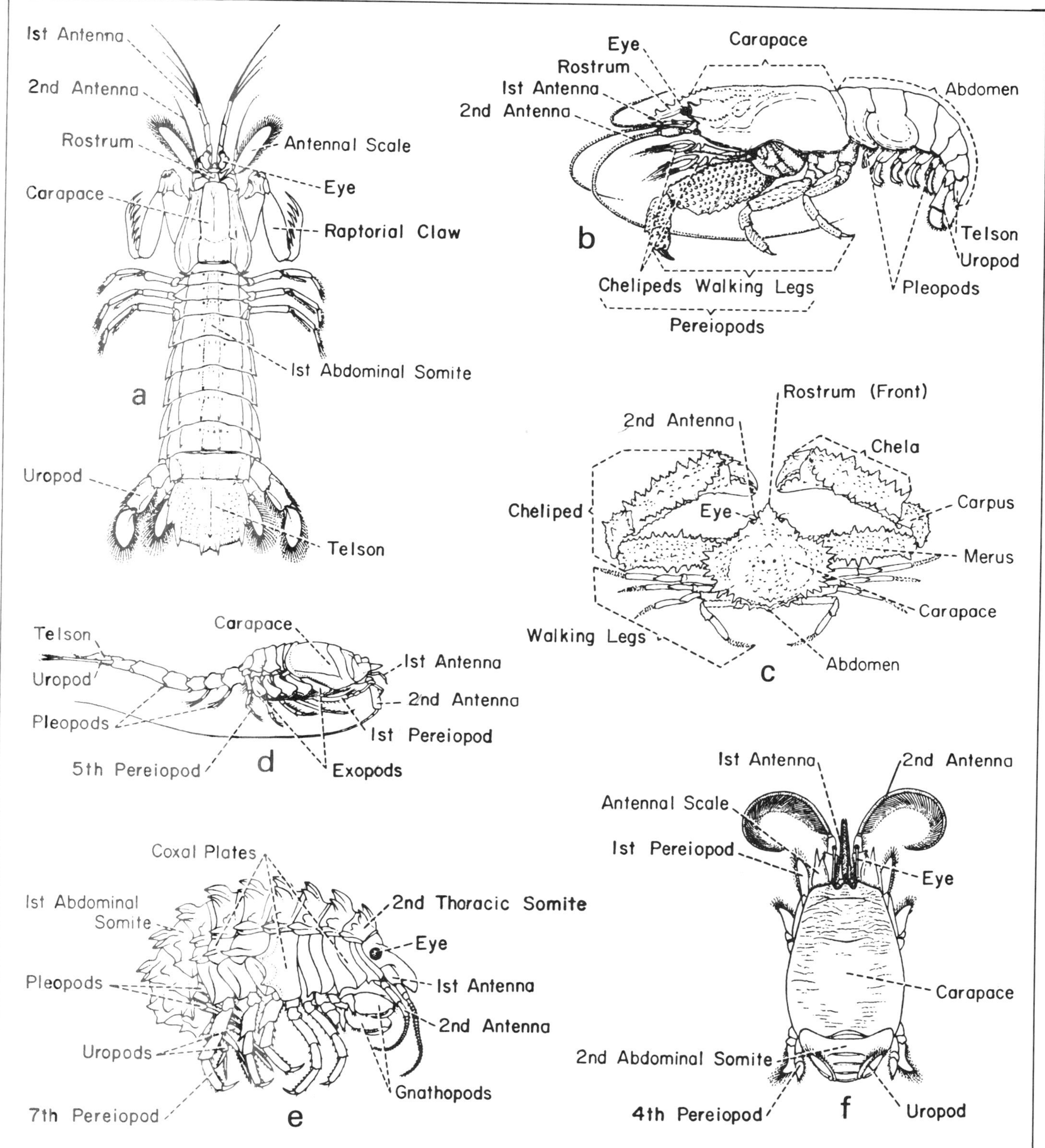

15-34. Crustaceans. *(a)* Stomatopod, *Squilla empusa* (redrawn from Rathburn). *(b)* Caridean prawn, *Atya crassa* (redrawn from Bouvier). *(c)* Oxyrhynch crab, *Parthenope pourtalesii* (redrawn from Smith). *(d)* Cumacean, *Diastylis alaskensis* (redrawn from Calman). *(e)* Gammarid amphipod, *Pleustes panopla* (modified from Shoemaker. *(f)* Anomuran, *Emerita talpoida* (redrawn from Verrill, Smith and Harger). Crowquill pen and ink on Bristol board, by Fenner A. Chace. From *The Physiology of Crustacea* (© 1960 Academic Press).

When the carapace of the animal is too hard to penetrate or doing so might damage the animal in a scientifically significant place, use the pins like tent pegs—stuck into the wax bottom two at a time to form Xs—and use thread or human hair as guywires over the specimen.

Lead birdshot or glass beads can be very useful in place of pins for larger animals. A bed of shot can be excavated or piled up in order to level off the animal, which then can be weighted down with pairs of weights (birdshot beanbags for larger animals, bolts or nuts for smaller ones) attached to each other by a length of thread passed over the animal in an unobtrusive place. The slack is rolled up around one of the weights. Bolts can be used to buttress either side of medium-sized specimens, such as small shrimp, and obliquely quartered and flattened birdshot can do the same for very small specimens such as ostracods. This permits observation by transmitted light around and through the specimen, which is between the weights, not on top of them.

Half-bury the large animal distorted and made brittle by Formalin in a shallow glass dish of birdshot, adjusting it as needed for different views and taking care not to damage it.

For very tiny specimens that will not sit firmly on the bottom of a container, follow suggestions for propping specimens given under Care and Handling of Specimens, at the beginning of this chapter. Alternatively, dip a dissecting needle or probe into liquid dishwashing detergent and then into the specimen's liqu
will preci
posed to
the dish.
the scient

Occasi
"feel" a
area to
bony shel
sure from
dissectin
lodge d
mals. A
be made
stiff, tap
with nail
end of a
or match

The d
taceans
nominall
times qu
rical as
tive and
illustrati
must b
chapter

INSEC
Elaine

The
entomo
becaus
sects a
than in
or pla
celled
econor
their i
mand
28, C-

Instr

In
(stere
items
brate
lustra
boxes
speci
speci

Richar
sects.

15-35. Female external genitalia of the shrimp, *Metapenaeopsis smithi*. Note that, unlike in most taxonomic illustrations, cast shadows have been shown. Technical pen and ink on Cronaflex, by Maria M. Dieguez (Farfante), courtesy of Isabel Perez Farfante.

A combination of instruments and tools might be used for some insects to achieve an accurate preliminary drawing. For example, in the case of a large specimen, such as a dragonfly, with complex wing venation, the body could be drawn with a grid, camera lucida, or dividers, but the wings might be mounted and projected from a microprojector, a photographic enlarger, or an opaque projector to the correct size so that the venation could be traced. The wing bases and general shape and size should be drawn with the body so that the wing drawing will be attached correctly in the final composite drawing. Scales should be projected with each rough drawing.

Anatomy

Insects are the only winged invertebrates. Arthropods often confused with Insecta include the Arachnida (spiders, mites, ticks), Myriapoda (millipedes), and Chilopoda (centipedes), as well as smaller groups. Arachnida have a cephalothorax (fused head and thorax) and possess four pairs of walking legs (figs. 15-36a; see C-10). They also have simple instead of compound eyes and no antennae. Myriapoda have a distinct head with antennae, plus many body segments, most of which bear one pair of legs. Millipedes appear to have two pairs of legs per segment; however, each "segment" in fact consists of two partially fused segments. These other groups can be treated for illustration like insects.

The adult insect usually is divided into three main parts: head, thorax (often bearing six legs and one or two pairs of wings), and abdomen (see fig. 15-36b). Further body divisions occur in all parts of

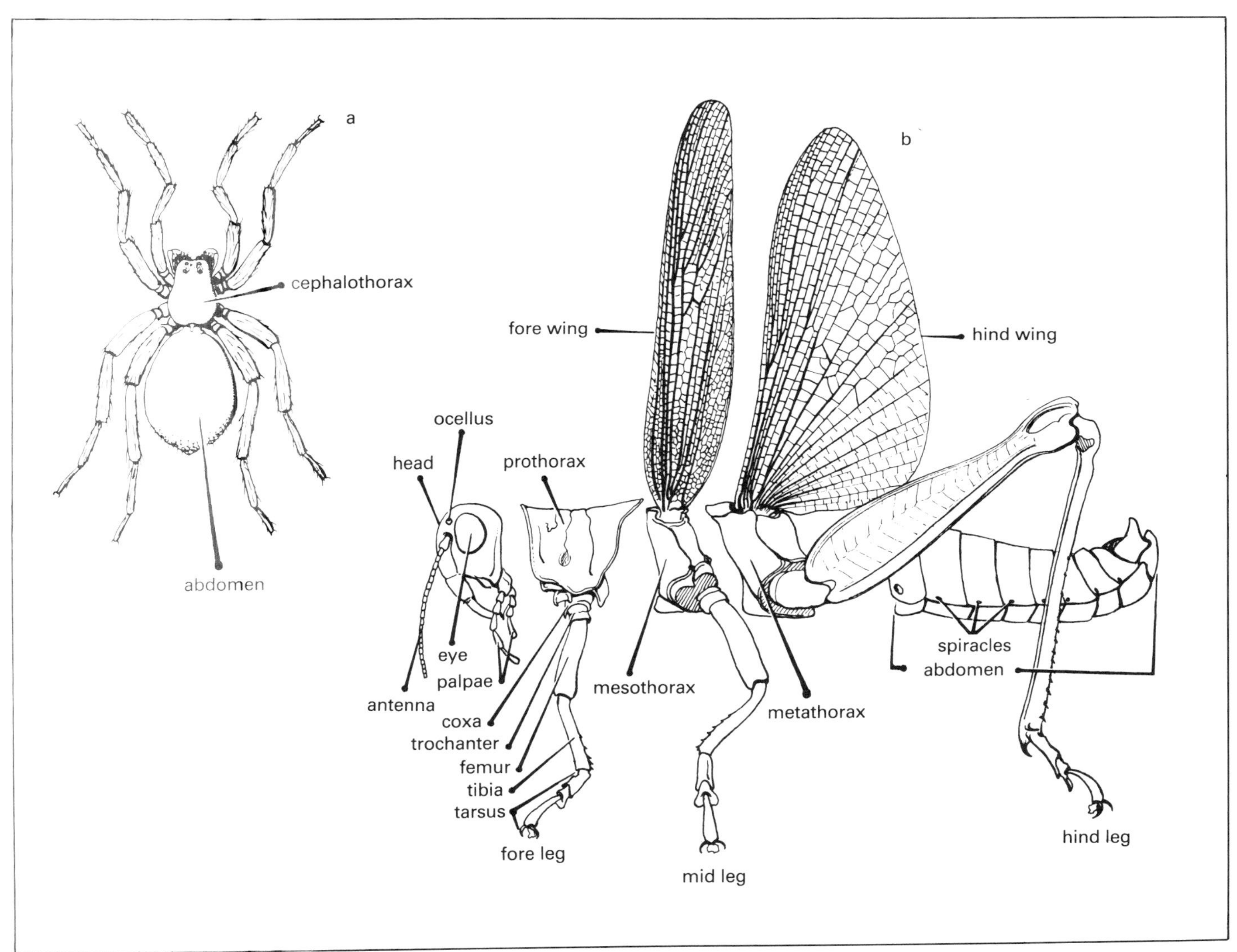

15-36. Some external features of Arachnida and Insecta. *(a)* Arachnid, spider—showing fused head and thorax, the cephalothorax. *(b)* Insect, grasshopper—exploded lateral view to isolate parts. Crowquill pen and ink on Bristol board, by Arthur Cushman. From *Insects* (USDA Yearbook of Agriculture, 1952).

the insect; the head has various plates, the thorax is subdivided into three main segments plus some plates, and the abdomen has six to twelve segments, depending on the group and life stage. Telescoping of the abdomen permits distortion, so that a dead insect may have an abdomen that is abnormally extended or twisted (fig. 15-37). The dorsal part of a segment is a tergum; the ventral part of a segment is a sternum. Connecting the terga and sterna laterally is the pleural membrane.

Each thoracic segment has one ventral pair of legs, and the meso- and metathorax bear the adult's wings or wing remnants. Some larvae (Lepidoptera) possess leglike projections on their abdomens (called pro legs), but these are not truly jointed legs. Another external feature to note is the series of spiracles, openings in the lateral body wall where internal trachea connect and through which oxygen is conveyed (see fig. 15-36b). Usually there are two pairs of spiracles on the thorax and a pair on many abdominal segments.

The features discussed below are especially important in insect illustration; some differentiate species. Other features may be important in certain groups. In all cases, the general shape, proportional relationships, and connections should be rendered carefully.

Bristles and Pubescence

Hair number, size, location, shape, and angle vary consistently. The chaetotaxy (arrangement and nomenclature of bristles and setae) of certain insects has been carefully worked out and must be depicted very accurately (fig. 15-38). An insect hair is called a seta (plural, setae). Setae include bristles (stouter setae) and scales (modified setae), and are set in sockets that usually should be indicated (fig. 15-39). Microtrichia (aculeae) are very tiny, hairlike structures that are not socketed and therefore are not setae. Significant bristles are often

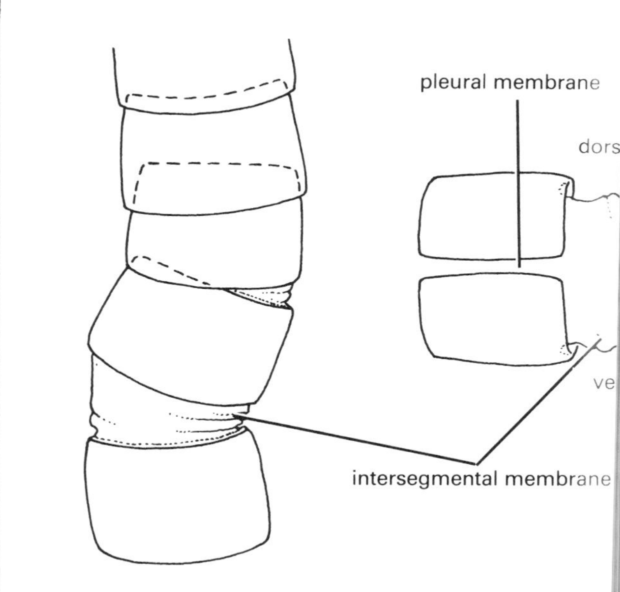

15-37. The ability of insect segments to telescope can result
and ink on Bristol board, by Elaine R. S. Hodges.

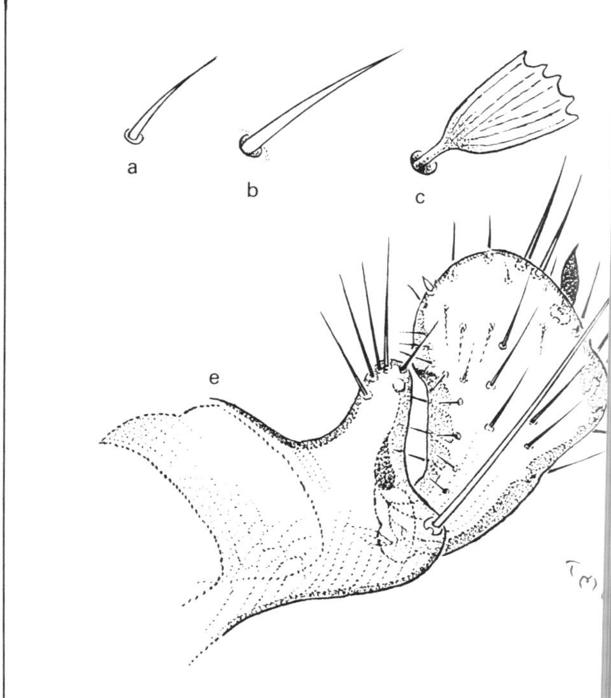

15-39. Types of setae: *(a)* typical seta; *(b)* bristle; *(c)* scale
(d) barbed seta, seen in bees; *(e)* example of several kinds
of a flea. Pen-and-ink on vellum-finish Bristol board, by Th
the *Journal of Medical Entomology*, vol. 4, no. 3, 1967. Co

Facing page:
15-38. Chaetotaxy of mosquito larva. Left side of vertical
ventral view. Technical pen and ink on Bristol board, by T
Contributions of the American Entomological Institute. Co
Walter Reed Biosystematics Unit, and Henry Townes.

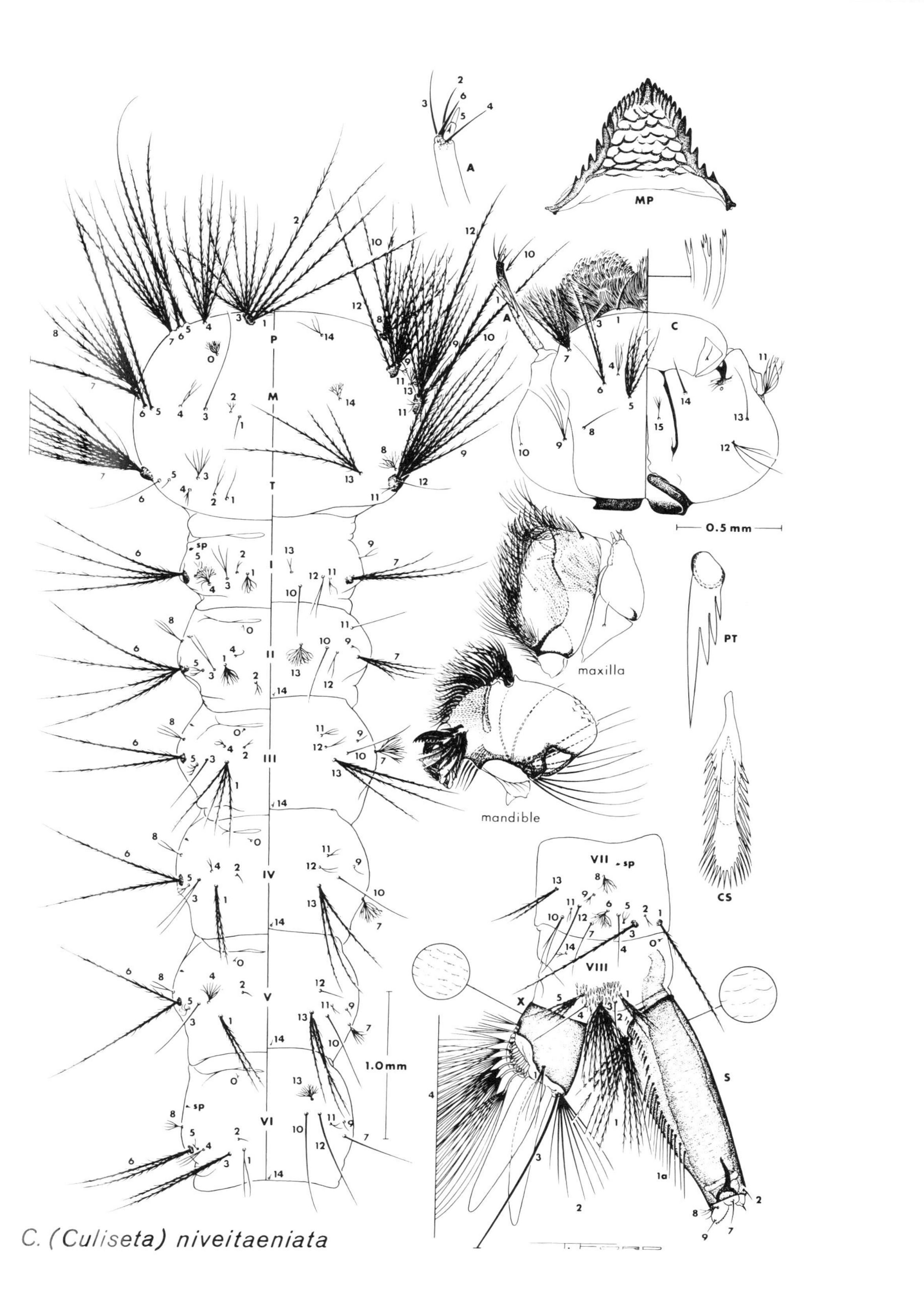

C. (Culiseta) niveitaeniata

sparse. When bristles, scales, or hairs are dense, there is no need to draw each one, since the reduction in publication might make a mass of setae appear as an undefined blob. It is more important to show the overally appearance of the setal mass, with the front ones and any isolated setae detailed. Sometimes setae reflect light and appear to be a body edge or division. Shifting microscope lights will help to clarify structures.

Sculpturing

In slide-mounted specimens, a double edge frequently appears to be outlining body parts; this double line marks the thickness of the exoskeleton and may not need to be drawn as double. Sclerotized areas can be rendered with lines instead of stipples to convey their hard quality, but care must be taken that the lines do not look like sutures or surface sculpturing. The exoskeleton frequently bears a variety of elev
some of wh
and taxono
example, th
number, an
of grooves
elytra, the
flies.

Wings

Venation
tion, curva
of veins ar

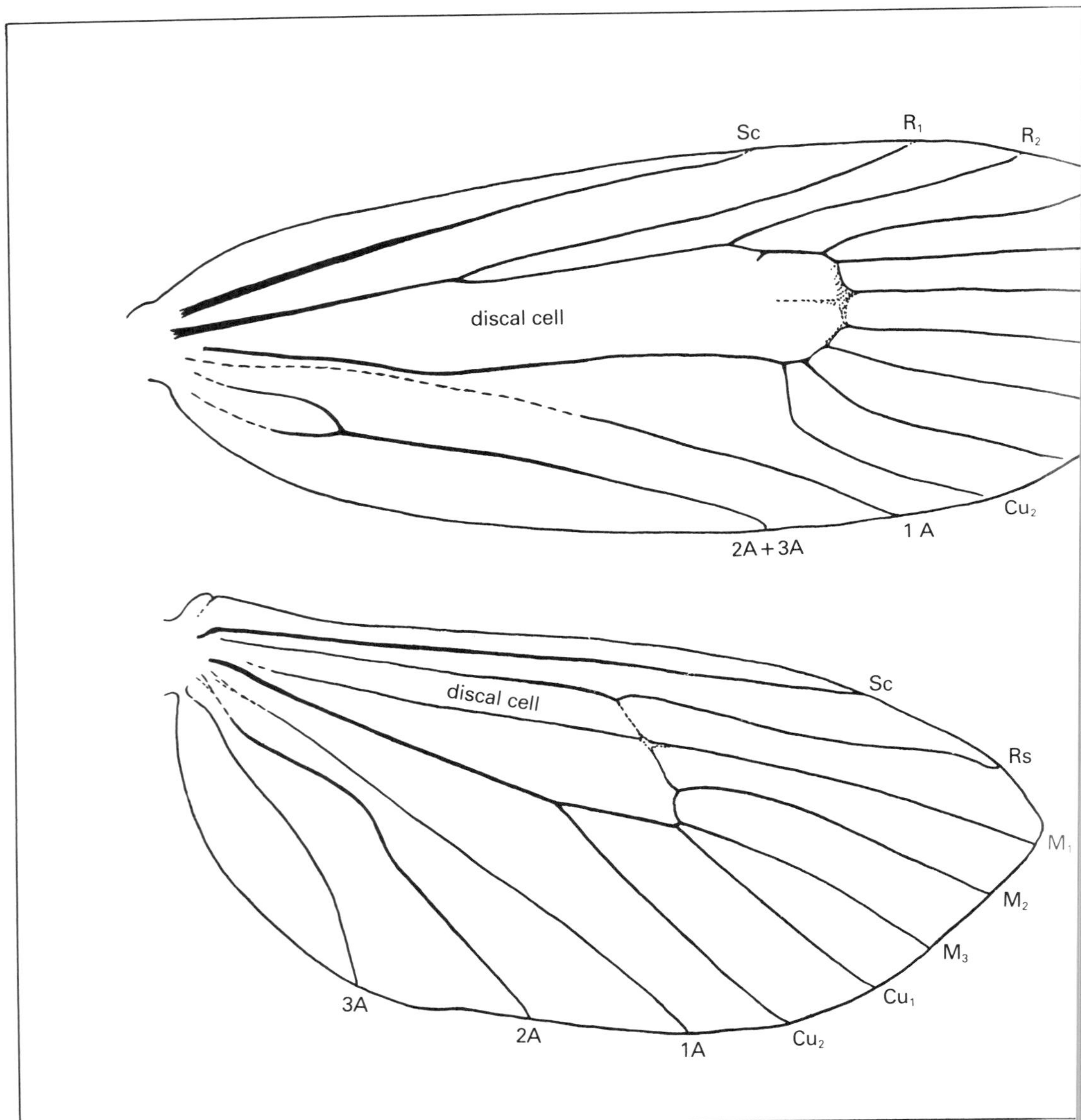

15-40. Wing venation. Lepidoptera fore and hind wings labeled using the Comstock system. Dashes represent vestigial vein extensions. Hunt 104, Gillott 659 pens and ink on Bristol board, by Elaine R. S. Hodges. From Gelechioidea: Oecophoridae, by Ronald W. Hodges, in *Moths of America North of Mexico*, Fascicle 6.2 (Wedge Entomological Research Foundation, 1974).

important in classification to family level than any other single character. Spaces between the veins are termed cells. Veins and cells are labeled with numbers, names, or letters, depending on the system being used (fig. 15-40). See various wing constructions in textbook keys. On specimens note whether certain veins meet or whether they reach the wing margin, and make sure that the venation on both wings matches. Incorrectly drawn venation is a common error in illustrations. The arrangement of setae and scale patterns on the wings also is important when these are present.

Wing venation is most easily seen if the wings are mounted on slides after being bleached (in liquid bleach) and having scales (if present) removed. The scientist will do the preparation and mounting. On the pinned insect with scaly wings (such as Lepidoptera) the veins are more easily seen from the underside. If a slide of the wing is not available, a drop of alcohol (any strength) carefully applied with an eyedropper to the dry wing surface makes the venation stand out. The alcohol evaporates, leaving the dry insect unharmed. Nonetheless, it is a good idea, as always, to obtain permission from the scientist before wetting the specimen.

Note that some insects have structures that permit fore and hind wings to connect. Bees have a series of hooklike hamuli on their hind wings (see fig. 27-6). Some moths have a clump of hairs called a frenulum on the base of the costal (top or anterior) margin of their hind wings, which slips into a pocketlike retinaculum on the underside of the fore wing. The frenulum looks like a hook on the male because the hairs are fused, forming a point. On the female the hairs are separated, like an unpointed paintbrush.

Antennae and Tarsi

The number of parts, the exact shapes, and the size relationships of antennae and tarsi are important and should be noted carefully by the illustrator. In some cases, antennal form is distinctive for families.

Tarsal structure is second in importance only to antennal form in many insects (such as beetles and true bugs) for identification to family. The subsections (tarsomeres) of the tarsus on each pair of legs are referred to as the tarsal formula. It is expressed in three parts, indicating the number of segments each in the fore legs, mid legs, and hind legs. For example, 5-5-4 means tarsi of the fore and mid legs have five segments, and the tarsi of the hind legs have four segments. Sometimes one segment of the tarsus is hidden by another segment, but it still should be found, counted, and illustrated, if possible (fig. 15-41).

Genitalia

This is sometimes the only structure that differentiates species and therefore is probably the most frequently illustrated insect part in taxonomic papers. The male genitalia usually show most variation and therefore are most used. Genitalia are dissected by the scientist, often put through a series of chemical baths to dissolve muscles, stained, and then mounted on microscope slides, placed in alcohol or glycerin, or embedded in glycerin jelly or other medium for drawing. Genitalia, although consisting basically of a cylinder supporting more cylinders, look flat when mounted on a slide and viewed through a compound microscope (figs. 15-42, 15-43, 15-44). Complex genitalia appear very different in dorso-ventral, lateral, and three-quarter views. The latter two positions clarify relationships of parts (see figs. 5-25, 15-43c). Genitalia are customarily drawn with the base down, as though the insect's head were at the bottom of the page, tail at the top. However, the reverse also is used (see fig. 5-9).

A trick that may help clarify genitalic structure (and perhaps other insect anatomy) is to use cutout pieces of fabric or paper to fold and roughly approximate anatomical connections. An invaluable reference for understanding structure and terminology of insect genitalia is *A Taxonomist's Glossary of Genitalia in Insects*, by S. L. Tuxen (see Bibliography). Each insect order has its own terminology, and it is difficult to establish homologies among the groups.

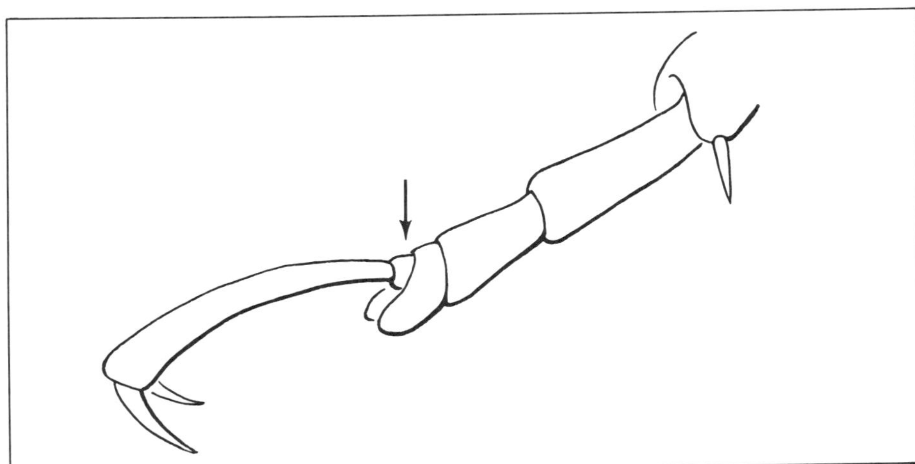

15-41. Tarsus of beetle showing reduced fourth segment, partially hidden by third. Modified from pen-and-ink drawing on Bristol board, by Richard E. White.

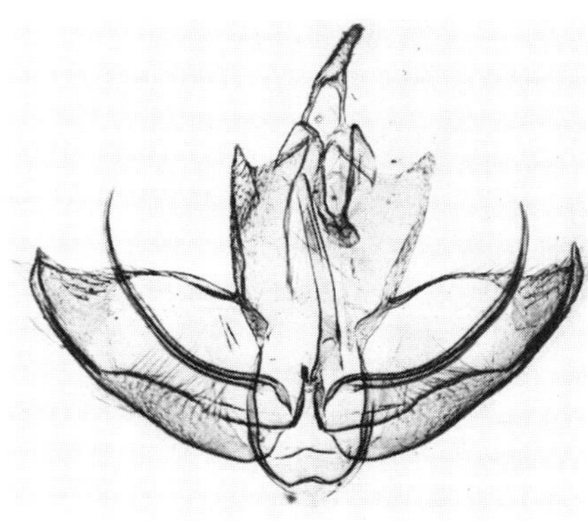

15-42. Microscope slide preparation of lepidopteran male genitalia, *Fabiola shaleriella*, the same specimen drawn in figure 15-43*(a)*. Courtesy of Ronald W. Hodges. Photo by Vic Krantz, Smithsonian Office of Printing and Photographic Services.

Right:
15-44. Coleoptera male genitalia (lateral view) rendered in carbon dust on Video board, by L. Michael Druckenbrod, showing its cylindrical form. Courtesy of Bob Gordon.

15-43. Examples of insect genitalia. Cylinders upon cylinders, sometimes flattened, form the basic structures. Stipples differentiate layers in *(a)* and *(b)*; dashes are used in *(c)*. Dashed ellipses indicate the cylindrical shapes. Lepidoptera (moths—ventral views) are shown in *(a)* and *(b)*, Coleoptera (beetle) in *(c)*. *(a) Fabiola shaleriella* male and *(b) Martyrhilda nechlys* female. Hunt 104 pens and ink on Bristol board, by Elaine R. S. Hodges. From Gelechioidea: Oecophoridae, by Ronald W. Hodges, in *Moths of America North of Mexico*, Fascicle 6.2 (Wedge Entomological Research Foundation, 1974). *(c) Cylloepus barberi* (male ventral and lateral views). Gillott 170 and 659 pens and ink on Bristol board, by Young T. Sohn. Courtesy of Paul J. Spangler.

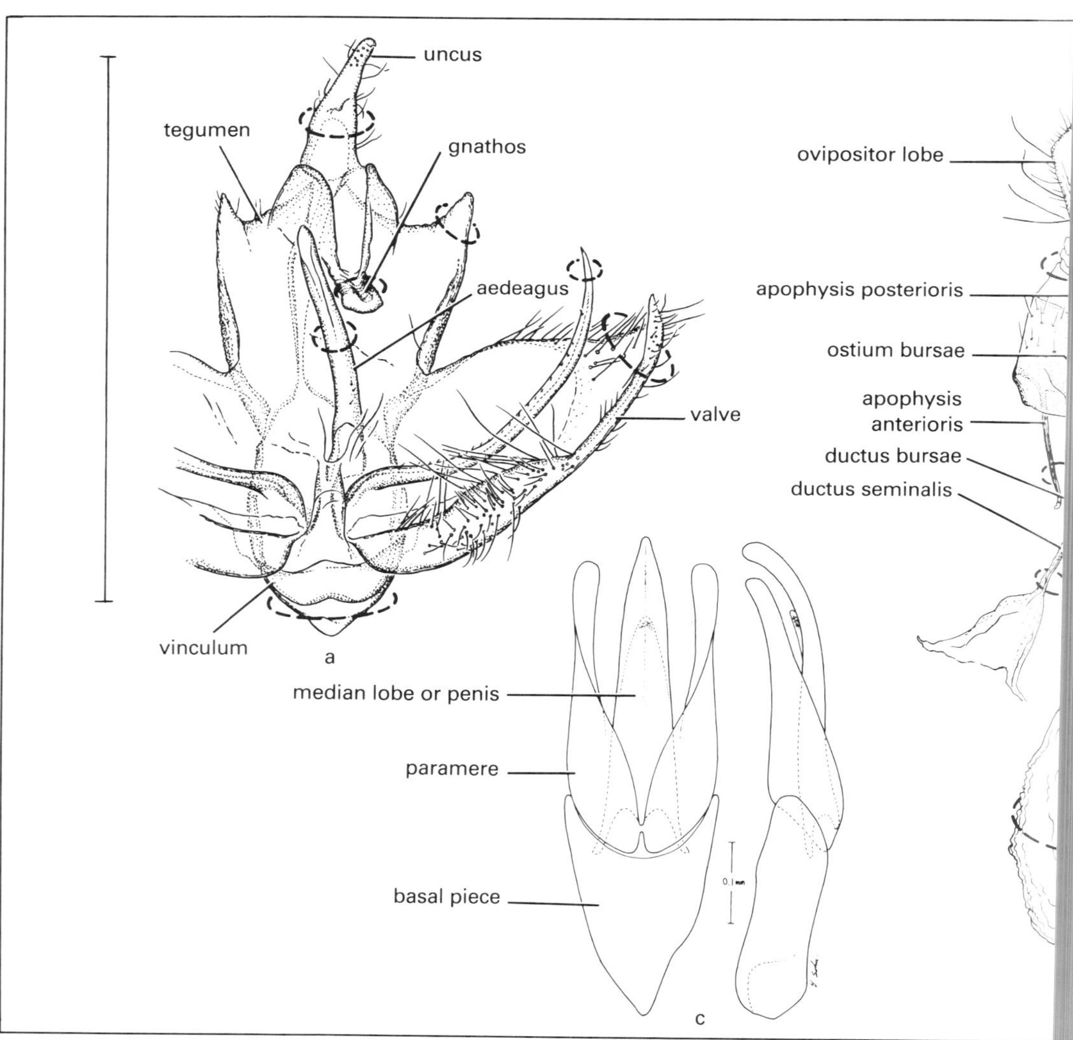

Care and Handling

Insects may be stored dry, in liquid, or mounted on microscope slides. When the insect is not in use (especially overnight) it should be kept in a protected place and covered to prevent dust accumulation, accidental breakage, and infestation by live insects or mice. Some suggestions are provided here for mounting techniques that are normally the responsibility of the scientist. The artist may want to collect insects to practice mounting and manipulation of specimens. When handling museum or other valuable material, always check with a specialist about the safety of a procedure.

Dry Specimens

Dried insects are usually mounted on insect pins (thinner and longer than sewing pins) or minutens (very thin, short pins) or are pointed—glued to the tip of a paper point (fig. 15-45). Pinned insects are stored in boxes whose bottoms are lined with soft material firm enough to hold pins—finely textured foam, for example. Some insects such as dragonflies are stored, with wings folded back, in envelopes to save space.

Mothballs (naphthalene or PDB—paradichlorobenzene) are used in insect storage drawers to cover the odor of dead insects, which attracts pests. PDB may kill insect pests as well. The mothballs or flakes should not be loose (they might knock into specimens) but should be put in a small punched or screen-covered container or wrapped in paper, either one pinned into the box. Work in well-ventilated areas and avoid excess exposure to either chemical.

Dry specimens require careful and special handling because of their fragility.

1. Open storage containers slowly so that a sudden rush of air does not rip off wings.
2. When handling an insect pin, always be aware of where your fingers are to avoid knocking off an insect leg.
3. Always hold the substrate into which the pin is inserted with one hand while inserting or removing the pinned insect with the other hand to prevent the pinning block from flipping up and breaking the specimen.
4. When removing a pinned insect from its box, balance your hand or free fingers on the box edge to minimize wobble. In pushing the pin back into the box, avoid using too much pressure; release the pin gradually so that it does not spring loose and send the insect flying. Some entomologists find it helpful to use pinning forceps with ridged jaws in handling pinned insects (see fig. 2-7). These facilitate working in a crowded box of specimens, but their manipulation requires practice. Good pinning forceps that hold a pin securely may be difficult to locate; try before buying.
5. When studying a dried specimen under the microscope, make sure it will not hit the objective or stage. Larger insects are especially prone to damage.
6. To examine the underside of a pinned insect, insert the pin head upside down into plasticine or another soft but firm substrate. Make sure the insect will not touch the plasticine. Carefully clean the plasticine from the pin head when the pin is removed.

Under the microscope, the dry insect is inserted into a specimen holder. This frees the illustrator's hands for drawing and holds the specimen steady. A simple pinning block can be made from wood or heavy board onto which plasticine is pressed or cork mounted to hold the pinned insect (fig. 15-46). Plasticine has the advantage of holding the insect pin rather securely even after it has been adjusted. Be careful to keep the microscope light far enough away so that its heat does not soften or melt the plasticine.

15-45. Ways of pinning dried insects: *(a)* pin inserted through specimen; *(b)* double-mounting—specimen is on a minuten, which is in turn inserted in another material that is itself pinned; *(c)* pointing—one side of the insect is glued to the tip of a paper point. Photo by Vic Krantz, Smithsonian Office of Printing and Photographic Services.

15-46. Specimen holders: *(a)* acrylic specimen rotator (made by Dave Meyersburg); *(b)* balsa-wood pieces nailed together; *(c)* plasticine shaped and pressed into cardboard. Photo by Vic Krantz, Smithsonian Office of Printing and Photographic Services.

Insect pins can slip from softened material, resulting in the specimen's burial in plasticine. Always turn down the microscope lights when leaving the work for more than a few minutes. (Turning the lights off and on too much reduces the bulb's life.)

Commercial specimen holders called microscope stages may be available in some biological supply catalogs; these permit rotation of the specimen under the stereoscope without repeated handling of the pin. They use soft cork in a small holder for the specimen. The cork wears out from multiple pinholes, but it can be replaced with clay or pieces of firm eraser. An older type of holder rotates the specimen in more than one direction (see fig. 15-46a).

Wet Specimens

Soft-bodied insects that may shrivel if dried are generally stored in 70 to 75 percent alcohol. This includes adults of certain insect orders and nearly all immature insects. Alcohol toughens tissue but also makes the insect brittle. Dissected parts of insects, especially genitalia, are sometimes stored in small vials of glycerin attached to the pin with the dried whole insect. Water is never used for storage because these animals would decay in it. Specimen study in water may be helpful, however, because some soft specimens retain their true shape in water but contract in more dense media, such as glycerin.

Insects may need to be transferred from water or alcohol into glycerin during the drawing process because the greater viscosity of glycerin keeps the specimen from moving as much. Alcohol and water disperse in glycerin so no special steps need to be taken. However, certain insects should not be transferred directly from

water to
parts ma
draws wa
should g
ing perc
process i
tist, as is
cedures,
been giv
specimen
men sho
to preve
forming
The h
liquid an
the begi

Living o

It is ra
a live ins
times th
insect in
present
changes
of a live
help to

quickly with a grid or camera lucida while the microscope lights are cool. Warmth makes insects move faster. Anesthetizing the insect in the freezer or with cyanide or ethyl acetate may keep it still for a few minutes, long enough for the preliminary drawing to be accomplished.

Freshly killed and mounted specimens are easier to draw than older, dried insects because the appendages are flexible and can be positioned easily. Either prop the body and appendages in the desired attitude at this time or wait some hours until the freshly killed insect stiffens a bit. Then appendages can be moved into desired positions and will stay there. Adults of certain groups, such as beetles, store well in alcohol and can be taken from the alcohol and mounted. Entomology texts and *A Field Guide to the Insects of America North of Mexico*, by D. J. Borror and R. E. White (see Bibliography) illustrate how different orders of insects should be pinned.

Appendage Illustration

Insects frequently have the appendages bent, curved, or pushed in close to the body, making it difficult to draw parts or to see the ventral side of the insect. After the body is drawn, it is sometimes possible to draw the appendages one part at a time. Position the insect so that the first part (closest to the body) is in a good position under the microscope. Draw this, then move the specimen until the next section is in the correct position and draw it, connecting it to the first section of the appendage. Repeat this process with the rest of the appendage. Doing this accurately requires knowledge of insect anatomy so that the same view of each section is maintained. The connection to the body must also be accurate (see figs. 2-28, 2-29, 2-30, 2-35). Groups of insects differ greatly in the normal attitude of the legs and in the extent of the femur visible from a dorsal view.

If the appendages cannot be drawn in sections and must be repositioned, ask the scientist if the specimen can be relaxed or if the appendage can be broken off and mounted separately. Usually the scientist will handle these tasks. Relaxing is done by placing the insect in a closed jar made humid by a wet sponge under paper on which the insect is placed or pinned for several hours or overnight until its appendages move easily. To prevent fungal growth overnight, naphthalene is added to the relaxing container. Another method is to hold the insect or its appendage with forceps in a jet of steam from a kettle of boiling water until it becomes flexible. This is safe only with relatively tough specimens such as beetles. A drop of saliva or household cleaning detergent placed on an appendage with the tip of an insect pin also will soften the joint after a few minutes so that it can be moved to a new position. Never touch a dried specimen with your fingers unless it has been relaxed first.

If you must break off an appendage (with the permission of the scientist), put a drop of saliva at the appendage base to prevent it from flying off when it is broken with a fine-pointed forceps. This may have to be done under the microscope. Mount the appendage on a slide with a cover slip or on a drop of saliva on the flat of the "point" holding the entire insect or on the insect label where the appendage can be seen. Wait until it softens a bit, then adjust its position for drawing. After the drawing is completed, you or the specialist should glue the appendage to the point or label or prepare a permanent slide mount to preserve it. Clear fingernail polish or white glue can be used to mount the appendage. Gently touch the appendage to the sticky surface so that the specimen does not sink into it and thus become harder to study. *Never* break parts off a type specimen.

Conventions

Different conventions are followed in illustrating different orders of insects and for different purposes. When the illustration is meant to show a lifelike appearance, the approach is straightforward: the illustrator must know how the insect would look standing, flying, and in other natural postures. Photographs of living insects are a helpful supplement to observation, as are books on insect flight (*Borne on the Wind*, by S. Dalton, and *Insects in Flight*, by W. Nachtigall—see Bibliography). For scientific publications, the aim is to illustrate the insect's characteristics and relative proportions, so the whole insect usually is drawn artificially flattened. The animal's appendages should be arranged gracefully so that they look relatively natural. Construction and size of the appendages, or typical posture of the living insect, determines how these appendages should be arranged.

Dorsal Views

In a dorsal view of the whole insect, the antennae and legs are frequently shown in lateral positions, the antennae arching forward or around the body so as not to obscure the legs, the fore legs extending forward and the mid and hind legs directed backward (see figs. 8-2, 8-3). Sometimes one leg or antenna is turned to show a lateral or ventral view (fig. 15-47). Usually the body and its parts are drawn symmetrically. For pleasing attitudes of the legs, the angles between the segments (femur, tibia, tarsus) generally range between 90 and 150 degrees. Too great an angle makes the insect look as though it were stretching out, and it takes up too much space; too small an angle looks awkward. The appendages of certain groups of insects, however, should not be portrayed this way because for them it would be unnatural. As examples: nymphs of stream-dwelling may-

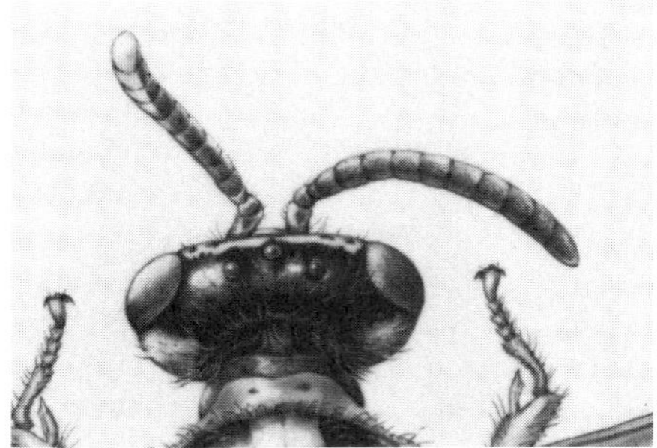

15-47. One antenna of a *Perdita* bee is turned back to show its lighter-colored underside. Graphite dust on Cronaflex, by Elaine R. S. Hodges.

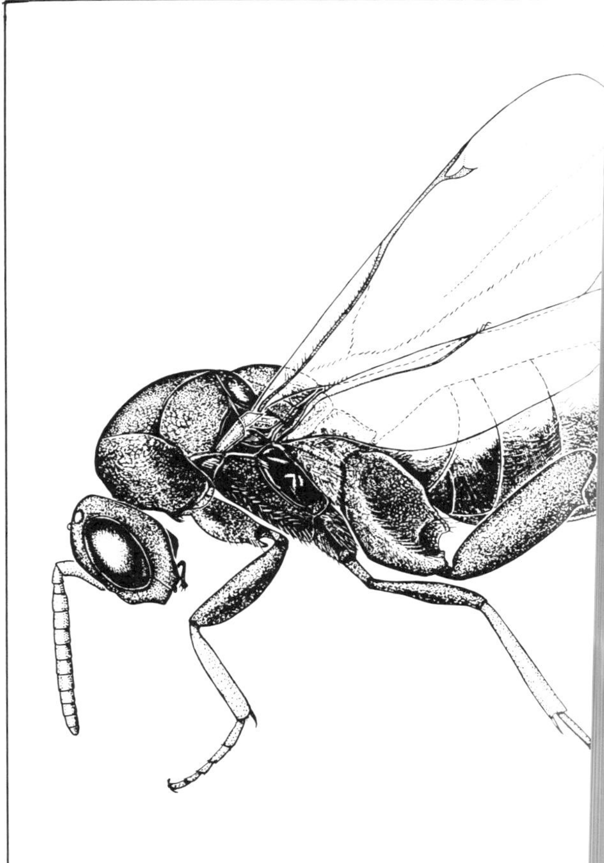

15-49. In lateral view, often one set of appendages only i
Chalcid wasp, *Monodontomerus obscurus.* Pen-and-ink o
Cooley. Courtesy of Eric Grissell.

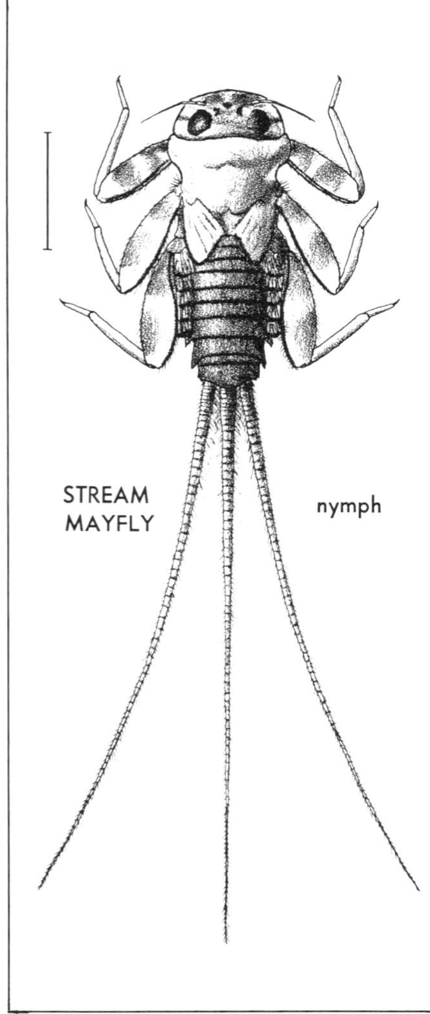

15-48. An example of an insect whose legs are arranged in positions different from the conventional dorsal view. Ink and Negro pencil on coquille board, by Richard E. White. From *A Field Guide to the Insects of America North of Mexico,* by Donald Borror and Richard E. White. © 1970 by Borror and White. Reprinted by permission of Houghton Mifflin.

flies typically have all of the legs directed forward (fig. 15-48); many aquatic insects hold their legs in an arcuate position; hind legs of leafhoppers are held against the body; insects with prehensile fore legs (such as mantids) often support themselves on the mid and hind legs only, directing the mid legs forward and the hind legs backward. Exceptions to the general rules may have to be made when drawing a very long-legged insect so as to conserve space and to prevent the drawing from becoming too large. Each appendage must be clearly visible after reduction in publication.

Lateral Views

Here the antenna is generally drawn arching up over the body or pointing forward, again not obscur-

ing the
otherwis
dages n
double
cates th
view of
femur i
tend to
may be
shorten
tened l
purpose

Combin

For
diagram
drawn
paper.
tailed
and on
(see fig
is usef
for wh

setae and their positions are important. Dorso-ventral drawings are used mostly for depicting mosquito larvae and pupae, scale insects, and mites, but they are also used occasionally for insect genitalia, abdominal color patterns, or other features. Another type of combination shows detail on one side but not on the other (fig. 15-50).

Reconstruction

The bilateral quality of most insects simplifies reconstruction of damaged appendages or parts, for if these are damaged or missing on one side, they may be whole on the other side. Additional specimens multiply the sources of information. Insects often are twisted, however, into positions where parts of the body are hidden by other parts, such as with tightly appressed legs, a bent head, a tumor, or an attached parasite. If the insect cannot be relaxed and repositioned and there is only one specimen, as is frequently the case, the illustrator must figure out how to represent the invisible. If the specimen is in pieces, there often are few clues as to how the whole insect or structure would appear. Experience and knowledge of insect anatomy are the illustrator's best tools for figuring out what that invisible part probably looks like. Consultation with the scientist may be necessary in the most difficult situations. Occasionally similar species can be used for reference to see how a particular body part is likely to be constructed, depending on what is in question. But characters of insect species vary so greatly that it cannot be expected that structures will be constructed alike, even in closely related species.

Body movement of insects occurs only at the areas where the segments meet, so if a specimen is twisted, this generally has little effect on the shape of the segments themselves. The specimen can be adjusted on paper by drawing the first body part, then shifting the specimen or paper to draw the next segment, and so on (see the Appendage Illustration section, above).

Sometimes the scientist does not want reconstruction. This usually applies to a holotype, which may be drawn in its actual condition. Reconstruction is not always drawn as though the specimen were perfect. The reconstructed part might be shown with a dashed or dotted line, especially if it involves interpretation or hypothesis rather than the simple copying of one side onto another (see fig. 1-1).

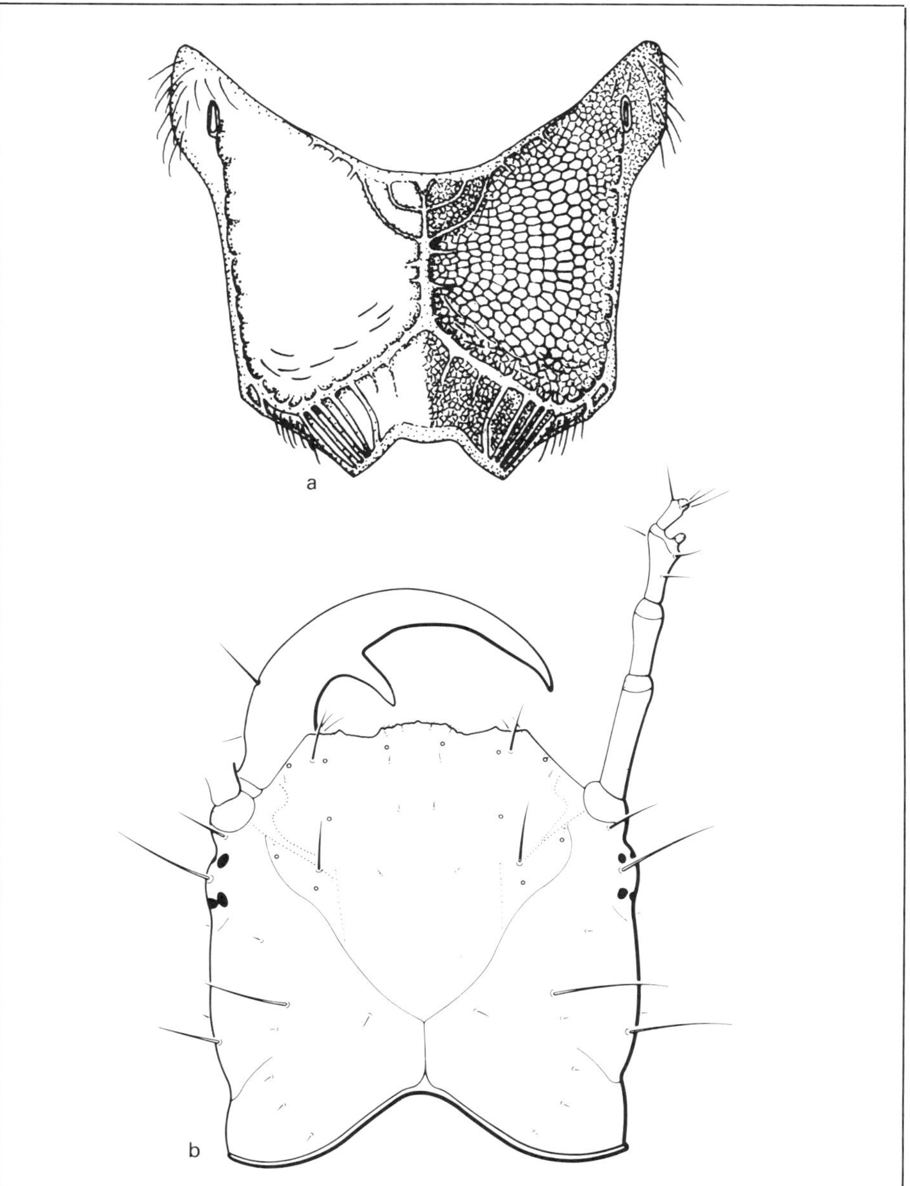

15-50. Symmetrical structures and details drawn only on one side to save time and to clarify underlying anatomy on the other side. *(a)* By showing texture on one side of this propodeum, structure and setal arrangement are clear on the other side. Chalcid wasp, *Pachytomoides megistus*. Technical pen and ink on Bristol board, by Linda Heath Lawrence. Courtesy of Eric Grissell. *(b)* Carabid beetle larval head. *Pterostichus moestus*, with one mandible and one antenna represented. Technical and crowquill pens on Cronaflex, by Go Sato. Reproduced by permission of the Minister of Supply and Services, Canada.

Special Problems

Rendering Eyes

Insects have simple or compound eyes, often both. Each simple eye (ocellus; plural, ocelli) possesses a single rounded corneal lens. On larvae, several simple eyes are lateral; on the adult, usually three are dorsal on the head. The compound eye is a collection of many "eyes," or ommatidia, each with its own corneal lens, the visible facet. Each ommatidium has a central linear core of sensory cells, the rhabdom, which

stretches i
the compo
the eye
thousands
facets.

It is in
facet of th
ceptual il
created w
tively few
subject ca
ties of th
ment of
relative si
identical.
be arran
The eyes
rendered
ideas are
and 15-52

"Actual-S

In son
pecially f
line or fig
sect's ac
the large
32). To a
tion that
drawing
drawing
the brac
represen
two tim
opaque
achieve
illustrati
a camer
duce ac
Field Gu
ica Nor
Field Gu
ica, wh
D. J. Bo
do this.
under
and pu
marked
size (pl
tual si
Lookin
line up
with th
increas
magnifi
drawin
paper r

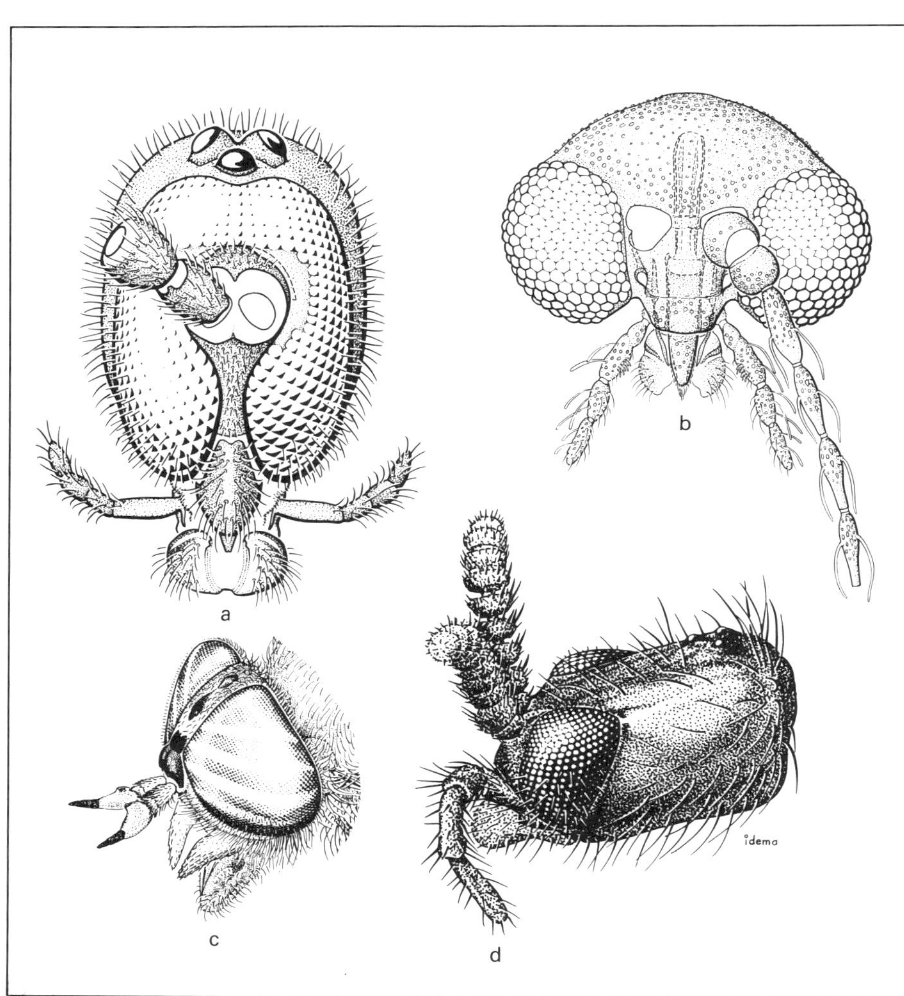

15-51. Methods of rendering insect eyes in line, by Ralph Idema. Each eye is begun by drawing two intersecting sets of faint concentric lines in fine H or HB pencil, following the natural direction of the specimen's facets. *(a)* Fine crowquill pen and ink on DuPont UC-7 drafting film. Pen nibs were widened by being filed off. The pencil sketch with the intersecting lines was placed under transparent film. At intersecting points, a small triangle was drawn to represent each ommatidium, in appropriate sizes to create highlight, shadow, and reflected light. The film is scratched like scratchboard. This is the fastest technique shown here. *(b)* Crowquill on Strathmore Bristol board, hot-press. Using the intersecting guidelines, the ommatidia are shown realistically with line thickness indicating shading. This method is best for large ommatidia. *(c)* No. 0 technical pen and ink on Bristol board. Little crosses are linked at each intersection of the guidelines. *(d)* Technical pens, nos. 0 and 1, on Bristol board with fine brush and zinc white acrylic paint. The entire eye was blacked out. Intersecting lines were drawn in fine HB pencil, barely visible. At intersecting points, a white dot was painted to represent each ommatidium in appropriate sizes to create highlight and shadow. From *Manual of Nearctic Diptera*, vol. 1, by J. F. McAlpine et al., Research Branch, Agriculture Canada Monograph no. 27, 1981. Reproduced by permission of the Minister of Supply and Services, Canada.

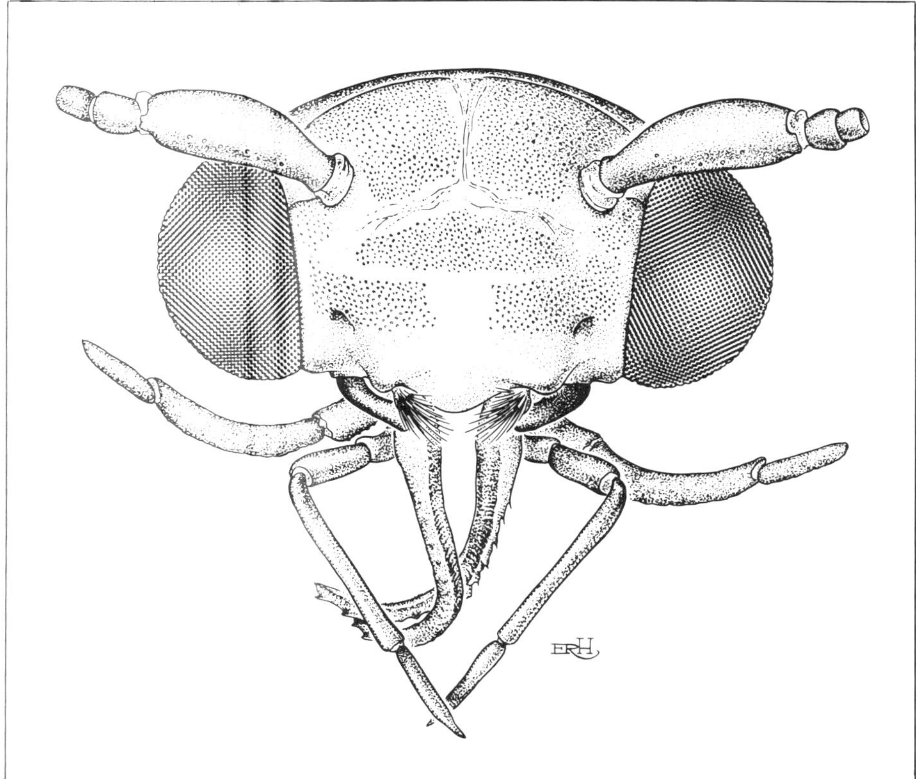

15-52. To produce a highlighted eye, two layers of shading film are overlapped and shifted against one another to produce a moiré pattern. The lightest part of the pattern is placed in the upper left or center of the eye—the highlight. After the eye's outline was inked, two small pieces of film were shifted until the proper size of moiré was found. One piece was then placed over the eye and the shape cut out, following the outline. The shape was peeled off and applied. This process was repeated with the second piece of film. Used were a sharp blade for cutting and jeweler's forceps to handle the film. Any film extending beyond the outline was cut away. Dots of ink or white paint fill in blank parts of the pattern. This example uses 32½-line, 20 percent screen for both layers; other patterns and combinations will produce different-sized highlights. Primitive moth head with scales removed. Hunt 104, Gillott 659 pens and ink on Bristol board, by Elaine R. S. Hodges. Courtesy of Donald R. Davis.

the drawing. Then outline the image of the drawing on the microscope stage. Obtaining an accurate reduction depends on the printer's reducing the drawing according to instructions.

Invertebrates include a huge number of very diverse animals, many of which are economically or medically important. As a result, there is a great demand for their illustration. Because these animals vary so widely in size, appearance, anatomy, and requirements for preservation, the techniques for handling and drawing them also vary. This chapter presents many suggestions for mounting, measuring, and drawing invertebrates, but with experience and practice, each illustrator and scientist will develop additional techniques.

16/Illustrating Fishes

Stanley H. Weitzman and Marion J. Dalen

The scientific illustration of fishes may be considered in two categories: drawings of complete fishes for descriptive and identification purposes in systematic ichthyology; and drawings of fish parts, such as histological or gross anatomical preparations for a variety of disciplines, including physiology, histology, functional and comparative anatomy, and phylogenetic studies in systematic ichthyology. The degree of descriptive accuracy and the emphasis on particular visible parts or subject matter depend upon the purpose of the drawing and may vary considerably according to the interest and descriptive intent of the research scientist directing or requesting the drawing.

Illustrations of whole fishes (figs. 16-1, 16-2) are prepared with the aid of accurate counts and measurements of structures on the specimen's body surface. The process often requires the use of a stereoscopic microscope, especially for small fishes, which may be drawn very much enlarged. In most cases, measurements cannot be taken and transferred directly to the rendering surface unless the fish is being drawn at actual size. In nearly all cases, some sort of special apparatus or measuring device—such as a camera lucida and microscope, photographic equipment, a reticle in a microscope eyepiece, or proportional dividers —is needed to transfer distances between points on a fish to corresponding points on a surface. Measurements taken optically and direct tracing of body profiles and structures such as can be done with photographic methods or a camera lucida attachment to a microscope (for fishes smaller than about 1.2 inches [3cm] in total length) are relatively easy to accomplish, although they do introduce a degree of optical distortion dependent upon the quality and kind of equipment being used. Such methods are not always possible, however, especially when the fish is preserved in a bent position. Drawings produced from measurements taken portional di paper as d are more those prepa by camera more expen illustrator a the subject.

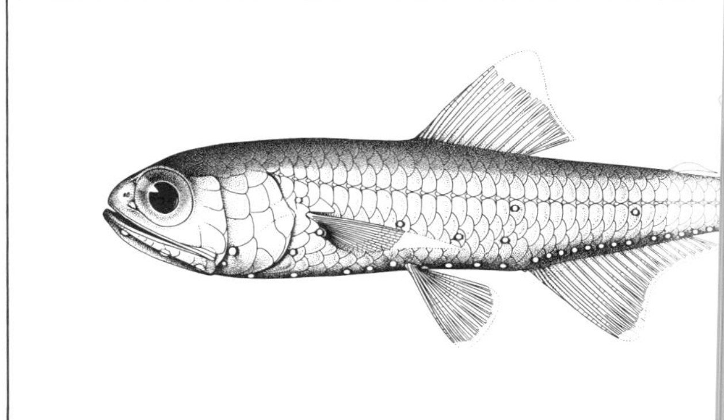

16-1. Variation in scale size and shape as discussed in the t of additional structures such as the photophores (white spots distributed on the body and lower jaw. The probable extent state is shown by dotted lines. California lanternfish, *Symbol* (Eigenmann and Eigenmann). Pen-and-ink on illustration bo 1906.

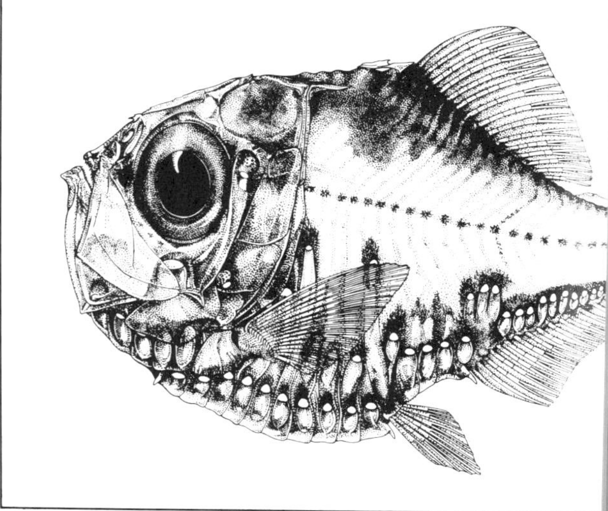

16-2. Location of bony head structures, body spines, photo special features of this deep-sea hatchetfish. Western Atla *laternatus* Garman. Pen-and-ink on Bristol board, by Mari

CONVENTIONS

Depiction of the distinguishing characters of closely related fish species often requires precise presentation of small differences in the number of scales, fin rays, teeth, bony prominences, soft fleshy papillae, skin flaps, barbels, color pattern, and the relative positions of jawbones, fins, and other body structures. All of these features are illustrated in drawings used for identification.

Usually scientific illustrations of fishes show them facing left. The fins are drawn expanded; the mouth may be open or closed. Exceptions occur for certain fish such as rays, which are flattened dorso-ventrally (fig. 16-3). For popular publications, the fish may be shown as though it were swimming or jumping, and in this case the body might be curved, foreshortened, pointed in any direction; the fins could be up or down, the mouth open or closed. Twisting the fish's body visually requires understanding how the skeleton is designed and therefore how it can realistically bend. Details such as scales and projections still should be accurate although it may not be possible or necessary to draw every scale as is done for research papers.

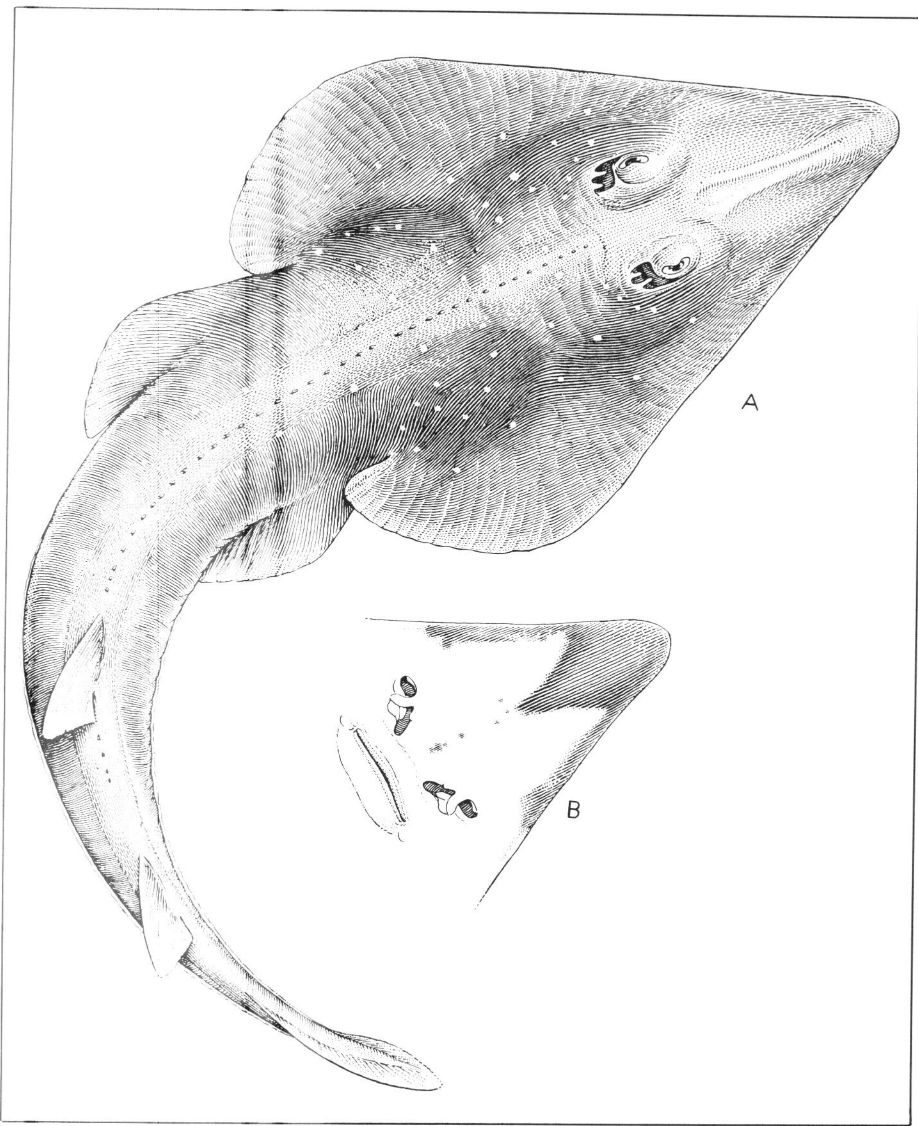

16-3. Some fishes, such as guitarfishes and rays, are dorso-ventrally compressed or flattened. Such fishes usually are drawn showing the dorsal and often the ventral surface of their bodies. In the case of the southern guitarfish or violet guitarfish, *Rhinobatos percellens* (Walbaum), shown here, the dorsal surface *(A)* and the ventral view of the mouth and snout *(B)* are illustrated because of their distinctive characteristics. The contours of the body are indicated by series of thin-thick-thin parallel lines using the eyelash technique described in chapter 5. Pen-and-ink on Bristol board, by E. N. Fischer, circa 1913.

THE ILLUSTRATOR

For the illustration of fishes, besides training in realistic drawing, pen-and-ink, and other techniques, courses in comparative vertebrate anatomy and general zoology would be helpful. A course in ichthyology, if available, would be ideal, but such training is likely to be too specialized for most schools. The artist must become familiar with the major parts of a fish and learn from the ichthyologist what other parts must be shown in any particular case (figs. 16-4, 16-5, 16-6).

INSTRUMENTS AND MATERIALS

Optical Devices

Stereoscopic microscope: for examining small fishes or parts of large ones.

Camera lucida.

Reticles: ocular micrometer or ocular grid; used as alternative to camera lucida to draw small fishes.

Adjustable illuminator: for stereoscopic microscope or for direct illumination of large fishes. A fiber-optic illumination system with at least two flexible light guides is best because it will not heat up the fish and increase the rate of alcohol evaporation.

Magnifiers: movable and adjustable large magnifying lamp and glass or other large magnifying

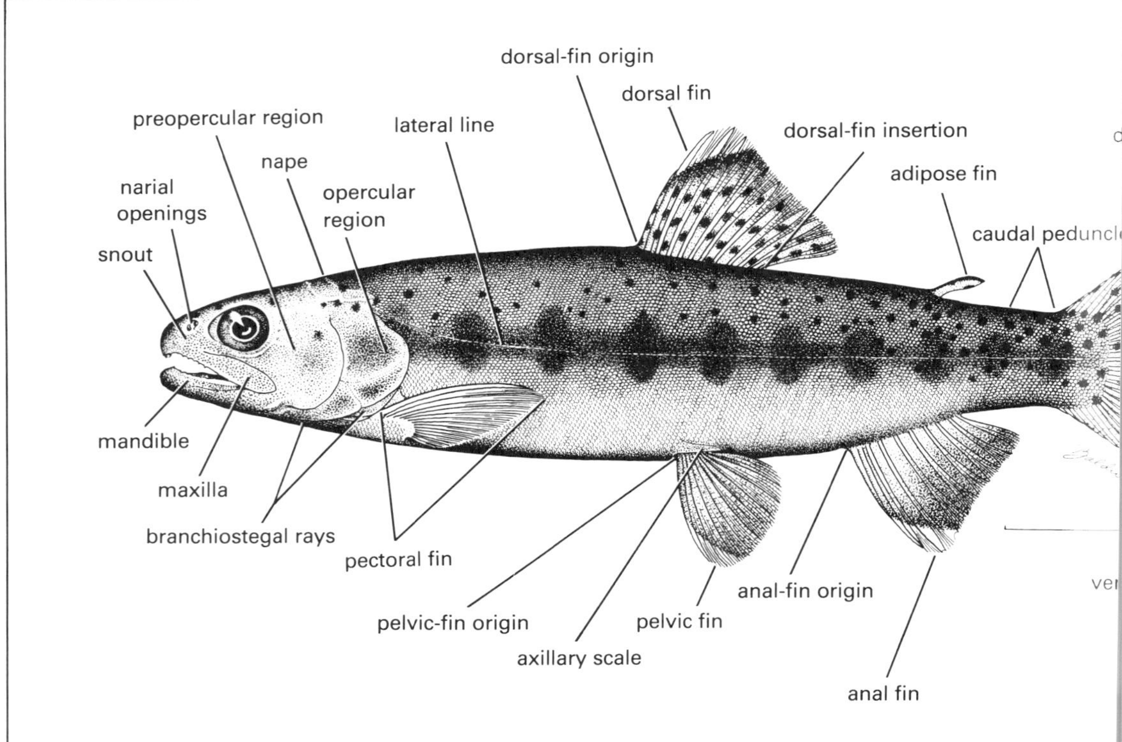

16-4. Certain of the important external parts of a fish's body used in forming the base drawing. Some other fishes have two (or sometimes more) dorsal fins—the first or anterior one of spiny rays, the second of soft rays. The adipose fin is absent in many kinds of fishes. South Fork of Kern golden trout, *Salmo aquabonita* Jordan. Pen-and-ink on illustration board, by A. H. Baldwin, 1904.

glass for examination of large fishes.

Reducing hand lens: to study proportions of a large fish by reducing its scale for comparison with its drawing; also for judging how a drawing will look when it is reduced.

Opaque projector: to project photographic prints of small fishes, if used.

Slide projector: to project 35mm slides used to depict small fishes.

Measuring Devices

Proportional dividers: 10-inch (25cm) dividers, adequate for most subjects.

Specimen-handling Tools

Forceps: bottle (long) and jeweler's finely pointed (short) (see fig. 2-7).

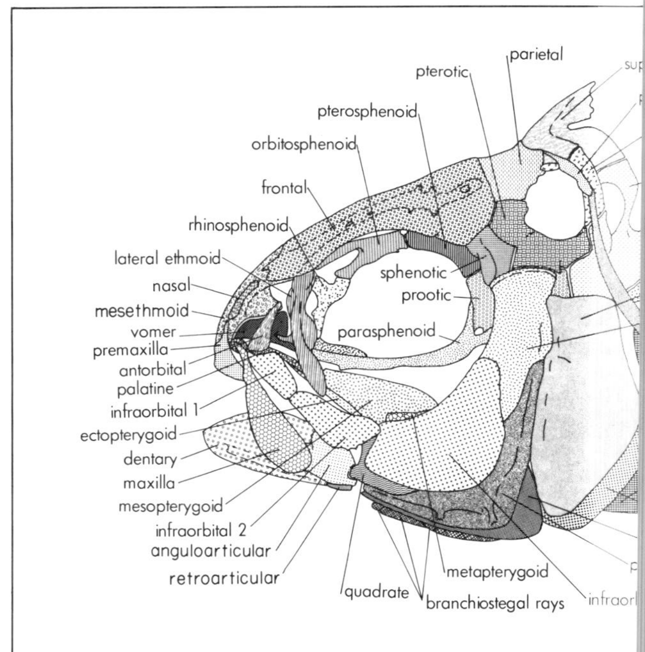

16-5. Simple cartoon illustration showing each skull bone wit of Cardinal tetra, *Paracheirodon axelrodi* (Schultz). Pen-and- patterned shading film by Stanley H. Weitzman, 1976, from a Sara Fink.

Specimen Props

Insect pins.

Styrofoam sheets, soft wood, silicone, wax: should be at least ½ inch (1.3cm) thick; to place in bottom of container as surface into which fish can be pinned.

Plasticine: for mounting fish.

Weights: to keep Styrofoam sheets from floating; pieces of nonrusting heavy metal are best.

Containers

Shallow pans.

Wetting Agents and Preservatives

Alcohol: 75 to 80 percent ethyl; 50 to 55 percent isopropyl, if needed.

Miscellaneous

Paper towels, cheesecloth, plastic wrap: moistened with alcohol; used to cover wet specimens.

CARE AND HANDLING OF SPECIMENS

Handle fish specimens, both whole fishes and their parts, with the utmost care. Usually their fins are fragile and break or tear easily. Other structures, such as spines, barbels, filaments, and the skin, can be damaged by careless treatment. Some fishes, even when well preserved, shed their scales easily. Remove fishes from bottles very carefully with long forceps. Manipulate fins or other parts either with the fingers or forceps, slowly and gently. Feel for stress and resistance when spreading fins. Never attempt to force a part of a fish into a position it will not take easily. Gain experience by handling common, easily available specimens before handling rare or important specimens such as types.

Anatomical preparations of fishes may be especially fragile. Although fish bones are usually strong, the soft connective tissues may be especially weak and prone to tearing. Bones of deep-sea fishes are thin and fracture easily. Soft parts of fishes, such as the contents of the abdominal cavity, may be damaged by an accidental poke with forceps, and the connective tissue holding them together may tear if the parts are lifted from the fluid enclosing them. They are best transferred from one container to another by "floating," that is, keeping them surrounded by fluid. If possible, ask the scientist-supervisor of the drawing project to manipulate fragile parts into position for drawing.

Whole fishes and their parts (except dry bones) must always be kept wet, and it is especially important to keep the fins damp at all times. Alcohol-preserved specimens will shrink while being drawn if the specimens are not kept wet. Of equal importance is that the alcohol-water mixture be maintained at a consistent concentration. When exposed in a tray, the alcohol evaporates at a faster rate than the water, thus reducing the concentration of alcohol in the fluid surrounding the fish and very soon in the fish itself. Adding more alcohol and water in the original proportions, which will now have a greater concentration of alcohol than is in the fish, will result in shrinkage of the fish's flesh as the fluid in the specimen and the surrounding fluid gradually equalize concentrations, drawing water out of the fish. Shrinkage can reach serious proportions in a short time—a few minutes for many small fishes. To prevent shrinkage it is necessary to replace the alcohol in the tray frequently while drawing—about three times a day for large fishes and about twice an hour for small fishes. It is very difficult to reconstitute or hydrate a fish without destroying its color or chemically damaging it in other ways. The problem of shrinkage is one of the ichthyologist's greatest concerns. Fishes being drawn are often important specimens, ones that cannot be replaced. Without experience with alcohol-preserved

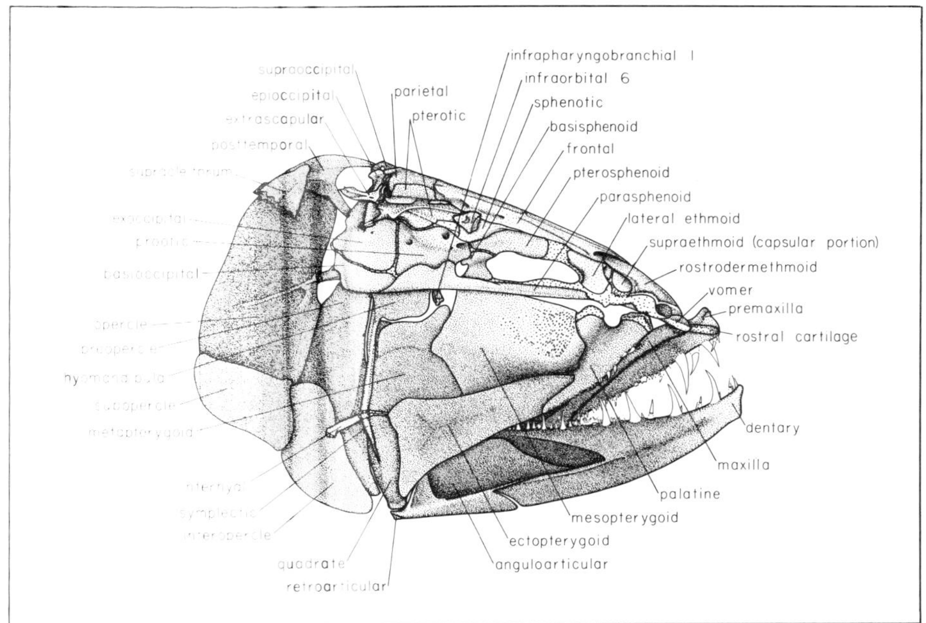

16-6. A stippled skull diagram of a pelagic ocean fish showing the internal side of the face bones of the head and the lateral external surface of the cranium. Drawing prepared from a specimen in which the muscle was digested by trypsin, the bones stained with alizarin red S, then the specimen placed in glycerin to clear the soft connective tissues. The drawing was made to show joints clearly. Oceanic stomiiform fish, *Diplophos taenia* Gunther. Pen-and-ink on Bristol board, by Sara Fink, 1976.

fishes, the danger of shrinkage is significant.

Scientific fish specimens usually are kept in 75 to 80 percent ethyl alcohol, but older specimens are sometimes in 50 to 55 percent isopropyl alcohol. The latter is a fluid that is no longer recommended since at the concentration used it is not a good preservative. Nonetheless, switching to an ethyl alcohol solution will cause shrinkage and should not be attempted without the advice of an ichthyologist.

As a general rule, insist that the fish provided for drawings not be in a Formalin solution, since breathing or working close to Formalin vapors is damaging to the lungs and mucous membranes, and in a short time it begins to preserve the skin of the fingers. Note that this rule may have to be broken in the case of larval fishes and soft-bodied specimens, such as those of the family Liparidae. If Formalin cannot be avoided, work in numerous short sessions rather than fewer long ones and take precautions to reduce evaporation, such as using fiber-optic lighting and, when using a microscope, covering specimen and microscope body with a clear plastic bag as described under Care and Handling of Specimens in chapter 15.

Care of Larval Fishes

Larval fishes are especially delicate and pose special problems. They are often preserved in buffered Formalin solution to prevent dehydration and are best drawn fully immersed in the preservative. They should not be exposed to air, and introducing them to alcohol may cause serious shrinkage. If the ichthyologist permits their being kept in water during illustration, return them to the Formalin solution between drawing sessions. Since this transfer may adversely affect the water content of their bodies, it is not advisable to attempt such changes too frequently. Extreme care must be taken with soft-bodied fishes. Some are so delicate that handling them with forceps will tear their skin and muscle tissue; instead, float the specimens from one container of fluid to the next.

Damaged Specimens

Most preserved fish specimens have sustained some fin or scale damage. The selection of the fish to be drawn is the choice of the ichthyologist, who, it is hoped, will provide specimens with the least damage and that are not bent out of shape. Whenever possible, extra specimens should be available to the illustrator for reconstructing damaged parts, but reconstruction should be done only with the agreement of the ichthyologist. Often sex or state of maturity of the fish or both will dictate the final choice of the fish to be drawn.

PREPARATION OF WHOLE FISHES FOR DRAWING

Mounting

Place into a pan, dish, or tray of suitable size a flat piece of thick Styrofoam a little larger than the fish in length and height, and thicker than the fish is thick. Use more than one layer of Styrofoam if the fish's body is thicker than any single available sheet. Place the fish on the Styrofoam with its head pointing to the left as you face it (see figs. 16-1 and 16-2). Weights may be necessary to keep the Styrofoam from floating. It is important that the median (sagittal) plane of the fish be parallel to the plane of the Styrofoam surface. This may be accomplished by building up plasticine clay around the right (down) side of the fish's body, supporting it in position. A more satisfactory method is to gouge out a portion of the Styrofoam's surface, in negative relief of the right half of the fish's body. When the fish is placed in the resulting depression, the sagittal plane through the length of th
to and near
surface of t
When a fish
dorsal, anal
on the ung
face. The fi
pinned dir
surface. If
curled, pla
on the head

Pinning Fi

Ordinari
a folded or
muscles
ments, the
tissue, an
and fixed
rays tightl
must, how
pinned in
suring and
ideal for t
damage
slightly. A
stain the f
pins as a
fin erect (

In pinn
hardened
use force
ray dorsa
basal arti
to the fis
ing the fi
of the fin
end of th
the mem
terior ra
more pin
the ray.
the next
manner
membra
this ray
more pi
der of th
ray in
riorly un
pinned
spread.
any, an
clearly.
peat this
fully. I
spreadi

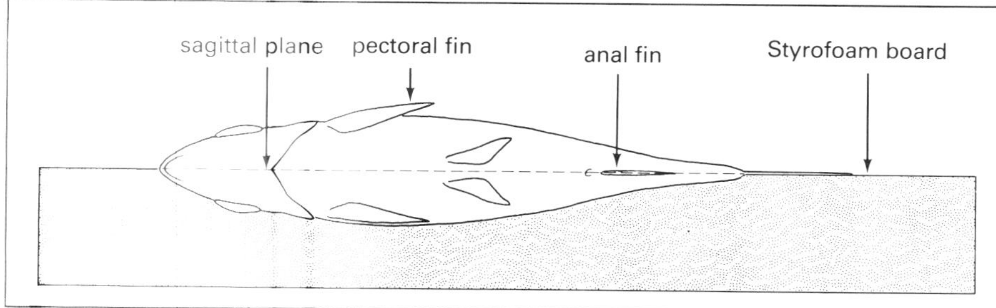

16-7. A fish mounted in a carved-out Styrofoam board. Shading film and pen-and-ink on Bristol board, by T. Britt Griswold.

16-8. Cichlid fish, *Cichlasoma severum* Heckel, with its dorsal fin pinned erect. The anal and caudal fins are collapsed. The dorsal fin anteriorly consists of several spiny rays. The posterior part of the fin, that dorsal to the tail fin, consists of nonspiny soft rays. Photo by Stanley H. Weitzman.

posterior ray first and work anteriorly, gently pushing each ray until all fin rays have been moved again.

When the dorsal fin is drawn, remove the pins by pulling the anterior pins first and successively pulling them posteriorly; pulling the posterior pins first increases the chance of tearing the fin.

Caudal fins generally require many pins to hold them open. If a caudal fin is delicate, the pinning procedure described for the dorsal fin should be used, starting at the middle of the fin between the lobes and working dorsally and ventrally; otherwise follow the procedure suggested here. Put one pin at the base of the long first dorsal ray of the dorsal caudal-fin lobe and the same for the first long ray of the ventral caudal-fin lobe. Place one pin near the ends and between the two longest and thickest rays of the dorsal and ventral lobes of the fin.

Keeping Specimens Moist

Once the fin is in place, pour in enough alcohol to just cover the supporting clay or Styrofoam. Keep the Styrofoam from floating by using weights if necessary. Keep the specimen wet between measurements with several thicknesses of wet cheesecloth or absorbent but strong paper towels. If it takes several days to draw the fish, return it to its bottle after each drawing session. Because of orthographic projection problems, discussed below, it is best to keep the fish mounted until the base drawing is completed. It may be kept in the tray and covered lightly first with an absorbent cloth soaked in preserving fluid and then with a plastic sheet. If the tray is deep enough, the specimen may be covered with preserving fluid between drawing sessions, but the fish should be prevented from floating out of position by mounting it with pins.

DRAWING A WHOLE FISH BY TRIANGULATION

John Ridgway, in *Scientific Illustration* (see Bibliography), noted that a complete fish drawing probably represents the most work per square inch of illustration for any organism except other scaled vertebrates. This is because scales and other details of a fish's body must be accurately delineated, not merely sketched.

Fishes approximately 1½ inches (3cm) or more in total length can be drawn by triangulation with proportional dividers, the size of the image either enlarged or reduced to a convenient size for publication, about 8 to 10 inches (20 to 25cm). This method produces a drawing from which measurements can be taken by the reader and compared with an actual specimen for identification purposes.

Other methods are discussed in a separate section. These are primarily optical methods, described for fishes of less than 1½ inches (3cm) in length, and a "direct transfer" method, for specimens more than 6 inches (15cm) in length.

Measurements

A series of measurements are taken from a whole fish and transferred to paper, either directly without change or multiplied or divided by a factor to yield the desired size for publication. Before beginning, take time to become acquainted with anatomical terms (see fig. 16-4), the body shape, placement of the fins in relation to each other, and the color pattern; attempt to gain a mental image of the fish before measuring and drawing.

All measurements used for drawing will be straight-line measurements between two points on the fish. These measurements are the same ones traditionally used by ichthyologists for the statistical studies of body proportions.

Some of the more common measurements are:

Standard length (abbreviated SL): a line between the snout tip and the caudal-fin base. The caudal-fin base is a point located at the anterior termination of the middle caudal-fin rays. This point is internal, enclosed by muscle tissue and scales, and ordinarily cannot by seen externally. The termination of the fin rays can be located by noting a crease caused by folding the caudal fin.

Fork length: the distance between the snout tip and the midpoint of the posterior border of the caudal fin.

Head length: the distance between the snout tip and the most posterior tip of the opercular border.

Upper jaw length: the distance between the snout tip and the most posterior tip of the maxilla.

Body depth: a vertical distance between the highest point on the back (often at the dorsal-fin origin) and the profile of the belly below.

Many other distances or measurements will be taken for drawing purposes and will be explained as they are taken. Ask the scientist whether any other measurements should be made.

Fish Delineation

Whole fish drawing by delineation is a method of transferring measurements taken from a fish to a piece of paper. The procedure outlined is a form of triangulation. The relative positions of the first two points, A and B, seen in figure 16-9, are established by taking direct measurements with proportional divid
transferring
case, points
tremes of fo
length is o
third point,
established
dius A (the
tance snout
and radius
fin origin to
length mea
equals dista
equals dis
these two a
a line drawn
B. Radius
from point
point B. Th
and B locat
the point of
fin. This pri
point from t
continued.
ously estab
needed ad
drawing are

Errors in
paper show
in point-to-
drawing. T
any two poi
ing by trian
be proporti
equivalent
Differences
these dist
points bein
rived at by
ample, in th
given abov
lished by t
pose a sim
of the pelvi
tablished
points A an
BD. If all h
the distanc
the drawing
be proporti
not, an err
of the pr
graphic pro
cause.

To unde
the process
necessary

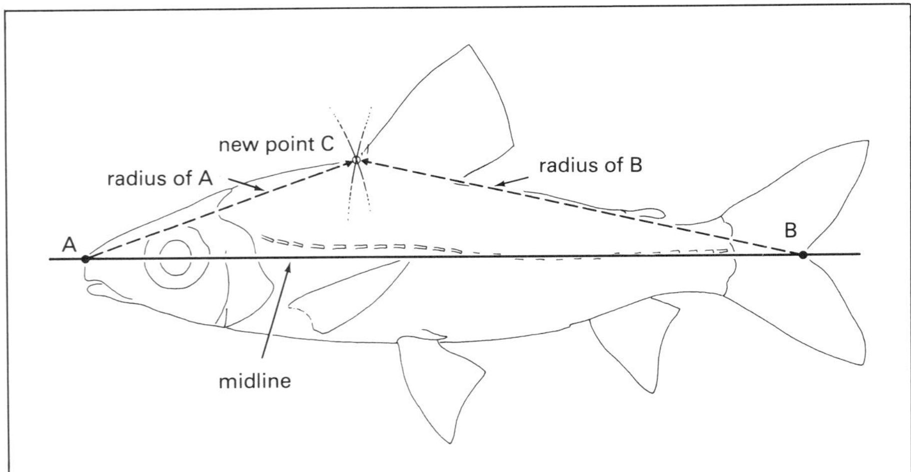

16-9. The process of triangulation for locating a new point on the drawing. The established measurement, A to B, represents the distance between two structures (points) previously located on the fish to be transferred to the drawing. The radii, AC and BC, represent the distances between each of these previously located structures on the fish and the drawing and a third, new structure selected on the fish to be transferred to the drawing. These two radii are transferred from the fish to the drawing, and the new point C, where the arc of each new radius intersects, will represent the proper location of the newly measured structure. Pen-and-ink on Bristol board, by T. Britt Griswold.

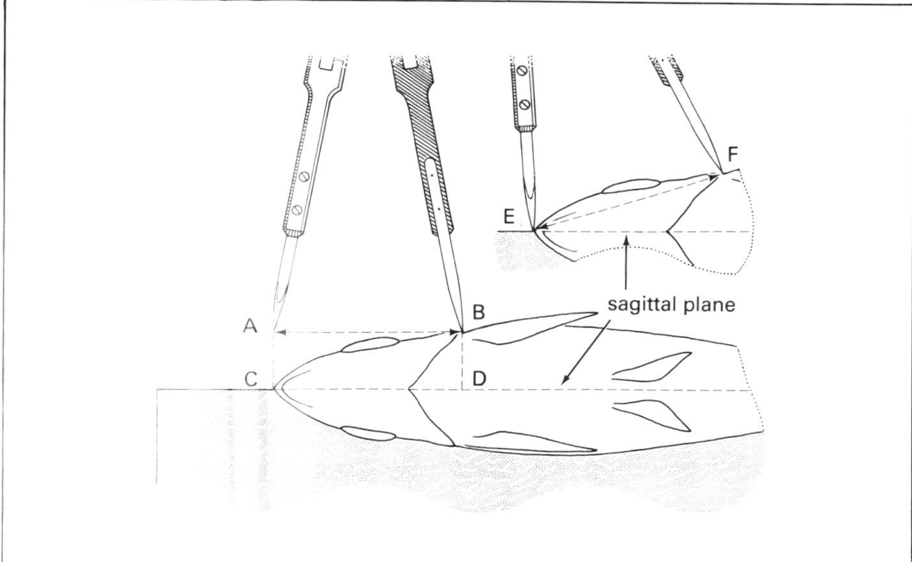

16-10. Correct and incorrect ways to measure the snout-to-pectoral-fin-origin distance. In all measurements, the divider points must be held parallel to the sagittal plane of the fish. The median long axis of the fish lies in the sagittal plane and contains points C and D. The distance between points A to B and C to D must be equal. Distance A to B gives the correct measurement to be transferred to the drawing. Distance E to F will be too long and give an incorrect distance. Pen-and-ink and shading film on Bristol board, by T. Britt Griswold.

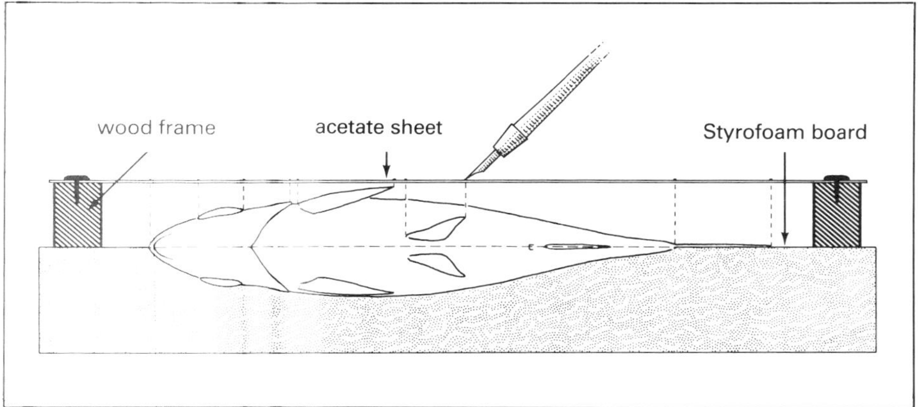

16-11. A clear acetate sheet stretched on a wooden frame over the surface of the fish may be used for locating points for measurement of fish in preparation of a base drawing. The acetate sheet must be in a single uncurved plane and not allowed to sag; the sheet should be parallel to the sagittal plane of the fish. Pen-and-ink and shading film on Bristol board, by T. Britt Griswold.

triangulation proceeds as governed by the concept of orthographic projection. For purposes of this discussion, orthographic projection may be defined as a transfer of an image along parallel lines from one area in space to another. In our case, the parallel lines project through the points we have chosen on the fish and these parallel lines are all perpendicular to the sagittal plane of the fish (fig. 16-10). This remains true even though the proportional dividers change the distance between these parallel lines by a constant factor. The radii as described above must equal the shortest distance between any two of the parallel lines passing through our chosen points—for example, radius AB or BC. This means that all radii taken in triangulation must be parallel to the sagittal plane of the fish and perpendicular to our parallel lines projecting through the selected points on the fish. Figure 16-11 shows a device to ensure this. If a radius is not parallel to the sagittal plane of the fish, it will be too long and the point transferred to the paper will be in error. Unfortunately, such errors are easy to make and can be time consuming to correct.

In taking measurements to be used as radii, it is absolutely necessary to keep the points of the proportional dividers equidistant from the sagittal plane of the fish. (See Proportional Dividers in chapter 2.) If a point or a series of points on the paper are inaccurately placed with respect to other points, it will be necessary to remeasure radii in the manner described above, rechecking all original and transferred measurements until those inaccurately taken are discovered and corrected.

Steps in Fish Drawing by Triangulation

The following steps in preparing a fish drawing are based on the kind of fish, such as a trout or perch, that illustrators are most frequently requested to draw. Unusual but by no means rare fishes provide special problems that the experienced artist may find challenging. For example, box fishes or pipe fishes have unusual shapes that may require special measuring and drawing techniques worked out by the artist based on previous experience and experiment.

Establishing Body Axis, Standard Length, and Fork Length

Lightly rule a pencil line across the center of the paper. This line will become the horizontal body axis, sometimes called the midline of the fish. The required length of the finished drawing should be marked by placing two small ink dots on this line, the dots being the required distance apart. Next, set

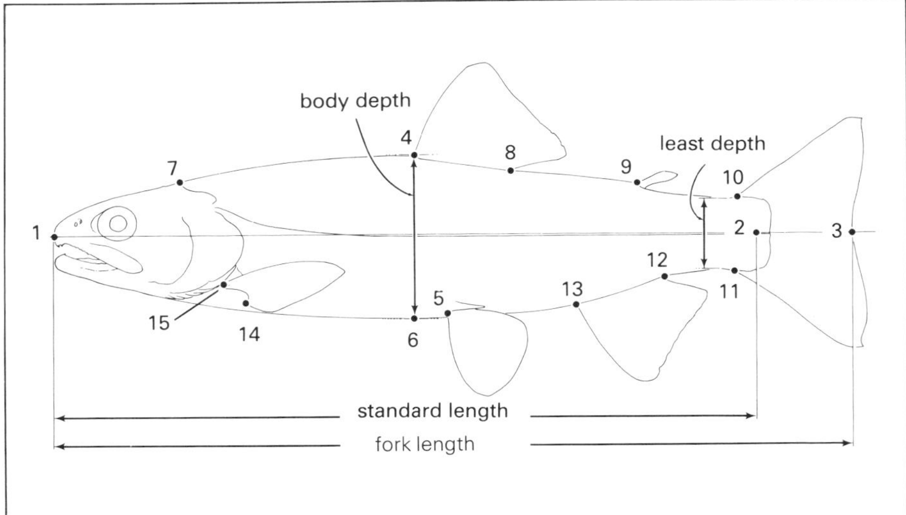

16-12. Traditional points for measurements that establish the shape of a fish: (1) anterior tip of snout; (1–2) standard length; (1–3) fork length; (4) dorsal-fin origin; (5) pelvic-fin origin; (4–6) greatest body depth; (7) nape; (8) dorsal-fin insertion; (9) adipose-fin origin; (10) anterior base of dorsal lobe of caudal fin; (11) anterior base of ventral lobe of caudal fin; (12) anal-fin insertion; (13) anal-fin origin; (14) pectoral-fin insertion; (15) pectoral-fin origin. Pen-and-ink with dry-transfer symbols and arrows on Bristol board, by T. Britt Griswold.

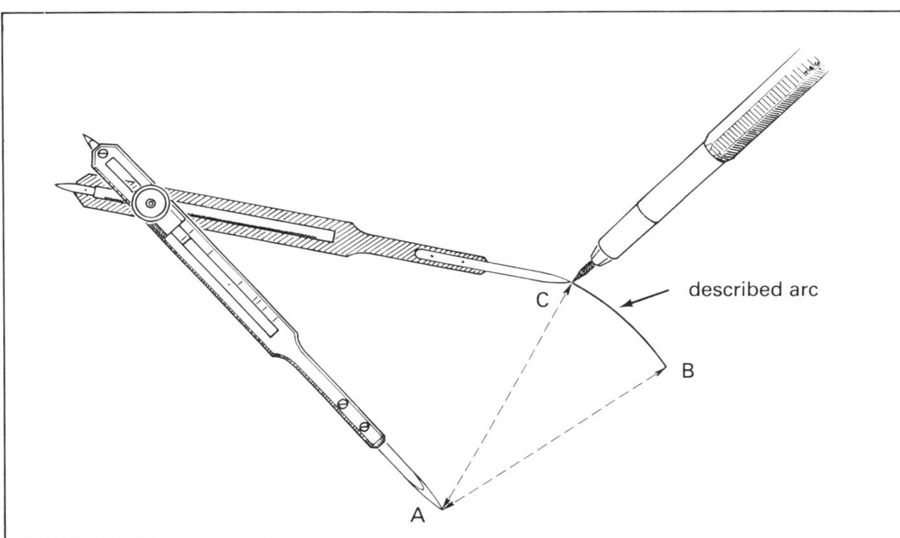

16-13. Describing an arc to establish a point from other known points on the drawing. Lines AB and AC are the radii and represent the enlargement of the measured distance between the short points of the divider. Curved line BC represents the arc. A pencil is used to follow the moving point of the divider. Pen-and-ink on Bristol board, by T. Britt Griswold.

the factor used for the proportional dividers so that the total length (snout tip to most posterior end of the caudal-fin lobes) of the fish is drawn within those two dots. Several attempts may be necessary to find the proportion that corresponds precisely with the required length of the drawing. Then tightly fix the locking thumbscrew on the dividers and keep it tight until completion of the drawing. Record on a corner of the drawing surface the proportional reading shown on the side of the dividers (see figs. 2-13, 2-16).

Next, usin
viders as set
dard length a
the horizontal
snout tip at th
ting the post
surements fal
the horizontal
a small ink d
16-14 show th
measuring. T
dots represen
eight addition
have establi
points on pa
specimen oth
locate specifi
them to the
tion as descri
tions given b
is being enlar

Establishing

Use the s
viders to mea
tip of the sno
of the first (a
of the fish (d
two points ar
and therefo
can be direc
tion for ort
With one lon
on the paper
designated a
locate on th
tip of the di
mate propor
base of th
Mark this r
describing a
cil (fig. 16-13
Repeat th
the distance
base of the
the posterio
inked in as
middle of th
take the mea
imen with t
viders. Then
the dividers
at the pos
point, place
the dividers
region of the
Again desc

crossing the first arc. The point of intersection establishes the point of the dorsal-fin origin on the paper (see fig. 16-9).

Establishing Pelvic-Fin Origin

The next step is to measure from the snout tip to the anterior base (origin) of the first pelvic-fin ray; but because these two points are not on the same plane, compensation must be made (see previous discussion of orthographic projection). Do so by raising the tip of the dividers at the snout tip toward you and along an imaginary line extending through the snout tip perpendicular to the sagittal plane of the fish. The distance raised should equal the distance that the pelvic-fin origin is elevated above the same sagittal plane. This will make the measurement parallel to the sagittal plane and therefore accurate (see fig. 16-10). It is, of course, difficult to "eyeball" such measurements. Slight differences in the elevation of the two points being measured from the sagittal plane may make little difference in accuracy if the radius being taken is long. If, however, it is short and the elevation differences are relatively great (such as they would be in taking a radius measurement between the snout tip and the nearest point on the rim of the eye), the error in point placement would be relatively great. Even with short elevation differences and a long radius, every effort should be made to be as accurate as possible. Although it is difficult, experienced artists can sometimes compensate for elevation differences by eye, without measuring the differences (see fig. 16-11). Once the snout-tip-to-pelvic-fin-origin measurement is taken with the short end of the dividers, describe an arc on the paper from the snout tip to the region of the pelvic-fin origin using the long end of the dividers.

Next, measure the distance between the point at the posterior end of the standard-length measurement and the point at the base of the first pelvic-fin ray. Again, compensate for orthographic projection. Transfer the compensated measurement to the paper. Describe the second arc so that it intersects the arc from the snout to the origin of the first pelvic-fin ray. The intersection establishes the location of the origin of the first pelvic-fin ray on the drawing.

Body-Depth Measurements

In their statistical comparisons of body form, ichthyologists use a body measurement called *depth at the dorsal-fin origin*. A second and often different measurement, called *greatest body depth*, may be used instead. Each is taken at right angles to the horizontal body axis and represents the vertical distance between the dorsal and ventral body profiles at the point they are taken. In figure 16-4, the greatest depth and the depth at the dorsal-fin origin are identical. In figure 16-1, however, the greatest depth occurs anterior to the origin of the dorsal fin.

Aside from these two, other ichthyologically important depth measurements must be taken and accurately depicted on the finished drawing, among them *least caudal peduncle depth* and *depth of the head at the nape*. Other depth measurements required to establish body profile vary according to the kind of fish being drawn.

To establish a depth measurement from a previously established point, such as the dorsal-fin origin, draw a light pencil line perpendicular to the body axis line through the dorsal-fin-origin point and above and below the body axis line. Then, use the short end of the proportional dividers on the fish to measure the greatest vertical body depth at the dorsal-fin origin. Transfer this measurement to the drawing with the long end of the dividers placed along the vertical line that passes through the dorsal-fin origin, one end of the dividers being placed on the dorsal-fin-origin point.

Nape

Measure from the tip of the snout to the point on the dorsal side of the fish that is at the dividing line between the head and body in the sagittal plane. The area near this point is called the *nape*, and it may be recognized because in many scaled fishes the squamation (pattern and distribution of scales) begins here, just at the termination of the smooth skin over the bones of the head. In some fishes with scales on the head (see fig. 16-1), the dividing line is not distinguishable. In such cases, any bony prominence at the posterior region of the head and in the sagittal plane will serve the purpose of locating a point in this region of the fish. With the snout-nape measurement as a radius, describe an arc on the paper in the region where the nape should be, using the snout tip as the center. Next, measure the pelvic-fin-origin-to-nape distance and, using this distance as a radius centered on the pelvic-fin origin, describe an arc on the paper that intersects the one just made. The intersection will locate the nape. An immediate check can be made on the nape location by measuring the dorsal-fin-origin-to-nape distance on the fish. Use that measurement as a radius centered on the dorsal-fin origin to describe an arc in the nape region. If all measurements are correct and if all three centerpoints were previously located correctly, all three arcs should intersect at the same or very nearly the same point. If the third arc intersects in a different place than the other two, the error is probably due to a problem in orthographic projection. Repeat measurements until all these arcs can be made to coincide. The seven basic points may be checked against one another using various combinations of three radii at each point. There should be a discrepancy of no more than 1/32 inch (0.75mm) if all measurements are accurate. It is especially important that this first series of points be accurately placed because these will be used in part for verification of later point locations. An error of even 1⁄16 inch (1.5mm) in a 12-inch (30.5cm) drawing can contribute to serious later errors. If all is well, proceed to the next steps.

The following additional points should be located by triangulation: the dorsal-fin insertion, the adipose-fin origin, the anterior bases of the dorsal and ventral lobes of the caudal fin (where the rays enter the body), the anal-fin insertion and anal-fin origin, and finally the pectoral-fin insertion and origin. These additional eight points on the paper can be located by triangulation using the previously verified points as radial centers. All the new points should be verified by the intersection of at least three radial arcs.

Sketching the Body Profile

There are now fifteen dots on the drawing representing the locations just described above, as shown in figure 16-12. These dots can now be connected by a light pencil line. Look at the fish and draw the profile of the head from the snout tip to the nape point, then to the dorsal fin insertion, and so on, until the entire profile of the body is filled in. Attempt to make the profile look correct with the eye. At this time, only those points verified by triangulation will be really accurate. Other points along the sketched profile can be verified by further measuring the fish and by triangulation. Each kind of fish will require a somewhat different series of points to produce an accurate body profile. Train your eyes to see and question proportional discrepancies in distance between the fish and the drawing. Even slight differences noted by eye should be checked by the proportional dividers. Necessary adjustments should be made on the drawing. Constantly check prominent points as the work proceeds.

Lateral-Line Placement

From the nape, measure to the point of origin of the lateral line, usually located near the most dorsal part of the opercular opening. Use this measurement as the first radius in locating the lateral-line origin on the paper. Take the next radius from the snout tip of the fish to the lateral-line origin, and the third radius from the pectoral-fin origin to the lateral-line origin. The intersection of these three radii on the paper will locate the lateral-line origin. Next draw in the lateral line from its point of origin to the point at the midbase of the caudal fin. Note the relationship of the lateral line to the body axis line as originally drawn. Some fishes have strongly curved or sometimes interrupted lateral lines, and it may, therefore, be necessary to establish several points of reference for the lateral line on the body. Some fishes have no lateral line. If there is one, use triangulation to check the location of points along the lateral line against established points. In the trout (see fig. 16-4) there is a slight downward curve from the anterior point of the lateral-line origin and a slight upward curve just anterior to the base of the caudal fin.

Dorsal Fin and Anal Fin

The anterior (origin) and posterior points of the basal border of these fins are already established. At this point it is important to verify the basal lengths of those fins by taking measurements from the fish with proportional dividers (fig. 16-14).

The fin to be drawn should already be pinned erect. If it is not, do it now. The procedure for drawing the dorsal fin and anal fin is the same, so only the dorsal fin will be described. For the sake of brevity, the word *measure* here means to take the measurement from the fish with proportional dividers, use that length as a radius with the verified point as the center, and describe an arc on the paper in the approximate region of the distal

end of the me
Begin by m
the first (ante
anterior base
the origin of
measure from
short ray to t
unbranched r
lar to that us
ray, measure
branched ray
rior dorsal-fin
measurement
triangulation
lished points
the outline of
newly establ
the rays, mea
tween them a
these counts
drawing. Dra
careful to dep
branching pa
the same wit

The pector
be drawn in a
all the fins, m
or region on t
fin that is
short, or espe

Pectoral Fin

The pector
problems fo
other fins on
pinned befo
cause pinn
scales. Mea
length from t
to the tip of
first ray is
slightly shor
ray. Observe
sal border of
paper. Sprea
from the tip o
fin ray to the
ray, and from
fin ray to th
posterior fin
base of the p
base of the
Establish the
ing. Outline
the almost c
base of the
and indicate

the origin of each ray at the base. Then draw in each ray, indicating the points at which it divides into branches, as in the fins in figure 16-2.

In the trout (see fig. 16-4), the origin of the pelvic-fin rays will be from the ventral border of the small skin flap, which now should be drawn in. Note that not all kinds of fishes have fleshy skin or scaly flaps (auxiliary processes) at the base of the pelvic fins.

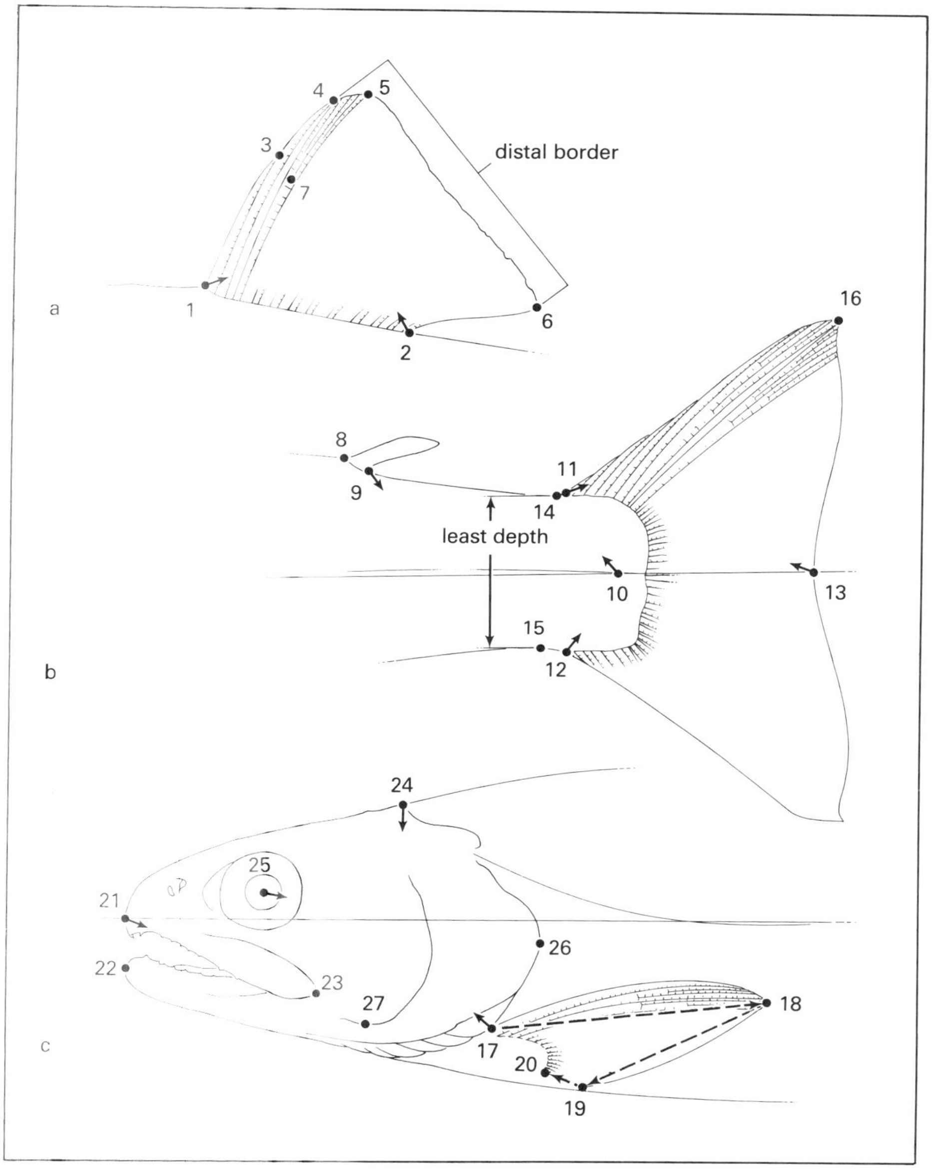

16-14. Fin and head measurements. The dots with solid arrows represent points on the fish used to locate other points by triangulation. The dashed arrows on the pectoral fin show the sequence of measurement on a spread fin. *(a) Dorsal fin:* (1) dorsal-fin origin; (2) dorsal-fin insertion; (3) anterior short ray tip; (4) longest anterior unbranched ray tip; (5) anterior branched ray tip; (6) most posterior ray tip; (7) major branching of a ray. *(b) Caudal peduncle and fin:* (8) adipose-fin origin; (9) adipose-fin insertion; (10) midbase of caudal fin; (11) anterior base of dorsal lobe of caudal fin; (12) anterior base of ventral lobe of caudal fin; (13) posterior point of fork-length measurement; (14) lowest point on dorsal border of caudal peduncle; (15) highest point on ventral border of caudal peduncle; (16) distal tip of dorsal caudal lobe. *(c) Head and pectoral fin:* (17) base of first pectoral ray; (18) tip of longest pectoral ray; (19) tip of shortest pectoral ray; (20) base of last pectoral ray; (21) anterior tip of snout; (22) anterior tip of mandible; (23) most posterior angle of maxillary bone; (24) nape; (25) center of eye; (26) most posterior point of opercle; (27) most ventral point of preopercle. Pen-and-ink with charting tape and dry-transfer symbols and arrows on Bristol board, by T. Britt Griswold.

Adipose Fin

The adipose fin is short and very short-based. The length of its base and its height should be established by triangulation and the fin sketched from these measurements. Many fishes have no adipose fin. A very few fish species have rays in the adipose fin.

Caudal Region

The caudal peduncle is usually the narrowest part of the fish near its tail fin. At this time you already should have two dots representing the least depth (the least vertical distance) of the caudal peduncle. If the distance between the dots is not the peduncle's narrowest depth, then that distance is the depth at the basal part of the anterior dorsal and ventral procurrent caudal-fin rays.

Details of the shape of the caudal peduncle may be established in the following ways: from the posterior base of the adipose fin and the mid-base of the caudal fin, measure to where the caudal peduncle makes an upward or dorsal turn to form the shape of the caudal fin or tail. From this point and from the mid-base of the caudal fin, measure vertically downward (ventrally) to the point where the ventral border of the caudal peduncle makes a similar downward turn. If you have done this correctly, you have measured and transferred to the drawing the least depth of the caudal peduncle.

Caudal Fin

Ichthyologists divide the rays of the caudal fin into dorsal and ventral procurrent rays and principal caudal-fin rays. The principal rays are all of the branched rays plus one dorsal unbranched ray and one ventral unbranched ray (fig. 16-15).

The origin of the procurrent dorsal and ventral procurrent caudal-fin rays has been established and

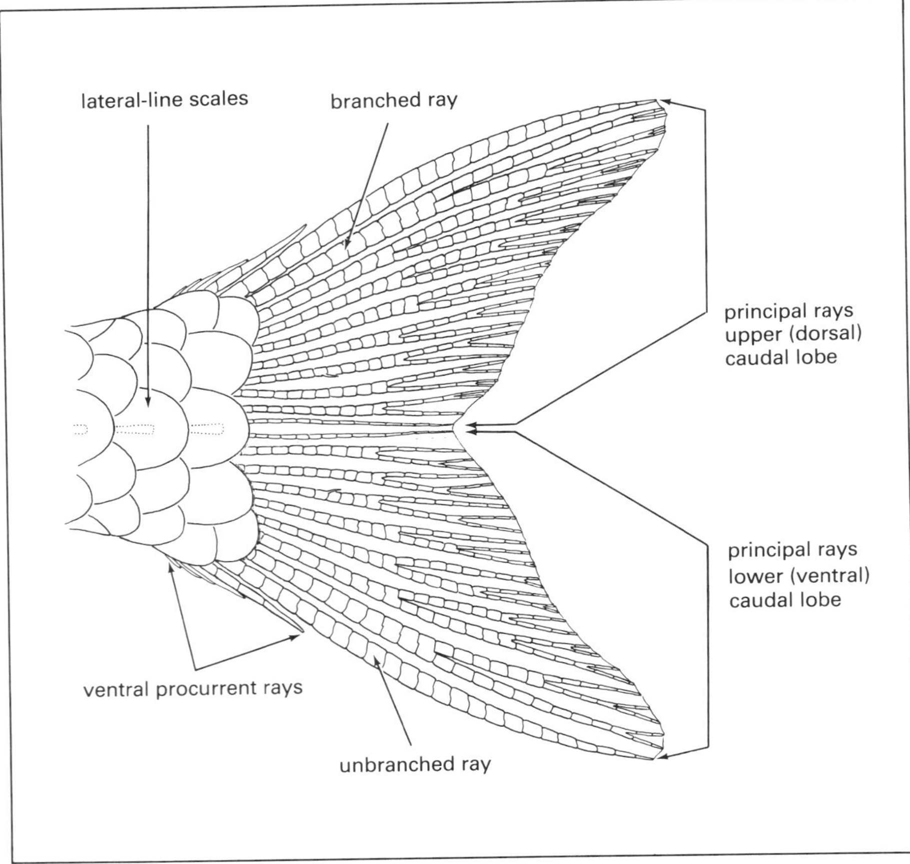

16-15. The caudal fin of a fish showing procurrent and principal caudal-fin rays, scales, and lateral-line scales. Pen-and-ink on Bristol board, by T. Britt Griswold.

verified as described above. The profile of the caudal fin should now be established. The fin should already be pinned in a spread condition. Measure, establish, and verify by triangulation the distal tips of the two caudal-fin lobes by measuring them from the caudal peduncle base and from the origins of the procurrent caudal-fin rays. The fork-length measurement, already established early in the drawing, is based on a direct snout-tip-to-fork-length measurement along the horizontal axis. Its placement thus should be accurate, and it is a valuable point for verifying the position of other points in the caudal region. If all points are now accurate, the profile of the fin can be drawn and verified by triangulation with additional measurements when needed. Using the method similar to that described above for drawing the dorsal and anal-fin rays, add the caudal-fin rays to the fin. Count the rays and make a mark on the drawing for each ray at the base of the caudal fin along the posterior curve of the caudal peduncle. Measure every fin ray and the points at which each branches. Some fishes have more rays in the dorsal lobe than in the ventral, some have more in the ventral lobe, or the count may be the same in both lobes. All fin-ray counts are very important. Remove the pins as soon as the counting, measuring, and drawing is completed. Once the fins are drawn, the skin-covered muscle attachments to the fin-ray bases may be drawn, if visible.

Damaged Fins

If the specimen is damaged, has broken fin rays, or is lacking a fin or two, you ca
ders by takin
surements fro
approximately
caudal, dorsa
perhaps the r
aged parts. F
lobe of the fi
diagonally. S
men that ha
caudal-fin lob
est ray with
viders and. k
measuremen
on the same
to this meas
the distance
first pelvic-fi
first anal-fin
distance on
drawing. Th
constructed
caudal-fin ra
rays and f
tances on th
of the fin
method can
for a variety
of the fish b
be done or
the ichthyo
specimens
be importa
males may
ently from
not be use
of males.
ent from
These kind
evaluated
reconstruc
attempted

It is up t
cide if rec
Other alte
broken pa
dashed or
1, in whic
with parts
damaged

Belly Pro

At this
more acc
profile, e
The grea
ready be

fied. Now measure from the point on the nape to a point on the forepart of the belly profile, vertically below the base of the first pectoral-fin ray. The body profile in the trout, for example, makes a slight concave curve at this point (see fig. 16-4). Describe an arc. To establish this point further, measure to the same point from the tip of the snout. Measure from the already verified base of the first pectoral-fin ray and from the base of the first pelvic-fin ray to the body profile vertically below the pectoral fin. This should determine the depth of the body at the nape region. Draw a continuous line, observing the curves and shape of the belly line from the base of the last anal-fin ray to the point on the forepart of the belly.

Mouth

Fishes vary in the relative protrusion of the upper and lower jaws. In some species, the upper jaw protrudes beyond the lower; in others, the lower jaw protrudes most. Some kinds of fishes have highly modified vertical mouths; others have highly modified ventral ones. Mouths and heads may be very specialized in some fishes, and considerable judgment and experience will be required in measuring and drawing these.

In the trout (see fig. 16-4), the snout and lower jaw protrude about equal distances. If the scientist wants the mouth to be drawn open, a measurement must be taken from the anterior tip of the snout to the anterior lip of the mandible (lower jaw) to establish the gape, or distance of mouth opening. In drawing a fish, try to select a specimen for drawing with the mouth preserved in a position that the ichthyologist wants shown so the mouth can be drawn as is.

It can be difficult to draw the mouth differently from the way it is preserved on the fish. To do it usually requires readjustment of all movable mouth parts relative to the head, and often of the head relative to the body, none of which should be done without discussion with the scientist. Such readjustment usually leads to distortion of the head parts.

If the mouth is to be drawn closed, the snout-tip-to-mandible-tip measurement may be eliminated or used, depending on the mouth structure. In the trout, measurements for the mouth should be taken as follows: from the anterior tip of the mandible, measure to the most posterior corner or angle of the maxillary bone. Compare the jaws shown in figures 16-1, 16-2, 16-4, 16-16, and 16-17a of whole but very different fishes with those of the skulls of the fishes in figures 16-5 and 16-6, which also are very different from each other. Notice the different positions of the jaw bones (premaxilla and maxilla of the upper jaw and dentary, anguloarticular, and retroarticular of the lower jaw or mandible) in figures 16-5 and 16-6.

Make a small arc in the drawing at about where the posterior end of the maxilla should occur. Use the nape on the dorsal profile of the fish as the point from which to check the posterior position of the maxilla. Then measure the width of the maxilla near its posterior border. From this last measurement point, draw in the entire upper jaw, taking measurements as needed from different points along its course to ensure accurate dimensions.

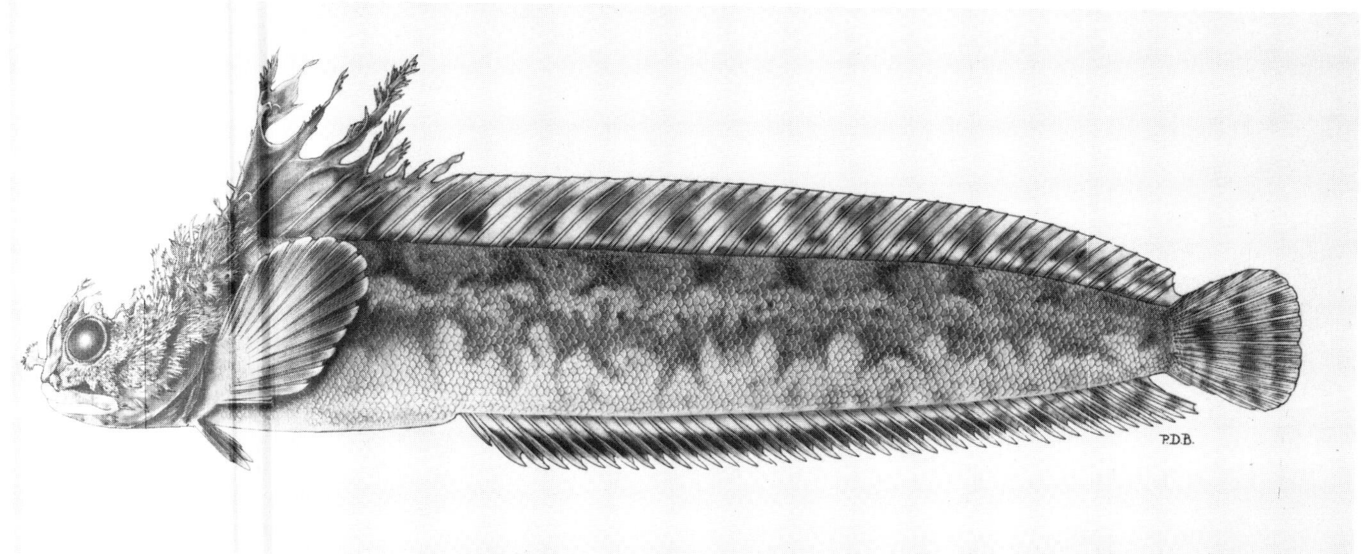

16-16. Thick matted cirri on the sides and top of the head are a special feature of the Matcheek warbonnet, *Chirolophus tarsodes* (Jordan and Snyder). Carbon dust with pen-and-ink line on Anjac board, by Patricia Drukker Brammall, 1973. Reproduced by permission of Dr. Alex Peden and the British Columbia Provincial Museum.

From this same point at the posterior end of the maxilla, carefully draw in the entire lower jaw. Continue the profile line from the established point below the pectoral fin to the anterior tip of the mandible.

The entire outline of the fish is now complete. It should compare favorably with the profile of the specimen. If it does not, remeasure the incorrect areas and adjust lines appropriately.

Eye

With the proportional dividers, locate on the drawing by triangulation the center of the eye, and use it as a point source. The pupil of many fishes is slightly elliptical, and its anterior border may be slightly pointed. Measure from at least four different directions to be sure the eye is accurately located. Draw in the pupil, then the whole eye and its outer rim, measuring each carefully from the center of the eye. Make checks at points on these lines from previously established points on the drawing. Then directly check the vertical and horizontal diameters of the eye. Constantly check points on the fish and on the drawing with the proportional dividers to maintain accuracy as you proceed.

Opercle

Measure from the tip of the snout to the farthest posterior point of the opercle and establish the latter point on the drawing. As always, compensate for orthographic projection. Check the placement of this point by measuring from the nape, from the point at the base of the first pectoral-fin ray, and from the center of the eye. Establish several points along the opercular border and branchiostegal rays in a similar manner and then draw the opercular border and branchiostegal rays, as in figure 16-4.

Next, measure from the center of the eye to the farthest ventral point of the preopercle and establish that point on the drawing. Check the point with measurements from the nape point and the point at the base of the first pectoral-fin ray. Complete the entire head portion, drawing in the opercular details.

Narial Openings and Other Miscellaneous Head Structures

Nares (nostrils) are present in some form in all fishes. Some fishes have other structures on the head (and body), such as spines, cirri, and light organs, that must be accurately located, measured, and drawn (see figs. 16-1, 16-2, 16-16).

Locate and draw in the narial (nasal) opening by triangulation from nearby points. In the head, be sure that the branchiostegal rays are counted and measured and that the nares are positioned correctly. Prominent bones and such structures as head pores and barbels should be delineated and added in many kinds of fishes.

SQUAMATION (SCALE ARRANGEMENT)

Drawing scales is a slow, exacting procedure. Besides being carefully delineated, each scale and its row must be precisely located. Scales also are counted on most fish. Very small scales, such as those on trout and salmon, are often not all drawn in, but simply indicated at important areas. The number of scale rows between the dorsal fin and the lateral line and between the lateral line and the pelvic-fin or anal-fin origins are sometimes illustrated. Figure 16-17 provides an example of scale-row counts. In many fishes, as in figures 16-1, 16-4, 16-16, and 16-17, all scales are drawn. In figure 16-2, the easily shed scales are not drawn because they were removed by the action of the net when the fish was caught. In figure 16-4 the scales were drawn even though they are very small.

It is a good idea to make a separate drawing of the scales on a trac-

ing-paper ove
drawing will
erasures as s
rected. Begi
scales and re
the bottom o
Count the sc
length of the
figure at the
Count and re
scales on the
to the base
Next count
base of the d
base of the
the anterior l
and from th
base of the
horizontal sc
of the first d
to the base
ray, and not
lateral line. I
fin origin wi
fin and in t
nient to cou
tween the d
origins. Cou
rows from
the midline
the pelvic fi
horizontal s
part of the
the midline
the midline
file. Identif
zontal scale
lateral-line
Be sure to r
count at th
drawing.

Place a
over the b
the body of
of the hea
trout (see f
scales on
the lateral l
of the scal
note that t
and often
parts of the

On som
pores are v
1 and 16-1
lateral-line
depicted. T

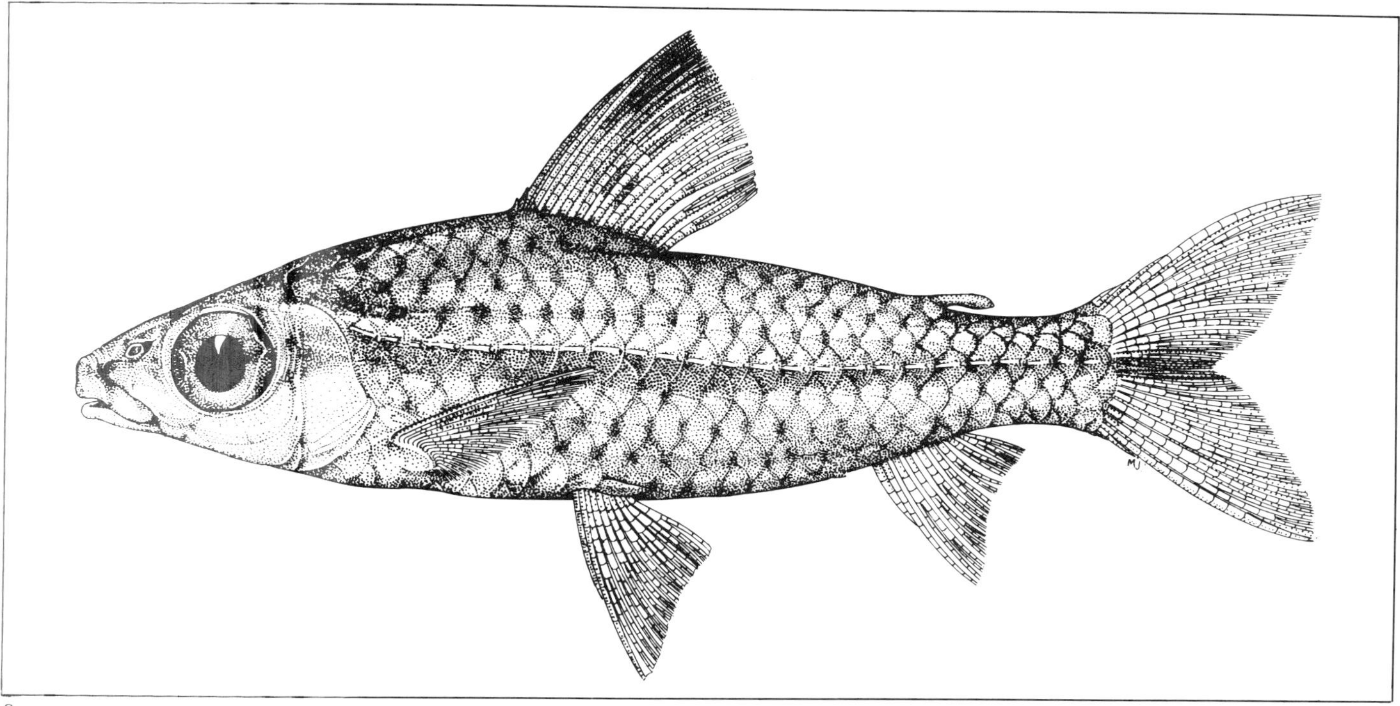

a

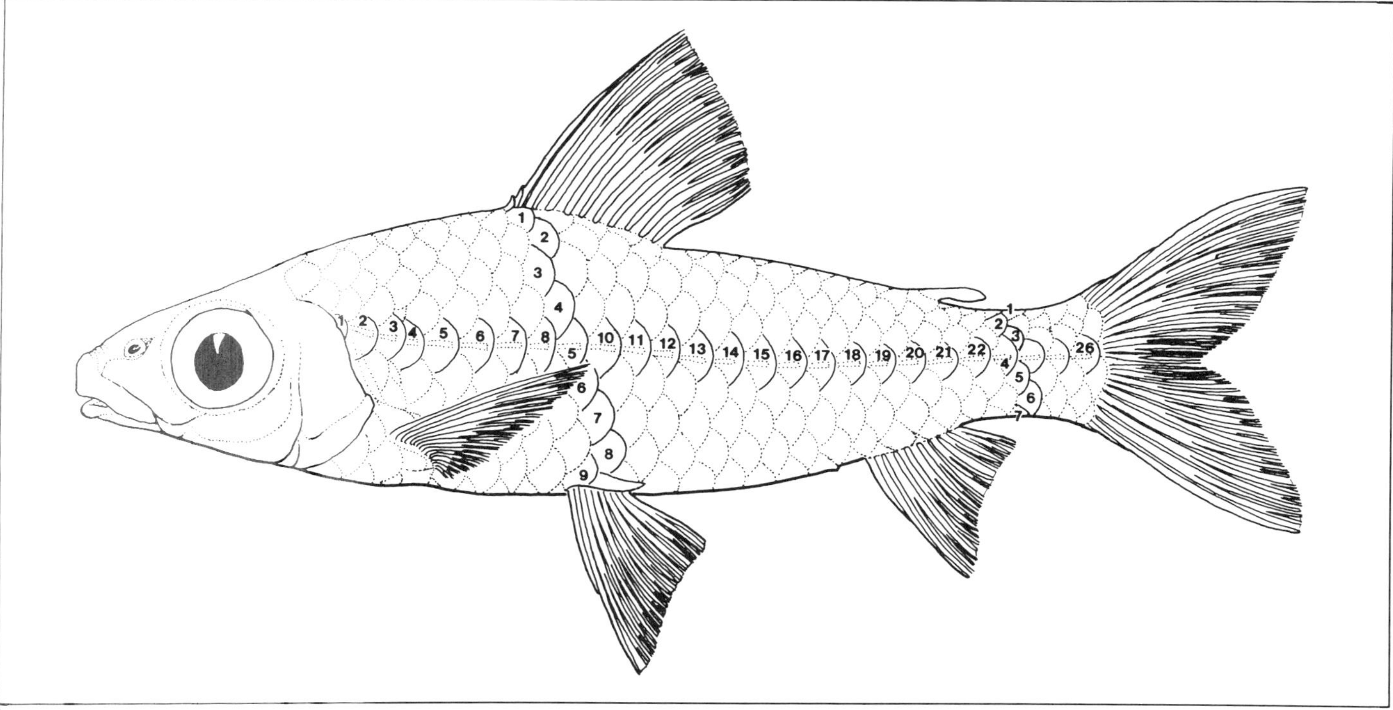

b

16-17. *Caenotropus maculosus* (Eigenmann), headstander tetra from Guyana. *(a)* Fully rendered pen-and-ink drawing by Marion J. Dalen on kid-finish Bristol board, 1966. *(b)* Sketch of the same specimen showing the nine horizontal scale rows between the dorsal-fin origin and the pelvic-fin origin, twenty-six lateral-line scales, and seven of the horizontal scale rows around the narrowest region of the caudal peduncle. Scale rows 1 through 7 at the caudal peduncle are scales visible on the left lateral side. These include scales number 1 (on the dorsal surface) and number 7 (on the ventral surface of the caudal peduncle). There are five additional scales on the opposite (right) side, for a total of twelve scale rows around the caudal peduncle. Pen-and-ink on tracing paper, by T. Britt Griswold, based on drawing by Marion J. Dalen.

terior termination of each tube in each scale. The pores are not easily seen on trout and salmon, but in most cases they are visible enough to be indicated on the drawing, even though rather diagrammatically, as in figure 16-4, in which the lateral line is represented as a pale horizontal line through the dark pigment spots on the sides of the body.

Starting at the origin (anterior end) of the lateral line, mark off the correct number of scales to the posterior end of the lateral line. Note and compensate for changes in scale size along the lateral line. Measure a few of the scales at the anterior end of the lateral line and then intermittently on to its posterior end. When these scales are marked off, shape them. This is a guide to fitting in the entire scale pattern.

The scale pattern of the least cisco (fig. 16-18) will be used to illustrate the procedure for drawing scales. It is best to begin by drawing a diagonal, slightly S-shaped, line matching the curvature of the scale rows on the fish. Begin it at the base of the first dorsal-fin ray and continue to between two of the scales on the lateral line. The line follows the border of a diagonal scale row, which includes the first scale at the anterior base of the dorsal fin. Continue this curved line ventrally to the belly, using triangulation to establish points on the drawing along this line. Continue establishing the curved lines

of the fish's
nape, chec
triangulatio
scales in o
the counte
base of the
posterior d
pose fin. D
base of th
there to t
caudal-fin
mation ab
first esta
row lines
the part o
dorsal-fin
counts and
the scale
from the d
lateral lin
the lateral

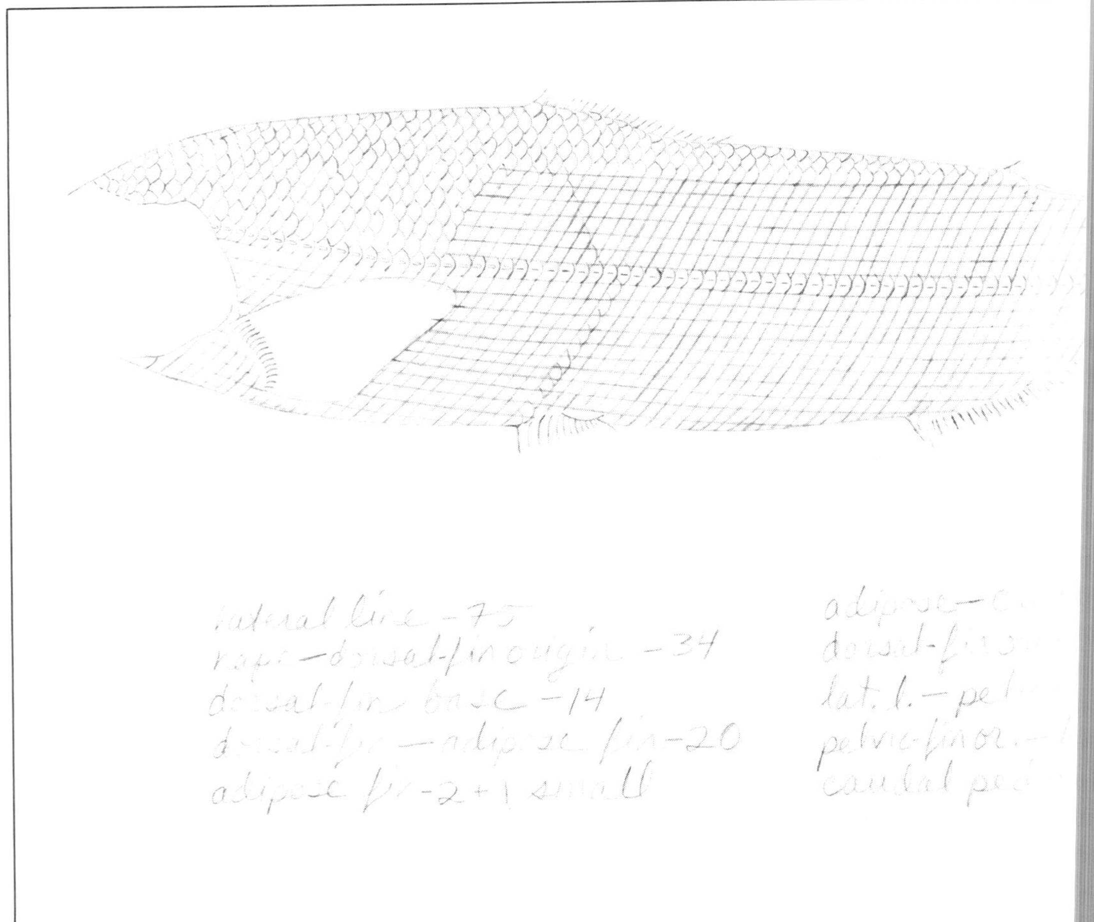

16-18. Preliminary layout of the scale pattern in the body region dorsal to the anal fin, the caudal peduncle, and tail fin. Note artist's scale count beneath drawing. The other body scales have been sketched and are ready for transfer to paper for the final drawing. Least cisco, *Coregonus sardinella* Valenciennes. Pencil on illustration board, by Sara Fink.

pelvic-fin origins, must be placed accurately by measurements.

A procedure similar to that used in illustrating the dorsal part of the body should be used for the ventral body half. Here the pelvic fin, anal fin, and lateral line should be used in establishing scale rows and scale counts. The rows on the belly anterior to the pectoral fin may not match the rows dorsal and posterior to the pectoral fin. Count the diagonal and horizontal rows along the base of the pectoral fin and indicate them as on the rest of the body.

Often there are slight irregularities in the squamation pattern. There may be an intercalated (extra) scale, or scales, here and there. Intercalated horizontal or diagonal scale rows may occur. In figure 16-18, an extra diagonal row occurs near the ventral body profile between the pelvic and anal fins. The artist should consult the ichthyologist about the inclusion of "extra" scales or scale rows.

It is best to take one row at a time when drawing and shaping the scales. It cannot be emphasized too much that the scale rows must be correctly positioned along the lateral line and at other points by triangulation from established body points. Constantly check counts against measurements on the fish and on the drawing. Note that scale-row positions are not always like that shown in figure 16-18. Compare the scale patterns in figures 16-1, 16-4, 16-16, 16-17, and 16-18, and note the differences. Scale shape or profile and other structures such as lateral-line pores may be shown in inset drawings, as in figure 16-1.

If the preliminary drawing and scale pattern are drawn on separate sheets, the scale-pattern drawing should be attached to the preliminary drawing as a removable overlay so that the scientist can check the scales in their proper position. Although the scale pattern may be transferred to the preliminary drawing, it may instead be transferred to the final drawing to save time. Transfer the lateral-line scales first, indicating the lateral-line pores as you go.

OTHER METHODS OF DRAWING FISHES

Drawing Whole Fishes by Direct Transfer of Measurements

Fish specimens more than 6 inches (15cm) in standard length can be drawn by using direct measurements. This method avoids time-consuming triangulation procedures. Tack a clear, strong plastic or acetate sheet to a frame just larger in linear dimensions than the fish and deep enough so that the plastic does not touch the fish (see fig. 16-11). The plane of the acetate sheet must be parallel to the sagittal plane of the fish. Ink black dots onto the sheet vertically over the appropriate points of measurement on the fish. Once you have located all desired points on the acetate sheet, remove it, place it on a light box, and trace the points directly onto drawing paper.

Other methods for transferring measurements from specimen to paper may be found in chapters 1 and 2.

Drawing Small Fishes and Parts

Small fishes and parts, less than about 1¼ inches (3cm) in total length, are too small to be drawn accurately by use of proportional dividers. These are best done with a camera lucida or a photographic process such as slides. Other possible choices are an ocular micrometer in the ocular of a binocular microscope and an ocular grid, although many grids do not cover a large area of the field. A grid, ideally, must be large enough to cover the entire object being drawn so that there is no need to move the object while drawing. If an ocular micrometer is used, take appropriate measurements from the fish viewed under the microscope and multiply each by a constant based on the magnification required for the drawing. Plot the resulting measurements on a separate piece of paper.

In microscope drawings, the requirements of orthographic projection make it imperative that the sagittal plane of the fish's body be held perpendicular to the optical axis of the microscope. To ensure consistent measurements and allow production of a drawing nearly meeting the requirements of an orthographic projection, the specimen must be mounted rigidly on a movable platform that will maintain it in a single plane even though the platform is moved about under the microscope's objective. If the fish may be pierced, it can be pinned in place with three or four insect pins into a block of Styrofoam, relatively soft wood, or in a plastic box with a layer of silicone (Silastic) on its bottom. The pins should not be parallel or the specimen may slide along the pins and move out of position. Do the pinning under the direction of the ichthyologist, taking care not to pierce bones of the body and head.

Microscopes focus essentially in one plane, so any given focus on an object records distances accurately and clearly only in the plane of focus. Therefore it is difficult or impossible to measure (or draw using a camera lucida) those parts out of focus. Changing from one plane of focus to another shifts the optical system and somewhat changes the magnification. This can make it difficult to follow or measure lines, such as joint lines between bones or borders of jaws, that are not all in the plane of focus. This problem is to some extent resolved in the photomicroscope by using a relatively high f-stop and gaining depth of field. Relatively easy establishment of the important outlines of a fish or its parts may be achieved by taking a picture, using either color or black-and-white positive film, of an object under the microscope, developing the film, and then projecting it.

If a stereoscopic microscope with a diaphragm is available, use that to increase depth of field by stopping down the diaphragm without adjusting the focusing knob. If one is not available, measurements will not be exact and it is best to compromise by focusing on the mid-distance between the two points in different planes of focus. Although not precise, such measurements will be much more accurate than those taken from small fishes using proportional dividers. With experience, the illustrator should be able to make small adjustments by eye.

Photographic or camera lucida delineations can pose a serious problem if a drawing is being patched together from two or more camera or microscope fields (separate views of the object). Parts of the subject may not correctly align or fit together when two or more fields are combined to make a single drawing. If the drawings are done in the center two-thirds of the field of view, the distortion may be reduced enough so that patching can be accomplished more easily. In any photographic or optical delineation for drawing purposes, care must be taken to have the "face" or flat surface of the subject at right angles to the long axis of the lens system.

Parts of fishes are drawn in a manner similar to that used for other organisms as described elsewhere in this book. The following comments are added here to help the artist in working with fishes.

Photographic slides, films, or prints can be projected for tracing the outlines, important points, and structures of small whole fishes or parts of fishes. The optical distortions created by such procedures usually are relatively minor and unimportant. The delineation of parts is more varied in scope and intent than that of whole-fish illustration. These drawings may vary from cartoons (simple outline drawings), often used in functional morphology and sometimes in comparative morphology (see fig. 16-5), to complicated drawings of anatomical parts presented in detail (see fig. 16-6).

RENDERING

The technique of final rendering is ultimately determined by the scientist and the budget. Often the cost of reproduction will dictate the rendering method. A technique that permits fine detailing is necessary, a fact that may preclude the use of coquille board or other rough drawing surfaces. Pen-and-ink drawing with stipple to show color pattern and shading may be cheapest, and most fish illustrations for research papers are done this way. However, some artists work faster with other techniques. Sometimes ink line-and-stipple drawings tend to be too dark. This is especially true if many fine scales are present. Fin rays should always be inked with the finest

lines that
being lost
may be too

Occasion
carbon dus
used to ren
and 6-6). I
tailed wat
produced b
various ex
new speci
other anim
ings are f
Fishes at t
tion's Nati
History. U
these exqu
were publi
of color p
hibited in
showing s
duced by
tion Pre
popular p
dered in
that permi

Fishes s
backs, ce
16-2), and
have very
structures
method c
above app

Each fis
lenges. O
miliar with
drawing f
tiple step
measurem
for the m
varied b
diverse st

17/Illustrating Amphibians and Reptiles

David M. Dennis and Kraig Adler

Amphibians and reptiles are two animal groups that are rather small when compared to fishes and insects, yet they are intensively studied, especially in the fields of behavior, ecology, anatomy, physiology, and systematics. Accordingly, artists are frequently called upon to illustrate them and may be confronted with numerous problems. Only a few artists today specialize in drawing these animals, and as a result many of the illustrations published recently by other artists are lifeless or inaccurate. Indeed, it is a source of acute embarrassment to note that the drawings of amphibians and reptiles made in the nineteenth century (fig. 17-1) are often better than those of the present century, particularly drawings by the English artists Edward Lear, G. H. Ford, John Green, and those of the great Sowerby clan, even though these illustrators worked with far less sophisticated equipment and did not have the photographic aids employed in making drawings today. But such artists usually were amateur naturalists themselves and thus very careful observers.

17-1. An outstanding nineteenth-century illustration of a tortoise, drawn by James de Carle Sowerby and transferred to stone by Edward Lear; first published in 1872.

For examples of excellent drawings of amphibians and reptiles, the reader is referred to these publications, listed in the Bibliography: color and black-and-white—*A Field Guide to the Reptiles and Amphibians of Britain and Europe*, by E. N. Arnold and J. A. Burton; *The Hylid Frogs of Middle America*, by William E. Duellman; *The Encyclopedia of Reptiles and Amphibians*, edited by Tim R. Halliday and Kraig Adler; color—*Fitzsimons' Snakes of Southern Africa*, by Donald G. Broadley; *A Field Guide to Western Reptiles and Amphibians*, 2nd ed., by Robert C. Stebbins; black-and-white—*Amphibians and Reptiles of Western North America*, by Robert C. Stebbins; skulls—*Snakes: A Natural History*, by H. W. Parker and Alice G. C. Grandison. Most of the remaining books listed in the Bibliography are useful for background information on amphibians and reptiles, in addition to *The Encyclopedia of Reptiles and Amphibians*, mentioned above.

THE ILLUSTRATOR

Illustrators of amphibians and reptiles are of two basic types: professional artists who learn secondarily to draw amphibians and reptiles and professional biologists specializing in herpetology who are usually self-taught artists. Professional biologists are more likely to be university-educated, but formal training is not as important as actual experience with animals: seeing them in natural settings, observing them close up, and watching their behavior. The better illustrators of amphibians and reptiles, including most of those whose drawings are published in the works cited above, are in the second category. Perhaps this is true because illustrators of amphibians and reptiles must be willing to work with actual specimens, living or dead, and some kinds—for example, snakes—are loathsome to many persons. Because many features of subtle shape and color do not preserve well—if at all—in museum specimens, illustrators of amphibians and reptiles often must also be good photographers and be able to photograph subjects in zoos or in the field, or have access to such photographs. Ideally, such an illustrator must be familiar with an animal's behavior in order to draw it in a lifelike pose and, if it is to be illustrated in a natural habitat, must know that habitat. All too often, a specimen is drawn against a habitat that is not typical for the species. Courses in vertebrate zoology, comparative anatomy, and herpetology would benefit the illustrator.

Above all, the illustrator must know the animals and must see every detail in order to draw. Despite their often small size, amphibians and reptiles have a wealth of surface features that must be drawn accurately and in a lifelike way. Probably the most common artistic error is the incorrect placement of the animal's eye. There must be extreme attention to detail. Indeed, the best herpetological artists often see detail missed by the scientist and sometimes are even invited by them to coauthor the publication being illustrated.

In the quest for knowledge of amphibians and reptiles, there is no substitute for intensive observation of living specimens, in zoos or in the field. Edward Lear, the great Victorian animal artist, one of whose specialties was drawing turtles, spent long hours at the London Zoo, patiently watching and sketching. In fact, his major benefactor, Lord Stanley, first discovered him while he was sketching animals at the zoo.

In addition to personal observation, the illustrator should seek information from other sources. The scientist who commissions the work is one good source; a reference library where photographs, slides, or published color illustrations are available is another. Many species have never been illustrated in color, so the artist must obtain color slides or published descriptions. Finally, careful judgment and attention to detail are essential, for embarrassing mistakes can occur. As a case in point, a drawing of the tuatara, a species of reptile that looks superficially like a lizard, was once used on the dust jacket of a book on lizard ecology! Illustrators cannot always depend on scientists and editors to catch errors.

In many instances the scientist will determine what is to be drawn: the species, pose, medium, and size. Some scientists will have very strong ideas concerning their needs, whereas others will have very little notion as to what they want. In the latter case especially, the artist must question the scientist to determine what function the drawing will have. For example, a drawing that serves merely to show general body form may not require much surface detail and the artist can avoid wasting time on pattern and shading. Adding a pattern may even distract the reader from the purpose of the drawing, just as so-called disruptive coloration in nature serves to camouflage an animal from being seen clearly by a predator. Thus, before a drawing is begun, the artist and scientist must discuss the function of the drawing, perspective, size, and other relevant details. A rough sketch is often made at this stage so that both parties can more easily visualize the finished product and avoid misunderstanding. If the final product is a simple line drawing requiring little time investment, the illustrator can proceed to the final drawing, but if the final product is to be a time-consuming watercolor portrait, then the artist is well advised to go through perhaps several stages of preliminary sketches before doing the final painting. This allows the scientist to change instructions without costing the artist too much time.

INSTRUM[illegible] MATERIA[illegible]

Optical De[illegible]

Stereoscopi[illegible]

Reducing [illegible] more of a [illegible] under the [illegible] scope.

Camera luci[illegible]

Indirect opa[illegible] larging or re[illegible] specimen, w[illegible] the projecto[illegible] can be enlar[illegible]

Camera: 35[illegible] to photogra[illegible] film.

Macro lens[illegible] photographs[illegible]

Slide proje[illegible]

Measuring[illegible]

Metric rule[illegible] (6-inch) and [illegible]

Proportion[illegible] (20cm) or 10[illegible]

Grid: used [illegible] available.

Specimen-[illegible]

Forceps: sh[illegible] (bottle) type[illegible]

Dissecting [illegible] insect pins, [illegible] (see fig. 2-8)[illegible]

Specimen [illegible]

Insect pins.[illegible]

Plasticine c[illegible]

Containers[illegible]

Tray with [illegible] **bottom:** for [illegible] fluid.

Aquarium, dishes: clean glass, for live specimens: other dishes for small preserved specimens.

Wetting Agents and Preservatives

Alcohol: 70 percent (reptiles) and 65 percent ethanol (amphibians).

Formalin: 10 percent, buffered (but not with borax, which will remove pigment).

Miscellaneous

Cheesecloth: to be soaked in water and used to cover specimens between drawing sessions.

Rubber gloves: for working with live specimens or Formalin.

CLASSIFICATION

Although amphibians and reptiles usually are considered a single disciplinary study (herpetology) and are studied by the same people (herpetologists). phylogenetically they represent two quite distinct classes of vertebrates that have evolved separately for at least 340 million years. Not surprisingly, they are physically very different from each other, and each class has diversified into an often bewildering array of forms that presents a special challenge to the artist.

Amphibians, of which there are 4,015 species known, are divided into three orders: Urodela (salamanders and newts, 358 species), Anura (frogs and toads, 3,494 species), and the Gymnophiona (caecilians, 163 species of little-known legless creatures). The 6,547 known species of reptiles are divided into four orders: Chelonia (turtles and tortoises, 244 species), Crocodylia (crocodilians, 22 species), Squamata (lizards, worm lizards, and snakes, 6,280 species), and the Rhynchocephalia (the lizardlike tuatara, with a single living species). It should be immediately clear to the illustrator that amphibians and reptiles represent a spectrum of body forms, surface textures, colors, and patterns more diverse than in many other groups such as birds, for example, all of which are covered with feathers.

The physical characteristics used in the classification of amphibians and reptiles that are of interest to the illustrator are here divided into external and internal structures. The accompanying figures illustrate many of these structures and the perspectives or views conventionally used in herpetological publications. The most important characters are labeled. Since the illustrator must know the basic anatomy of the animals being drawn, the terminology for the major structures, and the techniques for taking standard measurements, these aspects are covered first.

In addition to structural features, color and patterns (fig. 17-2) are key characteristics, of course, but they can be misleading. It is very important to understand that amphibians and, to a lesser extent, reptiles change color and patterns as they age, from season to season, and with changes in temperature. To compound this problem, color and pattern are often different between males and females (sexual dimorphism) and from individual to individual within a given population. Also, there may be two or more discrete color phases (polymorphs) within a population. The scientist must provide guidance as to accurate representation, but sometimes several individual specimens must be illustrated to show the range of colors and patterns. Preserved specimens drastically change color, lose patterns, and generally become dark. Very old preserved specimens can even fade to white, especially if exposed to light. Preservation fluids may also cause dehydration or bloating to the extent that the specimen no longer resembles the living creature. Wherever possible, therefore, live specimens, color photographs, or color slides of living animals should be used.

Amphibians

The most obvious difference between amphibians and reptiles is that amphibians are externally scaleless and usually have a moist skin that is glossy, whereas reptiles are covered with dry, horny scales

17-2. Color pattern of leopard lizard, *Gambelia wislizenii*. Pen-and-ink on Albanene tracing paper, by Karen Schmitt.

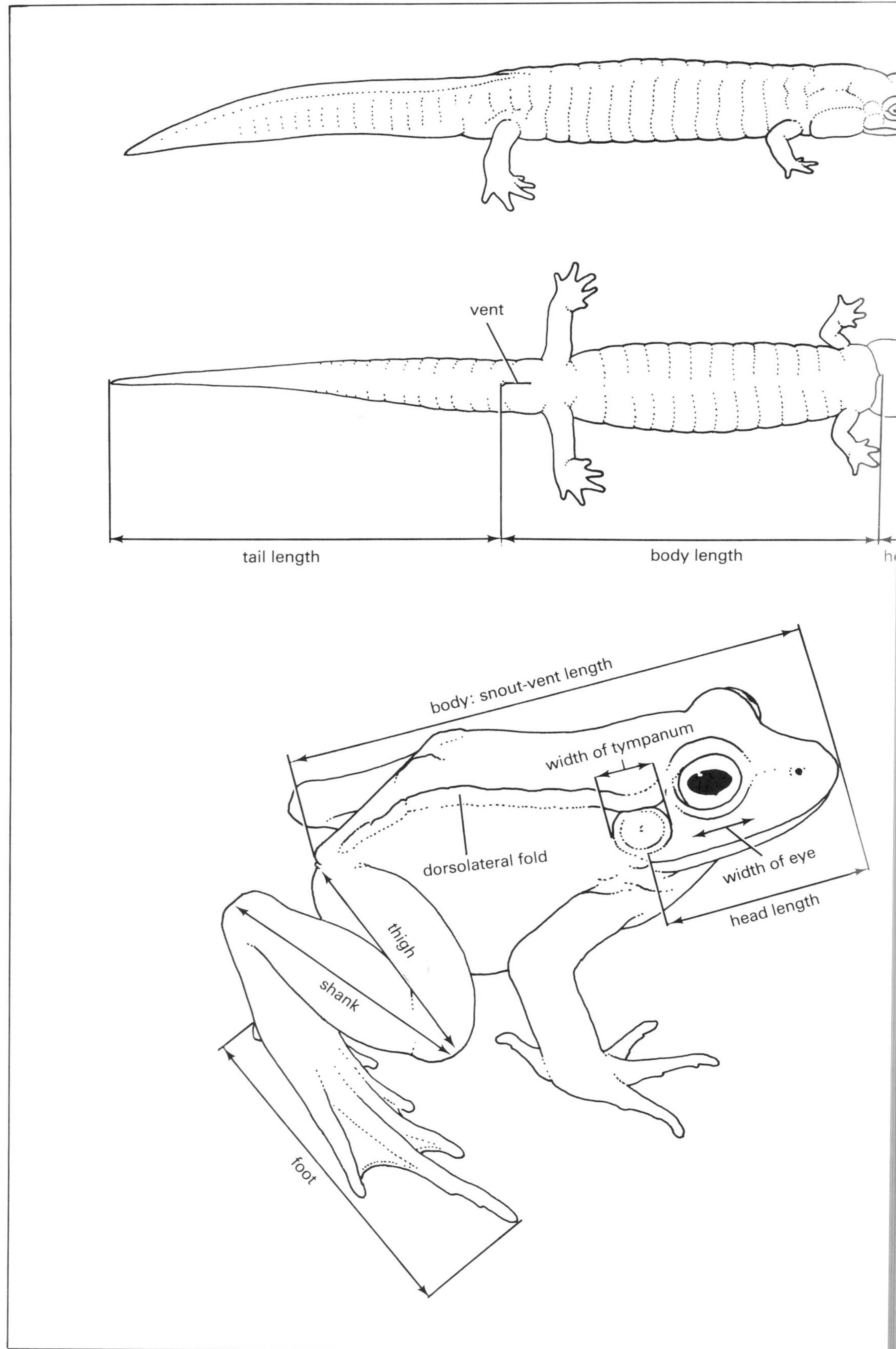

17-3. Standard measurements of salamanders and frogs. No. 1 technical pen and ink on Strathmore Bristol board, by David M. Dennis.

and plates. With the exception of the wormlike caecilians of the tropics, amphibians are easily recognized as either salamanders or frogs by the presence or absence of a tail (fig. 17-3). The overall shape of each species is important, particularly so because they lack external scales, which otherwise could be used to identify the species. Thus, in these animals subtle shapes and features such as skin folds, flaps, warts, crests, and proportions are vitally important for classification and must be drawn accurately. Figures 17-4 through 17-7 show some of the surface structures commonly used in identification.

Salamanders (Urodela)

Technically, all urodeles are salamanders, but members of some groups are called newts, mudpuppies and waterdogs, amphiumas, sirens, and olm. In salamanders, the presence and number of costal grooves are primary taxonomic characters and even the branching of grooves in the angle of the arm or leg can be of key importance (fig. 17-4). The areas between the grooves are called costal folds (technically, intercostal spaces). When the limbs of a salamander are folded against the body (appressed), the number of folds between the digits is an indicator of the relative length of limbs to body length. The extent or absence of a tail fin also is important. Only some species have parotoid (also spelled paratoid or parotid) glands on the nape. The cloacal swelling shown in fig. 17-4 occurs in males only during the breeding season. In the family Plethodontidae, the largest family of salamanders in number of species, there is a groove (nasolabial) between the nostril and the margin of the lip (fig. 17-5), often terminating on a protuberance called a cirrus (plural, cirri). Cirri are more pronounced in males and play a role in courtship, as does the mental "gland," which is not a single gland but a cluster of tiny

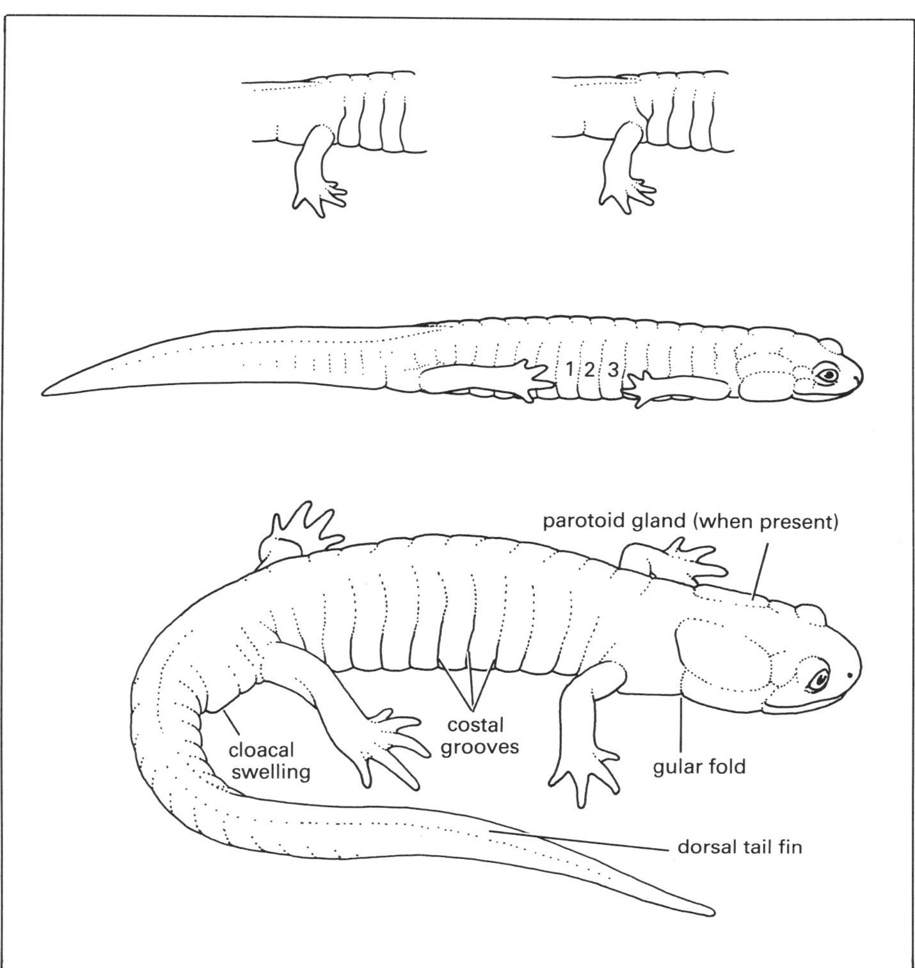

17-4. General anatomy of salamanders: the top and center drawings show two variations in costal grooves. The Y-shaped fold on the right is counted as two grooves. The number of intercostal spaces between tips of appressed limbs, shown in the center drawing, is used as a character. Pen-and-ink on Bristol board, by David M. Dennis.

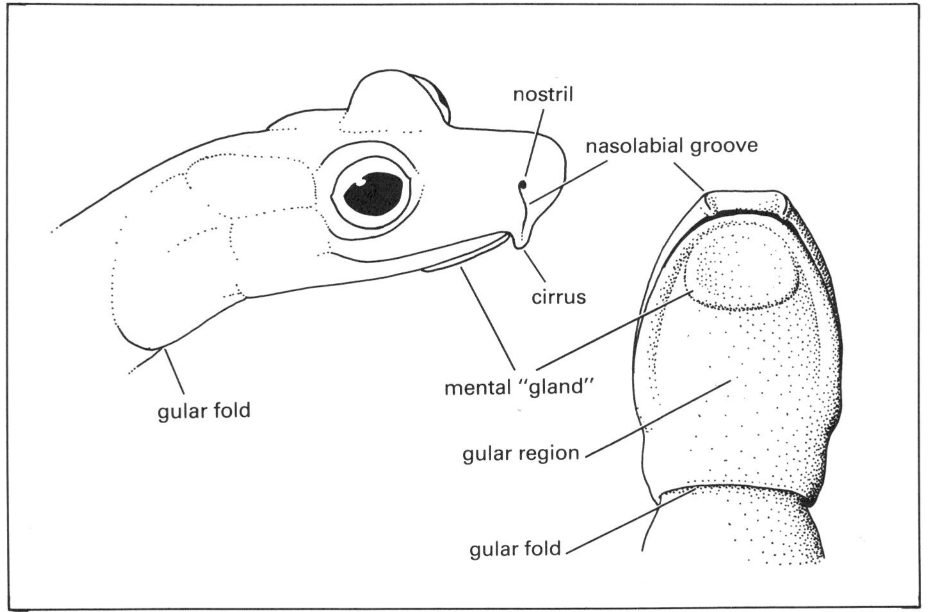

17-5. Salamander head. Pen-and-ink on Bristol board, by David M. Dennis.

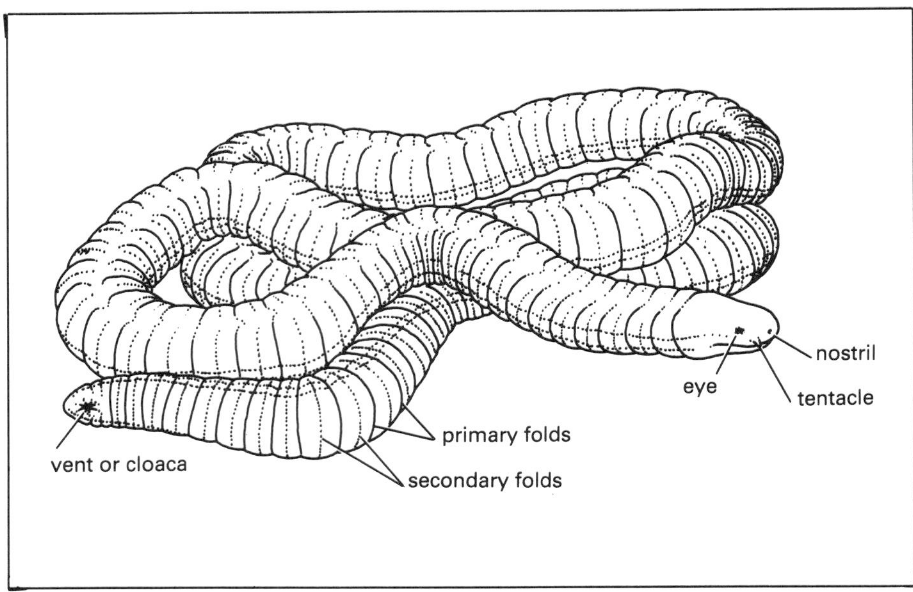

17-6. General anatomy of caecilians. Pen-and-ink on Bristol board, by David M. Dennis.

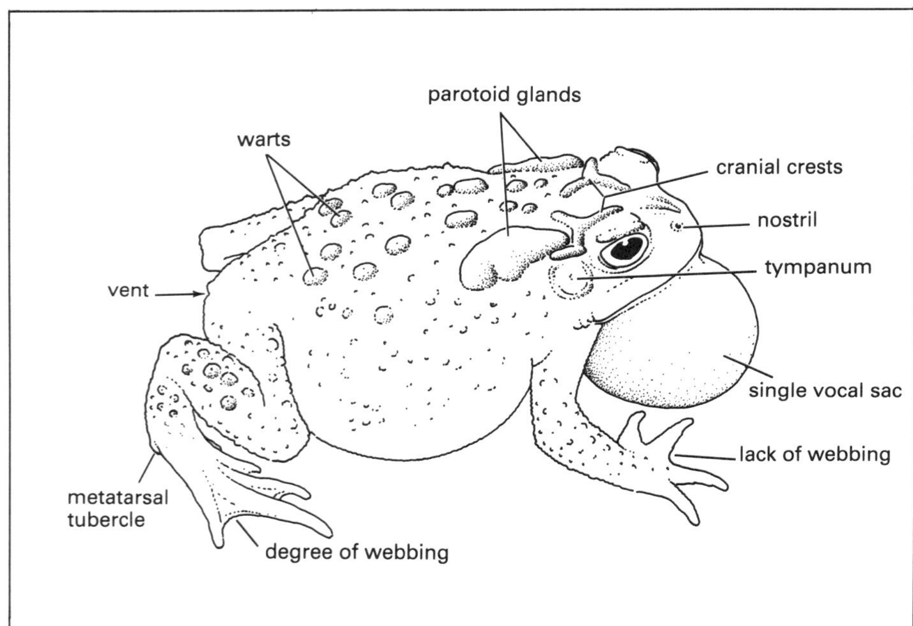

17-7. General anatomy of frogs. Pen-and-ink on Bristol board, by David M. Dennis.

glands located on the chin in males of many species. The mental gland varies among species in size and shape and also can vary seasonally.

Caecilians (Gymnophiona)

Caecilians are wormlike in general appearance (fig. 17-6), have a terminal anus, and have both primary and more faint secondary folds that alternate along the entire body. The eye is covered with skin and thus often overlooked, and there is a retractable tentacle between the nostril and eye. Scales—unique among the living Amphibia—are buried deep in the skin.

Frogs (Anura)

Technically, all anurans are frogs, although members of some more terrestrial groups are called toads. Frogs
surface fea
Cranial cres
tween and b
and some
glands of to
fluids; their
from specie
number, an
conical) of
characters f
urans, as a
The tympar
sent, depen
presence ar
are also imp

Reptiles

Unlike an
covered wit
both. These
shape, surf
rangement
of each spe
rangement
may seem c
tunately, a
ment that ca
by referenc
and 17-11 th

Turtles (Che

The shell
tortoise con
overlying bo
shell (carap
(plastron). N
there are fiv
midline and
side. With
or two spec
dividuals, th
tern, altho
(softshell tu
back turtle)
Note also t
measured a
tween the fr
scute (or, if
between the
to the sutur
of marginals

Crocodilians

Crocodilia
crocodiles, a

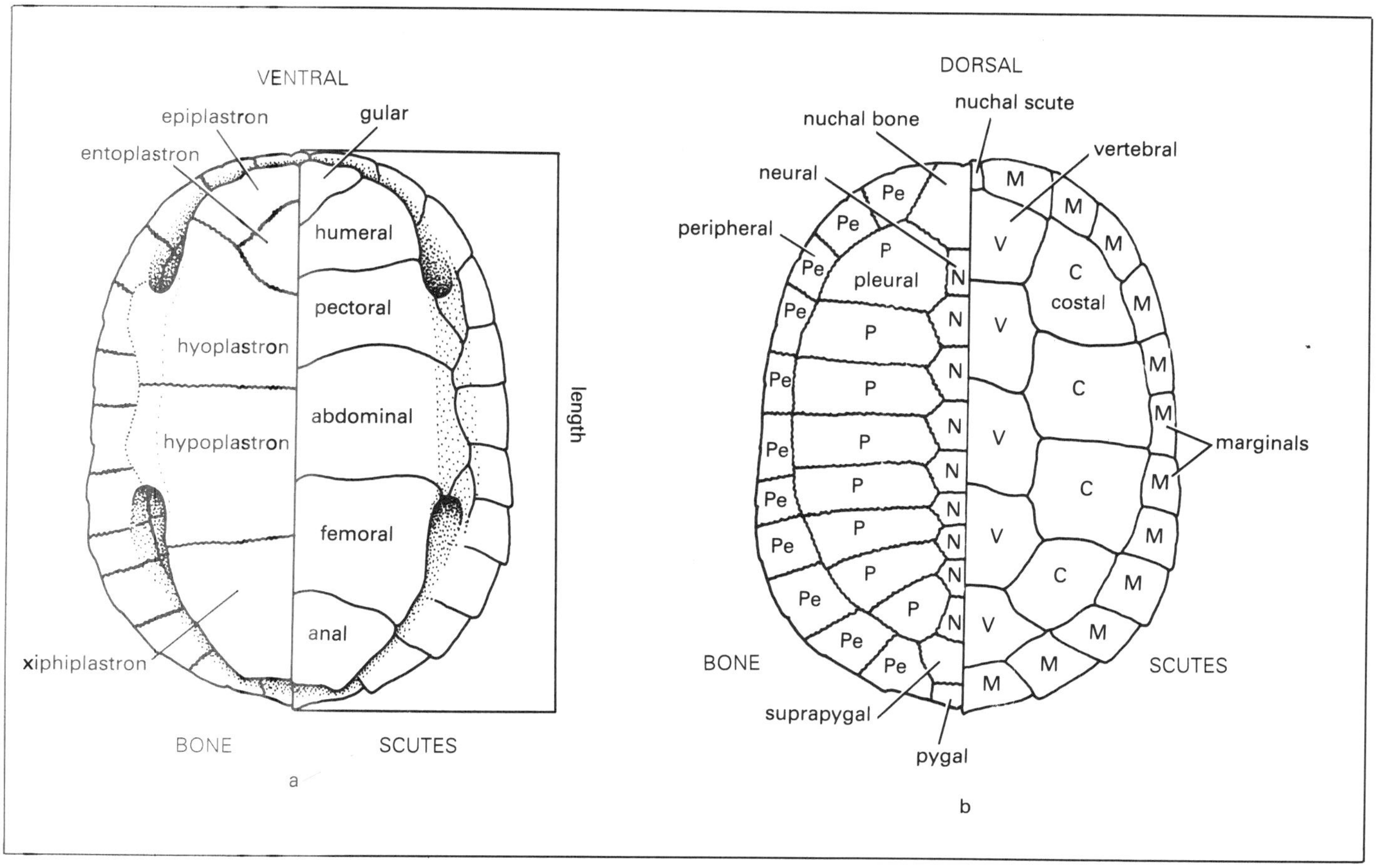

17-8. Scutes and bones of turtle shell: *(a)* plastron; *(b)* carapace. Note that the seams between the major scutes lie beneath and between the seams that are between major bones. This condition has evolved to strengthen the turtle's shell. Pen-and-ink on Bristol board, by David M. Dennis, adapted from "Turtles from Archeological Sites in the Great Lakes Region," by Kraig Adler, in *Michigan Archaeologist*, vol. 14, 1968.

gharials (gavials)—have a wealth of distinguishing features (fig. 17-9). The shape of the snout and whether the teeth in the lower jaw fit into depressions in the upper jaw (as in alligators) or not (as in crocodiles) are important characters. Note especially the skin-covered bony plates (osteoderms) on the neck, which vary in size and arrangement from species to species.

Lizards and Snakes (Squamata)

Lizards and snakes, despite their superficial differences, are closely related. Lizards possess legs (fig. 17-10), but these may be reduced in size or absent altogether in some species. The scales on a lizard's head are numerous, with larger plates down the midline and

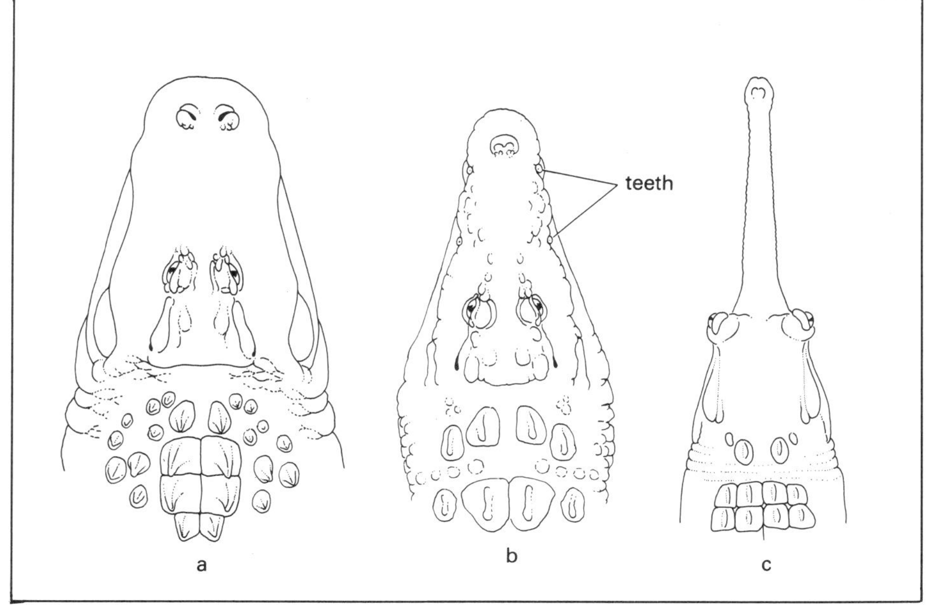

17-9. Heads of crocodilians: *(a)* alligator; *(b)* crocodile; *(c)* gharial. Pen-and-ink on Bristol board, by David M. Dennis.

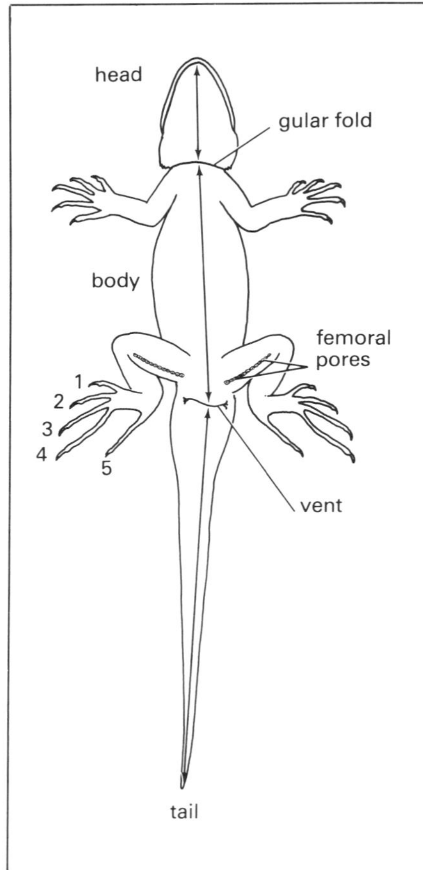

17-10. Ventral view of lizard, showing standard measurements. Pen-and-ink on Bristol board, by David M. Dennis.

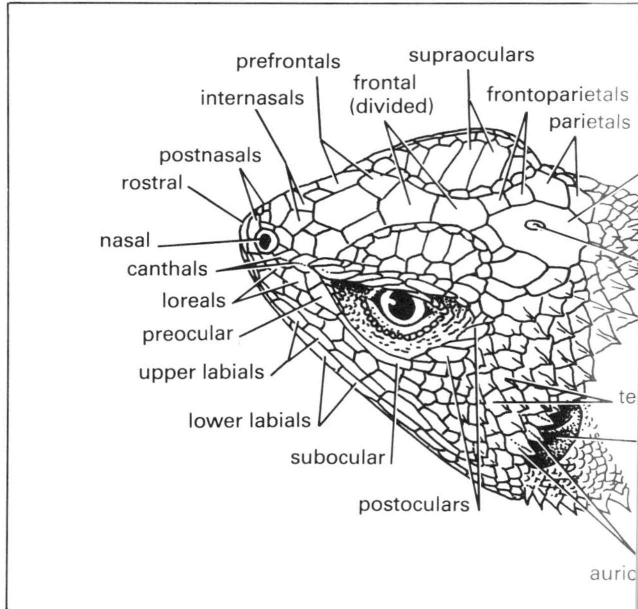

17-11. Scalation of lizard head. Pen-and-ink on Bristol board.

rows or circlets of smaller scales along the lips and around the eyes and nostrils (fig. 17-11). In many species there is a tiny light-receptive structure, or "third eye," in the center of the interparietal scale. Lizards almost always have eyelids and external ear openings. By contrast, the scalation on the head of most snakes (fig. 17-12) is much simpler. The number of scales is fewer, and there are never any eyelids, external ear openings, or third eyes. The underside of the tail of snakes has one or two rows of subcaudal scales (fig. 17-13), depending upon species. The anal scale is divided or not. The relative length and taper of the tail differentiate the sexes externally.

The scales on the bodies of lizards and snakes are arranged in regular transverse or oblique rows

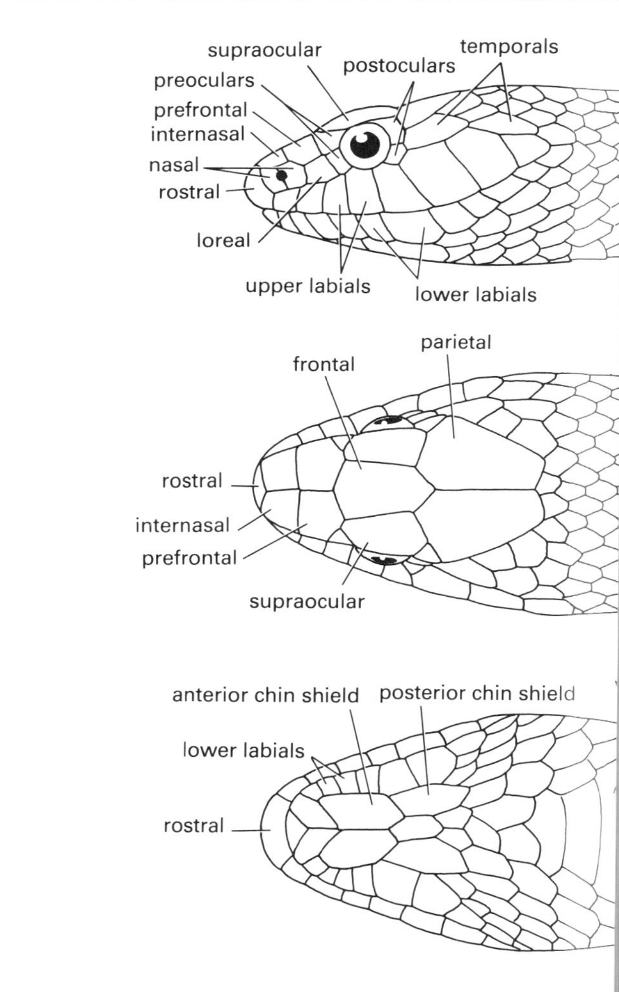

17-12. Scalation of snake head. Pen-and-ink on Bristol board.

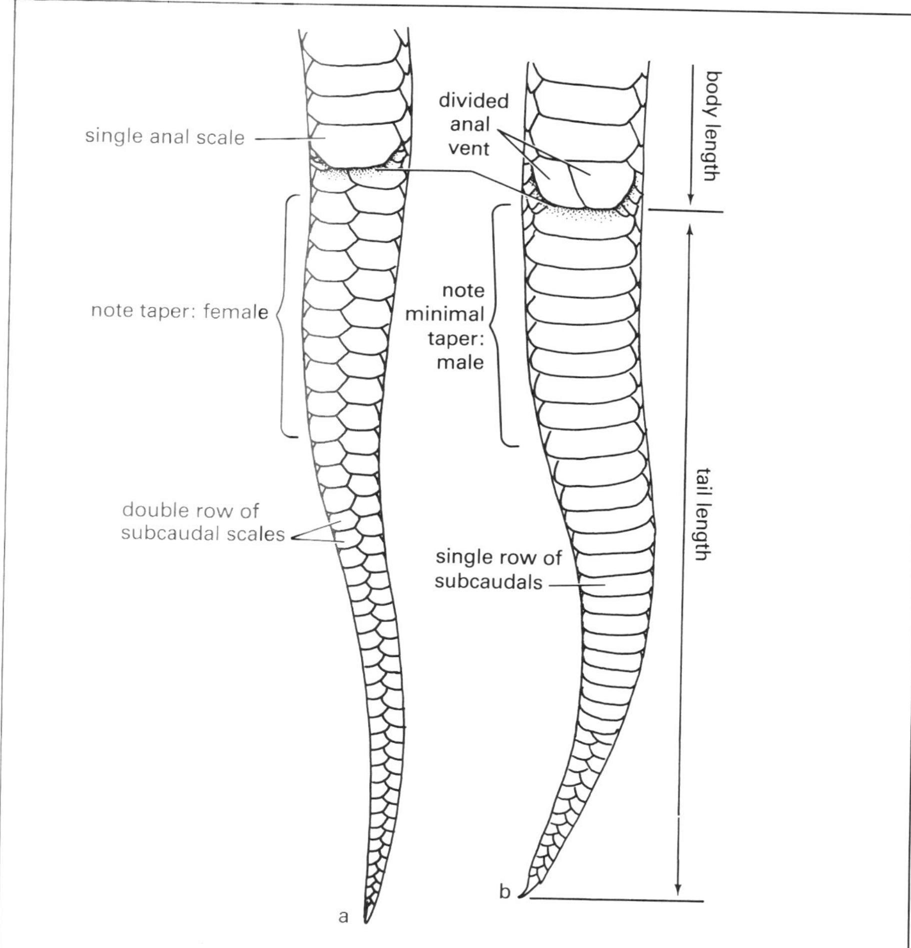

17-13. Ventral view of snake tails, showing standard measurements and differences in scalation and taper: *(a)* female; *(b)* male. Pen-and-ink on Bristol board, by David M. Dennis.

(fig. 17-14). Some scales have a longitudinal ridge down the center (keel), whereas others are smooth. In some species there are tiny holes in the scales (apical pits), which are sometimes so small that they require high magnification to see; in some species their presence can be confirmed only by examination of a shed skin. Some kinds of lizards have an irregular pattern of scalation (granular), with larger scales interspersed seemingly randomly. Normally the scales are overlapping so that skin does not show between them, but if the skin is stretched—for example, when a hognose snake or a cobra spreads a hood—it can then be seen. This skin is often brightly colored or black and sometimes creates a pattern that is invisible when the hood is relaxed.

The pattern of scales on the body is very regular and numbers are assigned to the different scale rows. Indeed, it is so regular that illustrators have even developed printed patterns, one for each different standard number of dorsal longitudinal scale rows (for example, twenty-one rows in fig. 17-15), allowing them simply to add the color pattern typical for a given

17-14. Basic types of scales found on the bodies of snakes and lizards. Top, left to right: snake scales—keeled with apical pits (arrow); keeled; smooth. Bottom, left to right: lizard scales—mucronate, granular, cycloid. Pen-and-ink on Bristol board, by David M. Dennis.

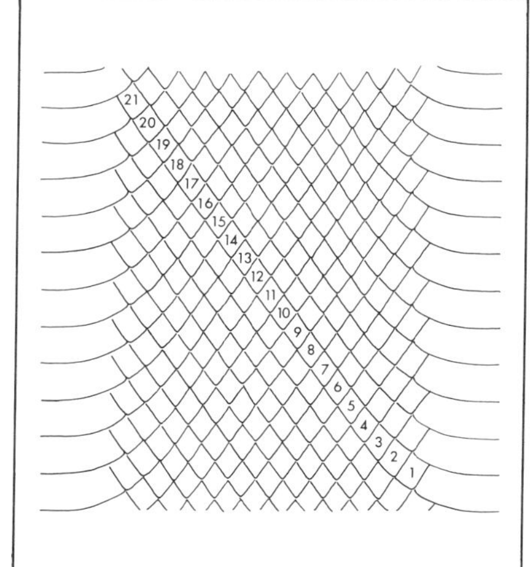

17-15. Dorsal scales of snake body, showing how rows are numbered. To each side are the broader ventral scales, here cut down the midline to allow the entire skin to lie flat. Pen-and-ink on Bristol board, by David M. Dennis.

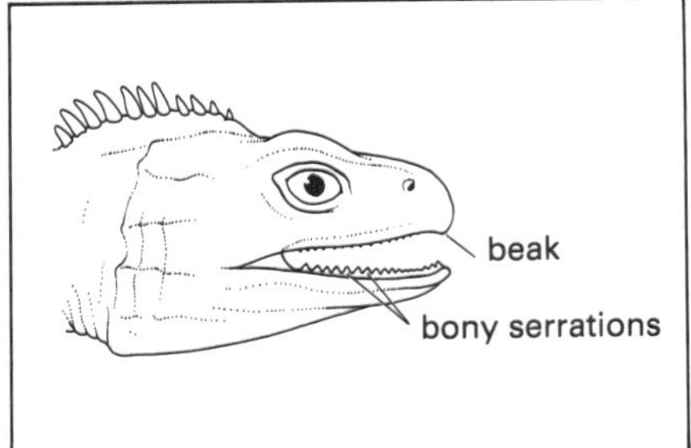

17-16. Head of tuatara. Note that the bony serrations of jawbone are not teeth. Pen-and-ink on Bristol board, by David M. Dennis.

species over the printed pattern and thus speed their work. However, because snake bodies taper at both ends, certain rows of scales drop out and herpetologists have developed complex scale formulas to describe the scalation of an entire individual. These formulas are of minimal importance to the artist, who will simply draw what is seen.

Tuatara (Rhynchocephalia)

During the Mesozoic era, members of this order were found throughout the world, but today only a single species—the tuatara—survives, in New Zealand. It is lizardlike in body form (fig. 17-16), with a dorsal crest and a beaked snout; most of the distinctive characters are skeletal.

Special External Characteristics

The shape and ornamentation of the hands and feet are important amphibian characters and therefore are frequently illustrated. For example, the hands and feet of frogs often have toe pads, and these vary in size and shape (fig. 17-17). Likewise, the extent of webbing varies among species or may be lacking altogether. Subarticular tubercles vary by species in number, shape, and size. Nuptial excrescences, a secondary sex character of males, consist of small horny spines on the hands or sometimes on the chest of many frogs and on the inner surface of the hind legs of some salamanders. These are present only during the breeding season and serve to allow the male to maintain a firm grasp on the female. In salamanders (fig. 17-18), the length of the digits and the degree of webbing on the hands and feet differentiate many species.

The eyes of amphibians and reptiles vary in the shapes of the pupils (fig. 17-19). Most species have round pupils, but others have pupils that are vertically or horizon-

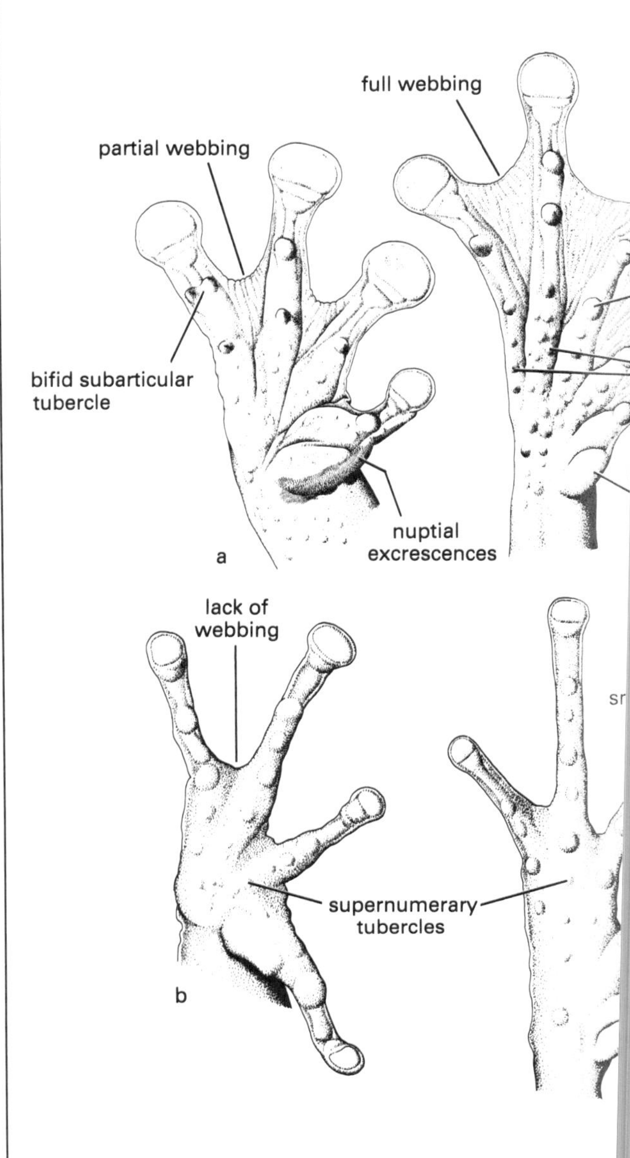

17-17. Hands *(a)* and feet *(b)* of frogs. Pen-and-ink on Brist
Dennis.

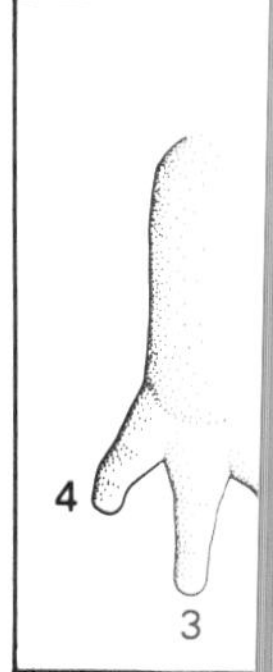

17-18. Han
ferences in
ink on Brist

tally elliptical. More curious, a few species (such as some gecko lizards) have an elongate pupil that, when closed, permits light to enter through multiple tiny "pupils," all of which project to the same spot on the retina, thus increasing stimulation in animals that are active under low light conditions. The colored part of the eye (iris) in amphibians and reptiles is often bright or metallic in color or has a fine network of reticulations. Thus, drawing the eye requires special care in order to do it accurately and to make it lifelike: ideally, it should be done with a live specimen.

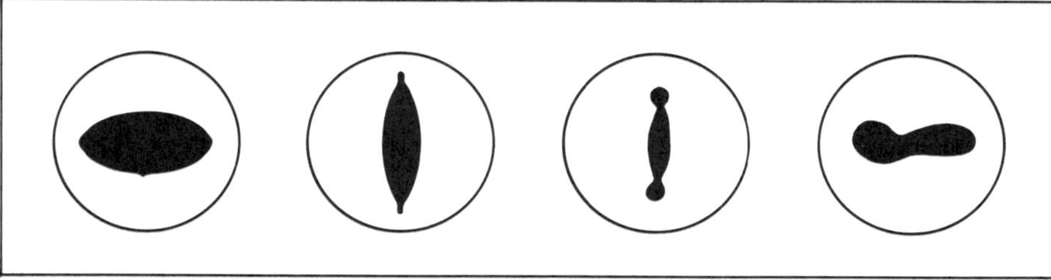

17-19. Eyes of amphibians and reptiles. Left to right: tree frog, crocodile, gecko lizard, vine snake. Pen-and-ink on Bristol board, by David M. Dennis.

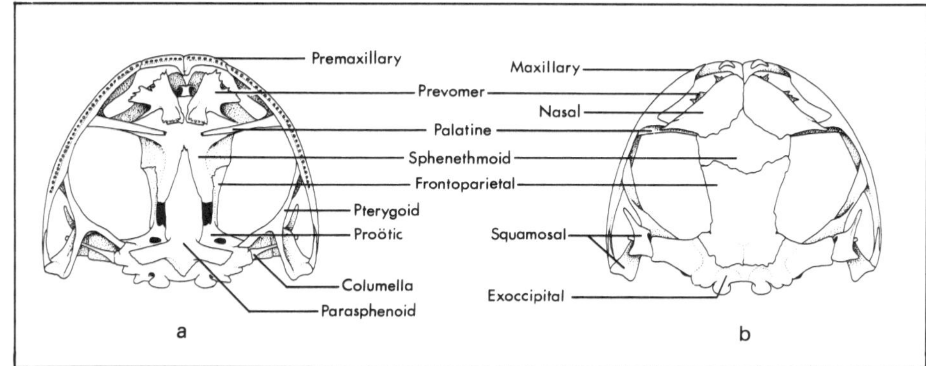

17-20. Ventral *(a)* and dorsal *(b)* views of frog skull. Pen-and-ink on Bristol board, by David M. Dennis.

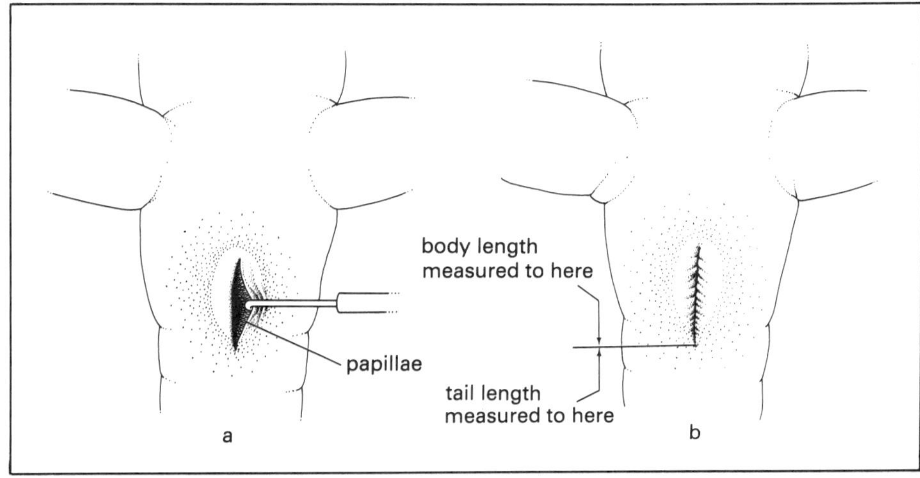

17-21. Vent of male *(a)* and female *(b)* salamanders. Pen-and-ink on Bristol board, by David M. Dennis.

Internal Features

The artist sometimes is called on to illustrate internal features, particularly the skull and skeleton. Dissections are provided by the scientist. The standard views used for amphibian and reptile skulls are shown in figure 17-20. Some skulls and skeletons, especially among the Amphibia, have large amounts of cartilage in them, and it is usually important to differentiate between cartilage and bone. This is often done by stippling the cartilaginous areas. The cloaca—the common chamber into which the digestive, urinary, and reproductive tracts discharge their contents, the opening of which is called a vent—is an important feature to illustrate in salamanders, and fortunately, it can be observed without dissection (fig. 17-21). Those of breeding males are lined with papillae, but those of females are grooved. The vents of immature individuals may show no sexual dimorphism.

The sperm of most salamanders is transferred to the female in a small packet that is usually situated on a pedestal deposited on the ground by the male. This compound structure is called a spermatophore. It has a characteristic shape in each species (see fig. 17-29) and is often illustrated.

All reptiles practice internal fertilization, and the sperm usually are introduced into the female's cloaca by means of a penis. The penis is a single organ in turtles and crocodilians, but in lizards and snakes it is paired (hemipenis or, plural, hemipenes) (fig. 17-22). It is everted (turned inside out) after cloacal contact is made. This structure has a characteristic shape and ornamentation in each species and it therefore is often illustrated. When everted, it is easy to see the spines or other structures that serve temporarily to anchor the organ in the female. Ideally, these structures should be illustrated in the everted state, but when an everted specimen is unavailable, the illustrator must draw the penis or hemipenis in the noneverted state. Everting must be done, usually by the scientist, just after the animal is killed and before preservation.

The tongues of amphibians and reptiles also are frequently illustrated (fig. 17-23). These vary in place of attachment, size, shape, and surface texture. They can be observed by cutting the angle of the jaw and opening the mouth, but

17-22. Hemipenes of a snake in *(a)* noneverted and *(b)* everted positions. The noneverted hemipenis has been dissected and split open. *(a)* Redrawn from The Classification of the Ophidia, by E. D. Cope, in *Transactions* of the American Philosophical Society; vol. 18, pp. 186-219 (Philadelphia, 1895). Pen-and-ink on Bristol board, by David M. Dennis.

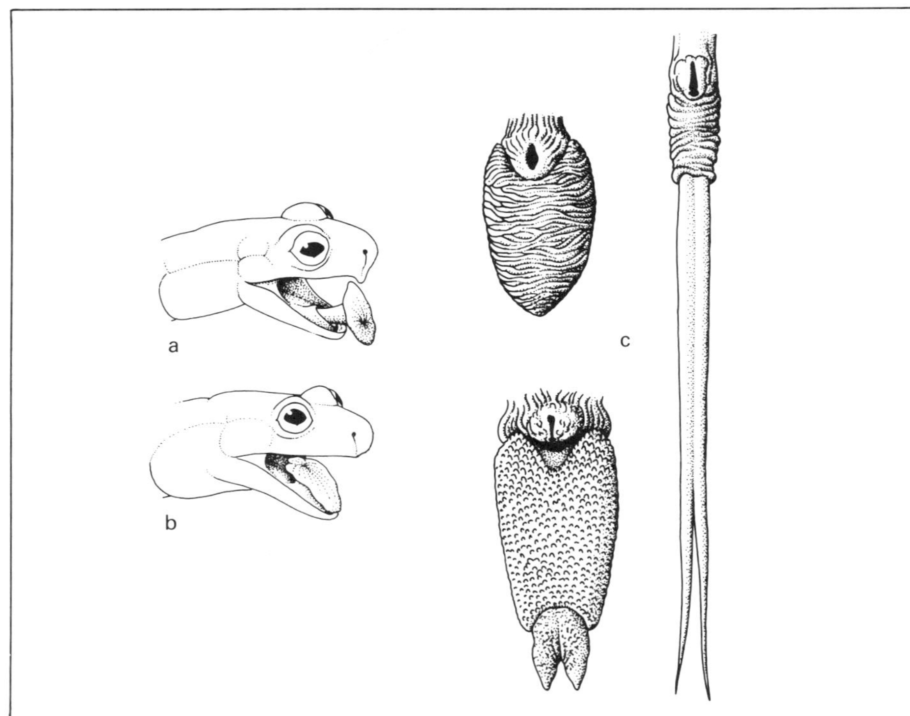

17-23. Tongues of amphibians and reptiles. Two types of salamander tongues: *(a)* stalked extensible tongue; *(b)* nonextensible tongue attached in front. (c) Some variations in lizard tongues (redrawn from Sauria, in *The Fauna of British India, Reptilia and Amphibia*, vol. 2, by Malcolm A. Smith (Taylor and Francis, London, 1935). Pen-and-ink on Bristol board, by David M. Dennis.

since damag
occur in the
best to hav
the dissecti
phibians li
mouth, uns
reptiles, e
snakes, are
sheath. Th
was preser
tended, it
without son

The toot
quently illu
of taxonom
17-27).

Developm

The eggs
tiles have
shapes an
17-24). Th
encased w
of gelatino
all shape c
from spec
reptiles d
phosis an
the egg a
embryos c
become f
metamorp
many feat
for each s
phibian la
mary kin
today in
and, cons
frequently

Larvae of

The ac
ders rese
lids, tong
features a
17-25). Th
ent speci
correlatin
habitat.
metamor
adult sta
salamanc
just behi
involved
number
varies fro

Larvae of Frogs

In contrast to those of salamanders, frog larvae (called tadpoles) are distinctly different from the adult morphology (fig. 17-26). The most obvious difference is a large, powerful tail, which serves to pro-

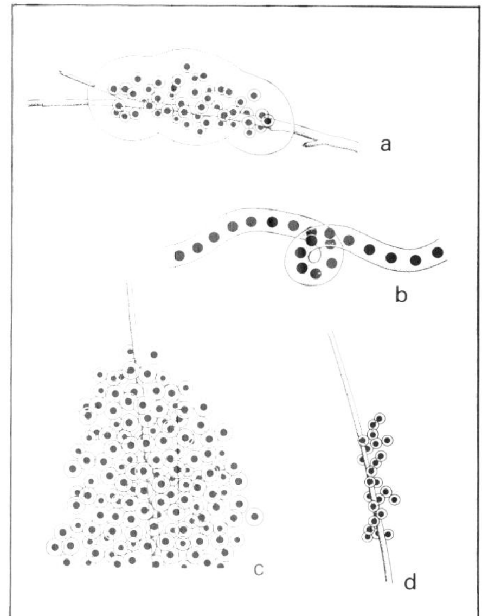

17-24. Eggs (technically, embryos) of amphibians. Note the differences in clutch arrangements: *(a)* spotted salamander; *(b)* toad; *(c)* ranid frog; and *(d)* hylid frog. Pen-and-ink on Bristol board, by David M. Dennis.

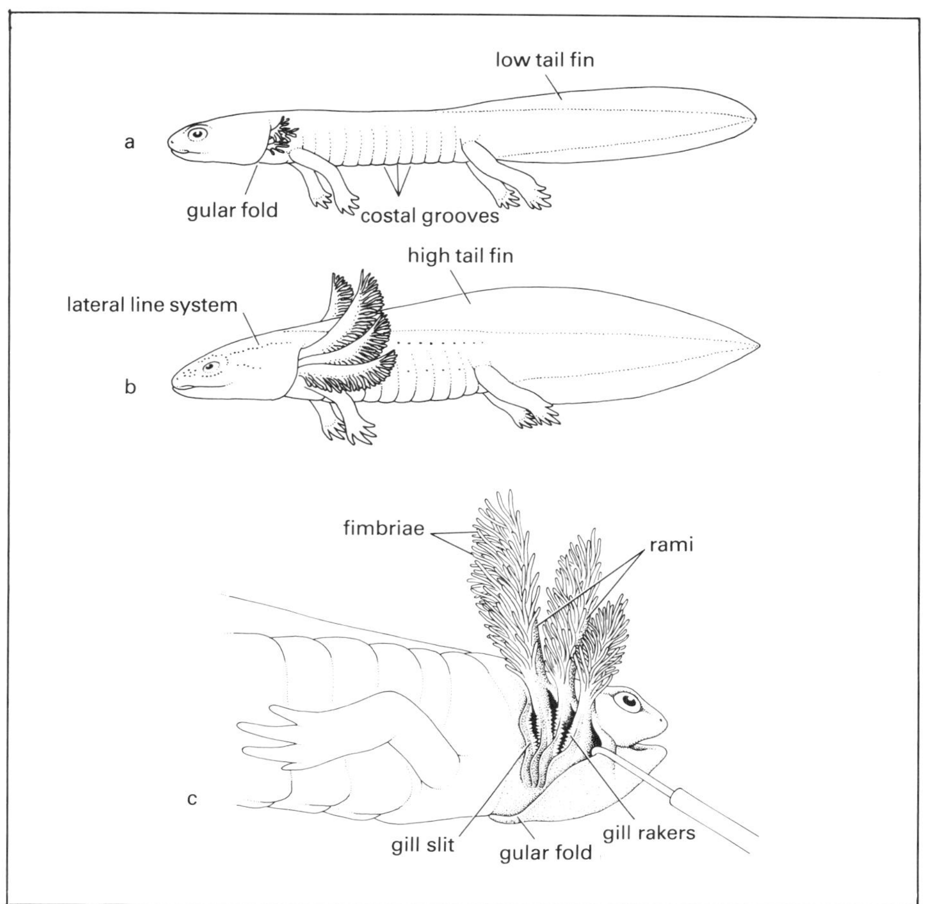

17-25. Salamander larvae: *(a)* stream type with small gills and low tail fin; *(b)* pond type with large gills and high tail fin; *(c)* close-up of gills showing fine structure. Pen-and-ink on Bristol board, by David M. Dennis.

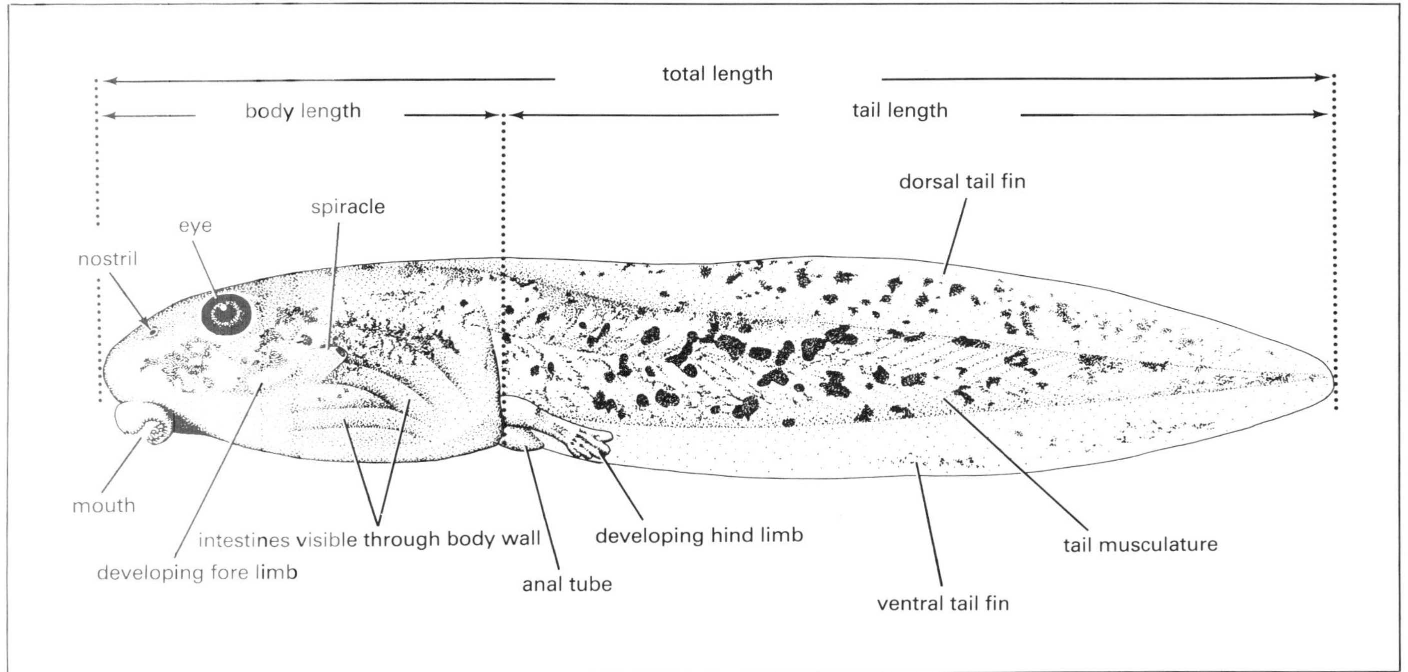

17-26. Surface structures of frog larva (tadpole). The developing fore limb is covered by an overgrowth of skin (operculum). Pen-and-ink on Bristol board, by David M. Dennis.

pel them through the water. Tadpoles have gills but, unlike those of salamander larvae, they are internal, being gradually covered over time by an overgrowth of skin called the operculum; thus, in fact, in the very youngest tadpoles the gills are momentarily still external. The water enters the mouth, passes through the gill chamber, where food is extracted and gases are exchanged, and passes out the spiracle opening. The arms develop inside the gill chamber. The eyes lack eyelids. The overall shape of the tadpole varies together

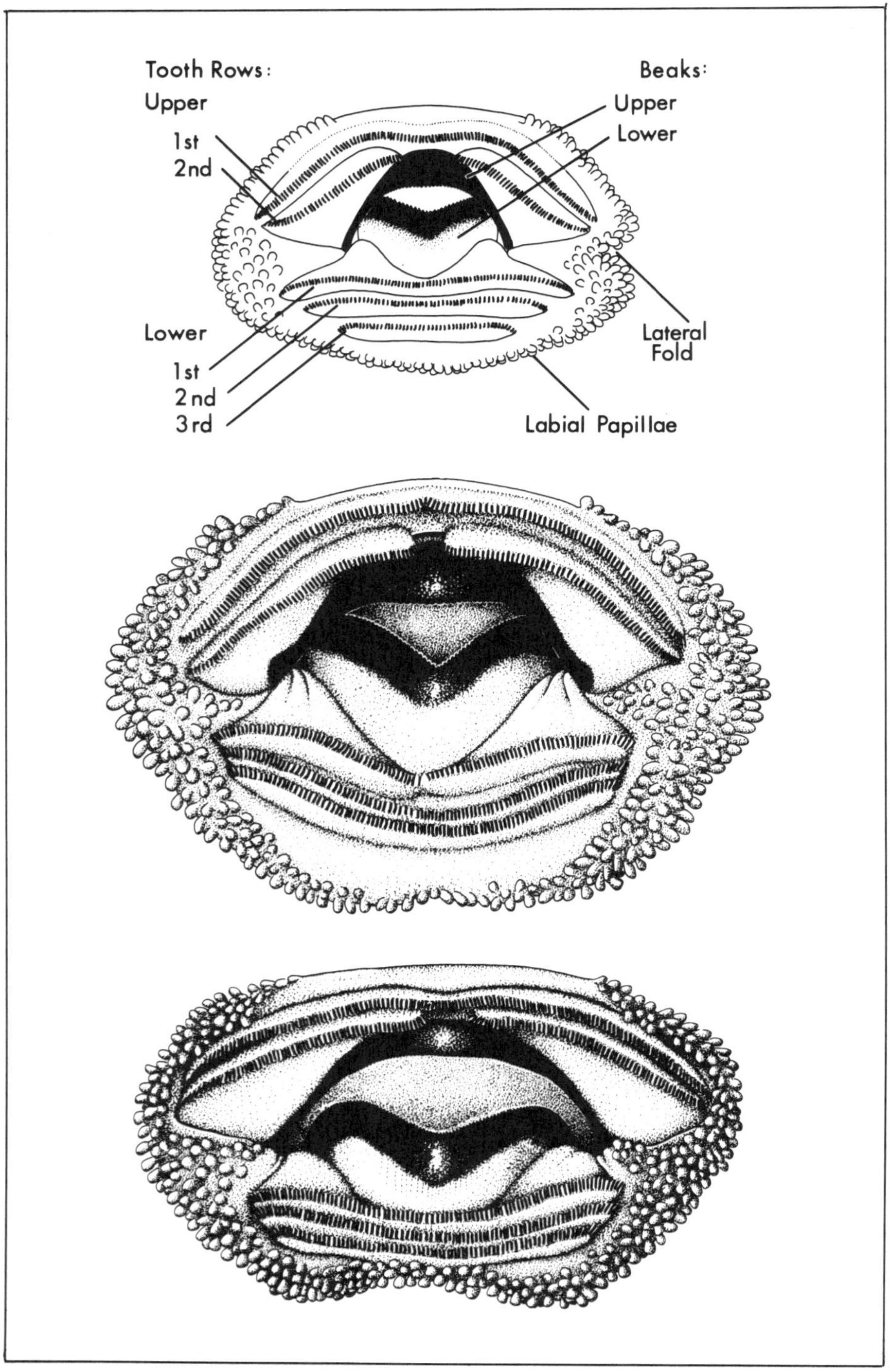

17-27. Mouthparts of frog tadpoles of three different species, showing variation in tooth rows. Pen-and-ink on Bristol board, by David M. Dennis.

with size an
as well as th
the tail fin. T
acle may be
sometimes
mouth parts
are also quit
and, althoug
often are ref
bear no deve
to the teeth
sition of the
characters i
number and
(and whethe
or not), nun
of papillae
even absenc
size and sh
these featur
in classifyin
families.

Behavioral

Illustrator
previously d
preserved
sionally they
amphibians
various acti

17-28. Inflate
paired; *(b)* sir
board, by Da

17-29. Courtship sequence of salamander: *(a)* female does the courtship "tail walk" behind the male while he deposits the spermatophore; *(b)* circling movements; *(c)* enlargement of spermatophore. Pen-and-ink on Bristol board, by David M. Dennis.

vocal sacs of frogs vary in shape and location according to species, genus, and family (fig. 17-28), but these cannot be drawn accurately from preserved specimens. Color slides or photographs of calling males are the best sources of information for such a drawing, but motion pictures or published descriptions also can be used, at least to supplement the color slides. Courtship sequences are species-typical and often illustrated (fig. 17-29). Depending upon the scientist's request, it occasionally may be necessary for the artist to improvise where no photographs are available. To do so, published descriptions of the behavior and actual specimens must be combined as references to create the desired result.

CARE AND HANDLING OF SPECIMENS

If live animals are to be drawn, it is the responsibility of the scientist to provide suitable containers for them and instructions for their care. In addition, precautions for working with venomous or otherwise dangerous amphibians and reptiles should be given by the scientist. Aside from venomous snakes and lizards, some other snakes produce a toxic saliva that, if injected in a bite, can cause respiratory or other problems for the person bitten. Several species of frogs and salamanders produce toxic skin secretions that, although probably never fatal unless swallowed or injected, can produce extreme pain if rubbed into the eyes or an open wound. It is advisable to wear rubber gloves when handling such amphibians or to wash the hands thoroughly after handling them. If the scientist does not mention any potential hazards, ask whether any exist.

Drawing live specimens has some redeeming features: since their metabolism is largely temperature-dependent, amphibians and reptiles, when shaded, often sit motionless for hours and, with care, can even be chilled in a refrigerator in order to give the artist or photographer a more cooperative subject!

Preserved specimens are usually stored permanently in ethanol (ethyl alcohol), after being fixed in Formalin (formaldehyde). Sometimes they are stored permanently in Formalin. Normally, reptiles are kept in a solution of 70 percent and amphibians in 65 to 70 percent ethanol in order to prevent decay. Isopropyl (40 to 55 percent) is also used sometimes, but specimens should not be transferred from one kind of alcohol to the other, as damage can result. Methyl alcohol should never be used. Ask the scientist what the preservative is and whether the specimens can be removed from the storage fluid during rendering. Amphibian eggs and larvae are best stored in 10 percent Formalin and never should be put in alcohol. Further details of preservation techniques and storage appear in *A Guide to Preservation Techniques for Amphibians and Reptiles*, by George R. Pisani, and *Herpetological Collecting and Collections Management*, by John E. Simmons (see Bibliography). Formalin and Formalin fumes can be very irritating to hands and eyes, and protective measures should be taken if exposure is to be for an extended period. The workroom should be well ventilated. (See Care and Handling of Specimens in chapter 15 for suggestions.)

To prevent drying, amphibians and reptiles should be covered with cheesecloth soaked in alcohol, leaving uncovered only the area being drawn. The cheesecloth should be soaked often. Amphibians, especially larvae, are extremely delicate; most have a thin skin that can easily be torn or rubbed away. Tails are easily broken and gills and tail fins damaged. To compound this problem, amphibians dehydrate rapidly, especially those preserved in alcohol. Thus, it is best to submerge larvae in water while drawing them (fig. 17-30), to prevent drying out but also to lift the gill filaments and the

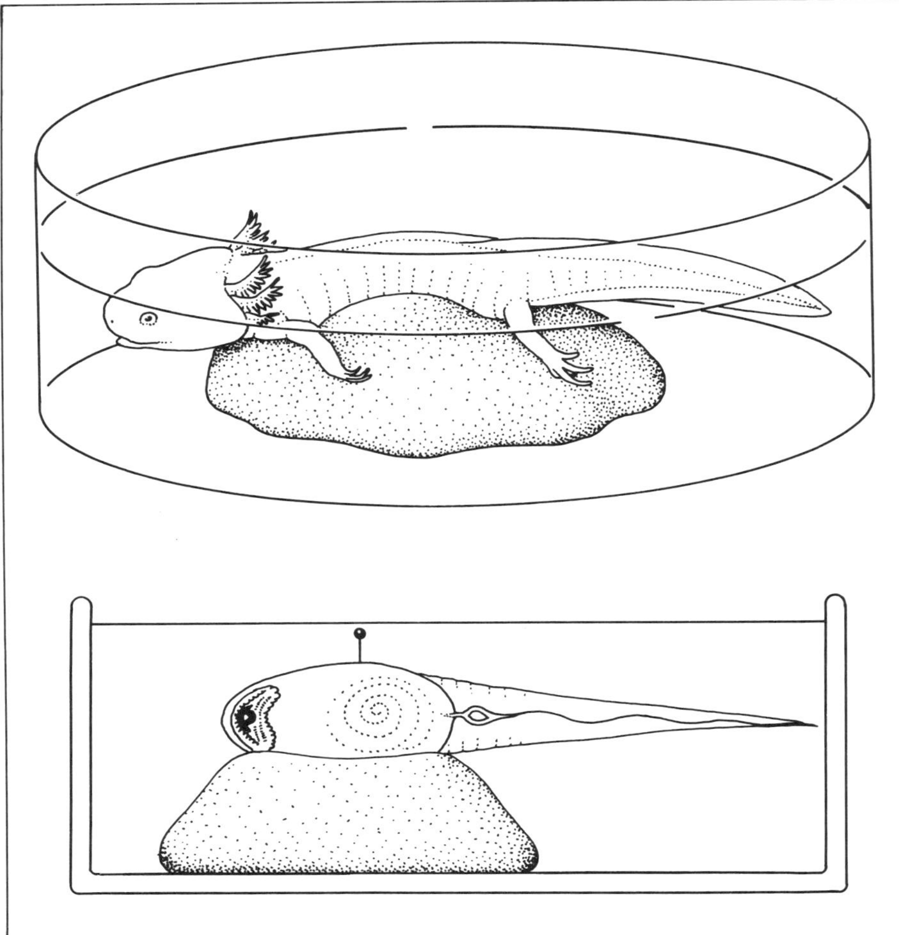

17-30. Positioning techniques for amphibian larvae and small delicate reptiles, using an insect pin and modeling clay. Note that water level is above head of insect pin. Pen-and-ink on Bristol board, by David M. Dennis.

tail into more natural positions. This technique also reduces surface reflections, which sometimes interfere with visibility.

Hold the specimen in position with an insect pin and plasticine clay. The clay can be molded into a holding platform that approximates the shape of the specimen. Pins should be inserted in a specimen only with the permission of the scientist. Reptiles also can be positioned in this way, especially small, delicate specimens that are prone to dehydration. Even large reptile specimens can dry out and be damaged if not kept moist. All specimens must be replaced in the appropriate preservative when not being drawn.

Specimens are sometimes missing tails or, less likely, toes and other parts of the anatomy. Whether or not the missing part is inferred depends on the function of the drawing. If the illustration is for general purposes, a missing toe can be reproduced from its symmetrical counterpart and tails can be approximated from other species or published illustrations. However, if the drawing is to represent a particular specimen, such as a holotype or other unique specimen, then the animal must be drawn as is, including all imperfections. Ask the scientist for guidance.

Standard Measurements

The artist is rarely if ever called upon to measure specimens, alive or dead. If necessary, specimens are best meas
ing them agai
intervals. Liv
to straighten
to crawl along
in a V-shaped

Many of th
chapter depic
fine termino
structures, a
showing how
be made are
scientists.

SPECIAL T
MEDIA

The scient
ing size (for
spective), bu
chooses the
tain an accu
lucida and
transparenci
simple obse
cida and mi
drawing ve
cially skull
penes), wh
positioned
shadows th
sualize imp
(see chapter
slides are e
taining accu
tion. They
depicting h
tions. The
take these
entist may
slides are u
ence, often
directly on
which fac
drawing of
vices in ch

Several
illustrating
tiles, depe
the scient
will be in
color, wat
rately depi
of color
Acrylic pa
ing the ad
proof after

the illustrator to work with both transparent and opaque techniques on the same illustration.

Because the skin of most amphibians is moist and the scales and scutes of reptiles are often very smooth, they typically produce reflection highlights that must be reproduced accurately if the drawing is to be lifelike. These highlights also help to impart a three-dimensional aspect to the specimen (see fig. C-17). The highlight on the eye is critical, although often overlooked. Remember, however, that such highlights are produced primarily by direct lighting, such as sun- or moonlight, and not by diffuse lighting. Thus, on an animal depicted in a shaded forest or under water, these highlights will not appear as distinctly, if at all. Sometimes it is necessary to exaggerate the highlight to make the drawing look lifelike or, conversely, diffuse or reduce the actual highlight so that the pattern can be seen (see Highlights in chapter 4).

Good illustrations of amphibians and reptiles demonstrate how attractive these animals can be with their range of colors from subtle to brilliant and texture from dry and scaly to wet and smooth. Unlike most other vertebrates, some amphibians inhabit both aquatic and terrestrial environments at different stages of their lives, changing structure dramatically to suit each habitat. Many amphibians and reptiles change color and structure of certain body parts just during sexual displays. Such physical variation adds interest and challenge to their illustration.

18/Illustrating Birds

Nancy R. Halliday

Birds confront the biological illustrator with a different set of problems than do most other zoological classes because assignments often require drawings of whole animals in lifelike poses. In addition to an understanding of the basic principles of drawing, the artist must completely understand avian anatomy for illustrations of birds to be successful. The literature is clogged with drawings of poorly balanced birds with appendages that appear to be broken in every conceivable manner prepared by those who have not made the effort to acquire this understanding. Many illustrators today merely copy photographs and finish their work with flawless illustration techniques. The results are dazzling in surface detail but woefully lacking in comprehension of the body underlying the feathers. Indeed, some of the most convincing drawings are simple but charming figures prepared by professional ornithologists self-trained in art who have become intimately acquainted with their subjects by countless hours of bird-watching in the field. It is hoped that this chapter will have some effect on improving the quality of bird illustrations made by biological illustrators.

INSTRUMENTS AND MATERIALS

Optical Devices

Stereoscopic microscope: to view details and very small parts such as internal organs and bones or tiny birds such as hummingbirds.

Reducing objective.

Camera lucida.

Reticle: ocular grid; used instead of camera lucida.

Magnifiers: hand lens or other type (see Magnifiers in chapter 2).

Binoculars: 7 × 35 size; for bird-watching, of enormous importance for understanding bird anatomy and behavior, both of which affect the stance of a bird.

Camera: 35mm single-lens reflex.

Slide projector: for 35mm slides.

Measuring Devices

Rulers: Metric, clear plastic, 15cm (6 inch), 30cm (12 inch), and larger.

Proportional dividers: 8 inch (20cm) or larger; for transferring measurements from specimen to drawing surface (see Proportional Dividers in chapter 2).

Specimen-handling Tools

Forceps: short (jeweler's) for handling tiny parts, long (bottle) for removing specimens from alcohol (see fig. 2-7).

Dissecting needles, probes: to tease apart anatomic dissections. Usually these are metal (see fig. 2-7).

Specimen Props

Insect pins: stainless steel to prevent rusting in fluid; for propping alcohol-preserved or dry specimens in place.

Wooden blocks, erasers: for propping dry specimens.

Containers

Dish or tray with wax bottom: for alcohol-immersed specimens or dry specimens to be propped with pins. If made
be placed dir
wax.

Tray or box
for carrying s

Wetting Ag
Preservativ

Alcohol: in
match those
usually 70 pe

Miscellane

Paper towe
covering wet
periods betw
Use pins in w
specimen.

Plastic wrap
mens, retaini

BASIC ANA

Internal

Since it is
stand the bi
order to mak
us begin wi
tween the ba
a bird and a
in figure 18-
tion into the
vided by figu
remarkable f
bones in the
essary for t
ments of
originally ma
reason all
hummingbir
ostriches, ar

Study the
ready in the
sion and re
Teeth were

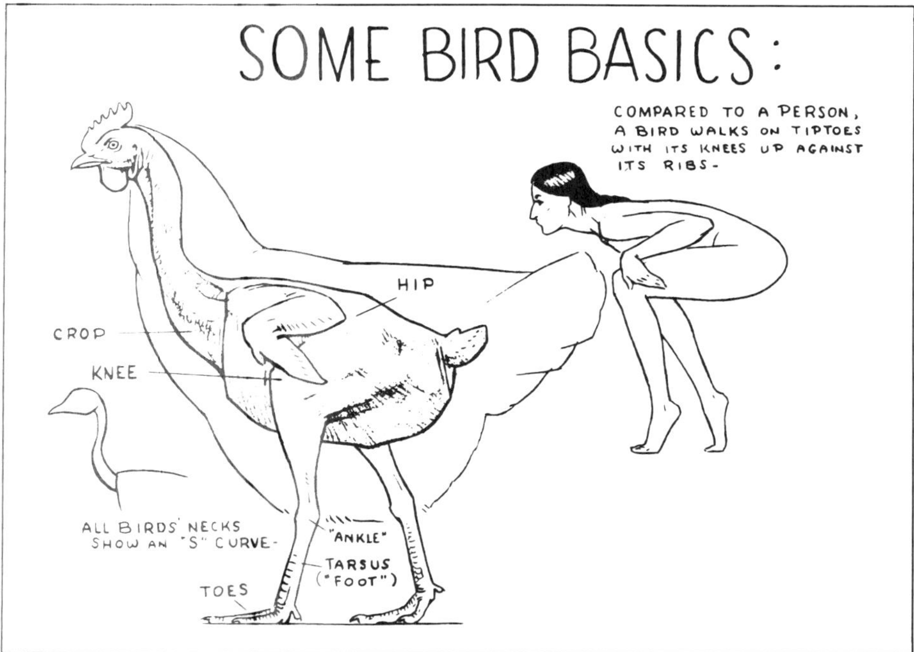

18-1. Comparison between the normal posture of a bird and a human in a bird's position. This is the type of body structure hidden beneath birds' feathers. Pencil on bond paper, drawing and description by William D. Berry © 1976. Courtesy of Mrs. Elizabeth Berry.

sary weight early in avian evolution, and the bones of the skull have become so fused that some sutures cannot be seen. Only one occipital condyle (a locking mechanism between skull and neck) is present in birds, compared to two in mammals; this arrangement and the flexibility of their long necks sometimes allow birds to rotate their heads 180 degrees. Mobility of the head, beak, and neck is essential to an animal that has sacrificed the food-gathering capabilities of its forelimbs to flight, and certain bones and joints in the head and neck have been retained for this freedom of motion. Note that the lower jaw articulates with the upper by a small intermediate bone called the quadrate; the separate motion of these two bones allows a wide gape. Furthermore, the upper jaw, or mandible, is hinged to the skull and can move independently of it by the pushing and pulling action of a thin, bar-shaped bone named the jugal, attached at one end to the upper bill and at the other to the quadrate. Birds can therefore use their bills to manipulate food with almost finger-like dexterity. The neck vertebrae, saddle-shaped at each end for the greatest possible movement, permit great mobility of the head. Unlike mammals, all of whom possess seven cervical vertebrae, birds may have from thirteen to thirty-five. The S-shaped curve seen in long-necked birds is also present in the smallest forms; even birds such as finches can extend their necks, usually completely hidden by feathers, for a surprising distance if a long reach is needed.

In contrast to the flexible neck vertebrae, the rest of the axial skeleton, from the pectoral girdle to the base of the tail, is shortened and strongly fused, thereby concentrating the bird's weight at the center of the body for more stable flight and providing a rigid support for the limbs. The pelvic girdle represents the most extensively fused area of the spinal column. Not only are vertebrae welded to one another in this region but also to the pelvis itself to produce a thin, light, rigid roof of bone, the synsacrum, which acts as a strong brace for the standing bird and as a perfect shock absorber during landing.

The forelimbs of birds have been greatly modified for their function as wings. The first bone of the forelimb, the humerus, is joined to the pectoral girdle by a ball-and-socket joint, as in humans, allowing the greatest possible rotation, but at the next joint outward, the true elbow, motion is restricted to only one plane to act as a bracing factor for the wing in flight. The next part of the wing, the forearm, presents an interesting question: if the avian skeleton is so characterized by reduction in bones, why does the bird retain both a radius and an ulna? These two bones together form opposite sides of a parallelogram that automatically opens and closes elbow and wrist joints in synchrony (fig. 18-3). Therefore, the wrist cannot open or close unless the elbow also opens or closes. Reduction is evident in the wrist bones (only two are present) and especially in the hand, so altered that it is hardly recognizable as such. Only three fingers remain, two as mere stubs. Figure 18-4 compares the bones of the arm, hand, and fingers of a human to that of a bird. Note that the patagium, the thin membrane that stretches between the bird's shoulder and wrist to form the leading edge of the wing, effectively conceals the V-shape formed by the humerus and radius-ulna. The elbow joint is usually visible in only the larger, long-winged birds, in which the elongated humerus positions the elbow well out from the body itself. Knowledge of the internal structure of the wing is invaluable to the illustrator not only in understanding the mechanics of motion but also in determining the placement of thicknesses caused by the underlying skeleton and its attached musculature.

The heavy muscles needed to drive the bird in flight are inserted on the deep keel of the breastbone; the stout coracoid bone, absent in mammals, acts as a compression column against the powerful forces activated by these muscles. Two

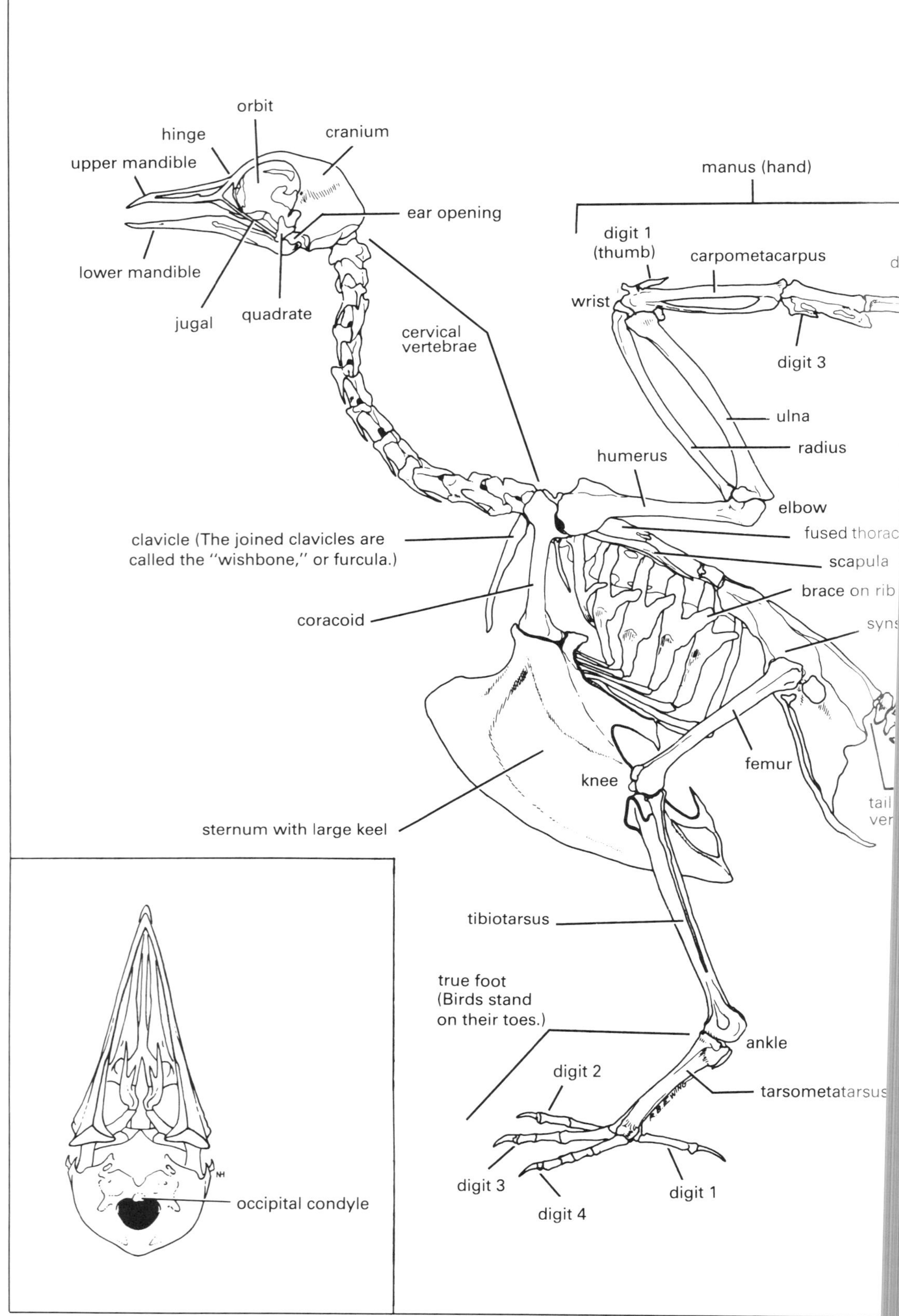

18-2. Skeleton of a common pigeon. Pen-and-ink, by R. B. Ewing. From *Ornithology in Laboratory and Field,* 4th ed., by Olin Sewall Pettingill, Jr. (© 1970, Burgess Publishing). Inset shows ventral or underside view of bird skull. Pen-and-ink on Satin Design paper, by Nancy R. Halliday © 1986.

other paired bones, the scapula and the clavicle (the latter commonly called the wishbone), form the remaining braces binding the wing to the bird's body.

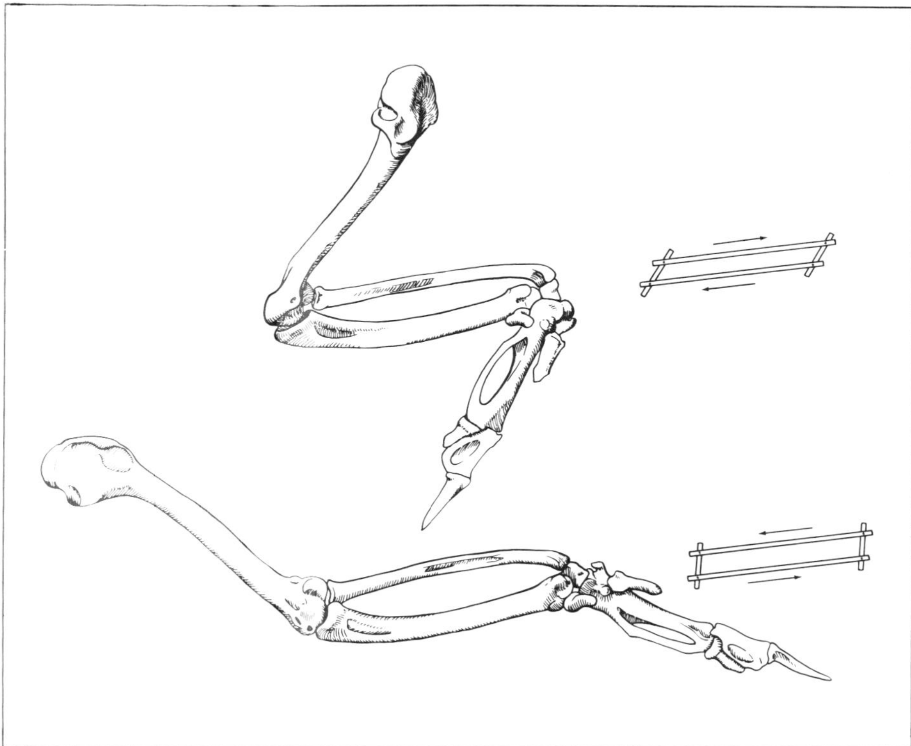

18-3. Use of a parallelogram to explain how a bird (pheasant, *Phasianus*, in this case) extends the elbow and wrist in unison, the one joint automatically following the other. Pen-and-ink. From *Analysis of Vertebrate Structure*, 2d ed., by Milton Hildebrand (© 1982, John Wiley and Sons).

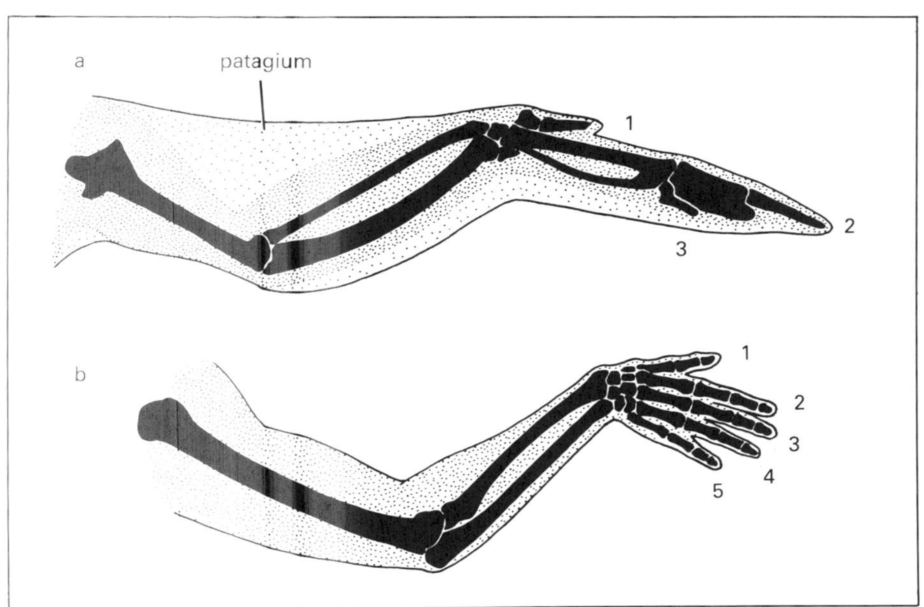

18-4. Comparison between *(a)* the wing of a bird and *(b)* the arm of a human. Pen-and-ink on Satin Design paper, by Nancy R. Halliday © 1982.

The legs of birds have not undergone as much differentiation from the basic tetrapod plan as have the wings. However, so much of the leg is hidden under the feathers that one must carefully study the bones to understand their placement in the living bird. A common error in many bird illustrations is incorrect placement of the legs. Figure 18-2 reveals the location of the true knee, a joint usually lost to view in all but some of the large flightless birds when they raise their floppy wings for cooling or display. The next joint proceeding down the leg is the true ankle. This is the part of the leg that becomes visible as that limb emerges from the body, and the ankle properly bends in the same direction as in all four-legged animals (tetrapods). We should expect to find a number of small ankle bones (tarsals) at this joint, but every one has been fused into one or the other adjacent leg bone for economy of weight. Thus, the tibia has been renamed the tibiotarsus and the metatarsal the tarsometatarsus. The number of metatarsal (true foot) bones has been reduced from five in the ancient condition to one in the bird. (The toes will be discussed under Taxonomic Characters.) If bird illustrators will remember that the three major leg bones of a bird form a sharp-cornered S originating at the joint of the femur with the synsacrum, it will result in a welcome extinction of the broken-legged bird drawings so common in the literature.

Study the placement of the feet under the bird. The massive flight muscles and the viscera are concentrated in the central area of the short body below and slightly to the rear of the wing. For proper balance, the feet are always placed directly below this area of greatest weight. Note also how extremely short the tail bones are. Most beginning bird artists place the feet too far to the rear, thinking that the tail, which is mostly composed of feathers, has weight. This general rule is violated by certain birds specialized for swimming and diving such as loons; their feet are displaced so far to the rear to act as more efficient paddles or rudders

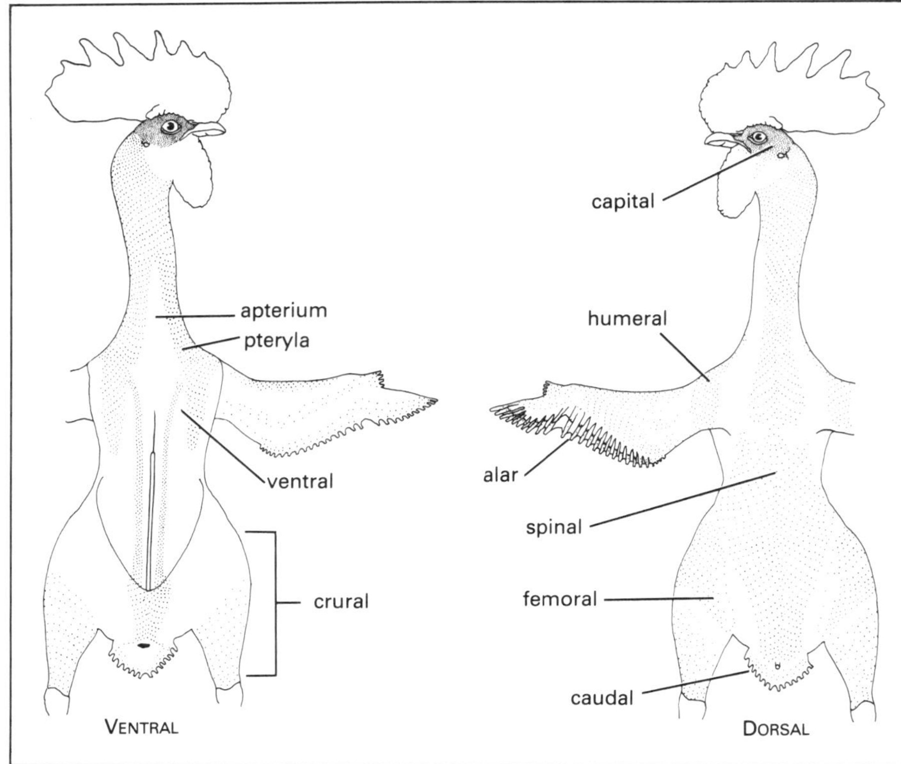

18-5. Feather tracts of a domesticated chicken. Pen-and-ink, by Margaret La Farge. From *The Audubon Society Encyclopedia of North American Birds*, by John K. Terres (© 1980, Alfred A. Knopf).

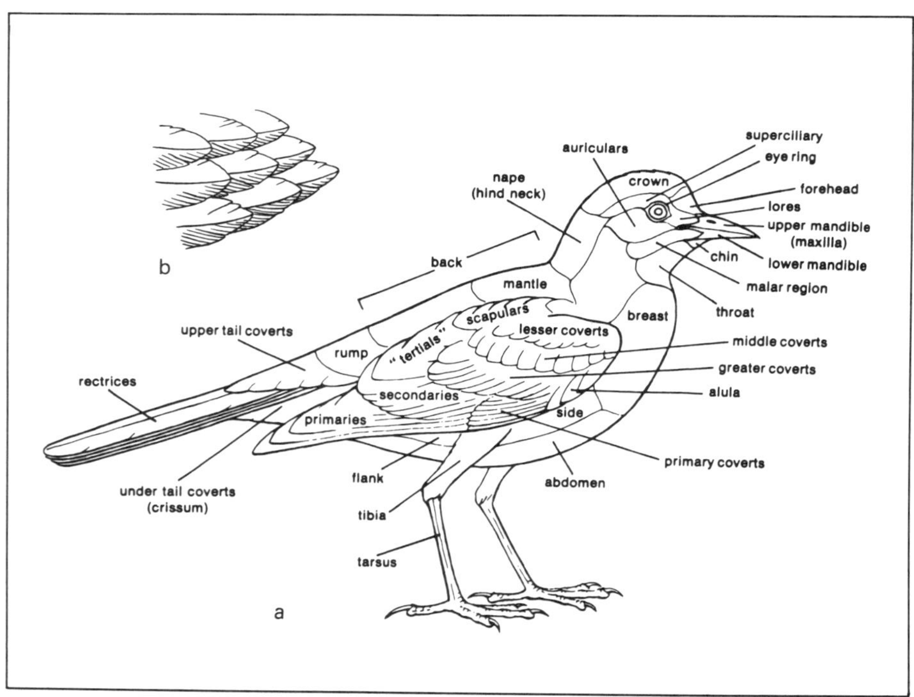

18-6. (a) Diagrammatic topography of a songbird. Pen-and-ink by R. V. Keane. From *Manual of Neotropical Birds*, vol. 1, by Emmet R. Blake (© 1977, University of Chicago Press). *(b)* "Rule of the Feather: Front Overlaps Back; Upper Row Overlaps Lower." © W. D. Berry, 1976. Pen-and-ink on Satin Design paper, by Nancy R. Halliday, after Berry.

that the birds
at all. Some
their tarsi wh
vertically the
ther to the r
set. Penguins
cated at the
body, have fi
lem by plod
upright, hum

External

After the s
next most im
mining the
feather mass
ment.

Feathers d
bird's body (
such as the p
specific trac
gular, pteryla
skin in betw
lar, apteriu
feather"). F
the pterylae
a chicken.
tion of feath
feather regio
pography of
figure 18-6.
know these
thoroughly,
being quite
terns often
Watching a
preening is
illustrator, f
and raise or
as it smoo
feathers.

Figure 18
a flight feat
are larger
body, or co
equipped w
shaft. Thos
are called r
tail rectric
feathers of
originate fr
daries, shor
the primari
arm, specif
the thumb
seven shor

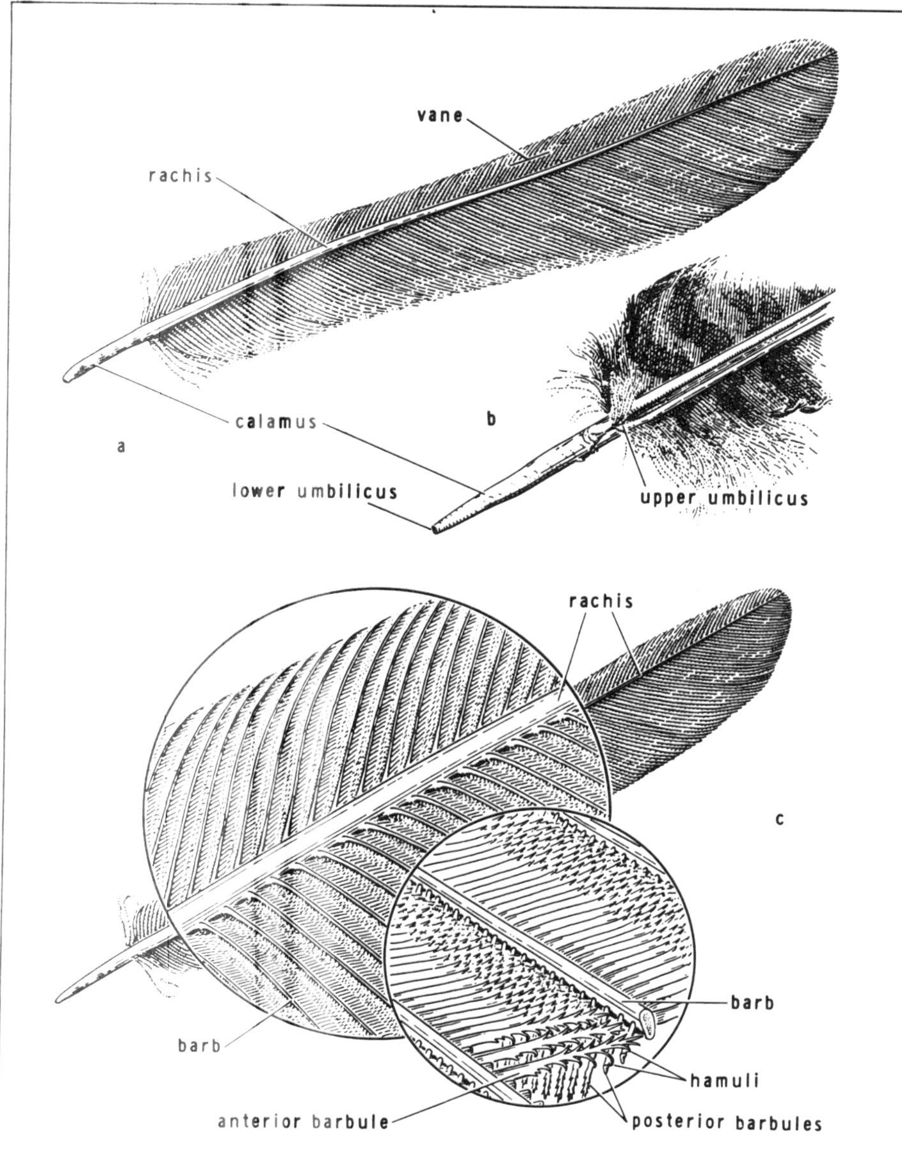

18-7. A typical flight feather and the nomenclature of its parts: *(a)* general view; *(b)* detail of base of feather; *(c)* detail of vane. By pulling a torn feather through its bill, a bird rehooks separated barbules and the feather is instantly mended. Pen-and-ink, by Dr. George Miksch Sutton. From *Fundamentals of Ornithology*, 2d ed., by J. Van Tyne and A. J. Berger (© 1976. John Wiley and Sons).

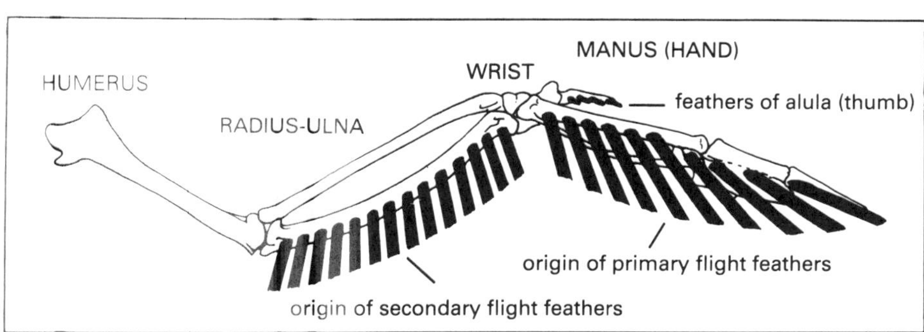

18-8. Derivation of major flight feathers on the wing of a generalized pigeon-dove. Insertion of the feather shafts is indicated in black. Pen-and-ink on Satin Design paper, by Nancy R. Halliday © 1982.

miniature wing in themselves—the alula. (The alula has a special function in flight that will be described later.) Figure 18-8 provides an explanation of the derivation of the flight feathers on the wing. Rows of shorter covert feathers overlap the bases of the primaries and secondaries (fig. 18-9). Note that the row called the middle wing coverts overlaps in the opposite direction from the other wing feathers. A wing stripe, if present, will often be located on this row. Axillaries (not pictured) are a group of somewhat elongated feathers growing from the armpit region to cover the space between body and elbow when the wings are spread.

The number of primaries varies from nine to twelve but is usually constant within a taxonomic group. It is very important for the illustrator to count the primaries; if the number is incorrect for the bird illustrated, an ornithologist will find that mistake almost immediately. The first primary is the one most proximally located on the wing, and the last (near the alula) may be so reduced in size in certain birds that it must be searched out.

Secondaries are counted in the opposite direction, and the number varies widely depending upon the length of the forearm, but the total is still constant within a taxon. (See figure 18-9 for numbering sequences of primaries and secondaries.) The last three secondaries (those closest to the body) may be differentiated from the others and are called tertials. Tertials may be shorter than the other secondaries (see fig. 18-9) or elongated, as in ducks and shore birds. *The Birds of North and Middle America*, by Robert Ridgway (see Bibliography) is a good source of feather counts for birds from this area.

When not in use, a wing folds neatly against the body in the form of a tight Z. The layering of feathers in a folded wing is often confusing, for in a short-winged bird, primaries can seem to disappear completely under the secondaries.

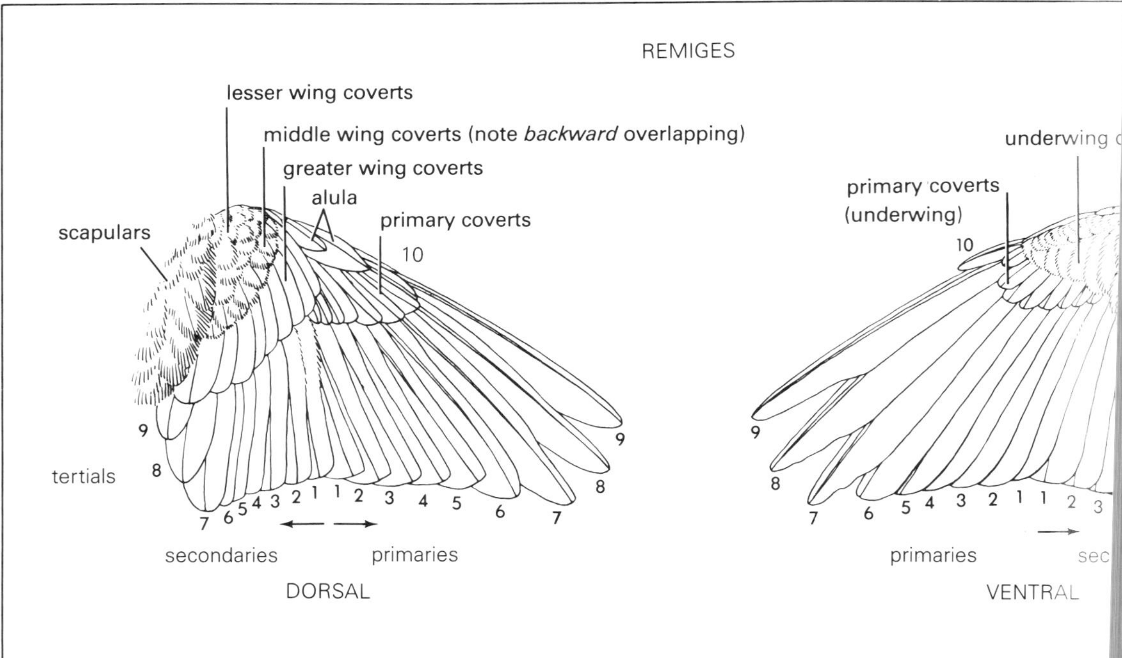

18-9. Topography of a bird's wing (Swainson's thrush). Note which way the feathers overlap. Pen-and-ink on Satin Design paper, by Nancy R. Halliday © 1978.

In other bird
pulars, and
thoroughly
that only the
portion of th
ble. The stri
often adorn
aid in dete
the wing is
Figure 18-1
description

The follo
the drawing
draw the ov
Then draw
separating
the second

18-10. How a
son's thrush).
Wing partly f
gether like a
secondaries.
well folded u
primary cove
ink on Satin
Halliday © 1

extending from the bend of the wing (wrist) to the rear edge, the angle formed where the primaries and secondaries meet (see figs. 18-8, 18-9). The curve of this line should arch (slightly) toward the wing's apex. Draw the outlines of all the feather tracts (coverts). Then the individual feathers will fall into place (see fig. 18-18). When drawing individual feathers, keep in mind their origin; they will radiate out like a fan from supporting bones.

Rectrices are usually twelve in number but may be as few as six or as many as thirty-two. Whatever their total, the number is always even (fig. 18-11). Look at the placement of the main shaft on both the rectrices and the primaries and note that it gradually migrates toward the leading edge in the outermost feathers. These offset shafts not only strengthen the leading edges and reduce wear but also allow the feathers to function as more efficient airfoils in flight.

If at all possible, an illustrator should handle a freshly killed bird to be able to manipulate the wings and tail and understand the functional feather groups.

TAXONOMIC CHARACTERS

Let us turn our attention to those particular taxonomic indicators that an illustrator is likely to encounter in preparing drawings of birds.

Beaks

Beaks of birds exhibit such a bewildering variety of shapes and sizes in response to various methods of obtaining food that an examination of each kind is not practical here. There are, however, certain characteristics that birds' beaks have in common. Figure 18-12 illustrates the major components of a bird's beak.

A bird's beak, or bill, is actually a horny sheath, the rhampotheca, formed around the bone of the mandible itself; the precise shape of that bill is very important in achieving a likeness of a particular species. Nostrils are located on the upper mandible, and their placement can be used in classification. Parrots and birds of prey possess a fleshy patch of skin called the cere (see fig. 18-21) in which the nostrils are situated at the base of the beak, and in one order of seabirds the nostrils are encased in tubes on the bill. Certain kinds of thin, hair-like feathers called rictal bristles

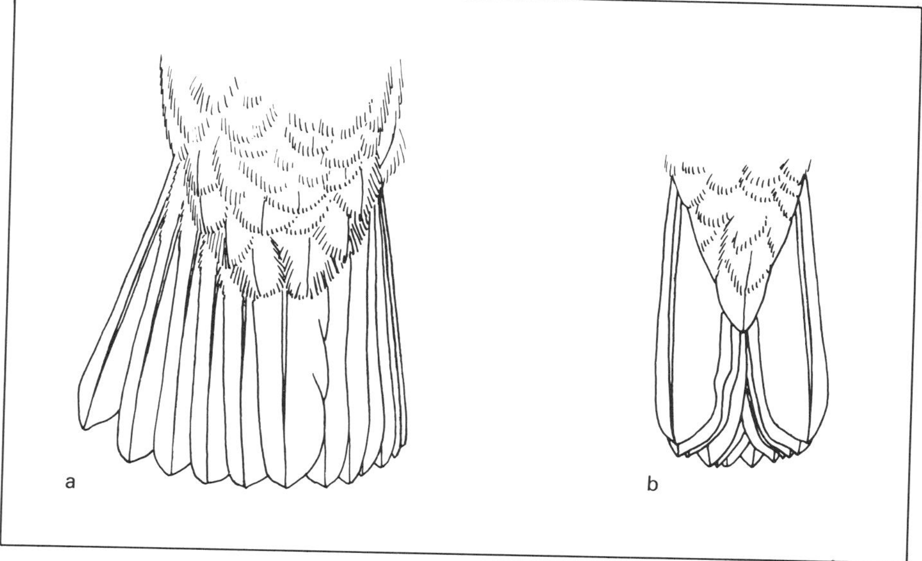

18-11. Rectrices (Swainson's thrush): *(a)* dorsal view (left side spread); *(b)* ventral view. Note which way the feathers overlap. Pen-and-ink on Satin Design paper, by Nancy R. Halliday © 1982.

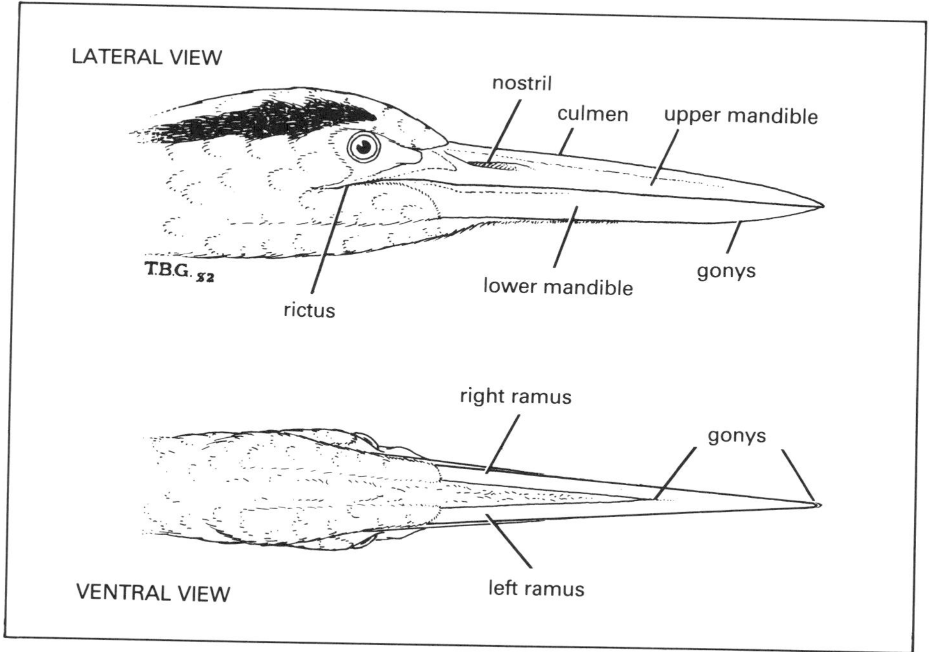

18-12. General features of a bird's beak as exhibited by a heron. The culmen is the ridge along the top of the upper mandible. The gonys is that portion of the lower mandible formed by the juncture of the two rami (branches) that connect the lower mandible to each side of the skull. Pen-and-ink on Bristol board, by T. Britt Griswold, partially based on drawing in *The Audubon Society Encyclopedia of North American Birds*, by John K. Terres (© 1980, Alfred A. Knopf).

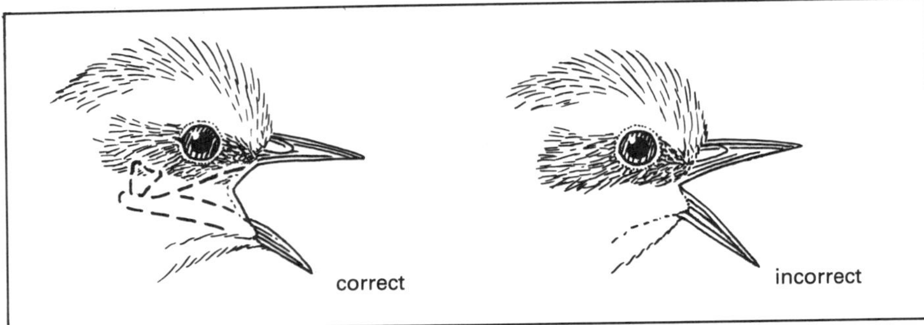

18-13. How a bird's bill opens. Left: correct (after photograph of golden-winged warbler, by A. A. Allen); right: incorrect. The dashed lines indicate the jugal and quadrate bones and the continuation of the lower mandible beneath the feathers and skin. Note that on the correct drawing the cheek skin (called the *rictal commissure*) stretches to accommodate the gape. Pen-and-ink on Satin Design paper, by Nancy R. Halliday © 1982.

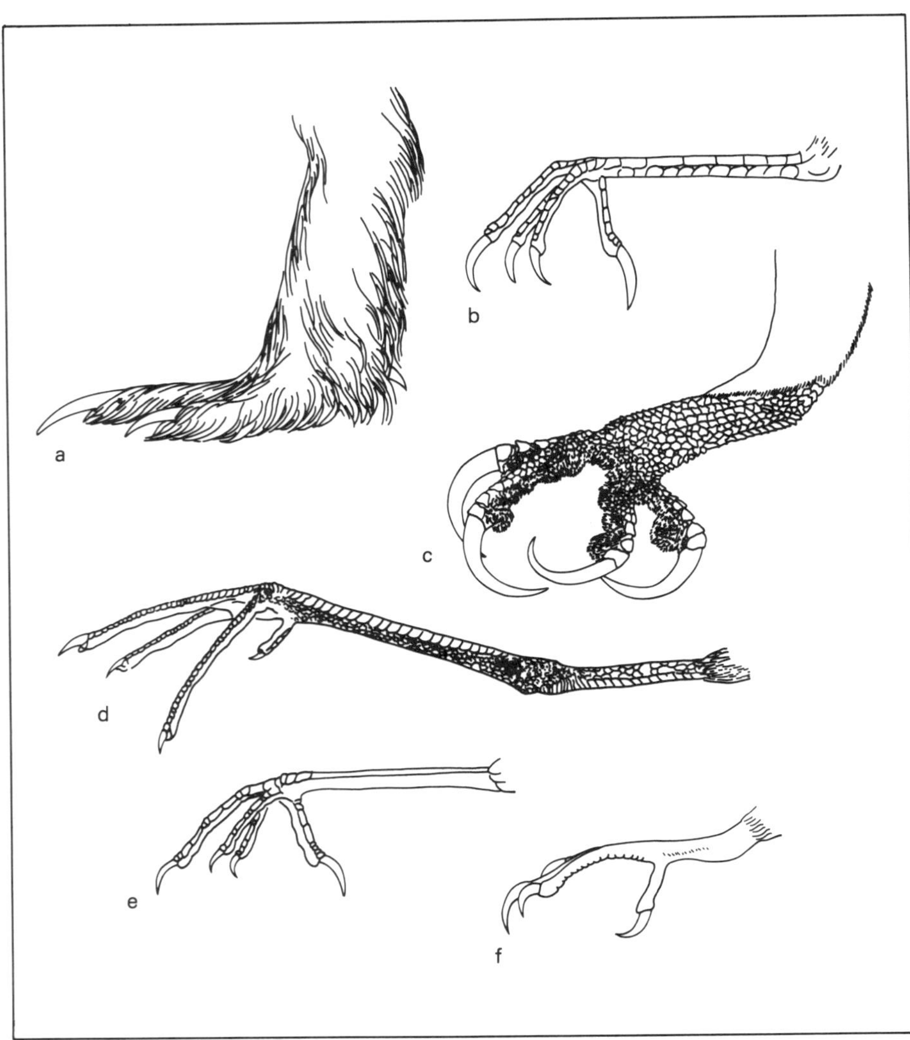

18-14. Types of covering on the tarsus of birds: *(a)* feathered (willow ptarmigan); *(b)* scutellate (ant bird); *(c)* reticulate (osprey); *(d)* scutellate-reticulate (dowitcher); *(e)* booted (thrush); *(f)* scaleless (green kingfisher). (Birds' legs are not drawn to scale.) Courtesy of U.S. Museum of Natural History. Redrawn, in pen-and-ink on polyester film, by Irene Jewett. From *The Birds of North and Middle America*, by Robert Ridgway (U.S. Government Printing Office, 1907–50).

grow at the
some birds t
sects.

A commo
birds with op
placement o
of the two r
often depicte
point where
emerge from
But a reexar
will reveal
lower jaw (
more than h
tire skull (fig

Feet and T

The basic
number of
five on eac
good examp
ber of toes
four—three
hind. But v
stance, ost
to a cursori
ening the
number of
ing forward
but three
vary in nu
ment. The
level with
the tarsom
ilies of bird
outer of th
toes may
temporaril

It is n
which toes
evolution o
versed on
of phalang
toe is diff
and rarely
(the back
two phala
(the insid
langes; to
est), fou
number f
phalanges
(outermos
more than
the joint
phalanx p

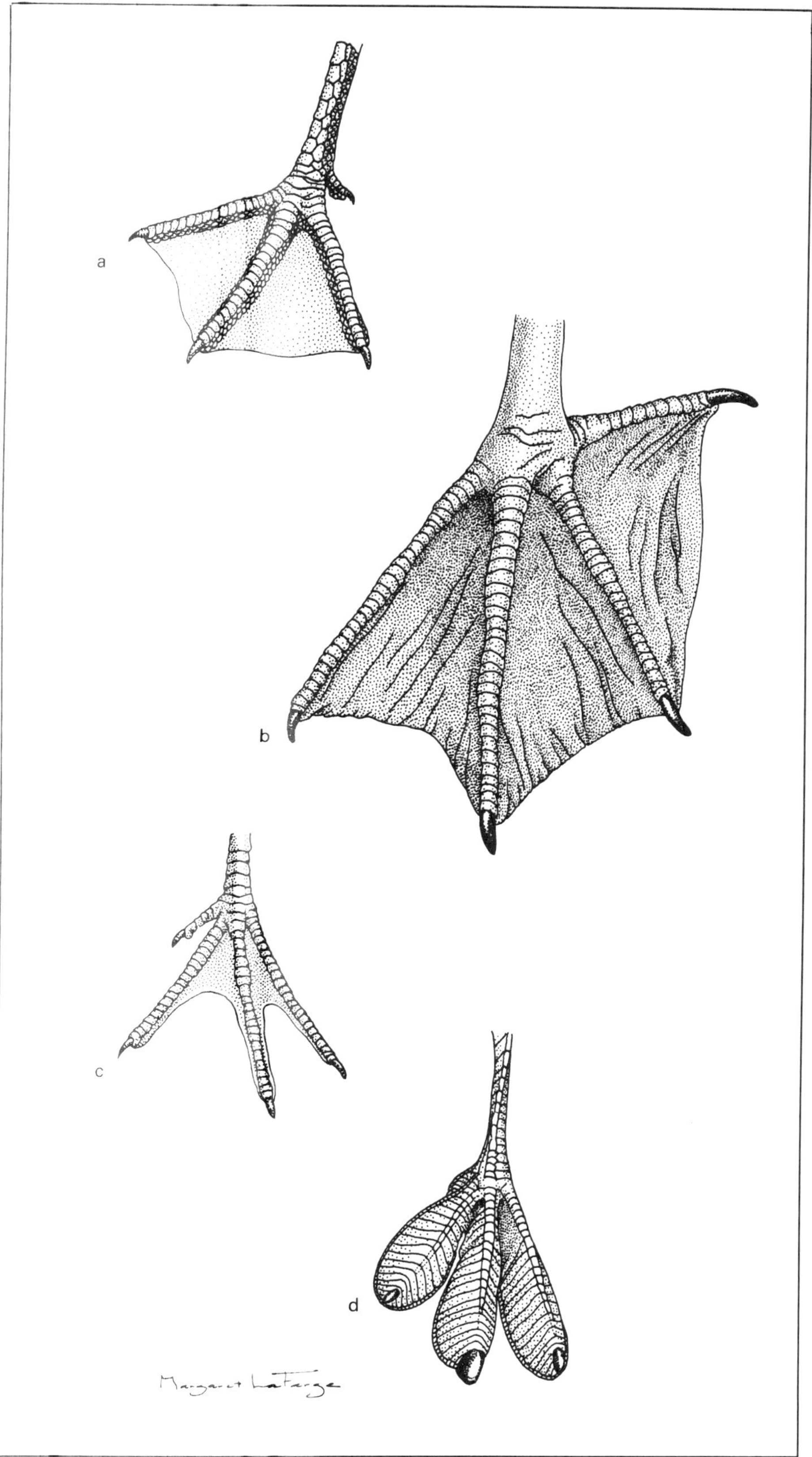

18-15. Types of webbing on birds' feet: *(a)* palmate (mallard); *(b)* totipalmate (pelican); *(c)* semipalmate (willet); *(d)* lobate (grebe). Pen-and-ink, by Margaret La Farge. From *The Audubon Society Encyclopedia of North American Birds*, by John K. Terres (© 1980, Alfred A. Knopf).

independently and greatly increases the grasping force of the foot. Illustrators not familiar with the bones in birds' feet have often depicted the rear toe curling, many-jointed, around a limb, but since the rear toe is made up of only two phalanges and one of these is merely the nail, it simply cannot coil serpentlike around its perch. Study figure 18-2 and memorize the phalanges; these little bones and their joints are clearly visible through the scaly covering on a bird's foot.

This covering may be arranged on a bird's tarsometatarsus in four different ways. The foot also may be entirely without scales or clothed instead in feathers (fig. 18-14).

Webbing on the three front toes of a duck's foot is familiar to all of us, but other water birds have developed variations on this swimming aid, and certain birds that never swim at all (the chicken family, for instance) possess a partial webbing between their toes. Figure 18-15 depicts all four types of foot webs.

Other Taxonomic Characters

Occasionally a scientific illustrator will be asked to make drawings of specialized anatomical parts used in systematic research—for example, arrangements of palate and nasal bones; types of sterna; muscle and tendon attachments; syringeal muscles (which operate the voice box, or syrinx); patterns of arteries; intestinal convolutions; variations of uropygial (oil) glands; tarsal scutellation (in passerine birds); and other kinds of feathers not mentioned previously, such as down and filoplumes. It is not within the scope of this chapter to explain in detail this long list of infrequently illustrated features. *Fundamentals of Ornithology*, by Josselyn Van Tyne and Andrew J. Berger (see Bibliography) provides a description and illustration of all the structures mentioned. Since many of these features are small and may be difficult to discern in the dissected specimen, a thorough briefing by the scientist is essential.

BIRDS IN THE FIELD

The study of bird behavior is becoming increasingly important in the twentieth century. The illustrator may be asked to record an action for which a camera was not available, with word descriptions serving as the only model. Familiarity with birds is essential in performing such an assignment.

No better way exists to understand the behavior, movements, and physical makeup of birds than by watching the living creatures in their natural environment and then sketching what is seen. Birds are among the most manifest of animals; most are diurnal, noisy, and conspicuously mobile. In addition, many are also quite colorful. Planting trees and shrubs that shelter or feed birds, and providing water year-round and food in winter when natural edibles are scarce, will easily attract birds for study.

Many avian families can be recognized quickly by size and silhouette alone. The patterns of color on the body are another "trademark" to note. Manners of locomotion—such as walking versus hopping, gliding versus flapping, or how much of the body of swimming birds appears above waterline—provide other clues to identification. Sometimes particular kinds of standardized behavior, such as tail bobbing, instantaneously give away a bird's identity. The type of habitat in which the bird occurs is also usually significant. With practice in quick processing of this information, an experienced birdwatcher can identify a feathered subject at first sight when it is only a speck in the sky to an untutored companion. The bird illustrator must be able to distill these visual characters as easily as the birdwatcher.

For viewing living exotic species, visits to the zoo are invaluable. Some of the larger zoos maintain flight houses in simulated habitats as natural as possible for their avian captives, but be warned that birds in confinement are often altered from their natural appearance in the wild. Old age and long captivity can produce excessive growth of the beak or of the claws and of scales on the feet. Primary feathers may be cut or the entire hand removed to prevent escape by flight. Birds will not often preen as carefully in captivity as in their natural state, so be prepared to see feathers out of place. Injuries and cripplings are also common in zoos.

In drawing birds from life, begin, as in drawing any subject, with the larger forms first—in this case, the egglike shape of the whole body. Record quickly but carefully the proportions of the other parts in relation to the body—size of head and lengths of bill, neck, wings, tail, and legs. If the model has not flown away, begin to draw the details within the larger forms—the major feather masses and color patterns. Only at the very last should individual feathers be delineated. Sketching a live animal as active as a small bird is not easy, but nothing else will force you to look so carefully for what is essential—the basic form and its attitude (see chapter 20). Beware of the subconscious tendency to underemphasize distinctive features in order to avoid the difficulty of working with unfamiliar proportions; do not be afraid to draw as they are the skinny neck of a heron, the oversized bill of a toucan, or the sprawling feet of a falcon.

FLIGHT

Because birds are designed to fly, although some have evolved secondarily to fit aquatic or terrestrial environments, the illustrator

may be aske
flight from ph
blurred) or ev
This task bec
unless the illu
aerodynamics
capabilities
move in ways

A cross se
reveals a stre
an airfoil that
in front (esp
body), conve
cave below.
trailing edge
attached to t
convexity on
ers of feather
to only the re
trailing edge.
ing of this sh
the bones of
has weeded o
can make a
drawing of a
mention a w
plex motions

The curv
wing is calle
over it take
rear than ai
ing in a net
above the w
sure benea
the force th
aloft. An in
to back thr
parison to
stream is c
If the lead
turned up
and some
angle of a
this angle
degrees, t
smooth fl
and the bi
ever, are
gency. Ra
miniature
thumb, fo
creased sp
tween the
thereby r
regular us
flight, tak

Taking

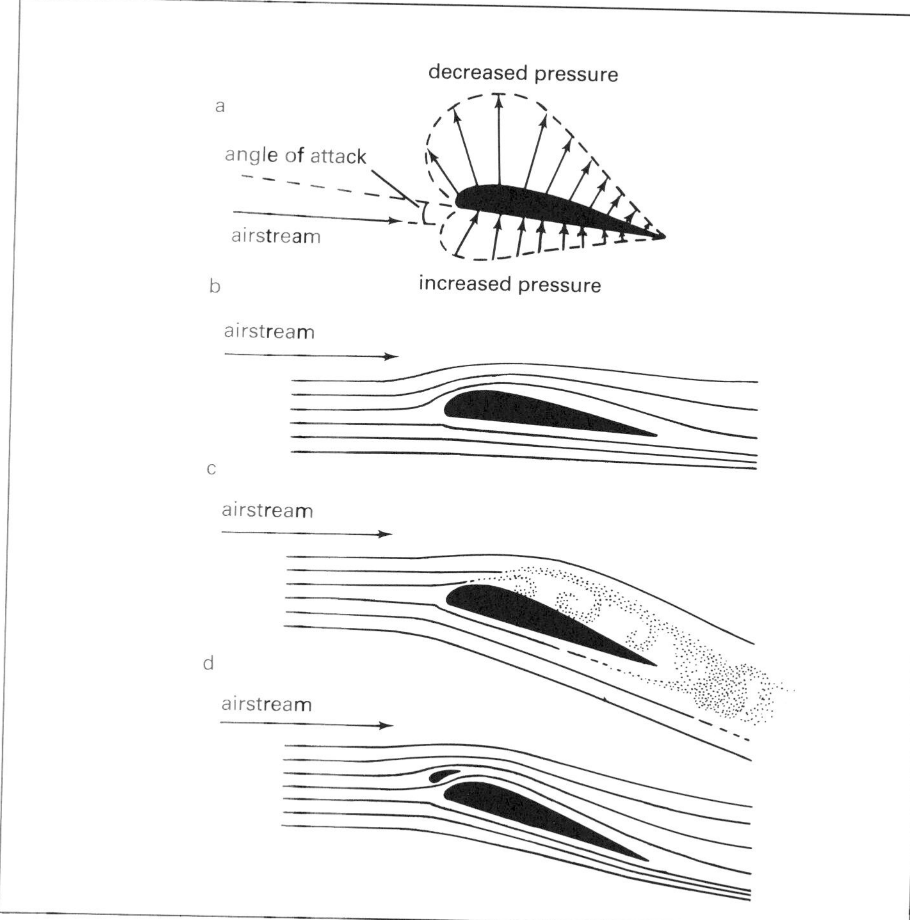

18-16. Airfoil design: *(a)* air pressure brought about by air passing over airfoil (courtesy of Dover Publications, Inc.). Correction of turbulence by alula: *(b)* in normal flight at a low angle of attack, the air streams smoothly over the upper surface of the wing and creates lift. *(c)* At too steep an angle of attack, air passing over the wing becomes turbulent, lift disappears, and a stall develops. *(d)* A wing-slot, the space between the alula and the wing, may prevent stalling turbulence by directing a layer of rapidly moving air close to the upper surface of the wing. Pen-and-ink on Satin Design paper, by Nancy R. Halliday.

great effort and control. In leaving the substrate, legs supply the initial push, then the wings are brought into play, beating rapidly in large-amplitude strokes. Birds cannot push backward against air for propulsion—air is too thin a medium; instead, the wings are thrown far forward into the wind on the downstroke, forcing as much air as possible over the upper surface to produce the critical lift needed to rise. Therefore, the wings are beating on a more or less horizontal plane. Furthermore, because lift is always generated at a right angle to the airstream, the hand portion of the wing (the manus) with its primaries is twisted down at a forward-facing angle, allowing lift to operate in that direction (fig. 18-17). The secondary region stays in a horizontal position to hold the bird aloft. The force of the downstroke is so great that the tips of the primaries turn up. The primaries, then, act exactly as the propellers on an airplane engine in providing forward motion.

The backstroke on takeoff must not interfere in any way with the lift attained on the downstroke. Small birds fold their wings close against the body and twist the manus so that the leading edges of the primaries are turned upward; air then slips easily between the feathers. The process is similar to the operation of a venetian blind (fig. 18-18a). Larger birds are too heavy to waste energy on a passive recovery stroke; on their upstroke the humerus is rotated forward and the wing partly flexed so that the wrist points upward; then the manus is turned outward and vio-

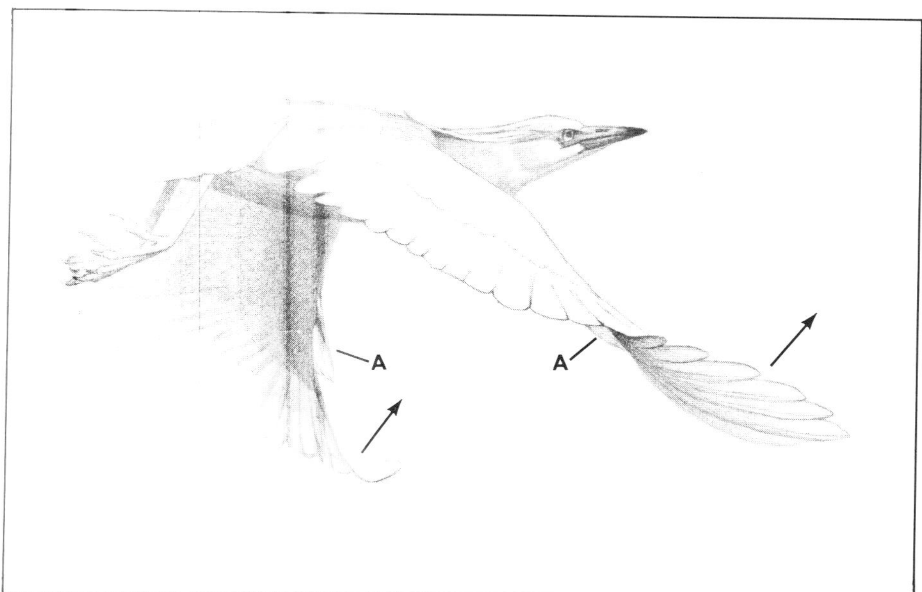

18-17. Downstroke of the wing demonstrating forward twisting of the primaries. Arrow represents lift. The alula *(A)* is raised during slow flight. Notice that the wing is thrown far forward during takeoff to "grab" for lift from the airstream. Graphite pencil on Clearprint paper, by Nancy R. Halliday, from photo in *Bird Flight*, by Georg Rüppell (Van Nostrand Reinhold, 1977).

a

b

18-18. Backstroke of the wing during slow flight. *(a)* Small bird (chickadee) employs a venetian-blind technique. Photo by H. C. Johnson from *The Life of Birds*, 2d ed., by J. C. Welty (W. B. Saunders Company, 1975). *(b)* Larger bird (pigeon) uses rapid back-flick of primaries. The wrist is flexed and the primaries travel backward at a positive angle of attack, producing lift as represented by arrow (A = alula). Larger birds use this technique when taking off, landing, and flying slowly. Graphite pencil on Clearprint paper, by Nancy R. Halliday, from photo in Georg Rüppell, *Bird Flight* (Van Nostrand Reinhold, 1977).

lently flung backward, forcing the primaries to travel backward at a positive angle of attack, yielding even more lift than on the downstroke. The tips of the primaries now bend inward (fig. 18-18b). At the top of the upstroke, the wing is quickly snapped back into position for the next downstroke.

Once the bird is airborne, wing beats become more shallow and more vertical. Only minimal downturning of the primaries is necessary for forward motion. Small birds fold the legs so that the feet are pointing forward, hidden under the feathers of the abdomen. Larger birds hold the legs straightened under the body with the feet pointed backward.

In preparing to land, the tail is spread and lowered and the body and wings are tilted upward to offer air resistance. Waterfowl with small tails hold their webbed feet well out from the body to act as effective air brakes. Wing beats are similar to those used in takeoff, but of course the procedure is reversed. Alulae are raised.

Most waterfowl do not enjoy the luxury of dropping off a high perch to become airborne. The so-called puddle ducks have large enough wings in relation to their body weight that they can take off straight up, but others with shorter wings must run across the surface of the water for some distance before becoming airborne. Large birds that use long runways need not make use of the violent back-

flick on tal
waterfowl t
ski to a sto
rear-positio
water on th

Hovering
flight that e
stationary
held vertica
rapidly in
upside up
and then r
upside do
stroke, so
straight up
lar to scu
steady in
mingbirds
kind of flig
hawks and
their prey u

Birds' wings have evolved into four major shapes to meet the demands of different kinds of flight (fig. 18-19). Birds that fly slowly will have camber well developed, as in the elliptical wing and the slotted high-lift wing; in addition, the primaries will be narrowed at their tips (known as slotting) so that each acts as a kind of alula to prevent stalling. The elliptical wing is restricted to birds that fly in densely forested areas where large wings would be a handicap. The longer, slotted, high-lift wing is possessed by soarers. Maneuverability is of utmost importance to both these types. Fast flyers have sacrificed maneuverability for speed; their wings are long, tapering, and pointed. In the high-aspect-ratio wing, the arm bones have been elongated to support a larger number of secondary feathers than in any other kind of bird. In fact, the wing is so long that it cannot withstand the stress of flapping flight. This shape has evolved for high-speed soaring over oceans. The high-speed wing is found in birds that feed while in flight or make long migrations. Because flight is swift, primaries are not slotted and camber is shallow in both pointed-wing types.

Flight is a complicated procedure. An illustrator of birds can benefit greatly by watching at every opportunity the maneuvers birds make as they take off, fly, and land. *Bird Flight*, by Georg Rüppell (see Bibliography) is highly recommended for further study.

18-19. The four general types of wing shapes: *(a)* elliptical wing (wren); *(b)* high-speed wing (snipe); *(c)* slotted high-lift wing (eagle); *(d)* high-aspect-ratio wing (albatross). (Wings are not drawn to scale.) Pen-and-ink on Satin Design paper, by Nancy R. Halliday © 1982.

Other Kinds of Locomotion

Water can provide as effective a medium for locomotion as can air. A number of diving birds, such as penguins and alcids, use their wings to achieve high swimming speeds, literally flying underwater. Other divers will use feet alone or a combination of feet and wings. Alulae also can be protruded from folded wings to act as lateral stabilizers under water. Some water birds paddle their feet alternately when swimming but use them synchronously while diving.

Locomotion on land consists of two methods: walking, in which one foot is placed in front of the other, and hopping, in which both feet touch and leave the substrate at the same time. Hopping seems to be an adaptation for tree-dwellers, whereas birds that spend most of their time on the ground have developed the cursorial habit of walking (or running).

DRAWING FROM SPECIMENS

If only all bird illustrators could at least see, if not sketch, in life every bird they are asked to draw! Such is rarely the case, and illustrators must be content with whatever material they and the ornithologist can find. This usually includes bird skins, photographs, sometimes motion pictures, other artists' renderings, and word descriptions. Mounted birds alone are not safe subjects. The illustrator may inadvertently perpetuate a taxidermist's mistake.

Unless it is absolutely impossible to obtain one, do not attempt to draw a bird without a specimen (a bird skin or a study skin). It may be the only actual contact with the animal. A study skin is prepared by first peeling the skin, feathers intact, from the body, then fitting it around a cotton or straw body and sewing it up. The beak usually points forward, the tail backward; legs are crossed over the under-tail coverts, and the wings are tightly folded against the body and cannot be moved (fig. 18-20). A tag with vital scientific data is attached to one leg by a string. Written material on the tag will supply valuable information to the illustrator; for instance, the date may indicate that the bird was in molt, which means that key feathers may be worn or faded, absent, growing in, or new. Also the original colors of eyes, feet, and bill are often written on the tag. Bird study skins are normally laid on their backs in drawers within specimen cabinets. For better fit, skins of larger birds may have the neck drawn along the side of the body with the head pointed down. Birds with high crests may have the head turned to prevent crushing that feature. Occasionally, spread wings may be preserved as specimens.

Keep in mind that the few bones retained in the specimen—that part of the skull attached to the beak and the few wing and leg bones that would be too difficult to extract—are not enough to maintain the natural shape of the bird. The illustrator should not expect the specimen to bear any close resemblance to the appearance of the bird in its living state except in general size. Also, feet and toes will lose the softness and fullness of life and become quite shriveled. Colors may have faded. For this reason, it is wise to examine a series of bird skins. If color seems to vary among birds of the same sex and the same approximate age taken at the same time of the year, choose the newest specimen. Only the illustrator's knowledge of birds and artistic skill can restore this little mummy to life again.

Occasionally, however, an illustrator is asked to draw a study skin exactly as it appears (see fig. 18-20). The proper orientation on the page is: dorsal and ventral views—bill pointed up, tail down; lateral view as a companion to the others—same as above; lateral view alone—bird on its back, bill pointing left.

Measurement

Standard measurements for bird specimens are given in figure 18-21. Figure 18-22 demonstrates additional measurements that may be very helpful. Since bird skins may be stretched during preparation, it is advisable to measure several or to compare them to a live bird or undistorted photograph (see Drawing from Photographs, below).

Measurements of the eye are usually not important taxonomically, but they are indispensable to the illustrator. One of the most common errors in bird drawing is incorrect placement of the eye, both horizontally and vertically. The eye should be in line with the upper bill.

Care and Handling of Specimens

Some words of caution are appropriate in handling specimens.

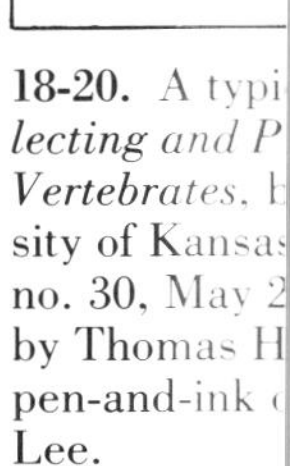

18-20. A typi[...] *lecting and P*[...] *Vertebrates*, [...] sity of Kansas [...] no. 30, May 2[...] by Thomas H[...] pen-and-ink [...] Lee.

The skin o[...] with the fe[...] becomes i[...] age. Man[...] have alrea[...] amputatio[...] out. Care [...] damage.

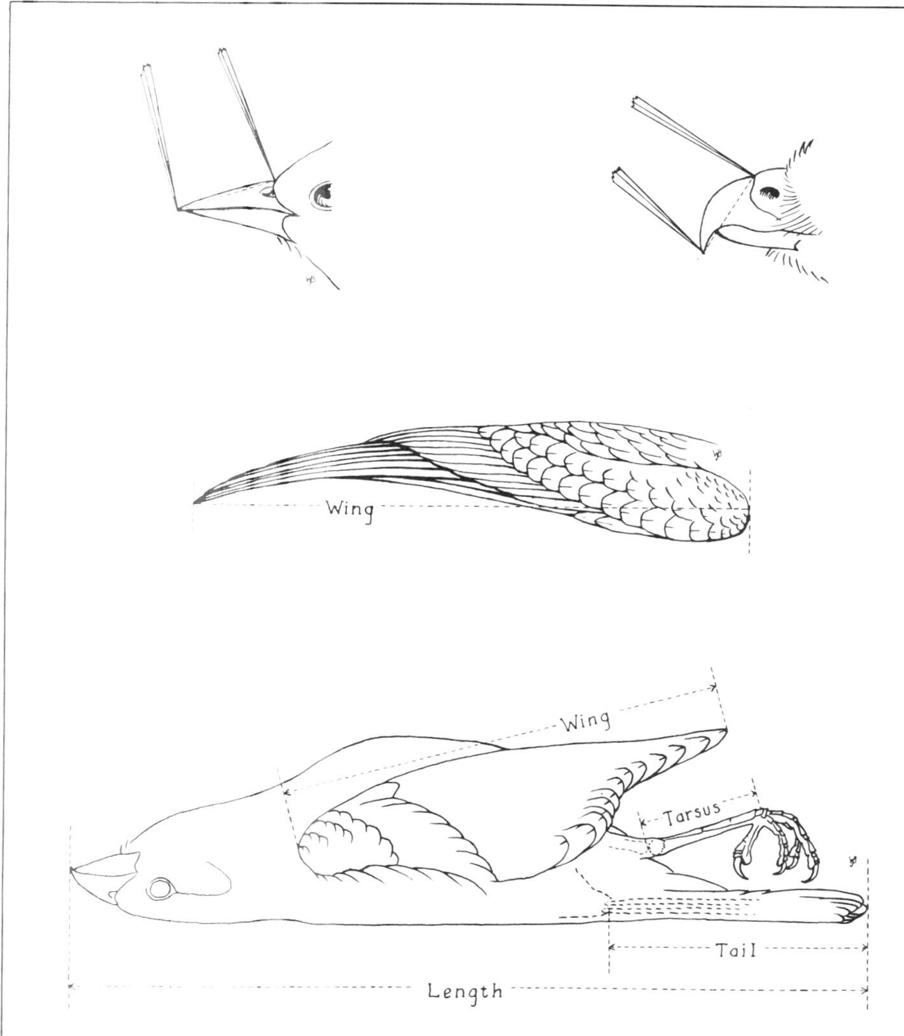

18-21. Standard measurements of birds. The wing and the total length are usually measured with a ruler; all of the other measurements can be obtained with dividers. The tail is measured from the base of the longest feather to its tip. Pen-and-ink. From *Ornithology in Laboratory and Field*, 4th ed., by Olin Sewall Pettingill, Jr. (© 1970 Burgess Publishing).

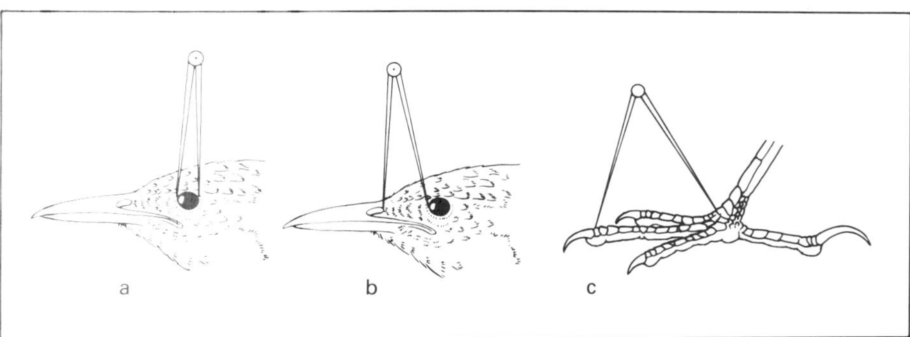

18-22. Additional measurements of birds: *(a)* eye; *(b)* lores; *(c)* toe. The eye measurements shown help establish the location of the eye. All the toes are measured as demonstrated for the middle toe, from the juncture of the toe with the leg to the end of the toe, minus the claw. Redrawn in pen-and-ink on polyester film, by Ken Lee, from "Bird Measurements," by Baldwin, Oberholser, and Worley (*Scientific Publications of the Cleveland Musuem*, vol. 2, 1931).

Never hold the specimen by its bill, feet, or tail; rather, gently grasp the specimen on either side of the body with fingers or hands, depending on the size of the bird. Avoid excessive handling to prevent depositing skin oils on the feathers. Some of the very smallest study skins have been placed on a stick, and they should be handled only by that stick. Use a tray or box to carry bird skins from one place to another. When using pins to prop a specimen in place, do not stick them into the specimen. Protect feathers from the color-fading effects of direct sunlight. If you plan to keep the specimens for any length of time, include a small amount of paradichlorobenzene (PDB) or naphthalene (both sold as mothballs) along with them to prevent possible insect attack. Avoid breathing either chemical for extended periods. Since arsenic was used in the past as a deterrent to insects, the illustrator should wash hands after handling older bird specimens. (See Study Skins in chapter 19 for other handling tips.)

Another less common method of preserving birds is to immerse the entire creature in alcohol; this is usually done when it is desirable to save the internal organs. More commonly, the internal organs alone are preserved in alcohol. The procedures for drawing such specimens are the same as those used for invertebrates (chapter 15) and amphibians and reptiles (chapter 17). If you must remove the specimen from the jar, keep it moist at all times with either water or the exact kind and concentration of alcohol in which the whole bird or organs were preserved. (Changing to another kind of alcohol can cause irreparable damage to specimens.)

Dry skeletons are also frequently prepared as adjuncts to study skins, and these are usually disarticulated and extremely fragile. Although museum policy generally does not allow specimens to be loaned to individuals, an independent illustrator can arrange to visit a research collection and work with bird skins on site. It therefore behooves a bird illustrator to maintain a healthy working relationship with one or more professional ornithologists.

DRAWING FROM PHOTOGRAPHS

Photographs can be useful in conjunction with bird skins, but great care must be exercised in their interpretation. The technical problems of distortion and freezing the subject in an awkward moment become especially critical with small and fast-moving creatures.

In addition, birds that are photographed under artificial conditions are often so stressed that they compress their feathers tightly to their bodies, crouch, and point their beaks upward in an attitude of extreme fear. However, photographs can supply valuable information, such as soft-part colors, if this data is not written on the specimen tag. Photographs can sometimes be relied upon to furnish basic posture and such details as facial expression and toe placement that may not be evident from a specimen. However, unless the illustrator is thoroughly familiar with bird anatomy, taxonomy, and behavior, photographs will tend to mislead rather than aid. Perhaps the most annoying sign of an inexperienced bird illustrator is the mindless copying of photographs with every accidental feature, such as out-of-place feathers, emphasized just as the camera caught it, while important anatomical characteristics are left undelineated.

On the other hand, photographs are the only means of securing an image of the details of bird flight. Even if a still photo or motion-picture frame is blurred from the fast action of the wings, an illustrator can extract a surprising amount of information if his or her knowledge of birds and their movements is solid (see Flight section, above).

RENDERING TECHNIQUES

Pen-and-Ink

Although pen-and-ink stipple is probably the most commonly used technique among illustrators, in bird illustrations it may produce the effect of an avian stone statue rather than a living creature. In general, line sh[illegible] fective techni[illegible] birds in ink, f[illegible] be composed [illegible] spection. Brus[illegible] well as pens. [illegible] lines must ru[illegible] tions as the fe[illegible] of crosshatchi[illegible] of personal pr[illegible]

a

c

b

18-23. A selection of pen-and-ink drawings. *(a)* Yellow-breasted chat, by Dr. George Miksch Sutton. From *Oklahoma Birds: Their Ecology and Distribution,* by George Miksch Sutton (© 1967, University of Oklahoma Press). *(b)* Cuban macaw, by D. M. Reid-Henry. Courtesy of Smithsonian Institution Archives. *(c)* Anna's X Costa's hummingbirds, by Nancy R. Halliday. From "Hybridization in *Calpyte* Hummingbirds," by S. Wells, R. A. Bradley, and L. F. Baptista (*The Auk*, vol. 95, 1978). Note the deceptively simple parallel-line technique used by Sutton. Rendering a bird and its background in the fewest possible lines is far more difficult than it appears. Reid-Henry makes liberal use of crosshatching and achieves a remarkable three-dimensional effect with his drawings. Note the different textures in his rendering of the feathers, bill, feet, and branch. Contrast between the glossy and soft feathers in the hummingbird was made by placing lines closer together or farther apart and by outlining the glossy feathers to make them appear "harder." All three of these illustrations show birds in relaxed and naturalistic poses, yet all were made to accompany scientific texts.

Miksch Sutton, one of America's most venerable bird artists, chose to use parallel lines only, while D. M. Reid-Henry, an Englishman and one of the most successful pen-and-ink illustrators, cross-hatched liberally (see figs. 18-23 and 5-32). Accessory features in the drawing, such as plants or background, must not detract from the bird itself.

Color

Birds are among the few biological subjects regularly depicted in color for field guides and on occasion for publication in scientific journals. The usual media are transparent watercolor, tempera, gouache, and acrylic (see figs. C-3, C-6, C-23). The style and application of color will depend upon the artist's abilities and the publisher's needs.

The variety of color patterns over a bird's body, whether for camouflage or to attract a mate, can be so bewildering that the illustrator may become lost in the maze, producing a painting that resembles little more than a patchwork quilt. Every color, however, has a value (or tone) in relation to every other color (see fig. 4-63). A simple solution to the beginner's infatuation with isolated colors is to translate those colors into black-and-white relationships by squinting at the bird until details are lost and an overall impression becomes clear. As an object in space, a bird also has a tonal relationship to its surroundings; this should be observed if the latter are to be included in the painting. Again, squinting at the bird in its natural environment will determine whether it is generally lighter or darker than its surroundings. This contrast should be emphasized.

Of course, disrupting the form is the purpose of natural camouflage. Even brightly colored birds are counter-shaded—dark on top and light below—so that natural light conditions will negate both, resulting in an apparent loss of dimensionality (a black cap on a sunlit bird is actually lighter than the shadows on its white belly). Nevertheless, as a three-dimensional object, a bird's form will be defined by light and shadow (see chapters 4 and 20.) In naturalistic painting, all actual colors (called local colors) must be subordinated to the form and the light and shadows falling over that form. Sunlight will bleach colors; shadows will darken and may intensify them. All areas that catch sunlight will also be warmer in color temperature; shadows, on the other hand, will be made cool from reflected blue sky light. A backlight *within* the shadow will be warmest of all, however, because it is caused by reflected sunlight. More specific information on painting birds in natural light is given in *To a Young Bird Artist*, by George Miksch Sutton (see Bibliography).

By paying attention to tone and color as they occur in nature, an illustrator can dramatically heighten a sense of three-dimensionality in artwork on paper.

Field guides often demand a simplified commercial treatment accentuating colors and patterns. The birds are usually idealized and portrayed as vignettes with local color emphasized and highlights and shadows minimized. A common practice is to place many birds, often standardized in the same lateral view for comparison, on one small plate. Roger Tory Peterson's well-known *Field Guide to the Birds* is a good example, especially the early editions (see Bibliography). The occasional color plate in a scientific journal such as *The Wilson Bulletin* and *The Living Bird* usually calls for more of a portrait treatment, often with background material included. Bird illustrators should examine issues of these journals. Finally, modern large-format books on birds of a particular family or of a specific region recall the magnificent hand-colored volumes of the

past century
talents of an
velopment o
rendering of
and shadows.
lavish backg
the latter (s
Portraits of
Selected Pain
Miksch Sutto
—*A Monogra*
lidae, by S.
trated by J. F
and *Parrots*
seph M. Fo
William T.
their great e
books can be
endowed or
but their ex
search. Mor
paintings
Fuertes, cons
illustrator of
Birds of Ame
bert Pearso
John James
bird illustrat
rate in detail
sign, have be
ornithologists
postures. A
dead specim
up with wire
his flamboya
critique by
"Beauty and
ing Bird (see

In summa
practice com
produce suc
tions. No an
will cover up
drawing. Obs
dle freshly
mounted ske
work of est
tors. As Jos
nineteenth-c
said, "There
finishing sch
remains a stu

19/Illustrating Mammals

Charles O. Handley, Jr.

Popular publications depict whole mammals in lifelike poses or use diagrams of organs, systems, external parts, or entire animals to explain form, function, and processes. Backgrounds include the stark white page, flashy colors, a few symbolic accessories, or complex habitats (see figs. 20-1, 20-3, and 20-5). Illustrations of mammals in technical publications are more specialized and precise. They generally fall into four categories: teeth, skulls, and bones; anatomical dissections; external parts; and whole animals. Illustrations for text and reference books fall between the popular and the technical styles.

Photography has usurped some of the turf of the illustrator. As photographic equipment and techniques have improved, the traditional reliance on drawings of mammals has lessened. Now, even a drawing is likely to have been based at least in part on photographs, movies, or video recordings, which are invaluable aids.

Whether a mammal is photographed or drawn depends on a number of factors. For example, it is especially difficult to equal in drawings the best photographs of teeth (fig. 19-1). Few photographers, however, have the skill or time for such exceptional work. Consequently, drawings often are the better choice for depicting teeth, especially when certain features need to be emphasized (fig. 19-2). When several toothrows or skulls are compared, photographs may be the best solution, but drawings are better for showing cranial details (fig. 19-3). The problems of depth of field and highlighting make it difficult to produce superior photographs of skulls (fig. 19-4), and because of reflection from moist surfaces and complexity of structure, drawings of anatomical dissections usually are preferable to photographs. In such sketches, superfluous details can be ignored, important features can be emphasized, and the three-dimensional impression of layering, difficult in photography, can be achieved easily (fig. 19-5). Similarly, in illustrating details of external parts such as ears, nose, or paws, drawings are preferable for control of detail (fig. 19-6).

Drawings of whole mammals can include impressions of still life (fig. 19-7) and animation (see figs. 20-1, 20-3, 20-5, 20-7 and 20-13). Capturing a subject in action is perhaps the most challenging form of mammalian illustration. It requires more background research, observation, preliminary posing, and sketching than any other form of illustration (fig. 19-8). There may be the added problem of fitting the animal naturally into a back-

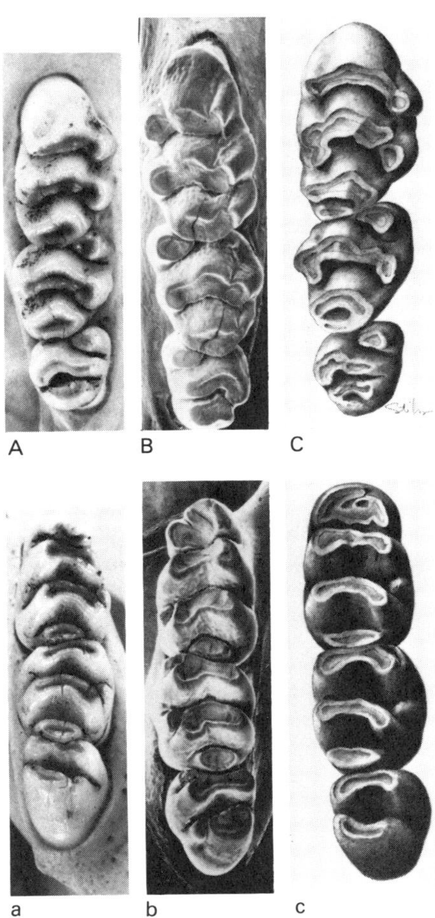

19-1. Occlusal views of teeth of rodents. Right upper *(A)* and right lower *(a)* molars of *Leopoldamys*. Photo by Peter Goldberg and Jim Coxe. From G. Musser, *Bulletin of the American Museum of Natural History* 168:263, 1981. Left upper *(B)* and left lower *(b)* molars of *Rattus*. Scanning electron micrographs by Robert J. Koestler, printed by Richard Sheryll. From G. Musser and C. Newcomb, *Bulletin of the American Museum of Natural History* 174:576, 1983. Right upper *(C)* and right lower *(c)* molars of *Margaretamys*. Pencil on illustration board, by Fran Stiles. From G. Musser, *Bulletin of the American Museum of Natural History* 168:284, 1981.

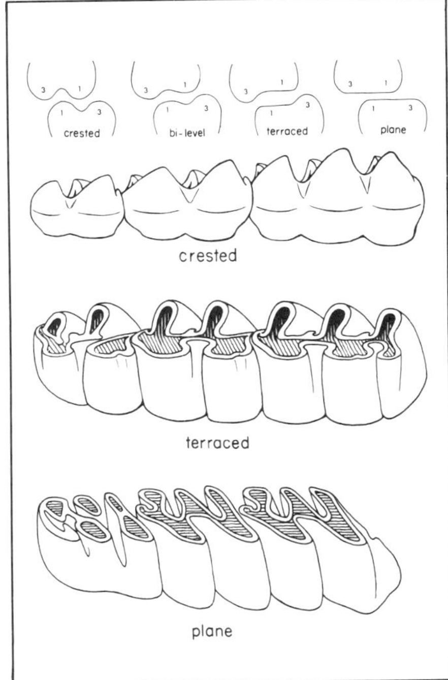

19-2. Schematic drawings of rodent teeth, emphasizing differences in the occlusal surface. Pen-and-ink, by E. J. Pfiffner and Marion Pahl. From P. Hershkovitz, *Fieldiana: Zoology* 46:87, 1962.

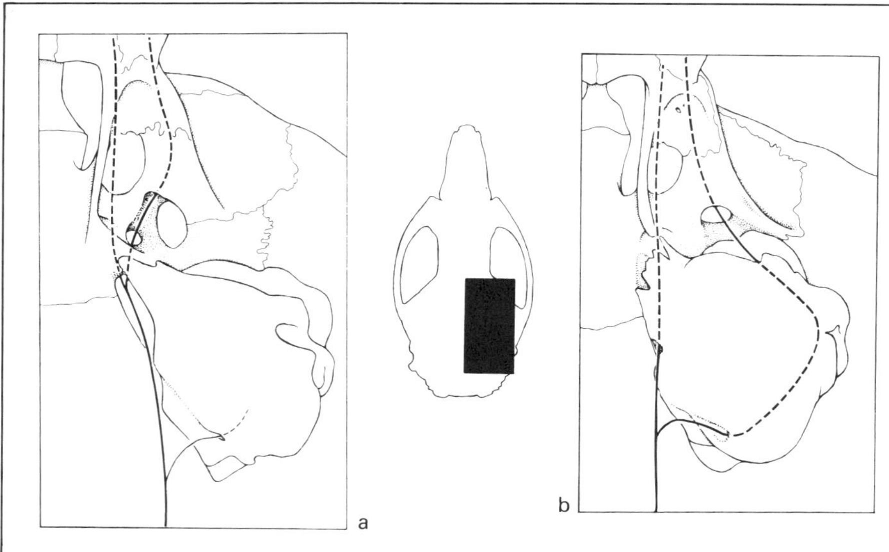

19-3. Diagrams illustrating the pathways of the carotid artery in skulls of rodents: *(a) Apomys; (b) Rattus.* Pen-and-ink on illustration board, by Patricia Wynne. From G. Musser, *American Museum Novitates* 2746:6, 1982.

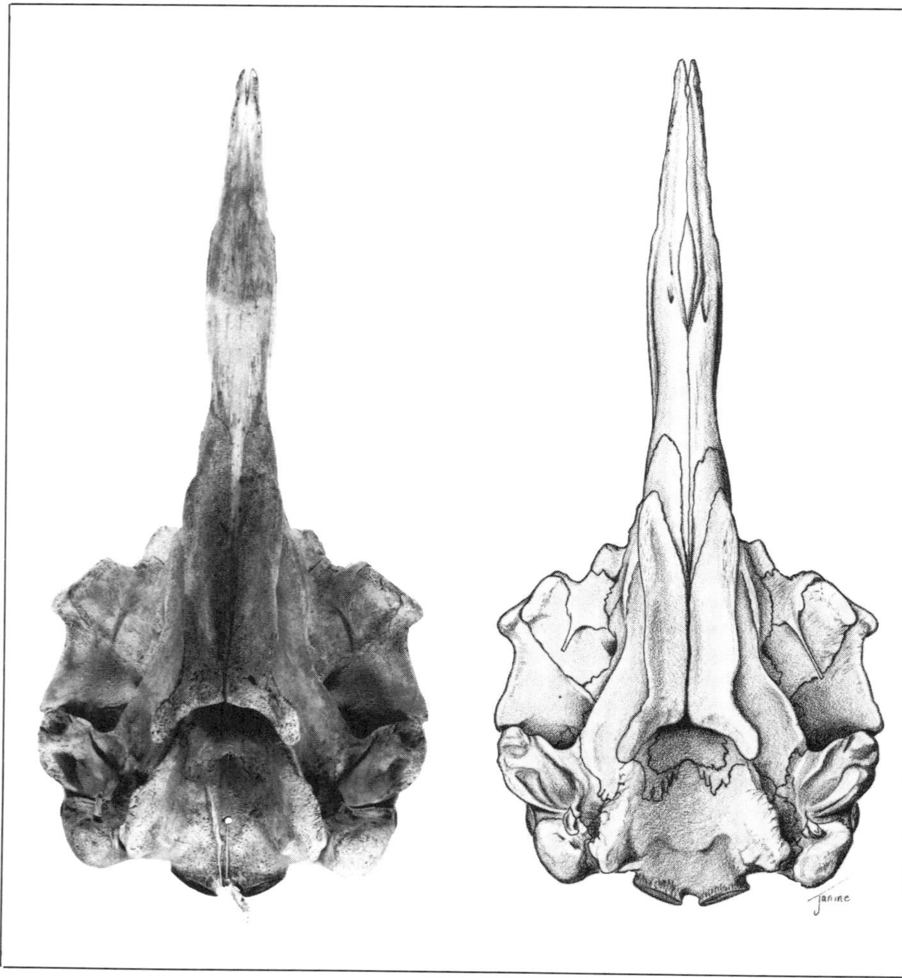

19-4. Photograph and drawing of the ventral aspect of the skull of a beaked whale (*Mesoplodon densirostris*). Photo by Vic Krantz. Carbon pencil on coquille board, by Janine Higgins.

ground, neit
the animal a
(See chapter
ation of this

THE ILLU

The most
of mammals
They may
mammals,
them at ever
behaviors, a
titudes. Or
mal training
not unusual
artist and l
ground nee
mammals.
ogy, zoolog
omy, natur
behavior a
Technical
ticularly fr
tion, osteol
anatomical

How mu
to know d
scientist w
probably
and other
vide instru
to illustrat
turn. On t
trator work
editor prob
sufficient—

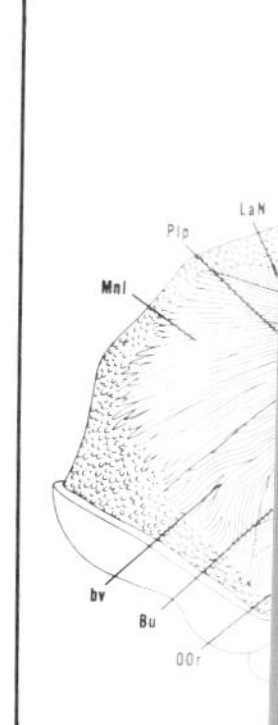

19-5. Later
of a dugong.
after the su
moved. Pen
and J. P. L
Smithsonian
226:38. 1977

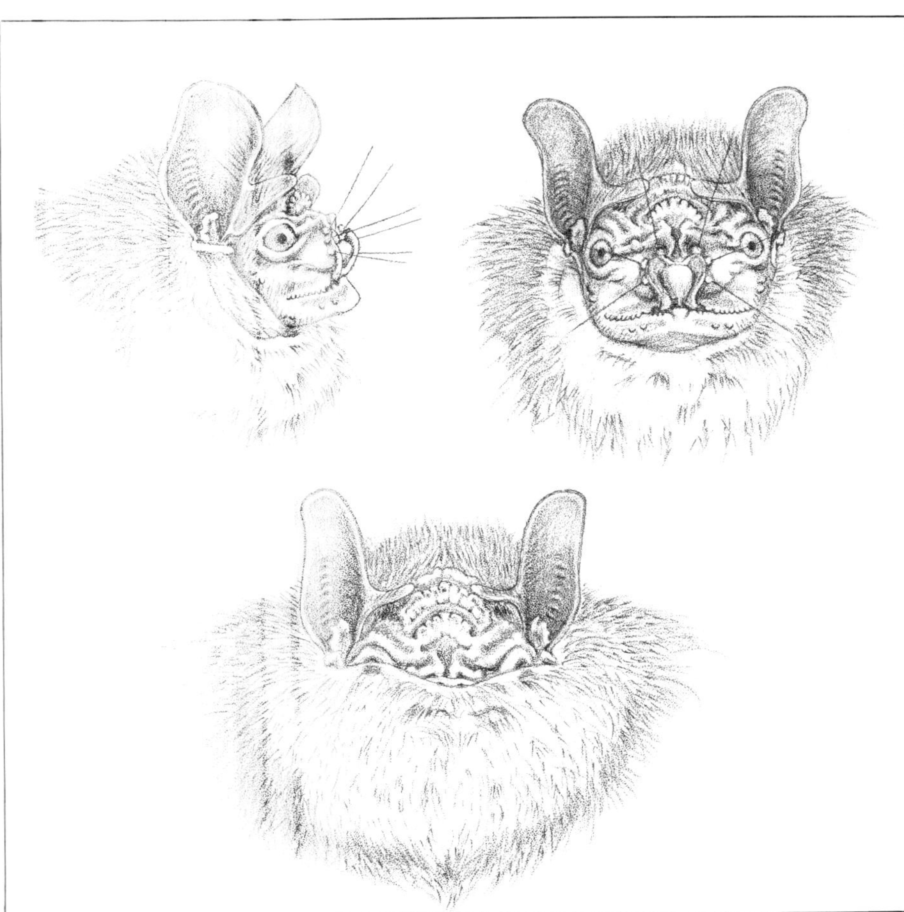

19-6. Illustrating details of external morphology: face of tropical bat *Centurio senex*. Pencil on coquille board, by Nancy Moran.

19-7. Still-life drawing of a whole animal. Dorsal view of tropical bat *Centurio senex*, with one wing extended. Pencil on coquille board, by Nancy Moran.

need to know more and be able to proceed with a minimum of advice.

If for no other reason than to be informed, the illustrator of mammals ought to know at least a little about the subject—what mammalogy comprises, what a mammal is, and what the rudiments of classification are. The science of mammalogy includes a variety of disciplines, the most basic of which is systematics. Others, such as paleontology, zoogeography, ecology, and demography, examine the historical perspective and distribution and relationships of mammals in time and space and within ecosystems. Studies of what mammals do come under the broad heading of natural history and include behavior (ethology), reproduction, food habits, locomotion, and communication. Disciplines such as anatomy, physiology, and genetics look within the mammal to contemplate form and function.

19-8. Sketches of a wolverine in motion. Shadows define the form of the active subject. Pencil on cold-press paper, by Wayne Trimm.

The illustrator of mammals needs versatility, patience, good humor, and a willingness to conduct personal research, if necessary, to develop background and a feel for the subject. Normally, personal art equipment and supplies will be required. Ideally, the illustrator will work where the subject matter, references, and technical support reside. This could be in a research laboratory, museum, zoo, city park, or almost anywhere, depending on the subject. Or the illustrator might work in his or her own studio with borrowed specimens and whatever aids are available. The client—administrator, scientist, editor—might provide specimens, detailed instructions, background, equipment, and supplies, or only an idea, to be developed and fleshed out by the illustrator. Depending on whether specimens are alive, preserved, whole, or dissected, they might be handled or only observed, close at hand or at a distance. The work might be in an air-conditioned laboratory, in a sweaty environmental chamber, or in a smelly paddock. There is no standard environment for mammalian art!

INSTRUMENTS AND MATERIALS

In addition to the art materials required for the chosen media and techniques, the illustrator of mammals most likely will use many of the tools and materials listed here. The choice depends on the size and condition of the specimen.

Optical Devices

Stereoscopic microscope: with 10× ocular and zoom or objectives approximating 6×, 12×, and 25×. Because parts of mammals to be illustrated vary so much in size, a fixed-objective stereoscopic microscope is almost useless.

Reducing objective: 0.5×, for increasing working distance between objective and subject.

Camera lucida.

Reticle: ocular micrometer.

Camera: 35mm single-lens reflex.

Camera adapter: to attach camera to microscope; essential for photographing teeth and other small parts.

Slide projector, desktop slide viewer: for 35mm slides.

Videocassette recorder (VCR): to view videocassettes of animals in action, or to study video-recorded procedures.

Measuring Devices

Rulers: metric, metal; 150, 300, and 1,000mm sizes, mostly for measuring fresh whole small mammals. Metal is necessary for accuracy; plastic or wood may shrink or expand.

Retractable steel tape measure: various lengths as needed, for measuring large mammals such as ungulates and cetaceans, and large skulls.

Calipers: digital, dial, or Vernier—in order of preference; for measuring skulls, teeth, and bones. A small pair (over 130mm) for small species is most versatile (see fig. 2-19).

Anthropometer: giant caliperlike device for measuring very large skulls and bones.

Dividers: various sizes, used with steel tape measures for measuring large skulls and other objects.

Craniometer: microscope with a measuring device on a mechanical stage.

Special devices: of limited utility; have been developed to measure such dimensions as incisor arc, basicranial skew, and facial attitude.

Proportional dividers: for transferring measurements to drawings (see chapter 2).

Specimen-

Forceps: sh
nipulating
straight ve
shown in figu
removing sp
tainers and f
imens.

Scissors.

Scalpel.

Specimen

Dental wa
based mode
or clay to
board cards
for mounting
and teeth fo

Black cards
faces for exa
bones. The
laroid film pa
purpose.

Microscope
for strips of
ing specime

Containers

Trays, pans

Jars: glass o

Wetting Ag
Preservati

Alcohol: eth

Formalin.

Aerosol sol
sulfosuccina
softening a
parts.

Miscellane

Hand towe
when worki

Cloth: to be
over wet s
them from c

Rubber glo

Barrier cream: such as No. 311 Protective Cream (West Chemical Products, Inc.—see Appendix) to protect hands from preservatives on wet specimens.

Compressed air, hair blow-dryer: for blowing off moisture from wet specimens for brief observation of hair characteristics.

Plastic bags: to hold wet specimens.

Fumigant: Vapona strips, paradichlorobenzene (PDB), naphthalene flakes to protect dry specimens from insect pests.

MUSEUM SPECIMENS

Sometimes an artist will be provided specimens from a research colony or other private source, but ordinarily the best source of information for illustration of mammals is a museum, particulary a large museum. However, only a few museums have collections that are worldwide in scope. The largest in North America, with collections of over 50,000 mammal specimens, are the U.S. National Museum of Natural History (Washington), the American Museum of Natural History (New York), the University of California Museum of Vertebrate Zoology (Berkeley), the University of Kansas Museum of Natural History (Lawrence), the University of Michigan Museum of Zoology (Ann Arbor), the Field Museum of Natural History (Chicago), the Harvard University Museum of Comparative Zoology (Cambridge), the Royal Ontario Museum (Toronto), and the Carnegie Museum of Natural History (Pittsburgh). There are many other excellent museums whose collections of mammals are smaller and often regional in scope. See "Collections of Recent Mammals in North America," by J. R. Choate and H. H. Genoways (*Journal of Mammalogy*—see Bibliography) for an annotated list of all the museums of North America.

Great mammal collections in other parts of the world are in the British Museum (Natural History) (London), the Zoological Museum of Moscow University (Moscow), the Mammal Research Institute (Bialowieza, Poland), the Zoologische Museum (East Berlin), the Zoological Institute (Leningrad), the Zoologische Staatssammlung München (Munich), the Museu Nacional (Rio de Janeiro), the Rijksmuseum van Natuurlijke Historie (Leiden), the National Museum of Zimbabwe (Bulawayo), and the Forschungsinstitut und Natur-Museum Senckenberg (Frankfurt am Main). For an annotated list of all the collections of mammals of the world outside of North America, see "Collections of Recent Mammals of the World, Exclusive of Canada and the United States," by H. H. Genoways and D. A. Schlitter (*Annals of the Carnegie Museum*—see Bibliography).

Specimens of mammals may be prepared in a number of ways in museums. Some are for display, others for study. The conventional exhibits mount has the tanned skin of a mammal mounted on an artificial body of fiber, plaster, or plastic. A freeze-dried specimen, on the other hand, lacks only its eyes (replaced with glass) and body fluids. (Every trace of moisture is removed from the specimen by sublimation in a vacuum in subzero temperature, so that it retains its original size and shape.) In research collections, specimens are kept as study skins (flat, tanned, or stuffed in a compact form) accompanied by the clean, dry skull; as skeletons (entire or disarticulated); or entire, frozen or in a fluid such as alcohol or Formalin.

Exhibits Specimens

Although the public exhibits of museums are showplaces for whole-body lifelike mounts and freeze-dried specimens that would appear to be valuable resources for illustrators, the quality of these specimens varies with the ability of the taxidermists who prepared them. Exhibits taxidermy is an art, but, unfortunately, not all taxidermists are good artists. Consequently, poses, attitudes, and expressions, as well as color, in exhibits specimens should be used as the basis of illustrations only with great caution.

It is seldom necessary to handle exhibits specimens. As a matter of fact, it is best not to touch them at all. They are fragile, and the ears, especially those of freeze-dried specimens, are brittle and easily broken.

Frozen Specimens

A frozen specimen (not freeze-dried) is exceedingly brittle and must be handled with great care to avoid breaking legs, tail, or ears. Unless the specimen is to be thawed completely and prepared for some other type of permanent storage, observations must be made quickly. Thawing and refreezing will soon ruin a specimen for any subsequent preparation. A frozen specimen should be carefully sealed in a plastic bag before it is returned to the freezer. Otherwise it will gradually freeze-dry.

Study Skins

The illustrator can use study skins for information on coloration, fur length and texture, size and proportions, and individual, sexual, age, seasonal, and geographic variations. Three or four useful measurements (fig. 19-9) and sometimes valuable habitat data appear on the specimen label.

Artists using a skin collection must cope with the disagreeable effects of a fumigant. A fugitive fumigant such as Dowfume presents no problem and little hazard, for it escapes when the specimen storage case is opened and quickly dissipates to nontoxic concentrations in the air of the room. On the other hand, a residual fumigant such as Vapona, paradichlorobenzene, or

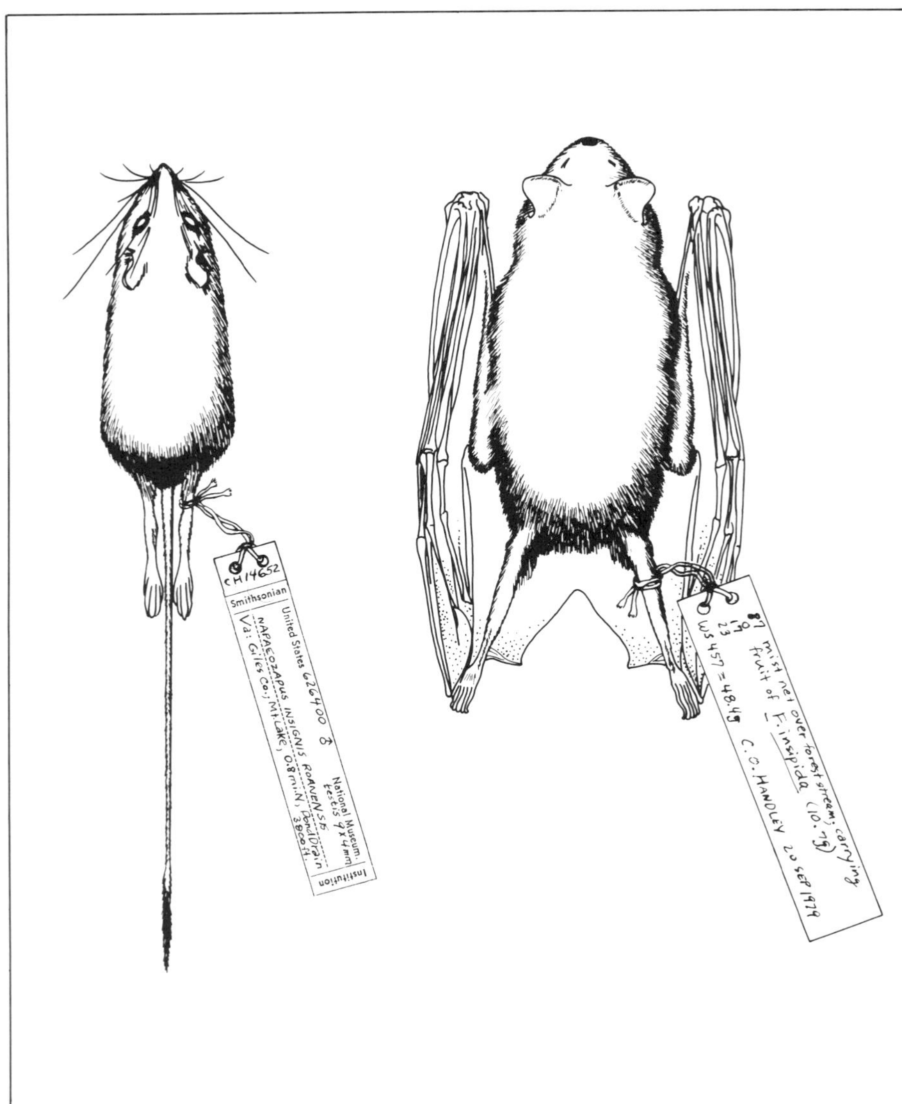

19-9. Study skins of a woodland jumping mouse (*Napaeozapus insignis roanensis*) and common fruit bat (*Artibeus jamaicensis*). Valuable data may be found on specimen labels. On the front of the label are the sex, reproductive information, scientific name, exact collecting locality, museum number, and collector's field number. On the back are measurements, weight, ecological data, collector's name, and date of collection. Redrawn with pen-and-ink on film, by Irene Jewett, from Smithsonian Institution Information Leaflet no. 380.

naphthalene may irritate the nasal passages and throat or lead to even more serious reactions if the charged air of the storage case is breathed for a prolonged period. Thus, it is best to select specimens as quickly as possible and close the storage case immediately.

A number of commonsense rules apply to the use of study skins. Chapters 18 and 20 mention some of a general nature. Here are some others, both general and specific, for mammals:

1. Wash hands before going to the collection to avoid transferring skin oils and other dirt to specimens.
2. Wash hands after handling specimens to remove residual chemicals from specimen preparation, tanning, or fumigation.

skull will be found its mandibles, original labels, and sometimes loose teeth and broken parts. Remove a skull from its container onto a sheet of paper. Watch for loose parts and carefully return them to the container. All skulls, even the largest and seemingly most indestructible, have fragile processes or parts that can be broken by careless handling or dropping. Every skull should be handled as though it were very fragile and would break easily. It is preferable to use a whole skull, but if it is necessary to handle a broken skull, exercise great care to avoid further damage. Do not attempt to repair a broken skull or glue in loose teeth.

Delicate skulls are regularly damaged by people trying to measure them with oversize calipers. Very small skulls and teeth should be measured with an ocular micrometer on a stereoscopic microscope or with a craniometer, a microscope with a measuring device on a mechanical stage (S. Anderson, *Journal of Mammalogy* 49:221, 1968).

Rather than risk damage to a skull by holding it for examination, gently mount it in the desired position on a strip of dental wax or a microcrystalline-based modeling clay such as ivory Leisure Craft Clay (see Appendix). Do not risk breaking the skull by pressing it too forcefully onto the mount. When work has been completed, carefully remove any particles of wax or clay that may cling to the skull and return it to its container. Take care that the top of the container does not touch the skull when it is pressed down for closing. Verify that skull, mandibles, and container all are matched correctly (bearing the same catalog number) before returning them to the collection.

Skeletons

Rules for handling skulls apply also to skeletons. In addition, always verify, before removal from its container, that each bone has a catalog number on it. If it is necessary to separate articulated bones, do it carefully with a scalpel or ask a member of the curatorial staff to do it. Verify that all newly separated bones are numbered before laying them out for use.

Wet Specimens

Using wet specimens for illustration often leads to better results than using dry ones, but special problems do exist. Smaller specimens are sealed in jars or small tanks, larger ones in tanks or vats. Use of large specimens must be planned in advance, for it may be necessary to bring in a group of laborers to remove a heavy, bulky specimen from its storage vat. The lids of tanks and vats often are sealed with petroleum jelly, which must be kept off the specimens.

Specimen storage jars may have friction tops or rubber gaskets and pressure seals. It can be very difficult to loosen a friction-type lid. Tap it gently—first on one side, then on the other—with a small leather, plastic, or rubber mallet. Work at a sink and be prepared for the possibility that the lid or jar might break.

Steady upward pressure on the exposed rim of a rubber gasket usually will be necessary to pry off the lid, probably damaging the gasket, and possibly the bottle or lid as well. Any damaged part should be replaced immediately. The safest and easiest course is to ask an experienced person, such as one of the curatorial staff, to loosen the lid. Some jars are permanently sealed; their contents should be viewed through the glass, and no attempt should be made to remove a specimen from such a jar.

The preservative on a wet specimen will temporarily dehydrate an investigator's hands. This annoyance can be reduced or avoided by handling the specimen only briefly, washing the preservative from the specimen with water before it is handled, anointing the hands with a barrier cream, wearing rubber gloves, handling the specimen with forceps, or viewing the specimen through the glass wall of its container.

Greatest concern must be exercised for the specimen. It must not be permitted to dry out while exposed to air. Drying can be retarded by draping the specimen, except for the part being examined, with a cloth or paper towel dampened with water or preservative. Also, the specimen should not be brought close to hot working lights for more than a moment. If at any time the specimen appears to be drying, it should be immersed immediately in water or put back into its preservative. Ears, lips, and eyelids are particularly susceptible to drying.

To restore a specimen momentarily to a lifelike appearance or to examine coloration or distribution of hair, it is necessary to dry all, or preferably part, of it. Compressed air, if it is available, is best for this purpose, but be careful not to blow off hair or rip open the specimen with strong blasts of air. A weak, steady stream of air is best. Be sure to let air trapped in the nozzle escape for a second or two before directing the stream toward the specimen. Drying also can be achieved, but with more danger to the specimen, with a hair blow-dryer set at lowest heat. Of course, the skin of the specimen will dry as well as its hair. Thus, observations must be made quickly so that the specimen can be returned immediately to liquid storage. In or out of its container, a wet specimen should not be subjected to prolonged exposure to daylight. The curatorial staff should be notified if the fluid level is low in a storage container. Alcohol from one jar of specimens must not be poured into another jar of specimens, because of the possibility of mixing ectoparasites and confounding subsequent entomological studies.

CLASSIFICATION

Mammals (class Mammalia) were derived from the Reptilia in the early Mesozoic, about 200 million years ago. Mammals are distinguished from the ancestral reptiles and from all other animals mainly by possession of hair and milk (both products of skin glands) and direct articulation of the lower jaws and the skull (squamosal-dentary joint).

Living mammals are divided into major categories primarily by their reproductive biology. The egg-laying monotremes (platypus and echidna) are the only living members of the subclass Prototheria. All other living mammals belong to the subclass Theria, which includes the typically nonplacental, sometimes pouched marsupials of the infraclass Metatheria and the placental infraclass Eutheria. Most living mammals are eutherians (sixteen of the eighteen living orders). These orders are distinguished primarily by morphological characteristics related to locomotion and food habits.

Mammalogists have traditionally used tooth characteristics, shape and proportions of the skull, and external morphology as their main tools in species-level classification—thus, "skin and skull taxonomy." Less attention has been paid to the postcranial skeleton and internal soft parts, such as digestive tract, glands, muscles, nerves, blood vessels, and reproductive system. Recently, however, there has been an explosion of interest in soft anatomy, karyotypes (morphological characteristics of the chromosomes of a cell), chromosome banding, protein chemistry, immunology, and behavior as aids to classification.

Morphology

Because of their usually somber coloration, mammals may appear to be monotonously similar to one another. To portray them well, the illustrator must go beyond superficial similarities and understand how function influences the shape of body parts, creating great variations among mammals. Many of the variations can be correlated with behavioral adaptations. Striking examples of this relationship can be seen in locomotor adaptations, as well as in others associated with feeding, defense, sex, and the environment.

The earliest mammals were terrestrial and had a flat-footed (plantigrade), ambling (ambulatory) gait. Mammals that have retained this basic, prin usually ha and mobil that permi (fig. 19-10) has the ad versatility, slowness. tigrades and many marsupials limbs of evolved fr ambulator changing 19-12).

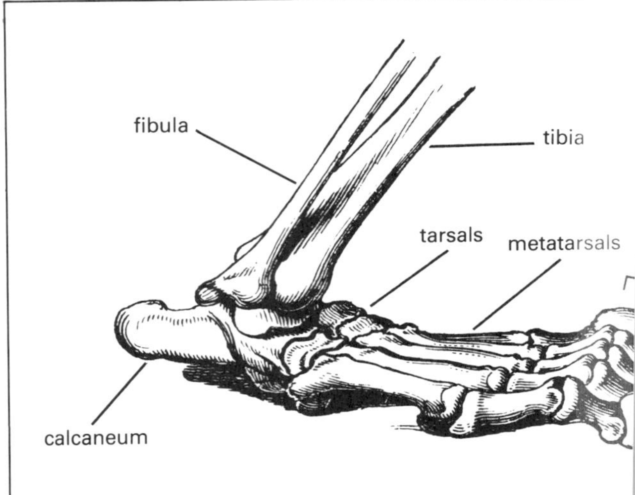

19-10. Plantigrade foot of a bear. Pen-and-ink. Artist unknow *Anatomy of Vertebrates* 2:289, 1866.

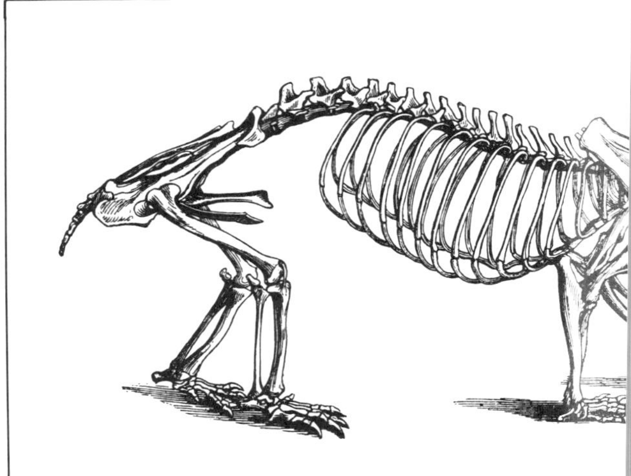

19-11. Skeleton of a wombat, an ambulatory plantigrade. Pe From R. Owen, *On the Anatomy of Vertebrates* 2:330, 1866.

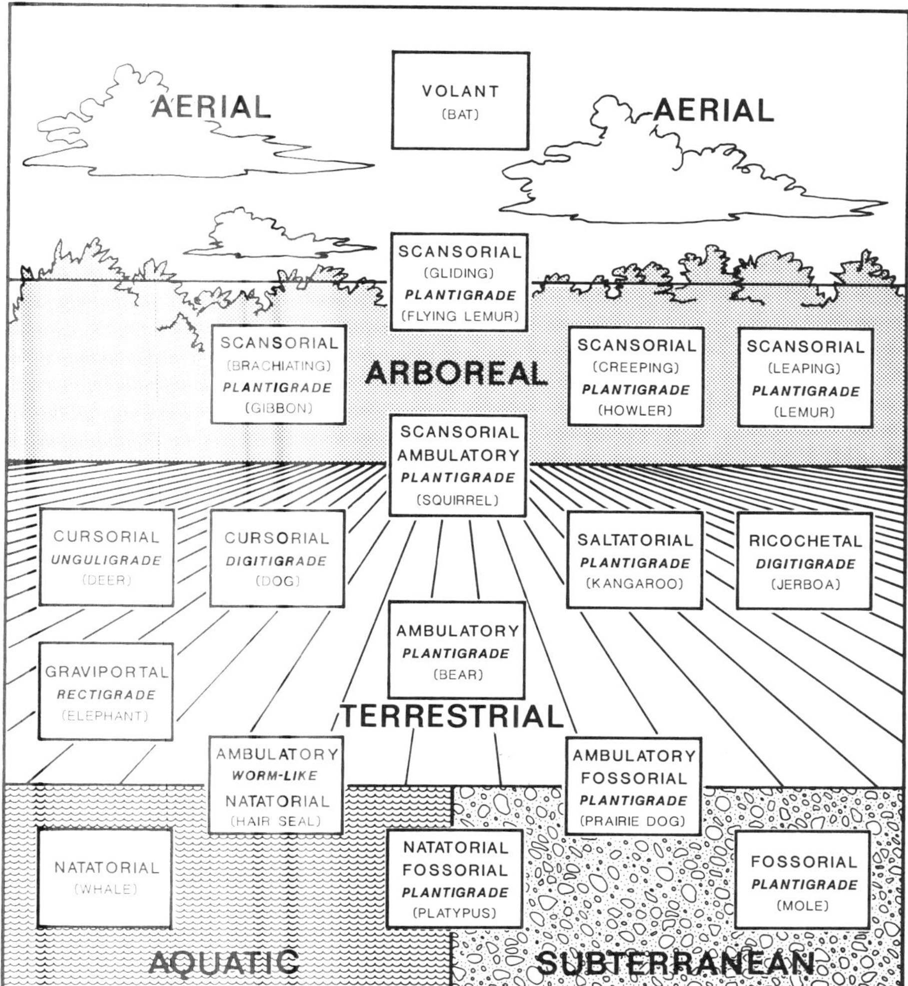

19-12. Classification of mammalian locomotion. Pen-and-ink and shading films on film, by T. Britt Griswold.

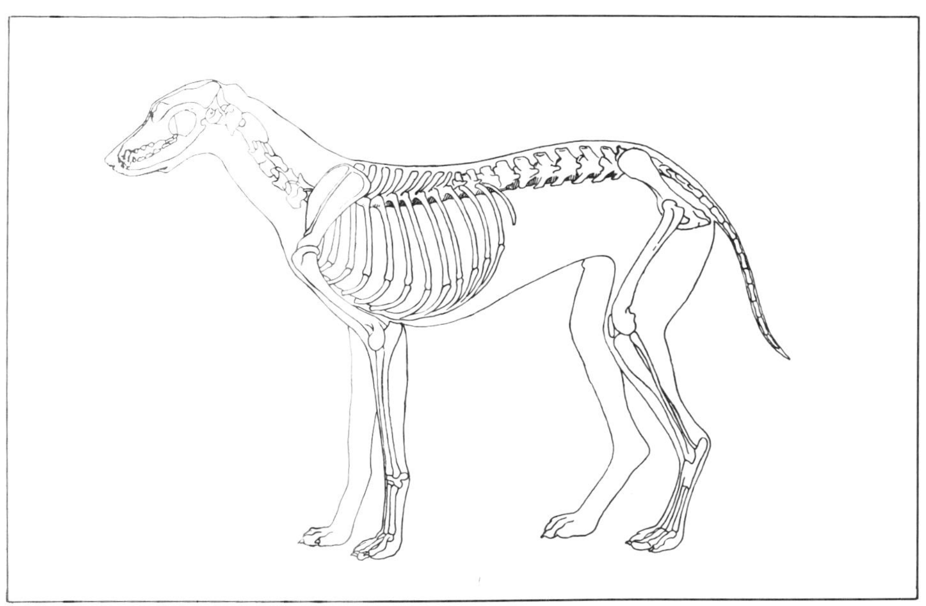

19-13. Skeleton of a dog, a digitigrade mammal. Pen-and-ink. Artist unknown. From M. Weber, *Die Säugetiere* (Verlag von Gustav Fischer in Jena, 1:110, 1927).

Climbing (scansorial locomotion) requires little anatomical modification from the basic type. Limbs and phalanges may be longer, the foot shorter and broader, claws sharp and recurved, joints at shoulder and hip usually flexible, tail long and bushy or prehensile, and eyes more anteriorly oriented (often binocular). Tree squirrels, some mice and rats, and many primates and marsupials are scansorial.

Other mammals stayed on the ground but abandoned the slow ambulatory gait in favor of a speedier, though less stable, cursorial (running) gait. Gradually limbs moved under the body, functional fingers and toes were reduced in number, and joints of the lower extremities were modified to limit movement mostly to a fore-and-aft plane. Thus evolved, these mammals walk and run on their toes (digitigrade) (fig. 19-13). Cursorial digitigrade mammals include dogs, foxes, cats, weasels, and mongooses.

From this grade have developed extreme specializations for speed: limbs locked into fore-and-aft movement with tongue-and-groove joints in the lower extremities, functional toes reduced to two or one on each limb, claws replaced by hooves, and humerus and femur buried in muscles in the body (fig. 19-14). Hoofed mammals such as horses, gazelles, pigs, and deer are ungulates. They walk and run on their toe nails. They display unguligrade locomotion.

In contrast, the limbs of elephants are graviportal—adapted to supporting great weight (fig. 19-15). They are straight and pillarlike, joints are flattened to limit movement in all planes, and digits are arranged in a proplike circular pattern and buried in flesh.

Elongation of hind limbs and tail and shortening of fore limbs are associated with saltatorial locomotion—traveling by leaps and bounds—an energetic improvement on four-footed running. Kangaroos and

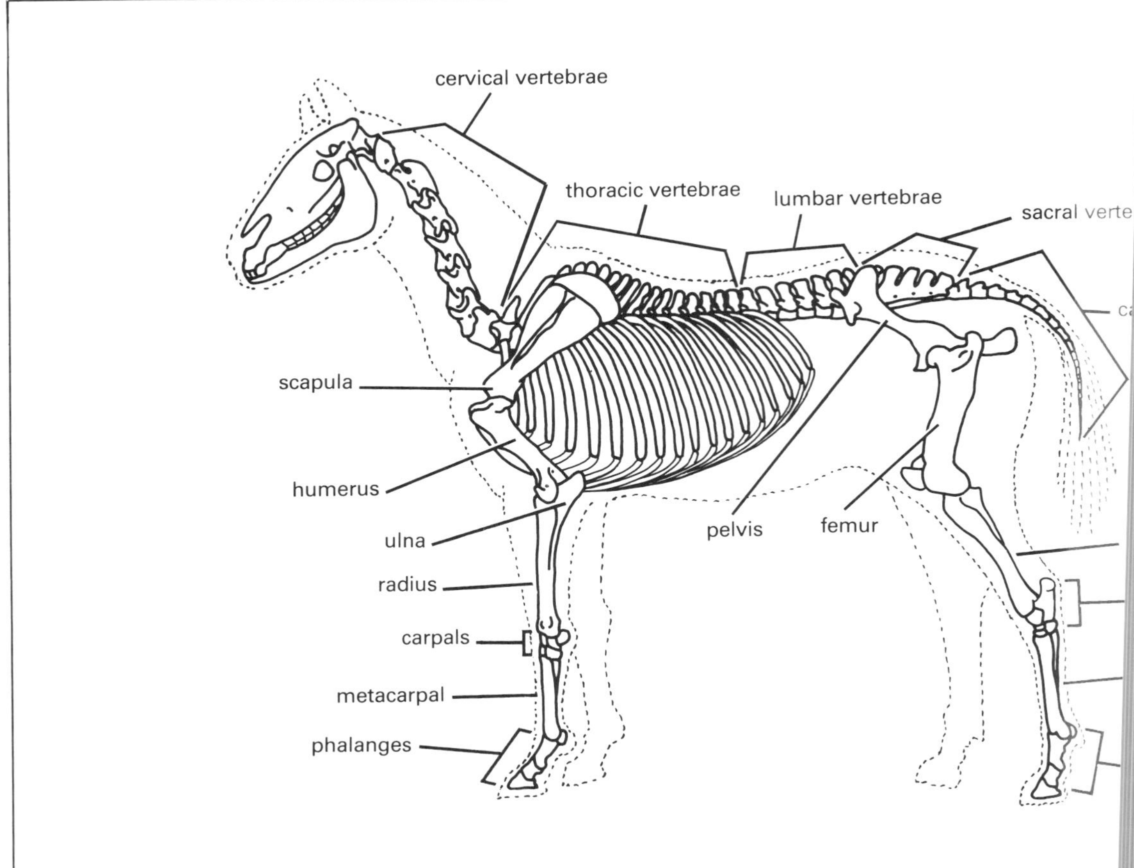

19-14. Skeleton of a horse, an unguligrade mammal. Pen-and-ink on film, by Irene Jewett, redrawn from S. Sisson, *The Anatomy of Domestic Animals* (W. B. Saunders Company, 1927).

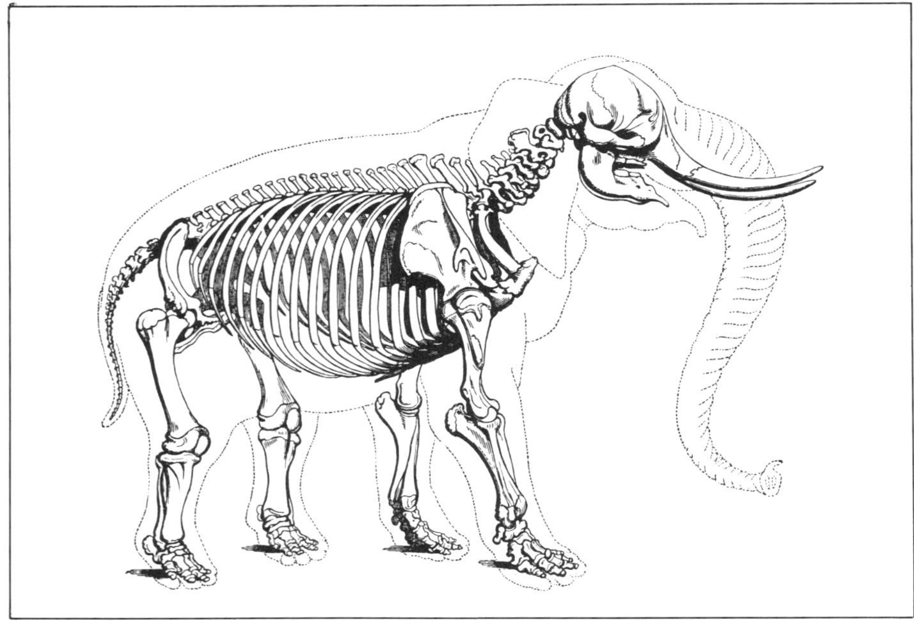

19-15. Skeleton of an elephant, a graviportal mammal. Pen-and-ink. Artist unknown. Redrawn, with outline added with pen-and-ink on film, by Jo-Ellen Trecartin, from R. Owen, *On the Anatomy of Vertebrates* 2:282, 1866.

wallabies a
cochetal m
kangaroo ra
a further r
that permi
bounds. In
the body is
often tassel
(fig. 19-16).
Morphol
various kin
are impres
matic, how
tions in l
permit oth
such as bu
flying. Rem
be traced b
that was sr
grade, sor
terrestrial.
The mo
of the fos

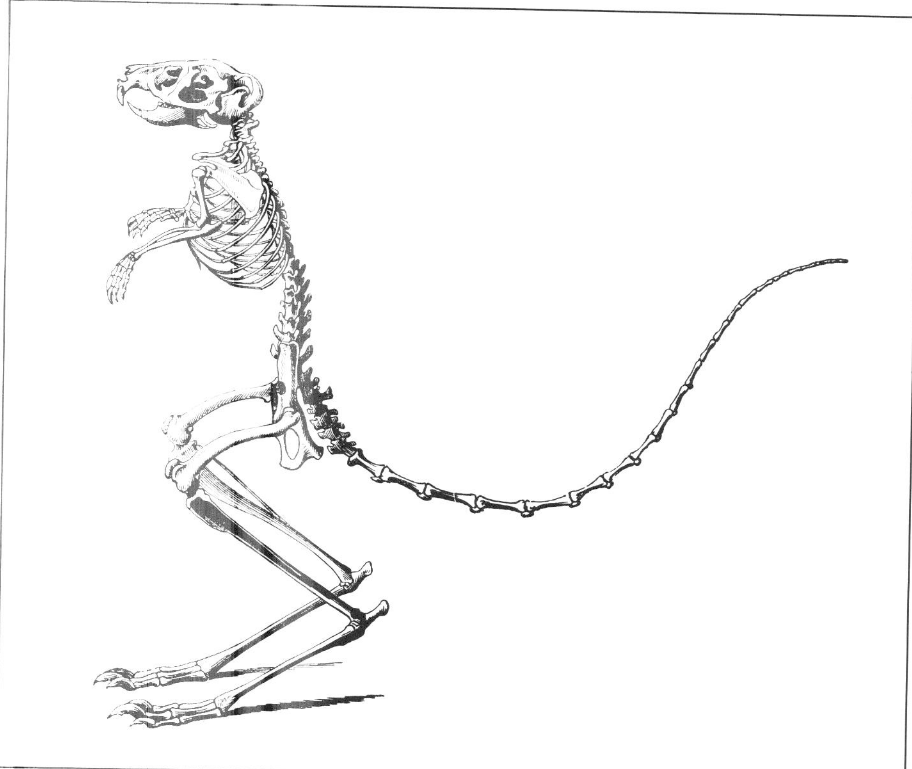

19-16. Skeleton of a jerboa, a ricochetal rodent. Pen-and-ink. Artist unknown. From R. Owen. *On the Anatomy of Vertebrates* 2:366, 1866.

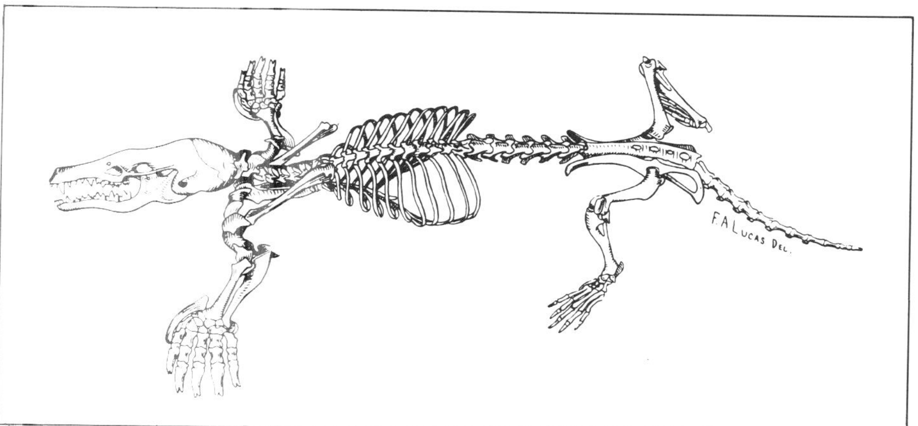

19-17. Skeleton of a mole, a fossorial mammal. Pen-and-ink, by F. A. Lucas. From R. T. Hatt. *Guide to the Hall of Biology of Mammals*, American Museum of Natural History Science Guide 76:32. 1946.

adapt them for digging in the earth and for traveling through the dark, narrow confines of their tunnels (fig. 19-17). They feature a body tapering at both ends: short neck; short, powerful fore limbs that project outward from the sides of the body; large, shovellike forefeet; velvety, reversible fur; and reduced ears, eyes, and tail (senses of smell and touch greatly magnified; sight and hearing reduced). Other burrowers such as pocket gophers, ground squirrels, and armadillos are less specialized than the moles.

In spite of profound modifications in the body of the natatorial (aquatic) whales and porpoises, all organs of their terrestrial ancestors are present, although some are vestigial. They have a streamlined, almost hairless, body sheathed with blubber (replacing hair as a heat-retaining mechanism—necessary because water is such a good conductor of heat), a neck shortened by fusion or shortening of the cervical vertebrae or both, a skull telescoped to place the nostrils on top of the head, and a thorax and lungs strengthened to withstand great pressure (up to a ton per square inch) without air leakage. Lips, eyelids, external ears, hind limbs, and skin glands have been virtually eliminated; bones of the arm have been shortened; digits are encased in skin and tough connective tissue to form a paddle (fig. 19-18); and the hind end of the body has been modified into boneless flukes for propulsion.

Among vertebrates, the air is almost exclusively the realm of birds. Nevertheless, the flight adaptations of bats, the only mammals capable of flying, are so good that many bats are more agile in flight than any bird. Modifications for volant locomotion include a forward shift of the center of gravity (through enlargement of the thorax and diminution of the abdomen and hind extremities), enlargement and ventral keeling of the sternum to support strong pectoral muscles, strengthened shoulder joint, elongated forearm, and enormously elongated and webbed fingers forming a wing (fig. 19-19).

Although morphological modifications related to locomotion are profound, other behavioral adaptations are notable as well. Many anatomical characteristics are associated with feeding behavior, for example: the elongated neck and fore limbs of the giraffe, a tree leaf browser; the baleen and cavernous mouth of the filter-feeding whales; and the great claws that enable anteaters to rip open termite nests. The concealing coloration of many predators facilitates stalking; the long face of horses al-

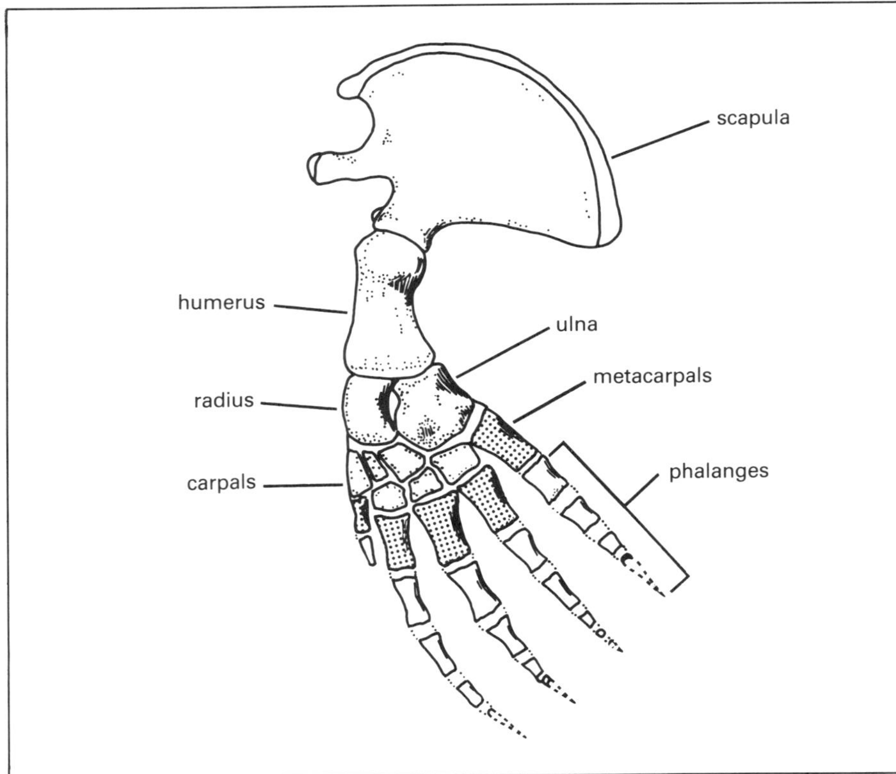

19-18. Fore limb of a cetacean, a natatorial mammal. Pen-and-ink on film, by Irene Jewett and Jo-Ellen Trecartin, redrawn from A. B. Howell, *Aquatic Mammals* (Charles C. Thomas Publisher, 1930).

lows watchfu
long grass.
Some modi
at least in pai
Most of these
Large size is
hippo, elepha
deter attacks
appear to be l
is (aardwolf).
(skunk) or cor
ruptive color
concealing in
pearance (ze
Thick hide,
woolly hair m
tors (rhino, c
spines (porcu
rec, echidna
and carapace
active repelle
Claws (cats
horns (bovids
and hooves (c
tive defense.

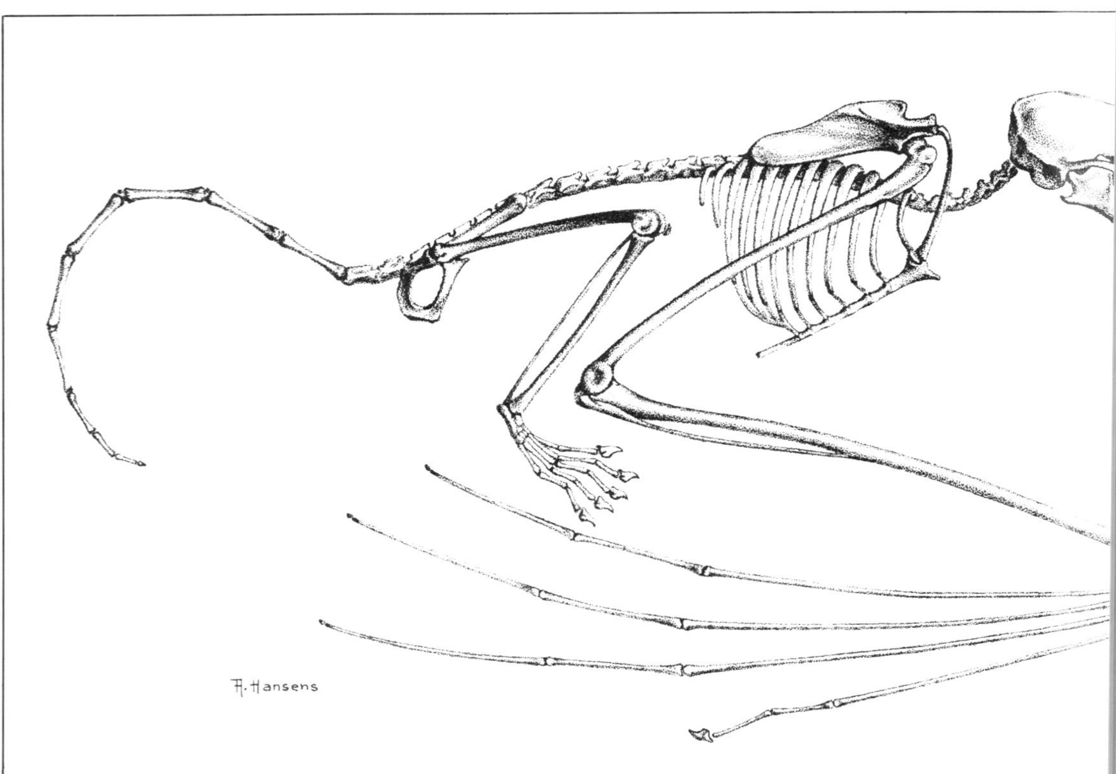

19-19. Skeleton of a bat (*Icaronycteris index*, from the Eocene of Wyoming), an aerial mammal. Lithographic crayon on coquille board, by Aline Hansens. From G. L. Jepsen, in *Biology of Bats*, vol. 1, edited by W. A. Wimsatt (Academic Press, 1970).

19-20. Enlarged nose of proboscis monkey, a sexual adornment (lower, female; upper, male). Carbon pencil on Video board, by Alice R. Tangerini.

19-21. Adaptation to cold and hot climates. Small, furry ears of the arctic hare and large, naked ears of the desert jackrabbit. Black Prismacolor pencil on coquille board, by Nancy A. Payzant.

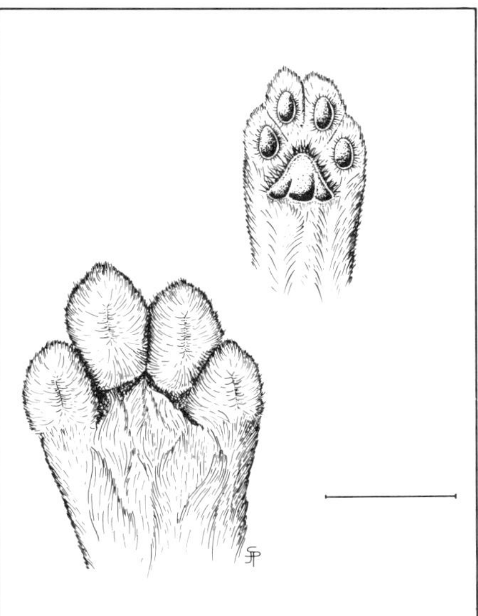

19-22. Left forepaw of bobcat (top) and lynx (bottom). The large, heavily furred feet of the lynx facilitate travel over deep snow, while the smaller, short-haired feet of the bobcat are adapted to snowless terrain. Pen-and-ink on Bristol board, by Stasia Penkoff.

When a morphological feature is exaggerated in one sex but not in the other, it probably has sexual significance. Skin glands and skin coloration often communicate sexual messages. Coloration of the hairy coat may distinguish the sexes (saki, nilgai) or the dominant male from other males in a herd (black buck). Manes and beards are primarily sexual adornments. Antlers, horns, and tusks may be badges of sex as well as functioning in defense. Unusual enlargement of the snout is peculiar to males in a few species (elephant seal, proboscis monkey) (fig. 19-20). Large size may make males more attractive in courtship or confer an advantage in sexual combat.

Factors in the environment—climate, substrate, and vegetation, to name but a few—also mold body form. Take, for example, heat and cold. As size increases, volume grows more slowly than surface area. Therefore, it is physiologically advantageous for mammals to be larger in cold climates, smaller in hot. Extremities such as ears, however, are smaller and more furry in cold (to lessen heat loss and reduce risk of freezing), larger and more naked in heat (fig. 19-21).

Most mammals prefer to travel on firm ground. Those that frequent other substrates often have specialized feet. In snow, lynx and snowshoe hare have broad, heavily furred feet (fig. 19-22) and caribou have broad, splayed hooves. Similar adaptations assist marsh-dwellers (several species of deer and antelopes) and species that travel on loose sand (camel, jerboa). Rock-hoppers such as klipspringer, chamois, and mountain goat have hooves specialized for nonskid traction.

Trees and forests obviously bring about climbing and browsing specializations, along with body form adapted to quick movement through narrow spaces. Bodies tend to be narrow (wisent) or tear-shaped (duiker, tapir, agouti, paca). Grassy plains, on the other hand, evoke burrowing and grazing adaptations and long, thin limbs suitable for speedy locomotion.

MEASUREMENTS

In spite of great variety, the measurements of mammals can be sorted into a few broad categories: external measurements from fresh or preserved specimens, cranial measurements made on cleaned skulls, and measurements of postcranial bones and various organs. The illustrator must understand measurement definitions and conventions in order to measure specimens or use measurements from literature accurately to establish scale and proportions in drawings.

External Measurements

External measurements of a fresh specimen are recorded on the specimen label, usually in metric units. Measurements of mammals are always straight-line distances, even in the largest species (never following body curves) (see fig. 2-14). Four or five measurements commonly are recorded on specimen labels (fig. 19-23). Since they are always recorded in the same order, the measurements are listed without identification on the labels. They may be listed in vertical columnar form or consecutively (horizontally). Measurements that are incomplete are enclosed in brackets. The order is as follows:

1. *Total length:* distance from tip of snout to tip of last tail vertebra, not including terminal hairs.
2. *Length of tail vertebrae:* distance from base of tail to tip of last caudal vertebra.
3. *Length of hind foot:* distance from heel to tip of claw of longest toe. O
erature,
sometime
tials c.u..
—with cla
4. *Length of*
tance fro
to tip of e
5. *Weight.*

Labels of
before 1930
measuremen
total length.
Since then,
the universa
and many
weight as we

On larger
shoulder so
This is the
length of t
from tip of
highest poin

In Europ
elsewhere.

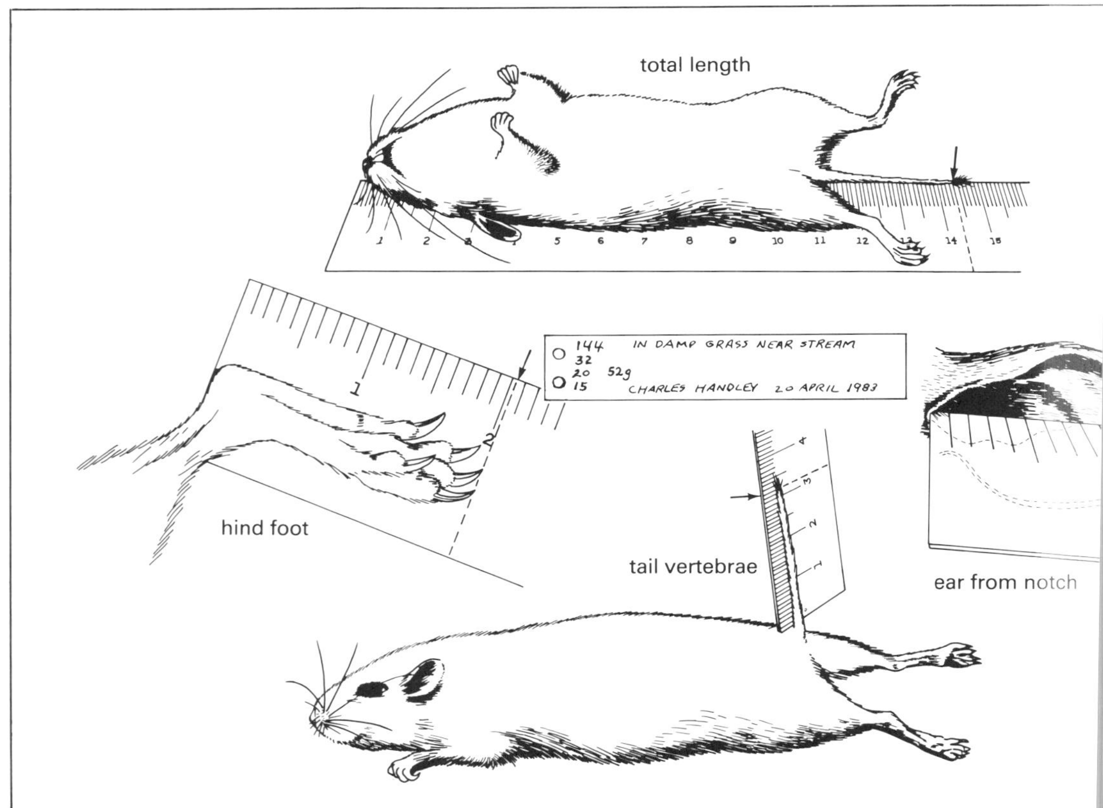

19-23. Taking and recording external measurements from a fresh specimen, North American style. Pen-and-ink on film, by Irene Jewett, redrawn from Smithsonian Institution Information Leaflet no. 380.

measurements may not be taken exactly as they are in North America. Furthermore, these measurements have varied to some extent from country to country and from time to time. Thus, external measurements on labels and in literature must be used with caution unless their definition is known or until equivalence can be established. The standard European measurements are:

1. *Length of head and body:* distance from tip of snout to base of tail (or to anus).
2. *Length of tail:* distance from base of tail (or from anus) to tip of last tail vertebra (or to end of tail hairs). Theoretically, the North American total length measurement can be obtained by adding head and body length and tail length, unless terminal hairs have been included in the tail measurement.
3. *Length of hind foot:* always measured from extremity of heel to tip of longest toe, not including claw (s.u.—*sine ungulus*). Thus, European hind foot length never can be interchanged with its American equivalent.
4. *Length of ear:* now measured from tip to notch at base, as in North America; formerly measured from tip to crown of head.

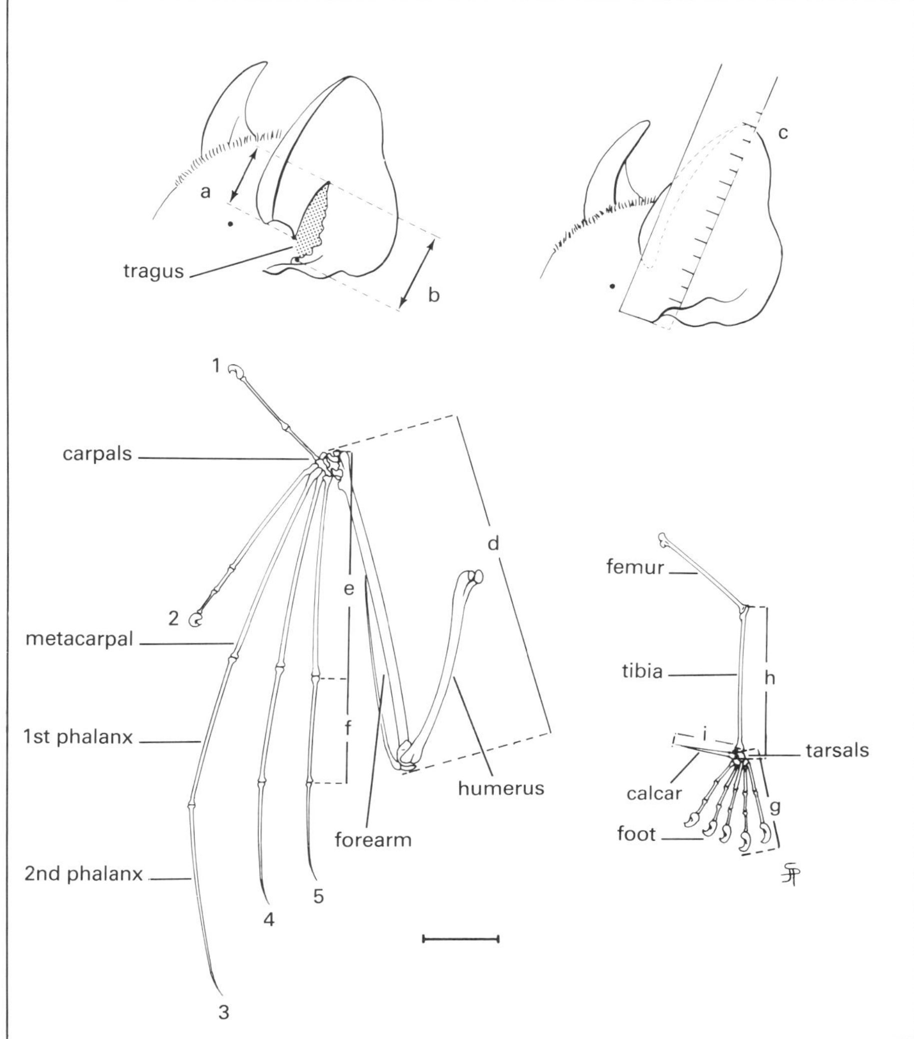

19-24. External measurements peculiar to bats: *(a)* and *(b)* two ways of measuring tragus; *(c)* length of ear; *(d)*, *(e)*, *(f)* wing; *(g)*, *(h)*, *(i)* leg and foot. Pen-and-ink on Bristol board, by Rosemary Calvert (ears) and Stasia Penkoff (wing and leg).

External Measurements of Bats

Some measurements are unique to bats (fig. 19-24). Wingspread and length of tragus (the small bladelike appendage at the anterior base of the ear) can be taken accurately only on fresh specimens. The others, all measurements of bones, should be taken only on preserved specimens. (Because of shrinkage in drying, the same measurements taken on fresh specimens are not exactly comparable.)

1. *Wingspread:* distance between tips of fully extended wings.
2. *Length of tragus:* distance from anterior base of tragus to tip—actually the "length of the tragus blade" (fig. 19-24a). Also, sometimes measured from tip of tragus to lowest point of foliations at base—actually the "total length of the tragus"—blade, plus foliations (fig. 19-24b). Method of measuring should be stated.
3. *Length of ear* (fig. 19-24c): measured from tip to notch, as in other mammals.
4. *Length of forearm* (fig. 19-24d): greatest length of radius-ulna, including carpals (extremity of wrist to extremity of elbow). Caution: always verify that the forearm is complete and not broken. Feel the elbow. It is helpful if the specimen preparator leaves part of the humerus attached so that it can be felt.
5. *Length of metacarpal* (fig. 19-24e): greatest length of metacarpal, including carpals (3, 4, and 5 customarily are measured).
6. *Length of phalanx* (fig. 19-24f): greatest length of each individual phalanx, joint to joint. On each finger these are numbered from the inside out.
7. *Length of hind foot* (fig. 19-24g): greatest length of fully extended, flattened foot, from tip of claw of longest toe to inner

edge of calcar at junction with tibia.

8. *Length of tibia* (fig. 19-24h): greatest length of tibia, from knee to outer edge of calcar at foot. Usually the head of the tibia can be seen through the skin at the knee. If it cannot be seen, use a sharp scalpel to slice the skin carefully at the knee until the head of the tibia is exposed. Do this only with permission of curatorial staff.
9. *Length of calcar* (fig. 19-24i): greatest length of bony calcar, not including cartilaginous extension, from tip to edge of tibia at base.

External Measurements of Cetacea

Because the external form of whales and porpoises is so different from that of other mammals, an entirely different set of sixteen external measurements is used to describe them (J. G. Mead, *Cetacean Data Record*, Smithsonian Institution Form SI-2367, 1980) (fig. 19-25). All measurements except 12 through 16 are taken in a straight line parallel to the body axis; 12 through 16 are taken point to point.

1. Snout to apex of melon
2. Snout to center of eye
3. Snout to angle of mouth
4. Snout to anterior insertion of flipper
5. Snout to end of ventral grooves
6. Snout to genital slit (center)
7. Snout to anus (center)
8. Snout to notch of flukes (total length)
9. Snout to insertion of dorsal fin
10. Snout to tip of dorsal fin
11. Fluke notch to anus (center)
12. Maximum girth
13. Flipper length, anterior
14. Flipper width, maximum
15. Fluke width
16. Dorsal fin height

Cranial Measurements

In studies of classification and relationships, the skull often is more valuable as a reference than the skin. It varies in overall size and shape, and it is composed of about three dozen bones that individually vary in size and shape. It has numerou
tions, crests,
fossae and f
vary in size.
Most import
teeth, signifi
classification

Some of th
described by
words, and
mented adec
ments alone
some sort ca
scribe most
sequently, c
are routinely
works, and
able (*A Man*
A. F. DeBlas
see Bibliogra
ever, a few f
measuremen
dard impres
terms of it
width (fig. 19

1. *Condylob*
extremes
(the kno
vertebra)
premaxil
2. *Greatest*
posterior
usually s
praoccip
point of
maxillae.
sals (in w
as occipi
times me
sors.
3. *Maxillar*
Alveolar
veolus (t
riormost
alveolus
lary toot
carnivor
(b) Cro
point of
point of
vores). I
(marsupi
4. *Zygomat*
distance
zygomat
5. *Interorbi*

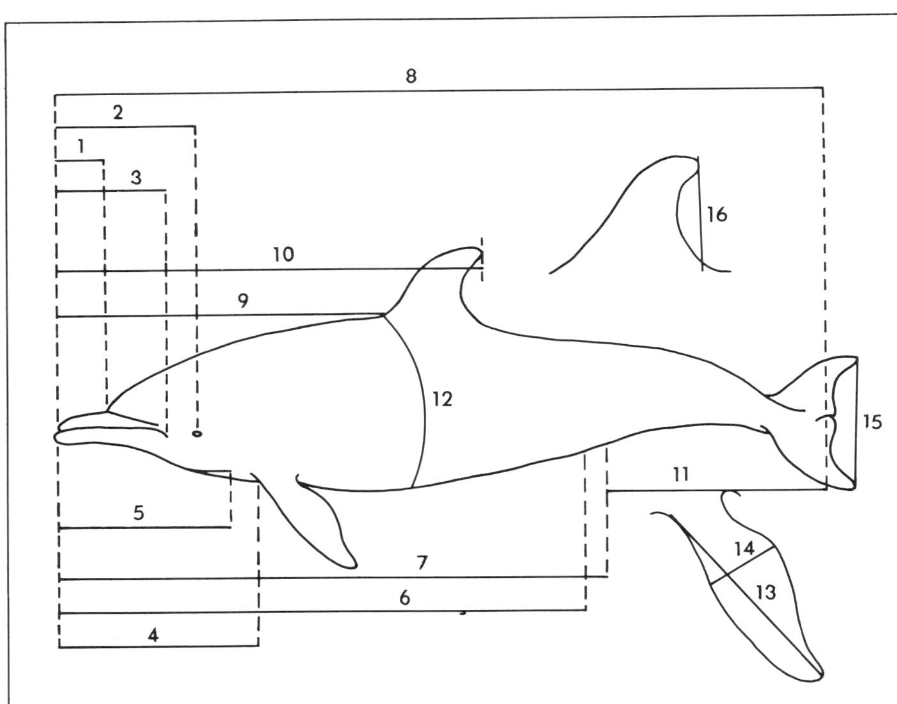

19-25. External measurements of Cetacea. Pen-and-ink on film, by Irene Jewett, redrawn from K. S. Norris, *Journal of Mammalogy* 42:475, 1961.

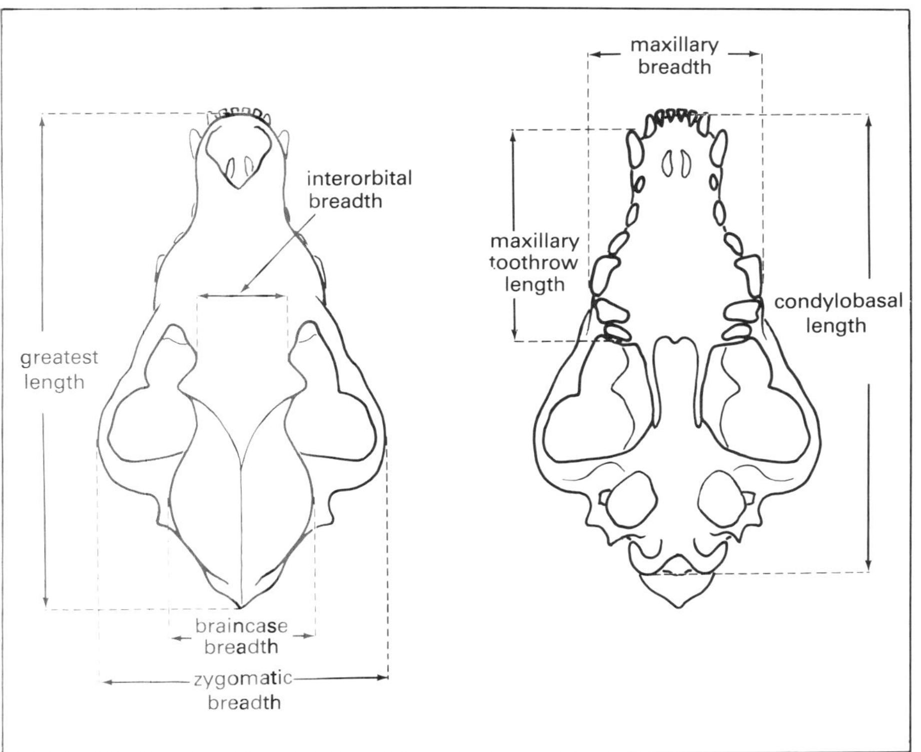

19-26. Cranial measurements on skull of a dog. Pen-and-ink on Bristol board, by T. Britt Griswold.

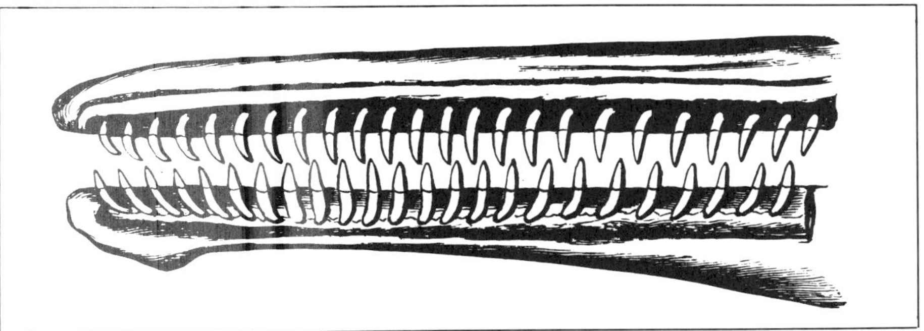

19-27. Homodont dentition of a porpoise. Pen-and-ink. Artist unknown. From W. H. Flower and R. Lydekker, *An Introduction to the Study of Mammals, Living and Extinct* (Adam and Charles Black, London, 1891).

tance across frontals, between orbits.

6. *Maxillary breadth:* greatest distance between outer edges of alveoli of cheek teeth (bats, rodents, marsupials) or between tips of maxillary processes (insectivores).
7. *Braincase breadth:* greatest distance between outer edges of braincase, or between other points (such as mastoid processes) that give an equivalent measurement.

Tooth Nomenclature

Since teeth are extremely varied in mammals, it is not surprising that they are much used in classification. Furthermore, they are so hard that they survive the ravages of time better than most other parts of the body. As a consequence, the best and sometimes only fossil remains are teeth. They also reveal much about the habits of their bearers. Thus, teeth are used by neontologists and paleontologists alike, both for classification and reconstruction of behavioral and ecological patterns.

In mammals, teeth occur only in the premaxillae, maxillae, and mandibles—never in other bones of the palate. They are always marginal, in a single row, and they are thecodont—that is, they are rooted in an alveolus or pit. Most mammals are heterodont—their teeth have varying shapes and functions. Only the armadillos, porpoises, and toothed whales are homodont, with teeth all alike or varying only in size, as is characteristic of fish, amphibians, and reptiles (fig. 19-27).

Characteristically, the complete mammalian dentition includes four distinct kinds of teeth. At the anterior end of the toothrows are the incisors, which are typically small and function as nippers. Next are the canines, one in each toothrow. Usually long, slender, and dagger-like, the canines grasp, pierce, and rip. In modern mammals, the anterior teeth—incisors and canines—are always single-rooted and relatively simple-crowned. On the other hand, the cheek teeth—premolars and molars—may have several roots and quite complex crowns. Generally, the premolars have a shearing function, while the molars are for crushing or grinding mastication.

The various categories of teeth are designated by the letters I, C, P, and M. Individual teeth are numbered from front to back in the jaw (fig. 19-28). Thus, the full (or ideal) placental dentition includes on each side of the face three pairs of incisors above and below, a canine in each jaw, four pairs of premolars, and three pairs of molars above and below—twenty-two teeth on each side, forty-four teeth in all:

$$\mathrm{I}\ \frac{123}{123}\quad \mathrm{C}\ \frac{1}{1}\quad \mathrm{P}\ \frac{1234}{1234}\quad \mathrm{M}\ \frac{123}{123}\quad \times 2 = 44$$

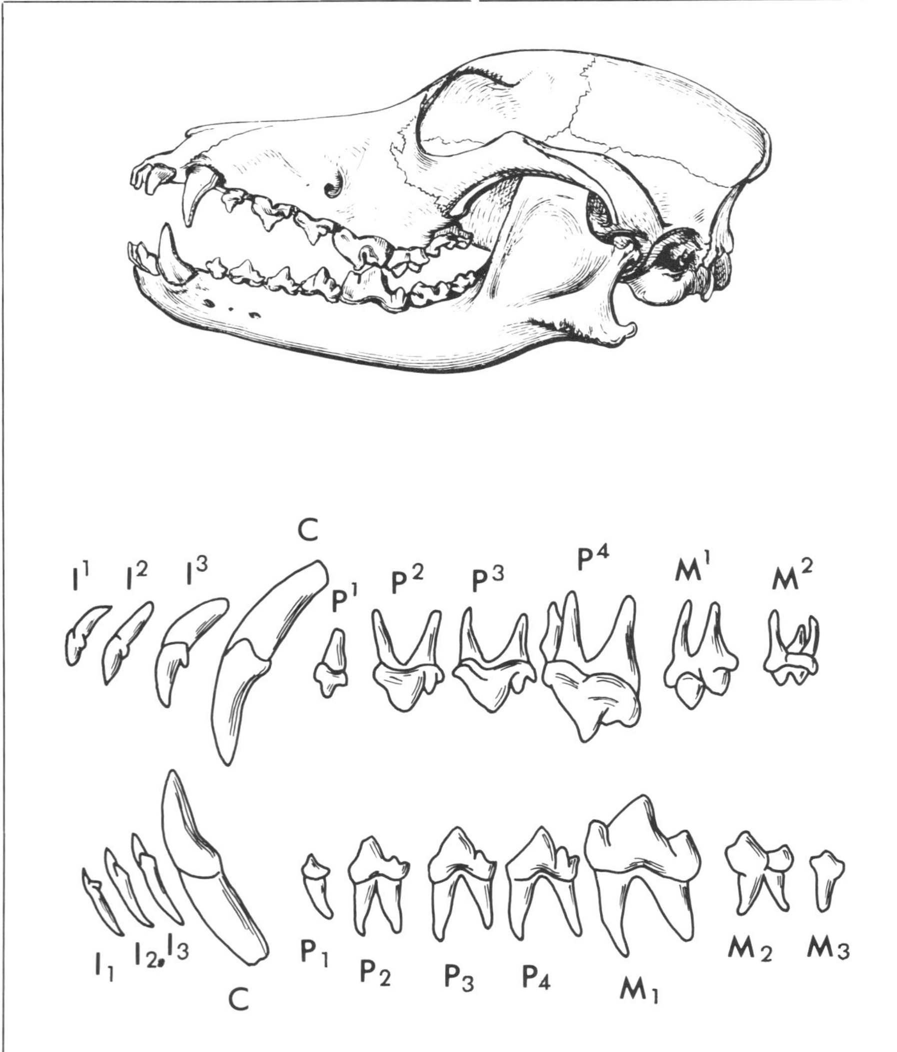

19-28. Heterodont dentition of a dog. Pen-and-ink on film, by Irene Jewett, redrawn from W. H. Flower and R. Lydekker, *An Introduction to the Study of Mammals, Living and Extinct* (Adam and Charles Black, London, 1891).

Using these numerical designations, there are several ways of distinguishing individual teeth. Any of the following notations are acceptable. The second upper incisor could be I$\underline{2}$, I^2, or I2; the second lower incisor, I$\overline{2}$, I_2, or i2.

Another method of describing a dentition considers only the total of each category of tooth, not the exact sequence of individual teeth. With this method, the complete eutherian (placental) dentition appears as:

$$\mathrm{I}\,\frac{3\text{-}3}{3\text{-}3}\quad \mathrm{C}\,\frac{1}{1}\quad \mathrm{P}\,\frac{4\text{-}4}{4\text{-}4}\quad \mathrm{M}\,\frac{3\text{-}3}{3\text{-}3} = 44$$

Since the teeth normally are the same in the right and left sides of the mouth, this also can be written as:

$$\mathrm{I}\,\frac{3}{3}\quad \mathrm{C}\,\frac{1}{1}\quad \mathrm{P}\,\frac{4}{4}\quad \mathrm{M}\,\frac{3}{3} \times 2 = 44$$

Or, in even more abbreviated form:

$$\frac{3\text{-}1\text{-}4\text{-}3}{3\text{-}1\text{-}4\text{-}3} \times 2 = 44$$

This dental formula is a shorthand way of describing a mammal's dentition.

The ideal placental formula is

found only am
moles. The Af
and some arr
and porpoises
formula, but
mammals hav
even are edent
altogether (ir
pangolins, so
New World an
a formula of

3-1-4-
3-1-4-

human being,

2-1-2-
2-1-2-

gray squirrel,

1-0-2-
1-0-1-

and a house

1-0-0
1-0-0

The primitive
mula is assu

5-1-3
4-1-3

With so m
surprising th
vocabulary
teeth. Orient
in tooth nome
before the lit
can be used
prehensive
Manual of
DeBlase and
liography).

COLOR C

Papers o
mals descri
of a color
dards and C
Robert Ridg
in spite of its

standard most often used. This is because it was developed for biologists and has so many hues and shades (1,115 in all, covering the whole spectrum). It is particularly useful to mammalogists because of the extent of the gray–brown–orange range. Unfortunately, good copies of Ridgway are becoming scarce, and many taxonomists do not have access to it. Consequently, other less-adequate standards, such as A. Maerz and M. R. Paul's *A Dictionary of Color*, the *Munsell Book of Color*, and the *Atlas de los Colores* by C. Villalobos often must be substituted. The National Bureau of Standards has produced a dictionary of color terms and an array of accurately reproducible color chips, but only 267 colors are represented, and only about 50 of these are potentially useful to mammalogists. Inasmuch as it is truly priceless, Ridgway's guide, when it is available, should be used with even more care than the specimens.

When making comparisons, the plates of any color guide should be masked to protect them from accidental soiling and scratches. The mask should be black and should have an opening only large enough to expose one color at a time. Not only does the mask protect the plates from mechanical damage, it also reduces confusion and distraction by hiding the other colors of the array from view until each in turn is used for comparison.

Ordinary room lighting seldom is adequate for accurate determination of color of pelage (hairy coat). Descriptions and comparisons should be made in natural north light or in artificial light adjusted to simulate daylight (such as Examolite).

In making color comparisons, allow for variation. Users of museum collections must seek out the average and be wary of extremes in determining color. Seldom are all specimens in a series alike. The pelage of young animals commonly differs from that of older individuals, and females often differ from males.

Seasonal variation is most troublesome. As a rule, fresh pelage immediately following a molt is brighter and darker, sometimes dramatically so, than old, worn, faded pelage preceding a molt. Bats that roost in small quarters with poor air circulation are subjected to chemical alteration of pelage coloration. The ammonia-charged atmosphere of the roost quickly changes grayish or blackish hair of fresh pelage to brown, orange, or yellow. In the next molt, the bat temporarily regains its darker coloration. So striking is the change that, until recently, many bats were thought to be dichromatic! Another factor responsible for an apparent seasonal change in color is hair length. In many species, hair becomes longer and more fluffy in winter, usually rendering the animal paler.

Vicissitudes of preservation and storage can bring about alteration of color that will confuse the unwary. Fortunately, there are clues that warn of such changes. "Foxing," or reddening of the pelage, resulting from exposure to sun or chemicals, is the most common modification. Beware of unusually bright, reddish, possibly shriveled or warped specimens from particularly rainy localities. To keep the specimens from rotting, the collector may have resorted to sun-drying. If a specimen was already rotting at the time of preparation, alum may have been applied to set the hair. The result would be a reddened, hardened specimen, probably with patches of hair missing. Also, a fumigant such as paradichlorobenzene (PDB) may fox all the specimens in a storage case if too much is used or if the case is carelessly placed where it can be heated by sun rays or a radiator. Most older museums contain once-valuable old dismounted exhibit specimens in their research collections, faded to a pitiful pallor by decades of exposure to daylight.

The color of specimens brought from the field as dry, flat skins to be soaked, relaxed, and stuffed later in the museum may change so drastically in the soaking that they become useless for color comparison. Entomologists sometimes cause modifications in pelage color by washing fresh specimens in a detergent solution to dislodge ectoparasites. In the process, hair oils are removed and changes in coloration result. Collectors should always indicate washing or exposure to sun on specimen labels.

RECONSTRUCTIONS

It is common in paleontology to reconstruct missing parts of skulls, skeletons, or teeth, but only rarely are these parts missing or incomplete in Recent mammals. When they are, the techniques of reconstruction employed in paleontology can be applied (see chapters 13 and 14).

In cases when neither whole specimens (in fluid or frozen) nor photographs are available for a species of Recent mammal represented in collections only by skins, skulls, and/or skeletons, a reconstruction must be attempted. Size and proportions can be inferred from the skin, skeleton, label measurements, or published measurements. If a skin is available, it will provide information on length, distribution, and coloration of fur. Soaking with a wetting agent such as dioctyl sodium sulfosuccinate (aerosol solution) will soften and relax ears, lips, snout, hands, feet, and wings so that their shape and characteristics can be examined. Of course, permission from the curatorial staff should be obtained before wetting a specimen.

The skull will reveal size of the eye, dimensions and shape of the snout, and position of the ear. Comparison of the subject skull with those of related species for which whole specimens or photographs are available will reveal which can be used as models for various parts—for example, the eye of one, the snout of another, and perhaps the mouth of a third. The illustrator must, however, be very cautious in using other species as references for reconstructions.

MAMMAL LITERATURE

The literature of mammalogy is not as large as that of some other sciences, but it is quite scattered. Nevertheless, a good background knowledge can be obtained from a few journals devoted exclusively to mammalogy, including *Journal of Mammalogy*, *Mammalia*, *Mammal Review*, *Säugetierkundliche Mitteilungen*, and *Zeitschrift für Säugetierkunde;* from a few journals devoted to mammal specialties, such as *Folia Primatologica*, *Primates*, *Carnivore*, and *Investigations on Cetacea;* and from a few excellent books, most of them still in print (see Bibliography).

There is considerable variety in the field of illustrating mammals. Artists familiar with mammalogy, anatomy, and natural history are likely to get more out of their work and produce superior artwork. Even a brief glimpse of the disciplines mammalogy comprises, the origin of mammals, mammalian characteristics, the rudiments of classification, and an appreciation of variation in body form and func-

tion and its co
ior and envi
should be hel
beginning to v
Two of the
sources availa
erature (perio
museums (spe
advisers). To r
seum opportu
should know h
specimens pr
ways, and ou
in taking and i
ments of spe
the nomencla
color compari
contriving rec

20/Illustrating Animals in Their Habitats

Trudy Nicholson, Patrick J. Lynch, and Wayne Trimm

Illustrating animals in their habitats, or wildlife illustration, differs from other more formal scientific illustration disciplines because, in addition to portraying the animal's physical form, the wildlife artist must convey a sense of the vitality and essence of the animal, much as might be experienced in the field. In contrast to photographs that capture only a fleeting moment in an animal's life, a wildlife illustration should be a summation of the artist's informed impressions of the animal's typical stances, behaviors, habitat, and anatomy. The illustrator has the freedom to transcend the vagaries and arbitrariness of an individual animal in a particular situation, to bring to the audience a more profound insight into the ecology of a species. The illustration may be used to promote conservation, to spotlight endangered species. Wildlife artwork is often used in publications to balance the spontaneity of color photography with a more reflective, balanced view of the subject, or to depict behaviors and situations not easily photographed (fig. 20-1; see figs. C-3, C-9). This often entails long hours of field observation and library research on the life history of the subject animal. Although the conventions of wildlife artwork place heavy demands on the drawing and painting skills of the artist, the ability to render anatomic detail is just the beginning of the process. To be truly successful, wildlife artwork must go beyond the particulars of visual fact to convey a sense of the animal's character (fig. 20-2; see figs. C-6, C-16, 11-2, 11-9, 18-23).

FINDING WORK AS A WILDLIFE ARTIST

As a profession, wildlife illustration is dominated by freelance illustrators, most of whom also do other types of commercial or scientific illustration. Full-time, salaried jobs in wildlife artwork are very rare and much sought. These jobs are usually offered by large natural history museums, the U.S. Department of the Interior, county or state park and environmental offices, natural history magazines, zoos, or aquariums that have a constant, long-term need for animal illustrations. For most wildlife illustrators (particularly those at the beginning of their careers), the freelance market for animal illustrations is the most practical route to a job that involves painting or drawing animals.

The majority of freelance work in natural history illustration is done for publishers of scientific books, educational texts, and natural history books for general audiences. Wildlife artists who specialize in these markets must have a good understanding of the needs of art directors and authors and be able to deliver on short notice publication-quality illustrations of a wide variety of natural history subjects. The availability and relatively low cost of color photographs has largely eliminated the market for elaborately rendered color wildlife art as a routine part of many publication projects—such illustrations are simply too expensive for most budgets. The typical freelance job will more likely be a black-and-white line (or color mechanical) drawing explaining some point of animal behavior, ecology, or anatomy (fig. 20-3; see figs. C-35, 9-8, 20-13). In addition to wide knowledge of natural history, artists specializing in book illustration must have a solid understanding of line-art and color-separation techniques (see chapter 27). There is a continuing (if smaller) market for more complex, very detailed color art of wild animals, but the competition for these choice assignments is fierce. Artists new to the market would do better to concentrate on the more routine illustrations while building a portfolio containing a range of illustration styles and techniques.

Magazines specializing in natural history, outdoor sports, and scientific subject matter have a continuous need for good natural history illustrations and form the next-largest market for the freelance wildlife illustrator. The budgets for individual illustrations are typically more generous in magazine illustration, and elaborate color artwork commissions are therefore more routine. Illustrators interested in pursuing magazine illustration must be particularly conscious of the current stylistic trends in both natural history and general editorial illustration. The best guide to the types of illustrations most often required are the pages of the magazines themselves. As in book illustration, most magazine art is commissioned to expand upon the text of the articles, not to decorate them. In addition to excellent artistic technique, this requires the illustrator to bring strong conceptual and explanatory skills to these proj-

20-2. Great gray owl in American elm, *Strix nebulosa* in *Ulmus americana*, painted from slides and photographs taken by Art Borkent at Amherst Island, Ontario. The tree and sky were modified to present a balanced composition and further enhance the impression of a windy day. Transparent watercolor on smooth Arches paper, by Barry Flahey. (Original is in color.) © Barry Flahey, 1982.

Facing page:
20-1. Golden lion tamarins, *Leontopithecus rosalia*. The tamarins were drawn from observation, sketches, and photographs of tamarins in the captive breeding program at the National Zoo in Washington, DC. The habitat was drawn from photographs and information in *Wildlife of the Forests*, by Ann and Myron Sutton (Harry N. Abrams, 1979), and supplemented by magazine photographs and videotaped television programs. Ink on scratchboard, by Trudy Nicholson © 1986.

ects (see fig. 20-11). Since most magazines have a distinctive editorial style in illustration, they will hire only those illustrators who have researched the magazine and understand the art director's needs.

Jobs with natural history institutions can be particularly rewarding because of the opportunities they afford the artist to work closely with museum curators and exhibit designers, scientists, and zoo professionals in the creation of educational materials for the public. Some illustrators receive their initial commissions as an outgrowth of active involvement with local natural history projects and naturalists, but many museums have not been able to establish relationships with skilled wildlife artists. It is always worth approaching local natural history institutions for freelance work. Federal and state agencies—such as the U.S. Fish and Wildlife Service; departments of agriculture; state environmental, agricultural extension, and conservation agencies; state parks; and the National Park Service—also commission wildlife artwork to illustrate their publications and public exhibits.

The widespread appeal of animal artwork gives the wildlife illus-

20-3. Round-tailed muskrat, *Neofiber alleni*. The muskrat was sketched from a live captive collected by the artist. The habitat plants were sketched and photographed in the field, and the final drawing was composed and finished in the studio. Ink on scratchboard, by Nancy R. Halliday © 1983.

20-4. Lion-tailed macaque, *Macaca silenus*, in motion. Sketcl zoo and rendered later in the studio. Pencil on paper, by Lois

trator a range of alternatives to conventional commercial publication markets and institutional commissions. Many successful wildlife illustrators earn a living solely through sales of original artwork, specialty items such as greeting cards and posters, or by selling limited-edition prints of their work. Most illustrators earning the majority of their income through wildlife artwork sell original artwork and prints through galleries and wildlife art shows. They also do a variety of book, magazine, institutional, and other work, supplementing this income with other commercial or scientific illustration jobs during the inevitable "dry" periods all freelancers must face. Federal and state duck-stamp competitions provide exposure and success for a fortunate few (see fig. C-23). The rules and contracts for all competitions should be read carefully before entering.

Career Training for Wildlife Illustration

Although there are no formal programs or degrees in wildlife illustration, most experienced natural history illustrators share similar backgrounds. Because the conventions of wildlife art are extremely representational (almost photorealistic) and so much depends on the illustrator's ability to capture subtle nuances of detail and animal character, wildlife illustrators must be very accomplished draftsmen and painters (fig. 20-4; see figs. C-3, C-16, 5-32). Most professional natural history artists have extensive formal training in commercial or fine art and may supplement these artistic skills with formal training in biology or natural history at the college level. Most also have years of experience in study-

ing and obse
formal trai
however, n
the field if
undertake a
self-educati
coming inv
community
thusiasts an
studying th
illustrators.
the Guild
Illustrators,
hold works
educate ill
natural hist
tration. An
the Society
Appendix).

tors are also active bird-watchers, environmentalists, or conservationists.

INSTRUMENTS AND MATERIALS

Most of the tools and equipment unique to wildlife illustration are used to make sketching and collecting information in the field easier for the artist. Field experience is the best teacher for deciding how best to support and carry equipment for the individual artist. Most illustrators eventually decide to travel light, taking along only the minimum amount of drawing tools and paper to enhance mobility and avoid distractions during field observation of animals. Items to be avoided include anything that makes a lot of noise and shiny metallic objects such as pens or metal clipboards that can flash in the sunlight. Colorful or dark sketchbook covers, clothing, and tools will often draw unwanted attention from bees and wasps. Avoid black, bright red, yellow, orange, or green; safer colors are pastels, white, and khaki. Because wildlife sketching and field observation entail long periods of sitting or standing in one place, items such as insect repellent, sunscreen, and suitable field clothing are even more essential to the wildlife illustrator than they might be to a moving hiker or birder.

Weather can be an important determining factor in selecting media for field use. (See below for further details on selecting media when working outside the studio.) In the studio, most wildlife illustrators rely on standard illustration tools covered elsewhere in this volume under the chapters on various illustration techniques.

Large amounts of useful visual information can be quickly collected with a camera to supplement written notes and field sketches of animals and their habitat. Although it is not possible to walk up to a wild bird and take its picture, it is possible to take a picture of the branch where it sat and thereby collect more information in a split second than hours of habitat sketching might produce. Drawings are still invaluable, however, for recording details not likely to show in a photo, such as leaf venation.

Optical Devices

"The Glass of Fashion," by C. A. Berman (see Bibliography) is an excellent discussion of binoculars and other optics for naturalists in the field.

Binoculars: 7 × 35 (7 power, 35mm object lens diameter) or 10 × 50 lightweight optics made by major camera manufacturers, principally Nikon and Leica. Avoid the small, inexpensive field glasses sold for sport or theater use, as their optics and alignment are generally not adequate for heavy use and will result in strained eyesight when used for long periods. They also impart a strong color cast (usually blue) to the subject due to cheap glass or inadequate antiflare coating of the optical elements.

Spotting telescope: 20- to 25-power, with sturdy tripod. Good-quality spotting telescopes are often sold with a choice of eyepieces that determine the magnifying power and field of view of the telescope. Select the brightest 20- to 25-power eyepiece available from the manufacturer and avoid the generally inferior zoom optics. Eyepieces with a higher power produce a field of view too dark and narrow for most tastes. A spotting telescope mounted on a sturdy tripod is particularly useful to the artist in situations where the subject is stationary for a period of time, making it easy to shift the eyes from subject to paper and back again without constant reorientation of binoculars. This also frees both hands for sketching and supporting the paper.

Magnifier: hand-held magnifying lens or loupe for examining slides and small subjects.

Camera: 35mm single-lens reflex (SLR); should allow manual exposure metering.

Telephoto lenses: 300 to 500mm; in general, the longer and better, but lenses longer than 400 mm are difficult to hand-hold and must be mounted on a tripod for acceptable results.

Macro lens: 50mm or 100mm fixed focal length (these are not "macro" zoom lenses) for close-up photography of small subjects as well as general use.

When buying a camera for the first time, seriously consider substituting a 50mm macro lens for the 50mm "normal lens" usually sold with the camera body. In addition to being a much more useful field lens, a 50mm macro is a perfect lens for photographing artwork for the portfolio. Novice photographers often assume that a long telephoto will answer most of the problems in getting good, tightly cropped photographs of wild animals. Telephoto lenses do help compensate for the typically long working distances between photographer and a wild subject, but in spite of their huge size, these long-focal-length lenses still require the photographer to be quite close to most small animals to get acceptable results. For example, to get a full-frame photograph of a songbird using a 400mm lens, the photographer will still need to be about twenty feet from the bird. This is much closer than most wild birds ordinarily will allow. (For further information on wildlife photography, see Bibliography.)

Slide viewer, projector: for viewing reference slides in the studio. Slide projectors with a television-sized built-in viewing screen, such as the Kodak Ektagraphic 460, are particularly convenient for use on or near the drawing board (see figs. 2-36 and 2-37).

Videocassette recorder (VCR): for recording television sequences depicting animals in action.

Surfaces

Sketching paper, film: appropriate to media being used. Use good-quality surfaces. See chapter 3 and chapters relevant to chosen technique.

Plastic sketch pad: for underwater work (see text and fig. 20-12).

Media

Graphite pencils: variety of hardnesses and thicknesses.

Colored pencils: for color sketching.

Pastels: for color sketching, oil pastels are a must for underwater work.

Watercolors: pan-type cakes or tubes, with a folding watercolor palette box.

Acrylic paints: tube or liquid colors stored in small airtight containers for easy transport. For large quantities, small plastic margarine tubs are excellent. For less frequently used colors, plastic 35mm film cans work well. Paints are premixed and kept covered except when actually in use. In hot weather it is best to mix the colors first on the palette and apply large areas of color as quickly as possible (see chapter 10).

Oil paints: used for underwater painting; very adaptable but generally so slow to dry that they are apt to smear when transported. This problem can be reduced with special carriers for wet canvases or by using Copal varnish, alkyd medium, or some other rapid-drying agent.

Tools

Pencil sharpener.

Erasers: Kneaded or other types, according to preference.

Brushes: sable rounds or acrylic brushes, as needed.

Miscellaneous

Workable fixative: for pastels or pencil work.

Canvas bag, daypack: large enough to transport art materials into the field.

Field palette box: for transporting tube or cake watercolors or acrylics. Some palette boxes have lids adapted for carrying wet canvas-covered boards and act as both carrying case for supplies and as a field easel when opened.

Clipboard: large enough to comfortably hold a sketch pad. Make a clip to fasten it to the strap of the materials bag.

Small containers: useful for all water media, particularly quick-drying media such as acrylic.

Wetting agent: Photoflo (available at photo supply stores) or glycerin, to slow, but not prevent, freezing of water supplies for watercolor or acrylic painting in cold weather.

Lead strips: for weighting tools under water.

Field easel: or watercolor table, lightweight aluminum. Rig a shoulder strap for carrying.

Camp stool: small folding stool with canvas sling seat, to make a long field session much more comfortable.

Paper towels: for cleanup, for handling fast-drying paint in hot weather; cover the palette with a water-soaked paper towel to keep paints wet; put paint on towel.

Personal items: insect repellent, sunscreen, hat with sun visor. Good-quality sunglasses with neutral-density glass lenses (such as Bausch & Lomb RayBans) can relieve the eyestrain of a long session in the sun, summer or winter.

Standardized color reference chart: to compare the colors of the

observed o
against a kr
later referen
though a st
selection ch
specialized c
the *Natura*
Frank B.
raphy), con
useful to the

REFERE

If an illus
ing to an i
illustrator
search man
animal's a
ecological
gratory hal
own and ot
hunting, th
nest, or fin
clues to ai
mal authen
lustrator c
history of
the artwor
sentation
search f
should ref
ciation of
lates to
addition
such as ph
of the ani
to locate i
tory of th
larly imp
for a "fu
tation of
(fig. 20-5
cases it i
research
other en
that mak
of the
Conscien
imal's lif
details th
piece of
animal il

Photog Materia

The v
photogra

20-5. Coyote. *Canis latrans*. The coyote was drawn from photographs of wild coyotes temporarily confined at the Living Desert Reserve, California, and sketches of domestic dogs, which provided the fine texture and detail that were unclear in the coyote photographs. Habitat information and photographs were found primarily in *God's Dog: A Celebration of the North American Coyote*, by Hope Ryden (Viking Press, 1979). Ink on scratchboard, by Trudy Nicholson © 1984.

est single influence on wildlife illustration since the invention of binoculars and spotting telescopes. Photographic references have profoundly influenced the accuracy and variety of animal illustration, revealing details of anatomy, behavior, and ecology. Vast numbers of animal species, some now extinct, have been photographed alive. In the past, this wealth of detail and nuance could be obtained only by illustrators willing and able to spend long hours in the field carefully observing and sketching the behavior of the animal in its natural habitat. The stop-action advantages of photography make visible transitory facets of animal motion that the eye cannot detect when observing living animals. Moreover, details of anatomy may be revealed that might otherwise be lost in fleeting field observations.

Limitations of Photography

With all of the advantages photography affords, the wildlife illustrator must also be aware of its shortcomings to avoid incorporating photographic artifacts (optical distortion, color shifts) and misleading information into the finished illustration. While photographs may not "lie," they often give a very biased version of the truth where color is concerned. The color films most often used in wildlife photography are the so-called daylight-balanced films, calibrated to produce accurate renditions of color when used outdoors on a clear, sunny day. The color of sunlight is strongly affected by atmospheric conditions and the angle at which the solar rays strike the earth, however. The light of a clear dawn or dusk is warm and reddish because of the proportionately greater amount of atmosphere the sun's rays must penetrate when the sun is low in the sky. Cloudy days have a cool, bluish look because the long-wavelength reds and yellows are inhibited by atmospheric moisture and the short-wavelength blue light is scattered throughout the sky. Although we are all aware of the variable quality of the sun's light, we are seldom acutely conscious of it because we tend to adjust the colors our retinas receive automatically to what we "know" to be true. Color films do not, of course, have the ability to adjust the quality of the light forming the image upon them to our notions of what the "real" colors of the scene were. Thus, a "brown" sparrow may look burnt sienna brown when photographed at dawn or raw umber brown if photographed on an overcast day. Shadow areas in a photograph may appear unnaturally bluish in color photographs, again because of the greater traveling power of the short-wavelength blue end of the spectrum. (The red-yellow wavelengths tend to be absorbed by the objects they fall upon and are less able to bounce out of the shadow areas.)

Virtually all published color photographs are printed from transparency (color slide) film, which has a rather limited ability to reproduce scenes containing a wide range of light intensities. The shadow areas of the picture may look unnaturally dark and the highlights excessively bright. Artificial contrast tends to be less of a problem in black-and-white photographs, but the overall contrast of any published picture is highly dependent on the care with which the photo was color-separated, screened, and printed. Whether source photos are black-and-white or color, be aware of the distorting effect photographic contrast can have on the subject's color tones and modeling.

The type of lens used by the photographer can have a dramatic effect on the way an animal subject is rendered on film. Telephoto lenses—the type most often used in wildlife photography—tend to flatten or compress spatial relationships, causing objects distant from each other to appear closer together and more flat than they actually are. This distorting effect of telephoto lenses is often used by photojournalists to emphasize crowded conditions such as traffic jams and city streets at rush hour, where the flattening effect of the telephoto exaggerates the congestion of cars and people. The same effect occurs in animal photography done with telephotos. The modeling of the animal may be reduced or even lost, making the animal appear more like a cardboard cutout than a three-dimensional object in space.

When using photographs as references, try to collect as many different photographs as possible for a more complete view of the animal's color, anatomy, posture, and other characteristics, as well as atmospheric effects. A photograph represents just an instant in an animal's life. It may capture an uncharacteristic pose, or the animal itself may not be truly representative of its species. It is always wise to supplement photographic source material with direct observation of the animal or preserved specimens to avoid mistakes.

Bearing these warnings in mind, the artist has available many sources for c
references.
magazines (s
Material, be
rial from the
lected by zo
and catalogu
tions and un
ments. If th
of the proje
from photo
Bruce Colem
or Photo Re
as referenc
of very rare
history sub
addresses).
lustrators n
collected
clipped fro
sources ar
They also
sources of r
material su
ralists, par
fessors,
fishermen.
pant in the
ural histo
enthusiasts
specializin
one person
maintain t
sources,
knowledge
wildlife a
Take full a
sources th

Video Re

As vi
(VCRs) h
place in
area of po
has opene
tors. Pop
science p
series *Na*
able sour
habits a
Video ref
cially use
tions, typ
habits of
The vide
rerun to p

lar sequence. Video cameras such as Canon have adapters for viewing color negatives as color positives on a TV monitor screen. Many wildlife illustrators now maintain video libraries of nature programming to supplement their conventional libraries and clip files. Many nature programs are also available through museum shops and video retail and rental stores; these should be considered when approaching any wildlife illustration project if the animal subject is likely to have been filmed in the past.

Copyright Considerations

In using photographs or video material as the basis for developing an illustration, it must be remembered that these media receive the same copyright protection as any other art medium. Copying a photograph exactly is legally and ethically plagiarism unless permission to copy has been granted by the copyright holder. The natural history community of authors, artists, photographers, and publishers is a small world. Novice illustrators are often shocked at how readily artwork copied from published photographs may be recognized and rejected by publishers and art juries (see chapter 28).

Library Reference Material

The importance of a good natural history library to the working wildlife illustrator cannot be overemphasized. When faced with the inevitable press of publication deadlines, the artist can save a tremendous amount of research time by pulling most of the needed references from his or her own library. Books that are fully indexed and give the scientific names of each animal illustrated are the most helpful. Many of the types of books most useful to wildlife artists can be purchased at discount by regularly visiting large bookstores and scouring the "remainder" piles for natural history subjects. Used-book stores are another source of inexpensive reference material. A selection of field guides is always useful for quickly pinning down the most salient field marks of an animal, its habitat, and general behavioral traits. The recent popularity of photographic field guides makes it possible to acquire inexpensively at least one color photograph of nearly every commonly encountered animal in North America. Most wildlife illustrators eventually specialize in one group of animals (birds, mammals, fish) and collect extensive reference material in just that one area, making the expensive task of building a comprehensive library a little easier.

Many books containing photographs of living animals and their habitats can be located by looking in the index file of the public or university library under the common name of the animal. Unfortunately, many useful source books have more general titles and will not be found in this way. Browsing will often turn up valuable references that would not be located merely by a search in the card catalog. The most likely locations for such books are under "Zoological Sciences" (Dewey Decimal System numbers 590 to 599), but other possibilities include "Sciences of Earth and Other Worlds" (550 to 559), "Life Sciences" (580 to 589), "Agriculture and Related" (630 to 639), "Photography and Photographs" (770 to 779), and "General Geography" (990 to 999). Children's books are often an excellent source of visual references because they tend to be more heavily illustrated than books for adult audiences. Most public and university libraries also stock magazines that may be useful to the wildlife illustrator. Among them are *National Geographic*, *Smithsonian*, *Audubon*, *Oceans*, *National Wildlife*, *International Wildlife*, *Natural History*, *Zoo News*, and *Ranger Rick*. The *Reader's Guide to Periodical Literature* indexes articles about specific animals. Most natural history museums and zoos maintain libraries that welcome the interested public and may be able to offer specific guidance in researching an animal or plant.

In anticipation of future rush assignments, many artists often start their own "card catalogs" of valuable library materials to shorten the time spent in research as much as possible. Knowing how and where to locate reference sources quickly is a large part of being a professional illustrator.

Using Preserved Animals

Photographs can supply a great deal of information on the typical postures and general surface details of animals, but they often fall short in providing the precise surface colors, textures, and detail necessary to complete an illustration. Preserved animals are an excellent source of information on these surface details, but they must be used with care to avoid incorporating misleading information into the finished art. Some animals preserve well in alcohol or Formalin, others quickly lose their natural shapes and colors when preserved in fluid. Liquid preservatives, light, the passage of time, and death itself alter the color intensity of most soft-bodied animals. Other sources of information should therefore be checked to determine typical color patterns in the living animal. Insects (particularly beetles) often look very lifelike when pinned for collections and sometimes retain their brilliant natural colors.

The superficial similarity of preserved specimens to the living organism may be misleading, however. The positions of legs, antennae, and other body parts should be compared with photographs or observations of the living animal to be sure no artifacts—dirt, discoloration, distortion—of the preservation process are incorporated as details in the finished art. Animals that are usually stuffed for preservation (birds, small mammals) must be examined carefully, as the process of skinning and stuffing usually distorts the overall bulk and length of the animal's body. Subtle details of the animal's body contours are usually lost in the preservation process and should be checked against living animals or photographs. Feathers and fur usually retain their color for years after the death of the animal, but the color of soft parts of birds and mammals quickly fades after death. These ephemeral details are often noted on the identification tag attached to the specimen. For practical reasons, the wings of preserved birds are almost always folded close to the body, making the details of wing patterns difficult to observe.

Extreme care must be taken when handling any preserved animal. Preserved birds and small mammal skins are extremely brittle whether dry or in fluid and should always be handled with great care to avoid ripping off body parts. Never try to unbend a wing or leg to get a better view of it. If the specimen was borrowed, check with the owner to find out if the animal may be removed from its container, and to determine proper procedures for handling and storing the specimen. Many preserved animals can be irreparably damaged through improper handling. (See pertinent chapters for more information about each animal or plant group.)

Regardless of the type of animal or how it was preserved, certain details of the specimen's origin should always be checked to be sure it is representative of the subject species. The age, sex, and location and circumstances of collection all play a part in determining the value of a particular specimen as a reference source. Many animals have distinctive geographic races or alternate color phases. Note whether the specimen is from an appropriate location, if this matters to the client. Specimens are often collected for preservation if they exhibit distinctive or unusual characteristics—be sure the specimen is typical of the species and not a variant individual. Most animals are sexually dimorphic, and these differences are sometimes quite subtle. Any questions about the suitability of a specimen should be checked against other reference material or referred to the client for additional information.

Museums of natural history usually maintain large collections of preserved animals and are often willing to extend viewing and borrowing privileges to serious students of natural history. (See chapter 19 for some museums with large collections.) Curators and museum technicians are usually quite helpful in finding specimens and answering questions. Other possible sources of preserved specimens are university biology departments, regional parks and nature centers, and state or federal agencies involved with ecology or wildlife management. Local taxidermists can also be a valuable source of information and guidance on the local wildlife and collections of natural history material in your area.

OBSERVATION AND FIELD SKETCHING

To achieve that indefinable but necessary "spark" of life and authenticity in wildlife illustration, there is simply no substitute for long, careful observation of wild (or even domestic) animals in their natural habitats. Photographic or preserved references, however many or varied, cannot impart a full sense of the living animal and its characteristic movements and gestures (fig. 20-6; see fig. 19-8).

Unfortunately, not every animal the professional artist must illustrate can be observed in its natural habitat, so the illustrator must look to other sources of information on

the behavior
clues to enli
The graceful
ing across the
markably sim
domestic cats
suburban ba
tered behavi
may be an eve
cats than the
large cats co
not possible t
animal you m
find a relate
study its habi

Observatio
developed th
the best way t
thumbnail ske
to which you
sketching th
quality of obs
the artistic
teaches the a
and simplify
characteristic
mal. Watchin
moves its he
makes it look
(fig. 20-7), or
lated motions
will help the
stand the n
expressions of
may be easy
movements, i
practice to
and translate
into accurate

Breaking
down into its
shapes can he
mental image
while transfer
to paper (fig.
many animals
are roughly e
be oval, roun
lar, or square.
create shado
geometric sha

A thorough
imal anatomy
ing the play
contours (fig.
18-17, 18-18,
body form has

20-6. A spider monkey, sketched quickly in a zoo. Notes on the sketch provide reminders of the color and other details for later, more complete rendering. Graphite pencil on paper, by Lois Sloan © 1983.

20-7. Quick field sketches in pencil of an eastern gray squirrel, *Sciurus carolinensis*, by Clare Walker Leslie © 1979, drawn on a clear day in New England. From *Nature Drawing: A Tool for Learning*, by Clare Walker Leslie (Prentice-Hall, 1980).

lution and the animal's role in the ecosystem. The movements and characteristic poses of a particular species are intimately related to its internal structure. When correctly rendered, the reflections of the animal's internal anatomy on its external form impart a strong sense of reality and liveliness to the finished artwork. Establish form first, regardless of the subject matter. Simplifying the animal's form into basic masses is also a constant reminder that animals are three-dimensional and must always be understood as such to convey their body shapes convincingly. In concentrating on surface detail over body form, novice illustrators tend to create flat "feather maps" (or "fur maps"), rich in extraneous detail but unsuccessful as representations of living animals.

Training for Field Sketching

One of the most common problems in field sketching of wildlife is how to make usable drawings of rapidly moving subjects such as running animals, jumping fish, and flying birds. With surprisingly little practice, it is possible to remember an amazing amount of detail of a moving animal if the artist does not overload the mind with too much information. Look at the subject with a quick glance, freezing in the mind a specific image. It is somewhat like viewing a single frame of a moving picture. Watching longer than is absolutely necessary to capture a mental image will yield too much information to sort out.

Aside from actually practicing this technique in the field, the artist can train the eye and hand at home. Project an image of some form of wildlife on a screen (video or slides work equally well), leaving it on for less than a second, then draw the subject from memory. Another practice technique that requires no projection or video equipment is the use of flash cards. Paste photographs of wild animals on one side of 5- by 7-inch index cards. Randomly mix the cards face down on a table, then select one and glance at it very briefly. Replace the card and try to draw as full a picture as possible of what you saw without further reference to the card.

A technique that is very useful both as a training exercise and in the field is "contour" drawing (fig. 20-10). Generally this is done looking not at the drawing surface but

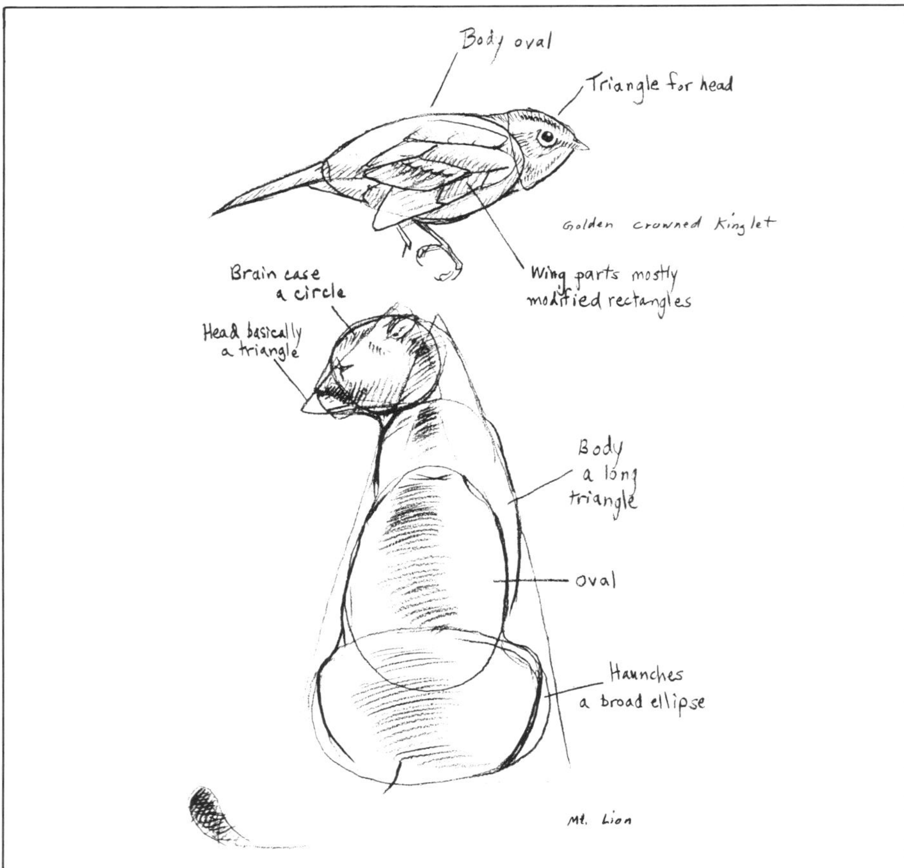

20-8. Body forms are reduced to simple geometric shapes used as construction lines. Graphite pencil on paper, by Wayne Trimm © 1983.

20-9. A broad s
der shapes quic
same pencil ca
paper, by Way

20-10. Contour drawing of a young opossum. Graphite pencil on paper, by Wayne Trimm © 1983.

intently at the subject. Where the pencil or pen is put down on the surface becomes the place to begin the drawing of the subject. The pencil should never leave the drawing surface but respond to visual messages relayed to the muscles of the hand. The eye follows the shape and contour of the subject, the hand keeping pace with one continous line. Lines may be retraced to reach new areas, sometimes resulting in a line on paper where there is no comparable line on the subject. Start off with simple subjects, such as tumblers or

bottles, unti
tion is devel
to more co
jects. This
important i
animal life.
reasonably
and it *is* pos
subject mor
personality
important i
cies.

Capturing
Details

In drawi
is more in
mood or c
than to con
of its surfac
in a positio
drawing in
cluded. bu
have severa
emphasize
and "gesta
detailed ske
fig. 20-7). I
the studio
but that sp
difficult to
ory and p
all field ske
should be
tion of the
11; see figs.

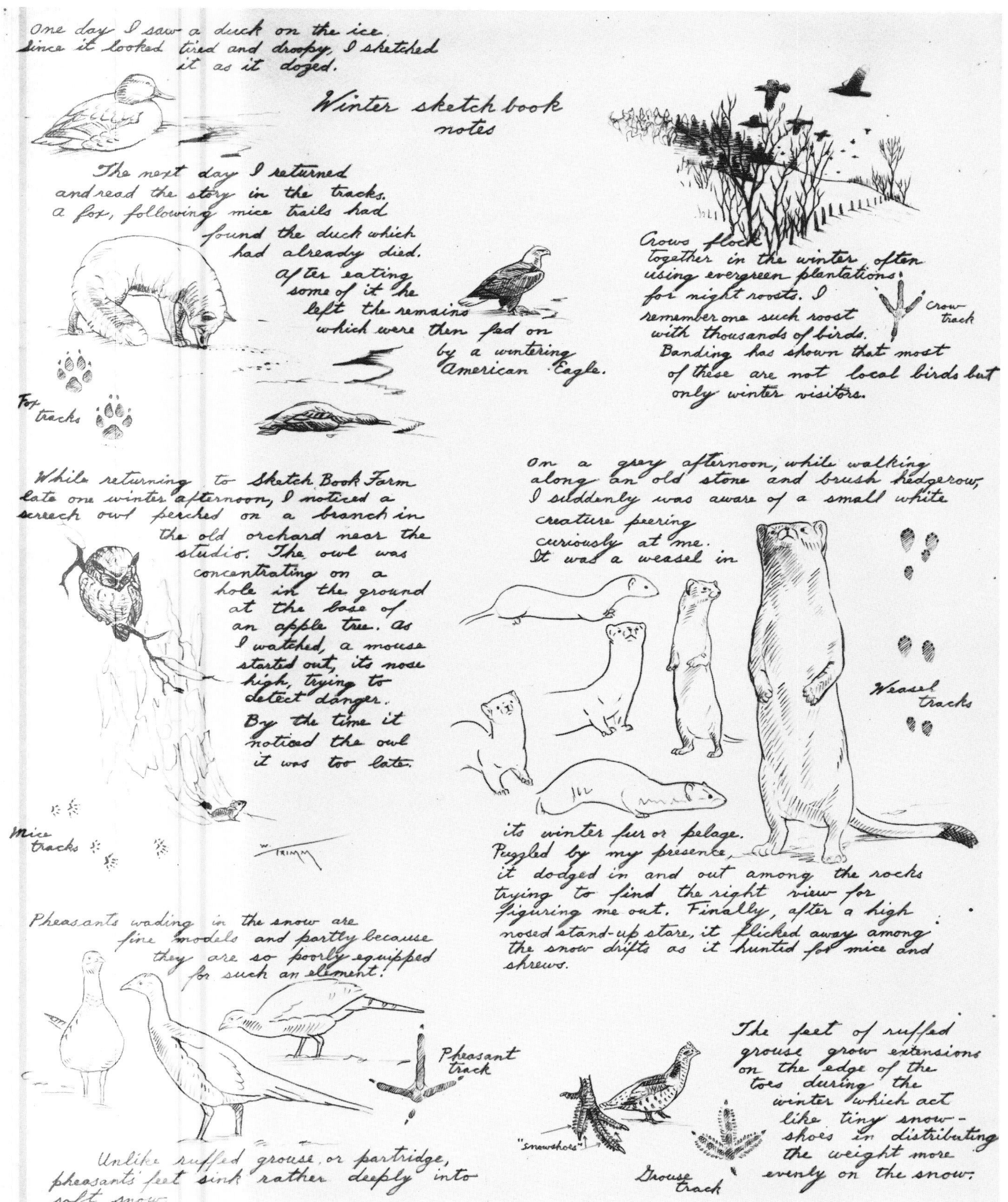

20-11. Winter sketchbook notes. Drawings accumulated from field sketches and arranged to form a story. Graphite pencil on Grumbacher three-ply cold-press paper, by Wayne Trimm. From *The New York State Conservationist*, December-January, 1975–76.

are so obvious at the time that they may seem unimportant. Write them down. Time erodes even the best memories, and your field sketches are a long-term investment in your profession.

Zoos are an excellent place to sharpen observation skills and provide a wide variety of animals to sketch and study (see figs. 20-4, 20-6). But because captive animals usually behave differently from their wild counterparts, they often show evidence of captivity in their anatomy as well. Captive predators such as lions or bears will often have more fat and less muscle tone than exhibited by predators in the wild. Close confinement and the zoo diet seem to dull the urge to maintain fur and feathers in captive animals. The colors of some animals, particularly tropical birds, often will be much duller because of items missing from their zoo diet. Some problems of captivity can be more subtle; the beaks and claws of captive birds often show unnatural wear or growth patterns due to mechanical damage from cages or lack of proper exercise. In zoos that provide adequate roaming space for the animals, it is sometimes difficult to get close enough to the animal to see details clearly, so it may be necessary to supplement zoo sketches with photographs even when an animal can be viewed in captivity (see figs. C-9, C-23, 20-1).

The ability to convey various surface textures and details in animal artwork is essential. The textures of an animal's fur, eyes, tongue, teeth, claws, skin, feathers, beak, and shell all vary, and the rendering of these many surfaces is not easy. It takes considerable practice to convey in the same medium the moist, smooth surface of the eyes; the matted effect of fur; glistening, hard teeth; and the rough, papillated tongue. Study the fur of a long-haired dog as opposed to that of the smooth, short-haired cat or rabbit. The more uneven or matted the fur, the more uneven or matted are the shadows within the fur. The textures and surface details of animals available nearby may be similar to those of unavailable animals. Thus, practice in duplicating the textures of a domestic dog may help in illustrating a coyote (see fig. 20-5). Many rendering techniques useful to the wildlife illustrator are explained elsewhere in this volume under the sections on various media and techniques.

Underwater Field Sketching and Painting

With the increasing interest in marine and freshwater environments, illustrators specializing in these subjects are often taking field sketching and painting equipment under water to better understand aquatic animals in their native habitat. The artist must first learn to use scuba equipment competently (a scuba license is strongly recommended). Then a suitable graphic medium for underwater work must be chosen. It is possible to set up a metal easel and white plastic painting board to work with oils under water. The paint must be used as pure pigment from the tube, with no extender such as linseed oil or turpentine. Painting knives are best as applicators, but brushes will work if they are weighted. Strips of lead can be wrapped around pencils, pastels, and brushes so they will sink instead of floating upward if dropped. A floating brush or pencil caught in the surface water movement can disappear very quickly. When working in tidal water or other situations with a strong current, anchor or tie the easel in place (fig. 20-12).

Supplies might include an 8- by 10-inch (20 by 25cm) white plastic sketchbook, regular graphite pencils (weighted), Craypas or other oil pastels, and occasionally water-soluble pencils (also weighted). The surface of the plastic sketchbook must be rough enough to hold the media; if it does not have a tex-

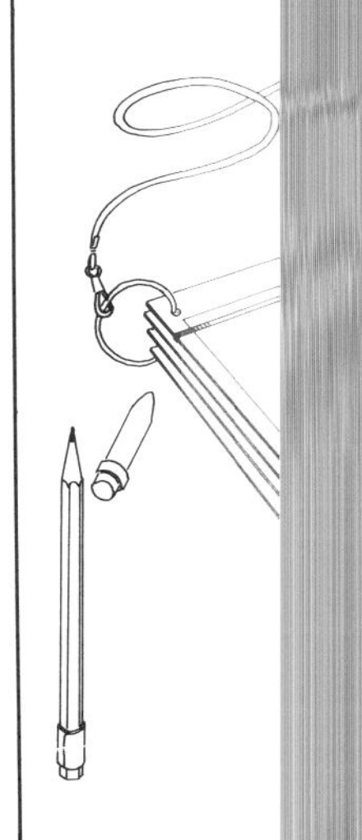

20-12. Underw
weighted oil pa
ink on illustrati
Trimm © 1983.

ture, sandpa
angle strokes
rough enougl
salt from filli
ducing their
ter films wi
such as Dur
underwater
be fastened
book with r
entire pad at
diver's weig
faces should
or salt wate
will remain
the media in
on location u
pencils, oil p
on the botto
in a conver
ment, weigh
look like l
glowing in t
be careful th
does not try
problems fr
servers is sli
and other s
watch, appa
but do no h
sometimes s
they see thei
face mask
cases, the ba

their territory against an imagined fish rather than a real diver.

The drawing techniques for underwater subjects are the same as those for dry-land fieldwork. As mentioned above, keep work simple and stress the personality and character of the subject rather than its details. As for color, the human eye sees underwater color more accurately than a color camera, catching subtle details rarely captured on film. Somehow the eye "corrects" for the distortion in color, which film cannot do. A problem unique to underwater sketching is that of the subject being so interesting that the diver may overstay the air supply. Luckily, most modern scuba tanks now give a warning when the air supply is getting low.

APPROACHES TO WILDLIFE ILLUSTRATION

The actual working process and the stylistic approach in the creation of wildlife illustrations is largely determined by the medium for which the work is intended, the economics and schedule of the job, and the reason the artwork was commissioned. Because animal illustrations are used in so many different contexts, no general rules apply in the creation of wildlife artwork. Wildlife illustration differs from other disciplines of scientific illustration primarily in the nature of the research and the natural history knowledge the wildlife illustrator must bring to the project, rather than in any specific illustration style or art medium unique to animal illustration. There are, however, broad stylistic trends that can be identified in modern wildlife illustration and certain approaches to composition and presentation that recur constantly in wildlife art. Wildlife illustration is almost by definition a representational genre, where the illustrator usually must re-create as closely as possible the physical form and surface details of the subject. Nevertheless, the illustrator is not a substitute for a camera, and within the constraints of realism, there are a number of distinct approaches to illustrating animals and their environment.

In "Of Animals and Art," his essay on the works of the Swedish wildlife artist Bruno Liljefors (see Bibliography), the distinguished wildlife artist Don Eckelberry identified two fundamental approaches to wildlife art and illustration as "objective realism" versus "intellectual realism." In an "objective" approach to realism, the artist emphasizes the quality of light and color in a manner much akin to impressionism. This way of looking at the world is held to be "objective" because in our actual experience we do not really see the mass of details that make up a scene in nature, concentrating instead on the overall impression made by the animal and its environment on our senses. Here the ability to capture the "gestalt" of the animal and its relationship to the environment is much more important than rendering reality in exhaustive detail. The success of an "objective" approach lies primarily in the ability of the artist to capture the most characteristic features of a wild animal, much as a good portrait seeks to define the character of the subject as well as his or her physical appearance. "Intellectual" realism is much more akin to straightforward natural history and scientific illustration, where the artist knows "intellectually" that certain details of form and color are present in the subject and painstakingly renders them all, hoping to simulate the experience of having the animal in front of the viewer to examine in careful detail. Neither approach to realism is more legitimate than the other, and few wildlife illustrators choose one approach to realism exclusively, often using both in their works to control the attentions of the audience. A highly detailed rendering of the principal subject in an illustration can focus the viewer's concentration on the animal while a more impressionistic handling of the surrounding environment can prevent these ancillary details from overwhelming the point of the illustration.

Composition

The problems of composition play a major role in the creation of wildlife artwork, where the illustrator must often orchestrate many subject and background elements into an aesthetically pleasing arrangement. Such principles of composition as asymmetry and perspective are, for the most part, outside the scope of this volume and should be studied carefully through art courses or books exclusively devoted to the subject. A few basic points of particular interest to animal illustrators can, however, be made. Having the heaviest part of the composition—the larger and darker masses and the bulk of the detail—at the bottom of the illustration gives a satisfyingly balanced and solid feeling to the viewer. For instance, composition elements are concentrated at the bottom of figure 20-3, and a simplified, linear rendition of water fills the arc created by the muskrat's nest, further stabilizing the composition. In figure 20-5, textural details lead from the coyote's body into the vegetation along the bottom of the drawing, balancing the darker masses of cactus and sky at the top of the drawing. Note that the coyote is concentrating on something outside the frame of the drawing. This device is often used to give liveliness and a sense of psychic tension to wildlife artwork. Strong, angular lines in figures 20-1 and 20-13 convey action or tensions of a fleeting pause in action, whereas strong verticals and horizontals in figures 20-2 and 20-5 give a more harmonious feeling to the composition. (See fig. 5-32 for another example of textural, vertical, and angular elements integrated into a complex composition. See also figs. C-3, C-6, C-9, C-23, 4-56, 5-18, 5-29, 9-8.)

20-13. A solitary black-backed jackal and three spotted hyenas feed on an old giraffe kill. Strong diagonals from the necks, muzzles, and fore legs of the hyenas through the carcass, opposed by diagonals of the jackal's fore legs, impart a feeling of action. Pencil, by Richard Orr/Linden Artists Ltd. From *The Hunters*, by Dr. Philip Whitfield. Book designed by Marshall-Editions Ltd. (Hamlyn Publishing Group Ltd. [U.K.] and Simon and Schuster, 1978).

Lines, light and dark areas, and contrast in detail can be used to focus the viewer's attention. Note in figure 20-2 that the painting has been almost halved by the dark tree on one side and the light sky on the other. The owl is framed by extreme contrast between these two elements and is further highlighted by the line of the branch it is sitting on. Note the harmony in textures between the rough bark of the tree and the patterned feathers of the owl. This device both knits together aesthetically the contrast elements of the painting and makes a powerful statement about the owl's adaptation to its habitat. In figure 20-5, the coyote's dark head is literally highlighted by the moon. In figure 20-1, the straight vertical line of the nearer tamarin's tail and the highly rendered curved branch it sits on bring the viewer's eye from the complex, dark masses of vegetation at the bottom to the light, delicate tamarins above. The animals make up the largest light area in a composition of dark, angular elements that create contrast for the white-haloed tamarin heads. The dark background elements recede further through the softening of their details, implying distance behind the highly rendered tamarins in the foreground. Contrast in rendering, in light, and in linear elements focuses the viewer's eye on the animals. The arc of water in figure 20-3 is a counterpoint to the reversed arc of white space above the muskrat, centering the animal between the arcs. Note how the lotus pod on the lower right balances the mass of leaves on the middle left, and how curved leaves lead the eye from the vegetation on the left toward the muskrat.

Many wildlife illustrations "vignette" the animal against the (usually) white field of the page, often with some environmental details such as a branch or vegetation to "ground" the animal (see figs. C-16, C-23, 5-18, 5-20, 20-4, 20-13).

In illustrati
part of the
head in an
background
at all (fig.
These vign
popular wit
tors, and b
they do not
cost) of pai
and they fo
tion sharply
surface det
type are co
give the r
look at the
of its beh
through ph
guides, bo
tory of a
groups of
articles are
manner, u
ing photogr
text furthe
wildlife illu
draw the re
point to ph

Media and Rendering Techniques

In color wildlife illustration, water-based media such as watercolor and gouache predominate, principally because these media lend themselves to the highly detailed styles of rendering that are currently popular in wildlife art (see figs. C-3, C-9, 20-2). This may be a stylistic holdover from the prephotography beginnings of wildlife illustration, where the portability of water-based media made painting in the field possible. In any case, the relatively uncomplicated field and studio techniques and tools of watercolor and its quick-drying nature are perfectly suited to most natural history and scientific illustration projects. Acrylic paints are also widely used in wildlife illustration and are highly regarded for their ability to mimic both watercolor and more elaborate oil techniques. Because acrylic paints are impermeable once dry, true glazing techniques may be used to modify subtly paintings that otherwise look very much like conventional watercolors. (See chapters 9 and 10 for further information on the techniques of watercolor and acrylic illustration.) Colored pencil and other media also are effective (see figs. C-6, 7-8).

The most popular black-and-white techniques in wildlife illustration are pen-and-ink drawings done on heavy drawing paper, Bristol board, or scratchboard. In figures 20-1, 20-3, and 20-5, the long tonal range possible in scratchboard work has been exploited to full effect, using many dark elements in the compositions that would be difficult to render without the ability to scratch texture and detail into the masses of black (see also fig. 5-20). Pencil also is used frequently, both for its loose, informal look of sketches (see figs. 19-8, 20-4, 20-6) and the ability to render in great detail gradations in tone and texture (see figs. 6-4, 11-2, 20-13). Wash and mixed media produce loose or tight results (see figs. 9-2, 9-8, 11-9).

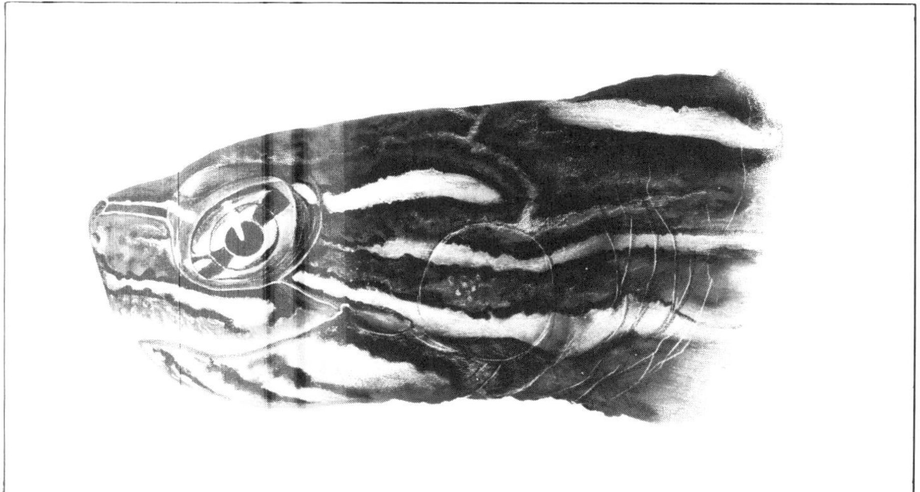

20-14. Vignetting of head of Eastern painted turtle. Airbrush, watercolor, and carbon pencil on no. 1 Ross board, by William L. Brudon © 1976.

Although the ancestry of wildlife artwork reaches back to the Stone Age and probably farther, the notion of illustrating an animal as a complex fellow creature worthy of serious aesthetic attention in its own right (and not just as a curiosity or symbolic reference) is a relatively new one. For the natural history catalogers of the nineteenth century and the romantic artists who portrayed animals in allegories of human nature, the animal kingdom was alternately viewed as a resource to be exploited and as a dark reflection of man's passions and conflicts. With our newfound appreciation of the earth's environment as a complex interdependent system of plants and animals adapted by evolution to their ecosystems, perhaps we can finally understand and portray animals with the respect and dignity they deserve.

21/Illustrating Humans and Thei
Artifacts

Elizabeth Morales-Denney and
Jennifer Loynd Cowherd

One of the key concerns of the anthropologist and archaeologist is the accurate and controlled collection of data and the subsequent translation of this data, so painstakingly documented in the field, into the published form. The scientific illustrator plays a vital part in this process.

Anthropology is the study of cultures and is traditionally divided into four subdisciplines; sociocultural anthropology, physical anthropology, linguistic anthropology, and archaeology. The sociocultural anthropologist focuses on the patterns of everyday life in existing societies. Ethnography is the data-gathering part of this subdiscipline —that is, fieldwork in a specific society. The physical anthropologist is interested in human beings, both ancient and contemporary, as biological organisms: how human physical variation changes over time and throughout the world, and the interplay of environmental factors. Common interests unite the physical anthropologist and the paleontologist, who is also interested in the evolution of life forms, especially that of early man. Linguistic anthropology is the study of existing and dead languages. Sociocultural linguistics, a dominant subfield, looks at the connection between linguistic diversity and social stratification within a single group. The archaeologist, sometimes called a paleoethnographer, focuses on the material remains of extinct cultures. With the knowledge of ethnographic theory borrowed from the sociocultural anthropologist and the controlled excavation of remains, the archaeologist can piece together by analysis of human, plant, and animal remains, manufactured items, house structures, and so on, a description of life in a community that once occupied a particular site.

The four subdisciplines of anthropology share the same goal: the study of sociocultural systems, how cultures evolve over time and throughout the world. These scientists accomplish this goal by combining their data to create a more complete picture of these processes.

The role of the illustrator takes on many forms to adapt to the different demands of these subdisciplines. In general, it would be advantageous for the illustrator to have a background in anthropology. Many universities offer courses in physical anthropology, linguistics, and archaeology that are helpful, enabling the illustrator to gain overall knowledge and understand general practices—talk the same language as the scientist. It would also be helpful to spend a few field seasons working with an ethnographic project or archaeological excavation that would introduce the illustrator to digging and recording in the field and to the laborious work in the lab, cleaning and cataloging gathered material. This kind of experience will help the illustrator appreciate the rigors of fieldwork and the nature of the objects being studied, as well as to understand his or her role in the overall research project.

THE WOR
ANTHROP
ARCHAEO
ILLUSTRA

Elizabeth M

The illus
upon to wo
subjects in
The socioc
may ask t
from previo
in museum
upcoming
tional mate
university,
for exhibiti
often is do
search area
limits to th
illustrator
large-scale
color or col
and-white c
required (fi
entist can
material to
is usually t
contempora
tures or wh
doing dom
ology. In so
tural anth
from the fie
wares, whi
the more
objects in
as models
home. This
excellent

George Robert
the work of an
illustrators.

21-1. Feather- (egret, heron, parrot, and macaw) and-mussel-shell necklace, Carajá Indians, Brazil. Watercolor on Arches watercolor paper, by Elizabeth Morales-Denney © 1984.

Some anthropological illustrators are called upon to draw many maps (see chapter 25).

The most difficult and most exciting work is done in the field in collaboration with the sociocultural anthropologist or with an archaeologist on an excavation. Typically, the sociocultural anthropologist will collect data on a foreign culture by living among a group of people for a short period of time, observing activities on a daily basis and conducting interviews with consenting members (informants). The illustrator may be asked to join the scientist in the field to draw maps of village layout, house structures, and objects of the material culture, such as cooking implements, clothing, jewelry, and the like, or people performing everyday tasks, such as methods for carrying heavy objects. The sociocultural anthropologist may also want drawings of individuals or groups in motion, such as during dances or religious ceremonies. Finally, the scientist undoubtedly will need charts and graphs depicting status hierarchies, kinship organization, and so on. If working conditions are poor or if time is limited, the illustrator may prepare comprehensive pencil roughs and with the aid of photographs complete the work at home.

When working with a physical anthropologist, the illustrator will be asked to concentrate on faunal material: human and animal bone. This scientist is looking for evidence of human prehistory and evolution as recorded in bone—changes in cranial capacity, effects of climate and diet on bone development and therefore body size, regional variations ("race"), and evidence of prehistoric diseases as detected in bone deformities. The illustrator must produce anatomically precise drawings of faunal material to document this work (see chapter 13).

The linguist also gathers data by doing fieldwork in different cultures, making tape recordings and copies of the written form of languages. The linguist will call upon the illustrator primarily for charts and graphs depicting theories of language structure as well as of the evolution of modern languages from prehistoric languages, maps illustrating language spread, and perhaps illustrations of facial and body expressions to augment the recordings.

At a large-scale archaeological excavation, the illustrator will be hired by the archaeologist to provide topographic maps, field plans, balk section diagrams, and detailed illustrations of all artifacts excavated during the field season. In countries with strict patrimony laws, artifact illustrations must be done in the field. Established in many countries in recent years to curtail the export and sale of valuable objects of a country's cultural heritage, patrimony laws forbid anyone from removing artifacts from the country of origin. Some countries will allow scientists to take home excavated material for a specified period of time, typically a year or two, for research, in which case the illustrator is under less pressure to complete the work in the field. The archaeologist may also want hypothetical reconstruction drawings of damaged artifacts or architectural structures. In addition, the illustrator may be asked to produce illustrations for other team members, such as drawings of floral material (plants, usually preserved seeds and pollen) for a paleobotanist. At an excavation, work is usually done in a temporary field lab set up near the site.

Clean, sheltered work areas are essential, not only for some of the illustration but also for some of the registration, conservation, and photography, as well as for the safe storage of artifacts and these records. A number of considerations (including time and local laws) will determine the degree of completion necessary on location for the illustrations. Because there is always the possibility that another person may need to do follow-up illustrations from the field drawings, complete, explicit information should always be included.

Finally, all of these scientists may require the illustrator's assistance in the design, layout, and production of site reports and field notes into camera-ready material for publication.

Although photography plays a very important role in the collection of data in the field, scientific illustrations are often superior to photographs for recording visual information. Good illustrations will eliminate confusing shadows, highlight diagnostic features, separate and show clearly objects that are hidden or inaccessible in nature (such as rollouts—see Rollouts, below—and pottery profile drawings), simplify objects with diagrammatic line drawings to highlight structural form or complex iconography (such as line drawings from rubbings), enlarge greatly without loss of detail (such as enlargements of weaving patterns), and show an artifact devoid of unwanted dirt or cracks. In addition, line art costs less to publish than photographs. Nonetheless, photographs are indispensable reference tools for the illustrator, and, indeed, many good illustrations are done solely from photographs taken in the field.

INSTRUMENTS AND MATERIALS

Some items on the following list are needed for field activities, such as measuring an excavation in order to produce a field plan. Some of these items are necessary for other aspects of the excavations and might be shared among the staff. Other materials are used for producing preliminary drawings in the studio or laboratory, whether in the field or at home. Not all of these materials are needed by every illustrator in every situation. These are used in addition to those general materials used for any illustration. With regard to surfaces and media, a few suggestions specifically for archaeology follow.

In the field, drawings and supplies may be affected by the climate (rain, humidity, sun). Use frosted polyester film and waterproof ink whenever possible. Graph paper or gridded film simplifies the drawing of field plans. For rubbings, HB graphite sticks are needed. To write on the plastic strips used to produce rollouts, a laundry marker or ink that will adhere to plastic is necessary. Because of the difficulty or impossibility of obtaining supplies or replacements in the field, bring extras of small items such as technical pen points and knife blades.

Optical Devices

Stereoscopic microscope: rarely needed.

Camera lucida: if microscope is used.

Magnifier: h
lens.

Opaque pr
enlarging an
as well as dr

Camera: 35
with black-a
color slide f
archaeologic

Lenses: 50m

Measuring

Rulers: cle
12 inch (30c
ones as nee
and drawin

Triangles:
two 12 inch
plastic for
suring pots
angles.

One-meter

Retractabl
2- and 6-m
the locking
end readin
to hook on

Proportio
(25cm).

Reverse
measuring
chapter 2)

Carpente
tour gaug
duplicatin
chapter 2)

Line lev
type with

Plumb b

Large bal

Metal or
nails: to
at the site

Magnetic
determini
tion.

Graphic

Drawing

Templates: assortment of circles, squares, rectangles, ellipses, as needed.

Drawing board: sturdy plastic or other lightweight material.

Letter clips: large; to attach paper to board.

Light table: to use in home studio, not in the field.

Tape: masking, artist's (opaque white), transparent.

Specimen-handling Tools

Clear acetate or polyester (.003 or .005 mil), clear plastic kitchen wrap: for producing rollout illustrations.

Toothbrushes, wide and narrow stiff paintbrushes: to clean crevices in artifacts and to clarify balk stratigraphy.

Stainless dental picks: to clean crevices.

Specimen Props

Fabric, kneaded rubber erasers: materials that will not damage the specimen's surface. The edge of the specimen's container and other materials may be suitable. What is used depends on the specimen's size.

Miscellaneous

Knives: mat knife and selection of blades, pocketknife.

Small notebook: for notes in the field.

Plastic atomizer: for spraying balks with water.

Backpack, shoulder bag: for carrying supplies.

Stiff portfolio.

Supply box.

Gloves: cotton, for handling artifacts while illustrating.

Clean rags.

SUBJECT MATTER AND TERMINOLOGY

Although the four subdisciplines of anthropology place a wide range of demands on the illustrator, many of these demands can be met with skills general to the field of scientific illustration. Artifact illustration and excavation illustration, however, are uniquely anthropological and archaeological and require special skills and knowledge. It is upon those areas, therefore, that this chapter will focus.

An artifact is any object that has been modified by humans. Artifacts are often called manufactured items and are the tangible goods of any society, past or present. A rich source of artifacts for the archaeologist are middens, ancient garbage dumps. The most pervasive of all artifacts are lithics, objects manufactured from stone. All known cultures, especially prehistoric cultures, used stone to manufacture tools and weapons, such as projectiles ("arrowheads" and spearheads), scrapers, and mortars; jewelry such as pendants and beads; pipes; and large structures such as carved monuments and buildings. Other artifacts from preindustrial societies may include clay pots and figurines, basketry and netting made from plant fibers, woven textiles, and numerous other objects that help define the culture, so-called ethnographic material (fig. 21-2).

21-2. Parrot-feather-and-tortoise-shell rattle, Carajá Indians, Brazil. Ink line and stipple on Vidalon tracing paper, by Elizabeth Morales-Denney © 1984.

A feature is an artifact found during excavation that cannot be removed from its position in the unit (the open pit) without destroying it. For example, a hearth would be a mere collection of fire-cracked rock if the rocks were removed from their relative positions (typically a crude circle or rectangle). Similarly, a burial (human bone surrounded by grave goods) is more significant in situ. Usually the feature is rendered schematically by the illustrator in situ as part of the level plan, and more realistic and detailed treatment of individual parts, such as the grave goods, is done by the illustrator after the feature is removed from the unit and is in the lab or studio (see Excavations, below).

CARE AND HANDLING OF SPECIMENS

In many cultures, the objects of everyday use typically are made of fragile materials such as bone, wood, shell, clay, feathers, leather, and plant fibers that easily deteriorate over time and with use. Excavated artifacts are often doubly fragile by virtue of the age of the materials and the effects of water and minerals in the ground. The illustrator will be handling these artifacts in the course of preparing a drawing and should be aware of some basic rules and procedures.

In the field lab, objects will be bagged and stored by unit and level (depth in unit). These bags may be identified with a code such as "Unit 2, Level: 20–30cm." Fragile pieces may have their own protective bag or box within the unit/level bag. At this stage, artifacts have not been treated by a conservator and do not have catalog numbers painted on them. The catalog number is the only way to cross-reference the material to the written field notes and, hence, keep track of hundreds of pieces gathered during a field season. Do *not* mix up the contents of different bags. Loss of context, or provenience, is a serious matter, and the one mistake made most frequently. In archaeology, the exact location of artifacts relative to all other artifacts, and the natural stratigraphy in the unit is of utmost importance —often more important than the objects themselves. For example, a unit/level with a dense grouping of unretouched flint or obsidian flakes, or debitage, may be evidence of a flintknapping workshop. Each individual flake holds far less importance than the cluster as a whole. Similarly, if a high percentage of all subsurface artifacts in a unit two meters deep are found in one thin layer—say, 30 to 40cm—this information may indicate the locale of a living floor, the actual floor of a structure or dwelling. Field-lab storage is temporary, and artifacts will either return home with the crew or remain in the country of origin, perhaps to be shipped to university or museum storage rooms there.

In the museum, artifacts can be stored by type (for example, all baskets of cane together), by culture (all Tlingit material together), or by donor (all Dr. Smith's temporary loan together). Usually the curator will retrieve all artifacts and return them to their padded drawers and shelves. Browsing among the shelves is usually not appreciated. Do not remove any tags or labels from objects during illustration, even for a few moments.

Do not expose artifacts of plant fibers or painted surfaces to a strong light or heat. A drafting light set too close will be too hot. Paint will fade, textile fibers become weakened, and feathers will singe. Do not wash or moisten any artifact unless given specific permission to do so. There is a great urge to put a soiled pottery sherd under a faucet to clean it or heighten the color contrast, but many objects have surfaces with paint that can dissolve in water, and faint traces of paint that cannot be seen except under a magnifying glass (fugitive
paint) will be l
more, what
smudges, esp
basketry cont
remains of fo
valuable clue
gist.

Handle obj
sible. Natural
and salt on fi
surfaces, so c
ommended. N
whether an a
put tape on a
position. Bal
safely on ma
the specimen
And, even th
natural thing
pot by its ha
tifacts with
course, mak
drop anythin
ken, do not
together. Sp
vation techn
ployed by an

Etiquette i

When tra
pologist, rem
visitor, and
community.
deportment i
portant. All
traveling ab
in mind that
a people is p
dignity. As
about local
have strict,
boos regardi
tain things.
touch, phot
undue inter
the anthrop
example, he
it would be
for a strang
est in, or
clothesline.
considered
dignity to
flag. In som
be so prot
they cannot

scribed members of a group (such as some southwestern United States Kachina dolls). Never photograph anyone without permission, as it is very offensive in many cultures. (The Masai in East Africa, as well as other peoples elsewhere throughout the world, are convinced that one's soul is jeopardized by a camera.)

Analysis of Specimens

The best anthropological illustration is done by an informed artist. The illustrator should have some knowledge of the culture that produced the artifacts to be illustrated, so that the more common objects of everyday use can be identified. The function of the artifact (if it is known) can help the illustrator draw it accurately and naturally. The anthropologist should explain critical or diagnostic features of an artifact or class of artifacts. For example, the drilling on Costanoan olivella shell beads and the shape of Peruvian Moche pot spouts are very important diagnostic features of these types of artifacts insofar as minor variations of these features are used to seriate these objects (place them in an evolutionary scheme based on stylistic changes).

Anthropological illustration is different from other specialties in scientific illustration in that most of the specimens are natural materials modified by a human touch. A good analysis and rendering of these specimens should reveal the nature of the raw material, the processes of manufacture, and the subsequent signs of use. It may help to examine specimens under a magnifying glass to differentiate decay, corrosion, faded pigment, subtle carving, accidental scars, and tool marks. Extremely small items, such as minuscule beads or wisps of fabric, can be drawn only from enlargements of photographs taken through a microscope or directly from the microscope.

CONVENTIONS

Anthropological illustration follows the standard conventions for scientific illustration, such as light source from the left and the inclusion of a scale (usually metric). Archaeologists typically arrange artifactual material such as stone tools into either functional or stylistic assemblages. Hence, the illustrator may be asked to combine such objects into one drawing. Established conventions should be followed in the page orientation of these assemblage illustrations. For example, projectiles of any kind are usually arranged with their points up (fig. 21-3). In drawings of stone tools, the striking edges generally are shown pointed down. For both stone tools and projectiles, side views, profiles, and reverse views customarily are shown on the right side of the front view, with cross sections and end views placed below and top views placed above.

Because of ease in reproduction, most drawings are done in ink stipple or ink line. Certain techniques have become standard for certain raw materials; pressure-chipped tools of hard and shiny stone (such as jasper and obsidian) are typically drawn in parallel line, whereas porous and grainy stone and bone implements are stippled. Pencil techniques sometimes are used for more decorative drawings where the artifact is being shown as a type and a looser technique is sufficient. Carbon dust can be used successfully instead of parallel line for very hard surfaces (figs. 21-4, 21-5, 21-6, 21-7).

Magnification of an important area, such as the tip of a stone blade or cordage detail, is frequently necessary. This enlarge-

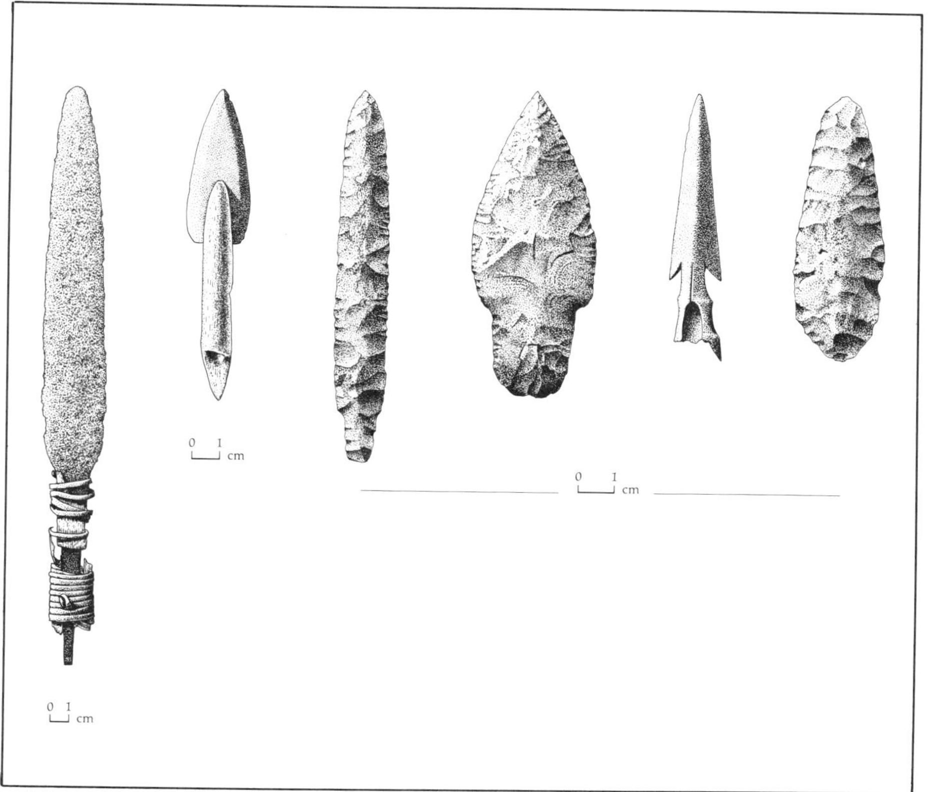

21-3. Projectiles. Left to right: knife—iron blade with wood and leather handle; end-bladed harpoon head—antler bone with slate point; arrow point—chert (variety of silica); lance point—chert; self-bladed harpoon head—antler bone; biface (tool with two sharpened edges)—chert. Barter Island sites, northeast coast of Alaska, ca. A.D. 1700. Pen-and-ink stipple on Satin Design paper, by Norman Frisch.

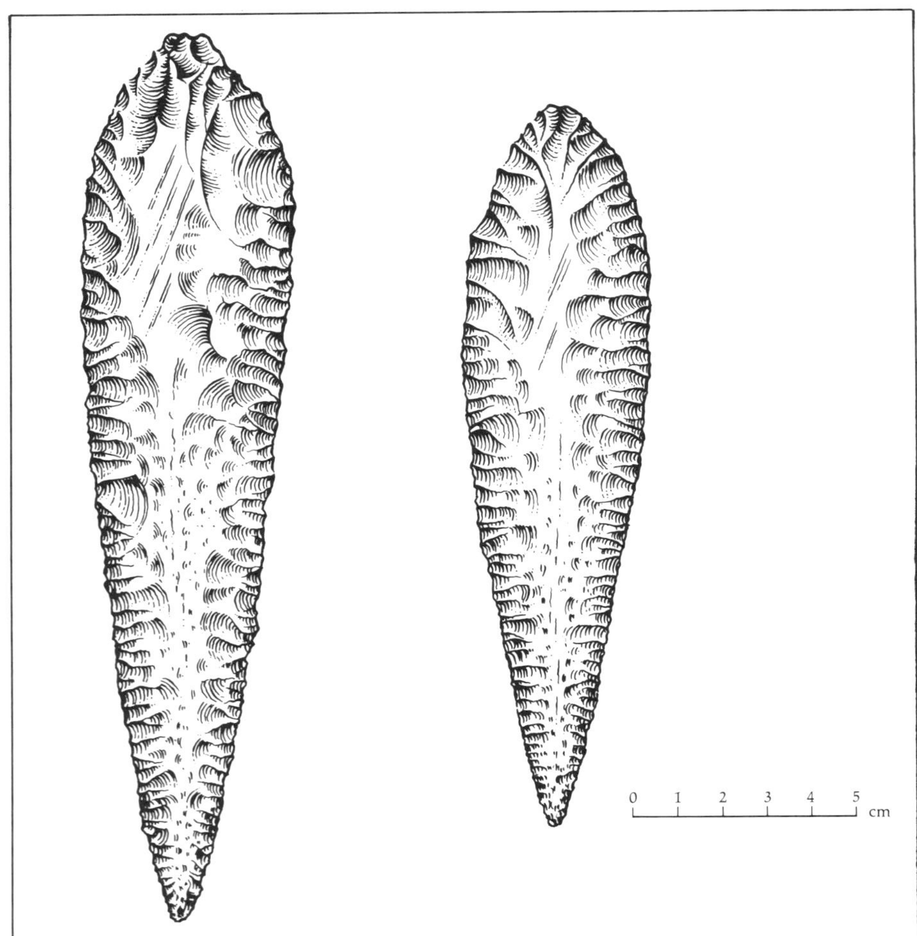

21-4. Obsidian projectiles, Costanoan Indians, California. Ink parallel line using flexible pen tip on Bristol board, by Elizabeth Morales-Denney.

ment can be
adjacent to
whole specim
sponding area
can appear wi
if the area of
sentative of t
in the cordag
part of the rir
sack and a fe
pattern used
and 21-9).

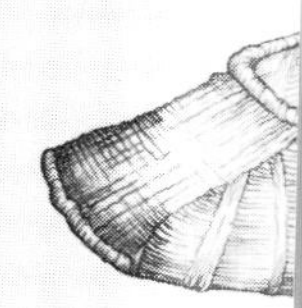

21-6. Plant-fib
Karok Indians
cil on Vidalon
Morales-Denn

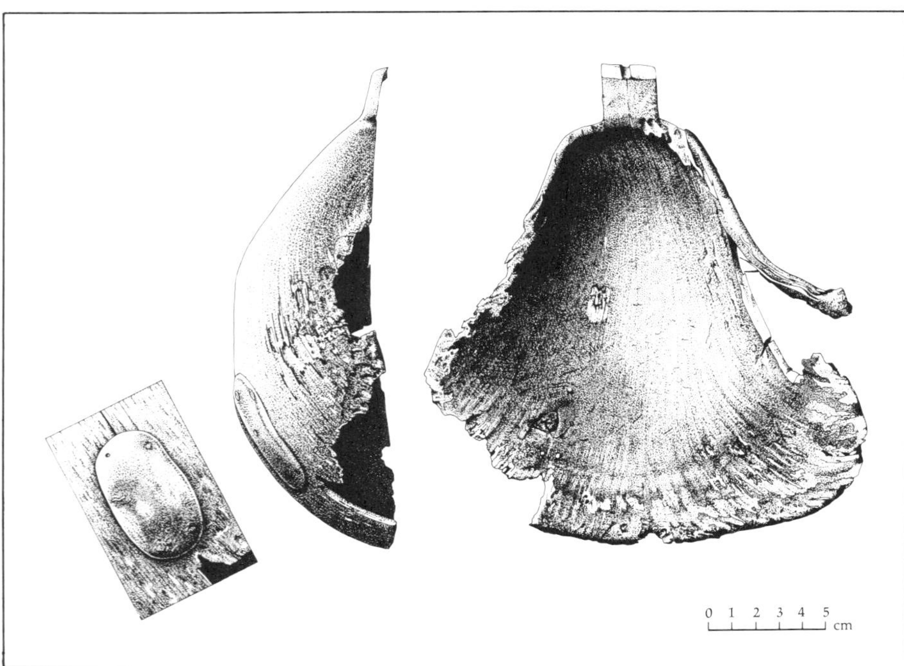

21-5. Musk-ox-horn ladle, Barter Island sites, northeast coast of Alaska, ca. A.D. 1700. Pen-and-ink line and stipple on Satin Design paper, by Norman Frisch.

21-7. Obsidi
Slope of Alas
bon dust on
Frisch.

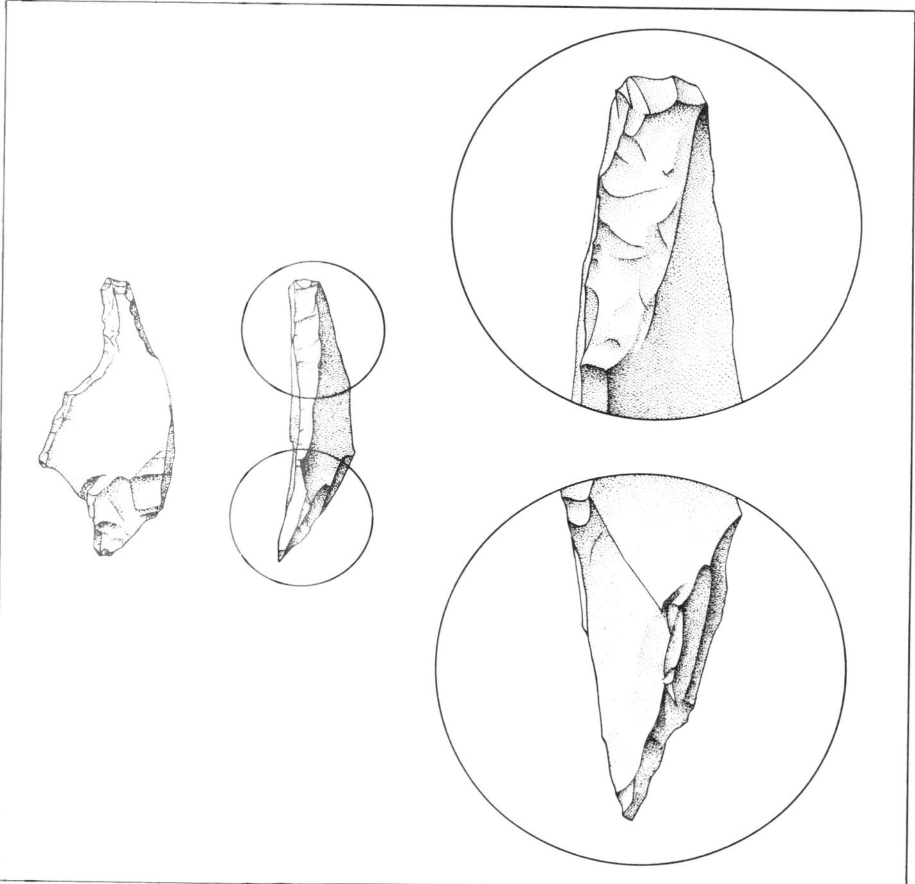

21-8. Stone tool with magnification of important areas. Pen-and-ink stipple on Bristol board, by George Robert Lewis. From *Early Formative Period of Coastal Ecuador*, by Betty J. Meggers, Clifford Evans, and Emilio Estrada (Smithsonian Institution Press, 1965).

TECHNIQUES AND PROCEDURES FOR ILLUSTRATING ARTIFACTS

Aside from the general standards in techniques to follow in meeting the usual challenges, the experienced illustrator will develop expedient variations on standard methods or may even devise completely original techniques as the subject matter demands. An example of such inventiveness is the so-called exploded view of composite objects in which the subject is shown as dissected or opened to reveal in the drawing its otherwise hidden inner form. Similar problems can be solved in illustrating complicated machinery or closed architectural structures as though fully or partially transparent (fig. 21-10).

The limitations of working in a foreign culture or at an excavation require the illustrator to devise the most efficient procedures to solve the problems that arise.

Described below are specific techniques and procedures to follow for several types of specimens unique to anthropology.

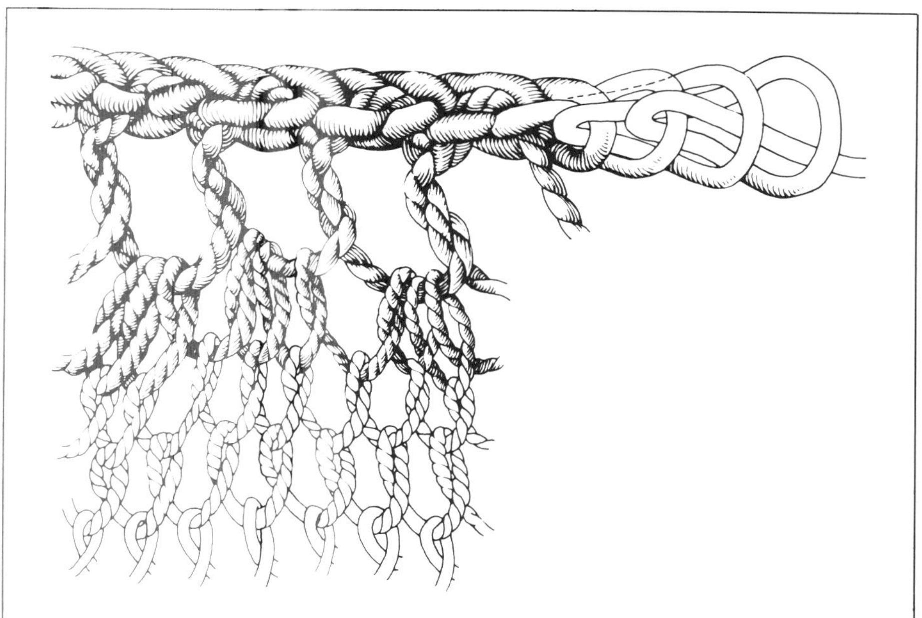

21-9. Milkweed-fiber carrying sack, Konkow Indians, California. Detail drawing by Jo Ann Moore, inked by Brigid Sullivan, pen-and-ink on Satin Design paper. From *Handbook of North American Indians*, vol. 8, *California*, Robert F. Heizer, ed. (Smithsonian Institution Press, 1978).

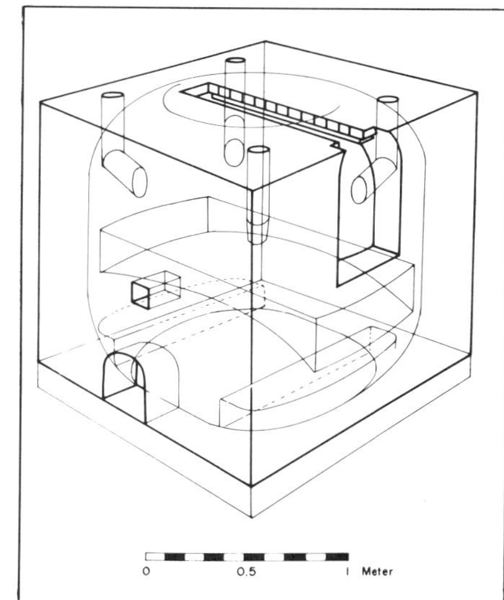

21-10. "Transparent" three-dimensional view of a Pakistani pottery kiln. Pen-and-ink on Cronaflex, by George Robert Lewis. From *Traditional Pottery Techniques of Pakistan*, by Owen S. Rye and Clifford Evans (Smithsonian Institution Press, 1976).

Rubbings

Graphite rubbings enable the illustrator to locate and delineate the raised areas of low-relief decoration on stelae (upright stone slab monuments) or incised lines on stone and bone implements. To make a rubbing of low-relief decoration, cover the area involved with very thin paper (ordinary onionskin or tracing paper) held in place with the fingers or taped to unmodified sections of the stone. (Do not apply tape to carved areas.) Lightly rub a medium-hard graphite stick across the tissue in all directions, producing a negative imprint of the raised areas (fig. 21-11). Then trace this as a positive ink drawing onto film. To ensure accuracy, make reference to the original or photographs (fig. 21-12).

The ink drawing renders schematically only the outline of the raised surface. Use stipple to define the background, or recessed, plane. This process becomes complicated when the monument is badly eroded or pitted. In such a case, it is difficult to pick up the design on a rubbing or to make out the remaining relief even with low-angled (raking) light. On such pieces, the illustrator should indicate the degree of certainty of carving on the surface by a system of ink line and stipple that can be decoded by the reader. Ian Graham, a specialist in Mayan stela illustration, suggests this system: a solid line indicates definite carved edges; a dashed line indicates eroded and possibly displaced edges, with the spacing between dashes relative to the degree of erosion. In the recessed areas, the density of stipple is also relative to the likelihood that an area once may have contained a raised feature now eroded to only a slight impression. For instance, on Mayan carved stelae, a badly eroded area above a human figure might be lightly stippled because the existence of a headdress, eroded to a vague image, is very likely, since it is known that nearly all Mayan figures on stone monuments (of which there are many) wear headdresses (except slaves, which are usually naked too). The light stipple does not attempt to reconstruct the headdress; it simply alerts the reader to a possibly significant, although now unrecognizable, area of badly eroded carving (*Corpus of Maya Hieroglyphic Inscriptions*, by Ian Graham—see Bibliography).

21-11. Colonial-period tombstone, Boston, Massachusetts, ca.
rubbing on paper, by Elizabeth Morales-Denney.

21-12. Schematic drawing of tombstone rubbing shown in figu
vellum paper, by Elizabeth Morales-Denney.

Rollouts

A rollout
sion of paint
a round obj
21-13). It is a
jection. Roll
is important
phy on a v
shape. Obv
geometric
some Amer
dian pottery

out because the reader has the cognitive ability to predict the appearance of a repetitive pattern on unseen sides.

Two-dimensional rollouts can be created by lightly taping together strips of clear plastic around the surface of the object vertically, like sections of an orange, and then using a marker or ink to trace the decoration onto the plastic. Be sure that the tape touches only the plastic, not the pot surface. Any clear malleable plastic, such as dry-cleaning bags or kitchen wrap, can be used. After tracing, carefully remove the plastic strips and tape them flat in sequential order on a board. The resulting crude rollout design will form an uneven row with elliptical spaces left between the strips. Trace a finished drawing from this rough preliminary. These tracings will be rough, and reference to the original is recommended when rendering the finished drawing.

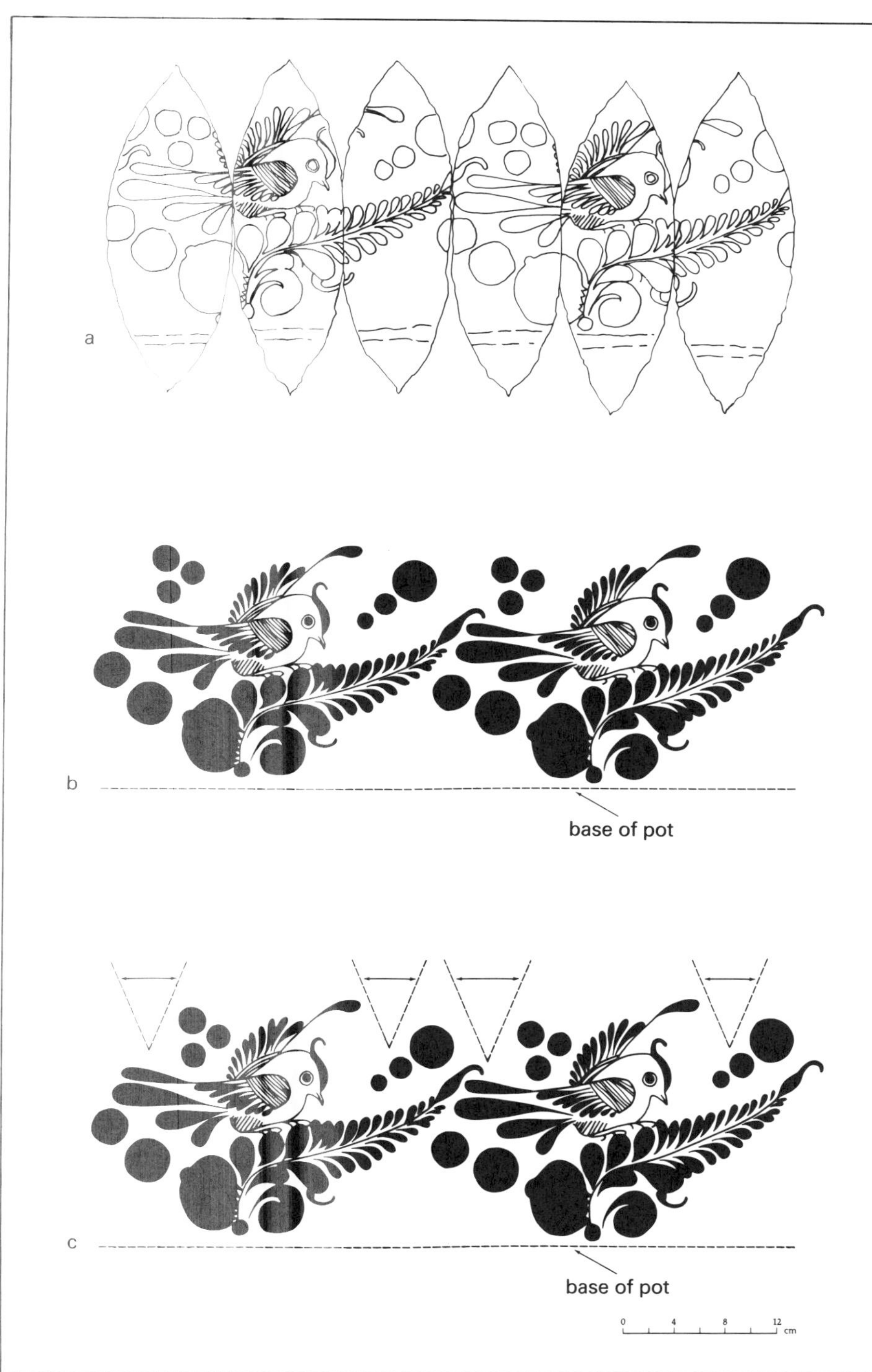

21-13. Rollout of iconography on a vase, Morelia, Mexico: *(a)* rough tracing taken directly from vase; *(b)* more refined illustration of the rough, with motifs spaced at the top to fill in blank areas; *(c)* dashed lines indicate blank areas. Pen-and-ink on polyester film, by Elizabeth Morales-Denney.

Rollouts create a problem, in that the relationship of objects in a design at the very top and sometimes at the bottom may be distorted, depending on the curve of the vessel. This distortion can be corrected by slightly enlarging the motifs at the very top and bottom to fill in the blank spaces and bring the motifs closer together (as in a Mercator projection of the continents, which exaggerates the size of northern- and southernmost landmasses), or by slightly respacing motifs to fill in the blank areas, just as the circle motifs are respaced to float more evenly in the blank areas (fig. 21–13). If either of these is done, the reader should be informed in a footnote. A third possibility is to indicate in dashes how the iconography articulates across the blank spaces created by flattening out this sphere, also shown in fig. 21-13.

Color Coding

Color coding an illustration for black-and-white reproduction is done with shading films in several patterns or percentage dot screens. A light dot pattern such as a 20 percent screen can be used for pale colors, a medium dot screen for darker colors, and so on. Additional colors can be indicated with other patterns. All color-coded drawings must contain a key. Color coding also can be done by hand stippling (fig. 21-14).

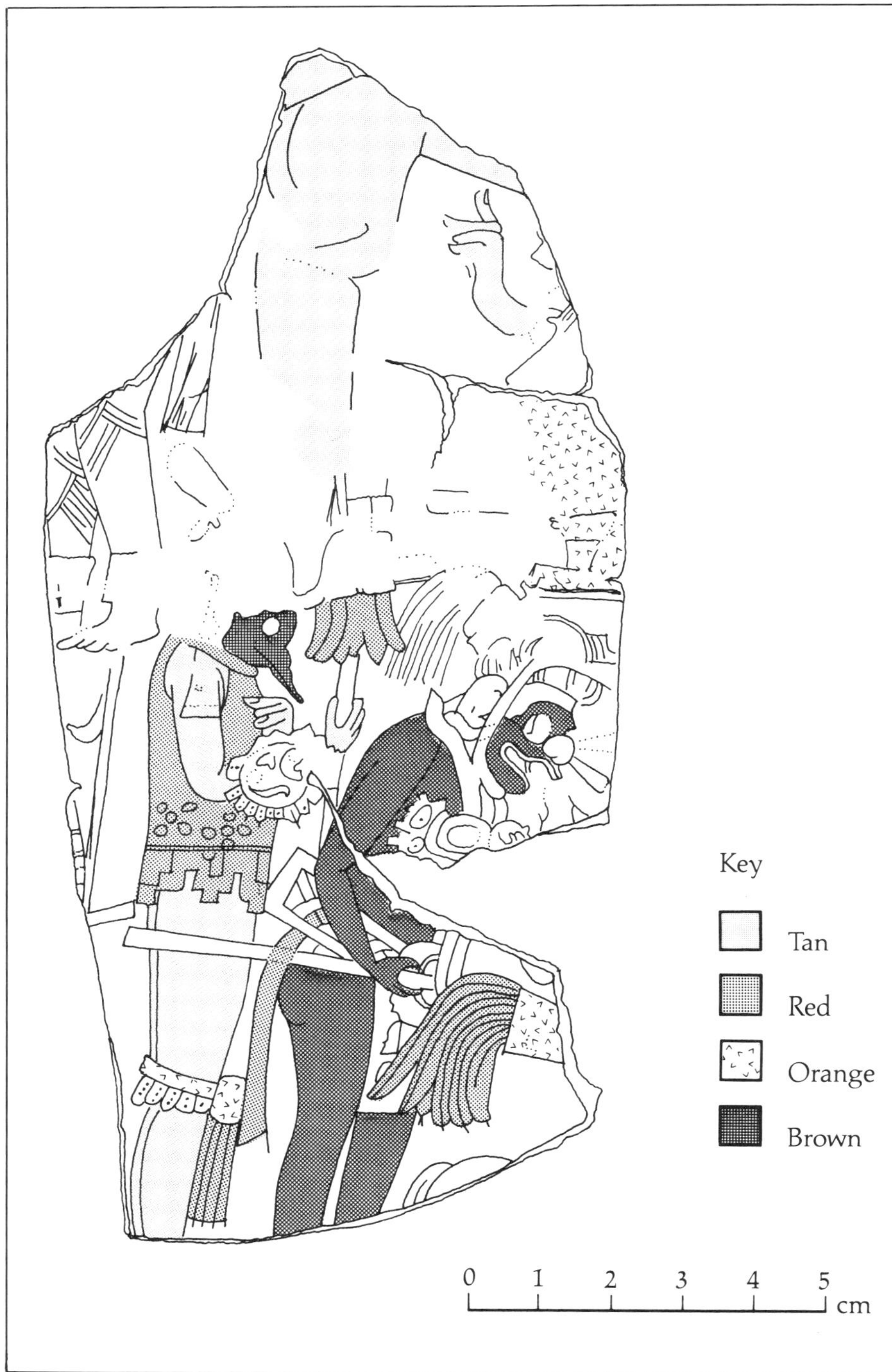

21-14. Color-coded drawing using shading films. Mayan polychrome pottery sherd. Polol site, Guatemala. Ink line and shading film on Dura-lene film, by Elizabeth Morales-Denney.

Pottery Profiles

The standard profile drawing of whole ceramic vessels combines both an interior and an exterior view. In one method of delineating the external contours, the pottery object is placed on graph paper on its side within the right angle created by two wooden panels hinged to each other (constructed in a convenient size by the artist). Either the rim or the base of the pot, whichever is largest in diameter,

must be held
panels, while
touches the ot
sition, the ves
dimension wi
exactly perpe
paper surface
its outline car
graph paper v
ing triangle se
dicular to th
touching the
the triangle
pot, these po
then connec
line to produ
complete out

Sometimes
lay a pot on
Whitney Pov
the following
tical measur
triangles anc
ers. Tape a
and tape th
back so the
up. With t
against the
use the oth
tally to me
Then plot
points that
the profile
main mea
height and
(which can
ing a ruler
ing). Halve
draw in the
Do not take
set interval
at every 10
the vessel
best to mea

Another
drawing of
a pot is v
(carpenter's
posed of a
comb of m
pressed aga
sel, one sm
produce a t
2-21).

Drawing
sels are di
solid or a

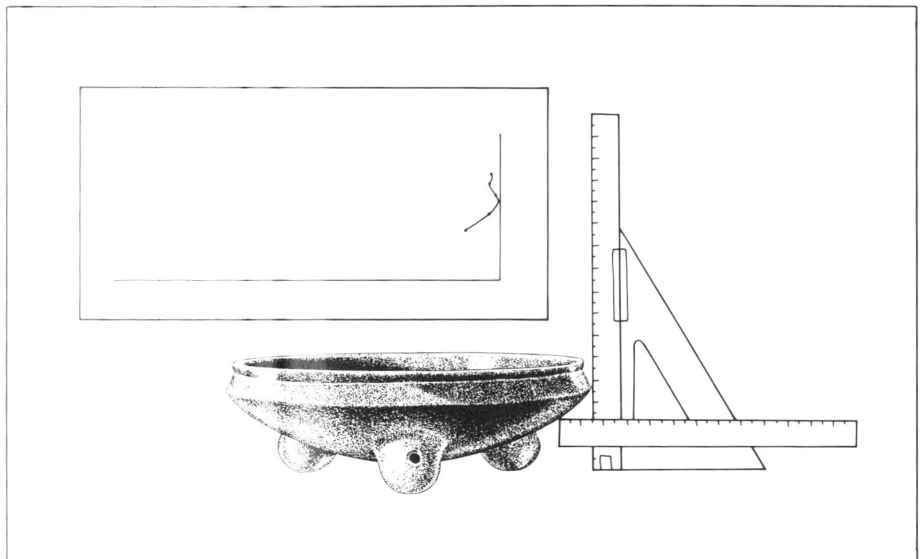

21-15. Triangle-and-ruler apparatus for drawing pottery profiles. Pen-and-ink on film, by Whitney Powell-Cummer. Reprinted from the *Proceedings* of the GNSI 1986 International Conference.

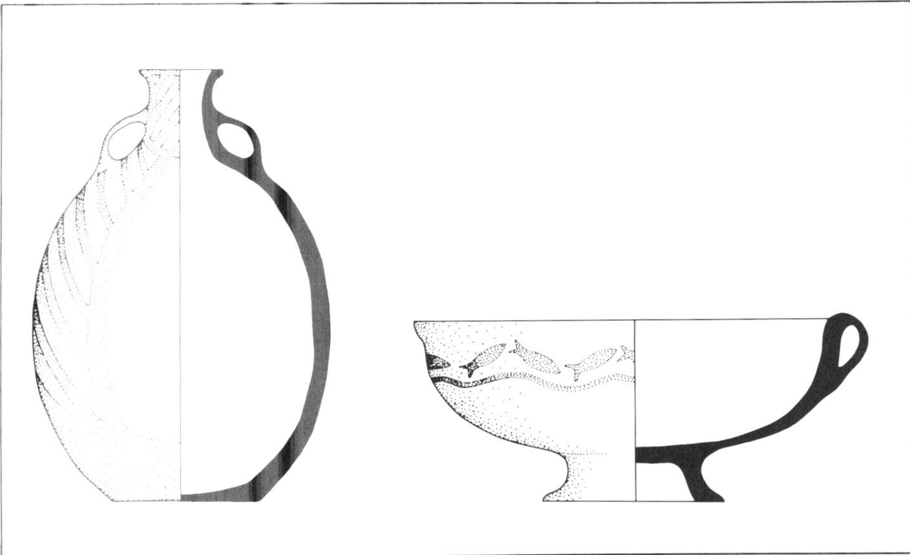

21-16. Profile drawings of pottery jar and bowl. Pen-and-ink on Dura-lene film, by Elizabeth Morales-Denney.

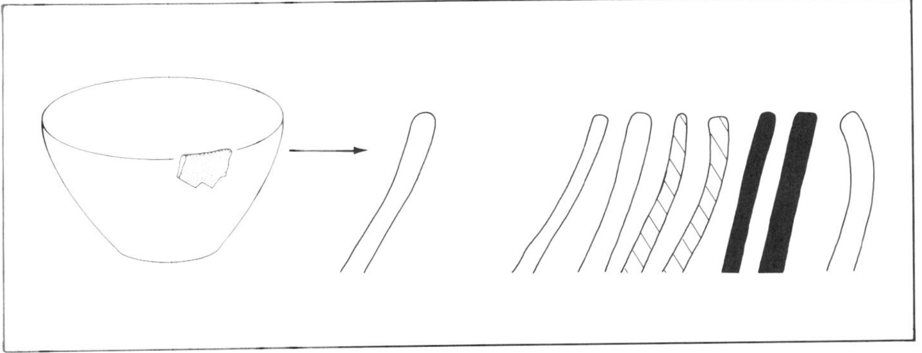

21-17. Profile drawings of related groups of pottery sherds. Pen-and-ink on Dura-lene film, by Elizabeth Morales-Denney.

from the rim to the base, separating the normally rendered exterior view from the more diagrammatic interior view. American convention has the interior view on the right; British publications require it on the left. If the object has only one handle, this feature should be shown in profile on the side with the interior view (fig. 21-16).

To determine the internal contours of pottery vessels (when the diameter at the top opening is large enough to permit a probe with instruments), insert reverse calipers and a ruler (see fig. 2-20). The thickness of the vessel walls is usually shown in solid black if moderately thin and crosshatched if thick. Certain specimens are so structurally complex, narrow-necked, or thickly corroded that only X-ray photographs, provided by the scientist, are likely to reveal their actual form.

Potsherds

Well-planned and accurate drawings of even the most nondescript potsherds (broken pottery parts) can help to establish their scientific importance. Easily identified rim and base sherds are referred to as diagnostic because their integral stance in the original unbroken vessel can be redetermined in simple profile drawings. Deciding on the proper stance for base sherds is not difficult, since they can be set firmly and evenly on a flat surface. Rim sherds, however, often require some manipulation to be positioned at the correct angle for illustration, which is only then assured if no line of light can be seen under their smooth edges when pressed against a flat surface. Draw preliminary pencil sketches of related groups of sherd profiles on graph paper in horizontal rows and then trace them in ink (fig. 21-17). Add labeling, measurements, and ornamental details as requested by the scientist. The full diameter of bases and rims of incomplete vessels can be reasonably estimated by matching the curve of sherds to a chart of concentric circles. Base sherds should be held flat on the chart and rim sherds should be held vertically so that they are resting upside down on the rim edge. If the curve of the sherd matches the curve of one of the circles on the chart, it can be assumed that the rim or base of the entire pot had about the diameter of that circle before it was broken (fig. 21-18).

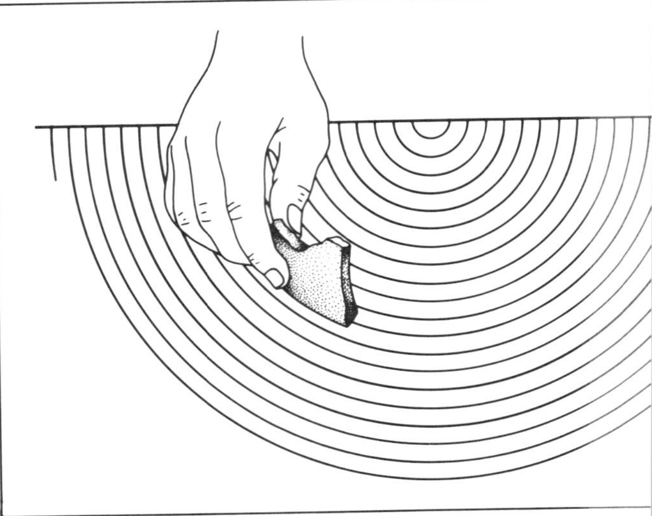

21-18. Matching the curve of a rim sherd to estimate the diamet
Pen-and-ink on Cronaflex, by George Robert Lewis. Courtesy of

Restoration and Architectural Reconstructions

A controversial issue in anthropological illustration is whether or not the artist should take the liberty of completing missing parts of an artifact in the drawing. And, if the artist does attempt to do this, what rules should govern such liberties. Obviously, the solution to this problem needs to be arrived at on a case-by-case basis. There are no overall rules or guidelines. One of the crucial issues is to decide the degree of completeness an artifact must possess for the illustrator to add the missing parts. These decisions are made by the specialist. Illustrators are not required, and should not attempt, to embellish an artifact with hypothetical parts, however natural or appropriate the addition may seem. Some restoration can be done if it can be determined that the missing pieces are part of a symmetrically decorative scheme, or when the artifact has many identically made twins within that particular culture and time period. For example, it is known that much of the elaborate pottery of Precolumbian Peru was made from reusable molds that produced many identical vessels. When there is insufficient evidence for authentic restoration, dashed lines can suggest possible form.

Extraneous surface characteristics are often purposefully omitted in anthropological illustration, although their deletion depends on the needs of the scientist. Cracks are frequently deleted from pottery that has been glued together in the lab, whereas cracks and chips made by the people who used the pottery (determined by dating methods) are always included in the drawing because this is visual information for the reader inter-

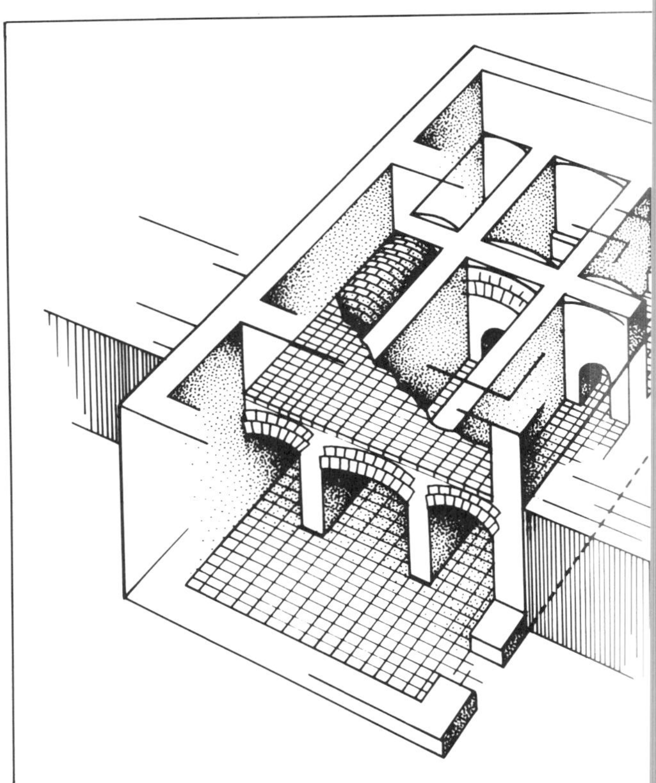

21-19. Reconstruction from photographs of ruined mud-brick
Cronaflex, by George Robert Lewis. Courtesy of G. W. Van B

ested in ho
whether it w
monial ware
and will sh
wear.)

The illustr
urge while d
crooked pott

sloppy paint application, realign an asymmetrical projectile, and generally eliminate signs of poor or hasty workmanship by the creator of the specimen. Resist this urge. The fact that an artifact may have been created swiftly or carelessly may have very significant social implications in terms of its value and use within that culture. An idealized restoration would produce a prettier drawing but make these clues unavailable to the reader.

Architectural reconstructions involve the conceptualization of structures through consultation with the scientist, analysis of site plans, and measurements of photographs of ruins and undamaged prototypes. These architectural drawings most often are rendered schematically and in orthographic projection (fig. 21-19).

Occasionally architectural reconstructions are done quite realistically, in full color with inhabitants doing everyday tasks. These more creative approaches to archaeological illustration are often part of museum exhibits and are sometimes used decoratively in special scientific publications.

Cultural Settings ("Scenes")

Illustrations of cultural settings in the field usually include people doing everyday tasks, performing in elaborately costumed ceremonies, using tools, and so on. Most of the time these scenes are staged by the anthropologist in cooperation with the informant and other members of the group. If the culture being studied does not prohibit them, photographs are the best material to work from.

At home, scale up the image using photocopy enlargements of the prints or projection of slides. These scenes generally are drawn in simple, clean ink line. Often a drawing of this kind will accompany a more realistic detailed drawing of the object being carried or worn (fig. 21-20).

EXCAVATIONS

Jennifer Loynd Cowherd

Illustration for an archaeological project is a two-step process that begins at the excavation site and moves into the studio after the completion of a field season. The illustrator, whose job usually requires a combination of artistic and drafting skills, is considered a member of an expedition's technical staff of specialists. Compensation can include undergraduate or graduate school credits, travel expenses with food and lodging at the site, and/or a salary. Classical sites with extraordinary architecture may employ a professional architect.

During an excavation project, dialogue among the expedition director, each field supervisor, and the illustrator determines a priority list for drawings. It is the illustrator's responsibility to provide input

Whitney Powell-Cummer contributed to the text on excavations.

21-20. Illustration of a cultural setting: costumed participant in a ceremonial dance, Carajá Indians, Brazil. Figure is wearing the feather necklace from figure 21-1 and holding rattle from figure 21-2. Pen-and-ink on Dura-lene film, by Elizabeth Morales-Denney.

concerning which features lend themselves best to a drawn record and to make judgments about a timetable, so that the director can establish work assignments. The illustrator should have at least a general understanding of the history and special characteristics of the subject matter (such as an architectural feature's construction method, original function, and style) and be well informed about the recording procedures used in field notes and in the registration book. Projects generally adopt a grid type of classification system for record keeping.

Accuracy is paramount. Field drawings, completed on graph paper or film, provide all pertinent information that will appear in the final format, and hence need only to be transformed into publishable form in the studio. Notations of site name, field name or number, unit or square number, locus number, drawing scale, date, and illustrator's initials should be lettered on each drawing. Seemingly obvious information, such as the name of the site, might not be so apparent years later in the context of an office file.

Three basic types of illustrations are drawn on location: the field plan or top plan, the balk section or profile, and the subject in situ. Additionally, survey work includes preparing topographic plans that define a site's relationship to its environment. It is assumed that topographic maps of the site and its environs have been secured prior to any excavation. A primary surveyor's benchmark must also have been established and a baseline (which is usually aligned with either true or magnetic north) originating from this benchmark defined for reference for all future field grids. From this primary benchmark, surveying procedures should have established additional benchmarks readily available for reference in each field under excavation.

21-21. Aerial view of an excavated field at Bab Edh-Dhra, Jordan; excavations sponsored by the American Schools of Oriental Research. Photo by R. Henry Cowherd. Courtesy of R. Thomas Schaub and Walter E. Rast.

Field Plan

The field p
than a topogr
tire site. It des
cavation area
delimited in re
surface struct
and divided
bered units by
excavation.
field plan is t
tural structur
cant features
unit to unit.
from a groun
within the wa
it sometimes
sociations an
21-21, 21-22).

Field plan
soon as exca
way. The fie
ent the illu
initial conce
uncovered. I
porarily inte
digging, plan
be illustrate
tating every
to field, pr
each plan wh
tion. Illustra
and artifact
a completion
excavation p

Drawing s
cided upon i
expedition d
be consisten
as balk se
site. The s
times calle
is reproduc
paper. Nex
vated strips
Balks corre
surveyor's
excavation
gates, door
forms, as w
tic, and in
then drawn

Such rep
plished w
methods a
ments. At

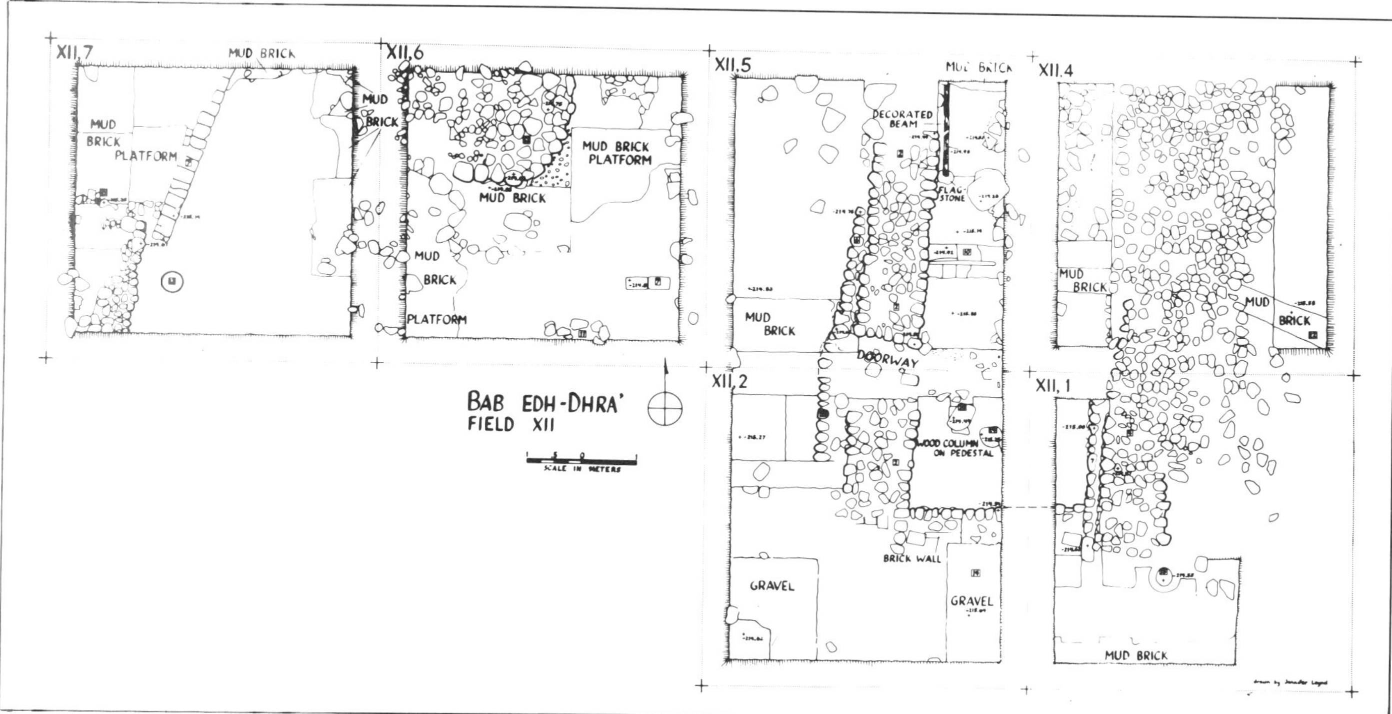

21-22. Field plan of the field in figure 21-21. All elevations are negative numbers because the site is located below sea level, and locus numbers are distinguished by having been enclosed in a box. Pen-and-ink on film, by Jennifer Loynd Cowherd. Courtesy of R. Thomas Schaub and Walter E. Rast.

assistant is helpful for holding and stretching meter tapes as well as to call off measurement figures as they are plotted.

Primary Measuring Methods

1. Iron stakes at the corner of each unit of the grid provide a known point, both in the field and on the graph paper, from which to measure. If more stakes need to be added, the following principle can be applied. Any baseline of 4m will form a right triangle with a 3m side and a 5m hypotenuse. Swing measuring tapes from each end of the baseline until this situation exists. Then extend the right angle as needed. Strings tied to each stake lie along the center of each balk and form perpendicular lines along which measurements can be taken. Obvious measurements to begin with are the points where features intersect the string lines or the balks.
2. When a feature does not cross the surveyor's grid or extend into any balks, measurements are taken with the surveying procedure of triangulation. If points A and B represent two corners of a unit, plot the position of point C, isolated within the unit, by measuring the length of lines AC and BC (fig. 21-23). After calculating A to C with a tape measure, represent the same distance on the plan by an arc made with a drafting compass. Describe another arc for distance B to C. The two arcs intersect at point C.
3. In the case where features are located at varying elevations, measurements can be read along a meter tape made horizontal with the use of a small liquid-bubble-type line level hung from a string. Plot the significant feature at the point of intersection with a string attached to a plumb bob (fig. 21-24).
4. Once the orientation of a feature is correctly established on the graph paper in relation to the surveyor's grid, draw individual stones or bricks with the aid of a meter tape attached by clothespins to a string stretched along that feature. After obtaining permission from the field supervisor, step carefully along the top of an architectural struc-

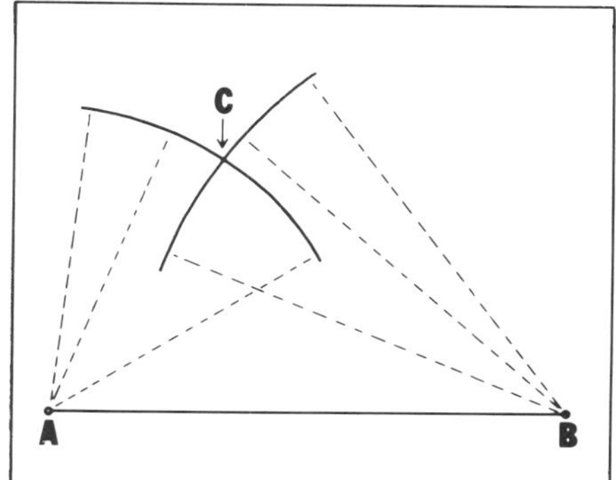

21-23. Triangulation: the positions of points A and B are known. An arc is drawn from point A to the distance of point C. Point C is located at the intersection of the two arcs. Pen-and-ink on film, by Jennifer Loynd Cowherd.

ture, looking directly down upon it while drawing. Include protruding lower courses in the field plan. Map (with a broken line or grayed area) less clearly defined features such as mounds of rubble or vague refuse dumps.

5. With two 2m and two 1m slats of wood, a few nails, and some string, a simple portable miniature grid can be constructed to facilitate drawing complex flat patterned areas of paving, foundation, postholes. Each square in this device corresponds to one printed on the graph paper. Caution: to avoid distortion, view the grid from directly above, in a line from eye to subject perpendicular to the grid (fig. 21-25).
6. Finally, highlight the line defining the top course or the outer

edge of ea
ture in wid
in ink on
Print eleva
field plan.
local field
method de
24. North
field plan.
netic com

Underground

An underg
as a tomb,
similar purp
slightly diffe
of its lack of s
Architecture
mal, and ar
21-26, 21-27)
taut between
the floor of t
tablish a str
through the c
Begin the pl
line represen
be pinned t
surements f
first to the p
ber and the
tures. A s
situated per
nal may be c

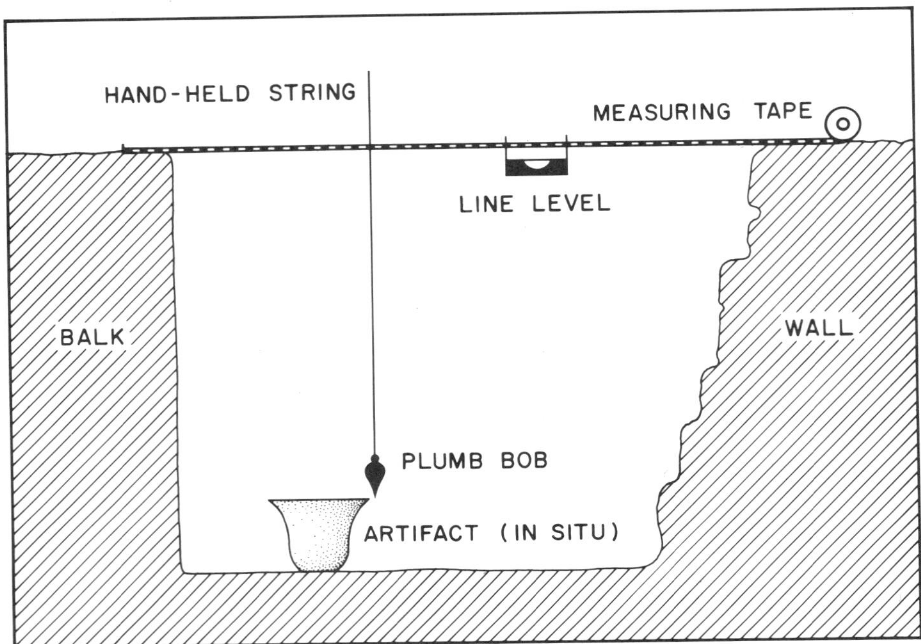

21-24. Features located at different elevations are measured for a field plan with a horizontal meter tape and a plumb bob hung from a string. Pen-and-ink on Cronaflex, by George Robert Lewis.

Each c
should be e
tive field su
explanatory
bers can b
tures. With
loci, which
here as feat
field notes.
made or al
has been
given a loc
field plan i
information
simplificati
can be add
field plan
using trac
situations
larly large
desirable t
map on the

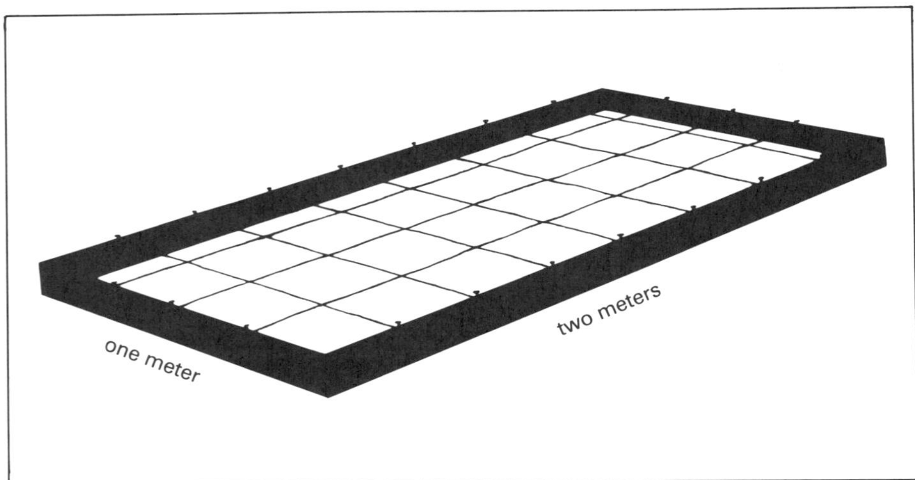

21-25. Wood-framed grid to aid in the observation of an area with complex flat patterns, such as is found in square 6 of the field plan in figure 21-22. Pen-and-ink and shading film on film, by Jennifer Loynd Cowherd.

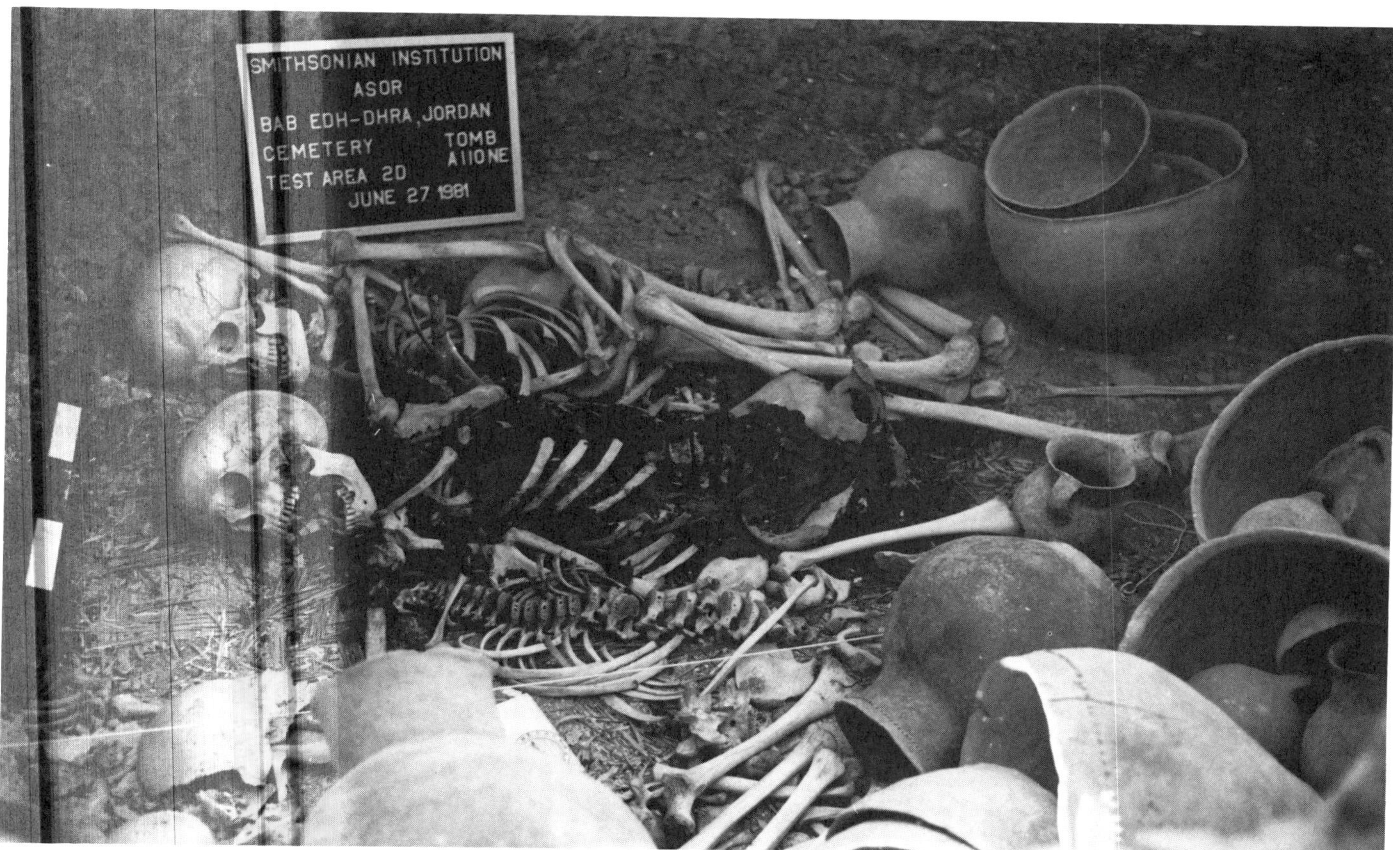

21-26. Photograph taken through opening into tomb. Tomb ceiling was too low to photograph contents from directly overhead. Photo by Dr. Bruno Fröhlich. From "Excavations of the Early Bronze Age Cemetery at Bab Edh-Dhra, Jordan, 1981," a preliminary report by Bruno Fröhlich and Donald J. Ortner, the *Annual of the Department of Antiquities*, Hashemite Kingdom of Jordan, 1982, vol. 26.

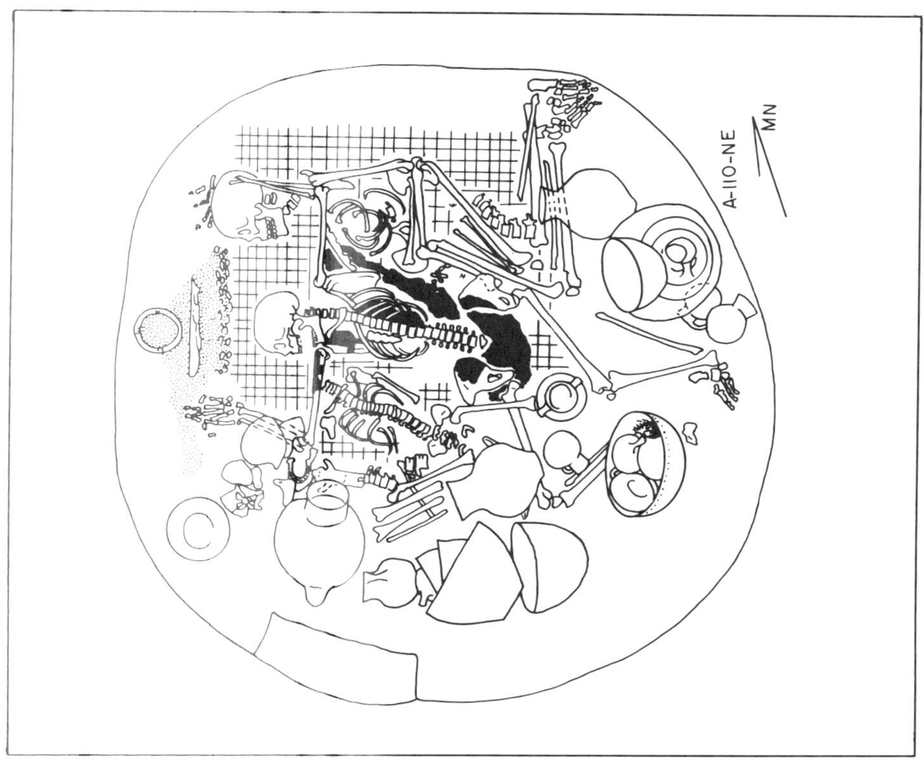

21-27. Drawing of tomb scene shown in figure 21-26, Bab Edh-Dhra, Jordan. This tomb contained the remains of three people: a man (top), a woman (with jaws agape), and a child lying in the crook of the woman's right arm (only the vertebral column of the child is easy to see). Black areas indicate cloth still clinging to the skeleton. The hatched pattern indicates the reed matting beneath the skeletons. The bodies were surrounded with stacks of pottery before the tomb was sealed. Some of the pottery appears to have toppled over in an earthquake. The overhead drawing was obtained by stretching a string across the width of the tomb, nailing it down, and then stretching a second string at a right angle to the first. Points were then drawn by triangulating from these two strings. This is a very slow, laborious process, but results are quite accurate. Pen-and-ink on Cronaflex, by Ellen Paige. From "Excavations of the Early Bronze Age Cemetery at Bab Edh-Dhra, Jordan, 1981," a preliminary report by Bruno Fröhlich and Donald J. Ortner, the *Annual of the Department of Antiquities*, Hashemite Kingdom of Jordan, 1982, vol. 26.

Balk Section or Profile

Each balk cuts a cross section through layers of soil and debris as they have been deposited chronologically. The purpose of a balk-section illustration is to diagram this horizontal stratigraphic record that exposes the time sequence associated with features found in the vertical excavation process (figs. 21-28, 21-29).

Rarely are the layers in a balk clearly discernible; therefore, the section drawing should be done in collaboration with the excavator of that particular unit, who is familiar with its subtleties. In a particularly difficult reading, it is judicious to have the excavator or field supervisor score the strata with a trowel.

21-28. Balk section prepared for illustration. Horizontal strin a cloth tape is attached. Measurements are taken above and metal tape measure. Photo by R. Henry Cowherd.

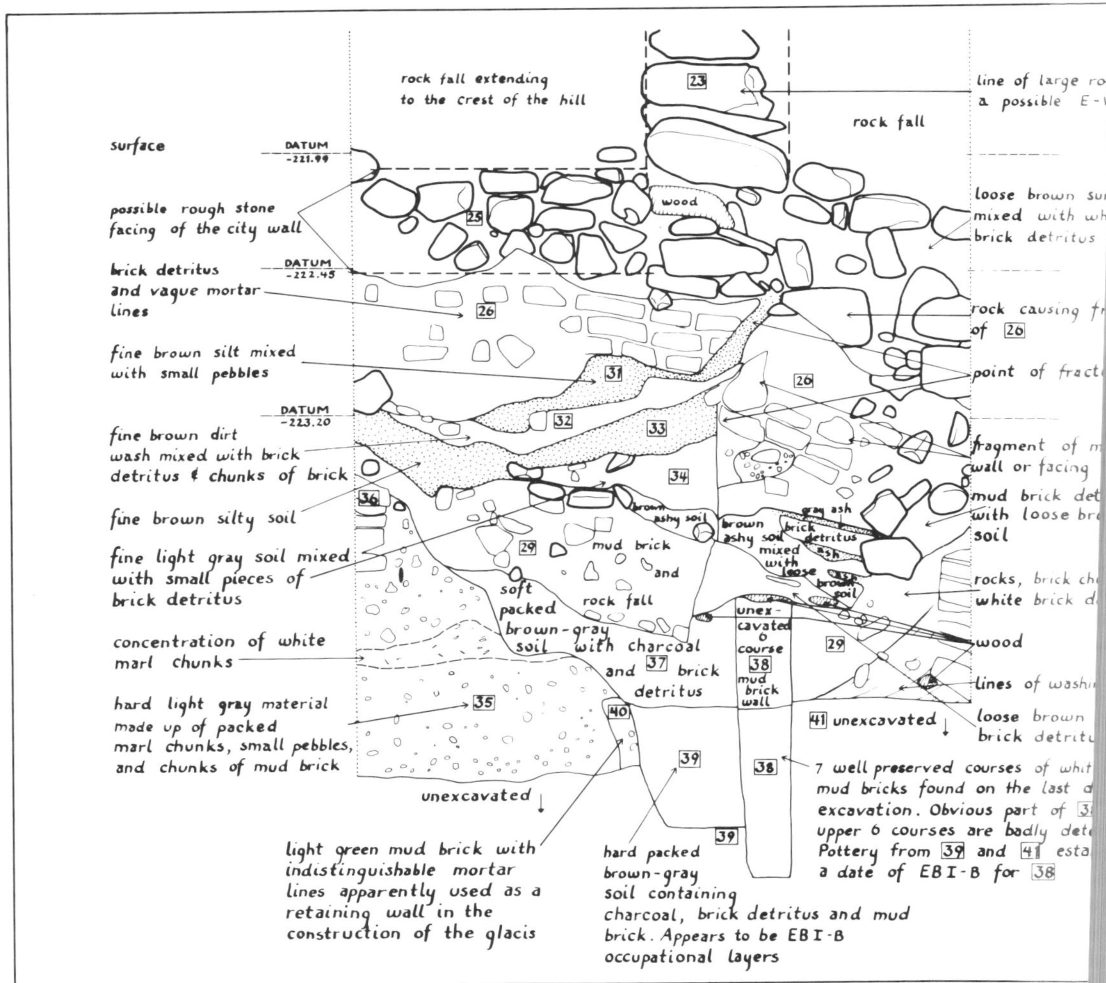

21-29. Balk section illustration. (This balk is virtually inaccessible for a photographic overview.) Pen-and-ink on film, by Jennifer Loynd Cowherd. Adapted from a preliminary drawing by David McCreery. Sponsored by the American Schools of Oriental Research. Courtesy of R. Thomas Schaub and Walter E. Rast.

To eliminate interference from the glare of the sun, make observations for the drawing when the significant side of the balk is in shadow. The layers also can be more clearly differentiated by spraying the balk with water from a plastic atomizer.

In choosing the drawing scale, try to match that of the field plan. A larger scale, however, may be necessary to accommodate a greater quantity of information.

Establish a horizontal datum line on the profile of the balk, again with two nails and a taut string with a meter tape pinned to it. Begin the section illustration with this line drawn to scale on millimeter graph paper. Measure and depict strata above and below the datum. Deep balks are more easily read and drawn with the inclusion of several datum lines. Derive the elevation of the datum by calculations from that field's benchmark. Label each balk layer in the illustration with a concise, printed description (see fig. 21-29). In addition to the aforementioned drawing identifications, note the general direction toward which one faces to view the balk—that is to say, a west balk forms the west side of its square and faces to the east.

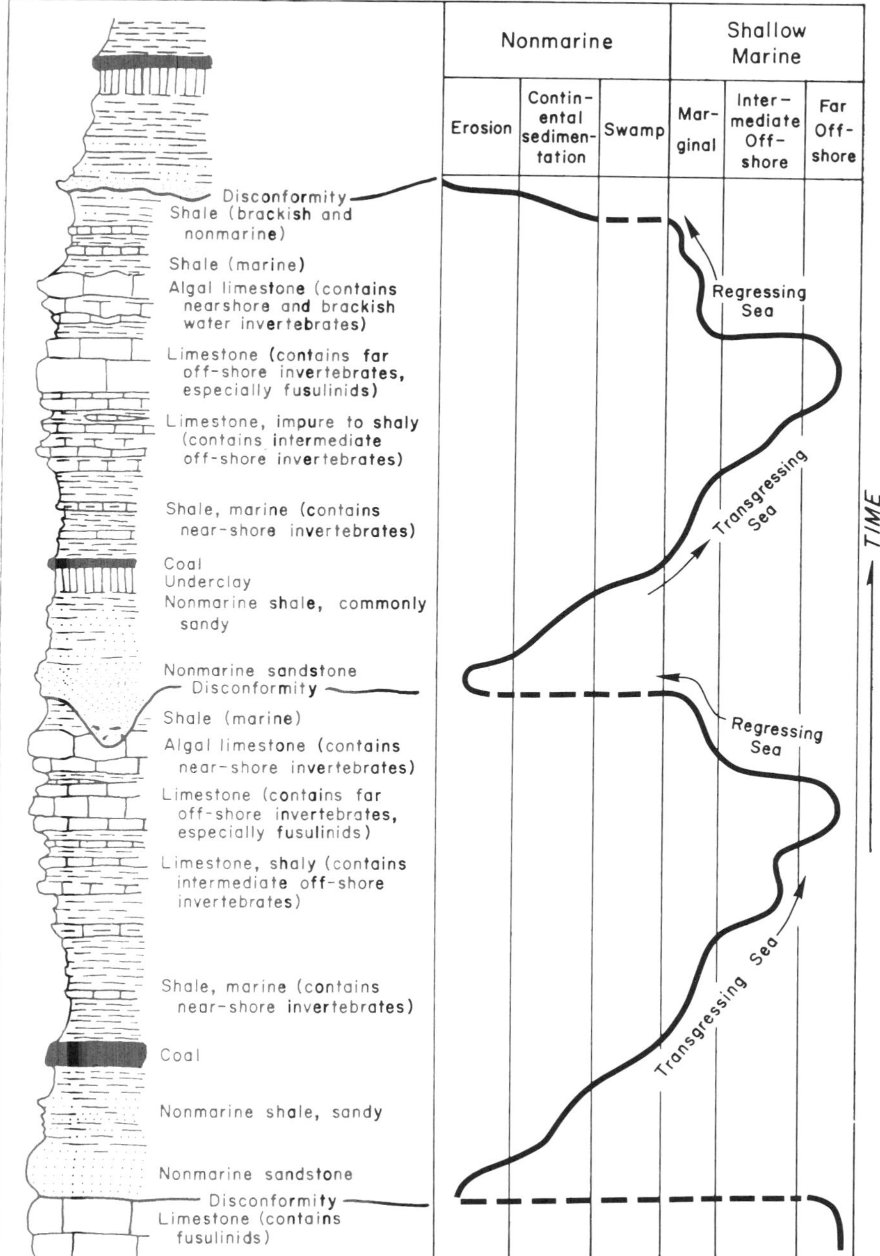

21-30. This geologic section is keyed to the graph on the right showing changes in environment with time. Technical pen and ink, flexible charting tape, Leroy lettering and Geotype dry-transfer lettering, on Albanene polyester film, by David Crouch. From J. C. Crowell, in *American Journal of Science*, vol. 278, 1978.

Later, in the studio, balk sections may be rendered naturalistically or stylistically. Naturalistic symbols somewhat resemble their appearance in nature. Here, strict junctions between layers often are not shown; one kind of material is blended into another. A naturalistic section should still have a key; visual recognition of natural elements is not enough (fig. 21-30).

In stylized sections, abstract symbols differentiate the strata. Junctions between layers are usually marked by a continuous, rather bold line. Each layer should contrast sharply with those above and below it (fig. 21-31). For either type of section representation, a key can be placed outside the drawn area, or labels can be placed within the sections or next to them as space permits. Another solution is to draw an overall plan of a complicated or large section in the stylistic manner, laying out the major areas, and then repeat a series of smaller, more detailed, naturalistic sections.

Balk section drawings provide the third dimension to complement field plans. Always cross-reference sections and plans of an area by labeling both similarly, for example, using a-a or b-b on the section and plan (fig. 21-32). Identify the part of the plan drawn in section with a title, such as "West Profile, Trench 11a, North-South." Indicate positions of significant finds in drawn sections, if possible. Each illustration section should have on it the site and field names, unit

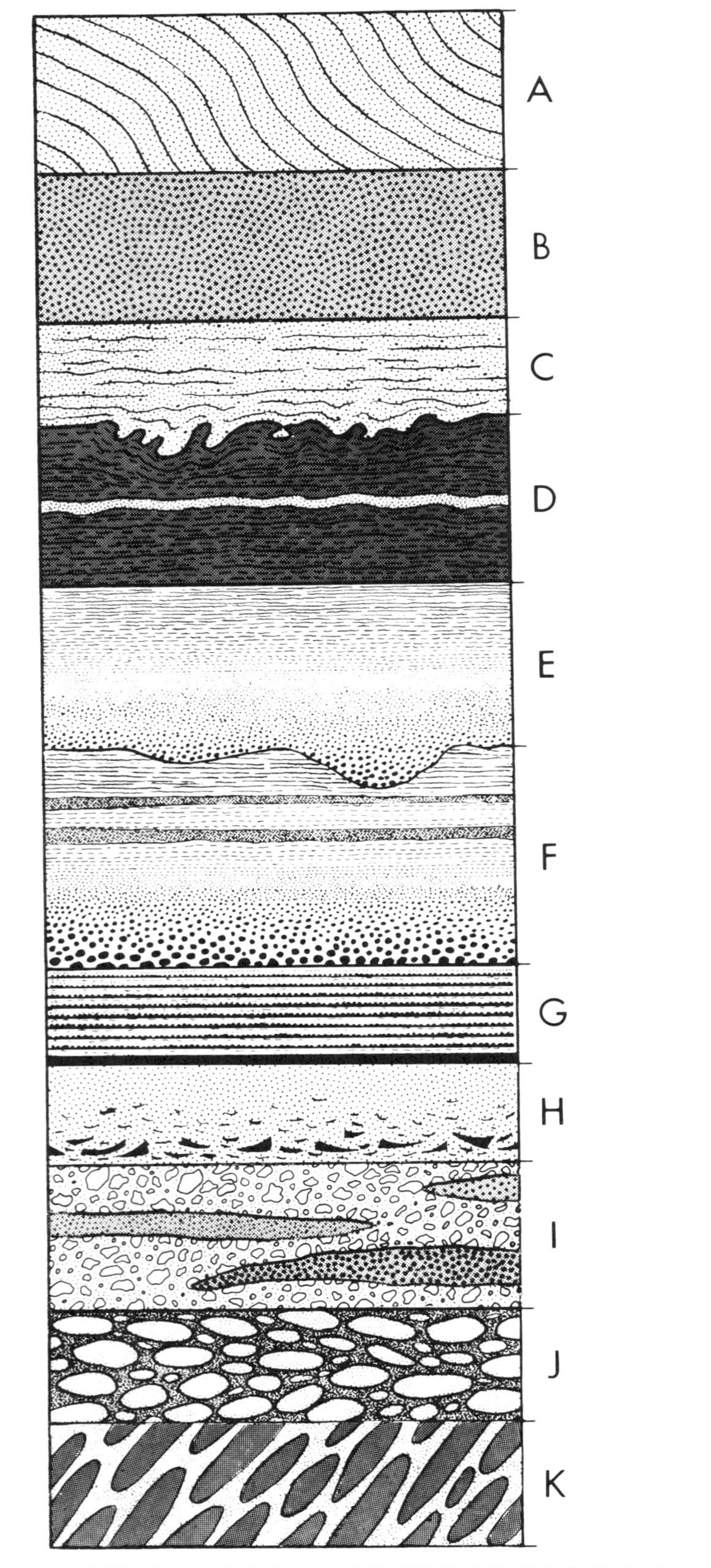

21-31. Stylized geological section. Pen-and-ink with shading films on tracing paper, by Terry L. Chase. From ***Environments Through Time: A Laboratory Manual in Historical Geology***, 2d ed., by R. L. Anstey and Terry L. Chase (Burgess Publishing, 1979).

numbers, da
initials or na
rections.

Block diag
illustrate sec
sions (see fi
40). Techniq
and charts a
sections (see
type of secti
structed pro
21-33).

Subject in

An archa
tifact in situ
task for the
because it
from its pl
fully record
of this kind
to general
methods. A
probably w
that is not
image of a
painting o
relief is bes
matic line
upon the
working c
drawing n
from obs
ment of th
ing photog
artifact of
measured
manner a
tific illust
and 2). N
on the dra
field or to
possible,
under var

Large,
reach fea
lustrated
tographic
prints. T
size, the
taken in
to avoid
edges. T
traced, c
ink on a
overlay

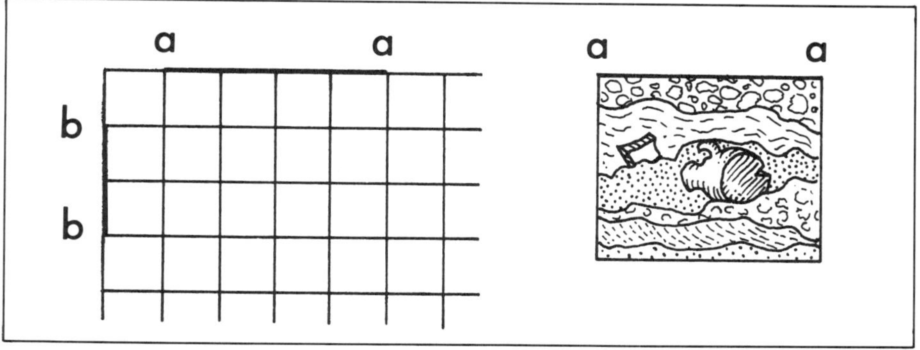

21-32. Cross-referencing site plan and section drawing. Left: bird's-eye view of diagrammatic site plan through a grid, with sections a–a and b–b labeled; right: view of the soil cross section a–a from within the excavation site, showing artifacts within the stratification where they were found. Technical pen and ink on vellum paper, by Elaine R. S. Hodges.

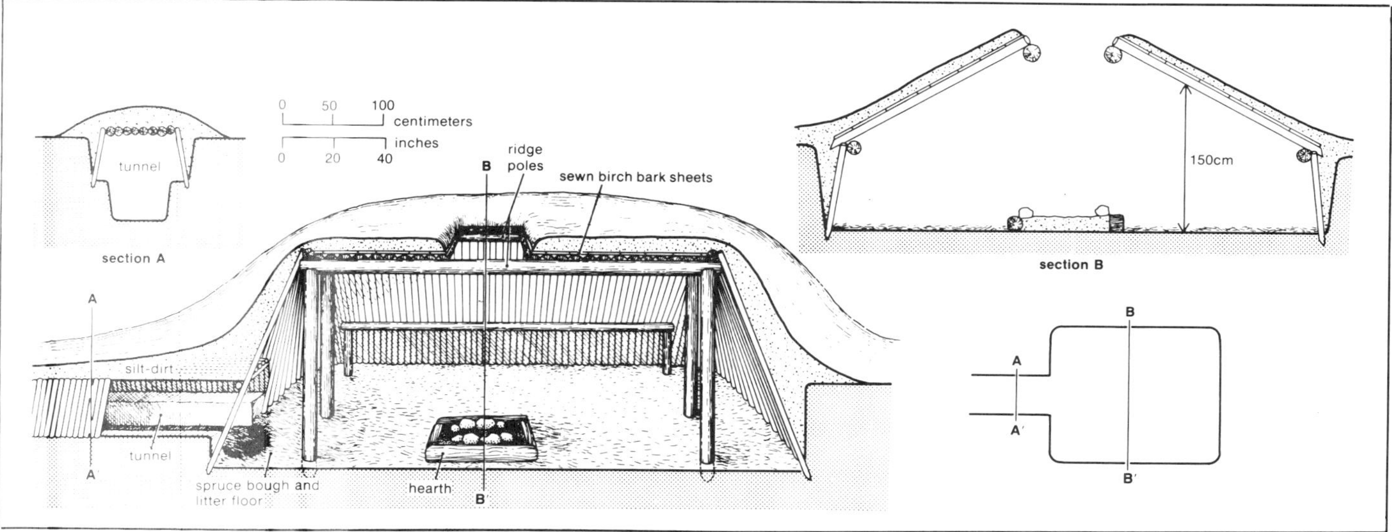

21-33. Profile of structure. Pen-and-ink on Satin Design paper, by Jo Ann Moore. From *Handbook of North American Indians*, vol. 6, *Subarctic*, June Helm, ed. (Smithsonian Institution Press, 1981).

THE FINAL RENDERING

In the studio, drawings most often are prepared for publication with ink on polyester drafting film, but other media and surfaces may be used, depending on what best represents the specimen and how the publication will be printed. Chapters in part 2 of this book provide instruction in the techniques that might be used. Some of the drawings will be either somewhat or entirely diagrammatic. To avoid confusion, when depicting a superficially imposed line such as a grid or datum, it is a helpful practice to use dots and dashes consistently, instead of a solid line. Shading films that provide the illusion of grays are useful for distinguishing certain areas or types of features. Transparent overlays might be used to clarify the relationship among different phases or time periods.

Frequently it is desirable to convert the final illustrations for slide projection, film, or videotape, in which case white or color on black works far better than the opposite. This may be obtained by reproducing the original artwork on high-contrast negative slide film.

The illustrator for anthropology and archaeology must have a clear concept of both the process from field drawing to publication and the scientific purpose for the illustrations, especially when working in the field. The evaluation of specimens and data following any field expedition involves considerable cross-referencing by the anthropologists and archaeologists among the field notes, registration book (record of artifacts), photographs, illustrations, and other research sources. Drawings are an integral part of this recording procedure and must readily complement both written descriptions and photographic images. The visual record in photographic form has the advantage of being without human interpretation, whereas the advantage of the drawn form is precisely its interpretative aspect, especially anthropological reconstructions. Anthropological and archaeological illustrations are a point of reference for analysis in research publications and in the expedition director's report and will continue to serve as significant documents for future evaluation.

22/Illustrating Medical Subjects

Patrick J. Lynch

Medical illustration, an ancient profession, is inextricably linked to the development of direct observational techniques that brought medical practice out of the dark ages of superstition and mistaken adherence to unproven theory. The foundations of modern medical science are usually traced back to the great Italian anatomist Andreas Vesalius, whose masterpiece of 1543, *De Humani Corporis Fabrica,* is principally remembered for its stunning woodblock illustrations produced in Titian's workshop. Prior to Vesalius's work, medical texts were largely unillustrated, and those plates that did accompany the text usually were copied from earlier works, with no reference to the actual dissection of human bodies. Vesalius and his artists scrupulously adhered to the visual facts that they could establish through direct observation of cadavers and in so doing demonstrated both the value of original research and the need for effective visual communication in medical science.

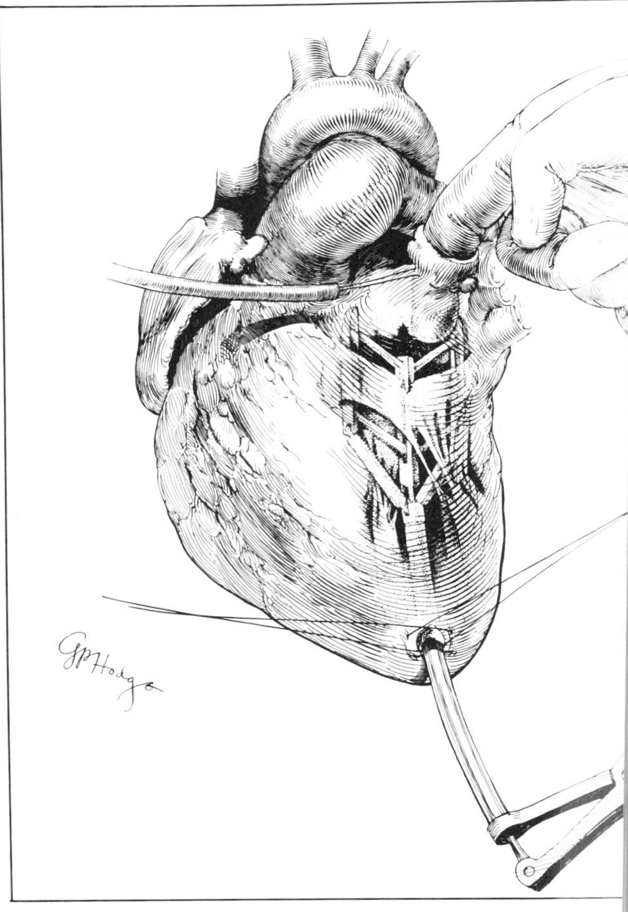

22-1. A classic medical pen-and-ink drawing of a transventr
stenotic mitral valve of the heart. The dark areas of the hear
painted black with several dilute coats of black drafting ink;
then scratched into the painted portions. Gillott 291 pen and
by Gerald P. Hodge. Courtesy of the University of Michigan

THE ILLUSTRATOR

The modern profession of medical illustration is quite varied, encompassing the production of anatomical and surgical illustrations as well as medical sculpture, commercial artwork for medical advertising, medical-legal artwork, medical exhibit and brochure design, the production of prosthetic devices, and many other subspecialties.

The medical illustrator may conduct a practice within large academic research or teaching institutions or be a freelance artist serving both science and commercial clients. Most academic medical illustrators have faculty or professional staff positions in schools of medicine, allied health professions, or in veterinary medicine. The staff artist's job is primarily the illustration of research papers and medical and surgical texts by faculty members (fig. 22-1; see figs. C-33, 4-12, 5-2, 5-23, 8-1, 9-15, 11-1), illustrating teaching materials produced by the university, and creating speaker support materials in a wide range of biomedical disciplines. In departments offering a comprehensive range of a
medical ill
ularly vers
tise in gr
graphics.
scientists.
poster sh
medical a
biocommu
composed
ists, me
video sp
structiona
staff medi

Medical

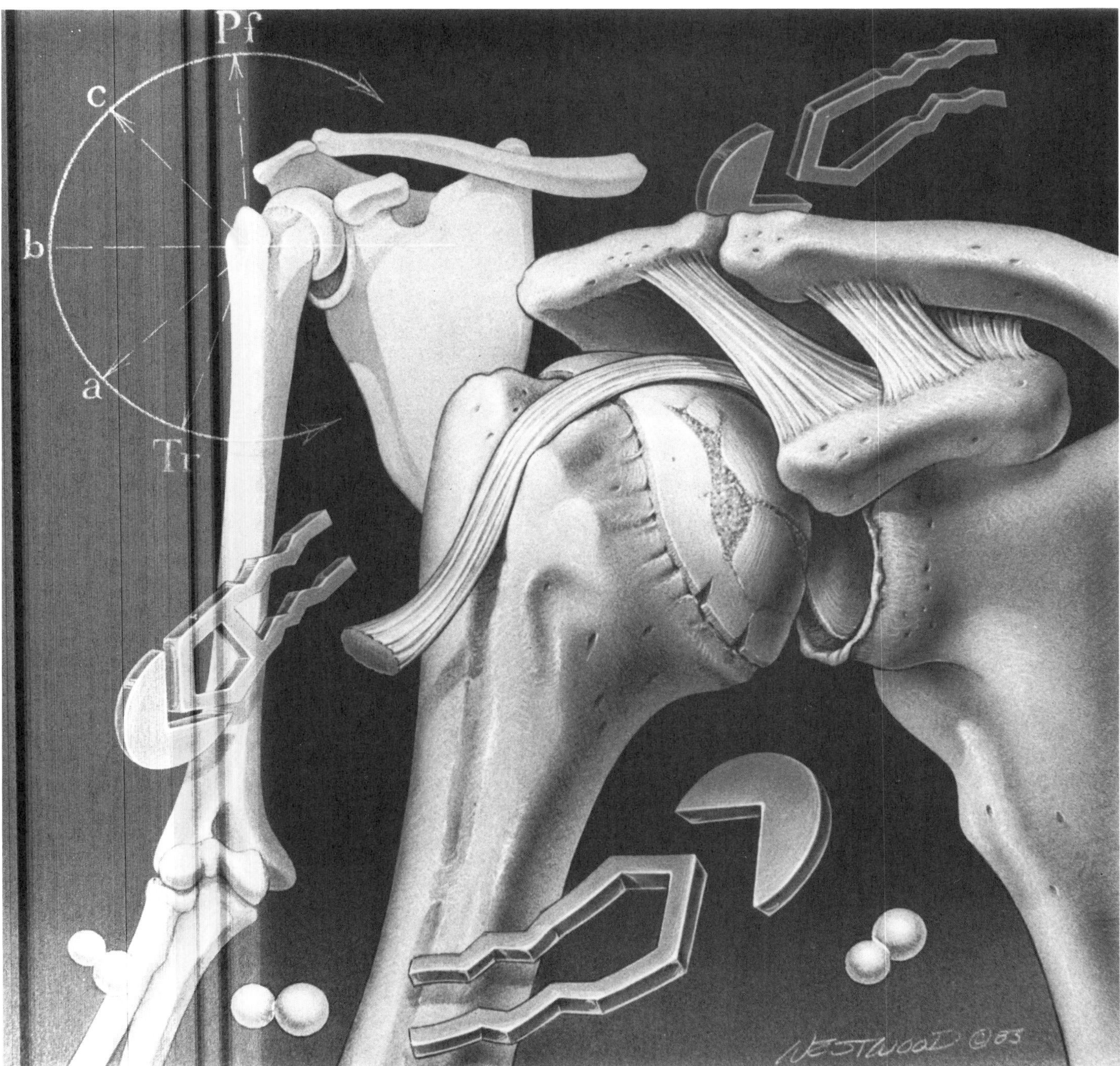

22-2. "The Painful Shoulder." Visually dramatic medical illustrations such as this are more often used to draw the viewer's attention than to instruct. This full-color painting appeared as a magazine cover for *Postgraduate Medicine*, illustrating arthritis of the shoulder joint. Airbrush, watercolor, and colored pencil on Crescent no. 110 illustration board, by William B. Westwood. Art direction by Tina Adamek.

lance careers work primarily for a variety of commercial clients, including pharmaceutical companies, publishers of medical and scientific books, medical equipment manufacturers, lawyers, advertising agencies, and private physician/authors (see figs. C-11, C-19, C-24, 5-38, 9-4). Freelance medical illustrators have become increasingly active in providing the legal community with courtroom exhibit materials used to explain the often complex physical and social ramifications of accidental injuries and medical malpractice. Medical-legal illustrators must be fully versed in the rules of evidence and the legal customs that apply in such potentially emotional situations. The commercial art arena demands top-notch skills in illustration technique and style, and is no less demanding of the medical

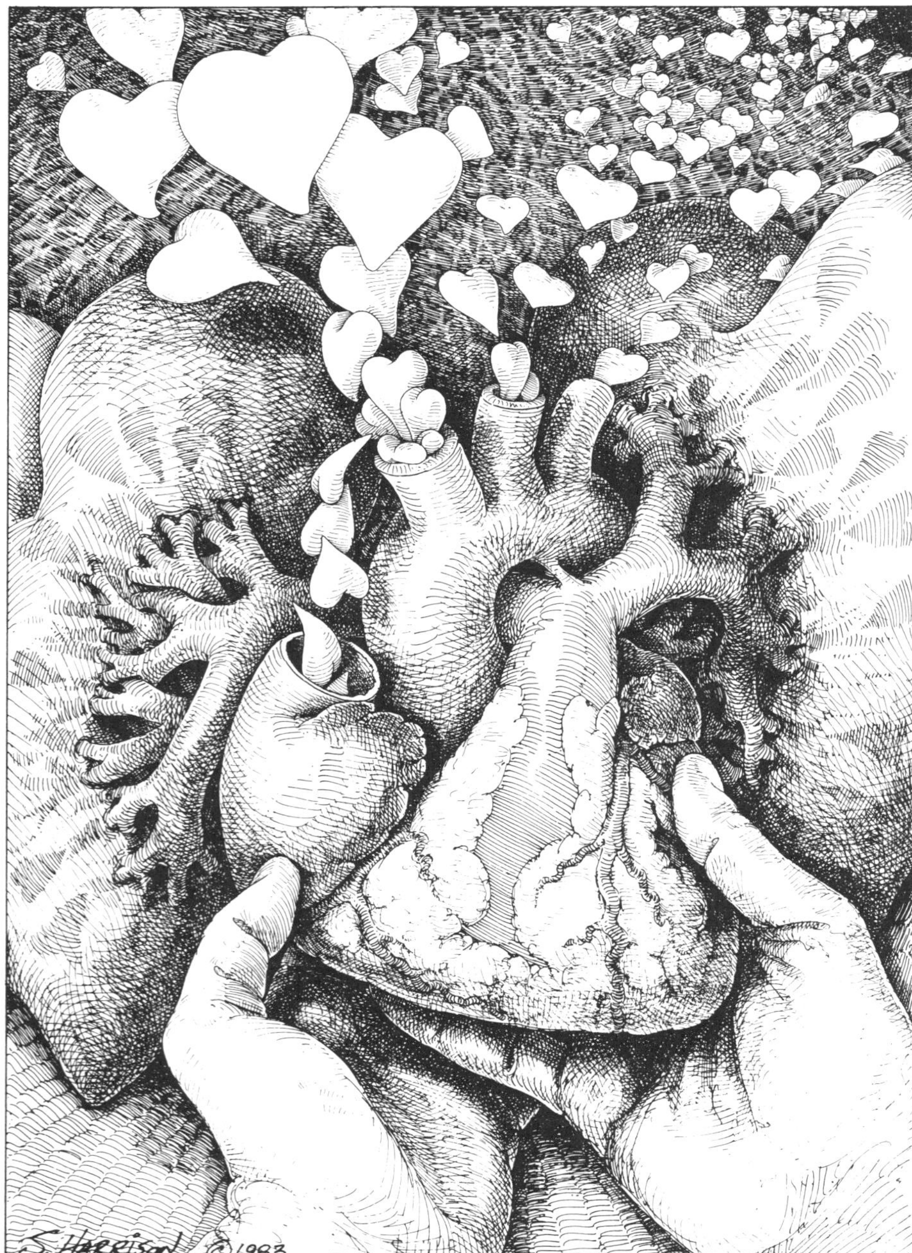

22-3. "Keep in Touch with Your Heart." Medical artists often choose a more commercial illustrative style when working for editorial markets. This drawing was used as cover art for KAET-TV's (Phoenix, Arizona) magazine *Under Cover*, promoting the first live telecast of open-heart surgery by Dr. Edward B. Dietrich. Technical pen (2 × 0 through 4 × 0) and ink on Crescent no. 300 illustration board, by Steven J. Harrison.

and scientific knowledge of medical illustrators. Figure 22-2 and 22-3 are reproductions of two cover designs done by medical illustrators for commercial clients. Although the style of these pieces differs from that customarily used in academic illustration, both convey the client's message with visual flair and a degree of anatomic detail that one could not expect from the general commercial illustrator. Most independent medical illustrators have their businesses in areas of the country where there are many commercial clients, medical magazine and book publishers, and advertising agencies.

A few medical illustrators become specialists in the design and

22-4. *Fetlock Joi*
sculpture used fo
omy to veterinar
caulking compou
pound over actua
E. Hosmer © 19

manufacture
medical mod
anatomical tr
ulators used
professionals.
horse fetlock
instruct vet
equine anat
thetic design
most deman
subspecialtie
tion, where
tomical and
design repla
(such as eyes
tures) lost th
ease. The
unique comb
anatomical k
by forensic
gators to re
ance of u
accident vi
have decom
ery. By usin
pally the sk
forensic arti
approximatin
features (see
22), or use t
studying the
portrait of th
pier use of

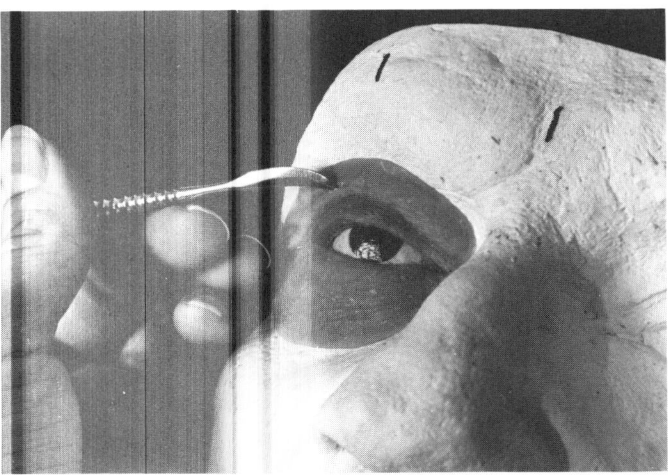

a

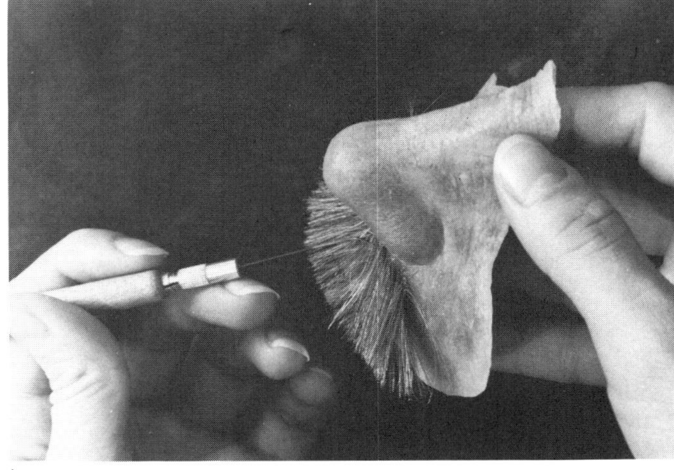

b

c

22-5. Replacement prostheses made of MDX4-4210 silicone rubber, intrinsically tinted. *(a)* Wax model of an orbital prosthesis being sculpted on a stone reproduction of a patient's face. *(b)* Final coloration of a complex nasal prosthesis illustrating application of a mustache for camouflage. *(c)* Patient wearing final complex nasal prosthesis. Photo submitted by Susan Habakuk and Greg Gion, Maxillofacial Prosthetics Clinic and Training Program, Center for Craniofacial Anomalies, University of Illinois Health Science Center, Chicago.

medical illustrators have become involved in the search for missing children. The face of a child changes rapidly (but predictably) as years pass, complicating the search for children long missing. Using as starting points old photos and data on how various parts of the face mature, the medical artist can produce a "current" portrait of the child as he or she might now look, often using computer graphics. A number of children have been located using these unique portraits.

In 1911 the German immigrant Max Brödel (see fig. 8-1) started the first school of medical illustration in the United States at Johns Hopkins University, where the program continues today. Contemporary medical illustrators generally have completed a two- to three-year master's degree program at an accredited school of medical illustration, comprising training in normal and pathological human anatomy (including cadaver dissection), physiology, embryology, histology, medical and surgical procedures, as well as instruction in a range of illustration techniques. In addition to this core curriculum, most programs offer additional courses in such subspecialties as the production of medical prosthetic devices, the construction of three-dimensional models and patient simulators, production methods in film and video, computer graphics,

and video, computer graphics, instructional design, biocommunications management, biological illustration, and advanced still-photography courses. The Association of Medical Illustrators (A.M.I.) has established standards and accreditation procedures for schools offering medical-illustration degree programs. (For further information on A.M.I. and schools of medical illustration, see Appendix.)

INSTRUMENTS AND MATERIALS

Unlike many fields of scientific illustration, which require extensive handling and dissection of specimen material, medical illustration requires few tools and materials other than the standard ones found in most art studios and those particular tools most appropriate to the illustrator's favorite media.

A few items, however, are peculiar to medical illustration because drawings or photographs must be produced in an operating or hospital room. In these situations, few tools should be carried, primarily because of the need for cleanliness and speed. All materials used in the operating room should be easy to hold securely to minimize the chance of dropping them. Nothing should flap loosely.

Optical Devices

Not all medical illustrators need microscopes, and often one is provided in cases where a freelance illustrator is requested to draw a microscopic specimen. If a microscope is required, it is most likely to be a compound one.

Compound microscope: to draw tissue sections, cells, microscopic organisms, or other slide-mounted material.

Camera lucida.

Camera: 35mm single-lens reflex; should have a manual operation mode for close-up photography.

Motor drive or autowinder: recommended for quick shooting in the operating room.

Macro lenses: 50mm or 100mm fixed focal length.

Shoe-mount electronic flash: ISO 25 guide number of about 50. Must have a manual mode of operation, a socket for PC cord (that attaches flash to camera), and optional high-voltage power supply, such as a 510-volt battery pack to prevent recycling delays in the operating room.

Surfaces

Tracing or other smooth drawing paper: on a firmly backed pad that permits pages to be quickly flipped but does not flop around during drawing. Ideal is a pad that is spiral-bound or has sheets securely glued at the top or side so that sheets can fold all the way back. About 9 by 12 inches (23 by 30cm) is a convenient size.

Media

Pencils: many soft graphite (HB, H, 2H). In the operating room, sharpening is impossible, and no erasing should be done because crumbs could be a serious hazard.

Miscellaneous

Anatomy book: for reference; can be consulted during slow periods in the operating or examining room.

TECHNIQUES

Because of the wide range of uses and reproduction media for medical illustration, no general rules apply in the selection of suitable working surfaces and working media. Some combinations of working surfaces and tools are so appropriate to the needs of the profession, however, that they have come to characterize the typical look of some areas of current medical illustration.

Black-and-W
Tone

The majorit
done in pen-ar
duction becaus
ably and is in
The most popu
medical pen-a
white scratchb
ester drafting
weights of hot-
finish) Bristol b
pen-and-ink c
with dip pen
steel crowquill
lott 290, 291, 6
This type of f
lows the artist
of the drawn
duces the clas
lel-line shading
modern medic
trations (see fig
rendering of r
can be "loose
fine-arts appro
omic illustratio
lash, crosshat
inking styles a
(see figs. 5-2,
figures there is
suggesting no
since literal rea
or required.
pens such as t
sometimes use
tire illustration
often used in
constant line w
graph gives c
ameter of the c
Many medic
tined for blac
duction are c
tone with gra
chrome waterc
dust technique
covered elsewh
Working meth
faces used dif
employed in o
tific illustration

Color Media

Color techni
cal illustration

dardized in style and the overall look they produce than medical pen-and-ink styles. Certain combinations of surfaces and media, however, predominate here as well. Airbrush techniques with watercolor, dyes, or acrylic pigments are used very heavily, particularly by illustrators in the more commercial areas of the profession. Usually the airbrush painting is combined with conventional brush techniques, colored pencil, and lead pencil drawing to produce mixed-media illustrations, though a few medical artists use airbrush exclusively in their work (see chapter 11 and figs. C-24, C-33).

In addition to the standard white surfaces used in most airbrush work (principally various weights of Bristol board), many medical artists use colored paper surfaces such as Canson Mi-Teintes, Color-Aid papers, and colored mat board (see figs. C-31, 10-1). Color grounds are particularly well suited to artwork destined for color slides and video, where the glaring effect of a white background is unacceptable. Many traditional watercolor, gouache, and acrylic techniques are also used frequently in medical illustration (*The Johns Hopkins Atlas of Functional Human Anatomy*, by L. Schlossberg and G. Zuidema—see Bibliography). Colored pencil drawing (see fig. C-19) has recently become popular as artists look for faster means of producing color art. Further discussions of color techniques in medical illustration appear in the *Journal of Biocommunication:* "Gouache for Scientific Art" and "Colored Pencils for Scientific Illustration," both by Gerald P. Hodge; "On the Use of Color in Medical Illustration," "The Use of Color in Medical Illustration II," and "The Use of Color in Anatomical and Surgical Illustration," all by David Mascaro (see Bibliography).

Cel Painting

Techniques adapted from animation cel painting are popular in medical illustration. In one variation of the technique, a conventional pen-and-ink drawing is done on clear acetate or polyester cels, then photographed to preserve this stage for use in print or journal publication. Line art done on other grounds also may be photographically or electrostatically transferred to clear acetate. To convert the line drawing to a full-color piece suitable for 35mm slides or film, the illustrator may paint in color on the reverse (back) side of the acetate with special cel animation paints or ordinary acrylic jar paint (fig. 22-6). This backpainting may range in complexity from simple fields of flat color to elaborately airbrushed or brushed color renderings that form a true painting on the cel (see fig. C-34). When the finished painting is placed on a colored background field and photographed, the process results in color slide, film, and video reproductions that are more visually dramatic than other color-conversion methods, and this gives the client additional uses for line artwork commissioned primarily for print.

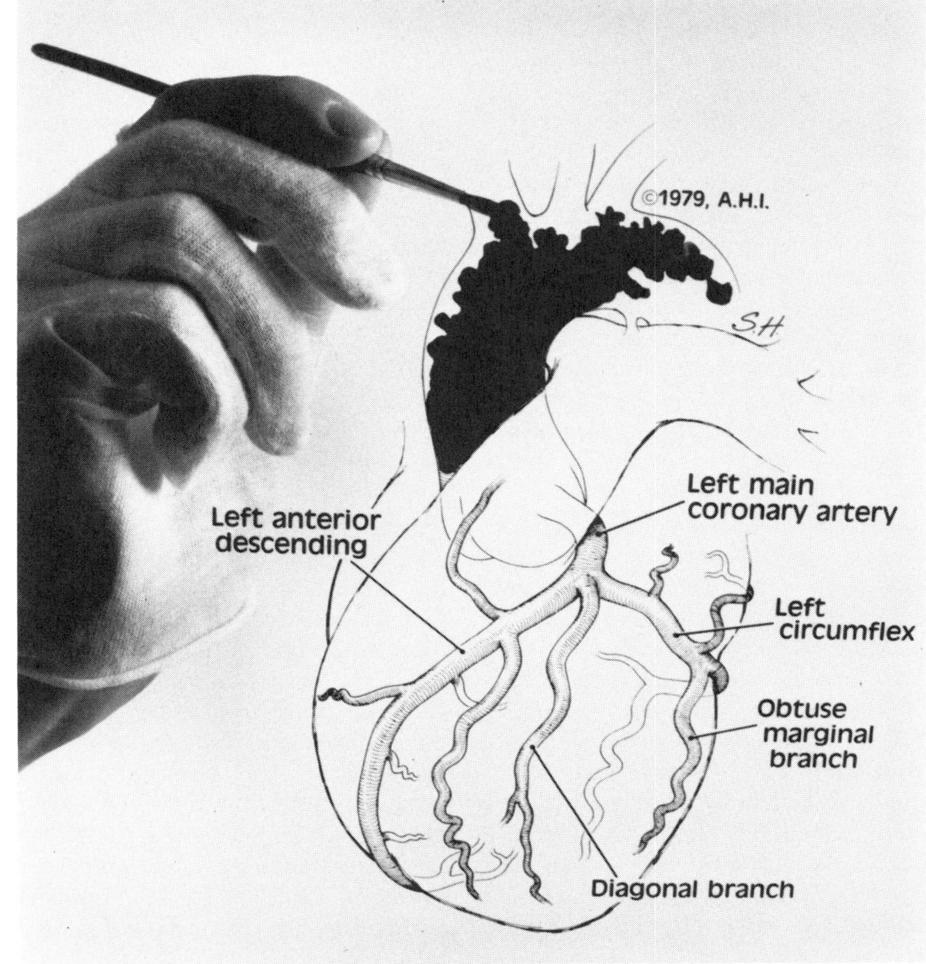

22-6. Cel animation technique adapted to produce artwork for slides, film, and video. The original illustration, a pen-and-ink drawing on illustration board by Steven J. Harrison, was photographically transferred onto clear film. Cel vinyl acrylic paints are then flowed or "puddled" (rather than heavily brushed) onto the back of the film to produce full-color art. The finished cel painting is then laid over a suitable color background for photography. Photo courtesy of Steven J. Harrison.

Paintings on acetate also may be used to modify conventional medical paintings. Variations or additional steps in the procedure are painted on acetate and laid over the original painting, avoiding costly repainting of repetitive subject matter. (See Backpainting in chapter 10; chapter 11; and "Cel Vinyls: Materials and Methods," by S. Harrison—see Bibliography—for a more complete description of acetate painting techniques.)

Computer Graphics

In recent years, computer-graphics systems of various kinds have had a major impact on medical illustration ("Computergraphics in Biocommunication," by H. Smith—see Bibliography). Currently used primarily to create images destined for video and color slides, the systems now widely available cannot yet create full-color images for print comparable in quality to those produced by traditional means. When reproduced by four-color offset lithography, most computer-generated images suffer from a distinct lack of sharpness, limiting their application to media where this characteristic is less noticeable, such as videotape. In spite of this drawback, computer-graphics techniques have made major inroads into the production of medical imagery.

The ease with which computer-generated images can be created, copied, moved, and modified has led to major changes in the way animated sequences for film and video are produced. Computer-generated animation is rapidly replacing conventional cel animation techniques, where each movement of the subject had to be hand-drawn and painted on individual animation cels. Most "in-house" medical-illustration departments have installed some type of computer equipment to generate graphs, charts, and diagrammatic images as well as "freehand" medical artwork for color slides and video (see chapter 24). The speed with which these systems can produce such graphics may greatly ease the workload of the average medical-illustration department. Some high-resolution systems also can produce high-contrast line images suitable for submission to publishers, but this technique is largely limited to graphic (diagrammatic or chart) images, not true medical artwork. The recent introduction of low-cost laser printers has placed most typographic and page-composition applications within the financial range of even small medical-illustration departments and studios. Page-composing systems allow the graphic designer to put together full pages of text, graphics, and diagrammatic artwork within the computer memory. These electronic "mechanicals" then may be printed out using a laser printer, or sent to a typesetting machine for better-quality output.

Because of rapid improvements in imaging technology, the current resolution limitations of computer-generated images soon will disappear. Most informed observers view this prospect as simply adding to the range of techniques available to the medical illustrator, not as a possible threat to the profession or to the viability of most current illustration techniques. As the technology matures, the dividing line between analysis images created by other medical professions—such as CAT-scan or Nuclear Magnetic Resonance (NMR) images—and those images created by medical illustrators will likely merge, giving the medical illustrator yet more tools and options with which to create medical artwork. The advent of more moderately priced three-dimensional computer-graphics systems will add an entirely new medium to the field of medical illustration. Already such systems are being used to design and sculpt (through robotics) medical models and prosthetics from data acquired by CAT-scan and NMR imaging.

REFEREN

Most med
tain extensiv
literature, w
time would
library (assu
These print r
mented with
preserved
medical mo
tion (a rare
graphs colle
illustrator. S
some advan
freelance
choose to w
where a wea
rial is availab

Anatomy R

Assuming
plied some
(such as pho
published m
in researchi
tain good an
anatomy atl
(see Bibliogr
ographical
Anatomy, by
Anatomy of
ited by C.
Atlas of Hu
by H. Ferne
Photographi
as *Color Atl*
by R. McM
(see Bibliog
although m
graphed are
specimens.
McMinn and
tains excelle
tic injection
systems of
other areas
Cross-sectio
Atlas of Se
omy, by J. K
Bibliography
studying the
lationships
structures,
NMR refere
the illustrat

histological atlas, such as *Sobotta/Hammersen, Histology, Color Atlas of Microscopic Anatomy*, by F. Hammersen (see Bibliography) should be present in the medical illustrator's basic library. Most medical illustrators own a variety of atlases, because each has its particular strengths and unique materials. In addition to atlases, standard anatomy texts such as *Gray's Anatomy* or *Clinically Oriented Anatomy*, by K. Moore (see Bibliography), are necessary to clarify information best presented in descriptive text, such as the precise origins and insertions of muscles, major vessels supplying a particular body region, and other details not readily obvious from illustrations. The American and British volumes of *Gray's* are quite distinct both in illustrations and text, and the British volume has extensive material on histology and physiology as well as standard gross anatomy. An especially good reference is the *Pocket Atlas of Human Anatomy*, by H. Feneis (see Bibliography).

Although limited primarily to the musculoskeletal system, art anatomies such as *Atlas of Human Anatomy for the Artist*, by S. Peck (see Bibliography) make valuable references to proper proportion and surface anatomy when depicting figures. *The Human Body*, by E. Ruby (see Bibliography), is an artist's photographic reference book of nude male and female figures in poses potentially useful to the medical illustrator. This book has good photographic references to facial features (child, adult, and geriatric; male and female) and typical hand and foot poses.

Surgical References

If the illustration is of a surgical subject, texts on surgical technology such as *Surgical Technology, Principles and Practice*, by J. Fuller (see Bibliography), are particularly good for establishing the standard procedures in a particular surgical discipline, the most commonly used instruments, and the major anatomical landmarks used in the operation.

Technique in the Use of Surgical Tools, by R. Anderson and R. Romfh (see Bibliography), is a valuable guide to the proper use of surgical tools, well illustrated with photographs. This small volume is especially useful for establishing the proper hand positions in depicting the use of scalpels, scissors, and other surgical tools. Surgical-instrument sales catalogs are frequently changed and updated by the manufacturers, so most hospitals have outdated catalogs they may be happy to pass on. *Basic Surgery*, by C. Donner and J. McCredie (see Bibliography) is a good general introduction to a wide variety of surgical disciplines, heavily illustrated with excellent line artwork and a small color section on surgical anatomy.

Miscellaneous References

Melloni's Illustrated Medical Dictionary by I. Dox, B. Melloni, and G. Eisner (see Bibliography), does double duty as a superb reference source to medical pen-and-ink technique. The *CIBA Collection of Medical Illustrations* (see Bibliography) and the CIBA Clinical Symposia series of pamphlets contain excellent anatomical plates as well as plates depicting the most commonly encountered surgical and medical problems. These CIBA publications are highly regarded throughout the medical community and often form the nucleus of a medical illustrator's library. *Illustration, Its Technique and Application to the Sciences*, by Carl D. Clarke, is one of the few volumes ever to deal extensively with the history, techniques, and media of medical illustration. Although somewhat dated, it still contains much information relevant to the concerns of current medical illustrators (see Bibliography).

After a number of years of work in the field, most medical illustrators have collected an extensive clip file, or "morgue," of their old anatomy sketches, drawings of figures, hand positions, various instruments, and other reference material left over from previous works. These old sketches are tremendously useful in building up new drawings of similar material and should be carefully preserved and organized for quick referral. In addition to collecting old sketches, many illustrators use slow periods to build up their clip files, an investment of time well worth the effort when faced with the inevitable rush jobs to come.

In addition to these basic resources, the medical illustrator would of course seek out any other pertinent material available in medical books or journals. Surgical atlases are particularly useful for clarifying procedures in unfamiliar operations. Copies of relevant journal articles can usually be obtained by writing to the author of the article and requesting a reprint. All medical illustrators, particularly those seeking commercial work, should pay close attention to artwork published by the major medical and surgical journals, as well as any scientific art published in the popular press and magazines. In addition to files of their own work, many illustrators maintain files of the work of other illustrators for inspiration when dealing with difficult problems. Many physicians do not keep their old journals and magazines and may be happy to pass along back issues. Ironically, those journals least likely to be bound for the library are medical "magazines," which publish the most artwork (and have the most illustrated advertisements).

APPROACHES TO MEDICAL ILLUSTRATION

The working process in medical illustration differs from other fields of bioillustration primarily because of the problems of working with human subject matter and the practical and ethical difficulties that complicate research for visual reference material. Of necessity, the medical illustrator often must work from reference materials that are much less direct than those available to other scientific illustrators. Frequently the procedure or condition being illustrated must be reconstructed from consultations with the client physician, photographs of patients or surgery, published reference materials supplied by the client, and research conducted by the illustrator (see figs. C-24, 9-1, 9-6). In addition to a working knowledge of a range of illustration techniques (as well as photography basics), the medical illustrator must be thoroughly conversant in medical terminology, human anatomy, the available reference materials, and the proper procedures for working in a medical and surgical environment. Rather than using any specific "tools of the trade," it is this training for working closely with other medical professionals that most distinguishes the medical illustrator from other scientific illustration disciplines.

Photography

Most medical illustrators will find a working knowledge of cameras and photography (particularly close-up and flash photography) to be extremely helpful in pursuit of their craft. A basic medical photography kit is needed for reference photographs, which frequently supplement or substitute for preliminary sketches of the subject. Both camera and flash must have a manual operation mode for successful close-up photography. The lenses most useful to the medical artist are macro lenses of 50mm or 100mm focal length. These macro lenses should be true (fixed focal length) macro lenses, not one of the popular but less capable macro zooms. The slight telephoto effect of a 100mm lens will ensure that proper subject proportions are maintained and give the illustrator the option of working from a greater distance without sacrificing too much detail in the subject. If the camera is to be used in surgical or clinical settings, where quick working time is essential, it should be equipped with a motor drive and a heavy-duty battery pack to speed the recycle time of the flash unit.

Any photo equipment used in the operating room should, of course, be checked to be sure no components are loose, dangling away from the camera, or dirty; however, the equipment does not have to be sterilized. Care should be exercised in using electronic flash in some surgical situations where flammable gases or chemicals are in use.

Procedures for photography in the operating room will vary from one hospital to another. Any doubts about the suitability of a particular piece of photo equipment should be resolved with the operating-room staff before bringing it into the operating room. More information on medical and close-up photography techniques and equipment appears in Eastman Kodak's *Biomedical Photography* and in *The Manual of Close-up Photography*, by L. Lefkowitz (see Bibliography).

Conceptualization

Photography long ago removed the need to record the raw visual facts in medicine. Most modern medical illustrations record a conceptual process that may be quite removed from what the physician will literally see during a patient examination or surgical procedure. The goal of good medical artwork is to illustrate the concepts and facts the medical audience must understand to appreciate the ideas the author is trying to communicate. According to Dr. Frank Netter, a widely recognized physician and illustrator, "The difficult thing

about makin
not the pain
the study, t
planning, in
ture that sa

Although
medical illus
trated than
certain char
cal illustrati
lustrator's jo
hierarchy, in
mary import
the illustrati
potentially c
deemphasize
The medica
ability to org
ical and phy
figures that
standable to
thetically pl
design (see
22-3).

A medic
ideally comm
the target au
sive labeling
trated.

Convention

In largely
tions, extra
will more o
message tha
conducted
McConathy
of Thoracic
ography) sh
disliked st
renderings,
was more h
photographi
tor's favored
of the job,
usually dict
ishing retur
piece.

Much of t
ating a succ
tion is in kn
reality in gr
move towar
or conceptu
22-7, the ar
tray only the

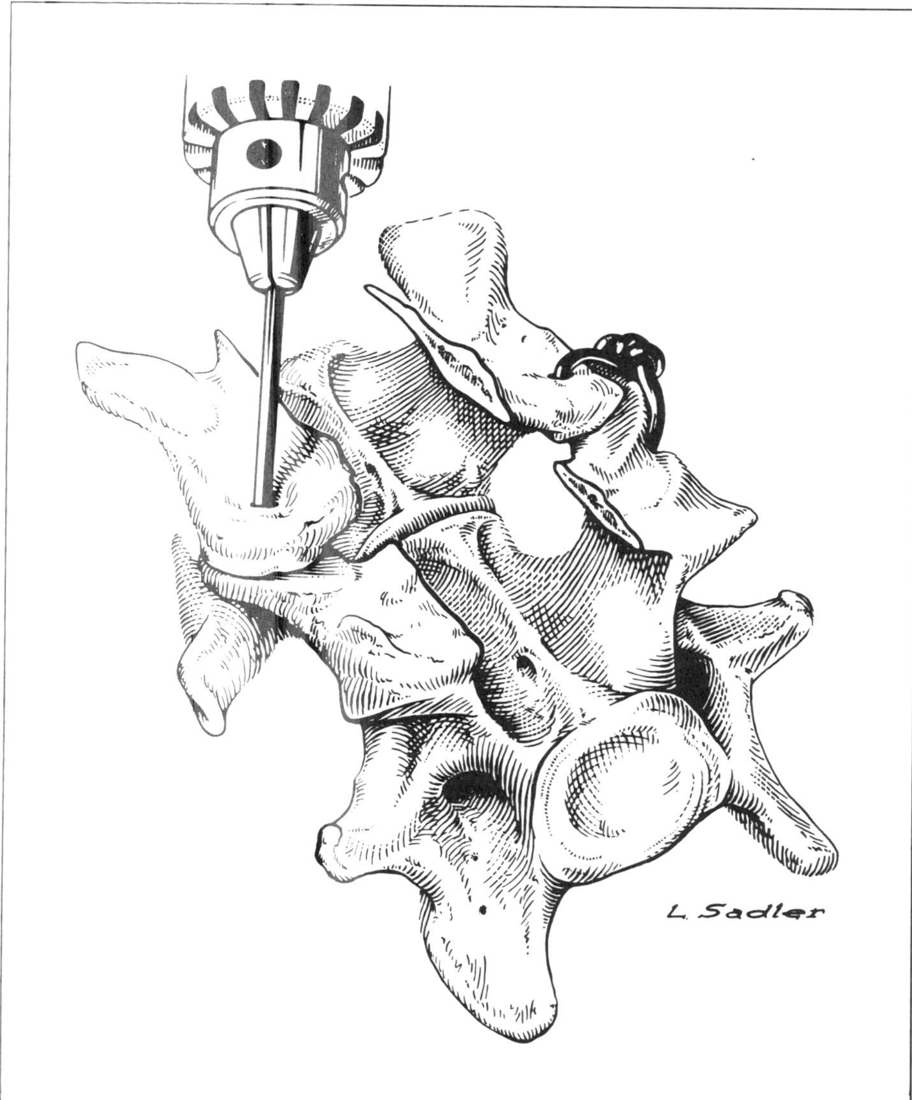

22-7. Conceptual drawings such as this are often used in medical illustration to highlight only the most important features of a procedure, particularly when the initial stages of the operation are well understood by the audience. Note that the artist has rendered the drill with drafting tools, visually separating it from the surrounding hand-drawn organic structures. "Laminectomy in the Dog," pen-and-ink on scratchboard, by Lewis L. Sadler.

and procedural elements of the surgery. Although far removed from what a veterinary surgeon might actually see during a laminectomy, the drawing conveys the essentials of the procedure succinctly. Alternatively, most observers would consider figure 22-8 a very realistic treatment of the subject. But here, too, the artist has eliminated much of the messy, confusing reality of heart surgery that a photograph might include, while conveying the most important elements of the actual visual experience to the audience. Both figures carefully organize visual reality to convey their client's message concisely. Neither approach is more legitimate, and each method has its place in a medical illustrator's range of stylistic options.

In general, all structures in a medical illustration should be shaded according to scientific illustration convention, where the main light source usually comes from the upper left-hand corner of the plate. Unlike most fields of scientific illustration, measurement scales rarely are incorporated into medical illustrations unless specifically required. The illustrator should be sure the orientation of structures in the drawing is immediately clear to the audience, independent of any captioning or labeling.

When illustrating complex subject matter, illustrators often establish visual keys to the nature of various objects portrayed. For example, all nonorganic or theoretical elements (such as tools, planes of dissection, motion arrows) might be drafted with French curves or templates to give them a hard, smooth look, and all organic elements drawn freehand. These subtle but useful visual aids can greatly speed an audience's appreciation of the author's message, but they must be used consistently to be effective. Figures 22-7 and 22-9 both demonstrate this principle; note that in both cases the instruments are not drawn freehand and stand out readily in spite of visual similarities to some of the organic structures that surround them.

Generally, when multiple illustrations are done, every effort should be made to keep the viewpoint and style of rendering consistent from one drawing to the next, regardless of any aesthetic advantages a temporary change in rendering style might bring.

Landmarks or important structures that are not actually visible during the procedure are often "ghosted" in to further orient the audience (fig. 22-10; see fig. 22-1). This is particularly important in surgical art, where what is actually visible within the surgical field may not be enough to communicate readily the message of the illustration, even to audiences of experienced surgeons.

Interaction with the Client

Often the client will arrive with nothing more than a few simple sketches of the subject to be illustrated. The initial conference should establish the purpose of the illustration; what references the client may be able to supply; the medium, style, and viewpoints in which the subject will be presented; and other basic facts. Next the medical illustrator must begin to flesh out these concepts. This initial research usually will be conducted quite independently of the client. The working reality of the profession is that few physicians (or commercial clients) have the time or inclination to guide the artist through the more basic aspects of human anatomy or medical terminology. More often than not, the client will expect the medical illustrator to supply these details to the artwork without extensive consultations. This is not to suggest that

interaction v
cally discou
cian or art d
to depend c
judgment of
to contribut
content and
ished wor
professional
cal illustrato
with coauth
lustrated w

Drawing t

Although
portunity a
vent it, an
procedure
would of co
able. Whe
present the
graphs and
ble to
illustrators
particularly
ating room
gical proce
rapidly to
static sub
tempted, t
quickly, p
thumbnail
omy and
beled. If
instead (b
profession
present).
mented b
parts of
graphed.
may be an
quantities
tail. Even
able to
going on i

Ideally
ence bet
geon will
the proce
or proble
will not
whole o
should an
be calle
time, av
spent in

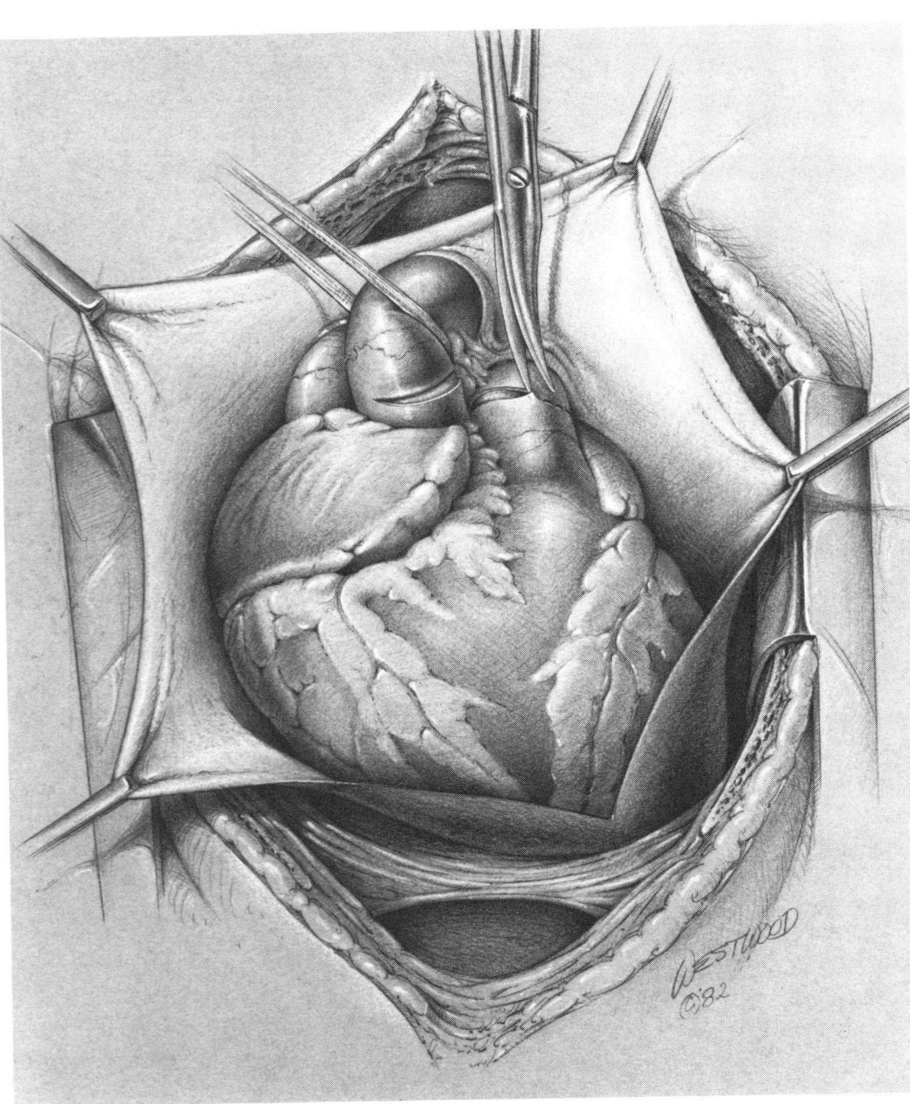

22-8. Portraying complex surgical techniques in a very representative manner is perhaps the greatest challenge to the surgical illustrator. Although quite realistic, this illustration is much more instructive than a photograph would be. The artist has chosen to represent only those aspects of visual reality that reinforce the client's message, and has removed or ignored all potentially distracting elements. "Denervation of the Heart," an operation to sever the sympathetic nerves in the adventitia of the aorta and pulmonary artery to control arrhythmia. Carbon and Conté pencils on gray charcoal paper, by William B. Westwood. Winner of the Max Brödel Award for Continuous Tone Illustration, Association of Medical Illustrators meeting, 1982.

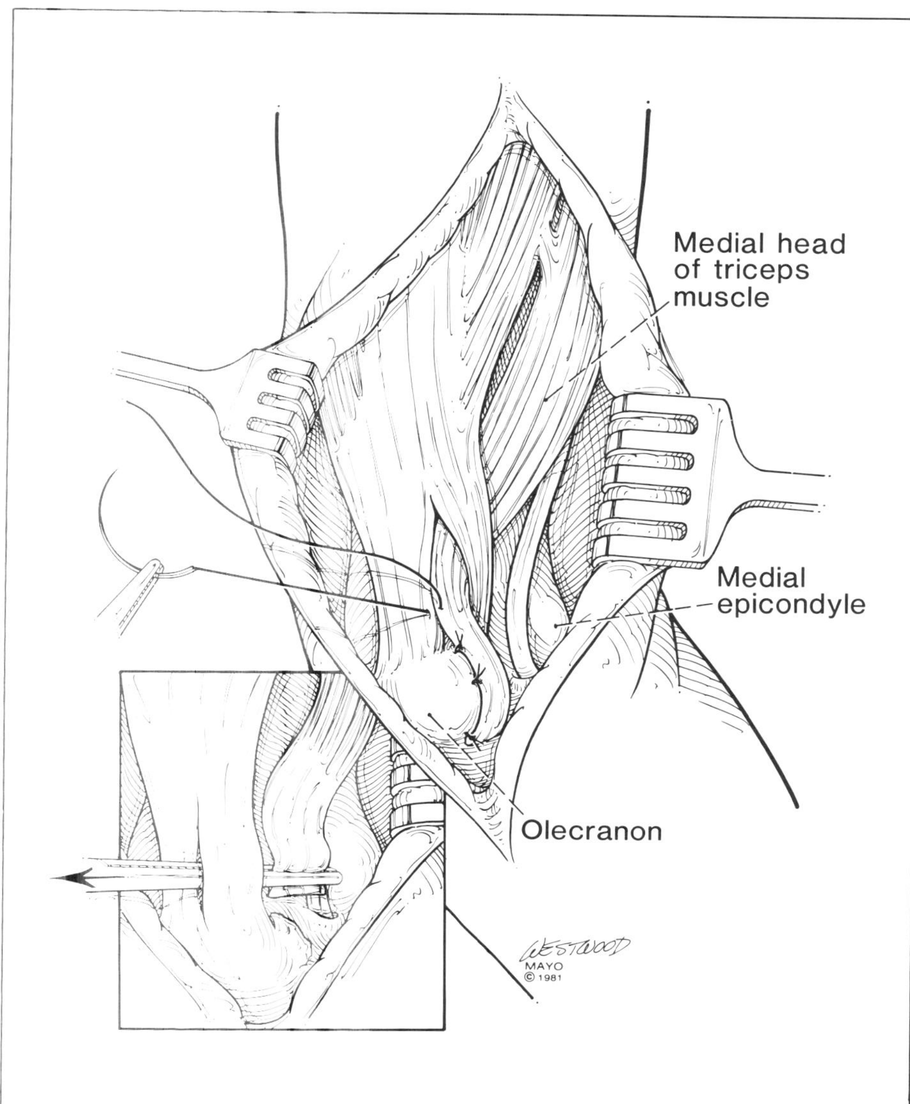

22-9. Schematic surgical drawings such as this are often used to demonstrate procedure and technique. Here again the artist has chosen to render arrows and surgical instruments with drafting tools, to differentiate them from hand-drawn organic structures. The figure is from a series illustrating management of elbow injuries. "Repair of Torn Triceps Muscle," a surgical textbook illustration in pen-and-ink on Dietzgen drafting film, by William B. Westwood. Courtesy of James H. Dobyns, Mayo Clinic.

When it is possible to view a surgical procedure or the examination of a patient, the needs of the illustrator obviously must be subordinate to the health and welfare of the patient involved. In clinical situations, the medical illustrator is no less obligated than any other member of the medical staff to observe proper procedure and appearances. One need only imagine oneself in the role of the patient to understand the discomfort the sudden arrival of a stranger (in street clothes, perhaps with camera or sketchbook) could cause in the examining room. Such visits should always be mediated by the physician. The illustrator should be fully prepared to explain the purpose of the visit, to follow hospital or clinic policies regarding photography, and to guarantee the confidentiality of any reference material obtained.

Surgical technology texts may be useful in learning proper operating-room conduct, but much of the illustrator's success in this delicate area will depend on the rapport established with the surgeon and the operating-room staff. Good communication between the illustrator and the operating-room staff is essential to avoid complicating the staff's job. Usually most of the interaction with operating-room personnel will be through the circulating (nonsterile) nurse, who can communicate the illustrator's arrival to the surgeons, answer questions about where to set up photographic equipment, help in setting up footstools, and address other basic concerns.

Because so often it is impossible to view every surgical procedure to be illustrated, the medical artist should make the most of each opportunity to visit the operating room, to gain experience in the appearance of tissues and organs in surgical settings. The shapes and textures of frequently rendered tissues—such as large and small vessels, subcutaneous fat, bone, internal organs, and other structures—should be carefully studied to lend authenticity to future illustrations.

Final Steps

Once adequate references are available, the preliminary sketches are done. At this stage, the artistic craft of medical illustration differs little from other fields of scientific illustration that require tight, reproducible originals suitable for the medium in which the artwork will appear. Regardless of the illustrator's particular working style or chosen medium, these preliminary drawings should contain as much detail as is practical to add. Any remaining questions about points of anatomy, instruments used, the precise colors or textures of tissues, labeling, or additional views required should be clarified before any final rendering is done.

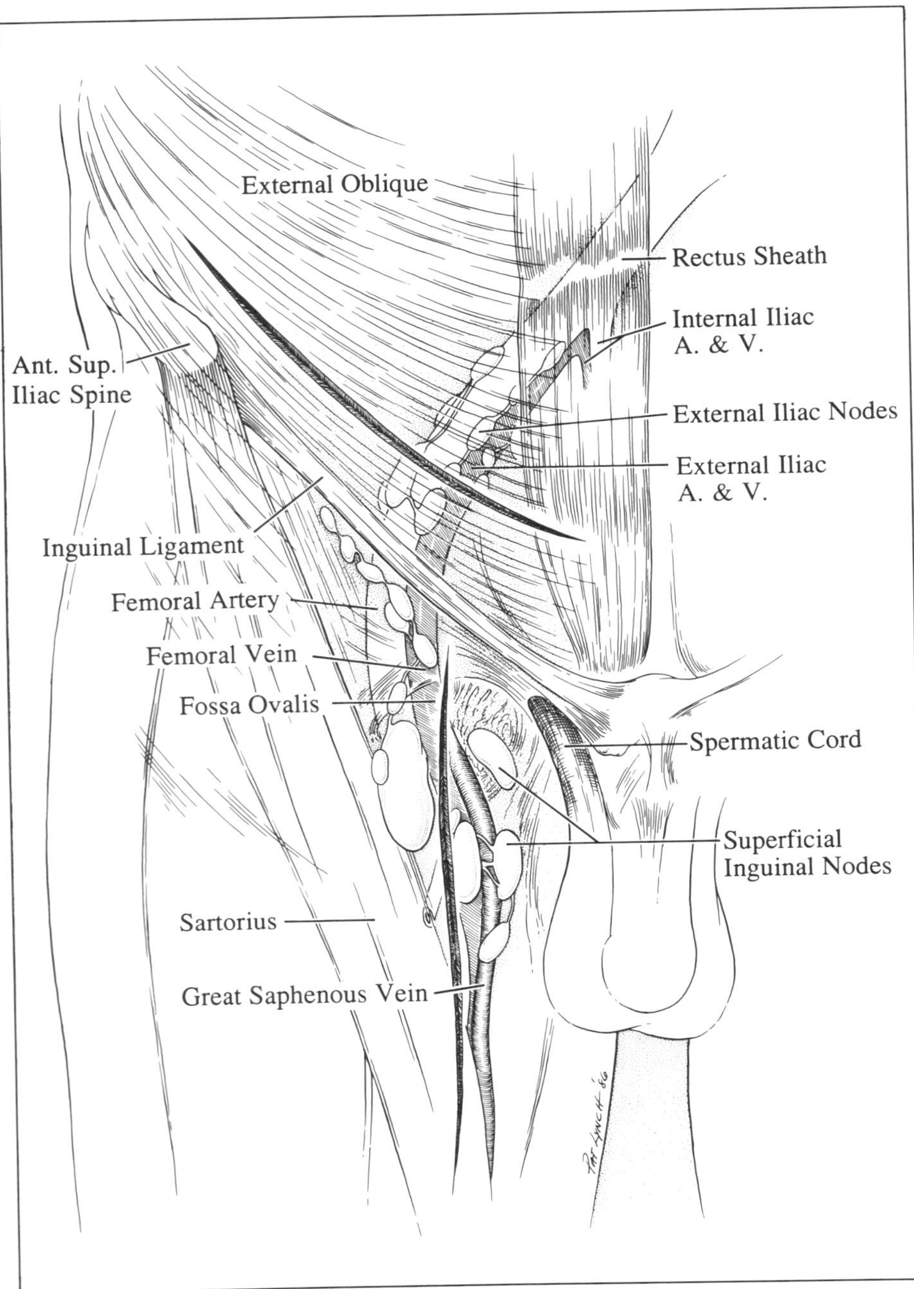

22-10. In situations such as that illustrated here, where incisions must be made relative to structures that are not visible, the underlying anatomy is often "ghosted" in to orient the audience. "Radical Groin Dissection, Placement of Incisions," one of a series of figures depicting the operation. Pen-and-ink on Herculene drafting film, by Patrick J. Lynch. Courtesy of Dr. Stephan Ariyan, Department of Plastic and Reconstructive Surgery, Yale University School of Medicine.

A medica
that literall
would be no
cent photog
illustration i
exercise no
gram. Ironi
often in kn
than what t
lar visual in
anatomical
nature of m
which is
tively the
the most
media, be
elaborately

Part IV
Beyond Basics

Chapters in this section discuss topics that provide valuable background information relevant to scientific illustration. For instance, since most subject areas require use of a microscope, it is essential for the illustrator to understand how to make the best use of this instrument. That is the thrust of chapter 23, Using the Microscope, which explains basic microscope optics. The complexity of the instrument requires that it be discussed in greater detail than other instruments covered in chapter 2.

Not all scientific illustration involves drawing specimens. The depiction of research results often is in diagrammatic form; many days may be spent drafting charts, graphs, or maps. Because the future of chart and graph production includes computer graphics, this technology is discussed in that context, in chapter 24. With appropriate software, computers can also produce maps.

Although most scientists need maps only occasionally to plot distribution of plants and animals, certain subject areas, anthropology among them, use maps extensively. Black-and-white base outline maps, obtained from the U.S. Geological Survey and other sources, are handy for affixing symbols that represent different species or other data. But when no base map can be found to suit the needs of the job, the illustrator must create a map. Conventions have been developed for consistency, legibility, and convenience for designing maps, and these are described in chapter 25.

Obtaining slides for publication, lecture display, portfolio, files, and exhibit entries need not require the services of a professional photographer. The scientist and illustrator who understand how to produce slides of artwork may be able to avoid that frequently large expense, and even those who do use a professional can profit from an understanding of what is involved. Chapter 26, Copy Photography, explains how to produce or ensure a photographer produces the best-quality results. Skill in photography is a valuable adjunct to scientific illustration in those disciplines and instances in which the illustrator must photograph specimens as part of the drawing process. In paleontology, for instance, reference photographs are often taken to aid in reducing a huge skeleton to manageable size. Reference photographs are also of value to the medical illustrator. The illustrator may be expected to be able to take the photograph, enlarge or reduce the negative, and print it. Although specimen and darkroom photography are not taught in this book, they can be learned from Kodak and other publications, courses, and practice.

Basic to all scientific illustration is reproduction of the drawing in print to communicate scientific findings. In order to prepare drawings that will reproduce well, the artist and scientist should understand what happens in the printer's shop, what technological limitations prevent perfect duplication of the original, and what can be done to produce the best results possible. Chapter 27 suggests solutions, along with a description of the printing process.

23/Using the Microscope

Kenelm W. Philip

In order to be able to illustrate very small specimens, the artist must know how to operate a variety of optical instruments. This chapter will discuss the compound microscope and the stereoscopic, or dissecting, microscope. Associated instruments (microprojectors, camera lucida attachments, and opaque projectors) are covered in chapter 2.

Basic principles are described for the compound microscope, primarily because it is a more complex system than the stereoscopic microscope and requires more understanding to use effectively. For homologous parts, the same information applies, although the lens systems in the compound and stereoscopic microscopes differ. Learning the principles of microscopy, even on an elementary level, can help the scientific illustrator adjust the microscope to show as much detail as possible. Such knowledge will also aid the illustrator in choosing an appropriate microscope for the task at hand.

Because a specimen seen under a stereomicroscope can look quite different when viewed through a compound microscope, a better understanding of some slide-mounted specimens may be gained through the use of both instruments.

Camera lucida attachments, eyepiece micrometers, and other accessories are available for both compound and stereoscopic microscopes.

BASIC PRINCIPLES

A properly shaped block of glass can use the bending of light rays to form an image of some real object; such devices are called lenses. Lenses are positive if the center is thicker than the edge and negative if the center is thinner than the edge (fig. 23-1). The focal length of an idealized thin lens (a lens whose thickness is negligible compared to other parameters of the system) is defined as the distance from the lens to the point at which rays of parallel light (from a point source infinitely far away) would cross the optical axis (a line through the center of the lens perpendicular to the plane of the lens) after passing through the lens (fig. 23-2). This intersecting of rays forms an image of the distant point source.

Images are of two kinds. For a distant point source, a positive lens will form a real image—a piece of photographic film placed at the focal point F would be exposed by the light converging to the optical axis. In the same circumstances, a negative lens would form a virtual

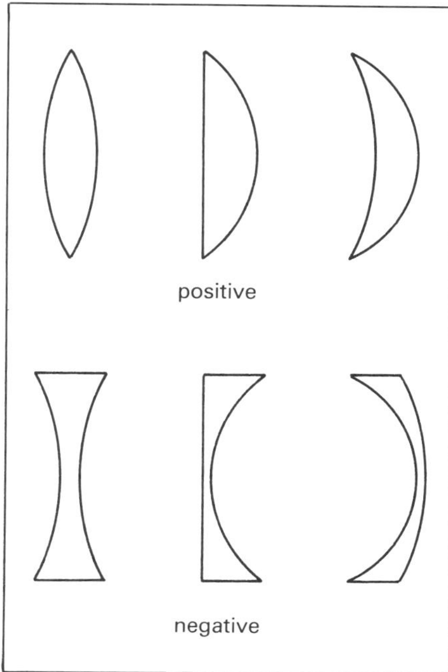

23-1. Positive and negative lenses. Pen-and-ink on bond paper, by Kenelm W. Philip.

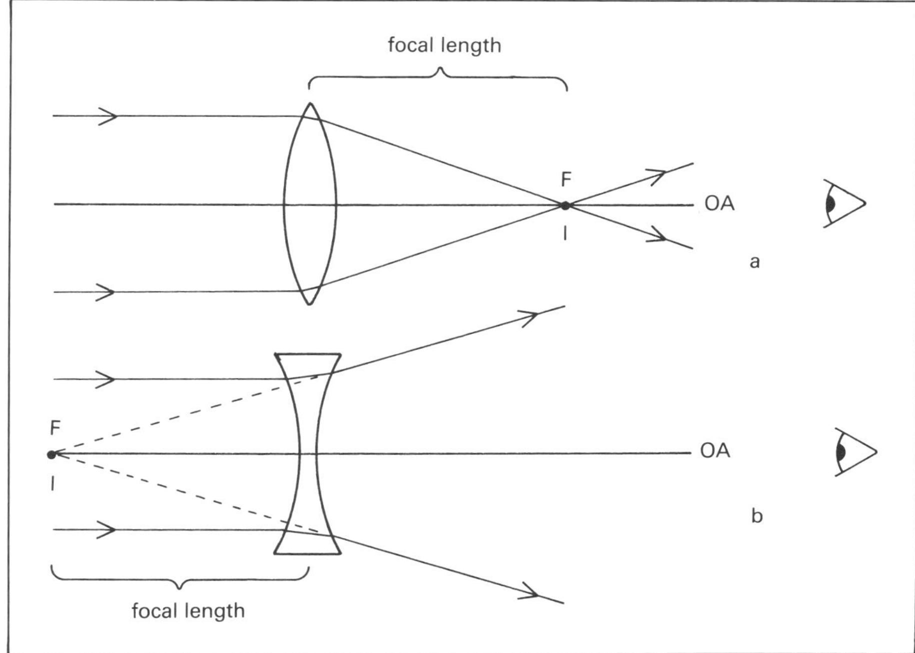

23-2. Focal length and focal points of ideal thin lenses. F is the focal point; OA is the optical axis. *(a)* The observer (to the right) sees a *real* image at I; *(b)* the observer sees a *virtual* image at I. In both cases, the image of an infinitely distant point lies at a focal point (F). Pen-and-ink on bond paper, by Kenelm W. Philip.

image—an eye to the right of the lens would see an apparent image at the point F to the left of the lens, but there are no light rays converging to that point, and a piece of film placed there would not receive an image of the light source. Note that real and virtual images are not necessarily produced by positive and negative lenses, respectively. Under the appropriate circumstances, either kind of lens can yield either kind of image.

A simple magnifying glass (fig. 23-3) is an example of a positive lens forming a virtual image. The image is moved back so the eye can focus on it, while the object is brought very close to the eye, yielding a magnified view compared to what the unaided eye could achieve at its distance of closest focus.

A magnifying glass can be made to magnify by 100 diameters or more, but such a lens is tiny and difficult to use. The microscopes made by Antoni van Leeuwenhoek in the seventeenth century were simple microscopes of this type. Using an object lens (objective) to produce an enlarged real image of the specimen and an eye lens (ocular or eyepiece) to then magnify this real image makes an instrument (the compound microscope) that is much easier to use and considerably more powerful than a simple microscope.

Magnification is not actually the most important property of a microscope, since an optical system can have empty magnification—magnification that reveals no additional information about the specimen. The essential quality of a microscope is its resolution, its ability to form distinct images of two very close points on the object.

Practicable lens systems have a number of aberrations that degrade image quality, and the wave nature of light sets limits on the ultimate resolution of any given optical system. Achieving high resolution and other desirable features at a reasonable price while balancing the effects of various aberrations is the task of the optical designer.

INTRODUCTION TO THE COMPOUND MICROSCOPE

An analogy between the compound microscope and a slide projector may help in explaining how a microscope forms an image of a specimen and underscores the importance of the illumination system to its proper functioning. (*Microscopy from the Very Beginning*, by F. K. Moellring—see Bibliography—includes a fuller treatment of this analogy.)

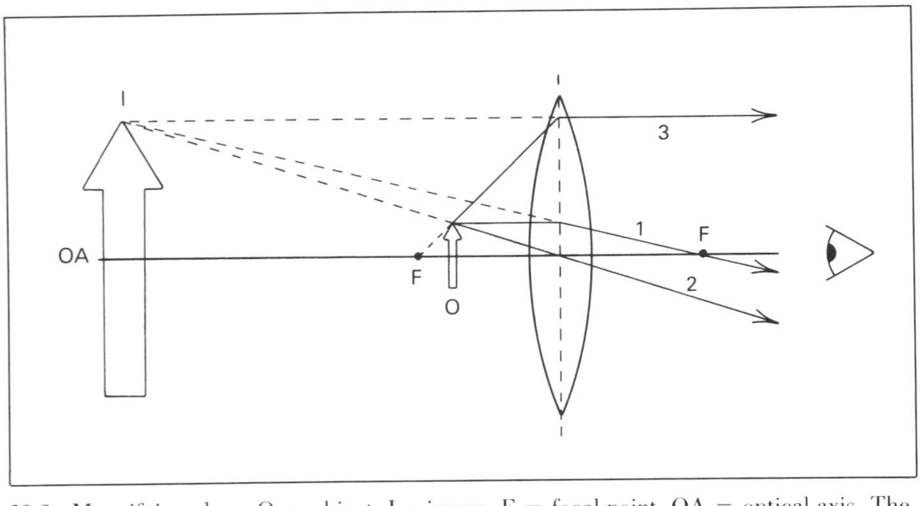

23-3. Magnifying glass. O = object, I = image, F = focal point, OA = optical axis. The image (I) is enlarged, erect, and virtual. Pen-and-ink on bond paper, by Kenelm W. Philip.

compound microscope arranged horizontally—what is normally called a microscope is merely the right-hand portion of the figure, without the lamp and condenser. A complete compound microscope (not the low-power stereoscopic microscope, which usually lacks a substage condenser and is often used for opaque specimens with reflected rather than transmitted light) must contain at least the following optical components: lamp (bulb, condenser, diaphragm); substage condenser (with diaphragm); slide, specimen, and cover slip (all optical components); objective lens; eyepiece (field lens and magnifier). The single condenser in the slide projector analogue above is replaced by two condensers in a real microscope, one at the lamp and one below the stage, in order to achieve better control over the illumination of the specimen (see Illumination for the Compound Microscope, below). In addition, a microscope has various mechanical components designed to align the optical components along a single optical axis and permit the necessary focusing motions. (See fig. 23-12 for diagrams of two representative styles of microscopes, with the various components identified.)

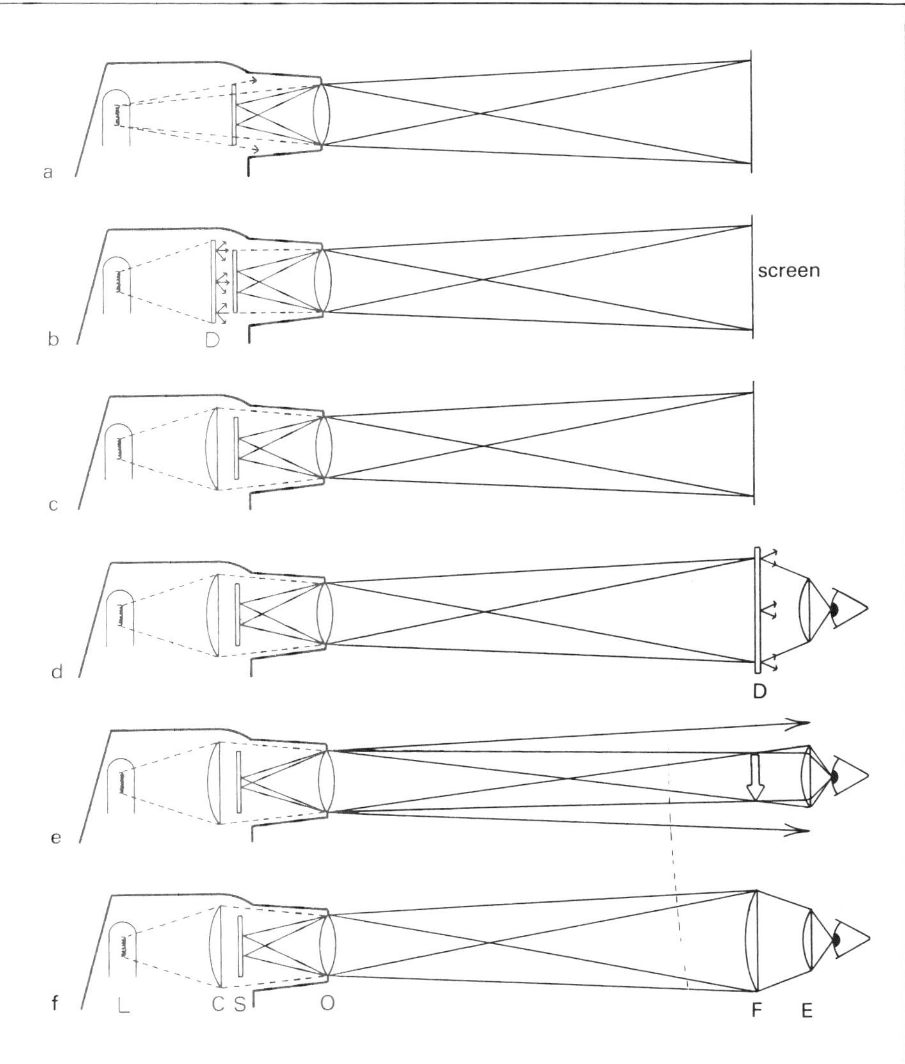

23-4. Developing a compound microscope from a slide projector: *(a)* lamp, slide, objective lens, and screen; *(b)* lamp diffuser added; *(c)* lamp diffuser replaced with lamp condenser; *(d)* screen replaced with diffuser, eye lens added; *(e)* diffuser removed, eye lens used to examine aerial image; *(f)* field lens added, yielding a working microscope. D = diffuser, L = lamp, C = lamp condenser, S = slide (photographic or microscope), O = objective lens, F = field lens, E = eye lens. Pen-and-ink on bond paper, by Kenelm W. Philip.

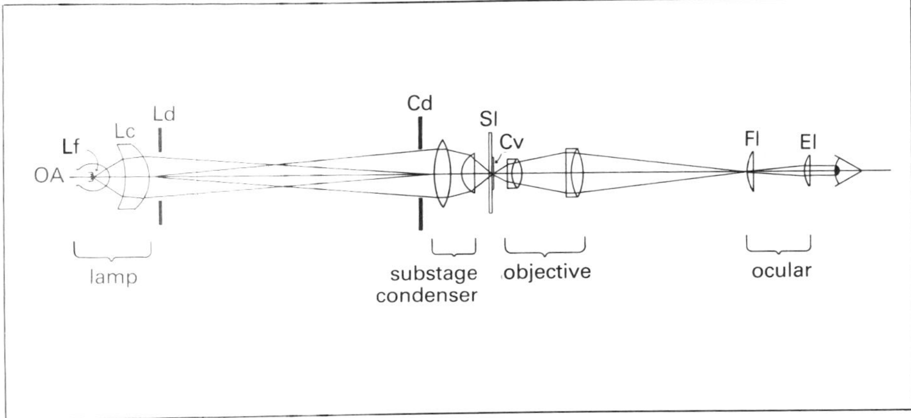

23-5. Complete optical train of compound microscope, arranged horizontally for comparison with figure 23-4. OA = optical axis, Lf = lamp filament, Lc = lamp condenser, Ld = lamp diaphragm, Cd = substage condenser diaphragm, Sl = slide, Cv = cover slip, Fl = field lens, El = eye lens. Light rays are shown for points on the optical axis in the filament, and in the plane of the lamp diaphragm. The lamp filament is imaged onto the substage condenser, the lamp diaphragm is imaged into the specimen plane, and the specimen is imaged (real image) at or near the eyepiece field lens. The eyepiece then forms a magnified virtual image lying some distance to the left, within the focusing range of the observer's eye. In most microscope systems, mirrors or prisms (not shown here) are introduced to allow the optical axis to fold into a smaller space. Pen-and-ink on bond paper, by Kenelm W. Philip.

Transmitted-Light Microscopy

Specimens on microscope slides usually are examined by transmitted light. The specimen is placed in a transparent mounting medium chosen for its optical properties and covered with a thin cover slip. If the specimen is not naturally translucent, it is either treated with a clearing agent to ensure at least partial translucency or cut into slices so thin that they are to some extent translucent. Permanent mounts are made in various proprietary substances that hold the specimen firmly in place. (The name notwithstanding, it is *not* recommended to store permanent slide mounts of large specimens on edge, since many so-called permanent mounting media will allow slow motion of the cover slip and specimen over long periods of time.) Temporary mounts may use water, glycerin, and other liquids or gels.

The most commonly used transmitted light method is bright-field microscopy, where the contrast in the image is formed by differential absorption of light in various parts of the specimen. The specimen appears on a uniformly illuminated field, its structure revealed by contrasts in color and intensity. Many specialized methods have been developed for staining (selectively dyeing portions of) otherwise transparent specimens so they will exhibit contrast in bright field. Living material and certain unusually transparent objects will often require other methods, such as dark-field illumination (see Substage Condenser, below, or *How to Use a Microscope*, by W. G. Hartley—see Bibliography) or phase contrast, which produces enhanced contrast by introducing a small phase shift between the direct illumination and the rays scattered by the specimen (refer to *Progress in Microscopy*, by M. Françon—see Bibliography). Inexperienced microscopists often attempt to push bright-field techniques too far when viewing material of low contrast. It is possible to increase materially the contrast in the bright-field image of a low-contrast specimen, but only at the expense of resolution—and if the contrast is very low, other methods are far superior to bright field. Phase contrast requires special optical components, but dark-field illumination may be obtained on almost any microscope, yielding a striking self-luminous image on a black field.

The Objective

Let us consider major components of the microscope individually, starting with the objective lens and cover slip, together the most critical portion of the microscope.

An objective may be characterized by five major parameters: the mechanical tube length, power, numerical aperture, optical medium, and color correction.

Mechanical Tube Length

The mechanical tube length is the distance from the bottom of the nosepiece (the shoulder where the objective screws into the nosepiece) to the upper end of the microscope tube. Tube length is now standardized at 160mm, but older Leitz microscopes used 170mm. Tube length is not an arbitrary parameter. Any objective has been optically corrected to work with a fixed tube length, except for the so-called infinity corrected objectives used on some modern microscopes, which do not require a fixed tube length.

Power

The power, or linear magnification, of an objective is approximately equal to its focal length divided into the tube length. Most modern objectives have the power (40×, or 40, for example) engraved on the barrel, but older objectives will give the focal length instead.

Note that m
to ensure tha
tives of diff
cal; that is,
in focus as
on the micro
objectives (1
parfocal with

Numerical A

The N.A.
single most
because the
imen plane i
to N.A. (fig.

The best
necessarily
with the hi
implies ver
very critical
(air) objecti
ditions disc
N.A. is the
resolves the
general rule
highest pow
and eyepie
should be u
tive is 100
very fine ob
about 750
light micros
empty and
in the subj

For visu
lower limit
mined by t
magnificati
250 times
leaving th
enter the
selecting a
an objecti
nification
eyepiece a
tions falls
to 750 tim

Since
can have
jectives, it
conclude t
mersion i
power. Th
an equally
oil immer
come the
incorrect

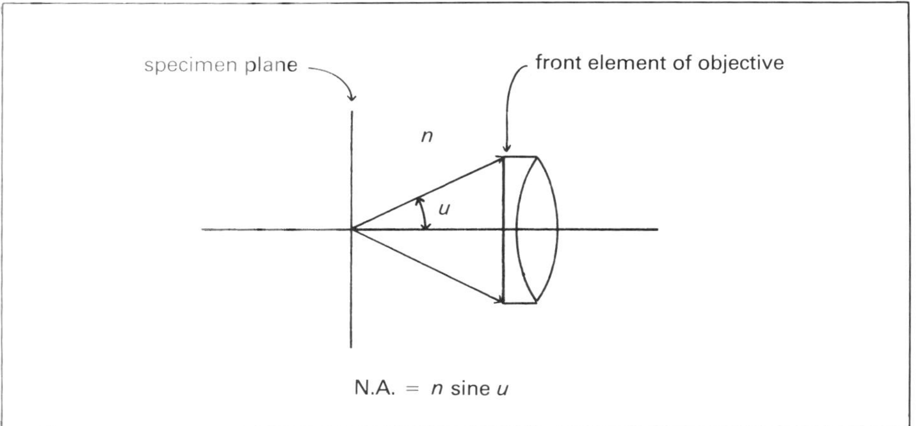

23-6. Definition of numerical aperture (N.A.). N.A. equals the sine of half the angle *(u)* subtended by the objective front lens (as seen from the specimen), times the refractive index of the medium *(n)* between the lens and the specimen. Pen-and-ink on bond paper, by Kenelm W. Philip.

removing the objective's dependence on that parameter. It should be noted here that the advantages of oil immersion may be achieved only if the entire light path from the slide to the objective is optically homogeneous.

Optical Medium and Immersion Objectives

Only two optical media are now in common use: air and oil. Water-immersion objectives are occasionally used in biological work, and special high-refractive-index immersion media have been used in the quest for higher resolution. Either water immersion (without a cover slip) or oil immersion (with a cover slip) provides an optically uniform path from the objective to the specimen and allows higher N.A. than can be obtained in air, while making the system free from introduced spherical aberration (see below).

Color Correction

To this point the objective has been considered as just a lens, without considering the constraints on an optical device that is designed to achieve magnifications up to 100 diameters and resolution to 0.2 microns. In practice, a high-power microscope objective is composed of a number (perhaps four to twelve) of component lenses, or elements. One reason for the number of elements is that the most basic optical parameter of glass—its refractive index—varies with the wavelength (color) of light. The refractive index *(n)* is the ratio of the velocity of light in a vacuum to its velocity in an optical medium, and it is a measure of the ability of a substance to change the direction of a light ray crossing its surface (approximate values: $n = 1.00$ for air, 1.33 for water, 1.51 for glass). A change in refractive index with color will make the focal length and magnification of a lens a function of color, but by using different types of optical glass in a multielement lens, these chromatic aberrations may be greatly reduced.

Objectives are now made in three degrees of color correction: achromats, fluorites, and apochromats. Achromats have the same focal length at two selected colors and may deviate widely for violet and red light. Apochromats are corrected for three colors, spanning most of the visual range, but are much more expensive than achromats. Fluorites (so named because they use fluorite elements, also called semi-apochromats) have an intermediate degree of correction between achromats and apochromats and are superb general-purpose lenses. Fluorites and apochromats require compensating eyepieces to remove residual chromatic difference of magnification.

There are two additional lens aberrations that should be discussed here: field curvature and spherical aberration. Both of these affect the performance of all objectives, and spherical aberration is the one lens aberration that microscope users can exacerbate or ameliorate by their own actions.

Curvature of Field

Normal objectives, whether achromats, fluorites, or apochromats, will exhibit marked curvature of the surface at which the image is in sharp focus (and apochromats will normally have more curvature than achromats). It is necessary, therefore, to refocus the objective whenever a different annular zone about the optical axis in the specimen plane is to be examined. If the center of the field is in sharp focus, the edges will be blurred, and vice versa. With thick specimens, this aberration may not be noticed, since some portion of the specimen may be in focus at any distance from the optical axis. For critical work on very thin specimens, however, the illustrator may find only a small region of the specimen in sharp focus at one time. If continual refocusing presents a problem, use a planapochromat, or flat field objective, which utilizes more elements to reduce the field curvature. These very expensive lenses are intended primarily for photomicrography, and for critical visual work they may not be quite as sharp at the center of the field as a good apochromat, since all optical design involves compromise.

Spherical Aberration

This is the most important lens aberration from the microscope user's viewpoint, because it can be introduced into the system by incorrect thickness of the cover slip and mounting medium (fig. 23-7). It produces an overall lack of sharpness in the image, which cannot be dealt with by careful focusing on

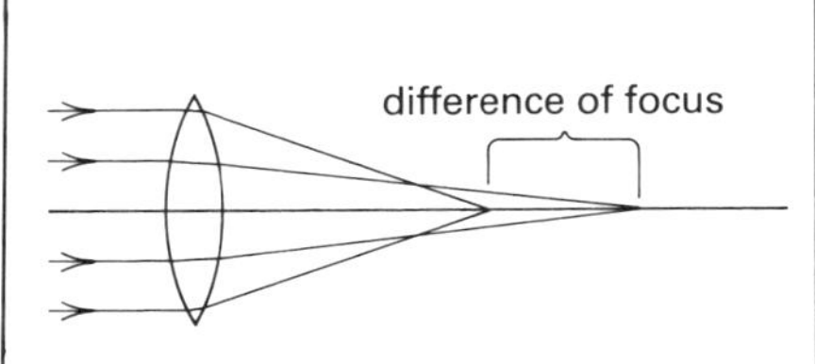

23-7. Spherical aberration for a simple lens with spherical surfaces. The outer rays are focused closer than the inner rays (spherical undercorrection). Pen-and-ink on bond paper, by Kenelm W. Philip.

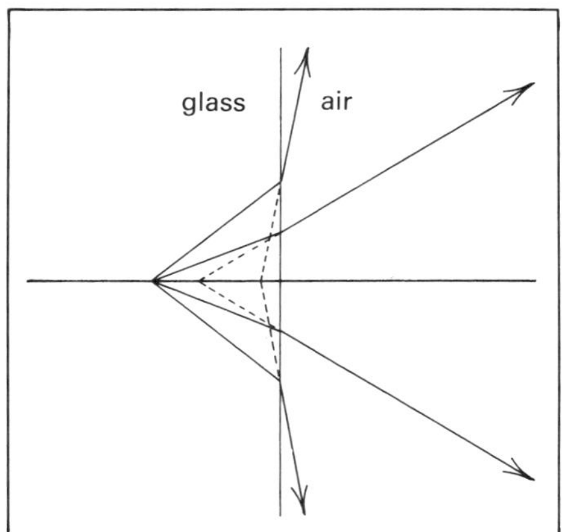

23-8. Spherical aberration in a cone of rays going from a glass block into air. Pen-and-ink on bond paper, by Kenelm W. Philip.

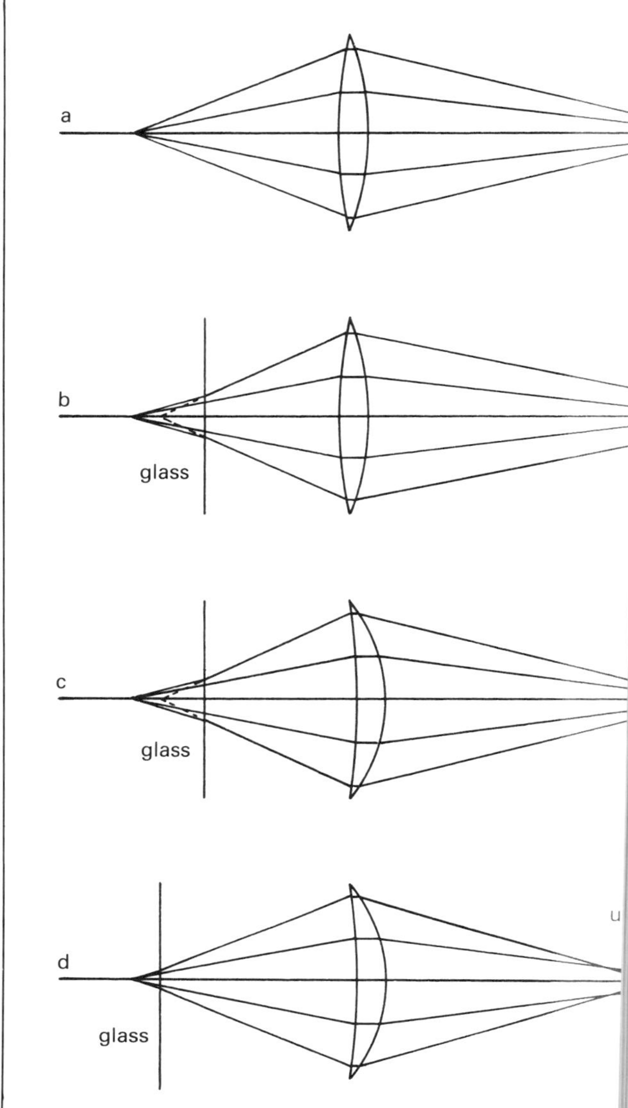

23-9. Spherical aberration—compensation versus cover-slip corrected for spherical aberration, object in air; *(b)* object in which produces spherical overcorrection; *(c)* bending lens co aberration caused by that particular thickness of glass; *(d)* th spherical undercorrection. Pen-and-ink on bond paper, by K

the area of interest. It is the responsibility of the user to keep introduced spherical aberration from degrading the performance of the system. Designers have been able to correct for this aberration in multielement lens systems, but the cover slip is one of the optical elements of the system, and its thickness is critical. Consider a source of light rays inside a glass block (fig. 23-8) and examine the cone of rays escaping through the surface of the block. The oblique rays will be more highly refracted, as shown, and an observer outside the block will not see a sharp image of the source. The marginal rays seem to originate from a point nearer the surface than the inner rays. (Note that spherical aberration can occur without involving spherical surfaces.) If these rays then enter a lens, they will not be brought to a true focus unless the lens has an equal and opposite spherical aberration. Figure 23-9 illustrates the effect of the cover slip and mounting-medium thickness on the spherical aberration of an objective and suggests ways lens designers can compensate for this aberration.

Use of Cover Slip and Oil Immersion

Most objectives are designed for a single object distance, a single image dist thickness medium o cal design these valu length of thickness U.S. make ropean an

Cover s eral thick 0.12mm; no. 1½—(0.18 to 0.2

With objectives of N.A. less than 0.5 (which means all objectives of power 20× and lower), there should be no visible effects from variations of cover-slip thickness unless the amount of mounting medium between the slip and the specimen is thicker than the cover slip. For dry objectives with N.A. between 0.65 and 0.95 (most 40× and higher power nonimmersion objectives), a small deviation from the 0.18 or 0.17mm value for the combined thickness of cover slip, mounting medium and specimen down to the level within the specimen being examined will produce a noticeable degradation of image quality.

If the objective has a correction collar that introduces controlled amounts of spherical aberration, it is possible to run through the range of adjustment, focusing for the best image quality at each setting of the collar, and select the setting that yields the sharpest image. If the 40× dry objective lacks a correction collar and there is reason to suspect image degradation from spherical aberration, a 50× oil-immersion objective should be used with the manufacturer's recommended type of oil. Under so-called homogeneous immersion there is a continuous optical medium, of refractive index equal (or nearly equal) to that of the cover slip and mounting medium, from the front element of the objective to the specimen. And the thickness of the cover slip and mounting medium is no longer critical as long as it does not exceed the working distance of the objective (distance between the front lens of the objective and the plane of focus in the specimen).

Objectives of higher power than 40× are almost always (with some rare exceptions) oil-immersion objectives, although water-immersion objectives may also be found. Since the N.A. of an objective is limited by the refractive index of the medium between the specimen and the objective, high-power objectives must use oil immersion, even aside from spherical aberration considerations, in order to achieve the resolution appropriate to their magnification.

In those rare cases where the illustrator may have some control over the preparation of microscope slides, ensure that there is the correct 0.18 or 0.17mm thickness from the top of the cover slip to the important level of the specimen. Cover slips thicker than the no. 1½ size should never be used. Very thin preparations in direct contact with the cover slip need no. 1½ slips; thicker preparations should use no. 1 slips (or even no. 0).

The Eyepiece

The eyepiece, or ocular, is the second stage of magnification in the compound microscope. Three points about it are important to the illustrator.

First, apochromatic objectives are left with some chromatic undercorrection, so compensating oculars must be used. These are deliberately overcorrected to counteract the residual aberration of the objective, and are usually marked "compensating" or "K." In practice, these are nearly universal oculars, since they may be employed with all apochromats and fluorites, and achromats above N.A. = 0.65 (which also have residual chromatic undercorrection). Nikon CF objectives (introduced in the 1970s) have no residual chromatic aberration and must be used with CF eyepieces.

Second, illustrators who must wear eyeglasses at the microscope should insist on high-eyepoint eyepieces, which are far more practical to use with glasses than the standard eyepieces. Several manufacturers make compensating wide-field high-eyepoint oculars; these are expensive but a joy to use, and they probably produce less eyestrain under long use. Wide-field eyepieces give the viewer a larger angular field (less appearance of looking down a narrow tube) and show a larger area of the specimen.

Third, oculars are available over a wide range of magnifications, from 2× to 50× or greater for special purposes, although most are between 6× and 15×. When selecting an eyepiece for a given application, remember the criteria for the upper and lower limits of total magnification (750 and 250 times the N.A. of the objective).

When using a microscope, take care that the accommodation muscles of your eyes are relaxed. To test this, focus on a distant object with one eye (using a mirror if needed) and simultaneously look into the ocular with the other eye (assuming both eyes are, or have been corrected to be, similar). If the microscope must be refocused to allow both the distant object and the microscope field of view to be in simultaneous sharp focus, the possibility of eyestrain exists. The virtual image seen through the eyepiece should lie at the greatest distance at which your eye can focus. Train your eyes to relax and focus for distant objects when using a microscope.

Eyeglasses pose special problems. If you have astigmatism, you must wear glasses at the microscope. If you are nearsighted, you may dispense with glasses, but at a price: different power objectives will no longer be precisely parfocal, and you will thus have to refocus whenever you change power. Also, you will introduce some additional aberrations into the image by focusing the objective slightly away from its design distance from the specimen. It is therefore recommended that nearsighted people use high-eyepoint oculars and wear their glasses.

The Substage Condenser

The substage condenser is the most misused component of the microscope. Generations of students have discovered or been taught that the substage condenser diaphragm can be used to control the intensity of the illumination in the image. All too many have been told that this is the function of that diaphragm, which is totally incorrect. The substage condenser diaphragm controls resolution and contrast in the image. Image brightness should be controlled with a rheostat or variable transformer at the lamp or with neutral-density or crossed polarizing filters.

The substage condenser controls the angle of the cone of illumination impinging on the specimen. Theoretically, an objective will achieve its full resolution only when the specimen is illuminated by a cone of light that fills a solid angle having the same N.A. as the objective (fig. 23-10a). When the cone is reduced to a narrow pencil of nearly parallel light (fig. 23-10c), the resolution of the objective is (theoretically) halved.

If resolution were the only factor to be considered, the user would always open the substage condenser diaphragm to at least the N.A. of the objective in use. As the N.A. of the illumination increases, however, there will be more stray light in the system, and scattered stray light (glare) reduces contrast. Resolution is useless if the contrast is too low to show the resolved detail. Conversely, contrast is useless if the resolution is too low to show the details of interest in the specimen. Resolution must continually be balanced against contrast, and the best setting of the substage condenser diaphragm will depend on a number of factors, including the inherent contrast of the specimen and the optical quality of both condenser and objective.

A good starting point is the Nelson three-quarter cone: remove the eyepiece and look down the tube at the back focal plane of the objective. In a properly set-up instrument, you will see an image of the substage condenser diaphragm. Adjust the diaphragm until the radius of the bright circle is three-fourths the radius of the back lens of the objective (fig. 23-10b). (If you cannot obtain such a three-quarter cone with the substage condenser diaphragm fully opened, either the N.A. of the condenser is too small for the objective or the instrument is not adjusted properly.) For high-quality objectives and well-stained preparations, it is sometimes possible to go to a nine-tenths cone without serious loss of contrast, whereas with more transparent specimens and poorer objectives, it may be necessary to drop back to a one-half cone. If a narrow pencil of light is required for sufficient contrast to show the specimen at all, the preparation is inappropriate for bright-field microscopy, and dark-field, phase, or other such methods should be used. The three-quarter cone may provide lower contrast levels than may seem comfortable, but there is a significant increase in resolution over narrower cones of illumination.

When examining specimens of low inherent contrast, inexperienced microscopists invariably nearly close the substage dia-

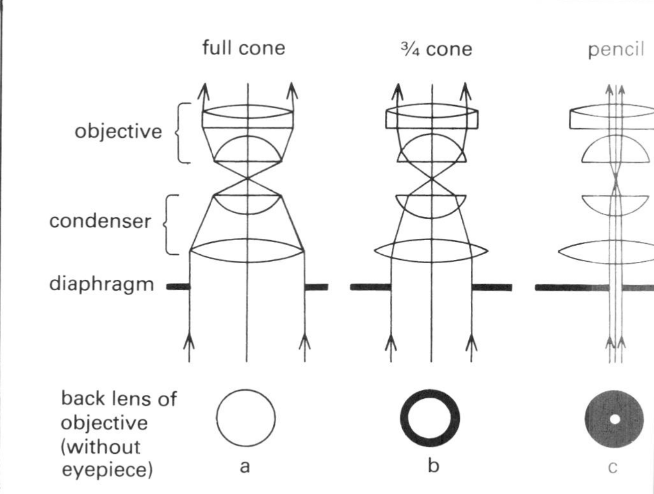

23-10. Illumination of objective as controlled by the substage co
full cone, diaphragm open; *(b)* Nelson ¾ cone; *(c)* narrow pencil
closed; *(d)* low-power dark field, diaphragm fully open with cent
of objective less than N.A. of central stop, which is less than N.
circle at the bottom of each figure shows what is seen in the bac
with the eyepiece removed. Pen-and-ink on bond paper, by Ken

phragm to ol
trast—which
along with
and the produ
tures in the ir
in the specim

The subst
phragm shou
the objective
with a diffe
cases, the su
self will hav
order to matc
used. No si
length can p
N.A. needed
large illumin
high-power
condensers.
may be remo
working with

Low-Power D
Illumination

Low-powe
tion is a usef
a hollow con
outside the
(see fig. 23-1
would be ef
tion, open
phragm fully
finger carefu

condenser diaphragm (or filter holder, if present) to block the direct rays from the light source. If the resulting image appears to be an improvement, obtain low-power dark-field stops (opaque-centered glass circles that mount in the substage filter carrier) for the microscope and follow the maker's instructions for use. Dark-field illumination has one defect: any out-of-focus dirt on the cover slip or in the preparation will produce luminous blurs in the field of view. The preparation should, therefore, be scrupulously clean.

Some 50× oil-immersion objectives have an internal diaphragm that controls the N.A. They are superb for the higher-power applications of low-power dark-field, since the variable N.A. allows compensation for the precise diameter of the dark-field stop and thus optimizes illumination.

Optical Correction of Condensers

Condensers are available in different degrees of correction, ranging from the simple Abbe illuminator to systems almost as good as objectives. For all objectives, well-corrected condensers reduce glare, but the Abbe condenser is unsuitable for objectives with N.A. greater than 0.7 because of its severe spherical aberration.

Illumination for the Compound Microscope

Koehler illumination has now become standard for the compound microscope, and substitutes should not be tolerated. Most modern microscopes come with built-in illumination on Koehler principles; separate microscope lamps utilizing this method may be obtained for microscopes lacking integral illumination.

Good illumination for bright-field microscopy ensures that each point in the specimen receives light coming from an identical and even distribution of directions about the optical axis (the converging cone of light in fig. 23-10). The best way to do this is to place the image of a uniform source of light into the specimen plane. You may have noticed that a magnifying glass with a small light source behind it can appear filled with light if the eye is at the right point; Koehler illumination relies on this fact and images the lamp condenser into the specimen plane. A small lamp filament can thus evenly illuminate a large area of the specimen (fig. 23-11).

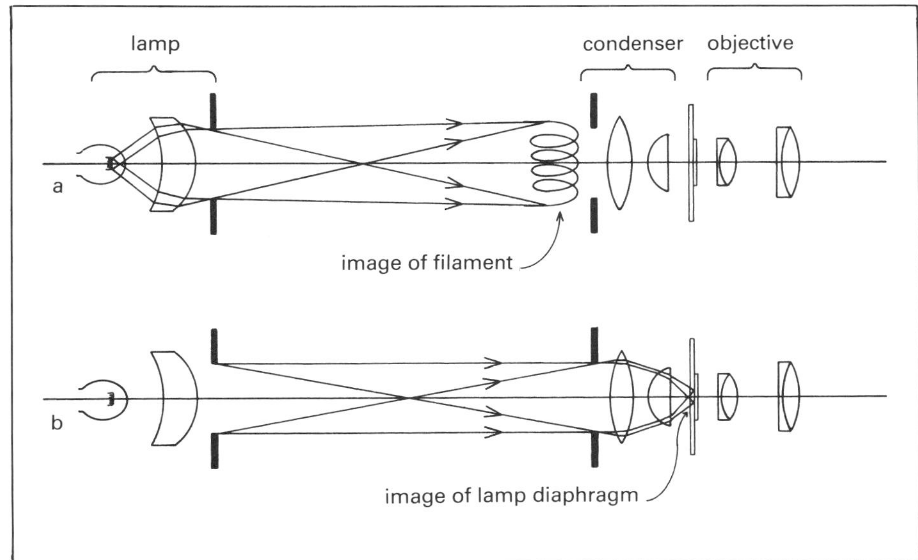

23-11. Koehler illumination: *(a)* image of lamp filament focused on the plane of the substage condenser diaphragm, filling the condenser aperture; *(b)* image of lamp diaphragm thrown into specimen plane, delineating visible field. Pen-and-ink on bond paper, by Kenelm W. Philip.

In figure 23-11a, the lamp condenser throws an enlarged image of the bulb filament on the plane of the substage condenser diaphragm. This image should be at least as large as the maximum diameter of the fully opened diaphragm, to fill the aperture of the substage condenser with light. The substage condenser is then used to focus an image of the lamp diaphragm on the specimen plane (fig. 23-11b). The lamp diaphragm sets the size of the illuminated area of the specimen. The light-filled aperture of this diaphragm is the uniform source of light that is imaged on the specimen plane to light the specimen evenly.

If the microscope has built-in illumination, following the manufacturer's instructions normally will yield Koehler illumination. (If you have a separate lamp, see section on Operating Procedures, below, or *How to Use a Microscope*, mentioned under Transmitted-Light Microscopy, above).

Filters

Microscope lamps produce light from the near-ultraviolet (UV), through the visible, into the infrared (heat) wavelengths. Because heat radiation may be damaging when focused on a specimen, many lamps accept a heat-absorbing filter (but *all* light wavelengths will produce heat when absorbed). Light from a tungsten-filament lamp tends to be too strong in the red for visual comfort in extended observing sessions. A daylight filter will produce a more pleasing quality of light and cut off wavelengths that achromatic objectives focus at the wrong distance. A green filter added to the daylight filter often improves image quality, especially with achromats. It also helps compensate for a major shortcoming in controlling brightness by the lamp voltage: the reddening of the light as the voltage is lowered. Daylight and green (and other color) filters may be obtained to fit the lamp or the substage condenser filter carrier.

Ultraviolet and blue light permit higher resolution because of their shorter wavelength and are used in photomicrography, but light strong in the blue and near-UV can cause eye fatigue. If you are using a mercury-vapor lamp, obtain a filter to block all UV and some of the blue light to protect your vision.

Filters may also be used to increase contrast in the specimen, following the same rule as in photography: a filter that passes wavelengths of color A and blocks wavelengths of color B will lighten color A and darken color B. Careful selection of filters can materially improve the contrast of specimens that have distinct (even if faint) colors.

Incident Light

Under some conditions, it may make sense to try overhead illumination (incident light) for opaque objects viewed under low powers. A high-intensity spot illuminator or fiber-optic lamp (or pair of lamps) may be used, mixed with transmitted light if desired.

Operating Procedures

Having discussed the individual components of the compound microscope, we should now put everything together.

The Assembled Instrument

Figure 23-12 shows two microscopes, with all their major parts labeled. Neither of these exactly depicts any single brand of microscope, but figure 23-12a is like many older instruments, whereas figures 23-12b is typical of modern design. Both figures show standard research microscopes; many specialized instruments bear little apparent resemblance to these.

The low-mounted concentric coarse and fine focus controls of the later instrument are an improvement over earlier models. They are easier to manipulate without strain (and a microscopist's hand is seldom far from the fine-focus knob). Furthermore, focusing by moving the stage rather than the lens tube allows rigid support of the objective, tube, and eyepiece. It is possible to use a heavy eyepiece camera without straining the focusing mechanism or having the focus creep out of adjustment during use.

In many microscopes of this general type, components may be quickly replaced with other versions of themselves or various accessories, so the entire instrument can be rapidly converted to do different tasks. The instrument in figure 23-12b has an integral illuminator in its base, which is a mixed blessing. It is very convenient, but a mirror and external lamp provide a more versatile system if you know how to adjust them properly.

All the components discussed above are identified in figure 23-12. You should be able to locate them in units of unfamiliar design with a little thought after comparing the two instruments illustrated.

Setup Procedures

Below is a list of the steps in alignment and adjustment of a compound microscope. Supplement the list with careful study of the manufacturer's manual for your instrument. If your attempts to align a microscope are unsuccessful, try a different objective. Objectives are delicate, and an element can be jarred out of alignment. No adjustments will solve that problem (and the misaligned objective should be repaired if possible, or else discarded). If you encounter difficulties that these procedures do not alleviate, a very helpful table, entitled "Troubleshooting problems in visual microscopy," appears in "Visual Microscopy in Diagnostic Cytology," by G. W. Gill (see Bibliography).

1. Center th
lamp bulb
of the lamp
2. If the lamp
the microsc
the lamp
stage cond
3. Focus the
moving its
to throw a
ment into t
stage con
The lamp c
to be clos
sharp ima
Use a pie
substage
phragm to
4. Check that
ament fills
substage
change th
the lamp c
5. Use a 10
down the
diaphragm
and set
denser foc
travel.
6. Remove t
your eye c
top of the
back of th
the subst
phragm (if
image is v
the objecti
7. If the micr
condenser
use them
of the dia
of the obje
8. Replace th
test slide
isolated.
on an othe
you may
specimen
scription.
ter) on the
it.
9. With the
diaphragm
close dov
phragm un
of view, t
stage cond

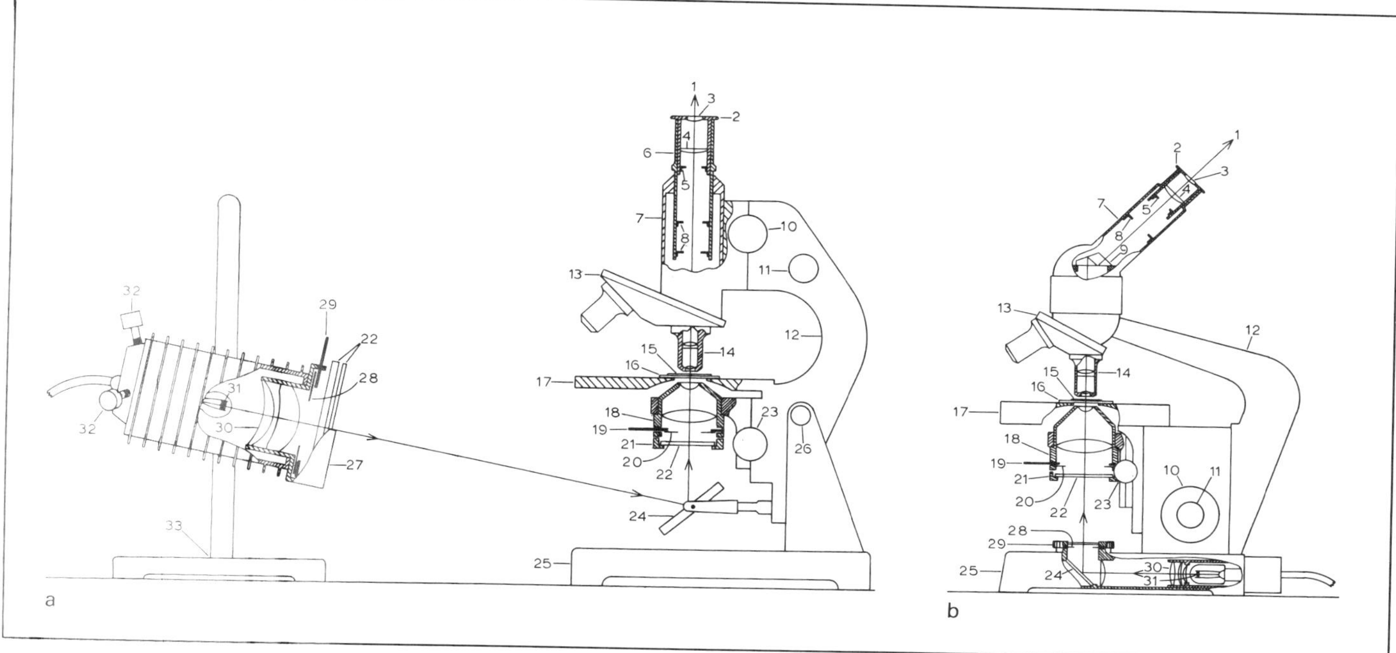

23-12. Compound microscopes: *(a)* older-style instrument, with separate lamp; *(b)* newer-style instrument, with built-in illuminator. Mechanical details have been simplified, but most components mentioned in the text are numbered. (1) optical axis; (2) eyepiece (ocular); (3) eye lens; (4) field lens; (5) field diaphragm; (6) drawtube; (7) body tube; (8) antiglare stop; (9) prism; (10) coarse-focus knob; (11) fine-focus knob; (12) arm; (13) revolving nosepiece; (14) objective; (15) cover slip; (16) slide; (17) stage; (18) substage condenser; (19) substage condenser diaphragm lever; (20) substage condenser diaphragm; (21) substage condenser filter carrier; (22) filter; (23) substage condenser focus knob; (24) mirror; (25) base; (26) inclination joint; (27) lamp filter carrier; (28) lamp diaphragm; (29) lamp diaphragm lever; (30) lamp condenser; (31) lamp filament; (32) lamp centering screws; (33) lamp stand. Pen-and-ink on bond paper, by Kenelm W. Philip.

sharpest possible image of the lamp diaphragm. Do not change the focus of the objective during this procedure—it should remain focused on the objects on the test slide.

10. Open the lamp diaphragm until the field of view is nearly filled with light and touch up the mirror position—or the lamp diaphragm centering if the microscope has a built-in illuminator—until the diaphragm image is precisely centered on the field of view. Then open the lamp diaphragm to just beyond the edge of the field.
11. If illumination is not quite even over the field, try a *small* change of the substage condenser focus adjustment to see if that yields any improvement.
12. Remove the eyepiece and again inspect the back of the objective. Set the substage condenser diaphragm to a three-quarter cone.
13. Replace the eyepiece. Replace the test slide, if used, with the preparation you intend to examine. Refocus the objective and inspect the field of view. Change the substage diaphragm opening as required to obtain the best visibility of the preparation (open to as much as nine-tenths cone for thin, heavily stained specimens, close to one-half cone or so for highly transparent specimens).
14. If in step 13 you closed down the substage condenser diaphragm, remove the eyepiece and check cone angle in back lens of objective (see fig. 23-10). If you had to close down to well under a one-half cone in order to see any detail in the specimen, try dark-field or phase/interference/modulation contrast methods. Check the cone angle for whatever adjustment is made to develop a feeling for the sort of image each cone angle produces with different specimens.
15. If you need higher power, switch to the appropriate objective and repeat steps 6, 7 (if needed), 8 (but do not return to the test slide unless your preparation is very dense all over—just move to a relatively unobstructed part of your preparation), and 9 through 14. Run through that series of steps *each time* you move to a higher power.
16. If you go from step 14 to a lower power that is in the range 1× to 5× or so, use a low-power condenser if available, focus it to throw the lamp diaphragm image on or near the front lens of the objective, and when you follow steps 6 through 14, note that for low-power condensers the functions of the lamp and substage

condenser diaphragms will be to some extent interchanged.

17. If you go from step 14 to dry objectives of powers in the range 20× to 60×, and you have any doubts about spherical aberration, use the correction collar to improve the image or change to a 50× oil-immersion objective.

Going through so many steps merely to change power may seem a waste of time, but they quickly become second nature and may be done rapidly. Considering that you intend to spend hours making a drawing, it is well worth a minute to get the best image from the instrument.

Operating Hints

Always focus *up* when changing to higher powers with an unfamiliar objective, after you have set the objective as close to the cover slip as possible while looking from the side. Happily, many modern microscopes have parfocal objectives. For parfocal objectives, the specimen should still be nearly in focus after you change to a higher power, so you can simply touch up the focus and carry on. If you go to a higher power and find nothing to focus on (even after moving the slide), you can close down the lamp diaphragm (also close the substage condenser diaphragm somewhat) and obtain an image of the diaphragm for your preliminary focusing (provided the lamp diaphragm was previously set accurately into the specimen plane). Many modern objectives are supplied in spring-loaded retracting mounts that prevent them from being jammed forcibly against the cover slip. Avoid utilizing this feature, since one small piece of grit on the cover slip can still do irreparable damage to your objective. The working distance (from objective front lens to plane of focus in the specimen) of higher-power objectives can be less than 0.1mm, so take care.

To immerse an objective, place a small drop of immersion oil on the cover slip at the spot where the beam of light from the substage condenser is focused. With an objective *known* to be parfocal with the previous objective, it is then possible to rotate the nosepiece slowly to bring the oil objective into position. The oil should make good contact with the front lens of the objective and be free from air bubbles. Some detail in the specimen should be visible for fine focusing.

With an objective not known to be parfocal, rack up the coarse focus. With the objective and slide dry, swing the lens into position and, watching from the side, lower it until it nearly touches the cover slip. Swing the lens aside, put a drop of immersion oil on the cover slip, and swing the lens back. Then focus slowly away from the slide (up) while looking through the eyepiece for the image to appear.

When you are through observing, clean the oil promptly from both objective and slide. Use *only* lens tissue, barely moistened with xylene (also called xylol) or Histoclear, available from chemical and biological supply houses. Do not inhale the fumes, and dispose of the lens tissue promptly. Modern immersion oils are nonhardening (unlike the old cedar-wood oil, which dried rock-hard on the objective), but in time they can work into the objective and loosen the lens cement. In the meantime, a layer of oil on the lens picks up dust.

Authorities appear to agree that users of monocular microscopes should keep both eyes open and learn to ignore the image from the eye that is not being used. A subdued level of room illumination may help (but an illustrator must be able to see the drawing).

If you take photomicrographs, note that the accommodating ability of the human eye makes it less sensitive to small focus errors than is a photographic plate. The adjustments mentioned above are even more critical for photography than for visual work.

THE STERE
MICROSCOP

The stereo
serves a diffe
compound mi
mally used
whole objects
lower powers
with the com
and it gives
view of the
however, capa
nification that
the compoun
its objectives
N.A.

The stereo
low-power b
consists of t
scopes moun
single stand
image to one
instrument is
ing microsco
for an instru
6× to 20×
mounted or
rests. Note:
microscope
the instrume
this chapter
instruments
pound micr
optical train
means the
verted as it
pound m
microscope
from slight
form a ster
The comb
gence of th
specimen
cation ma
scopic eff
more than
objectives
iting the
100× (us
rule). Som
plementar
able obje
magnificat

Figure
trains of t
eomicrosc

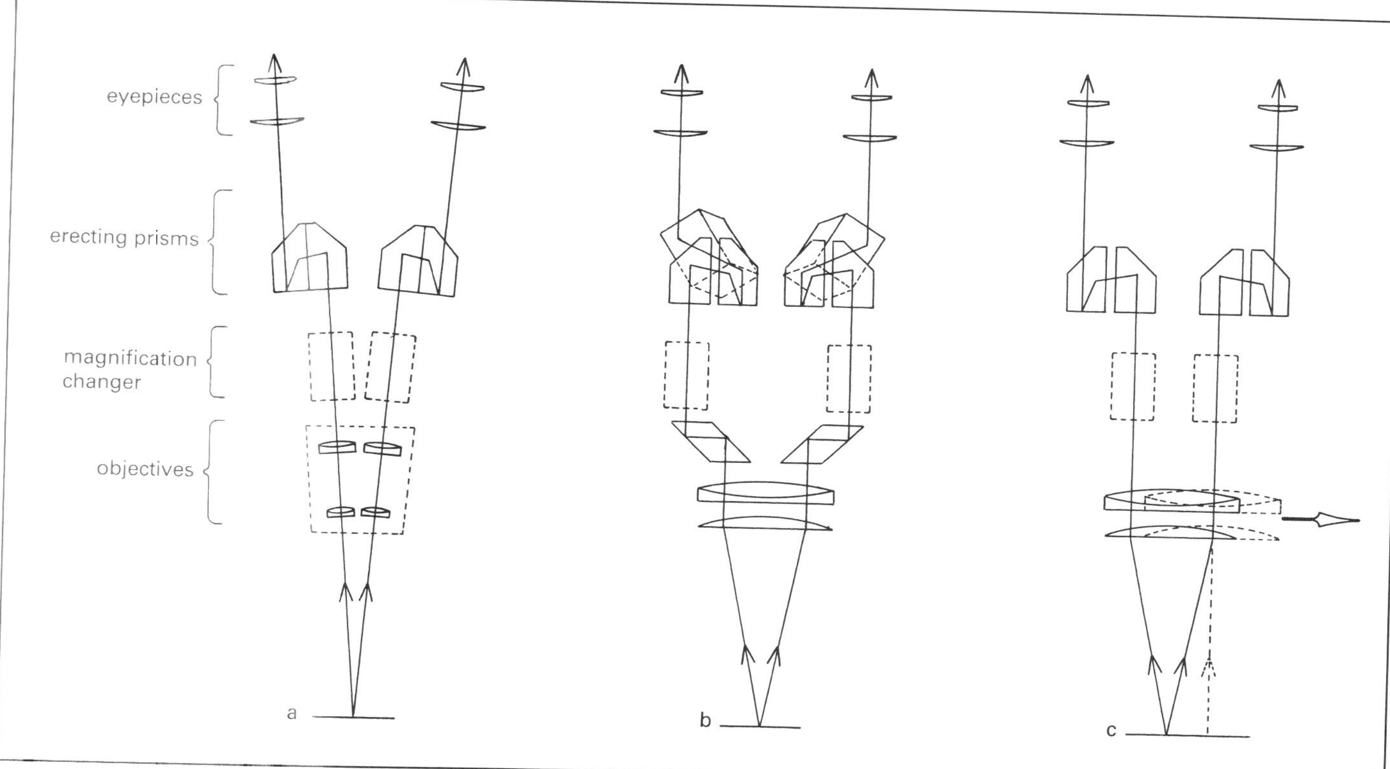

23-13. Optical components of low-power stereoscopic microscopes seen from front or rear: *(a)* twin objectives, magnification change by interchanging objectives or by internal unit; *(b)* single objective, magnification change by internal unit; *(c)* single objective, with provision for centering objective under one optical axis to put the light centrally through the objective and give a true vertical view of specimen. Pen-and-ink on bond paper, by Kenelm W. Philip.

the basic plan exist. Figure 23-13a is an old system, still in production by many makers. Magnification is changed by replacing the paired objectives with sets of higher- or lower-power objectives, or by internal devices. The set of paired objectives may be mounted in a revolving drum or sliding mechanism for convenient changing. Internal units are zoom optics, with a 4:1 or even 7:1 range of magnification, or sets of lenses in a drum or slide to modify the objective magnification. The focal planes of the two objectives are at an angle to each other, and at high magnifications only a narrow central band on the specimen is in focus for both eyes at the same time.

In figure 23-13b, a single large-diameter objective handles both beams of light. The magnification changer is an internal unit. The two focal planes coincide. Figure 23-13c shows a refinement of the single-objective instrument. The objective may be shifted laterally to yield a monocular instrument that looks *vertically* at the specimen, avoiding the distortion produced by off-center passage of light through the single objective in this type of microscope. All stereoscopic effect is lost, but the resulting freedom from distortion may result in a more accurate rendition of certain specimens.

Wide-field, high-eyepoint eyepieces sometimes come as standard equipment, which is useful for eyeglass wearers but may cause problems for other people, since the correct eye placement is so far back from the eyepiece. Eyecups (plastic devices that fit over the eyepiece, blocking extraneous light and holding the eyes at the proper distance from the lens) will help, and they should be used with high-eyepoint eyepieces if you do not wear glasses. Eyepiece powers may run from 5× to 20×, but the higher powers must give images of poor quality owing to the low N.A. of the objectives. At the cost of halving the working distance, you can use supplementary 2× lenses over the objectives to obtain higher power. Such a lens doubles the working N.A. of the objectives. There are 0.5× supplementary lenses that will double the working distance and reduce magnification. Other magnifying and reducing lenses are available.

Illumination for the Stereoscopic Microscope

Stereoscopic microscopes are most often used to examine opaque objects by incident light. The instrument may also be used for translucent specimens with transmitted light if it has a transillumination base with a light source or a mirror for use with an external lamp. Some makers supply a darkfield system that produces striking images with biological material too transparent for either incident light or normal transmitted-light methods. With any light source, experimentation with the lighting will help resolve various details of the specimen. Lamps may be adjusted to achieve pinpoint lighting or more diffuse effects, and the angle of the light can make a difference.

Vertical illuminators are available from some makers. They produce a collimated beam of light (parallel to the [mean] optical axis of the microscope) that allows the observer to examine the interior of deep holes in the specimen.

Proper illumination of (often highly reflective) three-dimensional objects can be a major problem. Refer to Kodak Technical Publications N-12A and N-12B *(Close-up Photography* and *Photomacrography)* for much useful information (see Bibliography). *The Practical Use of the Microscope*, by G. H. Needham (see Bibliography) has an excellent description of a homemade, tapered Lucite rod illuminator for both incident and transmitted light. Quartz halogen lamps illuminate very well. To subdue specular reflections, a white diffuser can be made from a cylinder of paper or plastic (watch for overheating) placed around the specimen with the top opening under the objective. Frosted filters placed in front of microscope lamps also diffuse light. Ring fluorescent illuminators provide even lighting for some situations.

Fiber-optic illuminators are now available, and they provide flexible light paths. A fiber-optic illuminator consists of a high-intensity light source coupled to a somewhat flexible lightpipe consisting of a large number of glass fibers bound together. The end of the lightpipe emits bright light through a small aperture, which can be placed just where the light is needed (within the limits of the flexibility of the lightpipe) (see Microscope Lighting in chapter 2 and fig. 2-25).

Backlighting a specimen with a transillumination base or by reflecting light off white paper under the specimen will give a sharp silhouette. This procedure may show details that are obscured under direct lighting.

At least two manufacturers (Olympus and Wild) make a twin-iris diaphragm that fits between the oculars and the objective, permitting adjustment of light and contrast as with the compound microscope.

CARE AND MAINTENANCE

A microscope should last almost indefinitely. Leave periodic lubrication and repair of serious problems to a trained repairer. If any adjusting slide or pivot on the instrument becomes stiff or loose, send for the expert unless you are skilled enough to know what is wrong. The problem may not be what you think it is. *Never* force any controls.

Short of being dropped or hit, the main hazard is dust on optical surfaces or the sliding metal surfaces of focusing tracks. Always keep a dust cover on the instrument when it is not being used, and remove any visible accumulation (use a small blower or grease-free camel-hair brush rather than indiscriminate wiping). Avoid direct sunlight and sudden, extreme changes of temperature. If a microscope is cold, warm it gradually in its case or under a cover to avoid condensation.

Keep your fingers off the glass surfaces; clean off accidental finger marks with lens tissue. Do not use alcohol on objectives — it can attack the cement between lens elements. Lens tissue and cotton swabs (Q-tips) *barely* moistened in Kodak Lens Cleaner, SP Lens Cleaner, or Histoclear removes grease.

Visible spec
the field of view
dirt on the optic
be tracked to
little thought a
Blotches caus
piece lenses wi
if the eyepiec
that vanish wh
made in subst
probably com
lamp condens
at the lamp. D
on other surf
objective) wi
contrast, glar
and loss of lig
may have tr
their glasses.
stage conde
closed down
which will exa
dust anywher

When work
microscopes.
vices and s
are often cha
these device
curely. If loo
the specimen

The light
complex inst
who utilize
little or no tr
croscopy an
instrument
knowledge
Such an att
handicap.

This chap
come that h
reader with
the light mic
system: and
of care and
knowledge
use a micro
achieving t
into the inst

24/Charts and Diagrams

Patrick J. Lynch

Pick up any current scientific book or journal and flip it open. The odds are overwhelming that the first graphic you find will be a chart or diagram, not a representational drawing. Do the same with a science book from the 1800s and the odds are almost exactly reversed. Modern science is, at heart, a quantitative business. The beauty of the classic nineteenth-century illustrated monograph remains today, but the science behind it was essentially a descriptive and anecdotal affair, not much given to quantifying results precisely and statistically proving opinions. What modern science may lack in visual charm it more than makes up for in accurate, reproducible results, backed up by reams of statistical data.

Charts and diagrams are a fundamental part of the process in modern scientific communication, and they form the vast majority of scientific graphics produced. The ability to design and draft charts and diagrams is an essential skill for any scientific illustrator, particularly for artists just beginning their careers. Novice illustrators often ignore the importance of a good chart section in their portfolios, concentrating on the more exotic subjects and media and ignoring the one skill area that is most likely to produce an entry-level job in scientific illustration. In large institutional biocommunications departments, the ratio of charts and diagrams to representational drawings is often ten to one or more, so a good chart artist may be much more sought than even a promising illustrator.

TERMINOLOGY

The terms *chart* and *graph* are used interchangeably in this chapter, as no firm distinguishing definitions exist for either. Both terms refer to the graphic display of quantitative information. The line between various types of diagrams is even fuzzier. Diagrams generally represent the relationships of component parts in a process or structure, but again, no hard and fast rules apply to the definition of *diagram* either. However vague some of the language may be, chartmaking has its own distinctive terminology, and biomedical chartists need to have a firm grasp of chart structure, terminology, and proper use to participate fully in the design of scientific graphics (fig. 24-1). This is particularly true in an age when

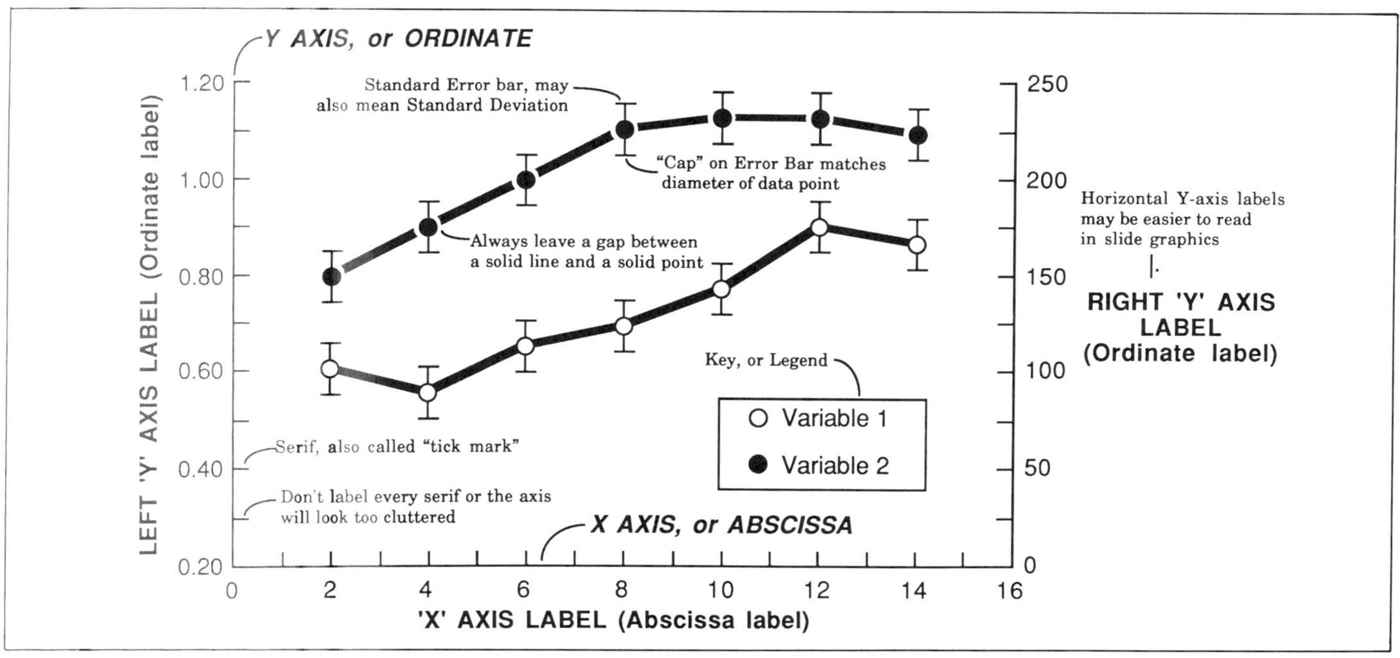

24-1. A typical scientific line graph, illustrating some of the terminology used to refer to the parts of data charts. In this example, two Ys (vertical axes) are used, one for each of the variables plotted. Created on a Macintosh II microcomputer with Cricket Graph and MacDraw software, and printed on a 300-dot-per-inch Apple LaserWritter laser printer, by Patrick J. Lynch.

computers are being used to construct most statistical graphics and the illustrator may have to create charts from nothing more than lists of numbers from a client's data files. Luckily, most chart terminology is fairly straightforward, and most of the unique terms refer to the axes defining the grid against which data are plotted, or special types of graphic formats.

The simplest line, scatter, and bar charts have two axes, or lines, that give the viewer reference marks against which the data points are compared. The vertical axis (typically on the left; see fig. 24-1) is most often referred to as the Y axis, but it may also be called the ordinate, value, or independent axis. The horizontal axis is usually called the X axis, or sometimes the abscissa, category, or dependent axis. In biostatistics, the Y axis is almost always a continuously variable arithmetic (even increments) or logarithmic progression of numbers, but the X axis may be either another continuous scale of numbers (as in a time scale) or a series of discrete categories arranged along the line (as in parts of a country).

Types of Charts and Diagrams

So many variations or combinations of chart types are used in scientific graphics that a listing of every known permutation would be impossible. The following are descriptions of the most frequently encountered chart and diagram types and their basic functions.

Line charts are used to portray the continuous movement or change in a measured variable, typically against a time scale (fig. 24-2). Line charts are best for showing the trend in a set of data over time, but they are less effective in comparing amounts of two variables. These are also referred to as curve or fever charts.

Bar charts are best used to compare the amount of a variable at particular points, or to compare the

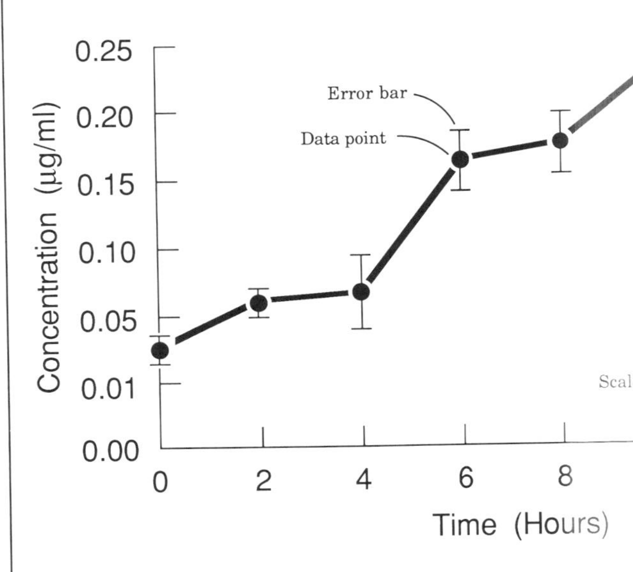

24-2. Line charts, or fever charts, are the most commonly us science graphics. In charts that include error bars, each data represents the mean (average) of a group of observations. Th of the standard error (or, sometimes, the standard deviation) group of observations. Scale breaks are a common feature of compress a wide range of values into a smaller visual scale. microcomputer with Cricket Graph and MacDraft software, per-inch Apple LaserWriter laser printer, by Patrick J. Lync

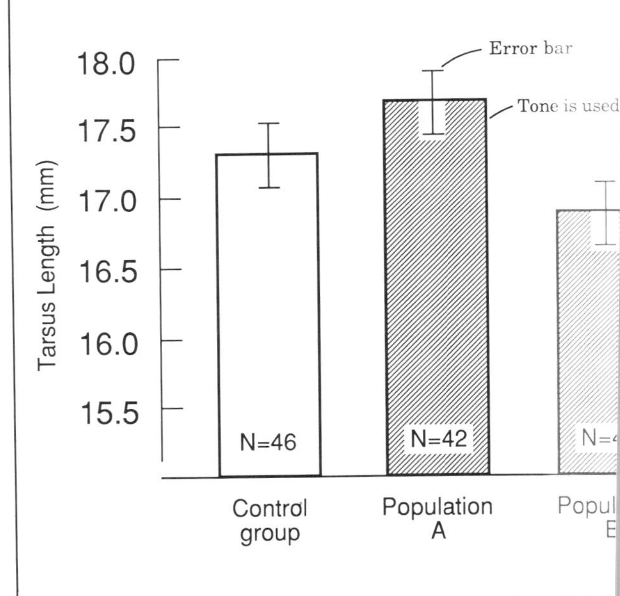

24-3. In bar charts that include a control variable, the cont stand apart from the experimental variables. Terminology would call this example a column chart, because of the ver Note that bar charts may also include error bars. The N nu shows how many observations were used to compute the m height of each bar. Created on a Macintosh II microcompu and printed on a 300-dot-per-inch Apple LaserWriter laser

amount of one variable to another (fig. 24-3). Bars are less effective in emphasizing the trend in a variable over time. Bar charts may be horizontally or vertically oriented. Terminology varies here: bar charts are sometimes distinguished as bar (horizontal boxes—fig. 24-4a) and column (vertical boxes—fig. 24-3). Histograms are bar charts that represent frequency distribution data (fig. 24-4b). (See also the discussion of stacked bars, below.)

Scatter graphs or scattergrams are used to plot individual data points in relation to one or two axes (fig. 24-5). Scattergrams are used to prove or disprove statistical hypotheses or to emphasize the range of individual data points over a scale. Most scattergrams also incorporate mean value markers (single-axis scattergrams) or regression lines (double-axis scattergrams).

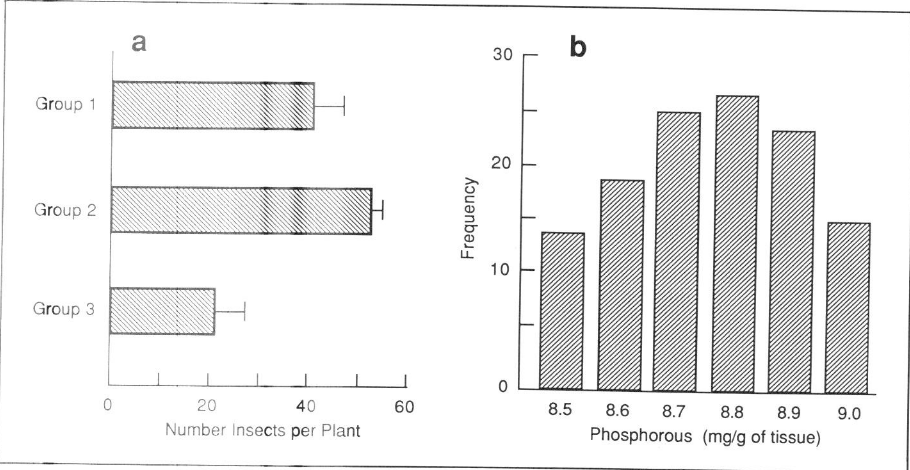

24-4. Two other common types of bar charts: *(a)* horizontal bar chart, where the Y (ordinate) axis has been shifted to the bottom of the graph; *(b)* histogram, a type of bar chart used to emphasize the frequency of observations within each of a number of categories along a continuous scale. In this example, it is easy to see that most of the samples studied contained 8.8 milligrams per gram of phosphorous. Created on a Macintosh II microcomputer with Cricket Graph and MacDraw software, and printed on a 300-dot-per-inch Apple LaserWriter laser printer, by Patrick J. Lynch.

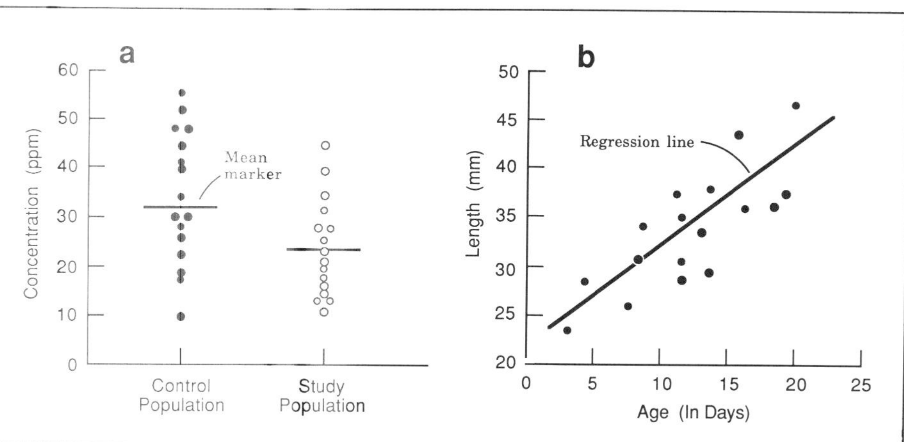

24-5. Two common types of scatter charts. *(a)* A single-axis scatter chart, where the data points are arrayed along a single (vertical) scale measuring one variable. In single-axis scatter charts, a bold horizontal line is often used to indicate the mean value of the observations. *(b)* A double-axis scatter chart, where the values are compared against two scales to show a relationship between one variable and another. In this example, length (of wings, in this case) and age are clearly related. The regression line typically splits the scattered points into equal groups above and below along a statistically determined angle (slope), and is used to indicate the degree of relationship between variables. Created on a Macintosh II microcomputer with Cricket Graph and MacDraft software, and printed on a 300-dot-per-inch Apple LaserWriter laser printer, by Patrick J. Lynch.

Pie graphs and stacked bar charts are best used to illustrate the component parts or percentages of a whole, where the values must add up to 100 percent. Pie charts are the least efficient means of charting small data sets and are not often used in the "hard" sciences, but they are common in business, social science, and general information graphics (fig. 24-6). A variation on this theme is the stacked bar chart (more common in science), in which component values are illustrated as blocks within a bar (fig. 24-7). Multiple stacked bars are often more space-efficient than multiple-pie charts when comparing the component parts of several variables. Neither stacked bars nor pies are effective if too many component parts are singled out for display. In either case, about five component categories would be the maximum before visual confusion sets in.

Tables are used to organize numeric or other data without graphic plotting; they are best used to emphasize the actual measured values of a small data set. Large or complex tables are appropriate for print media but are ineffective in slide or video graphics, where the audience's attention span and viewing time are short.

Diagrams are graphic attempts to simplify and order a process or structure so that its component parts or stages may be readily understood (fig. 24-8). Diagrams may emphasize the flow of processes over time (as in a laboratory procedure) or portray a hierarchical order of relationships (as in a business organization chart). Some authors prefer to define many types of diagrams (such as flowcharts, organization charts, time lines), but these are just arbitrary marks on a

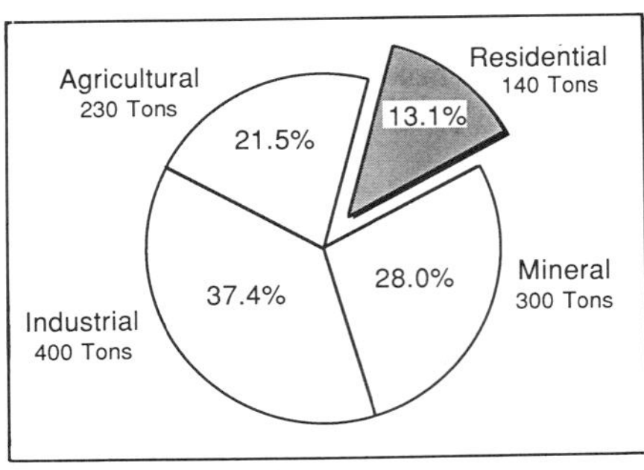

24-6. Pie charts are a simple way to illustrate the proportional relationships of component parts of an observation. Here the object was to highlight the residential value in a slide graphic. A heavier fill was used in that slice of the pie, and the residential component is further highlighted by pulling that slice away from the other components and giving it a drop-shadow. Although three other components are illustrated, their relative contributions are deemphasized by filling them all with the same light-gray tone pattern. Created on a Macintosh II microcomputer with Cricket Graph and MacDraw software, and printed on a 300-dot-per-inch Apple LaserWriter laser printer, by Patrick J. Lynch.

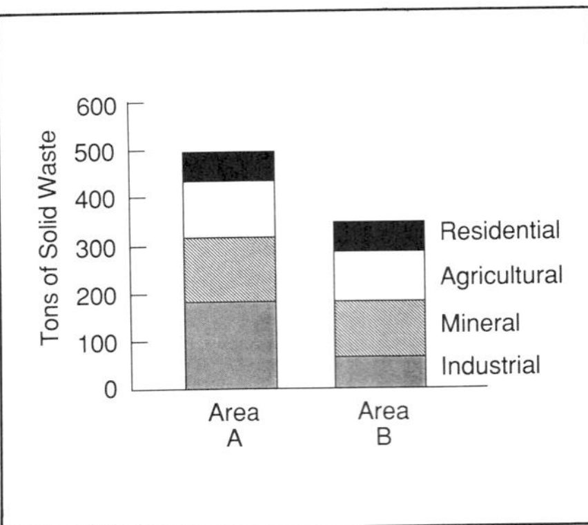

24-7. Stacked bars are often used as space-efficient replacements for multiple pie charts (two pie charts could illustrate the same data shown here). Note how the black fill of the residential value dominates the other fills, focusing the viewer's attention on that component of the total. This chart was designed as a slide graphic, with a simple layout, extra-large lettering, and bold fill patterns to distinguish the variables readily. Created on a Macintosh II microcomputer with MacDraw software,and printed on a 300-dot-per-inch Apple LaserWriter laser printer, by Patrick J. Lynch.

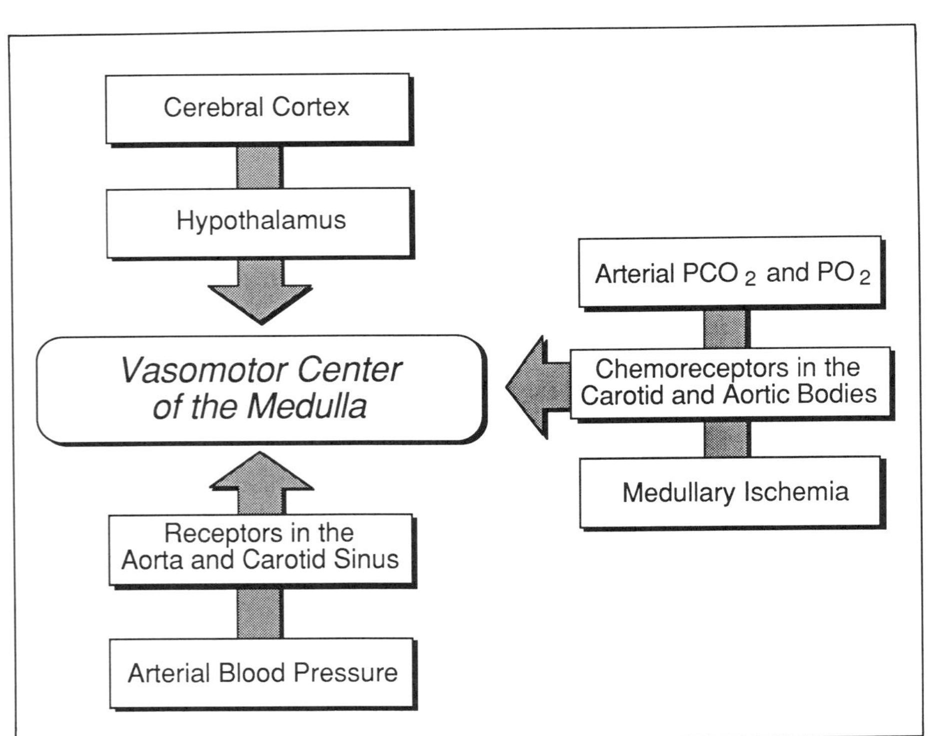

24-8. Diagrams are used to simplify and explain the relationships of component parts of an organization or process. Here the basic mechanisms controlling blood-vessel diameter and blood pressure are organized into a flow chart, reducing a complex set of neurochemical processes into a simple graphic. Diagrams may also show the flow of processes over time (as in a project chart) or the hierarchical relationships of components (such as a business organization chart). Created on a Macintosh SE microcomputer with MacDraw software, and printed on a 300-dot-per-inch Apple LaserWriter laser printer, by Patrick J. Lynch.

graphic cont
stract box-a
representati
corporates d
Special f
veloped to n
ticular scie
example, *cl*
used in tax
phylogeneti
or animal gr
type of *picto*
tions of pott
against a tin
agrams (fig.
rigid set o
used to illus
interactions

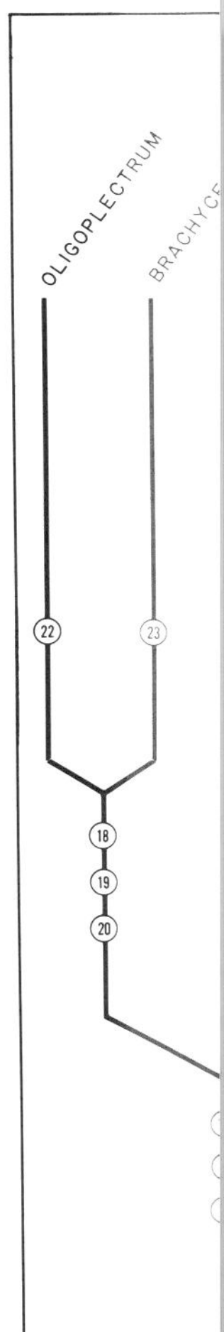

24-9. A clad
thetical phyl
trichopteran i
and numbers
were used by
tesy of Olive

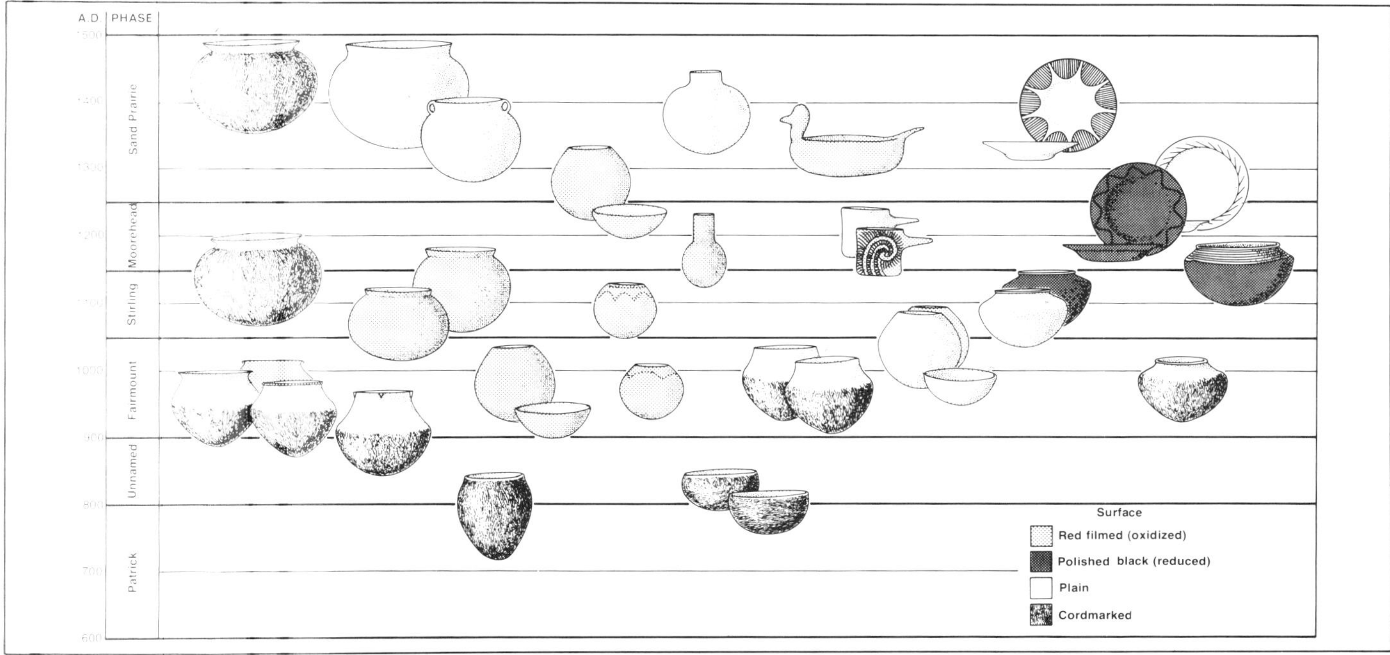

24-10. Pot profiles distributed on a chart illustrate the trends in form and finish of ceramics in a particular area over time. Showing the actual objects adds visual information and interest to the chart. Pen-and-ink stipple and line with two densities of shading film rendered the textured pots, by Jo Ann Moore. From the *Handbook of North American Indians*, vol. 15, *Northeast*, Bruce G. Trigger, ed. (Smithsonian Institution Press, 1978).

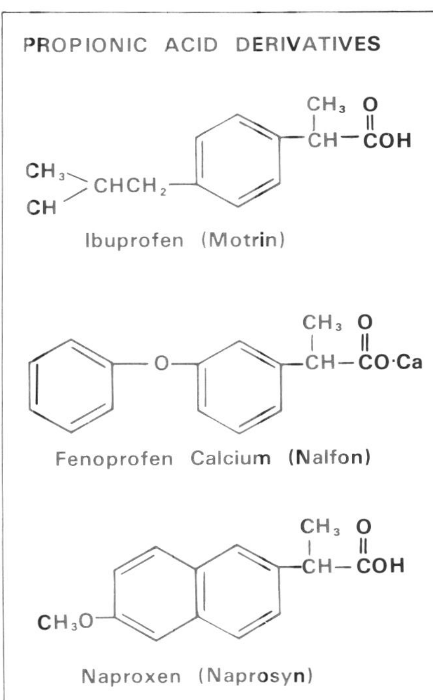

24-11. Diagrams of organic chemical structures must follow a rigid set of graphics conventions to allow orderly comparison of biochemicals and ready identification of common component parts of complex molecules (such as the hexagonal benzene rings shown here). Pen-and-ink with Compugraphics typography, by Judith Guenther.

INSTRUMENTS AND MATERIALS

Producing charts and graphs by conventional methods requires little in the way of special equipment and supplies. Details of the basic studio materials used can be found in chapter 2. If computer graphics are used, a computer and special software will be required. These are discussed in detail later in this chapter.

Surfaces

Vellum, rag tracing paper: can be used both for preliminary drawings and for final rendering. Preliminary art can be placed under these translucent papers and traced easily. Transfer lettering, charting tapes, and symbols stick to the surface well. Erasure, however, is difficult on rag tracing paper because the ink tends to soak below the surface sizing. Use good-quality papers such as Keuffel and Esser Crystalene and Albanene, or Canson Vidalon.

Graph paper: a selection in various grid sizes; essential for replotting data graphics and very useful for designing some types of diagrams. A basic selection should include, in addition, log and semi-log (log scale on one axis only) grids, polar grids (for pie charts and circular diagrams), and vellum tracing paper printed with a nonrepro blue grid for general layout tasks.

Bristol board: smooth plate-finish or hot-press; excellent drawing and drafting surface, more durable than rag tracing paper. When used on a light table two-ply Bristol board is translucent enough to trace from a tracing-paper sketch taped underneath. The porous surface holds transfer lettering, symbols, and tapes well but absorbs ink, making corrections tedious. An electric eraser is essential for clean erasures.

Illustration board: such as Crescent or Strathmore hot-press boards; has the same advantages as Bristol but is too opaque for light-box tracing. It is useful in situations where the final art will be used directly by the client, as in poster sessions.

Drafting film: an excellent all-around drafting surface for charts, diagrams, and line illustrations. Tracing and erasure are easy, but all lines must be drawn opaquely, since gray lines will suffer even more in photography, as the drafting film acts like a miniature light box, piping light behind the inkwork and further lightening poor linework. It is not suitable for most direct uses of finished artwork (as in poster shows).

Acetate: for color-separation overlays; masochists occasionally do whole drawings on it.

Media

Ink: see chapter 5.

Pencils: leads in holders, mechanical pencils, or wood-encased pencils; preferably medium to hard grades (H to 3H) for fine linework; nonrepro blue pencils or pens.

White paint, ink: for quick touchups.

Tools

Technical pens: the most widely used sizes range from 0.25mm (no. 000 Rapidograph) to 1.4mm (no. 4 Rapidograph). Technical pens are preferred over dip pens for charts, diagrams, and other technical graphics because they maintain a consistent line width (see chapter 5).

Pencil sharpener, lead pointer.

Drafting knife: light X-Acto bladeholders with no. 11 blades. This is the most generally useful cutting tool, but some illustrators prefer a swivel knife for cutting curves or intricate patterns in film. Surgical scalpels are especially useful for tape work, as their blades are much sharper and last longer than conventional art knives.

Erasers: various types, including an electric eraser, pencil-shaped erasers, and specialized erasers (depending on the drawing surface, media, and individual preference).

Erasing shield.

Cleaning pads, drafting powder.

Parallel rules, straightedge, drafting machine: to produce parallel and perpendicular lines squarely. A T square is inexpensive but will slip constantly unless held firmly in place; a straightedge mounted on the drawing board is cost-effective and versatile; most expensive is a drafting machine. The better parallel rules have stainless steel edges for safe cutting and tension adjustments (or locks) to prevent slippage.

Rulers: at least one good metal or plastic ruler with inch and metric scales, and the zero mark set in from the edge. Multiscale graphic-design rules (with picas, points, type sizes) are also very useful.

Drafting compass: good quality, capable of holding a technical pen (see chapter 2).

Triangles: for general drafting; a series of three to four 30°/60° triangles in sizes from 6 to 16 inches (15 to 40cm); an adjustable triangle is also useful. Select good-quality clear or gray triangles with beveled or raised edges. For intricate linework, a tiny 3- to 4-inch (8 to 10cm) 30°/60° triangle is handy for maneuvering around wet ink areas. For poster session work, a very large 18-inch (45cm) 30°/60° triangle is useful for layout and checking the squareness of large graphics. Check the edges for rough or damaged areas.

French curves: to draft smooth curves in charts and diagrams. A wide selection of sizes is helpful; choose both small curves with tight circumferences and long "ship," or "aircraft," curves for larger work. Some illustrators prefer adjustable curves. Unfortunately, many good

curves are r
drafting. To l
ing under the
described in c

Templates: (
various sizes
one circle te
small circles
circles just fo
and a small te
of geometric s
or for drafting

Burnisher: fo
film, transfer
bols. The bes
plastic blades
handle that a
the blade to b

Dust remove
other nonsme
scribed in ch

Small blow
amazing amo
days by dryin

Lettering a

Lettering eq
templates, s
tering syster
graph symbo

Dry-transfer
least expens
to standard t
as Helvetica
bels are sh
transfer lette
than most p
is easier to
labels when
acter labels
numbers-in-
diagrams. K
and black le
and font for
photographs
impose both
to drop-sha
clarity.

Symbol she
and energy l
to draft repe
and other sta
Arrowhead

need to draft arrowheads at the ends of lines. Symbol sheets are invaluable for drafting complex line charts with many different data symbols. Some small geometric symbols and arrows are also available as transfers on long tapes, a space saver in crowded tool drawers.

Charting tape: available in widths from 1/32 inch to 1 inch (1mm to 2.5 cm), in both glossy (not generally used in drafting) and matte surfaces (best for reproduction drafting work), and a range of colors for producing color charts and diagrams directly. Line graphs or diagrams requiring different line patterns are also easy to produce with patterned tapes instead of inking the lines by hand. "Crepe" charting tapes can also be bent to follow all but the tightest curves for chart and diagram work.

Tone shading film: self-adhesive tone film, such as Letratone or Formatt sheets, for most types of black-and-white chart and diagram work. The areas that they cover may be called "tone fills." The most useful patterns are 27- to 42-line dot screens (number of dots per inch) in 20 to 40 percent densities (ratio of black to white), and linear fill patterns in the same density range.

Rubylith, Amberlith masking film: useful for blacking out large areas on line artwork (such as bars on a bar chart); essential for creating color-separation overlays for mechanical-color artwork.

Miscellaneous

Waxer: best is a sheet-fed automatic waxer, but a small hand-held waxer will do. A good "high-tack" hot wax will hold even photographs and stats to mat board for poster show use.

Rubber cement: not suitable for anything that needs to last longer than a few months; see Adhesives in chapter 2 for additional information and options.

Rubber-cement thinner: very flammable. Use very small quantities and store in a tightly sealed can or dispenser.

Rubber-cement pickup.

Tape: artist's masking tape, transparent Scotch nos. 810, 811.

Calculator: useful in replotting or rescaling chart data, fitting blocks of text, and other common mathematical problems in graphic design.

Registration marks: on transfer sheets or in rolls for overlay work.

CLIENT INTERACTIONS

The Initial Conference

More often than not, it is the author/scientist who is responsible for most of the decisions regarding format in the production of a scientific graph or chart. It is the illustrator's job to work with the client to ensure that the final graphic is aesthetically and technically suitable for all of the presentation media in which it may be used. In typical circumstances, most of the basic structural decisions (such as which graph format to use or how many variables are to be plotted) will have been made before the graphic reaches the illustrator. In most instances, data graphics will arrive as pencil plots on graph paper, with the lines or bars drawn accurately against the grid and the X and Y scale angles already defined by the client. In the initial conferences with the scientist, the illustrator should discuss each part of the hand-drawn graph, clarifying all handwritten labels, numbers, and other text, and identifying any plotted or written material that will not be incorporated into the finished graphic.

One of the most important determining factors in the design of charts and diagrams is the final presentation medium for the graphic, as this will fundamentally affect most of the design decisions. Factors such as image reduction in the final printed version, the media in which the graphic will be used, and the particular requirements of individual journals and publishers must be taken into account before designing any chart or diagram. In science graphics, it is not unusual for the same chart to be used in a journal article, a slide presentation, and a poster show. Each of these eventual uses must be considered, as each may place different demands on the final drawing. Clients should be questioned about the eventual destination of the graphic and reminded if necessary that they may wish to use it in several different formats. This is especially important if the client wants both a color version of the graph for slides and a black-and-white version for publication and poster sessions.

Planning the Graphic

Beyond these basic design considerations, it is usually up to the illustrator to apply his or her graphics experience and expertise to transform a rough plot into a finished, publication-quality chart. The client's original plots need not be traced slavishly. In fact, clients will often use space within the graph inefficiently, use symbols or patterns inconsistently, repeat unnecessary labels in multipart graphs, or include labels and marks from the process of plotting the data that do not belong on the finished graphic. For example, when plotting out a data set on graph paper, most people will label every major division along each axis for easy reference, and use tick marks liberally along the axis line. Many of these labels and tick marks can be eliminated during drafting to clarify the axis labels and avoid unnecessary visual complexity. Although many of these graphic-design decisions are routinely accepted as the graphic artist's prerogative, the illustrator should be especially careful to check these style changes with any new client.

In diagrammatic graphics, the illustrator usually plays a much greater role in the design process than is typical in science charts or graphs (fig. 24-12). It is essential to have the client thoroughly explain the process or situation to be illustrated, independent of any sketch that has been produced. Nonartists often have a difficult time graphically organizing their thoughts, and the rough diagrams they produce are often misleading or poorly designed. The artist should explore each step in the process with the client—adding, subtracting, or changing elements as needed to clarify the work further. Unlike graphs or charts, complex diagrams often will go through several design revisions before final inking. At each stage, the client should be consulted on major revisions and asked to comment on pencil comprehensives of the work in progress.

Checking the Graphic

After the graphic has been completed, it must be carefully proofed by the client for any typographic errors, errors of interpretation or emphasis, and procedural errors such as incorrect keying of the variables. When dealing with complex charts and diagrams, even the most conscientious illustrator may miss subtle errors after looking at the work a long time. If the illustration must go to photography without the client's final proof, try to have a co-worker proof it for errors.

STUDIO METHODS

Conventional studio charting techniques and computer-graphics techniques ar
most chart a
methods to ge
and diagrams.

Conventiona
Technique

Methods of
or diagram wi
the rendering
chosen, but
many standa
final sketch or
down to the dr
to the under
paper or film
ness of the
paper before
and to the boa
ing tape (a lo
or Scotch no.
tear paper or
moved. Clean
sary with d
surfaces) or a

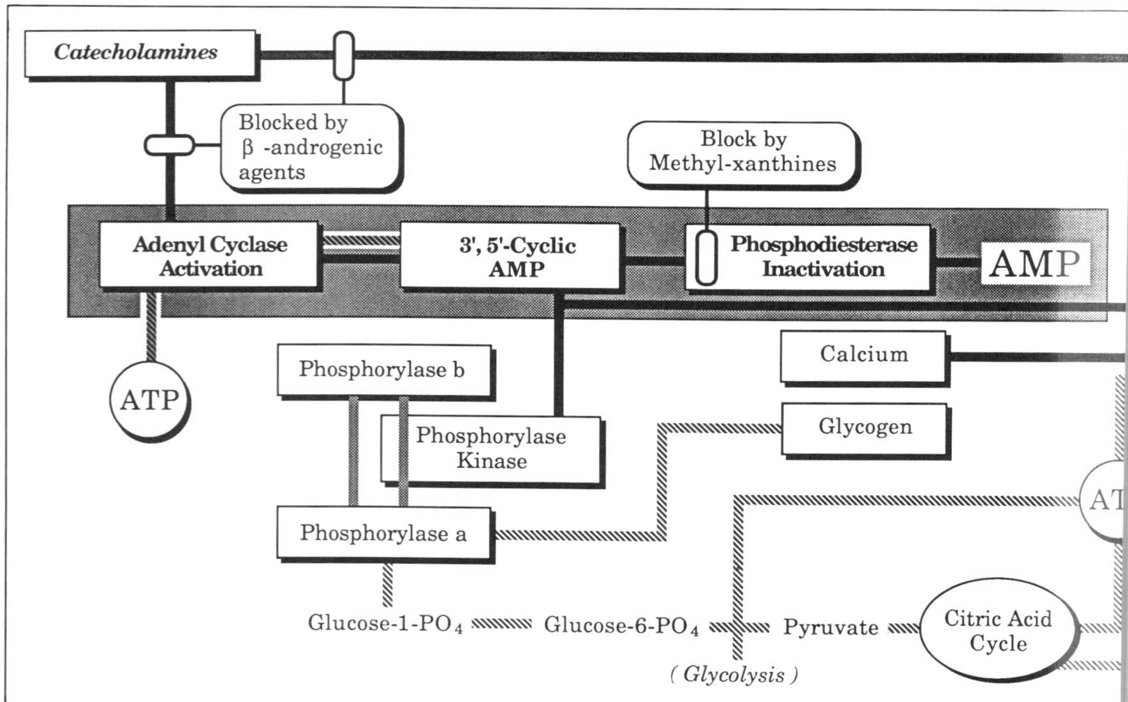

24-12. Complex diagrams may require much more consultation with the client than is typical with most scientific charts. Such diagrams, with many subsections and component parts, lend themselves especially well to computer-graphics systems, where the positions of graphic elements, fill patterns, and text blocks may be changed easily to suit the wishes of the client. Created on a Macintosh II microcomputer with MacDraw software, and printed on a 300-dot-per-inch Apple LaserWriter laser printer, by Patrick J. Lynch.

drafting film only). Use drafting powder sparingly if many transfer symbols or charting tapes are to be used. Beware of fingerprints on all surfaces, particularly on drafting film. Clean off any fingerprints on films with rubber-cement thinner, but note that this liquid is highly flammable and needs to be handled with care. To avoid further fingerprinting, keep hands scrupulously clean and use a piece of paper under the palm (or wear cotton gloves) when inking lines or laying in symbols.

Whether the lines are to be drafted with technical pens or charting tape, try to organize the work so you are moving across or down the drawing in a single direction, doing all the horizontal or vertical lines in one pass to avoid working over wet ink or disturbing previous tape.

Drafting with Technical Pens

When drawing with technical pens, do all linework first, before applying any tone film necessary to key the variables or shade diagram elements. Try to hold the technical pen at a constant angle and move it at a constant speed that is slow enough to ensure a clean, opaque line. Regardless of the drawing surface used, keep a wet paper towel handy and wipe off the pen point after every two or three strokes (more often when drawing long lines) to clean off dust and fibers that may foul the point and ruin the lines. When it is necessary to work over wet ink, try using a large oval template or an ink riser (see chapter 2) to act as a platform for a triangle or template. Place the opening of the oval around the wet area and lay the triangle over the template. Take care not to bend the template down into the wet ink.

Tone films such as Letratone have a high-tack adhesive, so apply them before adding any waxed labels or transfer symbols; otherwise, the film may lift off these pieces as excess film is trimmed and removed. If stray wax from the labels covers an area to be drawn over, first wash the area with rubber-cement thinner to remove the wax or it will ruin the linework by causing the ink to bead up. If any small overhangs, bumps, or breaks in the linework need to be scraped off, do it with a hand-held no. 11 or no. 16 X-Acto blade just before the drawing is finished. Scraping with a blade leaves a clean edge but roughens the drawing surface, making it difficult to draw over that area again cleanly. Pencil guidelines are best drawn with graphite leads, not nonrepro colored pencils, which leave a waxy surface that will cause ink to bead up. Use a soft plastic or kneaded eraser to remove graphite guidelines. Take care not to scrub the surface of ink lines too hard or the ink will "gray out" and fail to reproduce properly.

Drafting with Charting Tapes

The above process is reversed when charting tape is used to do linework. Apply tone film first, to prevent its adhesive from pulling off lines and labels later on. Then do any penwork necessary, to avoid catching the edges of charting tape with templates or triangles. After the tone and any inkwork are completed, begin stripping in all other linework with the tape. Do not overstretch charting tape, or the tension will produce bowed or wavy lines. At perpendicular (90-degree) junctions between two tape lines, overshoot the ends on both lines, then cut a 45-degree line across the joint to produce a clean, mitered intersection (fig. 24-13). If any gap remains after mitering, just touch the point of a technical pen to it to fill the gap with black ink.

For line-art originals done with charting tape, use nonrepro blue pencils to make guidelines, because in most instances they will not need to be erased. Erasing guidelines under and around chart tape is a risky business.

Using Tone Film and Transfer Symbols

Tone film and transfer symbols must be burnished hard to remove air bubbles and to prevent small symbols from falling off the chart during later handling. Some artists prefer to use a fixative to set the transfer symbols or letters in place, but this is not necessary if the symbols are well burnished to the sur-

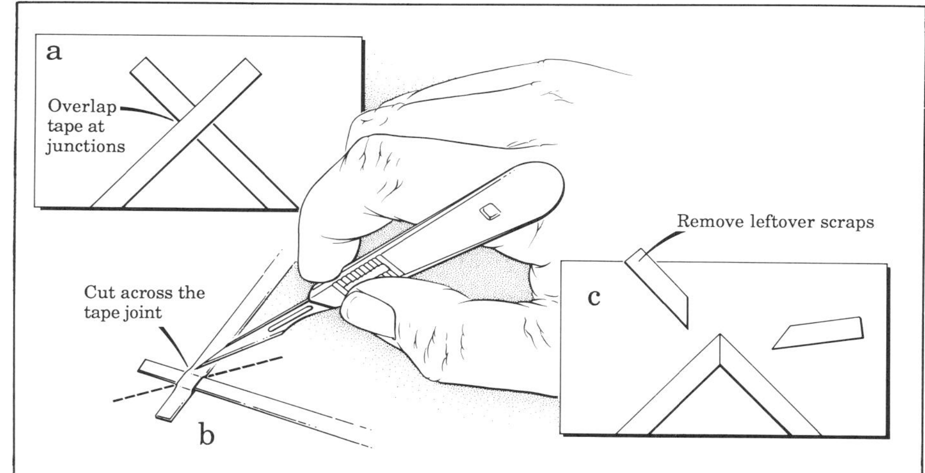

24-13. To make a clean joint between two sections of charting tape, first overlap the ends of the tape *(a)*. Using a series of two to three light strokes of the knife, cut a mitered joint through the intersection *(b)*. Too heavy a cutting stroke will pull the tapes out of position and make a straight cut more difficult to produce. If the tapes are fairly wide (3mm or more), use a cutting triangle to guide the knife blade and hold the tapes in place. Trim off the remaining scrap ends *(c)*. Hunt 100 crowquill pen, technical pen, and ink on Herculene film, by Patrick J. Lynch.

face. Any air bubbles remaining under tone film can be lanced with the end of an X-Acto blade and then burnished flat. Unburnished bubbles may photograph differently from the burnished film around them, so do not ignore them. After some use, burnisher blades will wear to a sharp edge and may inadvertently cut into the surface of the drawing or break up transfer symbols. Use a fine whetstone to reshape the blade and round off sharp corners. For burnishing small pieces of text or film, try using a tracing-paper cover sheet between the burnisher and the film to prevent the edge of the burnishing tool from catching on the edges of the film sheet or symbol.

If pen lines are drawn over the edge of a tone-film area, the ink will probably bleed under the film edge and ruin it, so try to complete all linework before laying down tone film. If you must add a line over an area of tone film, always draw the line from the center of the tone film down onto the drawing surface; working from the drawing surface up onto the tone film risks the pen catching the edge and leaving even more ink to bleed under the film. When cutting tone film edges over ink lines, do not cut any deeper than is necessary to score the film or the blade will carve a visible line into the ink line below. Most tone films and symbol sheets or tapes will last for several years under normal room temperatures and humidity, but they do not last forever. Discard any old sheets with symbols and letters that crack constantly during transfer and do not burnish down in one piece.

Typographic Options

Typography is often the most problematic element in chart and diagram production. Good type is expensive, and the inexpensive alternatives tend to be tedious to use and economically inefficient. In the past, the only inexpensive alternatives were drafting labels produced with scriber-and-template sets such as the Leroy system, press-on transfer type such as Chartpak, and stamped lettering produced by Kroy or Merlin lettering machines. For small graphics with short labels, Leroy lettering is still a viable (though less attractive) option. The Leroy templates and scriber can be used with virtually any technical pen. Transfer lettering is best used for very short labels, short lines of an unusual display font, or single-character labels and call-outs on diagrams and photographs. Most widely used typefaces and type sizes can be purchased as transfer letters, but matching the look of professional-quality typography with hand-set transfer letters is tedious and nerve-racking at best—many would say impossible. For larger amounts of type, Kroy and Merlin lettering systems can generate labels and short pieces of text on adhesive-backed tape. These systems are faster and produce attractive type but still are not suitable for creating large volumes of type or the long blocks of set type necessary for poster sessions and displays.

Laser-printed typography has gained wide acceptance in the scientific and technical graphics fields within the past few years, mainly because of the low cost of laser-printer type as compared to full-resolution phototypesetting. Most office computers can be used to generate text on a 300- to 600-dpi (dot-per-inch) laser printer, and laser printers can cost as little as one-thirtieth the price of a low-end phototypesetting machine (1200 to 3600 dpi resolution). At 300 to 600 dpi resolutions, laser printer text is suitable for all but the most demanding scientific charting tasks and is virtually indistinguishable from conventional phototypesetting once it is reduced and offset-printed. In addition to producing labels and short pieces of text, laser printers are capable of generating long blocks of type with full control of all typesetting param-

eters such as
kerning, and
laser printers
likely to be
source of ty
technical grap

Full-resolut
is the standa
other type-ge
judged. Alth
good phototy
dispensable
graphics stud
ficient quanti
economical
good type h
must be able
the typograph
lays for corre

Computer-

A revoluti
gram graphic
computers ha
many areas
duction. Mos
now able to
chart or dia
able to gene
rable in quali
inals. Most
quickly gene
charts and di
puter is n
trained eye
However ca
computers a
the chart arti
to be used o
applying the
design stand
tional charts
tunately, ma
systems ach
speed advan
many of the
would ordina
lustrator. Th
tually every
design and
follow the a
preferences
graphics pro
of "idiot box
the market.

Computer Hardware

The development of the microcomputer from a hobbyist's toy into a standard piece of office equipment has brought with it the capability to design professional-quality charts on most of the major types of personal computers. It is beyond the scope of this chapter to describe in detail the particular brands and features of personal computers currently in use, and those details change almost daily anyway. The dominant factors in evaluating the computer as a graphic-design tool are the quality and resolution of the equipment used to get graphics out of the computer (output devices) and the ease of use and capability of graphics programs running on the computer (graphics software). Because high computing speed, large amounts of memory, and adequate storage equipment are now commonplace, it is the capability of the output devices and graphics software that largely determines how useful a computer will be in solving any graphic design problem.

Graphics Software

It is the job of a software program to aid the artist in translating the raw data from a client's files, sketches, or notes into a finished graphic suitable for professional use. Although computer equipment (hardware) often gets more attention than the programs that run on it, the software is the key element. If the software is badly written or incapable of producing the desired results, having the world's fastest computer will only bring on the frustration sooner. Whenever possible, choose the software first, then decide what hardware to run it on.

Charting software is designed to accept all the basic data and design details for the chart. It then plots out the chart—first on the computer screen for analysis and proofing, then on an output device for final use. Two major ways of working with charting software have evolved. Command-driven charting software obligates the artist to memorize and use a large number of specific commands and data formats to create a detailed description of the chart to be generated. Although difficult to master at first, many command-driven programs are among the most capable and versatile charting systems. A skilled operator can swiftly give only those commands most appropriate to the chart at hand without wading through a host of irrelevant prompts and questions from the software. Since the details of virtually every part of the chart must be specified, virtually every aspect of the chart remains within the control of the illustrator.

Menu-driven charting software is popular because it is generally much easier to use than command-driven software. The computer guides the artist through a series of prompts and questions to get a description of the chart, then plots it out on the screen for review. Although easy to learn, many menu-driven programs frustrate experienced artists by taking away too many of the design decisions and forcing the artist to spend time changing inappropriate design elements (if they can be changed at all).

Fortunately, within these two extremes of software design are many capable charting programs that can save the working illustrator enormous amounts of drafting time. Only a careful evaluation of the software, using actual design problems from your work, can weed out the sheep from the goats. Both charting-software design philosophies have their strengths and weaknesses, and the final choice of which is best often is simply a matter of personal preference.

Most charting software is written for use in business settings and often has few provisions for the formats and graphic details common in scientific and technical charts. Standard science chart elements such as error bars, log scales, regression lines, Greek or mathematical symbols, and multichart formats may be impossible to create in many popular business charting programs. Computer systems designed to produce color-slide charts often do not include the ability to translate a color graphic into a black-and-white version suitable for publication in science journals or books. A slide that distinguishes all the data lines or bars by color will be useless when converted to black-and-white art without the provision to add different tone patterns, line patterns, and symbols to differentiate the variables. Scientific clients can rarely afford to commission two or three versions of their graphics (one for color slides, one for line art, one for posters). The suitability of a particular computer system for science graphics often hinges on the ability of the software and hardware to produce variations of the graphic for each use desired by the client. Before purchasing computer hardware and software for science graphics, check to be sure the system offers sufficient design and output flexibility to meet all of your typical client's needs.

Output Options

It is the output device that largely determines the visual quality and resolution (sharpness) of the computer graphic, and as such tends to be the most costly part of most computer design systems. While any method of extracting a graphic from the computer can be considered an output device, options such as dot-matrix printers or cameras that simply photogragh the display screen produce such bumpy, jagged linework that they are unsuitable for professional graphic use. The most commonly used output devices for graphic design professionals are described below.

Pen plotters at one time were the only method of obtaining a high-quality printed graphic from a computer system (fig. 24-14). The pen

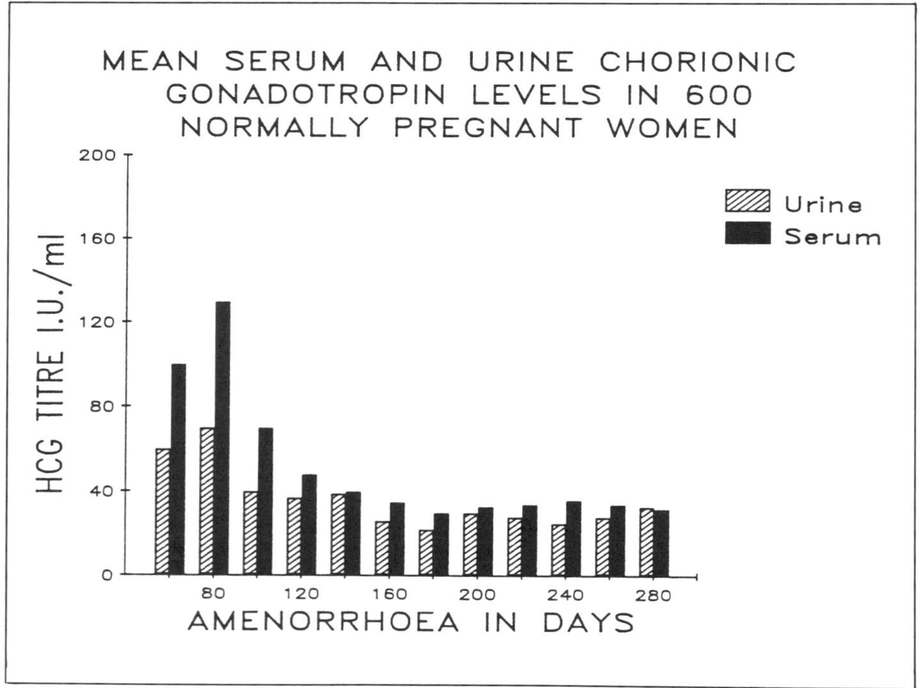

24-14. Pen-plotted bar chart created on an IBM-PC/XT microcomputer with ChartMaster software, and plotted on a Hewlett-Packard 7475 plotter, by Patrick J. Lynch.

plotter mimics conventional drafting methods by moving a technical or felt-tipped pen over the surface of a sheet of paper, tracing out the graphic according to instructions received from the computer. Small four- to eight-pen plotters are the least expensive "high-quality" output option, and the larger pen plotters can draw charts and diagrams on paper sizes big enough for direct use in poster presentations. Pen plotters can produce line graphics suitable for publication and good-quality color plots for slides or direct use, but they are slower and require more operator attention than other output options listed below. They are also limited to graphics built up from straight and curved lines only, and they cannot print out finely shaded dot screens or halftone images.

Laser printers resulted from a marriage of office copier technology and microcomputers. Laser printers are capable of producing near-typeset-quality text and linework comparable to conventional drafting methods (see figs. 24-1 through 24-8, 24-12, 24-16). In conventional office copiers, a series of lenses and mirrors focuses the reflected image of the original onto a light-sensitive photoelectric printing drum, where the pattern of light and dark produced by the original determines which parts of the drum surface pick up and print toner material onto the copy paper. In a laser printer, the image on the photosensitive drum is produced by a computer-controlled laser beam tracing out the patterns of the electronic "original" stored in its memory, producing an image on paper very similar to a high-quality xerographic copy. Because laser printers produce graphics on plain paper, laser-printer output is easy to integrate into conventional charting methods. Many studios now use laser printers as an inexpensive substitute for phototypesetting equipment as well as a computer-graphics printer. Laser-printed text is output on smooth, heavy (50- to 60-pound) offset paper and run through a waxer just as is done with phototype sheets.

Or the text
adhesive-back

Not all las
to profession
however. Ma
designed just
ple low-resol
printers inco
scription lang
Script, can f
design tool. T
of laser print
ity in graphi
them one of
put devices
tion.

Film rec
means of p
from compu
offering imag
of conventio
In a film re
type of high
used to displ
pose it to c
film in a ca
the unit. Al
monochrome
series of co
generate all
ors specified
graphic wa
corders sui
use must ha
tion of 2048
picture elen
be able to
pixels ("4K
work. Film
ited to pro
Many stu
printer for t
will film-r
"negative"
(at 4K reso
"negatives"
darkroom
black-and-
distinguish
tographs o
(see fig. 24-

Direct V
puters are
video outpu
dard NTS
Standards
States vid

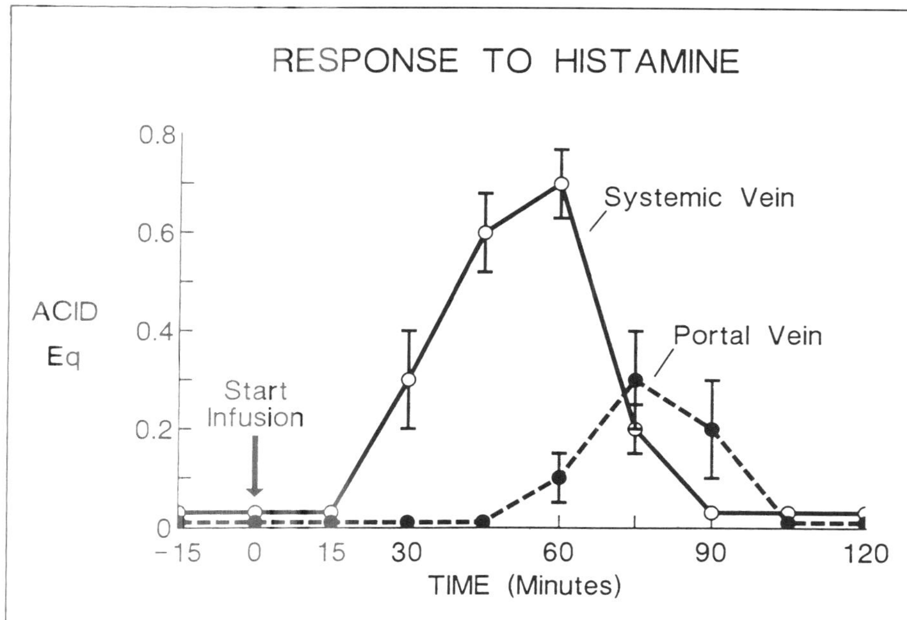

24-15. Black-and-white film-recorded line graph created on a Management Graphics TTS-Plus computer-graphics system, by Patrick J. Lynch.

(Phase Alternation Line, used in Great Britain and Germany), although special equipment such as an NTSC encoder may be necessary to produce a clean, stable video image. Graphics created on the computer can be transferred ("dumped") to videotape directly or routed through a video editing system and combined with live video or other program material.

AESTHETICS AND DESIGN

The design of charts and diagrams is often considered a backwater in scientific illustration, drawing much less attention than other, more exotic subject matter—in spite of the fact that scientific illustration as a whole is overwhelmingly composed of data graphics and diagrams. A quick survey of the charts and diagrams in virtually any scientific journal will confirm the lack of attention given data graphics by many experienced scientific and medical illustrators, although, to be fair, many graphics are also produced by the scientists themselves or by lab technicians. When charts and diagrams are relegated to the least experienced members of an illustration staff (or to nonillustrators), the results are often poorly designed graphics, however carefully they may have been drafted. Even the most humble chart or diagram deserves the same attention to design principles and aesthetics that would be routinely accorded to more representational illustrations.

Basic Design Principles

Regardless of the subject matter or structure of the particular chart or diagram, basic principles of graphic design apply to all data graphics. Charts and diagrams depend heavily on orthogonal linework: horizontal and vertical lines that meet at 90-degree angles. These line grids tend to be monotonous and inherently confusing if no visual hierarchy or dominance relationships are established to help the eye separate the different elements of the chart. The various parts of a chart should always be drawn in line widths that reflect their relative importance to the data message. Axis lines and ticks, error bars, boxes around text, and the linework in tone fills should always be distinctly lighter than the lines that actually represent the data lines and points in line graphs, bar boxes in bar graphs, and arrows indicating the flow of events in diagrams. Without visual contrast in the linework, the message of the data may be overwhelmed by ancillary elements in the chart. In general, the overall linework in a chart should be as light as possible, given the presentation medium and reproduction size intended. Overly heavy chart linework (particularly in the axes and ticks) looks clumsy and inappropriate when matched with good typography in a journal or other publication.

Do not confuse visual complexity with authority in science graphics. Superfluous linework—such as grid lines in the interior of the chart, boxes around the chart, and minor tick marks on the axes—should be pared away, leaving only the most essential and functional linework to orient the viewer. Numeric labels along axes should be trimmed to only the most essential divisions—ideally, no more than five to seven number labels on the average chart axis. In multichart formats that share a common X or Y axis, eliminate any redundant axis labeling to simplify the chart.

In line charts, the data points should always stand out from and dominate the connecting linework, since the data points are the actual data and the connecting lines are usually just a visual device to show trends and continuity. Symbols and connecting lines should dominate all other elements of the chart. Choose a symbol diameter about twice the width of any connecting lines. The connecting line should never run directly into a solid (filled-in) data-point symbol, or the visual distinction of the points may be lost (see fig. 24-1). Geometric symbols such as circles, triangles, squares, and diamonds make the most distinct data points; X marks tend to get muddy looking in reproduction and are too easy to confuse with the connecting linework.

Error bars should be the narrowest lines on the chart, to avoid dominating the data points themselves and to leave adequate white space between the point symbol and the "cap" of the error bar in small error ranges. The end "caps" on error bars should match the diameter of the point symbols.

Every data point measured should be visible on the chart. Points that occur too close to each other to be plotted at their literal positions on the grid should be "bumped" slightly apart to show two distinct symbols, even at the expense of slight data inaccuracy. Never run one data line over another without breaking one of the lines to indicate which line is on top, just as is recommended for ink drawings in chapter 5 (under Basic Techniques). Lines that run together will lose their distinction and directional quality without such small but important visual cues.

Bar charts can be the simplest type of chart to draft, but that very simplicity often leads to visual monotony or confusion if the chart is not designed well. Charts with many bars evenly spaced can confuse the eye, causing the distinction between each bar and the surrounding white spaces to be lost. Try to avoid making the space between the bars the same width as the bars themselves. The lines forming the box for each bar should be the heaviest on the chart, dominating all other linework. When the chart includes error bars that extend into the bar space, always cut away any tone fill within the bar to leave a white field around the error bar. Any text within a tone-filled bar should also be boxed against a white field; if it is not, the whole area will fill in and become illegible in reproduction.

Tone Fills

Tone-fill patterns such as Letraset and Formatt films are essential to the chart artist. They are used for separating variables in bar charts, distinguishing different parts of a diagram, and adding visual interest or tonal contrast in graphics that might otherwise be dull or confusing. Inappropriate or obnoxious fill patterns are also the single most common egregious element in badly designed charts. Heavy linear tone patterns, wavy line patterns, checked patterns, polka-dotted patterns, basketweave patterns, and other silly fill patterns routinely show up in science graphics, in spite of the annoying moiré effects they produce. Unfortunately, computer-graphics software has perpetuated this trend by allowing an almost unlimited number of fill patterns to be introduced into a graphic with the punch of a few keys. The appropriate use of tone-fill patterns is one of the most visible marks of graphic sophistication in chart design.

To avoid optical "shimmering" (moiré vibrations) and inappropriate visual dominance over other elements of the chart, try to choose tone patterns that are visually quiet and composed of light lines or dot patterns. Line and dot patterns of moderate density are the most useful. Heavy linear patterns should be used only for very small areas, or they will produce moiré patterns in the chart. Remember that tone fills reduce along with the graphic; if too light (or too dark) a fill pattern is chosen for a chart that will be greatly reduced, it may become too fine, uneven, or block up in its final form. On the other hand, many coarse fill patterns become quite attractive when viewed at the final reduction size. Use a reduction lens or an office copier with reduction capabilities to aid in selecting tones.

When the chart contains several variables to be keyed out, remember that white and black are also available as "fills." In bar charts that include a research control variable, the control bar usually is left unfilled, or white. Filling a bar with

black gives t
nance over th
black fill with
propriate em
tion is simply
bar individua
a multipatter
avoid confu
screen patte
density by
When repr
screens lose
and may loo
other to retai

Color

Now tha
systems are
place, the c
chart and
brought a n
ence graphi
ables in a c
more distinc
terns, and
grounds are
audience's
background
the past.

With the
ever, have
lems. Scie
conservativ
reluctant to
of their pee
looks too fla
oversaturat
add visual
the powerfu
fully chosen
legibility o
bright colo
fect that b
tracting
unfortunat
ing their ey
Try using
for most c
full-saturat
most impo
chart. Th
color char
tional gra
graphic n
undistract
backgrou

ments, and use bright-colored tape or fill patterns only where appropriate for maximum emphasis.

Typography and Labeling

Even the most carefully drafted chart will suffer if the typography and labeling scheme is poorly designed. Regardless of the method used to generate the labeling, certain design principles should be applied to all chart and diagram labels. Spell out as many of the labels as possible. Too many obscure abbreviations and mysterious codes will annoy and distract the audience. Wherever possible, labels should run horizontally, from left to right, as in normal written text. The only common exception to this rule is in labeling the Y (vertical) axis, where a long horizontal label would often waste too much space. Consider adding small notes or explanations right in the chart itself rather than referring the audience to the caption. In general, all labels should be large enough to be legible at final reproduction size, but avoid making the labels so large or heavy that they compete with the chart content for attention. Do not use boldface labels when you really need a larger font size. In many fonts, the boldface is less legible than the standard face and tends to fill in more in reproduction.

Use upper- and lowercase lettering for all but the most important titles in the graph. All-uppercase labels often command attention far beyond their relative importance in the chart and are harder to read as well. Text is read in letter groups (whole words) by pattern recognition, not letter by letter. The monotonous character height and width of uppercase text interferes with this process, slowing down the reader if the label is more than a few words long.

The convention in current scientific chart design is to use conservative, sans serif typefaces such as Helvetica for all labeling and text. This gives the chart a clean, modern appearance, and Helvetica is a reasonably legible typeface for general use. However, the notion that simple typefaces make simple reading is false. Most studies have shown that sans serif faces such as Helvetica are less legible than the traditional serif typefaces such as Times Roman or Century Schoolbook. The serifs add visual distinction to each letter form and to the word as a whole. Serif fonts can be especially useful when many small labels or dense blocks of text must be used in the graphic. Do not be afraid to violate convention in the cause of legibility and good graphic design.

Appropriate Design for the Presentation Medium

Each of the media commonly used in scientific communication has its own requirements for design and legibility in chart graphics. Often the needs of several media need to be balanced to allow the graphic to be used to its maximum potential, thus saving the client the expense of redrafting the chart for each new use.

Graphics for Publication

Charts and diagrams produced primarily for publication are less problematic than charts destined for other media. Charts done exclusively for publication rarely have titles, as this information belongs in the caption. As long as the platemaker and pressmen take reasonable care in printing a book graphic, very complex formats and fine linework generally will survive the reproduction process unscathed. Be aware that most science journals severely reduce data graphics, often to a width of one column. Since clients rarely know exactly how the editors of the journal will handle the charts, try to keep a selection of major science journals (scrounge back issues from clients) to refer to for style and usage information. Many of the less prominent journals cannot afford premium (or even reasonable) print quality, so plan the graphic accordingly for these destinations. Avoid overly fine linework or complex fill patterns, and be sure the client sends only top-quality photographs or photostats of the graphic (or the original art) with the manuscript.

Graphics for Slides and Overhead Projection

Since the audience for slide and overhead graphics can rarely exercise much control over the viewing time or viewing conditions, graphics for these media need to be especially easy to read and comprehend. Labels and linework should be larger and bolder than in other types of graphics. Use larger font sizes in preference to boldface text. Many computer-graphic systems allow the artist to "drop-shadow" text with black. The drop-shadows add contrast to the letter forms and help separate them from colored backgrounds. A quick test of slide legibility is to hold it close to a light box and try to read the text with your unaided eye. If you can read the text without too much effort, the people in the back row should be able to read it as well.

In order to take advantage of every bit of room available within the slide mount, slide graphics must be tightly designed within the 2:3 proportions of the 35mm slide format (fig. 24-16). Prepare a sheet with many concentric 2:3 rectangles drawn on it, and keep it handy for slipping over or under a work in progress to keep a constant check on the proportions of the graphic. Most projection facilities are set up for horizontal slides only. Vertical slides usually will spill off the top and bottom of the screen, obscuring those parts of the graphic. If you *must* create a vertical slide, try not to place essential information at the very top and bottom of the format. Remind the client to see the projectionist at the meeting about realigning the slide projector (or the screen). This is often possible if you warn the projectionist in advance about vertical slides.

Graphics for Poster Sessions

Poster-session graphics share many of the same problems of slide graphics. Viewing conditions at meetings are often crowded and chaotic, with little chance given to examine graphics and text blocks in detail. The graphics should be bold and simple. Text needs to be large enough so that the audience can read it comfortably from 5 or 6 feet away. Labels should be set in at least 18-point text (actual finished size), upper- and lowercase. Use generous leading (18-point type on 21 points of leading, or "18 on 21," works well) on multiline blocks of type. Graphics to be used directly in the poster should be done on a matte surface to reduce glare from overhead lights.

Graphics for Video and Film

These media are perhaps the most demanding when creating charts and diagrams. In addition to the problems of working within tightly defined proportions, both 16mm film and NTSC video have resolution limitations that will affect every aspect of the graphic design. Neither film nor video can display very fine distinctions of linework, complex fill patterns, or tiny text labels. Text should have extra-heavy drop-shadows to maintain separation from the background. Every nonessential chart element should be stripped away to leave only the simplest and most functional linework and labels. The whole chart may need to be redesigned if too many variables or observations are included in the chart. When viewed as original art, many good video and film graphics have a coarse, "cartoonish" look due to the simplicity of design and large, boldface text. Judge the graphic on the screen, not on the drawing board.

The color scheme for video must be very quiet and conservative, using mostly "grayed-out" pastels and avoiding large areas of white. The NTSC color video standard used in the United States simply does not have the capability to display many adjacent bright colors simultaneously. The video image will

"crawl" or sl
ders between
overall color
torted by in
color areas.
bright color v
to lessen the
actions and
The oldest jo
does not sta
sion Stand
stands for N
Color." Put
swatches to
(both on ta
lecting the
hook up an
computer-gr
the video co
schemes fo
can be bo
many inten
sual contras

Graphics
conform to
if precious
wasted. Th
height to w
16mm filn
graphic for
erous back
for fluctua
(the part o
the screen
video work
mation be
tions in vid

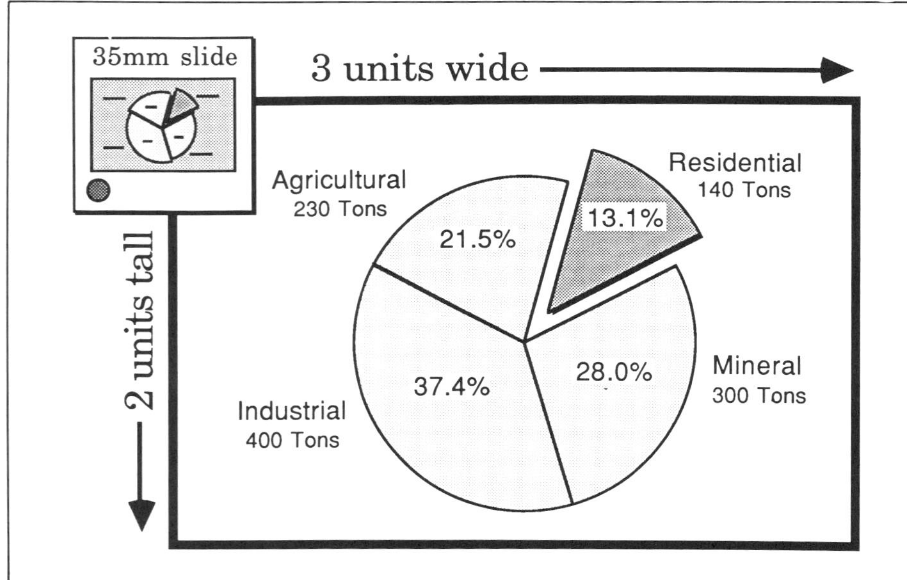

24-16. Ideal format for graphics created for a 35mm slide: horizontal layout in 2:3 proportions. Created on a Macintosh-Plus microcomputer with MacDraw software, and printed on a 300-dot-per-inch Apple LaserWriter laser printer, by Patrick J. Lynch.

When
view chart
chore to b
than an o
design ski
scientific
sult often
ecy: the w
dull and
diagrams
same atte
ciples tha
pieces wo
ing, poor
wound to
tific illust
the proce
cation.

25/Cartography for the Scientific Illustrator

Daniel G. Cole

Maps are one of the major means of conveying information on spatial distributions. A foremost consideration in cartography is that maps are the equivalent of paragraphs or pages about data and thus should have language (symbology) that relates to the elements or qualities represented; reveal the data at several levels of detail, from simple to complex; be closely integrated with the statistical or verbal descriptions of the data; provide a "good fit" between themselves and the environment represented; avoid distorting or misrepresenting the data; present many numbers and words in a small space; make large data sets coherent; encourage the eye to compare different pieces of data; serve a reasonably clear purpose while being easy to use, legible, and attractive; induce the reader to think about the substance rather than the methodology, graphic design, production, or technique; suit the data to the user's needs; and allow interaction with the user.

For many map readers, the search for information is largely haphazard—readers are often ignorant of what is most important or what should be read first. Their attention is diffused. The cartographer should direct the reader's attention, design the map to make readers see what is important and in the correct sequence, and make the map attractive enough that readers think about what they see. And, approaching the map as a reader, the cartographer must subjectively ask, "Does the map look good?" This chapter addresses these concerns while discussing the various elements of cartographic design and production.

THE CARTOGRAPHER

Academic requirements and training in cartography vary from university to university, but the following list of courses, usually offered by the geography department, gives an indication of the educational experience needed to be a well-rounded cartographer:

- Map Interpretation
- Introductory Cartography (pen-and-ink drafting)
- Map Projections
- Intermediate Cartography (darkroom technique and scribing)
- Phototypesetting
- Advanced Cartography (map design)
- Computer Graphics
- Computer Cartography
- Computer Programming (BASIC and FORTRAN)
- Geometry
- Statistics
- Surveying
- Photogrammetry
- Aerial Photographic Interpretation
- Remote Sensing
- Various regional geography courses

INSTRUMENTS AND MATERIALS

A well-equipped cartographic lab has the materials listed below. More sophisticated labs have darkroom equipment, such as a contact printer and a copy camera, and computer-graphics equipment. If a darkroom and camera equipment are available, negative line film, 35mm slide film, and overhead transparency film might be needed, depending on the jobs required.

Surfaces

Drafting film: frosted and clear polyester

Tracing paper.

Scribe sheets: plastic, color-coated film, such as Scribecoat.

Media

India ink: black.

Pencils: various degrees of hardness.

Graphic materials: shading film colors, tones, textures, and patterns; dry-transfer point and line symbols such as dots, triangles, open circles, squares, borders.

Tools

Technical pens: sizes 5 × 0 (.13) through 2 (.50).

Erasers: for ink, pencil.

Scribers: for etching lines on maps (fig. 25-1); rigid for smaller points, swivel for larger points.

Sapphire scribing points: sizes .002 inch through .030 inch.

Small magnifier (loupe): with micrometer scale for checking line widths.

X-Acto knife: with no. 16 or other blade.

Straightedge, T square.

Drafting compass: capable of holding a technical pen (see chapter 2).

French curves.

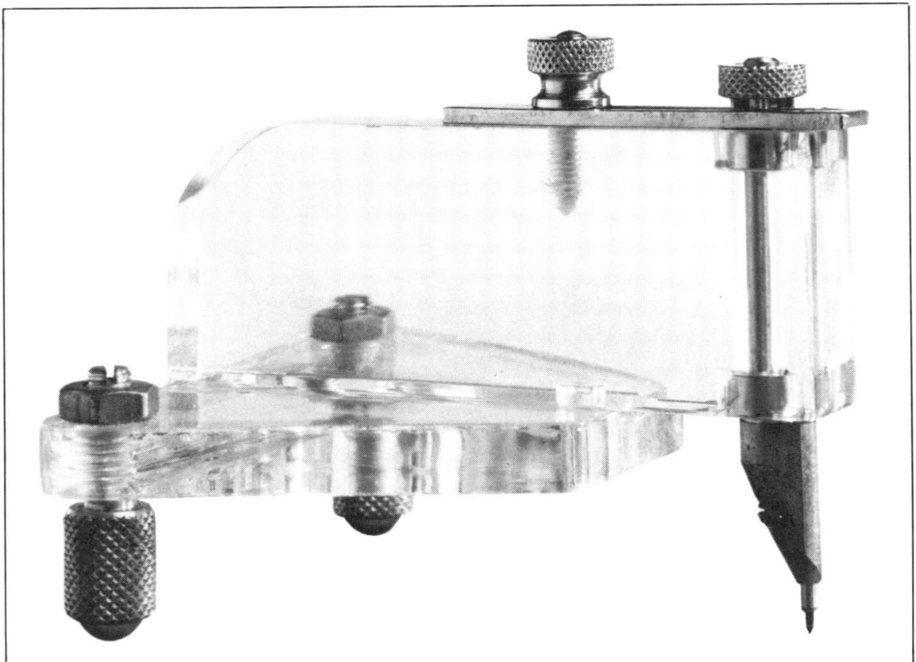

25-1. See-through dual/rigid swivel scriber with sapphire point. The rigid scriber option is recommended for thinner (≤.008-inch) lines, and the swivel scriber option is recommended for thicker (≥.008-inch) lines. Courtesy of Keuffel and Esser Co.

Railroad curves: very long curves for latitude and longitude grid lines. Various sizes provide consistent angles along their lengths.

Templates: circles, ovals, triangles, squares.

Miscellaneous

Masking film: dark red, such as Rubylith, Cut 'n Strip; light-sensitive, such as peel coat or Peelrite.

Registration punches and registry pins: to align successive overlays (see fig. 2-44).

Plate maker: or other device with brilliant light source (2500-watt pulsed xenon at distance of 24 inches [61 cm]) for exposing peel coat or Peelrite if used.

Photocopier.

TECHNIQUE

Traditionally maps for printed reproduction are rendered in pen-and-ink, then reduced photographically to produce a negative from which a plate is made; the reduction serves also to clean up the unevenness of the hand-inked line. This method is still in common use, especially among scientific illustrators who are called upon from time to time to produce maps but are not trained in the latest cartographic technology. The advent of the scriber with jeweled points (see fig. 25-1) has given the cartographer a tool that provides reliably consistent line widths and saves a step in the darkroom. With a scriber, the cartographer works at final size, the precise linework does not have to be cleaned up, and the scribe sheet on which the linework is done serves as a photographically opaque negative.

The next step, in either case, is the exposure of a series of sheets of light-sensitive film (peel coat, Peelrite) in a platemaker. A separate sheet is made for each color, screen, and/or screen angle to represent various features on the map. Pin registration (see fig. 2-44) ensures that each succeeding overlay is aligned with the one beneath it. Figure 25-2 illustrates how a chart of line negatives or scribe coats,

peel coats, a
used to disting
or quantitativ
chart such as
printer as a
color plates.
lows flexibilit
scheme if th
problems.

Maps inte
media other
(ozalid or di
pies, slides,
parencies—
in pen-and-i
but the meth
differ from t
or diazo ma
providing a
nal map. T
proved such
colors, rath
available. B
atively rapid
tortion caus
ozalid mach
copying me
phy have a
years with
multicolor
ducing cap
that arise w
light blue d
white copie
continuous-
pear washe

When m
plan for th
will take
most minu
only slow-s
With both
cies for ov
for a view
thirty feet.

Generaliz

Since n
scale of 1:
actual lan
volve vary
zation (th
and the
through s
scale dec
creases. T

ited by the width of the drafting point and by the human hand. Technical advances in drafting (scribing versus pen-and-ink or high-resolution computer plotting versus manual methods) permit greater detail and thus less generalization of coastlines, rivers, boundaries, and so on. But generalization, with or without technical advances, is desirable if only to decrease visual "noise." For example, including too many coastal nooks and crannies when drafting a map to be reduced not only makes the coastline look very messy and crowded, but also distracts from the map's content (fig. 25-3).

Scale is determined by the amount of area to be mapped in conjunction with the published size of the map. Scale may be very large (greater than 1:5,000), large (1:5,000 to 1:75,000), medium (1:75,000 to 1:1,000,000), small (1:1,000,000 to 1:100,000,000), or very small (less than 1:100,000,000). Larger scales allow for greater detail while depicting smaller areas, whereas smaller scales require greater generalization when depicting larger areas.

If the scale of a base map is unknown (1:x), proportionally compare identical ground distance between it and another map that has a known scale, such as 1:5,000. If the ground distance translates, for instance, into 1 inch (2.5cm) on the map with unknown scale and 2 inches (5.2cm) on the map with the known scale, the following equation provides the unknown denominator:

$$\frac{1 \text{ in.}}{1/x} = \frac{2 \text{ in.}}{1/5{,}000}$$

$$x = 10{,}0000$$

In addition to generalizing the physical earth's surface, cartographers must also generalize the statistical earth's surface. Here the generalization process starts with data compilation. First, a scientist or client selects the type of data; then the scientist or cartographer narrows the topic. For instance, mapping mortality of animals may be narrowed by cause, time period, species, age, sex, and unit area (town, county, state, region, nation). The next step is to decide what to do with the categorized raw data: the data must be generalized and simplified through classing, standardizing, and averaging processes. These generalizations reduce the precision of the data on the map; raw statistical data, which would be most accurate, usually is not mapped. For example, do not map the *number* of births or deaths; instead, use birth and death *rates.* A map is intended to show generalized spatial overviews of areas and topics. An exception is a dot map; for example, in taxonomic research, species-distribution maps show locations where single species were collected, although the exact number of individuals is not mapped. In most cases, however, where depiction of raw data is necessary, a table is a more suitable device than a map.

Overall, generalization is not the mere elimination of detail. Think of maps as containing data ink (the proportion of the map providing essential data and graphic information). On the other hand, maps also contain some nondata ink (redundant or extraneous information), such as the geographic grid or graticule on a thematic map. *The Visual*

Type of Material	Feature to be shown on Map	Instructions to Printer for Color Percentages to be used			
		Black	Cyan	Yellow	Magenta
Negative #1	cultural type	100%			
Negative #2	water type		100%		
Scribe coat #1	political borders	100%			
Scribe coat #2	land-water boundary		100%		
Peel coat #1	water		10%		
Peel coat #2	green forested areas		20%	20%	
Peel coat #3	urban areas				20%

25-2. Example of a color/screen tint specification chart.

25-3. Map features that are too detailed will merge in the process of reduction. Here, a copy is shown at 50 percent of the original. Generalization is needed. A portion of the coast of Greenland. Technical pen and ink on polyester film, by Daniel G. Cole.

Display of Quantitative Information, by Edward R. Tufte (see Bibliography), notes that cartographers need to maximize the ratio of data ink to nondata ink by generalizing the physical and data surfaces to minimize any superfluous linework, wording, or other information not essential to the map's message.

Keep in mind that generalization does have its limits: base map detail can be generalized to the point of nonrecognition and data can be generalized to the point of no differentiation. Further, because small-scale maps are more generalized than large-scale maps, never work with an enlarged small-scale map base, because the resultant linework would be too coarse. Conversely, if the base map being drafted is to be reduced, too much detail inevitably will coalesce into lines of black blobs. Overall, graphic and data generalization on maps is controlled by the objective, scale, graphic limits, and quality of the data.

Projections

No flat or even spherical map is distortion-free, but the aim is to choose a map of the earth's surface that minimizes distortion. This chapter will not examine the mathematical transformations of the earth's spherical geometry to the plane coordinate geometry of a flat map. For information on projections and their properties, see Bibliography (*An Introduction to the Study of Projections*, by J. A. Steers; *A Projection Handbook*, by J. A. Hilliard, U. Bosoglu, and P. C. Muehrcke; *Introduction to Map Projections*, by P. W. McDonnell; and "The Role of Projections in Modern Map Design," by M. L. Hsu).

An understanding of projections first requires comprehension of latitude and longitude determinations. Latitude is the location on the globe between either the north or the south pole and the equator.

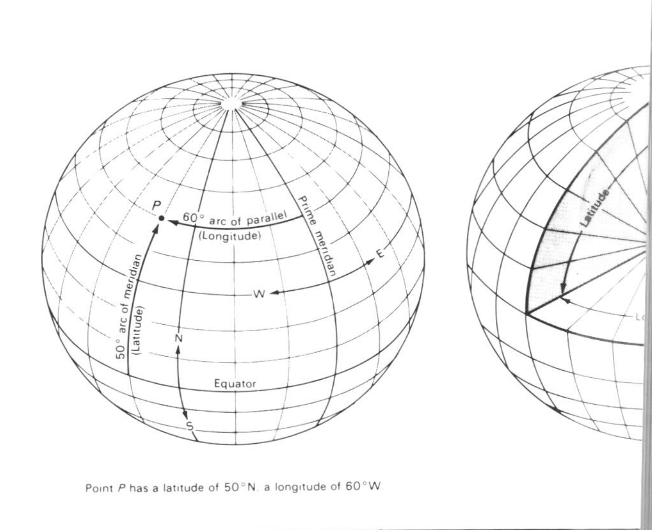

25-4. The complete geographic grid. Scribe sheet and peel coat
screen. From *Principles of Thematic Map Design*, by B. D. De
1985).

Each latitude line may be thought of as an imaginary plane passing through the earth parallel to the equator. With longitude, most countries recognize the meridian passing through the Royal Greenwich Observatory in England as 0 degrees—the prime meridian from which all other east-west points are measured. All points move through 360 degrees per day and 15 degrees per hour. Any vertical plane intersecting the earth's axis completely is a meridian, and its longitudinal angle is merely measured between the prime and the local meridian planes. All of the parallels and meridians together yield the geographic grid (fig. 25-4). In addition to latitude and longitude, great-circle arcs also must be considered. These arcs are defined by any plane fully bisecting the globe. The planes include the equator, meridians, and diagonals, each of which defines the shortest route between two points on the planet.

Projections are classed in one of three basic surfaces: azimuthal or planar, cylindrical, and conic (fig. 25-5). Each surface type is further broken down into three cases: simple or tangent, secant, and complex (for example, multiple planar). In addition, three basic projection

types fall in
three surfac
tance along
uniform), equ
ships for al
are maintai
(shapes of
served). Equ
types are
each other.

Many mo
types also o
modification
rupted proj
only is dist
critical area
wanted are
save space
distorted gr
turbing, it
many cases
ous value.

All of the
lowing poin
tion type c
often make
at large an
manner in
jected will
ments take
care should
projection.
able, and t
both distor
cartograph

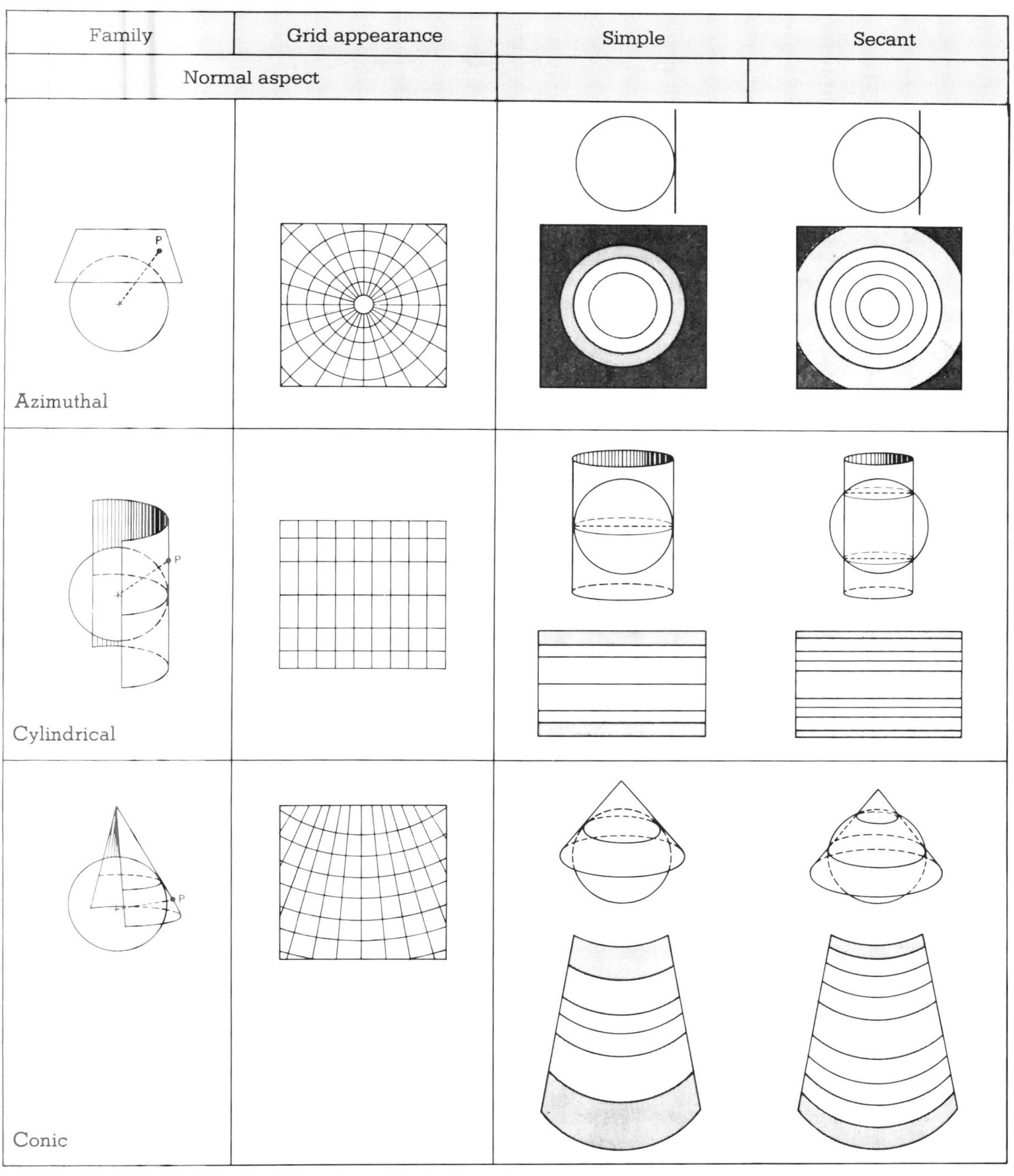

25-5. Projection families and patterns of deformation. Scribe sheet and peel coat with photomechanical screens. From *Principles of Thematic Map Design*, by B. D. Dent (Addison-Wesley, 1985).

two choices for a book, although a different projection may be chosen each time for other publications. In any case, balance the characteristics of the projection with objective(s) of the map.

Visual Balance and Layout

Because all features of a map are interrelated, the balance between different features must be carefully controlled. As J. S. Keates notes in

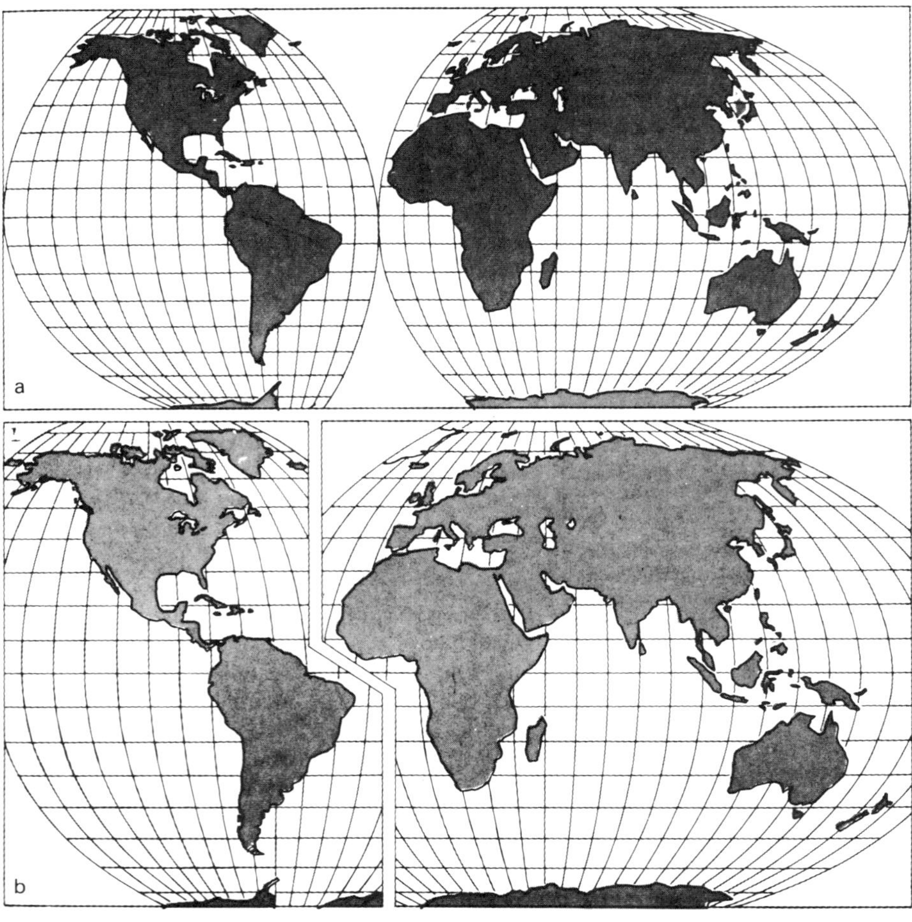

25-6. An interrupted flat polar quartic equal-area projection of the entire earth *(a)*. Deleting unwanted areas *(b)* obtains additional scale within a limiting width. The areas of concern could just as well be the ocean areas. Scribe sheet and peel coat with photomechanical screen. From *Elements of Cartography*, 5th ed., by A. H. Robinson et al. (John Wiley and Sons, 1984).

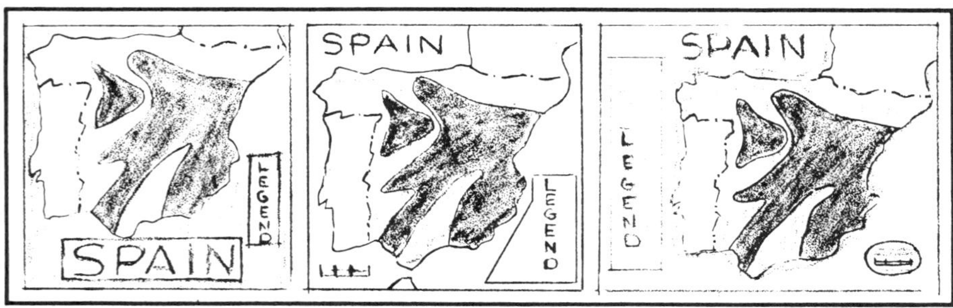

25-7. Preliminary sketches of a map, made in order to arrive at a desirable layout and balance. Pencil on tracing paper. From *Elements of Cartography*, 5th ed., by A. H. Robinson et al. (John Wiley and Sons, 1984).

Cartographic
tion (see Biblio
in principle to
ture at a diffe
features relate
in a map of th
in which there
between land
patterns, a de
of drainage wo
with simplified

Determine
balance by
sketches (fig.
isfied with th
arrangement
scale, legen
termed "perip
map depends
tion and basi
ious parts of t
shape of the
peripherals, t
of the map an
the reader's
area. Avoid s
heavy arrang
is used, posi
other periphe
tation also m
cially if the
shaped area
map somewh
the available
white space.
to allow free
peripherals:
the maximu
area and the
in "unused"
the map.

The direct
ences the ba
ing process
states of Ve
the peripher
along vertica
respectively.
with the ma
erwise result
taken up un
important, la
als parallel
leads the rea
tion desired.

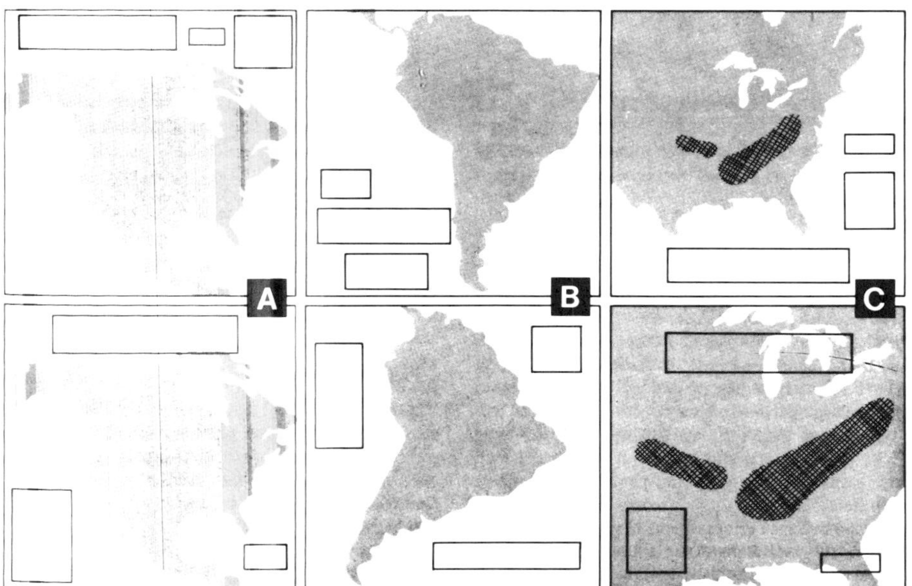

25-8. Adjustments of the map and peripheral elements. Scribe sheet and peel coat with photomechanical screen. From *Thematic Maps: Their Design and Production*, by D. J. Cuff and M. T. Mattson (Methuen, 1982).

25-9. Example of the figure-ground relationship: territory and approximate locations of Indian bands and subgroups in Quebec and Newfoundland. Pen-and-ink and photomechanical screen, by Judy Wojcik. From *Handbook of North American Indians*, vol. 6, *Subarctic*, June Helm, ed. (Smithsonian Institution Press 1981).

Figure-Ground and Visual Hierarchy

As early as 1951, A. H. Robinson, in *The Look of Maps*, (see Bibliography), recognized the need to borrow the figure-ground relationship from artists and make use of it. Since then, several papers have been written to explain the relationship between figure and ground cartography. In his article "Visual Perception and Map Design" (1968), Wood defines the use of figure-ground as analyzing maps on the basis of "receding planes," where each plane contains a specific selection of graphic information (see Bibliography). As the planes recede, importance decreases. For example, in figure 25-9, the locations of bands and subgroups are the figure (black symbols); the territory of the three main Indian groups is the secondary figure (medium tone); and the outside land area in this case is the ground (white). This gives a general idea of a visual hierarchy through the use of figure-ground. The division of map content into successive levels depends not only on contrast but also on color, line weight, and complexity. Progressively darker gray tones and colors, thicker line weights, and greater complexity are indicative of layers within the map hierarchy ascending to the subject study area. A note of caution: avoid making the figure so dark and complex that it becomes a black mess that the reader will disregard.

On the simplest level, merely establishing a figure-ground relationship between land and water is the most common problem. Figure 25-10 illustrates six different approaches: in *(a)*, no figure-ground relationship exists, making it difficult to distinguish between land and water; *(b)* shows all the land-based place names on land, using typography to identify land as the figure (not ground). Both *(c)* and *(d)* use patterned films to exhibit the figure-ground relationship, but these methods are not often used because they are visually noisy and unaesthetic. The most common methods of land/water differentiation are shown in *(e)*, drafted with pen-and-ink and *(f)*, produced with a photographic gray screen, although *(f)* is the method of preference because it is less visually noisy and has more continuity.

Using white for land when land is the study area (fig. 25-11) might seem to contradict the figure-ground relationship in figure 25-9. But highlighting the thematic information in white makes the study area more interesting. This method displays the fig ship in a visu chical manner.

Letter Design

The princip and visual hie to lettering. A

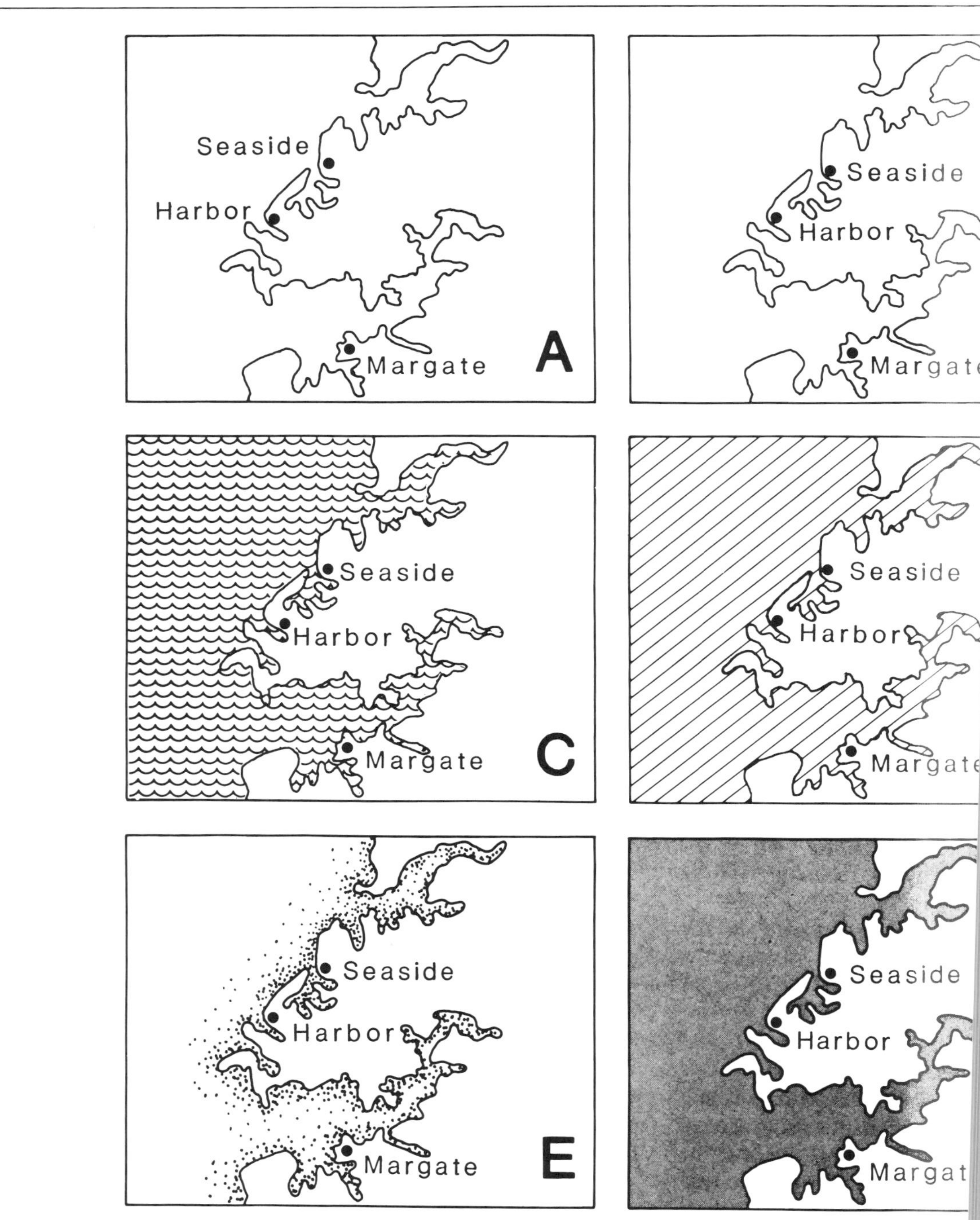

25-10. Factors in the differentiation of land areas from water. Pen-and-ink for linework and stippling, adhesive patterns, and photomechanical screen. From *Thematic Maps: Their Design and Production*, by D. J. Cuff and M. T. Mattson (Methuen, 1982).

25-11. An example of visual counterpoint. Peripheral dark areas highlight the lighter study area; within the study area, a hierarchy of white, gray, and black is used. Map designed and produced by Patrick Stocking using scribe sheet, peel coat, and photomechanical screens. From *Thematic Maps: Their Design and Production*, by D. J. Cuff and M. T. Mattson (Methuen, 1982).

is: big, black, bold letters assume more visual importance than small, screened, lightweight letters. But there is more to a map's verbal content than that. By employing style, form, size, color, contrast, and position, the artist shows a nominal hierarchy.

There are hundreds of styles of lettering to choose from—many inappropriate for most cartography, if only for reasons of taste. Letters are either serif or sans serif. Within each style are choices of weight and style—light, medium, bold, expanded, regular, condensed, upright, slanted, all uppercase (capitals), and uppercase along with lowercase (fig. 25-12).

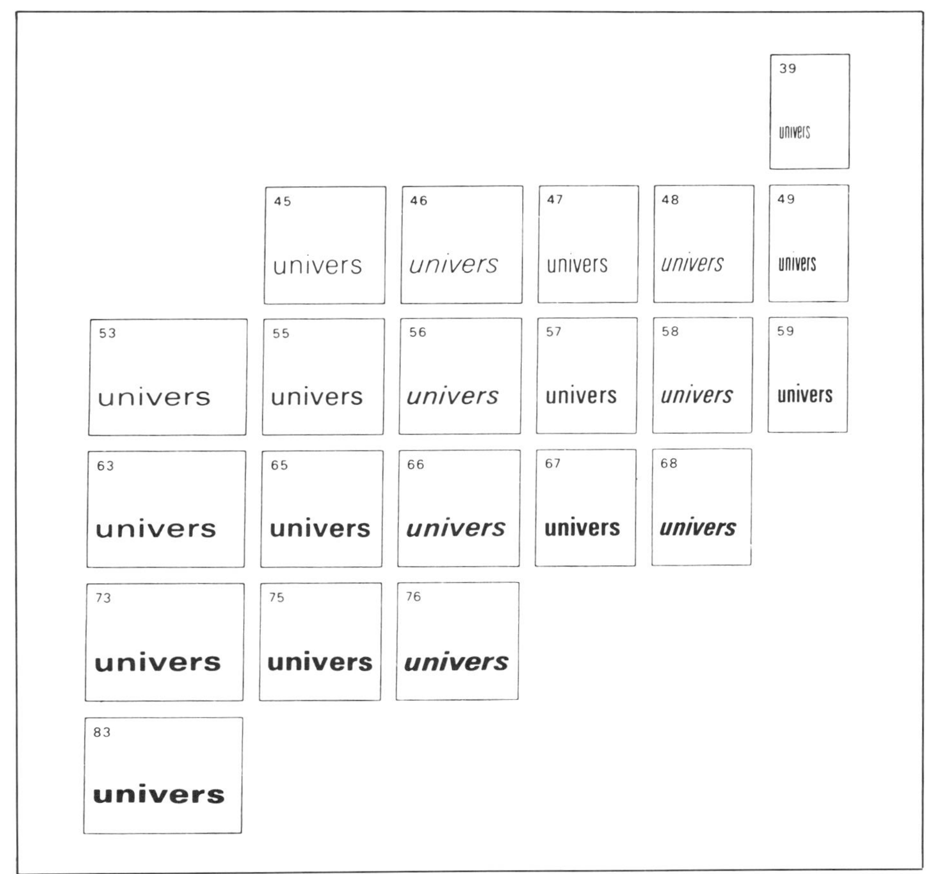

25-12. The complete Univers palette showing all possible weights and forms of this sans-serif typeface. From *A History of Graphic Design*, by P. B. Meggs (Van Nostrand Reinhold, 1983).

Although no hard rules for type selection exist in mapmaking, the fewer choices made, the more harmonious the appearance of the map. Maps are easier to read with one or two ordinary types as opposed to a variety of types, and the ease of reading is even greater when uppercase and lowercase letters are used instead of capitals alone. But usi
forms permits
graphical hier
ordinated thro
names are e
often, variatio
style are mor
create an orde
25-13).

Like the el
can be used t
information—
bolder forms
more importa
Understandin
pects of type
portant prior
Typography is
point size, wh
0.35mm or 1/
usable type fo
maps is 4 poi
tions set a c
such as 7 poi
determined b
size of the m
often require
can be read
least thirty fe
the final size
drafted map i
percent reduc
ters results in
medium or li
duced that n
fect.

Color and
to illustrate q
For example,
associated w
tures, green
and so on.

Integral to
sitioning, as
wording shou
cluded. Bec
there are sev
not to appea
and "Map" i
end" and "K
example, "M
ease" is inap
"Distribution
ease." The ti
changeable v
so if a figur
title should

		NATIONAL GEOGRAPHIC		NATIONAL ATLASES		ATLASES		
		Reference	Magazine	U.S.	Canada	CIA	Goode	Oxford World
WATER	Salt	CAP	Cplc	CAP	CAP*	Cplc	CAP*	CAP*
	Fresh	Cplc	Cplc	Cplc	Cplc	Cplc	Cplc	CAP*
LAND FEATURES	Other	CAP*	Cplc	CAP	—	CAP	CAP	CAP
	Peak	CAP*	Cplc	Cplc	—	Cplc	Cplc	CAP
	Range	CAP*	Cplc	CAP*	—	CAP	CAP	CAP*
CULTURAL	City	Cplc	Cplc	CAP*	CAP*	CAP*	* * *	Cplc
	Park	CAP	CAP	CAP	—	—	CAP	CAP
	Political	CAP	CAP	CAP	CAP	CAP*	CAP	CAP
THEMATIC	Notes	Cplc	Cplc	Cplc	Cplc	Cplc	Cplc	Cplc
	Legend Item	Cplc	Cplc	Cplc	Cplc	Cplc	Cplc	Cplc
	Legend Head	Cplc	Cplc	CAP	CAP	Cplc	Cplc	Cplc
	Title	CAP	* *	CAP	CAP	Cplc	CAP	Cplc

☐ Sans Serif
* CAP or Cplc, depending on map scale and status of feature.
** Lettering unique to map theme.
*** Cplc, CAP or Cplc, depending on status of feature.

25-13. Lettering conventions of some major mapmaking establishments. After *Thematic Maps: Their Design and Production*, by D. J. Cuff and M. T. Mattson (Methuen, 1982).

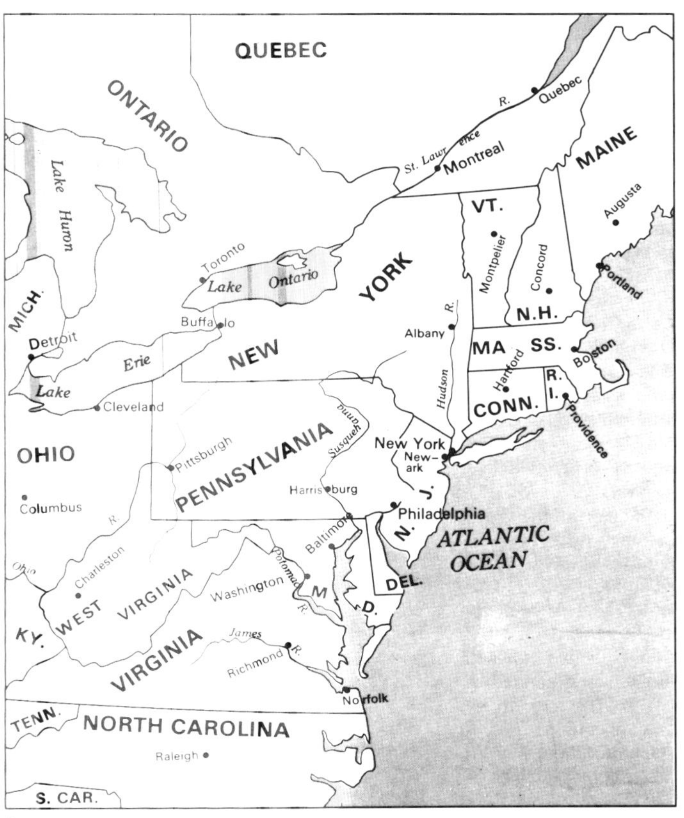

a

b

25-14. Map lettering. *(a)* Most of the general rules about positioning lettering have been violated in almost every instance on this map. *(b)* The same lettering as in *(a)* has been positioned to better advantage. Scribe sheet, peel coat, and photomechanical screen. From *Elements of Cartography*, 5th ed., by A. H. Robinson et al. (John Wiley and Sons, 1984).

used must be consistent with the symbolization and what is being mapped—for example, "Population Density of Deer within National Forests" would be an incorrect title if the map is actually of population size. Next, the legend should complement the title—given the above title, the legend ought to state "Deer per Square Mile." Last, the source and explanatory notes will not take up space needed for other items if they are included in the figure caption or placed in a corner of the map.

Positioning letters, numbers, and words on a map entails several rules (fig. 25-14) outlined in *Elements of Cartography*, by A. H. Robinson, R. D. Sale, J. L. Morrison, and P. C. Muehrcke, and in *Principles of Thematic Map Design*, by B. D. Dent (see Bibliography):

1. Place each name entirely on land or in water (or all in or out of the subject area).
2. Place each name parallel to the map border, grid, or other linear features such as rivers.
3. Do not curve the type unless necessary; when curving, keep the curve constant over the word.
4. Spread out the letters of a word (or words) labeling an areal feature within the feature.
5. Interrupt linework and data, not names or numbers.
6. Lettering should never be upside down or falling over.
7. Abbreviate as little as possible; do not hyphenate.
8. When labeling place names, observe the order of preference shown in figure 25-15.

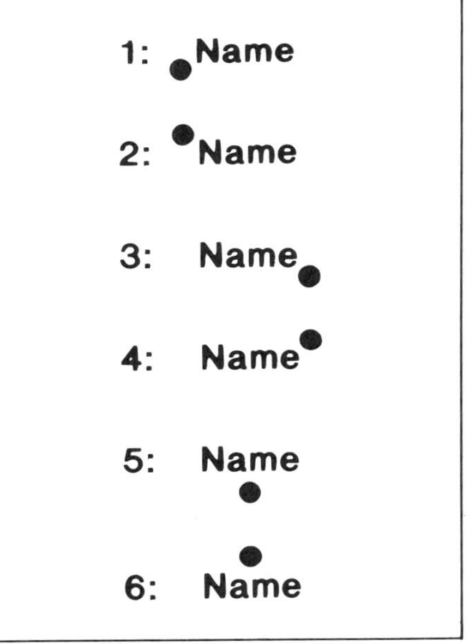

25-15. The order of preference in positioning a place name relative to its point location. The location of Name 1 has first preference, and the location of Name 6 has last preference, according to E. Imhof in "Positioning Names on Maps" (*American Cartographer* 2 [1975]): 128–44.

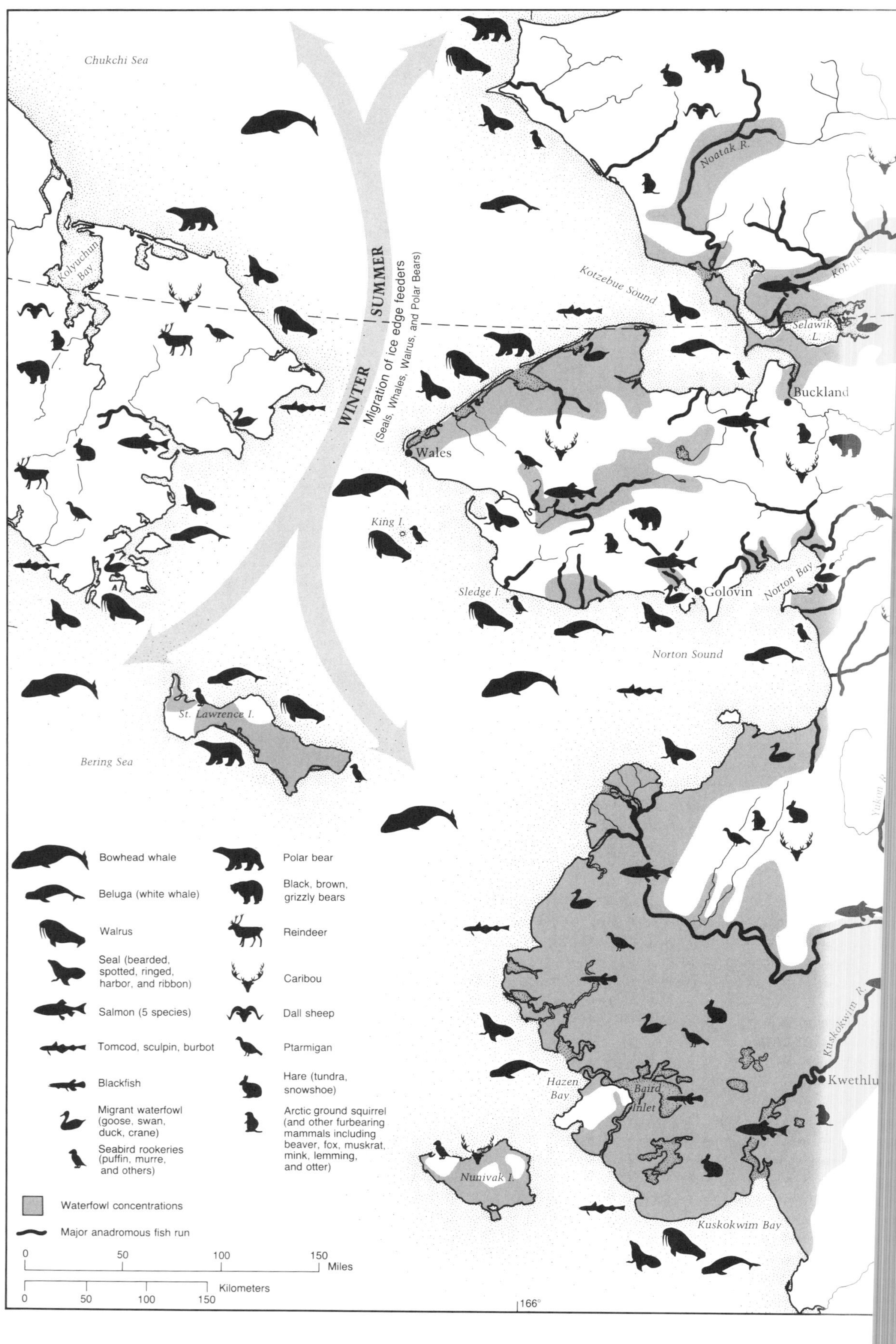
Chukchi Sea
Kolyuchin Bay
WINTER
SUMMER
Migration of ice edge feeders
(Seals, Whales, Walrus, and Polar Bears)
Noatak R.
Kobuk R.
Kotzebue Sound
Selawik L.
Buckland
Wales
King I.
Sledge I.
Golovin
Norton Bay
Norton Sound
St. Lawrence I.
Bering Sea
Hazen Bay
Baird Inlet
Nunivak I.
Kuskokwim R.
Kwethlu
Kuskokwim Bay
166°
Bowhead whale
Beluga (white whale)
Walrus
Seal (bearded, spotted, ringed, harbor, and ribbon)
Salmon (5 species)
Tomcod, sculpin, burbot
Blackfish
Migrant waterfowl (goose, swan, duck, crane)
Seabird rookeries (puffin, murre, and others)
Polar bear
Black, brown, grizzly bears
Reindeer
Caribou
Dall sheep
Ptarmigan
Hare (tundra, snowshoe)
Arctic ground squirrel (and other furbearing mammals including beaver, fox, muskrat, mink, lemming, and otter)
Waterfowl concentrations
Major anadromous fish run
0 50 100 150 Miles
0 50 100 150 Kilometers

Point Symbol Design

The symbology chosen must relate to the distribution being mapped. Place data and volume data both are represented by point symbols, be they abstract (dots, circles, squares) or pictorial. If merely showing the sites of, for instance, various animal types, pictorial symbology works well (fig. 25-16). The symbology used should be of sufficiently different shapes, tones, and colors to make them easily differentiated.

Using nonabstract symbology to depict quantitative data may not be wise because it is difficult for the reader to make size-value comparisons between different pictorial representations of even one species, if this comparison is important. Of the different abstract point symbol types and forms (black, white with black outline, gray with black outline), gray-toned circles have become the proportional symbol of preference in cartography (fig. 25-17). The circles used in the legend to portray particular values represented on the map should be different enough in size to easily distinguish visually.

The place data obviously need to be positioned in the correct geographic location. With qualitative pictorial data, leaders or arrows can be used to point out the correct position of, say, various animal silhouettes. But quantitative abstract data often do not allow that luxury, and overlap inevitably occurs. Mapping more than one variable with overlapping circles, squares, and triangles is likely to get quite messy. So a simple design alternative for a multivariate map is to make one map for each variable.

Drafting dot maps is an old and relatively simple means of illustrating volume data. *Elements of Cartography*, mentioned earlier, notes that there are three basic considerations when making a dot map: size, value, and location. Figure 25-18 shows the range of possible problems and the best solution *(e)*. If the dots are too small, they tend to disappear into the background *(a)*. If the dots are too large *(b)*, they give the map a heavy, gross appearance. If the value of each dot is too small *(c)*, the map becomes overly detailed and crowded. If the value of each dot is too large *(d)*, the map has a rather sparse appearance. To achieve a balance between size and value, take a square inch of the highest density area and within that space experiment with the dot size and value until overlapping has just begun. That process should provide the best overall dot map design *(e)*. At the same time, remember that if the map is not drafted at final size, some dots probably will merge when the map is reduced.

Precisely positioning dots when the value equals one is a goal for which the cartographer strives. Often, however, the value is greater than one, so the dots must be placed on mean locations. If, on the other hand, the data indicate, for example, the number of deer per county on a statewide map, then the location of the dots is constrained merely by physical and cultural phenomena—the dots ought not to be placed in cities or water bodies. Overall, the look of a dot map reflects the constraints of

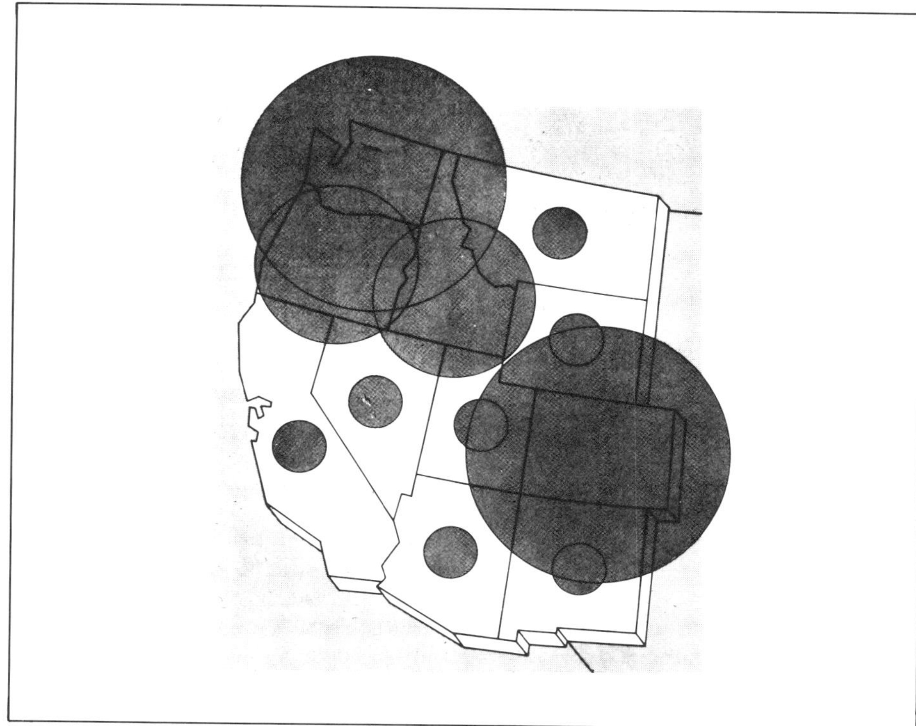

25-17. Example of use of gray-toned circle. Note that gray-toned circles can show full circle overlap as white circles can while portraying figure-ground as black circles can. Scribe sheets and peel coat with photomechanical screen. From *Thematic Maps: Their Design and Production*, by D. J. Cuff and M. T. Mattson (Methuen, 1982).

Facing page:
25-16. Pictorial map showing animal resources in western Alaska. All black lines and type were applied to Denril drafting film. Another polyester film served as an overlay on which photographic prints of the animals were applied after being waxed. This overlay was planned for 100 percent brown. To see and remove inked lines where they crossed an animal figure, the artist placed the overlay with animals under the inked map. Tone areas were created on a second overlay with Amberlith masks, indicating 30 percent brown for the areas of waterfowl concentration and 20 percent gray tone for the large migration arrow. By Molly Kelly Ryan. From *Inua: Spirit World of the Bering Sea Eskimo*, by W. Fitzhugh and S. Kaplan (Smithsonian Institution Press, 1983).

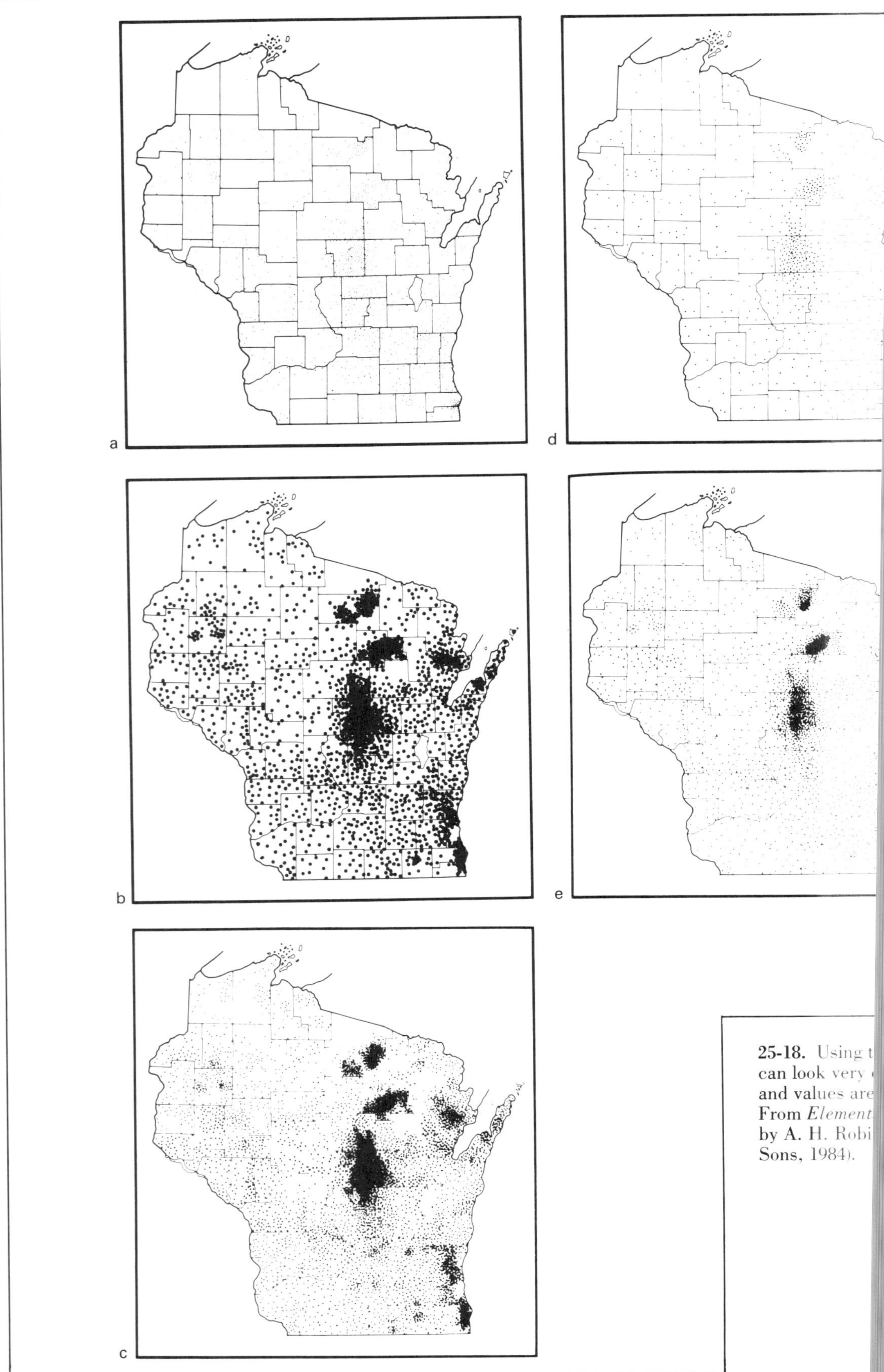

25-18. Using t
can look very
and values are
From *Element*
by A. H. Robi
Sons, 1984).

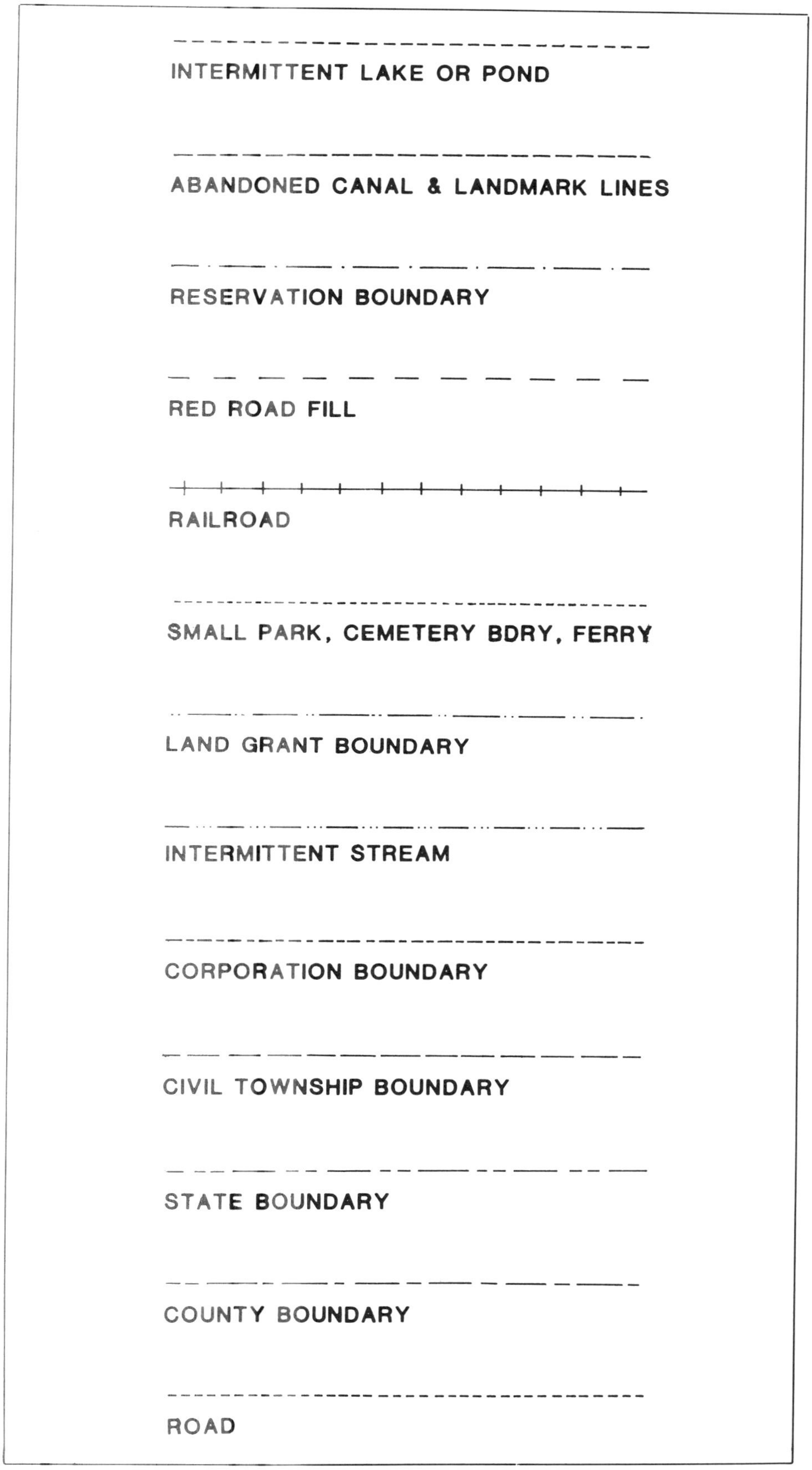

natural and human-related distributions while showing the data in an easily readable format.

Line Symbol Design

Like other symbols, line symbols create a visual hierarchy on a map. Line width denotes importance or rank—for example, thick lines for national borders, medium lines for state borders, and thin lines for county borders. The mapmaker can also alter the characteristics of the lines for different types of borders. The linework in figure 25-19 gives a guide to the lines used as standards for the U.S. Geological Survey (U.S.G.S.), but there is no profession-wide standard for nominal line types. Use the U.S.G.S. guidelines or work on a case-by-case basis. The important point is to be consistent within the particular publication.

Drafting linework requires the use of smooth straightedges and French curves and a steady hand when mapping any kind of boundary. If a latitude/longitude grid must be shown on the map, the best accessory is a set of railroad curves, because only they can provide a consistent angle across the entire curve.

Beyond the use of qualitative line symbols for political, land/water, and subject-area boundaries, roads, rivers, graticule, and map and legend borders, lines also transmit quantitative information. One type of data shown through line symbology is that of movement. Flow lines show the movement of goods, animals, people, diseases, and ideas between places. The lines may be either smoothly curving or angular, with the thickness proportional to the data and varying in width along any one line solely due to additions or subtractions from the flow. Whereas both maps shown in figure 25-20 deal with economic data, lines could be used similarly on maps concerning, for instance, river water volume or whale migration routes.

INTERMITTENT LAKE OR POND

ABANDONED CANAL & LANDMARK LINES

RESERVATION BOUNDARY

RED ROAD FILL

RAILROAD

SMALL PARK, CEMETERY BDRY, FERRY

LAND GRANT BOUNDARY

INTERMITTENT STREAM

CORPORATION BOUNDARY

CIVIL TOWNSHIP BOUNDARY

STATE BOUNDARY

COUNTY BOUNDARY

ROAD

25-19. United States Geological Survey linework guidelines for various boundary and road types. Technical pen and ink and Kroy lettering on Clearprint gridded vellum, by Alice R. Tangerini. Courtesy of the U.S.G.S.

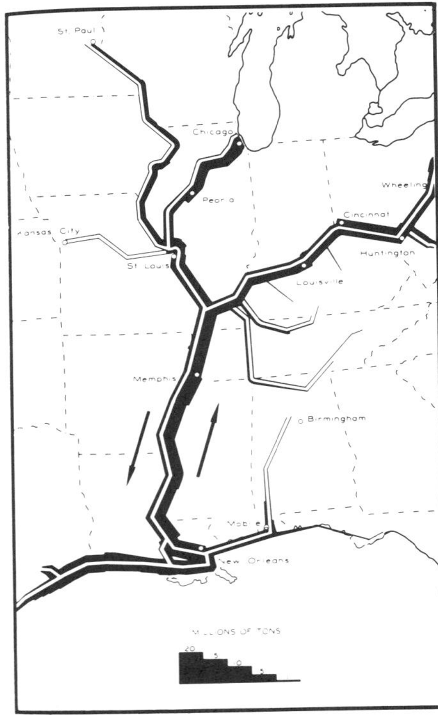

a

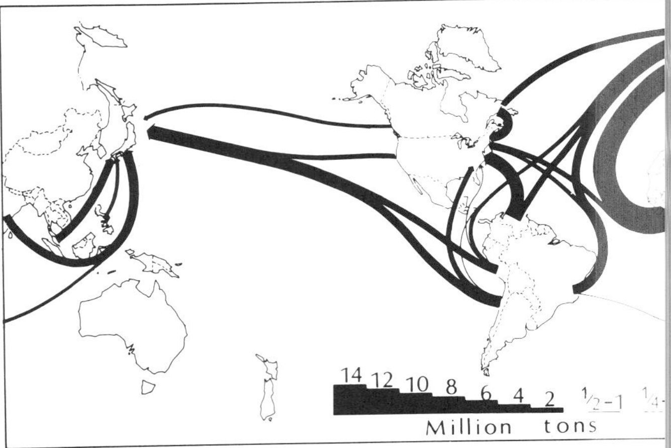

b

25-20. Examples of flow maps, both drawn with pen-and-ink. *(a)* *Commodity Flow*, by E. L. Ullman (University of Washington Pr… G. B. Lewis. From "Transport Costs, Freight Rates and the Cha… Geography of Iron Ore," by G. Manners (*Geography* 52 [1967]: 2…

The most common quantitative line symbol is the isoline, or isarithm, connecting points of equal value through a three-dimensional plane (fig. 25-21). And the most common isolines include the isobath (the depth below sea level), isohypse or contour (the height above sea level), isotherm (temperature), isobar (atmospheric pressure), and isohyet (precipitation). These are just a few of numerous terms; others include anything that varies across a statistical surface, such as isogene (density of a genus) and isospecie (density of a species).

Before an isoline map is designed and executed, the data must be collected. Proper data collection is equally important for other types of mapping, but the look of an isoline map is more profoundly changed as the data collection methodology changes. Figure 25-22 shows three different isoline maps of the same topic and area produced simply by increasing the number of data points and simultaneously increasing the accuracy of the display. A point of diminishing returns occurs when collecting

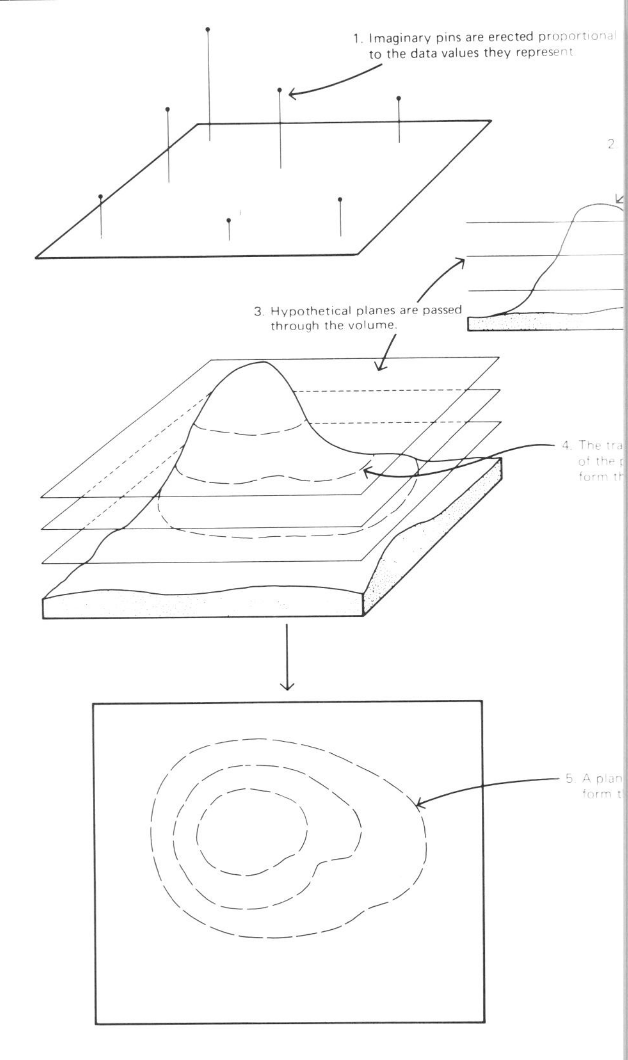

25-21. The conceptual development of an isarithmic map. Fro… by B. D. Dent (Addison-Wesley, 1985).

data, so a balance between cost and accuracy should be attempted. The scatter of data points affects the look and accuracy of maps of the same region and theme as well. Data points may be scattered in a random, clustered, or systematic array (or some combination thereof), any of which might be perfect for the job. Knowledge of the physical or statistical landscape being mapped would greatly help in the correct choice of the data scatter. More detailed information appears in *Elements of Cartography*, mentioned earlier, and in *Method Produced Error in Isarithmic Mapping*, by J. L. Morrison (see Bibliography).

After the data are received or collected, the next step is to plot the isolines. This process can be rather tedious since seemingly ambiguous problems such as that illustrated in figure 25-23a occur frequently. As is seen in figure 25-23b, however, the problem of isoline layout is easily resolved. With relatively few data points, plotting the lines by hand is appropriate; but more often a large number of data points exists, and then a computer can plot the lines more efficiently.

Design conventions for isolines suggest that each line be drafted relatively thinly; sometimes every fifth line is made thicker to serve as a reference line. Isolines should be labeled systematically and frequently enough to spare the map reader too much searching (fig. 25-24). On the other hand, closely spaced isolines need not all be numbered, so take care to avoid over- as well as underlabeling.

25-22. Three isoline plots of the same subject and location, but with successively more data points. The top plot uses 25 points, the middle plot uses 100 points, and the bottom plot uses 225 points. Computer printout from *Elements of Cartography*, 5th ed., by A. H. Robinson et al. (John Wiley and Sons, 1984).

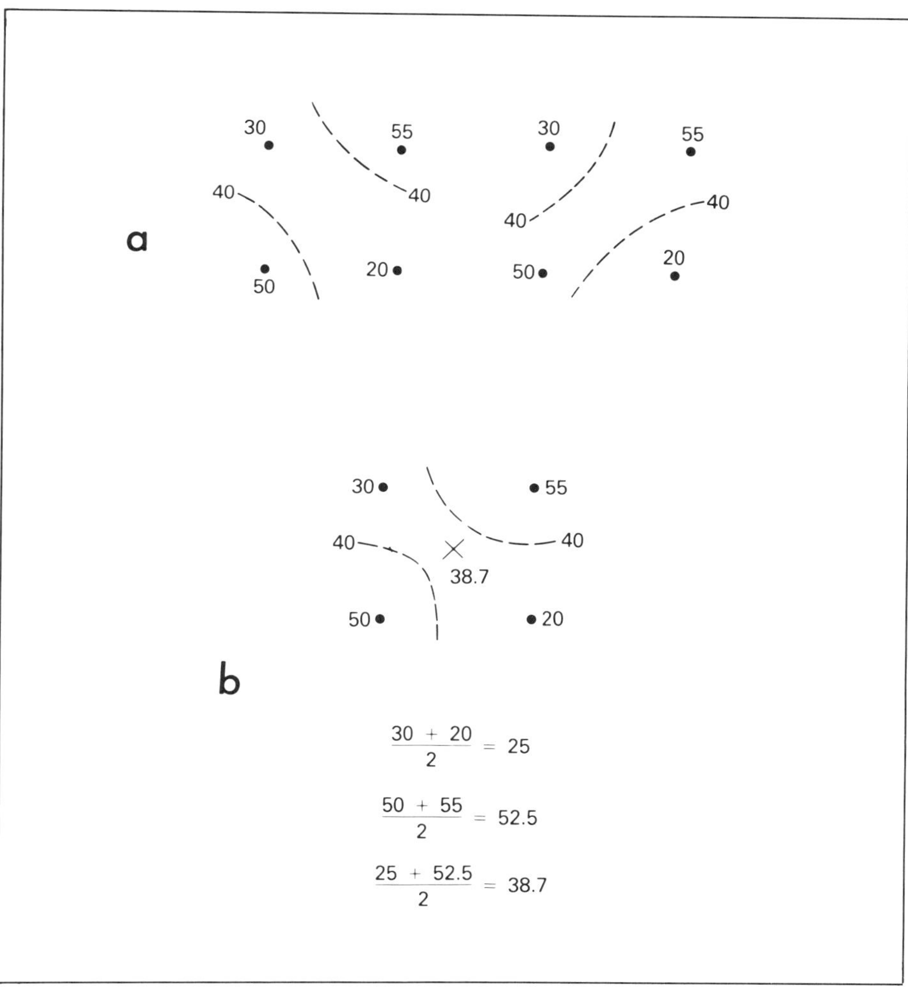

25-23. When two opposite data points have higher values (in this case, 50 and 55) than two other opposite points (20 and 30), arranged in a square pattern, two interpolations are possible *(a)*. The solution *(b)* lies in averaging opposite pairs to determine an intermediate value, then using that value to determine where the contour lines go. From *Thematic Map Design*, by B. D. Dent (Addison-Wesley, 1985).

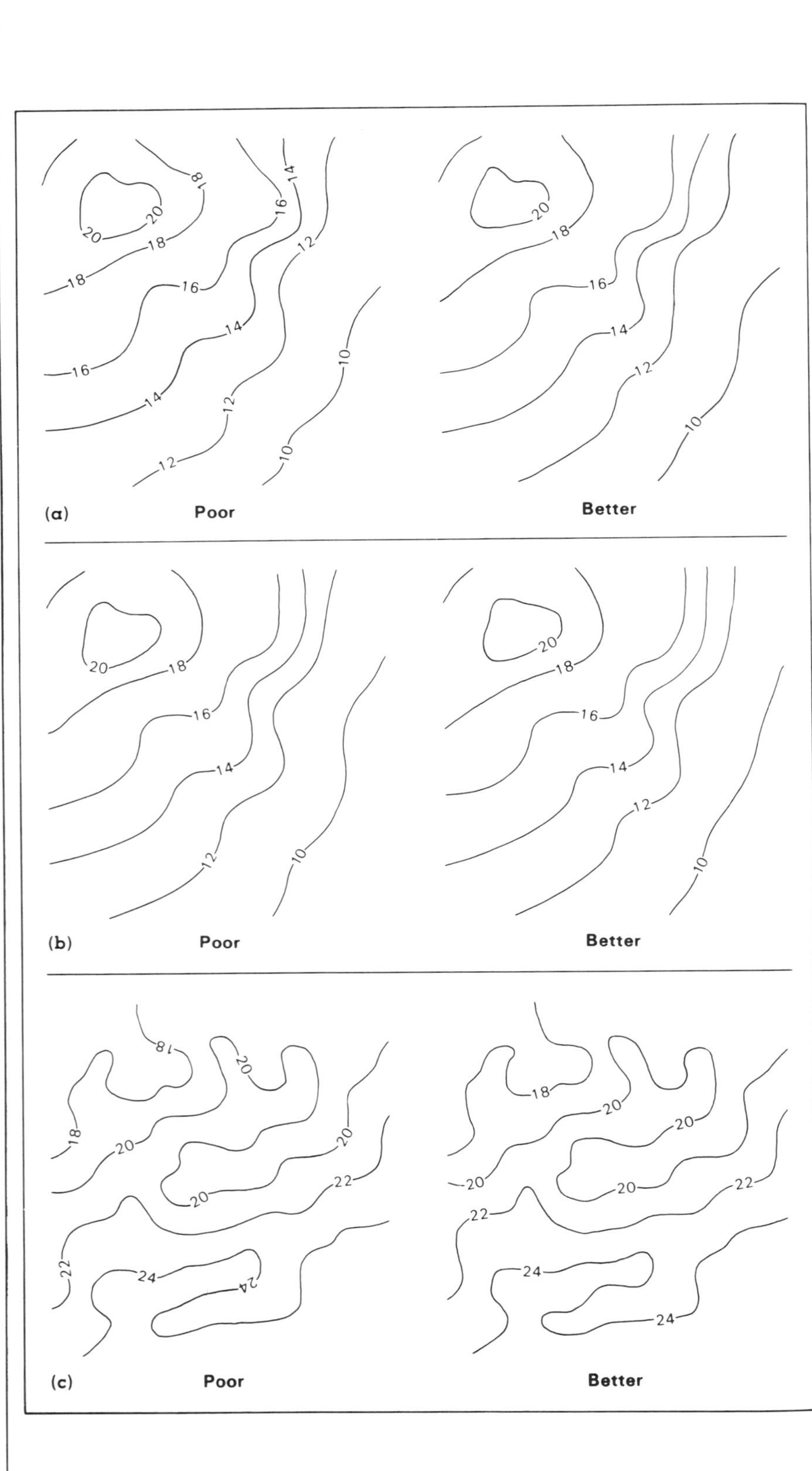

25-24. Design alternatives for labeling isolines. From *Thematic Map Design*, by B. D. Dent (Addison-Wesley, 1985).

MAPPING O

Areal Mappi
Data

The types o
topic include
cultures, lan
land covers,
ogy, zoogeogr
raphy. In ge
exist for por
categories of
ing a wide rar
patterns, anc
Colors are a
that may ofte
variations of
ure 25-25 por
numerous c
patterns avai
that are suit
gross-looking
tures, such a
lines and do
and money.
single patter
extra symbo
26).

Several ru
the use of to
ity of patte
qualitative m

1. Avoid usi
tones bec
as more
2. Use dark
regions t
from get
3. Use the
largest a
regions
map.
4. Moderat
map so
dominat

Unavoida
lapping sym
itative ma
methods of
25-27): inte
somewhat
cult to draf
which ofter
bol rather

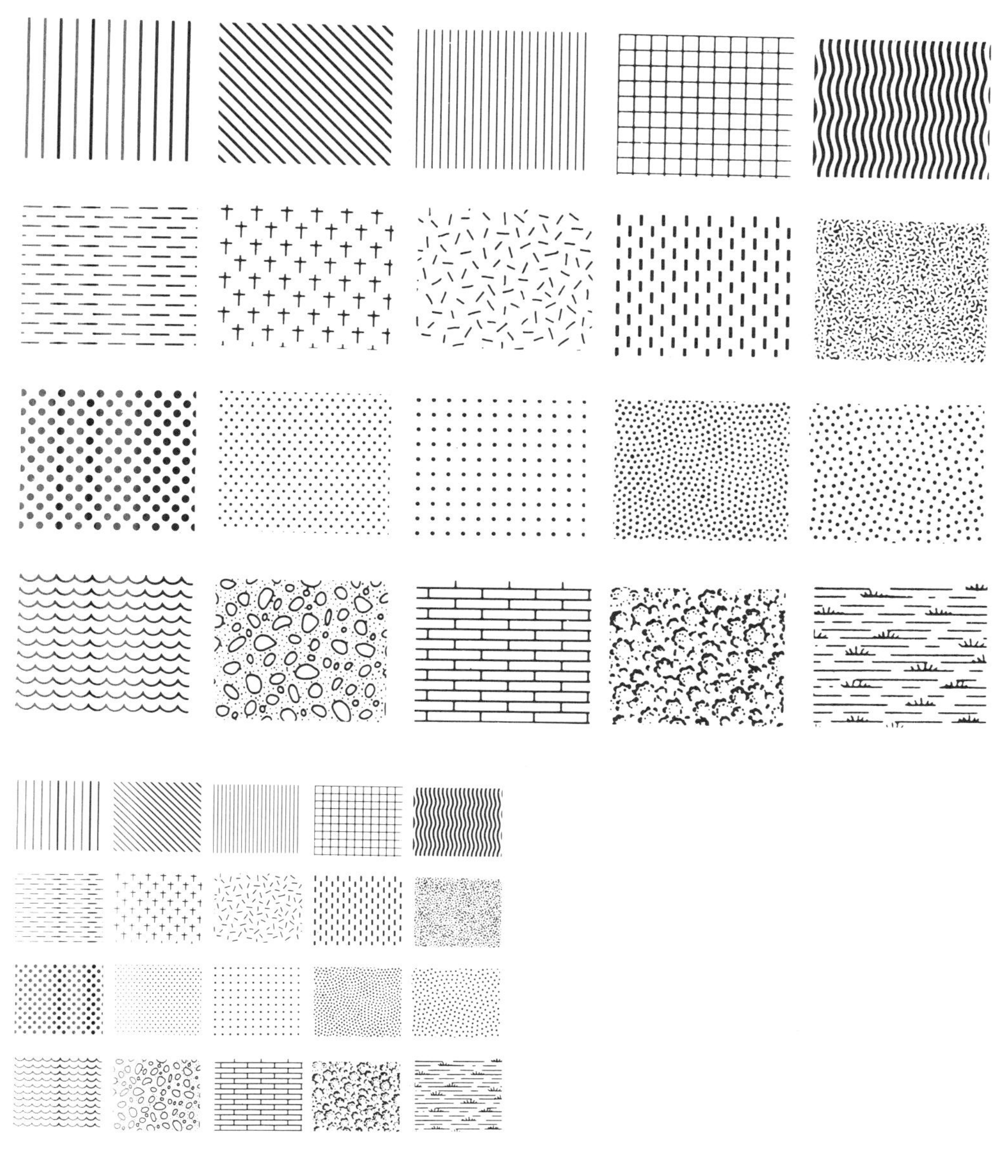

25-25. A variety of common patterns and textures at 100 percent and 50 percent reduction. These patterned shading films are available as preprinted adhesive sheets or in photographic negative forms. Layout by Alice R. Tangerini from shading film samples.

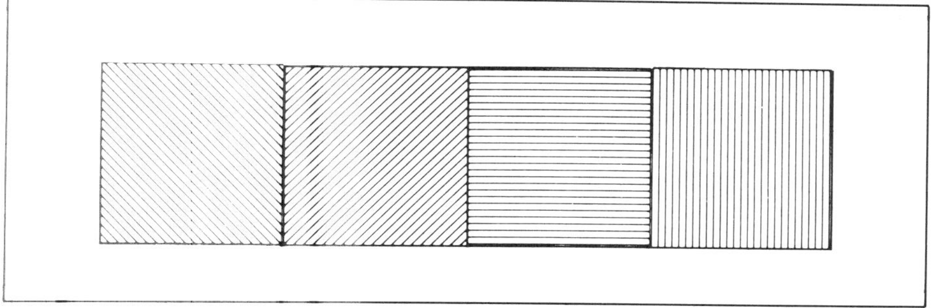

25-26. Reorientation of a single pattern. From *Elements of Cartography*, 5th ed., by A. H. Robinson et al. (John Wiley and Sons, 1984).

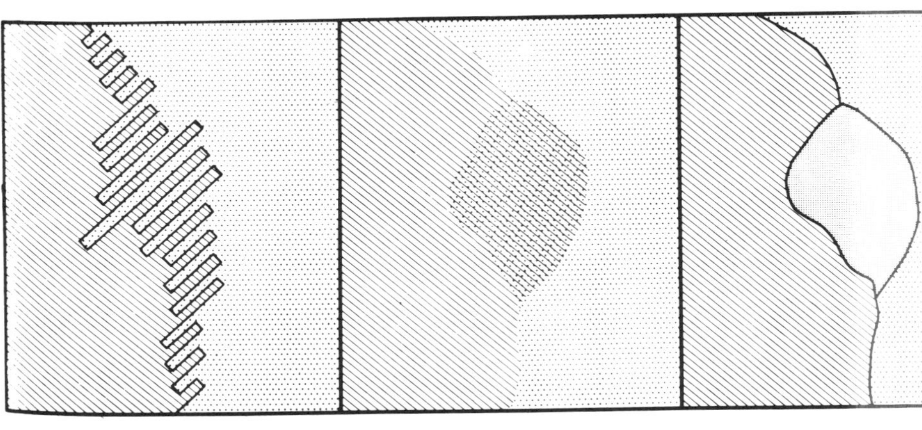

25-27. Several methods of showing geographical mixture or overlap with area symbols. From left to right: interdigitation; overlap of symbols; area of mixture symbolized. From *Elements of Cartography*, 5th ed., by A. H. Robinson et al. (John Wiley and Sons, 1984).

lapping; and the creation of a new symbol. The second and third options require adding extra overlap categories in the legend to lessen reader confusion. Unfortunately, if the map has more than just a few categories, the resulting legend will be quite large and complex. There are advantages and disadvantages to each method, so choose carefully for each situation.

Areal Mapping of Quantitative Data

Choropleth mapping is the statistical portrayal of quantitative differences between areal units. Before designing and producing a choropleth map, consider what to do with the data given. The use of raw data must never be portrayed. For example, if the data concern deer population, merely mapping the number of deer within a county or state is unacceptable. Instead, transform the data to the number per square kilometer or mile to indicate density. Transforming raw number data to ratio data allows greater accuracy and truthfulness with the graphic presentation of the data because different-size areas having identical distributions would be shown differently if raw data were used (fig. 25-28).

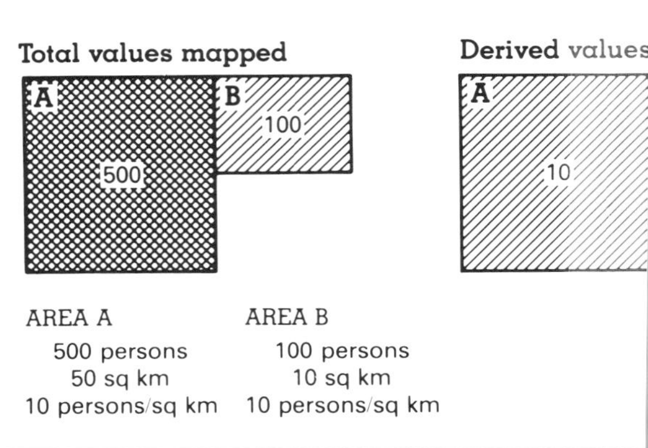

25-28. Mapping data totals masks even densities because the
From *Principles of Thematic Map Design*, by B. D. Dent (Ad

The next step involves classing the transformed data. The particular classing system chosen must be accurate and readable and reflect the distribution of the data. A number of classing methods exist, including equal interval (for example, 1 to 10, 11 to 20, 21 to 30), equal number (quantiles), and natural breaks. The first two methods are arbitrary regarding the data. Neither environment nor human-related activities often, if ever, fall into such neat categories. Rather, a more accurate method of data classification is to array the data and look for the natural gaps or breaks in the figures. These breaks become the points of class separa-

tion (such a
19, 19. 20.
one step fu
accuracy a
the numbe
classes wou
and 31 to
data in an
as 0 to 15.
would dist
tion of the
not only to
but also wh

Logically
lates to the
most gener
class, is t
least comp
ized map, c

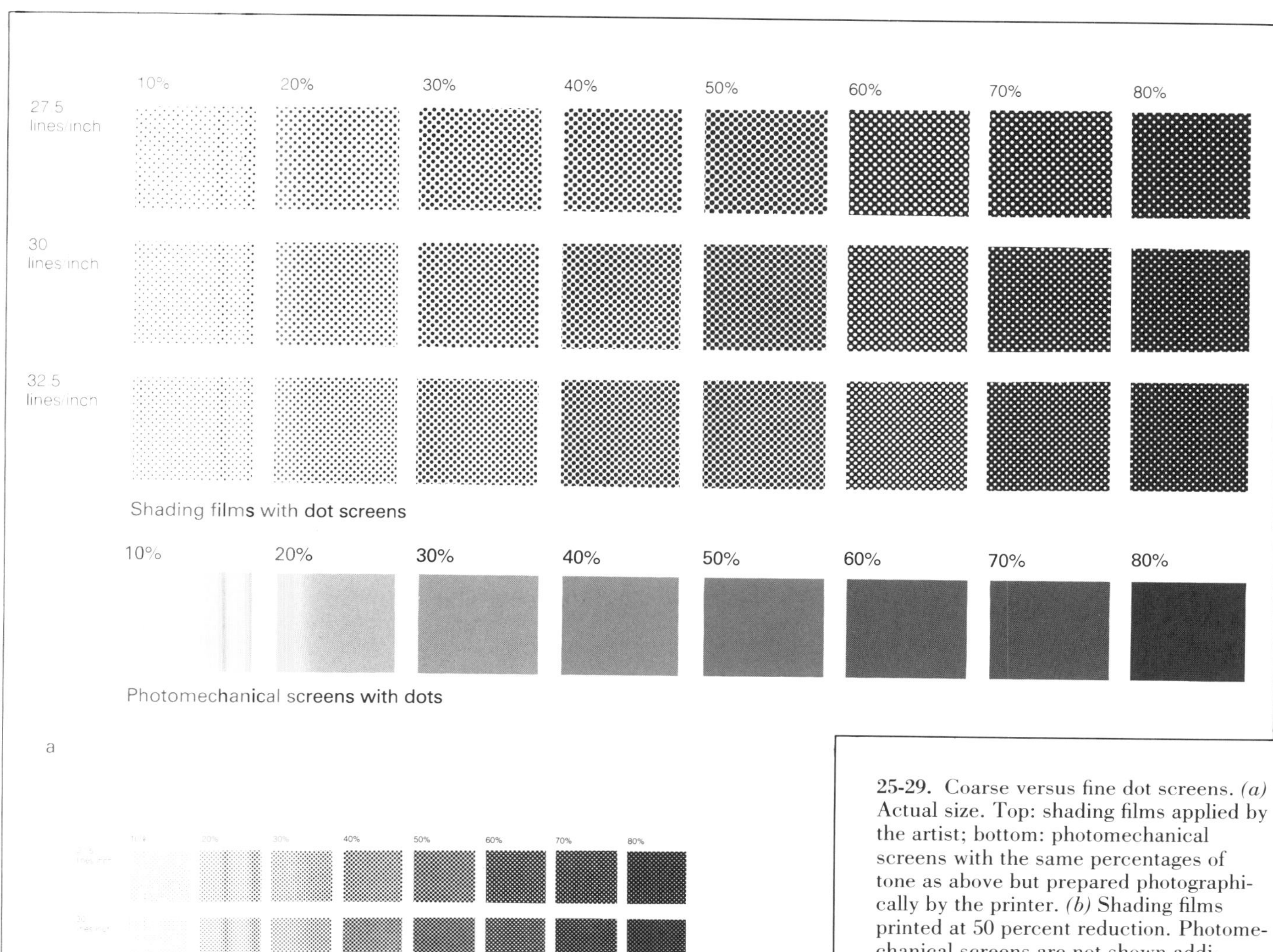

25-29. Coarse versus fine dot screens. *(a)* Actual size. Top: shading films applied by the artist; bottom: photomechanical screens with the same percentages of tone as above but prepared photographically by the printer. *(b)* Shading films printed at 50 percent reduction. Photomechanical screens are not shown additionally reduced because they would be prepared according to the artist's or designer's instructions to fit the finished reduction of the artwork, not reduced with it. In the higher dot percentages and line densities, the dots tend to merge. Layout by Alice R. Tangerini.

curate and most complex. If a classless choropleth map is desired, ignore the above paragraph on classing methodology; but a computer plotter or electrostatic printer will be required to produce such a map. The human hand and the photographic screening process are not so capable at this time. If, on the other hand, complexity and accuracy are to be balanced with generalization, the number of classes recommended falls into the range of five to seven.

Once the classing system and the number of classes are chosen, it is necessary to decide how to symbolize the data. Tones are preferred to patterns and textures for illustrating low to high volumes. Further, the finer the tone, the better; fine photomechanical dot screens (120-line or higher) are preferred to coarse preprinted adhesive dot screens (85-line or lower) (fig. 25-29). Cartographic convention dictates that light tones are indicative of low values and, conversely, dark tones indicative of high values. Five- or seven-class maps could have the following screen percentages, respectively: 0, 10, 30, 60, 100 and 0, 5, 15, 30, 50, 80, 100. Following the above guidelines for data classification and portrayal gives the overall map a more aesthetic professional appearance and also enhances its readability.

COLOR

Since the invention of color printing, colors seem to be used with reckless abandon to portray all sorts of data on maps. *Cartographic Design and Production*, by J. S. Keates (see Bibliography) notes that the "apparent need for more colors stems not from the complexity of map information, but from the cartographer's inability to make the most effective use of the available palette." So always decide first whether colors are necessary. A two-color choropleth map (black and one color) exhibiting changes in value is not often used because it merely provides an expensive way of showing what a black-and-white gray-tone map could show. But in other respects, colors are quite versatile in portraying a wide variety of data. For instance, using colors with patterns is a requirement in geologic mapping, which has voluminous categories.

Colors are of great help in further establishing a visual hierarchy. Think of a mass of black lines of varying thickness and tone symbolizing boundaries, rivers, coasts, roads, railroads, contours, and transmission lines. Now visualize those same lines in black, blue, red, and brown; the distinctions among them are more evident.

A number of considerations must be kept in mind when choosing colors:

1. Visibility, contrast, and figure-ground: dark and light colors should be used in the same manner as dark versus light gray tones.
2. Association of color with subject: blue = water, brown = land, green = vegetation.
3. Individuality of hues: hues such as blue, green, red, yellow, brown, black, and white should serve as classes while colors such as turquoise, purple, and orange can serve as class mixtures.
4. Final printing stock: if the paper is not pure white, it will alter the color scheme.
5. Convention: for hypsometric (color-coded contour) maps, colors progress from black-blue for very deep water to light blue for the shallows, greens for the lowlands, progressing through yellows and buffs for middle elevations to reds, purples, and finally white at the highest mountaintops.
6. Value and chroma: most colors when screened cannot be seen in as many tints as black, so caution must be exercised when using color on a choropleth map. If the quantitative range depicted is double-ended—that is, values progress in opposing directions—use a color scheme such as dark red to light red for decreasing positive numbers, white for zero, and light blue to dark blue for increasing negative numbers. If spectral colors are used, the wisest low-to-high-value progressions to use would be yellow-green-blue-violet or yellow-orange-red-violet, because these colors progress from light to dark and are associated with low-to-high values, respectively.

Overall, the choice of colors should be systematic in enhancing the display while avoiding garish color combinations and contrasts.

In choosing colors, the Pantone Matching System (PMS) printing colors frequently are warranted. For example, brown, which often is used to symbolize land, is a difficult color to produce through overlapping of colored inks by the printer. Specifying a particular PMS brown to the printer permits the use of a premixed ink. (Additional information on color production appears in chapter 27.)

RELIEF REPRESENTATION

Nine choices exist for portraying the physical landscape: simple contour (isoline), hypsometric contour, Tanaka
lief, hachured
physical profil
agrams, and bl

Isoline

A simple co
already has be
chapter. Addi
erations inclu
tour interval
abrupt chang
landscape) an
of a contou
U.S.G.S. has
index—every
thicker; inte
width of the
mentary—ver
dotted; de
ticks are adde
down-slope; c
represents se
lines for cliffs
interpolated—

Hypsometri

Designing
contour map
choices (or c
the vertical in
ods also may
and-white iso
ble. An equi
that required
map, is effec
elevation ra
variation. F
with supplem
applicable t
where areas
twice as ma
high ground
that vary w
slope are su
maps with w
progressive i
geometric) a
maps.

Tanaka

Tanaka c
for their inve
tween simple
relief maps. I

25-30. Map with illuminated contours of a volcanic landscape in Japan, by K. Tanaka. Courtesy of the *Geographical Review*, 1950.

25-31. A portion of a small-scale, vertically viewed map incorporating hill shading with pencil on stipple board, by John L. Ridgway (see fig. 25-32). From *Scientific Illustration*, by John L. Ridgway, 1938. By permission of Stanford University Press.

how this method makes use of theoretically illuminated and shaded contours. The illumination is always from the upper left or upper right corner, and typically at a 45-degree angle of height. The map has a gray screened background with white contours in the imagined sunlight and black contours in the shade. Ignoring possible shadows from hilltops to opposing valley sides enables the cartographer to blacken in those contours on the shaded sides of valleys by delineating the black-white contour divisions with a 45-degree angle triangle.

Shaded

Shaded relief, whether done with an airbrush or a pencil, requires training and skill (fig. 25-31). The most common shading method combines both slope and oblique shading. Here, the basic rule is that the steeper the slope, the darker the shade, while contrasting slightly the lee-side versus the "sunny"-side slopes. This method allows for some slight shading to represent slopes on the sunny sides and prevents features from being totally hidden by shadows on the lee sides.

First, decide upon the location of the light source both in terms of the light's elevation angle (zenith) and orientation angle (azimuth). Traditionally, the elevation angle is 45 degrees (lower for low terrain) and the orientation angle is from one of the top corners of the map. In this way, shadows fall toward the map reader, preventing topographic inversion that results when illumination comes from one of the lower corners of the map.

The skill to produce a shaded relief map, along with an excellent geomorphological understanding of the landscape, eludes most cartographers. A century ago, equations were worked out concerning light intensity reaching the surface. The equations were only theoretical until computers were invented. Now it is relatively quick and easy to produce shaded relief maps with computers. Automated shading requires elevation data from a data point array that is interpolated from contour maps or photogrammetrically interpreted from aerial photographs. Simply, the computer begins by calculating the gradient at each data point in the array. Given an illumination from the northeast, the computer determines the slope in a west-east direction and a south-north direction. Then, given the orientation and elevation angles, a gray tone for each data point is calculated and printed.

Hachures

Lines or strokes, called hachures, also are used to represent relief. Drafting a hachure map involves six basic rules, according to *Cartographic Methods*, by G. R. Lawrence (see Bibliography):

1. The hachures must be drawn in the direction of maximum slope.
2. Hachures must be arranged in rows, not down the entire slope.
3. The length and thickness of each stroke must approximate an equal drop in height—that is, a series of short, thick strokes illustrate a short, steep slope; longer, thinner strokes indicate a long, gentler gradient.
4. Spacing is uniform for any one slope class.
5. The thickness of each stroke must be constant for each slope class.
6. If the slope is illuminated, lines are less thick overall for "sunlit" areas (fig. 25-32).

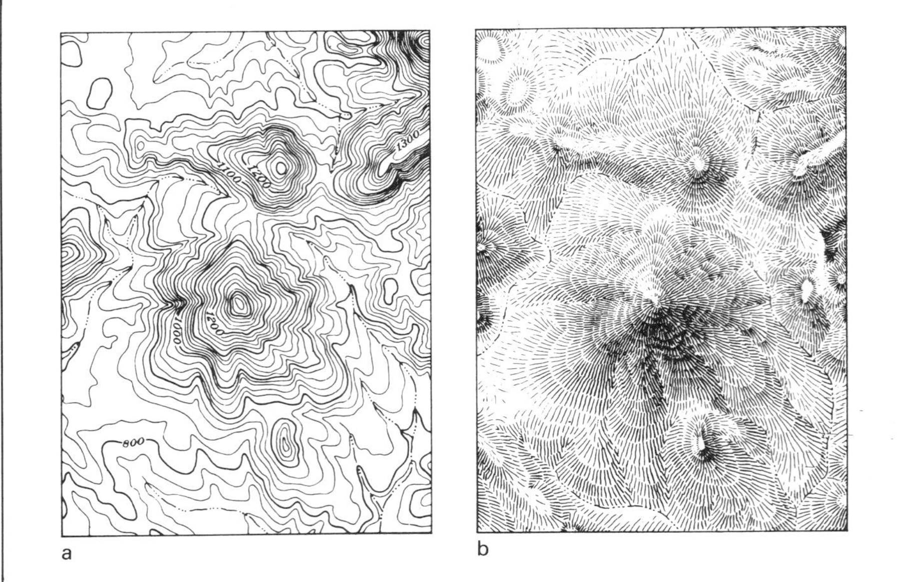

25-32. A section of a topographic map that portrays the land surface form with *(a)* contour lines and *(b)* obliquely illuminated hachuring. Pen-and-ink, by John L. Ridgway (see fig. 25-31). From *Scientific Illustration*, by John L. Ridgway, 1938. By permission of Stanford University Press.

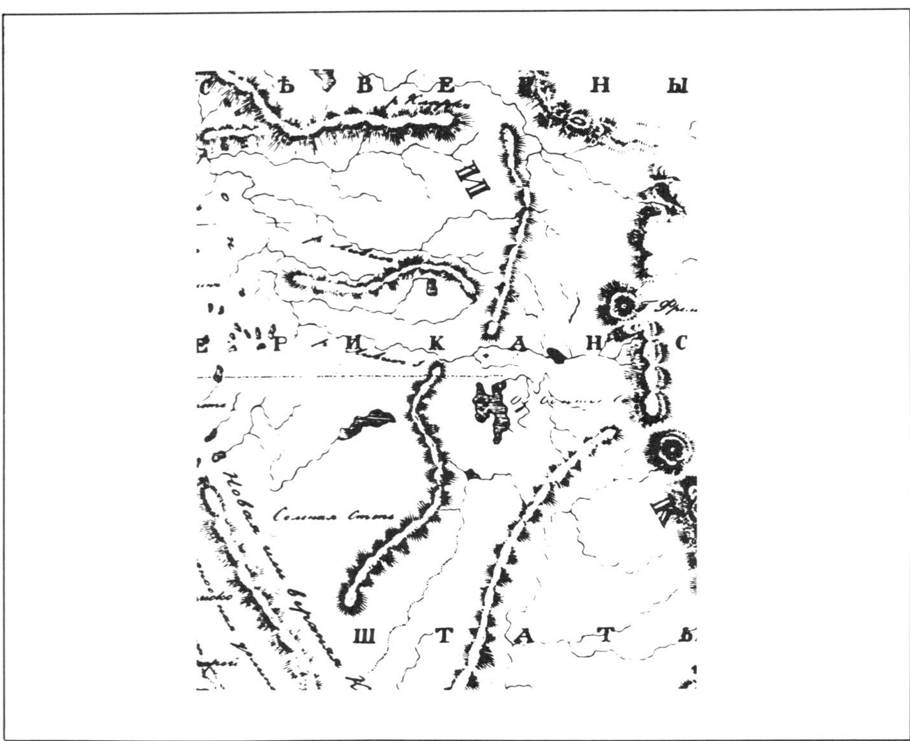

25-33. Portion of a "caterpillar" hachure map from an old Russian atlas of western North America. Pen-and-ink. From *Elements of Cartography*, 5th ed., by A. H. Robinson et al. (John Wiley and Sons, 1984).

Hachures are not as popular as they were a century ago, partly because their standing was degraded by the production of "caterpillar" maps, which give the reader no understanding of mountains' characteristics (fig. 25-33). In addition, hachures are not quantitatively measureable, but they can accurately portray slope.

Slope

A slope zon
tempt to portra
kind of illum
classes varying
one of three w
meters per ki
percentage slo
qualitative ter
ing, moderate,

Physical

Physical p
models exag
method usuall
smaller areas.
simply built by
races from ma
faces, gluing
applying a co
of varying th
painting the m
tion would be
dimensional m
haps for an ex

Physiograph

Physiograph
shaded relief.
of artistry as
comprehensio
landscape. Ve
siographic dia
tray the lands
an aerial ph
image, or they
cally emphasi
the landscape

Block Diagr

An incline
diagram has q
of applications
primary applic
ogy/geomorph
physiographic
above and ben
face. Other fie
block diagram
ogy, oceanog
architecture,
which provid
views of the su
isometric-orth

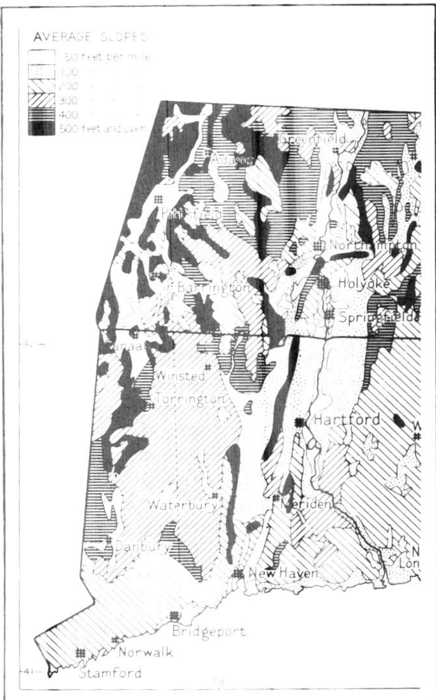

25-34. Portion of a slope zone map of part of southern New England. The areas of similar slope were derived by noting areas of consistent contour spacing on topographic maps. Adhesive patterns, pen-and-ink. Courtesy of the *Geographical Review*.

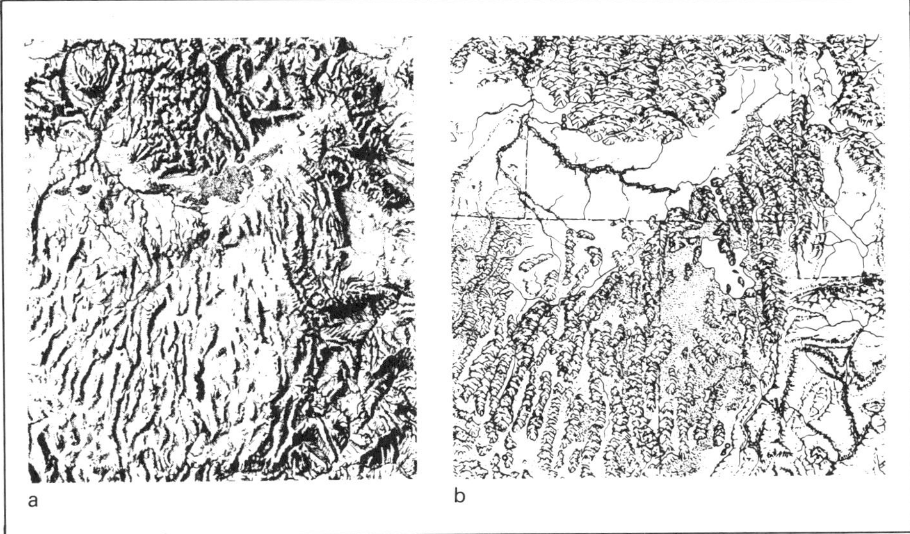

25-36. Physiographic diagrams. *(a)* A relatively realistic portrayal of the region around Great Salt Lake (just to the right of center) and the Snake River valley, drawn by R. E. Harrison for the *National Atlas of the United States*. *(b)* The same area from A. K. Lobeck, "Physiographic Diagram of the United States," which employs a schematic treatment to emphasize the geomorphic characteristics. Courtesy of Geographical Press, Hammond Company.

Below:
25-35. Portion of the experimental Richmond, Virginia, percentage slope map, 1:24,000, prepared by the United States Geological Survey. Scribe sheets, peel coats, and photomechanical patterns. From *Elements of Cartography*, 5th ed., by A. H. Robinson et al. (John Wiley and Sons, 1984).

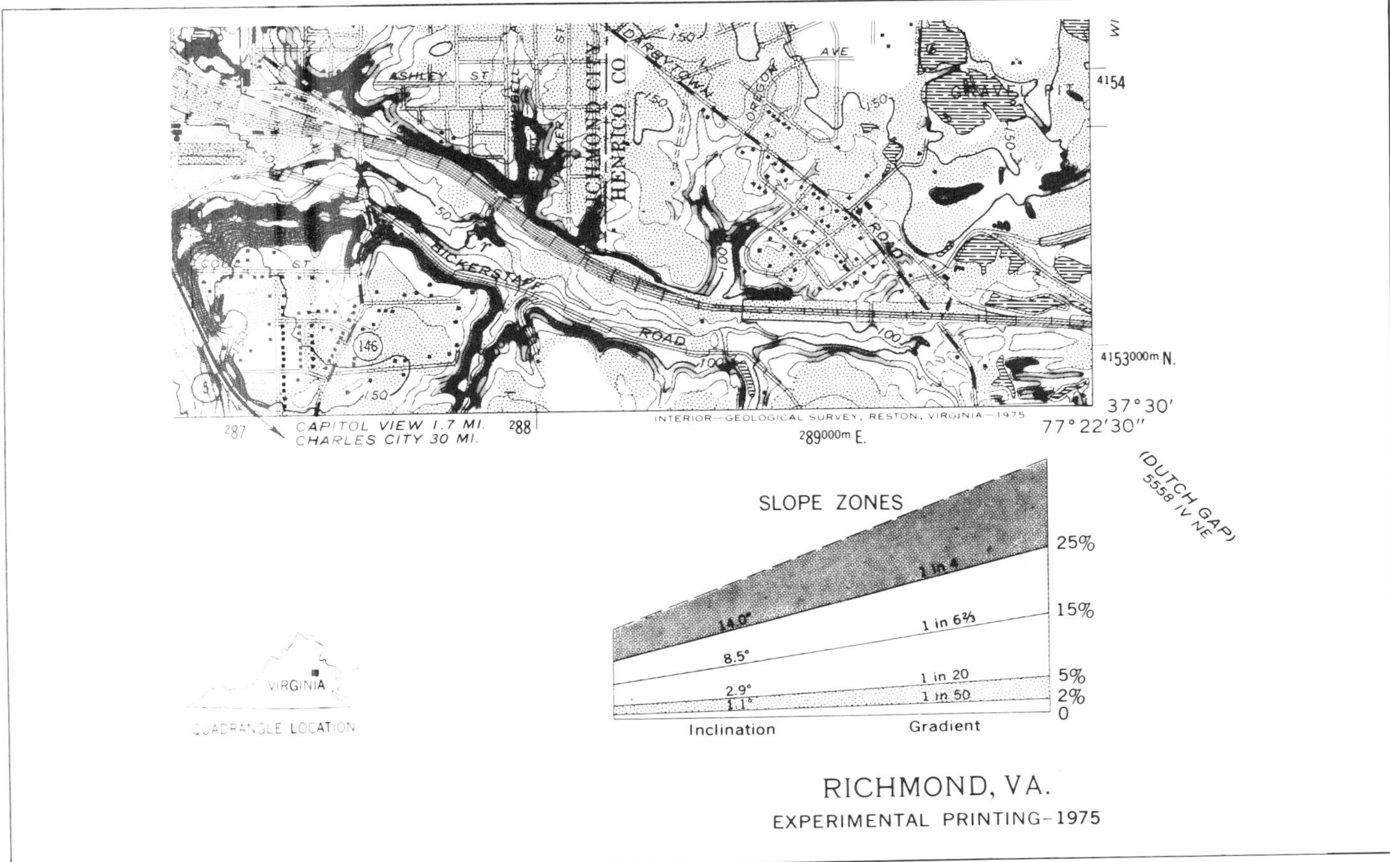

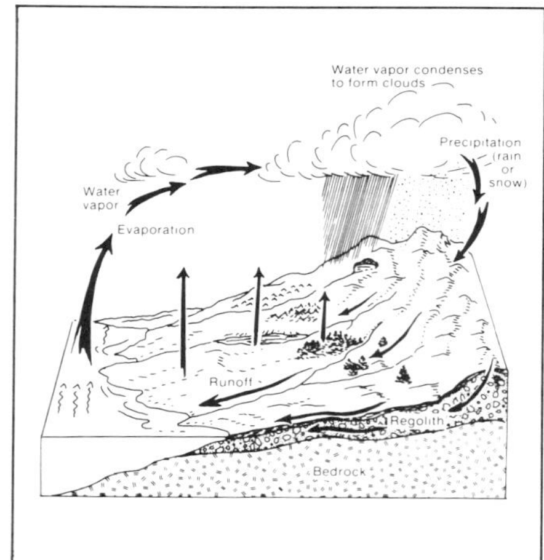

25-37. Block diagram illustrating the hydrological cycle. Technical pen and ink and shading film on Cronaflex film, by Rosemary Nothwanger © 1984.

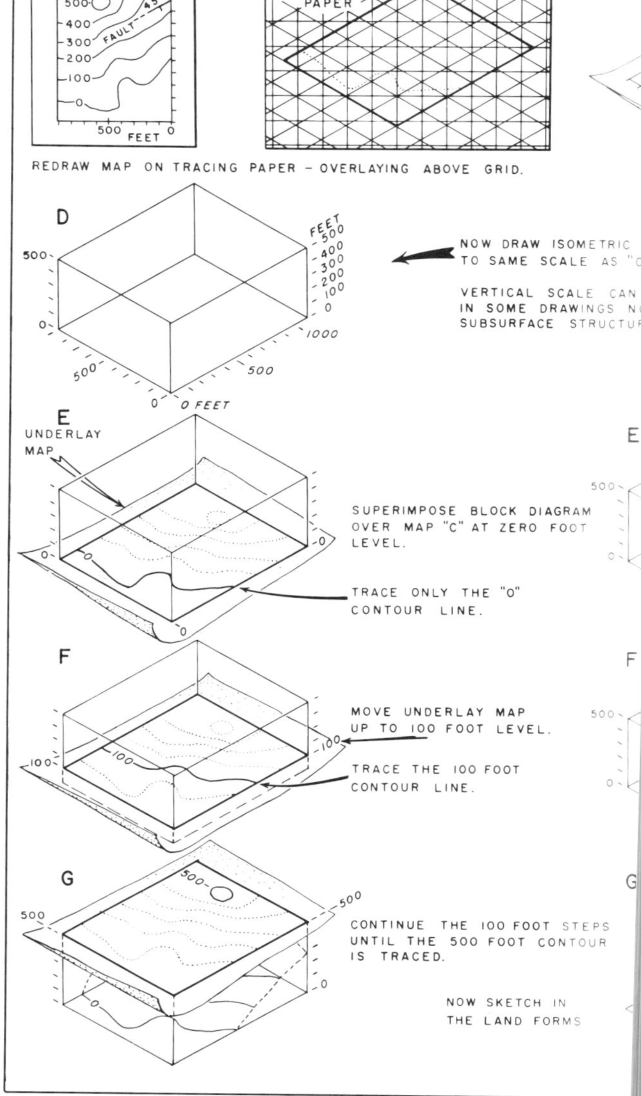

25-38. Construction steps of a surface portion of a block diagram. Pen-and-ink, by Donald B. Sayner. From *Drawing for Scientific Illustrations: Maps, Graphs, Diagrams*, by Donald B. Sayner and Gladys Bennett Menhennet (University of Arizona, 1969).

like figure 25-37, follow the step-by-step procedures outlined in figures 25-38 and 25-39. Whether transferring surface information to an isometric projection or subsurface information to the raised block diagram, it is necessary to work carefully, using the similar-squares (grid) method. With the possible exception of sketching the landforms, this entire procedure can be easily accomplished by any experienced draftsperson. Again, the computer will depict almost any surface phenomena while simultaneously altering the viewing distance, elevation, and orientation angles.

For a more accurate view of the landscape, a vanishing-point perspective is called for. This procedure necessitates the use of a Lawson Perspective Chart, as shown in figure 25-40 (see Bibliography). Except for the different look of the landscape, the methodology is much the same as outlined for the standard block diagrams. A block diagram with vanishing-point perspective is not used as often as standard block diagrams, even though it is more accurate, because items in the ba "shrunk" to

Some sc draw few m produce ma their care knowledge ventions to niques that efficient w graphic an make the cate its mes

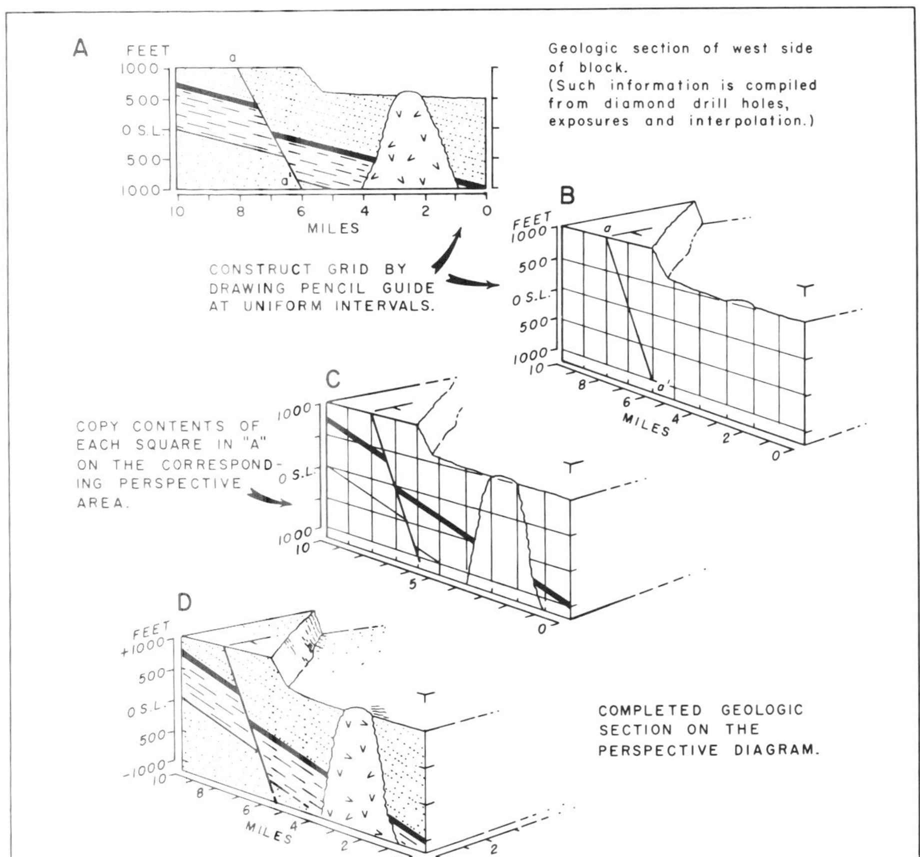

25-39. Construction steps of the side portion of a block diagram. Pen-and-ink, by Donald B. Sayner. From *Drawing for Scientific Illustrations: Maps, Graphs, Diagrams*, by Donald B. Sayner and Gladys Bennett Menhennet (University of Arizona, 1969).

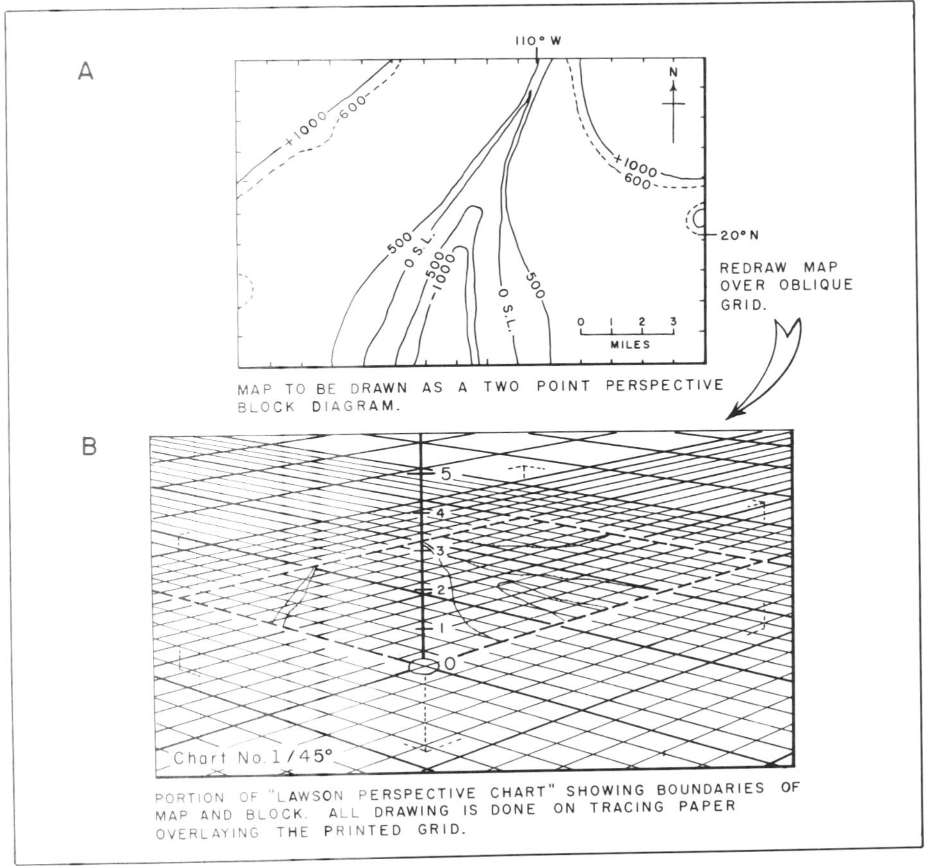

25-40. Construction steps of a vanishing-point perspective block diagram. Pen-and-ink, by Donald B. Sayner. From *Drawing for Scientific Illustrations: Maps, Graphs, Diagrams*, by Donald B. Sayner and Gladys Bennett Menhennet (University of Arizona, 1969).

26/Copy Photography

Chip Clark and Lloyd E. Logan

Of the numerous photographic techniques available to the scientific illustrator, those used most frequently are for the copying of original illustrations. These photographic copies often are intended for the artist's portfolio, for mailing to a prospective client, or for use in a presentation when the original art is unavailable.

The fundamentals of copy photography are straightforward and apply to all aspects of copying; other, more specialized techniques are discussed under Specific Applications, below.

EQUIPMENT

Camera: preferably 35mm single-lens reflex with built-in light meter. These versatile cameras offer superb image quality at modest cost.

Lenses: macro—preferred for copy photography. Not only do macro lenses focus closer than standard lenses, allowing better composition in photographing small original art, but they are designed to give their best results in this close-up range, whereas standard lenses are corrected for optical infinity. And because macro lenses are flat-field lenses, they provide a uniformly sharp focus across a flat plane, which is ideal for copying flat artwork. These features generally increase the cost of a macro lens compared to a standard lens, but the increased sharpness and reduced geometric distortion are worth the investment.

If macro lenses are unavailable, standard lenses can be used—with the introduction of some loss of sharpness, reduction of contrast, and distortion. A normal-focal-length lens (50mm) will probably yield the best results of any standard lens; avoid using the zoom lenses that have a "macro" setting; they typically have severely curved planes of focus and large amounts of geometric distortion.

Film: black-and-white—Kodak Technical Pan for linework, Kodak T-Max 100 and similar ones for continuous-tone art; color—Kodak VRG-100, Kodachrome 25, Kodak Ektachrome Professional 50 (EPY), Kodak Kodachrome 40 (KPA), depending upon the kind of lighting and whether prints or slides are needed (see Specific Applications below). Color slide film can be used to make slides of black-and-white artwork.

Copy stand: for proper positioning of the camera and artwork. A copy stand, designed for photocopying, is excellent, but equally good results can be produced by using a tripod and easel, or just a tripod and a wall.

Cable release: strongly recommended for minimizing vibration when making an exposure.

Kodak Gray Card: to determine the proper exposure. These cards are available in photographic stores for several dollars each—probably the last inexpensive photo accessory in the world.

Lights: to illuminate artwork. Photographic floodlights and light stands are best if a large volume of art is to be copied or future heavy use is anticipated. For the occasional photocopy project, sunlight or desk lamps can suffice.

Tripod: a sturdy one, for supporting the camera.

BASIC COP
TECHNIQU

Successful
involves thre
ment, comp
Regardless
simplicity of
these three
fied; the fo
with these fa
later section
niques and f
of illustration

Alignment

The artwo
a flat plane.
paper or
stated, the
camera mu
plane of the
be located fa
work so tha
focus the im
film. In pra
era must be
tical axis is
plane of the

In a ver
alignment i
stands are
camera sup
to the copy
fixed on th
with the l
down (perp
work on the

Although
ideally sui
copying, it
piece of equ
worth its co
alignment
stand is ea
sturdy trip
support, eit

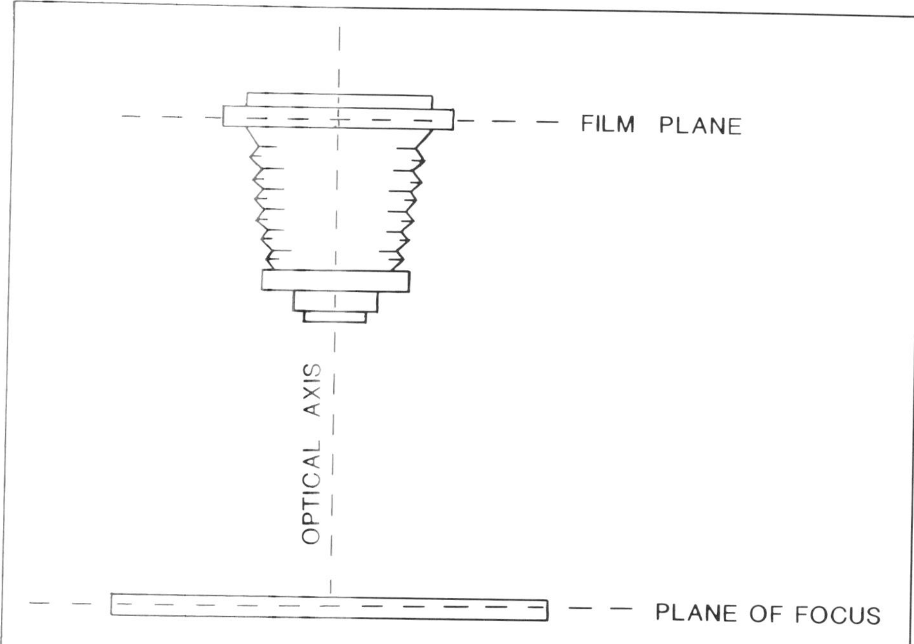

26-1. The relationship of the camera to the artwork. The camera's film plane must be parallel to the plane of the artwork. Technical pen on Denril polyester film, by Jennifer B. Clark © 1987.

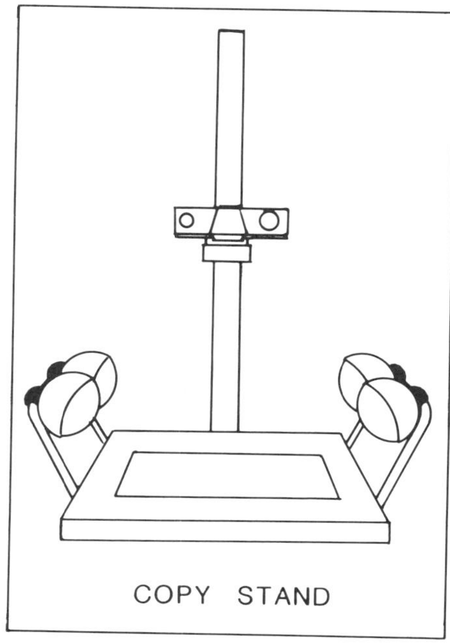

26-2. Camera copy stand with lights on each side of the artwork. Technical pen on Denril polyester film, by Jennifer B. Clark © 1987.

Tape the illustration to be copied to a board or easel or onto a flat wall; then arrange the camera on the tripod so that its optical axis is perpendicular to the center of the artwork. When alignment is perfect, the center of the camera's viewfinder screen should coincide exactly with the geometric center of the illustration, and the illustration should be symmetrical as seen through the viewfinder.

One easy technique for aligning the camera and artwork uses a flat mirror: if the mirror is placed on the copyboard where the artwork will be, the image seen through the perfectly aligned camera will be the center of the lens filling the exact center of the camera's viewfinder.

Any misalignment of the camera and artwork will introduce some degree of distortion into the photograph. For example, if the illustration was a square and the camera's optical axis was tilted from perpendicular (90 degrees) to 60 degrees, the square would record on film as a trapezoid. The focus would degrade across the image as well. The plane of focus would coincide with the plane of the illustration at only one point; everything closer or farther in the illustration from that one point would be out of focus.

Composition

In copy photography, especially with color slides, the image should fill the frame of the camera viewfinder. The photographic image should be as large as practical on the negative or slide, since the ability of films to record fine detail is dependent upon how much film area is utilized; the more film area an image covers, the greater the resolution of fine detail.

Composing the artwork in the viewfinder also will yield more aesthetically pleasing images. Mask off unwanted mounting board, type, and marginal notes by using strips of black or white paper or black velvet to produce a neat, uncluttered image.

Although images can be cropped and recomposed in the process of making the photographic print, efforts made to minimize blemishes and enhance composition in the copy photographic negative will further improve the final image. In color slides, the image seen through the viewfinder will be the exact image on the slide, since the film in the camera is processed and mounted in a slide mount directly, with no intermediate printing or processing step to allow corrections to be made. Color slides can benefit from masking of the original illustration with black velvet; the velvet reproduces as pure black in the final slide, leaving the image of the illustration floating in space, free of distracting borders, frames, or tape. If masking of the original art is impractical, the finished slide can be masked by the application of opaque tape on the slide itself, although this takes practice, steady hands, and often a new slide mount.

Exposure

The most difficult aspect of photography is the determination of the proper exposure. In copy photography, this is simplified by the use of the light meter in the camera and a Kodak Gray Card.

The camera's meter measures the intensity of the light entering the lens. By setting the proper value of the film's sensitivity to light (the ASA or ISO number of the film) on the appropriate dial of the camera, the light meter will display the proper settings of aperture (lens aperture, designated in f-stops) and shutter speed (designated in fractions of a second) to produce a proper exposure. A low ASA/ISO number means the film requires much more light to achieve proper exposure than a higher-number ASA/ISO film.

The light meter in the camera was designed and calibrated to produce correct exposures in most situations—taking pictures of "average subjects." This is when the Gray Card becomes indispensable; it is manufactured to reflect 18 percent of the light that falls upon it, which makes it identical to the reflectance of the "average subject." The Gray Card is thus a substitute "average subject."

In copy photography, the Gray Card is used to determine the correct exposure by placing it on top of the illustration to be copied and then measuring the light reflected from it.

Photographic Copying Procedure

Perfect copy photographs will result if the shot is set up with proper illumination, alignment, and exposure. Preparations for the shot take time, but the results are worth it.

Illumination

The illustration to be copied must be illuminated evenly; any variation in illumination will produce unevenness in the copy. The photographic process actually exaggerates unevenness, creating light and dark areas in the copy that the human eye could not detect in the original illustration. Even illumination is readily available outdoors on a sunny or lightly hazy day; indoors, it is necessary to use two lights of equal intensity, at equal distances from the artwork (usually located 45 degrees to each side of the camera's axis).

Preliminary Alignment

The camera should be affixed to the copy stand or tripod and positioned at the proper distance from the illustration to produce the desired composition, usually close enough to fill the viewfinder frame with the entire illustration.

Determining Exposure

A Gray Card placed directly on top of the illustration (with the gray side showing, of course) is subjected to the same illumination that will fall on the artwork. To determine correct exposure, turn on the camera's light meter so it will measure the light reflected from the Gray Card. Because many cameras meter any light that enters the lens, it is necessary to exclude any light but that reflected from the Gray Card. Do so by moving the camera from its proper location of perfect alignment closer to the artwork until the camera lens views only the Gray Card. During this operation, do not refocus the lens as the camera approaches the Gray Card; since the exposure determination does not involve focus, refocusing is unnecessary and will add a degree of error in the exposure. Also avoid casting shadows on the Gray Card, which would introduce large errors in the exposure.

Determining exposure in this way will provide a correct combination of aperture and shutter speed values for a perfect exposure. The correct settings represent a range of correct exposure values, however, any combination of which will produce a correct exposure. For example, one combination of aperture (f/8.0) and shutter speed (1/60 second) could produce as correct an exposure as another setting of values—f/5.6

and 1/125 sec
posure contro
speed, are ec
an increase
more light in
the aperture
—f/8.0 to f/5.
offset by a c
value (speed
ened to cut t
second). Th
and shutter s
tographer, a
consideratio

Lenses ha
ture at whic
macro lense
tures near f
are optimum
timum valu
rior sharpn
result.

Shutter s
second allo
the image.
avoided by
and copy st
release. Us
1/60 secon
mizes came

Taking the

Once yo
timum com
shutter spe
meter reac
reposition
illustration
artwork is
essary), ar
critical sha
release, tr
the film.

It is ad
correct ex
posures b
indicated
by changi
half f-sto
ensure tha
perfect, s
storage
chemistry
ton can in
the best e
extra film
bracket t

cheap insurance for producing a perfect negative or slide.

Multiples

If several illustrations of approximately the same size are to be copied, only one exposure measurement need be made. Once the proper exposure is set, the illustrations can be photographed and replaced by other illustrations: focus should be confirmed each time, but unless the lighting is changed or an illustration of a much larger or smaller size is introduced, no other exposure measurements need be made.

With black-and-white or color negative film (to make color prints), it is necessary to produce only one perfect copy negative. Any number of prints can be made from it by a competent photo laboratory. Color slides, however, are difficult to duplicate in any laboratory, and shifts in colors, sharpness, and graininess of the image frequently result. For this reason, when copying with color slide films, shoot many "original copy" slides of the illustration. Making multiple exposures in the copy camera is vastly cheaper than trying to obtain top-quality duplicates of a single perfect slide.

Reciprocity Failure

If the shutter times calculated for the proper exposure are in excess of one second, the shutter speed must be modified to compensate for a phenomenon called reciprocity failure. When films are exposed to faint light for relatively long times (seconds, usually) the light-sensitive silver-halide grains in the emulsion "forget" the total light they have received, resulting in underexposure of the film. To compensate for this reciprocity-failure effect, increase the exposure: the general rule of thumb is to double the exposure time for any exposure one second or longer. Therefore, a two-second exposure becomes four seconds, eight seconds become sixteen, and so forth. This rule applies to virtually all films in all long-exposure situations.

SPECIFIC APPLICATIONS

The choices of film, lighting, and processing are determined by the nature of the original illustration and the type of photographic copy desired as an end product. In some cases, the archival qualities of the copy will influence these choices, too.

Linework

Line illustrations are essentially black ink on white paper; there are no shades of gray, no tones, just black and white. Such an illustration frequently contains stippling or lines for shading, but no true grays.

By their very nature, line illustrations are "contrasty" and thus are copied best on high-contrast film. Kodak Technical Pan film, the current film of choice for line illustrations, is a black-and-white negative film suitable for prints. It has extremely fine grain structure, is capable of very high resolution of detail, and when developed in a high-contrast developer such as Kodak's D-19, produces a very high contrast negative. The negative can be used by a professional laboratory to make slides. The film is available from large photography stores in thirty-six-exposure rolls of 35mm film. It can be processed by any competent photo lab, or by the artist with the basic skills of home developing, using standard tanks and chemicals. Detailed information is available in Kodak pamphlet P-255.

Continuous Tone

Illustrations that contain gray values between pure black and pure white are called continuous tone. Some may contain a complete spectrum of gray values from a very pale off-white to a series of near-black, dark, rich tones. Any illustration that contains any gray values must be copied on continuous-tone film because the high-contrast films cannot reproduce intermediate values of gray; they can only record black and white.

The preferred films for continuous-tone copying are the normal black-and-white films used in everyday photography. The best results come from the fine-grained low-ASA/ISO films such as Kodak's T-Max 100. These films are processed in standard developers such as Kodak D-76 or Ilford ID-11 Plus.

This type of continuous-tone black-and-white film also is used when black-and-white negatives (and prints) are to be made from original color artwork.

Color

Copying color illustrations differs from copying black-and-white illustrations in one crucial detail: the light that illuminates the artwork must be matched with the specific color balance of the film. The standard measurement of this color balance of light sources and films in photography is called color temperature, given in degrees Kelvin (°K).

The Kelvin scale of temperature is borrowed from engineering and physics: the color temperature of a glowing object is a measurement of the temperature to which a theoretical colorless object would have to be heated to give off light of an identical color spectrum. Consider a sphere of black metal; if it were heated to higher and higher temperatures, it would begin to glow—first dull red, then orange, then yellow, and eventually white hot. As the temperature increases, more colors in the spectrum are added to the light; specifically, more blue light is added to the red, shifting the overall color balance toward neutral white.

Light sources in photography are described by their color temperature. A candle flame is very red, at a color temperature of 1600°K; household incandescent lamps are more yellow at 2600°K; and photographic studio lamps are whiter at 3200°K. Daylight, to which most color films are matched, is considered to be 5500°K.

The film used to copy color illustrations must be matched to the light-source color temperature, or the copy will be unacceptably off-color: blue, orange, or magenta.

Daylight

The simplest example of color copy is also the least elaborate and the least expensive: a daylight-balanced color film used outdoors in sunlight or in light overcast conditions. The illustration, fastened to a copyboard, should be placed in the light so that no shadows fall across it, and then copied as described earlier. Any daylight film can be used to produce prints or slides. Notice, however, that outdoor lighting is variable, and although full sunlight or lightly hazy sunlight is true 5500°K daylight, the light changes throughout the day and with cloud cover. True daylight conditions are found between 10:00 A.M. and 2:00 P.M.; times closer to sunrise and sunset are too red (lower color temperature), and overcast days are too blue (higher color temperature). Because of this variability of natural light, photographers have turned to using artificial lights in the studio and for copying as well.

Studio Lighting

Studio lights use tungsten filaments, as do household light bulbs. The color temperature is precisely controlled, usually 3200°K, which is much higher (whiter) than house bulbs and very close to the melting point of tungsten. For this reason, studio lamps have very short lives, usually less than twenty hours. By matching these lamps with tungsten-balanced color films, rated 3200°K, perfect color balance can be achieved in copying. Two commonly available photo lamps are the ECA, which is a 250-watt bulb, and the ECT, which is 500 watts. Both are rated 3200°K, fit in standard screw-base sockets, and cost only a few dollars each.

It is possible to use special color-correcting filters on the camera lens itself to match the film's color temperature to the lamps. For example, an 80A filter will balance 3200°K studio lamps to 5500°K daylight films, but this requires a much longer exposure, since the filter absorbs so much of the light.

Electronic flash units, although rated "daylight" balanced, seldom are corrected well enough to produce perfect color copies. Other difficulties, such as uneven light distribution and complexity of light metering, generally prohibit the use of flash units in this situation.

Fluorescent lamps are also unacceptable for copy photography; their light is not a continuous spectrum of colors, but rather a series of color spikes, which makes accurate color reproduction almost impossible.

Color Film

Several films for color copying are outstanding. For daylight-balanced films, Kodak VRG-100 will produce beautiful color prints, and Kodachrome 25 will make extraordinary color slides. Both of these films are low-ASA/ISO, requiring relatively large amounts of light for proper exposure, and both display the ultra-high resolution and lack of grain that characterize such slow films. For tungsten-balanced lighting, Kodak Ektachrome Professional 50 (EPY) is balanced for 3200°K, and Kodak Kodachrome 40 (KPA), although balanced for 3400°K, works very well at 3200°K.

ADDITION
CONSIDER
SPECIAL M

Archival Ph

If the long
the copied i
tion, steps ca
the archival
Black-and
negatives ca
chival perm
them with
elimination
ing step in
Perma-Was
photo stores
By chemica
ual fixer (hy
the lifetime
tended to
should be st
safe plastic
paper enve
buffered p
type D poly
Many arch
are availabl
sions Corp
New York.
(see Appen
Color in
less stable
since they
stable col
tually fade
be stored
tics, as wit
tives, and
dark in s
store colo
buffered p
Any color
if it is sto
and away
traviolet
made for c
time, but
traviolet l
blocking
by display
overall lig
tend the c
If the orig
has been

placement prints can be made after the first prints have faded.

The most stable color prints available at this time are those produced on Cibachrome materials. Using azo dyes and a plastic substrate instead of paper, Cibachrome prints should be stable for a century or so. They can be made commercially by specialty photo labs or at home using a photographic enlarger and color filters.

When archival permanence is desired in making color slides, Kodachrome films should be used. Kodachrome films are unique because the color dyes are added to the emulsion when processing occurs, not built into the film, as with Ektachrome and other types of slide films. This post-exposure dyeing uses much more stable color dyes than those that can be incorporated into the emulsion during manufacture. The result is that the processing of Kodachrome films is so complex and expensive that only a handful of labs, mostly Kodak labs, process them. Nonetheless, the lifetime of the color image is in excess of a century, whereas the expected life of the Ektachrome images is half of that.

All color slides should be stored in archivally safe plastic sleeves or pages: products for this purpose are generally made of polypropylene, polyethylene, or Mylar. Do not use vinyl or polyvinyl plastics. Maximum color stability can be achieved through dark storage in low humidity and at low temperatures.

Polaroid Instant Slide System

The Polaroid Corporation has introduced a series of three 35mm films that come with chemical processing modules. When inserted in a special developing machine (which cost about $90 in 1987), each module will process one roll of film yielding slides ready for mounting and projection. Processing takes only minutes at room temperatures and is clean, requiring no water or additional chemicals. On occasion, all three slide films may prove useful to an illustrator.

Polagraph is a high-contrast black-and-white slide film, well suited for line artwork. Polapan is a continuous-tone film producing black-and-white slides with a full range of gray values, which works well with continuous-tone black-and-white or color original art; its grain structure is similar to that of a high-ASA/ISO black-and-white film. Polacolor is an unusual film that produces full-color slides, but the film's black matrix produces images that are darker in appearance than those produced by regular slide films. The color accuracy of Polacolor, unlike regular slide films, is unreliable.

These Polaroid films are useful for projection, for quick copies on short notice, and for preliminary presentations, but their quality is not adequate for publication or portfolio use.

COPYING FOR PUBLICATION

If an illustration is to be used for publication and the original work is not available or adaptable to the printing process, efforts should be made to obtain the highest-quality photographic copy. This usually involves taking the original to a professional photographer with experience in copying artwork. By using 4- by 5-inch (10 by 12.5cm) or 8- by 10-inch (20 by 25cm) sheet film, color-corrected lenses, and custom laboratory processing, a photographer can produce copies virtually identical to the original illustration.

Evaluating Copy Photographs

Most unsatisfactory copywork is the result of an inexperienced photographer making errors in exposing, processing, or printing the negative. The majority of problems will fall into one of the five categories described below. Although they are primarily concerned with the black-and-white printed image, most aspects apply equally to color copying.

Excessive Contrast

Every attempt at copying generally results in some increase in contrast. The nature of the photographic emulsion causes a compression of the tone in the original art to produce the copy, and this compression is imperfect. Subtle tonal values are lost and the result is a reduced spectrum of tones, an increase in contrast.

In black-and-white printing, the normal increase in contrast can be controlled by printing the negative on a lower-contrast (softer) grade of printing paper, if necessary. Black-and-white photographic papers come in several grades of contrast, usually from grade 1 (the least contrasty) to grade 5 (the most contrasty). While normal images are generally printed perfectly on grade 2 papers (normal contrast), using a higher grade of paper will produce a more contrasty (harder) image; using a lower grade will soften the contrast below normal (fig. 26-3).

If the photographer has inadvertently used a high-contrast line film for a continuous-tone illustration, the result will be a very high-contrast image with the tones split into stark white or solid black (fig. 26-4).

Inadequate Contrast

Inadequate contrast may be caused by several factors. In printing, the paper contrast may be too low, the print exposure may be insufficient, or the developing time for the print may be too short. The negative itself may be at fault: the exposure could be too light (underexposed), or the development could be insufficient (underdevel-

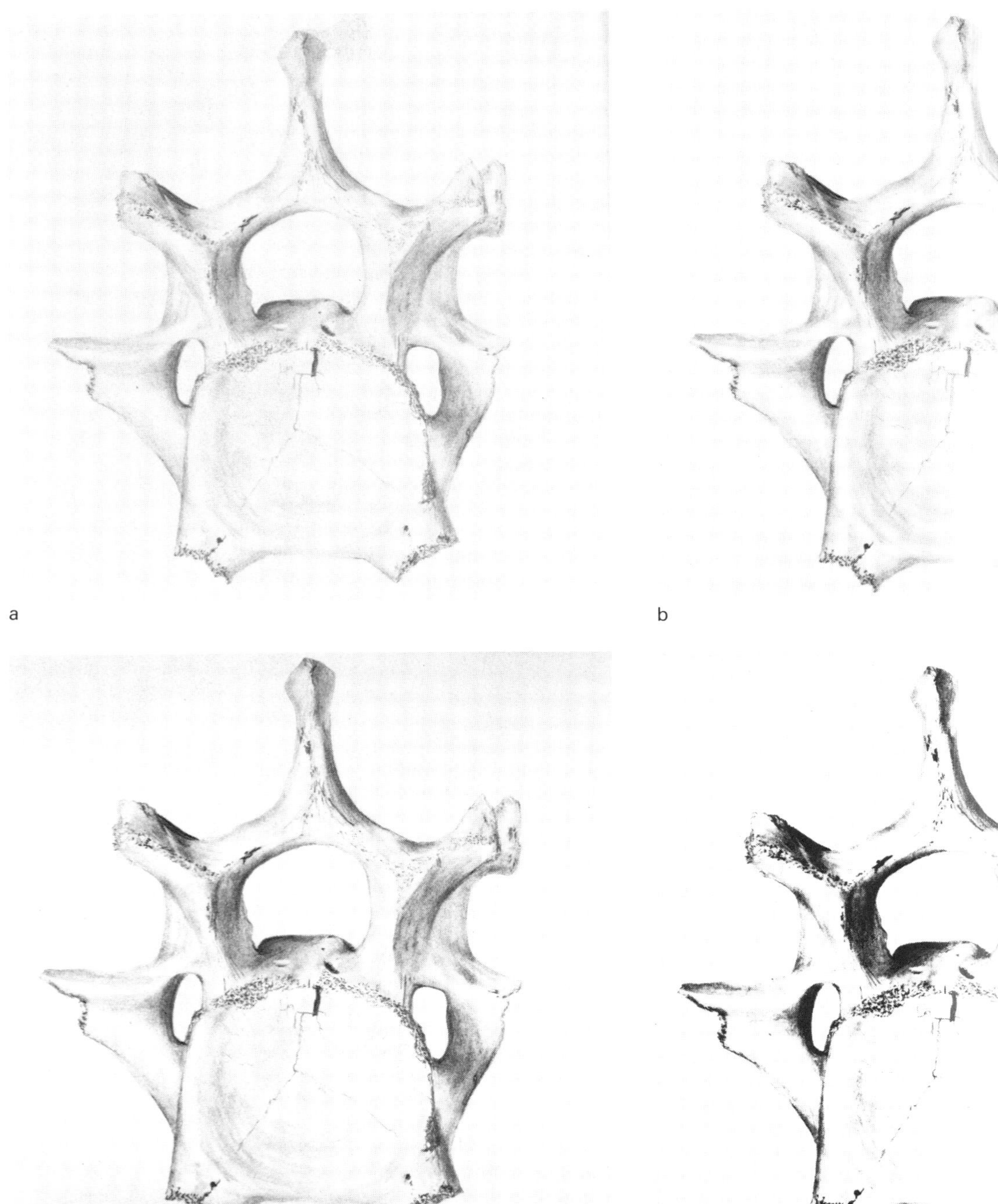

26-3. The effects of printing the same copy negative on three different grades of photographic paper: *(a)* paper grade 1, soft contrast; *(b)* paper grade 2, normal contrast; and *(c)* paper grade 3, higher than normal contrast. Cow vertebra, graphite pencil on Bristol board, by Jennifer B. Clark © 1982.

Bottom right:
26-4. Film error. High-contrast film used for the continuous-tone illustration shown in figure 26-3, resulting in a reproduction devoid of middle tones.

oped) caused by too little developing time, or overworked (exhausted) developer.

Finally, inadequate contrast may result if high-contrast (line) originals are copied onto continuous-tone film; but this is unusual, and it generally can be corrected by printing the negative onto a very high contrast grade of photographic paper.

Loss of Sharpness and Detail

Overall, lack of sharpness and loss of detail are caused by movement of the camera during the exposure (camera shake) or by movement of the enlarger during printing. Dirty lenses in the camera or enlarger will reduce the contrast of the image rather than the overall sharpness.

Occasionally, a copy is sharp but lacking in fine detail compared to the original artwork. If the contrast of the copy is similar to that of the original, the most likely cause is excessive reduction of the original. This condition is most commonly observed in stipple and scratchboard illustrations and occurs when the illustrator does not allow for the effects of reduction when executing the work. The fine details have coalesced into a mass instead of being perceived as independent points.

Uneven Lighting

Generally, uneven lighting results from incorrect placement of the copy lights when the image is being copied. Unevenness causes corners or other areas of the image to be too light or too dark. Vignetting (the obstruction of the lens) can cause similar uneven lighting. Generally, a lens shade or filter is to blame, but a misplaced condenser lens in the enlarger or a misaligned enlarging lamp creates the same effect.

Discrete Blemishes

Spots, lines, scratches, and blobs are the result of damage to the film during processing. Circular dark spots usually are caused by "air bells," bubbles of air sticking to the emulsion during processing, causing uneven development. Scratches usually are caused by rough handling of the wet film during processing. White spots and lines in the finished print generally are caused by dust or lint on the negative or photographic paper.

Most blemishes of this type cannot be corrected and require reprinting the negative or, in the worst cases, producing another copy negative.

Once an illustration has been created, the logical next step is to produce copies of it. Copies could include color slides and prints for use in the artist's portfolio, extra slides for submission to prospective clients or art competitions or for presentations by the artist to clients or general audiences. In all probability, the client who commissioned the artwork could use slides for presentations and, perhaps, enlarged prints for display in an office or exhibit. At the very least, a copy photograph is a record of the artwork.

This chapter was designed to guide the nonphotographer artist through the basic techniques of copy photography. It should enable the artist to produce good-quality duplicates of artwork and, with practice and experience, produce excellent copies.

As the artist's skill and confidence grow with experience in copying, the ability to make copies for myriad uses will be most rewarding.

27/The Printing Process

Arly Allen

The graphic artist is like a playwright. Both create a work of art but must rely upon others to produce it. The illustrator speaks not directly to the audience, but rather through the actions of others. The illustration, for good or ill, is transformed by the skill of the printer.

The printer is like an actor. Both bring the work of the creator—artist or playwright—to the audience, enhancing or obscuring it by their actions. The printer can make a success or a failure of the illustrator's work.

Success in the graphic arts depends upon the close cooperation of the illustrator and the printer. Neither can accomplish as much separately as they can by working together. This chapter is designed to describe the printing process as it relates to the production of scientific illustrations. The aim is to help illustrators work better with printers. By understanding the basics of the printing process and how that process affects the work they produce, graphic artists may be better able to prepare their art for reproduction.

THE END RESULT

Illustrations in a printed book or journal are of two types: line and halftone. Line illustrations appear as one single ink color, usually black lines on white paper; they have no printed tone in the background. Shading can be achieved only with crosshatching, stippling, and other line patterns. Typically, printed line illustrations have a stark, clean look. Graphs, charts, pen-and-ink drawings, and hand-drawn chemical or mathematical equations are normally produced as line illustrations (fig. 27-1). Halftones are so called because they reproduce the half or intermediate grays of photographs and tone drawings. A black-and-white halftone can produce a range of shadings from solid black through the grays to paper white (fig. 27-2).

Line illustrations are fixed in their position in the text early in the production cycle. They can, therefore, be easily proofed by authors and editors. Halftones, on the other hand, are not linked to the text until the very last stage of production. After galley proofs and page proofs are approved by the author (and sometimes proofs of illustrations by the illustrator), the final approval of halftone placement is normally given by the publisher through the use of a photographic proof, often called a blueline or ozalid. This proof shows the pages with the halftones in position. Although it would be ideal for the author to see this blueline to ensure that illustrations are correctly placed, there usually is no time for that. The illustrator and author should recognize this and seek to prevent errors by clearly marking and labeling illustrations for the printer. (In addition to information presented in this chapter, see chapter 1, especially Final Check, Corrections, and Last Steps.)

Line Illustrations

Line illustrations are produced in the printing process by making a single-exposure, high-contrast camera negative of the original artwork. The goal of the printer is to eliminate all background material photographically and to hold only the lines of the original drawing.

Since the spe
printer in prep
for printing is
the essential d
the wise illustr
with this in
negatives pre
lines best. De
drawings in g
ink or pencil c
as line illustra
of thumb for
keep the line
crisp, clean.
greater the c
lines of the
background
pared, the be
successful rep

Halftone Ill

The purpos
cess is the o
line process.
tone image.
seeks to reta
the original a
This include
the central
tones and
Unlike the p
illustrations.
background.
holds all bac
specific step
them (see
halftones).
pares mater
shades must
background
clean and e
possible, for
illustration
the central

Halftones
perimposing
in the came
graph thro

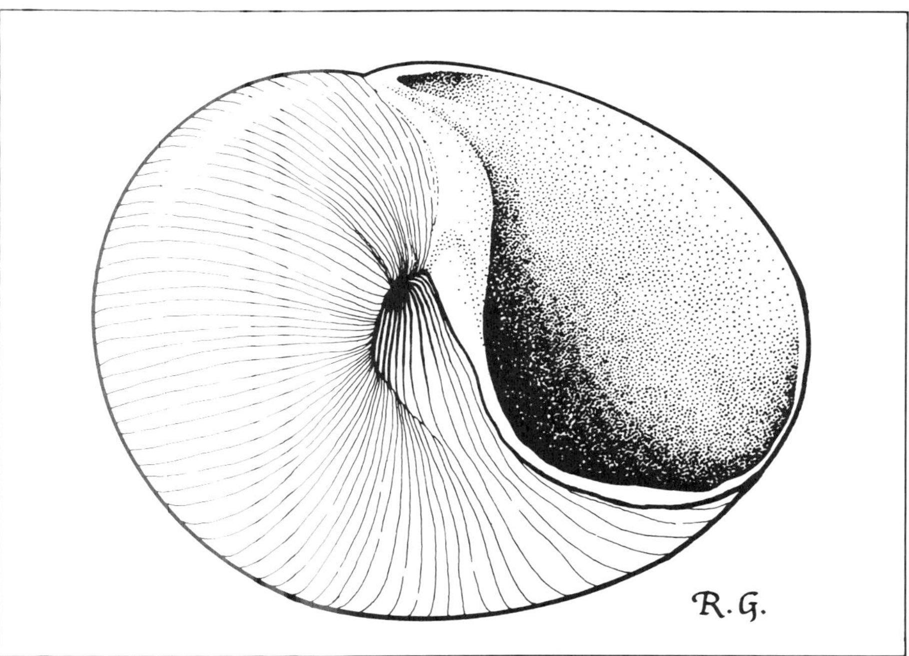

27-1. A line illustration. Shading with stipple also is line. Moon snail, *Lunatia heros*. Pen-and-ink on Bristol board, by Robert Jon Golder.

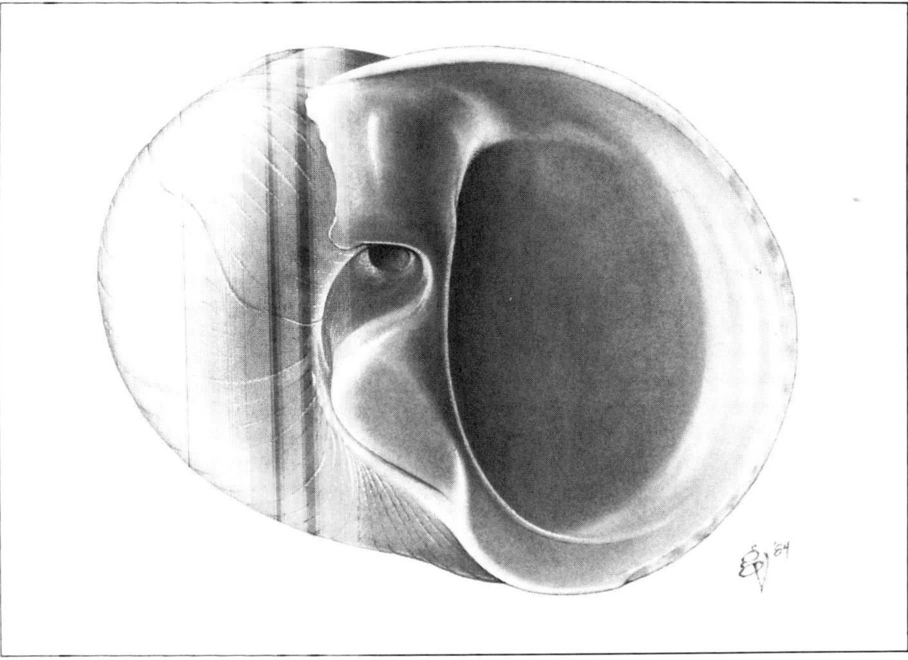

27-2. A halftone. Note that shading is possible for a range of tones from black to white. Moon snail. *Natica*. Carbon dust on Video board, by George L. Venable.

screen lines serve to break up the continuous-tone image of the original photograph or artwork into a series of discrete dots. (This dot pattern is the identifying characteristic of a halftone.) The dots are the printing image. They are of differing sizes: dots representing the darkest portions of the illustration are the largest and thus get the most ink from the press; they print as black or dark tones. Dots from the light portions of the illustration are smaller. They get less ink and are surrounded by more unprinted paper surface. Thus, they appear to the eye as lighter tones. Where the very lightest tones appear in the original illustration, depending on the printer's procedures, the printing dots simply may not exist. At this point, no ink will be printed and the paper will show through the halftone.

The halftone image is thus a *trompe l'oeil*. It tricks the eye into believing that it sees contrasting tones when in reality it sees dots of ink of contrasting size. The eye translates the pattern of large and small dots in the halftone into patterns of light and dark, which replicate the original image of the artwork or the photograph.

Halftone Screen

Many things affect the quality of the halftone reproduction. From the standpoint of the illustrator, however, the basic rule to remember is: the higher the halftone screen number, the closer to the original image the results are likely to be.

The halftone screen number is a measure of the number of vertical or horizontal lines scribed per inch of halftone screen. Low numbers (65 to 100 lines per inch) mean that the illustration is divided into a number of rather large or coarse dots. Typically, halftones printed in books and journals use screens ranging from 120 to 150 lines per inch. Finer halftone screens with still higher numbers are used for the best reproductions. High-quality photographs and artprints are normally printed with halftone screens ranging from 200 to 300 lines per inch. The 300-line-per-inch halftone screen creates a dot pattern that is so fine that it cannot be distinguished with the naked eye. At this level, the eye is tricked into believing that the printed image is a continuous-tone reproduction.

Often it may not be possible for the illustrator to know in advance what number of halftone screen

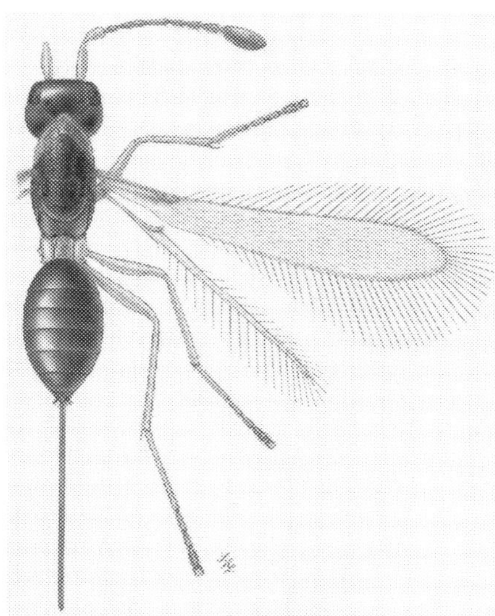

a

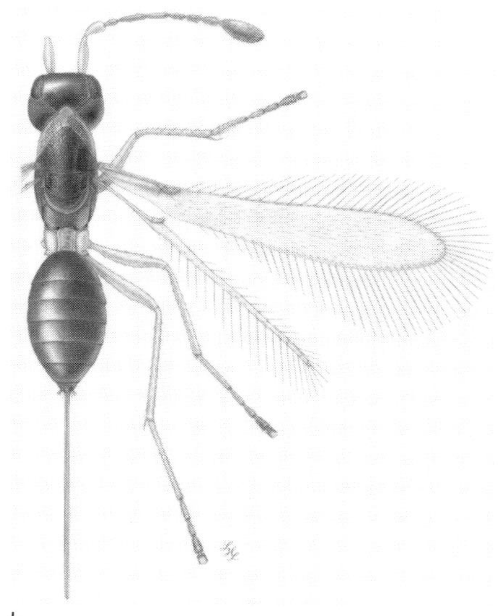

b

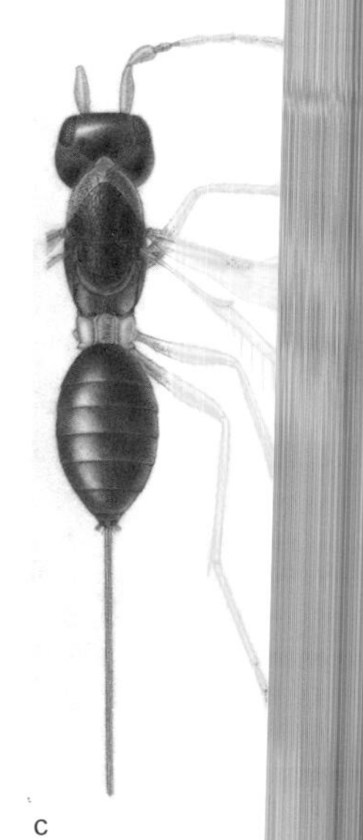

c

27-3. The effect of different screen patterns on a halftone. Detail can be lost if too coarse a screen is used. The finer the screen, the more detail that may be retained in the final printed illustration: *(a)* 85-line screen; *(b)* 120-line screen; *(c)* 200-line screen. Mymarid wasp, *Polynema ema*. Carbon dust on Cronaflex, by Linda Heath Lawrence. Courtesy of E. Grissell and M. Schauff.

will be used to produce an illustration. In this case, the next best thing is to know in what type of publication the illustration is likely to be printed. Since newspapers and books printed on uncoated paper typically use screens ranging from 65 to 120 lines, illustrations prepared for this type of reproduction should not contain subtle detail. Rather, they should focus on bolder, more clearly defined subjects. Furthermore, the background should not be dark; it should be lighter than the subject itself. The tones of the illustration should be in the middle range, and the artist or photographer should try to avoid having any critical detail in either the light or dark areas of the image (fig. 27-3).

Most journals, and many books, use screens in the 120- to 150-line range, and they may be printed on coated paper. This allows the reproduction of a much broader range of tones. In such cases, it is possible to reproduce an illustration with a light-colored subject on a darker background, as long as the background is not intended to be black. Detail should still be concentrated in the middle-tone range, although it is possible to reproduce detail in the lighter and darker areas if the image is defined carefully.

If the illustration is being prepared for an art book or for a journal well known for its attention to detail, the work may be reproduced using a 200- to 300-line-screen halftone. In this case, a full range of tone patterns is possible, from solid black to paper white. The subject matter can be very delicate, and the tone separation between the background and the subject need not be great to reproduce well. Very light subjects can be reproduced on very dark backgrounds, and vice versa. Delicate lines can be reproduced in either the lightest areas or the darkest areas of the illustration. Tone compression is not a problem, nor is loss of detail. The artist or the photographer can express the full range of his or her techniques.

PREPARATION OF ILLUSTRATIONS FOR PRINTING

The basic goal of the printer is to be invisible. The quality of the orig-

inal illustr
through in t
exactly as
duced. Unf
limits in pri
standing of
tors and sci
arise in the
A few key c
trators bett
for printing
proved resu

There are
ciated by m
is no subs
professiona
trations tha
printing pr
for printers
better repr
lustrations
medium an
as an afte
original illu
better for t
the origina
so grossly
unworkabl
of the c
printer, th
For examp
illustration
results in

fogged letters or symbols, and poorer printed results. The further the printer is removed from the original image, the less satisfactory will be the final result. These rules hold true for both line and halftone illustrations.

Line

The ideal line illustration is one drawn specifically for the book or journal to which it will be submitted. Since most books and journals are taller than they are wide, this means that most line illustrations should be designed with vertical as their longest dimension. Illustrations that are wider than they are tall can create production problems. This is truer with journals than with books, since the format of journals is fixed and illustrations will be forced to fit within the journal format. Typically, the journal format consists of two or more columns, so thought should be given to whether the illustration should be designed for a single column or more. The economics of journal production makes it desirable that line illustrations be reproduced in one column if at all possible. This means that the ideal line illustration not only will be taller than it is wide, but also basically simple in its design and content so that reduction to one-column width does not make it either illegible or unintelligible.

Book formats are more flexible. In some cases, the book design is dictated by the design of the illustrations. However, unless you know the format requirements, or unless the book publisher has indicated that the book's format will be decided after the illustrations are produced, it is wise to follow the design rules for illustrations submitted to journals.

The rules that follow are specifically keyed to journal production, with reference in special cases to book production.

Line illustrations should be drawn in india ink on Bristol board or other good-quality illustration board or film. Lines should be clear, clean, and crisp. Regardless of the final color of printing, the ink used should be black—not gray, brown, or blue. It should contrast strongly with the surface on which it is drawn. If drafting film is used as a substrate, drawing should be on only one side of the film, since distortion arises when both sides of the film are used in a line illustration. If a paper or board surface is used, the paper or board should be made of acid-free materials, since acidic papers yellow over time, reducing the contrast between the drawing and the background. Furthermore, since the background is eliminated in line reproduction, illustrations done on yellowed or dark backgrounds may suffer loss of detail and data in the reproduction process when the printer attempts to eliminate the background.

Scratchboard illustrations, or other line illustration techniques that create white images on a black background, pose production problems for printers. It is difficult to reproduce black backgrounds well, and this in turn can make the white image difficult to use. The conventional technique for reproducing line illustrations is based on black images on white paper. Before departing from this approach, consult carefully with the publisher or editor about the problems that might arise.

Line illustrations should be designed to be printed at two-thirds of their original size. This reduction helps to sharpen lines and eliminate minor imperfections in the drawing. Letters, numbers, degree symbols, and the lines of the illustration itself should be designed to be printable and legible when reduced. The internal complexity of the illustration also should be considered in light of a probable reduction in the printing process. The greater the complexity of the illustration, the greater the difficulty the reader may have when it is reduced. The use of broken lines in graphs, of open and closed symbols of the same shape, or of shading patterns that closely resemble one another, all create problems when line illustrations are reduced in the printing process. Simplicity of design is preferable to complexity. Simplicity leads to clarity in reproduction, and clarity leads to greater usefulness to the reader.

Illustrations in a series showing differences in size should all be drawn in the same proportion so that all can be reproduced at the same reduction. The dimensions of the largest drawing of the series should set the reduction percentages for the rest of the drawings. If the series is intended for reproduction in a journal, it is important to make sure that all data will be legible when the largest drawing is reduced to the eventual size. It is also desirable that the smallest illustration in the series not be significantly smaller than one column width. If it is, it may look unattractive in print.

When suggesting sizes of illustrations for reduction, it is safest to give the desired final size in inches (or centimeters) rather than in a percentage figure. The use of percentage figures can lead to confusion. For example, a reduction of 25 percent may be interpreted to mean "reduce the figure to 25 percent of its present size" rather than to 75 percent. When size is critical to the quality of reproduction, as in a series of illustrations, always discuss your views with the editor or publisher for best results. (See fig. 1-5 for an easy method of determining the size of the final reproduction.)

Illustration copy ideally should have the same dimensions as the manuscript, 8½ by 11 inches (21½ by 28cm). It may be somewhat larger if this size is too small to show what is needed, but no matter how large the illustration is when it leaves your studio, its size when reproduced will be smaller than the trim size of the journal or the book (see chapter 1). An illustration larger than 14 by 20 inches (35 by 50cm), including space for handling on the margins, will have to be reduced too much to retain details. Furthermore, oversize artwork is vulnerable to damage, particularly during shipment. If you have difficulty wrapping your illustrations for shipment, everyone else will too. Remember that the final printed illustration will be only as good as the copy the printer receives. Oversize illustrations are a sign of inefficient thinking. Simplify your design, and you will earn the thanks of your printer and the gratitude of your readers.

Symbols used in an illustration should be explained within it; do not leave them to be explained in the caption. Often the typesetter or printer may not have the particular symbol used in the illustration, and obtaining it may cost time and money and delay the production of the paper. To avoid this, include a key in the illustration explaining the symbols used.

Very fine dot patterns or very fine stippling should be avoided in line illustrations. When line illustrations are reduced, delicate dot patterns become difficult for printers to retain. When the dots disappear, the illustrations may be hard to understand. Compensate for the expected reduction by making the stipples large enough to remain visible at the reduced size; use a reducing glass to check this. Line patterns used for shading avoid the problem altogether. Be certain that all dots and patterns are solid black and not gray (see chapter 5).

Lettering (labeling) on all line art should be clean and open. Sans serif faces such as Univers, Helvetica, and Spartan are usually better than serif faces such as Times Roman or Baskerville. Sans serif faces have solid, clean lines that reproduce well in illustrations, whereas serif faces have delicate features that often do not withstand reduction well.

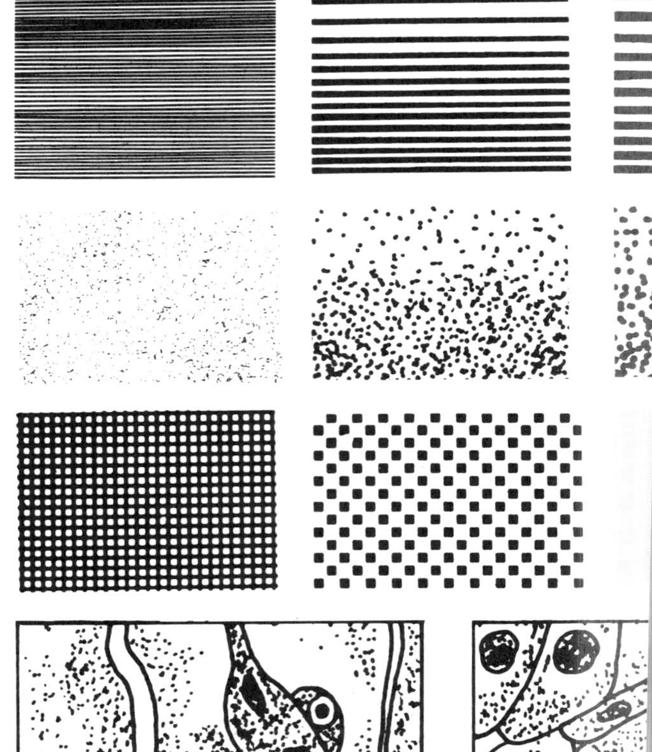

27-4. The appearance of different types of lettering and sha[...] drawings: *(a)* 100 percent of size; *(b)* reduced to 66⅔ percen[...] 33⅓ percent of size. (See also fig. 25–29.)

Excessively large or bold letters should be avoided on line copy. The function of labeling is to inform, not to shock the reader. Large, bold letters in the illustrations detract from the appearance of the page. In order to keep the

labeling i[...]
overpoweri[...]
or the rest[...]
tering size[...]
illustration[...]
enough to[...]
for a series[...]

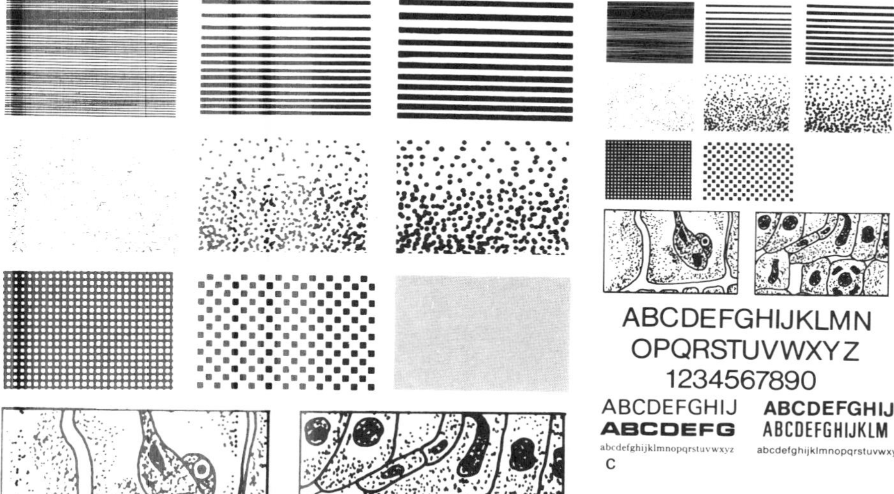

professional illustrator will recognize that unless all of the illustrations will be reduced exactly the same percentage for publication, the labels will vary in size from one printed illustration to another. To avoid this, the illustrator should request that the illustrations be reduced in the same proportion or plan for separate reductions by using different-sized type for different illustrations. In this last case, larger type should be used on illustrations with larger reductions, and smaller type should be used on illustrations with smaller reductions. The rule of thumb should be to have the labels proportional to the art itself so that no matter what the reduction, the type fits the figure (fig. 27-4).

Halftones

The ideal halftone is designed specifically for the journal or the book in which it is to be printed. It may be either an original glossy photograph or a tone drawing. The photograph or continuous-tone illustration should be submitted for printing at or close to the actual size it is to have in print.

The worst possible halftone is a matte-paper photograph of a previously printed halftone that requires significant enlargement or reduction for the new printing. Matte photographic paper dulls and softens the image of the halftone—in contrast to glossy photographic paper, which holds detail sharp and clear. Photographs submitted on matte paper will result in a blurred and indistinct printed image. The reproduction of a previously printed photograph may require the superimposition of a secondary halftone screen. In this case, detail is lost and a moiré pattern can result, thus degrading the image (fig. 27-5).

Line copy generally will benefit from some reduction; tone copy generally will not. Enlarging the illustration tends to soften the image and in some cases to make it appear grainy and uneven. Reducing the image photographically tends to compress the tone patterns and usually darkens the illustration. Further, it may lead to loss of detail. In order to avoid unsatisfactory halftone results, the illustrator should plan the original to be the same size as final reproduction, if it is known.

Cropping

Cropping is the process of blocking out nonessential parts of an original image to reproduce the essential parts. It is useful when only part of the original image is needed for the text. The actual process of cropping is done by the printer after an offset negative of the original art has been created. At that stage, the unnecessary part of the negative may be physically cut off and discarded or it may be covered with a light barrier that prevents it from printing. In this process, the printer is guided by instructions from the illustrator, designer, editor, or publisher. The conventional way of instructing the printer to crop an illustration is to place crop marks (short lines) at right angles on the edges of the illustration, being careful to keep those marks outside the area of the original copy that is to be reproduced (see fig. 2-42). Crop marks may be made with ink or grease pencil, as long as they are clear and clean. Messy marks mean trouble. They may spoil the illustration and confuse the printer. Crop marks also may be placed on an overlay sheet, as long as they are in register with the original illustration and do not transfer to the surface of the art. Do not ever crop the original art by cutting it yourself.

Cropping allows the reproduction of critical detail in an illustration at full size, when reproduction of the entire illustration would re-

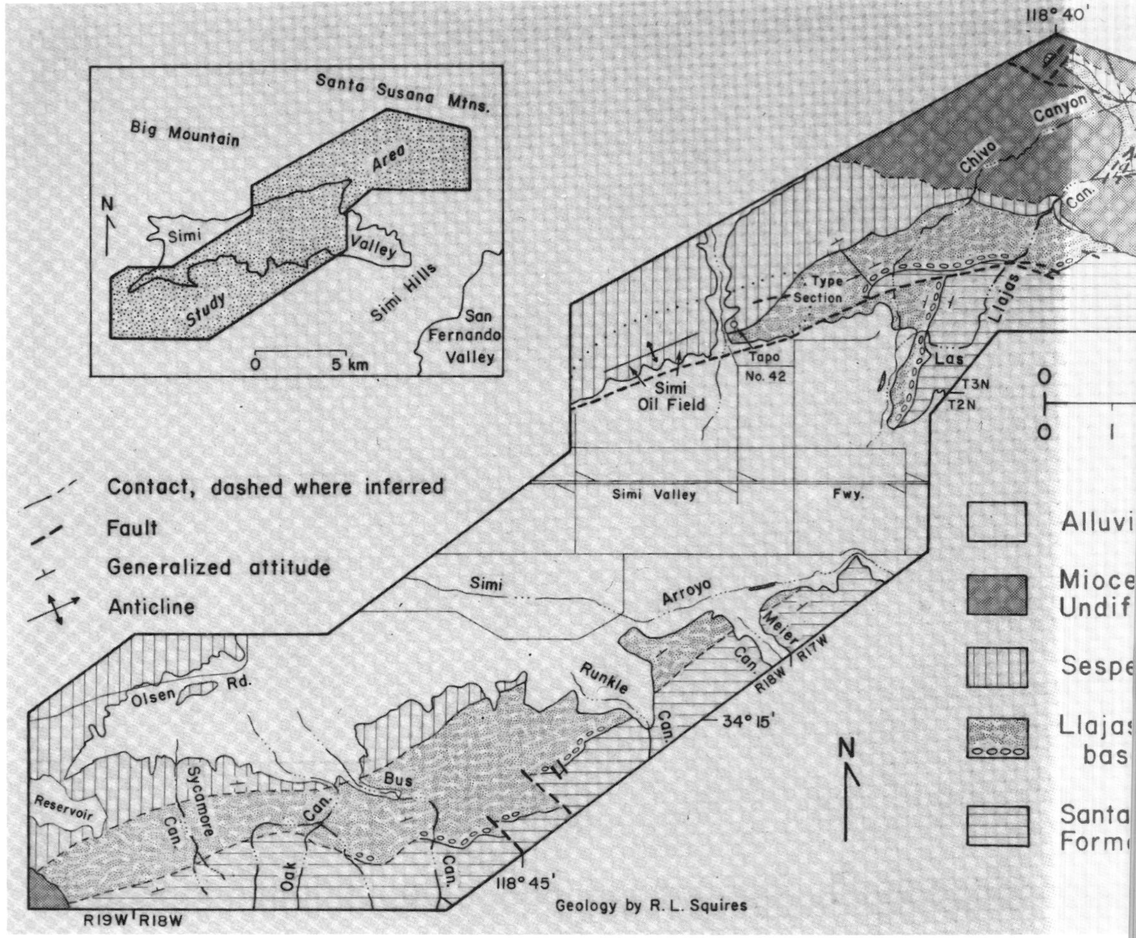

27-5. An example of a moiré pattern. An illustration, already printed with a screen, has been reshot with an additional screen. Where the dots do not match precisely, a visible dot pattern emerges. From "Megapaleontology of the Eocene Llajas formation, Simi Valley, California," by R. L. Squires, *Contributions in Science* no. 350 (Natural History Museum of Los Angeles County, 1984).

quire reduction and loss of detail. Cropping also permits the illustrator to focus the reader's attention on the area of specific importance, without distraction by other data. Although both line and halftone illustrations may be cropped, halftones are more commonly so treated.

Square Halftones

The standard halftone is distinguished from the line illustration by the fact that, because of its screen, the printing tone extends throughout the entire illustration, including the background. Unless otherwise instructed, some printers typically crop the edges of tone illustrations when printing them. This gives the printed halftone a square or rectangular shape to fit the page or the column (fig. 27-6; see fig. 2-45).

Dropout and Silhouette Halftones

In certain cases, an illustrator may wish to produce a tone illustration while eliminating the background. There are two ways to achieve this. The first is the dropout halftone, a photographic process in which the image is overexposed to the point that the background is photographically "dropped out." No detail is held in the background, so no halftone dot appears and no printed image occurs (fig. 27-7). The process is relatively inexpensive, but it is possible only when there is a considerabl[e] to[...] the image an[...] cause the dr[...] a lightening [...] tral image. T[...] detail in the [...] dropped out [...]

The silho[...] ground halft[...] than the dro[...] tone, but it a[...] the dropout [...] fig. 2-46). In [...] lith or Rubyl[...] hand (by the [...] one hired [...] placed in re[...] tion or its n[...] printing plat[...] Materials in [...]

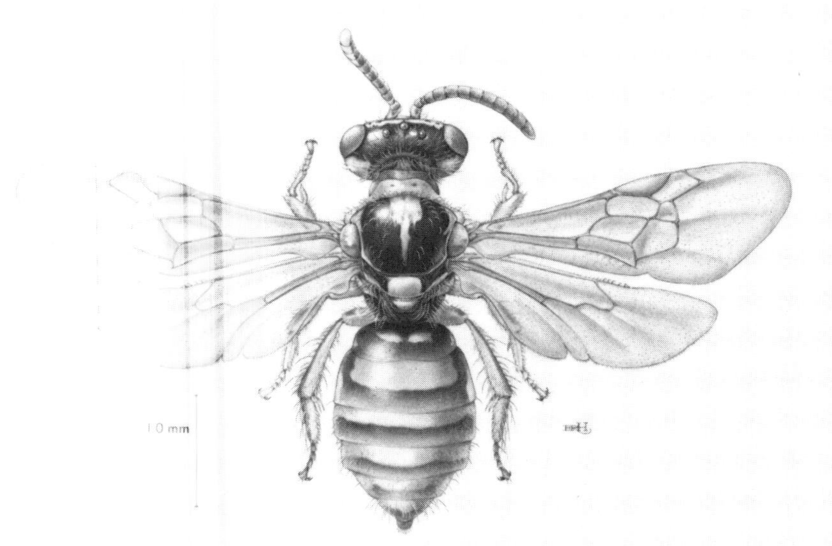

2). The mask prevents the background from being exposed on the printing plate, thus eliminating the dot pattern and preventing any printing image. Cutting out a silhouette of the central image of an illustration requires considerable skill and time. The more irregular the image, the more delicate the work involved. Thus, silhouette or cutout-background halftones are used for special projects, particularly where the tone values of the original image and the background are so close to each other that the dropout process is impractical.

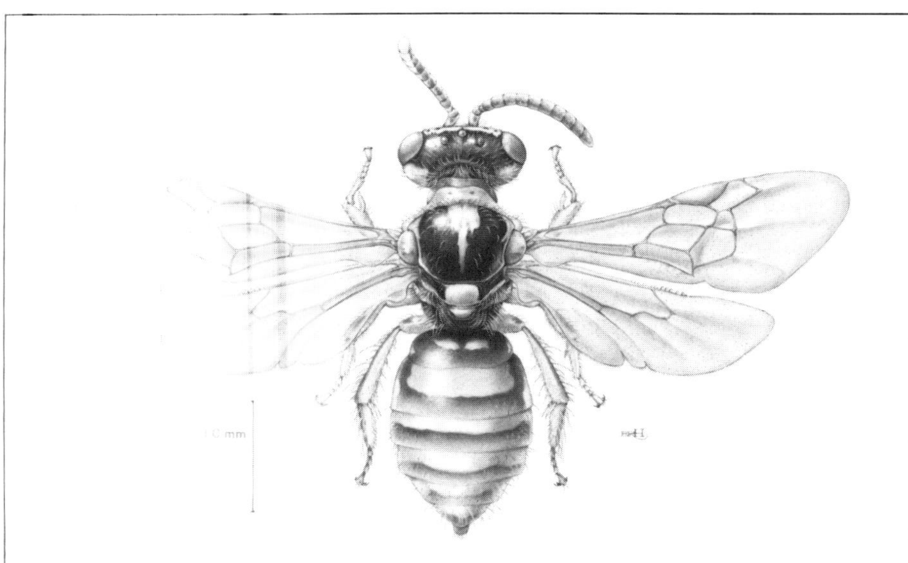

Top:
27-6. Square-finish halftone. A screen has put dots all over the illustration, including the scale and numbers.

Center:
27-7. Dropout halftone. The background of the original drawing is no. 00 Ross board, an old, slightly yellowed material. To the camera, the yellowish cast is close in tone to the lightest tones in the illustration. When the background drops out, so do these tones, unfortunately. Compare with figure 27-8.

Bottom:
27-8. Silhouette halftone. An Amberlith mask was cut to cover the image. A scale, numbers, and signature were applied to the Amberlith overlay, precisely over their counterparts on the drawing itself, and shot as a line negative along with the shape of the image. The scale, numbers, and signature were circled and marked on the overlay, using grease pencil, "shoot as 50% screen," so that they would appear gray in the reproduction and thus not contrast too harshly with the drawing. The entire drawing was shot as a halftone. Thus, two negatives—one line and one halftone—and a 50 percent contact screen were combined to make a single combination plate. On the line negative, clear windows appear wherever an image (drawing, scale, numbers, signature) was masked. Through the clear windows, the halftone images appear. Bee, *Perdita stathamae stathamae*. Graphite dust on no. 00 Ross board, by Elaine R. S. Hodges. Courtesy of E. G. Linsley, T. Zavortink, and R. J. McGinley.

In figure 27-8 the artist wanted to have the scale, numbers, and signature screened so that they would not contrast too harshly with the pale drawing. Normally it would be desirable to have these items appear black, and they would not be screened in order to retain crisp, clean edges (see figs. 27-11 and 27-12). There are several ways the printer can create the gray image of objects, like signatures, isolated in the background when the background is to be silhouetted away with an Amberlith mask. If the signature is masked by an identical tracing on the overlay, it will appear as a window in the line negative, just as does the drawing. However, since most material like signatures and scales on an overlay are intended to be printed as black lines, the printer may not treat these like the drawing but may instead print them as black lines unless told otherwise. The items that are to appear gray can be circled on the overlay and marked "Print as halftone," and they should appear just as they do on the drawing: almost black if they are black and gray if they are gray. Or they can be marked "50% screen," which is what was done with figure 27-8, so that the black scale and numbers would appear gray. A 50 percent screen is the darkest that the eye generally will perceive as gray and not black in the context of a gray image. The printer can make a third screened negative to sandwich with the halftone and line negatives or can tape a 50 percent screen negative under the window created in the line negative, resulting in only two thicknesses of full-size negatives to be sandwiched.

Mounting Tone Art

Quite often, several halftones need to be "ganged," or grouped together, to form a plate. Considerable controversy exists over whether or not such illustrations should be grouped together (ganged) and mounted by the illustrator. Printers and, as a result, publishers are divided. Book publishers often request that illustrations that are to be ganged be submitted unmounted and uncropped for publication. Their argument is that book design requires flexibility in layout and that illustrations can better be sized and placed together within the text when they are unmounted. Since cropping is related to sizing illustrations, uncropped illustrations also are preferred. In addition, some printers use laser scanners to produce black-and-white halftone negatives. Currently most of these machines have curved drums on which the illustrations are placed for scanning. Illustrations mounted together do not bend easily around scanner drums, so unmounted illustrations are preferred.

Journal printers and publishers, on the other hand, generally request that illustrations that are grouped together be mounted to protect them during handling, and also to ensure their proper arrangement. Journal production schedules are typically shorter than book production schedules, so there is less time for mounting illustrations in the editorial office.

There is also an economic argument. When a number of illustrations are mounted on a plate by the illustrator or author, the entire plate can be photographed as a single unit. When separate illustrations are submitted, each must be photographed separately and the negatives stripped together separately. Separately photographing and stripping each halftone allows each illustration to be selected for its own tone values, but the cost of production is much higher. The mounting system keeps down the cost of production and allows the illustrator or author to control the relationship of the figures, but it averages the tones of the illustrations together.

Generally speaking then, illustrations having several parts should be submitted t[illegible]
while those i[illegible]
should be sub[illegible]
To avoid probl[illegible]
vestigate the [illegible]
ence prior to su[illegible]

If you shou[illegible]
submit a num[illegible]
mounted in a p[illegible]
lication purpos[illegible]
rules to follow:

- Take care t[illegible]
the illustrati[illegible]
illustrations [illegible]
grounds an[illegible]
backgrounds [illegible]
separate pla[illegible]
and one for [illegible]
the illustra[illegible]
proper orde[illegible]
way, the ec[illegible]
does not res[illegible]
of image qu[illegible]
- If a numbe[illegible]
being moun[illegible]
make sure t[illegible]
the same t[illegible]
paper. Mix[illegible]
pers with gl[illegible]
fluorescent [illegible]
orescent o[illegible]
printing pr[illegible]
reproductio[illegible]
These and [illegible]
tion proble[illegible]
one type of [illegible]
is used thro[illegible]
- Mount illus[illegible]
gether as [illegible]
finish phot[illegible]
mounted fl[illegible]
tween them [illegible]
ette illust[illegible]
mounted c[illegible]
that space [illegible]
part of a fig[illegible]
other. Wh[illegible]
or silhouet[illegible]
to mount t[illegible]
or white b[illegible]
the highest [illegible]
the tones o[illegible]
Adhesives [illegible]
vice on mo[illegible]

White-Lining

When a number of square-finish photographs are mounted together to form a single figure or plate, it is common to have the printer add a thin white hairline between the photographs to separate them. Do not be tempted to add this white line yourself, since lines appearing on the original copy will be processed as part of the halftone and will have a halftone dot in them. White hairlines typically are added in the negative stage. They thus have no dot pattern and are sharp and clean (figs. 27-9, 27-10).

Lettering and Labeling Halftones

There are currently three schools of thought about the best method of lettering and labeling halftones.

1. *Labeling on overlay.* Using this system, each original image consists of two parts: the tone image itself and an overlay that carries any numbering or labeling that is to appear in the final printed result. The overlay sheet ideally should be some type of stable transparent or translucent material, such as polyester. It should carry register marks outside the image area that match a set on the edge of the tone image. Because the overlay is part of the printing image, it should have nothing on it, with the exception of the register marks, that should not print in the final illustration (see figs. 2-42, 2-43, 4-59b, 9-7). A second overlay, this one a paper cover sheet, should be placed over the film, both to protect the lettering and to carry other instructions.

 Labeling on the overlay requires two separate camera procedures. The tone image is shot as a regular halftone negative; the overlay is shot as a regular line negative. Using the register marks, the printer then places the two pieces in register and exposes them both on the same

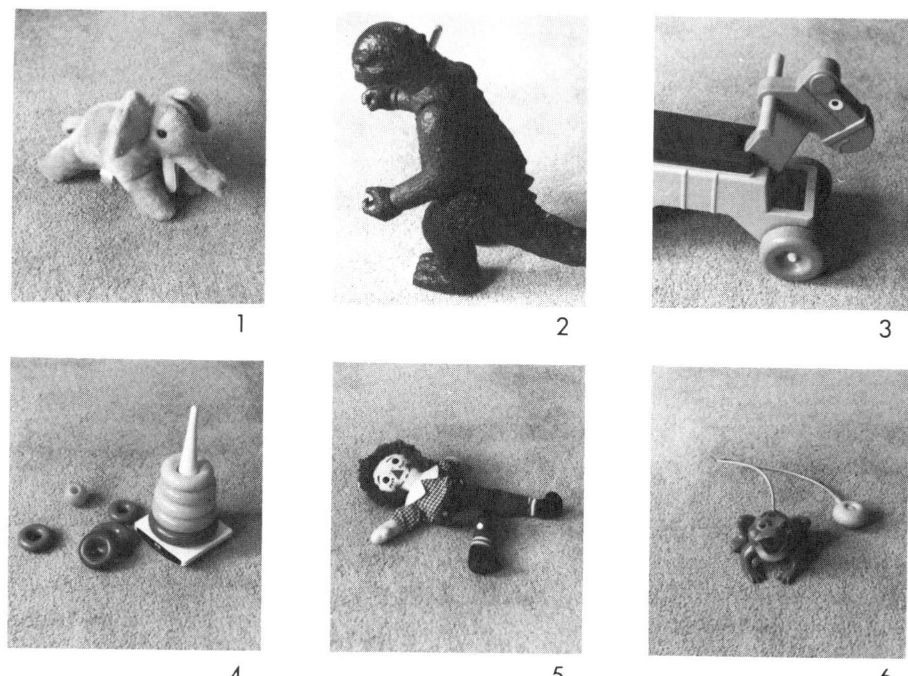

27-9. Poor design of a halftone plate. The identifying numbers have been placed outside the individual photographs, thus requiring a combination of two separate shots, a halftone and a line. Note the sacrifice of illustration to white space. The figures are smaller than their counterparts in figure 27-10, and the eye is drawn to the blank spaces between the figures.

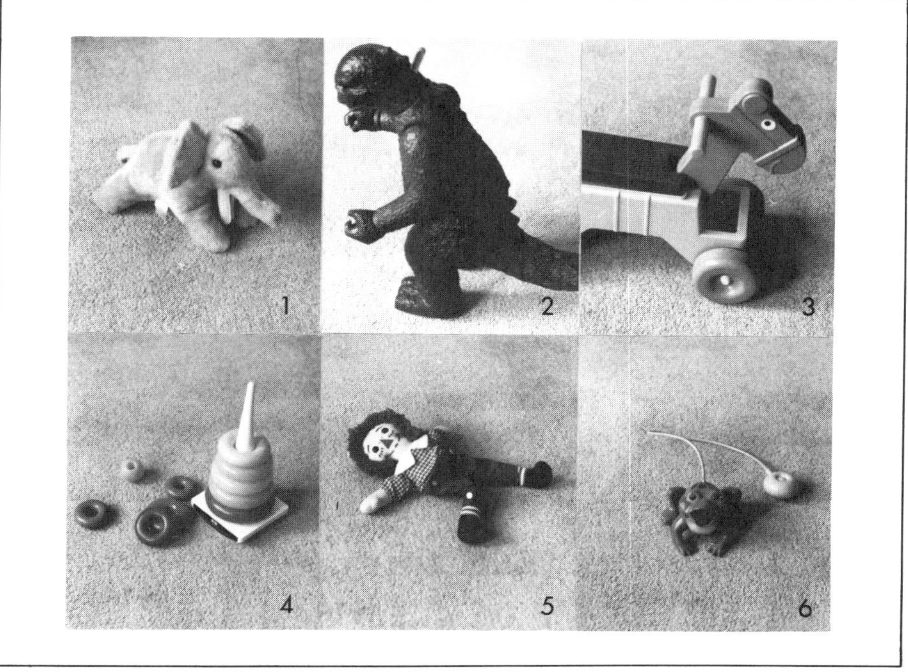

27-10. Correct design of a halftone plate for most scientific publications. The identifying numbers have been placed inside the individual photographs. The photos have been butted together to produce a single halftone. The total figure now requires only one camera exposure in place of the two required by figure 27-9. Hairlines are then cut between the numbered figures by the printer. The photos are larger than in figure 27-9, even though the two original plates are the same size. The cost to produce figure 27-10 is much less than for figure 27-9.

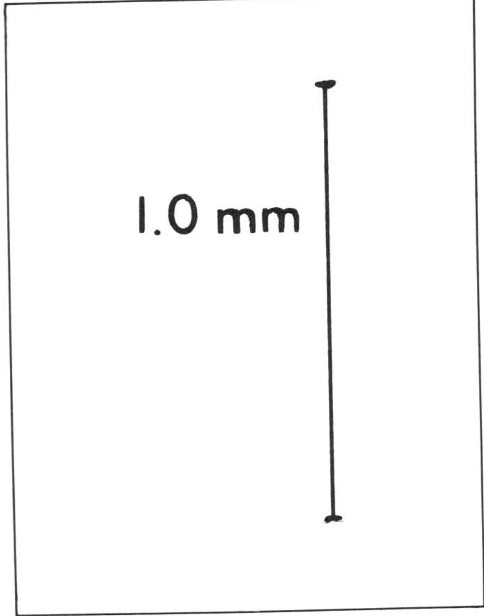

27-11. Enlargement of scale and numbers in figure 27-8 (without the 50 percent screen) to show that no dots are present over the lettering.

27-12. Enlargement of scale and numbers in figure 27-6. Note slightly ragged edges due to the dots from the halftone screen.

spot on the printing plate. This process is called a "double burn" of the printing plate, or a combination shot. The result is a halftone image with solid letters or numbers superimposed upon it (fig. 27-11; see fig. 27-8).

2. *Direct labeling.* In this case, all labels and numbers that are to appear in the halftone in print are placed directly upon the original image itself. These may include figure identification numbers, arrows, magnification scales, and any type of line copy that should be printed in the final illustration. Again, any special instructions that should not appear in print should be written on a paper cover sheet, which is also useful for protecting the letters on the surface of the original art.

   This type of illustration requires only one camera procedure. The illustration is treated as a normal halftone, and one negative is produced. The halftone negative is exposed to the printing plate. The letters in the final printed result have a halftone dot pattern in them (fig. 27-12; see figs. 27-6, 8-5).

3. *Labeling outside the image area.* In certain cases, it is desirable to have all labels and line information printed outside the halftone image area. This might be the case when all of the image area is important or when its appearance would be spoiled by having labels printed on it, as in the case of art illustrations or silhouette halftones. In this situation, some publishers want to have the labels set in type and placed next to the halftone image (see figs. 4-10, 15-45). More commonly, however, the labels are produced on an acetate or polyester overlay, as described in the first method above. The one difference is that all label material is designed to print outside the halftone area. The printed result is a combination of a normal halftone image and a line image (see figs. 27-8, 2-42, 2-43).

Before deciding which system to choose, the illustrator should check with the publisher or client. If this is not possible, a rule of thumb is that book publishers generally prefer overlay labeling because it is mor
publishers, on
to prefer direc
less expensive
labeling outsid
the subject ma

COLOR ILL

Color illust
the most attra
expensive of
tions. Because
the difficulty
color, the worl
printing long
white. New
tools, and bett
made color ill
mon in books
illustrators an
greater oppo
work reprodu
But althoug
there, so is
using color
ciently. This
some of the
that should b
using color in
There are
color printin
known as flat
commonly u
tions, and pr
used for tone
volve color se
of concern to
two, spot col
on the part o

Spot or Me
(Color Sepa

Spot color
tention on a
illustration.
with line ill
commonly f
widely used
and book p
may be used
as a tint. It i
cess, not a h
cess. Since
are used in
venient to u

(Chapter 25 provides additional information on creating these effects on maps.)

In a map that shows both land and water areas, the water area is commonly printed in a blue tint, made by printing spot color using a 20 percent to 40 percent screen. The dot pattern in the blue area is not likely to be the result of normal halftone screening; rather, it is from a percentage screen mechanically prepared by an illustrator using shading film (see fig. 25-29). The two parts of the map, the water and the land, are prepared by the mapmaker as two separate pieces of art, and the printer is instructed to shoot them separately as line illustrations. The printer makes two negatives, one with the outline of the land and the second with the screen tint of the water. The negatives are placed in register with each other and two separate printing plates are made. When printed, the land outline appears in black and the water area appears in blue. As long as the dot pattern in the screen used by the mapmaker is large enough, the printer will have no difficulty printing the screen tint area as a line illustration. Additional colors can be added to the map. Each additional color requires a separate overlay. With this method, there are three points to keep in mind.

1. Each overlay (or color) must register precisely with the other overlays. This is best assured when the artist uses a pin register system to keep all parts in perfect register (see fig. 2-44).
2. When dot patterns are used, they should be coarse enough to print easily. A 100-line-screen dot pattern should give good results with tints.
3. When several different densities of tints are to be used in one piece of art, try to have at least a 20 percent difference between the tint levels. A 20 percent, 40 percent, 60 percent, 80 percent range of tints will work. The tints at the extremes—10 percent and 90 percent—are often too light and too dark to be effective. The greater the contrast between the tints, the easier for the reader to understand the point. (This is true of gray tones as well as color—see fig. 25-29.)

Spot color can be used to produce any number of colors. Each color is unique and requires a separate printing operation. There is no natural blending of colors in spot-color reproductions, as can be done with process colors. Each color printed can be prepared exactly to match the requirements of the illustrator.

Certain standard colors do exist, however. The most common system is known as the Pantone Matching System (PMS), which offers a range of more than 500 ink formulas for standard ink colors, plus a number of special ink colors that can be obtained from ink manufacturers. In addition to standard inks, special inks can be used to create special effects. Metallic or fluorescent inks are available and require only one or two additional press runs beyond the normal black run to produce. The range available to the illustrator when using spot color is virtually unlimited; what is limited is the capacity of the printer to print as many colors as might be desired, since each color printed requires a separate printing operation.

Fortunately, spot color does lend itself to certain economies. When used to reproduce one-, two-, or three-color illustrations, it is generally less expensive than the alternative of process color. There is less camera time—if the art is provided in separate mechanicals by the illustrator—than when it must be separated by the printer. There is less difficulty in starting up the press run, since the register of spot color is often not as critical as process color. Nor is color balance as critical an issue: a slight imbalance in any color does not affect the other colors, since each is printed in a separate part of the illustration.

Different values may be represented by different screen densities, rather than different colors. For example, an illustration may be printed using both solid lines as well as screens of 20 percent, 40 percent, and 60 percent of a single color at only slightly more than the cost of printing the solid lines by themselves. Although each screen is photographed separately, all of the same color can be incorporated onto the same printing plate and printed in one pass. Since each screen may be specifically placed where the illustrator wishes it, this gives a wide range of possibilities at minimum cost. It should be noted that you should not apply screen over type or fine lines, as the addition of a screen breaks up the image of the type or line and makes it hard to read. Screens should be used only for large areas, while solid colors should be used for type or lines.

Preparing Spot Color

Spot color gives illustrators virtual control of the printing process. With that control comes the responsibility of creating the tools that the printer needs to make the process work. The illustrator must plan ahead. Since every color adds cost, it is useful to plan each step of the illustration for maximum color efficiency.

The first step is the base art. A finely detailed drawing with stippled or hatched shading may be drawn with pen-and-ink on any good drawing surface, but it is preferable that the base drawing and all the parts be prepared on a stable material such as polyester. In this way, the register will remain consistent despite changes in temperature or humidity. The base art should contain all the material that

Arwin V. Provonsha contributed to the text on preparing spot color.

will print in black. No other color should appear on this mechanical, nor should any material that should be black appear on any other mechanical. Registration marks are essential for aligning overlays. Sometimes it is useful to punch the base art to match a standard pin register system, if you know the printer uses the same system, and to prepare all other pieces of art to register on the same system. This helps ensure that each color will appear precisely where intended in the printed result (see fig. 2-44).

The second color should be prepared on a second polyester film, registered and taped on top of the first. Subsequent colors go on separate films, one to each, and are registered and taped over the ones before them. Finish with a protective paper cover sheet. Depending upon the subject matter, each separate color can be prepared as if it were a separate black-and-white line illustration, using the same techniques for linework. The critical difference is that register of all of the parts must be controlled at the drafting stage by the illustrator or they cannot be controlled at the printing stage by the printer. If this is done, then the printer can photograph each separate piece of art and find that the negatives register when it is time to make the printing plates.

Each layer should be clearly labeled for the printer, indicating the color and percentage screens to be used. Use a pressure-sensitive label on clear film well outside the printing area. Include names of the author and the publication as well as the illustration number.

When multiple tones of the same color are to be used, certain shortcuts are possible:

1. If the tones are separated spatially, individual overlays may be prepared for each value or all values may be included on the same overlay. Create a piece of positive art with solid areas where the spot is to be. Mark the screen percentage desired for each area on tracing paper placed over the plate. The printer will be able to handle the rest.
2. If different tones of the same color are adjacent to each other (for example, 20 percent, 40 percent, and 60 percent screens of blue), prepare one overlay that covers the entire area to be printed with blue ink; mark this overlay for 20 percent screen. Prepare the next overlay to cover the area to be printed with both 40 percent and 60 percent screening; mark this for 40 percent screen. Prepare a third overlay covering only the 60 percent screen area; mark this for 60 percent screen (figs. C-35, C-36). The printer will use a 20 percent screen for each of the overlays; however, each screen will be rotated slightly so the dots will form a rosette, giving the same percentage color but with better quality than if coarser screens were used for the 40 percent and 60 percent color. This procedure also gives good, crisp edges and avoids the problem of overlapping tones or white lines between values if the plates are slightly out of register.

Process Color

Spot color is used in line illustrations; process color is used for halftones. Simply put, process color is the printing of color using a halftone screen. The most common form of process color is four-color, but other options are two-color (duotone) and three-color. It is also possible to add more than four colors to process work to create special effects.

A duotone is a halftone printed from two separate negatives, one emphasizing the highlights or bright areas of the picture and the other emphasizing the shadows or darker areas. A duotone may be printed with two shades of black

ink (double-bla
black ink and
color. It thus r
camera negat
printing plates
press runs. A
ognized by th
visible in the h

Three-color
typically use t
ors: yellow,
cyan (blue). A
may be repr
three colors a
rated negative
photographing
times, using a
each time. E
negatives sho
color spectrum
made for eac
arate printing
each color. T
are printed s
that the eye i
ing that new
ated.

Four-color
are the most
procedure is
color, but bla
magenta, an
areas. The r
to each oth
densities in
the impressi
color in the o

Halftone Co

The halfto
cess color m
sion or refle
copy, the im
of light pass
ent film. C
slides, and
amples. Re
thing from
to the eye,
and drawing
the two typ
printing pro

Transmis
encies) is w
industry, i
and in comm
due largely

35mm camera, which can produce negatives or positive transparencies as original copy, and to the development of curved-drum laser scanners, which made it possible to produce high-quality color separations in less time and with less effort and expense than conventional graphic-arts cameras.

Reflection, or reflective, copy was widely used when separation was done by camera. As the camera has yielded to the scanner, however, reflection copy has fallen out of favor. This is unfortunate for both illustrators and printers, since in many ways reflection copy is much easier to use than transmission copy. Photography produces a film negative as original copy. Since the rule of thumb in the printing trades is that original copy is the best copy, it makes sense to use film (transmission copy) instead of photographic prints (reflection copy) in color work based on photography.

The opposite is true with the work of most illustrators, however. Most original tone drawings and paintings are designed as reflection copy, and most are prepared on boards too thick to curve around a scanner drum. This leaves two choices, neither of which is good. Either the illustration must be sent to a camera to produce color separations at greater expense or the illustrator must photograph the art and submit flexible transmission copy. Although the camera separations may give the best results, the publisher may opt for the film copy, since it can be processed on the scanner and is less expensive.

A third option is available, although for the illustrator this may be even worse than the other two: The original drawing is peeled off the mounting board so that it can be mounted on the scanner as original copy. Stories exist of production houses with full-time staff members whose only job is to strip illustrations off their backings.

This demonstrates the dilemma facing illustrators and printers today: most illustrators prefer to prepare reflection copy and most printers, given the option, would prefer to work with it. Yet the curved-drum scanner has created a technological trap for both that makes it difficult to use reflection copy.

Were it not for these problems, two characteristics would make reflection copy the preferred method. First, it is easier to read than transmission copy. This permits earlier agreement on the color tones that are to be matched in the negatives, in the proofs, and in the final printing. Since printing is an art and not a science, this agreement is critical. The sooner the illustrator, the publisher, and the printer agree on the color values, the less expensive the production process. The second advantage follows from the first. Since the final printed product is itself a piece of reflection copy, it is much easier to compare it to an original that is also reflection copy. A reflection original is much closer to what can be produced in print than a transmission original. Printers cannot match the tones created by light shining through film. They can come much closer to matching the tones of light reflected from photographic prints or artists' paintings.

Fortunately, a new generation of flatbed scanners and video digital cameras may soon solve this problem. As this technology becomes available, the form of the copy may no longer matter. What will matter is finding the form that gives the best working image of the original copy.

Responsibilities of the Illustrator in Using Process Color

The responsibilities of the illustrator when using process color are not as great as those to be faced when creating spot color. Generally speaking, the normal care required in the production of black-and-white halftones will be all that is needed. Yet care should be exercised, for the cost of producing color is significant, and the cost of the original color copy may well be significant too.

The one area where special care is needed is in the handling of transmission copy. Since transmission copy is currently more popular than reflection copy there are a few key points to keep in mind.

It is difficult to gauge the density of color in transmission copy, since the intensity of the light passing through it is subject to infinite variation. Unless transparent illustrations are viewed under carefully controlled conditions, such as on calibrated light boxes, colors thought to exist in the transparency do not appear in print, and vice versa. Since the color range of film is much greater than that of ink on paper, be prepared to compromise.

If it is not possible to reach agreement with your printer as to the exact colors in your illustration before the negatives are made, try to do so afterward. Ask for a prepress reflection proof. This may be a Cromalin, Transfer Key, Matchprint, or some other type of proof. Most color proofs, including press proofs, provide only an approximation of the final printed result. But this approximation is normally good enough to tell whether or not you will be satisfied with the end result. Usually this is the last chance you will have to exercise control over the appearance of your illustration. Be sure to take it. It is often very difficult to describe to a nonartist the color you wish to see in print. A simple way to do so is to circle the area on the color proof that is off and attach a piece of reflection copy showing the color you wish. The printer may not be able to match the color exactly, but at least he knows the color you are seeking and where you want it to appear.

If your illustration has been enlarged from its original size, or cropped in any way, be sure to check this in the proofing stage. Graininess caused by enlargement may be exaggerated by the dot pattern of the halftone. Cropping especially should be checked to make sure that nothing essential has been removed. This is particularly critical with transmission copy, since it is difficult to affix crop marks to transparencies in a way that can be retained through the production process. There is an ever-present danger that crop marks may be overlooked or misread with transparent copy.

The problem of cropping is made more complex if several transparencies are to be stripped together in one plate. If you plan to make one illustration out of several pieces, you might make black-and-white reflective prints of the transparencies, crop the prints or photocopies of the prints, and mount them to show the printer how the final illustration should appear. This will help prevent expensive mistakes.

Additional problems arise if you wish to add labels or numbers to your illustration. Although such things can be handled easily with reflective copy, they become very complex with transparent copy, particularly if the original transparency is smaller than the final printed result (as, for example, 35mm slides). Labels generally must be submitted separately and have to be stripped on at a later date. Careful discussion with your publisher and printer is advised.

Also remember that, whereas reflection copy is one-sided, transmission copy can be viewed from either side. It is not always apparent to the printer which side is the right one. Careful labeling helps, but the possibility still exists that the illustration may be flopped, yielding a reverse print. This is another reason for requesting a prepress reflection proof. In only this way can you be sure that it will print the proper way.

The illustrator preparing mechanicals for the production of spot color exercises as complete control over the printer as the painter does over the brush. The printer becomes an extension of the illustrator's hand, transferring to paper the colors and designs the illustrator has determined. This is not true of process color. The procedure of printing process color is not a direct repetition of the illustrator's work, but a re-creation of it by new and different means. The printer is not an extension, but a companion working with the illustrator. And just as the painter cannot capture the work of nature completely on canvas, neither can the printer capture completely the work of the painter on paper. Both are artists, and both share the frustrations of art, of striving for perfection and never reaching it. The printing of process color is the supreme test of the printer's art. It has unlimited possibilities, but achieving absolute perfection is not one of them. In seeking out a printer for your work, do not look for one who is perfect; look for one who is willing to strive toward perfection.

One of the
sional attitud
how your wo
of others. By
how the thin
the tasks of
make your ov
Illustrators w
learn how th
are often dis
sults. Those
often find the
effort. Print
their trade.
more than w
they process
problems th
visit a large
ularly prints
and-white ar
color, it wo
visit a firm t
aration for
make a visit
with rapidly
Explain the
and your c
By sharing
your job be
in less time

The que
gious. If yo
ity control
others will
nize that yo
the finest p
may adopt
will lead to
one.

Part V
The Business of Scientific Illustration

Professional artists—and illustrators are artists—often fail to realize they are in business as much as any independent lawyer, doctor, scientist-consultant, or performing musician. Generally they hate to deal with the problems of asking for money, figuring out a proper contract, retaining copyright, and planning insurance or retirement. Many just want to produce the best art they can and hope it will be appreciated aesthetically, intellectually, and financially. Unfortunately, hope will not pay the rent, and ignorance of sound business practice is a prescription for failure, particularly for the self-employed. The artist must think professionally and must obtain information about copyright, contracts, setting up a business, and presenting a portfolio that attracts clients—topics covered in this section.

Most scientists, publishers, art directors, and other employers see the scientific illustrator as a businessperson, a professional whose services they need. A few, unfortunately, fail to place a high value on scientific illustration. The latter group usually includes people who do not appreciate the training and expertise required to achieve accuracy and quality. Their attitude, sadly, is encouraged by the "Work Made for Hire" clause of the United States copyright law of 1978, which gives credit for creation of works of art to the employer rather than to the actual creator if the creator-artist has signed a work-for-hire contract. This and other dilemmas and how best to handle them are discussed in chapters 28 and 29.

A corollary to ensuring due and proper credit for work done is ensuring due and proper payment. In addition to other topics that have to do with business practices, chapter 30 examines what to charge or what fees to accept, for the artist does not always get to name the price. Often it may be a matter of choosing between accepting what the client is willing to pay or not accepting the job. Knowing what going rates are and how to realistically estimate the time that is likely to be involved in an assignment will aid the artist in the complex matter of payment.

Virtually all scientific illustrators will work on a freelance basis at some point in their careers. Therefore, these topics apply to all of them. Their clients also will benefit from information in these chapters, particularly those on copyright and contracts.

28/Copyright

William Hamilton IV

As of January 1, 1978, a new copyright law became effective in the United States. The law is generally much more favorable toward artists than was its predecessor, under the terms of which the work of artists was not placed on the same legal footing as that of writers and photographers. It is essential that professional artists know about this law and understand how it applies to them and their relationships with clients. It is the artist's responsibility as a professional to be able to both protect himself or herself and advise clients about the impact of this law upon the work and the uses to which it may be put. As a supplement to the information covered in this chapter, a Copyright Information Kit is available from the Copyright Office, Library of Congress, Washington, DC (see Bibliography). It includes copyright information forms and circulars explaining how the forms are used and how the Copyright Office operates. Changes in procedures and interpretations, as well as the law itself, may affect some of the information provided here.

It is wise to remember that transactions prior to January 1, 1978, generally remain subject to the provisions of the old law. Renewal terms are subject to extensions under the new law and may affect work done prior to 1978. Under the old law, the renewal term was twenty-eight years; under the new law, it is forty-seven years. In certain circumstances, works that have been lost to the public domain since January 1, 1978, are reclaimable. Those in the public domain prior to that date are not. The advice of an attorney regarding the particulars of this issue is recommended.

As soon as a piece of work has been produced in tangible form, the reproduction rights are covered by a statutory copyright, which means that its use is reserved to the artist by law, provided the work is original (not copied from someone else's work), creative, and possesses some aesthetic qualities. The copyright essentially reserves to the artist an entire collection of rights regarding the subsequent use of the work or restrictions thereon. By contract with the buyer of the work, the artist may divide up the ownership of these rights in any manner that is mutually agreeable. Two extreme examples of this would be the sale of one-time use in a particular publication and the sale of all reproduction rights.

Copyright has nothing to do with the ownership of the work itself; the law deals only with the reproduction rights for the work. The ownership of the art is something that should be agreed upon separately with the buyer. Most professional commercial artists do not sell the artwork itself, and most national publishers buy only limited use of artwork.

These points about ownership apply only to freelance or independent contractors working on nongovernment jobs. Material for federal government publications cannot be copyrighted, as they belong to the taxpayers and reside in the public domain. Work done for state governments may be copyrightable, but the laws of each state vary. Artists who are employees are covered under the "Works Made for Hire" clause of the law and retain no ownership of work produced within the course of their employment unless they have some other specific arrangement with their employer. This is also the case with writers and photographers working as employees. A more thorough examination of the work-for-hire issue occurs later in this chapter.

Works that are copyrightable include graphic, sculptural, or pictorial creations of either a two- or three-dimensional nature, be they fine, graphic, or applied art or photographs. Also included are prints, globes, charts, technical drawings, and models. Audiovisual programs are also copyrightable as a series of related images viewed by projectors or viewers, and included are the sound recordings accompanying them. Among the things that are not copyrightable are ideas (they must be in tangible form), names, titles, or short phrases, although a trademark or specific way of dealing with a name is copyrightable.

REGISTRATION OF COPYRIGHT

Although a piece of artwork theoretically is protected from the moment it is produced in a tangible form, there are a number of important advantages to registering the copyright with the Copyright Office. Registration can serve as proof of the validity of the copyright, and if an artist is dealing with an infringement, the registration is necessary for pursuing legal action. Registration also protects against some defenses that an innocent infringer may be able to use against the artist who may have used a defective copyright notice. An innocent infringer is one who does not know that the work is copyrighted, usually because the copyright notice has been omitted by the artist, client, or publisher. Registration also makes the artist eligible to receive attorney's fees, court costs, and "statutory damages" in cases where the artist's loss and the infringer's profit are hard to establish. (In order to qualify for statutory damages, registration must have been in effect within at least three months of publication.)

It is advisable to place a copyright notice on the work for any publication, whether or not it is registered. The notice should occupy a position on the original art either on the front (where it will be included in the reproduction) or on the back. The key criterion in placing the notice is whether it provides an ordinary user of the work reasonable notice that the work is protected. If the work is published in a book, notice should be either on the work, on the same page, or on the book's copyright page. If in a journal, it should be on the work or in the caption. If an entire book is illustrated by a single artist, copyright notice should be on the copyright page or any page prior to the main text or on the cover or title page.

The proper form for copyright notice is ©, copyright, or "copr"; the artist's name, initials, or symbol; and the year. It is wise for the artist or author to request, in writing, that publishers include a copyright notice on the artist's contribution.

It is possible, of course, to publish work without registering the copyright or having it carry a copyright notice. Should you do this and then later decide to register the work, you have five years from the date of publication to do so. By the same token, a work need not be published in order to be registered. It is worth noting that the Copyright Office does not judge the originality of the work nor does it ensure or define the artist's right. Registration is merely that: registration of *claims* to copyright. The rights themselves are ensured and defined by law.

Forms

The registering of copyright is a fairly simple matter with the forms included in the Copyright Information Kit. If the work is primarily graphic, sculptural, or pictorial, form VA should be used. If text is the predominating factor, form TX is appropriate. In the case of a contribution to a collective work, the form appropriate for the contribution—text or pictorial, not the entire collective work—should be used. Form PA is used for the registration of audiovisual works. Accompanying the form should be the fee as specified in the Copyright Information Kit and copies of the work being registered—one if unpublished and two if published. Registration becomes effective on the day an acceptable application —including copies for deposit, fee, and correct forms—reaches the Copyright Office. Mistakes on the application may be corrected by submitting form CA. The term of copyright is the life of the owner plus fifty years. Institutional (and works made for hire) copyright is for seventy-five years from publication or one hundred years from creation, whichever is shorter.

Group registration is the most economical way to register for a copyright if more than one piece of work is involved. A collection of unpublished work may be registered under a single title if the materials are presented in an orderly form, bear a single collective title, are entirely by the same person as the one claiming the copyright, or, if by different people, at least one person has contributed copyrightable material to each work in the collection. There is no limit to the number of works in a given group. In cases where the work has been published in several periodicals

during a twel
with a spot ill
it may still b
each contrib
copyright not
name (such as
lective works)
form GR/CP
collected pap
form VA. The
accompanied
copy of each
if unpublishe
the best editi
for deposit w
fice.

Deposit of C

Provisions
deposits of m
complete cop
"alternate de
where a grap
dimensional.
posit. In such
can be photo
parencies, ph
other two-di
tions of the v
viewed throu
should, in th
tration, be th
ample, 35mr
smaller than
7.6cm) nor
inches (20.3
reproduce th
original and
rightable con
title and the
of one or m
work should
the work has
position and
notice should
one piece of
This could
work, if it is
very large, sl
the copyright
a different se
garding what
deposited. C
visions of th
posit.

In some ca

published in the United States, copies also may have to be supplied to the Library of Congress. For published work, the normal fee and registration procedures cover this. For work registered previously as unpublished, registration should be updated within three months of publication with copies of the published work sent to the Copyright Office for Library of Congress deposit with the appropriate forms, unless the work falls into specified exempt categories. (This should be checked with the Copyright Office or on the copyright instruction forms.) The Register of Copyrights must request copies from you when the work is published, and you become liable for fines only if you have not complied within three months. Compliance with the registration procedures for published material should satisfy this requirement. This in no way affects the validity of the copyright.

RIGHTS

The rights that the artist, as the creator, possesses upon the creation of a piece of work and that are confirmed by the registration of the copyright with the Copyright Office, are stated by the law as follows: "The owner of a copyright has the exclusive rights to reproduce the work, sell and distribute the work, prepare derivative works, perform the work publicly."

The rights to reproduce the work, whatever the reproduction form, may be divided up and transferred in whatever manner is agreeable to the parties involved. All transfers of this nature should be written and signed by the copyright owner or his agent. It is important to realize that it is possible to lose all rights to a work and the art itself when there is no written agreement between artist and client. Federal district court decisions have reversed the assumptions about the new copyright law under which most artists had been working by ruling that a work-for-hire arrangement may exist between an artist and a client even when there is no written document to that effect. (In the past, artists understood that for work-for-hire to take effect, there had to be a signed contract stating that.) The issue is still open to interpretation, either through the courts or through clarifying legislation. In the meantime, artists must protect themselves with some form of written contract (see chapter 29).

It is generally in the artist's best interest, whenever possible, to sell only limited reproduction rights. This may not always be practical or even desirable in the cases of artists beginning in the field, of quite small jobs, or of work so specific that no financially rewarding reuse can be anticipated. It may be, however, that a drawing is made for a book that is expected to sell well and go through several editions, and from which derivative products may be obtained—all involving the artwork in question. It is only reasonable for the artist to expect to share in the financial rewards for the subsequent use of his or her work. This is not possible when all rights have been sold.

One-time reproduction rights are the basic unit of sale by freelance artists in the commercial sector. In most cases, the buyer does not need to obtain all rights to a piece of work. The artist should negotiate to sell only the rights that the client specifically needs and is willing to purchase. Such agreements should be in writing and signed by both parties.

Magazines, newspapers, and anthologies are considered to be collective works, and the law provides that "the copyright of each contribution is separate from the copyright of the entire collective work." (Unless the artist agrees in writing otherwise, he or she usually owns the copyright of the artwork and sells the owner of the collective work only such rights as are agreeable to both parties.) Again, it is wise to have some verifying document signed by all parties. In the case of magazines and newspapers, the rights sold are usually "first North American (publication) rights." If there is no written agreement, the owner of the collective work has the following rights: to use the art in the collective work for which it was bought, in subsequent revisions of that work, and in later collective works of the same series. It is assumed at this time that the buyer cannot use the art in other collective works except later editions of the same work.

Selling nonexclusive rights only ensures that the artist may sell the work elsewhere at the same time. Obviously it must be specified in writing what rights are being sold. Tad Crawford, auther of *The Visual Artist's Guide to the New Copyright Law* (see Bibliography), recommends a simple letter:

> This is to confirm that in return for your agreement to pay me $_____, I am transferring to you first North American rights to my work titled _________ described as follows: ___ _________ for publication in your magazine titled _________.

Such a letter should be signed by the seller (artist) and the buyer (owner of the collective work or authorized agent). See chapter 29 for more information.

WORK FOR HIRE

One aspect of the new copyright law that is disliked by artists is the "Work Made for Hire" clause. In effect, this clause says that the employer or other commissioning party owns the copyright in a "work made for hire" as if that party had in fact created the art (see fig. 29-5). This means that the artist working under such an agreement has no rights whatsoever in the use or reuse of the artwork. Most artists in the employ of public and private institutions are covered by this clause. And it means that copyrights on work done during an artist's hours of employment belong to his or her employer, be it an agency or an individual.

A freelance artist should be extremely wary of signing any contract or legal paper that contains a clause stating that the work created is done on a work-for-hire basis or in any other way implies entrance into an employee situation. Federal district court decisions have made it possible for a self-employed artist to be considered an employee with regard to ownership of copyright even if no work-for-hire or employment contract has been signed. This can occur because the new copyright law does not define the terms *employee* or *employment*, and that has allowed the courts to revert to the definitions of *employment* used by the old copyright law. The new law seemed to imply that a person could be regarded as an employee only if formally employed by someone (receiving salary, benefits, having taxes withheld) or if a work-for-hire agreement had been signed. The courts, however, in defining *employment*, have assumed an employee to be someone commissioned to do work at the behest of and under the supervision of the buyer. This means that an artist who agrees to create a piece of art to the specifications of the buyer—if the buyer may suggest changes as the art develops or cancel it altogether—has entered into an employee agreement with the buyer and is subject to the works-made-for-hire provisions of the copyright law.

This state of affairs can occur if there is no contract stipulating the relationship between artist and buyer. It is possible, in some cases, to negotiate a satisfactory work-for-hire situation. There may be addenda to the contract stipulating reuse payment, name credit, and so on. In such cases, the only thing the artist may end up signing away would be the right to reclaim the work after thirty-five years. (In all cases except work-for-hire, the creator has the right to terminate the grant of copyright during a five-year period thirty-five years from the date of the original sale.)

One trap used by some unscrupulous clients is to include nothing about work-for-hire in the contract or in negotiations but to send the payment check stamped on the back, "Negotiation of this check constitutes agreement that the work was done as a work-made-for-hire." If the illustrator wants to retain rights to the work, the only legally safe action is to return the check uncashed, along with a letter stating that there was no work-for-hire agreement, and that unless a check without this statement on the back is forthcoming, legal steps will be taken. This is an example of the importance of having a signed contract (presumably without a work-for-hire clause) to back up any legal action.

The work-for-hire clause is more than a complete transfer of rights; it includes ownership of the art itself and cannot be appealed. The artist who works under a work-for-hire arrangment is accepting the disadvantages of being an employee and receiving none of the benefits (such as retirement plans, medical coverage, security) that an employee ordinarily receives. Efforts by artists and other creators are underway to alter this part of the law.

COPYRIGHT INFRINGEMENT

The artist who finds that his or her copyrighted work has been used without permission may file for an infringement suit against the individual(s) involved. In order to win such a suit, the artist must be able to prove that he or she indeed owns the copyright to the work and that the infringer did indeed copy the work. In order to prove the first point, the artist need only produce the registration of copyright, since this constitutes proof of ownership.

Lacking regist
the artist may
ing personal de
in question. In
second condit
produce evide
ilarity of the
original and e
fringer had ac
key to the for
ordinary pers
works must c
copy of the o
for two peop
same subjec
ways.) In cas
tual damages
strate, the ar
"statutory da
$250 and $10,
infringed upo
is innocent, t
$100. Or, if it
tional, the av
as $50,000. I
may prevent
and dispose
Also, awards
and attorney

Fair Use

Not every
out express
ment. It ma
use." The ar
The four fac
ing it are: (1)
involved a p
character o
much of the
what effect t
value of the
ment, the k
nary person
believes tha
from the oth

As a pot
artist is wis
mind when
rials. Chang
execution a
piece of wo
new work a
aesthetic.
contracts h

in case of a copyright-infringement suit.

When work is used for nonprofit educational institutions, it is considered fair use—subject to certain legal restrictions on the number of copies made and the amount of material copied. Individuals wanting to use published material (such as photographs) for reference or teaching should familiarize themselves with fair-use restrictions. It is possible to gain permission to use a piece of work by obtaining a letter of permission from the copyright holder. The letter should specify how the work will be used and should contain the phrase "consented and agreed to" and be signed by the owner of the copyright.

This chapter is a brief introduction to the aspects of the new copyright law that apply to scientific illustrators. It is not intended to be a complete interpretation of or a final authority on the law. These await future test cases and the interpretation of the courts. Obtain the Copyright Information Kit from the Copyright Office and review it. For a more complete treatment of the law and how it applies to artists, read *The Visual Artist's Guide to the New Copyright Law* and *Legal Guide for the Visual Artist*, both by Tad Crawford (see Bibliography). It is to every artist's advantage to be thoroughly familiar with his or her rights and responsibilities under the copyright law.

29/Contracts

John W. Karapelou

Professional illustrators are for the most part in the business of selling some form of reproduction rights to original images they create. Notwithstanding consultation services, that is the illustrator's primary source of income. Therefore, apart from their role as visual communicators, they must be responsible businesspeople. Contracts are a normal function of doing business. They add a professional commitment to business arrangements and are a protection for all parties concerned (fig. 29-1)

A contract is essentially an agreement between two or more parties. For a contract to be binding and enforceable, it must fulfill four legal requirements: mutual consent; competent parties; lawful considerations; and valid subject matter.

The elements of "mutual consent" are the offer and the acceptance. The offer is a promise that becomes a legal obligation if accepted. It can be oral or written. Oral contracts are more difficult, but not impossible, to substantiate and do allow the artist a certain amount of legal recourse. Written contracts are much easier to enforce and therefore are preferred.

"Competent parties" means that the various individuals who are providing the mutual consent are legally qualified or fit to do so. This is particularly important when an individual is serving as an agent or representative for a corporation or organization. It must be established that such an agent (for example, an art director) is empowered to provide such contractual consent on behalf of his or her employer.

"Valid sub
there must be
in the agree
one cannot le
to commit an
intentional pl

"Considera
the parties t
one party to
not an oblig
consideration
by one party
service (prom

A contract
endorsed (sig
parties involv
feel intimida
ment submit
and signatur
most busines
and change.
rangements
first-draft co

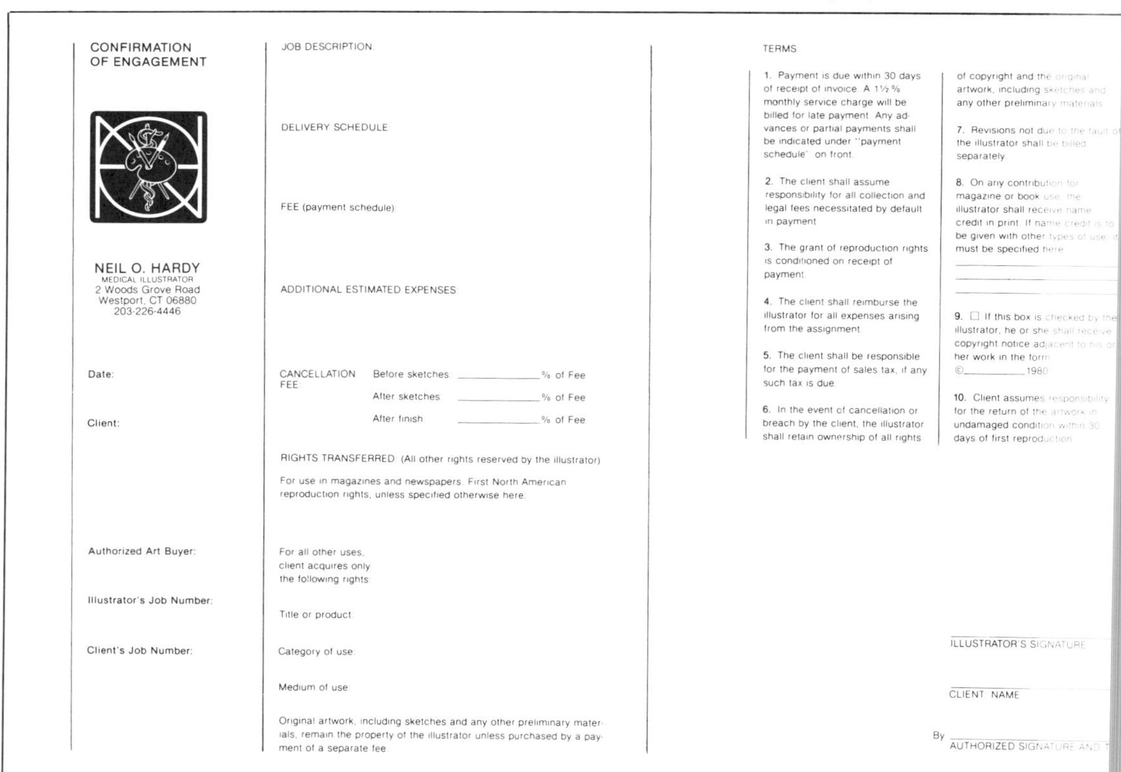

CONFIRMATION OF ENGAGEMENT

NEIL O. HARDY
MEDICAL ILLUSTRATOR
2 Woods Grove Road
Westport, CT 06880
203-226-4446

Date:

Client:

Authorized Art Buyer:

Illustrator's Job Number:

Client's Job Number:

JOB DESCRIPTION:

DELIVERY SCHEDULE:

FEE (payment schedule):

ADDITIONAL ESTIMATED EXPENSES:

CANCELLATION FEE: Before sketches: ______ % of Fee
After sketches: ______ % of Fee
After finish: ______ % of Fee

RIGHTS TRANSFERRED: (All other rights reserved by the illustrator)

For use in magazines and newspapers: First North American reproduction rights, unless specified otherwise here:

For all other uses, client acquires only the following rights:

Title or product:

Category of use:

Medium of use:

Original artwork, including sketches and any other preliminary materials, remain the property of the illustrator unless purchased by a payment of a separate fee.

TERMS:

1. Payment is due within 30 days of receipt of invoice. A 1½% monthly service charge will be billed for late payment. Any advances or partial payments shall be indicated under "payment schedule" on front.

2. The client shall assume responsibility for all collection and legal fees necessitated by default in payment.

3. The grant of reproduction rights is conditioned on receipt of payment.

4. The client shall reimburse the illustrator for all expenses arising from the assignment.

5. The client shall be responsible for the payment of sales tax, if any such tax is due.

6. In the event of cancellation or breach by the client, the illustrator shall retain ownership of all rights of copyright and the original artwork, including sketches and any other preliminary materials.

7. Revisions not due to the fault of the illustrator shall be billed separately.

8. On any contribution for magazine or book use, the illustrator shall receive name credit in print. If name credit is to be given with other types of use, it must be specified here:

9. ☐ If this box is checked by the illustrator, he or she shall receive copyright notice adjacent to his or her work in the form:
©______ 1980

10. Client assumes responsibility for the return of the artwork in undamaged condition within 30 days of first reproduction.

ILLUSTRATOR'S SIGNATURE

CLIENT NAME

By ______
AUTHORIZED SIGNATURE AND T

29-1. Sample contract. Courtesy of Neil O. Hardy.

sidered a proposal, with everything in it negotiable to some degree. If any party is uncomfortable with a portion of the proposed contract, that party should insist on changing that portion to one that is mutually agreeable.

It is wise to seek professional legal guidance on any contract the artist considers to involve a high degree of risk, particularly if the contract is proposed by a large corporation or publisher. Issues at risk could be such things as amount of money, investment of time on the project, extent of copyright stipulations or transfers, or limitations on project size. The greater the risk, the more likely the need for professional legal counsel. Try to find a lawyer who has had experience with the new copyright law, especially as it applies to illustrators. Shop around.

Once you have a written contract offer, read it carefully before you sign. Do not rely on previous correspondence or oral assurances concerning any points in the contract. The Parol Evidence Rule states "that where an agreement has been reduced to writing, which the parties intend as the final and complete expression of their agreement, evidence of earlier expressions is not admissible to vary the terms of the writing." In simple terms, a person is bound by what is signed, not by what might have previously been discussed. Notable exceptions are contracts signed under fraud or duress.

One of the major mistakes leading to defective contracts is the lack of specificity. If anything is capable of having more than one meaning, it should be reworded so that it can be understood to mean only one thing. If this means adding definitions, then add them to clarify the identity of the subject matter. For example, under a particular contract, the term *plate* might mean one illustration; under another contract, it might refer to four spot illustrations arranged in a particular image area. A *plate* may mean only one book-page plate to the publisher, whereas it might be composed of four illustration plates submitted by the illustrator. Do you get paid for four plates by your definition or for one plate by the publisher's definition? Be sure the contract is specific!

At the time the assignment of a potential project is being negotiated, it is appropriate to request and review the client's standard client-artist contract. If it is largely acceptable but requires one or more terms of agreement to be added or deleted, you can merely cross through disagreeable terms and type or handwrite additional terms directly on the original contract. Alternately, you can carefully cross through (delete) any items in the client-provided contract and affix a second typewritten sheet of addenda (additional terms) you prepare. In either case alterations are initialed by both parties and the contract signed in the usual manner. If, however, a contract provided by the client requires extensive and necessary revisions or is unacceptable, or if the client does not have a contract, submit your own contract for review. It is not important which negotiating party's contract form is used, only that the terms agreed to are mutually satisfactory.

TYPES OF CONTRACTS

The work situations that illustrators encounter will vary from job to job and client to client. A wide variety of contracts can be used for most situations. They range from a few simple sentences, as in a short letter of agreement (fig. 29-2), to a more complex, longer document

From: ______________________

To: ______________________

This memorandum constitutes a letter of agreement between ______________________ (Client) and ______________________ (Illustrator) for [number] full-color continuous-tone medical illustrations to be prepared for ______________________ (Publication).

1. The ______ [number] illustrations are to be used as full-page art for each section title page; to be reproduced as four-color halftone, vignette (where applicable), dropout halftone.
2. First North American Reproduction Rights only; all other rights reserved to Illustrator. For use in ______________ [Publication] only. Original art to be returned to Illustrator within thirty days of completion of production and publication.
3. Full name credit line for Illustrator on title page; Illustrator's initials or signature will remain affixed to each illustration.
4. All final sketches are due on __________ [date]. All final art is due on __________.
5. A fee of $__________ per illustration, for a total of $__________ (not including messengers or other shipping costs, which will be additional charges) to be paid within thirty days of delivery of all final art.
6. The Illustrator is to be provided with complimentary copies of ______________ [Publication] within thirty days of publication.

By signing below, the parties acknowledge and accept the terms outlined above.

______________________ Illustrator ________ Date
______________________ Client ________ Date

29-2. Sample of a relatively simple letter of agreement outlining all basic concerns: number and type of illustrations, rights granted, credits, dates, fees, and number of copies of the publication. The illustrator can develop a standard format that can either be drafted as a custom memo to a specific client or as pre-prepared forms with blanks (see fig. 29-1).

Name of Magazine
Illustration Contract

Illustrator or Agent: ____________________

This agreement, upon its acceptance and return by you, shall constitute a contract for artwork to be created by you or your agency and purchased by MAGAZINE.

You agree to create and execute the following commissioned original artwork for MAGAZINE:

Preliminary sketches of the artwork shall be submitted to MAGAZINE not later than __________ [date] and the completed artwork submitted not later than __________ [date].

As payment in full for the artwork and all other rights granted herein MAGAZINE will pay $__________ to you. Payment will be made upon completion of the artwork in a form satisfactory to MAGAZINE. MAGAZINE reserves the right to reject and refuse acceptance of commissioned artwork that is not in accordance with instructions and specifications communicated to you. MAGAZINE also shall have the right to edit, correct, adapt, exhibit, and publish or not publish the artwork. Artist shall be given first option to perform revisions whenever possible.

In return for the above-mentioned payment, MAGAZINE shall have North American and French editorial rights for one-time use and reserves the right to select the artwork for reuse as follows:

1. In its Chinese co-publication, at the flat fee of $__________ per color illustration and $__________ per black-and-white illustration;
2. In reproductions of inside editorial pages or the MAGAZINE cover (including the logo in original or updated form), without additional payment;
3. In literature or advertising promoting sales of MAGAZINE, upon additional payment of 50% of the original fee for each creative use. However, minimum payment will be $__________, and all usage will include your usual credit line.
4. In a poster, compilation or other editorial product to be sold by MAGAZINE, upon additional payment of 50% of the original fee for each creative use.

To facilitate reuse, MAGAZINE may retain a reproduction-quality duplicate transparency of the artwork. Original work shall be returned to you.

You will have the right to reuse or resell the artwork on a royalty-free basis. Such right of reuse or resale shall be subject only to the following conditions: (1) each republication of the artwork shall bear the following copyright symbol: "© [artist's name] for MAGAZINE; and (2) the artwork shall not be reused or sold for reuse in North America within a period of ninety days from the date of its original use by MAGAZINE unless individual permission is granted.

In the performance of this contract you are an independent contractor and are neither an agent nor an employee of MAGAZINE.

If you agree with the terms of this contract, please indicate in the appropriate space below.

Accepted: ____________________ Illustrator
Date: __________
Social Security #: ____________________
____________________ MAGAZINE
__________ Date

29-3. The sort of preprinted contract of average complexity that frequently is presented by publishing and agency clients. Note that the number and type of illustrations must be specified by the illustrator or art director. Also note the implication in the sixth paragraph that the client retains the right to stipulate the conditions for reuse of the art, even though the artist owns the original art and its copyright. If objectionable to the illustrator, such clauses can be crossed out and initialed by both parties before signing. Additionally, there is no mention here of complimentary copies or tearsheets for the illustrator; this would require a handwritten and initialed addition.

(fig. 29-3), as
client-artist ag
29-4). Falling i
of assignmen
statements on
assignment ag
the artist), a
(from the clie
contracts on
the selection
ity dictated b
of the work,
ship), and th
or another, t
the job: gener
specific art
deadlines, fe
ules, and tra

Generally,
of money, tin
ity, or any c
should be p
creasingly
tract. But for
letters and s
cient. Notari

CONTRAC

When det
involves mor
elements of
portant to
and specific
sult, illustr
routinely inv
terms of agr

- *An accur*
vices: to b
trator, in
illustratio
of comple
lustration
ect, estab
total illus
mum and
- *Basic fee*
client for
This can
a portion
a fee all
priced ill
on averag
(essential
cost per
type of il

1 Identification — Date ______

A. Illustrator: ______ B. Client: ______

2 Description of Job

A. Usage: ______

B. Style/Medium/Color: ______

C. Number of illustrations: ______

D. Size of illustrations: ______

E. Labels/Overlays/Other: ______

3 Estimated Fees

A. Estimated fees for work described in Section 2 only:

Preliminary art: ______

Final art: ______

Estimated total: ______

B. Expenses: In addition to the estimated illustration fees stated above, the Illustrator shall be reimbursed for out-of-pocket expenses such as photographic work, materials, copies, telephone toll charges, typesetting, postage, delivery, travel expenses, etc.

4 Corrections, Changes and Additions

A. The Illustrator shall not charge the Client for revisions or alterations made necessary by error on the part of the Illustrator.

B. The Illustrator shall not charge the Client for changes and corrections to first draft preliminary art.

C. Fees stated in Section 3 do not include Client changes, corrections or additions to second or subsequent draft preliminary art and to final art. The Client shall compensate the Illustrator for all such authorized corrections, changes and additions at the hourly rate of: ______

5 Payment Schedule

A. Upon authorization to proceed, the Client shall provide an advance payment of: ______

B. Subsequent payments: ______

6 Delivery Schedule

A. Preliminary art: ______

B. Revised preliminary art: ______

C. Final art: ______

D. Preliminary art shall be approved by the Client prior to the production of final art. Approval of preliminary art shall constitute agreement by the Client to accept final art unless final art is not substantially similar to preliminary art.

7 Grant of Rights

A. It is expressly agreed that the work created under this agreement shall in no way be considered work made for hire.

B. The Illustrator grants to the Client the following copyright license and use rights. All rights not specifically enumerated and transferred are reserved by the Illustrator: ______

C. A notice of copyright shall appear as follows in any publication of the illustration(s): ______

Authorized Signatures

Client ______ Date ______

Illustrator ______ Date ______

CLIENT AND ILLUSTRATOR AGREE TO ALL TERMS AND CONDITIONS SET FORTH ON BOTH SIDES OF THIS PURCHASE AGREEMENT

8 Payment

A. Net payment shall be made within 30 days of invoice date.

B. A 1.5% monthly service charge shall be applied to any balance due and unpaid for more than 30 days.

C. The Client agrees to pay any applicable state sales tax in addition to the Illustrator's fee and expenses.

9 Delivery Delays

The Illustrator's obligation to adhere to the delivery schedule is dependent upon the timely delivery by any/all vendors of the Illustrator and upon the timely delivery by the Client of authorization to proceed, required reference material or specifications, approvals of preliminary work and any agreed upon progressive payments.

10 Original Art

A. Original illustrations, including preliminary art, remain the property of the Illustrator.

B. The Client shall return to the Illustrator all final and preliminary artwork in good condition no later than 30 days following the Client's initial production use of the work as described in Section 2. The Client shall be liable for any loss or damage to originals.

C. The Client shall not alter the illustrations in any manner whatsoever without the consent of the Illustrator. In the event alterations are necessary, the Client agrees to offer any and all alteration work to the Illustrator on a right of first refusal basis at the Illustrator's hourly rate stated in Section 4C.

11 Credit Lines

A. The Illustrator shall receive name credit in print in any reproduction of any or all illustrations created under this agreement.

B. The Illustrator's signature shall appear in any reproduction of any or all of the illustrations created under this agreement.

12 Cancellation

A. In the event of cancellation, the Illustrator shall be compensated according to the fees stated in Section 3 for all preliminary and final artwork created by the Illustrator under this agreement as of the time of notification of cancellation. Unfinished illustrations shall be paid for at a prorated fee compatible with the fees in Section 3. The Client shall reimburse the Illustrator for all expenses (as stated in Section 3) incurred by the Illustrator as of the time of notification of cancellation.

B. In the event of cancellation, all preliminary and final art remain the property of the Illustrator and shall be returned to the Illustrator.

13 Re-Use

A. Illustrations created under this agreement shall not be used for purposes other than those stated in Section 7 without additional compensation to the Illustrator.

B. The fee for re-use shall be negotiated at the time of the request.

14 Subcontracting

The Illustrator may subcontract part of the preliminary and/or final illustration work at the Illustrator's discretion, providing that all work meets the specifications of the Client. All subcontracting fees shall be included in the Illustrator's fees stated in Section 3.

15 Warranty

The Illustrator warrants that all illustrations created under this agreement will be original, that the Illustrator has the full and exclusive right to grant the rights transferred and that none infringe upon or violate any right of third parties.

16 Agreement

This agreement is the entire agreement between the parties and supersedes all previous oral and written representations. It may not be amended or modified except in written form. This agreement shall be binding upon the undersigned, their heirs, successors, assigns and personal representatives, and reference within this agreement to "Illustrator" and "Client" shall include their respective heirs, successors, assigns and personal representatives.

17 Disputes

In the event that there is a dispute concerning this agreement and the Illustrator hires an attorney as counsel in the dispute, then the prevailing party in such a dispute shall be entitled to reasonable costs and attorney's fees to be paid by the other party.

29-4. Sample of a relatively comprehensive contract format presented by the illustrator. Note that this contract more extensively covers issues and concerns facing the illustrator and client than a simple letter of agreement. Contract designed by Palay/Beaubois, San Francisco.

pricing structure you feel is necessary to cope with project variability (see Setting Fees in chapter 30).

- *Essential deadlines:* for each stage of project completion by the illustrator. These may include dates for submitting sketches, storyboards, comps (comprehensive drawings), and final renderings for approval by the client.
- *Payment schedules:* to be met by the client at specific phases of project completion or within a fixed period of time upon completion of the entire job. On large jobs, it is sometimes customary for the client to pay one-third of the total fee upon consignment of the job, one-third upon receipt of sketches, and one-third upon receipt of final art. Similarly, for large jobs that involve an extensive commitment of time, the client will sometimes issue a monthly (or other fixed time unit) advance against the projected total fee for the job. However, government agencies may make payment only upon completion of project.
- *Definition of rights granted:* the new copyright law of 1978 largely defines the artist/author as the creator of an artistic or literary work, and in the absence of a written agreement to the contrary, the creator is considered the owner of the copyright. Therefore, transfer of copyright does not occur unless and until agreed to in writing by the illustrator (fig. 29-5), and it does not necessarily include ownership of the original art.

Recent federal district-court decisions have, however, apparently reversed the original intent of the 1978 copyright law by ruling that, in the absence of an agreement to the contrary, freelance artists or authors who accept commissioned assignments are considered employees who "work-for-hire." Work-for-hire can mean that the artist loses all rights to his or her work. Therefore, at this time it is very important that the freelance artist be protected against questionable work-for-hire interpretations by contractual agreements. (See chapter 28 for further information.) Specify the rights you are granting the client: first reproduction rights only, unlimited use, or exclusive rights. Define the area of intended use—for example, North America only, North America and Great Britain only, or the entire world. Establish the medium of reproduction in which the artwork may be used (magazine, textbook, commercial exhibit, television, 35mm slides); where in each medium it can appear (cover art, quarter-page inside); and how it will be reproduced (four-color, black-and-white, line conversions). Specify the exact publication intended for use. Include any agreem
use (such a
printings,
jackets, or r
subsidiary r
translations
another me

- *Ownership*
belongs to t
if freelance
tution if st
specified
This can b
cause man
assume th
paid for un
instance, i
of originals
fect access
sale of sub
rights, or f
as portfol
and gallery
- *Credit line*
tect the ar
nate redu

Dear ______________________

This letter of agreement commissions you to prepare ar
COMPANY ______________________
for delivery by COMPANY to client for the assignment.

The work to be prepared by you shall be considered wo
extent permitted by the copyright law of the United States
ownership and authorship in the work throughout the wor
PANY or its client.

You shall neither retain nor make any proprietary or othe
or services contributed or rendered to the Work, and you
owns any and all rights in such Work for use in all media c
including derived works, and the right to copyright the sar
in the name of its assignees, for the original copyright terr
extensions thereof.

COMPANY may use, change, add to, or delete from an
by you and you are not entitled to any authorship or other
with the use of the results of this assignment.

Further, this agreement is made with the understandin
prepare will not infringe on any copyright or personal or p
ers.

You will be paid a fee agreed upon by you and COMPA
completion of your work in accordance with the terms an
PANY's purchase order or the assignment.

Sincerely,

The undersigned is over the age of 21.
Accepted: ______________________ by ______
Date: ______________________ COMPA

29-5. A fairly typical work-for-hire contract. Note that price
illustrator could insert a fee and cross out offending portions,
contract, and then see whether the company would agree to

perceived value, which may be seen in the occasional omission of credit in published works. Be sure to specify in the contract the details of credit to be given. Indicate the content and placement of full-name (with title) credit on the book cover, book-jacket flap, title page, or acknowledgment, as well as individual credit lines, signatures, or initials juxtaposed to art.

- *Alterations:* changes made to the originals, or during the course of reproduction, that affect the image either in content or quality should require the illustrator's written consent. Alterations might include considerable enlargement, reduction, or cropping of the image; deletion of signatures or initials; changes on the original by another artist. Indicate whether you insist on the right to make changes that may be required in current or subsequent uses of the art (as for second editions).
- *Additional artwork:* requested after the contract has been signed. Clients may request additional uncontracted artwork and orally assure the illustrator of additional payment. This is not legally binding. Additional artwork should be covered in a separate agreement.
- *Provisions for termination of the project:* should the client cancel the project before it is completed. The illustrator should be paid for all artwork wholly or partially completed, based on average unit prices or at a prorated hourly fee compatible with the original fee structure of the project.
- *Incapacitation or death of illustrator:* if the illustrator is unable to fulfill his or her obligation because of incapacitation or death. The illustrator or the illustrator's estate should receive payment for all artwork wholly or partially completed under the same conditions as described above for termination of the project. The client should be allowed to arrange for another illustrator to prepare additional illustrations or to modify existing ones for which the illustrator has been paid. Beware of clauses that will hold the illustrator's estate responsible for the completion of the work. Since illustrators enter into personal-service contracts, which can be satisfied only by the artist, the estate would not be responsible for the completion of the work. Under limited circumstances, however, the estate might be held liable for damages.

A thorough and analytical review of any contract should reveal whether or not it contains all the terms you feel are necessary to protect yourself and your art as you engage in any business arrangement. If you feel that you are in over your head with a proposed contract, it is highly appropriate to request extra time to have it reviewed by a lawyer of your choice.

From simple letters of agreement to extensive multipage client-artist agreements, contracts are merely one of the many tools illustrators need for doing business. They are certainly nothing to fear.

30/Operating a Freelance Busines

Barbara N. Rankin and Elaine R. S. Hodges

The artist who chooses a career in freelance illustration not only is free to enjoy a personal choice of subjects or projects, but also must accept total responsibility for their successful execution and delivery. The freelancer usually works in a completely private environment, follows an unconventional work schedule, and works with other artists only on cooperative assignments.

Illustrators who are employed as staff within academic communities, medical schools, museums, and commercial establishments depend upon studio facilities provided with tools and raw materials, steady clients, and a regular paycheck. They can take for granted other benefits such as sick leave, paid holidays, insurance, and retirement plans. Freelancers, on the other hand, must provide these amenities for themselves.

Combining a staff position (full or part time) with freelance work is another option and can provide the best of both worlds if benefits come with the staff position. Freelancing on the side (or "moonlighting") has positive and negative aspects: increased diversity of work and additional income but also reduced free and family time and the increased pressure of deadlines.

Regardless of an artist's talent or technical abilities, the economic success of any freelance career is a direct result of self-discipline and the application of the practical skills required in small-business management.

STARTING OUT

No artist should consider a full-time freelance business career without careful preliminary investigation, especially in the area of financing. Enough cash should be initially available: perhaps enough savings to establish a studio with modest equipment and inventory, as well as enough to live on for six to twelve months, because many of the early activities involved in setting up a business are not income producing. The U.S. Small Business Administration (1441 L Street, NW, Washington, DC 20005) offers written advice and sometimes seminars for people starting small businesses, including occasional sessions for artists.

Potential Markets

The techniques for establishing markets for illustration are similar to those used in starting or relocating any business. The artist should research the area, determine the needs for illustration services, and contact the appropriate sources for assignments, whether in a familiar or new location. Review the local area with a map, then, if necessary, contact the chamber of commerce for information on the city, its suburban areas, educational institutions, hospitals, museums, industries, and organizations.

The reference department of any public library has market information, most of it updated annually. *Artist's Market*, *Literary Market Place*, *Publishers' Directory*, and *Gale Directory of Publications* are examples of such references. *Artist's Market* contains names and addresses of prospective clients from a variety of art-related industries, often including information about a client's specific art needs, contact person, and fees. *Design*

Career, by St
Talarico, offe
useful appen
Artist's Maga
umn listing p
of artwork wi

The yello
phone book
art and photo
agencies, pri
exhibit hous
photographer
tential sourc
scientific illu
contacts wit
torical societ
departments
vices; local
papers and
city, state,
mental prot
agencies: z
associations
preserves,
arboretums,
ological sup
agencies: a
tific books a

The med
prospective
universities
medical,
schools:
branches o
(American
American
Cross): go
book publi
and lay pe
cal magazi
and surgeo
in persona
maceutical
tising agen

When s
not overlo
signments
radius of y

trip may be worthwhile in establishing a long-term contract, which can be maintained later by telephone and mail.

Market availability may determine whether the freelancer can afford to pursue a specialized career or should concentrate on developing a diverse style of working. But since artists are involved in all forms of human communication, the ability to complete a wide range of assignments in a variety of illustrative techniques becomes a distinct asset readily appreciated by a prospective client. Some freelancers advocate accepting projects totally unrelated to the type of work they generally do in order to become established within a community. This exposure adds to the artist's general experience and can provide needed income.

The Small Business Administration reports that most new businesses do not make a profit for the first three to five years. To become financially solvent as rapidly as possible, seek assignments in your specialty first. Learning a new technique or subject area can be time consuming: you cannot, in good conscience, charge a client for your own education time when you have been hired as an expert.

Establishing Contacts

Once you have developed an appropriate list of organizations, the difficult job of landing assignments begins. There seem to be three accepted methods of client contact: personal referral from colleagues or previous clients, unsolicited letters of introduction, and personal interviews. The word-of-mouth reference is by far the most valuable recommendation, while the letter of introduction, even when accompanied with attractive samples, is much less effective. Unsolicited letters sent to scientists, publishers, hospitals, and lawyers engaging artists for court presentations tend to be largely unproductive.

With or without professional referral, the personal interview is an important opportunity to present yourself, while your portfolio is a showcase for your artistic abilities (see Portfolios, below). Create a businesslike impression enhanced by the careful choice of a wardrobe suitable for a business occasion.

At the conclusion of an interview, establish some means for the client to recall your meeting. Since art directors interview large numbers of artists, they cannot be expected to remember the work of each applicant. Therefore, it is wise to leave a current sample of your work with your name, address, and telephone number on file with the art director or client. A single-page résumé could be included with the artwork, but the professionally presented sample of your work remains the best introduction to your qualifications as an illustrator. Potential employers are more interested in what you can do than in your background.

After any interview, it is considerate to write a simple thank-you letter on your business stationery, which may result in your name remaining on file. You might also consider calling clients at reasonable intervals—for example, every three to four months—to inquire about the prospect of work. Be careful to differentiate between persistence and annoyance when calling contacts, and be very patient in waiting for responses to interviews or applications. In the case of some contacts it might take six months to years for the appropriate assignment to materialize.

Once you are called for a specific job, do everything possible to meet required deadlines. The first job done for any client is very important. You must impress the client with the professional quality of your work, your efficiency, and your promptness. If the first assignment is well done, the client is likely to seek more work from you. And even after the first job, it is unfair to the client for you to accept assignments when you know in advance that you cannot complete them within the allotted time. Dependability in all cases must be valued above your personal convenience. On the other hand, clients who habitually request work to be done on a "rush" basis should expect to pay for this extra service.

After the work is done, a bill or invoice must be submitted. For billing (as well as taxes), it is most important to keep good records. You may have a variety of projects completed for the same client; therefore, recording a detailed description of the individual assignment on each bill is essential to avoid confusion. Your conference and travel time are as valuable as studio board time and should be included in accounts for any project. Verifications attached to the bill's carbon copy (in your files) could include studio time sheets, hourly rate scales, records and receipts for materials, and itemized accounts for contract labor.

Setting Fees

Fees for commissioned artwork may be set by the artist or by the client. Even when the client names the price, it is a good idea to have in mind a fee you deem acceptable. Arriving at a notion of what is acceptable is largely a matter of experience coupled with a realistic sense of what the market will bear. Check with other illustrators about current fees for different types of illustrations in your local area. *Artist's Market* of the current year gives information about rates paid by various publishers for specific art spreads. The Graphic Artists Guild publishes *Pricing and Ethical Guidelines* (see Bibliography), a booklet listing average costs for various types of illustration, but these tend to reflect New York City prices and may be high for the rest of North America.

Most clients want an estimate of the total or cost per illustration, not the hourly charge. Use hourly prices as a guide, multiplied by the number of hours you estimate to complete a project. Many experienced freelancers suggest increasing—perhaps even doubling—that estimate in order to be realistic. Many jobs invariably take twice as long as estimated, and overhead costs must be taken into account: rent or mortgage, utilities, telephone, postage or messenger costs, supplies, and time for research, travel, correspondence, and consultation. Try to estimate in detail how much time and expense will be required for each item. Maintaining careful records of time and expense for jobs will provide a guide for future cost estimates.

The budget of the client must be considered. Obviously, clients are interested in paying as little as possible, but the nature of the client's resources should be assessed. It is unreasonable, for example, to charge a graduate student with a study grant of a few hundred dollars the same amount as an advertising agency with an illustration budget in the thousands of dollars. Biological scientists typically have very small budgets. In the medical and advertising fields, on the other hand, budgets tend to be quite a bit higher. Book and journal publishers' budgets may be in between. When discussing prices with a new client, it is wise to ask what the budget is and then decide if you can do the job for that price.

PORTFOLIOS

The portfolio is, by definition, a "portable case for carrying loose prints without folding," and as such has become a well-established means of introducing both artists and their abilities to prospective clients or employers.

Your portfolio is your personal service advertisement, so select the best examples of your work that illustrate your current abilities and interests. Student work and experimental projects should not be included unless you are currently working in this style. A piece that does not match your current expertise is a form of false advertising, and it may trip you up later should you receive an assignment based upon it.

Never apologize. Everything in your portfolio must represent your best efforts. Take time to choose your samples and design each unit or page with care. The subtle differences between a handsome, well-prepared presentation and a last-minute venture will be obvious to the viewer from the start. Your portfolio may be your first, and only, introduction to a client.

A selection of twelve to twenty pieces can demonstrate a variety of techniques and skills. Critically select featured items to match the specific client's interest in subject matter and style. An art director for a magazine that uses only black-and-white artwork will have little interest in full-color work, and a surgeon will not appreciate chemical diagrams rendered for a research radiologist. If you are interviewed by the same art director a second time, show a different collection of work. Sometimes employers are interested in seeing the progression of ideas from sketch to final published art. Therefore, if you have room, include a page of your sketching techniques.

Presentation

Be businesslike in presenting your materials, for many clues to your total professional ability are gathered from the examination of a portfolio. Let the client leaf through the portfolio, and do not volunteer elaborate explanations of various assignments unless requested to do so.

It is often helpful to provide a subject legend that includes the title, objective, media employed, mode of presentation (for publication or projection), and intended viewing audience of each piece. Include your name, address, and telephone number neatly and legi-

bly in your por
contents in cas

Keep severa
copies of a si
the portfolio.
leave your por
part of the da
"drop-off polic
lio must spea
not always be
contents. If yo
portfolio, requ

Be attentive
ple, keep sam
attractive ord
together simil
Be sure any
and trimmed
balanced, an
concise (see
to maintain
vertical form
a horizontal p
mat, or vice
one direction
come annoyi

Some illus
originals in t
they feel mo
interested in h
will reprodu
These artis
mainly of pu
Many artists
final publish
signments, r
clude sampl
journal repr
photocopy, p
reduced, of
be used as
tocopies.
photographs
oversized o
produced fo
photographe
for your stu
the job for t
then may b
folio as a s
slides. If s
carry a por
extra batte
cord) and b

Portfolio Types

Having considered the contents of portfolios, let us now examine their various styles and designs, apparent uses, and preparation. The simple fiberboard folder tied with strings, although practical for casual purposes, may suggest from its flimsy appearance that the artist is either fresh from art school or lacking in business experience. A leather case or other heavy material with zippered closings is not only more professional but also stronger and especially useful for carrying a sizable number of individually mounted pieces. Pockets in the portfolio can conveniently carry résumés, slides, and business cards.

Matting

When using original art in a portfolio, make certain the illustrations are clean (smudges and fingerprints are unprofessional). Mat the artwork to protect it from damage and use some form of backing. Cut the mat so that its opening is smaller than the artwork itself. A portfolio is especially attractive when all the mats are the same size. The illustration can be taped directly to the back of its mat or to a backing of mounting cardboard that is then hinged to the mat at its top edge (fig. 30-1). Regardless of how the mat is attached to a drawing, the backing of smooth cardboard or mat board will prevent holes from being punched accidentally through the artwork from the back. Acetate should cover both mat and artwork. The heavier weights of acetate or polyester look best, provide the most protection, and can be spread over the face of the piece and taped to its back (fig. 30-2). Another option is to secure the acetate to the mat with colored cloth adhesive tape neatly and evenly folded around the edges of the mounting materials. However, the tape edges may attract dirt and eventually look messy. If an original piece is in a friable medium

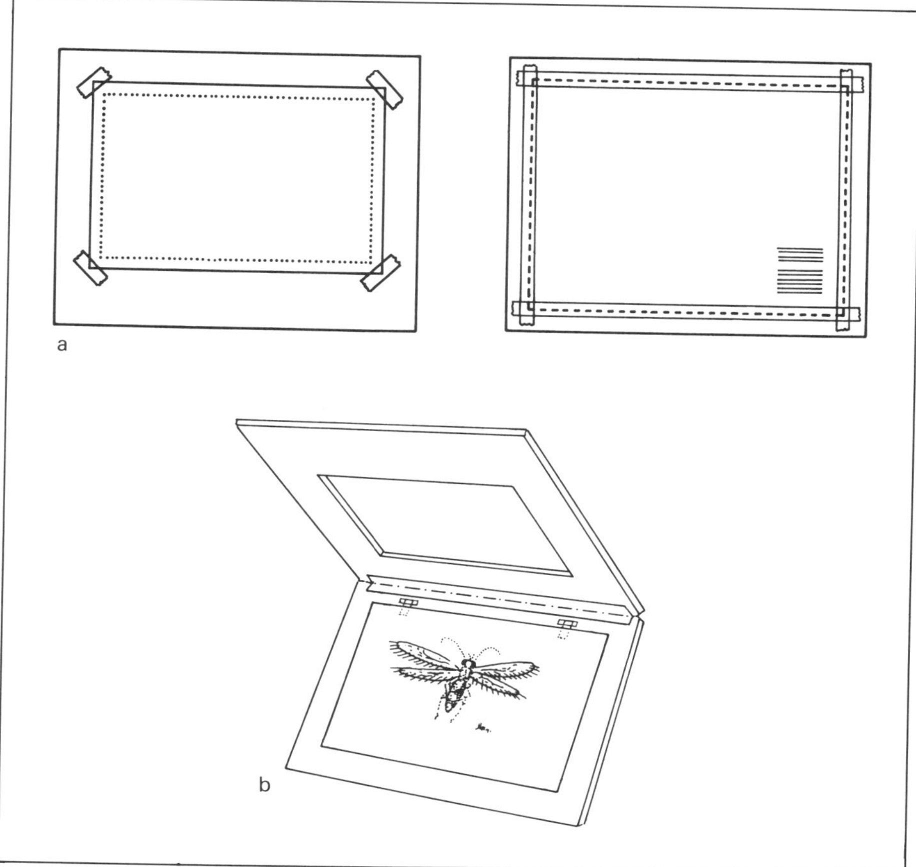

30-1. Matting drawings. *(a)* Attaching drawing to the back surface of a mat. The mat opening, represented by dotted lines, is smaller than the paper's outer dimensions. Tape a backing board (dashed lines), larger than the illustration but smaller than the mat board, to the back of the mat. Or a board the same size as the mat can be attached with double-sided tape. *(b)* Hinging mat to mounting board. The drawing is mounted on the board, preferably with vertical hinges. The mat opening is smaller than the outer dimensions of the drawing surface. Pen-and-ink on film, by Karen Schmitt.

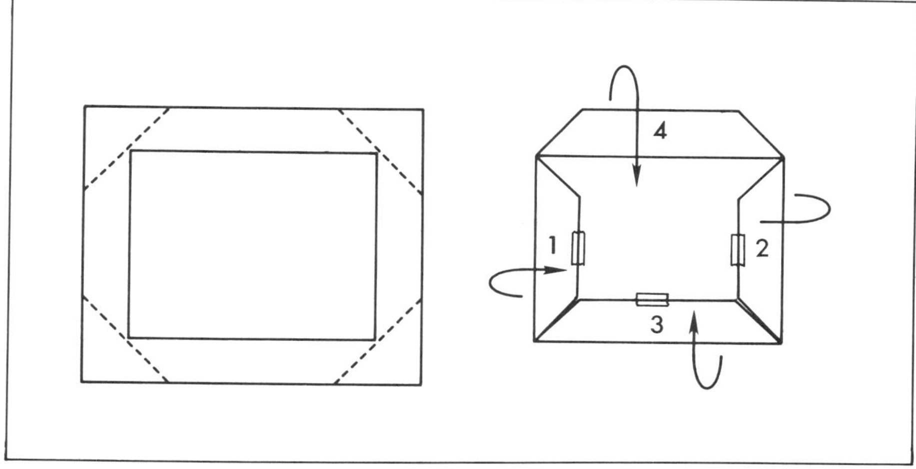

30-2. Covering a matted drawing. Cut a piece of acetate or polyester larger than the board to be covered. Cut corners of acetate as shown by dashed lines. Then fold opposing sides in order, first 1 and 2 (or 3 and 4), then the other sides, pulling each pair tight and taping to the back of the board in sequence. Use paper rather than acetate or plastic over carbon dust, charcoal, pastel, or soft pencil, unless separated from the surface by a thick or double mat. Pen-and-ink on film, by Karen Schmitt.

such as carbon dust or soft pencil, use a paper covering instead; static electricity from acetate or plastic may lift the medium off its surface.

Binders

If the portfolio consists of unmounted works, sketches, tearsheets, and photographs of larger pieces, a spiral presentation binder with acetate protectors can be used to display work attractively and professionally. Some binders are designed like loose-leaf notebooks, whereas others are intended to stand up on the desk like a flip chart. The choice of style depends largely upon the type of samples included (their physical sizes and shapes) and the intended market. In this type of portfolio, page design and neatness are important; one drawing per page is most effective.

Slides

Many graduate schools, the U.S. Office of Personnel Management (civil service), and employers request slide portfolios as part of an application. Carefully follow the client's suggestions regarding content, and make certain that you have professional-quality photographs of your illustrations to show them off to best advantage (see chapter 26, Copy Photography). Slides are easily assembled into a portfolio by using the 9- by 11-inch (22.5 by 28cm) soft polyester pages made for this purpose (available at most photography shops). Each page can hold twenty 35mm slides in individual pockets.

Occasionally, one or more slides might be removed from the page for closer examination or for projection. Label each slide with at least the copyright date and your name, so that it is not lost or returned by mistake to someone else's slide portfolio. You also may want to include where or how the work was published by indicating the information directly on the slide mount or by numbering the slides and providing a detailed legend on a separate sheet.

To ship pages of slides, reinforce both sides of the slide portfolio pages with cardboard and wrap securely with paper and tape before mailing in a large, flat envelope. Always include a cover letter in the mailing package, regardless of whether or not the client is expecting your samples. A business card slipped into one of the slide pockets is a nice touch. Your return address and a second mailing address label should be added to the inside package in case the mailing envelope is damaged or lost. Including a self-addressed, stamped envelope may ensure that your slides are returned to you.

THE ILLUSTRATOR'S STUDIO

Good studio management is the consequence of proper balancing of assignments, inventory, and billing. The institutional staff artist has many of these things provided, but the freelancer must rely upon personal resources. Although each illustrator develops a personal style of handling work, most projects seem to progress through the same logical steps—from the initial conference with the client to the delivery of the completed artwork. Establishment of priorities for the various stages of production is the essence of studio management. A wall chart or calendar can display at a glance assignments, stages of development, and projected deadlines for each client. A daily notation of priorities may be useful in scheduling jobs, and other lists help to maintain studio inventory of equipment, tools, and replaceable supplies.

Every artist should try to spend most of the workday at the drawing board instead of spending many hours on routine chores that accompany the average studio project (preparation for mailing, reordering of stock, or assembly of materials for billing). Organize work areas and group similar activ-
ities together t
the same time
photos together
ings to final sto
same color on c

Studio Layou

Assemble fu
ciency in mi
small studio, t
rate spaces for

- Flat area fo
matting.
- Flat area fo
ects and sk
ences.
- Illustration
space for m
mens: adja
and art sup
age; table,
shelf to di
ences: a pl
for referenc
while worki
- Desk area
used for e
drawings (
freestandin
- Office or ac
reference l
- Storage fo
pleted assi
drawers fo
large item
boards, pa
ing adhesi
drawings:
tical hang
neous ite
files shoul
val storag
and acid-f

Storage p
make findin
case of loss.
saves valual
habit of retu
cleaned an
again. Chap
most tools,
their use an
lustration, it
pared to wor
so the studi

ularly consist of a full range of supplies.

Equipment

Do not invest in sophisticated equipment that you will rarely use. Institutions (or the client) may be willing to lend such equipment or may require the work to be done at the client's laboratory because specimens cannot be removed. Consequently, locate sources of camera lucidas, microscopes, microprojectors, and copying machines for certain aspects of production rather than purchasing or renting them yourself. Unless the item is needed daily and is unavailable elsewhere, consider renting it.

Each addition to the studio should pay for itself within a reasonable time. Some major purchases that may be worth the investment if essential to increase workloads are microscope (stereo or compound or both), and camera lucida, opaque projector, copy machine, lettering machine, 35mm slide projector, instant camera for reference shots, and photostat copy camera. Obtain these only after a definite need for them has been established.

Any discussion of a working studio is incomplete without mention of its reference library. These are highly personal collections, enlarged gradually, which reflect the interests and education of their compilers. Anatomy, medicine, surgery, natural sciences, anthropology, world history, children's literature, and cartooning are some of the headings in one freelancer's library. Collect magazines and subscriptions to a variety of journals. A clip file or "morgue" should contain clippings and photographs of anything that can be used as a basis for future artwork. Also, guides to time management and various business practices, some of which are listed in the Bibliography, are essential to successful studio management.

OFFICE MANAGEMENT

Office management is an extension of studio efficiency. The "office" need not require a separate room, but its components should be isolated from the production areas. In simplest form, the office area should contain a typewriter, a computer, or both, plus storage containers for stationery (for billing and correspondence), assignments, accounts, studio inventory (permanent and replaceable), and business receipts.

Letterhead and Logo

Studio letterhead and business cards imprinted with your logo are useful forms of advertisement (fig. 30-3). The logo indicating your particular specialty should be eye-catching but uncluttered, and professionally to the point. Its design quality should reflect your taste, but consult a professional graphic designer if this kind of artwork is not your forte. On your business card include your telephone number (with area code) and full address with zip code. If the address is likely to change, include at least a phone number.

A studio letterhead that coordinates with or repeats the logo of the business card looks professional and is more likely to be remembered by a potential client. In the printing of business stock, putting the name and logo on a separate negative from the one with address and phone number will facilitate possible later changes. Other coordinated items might be invoice (possibly with separate colored carbon sheets attached) and adhesive-backed mailing labels. These labels also could be used on the backs of drawings or as studio identification in books. Rubber stamps can be ordered that give the artist's name and address or "Please return art to . . . ," "© John Doe, 19____," "Do not bend," and other phrases likely to be used repeatedly.

Storage and Filing

When the artist retains artwork, it should be kept in presentable condition—safe, clean, and readily accessible for reuse. Flat files or vertical files with hanging folders (alphabetized or otherwise labeled) are an effective means of storage. Protection from dust, sunlight, insects, water, extremes in temperature, and high humidity is essential. Any kind of strong flat cardboard box, such as that used for packaging photographic film or paper, is useful for this type of storage. For long storage of valuable artwork, archival-quality boxes and interleaving tissues are best (see chapter 3).

A standard filing cabinet for business files, separate from household expenses, might be subdivided as follows:

- Client and job records
- Employee records (subcontractors, agents, photographers)
- Invoices (outstanding and paid accounts)
- Expense receipts
- Art supplies (catalogs and product information)
- Bank statements (deposit receipts, canceled checks)
- Charge accounts
- Rent or mortgage (percentage of home used for office if office is not separate)
- Utilities and telephone (percentage used for business)
- Copyright forms and information
- Contracts
- General correspondence
- Organizations (correspondence, newsletters, directories)
- Public relations (résumé information, tearsheets, samples for portfolio)
- Education (workshops, courses)
- Studio insurance
- Retirement
- Equipment (warranties and instruction booklets)

In the files devoted to equipment, keep a detailed list of major

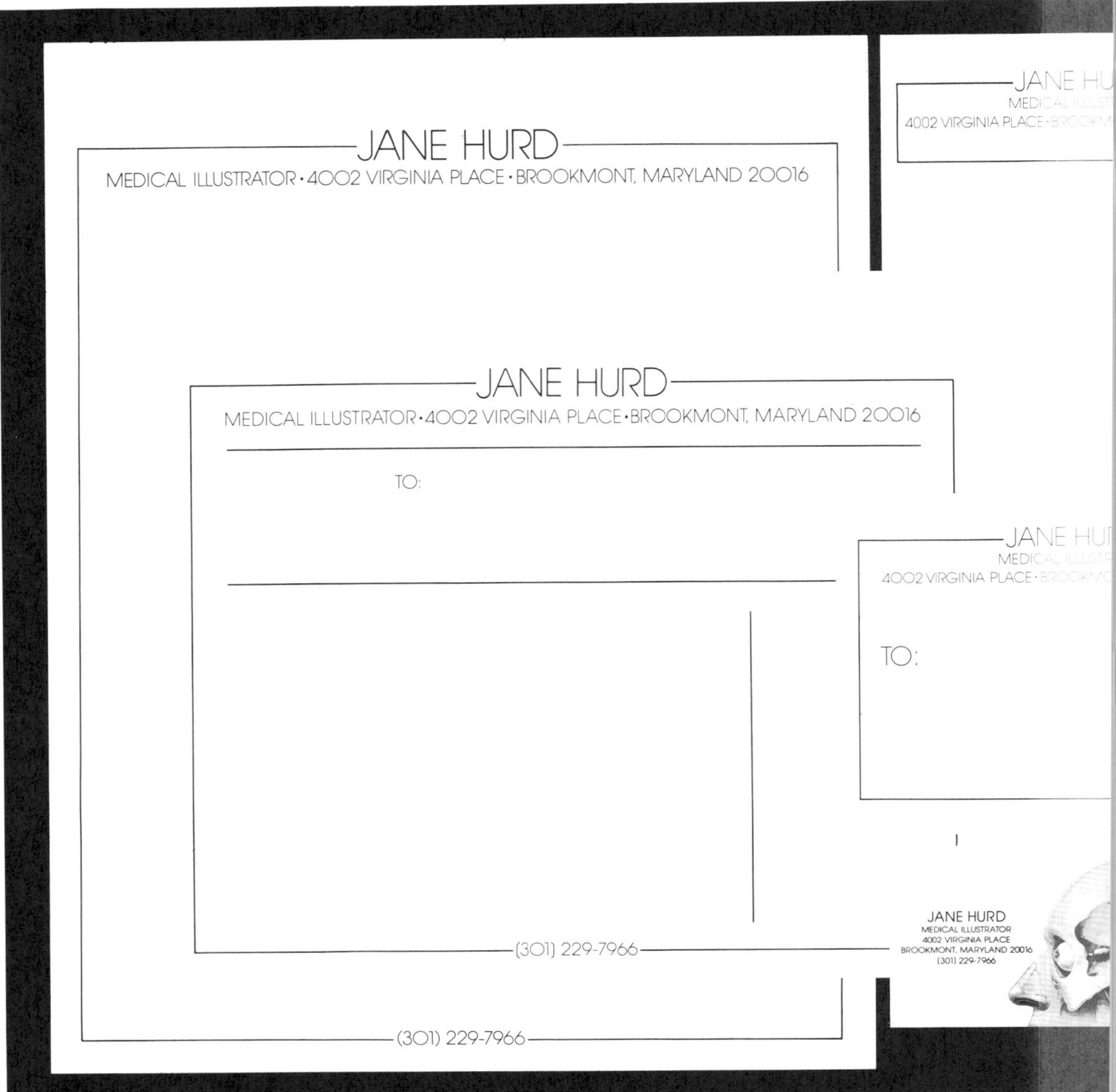

30-3. Coordinated business stationery: letterhead, envelope (no. 10 size), invoice form, mailing label, and business card. The invoice is in duplicate form with an attached yellow second copy. On the card, a drawing represents the illustrator's specialty. Courtesy of Jane Hurd.

pieces for insurance and tax purposes. Include type of equipment, model number, serial identification, purchase price, year of purchase, and a photograph. Place a copy of the studio insurance in a bank safety deposit box in event of fire or theft in the studio.

Maintaining Supplies

The studio inventory includes both permanent equipment and replaceable supplies. Monitor frequently used stocks, maintaining a studio "grocery list." For supplies used up rapidly, have one quantity in use, one in stock, and one on order. Consider purchasing items in larger quantities than needed at the moment for greater efficiency and cash savings, but keep in mind that impulse buying can ruin any budget. If you are easily tempted when faced with displays of supplies, you may find it advantageous to order by phone, having deliveries made by suppliers with whom you maintain [illegible] do frequent [illegible] cards to use [illegible] ness purchas[illegible] business exp[illegible] from persona[illegible] ords.

As the [illegible] creased offic[illegible] may deman[illegible] equipment: [illegible] be replaced [illegible] electronic m[illegible] or computer: [illegible] equipped with a variety of communication devices, such as an answering machine, subscriber long-distance network, call-waiting, and call-forwarding. These telephone devices and services are worthwhile investments in a business that depends upon artist availability.

INCOME TAX CONSIDERATIONS

The U.S. tax laws have been changing over the years, but various provisions always are likely to apply to small businesses such as freelance illustration. Keep informed about the latest tax law, in particular about what business-related deductions are allowed. Obtain copies of relevant Internal Revenue Service publications (see Bibliography). Income tax for self-employed persons is an estimated tax, paid in quarterly installments, taking the place of withholding tax by employers. These installments are due April 15, June 15, September 15, and January 15, and are filed on the Estimated Tax Voucher form (1040 ES).

It is very likely that any reasonable costs incurred in the production of illustrative materials for sale may be considered business deductions, including repair and purchase of equipment, inventory storage for retail business, and other expenses incurred in generating income. Therefore, both for accurate records of your business and for easy income tax preparation, keep careful running accounts of expenses. A running record will save you many anxious hours of assembling accounts at the last minute. Regardless of tax considerations, careful records will document the growth of your business and help in evaluating where changes in expenditures might be made if necessary. The three main categories of good accounts are (1) all receipts for expenses, listed earlier as part of the business filing system; (2) a diary of all meetings, travel, and business activities; and (3) ledger books on all expenses and income. Keep business checking and savings accounts separate from personal accounts to simplify the maintenance of tax records and to add credence to your business. All business income and expenditures should be channeled through the business accounts. Even charge accounts should be set up separately for the business to facilitate the tracking of business expenses.

Receipts

Receipts should be filed by the tax year, usually January 1 through December 31, with frequently recurring expenses (such as utilities) subdivided within the file. Receipts for equipment eligible for depreciation should be filed separately because the deduction in the past has been taken over a period of several tax years—for example, the equipment itemized in studio insurance inventory. Under the 1986 tax law, up to $10,000 in equipment purchases can be deducted (with certain limitations) in the year when purchased. To reduce taxable income in a given year, pay some bills shortly before the end of the tax year, and delay the delivery of income until after the beginning of the next tax year.

Diary

The diary should have space for recording the events of every day of the year. For every business meeting there should be a notation of "who, where, why, and when," together with all expenses incurred (mileage driven, taxi fare, parking, tolls, meals, and entertainment). If the artist buys a meal or drinks for clients or business associates, the cost may be at least partially deductible and should be recorded in that diary. Retain all associated receipts with notations of what they were for. Often, it is inconvenient to use checks or credit when purchasing small numbers of items. If such purchases have been taken out of your personal, nonbusiness money, as sometimes happens, note this; your business may write a check to reimburse you on a monthly basis, or by the end of the tax year. The diary is especially important for petty-cash expenditures for which receipts can be difficult or impossible to obtain (parking meters, photocopying machines, tolls, phone calls, and taxis). Develop the habit of recording these expenses daily. Trying to remember them a few days or a week later often is futile.

Ledger Books

The studio ledger books should contain two sections: Income and Expenses (or Credit and Debits). Within the income section, group clients according to university or institutional affiliation (if applicable) to associate the 1099 tax form you will receive from them at the end of the tax year. Besides sale of artwork or services, income may come from royalties, awards, grants, dividends from investments or rental properties, or other sources. The expense section should be broken down into at least twelve columns to provide enough space for entries. Each entry should show the date, payee, check number, and amount, with the amount being carried over to the right under the appropriate heading. Headings might include Rent, Utilities, Office supplies and postage, Professional services. Headings might match tax categories, such as those found on federal tax form 1040, Schedule C, Profit (or Loss) From Business or Profession. Keep every record and receipt that may be relevant so that you or your tax accountant will have all the information necessary when preparing returns. You or

---

Stanley Snyder and William Hamilton IV contributed to the text on income tax considerations.

your accountant will need to decide which items may be declared and which are likely to be disallowed under current law.

Deficits

In cases where an operating deficit occurs in a given year, the loss may be subtracted from gross income. When the loss wipes out other taxable income for that year, the remainder of the loss can be carried back to reduce taxable income from previous years, resulting in a refund of taxes paid previously and then forward to reduce taxable income of future years—thus reducing taxes in coming years. The Internal Revenue Service publication *Net Operating Losses and the At-Risk Limits* (see Bibliography) explains this subject.

To prevent the operation of a small business from being merely a tax shelter, the Hobby Loss Law requires that in order for a business to be considered legitimate, it must show a profit in any three years of a five-year period. Otherwise, it may be considered a hobby, and losses incurred from it may not be deductible. To some extent, by regulating the time of receipt of income or times of payment of expenses, profitable years may be created to satisfy the requirements of the law. In cases where this is impossible and the IRS challenges the profit motive of the artist, there are nine points that the artist must satisfy to prove a profit motive, even if there was no profit in three years out of five. Here careful, accurate records prove their value. The nine points are:

1. The manner in which the business is run. It must be businesslike, with careful records of receipts and expenses.
2. The expertise of the artist. Study in the field, professional recognition, prizes, professional memberships, critical recognition in articles or books, the use of professional equipment or techniques, or appointment to a teaching position based on ability are all indicators of expertise.
3. Time and effort involved in the pursuit of business—for example, the number of hours expended daily doing artwork or generating jobs.
4. Expectation that assets used in the activity will appreciate in value. This is not always applicable to artists.
5. The success of previous activities of either a similar or a dissimilar nature.
6. The history of the taxpayer's income or losses with respect to the activity. Is income increasing over the years?
7. The amount of profits, if any, compared to expenses. This applies only if the taxpayer is wealthy enough to gain tax benefits from a business that operates at a loss.
8. The need for funds. An independent income suggests that there may be no profit motive.
9. Elements of recreation or personal pleasure. Except in the case of travel expenses, this would not apply to artists.

Incorporation

Incorporating the individual as a business is sometimes recommended as a way to avoid liability in certain situations. Sometimes corporations have certain tax advantages over individuals. It is not expensive or complicated to incorporate oneself in many states. Check with an accountant or with the office in your state that handles incorporation to see whether this option is desirable. Incorporation does require regular (usually annual) reports and fees to the state and the designation of officers in the incorporated body.

Home Office

If your offic
home, you ma
of maintaining
requirements
eliminates su
part of the r
office must l
place of busin
business used
patients, cust
course of bus
for inventory
saler or retail
A portion
used *exclusiv*
basis to qua
place of busin
conducted a
the principal
by taking int
income earn
available at
portion of th
only for bus
with persona
guest room.
be marked o
tition. If clie
and exclusiv
the home, it
principal pla
ify for dedu
the sole fixe
payer's wh
ness, space
necessarily
area for inv
deduction.
Even if
done at hor
nizations sti
office dedu
two excepti
fice is for
employer. I
a home of
business e
ducted by a
exceed 2 pe
income.
When
home-office
ductible it
penses suc
walls as w

such as a proportionate share of electricity, gas, furnace repairs, and so on. Indirect expenses can be computed by figuring the ratio of business square feet to total square feet of the home or ratio of business rooms to total rooms, if the rooms are of approximately equal size.

One caveat: should you claim part of your own home as a home office, upon the profitable sale of this home, that portion claimed as a business expense ultimately could be subject to capital gains tax.

Employees

Sometimes the freelance illustrator must hire employees. These are most likely to be independent contractors such as a photographer, agent, or subcontracting illustrator, rather than a salaried employee. Under past law, if an independent contractor or employee was paid more than $600 in the taxable year, a 1099 form had to be filed with the Internal Revenue Service for that person. Current law must be checked. Social Security payments (a certain percentage of the employee's income) must be made for any regular employee, but the definitions, percentages, and salary limits under current law should be reviewed. By law the employer pays half and deducts the other half from the employee's salary, sending the total to the Social Security Administration. The employer can pay both halves.

If employees, contractors, interns, or others are working regularly in your office, purchase liability insurance.

INSURANCE

The biggest worry for any self-employed person is health insurance. Do not put off obtaining such coverage if you and your family are not covered by some medical plan. A catastrophic illness or accident can financially wipe out anyone, as well as relatives such as parents who would want to help. Major medical coverage is most pertinent here, but further medical coverage is also important. (The 1986 tax law generally allows self-employed persons to deduct 25 percent of health insurance costs.) Life insurance may also be valuable, especially for those with families.

Look for and try to avoid loopholes in any plan you investigate, such as noncoverage for preexisting conditions—although this is a common and perhaps unavoidable clause. Any individual insurance plan is expensive. There are group plans for artists through Artists Equity Association, the Graphic Artists Guild, and the Association of Medical Illustrators (see Appendix). Membership in the respective organizations usually is required in order to obtain the insurance.

Another type of insurance important to artists is coverage of artwork in the office and home, at exhibits, and in transit. Coverage should include theft or other loss, as well as damage from fire, water, accidents, and other causes. Government and private delivery services offer insurance up to a certain amount. If that is not high enough, or if the carrier will not insure original artwork, it may be necessary to have your own coverage. Check to see that your auto insurance will cover artwork being transported in your car.

Presumably clients, especially organizations, would have coverage for artwork while in use, and this is usually true—but not always—of exhibitors such as art galleries. Ask users of your work whether they have insurance coverage.

Unfortunately, the cost of such insurance has been escalating. Artists Equity provides a group plan for insuring artwork. Fire, tenant, or homeowner's insurance should be obtained for the studio or office. Liability coverage may be provided in some of these plans. It is possible that such plans will cover artwork, even in transit, and perhaps less expensively than fine-art insurance. Investigate a variety of plans and compare coverage and costs.

RETIREMENT PLANS

It is never too early to plan for retirement, especially for the freelancer who has no employer to provide a plan. The Social Security tax consititutes a mandatory retirement plan; the self-employed person pays both the employer's and the employee's contributions, a certain percentage of gross income, on a quarterly basis, along with the quarterly estimated tax payment. To obtain the maximum retirement benefit for any income level, payments must be made for at least forty quarters. Benefits are not paid until the claimant reaches a certain age, and there also may be a minimum number of quarterly payments that have to be made before the benefits can be claimed. Check current regulations through the Social Security Administration (see Appendix).

Two other retirement plans available to freelancers are Keogh and IRA (Individual Retirement Account). Both plans require that money be set aside in a retirement fund, which can be a trust, annuity contract from an insurance company, custodial account with a bank, United States bonds, bank certificates of deposit, or other investment accounts through investment companies such as mutual funds. There are hefty financial penalties for withdrawal before age 59½, with certain exceptions for disabilities or medical emergencies. Distribution from the account must begin by age 70½.

The Keogh plan is for self-employed people only. Up to a certain percentage of annual net income or a specific limit (25 percent or $30,000 in 1987) can be invested in a Keogh retirement fund, and the invested amount is deductible from gross income. The IRA is available to both employees and freelancers. Any amount up to 100 percent of income (not exceeding $2,000) can be invested, but as of 1987 it is tax-deductible wholly or partially only below a certain income level. However, if the person has no other retirement plan, payments to an IRA may be completely deductible. The current regulations regarding these retirement plans must be investigated. (Obtain Internal Revenue Service Publication 560, *Self-Employed Retirement Plans*—see Bibliography.)

Getting in the habit of regularly putting aside something for retirement, even if it is only a small amount, is important because worsening eyesight or shaky hands can force retirement for an illustrator. Social Security alone is not likely to provide a very good retirement income. The amount of retirement benefits from Keogh and IRA plans will depend on how judiciously they are invested. But according to published tables, starting investments early in one's career in safe, stable forms with dependable interest returns is bound to produce good results. It is up to the individual to research current investment possibilities. Articles on retirement plans appear frequently in business sections of magazines and newspapers. Business magazines such as *Forbes* and *Money* compare investment options and their latest interest returns. Accountants, investment lawyers, stockbrokers, and banks can provide advice, but remember that such information may be colored by the affiliation of the advice-giver. These same sources, plus the Internal Revenue Service, can provide you with current tax regulations.

MAINTAINING THE BUSINESS

The maintenance of a successful business requires continuous attention. In addition to handling established accounts, the artist must constantly develop skills and find new markets for using them. Again, the methods used to become established within a community are the same as those used to begin a career, to relocate it, or to expand it. Seeking assignments in a slightly different field from your own (if you have the daring and talent) can offer opportunities not previously considered—for example, keylining of brochures and pamphlets; spot line drawings or cartoons for local newspapers; illustrations for veterinarians, cooking schools, extension services, and horticultural societies; and publicity campaigns, including preparation of exhibits and posters for fundraising events by garden centers, theater groups, preparatory schools, and colleges.

A considerable amount of public interest can be generated by a gallery exhibition of your work. The illustrations or paintings shown need not be examples only of assignments; they could include a selection of fine art and sketches. A variety of organizations—such as universities, art schools, garden centers, museums of natural history, nature centers, and private galleries—would welcome exhibits of scientific illustration techniques. Medical artists might find their subjects suitable for university and medical school libraries, museums, professional organizations, and community colleges. Participation in professional societies and their exhibits exposes your work to colleagues who can recommend you for jobs that seem appropriate to your expertise.

Art directors are good sources of contracts. You can meet them at exhibitions and meetings presented by local art directors' clubs or the annual national shows, some of which result in widely distributed yearbooks mentioning all exhibitors' works (N.Y. Art Directors, the Society of Illustrators in New York, Chicago Art Directors, and the Washington Art Directors' Club are some major ones). The entry and hanging fees can be tax-deductible investments. Judge whether you should enter by comparing your work with that of previous successfu

In preparing
design and dist
tation, the art
business cards
Advertise the
priate notices,
ments to all of
and associates
showing one o
trations can b
tion visitors to
brochure. Busi
spective client
your studio l
ample supply
available to th
bition.

To present y
vantage, mak
play is hung
manner: well
framed, care
adequately lig
sible, decide
prices of indiv
cide which ite
for sale.

Another ex
creasing profe
give slide lect
or techniques
flyers announ
brochures an
the event, ar
future client
societies, art
sity graduate
ciate talks on
and they adv

Regardles
is pursuing f
sional recogn
ification from
the developm
dio is essen
overworked c
certainly app
world, where
activity resul
loss of inco
businesses
clothed" ove
ably the res
work and pe
that can be
warding.

Appendix

The Guild Handbook of Scientific Illustration
1995, Third Printing

Included here are sources and information not readily available, especially to those outside large metropolitan areas. The information is current as of early 1988, as far as could be determined. Usually, toll-free (800) telephone numbers are intended for orders only. Listings here are generally in the sequence in which their subjects are discussed at length in this book, but they are not listed by chapters because a number of topics are covered in more than one chapter.

ART SUPPLY SOURCES

Listed below are art suppliers that stock a wide variety of materials for graphics work or that have discounted prices. Some suppliers provide both advantages. Sale prices at the nondiscount stores sometimes can be better than the discounted prices. All of these suppliers produce catalogs, including sales brochures, and accept mail or telephone orders. Several have branch offices in other cities in the United States or in other countries, which may be more convenient than the central office listed here.

Alvin
P.O. Box 188
Windsor, CT 06095
(800) 444-2584
CT, AK, HI, Can.: (203) 243-8991

Arthur Brown & Bros., Inc.
2 West 46th Street
New York, NY 10036
(212) 575-5555
(800) 722-PENS

Art Supply Warehouse (discount)
360 Main Avenue
Norwalk, CT 06851
(800) 995-6778

Charrette
P.O. Box 4010
31 Olympia Avenue
Woburn, MA 01888-4010
(617) 935-6000

Daniel Smith, Inc. (discount)
4150 First Avenue South
P.O. Box 84268
Seattle, WA 98124-5568
(800) 426-6740
Fax (800) 238-4065

Dick Blick (discount)
P.O. Box 1267
Galesburg, IL 61401
(800) 447-8192
IL: (309) 343-6181

DMI Industries, Inc.
222 No. Woodward
Royal Oaks, MI 48067
(313) 546-2880
Fax (313) 546-5423

Jerry's Artarama, Inc. (discount)
P.O. Box 1105 AM
New Hyde Park, N.Y. 11040
(800) 827-8478
N.Y. (516) 328-6633
Fax (516) 328-6752

Utrecht (discount)
33 35th Street
Brooklyn, NY 11232
(718) 768-2525

Visual Systems, Inc.
1596 Rockville Pike
Rockville, MD 20852
(301) 770-0500

DRAWING SURFACES

Suppliers of additional drawing surfaces as well as matting materials are listed under the various types of conservation supplies.

Papers and Matboard

Aiko's Art Materials Import
3347 North Clark Street
Chicago, IL 60657
(312) 404-5600

RIS Paper
45-11 33rd Street
Long Island City, NY 11101
(800) 221-0655
(718) 392-8100

Neilsen-Bainbridge
17 So. Middlesex Avenue
Cranbury, NJ 08512
(800) 631-5414
NJ (609) 395-5550

Crescent Cardboard Company
100 West Willow Road
P.O. Box X-D
Wheeling, IL 60090
(800) 323-1055
(708) 537-3400

Crestwood Paper Company
Division of Wilmann Paper
Company
315 Hudson Street
New York, NY 10013
(800) 525-3196
NY (212) 989-2700
Fax (212) 929-7532

The Hollinger Corporation
3810 South Four Mile Run Drive
P.O. Box 6185
Arlington, VA 22206
(703) 671-6600

Paper Source, Ltd.
1506 West 12th Street
Los Angeles, CA 90015
(213) 387-5820

Rising Paper Company
Park Street
Housatonic, MA 01236
(413) 274-3345

Strathmore Paper Company
39 South Broad Street
Westfield, MA 01085
(413) 568-9111
(800) 628-8816

Opaque, Coated Surfaces

Ampersand
1500 East 4th Street
Austin, TX 78702
(800) 822-1939
Claybord

Geller Artist Materials
38 East 18th Street
New York, NY 10003
(212) 673-5500
Color-Aid

Medical Models Laboratory
P.O. Box 2651
Baltimore, MD 21215
(410) 358-9199
dull-finish stipple board

Graphics Arts Systems
19499 Miles Road
Cleveland, OH 44128
(800) 447-2349
(216) 581-9050
ColorMatch, clear polyester

United Process Boards
Arr-Jay Productions
12460 N.E. Marine View Drive
Kingston, WA 98346
(206) 297-4455
Ess Dee

Translucent Surfaces — Drafting Films

Borden and Riley Paper Co., Inc.
184-10 Jamaica Avenue
Hollis, NY 11423
(800) 221-1416; Fax (718) 454-0791
NY: (718) 454-9494
Denril

Bruning
1800 Bruning Drive West
Itasca, IL 60143
(800) 323-4827
(708) 351-6000
Bruning — Sure Scale

Deitzgen Corporation
250 Wille Road
Des Plaines, IL 60018
(800) 473-1270
(708) 635-5200
Ageproof

Koh-I-Noor Rapidograph, Inc.
100 North Street
Bloomsbury, NJ 08804
(800) 631-7646
NJ, AK, HI, Can.: (908) 479-4124
Rapidraw

James River Graphics
28 Gaylord Street
South Hadley, MA 01075
(800) 628-8935
MA, AK, HI, Can.: (413) 536-7800
JR 300, frosted on one side;
JR 330, frosted on both sides;
both formerly called Tecnifax

Graphics Arts Systems
(see Opaque, Coated Surfaces)

TOOL HOLDERS

ArtCadi Products
P.O. Box 5591
Lincoln, NE 68505
(402) 464-3504
"Drop-Lock" airbrush holder, other tool holders

SAFETY PRODUCTS AND INFORMATION

Art Hazards Information Center
Center for Safety in the Arts
5 Beekman Street
New York, NY 10038
(212) 227-6220
Publishes newsletter, has computer bulletin board

West Penetone Corporation
74 Hudson Avenue
Tenafly, NJ 07670
(800) 631-1652
(201) 567-3000
Protective Cream No. 311, for hands

Face Masks a

Daniel Smith, I
(see Art Supply S

Direct Safety Co
P.O. Box 50050
Phoenix, AZ 850
(800) 528-7405
AZ, AK, HI, Ca

LETTERING

Lettering r
brands of dry
lettering are w
ply stores. T
brands are har

Geographics, I
Box 1750
Blaine, WA 9
(206) 332-671
Geotype

MOUNTING

The clays l
than most
plasticines or
beads are ha
transparent a

Art Chemical
1019-29 Sala
Huntington, I
(219) 356-23
Klean Klay

Brick Yard H
4721 West 1
Speedway, IN
(317) 244-52
Permoplast n

Cataphote C
Microbeads
P.O. Box 236
Jackson, MS
(601) 939-46
Glass beads,
five-pound n
much for an
chase is reco

Leisure Craf
P.O. Box 16
Rancho Cuca
(909) 948-8
Leisure Craf

Sculpture House, Inc.
National Arts Building
30 East 30th Street
New York, NY 10016
(212) 679-7474
Jolly King plasteline

MICROSCOPES AND OPTICAL EQUIPMENT

All of these companies sell microscopes. Most microscope companies supply related optical equipment such as reticles, stage micrometers, and microscope lights. Some make camera lucidas. Special products are listed under the relevant company names. Many of these companies have primary offices in countries other than the United States and also maintain offices in Canada.

Bausch and Lomb
1400 North Goodman Street
P.O. Box 450
Rochester, NY 14692
(716) 338-6000
hand magnifiers

Fairfield Scientific
P.O. 369
Old Greenwich, CT 06870
(800) 637-8586
clip-on eyeglass magnifier
Hastings Triplex

Leica, Inc.
Rockleigh, NJ 07647
(201) 767-1100
microscopes

Nikon, Inc.
Instrument Group
1300 Walt Whitman Road
Melville, NY 11747
(516) 547-4200

Olympus Corporation
4 Nevada Drive
Lake Success, NY 11042-1179
(800) 446-5967
(516) 488-3880

Carl Zeiss, Inc.
One Zeiss Drive
Thornwood, NY 10594
(914) 747-1800

Microscope Fiber-Optics

Cuda Products Crop.
6000 Powers Avenue
Jacksonville, FL 32217-2279
(904) 737-7611

Dolan-Jenner
678 Andover Street
Lawrence, MA 01843
(508) 681-8000

Volpi Manufacturing USA
5 Commerce Way
Auburn, NY 13021
(315) 255-1737

Magnifiers — Visor Style

These magnifiers are like eyeglasses that fit over the head with an adjustable band around the back of the head. The eyeglass portion fits over standard eyeglasses or works without eyeglasses and moves up out of the way when magnification is unnecessary. The lenses are available in various magnifications, providing shorter or longer working distances. (More magnification means less working space.)

Bowen and Co., Inc.
1800 Chapman Avenue
Rockville, MD 20852
(301) 881-8910
Optivisor

Edroy Products Co., Inc.
P.O. Box 998
245 North Midland Avenue
Nyack, NY 10960
(800) 233-8803
NY: (914) 358-6600
Magni-focuser, Opticaid, other magnifiers

Microprojectors

Bausch & Lomb
(see Microscopes. Tri-Simplex is no longer made; old or used ones may be available.)

Ken-A-Vision
5615 Raytown Road
Raytown, MO 64133
(816) 353-4787

Opaque Projectors

Artograph, Inc.
2838 Vicksburg Lane North
Minneapolis, MN 55447
(612) 553-1112

BIOLOGICAL SUPPLY SOURCES

AMBI-American Biological Supply Company
2405 N.W. 66th Court
Gainesville, FL 32653
(904) 377-3299
Fax (904) 375-AMBI

BioQuip Products
17803 LaSalle Avenue
Gardena, CA 90248
(310) 324-0620

Carolina Biological Supply
2700 York Road
Burlington, NC 27215
(800) 334-5551

Edmund Scientific Corporation
101 East Gloucester Pike
Barrington, NJ 08007
(609) 547-3488

Fisher Scientific
711 Forbes Avenue
Pittsburgh, PA 15219
(412) 562-8300

Preiser Scientific
94 Oliver Street
St. Albans,WV 25177
(304) 727-2902

Thomas Scientific Company
99 High Hill Road
Swedesboro, PA 08085
(215) 988-0533

Ward's Natural Science
5100 West Henrietta Road
P.O. Box 92912
Rochester, NY 14692-9012
(800) 962-2660
NY: (716) 359-2502

LIGHTING FOR SPECIMENS, WORKING, AND DISPLAY

Light Impressions
(see pH Testing Materials)
fluorescent shields

Macbeth Corporation
405 Little Britain Road
New Winsor, NY 12553
(914) 565-7660
Examolite (simulates daylight)

Read Plastics
12331 Wilkens Avenue
Rockville, MD 20852
(301) 881-7900
Arm-a-lite FR 312W, fluorescent shields

Solar Screen Corporation
53-11 105th Street
Corona, NY 11368
(718) 592-8222
fluorescent shields

Venture Lighting
32000 Aurora Road
Solon, OH 44139
(800) 338-6161
MR 16 quartz halogen bulb with UV filter for track lights

pH TESTING MATERIAL

Applied Science Laboratory
2216 Hull Street
Richmond, VA 23224
(804) 231-9386

Conservation Materials, Ltd.
1275 Kleppe Lane, #10
P.O. Box 2884
Sparks, NV 89431
(702) 331-0582

E. M. Laboratories
5 Skyline Drive
Hawthorne, NY 10532
(914) 592-4660

Light Impressions Corporation
439 Monroe Avenue
Rochester, NY 14607-3717
(800) 828-6216
Fax (800) 828-5539

TALAS
213 West 35th Street
New York, NY 10001-1996
(212) 736-7744

University Products, Inc.
517 Main Street
P.O. Box 101
Holyoke, MA 01041
(800) 628-1912
MA: (800) 336-4847

ARCHIVAL STORAGE BOXES, COVER SHEETS

Conservation Resources, International, Inc.
8000 H. Forbes Place
Springfield, VA 22151
(703) 321-7730

The Hollinger Corporation
(see Papers and Matboard)

Light Impressions Corporation
(see pH Testing Materials)

Pohlig Brothers, Inc.
P.O. Box 8069
Richmond, VA 23223
(804) 644-7824

Spink and Gaborc, Inc.
11 Troast Court
Clifton, NJ 07011
(201) 478-4551

TALAS
(see pH Testing Materials)

University Products, Inc.
(see pH Testing Materials)

HUMIDITY INDICATORS

Micro Essential Laboratory
4224 Avenue H
Brooklyn, NY 11210
(718) 338-3618

Multiform Desiccant Products, Inc.
960 Busti Avenue at Niagara Street
Buffalo, NY 14213
(716) 883-8900
(800) 445-9890

TALAS
(see pH Testing Materials)

ADHESIVES

Archival-quality adhesives are sold by the sources listed below.

Light Impressions
(see pH Testing Materials)
C-35 applicator for applying 3M Positionable Mounting Adhesive no. 568 for drymounting without heat.

Archival Adhesives, Tapes

Conservation Materials, Ltd.
(see pH Testing Materials)

Light Impressi
(see pH Testing

Process Materi
109 West 26th
New York, NY
(212) 627-775

TALAS
(see pH Testin

STOCK PH

Animals, Anir
Scenes
17 Railroad A
Chatham, NY
(518) 392-55

Bruce Colema
117 East 24th
New York, N
(212) 683-52

Grant Heilma
506 West Lin
P.O. Box 317
Lititz, PA 17
(717) 626-02

Peter Arnold
1181 Broadw
New York, N
(212) 481-1

Photo Resea
60 East 56th
New York, N
(212) 758-3

Tom Stack &
3645 Jeanni
Colorado Sp
(719) 570-1

ACCREDI MEDICAL

Departmen
Illustrati
Allied Hea
Medical Ill
Program
School of C
The Medic
Augusta, G
(404) 721-
M.S. degre

Department of Biomedical Visualization
College of Associated Health Professions
University of Illinois at Chicago
1919 West Taylor Street, Room 213
Chicago, IL 60612-7249
(312) 996-7337
M.A.M.S. degree, 2.5-year curriculum

Art as Applied to Medicine
The Johns Hopkins School of Medicine
1830 East Monument
Suite 7000
Baltimore, MD 21205
(410) 955-3213
M.A. degree, 2-year curriculum

The School of Medical and Biological Illustration
1327 Jones Drive Suite 102B
The University of Michigan
School of Arts
Ann Arbor, MI 48105
(313) 998-6270
M.S. degree, 2.5 year curriculum

The Biomedical Illustration Graduate Program
University of Texas
Southwestern Medical Center at Dallas
5323 Harry Hines Boulevard
Dallas, TX 75235-8881
(214) 648-4699
B.F.A. Scientific Illustration
M.S. degree, 2-year curriculum

PROFESSIONAL ORGANIZATIONS

Some of these groups offer insurance benefits, as noted. Benefits may change, so check with each group for current information.

Artists Equity Association
P.O. Box 28068
Central Station
Washington, DC 20038
(202) 628-9633
hospital indemnity, major medical, life, Fine Art Studio Insurance

Association of Medical Illustrators
1819 Peachtree Northeast, Suite 712
Atlanta, GA 30309
(404) 350-7900

Biological Photographic Association, Inc.
115 Stoneridge Drive
Chapel Hill, NC 27514
(919) 967-8247

Graphic Artists Guild
11 West 20th Street, 8th Floor
New York, NY 10011
(212) 463-7730
health and disability, life

Guild of Natural Science Illustrators
P.O. Box 652
Ben Franklin Station
Washington, DC 20044
(301) 309-1514 Phone and Fax

Nature Artists Guild of the Morton Arboretum
Route 53
Lisle, IL 60532
(708) 719-2448

Society of Animal Artists
Salmagundi Club
47 Fifth Avenue
New York, NY 10003-4396
(212) 741-2880

Society of Illustrators
128 East 63rd Street
New York, NY 10021
(212) 838-2560
hospital indemnity, major medical, disability income, accidental death

COPYRIGHT

Copyright Office
The Library of Congress
101 Independence Avenue, S.E.
Washington, DC 20559
Public Information: (202) 707-3000
Forms Request: (202) 707-9100

INCOME TAX, BUSINESS PRACTICES, AND RETIREMENT

IRS-CADC
U.S. Internal Revenue Service
2402 East Empire
Bloomington, IL 61799
Information regarding publications (see Bibliography)

U.S. Small Business Administration
Central Office
Office of Public Communication
409-3rd Street, S.W.
Washington, DC 20416
(800) 827-5722
There are SBA field offices in 42 states, the District of Columbia, Puerto Rico, and the Virgin Islands. (See Bibliography for information on publications.)

U.S. Social Security Administration
(800) 772-1213
TDD (800) 325-0778
Missouri TDD (800) 392-0812
Regional offices all over the United States can provide information. Consult local telephone directory.

MAP SOURCES, SYMBOLS, AND SCALES

F. Forster Apparatebau
Randenstrasse 220
8200 Schaffhausen
Switzerland
053-577-97
Perspektomat

For U.S. Government paper or digital map inquiries, call
(800) USA-MAPS
(800) 872-6277

For maps of other countries, contact
MapLink
25 E. Mason
Santa Barbara, CA 93101
(805) 965-4402

Federal Map Products and Sources

Type	Publishing Agency
Aeronautical charts	Defense Mapping Agency National Ocean Service
Boundary information	
United States and Canada	International Boundary Commission
United States and Mexico	International Boundary and Water Commission
Census geographic area (1990)	Bureau of the Census
Census tract outline maps (1990)	Bureau of the Census
Climatic maps	National Oceanic and Atmospheric Administration
Coal investigations maps	Geological Survey
Congressional districts	Bureau of the Census
Electric transmission and generation facilities	Federal Power Commission
Geologic quadrangle maps	Geological Survey
Geologic investigations maps	Geological Survey
Geologic map of North America	Geological Survey
Geologic map of the United States	Geological Survey
Geophysical investigations maps	Geological Survey
Ground conductivity	Federal Communications Commission
Highways, state and county	State highway departments
Historical	
Reproductions from historical and military map collections	Library of Congress National Archives
Selected Civil War maps (reproduced from originals)	National Ocean Service
Treasure maps and charts (bibliography)	Library of Congress
Hydrographic information	
Bathymetric maps of United States adjacent and continental shelf	National Ocean Service
Nautical charts of U.S. coastal waters	National Ocean Service
Great Lakes and connecting waters	National Ocean Service
River charts	
Cumberland River	Corps of Engineers
Illinois waterway to Lake Michigan	Corps of Engineers

Federal Map Products and Sources

Type	Publishing Agency	Source
Hydrographic information		
Mississippi River (lower)	Corps of Engineers	Corps of Engineers, Vicksburg
Mississippi River (upper)	Corps of Engineers	Corps of Engineers, Chicago
Missouri River	Corps of Engineers	Corps of Engineers, Omaha
Ohio River	Corps of Engineers	Corps of Engineers, Louisville
Tennessee River	Tennessee Valley Authority	Tennessee Valley Authority
Foreign waters	Defense Mapping Agency	Defense Mapping Agency Topographic Center
Hydrologic investigations atlases	Geological Survey	Geological Survey
Hydrologic unit maps (by state)	Geological Survey	Geological Survey
Indian reservations	Bureau of Indian Affairs	Bureau of Indian Affairs
Land use and land cover maps	Geological Survey	Geological Survey National Cartographic Information Center(NCIC)
Map projections	National Ocean Service	National Ocean Service
Mineral investigations field studies maps	Geological Survey	Geological Survey
Mineral investigations resource maps	Geological Survey	Geological Survey
Minor civil divisions	Bureau of the Census	Superintendent of Documents
Moon/planetary maps	Geological Survey	Geological Survey
National atlas separate sales editions	Geological Survey	Geological Survey
National forest regions	Forest Service	Forest Service
National Parks		
Topographic maps	Geological Survey	Geological Survey
National Parks System	National Park Service	Superintendent of Documents
Natural gas pipelines	Federal Power Commission	Superintendent of Documents
Oil and gas investigations maps and charts	Geological Survey	Geological Survey
Orthophotoquads	Geological Survey	Geological Survey
Polar maps		
Antarctic	Geological Survey Defense Mapping Agency	Geological Survey Defense Mapping Agency Topographic Center
Arctic	National Ocean Service Defense Mapping Agency	National Ocean Service Defense Mapping Agency Topographic Center
Population distribution of the United States (1990)	Bureau of the Census	Superintendent of Documents
Soil survey maps	Soil Conservation Service	Soil Conservation Service
Space imagery maps	Geological Survey	Geological Survey
State maps (base, shaded, and topographic)	Geological Survey	Geological Survey
State maps (geologic)	Geological Survey and various state geological surveys	Geological Survey and various state geological surveys
Status maps		
Standard topographic mapping	Geological Survey	Geological Survey

Federal Map Products and Sources

Type	Publishing Agency
Status maps	
Intermediate-scale topographic mapping (county and quadrangle)	Geological Survey
Orthophotoquad mapping	Geological Survey
Storm evacuation maps	National Ocean Service
Time zones of the world	Defense Mapping Agency
Topographic map indexes (by state)	Geological Survey
Township plates (reproductions)	
Illinois, Indiana, Iowa, Kansas, Missouri, and Ohio	National Archives
All other public land states	Bureau of Land Management
Transportation maps (State)	Federal Railroad Administration
United States base maps	Geological Survey National Ocean Service Other government agencies
Urban Atlas (Selected Standard Metropolitan Statistical Areas)	Bureau of the Census
Water Resource Development Maps	Geological Survey
Weather Maps	National Weather Service
World Maps	Defense Mapping Agency National Ocean Service

Addresses of Government Agencies Producing Reference Maps

Defense Mapping Agency
Topographic Center
Office of Distribution Services
Attn: code 55500
Washington, DC 20315

Federal Communications Commission
Office of Public Information
191 M Street N.W.
Washington, DC 20554

Department of Energy
Office of Public Information
1080 Independence Avenue, S.W.
Washington, DC 20585

Federal Railroad Administration
Office of Public Affairs, RPD-1
400 Seventh Street N.W.
Washington, DC 20590

International Boundary Commission
United States and Canada
1250 23rd Street N.W.
Washington, DC 20037

International Boundary and Water Commission
United States and Mexico, United States Section
Post Office Box 20003
El Paso, TX 79998

Interstate Commerce Commission
Office of Public Information
Constitution Ave. & 12th Street N.W.
Washington, DC 20423

State Highway Departments
State Capitals

Superintendent of Documents
U.S. Government Printing Office
North Capitol and H Streets, N.W.
Washington, DC 20402

Tennessee Valley Authority
Mapping Services Branch
111 Haney Building
Chattanooga, TN 37401

U.S. Army Engineer District
Corps of Engineers, Chicago
219 South Dearborn Street
Chicago, IL 60604

U.S. Army Engineer District
Corps of Engineers, Louisville
Post Office Box 59
Louisville, KY 40201

U.S. Army Engineer District
Corps of Engineers, Nashville
Post Office Box 1070
Nashville, TN 37202

U.S. Army Engineer District
Corps of Engineers, Omaha
6014 U.S. Post Office and Courthouse Building
Omaha, NE 68102

U.S. Army Engineer District
Corps of Engineers, Vicksburg
Post Office Box 60
Vicksburg, MS 39180

U.S. Bureau of the Census
Subscriber Service Section (Pubs.)
Administrative Service Division
Washington, DC 20233

U.S. Bureau of Indian Affairs
Office of Public Information
1951 Constitution Avenue N.W.
Washington, DC 20245

U.S. Bureau of Land Management
Office of Public Affairs
Washington, DC 20240

U.S. Forest Service
Publications Office
201 14th Street S.W.
Washington, DC 20250

U.S. Geological Survey
Branch of Distribution
Box 25286, Federal Center
Denver, CO 80225

U.S. National Archives and Records Service
Cartographic Archives Division (NNS)
Pennsylvania Avenue at 8th Street N.W.
Washington, DC 20408

National Weather Service
U.S. National Climatic Center
Customer Service
37 Battery Park Avenue
Federal Building
Asheville, NC 28801

U.S. National Ocean Service
Distribution Division
Riverdale, MD 20737

U.S. National Park Service
Office of Public Inquiries
P.O. Box 37127
Washington, DC 20013

U.S. Soil Conservation Service
Resources Inventory and Geographic Information Systems Division
Post Office Box 2890
Washington, DC 20013

GEOLOGIC MAP SYMBOLS

COMMONLY USED ON MAPS OF THE UNITED STATES GEOLOGICAL SURVEY

Contact — Dashed where approximately located; short dashed where inferred; dotted where concealed

Contact — Showing dip; well exposed at triangle

Fault — Dashed where approximately located; short dashed where inferred; dotted where concealed

Fault, showing dip — Ball and bar on downthrown side

Normal fault — Hachured on downthrown side

Fault — Showing relative horizontal movement

Thrust fault — Sawteeth on upper plate

Anticline — Showing direction of plunge; dashed where approximately located; dotted where concealed

Asymmetric anticline — Short arrow indicates steeper limb

Overturned anticline — Showing direction of dip of limbs

Syncline — Showing direction of plunge; dashed where approximately located; dotted where concealed

Asymmetric syncline — Short arrow indicates steeper limb

Overturned syncline — Showing direction of dip of limbs

Monocline — Showing direction of plunge of axis

Minor anticline — Showing plunge of axis

Minor syncline — Showing plunge of axis

Strike and dip of beds — Ball indicates top of beds known from sedimentary structures

70 Inclined — Horizontal
Vertical — 40 Overturned

Strike and dip of foliation

20 Inclined — Vertical — Horizontal

Strike and dip of cleavage

15 Inclined — Vertical — Horizontal

Bearing and plunge of lineation

15 Inclined — Vertical — Horizontal

Strike and dip of joints

40 Inclined — Vertical — Horizontal

Note: planar symbols (strike and dip of beds, foliation or schistosity, and cleavage) may be combined with linear symbols to record data observed at same locality by superimposed symbols at point of observation. Coexisting planar symbols are shown intersecting at point of observation.

Shafts

Vertical — Inclined

Adit, tunnel, or slope

Accessible — Inaccessible

Prospect

Quarry

Active — Abandoned

Gravel pit

Active — Abandoned

Oil well

Drilling — Shut-in — Dry hole abandoned
Gas — Show of gas
Oil — Show of oil

Scales of National Topographic Maps Produced by the United States Geological Survey

Series	Scale	1 inch represents	1 centimeter represents	Standard Quadrangle Size (latitude × longitude)
7.5 min	1:24,000	2,000 ft	240m	7.5 × 7.5 min
7.5 × 15 min	1:25,000	2,083 ft	250m	7.5 × 15 min
Puerto Rico				
7.5 min	1:20,000	1,667 ft	200m	7.5 × 7.5 min
15 min	1:62,500	1 mi	625m	15 × 15 min
Alaska	1:63,360	1 mi	634m	15 × 20 to 36 min
Intermediate	1:50,000	3.2 mi	2 km	
Intermediate	1:100,000	1.6 mi	1 km	30 × 60 min
United States	1:1,000,000	4 mi	2.5 km	1° × 2° or 3°
State maps	1:500,000	8 mi	5 km	
United States	1:1,000,000	16 mi	10 km	4° × 6°
Antarctica	1:250,000	4 mi	2.5 km	1° × 3° to 15°
Antarctica	1:500,000	8 mi	5 km	2° × 7.5°

Source: *Principles of Thematic Map Design* by B. D. Dent. Reading, MA: Addison-Wesley 1985.

Bibliography

Some of the books listed are included, not because of their subject matter, but as excellent illustration examples.

Chapter 1. Generalized Steps in Scientific Illustration

Barlowe, Dorothea, and Sy Barlowe. 1982. *Illustrating Nature: How to Paint and Draw Plants and Animals.* New York: Viking Press.

Bethke, Emil G. 1969. *Basic Drawing for Biology Students.* Springfield, IL: Charles Thomas Publishers.

Clarke, Carl D. 1949. *Illustration, Its Technique and Application to the Sciences.* Butler, MD: Standard Arts Press. (Distributed by Pergamon Press, Elmsford, NY.)

Coineau, Yves. 1978. *Comment réaliser vos dessins scientifiques.* Paris: Gauthier-Villars. Bordas (in French). 1987. *Cómo Hacer Dibujos Científicos. Materiales y métodos.* Barcelona: Editorial Labor (in Spanish).

Dalby, Claire, and D. H. Dalby. 1980. *Biological Illustration*, *Field Studies* 5:307–21. (Available from The Leonard Wills Field Centre, Nettlecombe Court, Williton, Taunton, Somerset TA4 4HT, England.)

Herdeg, Walter. 1973. *The Artist in the Service of Science.* Zurich: Graphis Press.

Holmgren, Noel H., and Bobbi Angell. 1986. *Botanical Illustration: Preparation for Publication.* Bronx, NY: The New York Botanical Gardens.

Jastrzebski, Zbigniew T. 1985. *Scientific Illustration: A Guide for the Beginning Artist.* Englewood Cliffs, NJ: Prentice-Hall, Inc.

McCann, Michael. 1985. *Artist's Health Hazards Manual.* New York: Nick Lyons.

Mueller, Justus F. 1935. *A Manual of Drawing for Science Students.* New York: Farrar & Rinehart.

Papp, Charles S. 1976. *Manual of Scientific Illustration.* Sacramento: American Visual Aid Books.

Ridgway, John L. [1938] 1979. *Scientific Illustration.* Reprint. Stanford, CA: Stanford University Press.

Sayner, Donald B., and Gladys Bennett Menhennet. 1969–72. *Drawing for Scientific Illustrations.* Tucson, AZ: University of Arizona. (Set of four booklets: *Maps, Graphs, Diagrams*, 1969; *Professional Aids and Devices*, 1969; *Technique and Rendering*, 1971; and *Production*, 1972.)

Smith, Herb. 1975. *Handbook for Effective Audiovisuals.* Houston: Medical Illustration and Audiovisual Education, Baylor College of Medicine.

Wood. Phyllis. 1982, 1994. *Scientific Illustration.* New York: Van Nostrand Reinhold.

Zweifel, Frances W. 1961, 1988. *A Handbook of Biological Illustration.* Chicago: University of Chicago Press.

Chapter 2. Studio Basics

Dalley, Terence, ed. 1984. *The Complete Guide to Illustration and Design: Techniques and Materials.* Secaucus, NJ: Chartwell Books. (Available from Book Club Association, Smith/Doubleday House, 87 Newman St., London, W1P 4EN, England; or Graphic Artists Book Club, P.O. Box 429566, Cincinnati, OH 45242-9566.)

Gates, David. 1982. *Graphic Design Studio Procedures.* Monsey, NY: Lloyd-Simone Publishing Co.

Hebblewhite, Ian. 1986. *The North Light Handbook of Artist's Materials.* Cincinnati: North Light Books.

Hodge, Gerald P. 1988. Alkyd Paint for Scientific and Medical Illustration. *Journal of Biocommunication* 15(1): 19–21.

Richardson, Graham T. 1985. *Illustrations: Everybody's Complete and Practical Guide.* Clifton, NJ: Humana Press.

Chapter 3. Materials, Construction, and Care of Scientific Illustrations

Artist's Materials

Cohn, Marjorie B. 1977. *Wash and Gouache: A Study of the Development of the Materials of Watercolor.* Cambridge, MA: Fogg Art Museum and Foundation of the American Institute for Conservation.

Hunter, Dard. 1978. *Papermaking: The History and Techniques of an Ancient Craft.* New York: Dover Publications.

Meder, Joseph. 1978. *The Mastery of Drawing.* Translated and revised by Winslow Ames. 2 vols. New York: Abaris Books.

Mitchell, C. Ainsworth. 1937. *Inks: Their Composition and Manufacture.* London: Charles Griffin & Co.

———. 1968. *Papermaking: Art and Craft.* Washington, DC: Library of Congress.

Roff, W. J., and J. R. Scott, eds. 1971. *Fibres, Films, Plastics, and Rubbers: A Handbook of Common Polymers.* London: Butterworths.

Waters, C. E. 1940. *Inks.* Washington, DC: Government Printing Office.

Watrous, James. 1967. *The Craft of Old Master Drawings.* Madison, WI: University of Wisconsin Press.

General Introduction to Conservation

Clapp, Anne F. 1978. *Curatorial Care of Works of Art on Paper.* 3d ed. Oberlin, Ohio: The Intermuseum Laboratory (Allen Art Building, Oberlin, OH 44074).

Dolloff, Francis W., and Roy L. Perkinson. 1971. *How to Care for Works of Art on Paper.* Boston: Museum of Fine Arts.

Stuhrke, Richard A. 1977. The Development of Permanent Paper. In *Preservation of Paper and Textiles of Historic and Artistic Value,* ed. John C. Williams, p. 33. Washington, DC: American Chemical Society.

Environment

Clark, Nancy, Thomas Cutter, and Jean McGrane. 1984. *Ventilation, A Practical Guide.* New York: Center for Occupational Hazards.

Feller, Robert L. 1964. Control of Deteriorating Effects of Light on Museum Objects. *Museum* 17:2.

———. 1964. The Deteriorating Effects of Light on Museum Objects: Principles of Photochemistry, the Effect on Varnishes and Paint Vehicles and on Paper. *Museum News* 42 (June): 3 (technical supplement).

———. 1968. Control of Deteriorating Effects of Light on Museum Objects: Heating Effects of Illumination by Incandescent Lamps. *Museum News* 46 (May): 9 (technical supplement).

———. 1973. Thermochemically Activated Oxidation: Mother Nature's Book Burning. *Pennsylvania Library Association Bulletin* 28(6).

Stolow, Nathan. 1966. The Action of Environment on Museum Objects: I and II. *Curator* 9:3,4.

Thomson, Gary. 1965. Air Pollution—A Review for Conservation Chemists. *Studies in Conservation.* 10 (Nov.): 4.

Wessel, Carl J. 1970. Environmental Factors Affecting the Permanence of Library Materials. In *Deterioration and Preservation of Library Materials,* edited by Howard Winger and Richard Smith. Chicago: University of Chicago Press.

Insects and Mold

Gallo, Fausta. 1963. Biological Agents Which Damage Paper Materials. . . . In *Recent Advances in Conservation,* ed. Gary Thomson. London: Butterworths.

Gallo, Piero. 1963. Problems in the Use of Insecticides on Occupied Premises. In *Recent Advances in Conservation,* ed. Gary Thomson. London: Butterworths.

Meynell, G. G., and R. J. Newsam. 1978. Foxing, A Fungal Infection of Paper. *Nature* 274 (August): 466–68.

Torkelson, T. R., H. R. Hoyle, and V. K. Rowe. 1966. Toxicological Hazards and Properties of Commonly Used Space, Structural and Certain Other Fumigants. *Pest Control* (July).

Matting and Framing

Barrow, William J. 1960. *Permanence/Durability of the Book.* Vol. 4, *Spot Testing.* Richmond, VA: W. J. Barrow Research Laboratory.

Perkinson, Roy L. 1975. Unframing and Framing. *Museum News.* Part I, 53(8). Part II, 53(9).

Smith, Merrily. 1981. *Matting and Hinging of Works of Art on Paper.* Washington, DC: Library of Congress.

Weidner, Marilyn K. 1967. Damage and Deterioration of Art on Paper Due to Ignorance and the Use of Faul
in Conserva

Preparing C

Keck, Carolin
ing Your C
Nashville: A
for State ar

Stolow, Nath
Environme
Transit. Lo

Disasters

Spawn. Will
Water Con
brary Asso

Waters, Pet
for Salvag
Materials.
brary of C

Reference

American Pa
ation. 196
Paper. 3d
George Ba

Gettens, R.
Stout. 196
A Short
York: Dov

Mayer, Ral
Handbook
Technique
Press.

McCann, M
ware: The
tions in
Craft M
Watson-G

Winsor &
the Com
nence of
York: Wi

Chapter 4

Arnheim,
Thinking
of Califor

———. 19
ception.
Californi

Held. Ric
Image.

Readings from Scientific American. San Francisco: W. H. Freeman & Co.

Hess, Thomas B., and John Ashbery, eds. 1971. *Light in Art.* New York: Collier Books, Art News Series.

Mason, Peter. 1982. *The Light Fantastic.* Middlesex, England: Penguin Books.

Wilmerding, John. 1980. *American Light.* New York: Harper & Row; Washington, DC: National Gallery of Art.

Application of Color Theory

Birren, Faber. 1961. *Creative Color.* New York: Van Nostrand Reinhold.

Mascaro, David. 1983. On the Use of Color in Medical Illustration II. *Journal of Biocommunication* 10 (March): 30–38.

———. 1984. The Use of Color in Anatomical and Surgical Illustration. *Journal of Biocommunication* 11 (Nov.): 4–16.

Parramion, J. M. 1971. *Painting.* New York: Graphic Press.

Sargent, Walter. 1964. *The Enjoyment and Use of Color.* New York: Dover Publications.

Iridescence

Denton, E. 1971. Reflectors in Fish. *Scientific American* 224 (1): 65–72.

Ghiradella, Helen, Daniel Aneshansley, Thomas Eisner, Robert E. Silberglied, and Howard Hinton. 1972. Ultraviolet Reflection of a Male Butterfly: Interference Color Caused by Thin Layer Elaboration on Wing Scales. *Science* 178(4066): 1214–16.

Hillman, H. 1967. *The Art and Science of Color.* New York: McGraw-Hill.

Michelson, A. A. 1968. *Studies in Optics.* Chicago: University of Chicago Press.

Minnaert, M. 1954. *The Nature of Light and Color in the Open Air.* New York: Dover Publications.

Monroe, E. A., and S. E. Monroe. 1968. Origin of Iridescent Colors on the Indigo Snake. *Science* 159 (3810): 97–98.

Simon, Hilda. 1971. *The Splendor of Iridescence: Structural Colors in the Animal World.* New York: Dodd, Mead.

Chapter 5. Line and Ink

Bacon, C. W. 1951. *Scratchboard Drawing.* London and New York: Studio Publications.

Borgman, Harry. 1977. *Drawing in Ink.* New York: Watson-Guptill.

Brödel, Max. Brödel is best known for his medical drawings, though he did numerous zoological studies. His work is represented in many books, including the following: Cullen, Thomas S. 1916. *Embryology, Anatomy, and Diseases of the Umbilicus.* Philadelphia: W. B. Saunders. Kelly, Howard A. 1905. *The Vermiform Appendix.* Philadelphia: W. B. Saunders. Kelly, Howard A., and Curtis F. Burnam. 1922. *Diseases of the Kidneys, Urethers and Bladder.* 2 vols. New York and London: D. Appleton and Company.

Clarke, Carl D. 1939. Pen-and-Ink Drawings. In *Illustration, Its Technique and Application to the Sciences.* Baltimore: John D. Lucas Company.

Cutler, Merritt Dana. 1949. *Scratchboard Drawing.* New York: Watson-Guptill.

De Lahunta, A. 1977. *Functional Neuroanatomy and Clinical Neurology.* Philadelphia: W. B. Saunders.

Ellwood, Montague. 1927. *The Art of Pen Drawing.* London: B. T. Batsford.

Gilbert, S. G. 1965. *Atlas of General Zoology.* Minneapolis: Burgess Publishing Company.

———. 1973. *Pictorial Anatomy of the Dogfish.* Seattle: University of Washington Press.

Gill, Robert W. 1973. *Rendering with Pen and Ink.* New York: Van Nostrand Reinhold.

Guptill, Arthur L. 1976. *Drawing with Pen and Ink.* Edited by Susan E. Meyer. New York: Watson-Guptill. (Originally published in 1930 by Reinhold Publishing Corporation, New York.)

Jayne, H. 1898. *Mammalian Anatomy.* Philadelphia: J.P. Lippincott.

Miller, M., G. Christensen, and H. Evans. 1964. *Anatomy of the Dog.* Philadelphia: W. B. Saunders.

Pennell, Joseph, 1977. *Pen Drawing and Pen Draughtsmen.* New York: Hart Publishing Company and Da Capo Press. (Originally published in 1889 by Macmillan, New York.)

Raven, H. C. 1950. *The Anatomy of the Gorilla.* Edited by W. K. Gregory. New York: Columbia University Press.

Snodgrass, R. E. 1935. *Principles of Insect Morphology.* 1st ed. New York: McGraw-Hill.

Chapter 6. Pencil

Borgeson, Bet. 1983. *The Colored Pencil: Key Concepts for Handling the Medium.* New York: Watson-Guptill.

Calle, Paul. 1985. *The Pencil.* Cincinnati: North Light Books.

Herdeg, Walter, ed. 1973. *The Artist in the Service of Science.* Zurich: Graphis Press.

Hodge, Gerald P. 1985. Colored Pencils for Scientific Illustration. *Journal of Biocommunication* 12(1): 4–7.

Linsenmaier, Walter. 1972. *Insects of the World.* New York: McGraw-Hill.

Walker, Don. 1985. Drawing in Colored Pencil. *The Artist's Magazine* 2 (2): 68–73.

Chapter 7. Coquille Board

Allaben-Confer, Karen. 1979. Lukey—Foster Parent: A Study. GNSI [Guild of Natural Science Illustrators] *Newsletter,* December, 5–8.

Brudon, William L. 1979. Coquille Board Rendering. GNSI *Newsletter*, September, 6–10.

Gardner, Wes. 1984. Coquille Board for Drawing. GNSI *Newsletter*, Summer, 5–7.

Taylor, Lucy. 1980. More on Coquille Board Technique. GNSI *Newsletter*, May, 7–9.

Chapter 8. Carbon Dust

Drukker-Brammall, P. 1976. Carbon Dust Technique in Ichthyological Illustrating. GNSI [Guild of Natural Science Illustrators] *Newsletter*, May, 6–9.

Gast, Carolyn Bartlett. 1970. Carbon Dust on Cronaflex. GNSI *Newsletter*, March, 1–3.

———. 1973. Graphite on Cronaflex. GNSI *Newsletter*, April, 3–4.

———. 1974. Notes to be Added to Carolyn Gast's Earlier Technique Sheet on Carbon Dust on Cronaflex—March, 1970, and April, 1973. GNSI *Newsletter*, June, 5.

———. 1974. Comparison of Three Surfaces. GNSI *Newsletter*, November, 9.

———. 1978. Notes on Comparative Textures of Drawing Surfaces. GNSI *Newsletter*, Summer, 8–9.

Hodge, Gerald P. 1972. Notes for the Procedures, Carbon Dust on Ross Stipple Board #00. GNSI *Newsletter*, September, 5–6.

———. 1973. Notes for the Procedure, Video Paper Technique. GNSI *Newsletter*, February, 5–6.

———. 1973. Silver Point on Video and Media Papers. GNSI *Newsletter*, March, 3–4.

———. 1976. Substitute Papers for Carbon Dust Drawings. GNSI *Newsletter*, September, 4–5.

Lorraine, Helen. 1950. "Brödel Technique" for Halftone Reproduction. *Journal of the Association of Medical Illustrators* 12:38–39.

Nicholson, Trudy. 1974. Pencil on Frosted Acetate. GNSI *Newsletter*, November, 7–8.

———. 1978. New Dull-Finish Stipple Board. GNSI *Newsletter*, April, 3.

Page, N. 1970. Carbon Dust Technique. GNSI *Newsletter*, May, 2.

Stone, Peter. 1975. Yet Another Carbon Dust Surface. GNSI *Newsletter*, May, 4–5.

Chapter 9. Watercolor and Wash

Guptill, Arthur L. 1967. *Watercolor Painting Step-by-Step*. 2d ed. New York: Watson-Guptill.

Johnson, Cathy. 1986. Exploring the Properties of Pigments. *The Artist's Magazine* 3 (10): 56–61.

Kautzky, Ted. 1963. *Ways with Watercolor*. 2d ed. New York: Van Nostrand Reinhold.

Pike, John. 1973. *Watercolor*. 2d ed. New York: Watson-Guptill and London: Pitman Publishers.

Reid, Charles. 1973. *Portrait Painting in Watercolor*. New York: Watson-Guptill.

Szabo, Zoltan. 1974. *Creative Watercolor Techniques*. New York: Watson-Guptill.

Chapter 10. Gouache and Acrylics

Gouache

De Reyna, Rudy. 1969. *Painting in Opaque Watercolor*. New York: Watson-Guptill.

———. 1973. *Magic Realist Painting Techniques*. New York: Watson-Guptill.

Hodge, Gerald P. 1982. Gouache for Scientific Art. *Journal of Biocommunication* 9(3):10–14.

Mann, W. 1964. *Gouache Painting with Designers' Colors*. London: Winsor & Newton Ltd.

Winsor & Newton. n.d. "Designers' Gouache." Free brochure available in large art-supply stores.

Acrylics

Blake, Wendo *Guide to Acr* York: Watso

Brooks, Walter *of Acrylic P* M. Grumbac

Covino, Fran *Acrylics with* cinnati: Nort

Pellew, John *Landscape P* Watson-Gup

Taubes, Fred *Painting for* York: Watso

Acrylics Use Media

Unger, Joseph *Mixed Medi* son-Guptill.

Chapter 11.

Airbrush Dige enue. Port 2691.

Childers, R. New York:

Dember, S. *brush Tech cial, Techn Applicatio* lis: Bobbs-

Isham, Lawr plication o in Paleo GNSI [Gui Illustrators mer, 3–6.

Ito, Joel H. brush to D tic Film. October, 7

Marten, C. *brush Ma* VT: David

Martin, Judy *Guide to A and Mate* Chartwell

Maurello, S

plete Airbrush Book. New York: L. Amiel Publishers.
Misstear, Cecil, and Helen Scott-Harman. 1984. *The Advanced Airbrush Book*. New York: Van Nostrand Reinhold.
Paschal, Robert W., and Robert R. Anderson. 1985. *The Art of the Dot*. New York: Van Nostrand Reinhold.
Rubelman, S. D. 1982. *Encyclopedia of the Airbrush*. Vols. I and II. New York: Art Direction.
Sadler, Lewis. 1983. Airbrush Technique. GNSI *Newsletter*, (Part 1) Summer, 10–11; (Part 2) September, 5–6.
Shafran, A. 1968. *Airbrush Photo Retouching Manual*. Philadelphia: Chilton Book Company.
Tombs Curtis, S., and C. Hunt. 1980. *The Airbrush Book: Art, History and Technique*. New York: Van Nostrand Reinhold.
Vero, Radu. 1983. *Airbrush: The Complete Studio Handbook*. New York: Watson-Guptill.

Chapter 12. Illustrating Plants

Alexopoulos, C. J., and C. W. Mims. 1979. *Introductory Mycology*. 3d ed. New York: John Wiley and Sons.
Bailey Hortorium. 1976. *Hortus III*. New York: Macmillan.
Bold, H. C., C. J. Alexopoulos, and T. Delevoryas. 1980. *Morphology of Plants and Fungi*. 4th ed. New York: Harper & Row.
Bold, H. C., and M. J. Wynne. 1985. *Introduction to the Algae, Structure and Reproduction*. 2d ed. Englewood. Cliffs, NJ: Prentice-Hall. Prentice-Hall Biology Series.
Engler, A., and K. Prantl. 1887-1915. *Die Naturlichen Pflanzenfamilien*. 23 vols. Leipzig: W. Engelmann. (1924–52. 2d ed. 8 vols. [incomplete] Leipzig: W. Engelmann [in German]).
Esau, K. 1965. *Plant Anatomy*. 2d ed. New York: John Wiley and Sons.
Fitch, W. H. 1869. Botanical Drawing. *Gardeners' Chronicle* 1:7, 2:51, 3:110, 4:165, 5:221, 6:305, 7:389, 8:499.
Foster, A. S., and E. M. Gifford. 1974. *Comparative Morphology of Vascular Plants*. 2d ed. San Francisco: W. H. Freeman & Co.
Graf, A. B. 1982. *Pictorial Cyclopedia of Exotic Plants*. Exotica Series 4, International. East Rutherford, NJ: Roehrs.
———. 1978. *Tropica*. East Rutherford, NJ: Roehrs.
Hutchinson, J. 1973. *The Families of Flowering Plants*. 3d ed. Oxford: Clarendon Press.
Index Kewensis. 1893–1947. 2 vols. (16 supplements, to 1975). London: Oxford University Press.
Index Londonensis. 1929–31. Oxford. 6 vols. (one 2-vol. supplement, 1941; supplemental list 1921–35.) London: Oxford University Press.
Lawrence, G. H. M. 1951. *Taxonomy of Vascular Plants*. New York: Macmillan.
Smith, Gilbert M. 1955. *Cryptogamic Botany*. 2d ed. Vol. 1, *Algae and Fungi*. Vol. 2, *Bryophytes and Pteridophytes*. New York: McGraw-Hill.
Sporne, K. R. 1965. *The Morphology of Gymnosperms*. London: Hutchinson and Co.
Watson, E. V. 1971. *The Structure and Life of Bryophytes*. 3d ed. London: Hutchinson and Co.
Weier, T. Elliot, C. Ralph Stocking, and Michael G. Barbour. 1974. *Botany: An Introduction to Plant Biology*. 5th ed. New York: John Wiley and Sons.
West, Keith. 1983. *How to Draw Plants*. New York: Watson-Guptill.
Wherry, Edgar T. 1964. *Southern Fern Guide*. New York: Doubleday.
Wilson, Carl L., and Walter E. Loomis. 1967. *Botany*. 4th ed. New York: Holt, Rinehart and Winston.

Chapter 13. Illustrating Fossils

Fossil Plants

Banks, Harlan P. 1970. *Evolution and Plants of the Past*. Belmont, CA: Wadsworth Publishers.
Delevoryas, T. 1962. *Morphology and Evolution of Fossil Plants*. New York: Holt, Rinehart and Winston.
Taylor, T. N. 1981. *Paleobotany: An Introduction to Fossil Plant Biology*. New York: McGraw-Hill.

Fossil Invertebrates

Cushman, Joseph A. 1948. *Foraminifera: Their Classification and Economic Use*. Cambridge: Harvard University Press.
Finks, Robert M. 1965. Sponges. In *Handbook of Paleontological Techniques*, ed. Bernhard Kummel and David Raup. San Francisco: W. H. Freeman & Co.
Hueber, F. M., and H. P. Banks. 1979. *Serrulacaulis furcatus* gen. et sp. nov. a New Zosterophyll from the Lower Upper Devonian of New York State. *Review of Palaeobotany and Palynology* 28: 169–89.
Isham, Lawrence B. 1965. Preparation of Drawings for Paleontological Publication. In *Handbook of Paleontological Techniques*, ed. Bernhard Kummel and David Raup. San Francisco: W. H. Freeman & Co.
Moore, Raymond C., ed. ca. 1953–81. *Treatise on Invertebrate Paleontology*. Boulder, CO: Geological Society of America and Lawrence: University of Kansas Press.
Sohn, I. G., Jean M. Berdan, and Raymond E. Peck. 1965. Ostracods. In *Handbook of Paleontological Techniques*, ed. Bernhard Kummel and David Raup. San Francisco: W. H. Freeman & Co.
Todd, R., D. Low, and J. F. Mello. 1965. Smaller Foraminifers. In

Handbook of Paleontological Techniques, ed. Bernhard Kummel and David Raup. San Francisco: W. H. Freeman & Co.

Fossil Vertebrates

Colbert, E. H., and C. Tarka. 1960. Illustration of Fossil Vertebrates. *Medical and Biological Illustration* 10(4):237–46.

Jollie, M. T. 1962. *Chordate Morphology*. New York: Reinhold Publishing Corp.

Kummel, Bernhard, and David Raup, eds. 1965. *Handbook of Paleontological Techniques*. San Francisco: W. H. Freeman & Co.

Ostrom, J. H., and J. S. McIntosh. 1966. *Marsh's Dinosaurs*. New Haven, CT: Yale University Press.

Szalay, F. S., and E. Delson. 1979. *Evolutionary History of the Primates*. New York: Academic Press.

Chapter 14. Reconstructing Extinct Vertebrates

Bakker, R. T. 1975. Dinosaur Renaissance. *Scientific American* 237(10):58–78.

Behrensmeyer, A. K., and A. P. Hill. 1980. *Fossils in the Making: Vertebrate Taxonomy and Paleoecology*. Chicago: University of Chicago Press.

Chase, Terry L. 1979a. Illustration Techniques for Palaeontological Exhibits. In *Curation of Palaeontological Collections*, ed. M. G. Bassett. *Special Papers in Palaeontology* 22:189–208.

———. 1979b. Methods for the Preparation of Palaeontological Models. In *Curation of Palaeontological Collections*, ed. M. G. Bassett. *Special Papers in Palaeontology* 22:225–67.

Czerkas, S. M., and D. F. Glut. 1982. *Dinosaurs, Mammoths and Cavemen: The Art of Charles R. Knight*. New York: E. P. Dutton.

Farlow, J. A. 1981. Estimates of Dinosaur Speeds from a New Trackway Site in Texas. *Nature* 294:747–48.

Hotton, N., III. 1963. *Dinosaurs*. New York: Pyramid Publications.

———. 1965. Tetrapods. In *Handbook of Paleontological Techniques*, ed. Bernhard Kummel and David Raup. San Francisco: W. H. Freeman & Co.

Knight, Charles R. 1947. *Animal Drawing*. New York: Dover Publications.

Rensberger, B. 1981. Facing the Past. *Science 81* 8 (Oct.): 40–50.

Rixon, A. E. 1976. *Fossil Animal Remains: Their Preparation and Conservation*. London: Athone Press.

Romer, A. S. 1922. The Locomotor Apparatus of Certain Primitive and Mammal-Like Reptiles. *Bulletin American Museum of Natural History* 46:517–606.

———. 1966. *Vertebrate Paleontology*. 3d ed. Chicago: University of Chicago Press.

Rudwick, M. J. S. 1964. The Inference of Function from Structure. *Fossils, British Journal of Philosophical Sciences* 15: 27–40.

Shipman, Pat. 1981. *Life History of a Fossil*. Cambridge: Harvard University Press.

Sukhanov, V. B. 1974. *General System of Symmetrical Locomotion of Terrestrial Vertebrates and Some Features of Movement of Lower Tetrapods*. New Delhi: Amerind Publishing Co. Published for the Smithsonian Institution.

Chapter 15. Illustrating Invertebrates

General

Barnes, Robert D. 1987. *Invertebrate Zoology*. Philadelphia: Saunders College.

Bayer, Frederick M., and Harding B. Owre. 1968. *The Free-Living Lower Invertebrates*. New York: Macmillan.

Boolootian, Ri *Physiology* New York: Sons.

Buchsbaum, R *without Ba* University of

Corliss, John dom Protist *Biosystems* 1

Hyman, Libbi *Invertebrate* York: McGr

Jahn, T. L., E. Jahn. 1979. *Protozoa*. 2 Wm. C. Bro

Levi, Herbert Levi. 1968. *and Their* Golden Pre

Mann, Mary-J S. Hodges. croscopy as Illustrators. *munication*

Margulis, L., 1982. *Five trated Guid on Earth*. S Freeman &

Marshall, A. liams. 197 *ogy, Inve* London: N York: Am lishing Co.

Entomolog

Borror, D. J. C. A. Trip *troduction sects*. 4th Rinehart a

Borror, D. J 1970. *A F sects of A ico*. Boston

Chapman, P 1971. *Tort in N.Y.* Ge culture F March.

C.S.I.R.O. entific an Organizati

of Australia. Carlton, Victoria: Melbourne University Press.

Dalton, S. 1975. *Borne on the Wind: The Extraordinary World of Insects in Flight*. New York: Reader's Digest Press.

de la Torre-Bueno, J. R. 1973. *A Glossary of Entomology*. New York: New York Entomological Society.

Dominick, R. B. 1971–present. The Moths of America North of Mexico. Washington, DC: Wedge Entomological Research Foundation.

Eisner, T., and E. O. Wilson. 1977. *The Insects*. San Francisco: W. H. Freeman & Co.

Evans, H. E. 1984. *Insect Biology: A Textbook of Entomology*. Reading, MA: Addison-Wesley.

Linsenmaier, W. 1972. *Insects of the World*. New York: McGraw-Hill.

McAlpine, J. F., B. V. Peterson, G. E. Shewell, H. J. Teskey, J. R. Vockeroth, and D. M. Wood, coordinators. 1981. *Manual of Nearctic Diptera*. Vol. 1. Research Branch Agriculture Canada. Monograph no. 27. Hull, Quebec: Canadian Government Publishing Centre.

Matsuda, R. 1965. *Morphology and Evolution of the Insect Head*. Ann Arbor, MI: American Entomological Institute.

———. 1970. *Morphology and Evolution of the Insect Thorax*. Ottawa, Canada: Entomological Society of Canada.

———. 1976. *Morphology and Evolution of the Insect Abdomen*. New York: Pergamon Press.

Nachtigall, W. 1974. *Insects in Flight: A Glimpse Behind the Scenes in Biophysical Research*. (English ed.) New York: McGraw-Hill.

Snodgrass, R. E. 1935. *Principles of Insect Morphology*. New York: McGraw-Hill.

Tuxen, S. L. 1970 *A Taxonomist's Glossary of Genitalia in Insects*. Copenhagen: Ejnar Munksgaard. (Available from E. W. Classey Ltd., Oxleaze Farm nr. Uffington, Oxon SN7 7QS England, or S-H Service Agency Inc., P.O. Box 2000, Darien, CT 06820.)

White, R. E. 1983. *A Field Guide to the Beetles of America North of Mexico*. Boston: Houghton Mifflin.

Zahrednik, Jiri. 1978. *Field Guide in Color to Insects*. New York: Smith Publishing, Mayflower.

CHAPTER 16. ILLUSTRATING FISHES

Blaker, A. A. 1965. *Photography for Scientific Publication: A Handbook*. New York: W. H. Freeman & Co.

——— 1976. *Field Photography, Beginning and Advanced Techniques*. New York: W. H. Freeman & Co.

Dingerkus, G., and L. D. Uhler. 1977. Enzyme Clearing of Alcian Blue Stained Whole Small Vertebrates for Demonstration of Cartilage. *Stain Technology 52* (4):229–32.

Faber, D. J., and S. Gadd. 1983. Several Drawing Techniques to Illustrate Larval Fishes. *Transactions of the American Fisheries Society* 112:349–53.

Jastrzebski, Zbigniew T. 1984. Technique of Making Fish Illustration 3 and 4. *Environmental Biology of Fishes* 11(4): 276, 300.

———. 1985. Technique of Making Fish Illustration 5. *Environmental Biology of Fishes* 12(2):142.

———. 1985. Technique of Making Fish Illustration 6. *Environmental Biology of Fishes* 12(4):318–19.

———. 1985. Technique of Making Fish Illustration 7. *Environmental Biology of Fishes* 13(2):124.

Karstad, Aleta. 1987. Technique of Making Fish Illustration 28: Painting of Living Specimens. *Environmental Biology of Fishes* 19(1):78–79.

Ridgway, John L. [1938] 1979. *Scientific Illustration*. Reprint. Stanford, CA: Stanford University Press.

Schmidt, Kathleen A. 1986. Technique of Making Fish Illustration 19. *Environmental Biology of Fishes* 16(4):294.

Stone, Dayton Bryan, III. 1986. Technique of Making Fish Illustration 18. *Environmental Biology of Fishes* 16(4):267–68.

Werner, Marlene. 1985. Technique of Making Fish Illustration 13. *Environmental Biology of Fishes* 14(4):268.

CHAPTER 17. ILLUSTRATING AMPHIBIANS AND REPTILES

Adler, Kraig. 1968. Turtles from Archeological Sites in the Great Lakes Region. *Michigan Archaeologist* 14:147–63.

Arnold, E. N., and J. A. Burton. 1978. *A Field Guide to the Reptiles and Amphibians of Britain and Europe*. London: Collins.

Bishop, Sherman C. 1947. *Handbook of Salamanders*. Ithaca, NY: Cornell University Press.

Broadley, Donald G. 1983. *Fitzsimons' Snakes of Southern Africa*. Johannesburg, South Africa: Delta Books.

Carr, Archie. 1952. *Handbook of Turtles*. Ithaca NY: Cornell University Press.

Duellman, William E. 1970. *The Hylid Frogs of Middle America*. Monograph. Lawrence, KS: Museum of Natural History, University of Kansas.

Duellman, William E., and Linda Trueb. 1985. *Biology of Amphibians*. New York: McGraw-Hill.

Gans, Carl, ed. 1969 et seq. *Biology of the Reptilia*. Vols. 1–15. London: Academic Press, and New York: John Wiley/Interscience.

Goin, Coleman J., Olive B. Goin, and George R. Zug. 1978. *Introduction to Herpetology*. 3d ed. San Francisco: W. H. Freeman & Co.

Halliday, Tim R., and Kraig Adler, eds. 1986. *The Encyclopedia of*

Reptiles and Amphibians. New York: Facts on File, and London and Sydney: George Allen and Unwin.

Noble, G. Kingsley. 1931. *The Biology of the Amphibia*. New York: McGraw-Hill. (Reprint, 1954, Dover Publications.)

Parker, H. W., and Alice G. C. Grandison. 1977. *Snakes: A Natural History*. London: British Museum (Natural History), and Ithaca, NY: Cornell University Press.

Peters, James A. 1964. *Dictionary of Herpetology*. New York and London: Hafner.

Pisani, George R. 1973. *A Guide to Preservation Techniques for Amphibians and Reptiles*. Society for the Study of Amphibians and Reptiles, Herpetology Circular, 1:1-22. (A Spanish version, by Pisani and Villa, 1974, is also available from the same publisher.)

Simmons, John E. 1987. *Herpetological Collecting and Collections Management*. Society for the Study of Amphibians and Reptiles, Herpetology Circular 16: 1–72.

Smith, Hobart M. 1946. *Handbook of Lizards*. Ithaca, NY: Cornell University Press.

Smith, Malcolm A. 1935. *The Fauna of British India: Reptilia and Amphibia*. Vol. 2, *Sauria*. London: Taylor and Francis.

Stebbins, Robert C. 1954. *Amphibians and Reptiles of Western North America*. New York: McGraw-Hill.

———. 1985. *A Field Guide to Western Reptiles and Amphibians*. 2d ed. Boston: Houghton-Mifflin.

Wright, Albert H., and Anna A. Wright. 1949. *Handbook of Frogs and Toads*. Ithaca: NY: Cornell University Press.

———. 1957. *Handbook of Snakes*. 2 vols. Ithaca, NY: Cornell University Press. (Vol. 3, *Bibliography*, was published privately by the authors in 1962 and reprinted 1979 by Society for the Study of Amphibians and Reptiles, Oxford, Ohio.)

Chapter 18. Illustrating Birds

Austin, Oliver L., Jr. 1961. *Birds of the World*. New York: Golden Press.

Bent, A. C. 1919–58. *Life Histories of North American Birds*. 21 vols. Washington, DC: Bulletin of the U.S. National Museum.

Eckelberry, Don Richard. 1965. Techniques in Bird Illustration. *The Living Bird* 4:131–60.

Forshaw, Joseph M. 1973. *Parrots of the World*. Melbourne, Australia: Lansdowne Press.

Mengel, Robert M. 1980. Beauty and the Beast: Natural History and Art. *The Living Bird* 18:27–70.

Pearson, T. Gilbert, ed. 1942. *Birds of America*. Garden City, NY: Garden City Publishing Company.

Peterson, Roger Tory. 1980. *A Field Guide to the Birds*. 4th ed. Boston: Houghton-Mifflin.

Pettingill, Olin Sewall. 1985. *Ornithology in Laboratory and Field*. 5th ed. Orlando, FL: Academic Press.

Ridgway, Robert. 1907–50. *The Birds of North and Middle America*. Washington, DC: U.S. Government Printing Office.

Ripley, S. Dillon. 1977. *Rails of the World: A Monograph of the Family Rallidae*. Boston: David R. Godine.

Rüppell, Georg. 1977. *Bird Flight*. New York: Van Nostrand Reinhold.

Sutton, George Miksch. 1975. *Portraits of Mexican Birds: Fifty Selected Paintings*. Norman, OK: University of Oklahoma Press.

———. 1979. *To a Young Bird Artist—Letters from Louis Agassiz Fuertes to George Miksch Sutton*. Norman, OK: University of Oklahoma Press.

Terres, John K. 1980. *The Audubon Society Encyclopedia of North American Birds*. New York: Alfred A. Knopf.

Tunnicliffe, C[illegible] *Sketchbook o*[illegible] Holt, Rineha[illegible]

Van Tyne, Joss[illegible] Berger. 197[illegible] *Ornithology*.[illegible] John Wiley a[illegible]

Welty, J. C. [illegible] *Birds*. 2d e[illegible] B. Saunders[illegible]

Chapter 19. [illegible] Mammals

Textbooks

Cockrum, E. [illegible] *to Mammal*[illegible] ald Press.

Davis, D. E. [illegible] 1963. *Princ*[illegible] New York:[illegible] Corp.

DeBlase, A. [illegible] 1981. *A M*[illegible] *with Keys*[illegible] *World*. 2d[illegible] Wm. C. B[illegible]

Gunderson, [illegible] *ogy*. New [illegible]

Jones, J. K., [illegible] R. S. Hoff[illegible] *Readings*[illegible] rence, KS[illegible] History, U[illegible]

Van Gelder, [illegible] *Mammals*.[illegible] Scribner's[illegible]

Vaughan, T. [illegible] 2d ed. [illegible] Saunders.[illegible]

Synopses

Anderson, S[illegible] eds. 1967[illegible] *the World*[illegible] *lies*. New[illegible]

Corbet, G. [illegible] *A World L*[illegible] *cies*. Itha[illegible] sity Press[illegible]

Duplaix, N. [illegible] *World Gu*[illegible] York: Cr[illegible]

Grassé, P. [illegible]

Vol. 17. *Mammifères.* Paris: Masson et cie.

Honacki, J. H., K. E. Kinman, and J. W. Koeppl, eds. 1982. *Mammal Species of the World.* Lawrence, KS: Allen Press and Assoc. Systematic Collections.

Lawlor, T. E. 1979. *Handbook to the Orders and Families of Living Mammals.* 2d ed. Eureka, CA: Mad River Press.

Nowak, R. W., and J. L. Paradiso. 1983. *Walker's Mammals of the World.* 4th ed. Baltimore: Johns Hopkins University Press.

Simpson, G. G. 1945. The Principles of Classification and a Classification of Mammals. *Bulletin American Museum of Natural History* 85: 1–350.

Natural Histories

Bourlière, F. 1955. *Mammals of the World.* New York: Alfred A. Knopf.

———. 1970. *The Natural History of Mammals.* 3d ed., rev. New York: Alfred A. Knopf.

Carrington, R. 1963. *The Mammals.* Life Nature Series. (Distributed by Silver Burdett, Morristown, NJ.)

Grzimek, B., ed. 1972. *Grzimek's Animal Life Encyclopedia.* 13 vols. New York: Van Nostrand Reinhold. (Vols. 10–13 cover mammals.)

Sanderson, I. T. 1967. *Living Mammals of the World.* Garden City, NY: Doubleday.

References

Anderson, S. 1968. A New Craniometer and Suggestions for Craniometry. *Journal of Mammalogy* 49:221–28.

Choate, J. R., and H. H. Genoways. 1975. Collections of Recent Mammals in North America. *Journal of Mammalogy* 56:452–502.

Genoways, H. H., and D. A. Schlitter. 1981. Collections of Recent Mammals of the World, Exclusive of Canada and the United States. *Annals of the Carnegie Museum* 50:47–80.

Kelly, K. L. 1965. Standard Sample no. 2106. National Bureau of Standards Circular 553, Supplement (color chips). Washington, DC: U.S. Government Printing Office.

Kelly, K. L., and D. B. Judd. 1955. Dictionary of Color Terms. National Bureau of Standards Circular 553. Washington, DC: U.S. Government Printing Office.

Maerz, A., and M. R. Paul. 1930. *A Dictionary of Color.* New York: McGraw-Hill.

Munsell Color Company. 1929. *Munsell Book of Color.* Baltimore: Munsell Color Company.

Ridgway, Robert. 1912. *Color Standards and Color Nomenclature.* Washington, DC: published by the author.

Villalobos, C. 1948. *Atlas de los Colores.* Buenos Aires: El Alteneo.

Chapter 20. Illustrating Animals in Their Habitats

Angel, Heather. 1979. *Nature Photography, Its Art and Techniques.* Watford, U.K.: Fountain Press.

Barruel, Paul. 1954. *Birds of the World.* New York: Oxford University Press.

Bergman, C. A. 1981. The Glass of Fashion. *Audubon* 83(6):74–80.

Buchsbaum, Ralph, and Lorus Milne. 1960. *Lower Animals, Living Invertebrates of the World.* New York: Doubleday.

Dalton, Stephen. 1977. *The Miracle of Flight.* New York: McGraw-Hill.

Eckelberry, Don R. 1978. Of Animals and Art. *Audubon* 80(5): 105.

Grassé, P. P. 1975. *Larousse Encyclopedia of the Animal World.* New York: Larousse and Co.

Knight, Charles R. 1959. *Animal Drawing: Anatomy and Action for Artists.* New York: Dover Publications.

Lefkowitz, Lester. 1979. *The Manual of Close-Up Photography.* Garden City, NY: Amphoto.

Leslie, Clare W. 1980. *Nature Drawing: A Tool for Learning.* Englewood Cliffs, NJ: Prentice-Hall.

———. 1984. *The Art of Field Sketching.* Englewood Cliffs, NJ: Prentice-Hall.

Life Nature Library. 1961–65. Alexandria, VA: Time-Life Books.

Living World Books. 1962–73. Philadelphia and New York: J. B. Lippincott Co.

Menzel-Tettenborn, H., and G. Radtke. 1973. *Animals in Their Worlds.* New York: Madison Square Press, Grosset & Dunlap.

Muybridge, E. 1957. *Animals in Motion.* New York: Dover Publications.

The New Larousse Encyclopedia of Animal Life. 1980. New York: Larousse and Co.

Our Living World of Nature Series. 1966–70. New York: McGraw-Hill.

Photographing Nature. 1971. New York: Time-Life Books, Life Library of Photography.

Rayfield, Susan. 1985. *Wildlife Painting: Techniques of Modern Masters.* New York: Watson-Guptill.

Russell, Franklin. 1975. *Wild Creatures.* New York: Simon and Schuster.

Smythe, Frank B. 1975. *Naturalist's Color Guide.* New York: American Museum of Natural History.

Chapter 21. Illustrating Humans and Their Artifacts

Addington, Lucile R. 1986. *Lithic Illustration: Drawing Flaked Stone Artifacts for Publication.* Chicago: University of Chicago Press.

Adivasio, J. M. 1977. *Basketry Technology.* New York and Chicago: Aldine.

Dever, William G., and H. Darrell Lance, eds. 1978. *A Manual of Field Excavation*. New York: Hebrew Union College, Jewish Institute of Religion.

Dillon, Brian D., ed. 1985. *The Student's Guide to Archaeological Illustration*. Vol. 1 in *Archaeological Research Tools*, 2d rev. ed. Los Angeles: University of California, Institute of Archaeology

Donnan, Christopher. 1978. *Moche Art of Peru*. Los Angeles: Museum of Cultural History, University of California.

Evans, C., and B. J. Meggers. 1968. *Archeological Investigations on the Rio Napo, Eastern Ecuador*. Washington, DC: Smithsonian Institution.

Fladmark, Knut R. 1978. *A Guide to Basic Archaeological Field Procedures*. Burnaby, British Columbia: Simon Fraser University.

Graham, Ian. 1979. *Corpus of Maya Hieroglyphic Inscriptions*. Cambridge: Peabody Museum, Harvard University.

Haury, Emil W. 1945. *Excavation of Los Muertos and Neighboring Ruins in the Salt River Valley, Southern Arizona*. Cambridge: Peabody Museum, Harvard University.

Hayes, Alden C., and James A. Lancaster. 1925. *Badger House Community, Mesa Verda National Park, Colorado*. Washington DC: National Park Service, United States Department of Interior.

Heizer, Robert F., ed. 1978. *Handbook of North American Indians*. Vol. 8, *California*. Washington, DC: Smithsonian Institution.

Hester, Thomas R., Robert F. Heizer, and John A. Graham. 1975. *Field Methods in Archaeology*. 6th ed. Palo Alto, CA: Mayfield Publishing Co.

Hurley, William M. 1979. *Prehistoric Cordage*. New York and Chicago: Aldine.

Kenyon, Kathleen. 1966. *Beginning in Archaeology*. Rev. ed., with sections on American archaeology by Saul and Gladys Weinberg. New York: Frederick A. Praeger.

Kluckhohn, Clyde, L. W. Kluckhohn, and W. W. Hill. 1971. *Navajo Material Culture*. Cambridge: Harvard University.

Rye, Owen S. 1976. *Traditional Pottery Techniques of Pakistan*. Washington DC: Smithsonian Institution.

Tanner, Clara Lee. 1976. *Prehistoric Southwestern Craft Arts*. Tucson: University of Arizona.

Van Beek, G. 1969. *Hajar Bin Humeid: Investigations of a Pre-Islamic Site in South Arabia*. Baltimore: Johns Hopkins University Press.

Chapter 22. Illustrating Medical Subjects

Anderson, J. 1978. *Grant's Atlas of Anatomy*. 7th ed. Baltimore: Williams and Wilkins.

Anderson, R., and R. Romfh. 1980. *Technique in the Use of Surgical Tools*. New York: Appleton-Century-Crofts.

CIBA. *The CIBA Collection of Medical Illustrations*. 7 vols. Summit, NJ: CIBA Pharmaceutical Co.

Clarke, Carl D. 1949. *Illustration, Its Technique and Application to the Sciences*. Butler, MD: Standard Arts Press. (Distributed by Pergamon Press, Elmsford, NY.)

Clemente, C. 1981. *Anatomy: A Regional Atlas of the Human Body*. 2d ed. Baltimore: Urban and Schwarzenberg.

Clemente, C., ed. 1985. *Gray's Anatomy of the Human Body*. 30th American ed. Philadelphia: Lea and Febiger.

Donner, C., and J. McCredie. 1977. *Basic Surgery*. New York: Macmillan.

Dox, I., B. Melloni, and G. Eisner. 1979. *Melloni's Illustrated Medical Dictionary*. Baltimore: Williams and Wilkins.

Eastman Kodak Co. 1976. *Biomedical Photogr*
inar in Pri
Eastman Ko

———. 1979.
mation. Ro
man Kodak

Feneis, H. 19
Human Ana
Internationa
Chicago: Y
Publishers.

Ferner, H., a
eds. 1983.
Human A
Urban and S

Fuller, J. 198
ogy, Princ
Philadelphi

Hammersen.
Hammersen
Atlas of M
Baltimore:
enberg.

Harrison, S.
terials and
Biocommun

Hirsh, K., a
1986. Pic
Thoracic S
Biocommu

Hodge, Gera
for Scient
Biocommu

———. 198
Scientific
Biocommu

Koritke, J.,
Atlas of S
omy. Ba
Schwarze

Lefkowitz, I
Close-up
York: Am

McMinn, R
1981. *Co*
Anatomy.
Medical

Mascaro, D
Color in
Journal
9(1):10–1

———. 198
Medical
of Bioco
38.

———. 198
Anatomi

tration. *Journal of Biocommunication* 11(4):4–16.

Moore, K. 1985. *Clinically Oriented Anatomy*. 2d ed. Philadelphia: Williams and Wilkins.

Peck, S. 1982. *Atlas of Human Anatomy for the Artist*. New York: Oxford University Press.

Pernkopf, E. 1980. *Atlas of Topographical and Applied Human Anatomy*. Edited by Helmut Ferner. Baltimore: Urban and Schwarzenberg. (Originally published by W. B. Saunders, Philadelphia, 1963.)

Ruby, E. 1974. *The Human Body: A Photographic Reference for Artists*. New York: Van Nostrand Reinhold.

Schlossberg, L., and G. Zuidema. 1980. *The Johns Hopkins Atlas of Functional Human Anatomy*. 2d ed. Baltimore: Johns Hopkins University Press.

Smith, H. 1984. Computergraphics in Biocommunication: A Report on the Impact. *Journal of Biocommunication* 11(2):40–48.

Chapter 23. Using the Microscope

Curry, A., R. F. Grayson, and Geoffrey R. Hosey. 1982. *Under the Microscope*. New York: Van Nostrand Reinhold, and London: Blandford Books Ltd.

Eastman Kodak Co. 1969. *Close-up Photography*. Technical Publication N-12A. Rochester, NY: Eastman Kodak Co.

———. 1969. *Photomacrography*. Technical Publication N-12B. Rochester, NY: Eastman Kodak Co.

Françon, M. 1961. *Progress in Microscopy*. Evanston, IL: Row, Peterson, & Co.

Gill, G. W. 1981. Visual Microscopy in Diagnostic Cytology. *American Laboratory* 13(12):17–25.

Hartley, W. G. 1964. *How to Use a Microscope*. Garden City, NY: Natural History Press, American Museum Science Books.

Moellring, F. K. 1966. *Microscopy from the Very Beginning*. Oberkachen, Germany: Carl Zeiss.

Needham, G. H. 1958. *The Practical Use of the Microscope*. Springfield, IL: Charles C. Thomas.

Shillaber, C. P. 1944. *Photomicrography*. New York: John Wiley and Sons.

Chapter 24. Charts and Diagrams

Council of Biology Editors, Scientific Illustration Committee. 1988. *Illustrating Science: Standards for Publication*. Bethesda, MD: Council of Biology Editors.

Eastman Kodak Co. 1975. *Effective Lecture Slides*. Technical Publication S-22. Rochester, NY: Eastman Kodak Co.

———. 1983. *Legibility—Artwork to Screen*. Technical Publication S-24. Rochester, NY: Eastman Kodak Co.

Gray, Bill. 1976. *Studio Tips for Artists and Graphic Designers*. New York: Prentice Hall Press.

———. 1978. *More Studio Tips for Artists and Graphic Designers*. New York: Prentice Hall Press.

Herdeg, Walter ed. 1981. *Graphis Diagrams: The Graphic Visualization of Abstract Data*. Enlarged ed. Zurich: Graphis Press.

Lockwood, Arthur. 1969. *Diagrams: A Visual Survey of Graphs, Maps, Charts and Diagrams for the Graphic Designer*. New York: Watson-Guptill.

McGregor, A. J. 1979. *Graphics Simplified*. Toronto: University of Toronto Press.

Schmid, Calvin, and Stanton E. Schmid. 1979. *Handbook of Graphic Presentation*. 2d ed. New York: Ronald Press, John Wiley and Sons.

Simmonds, Doig, ed. 1980. *Charts and Graphs*. Lancaster, England: MTP Press, Ltd. (Falcon House).

Tufte, Edward R. 1983. *The Visual Display of Quantitative Information*. Cheshire, CT: Graphics Press.

White, Jan V. 1984. *Using Charts and Graphs: 1000 Ideas for Visual Persuasion*. New York: R. R. Bowker.

Chapter 25. Cartography for the Scientific Illustrator

Barnes, W. J. 1981. *Basic Geological Mapping* (Geological Society of London Handbook). New York: Halsted Press.

Bartz, B. A. 1970. Experimental Use of the Search Task in an Analysis of Type Legibility in Cartography. *Cartographic Journal* 7:103–13.

Castner, H. W., and A. H. Robinson. 1969. *Dot Area Symbols in Cartography: The Influence of Pattern on their Perception*. Technical Monograph #CA-4. Washington, DC: American Congress of Surveying and Mapping.

Crawford, P. V. 1971. Perception of Gray-Tone Symbols. *Annals of the Association of American Geographers* 61:721–35.

Cuff, D. J. 1972. Value versus Chroma in Color Schemes on Quantitative Maps. *Canadian Cartographer* 9:134–40.

———. 1973. Color on Temperature Maps. *Cartographic Journal* 10:17–21.

Cuff, D. J., and M. T. Mattson. 1982. *Thematic Maps: Their Design and Production*. New York: Methuen.

Deluca, J. P. 1980. *Pantone Matching System and Pantone Matching System Formula Guide*. Moonachie, NJ: Pantone.

Dent, B. D. 1985. *Principles of Thematic Map Design*. Reading, MA: Addison-Wesley.

Eckert, M. 1977. On the Nature of Maps and Map Logic. *Cartographica* 19:1–7.

Flannery, J. J. 1971. The Effectiveness of Some Common Graduated Point Symbols in the Presentation of Quantitative

Data. *Canadian Cartographer* 8:96–109.

Groop, R. E., and D. G. Cole. 1978. Overlapping Graduated Circles: Magnitude Estimation and Method of Portrayal. *Canadian Cartographer* 15:114–22.

Hilliard, J. A., U. Bosoglu, and P. C. Muehrcke. 1978. *A Projection Handbook.* Cartographic Laboratory Paper #2. Madison, WI: University of Wisconsin.

Hsu, M. L. 1981. The Role of Projections in Modern Map Design. *Cartographica* 18:151–86.

Imhof, E. 1975. Positioning Names on Maps. *American Cartographer* 2:128–44.

———. 1982. *Cartographic Relief Presentation.* Edited by H. J. Steward. New York: Walter de Gruyter.

Jenks, G. F. 1963. Generalization in Statistical Mapping. *Annals of the Association of American Geographers.* 53:15–26.

———. 1976. Contemporary Statistical Maps—Evidence of Spatial and Graphic Ignorance. *American Cartographer* 3:11–19.

Jenks, G. F., and F. C. Caspall. 1971. Error on Choroplethic Maps: Definition, Measurement, Reduction. *Annals of the Association of American Geographers* 61:217–44.

Keates, J. S. 1973. *Cartographic Design and Production.* New York: Halsted Press.

———. 1982. *Understanding Maps.* New York: John Wiley and Sons.

Kimerling, A. J. 1980. Color Specifications in Cartography. *American Cartographer* 7:139–53.

Lawrence, G. R. 1979. *Cartographic Methods.* 2d ed. New York: Methuen.

Lawson Perspective Charts. 1948. New York: Van Nostrand Reinhold.

Lobeck, A. K. 1958. *Block Diagrams.* 2d ed. Amherst, MA: Emerson-Trussel.

MacKay, J. R. 1949. Dotting the Dot Map: An Analysis of Dot Size, Number and Visual Tone Density. *Surveying and Mapping* 9:3–10.

McDonnell, P. W. 1979. *Introduction to Map Projections.* New York: Marcel Dekker.

Monmonier, M. S. 1977. *Maps, Distortion and Meaning.* Resource Paper #75–4. Washington, DC: American Association of Geographers.

———. 1982. *Computer Aided Cartography: Principles and Prospects.* Englewood Cliffs, NJ: Prentice-Hall.

Morrison, J. L. 1971. *Method Produced Error in Isarithmic Mapping.* Technical Monograph #CA-5. Washington, DC: American Congress on Surveying and Mapping.

Muehrcke, P. C. 1972. *Thematic Cartography.* Resource Paper #19. Washington, DC. Association of American Geographers.

Muehrcke, P. C., and J. Muehrcke. 1986. *Map Use: Reading, Analysis and Interpretation.* 2nd ed. Madison, WI: J. P. Publications.

Olson, J. M. 1981. Spectrally Encoded Two-Variable Maps. *Annals of the Association of American Geographers* 71:259–76.

Raisz, E. 1962. *Principles of Cartography.* New York: McGraw-Hill.

Robinson, A. H. 1986. *The Look of Maps.* Madison, WI: University of Wisconsin Press.

Robinson, A. H., and B. B. Petchenik. 1976. *The Nature of Maps: Essays Toward Understanding Maps and Mapping.* Chicago: University of Chicago Press.

Robinson, A. H., R. D. Sale, J. L. Morrison, and P. C. Muehrcke. 1984. *Elements of Cartography.* 5th ed. New York: John Wiley and Sons.

Shelton, J. S. 1966. *Geology Illustrated.* San Francisco: W. H. Freeman & Co.

Shortridge, B. G. 1979. Map Reader Discrimination of Lettering Size. *American Cartographer* 6:13–20.

Southworth, [...] worth. 198[...] *Survey and* [...] ton: Little, [...]

Steers, J. A. 1[...] *to the Stud*[...] don: Univ[...] Press.

Tanaka, K. 1[...] tour Meth[...] Topography[...] *cal Review*[...]

Taylor, D. R. [...] *in Contem*[...] Vol. 1. *The*[...] *porary Car*[...] John Wiley[...]

———. 1982[...] *porary C*[...] *Graphic*[...] *Design in*[...] *raphy.* Ne[...] and Sons.[...]

Thrower, N.[...] *Man.* En[...] Prentice-H[...]

Tufte, E. R. [...] *play of*[...] *tion.* Ch[...] Press.

Wood, M. 1[...] and Map[...] *Journal* 5[...]

CHAPTER 2[...]

Eastman K[...] *Lecture S*[...] cation S[...] Eastman[...]

———. 198[...] Technica[...] Rocheste[...] Co.

———. 19[...] *to Screen*[...] S-24. Ro[...] Kodak C[...]

———. 19[...] *cating in*[...] *Color.* T[...] 1. Roc[...] Kodak C[...]

Hart, Rus[...] *ing You*[...] North Li[...]

Keller, Kate, and Mali Olatunji. 1982. Preparing Your Portfolio. In *The Business of Art*, ed. Lee Evan Caplin. Englewood Cliffs, NJ: Prentice-Hall.

Chapter 27. The Printing Process

Allen, Arly. 1977. *Steps toward Better Scientific Illustrations*. Lawrence, KS: Allen Press.

Council of Biology Editors, Scientific Illustration Committee. 1988. *Illustrating Science: Standards for Publication*. Bethesda, MD: Council of Biology Editors.

Pocket Pal: A Graphic Arts Production Handbook. 1983. New York: International Paper Co.

Sanders, Norman. 1982. *Graphic Designer's Production Handbook*. New York: Hastings House.

Steinberg, S. H. 1979. *Five Hundred Years of Printing*. Rev. ed. New York: Penguin.

Stone, Bernard, and Arthur Eckstein. 1983. *Preparing Art for Printing*. Rev. ed. New York: Van Nostrand Reinhold.

Chapter 28. Copyright

Copyright Information Kit. (Available from Copyright Office, Library of Congress, 101 Independence Ave., S. E., Washington, DC 20559.)

Crawford, Tad C. 1978. *The Visual Artist's Guide to the New Copyright Law*. New York: Graphic Artists Guild. (Available from 11 West 20th St., New York, NY 10011.)

Crawford, Tad C. 1987. *Legal Guide for the Visual Artist*. New York: Madison Square Press.

Latman, A. 1979. *The Copyright Law*. 5th ed. (Available from Bureau of National Affairs, 1231-25th St., N.W., Washington, DC 20037.)

Rodewall, Fred C., and Edward M. Gottschall. 1971. *Commercial Art as Business*. 2d rev. ed. New York: Viking Press.

Samuels, Jeffrey. 1984. *Patent Trademark and Copyright Law*. Washington DC: Bureau of National Affairs.

Chapter 29. Contracts

Cochrane, Diane. 1978. *This Business of Art*. New York: Watson-Guptill.

Crawford, Tad C. 1987. *Legal Guide for the Visual Artist*. New York: Madison Square Press.

Graphic Artists Guild. 1988 (or latest edition). *Graphic Artists Guild Handbook, Pricing and Ethical Guidelines*. New York: Graphic Artists Guild. (Available from 11 West 20th St., New York, 10011.)

Chapter 30. Operating a Freelance Business

Caplin, Lee Evan, ed. 1982. *The Business of Art*. Englewood Cliffs, NJ: Prentice-Hall.

Colby, Jean Poindexter. 1967. *Writing, Illustrating and Editing Children's Books*. New York: Hastings House.

Conner, Susan, ed. 1988 (reprinted annually). *Artist's Market: Where and How to Sell Your Graphic Art*. Cincinnati: Writer's Digest Books.

Conran, Shirley. 1978. *Superwoman—For Everywoman Who Hates Housework*. New York: Crown Publishers.

Craig, James. 1983. *Graphic Design Career Guide*. New York: Watson- Guptill.

Crawford, Tad, and Arie Kopelman. 1981. *Selling Your Graphic Design and Illustration*. New York: St. Martin's Press.

Gold, Edward. 1985. *The Business of Graphic Design: A Sensible Approach*. New York: Watson-Guptill.

Heller, Steven, and Lita Talarico. 1987. *Design Career*. New York: Van Nostrand Reinhold.

Hoover, Deborah A. 1985. *Supporting Yourself as an Artist*. New York: Oxford University Press.

Lakein, Alan. 1974. *How to Get Control of Your Time and Your Life*. New York: Signet.

MacKenzie, Alec, and Kay Cronkite Waldo. 1981. *About Time! A Woman's Guide to Time Management*. New York: McGraw-Hill.

Scott, Dru. 1981. *How to Put More Time in Your Life*. New York: Signet.

Snyder, John. 1973. *Commercial Artist's Handbook*. New York: Watson-Guptill.

Studio Planning and Design. 1987. *The Artist's Magazine* 4 (12):60–75.

Tennov, Dorothy. 1978. *Super Self: A Woman's Guide to Self Management*. New York: Harcourt Brace Jovanovich.

Weaver, Peter. 1975. *You, Inc.: A Detailed Escape Route to Being Your Own Boss*. Garden City, NY: Doubleday/Dolphin.

Portfolio Preparation

Berryman, Gregg. 1985. *Designing Creative Résumés*. Los Altos, CA: William Kaufmann, Inc.

Marquand, Edward. 1981. *How to Prepare Your Portfolio*. 2d ed. New York: Art Direction Books.

Smith, Merrily. 1981. *Matting and Hinging Works of Art on Paper*. Washington, DC: Library of Congress.

Small Business

U.S. Small Business Administration, P.O. Box 30, Denver, CO 80201-0030. Most Small Business Administration publications are available for a small charge, but the following ones are free:

Business Development Pamphlet Order Form 115A

Business Development Booklets List—Form 115B

Your Business and the SBA—OPC-2

Taxes

Listed here are publications that might be most helpful for the freelance illustrator. They can be ordered at no cost from the Internal Revenue Service, Forms Distribution Centers: P.O. Box 12626, Fresno, CA 93778; P.O. Box 9903, Bloomington, IL 61799; P.O. Box 25866, Richmond, VA 23260.

Guide to Free Tax Services, Pub. 910.

Your Federal Income Tax, Pub. 17

Tax Guide for Small Business, Pub. 334

Travel, Entertainment, and Gift Expenses, Pub. 463

Tax Withholding and Estimated Tax, Pub. 505

Educational Expenses, Pub. 508

Miscellaneous Deductions, Pub. 529

Self-Employment Tax (Social Security), Pub. 533

Depreciation, Pub. 534

Business Expenses, Pub. 535

Net Operating Losses and the At-Risk Limits, Pub. 536

Accounting Periods and Methods, Pub. 538

Employment Taxes, Pub. 539

Tax Information on Corporations, Pub. 542

Deduction for Bad Debts, Pub. 548

Recordkeeping for Individuals and a List of Tax Publications, Pub. 552

Self-Employed Retirement Plans (Keogh or HR-10), Pub. 560

Information for Business Taxpayers, Pub. 583

Business Use of Your Home, Pub. 587

Individual Retirement Arrangements (IRAs), Pub. 590

Information Returns, Pub. 916

Business Use of a Car, Pub. 917

Index to Illustrators

Index

ABOUT THE EDITORS

Elaine R. S. Hodges is a scientific illustrator in the Department of Entomology at the Smithsonian Institution's National Museum of Natural History. She studied art at Pratt Institute and American University and majored in entomology at the University of Maryland. An illustrator and painter since 1956, Mrs. Hodges entered the field of scientific illustration at the Smithsonian in 1965. She helped found the Guild of Natural Science Illustrators, serving as its first *Newsletter* editor and later as vice-president and president. Mrs. Hodges has also lectured, taught, and written extensively on the field.

The board of editors includes Lawrence B. Isham, Marsha E. Jessup, and G. Robert Lewis. Lawrence B. Isham is a retired scientific illustrator who began scientific illustration in 1949 and worked in the Department of Paleobiology of the Smithsonian's National Museum of Natural History. He was a founder and first president of the Guild of Natural Science Illustrators. His B.S. and M.S. degrees in biology were earned at the University of Miami, Florida. Another past president of the GNSI and founder of its annual summer workshop, Marsha E. Jessup is Director of Media Resources for the University of Medicine and Dentistry of New Jersey, Robert Wood Johnson Medical School. She began medical/scientific illustration in 1967, earning her B.S. in zoology at Howard University and her masters in medical and biological illustration from the University of Michigan, Ann Arbor. G. Robert Lewis retired as scientific illustrator from the Department of Anthropology at the Smithsonian's National Museum of Natural History, where he still does freelance scientific illustration. A charter member of the GNSI, he studied art at the Maryland Institute of Art, American University, and the New School for Social Research. From 1947 to 1971, he produced works of art in stained glass, some of which are represented in various museums.

. . . and other Smithsonian museums.